HERBERT VON KARAJAN

Music advisor to Northeastern University Press
GUNTHER SCHULLER

HERBERT von KARAJAN

A Life in Music

===

RICHARD OSBORNE

Northeastern University Press
BOSTON

FOR HARRY

Published in England in 1998 by Chatto & Windus, an imprint of
Random House, London. Published in the United States of America
in 2000 by Northeastern University Press, by arrangement
with Random House UK.

Library of Congress Cataloging-in-Publication Data
Osborne, Richard, 1943–
Herbert von Karajan : a life in music / Richard Osborne.
p. cm.
Originally published: London : Chatto & Windus, 1998.
Includes indexes.
ISBN 1-55553-425-2
1. Karajan, Herbert von. 2. Conductors (Music)—Biography.
1. Title.
ML422.K22 O83   2000
784.2'092–dc21
[B]   99-059108

MANUFACTURED IN GREAT BRITAIN
04 03 02 01 00   5 4 3 2 1

CONTENTS

LIST OF ILLUSTRATIONS

Illustrations numbers 1–4, 6, 9–11, 14, 33, 39, 41, 42–44 are reproduced by courtesy of the Siegfried Lauterwasser Archive, Überlingen.

FOREWORD

Though this book is in no sense a work of joint authorship, it could not have been written in its present form without the meticulous research into Karajan's early career undertaken by the Swedish-born writer and scholar Gisela Tamsen (1922–1995).

The daughter of a German father and a Swedish mother, Gisela Tamsen was born and brought up in Stockholm where her father was a government-appointed inspector of the teaching of German in Swedish schools. An employee of the German government, he lost his job when he renounced his German citizenship in the late 1930s. During the war, he became involved with the anti-Nazi 'Kreisau Circle', a Christian-Socialist group, dedicated, not to the violent overthrow of Hitler, but to the planning of the moral regeneration of Germany after what it was believed would be Hitler's inevitable defeat. Gisela Tamsen worked with her father, occasionally acting as a courier. She met many refugees and musicians; and it was their reports of musical life in wartime Germany – of the careers of Furtwängler and Karajan in particular – which would later cause her to question much that she read about the subject in the postwar years.

She graduated from Stockholm University in 1948 with an honours degree in theatre and music history, and went on to study opera staging in Italy and Germany before returning to Sweden to work as a writer, editor, and broadcaster. Interested to build up a true picture of Karajan's early career, she spent many years researching archive sources in Germany and Austria, as well as making a detailed study of the Nazi Party's membership systems.

Though Miss Tamsen had long planned to write a book on Karajan, her passion was research. In this, she proved herself to be both brave and generous. A tireless correspondent, she took issue with numerous authors and journalists with whom she was more than happy to share her hard-won research. Few availed themselves of her offers.

Her help with the present volume was unstinting, but it was only after her death that I was able to appreciate the extent of her research: a body of painstakingly assembled documentation, including newspaper reviews of practically everything Karajan conducted in Ulm, Aachen, Berlin, and Vienna in the years 1929–55.

I am indebted to Christina Tamsen-Wall for allowing me early and exclusive access to the archive, to Britta Frieberg who helped order it, and to Ingegerd Östman-Smith who supervised the whole operation, first in Stockholm and later here in England.

Interviewer: Klemperer?
Singer: Un bloc de marbre.
Interviewer: Böhm?
Singer: L'intelligence.
Interviewer: Solti?
Singer: [pause] . . . très hongrois.
Interviewer: Bernstein?
Singer: La joie, la vie.
Interviewer: Karajan?
Singer: Le bon Dieu.

CHRISTA LUDWIG, *France Musique*, August 1995

You may not look with friendly eyes on everything Reinhardt did, or Toscanini, or Furtwängler, or Karajan. But it was always a tradition of Salzburg to caress a big personality, to take care of him. And in this age of democratising, of always looking downstairs rather than upstairs, this tradition should go on. For all their mistakes, we have to take care of these men. Karajan was not only a musician, he was a whole period. When I was a boy, he was already a period.

OTTO SCHENK

A child and a very wise old Chinese man, this was the extraordinary combination that was Herbert von Karajan.

MICHEL GLOTZ

A genius – with a whiff of sulphur about him.

SIR ISAIAH BERLIN

PART I
1908–1945

CHAPTER I

An atmosphere of war

May you be born into interesting times.
Old Chinese curse

It was shortly before eleven o'clock on the morning of 28 June 1914 that the leading car in the motorcade inexplicably turned off Appel Quay into Franz Josef Street.

The Governor, who was travelling on the jump seat of the royal car, shouted that they were going the wrong way. The chauffeur brought the black open tourer to an abrupt halt by the kerb in front of Schiller's delicatessen, the very place where Gavrilo Princip happened to be standing.

Princip later said that he aimed indiscriminately, bewildered by the sudden unexpected appearance of the car, and the fact that it was the Duchess Sophie, not the Archduke, who was on the side nearest to him.

By what malign chance, then, did both bullets find their mark? The first pierced the door of the car and the Duchess's right side; the second passed through the Archduke's collar, severing his jugular vein before lodging in his spine.

The assassination had been elaborately planned and might have succeeded earlier that same Sunday morning in Sarajevo had the bomb lobbed by one of Princip's accomplices not rolled off the folded-down hood of the royal car into the road, damaging the car behind.

It remains one of the most bizarre of twentieth-century assassinations, and the most momentous.

*

The two Karajan boys watched the battleship *Viribus Unitis* thread its way through the narrow channel near the small island on which they were holidaying. Funeral-bedecked, escorted by destroyers, the battleship was bound for Trieste. There the bodies of Franz Ferdinand and his wife would be transferred to the royal train for the final stage of their return to Vienna.

The small island on which the Karajans were staying was owned by the Kupelwieser family of Vienna. In an era before the advent of mass tourism, it was still possible for a well-to-do family to acquire an island or two for its private use. The Kupelwiesers – heirs to Schubert's great friend the painter Leopold Kupelwieser and long-standing friends of the von Karajans – had purchased the island across the water from the fashionable resort of Brioni, had planted and irrigated it, and turned it into a small paradise.[1]

The Karajan boys had arrived there with their mother, Martha von Karajan, for an extended vacation away from that unpredictable mix of torrid heat and torrential rains which is Salzburg in high summer. Wolfgang was rising eight, gangling and slightly unkempt. Heribert was six, smaller and sleeker, with a certain gamin charm. He had not previously seen the sea and declared it to be 'enormously impressive'.

The family had barely settled into their rooms when Martha's brother unexpectedly arrived with a message from her husband, Dr Ernst von Karajan. He had remained at home in Salzburg attending to his medical duties. Now 'something serious had happened'. It was imperative that his wife and children leave Brioni for a safer place.

Before they left, the family watched the water-borne cortège pass through the Fazanski channel. Karajan would later recall:

When my uncle saw these ships – I couldn't imagine why – he said: 'Now there'll be a war.' The word 'war' meant nothing at all to me, but I had quite a strange feeling all the same. In the way children do, I probably grasped the atmospheric feeling of the word rather than the drama itself. I noticed that the adults were afraid, and that communicated itself to me.[2]

The boys' uncle proved to be more prescient than many of his contemporaries. In Vienna, reaction to the Archduke's assassination was muted. He was not universally, or even widely, liked; and his morganatic marriage to the Duchess Sophie was a complicating factor when it came to the State obsequies, which were brief and low-key.

Yet Franz Ferdinand's death was a catastrophe in more senses than one. He had long been a moderating influence in the Austrian government, arguing that war with Serbia would mean war with Russia, the break-up of the fragile Austro-Hungarian empire, and the end of the monarchy. Now, ironically, his assassination threatened to provoke the very thing he most feared. Though Germany's Kaiser Wilhelm II had shared Franz Ferdinand's circumspection, he now shifted ground, urging a resolute response by the Austrians to Serb aggression, offering full German military backing in the event of Russian intervention.

The people, too, seem to have been hungry for war. Through the long days and balmy nights of the unusually fine summer of 1914, crowds massed in the streets in increasing numbers. The German Chancellor, Bethmann Hollweg, had feared that neither he nor the Kaiser would be able to carry public opinion with him in the event of Serb rejection of the Austrian ultimatum of 23 July. He need have had no qualms. On the evening of Saturday, 25 July huge crowds milled about the streets of Berlin awaiting the Serb response. When it finally came – a resolute 'no' – the crowds went wild. 'Es geht los!' the cry went up. 'It's on! The war is on!' Huge masses moved through Berlin's main thoroughfares singing Austrian and German marching songs. The Austrian embassy was besieged; the Austrian ambassador, Szögyény-Marich, was serenaded with a blustering rendition of 'Ich hat' einen Kameraden'.

On 30 July, the Russians mobilised. The following day at 1.00 p.m. the Kaiser announced a state of *drohende Kriegsgefahr* (imminent danger of war). The crowds again went wild.

*

After leaving Brioni, the Karajan boys did not immediately return to Salzburg. They travelled north to Styria, 'the green heart of Austria' as it is sometimes called, to the small town of Knittelfeld north-west of Graz. This was Martha von Karajan's home country. Her mother, Katharina Axterer, had been born there, and was to die there in 1944, aged 96. Martha's Serbian-born father, whom she barely knew (he died aged 46 when she was only three), was an agricultural accountant in Graz. Her sister had also settled locally, marrying Baron Leutzendorff, the owner of Schloss Prankh, a small estate near Knittelfeld. But she, too, had been widowed early. The baron had died in 1913.

The widowed baroness seems to have been as thrilled to have the Karajan boys staying with her as they were by the freedom the estate afforded them. They were halcyon days:

> Two lads that thought there was no more behind
> But such a day tomorrow as today,
> And to be boy eternal.[3]

For Heribert, though, happy days were accompanied by troubled nights. Though the word 'war' evoked as yet only 'atmospheric feelings', the idea of marauding Russian invaders was all too pressingly real. During his stay at Schloss Prankh, he fancied he heard shots in the woods at night. The assurance of the boys' nanny that if the Russians did arrive they would not advance beyond the Gasthof Dietrich was, not surprisingly, of little comfort to him.

The Russians didn't arrive. Yet fear of them was to haunt Karajan until well after the Second World War. In 1948, the year of the Berlin Airlift, he was actively making plans to bail out of Europe altogether.

One of the Baroness's recent acquisitions at Schloss Prankh was a newfangled player-piano. Heribert had started learning the piano proper at the age of three. Sibling rivalry had caused him to lurk, incubus-like, behind the curtains of the room in which Wolfi was already taking lessons.

5

By the age of four, Heribert had (in his own estimation) overtaken his brother; certainly, he was good enough to play in public, beguiling a charity audience in a Salzburg restaurant in 1912 with a pert rendering of a Mozart rondo.

Yet his aunt's player-piano, with its accompanying piano rolls, was something other. It was a Hupfeld Phonola, an 88-note cabinet player that would have been pushed up against the keyboard of the Baroness's own piano. This would not have allowed Heribert to listen to what one writer has described as 'original recordings by Rachmaninov and other great and important composers'.⁴ The Phonola, unlike the much rarer Hupfeld DEA, was not a reproducing piano; nor were Rachmaninov piano-roll recordings commercially available at that time. There were, however, hundreds of recordings being manufactured in the 'hand played' or 'machine cut' categories. These were relatively simple affairs. They reproduced the notes and allowed the player to pedal in a limited range of dynamic nuances. Here there was Rachmaninov in abundance: the C sharp minor Prelude and much else besides, music for which Karajan was to develop a lifelong passion.⁵

'It goes without saying,' Karajan later observed, 'that I spent many hours with this amazing apparatus.' Throughout his life he would talk of the latest advances in technology in a way that was almost proprietorial.

Fascinating as the player-piano was, the estate possessed another machine whose power was even more overwhelming to Heribert's six-year-old consciousness. In the grounds of Schloss Prankh there was a hut by a waterfall. In the hut was a generator, a water-driven turbine that provided power for the estate. Walking with the estate manager to unlock the hut (Heribert solemnly carrying the key) and switching on the turbine (Heribert helping plunge down the great lever) was an adventure beyond compare. The roar of the generator, light flaring out of darkness: a single gesture creating so powerful an effect. Even as an old man, Karajan would tell the story, as if still hypnotised by the memory. But, then, the old man knew what the six-year-old child could barely guess at: the existence of a profession in which a not dissimilar gesture could create epiphanies of sound and light as splendid as any known to man.

CHAPTER 2

Sunday's child

> Mozart was born in Salzburg, the birthplace
> of Herbert von Karajan.
>
> *Viennese joke*

Martha von Karajan worshipped her younger son. She called him her 'Sunday child', which, indeed, he was; born shortly before midnight on a grey, damp Salzburg Sunday, 5 April 1908.

> The child that is born on the Sabbath day,
> Is bonny, blyth, and good and gay.

Or so the old rhyme has it. An early Karajan biographer, resorting to astrology, claimed to see otherwise: a difficult personality and a stony way to the top.[1] In his later years, Karajan often gave the impression of harbouring a grudge against the past. Relentlessly ambitious and deeply convinced of his own worth and his capacity for work, he seems to have resented the fact that the route to the summit had, indeed, proved stony and long. This, and his natural inclination to characterise as 'gaslight' anything that happened as far back as the day before yesterday, had the effect of giving a slightly querulous feel to many of his memories.

Aside from the fact that he was the second child, his brother's junior by twenty months, and physically smaller, nothing has come down to us about his actual birth. Yet the birth of a child who subsequently turns out to be a musician is never without its particular interest. During the latter part of a mother's pregnancy, when the darkness is all-encompassing, the baby is conscious only of the sound and pulse of its mother's heartbeat, the larger rhythms of her breathing and moving, and the sound of her voice. Once the baby is born, the power of sight usually asserts its hegemony over all other senses. But this is not in the case with every child. There is evidence that, like many musicians, Karajan remained preoccupied with sound and rhythm: and to a degree greater than most.

As a young man, he would become famous for conducting with closed eyes. This was partly to avoid visual distractions, but as he would later explain: 'After I learn a score, at the end I try and forget what I have seen, because seeing and hearing are two such different things.'[2]

It would be untrue to say that Karajan had a deficient visual sense; he was obsessed with stage design and stage lighting. But as often as not the outcome of a hundred Karajan lighting rehearsals would be what the poet Milton calls 'No light, but darkness visible'. Several key works which held Karajan in thrall for most of his working life – Wagner's *Tristan und Isolde*, Debussy's *Pelléas et Mélisande* – inhabit closed worlds, womb-like in their darkness and seclusion.

Conversely, his astonishingly acute aural sensitivity was complemented by a deep and abiding fascination not only with the longer-term rhythms of a piece of music but also with the relation of the music's life-giving pulse to the pulse of his own heartbeat. Listening in St Moritz to the roughly edited tapes of a Beethoven symphony that had been recorded in Berlin, he was appalled by the sense he had of the tempi being wrong: until he realised that he was in the mountains where his heart-beat was faster.[3]

*

The child's name was entered in the baptismal register as Heribert Ritter von Karajan. The aristocratic title was genuine enough. Karajan's great-great-grandfather, Georg Johann Karajoannes, a cloth manufacturer of Greek-Macedonian origin, had been raised to the nobility by Friedrich August, Duke of Saxony, on 1 June 1792. The name 'Heribert', though, bordered on conscious archaism, a throwback to the Old German 'Hariberct', meaning 'bright host' or 'bright army'.

Heribert von Karajan remained Heribert von Karajan until political collapse and adolescent coyness caused him to modify his name in the 1920s. First, the family 'von' disappeared, outlawed in April 1919 in a purge of imperial titles under Austria's new post-war constitution. Then Heribert himself began to have doubts. Examine the typescript of his school-leaver's project (a first-rate dissertation, highly commended) on the internal combustion engine – *Moderne Verbrennungskraftmaschinen: ihre Wärmetechnischen und dynamischen Grundlagen* – and you will see that it is the work of Herbert Karajan. Check the signature beneath the photograph required by the Hochschule für Musik in Vienna in October 1927 and that, too, clearly says Herbert Karajan. Yet the boy who signs himself 'Herbert' registers for the university under the name of Heribert. Back home in Salzburg in 1929 it is Heribert who conducts Lortzing's folksy comedy *Der Waffenschmied* in the Landestheater, but Herbert who conducts Richard Strauss's *Salome* in the Festspielhaus (the opera's Salzburg première) and an orchestral concert in the Mozarteum.

Was a war of attrition being waged within the Karajan family, by Martha von Karajan, perhaps? There is no more jealous guardian of a child's name than its mother. Whatever the explanation, the offer of a job at the Opera in Ulm in Germany in 1929 appeared to resolve Karajan's problem. Since the new German constitution permitted the retention of old titles, no one minded a 'von', albeit an Austrian one.[4] In Ulm he became Herbert von

Karajan. For a while, whenever he conducted in Austria, he continued to observe the letter of Austrian law; but it was unequivocally Herbert von Karajan who first conducted the Vienna Philharmonic at a private concert in Salzburg in 1934.

As for his baptismal 'Heribert', that seems to have received a last public outing in the summer of 1933 when Karajan was invited to conduct the music for Max Reinhardt's production of Goethe's *Faust* in Salzburg's old Riding School, the Felsenreitschule. But perhaps that was a calculated effect; in the context of the medieval Faust story, 'Heribert von Karajan' sounds rather well.

*

Resemblances can be misleading. The parent we most resemble often changes down the years; and a physical resemblance by no means guarantees a temperamental one. Yet there is no doubt that, physically, Karajan came more and more to resemble his mother. Looking at photographs of Martha von Karajan one recognises the same small, wiry physique, the fine head, the strong, slightly protuberant nose, the clear eyes, the slightly cruel set of the mouth. There is also her powerful gaze and a purposeful tilt of the head that was to become one of her son's most striking mannerisms. Here, one feels, is a strong woman, and an ambitious one.

Whether she had any very highly developed artistic sensibilities is difficult to determine. It is rumoured that at coffee-mornings in Salzburg she boasted that she denied her sons fairy-tales on the grounds that such tales were not true. If this is so, it calls into question a quotation from Goethe which Karajan was fond of using about his parents: 'From my father I have my nature for the serious business of life; from my mother my cheerful nature, my pleasure in stories.'

Karajan often said that he considered his mother to be 'intuitively' musical, with a deep but generally well-disguised passion for music. (She seems to have been more open about her love for Wagner's music.) Unlike her husband and two sons, she had no practical skills in music; and yet there is little doubt that temperamentally Karajan had certain things in common with her. Though he was gifted technically in a way that she clearly was not, as a conductor he, too, could be said to be an intuitive musician rather than a ratiocinative one. As Karajan's friend and teacher Bernhard Paumgartner would later remark:

Everything Herbert does is musical. This is his great secret. As for the works to which he feels drawn: Herbert's strength always lies in those things he is particularly interested in at the time. He combines his gift with a certain intensity and depth, which however *he does not like to reveal* [my italics]. Here he is a little reserved, and this can lead to withdrawal, which is his difficult side.[5]

9

Curious as it may seem to anyone who did not know him personally, Karajan was an extraordinarily shy man. Martha von Karajan, too, was of a retiring disposition, though this was perhaps as much a matter of social conditioning as private temperament. Coming as she did from a good family, though a rather less distinguished one than the von Karajans, her role was that of wife and mother, a role she exercised with tireless efficiency. Heribert's piano teacher, Franz Ledwinka, described her as 'loving, good, and charming'. Heribert himself later said that she would willingly have cared for the whole world.

The photographs reveal that the father was taller than the mother, more Wolfgang's build, his face friendlier. It is a kind face and, in old age, a wise one. There is humour in the eyes and the gaze is calm. Here is a man, one senses, who knows there are more things in heaven and earth than are dreamt of in most of our philosophies. They make a fascinating pair. The mother Heribert resembled, loved, feared, and endlessly fought; the father whose gentle steadfastness was as much a rebuke to the wilder aspects of his youth as it would be the lodestar of his more mature years.

Ernst von Karajan was a doctor, and by all accounts a good one, a man with a human touch. As a practising surgeon he specialised in the treatment of goitres, those unsightly thyroid swellings of the throat that were commonplace a hundred years ago, particularly in certain country areas. Many of Ernst von Karajan's patients were local farming folk. As a young man brought up in the artistically vibrant village that was mid-nineteenth-century Vienna, he had wanted to be an actor. In the end, he followed his father, Hofrat Dr Ludwig Anton von Karajan, a distinguished doctor and a tireless worker for the reform of medical administration in the area of Lower Austria for which he eventually had overall responsibility. Ernst von Karajan also became a respected administrator: Senior Registrar at St Johann's Hospital in Salzburg, later Director of the Regional Health Authority. It was said he would have liked to teach medicine; sadly, academic recognition never came his way.

This tradition of public service in the family can be traced back to Heribert's great-grandfather, Theodor von Karajan (1810–73). He had entered the Austrian Civil Service in 1832 with a reputation (a badly fluffed Physics exam apart) as a brilliant academic. As an archivist in the Ministry of Finance he had been taken up by the department's director, the poet and playwright Franz Grillparzer, the man who had delivered Beethoven's funeral oration. It was Grillparzer who in 1841 helped engineer a position for Theodor – 'consistent with his academic background' – in the Imperial Library. In 1848 Theodor was elected to Vienna's Academy of Sciences; in January 1850 he was appointed Professor of German Language and Literature in the University of Vienna.

The physics exam apart, it was an effortless progress through the Austrian administrative hierarchy. But in 1851 a decree was passed banning non-Catholics from senior university positions. Theodor, who was a member of the Greek Orthodox Church, was not immediately affected. Yet he resigned in protest, a serious decision for a man with a wife and four children to care for. This act of self-determination did him no long-term harm. After two years during which he and his family lived off private capital, Theodor resumed his academic work. In 1866 he was elected President of the Vienna Academy of Sciences; and in 1869 he received a knighthood from the Imperial Household for 'loyalty and devotion, revealed in his work at every opportunity'.

Theodor had a wide circle of acquaintances among academic, theatrical, and literary folk, including the brothers Jacob and Wilhelm Grimm. He was also interested in music. A rare copy of Mähler's portrait of Beethoven (1815) hung in his drawing-room. His archive included letters written by Haydn to Maria Anna von Genzinger during the years 1789–92, an important correspondence that stimulated Theodor to write a celebrated monograph on Haydn's visits to London of 1791 and 1792.[6] That same year, 1861, he published an account of the life at the Viennese court of the poet and librettist Metastasio.[7] He also offered support and encouragement to a fellow academic and distinguished classical scholar, Otto Jahn, an amateur music-lover who had embarked on one of the great biographical projects of the age, a four-volume life of Mozart. The science of musicology as we understand it nowadays barely existed when Jahn was working on his epoch-making *W. A. Mozart*; yet it was precisely this need for a 'musicological' aspect to the researches that Theodor von Karajan seems to have urged upon Jahn.

Theodor's private, perhaps rather bookish, love of music was the start of a growing enthusiasm for music in the Karajan family. When Theodor's son Ludwig died in 1906, the obituary notices spoke of Ludwig's deep and abiding passion for music. He had no practical skills, yet there was a huge roster of works that acted as an emotional and spiritual salve for him: Bach's *St Matthew Passion* and *St John Passion*, the symphonies of Haydn, Mozart, and Beethoven, Mendelssohn's oratorios, the symphonies and songs of Schubert and Schumann. Above all, he loved Wagner's *Die Meistersinger*. He rarely neglected a chance to hear the opera and never ceased marvelling afresh at its manifold beauties.

Heribert never knew Ludwig, and Ludwig's wife, Heribert's paternal grandmother, died when he was four. As a child, though, he would play four- and eight-handed arrangements of symphonies by Haydn, Beethoven and Mendelssohn with his aunts, Ludwig's two daughters, occasionally making mild complaints about the arthritic fingers of the 'old ladies' (they were both in their fifties) and their over-cautious tempi.

Ludwig's passion for *Die Meistersinger* seems to have been shared by his son. In 1912 Ernst von Karajan took the four-year-old Heribert to a production of the opera at Salzburg's Landestheater. The child was allowed to stay for the overture and part of the first scene, long enough to glimpse a 'proud knight and his beautiful lady'. Back home, the proud knight and beautiful lady were rapidly assimilated into one of the elaborately coloured cardboard-cut-out theatres which the Karajan boys loved assembling and working.

*

Though Ludwig von Karajan had no practical musical skills, he had seen to it that his children acquired them. Ernst von Karajan played the piano and – the real joy of his life – the clarinet, more especially the basset horn and the bass clarinet. So it was that the Karajans' spacious apartment, looking out across the River Salzach to the Old Town beyond, became a gathering-place for Salzburg's chamber music fraternity. 'It was a home impregnated with music,' wrote one regular visitor, who also cherished its smartness and old-fashioned elegance (its *'biedermeierliche Vornehmheit'*). There were at least two pianos in the house, and a harmonium. This was allotted an unusual role when Heribert was invited to play Mozart piano concertos at musical evenings, his teacher Franz Ledwinka filling in the wind parts on the harmonium. Not that there was any shortage of wind players in the Karajan circle; works like Beethoven's Septet and Schubert's Octet were often included in the programmes.

As well as the musicians themselves, numerous guests were invited to these evenings. It is said that Heribert would often grimace at what he called 'their stupid applause'. (Years later, taking curtain calls in Salzburg, he would mutter to singers 'they haven't the faintest idea how good we *really* are'.[8]) Yet how proud he was when, after a particularly pleasing contribution, he was invited by his parents to stay up and join the adults for supper.

Inevitably, there were evenings when the Dr von Karajan would be called away to the hospital. Karajan later recalled:

There was never any question of us finishing when he went, or continuing while he was away. We all waited till he came back, even if this meant finishing in the early hours of the morning.[9]

The Karajans must have had tolerant neighbours. One session is reputed to have finished at four o'clock in the morning. A Dr Strohschneider lived beneath them and a dentist, Dr Schwabe-Schwabe, had his home and practice in the same building.

The chamber music evenings apart, Ernst von Karajan seems to have used the clarinet as a kind of therapy. Nothing gave him more pleasure than an evening away from hospital and home doing some illicit deputising in the pit of the Landestheater. Fellow musicians in Salzburg thought him fanatically keen.

*

Heribert was born into an age when fathers retained their patriarchal authority and, with it, a certain distance from their children. Professional men like Ernst von Karajan tended to marry later than is the custom nowadays. (Ernst was 36 when he married in September 1905, 39 when Heribert was born.) Marriage and the responsibilities of raising a family were conditions not lightly entered into. It was, in Karajan's own word, a 'hierarchical' world, one in which a father might reasonably address his son as 'Sie' rather than the more familiar 'Du'. That was certainly the form Ernst had used to his father, though there is no evidence that he had continued the custom in his own household.

Karajan told an early biographer that neither he nor his brother had any really close contact with their parents.[10] This is palpably untrue. With his mother the problem was all the other way. Her entire life was given over to her family. Yet this self-sacrificing spirit was offset by the emotional demands she made on those she cared for, something that Karajan seems to have shied away from.

As a boy, he fell seventy feet scrambling on Salzburg's Kapuzinerberg. He broke a leg in the fall and may well also have triggered the back trouble that would contribute to the tribulations of his later years. His mother's reaction on seeing her stretcher-borne son was relief that he was not more seriously injured, coupled with joy at the thought of his being confined to the house for several weeks to come.

This possessiveness irked Heribert beyond measure, complicating his relationship with his mother. In later years, several of Karajan's closest friends – among them, Raffaello de Banfield Tripcovich and Michel Glotz – spoke of the warmth of his friendship with their own mothers. Nor did he leave it at that. He would quiz both men incessantly on the bonds that held them and their mothers together.

The rigours of Ernst von Karajan's life as a surgeon-administrator meant that his dealings with his sons were more distant than their mother's relationship with them. Yet the boys lacked neither his physical proximity nor his steady interest in their well-being. He was in no hurry to parade them as prodigies, yet, as his diary entries reveal, he was keen to draw them quietly into the circle of his own music-making:

Sunday, 15 April 1917
Heribert's first participation in the family's eight-handed playing. Haydn's Symphony No. 103, *Paukenschlag*.

Thursday, 19 April 1917
Eight-handed. Mendelssohn *Scotch* Symphony, in which his [Heribert's] contribution showed excellent rhythmic and technical control.[11]

Like many music-lovers, Ernst von Karajan could not abide noise. He also needed time for calm reflection. Before performing an operation he would take a twenty-five-minute walk alone along the banks of the Salzach to the hospital. When things went wrong – mishaps or the kind of unforeseen complications that not even the most conscientious surgeon can guard against – he would remain silent for days afterwards.

Heribert inherited from his father this seriousness of purpose and would adopt similar methods: seeking solitude to prepare his work and compose himself mentally ahead of everything he did. Yet the air of seriousness that hung about their father often drove Heribert and Wolfi out of the parental home. Their particular friends were Edi and Igi von der Mauer, sons of a distinguished specialist Dr Hueber von der Mauer. (Edi later became Karajan's own doctor.) The von der Mauers were minor Tyrolean nobility. They were better off than the Karajans (they owned a motor car) and led a more free-and-easy life-style.

One thing that particularly tried Ernst von Karajan's patience was Heribert's scatter-brained treatment of personal possessions and his excitable, linguistically fractured explanations of their possible whereabouts. All his life, Karajan had a propensity for losing things and failing to explain their loss clearly. At times this bordered on the weird: sunglasses, watches, shoes, even on occasion his trousers. As a child, it was umbrellas, not the best thing to mislay in Salzburg. As Heribert begged the loan of yet another umbrella, his father would smile, make a sign of the cross over the replacement, and murmur '*Schon verloren* [already lost]'.

*

When he was not working, making music, or buying umbrellas, Ernst von Karajan spent time in the mountains walking, climbing, skiing and sailing. In 1880 Ludwig von Karajan had built himself a handsome villa at the western end of Grundlsee, a remote and to this day still largely unspoiled lake in the mountains sixty kilometres east of Salzburg. When Ludwig died the villa passed to three of his children. According to Heribert, who spent many of his childhood summers there, the house was subdivided into three, though how this worked is not clear. There were, for instance, three cooks, but only one wood-burning stove. It was an idyllic place, rackety children and family quarrels notwithstanding. Karajan would later recall:

This is where I began sailing at the age of six or seven. The wind came straight down off the mountains, as in the fjords. The beauty of it was something. Salzburg and Vienna were crowded, a mass of stone buildings. I didn't like the cities.[12]

'The Child is Father to the Man' says Wordsworth in his poem 'The Rainbow', which ends with a glimmer of apprehension at the idea of the vanishing idyll. That sense of loss was to be Karajan's problem too. He was a man who hated urban life, a shy man and, in the last resort, a solitary one.

His friend Michel Glotz would dub him 'a mountain man'.

'And what is a mountain man?' I asked.

'A man who likes loneliness, who doesn't like lies. A man who likes to be by himself, able to reflect on himself, on music, on the world.'

Bernard Haitink remembers a lakeside village south of St Moritz which in later years Karajan would often visit, mostly alone. He would spend a morning or an afternoon there: a walk around the lake, a bowl of soup and a platter of cold meats at the local inn, 'the old man alone with his own sense of perfection'.[13]

Ludwig von Karajan was in his mid-forties when he built the Villa Karajan on Grundlsee. He had just turned sixty when, in the autumn of 1895, he began to suffer from a 'nervous condition' that affected his walking and, eventually, practically all his physical functions. His son, Heribert's father, would also be stricken in old age, with Alzheimer's disease. A family friend, Count von Walderdorff, remembers driving Martha von Karajan to see Ernst in the nursing home to which he was moved shortly before his death in 1951. As they were leaving, Ernst beckoned to the Count: 'Thank you so much for coming. And with such a delightful lady! Tell me, who is she?'[14]

His father's end, and his grandfather's, would haunt Karajan. He feared that one day he, too, might lose his mind and physical capacities. Fascinated as he was by medicine and medical technology, he knew that research into the causes and treatment of mental illness was in many respects poorly advanced. So he opted for self-help, working on the not entirely implausible theory that rigorous mental activity is as good for the mind as regular exercise is said to be for the body.[15]

Music-making – learning scores, conducting from memory – was his primary mental activity. But this was not enough. He learnt languages and used them assiduously. However fluent a colleague or acquaintance might be in German, Karajan would invariably speak the language of his interlocutor. With his old friend from Trieste, the English-born, Italian-bred, French- and German-speaking Raffaello de Banfield, the situation was even more bizarre. In Trieste they would speak Italian; in Paris,

French; in Salzburg, German. (History does not relate what they spoke in Lebanon, in the hills above Beirut when the Berlin Philharmonic visited there in 1968.)

There was also Karajan's addiction to flying. Josephine Veasey remembers a conversation she had with him in New York in 1968 during rehearsals for *Das Rheingold*. Most of Karajan's serious training took place in the United States, and he had recently been learning to fly jets. She asked him why he was interested in mastering ever more complex aviation techniques.

'Because I don't want to end up like my father,' was his frank reply.[16]

It was a fear that extended beyond the grave. In Karajan's will, there is a clause stipulating what should be done in the event of an administrator or beneficiary of his musical estate becoming mentally incapacitated.

CHAPTER 3

Teachers' boy

'But piano lessons should not be – or not essentially or not first
and last – lessons in special ability, but lessons in m-m – '
   'Music!' cried a voice from the tiny audience, for the speaker
could simply not get the word out, often as he had used it before,
but kept on mumbling the *m*.

Thomas Mann, *Doctor Faustus*

The earliest memory to which Karajan regularly alluded – his hiding behind
the curtains, jealously auditioning his brother's piano lessons – enmeshes
music with the competitive urge. The fact that he quickly outflanked his
brother as a pianist, causing Wolfi to take refuge in the violin, was
both a blessing and a curse. For Heribert was not just talented, he was
extraordinarily talented, with all the stress that such talent involves. Where
there is school to attend, schoolwork to be done, bikes to be ridden,
footballs to be kicked, trees to be climbed, the additional burdens that
music imposes will always leave the musically gifted child running to catch
up with himself.

Academically, the young Heribert was a good all-round performer,
though not effortlessly so. Mathematics (a subject at which musicians
often excel) was never a strong point. Physically slight, though by no
stretch of the imagination the effeminate weakling some writers have
attempted to portray, he shone in most sports. He played soccer well
into his twenties, keeping goal ('There he was his own boss,' observed
his brother). He was a good enough tennis player to merit professional
coaching (there is a photograph of him in his tennis blazer that gives him
the look of a well-heeled English public schoolboy), and he was a superb
skier, for many years one of the best amateur skiers in Austria.

As for the piano:

I was naturally under a lot of stress from my piano studies alongside my school
work. I wasn't just plonking away. I played in public every year. On the one
hand, it isolates you; on the other hand, it gives you a satisfaction it would be
very difficult to get from any other source.[1]

Violinist Joshua Bell's father, a distinguished academic psychiatrist, has
spoken of the potentially calamitous effects a very gifted child can have
within a family that is unprepared for the intrusion; of the dangers to a
boy prodigy of a mother's over-involvement; and of the damage that can
be done, not by sibling rivalries, but by the very thing Karajan himself

alludes to: the isolation of the child within the family circle as a result of the punishing pressures of daily practice.[2]

Karajan claimed that as a child he did four hours practice a day, even in term-time. This is confirmed by the boys' nanny, Anna. Where Wolfgang – happy, extrovert, the very model of the easygoing Austrian, and mad keen on science – would often turn the house upside down with his games and scientific experiments, Heribert cut a more serious and taciturn figure. 'He was no problem at all in the house,' said Anna. 'He spent all his time playing the piano.' Away from home it was a different matter, yet as early as Heribert's tenth year it is possible to descry the shadow of the man: the work-obsessed perfectionist, shy, withdrawn, difficult to fathom.

*

Heribert had started attending classes at the Mozarteum in 1914, the year the institution moved to Richard Berndl's new *Jugendstil* building in Schwarzstrasse, a stone's throw from the Karajans' apartment. (A wrong note in a Mozart quotation carved on one of the cornerstones amused him hugely.) By 1917, he was working with three specialists on the Mozarteum staff: Franz Ledwinka (piano), Bernhard Paumgartner (composition and chamber music), and Franz Sauer (harmony). As a pupil and rising star of the Mozarteum, Heribert made regular appearances in the special Mozart Birthday Concert that took place every year on or around 27 January. In 1917 he played Mozart's *Rondo* in D K485, in 1918 the *Fantasia* in D minor K397, in 1919 the *Rondo* in D for Piano and Orchestra, K382.

Such judgements as have come down to us speak fairly consistently of great assurance both of manner and touch, and a preoccupation with beauty of sound born of an evidently precocious musical sensibility. (To play the D major *Rondo* K485 even half adequately, you need all these qualities and more.) Of the concert on 26 January 1918, a Salzburg journalist wrote:

After an opening devoted to the first movement of the serene and graceful Symphony No.29, Valerie Koller read aloud two letters by the musician [Johann] Schachtner who had spent many hours in Mozart's home and who related scenes from Wolfgang's sunny childhood with ingenuous clarity. To illustrate these letters, the young Heribert von Karajan appeared and, unaware of the chasms and lurking dangers, calmly and surely performed the *Fantasie* in D minor, from memory, with both grace and feeling.[3]

After which, like all participating students at Mozarteum concerts, Heribert was allowed just one curtain call before the packed audience.

He seems to have been fortunate in his teachers, not least because they mixed musical competence with a broader array of interests. Franz Sauer, his harmony teacher, is perhaps the least well-known outside the narrow environs of Salzburg itself, though recordings by him do exist. He was for many years the cathedral organist in Salzburg. He played in the inaugural production of Max Reinhardt's *Jedermann* in 1920 and was still active forty years later, playing the organ under Karajan's direction in the 'Gloria' from Mozart's C minor Mass during the inauguration of Salzburg's new Grosses Festspielhaus on 26 July 1960.[4]

Wolfgang von Karajan was also interested in the organ. Indeed, for a time in the mid-1950s he made quite a good living touring a programme with three semi-portable organs entitled 'The Art of Fugue'. The group called itself the Wolfgang von Karajan Organ Ensemble, the 'Karajan' part of the name printed – to Herbert's considerable annoyance – in extremely large type.

Wolfgang's specialism has tended to obscure Herbert's own interest in the organ, an interest which almost certainly goes back to his studies with Sauer. David Bell, an organist who played regularly for Karajan from 1975 onwards, recalls:

Karajan was very much an organist's conductor. He never took the organ part of any piece for granted. He always treated it as intrinsic and was meticulous about overseeing the preparation of the instruments we encountered in various concert halls. I don't know where he acquired his knowledge, but certainly he knew a tremendous amount about the subject.[5]

Bell recalls arriving with the Berlin Philharmonic in Lucerne where they were due to play *Also sprach Zarathustra*. Unfortunately, with over a hundred players on stage there was no room for the mobile organ console that normally sat in an alcove to the left of the stage. So Bell ended up attempting to play the organ from the back of an adjacent storeroom. With the door slightly ajar, it was just about possible to see the conductor:

I had a separate rehearsal with Karajan, who determined *everything*: all the registrations, the balance and power of the organ at my various entries. At the final full rehearsal and at the concert I could hear nothing of the organ sound at all. However, members of the orchestra assured me that we were in accord.[6]

Karajan came from a generation of musicians that was not averse to filling out the organ part in large-scale choral works. His interventions were never on the scale of those of Wood, Stokowski, or Sargent, but they were more substantial than is generally supposed. It takes a confident man to contemplate modifying the organ writing of a composer who was himself a great organist, but Karajan regularly asked for a number of small changes to be made in the organ part in Bruckner's *Te Deum*.[7] There were even bigger surprises in store for David Bell in Brahms's *German Requiem*, a work Karajan almost certainly studied with Sauer.[8] Bell was already using a deeper bass at several points in Brahms's score. He was totally perplexed, though, by glances from Karajan in rehearsal suggesting some kind of enhanced organ presence at points where his part was *tacet* [silent].

I was so surprised, when I got back to London I consulted Clem Relf [the Philharmonia Orchestra's librarian]. Did he know of an 'extended' organ part for the *German Requiem*? He certainly did: the 1913 Peters Edition, edited by Hermann Keller. In fact, it's a very tactful piece of work, nothing more than a set of suggestions as to how the organ part might be better adapted to work with a new generation of organs, halls, and orchestral instruments. It's fairly clear that this is the edition Karajan had in mind.[9]

Nor were the interventions confined to choral repertory. When Karajan finally came to perform and record Richard Strauss's *Alpine* Symphony in the early 1980s, he made it clear to Bell that he had serious reservations about Strauss's writing for the organ. ('He writes like a pianist!') In particular, Karajan was unhappy with the organ writing in the epilogue, 'Ausklang'. Here, a long, unbroken melody, mainly in unison, is played by a large wind section: four flutes, four clarinets, three bassoons and cor anglais, later joined by two oboes, horns, and trumpet. The organ supplies the harmony, then doubles the orchestral melody in octaves. Over a number of weeks and months, Karajan worked with Bell on developing the organ part to the point where it was providing a halo of sound around the melody, as well as a strongly supportive bass beneath it:

Karajan's objection to the organ score was that the manual parts were 'wastefully organised', with much ineffective doubling of the winds. The keyboard layout was practically rewritten, so that the organ provided a harmonic halo around the orchestral melody, necessitating the use of large Reger-type chords. Seamless hairpins were the aim, closely hugging the orchestra's dynamics.[10]

If Sauer taught Karajan rather more than elementary harmony, Karajan's distinguished piano teacher Franz Ledwinka awakened interests and expectations beyond piano playing. In a telegram Karajan sent to Ledwinka on his seventieth birthday in May 1953, he called him 'my distinguished teacher, whom I must thank for my complete musical education'.

As well as being a first-rate piano teacher, Ledwinka was also a composer, and an excellent conductor. He had no national or international reputation but, locally, he was highly prized, both within the Mozarteum and by the theatre director and impresario Walter Hofstötter, without whom concert and opera life in Salzburg outside the confines of the fledgling festival would have been more or less non-existent in the 1920s. According to Karajan, it was Bernhard Paumgartner who directed him towards conducting. But it was Ledwinka who noticed how his pupil's imagination was caught by the lure of orchestral sound.

*

Bernhard Paumgartner was thirty when, in 1917, he was appointed Director of the Mozarteum. At the time, the Mozarteum was more like a private school than a national academy, with Paumgartner as the energetic, well-connected, go-ahead young headmaster. It was not long before he was playing the roles of private tutor, favourite uncle, surrogate father, and eventually grown-up older brother to the two Karajan boys: to Heribert in particular.

Paumgartner died two days after the opening of the 1971 Salzburg Festival, the festival he had helped found in 1920 and which he had presided over since 1960. In his later years in festival time, he confined himself to conducting the 11 a.m. Mozart Matinées in the Mozarteum and an annual performance of Mozart's C minor Mass in the Abbey Church of St Peter where the Mass had received its first performance in 1783.[11]

He was a tall, heavily built man, slightly stooping, an imposing figure on the rostrum, undemonstrative, and if the truth be told a bit of a dull dog musically. But, then, he had always been an all-rounder: pianist, composer, conductor, biographer, Mozart scholar, amateur art lover, and universal acquaintance of the great and the good. His friends revered him as a polymath; his enemies (who by the mid-1930s included a number of leading Austrian Nazis) dubbed him a Jack-of-all-trades, a fixer, a local Pooh-Bah.

Both his parents were musicians. His father, Hans Paumgartner, was a pianist and critic; his mother, Rosa Papier-Paumgartner, was one of the leading mezzo-sopranos in Vienna in the 1880s, until a sudden deterioration in her voice, brought on perhaps by too rapid a return to the stage after the birth of her son, caused her to take up teaching in 1891.

Bernhard can barely have known his father; his parents separated in 1891 when he was three, and his father died five years later. The mother, though, was formidably well connected. To look through the list of her son's teachers is to make an inventory of some of the leading names in Viennese musical life at the turn of the century. He studied the horn with Karl Stiegler, the violin with the leader of the Vienna Philharmonic Jakob Grün (and later with Gustav Mahler's friend Natalie Bauer-Lechner), music history with Adler and Mandyczewski, conducting with Bruno Walter.

Rosa Papier also knew Mahler. In 1895 she had taken her star pupil, Anna von Mildenburg, to Hamburg to audition for him. Anna and Mahler became lovers, while Rosa and her own lover, Eduard von Wlassack, a senior figure in Vienna's theatre administration, played a crucial role in helping mastermind Mahler's successful bid to succeed Wilhelm Jahn as Director of the Vienna Opera. Once safely ensconced on the Opera Director's throne, Mahler gradually put a distance between himself and his former allies. In 1903, Rosa would write to Anna:

At one time [Mahler] spent hours in my waiting room, but now that he is married, he never comes to see me; he hasn't even introduced his wife to me, etc. You yourself wrote to me from Hamburg: 'He would walk over dead bodies', and you were right.[12]

One can only guess at the tales Bernhard Paumgartner passed on to the Karajan boys – one of them destined to be Director of the Vienna Opera – about Mahler and musical life in Mahler's Vienna.

For the Karajan brothers, Vienna around the year 1920 was a place for family visits to the opera, derring-do in hotel lifts (hand-operated in those days), and the booby-trapping of wash-basins in unoccupied bedrooms. Yet it is through the reminiscences of older friends and relations that many of us come imaginatively to appropriate and inhabit the age before our own. There is a sense in which Heribert would have 'known' Mahler's Vienna better than we might think.

Towards the end of his life, Paumgartner hazarded the idea that Karajan resembled Mahler in his music-making; not how he looked or ordered his affairs (though there are plenty of parallels there) but how the music sounded.[13] Alas, there is no way of proving this surmise. At the same time, Paumgartner prophesied – this was the mid-1960s – that in due course, and even at so late a date, Karajan would one day begin to conduct the music of Mahler. It was an accurate prophecy, though I suspect Karajan's route to Mahler – to late Mahler, in particular – was not through Bruckner (Paumgartner's suggestion) but through a complex series of journeys into various musical and spiritual interiors: Eastern mysticism, the music of Berg and Schoenberg, and (in the case of the Ninth Symphony) Act 3 of Wagner's *Parsifal*.

*

Paumgartner's first visit to Salzburg had been in 1906, the year of the Mozart festival arranged by the most prominent member of the fund-raising committee for the new Mozarteum, the soprano Lilli Lehmann. It was a famous festival. Mahler conducted *Le nozze di Figaro*; Richard Strauss conducted *Così fan tutte*, a rarity in those days. Even more of a rarity in German-speaking countries was *Don Giovanni* performed in the original Italian; a somewhat shambolic production, by all accounts, shakily conducted by Reynaldo Hahn.

In 1914, after a spell as a répétiteur at the Vienna Opera, Paumgartner was posted to a department of the military entitled 'Musikhistorische Zentrale'. His job was to continue the work that had been initiated by a 'Procedure of the Imperial and Royal Army' in 1905 to research the songs and marches of the Austrian imperial army in its various far-flung regions. (In the course of his researches, Paumgartner was to meet both Bartók and Kodály.) The researches were never published, but it is interesting to speculate how much of his enthusiasm for these old songs and marches Paumgartner passed on to his musically avid pupil. In 1973, Karajan amazed everyone by recording a remarkable double album of Prussian and Austrian marches with wind players from the Berlin Philharmonic. The marches ranged from such classics of the band repertory as *Alte Kameraden* to a gloriously cheeky Wagnerian pot-pourri, *Nibelungen-Marsch*, assembled by Gottfried Sonntag, bandmaster of the 7th Bavarian Infantry in Bayreuth. I once asked a producer at Deutsche Grammophon if Karajan had actually conducted the sessions. 'You bet he did,' was the reply. 'He loved the music and seemed to know a great deal about it.' The fact that at much the same time Karajan was also recording Alban Berg's *Three Orchestral Pieces* (1914), war-torn music, grimly prophetic of the catastrophes to come, may or not have been a coincidence.

On 6 September 1917, still in military uniform, Paumgartner took up his post as Director of the Mozarteum, a job his mother's tireless manoeuvrings had helped him secure. Within a fortnight, he found himself directly involved in the personal and political arguments that had once more broken out over the question of a festival in Salzburg.

For the best part of a century, Salzburgers had been notoriously remiss in honouring the name of Mozart, the city's most famous son. Finally, in 1887, a committee was formed to initiate the building of 'a temple of art' on the Mönchsberg, near the site of the present complex of Salzburg theatres; it would seat 1500 people and be used to stage 'perfect' performances of Mozart operas. Nothing came of it. In 1916 two oddball enthusiasts, Friedrich Gehmacher and Heinrich Damisch, whose idea of a high-quality music festival as a lure for the rich and famous had already been sniffily received by the powers-that-be at the Mozarteum, came up with a plan to build a theatre on waste ground to the north of the city, near the Pilgrimage Church of Maria Plain.

By now, though, the festival idea had been around long enough for it to be thoroughly bogged down in a mire of competing interests. Frustrated once more, not least by Lilli Lehmann, the two men issued and carried out a peculiarly Austrian kind of threat. They decided to create a new Salzburg Festival Society – in Vienna.

It was for this that they now sought Paumgartner's support. However, a new player had recently joined the game: the theatre director Max Reinhardt. And with him came two even bigger names: Richard Strauss and the poet and dramatist Hugo von Hofmannsthal, whose idea of a festival mixed the distinctive elements of places of religious and cultural pilgrimage such as Oberammergau and Bayreuth with the wider purpose of serving what he called 'the entire classical possession of the nation'.

Politically, Hofmannsthal was of the anti-*Anschluss* (union with Germany) persuasion. Aesthetically, though, he believed that the German-Austrian (*Deutschösterreich*) strand in Germany's cultural heritage was the authentic one. The spirit of 'Germanism' he wished to celebrate and enshrine in the new festival – helping, in the process, to redefine Austria's own cultural identity in war-shattered Europe – was 'German and national in the sense in which the great Germans at the end of the eighteenth and the beginning of the nineteenth centuries, the true teachers of the nation, thought of a national style'.[14] It was a non-military form of nationalism in which the works of men like Goethe, Gluck, Mozart, and Grillparzer would be the informing influences.

*

Reinhardt knew Salzburg of old, but had returned to it because of a property that had been advertised there: Schloss Leopoldskron, a semi-derelict eighteenth-century castle which he bought, renovated, and would eventually turn into one of Europe's most fashionable artistic meeting places. Having secured his base, Reinhardt had proposed to the Imperial Theatre administration in Vienna that a theatre be built at Hellbrunn on the outskirts of Salzburg.

His intervention opened up a split in the Festival Society. Where Damisch suspected Reinhardt's motives, Gehmacher saw no option but to hang on to the great man's coat tails. The problem was, no one knew precisely what it was that Reinhardt and Hofmannsthal had in mind. It rapidly became clear, though, that their thinking – in theory, at least – went some way beyond the production of de luxe theatrical and operatic events. 'Catholicism', 'community' ('*Volk*', one of Hofmannsthal's favourite concepts), and the 'spirit of the place' were ideas talked about a good deal, to the puzzlement of the locals, who saw the two men merely as Jewish entrepreneurs with internationalist ambitions.

But Reinhardt was true to his word. While the Festival Society busied itself with plans for a theatre in the grounds of Hellbrunn Palace, he went ahead during 1919 with plans for a Christmas production of an updated version of a medieval Mystery Play that had traditionally been performed at the village church of Hallein, a little way south of Salzburg. Paumgartner was invited to arrange the music, the proceeds of the production to be donated to a local children's charity. Frustratingly, the event foundered in the post-war austerity. Travel was difficult; hotels remained unheated for lack of reliable coal supplies.

None the less, the Hallein experiment had the virtue of concentrating people's minds. It was only a short step from there to the idea of bringing to Salzburg the spectacular reworking of the medieval morality play *Everyman* which Hofmannsthal had prepared for Reinhardt in Berlin in 1911.

Whether the idea was hatched by Reinhardt and Paumgartner over a cup of execrable coffee in a seedy Salzburg hotel (Paumgartner's version) or suggested by the Festival Society's formidably gifted business secretary Erwin Kerber over coffee with Reinhardt and his distinguished Viennese patron Hermann Bahr (the official version) is immaterial. *Jedermann* had its first staging in the Cathedral Square in Salzburg on 22 August 1920:

The performance began late in the afternoon. Passing clouds, the setting sun and the dusk all contributed light effects which would never have been possible in any theatre.[15]

It was not quite the birth of the Salzburg Festival as we now know it, but it was an important proposal of marriage.

CHAPTER 4

A Salzburg education

> That is the difference between good teachers and great teachers:
> good teachers make the best of a pupil's means, great teachers
> foresee a pupil's ends.
>
> Maria Callas

Increasingly, as the years went by, Paumgartner drew Heribert along in his own social and musical slipstream. Karajan would later recall:

He took me along again and again to orchestral rehearsals and let me sit alongside him – 'So that you get an idea what conducting is like'. And he also did his utmost to make sure that I eventually put it all to the test . . . He was more than a superior, he was an older friend. A man who was enormously open-minded about everything in life, whether it involved art or very practical things.[1]

Paumgartner's conducting engagements in Salzburg in the 1920s were legion, albeit in what was generally a rather repetitive repertory (in the official festival at least) of Mozart serenades and Mozart choral music. Yet as early as the age of thirteen, Karajan would have been able to hear Paumgartner rehearsing not only with the Mozarteum Orchestra but with such famous soloists as horn-player Karl Stiegler and pianist Elly Ney, whom Karajan himself would later work with. And there was choir work. The Karajan boys sang hymns and motets by Mozart in concerts in which leading players from the Vienna Philharmonic – Stiegler, the bassoonist Hugo Burghauser, and Karajan's future teacher the oboist Alexander Wunderer – starred in performances of serenades and divertimenti by Mozart.

Though Paumgartner spent a great deal of time conducting incidental music for the stage, he did not conduct a great deal of opera, not even his own *Die Höhle von Salamanca* which the Leningrad Opera Studio brought to the Festival in 1928. He was, however, immensely proud of the ambitious roster of operas the Mozarteum was able to perform under the aegis of a wonderful old theatre buff, Dr Carl Gross. The operas Gross put on ranged in seriousness and weight all the way from *Susanna's Secret* to *Tristan und Isolde*. One year, the composer Wilhelm Kienzl came to conduct his now largely forgotten smash-hit *Der Evangelimann* (1894); another year Gross staged a popular one-acter by the young Erich Korngold, *Der Ring des Polykrates* which Bruno Walter had premièred in Munich in 1916. How many of Gross's productions Heribert saw is not clear, though in 1929, after he had graduated from the Hochschule für Musik in Vienna, he conducted Lortzing's *Der Waffenschmied* for him.

The first opera Heribert heard in its entirety was Wagner's *Die Walküre* performed by a visiting company from Würzburg. As for his own early experience of the stage, this seems to have been confined to directing a school production of a twopenny-halfpenny farce entitled *Der Lügner und sein Sohn* by Arnold Scribber. Many years later Paumgartner would venture some gentle criticisms of his former pupil's abilities as a stage director – 'when it comes to movement about the stage, he has not yet reached the point where he should be'[2] – but Karajan's schooldays belonged to an era long before the age of 'director's opera'. What Karajan eventually learned about theatre direction, he learned on the job.

Heribert's horizons were widening all the time. Because of his father's position, the family suffered few of the physical hardships that beset many less fortunate Austrian families in the years immediately following the country's political collapse at the end of the Great War. This was a time when even the pampered heroes of the illustrious Vienna Philharmonic looked 'like grey shadows in their shabby dress suits, undernourished, and exhausted by many privations'.[3]

Nor does the Karajan family appear to have been infected by the anti-British feeling rife in post-war Austria. In the summer of 1924, the year of Wolfgang's eighteenth birthday, the two boys were sent to London for three months to learn English, staying first in a small pension whose owner Heribert seems to have instantly disliked, and later with a family. Money was a problem; midway through the stay Ernst von Karajan was obliged to send the boys a further £60.[4] It is said that Heribert came back speaking English like a native, a pardonable exaggeration, perhaps, though he later spoke excellent English – 'selectively articulate' was Walter Legge's phrase – with the kind of refreshingly idiosyncratic vocabulary that can make the English of an intelligent foreigner infinitely more vivid than that of many a semi-articulate native.

Nor was England the only place visited by the teenage Karajan. In 1967 he told Ernst Haeusserman:

[Bernhard Paumgartner] took my brother and myself to Italy in his car. These are all things which still influence me today. For example, the way in which he saw and was able to explain works of art; just as in his own books, which were immensely enriching coming as they did from a great reservoir of general culture.[5]

The artist often venerates his antitype and Karajan, with his nearly monomaniac interest in music, always revered the polymath. As for the phrase 'the way in which he saw', here is further evidence of the aurally preoccupied talent seeking elucidation of things visual from another source.

*

Between 1921 and the latter part of 1924, Heribert's early teenage years, the barely fledged Salzburg Festival was a sickly thing, half suspended from its nest. In addition to a small but vocal band of anti-Semites, whose hostility to Reinhardt and his friends had been evident from the first, the townsfolk themselves were none too happy. Though there were rich pickings to be had from the international carriage trade the festival instantly attracted, this was little consolation to Salzburgers who saw shop prices soaring, taxes rising, and their well-brought-up sons and daughters being exposed to the glitzy and cynical life-style of the young cosmopolitan set whose revolt against the bankrupt moral idealism of the First World War was now in full swing. (Karajan later told Roger Vaughan that 'sex was taboo' in his family's house.[6])

Most seriously, the Festival was short of money. Post-war inflation was now at a record high, with food prices soaring and even a simple postage stamp costing a four-figure sum. Though the 1921 festival had been reduced to six performances of *Jedermann* and fewer than a dozen concerts, the 1922 festival was surprisingly adventurous. The Vienna Philharmonic was on tour in South America but a small band of thirty-seven players stayed behind to accompany the Vienna Opera to the festival; about as many, in fact, as could be accommodated in the tiny pit of the Landestheater. It was an all-Mozart festival, with four operas and two concerts divided with scrupulous fairness between Richard Strauss and Franz Schalk, the Vienna Opera's bitterly warring co-directors.

Reinhardt's contribution to the 1922 festival was a new and spectacular show designed by Alfred Roller entitled *Das Salzburger grosse Welttheater*.[7] So once again the beautiful and the famous flitted across Salzburg's stages and squares and through the foyers of its drab provincial hotels, until street protests against rising prices precipitated a government decree requiring all tourists to leave the city by 3 September.

In 1923 Reinhardt produced Molière's *Le malade imaginaire* with the celebrated actor Max Pallenberg in the title role, the performances divided between Reinhardt's Schloss Leopoldskron and the Landestheater. But there was no music. And in 1924 there was no festival at all.

*

At which point, enter Franz Rehrl. It is rare to find a politician who can legitimately claim decisively to have influenced for the good the future course of a great artistic institution; but Rehrl, a dumpy, bespectacled wheeler-dealer of a man, must be accounted an exception. He saved the Salzburg Festival.

A Christian Socialist, Rehrl was Provincial Governor of Salzburg from 1922 until March 1938, when he was arrested and imprisoned by the Nazis. In the winter of 1924–5, tired of Strauss's dilettantism and the endless bickering of the various festival 'societies', Rehrl set in train a series of political and financial initiatives that not only saved the festival idea but laid sound foundations for its future.

The city of Salzburg is often talked of as a hotbed of Nazism in the inter-war years. But, as Rehrl's case shows, the day-to-day political reality was rather different. Members of the proto-Nazi German Nationalist Party did, indeed, hold a number of key positions in the city administration in the 1920s; but it was a fractious grouping. In 1923 the Nationalists raised a hue and cry sufficient to see off plans for a costly re-staging of *Das Salzburger grosse Welttheater*, encouraged by a vicious review of the show by Karl Kraus, the Jewish-born Viennese satirist who loathed Reinhardt and all his works. But actual political power in Salzburg lay with a coalition of interests between Rehrl's Catholic, conservative Christian Social Party and the Socialists, led by the politically moderate Robert Preussler, the Deputy Provincial Governor.

The real enemy in the eyes of Salzburg politicians was the now largely impotent administration in Vienna. It starved Salzburg of cash at a time of massive inflation and often seemed to be working to a radically different political agenda, not least over the long-standing question of union with greater Germany. The case for *Anschluss* had long been argued by academics and political theorists in Austria. In the nineteenth century, the argument centred on a shared language and culture. But there were economic lures, too, not least in Salzburg where the citizens, cheek by jowl with the German border, were all too well aware of the economic might of the German territories to which, until 1816, Salzburg itself had belonged.

By the early 1920s, the idea of *Anschluss* had become even more badly blurred. Austrian Social Democrats, the principal pro-*Anschluss* party, looked for a new political and economic union with Weimar Germany. This, though, was anathema to the federal government in Vienna, which was fearful of upsetting the victorious Allies. It was anathema, too, to that element within the cultural and intellectual élite – men like Hugo von Hofmannsthal – who took the view that the preservation of some kind of Austrian national identity after the humiliations of 1918 was crucial to the re-establishment of the old *Deutschösterreich* cultural order.

Salzburg was less equivocal. It was *Deutschösterreich* and pro-*Anschluss*. In May 1921 a plebiscite was held within the province of Salzburg itself. With all the principal political parties taking a pro-*Anschluss* line, the vote was overwhelmingly in favour. But it was little more than gesture politics. The federal government had already taken the precaution of declaring the plebiscite illegal.

*

And what did the teenage Karajan think of all this? What, indeed, had he been encouraged to think by his parents or his teachers in the local state grammar school where his performance in history was never less than creditable? There are adolescents who shun serious politics. But such opinions as are formed – in revolt against received opinion or in concurrence with it – are often forcefully held. Walter Legge once remarked that Karajan was uninterested in every kind of politics except the musical kind, of which he was a consummate master.[8] If by this Legge meant that Karajan was uninterested in party politics, it is undoubtedly true. Politics in the wider sense, however, interested him deeply since he was, at bottom, a natural conservative who feared all forms of politically manufactured change and the dangers and instabilities such changes, in his experience, inevitably brought. On the *Anschluss* question, there is evidence to suggest that he was exactly what we would expect him to be, given his social and family background: conservative *Deutschösterreich*, pro-*Anschluss*.

Part of the evidence is in the enrolment form he filled in each year for the University of Vienna's Faculty of Philosophy under whose aegis he studied between 1926 and 1928. The form itself is the product of a political culture which will be more familiar in some countries than in others; for in addition to asking details of the student's age, nationality, and place of birth, it also asks for a statement of *Volkszugehörigkeit* or ethnic origin. Almost without exception, Karajan's fellow students answered the question blandly and directly: Austrians wrote 'Austrian', Swiss wrote 'Swiss', Jews wrote 'Jewish'. By contrast, the Salzburg-born Karajan describes himself as 'German-Aryan'.

It is a provocative entry. 'German' rather than 'Austrian' or 'German-Austrian'. And what of the factually accurate but supererogatory 'Aryan'? Believing oneself to be one thing does not necessarily imply that one is actively opposed to the alternative, but it is easy to see how this might be construed as 'German, anti-Semitic'. If Karajan harboured such views, he kept them to himself. During his time in Vienna he had Jewish friends, patronised Bolshevik theatre companies, played jazz, and attended to all manner of 'degenerate [*entartet*]' art. What the yearly enrolments do suggest is a young man who is both at odds with a narrowly local vision of the provincial community from which he comes and yet, paradoxically, still firmly grafted to it.

*

Meanwhile, the wish of the Salzburgers to be part of a greater Germany, while at the same time fiercely resisting any form of 'foreign' interference in 'their' festival, was causing frustration among the intellectuals, idealists, and internationalists of the Reinhardt set who would vent their anger against the locals by referring to them as 'fat beer-swillers' and 'small-time bourgeoisie'. Franz Rehrl resembled both, but favoured neither. He closed ranks with Reinhardt; outflanked the various festival societies by bringing the festival under the direct control of the Provincial Government; wooed and won over key figures in leading banks and in the treasury and education departments of the federal government in Vienna; commissioned the conversion for theatrical use of the old Riding School; chivvied tour operators and railway companies; entrusted programme planning to the Festival's newly appointed President, Robert Hildmann; and in February 1925 sent his old school chum Erwin Kerber to Vienna to try to do business with the men of the Philharmonic.

The demands of the Vienna Philharmonic were predictably steep, ruinously so for the financial director of a festival which was seriously strapped for cash. Kerber demurred, and found himself thinking aloud about the possibility – 'not at all what we want, you understand' – of opening negotiations with a 'German orchestra'. Kerber did not name the orchestra but there can be little doubt that the orchestra he had in mind was Furtwängler's Berlin Philharmonic. The Vienna Philharmonic promptly capitulated.

For the young Heribert, all this was an education in itself. Great orchestras jockeying for position and great conductors, too: Strauss and Franz Schalk, Clemens Krauss, Toscanini, Furtwängler, and Bruno Walter. For better or worse, musical *realpolitik* of a bitter and often vindictive nature was the common coin of Austrian musical life in Karajan's teenage years. And with Paumgartner himself often in the thick of it all, Karajan was specially well placed to listen and learn.

Once a deal had been struck in February 1925, the Vienna Philharmonic held exclusive sway over the Salzburg Festival until 1957 when Karajan, in his joint role as Artistic Director of the Festival and Chief Conductor of the Berlin Philharmonic, brought the Berlin orchestra to play five concerts under five different conductors.

The Vienna Philharmonic's right to play for the opera, however, was never seriously challenged even in Karajan's time. And rightly so. Back in 1931, the English critic Neville Cardus wrote in the *Manchester Guardian*:

I will go so far as to say that no orchestra in the world can play the Strauss of *Der Rosenkavalier* with half of the Vienna orchestra's lightness and swiftness of touch, its pride and verve of melody, its richness and refinement of harmony, and its freedom and felicity of rhythm. For years I have lived on memories of the Vienna orchestra as I heard it in boyhood. I had begun to think lately that these memories of youth, like all the memories of youth, were heightened and sweetened by time – the pathos of distance! But this week I find that I have not at all idealised the Vienna orchestra; that, indeed, it is a more enchanting orchestra than on dark days in Manchester winters I have ever dreamed.[9]

For the 1925 festival, the Vienna Philharmonic played *Don Giovanni* under Karl Muck, *Le nozze di Figaro* under Schalk, and (controversial innovation) two performances of Donizetti's *Don Pasquale* under Bruno Walter. *Das Salzburger grosse Welttheater* was revived, playing to packed houses in the newly renovated Felsenreitschule, and Reinhardt introduced to the festival another of his big international smash-hits *Das Mirakel*, a pantomime – music by Engelbert Humperdinck – that had originally been commissioned for Christmas performances at London's Olympia Theatre in 1911. With Humperdinck now dead, it fell to Paumgartner to adapt and conduct the music, which he did in conjunction with one of the most talented of Reinhardt's many camp-followers, the 26-year-old Bulgarian composer and virtuoso pianist, shortly to become a friend of Heribert, Pancho Vladigerov.

In later years, Karajan offered several explanations of why he exchanged the piano for conducting. One was that he was advised both by Bernhard Paumgartner and by his piano teacher in Vienna, Josef Hofmann,[10] that the piano alone would not satisfy him. Another was 'an inflamed tendon' in one of his hands. Certainly, by the age of sixteen he was playing some fairly taxing pieces. At a concert in the Mozarteum on 5 March 1925 he gave an explosively fiery account of Liszt's First Piano Concerto. The following year he played Liszt's *Hungarian Rhapsody* No.12 at the equivalent concert. He was also playing a good deal of Brahms, and learning chamber music repertory, too: the César Franck Sonata, which he performed in public with Salzburg violinist Josef Schmalwieser.[11]

However, it was the work he played on 12 May 1926 that may well have been his pianistic Waterloo. It was Pancho Vladigerov's First Piano Concerto, a punishingly difficult piece which Heribert is said to have learned in fourteen fretful days.

CHAPTER 5

Vienna

> When I came to Vienna, I thought I'd hear only the very best
> concerts. But I had a good enough ear to realise that even the
> Vienna Philharmonic gave bad concerts.
>
> Herbert von Karajan, *My Autobiography*

In March 1926, Herbert successfully completed his end-of-school exams.
The question was, what next? It was a question that set off, not so much
a battle, more a phoney war within the Karajan family.

Neither of [my parents] could ever make up their minds. If there was something
to be done, then it was 'Ask your father!' And he would say 'Ask your mother!'
Then they would try to find a solution between them. In the end, things stayed
as they were. I felt so hampered by this as a boy that I said I'd find my own
solutions. You may not be aware of it at first, but this turns you into the kind
of person who says: I'd like things to be as decisive as possible.[1]

That suggests a condition brought about by nurture rather than nature.
But, then, Karajan added: 'I wasn't born to be ordered around', which is
rather different.

His mother would probably have agreed with the second diagnosis. Once,
when Heribert was still quite young, she had taken the two boys with her on
a visit to a fashionable spa on the Austrian-Swiss border. In all probability
she had embarrassed Heribert with talk of his musical prowess, but it was
her turn to be embarrassed when he flatly refused to play the piano for
their fellow guests. From this point on, the story exists in two versions.
In one, a well-meaning old gentleman offered Heribert a modest financial
inducement to play, which he declined with the words, 'No one can buy
me.' In the other, he was offered a bicycle, which he similarly declined,
only to find the offer being taken up by his brother who duly entertained
the guests and secured the bicycle.

It was a characteristic of both boys, in fact, that neither was readily
bought. In their different ways, both were fiercely independent. Wolfgang,
the brilliantly inventive electrical engineer, refused all his life to be beholden
to big companies or corporations. (The German electrical firm Siemens
offered him his own independent in-house research facility, but he declined.)
Similarly, Karajan seems to have spent the greater part of his life seeking the
one thing he believed would make him completely happy: absolute mastery
over his own destiny.

Neither boy had been a teenage rebel, but the end of childhood marked for both of them the start of individual quests for independence. Herbert set his sights high from the outset. Wolfgang remembered him saying at the age of eighteen or nineteen: 'The direction doesn't matter. Whether it's conducting, skiing, or motor-racing, I simply want to be the best.'² Herbert even contemplated invading Wolfgang's world of engineering. He was convinced that the days of the petrol-driven internal combustion engine were numbered and that he, Herbert, would invent its successor.

Nor were these technological fantasies discouraged by his parents. Better, they reasoned, study engineering with the prospect of a 'real' job, than risk pursuing the chimera of a career in music. His mother fretted over Herbert's musical ambitions, 'But if you go deaf? What then?' His father, who as a young man had sacrificed acting to medicine, advised compromise: pursue your musical studies in Vienna but get some kind of technological qualification at the same time. Herbert appears to have accepted the compromise but then reneged on the idea when he got to Vienna. Though he went through the motions of applying to the Technische Hochschule, there is no evidence of his having attended any lectures or completed any course-work. Music was his dream, his private kingdom. It was also his father's world – for all that the old man had advised him otherwise – and a refuge from the domestic anxieties of his all too intrusive mother.

Ernst von Karajan does not seem to have resented his son's rapid defection to the Hochschule für Musik. One of Herbert's landladies in Vienna remembers the father arriving at his rooms shortly before Christmas with a handsome radiogram. He also brought scores and records. Thereafter, she recalls, Herbert spent many hours in front of the radiogram conducting the records. When she enquired, as is the habit of landladies, what it was, precisely, that he was doing, he replied: 'I am practising. One day I shall be a very famous conductor.'

There can be little doubt that during Herbert's time in Vienna he was obsessed by the craft of conducting and the work of the conductors he heard there. Not that it was quite such a dazzling constellation of conducting talent at the Vienna Opera as we might be led to believe. (Or singing talent. Karajan remembered: 'People today enthuse about Slezak, Piccaver and Schmedes. But most evenings it was Josef Kalenberg who sang. And quite respectably, too.'³) In the years 1926–8, Furtwängler appeared at the opera once, Toscanini not at all. There was Strauss, of course. Strauss conducting one of his own operas was bound to be a red-letter day in the life of any aspiring young musician. Massimo Freccia, who was a student in Vienna at much the same time as Karajan and whose brother Vieri Karajan later came to know and idolise, recalls a performance of *Salome* that Strauss conducted in Vienna in the late 1920s:

The dimming of the lights brought silence. Complete stillness, suspense; everyone's eyes converged on the orchestra pit. Richard Strauss mounted the rostrum, and with a slight nod acknowledged the thunderous applause. I was expecting an exuberant personality, dramatic gestures to drive his musicians through the tumultuous pages of the score. But his movements were composed, calm, almost detached. An impassive gaze in the direction of the brasses would unleash a stormy crescendo, a benign glance to the strings would calm their ferocity. He was like an unruffled trainer in a cage of lions, certain to emerge without a scratch. He brought the performance to an overwhelming finale. After the last crashing chords he shook hands with the leader and left unperturbed, avoiding the customary appearance on stage holding hands with the cast.[4]

The man Herbert would have heard most frequently, however, was the conductor he heard most frequently at the Salzburg Festival: Franz Schalk. A Bruckner pupil and Mahler's former deputy at the Opera, Schalk was possessed of a middling talent: a 'conductor of authoritative craftsmanship' as the Viennese critic Julius Korngold liked to describe such men. Karajan is sometimes written up as a pupil of Schalk. It is true that he met him, and sat in on his rehearsals, relishing his dry humour and coffee-house jibes; but he never studied with him. Karajan belonged to that species of pupil – the most talented, often – who prefers to observe at a distance, the quiet boy at the back of the class who absorbs everything and says little. Naturally retiring, he would ask himself: 'What possible interest can I be to someone like that?' His relations with Clemens Krauss would be similarly circumspect.

Schalk, Heger, Karl Alwin: these were some of the regular conductors at the Vienna Opera during Karajan's time as a student. Stung by Richard Strauss's jibes about his lack of adventurousness, Schalk was dutiful in his attitude to new music, as Karajan would later be, to similarly muted acclaim. Heger programmed the Viennese première of Puccini's last opera *Turandot*, Stravinsky's *Oedipus Rex*, Ravel's *L'enfant et les sortilèges*, Korngold's *Das Wunder der Heliane*, and, most controversially, Ernst Krenek's *Jonny spielt auf*. 'A wicked Jewish-Negro besmirching of the State Opera, the world's leading place of art and learning' screamed the Nazi handouts, inviting 'Christian Viennese men and women, artists, musicians, singers, and anti-Semites' to stage a protest at the Opera. In the event, the production was a sell-out. Heger conducted, and though both he and Schalk loathed the piece, they spared no expense on the production, packing the stage with all manner of modern gimmicks: a train, a motor car, a radio, telephones, searchlights.

As a student, Karajan had particularly easy access to the State Opera. His father's younger brother Emanuel 'Max' von Karajan, a civil engineer by training, had been a senior house manager at the Opera since before the First World War. (He retired in the 1930s and died in Vienna in 1947 aged seventy-six.) He must have been a man of some consequence. Among his duties was the swearing in of new employees. In the heyday of the Vienna Opera, no one could work there without first swearing an oath of allegiance to *the house itself*.

For Karajan, every visit to the opera involved meticulous preparation. Though he was not the most gregarious of students, he had enough friends for his immediate needs. In particular, there were the play-throughs-cum-study-sessions Karajan and his friends would arrange ahead of any visit. These involved a couple of pianists providing a four-handed accompaniment, a conductor (more practice), and as much improvised singing as they could muster. There were also the debriefings:

After our visits to the opera, we always used to sit together until the early hours and discuss what we thought was right or wrong about the performance. A dubious undertaking, of course! But one thing is certain: in doing all this, we acquired an extremely accurate knowledge of the repertory.[5]

Herbert was generally well liked by his fellow students despite a *de haut en bas* manner that bordered on the autocratic. Curiously, this was something they found more endearing than intimidating: the well-heeled boy from the provinces with his old-fashioned manners and well-nurtured sense of self-esteem. Later, in Salzburg, he would occasionally unbend sufficiently to address his old university colleagues as '*Du*'. In Vienna, he addressed everyone as '*Sie*', a quirk that did not go unnoticed, though for the most part it was interpreted, not as arrogance, merely as a misplaced belief that Heribert Ritter von Karajan, scion of a famous Viennese family, had every right to exercise a degree of formality in his relations with his fellow students.

Though Karajan studied a full range of subjects at the Hochschule für Musik, the course he immediately enrolled for was conducting. Unfortunately, there was no conductor to teach it; Vienna's way, perhaps, of saying that conductors are born, not made. Karajan's professor in the conducting class was the tirelessly versatile Alexander Wunderer, the 49-year-old principal oboe of the Vienna Philharmonic and, between 1923 and 1932, the orchestra's Chairman. To all outward appearances, Wunderer was an easygoing Austrian. When the president of the Reichstag greeted the Vienna Philharmonic on the station platform in Berlin during the orchestra's 1925 German tour, Chairman Wunderer clambered off the train in his travelling clothes, complete with rucksack and climbing boots.[6] Yet it was Wunderer who brokered Furtwängler's coming to the Vienna Philharmonic in the late 1920s in the face of the conductor's extensive commitments to the Berlin Philharmonic and Leipzig Gewandhaus orchestras. Perhaps it was no bad thing having an orchestral chairman as one's conducting teacher.

The successful conductor is not simply a musician; he is also a manager of men.

There is little evidence of Karajan's having had very much social life in Vienna. His fellow students remember him as being more or less totally preoccupied with music and theatre. The snatched sandwich in the canteen, the cursory chat, the rapid return to a rehearsal or the next event in a crowded calendar. Certainly, there was a lot going on. Writing home on 3 November 1927, he told his parents:

Things are very active now on the concert scene. I often go to the Opera. Recently I heard Ernst von Dohnányi's piano recital; today I'm going to hear Verdi's *Requiem*, Furtwängler conducting, tomorrow there is a symphony concert by Clemens Krauss. For Friday Uncle Max has got me tickets to a performance of the important Moscow Artists' Union. On our evening they will be performing Maxim Gorky's *Nachtasyl*. Sunday, Fritz Kreisler is giving a matinée at the Opera, and I'm hoping to get a ticket for it. Recently, I did my very first conducting – Weber's *Euryanthe* Overture. After ten minutes, conductor and orchestra understood each other perfectly . . . I'm hoping for a second performance before Christmas. The orchestra and I are working on Bruckner's *Romantic* Symphony [No.4].[7]

In later years, when Karajan made his famously unexpected recording of works by Schoenberg, Webern, and Berg he talked about student riots at the Workers' Symphony Concerts that Webern used to conduct in Vienna in the 1920s. But there is no indication of his having been anything much more than an interested onlooker of the New Music scene, something that perhaps sheds some light on the one respect in which he was a less than model student at the Hochschule: his refusal to complete, let alone submit for examination, any of his own compositions.

Was this a fear of not doing well; a variation on his old fear 'What can I possibly say that would be of any interest to him'? Or a fear of failure? Or, possibly, of revealing too much about himself? Whatever the reason, it marks a certain limitation. As Christoph von Dohnányi has put it: 'In the last resort, it doesn't matter how good – or bad – a symphony by Klemperer is. The fact is, it is a process he has gone through and therefore a process which he is better able to grasp.'[8]

The more immediate problem for Karajan was that it was impossible to complete the conducting course without receiving a pass in all the prescribed subjects, including composition. Furthermore, when it came to composition, Karajan was not dealing with some hired help but with the Head of the Hochschule himself, Franz Schmidt. Schmidt was a composer, conductor, virtuoso pianist, and celebrated cellist. In Mahler's judgement, he was the finest of all the Vienna Philharmonic cellists, and in other people's he was an incomparable player of the cello within chamber ensembles. The Austrian-born music critic Hans Keller called him quite simply 'the most complete musician I have ever come across in my life'.

When I talk about 'the most complete musician', I am talking about a type of musician no longer extant: under the influence of the inescapable assault on our ears which contemporary civilization confronts us with, our power of aural concentration and our quality of listening have deteriorated to an extent which, *pro tempore*, make the birth of a Franz Schmidt impossible. What am I talking about? About the simple fact that he knew, and remembered, all music. Whatever you raised, whether it was a point about a tricky passage in the *Matthew* Passion or *John* Passion, in a Bruckner symphony and, yes, in Schoenberg's *Transfigured Night* or *Gurrelieder*, he would jump up, waddle across to the piano, and play the passage in question in an instant, perfect piano arrangement, stressing the inner part you happened to be talking about.9

Schmidt was also a man who venerated the improvisatory spirit in music. It was for this reason that he distrusted musicians such as Josef Hofmann (Karajan's piano teacher) and Karl Doktor, the viola player in the Busch Quartet.

Karajan always spoke warmly of Schmidt, possibly because in the confrontation over the composition exam it was Schmidt who backed down. Oddly enough, none of Karajan's fellow students seems to have been at all aggrieved by this. 'The conducting talent was so overwhelming,' one of them later recalled, 'it would have been absurd to fail him.'10

Not that Karajan got away scot-free. If the young man was unable to submit an original composition, Schmidt insisted, then he must at least demonstrate his skills as an orchestrator. Karajan duly obliged with a version for full orchestra of the opening movement of Beethoven's Piano Sonata in C, Op.2 No.3.

In the students' final conducting exam, Karajan once again insisted on doing things his way:

The programme consisted mainly of arias and duets; all we had to do was to accompany. I banked everything on being allowed to conduct the only work that was actually intended for the orchestra – the overture to Rossini's *William Tell*. The rehearsals were held in the presence of the entire professional staff; Franz Schmidt was the principal and took the chair. Those of my fellow students who had preceded me had gone through their paces and shown themselves to be as effective as was possible in the circumstances. Then I came and worked with the orchestra. We were expected simply to conduct the overture straight through, but even at that stage I was saying things like, 'Each trumpet on its own, please' and 'No, there is no rhythm in what you are playing'. I worked in this way for about ten minutes on the trumpets' first entry. Franz Schmidt then stood up and announced that the test was over. 'I believe, gentlemen, that we now know enough,' he said.11

It says a good deal for Karajan's sense of self-esteem that he took Schmidt's remark to be a compliment. Perhaps it was. Here at least, he must have thought, is a born rehearser. In later years, Karajan would advise the select band of young conductors whom he allowed to follow him on attachment: 'I cannot teach you how to conduct, but I can show you how to rehearse in such a way that, when you come to the concert itself, you will barely need to conduct.'

The graduation concert at the end of the conducting course took place on 17 December 1928. It left Karajan just enough time to pack his belongings and return to Salzburg for Christmas. Meanwhile, back in Salzburg, plans were being laid for his first professional appearance as a conductor.

CHAPTER 6

A leader of suggestive power

What is a conductor's gesture? It's merely the
prolongation of his musical will.

Walter Legge

Though Karajan had lodged in Vienna for the best part of two and a half
years, he had made numerous trips home to Salzburg. He had been at
home on Sunday, 22 May 1927 for a concert given by Furtwängler and
the Berlin Philharmonic in Salzburg's newly built Festival Hall. It was the
first time he had heard either Furtwängler or the orchestra he himself
would one day command. As for the programme, it was a feast fit to
set before any prince or Young Pretender: the Prelude to Wagner's *Die
Meistersinger*, Beethoven's *Eroica* Symphony, Strauss's *Till Eulenspiegel*,
and three of Brahms's *Hungarian Dances*.

They were stirring times. The day before the Furtwängler concert, the
American Charles Lindbergh completed his sensational flight across the
Atlantic, the first solo flight, and the first without radio. The response,
on both sides of the Atlantic, verged on the hysterical. In his book *Rites
of Spring*, Modris Eksteins suggests:

The modern sensibility was exhilarated. It was enchanted above all by the *deed*.
Lindbergh had not swum the Atlantic, nor rowed across it nor catapulted over
it. He had flown! Man and machine had become one in this act of daring. The
purpose was immaterial. The act was everything. It almost captured Gide's
pre-war vision of the *acte gratuit*, a perfectly free act, devoid of meaning other
than its own inherent energy and accomplishment. And Lindbergh had been
alone in his flight, completely alone, free of civilisation and its constraints, in
communion with the oceans and the stars, the winds and the rains. He flew
for no one, not even mankind. He flew for himself. That was the greatest
audacity . . . He was not the creation of an old world; he was the harbinger
of a new dawn.[1]

A Fascist dawn, as it happened; Lindbergh turned out to be a right-wing
ideologue and an enthusiastic supporter of Nazi Germany. In America
in 1940 Lindbergh's wife published a pacifist, anti-interventionist tract
entitled *The Wave of the Future*. In it, the Lindberghs argue that to resist
Nazism is to resist change, 'and to resist change is a sin against life itself'.

The idea of progress as a force it is morally wrong to resist had established
itself as a potentially virulent organism in the gut of the German body politic
well before the First World War. This, too, was part of the intellectual

baggage inherited by the young Herbert Karajan whose admiration for a man like Lindbergh must have been immense.

Other worlds were changing, too. Two powerfully emergent forces in mass entertainment, cinema and the gramophone, were in the process of being transformed by the advent of electrical recording. In 1925, Robert Wiene of Pan-Film, Vienna cajoled Richard Strauss into writing music for a screen adaptation of his opera *Der Rosenkavalier*. The film was premièred in Dresden and London in 1926, and reached Salzburg the following year.

And there was Cecil B. De Mille's *King of Kings*. If anything was likely to render obsolete Max Reinhardt's peculiar form of theatrical epic, it was epic cinema. Which is presumably how De Mille and the Machiavellis of his marketing department saw it. Reinhardt's show-piece Salzburg stage production in the summer of 1927 was Shakespeare's *A Midsummer Night's Dream*, for which he used Mendelssohn's incidental music (and the 19-year-old Herbert Karajan as his principal répétiteur). The production was upstaged, however, by *King of Kings*, which was given its European première in Salzburg during the festival.[2]

*

The years 1926–8 had seen the Salzburg Festival both establish itself and undergo a strange kind of paralysis. When Karajan returned home in the winter of 1928–9, the festival was again in crisis. Committees were being set up, reports written.

One report, an anonymous paper entitled 'The Case of Max Reinhardt', rehearsed objections that, fifty years on, would frequently be levelled at Karajan himself. Reinhardt, it was said, was attracting the wrong kind of people to the festival, monied Americans and the social élite. He was a great artist, but he was cold, ruthless in dismissing artists of whom he did not approve. He was also an immensely successful businessman, with business interests that fed in significant measure off the Salzburg Festival.

Franz Rehrl would have none of these criticisms. The following year a bust of Reinhardt was placed in the festival theatre and the square opposite was renamed Max Reinhardt Platz. Reinhardt was deeply touched. He wrote to Rehrl: 'I have learned during my life that it is as difficult to put into practice a work of art as it is to create one . . . I have also learned that in this life, gratitude is a rare commodity.'[3]

Rehrl was right; sniping at Reinhardt was a futile activity. He had more or less founded the festival (as Karajan would later found the Easter and Whitsun festivals) and the festival needed him as much as he, for the time being, needed it. The other reports were more practical, in particular a report drawn up by three influential locals: the politician Gehmacher, Paumgartner, and the cathedral choirmaster Joseph Messner.

Messner is an interesting figure, not least because he represented a body of 'local', old-fashioned musical values which the young Karajan was in revolt against and which the older Karajan would partly return to. Messner was born in Schwaz in the Tyrol in 1893. He studied music in Innsbruck and Munich, and in 1926 succeeded Franz Gruber (grandson of the man who wrote *Silent Night*) as Director of Cathedral Music in Salzburg. It is said that the revival of the old traditions of performing church music were especially close to his heart.⁴ And, indeed, we can judge for ourselves. Gramophone records exist of Mozart's *Coronation Mass* and *Requiem* recorded in Salzburg under Messner's direction during the festivals of 1930 and 1931.⁵ They are performances of considerable power, steadily paced, hefty, but with a quality of spiritual certainty about them that eludes many we hear nowadays. Even more interesting are recordings Messner made in the late 1940s or early 1950s of a number of Mozart's Sonatas for Organ and Orchestra with the Mozarteum Orchestra and Paul Walter.⁶ This is Mozart in lederhosen, the gait of the music-making unmistakably Austrian.

Paumgartner and Messner did not get on, but they respected each other's work and, for the most part, kept off each other's territory. Karajan, the Paumgartner protégé, knew Messner; indeed, Messner provided a character reference for Karajan during the post-war denazification hearings. But relations were never especially cordial. In the winter of 1948–9 Messner attempted to block a decision by the festival organisers to invite Karajan to conduct the Verdi *Requiem* at the 1949 festival. 'Opera conductors' who meddled with sacred music were not to his liking. The objection was ignored, but Messner seems to have made a point of his own by putting Rossini's *Stabat mater* – another work erroneously thought to be 'operatic' by the world at large – into the schedule of cathedral music for the 1949 festival.

*

It was against this background of old-fashioned values and a certain conservative provincialism that Herbert Karajan made his public début as a conductor in the Salzburg Mozarteum on 22 January 1929. He struck the city like forked lightning. 'It was like being connected up to an electricity pylon and having 40,000 volts run through us,' one of the players recalled with all the pride of a man who touched the pylon and survived.⁷ Not for Karajan a circumspect and geometrically correct beat; rather, the players found themselves galvanised into action by tremendous slashes of the baton.

The prospect of having the 20-year-old Herbert Karajan standing in front of them had not filled members of the Mozarteum Orchestra with unalloyed joy. They were not used to being treated as guinea-pigs by aspiring young conductors, and they were not inclined to make an exception for the son of Primarius Dr Ernst von Karajan. As for Dr von Karajan, he had merely promised to play the clarinet and underwrite any losses the concert might incur, though with the indefatigable Walter Hofstötter managing the business side of the evening there was not much danger of that. (Karajan's later claim that he underwrote the concert with his own money is a fiction, another paragraph in the epic tale of himself as a self-made phenomenon.) In the event, it was Karajan's skills as a rehearser that saw him through; in rehearsal he was as calm, as patient, as practical as any orchestral *routinier* could reasonably hope for.

The programme consisted of Tchaikovsky's Fifth Symphony, Mozart's Piano Concerto K488, and Strauss's *Don Juan*. The soloist in the Mozart was the 23-year-old Yella (Gabriella) Pessl, a girl Herbert had become friendly with at the Hochschule für Musik in Vienna. Pessl's real love was the harpsichord, an instrument Karajan was also learning to play at this time.[8]

Naturally, the local press had ears only for the young *wunderkind*. The *Salzburger Volksblatt* published one of those long, high-flown, often impenetrable reports that German provincial papers specialised in at the time. The prose is dense, the syntax convoluted, yet the essential judgements are sharp enough, with such observations as:

. . . a strong disciplined conductor's will with a capacity to assert itself . . . Stick-technique and posture calm. Not a declamatory conductor, but a leader of suggestive power . . . The work's construction laid bare . . . the primeval power of Karajan's musicality and the intuitive way in which he influences the orchestra . . .[9]

Herbert must have been in his father's good books, too, for it was around this time that he acquired a motor-bike, a Harley Davidson. After rehearsals, selected friends in the orchestra would be treated to a private inspection of the beast; the inspection over, Herbert would leap into the saddle and roar off through the streets of Salzburg 'like a hussar leading a cavalry charge'. The origins of this lifelong interest in high-speed locomotion can also be traced back to Paumgartner. He, too, was a motor-bike addict. Like the soldier-musician hero of Louis de Bernières's *Captain Corelli's Mandolin*, the two of them loved their motor-bikes as only true-born musicians can:

'Just listen,' he cried, 'it's metronomic. And you could play a tune to it. That tempo, it's perfect, not a beat missed, not a hesitation. It's a musical machine, bubble, bubble, bubble, and the exhaust, it sings.[10]

Paumgartner was not surprised by Herbert's success. He had always regarded him as a natural, a born conductor.

As far as Herbert's studies as a conductor are concerned, I think he had – how shall I put it? – very little technical instruction. He had a really great natural gift and . . . I think I even had a certain part in it – that part of his conducting skill developed from his sporting ability: movement, freedom of movement, and a capacity to relax. You see, there are so many conductors who would like to imitate Herbert, but they end up as couch conductors . . . In his case, the movements came about of their own accord, let's say from a thought process which transformed itself into something physical without being felt.[11]

The Karajans and their circle of friends had seen to it that the concert was well attended. Provincial Governor Rehrl, President of the Salzburg Festival, was given a seat of honour. He was so impressed by the concert, he summoned the young man and placed a laurel wreath around his neck. More important, though, was the response of a member of the audience who was not from Salzburg. His name was Erwin Dieterich.[12] He came from Ulm, and he came bearing gifts.

CHAPTER 7

A young bandmaster from Ulm

'A young bandmaster from Ulm called Karajan.'
'From Ulm?' exclaimed Reinhardt. 'How long has he been there?'
'Five years, Professor.'
'Five years in Ulm,' said Reinhardt with a regretful wave of the hand. 'Nothing will come of *him*!'

Erwin Dieterich, General Manager of the Stadttheater in Ulm, was on a scouting mission; the opera company in Ulm needed a new assistant Kapellmeister. It is unlikely that Dieterich was in Salzburg by chance. Since he had no funds to speak of, he was in search of a young man, a graduate, possibly, hungry for work. Whether Dieterich had trawled the music academies, received a tip-off, or merely kept his ear close to the ground is not recorded. The fact is, he came, he heard, and he offered the young man work.

The initial offer was based on the idea of a trial performance. Karajan was tempted. He desperately wanted to conduct; it was for this reason he had turned down the offer of bread-and-butter work as a house répétiteur with the Vienna Opera. None the less, he rejected Dieterich's proposal:

I told him, 'It's pointless. I'll come at once if you'll give me the chance to conduct a new production. At the end of the week you can tell me if you don't like me, and I'll go away with no hard feelings. But I myself would like to rehearse the work you want me to conduct.'[1]

Even though Karajan was only twenty, this is what we would now recognise as a typical Karajan response. A certain mindset is already evident.

Karajan admitted that he had never conducted a complete opera. On the other hand, he argued, he was already steeped in opera. He had studied, watched, and listened. He had observed at first hand some of its greatest practitioners. To the best of his abilities, he had made his calculations. 'The difference between a dog and a cat,' he used to say, 'is that a dog jumps out of a window, a cat looks before it jumps.' On this occasion, he had looked and was ready to jump.

Impressed by the young man's honesty and confidence, and by the logic of his arguments, Dieterich invited him to conduct Ulm's forthcoming production of Mozart's *Le nozze di Figaro* scheduled to open on 2 March.

*

The city of Ulm stands astride the Danube midway between Munich and Stuttgart. Karajan arrived there in the gloom of a late winter's afternoon towards the end of January 1929. Five years later, on a similarly dark and snow-bound January afternoon, there arrived in Ulm an English schoolboy who was to become a hero of wartime operations in Crete and one of the finest writers of his age. His name was Patrick Leigh Fermor. In *A Time of Gifts* he describes Ulm as he found it in the early 1930s.

A late medieval atmosphere filled the famous town. The vigorous Teutonic interpretation of the Renaissance burst out in the corbels and the mullions of jutting windows and proliferated round thresholds. At the end of each high civic building a zigzag of isosceles rose and dormers and flat gables lifted their gills along enormous roofs that looked as if they were tiled with the scales of pangolins. Shields carved in high relief projected from the walls. Many were charged with the double-headed eagle. This bird was emblematic of the town's status as an Imperial City: it meant that Ulm – unlike the neighbouring towns and provinces, which had become the fiefs of lesser sovereigns – was subject only to the Emperor. It was a Reichstadt.

Leigh Fermor began to explore the town in the midwinter gloom.

A flight of steps led to the lower part of the town. Here the storeys beetled and almost touched and in one of the wider lanes was a warren of carpenters and saddlers and smithies and cavernous workshops. Down the middle, visible through a few chopped holes, a river rushed ice-carapaced and snow-quilted under a succession of narrow bridges ... This part of the town contained nothing later than the Middle Ages, or so it appeared. A kind of crone outside a harness-maker's saw me peering down a hole in the ice. 'It's full of Forellen!' she said. Trout? 'Ja, Forellen! Voll, voll davon.' How did they manage under that thick shell of ice? Hovering suspended in the dark? Or hurtling along on their Schubertian courses, hidden and headlong? Were they in season? If so, I determined to go bust and get hold of one for dinner, and a bottle of Franconian wine. Meanwhile, night was falling fast. High up in the snowfall a bell began booming slowly. *Funera plango!* a deep and solemn note. *Fulgura frango!* It might have been tolling an Emperor's passing, for war, siege, revolt, plague, excommunication, a ban of interdict, or Doomsday: '*Excito lentis! Dissipo ventos! Paco cruentos!*'[2]

Had Leigh Fermor been so minded, he could have added to his sense of an all-embracing German medievalism that evening by attending Ulm's Theater der Reichsfestung where Wagner's *Lohengrin* was being played under the direction of Heribert Ritter von Karajan.

That was January 1934. And it was a production of *Lohengrin* which Karajan stumbled upon when he first arrived in Ulm in 1929. It was, he later admitted, a terrible shock after Vienna and Salzburg. The theatre was tiny and ill-equipped, the orchestra so small that such brass players as there were had to commute, fully costumed, between their on-stage and off-stage roles. For Mozart, though, a 500-seat theatre, tiny stage, and small orchestra are not necessarily disadvantages. Indeed, it was during his time at Ulm that Karajan came to cherish the skills of two composers whose scoring always seemed 'right', whatever the size of the orchestra: Mozart and Verdi. *Die Hochzeit des Figaro* – the Ulm performances were sung in German, in Hermann Levi's translation – was certainly a convenient work with which to launch a career in a small provincial house.

Throughout his career, Karajan tended to conduct *Figaro* rather rapidly. Comparing Fritz Busch's 1934 Glyndebourne recording of the opera with the recording Karajan made for EMI in Vienna in 1950, the founder editor of *Opera* Lord Harewood wrote:

Neither [Busch's] orchestra nor, in the final analysis, his cast is as good as Karajan's, but he is relaxed where Karajan is relentless, urbane where Karajan is demonic, and he gives the voices (and thus the music) time to speak where Karajan clips both short.[3]

In 1929, players in the Ulm orchestra also complained of quick speeds and missed beats. Indeed, Karajan himself admitted, in a letter to his parents at the time of the Ulm revival of *Figaro* in 1934, that back in 1929 he had been flying by the seat of his pants. And yet the critics were kind enough:

In Saturday's performance, which was a good one and which will be very good after a second repeat, the new Kapellmeister Herbert von Karajan introduced himself. He has the vitality, and apparently the necessary musical talent to explore a work in depth. The overture was brought out very sensitively, with the light and shade excellently distributed. When he and the orchestra are fully accustomed to each other, many further good and beautiful things are expected of Karajan.[4]

Within a week of the opening night of *Figaro*, it was announced that Kapellmeister Herbert von Karajan would be assuming new and more permanent responsibilities for the 1929–30 season at Ulm. Karajan telegraphed home with the news. The announcement was not conclusive proof of the wisdom of his choice of career, but it was a start.

Shortly after the announcement, Karajan conducted and played in a sparsely attended Sunday morning Mozart Matinée in Ulm. The audience loved it but the critical reception was less friendly. The critic of the *Schwäbischer Volksbote* expressed himself mildly surprised to find a bandmaster who was both a fine pianist *and* a man conversant with the essence of Mozart. The 'D minor Concerto for two pianos, originally for piano and string orchestra' [*sic*] was, we are told, remarkably well played. (It was, in fact, a two-piano version of the D minor Concerto, K466 played with great *élan* by Karajan and Otto Schulmann, the senior conductor at Ulm, who supplied the accompaniment.) This was the only praise the critic was willing to bestow. '*Eine kleine Nachtmusik* played at *this* tempo?' he remarked, not deigning to specify the offending tempo. As for Mozart's *Kegelstatt* Trio, this, he said, was palpably under-rehearsed. 'Does Herr von Karajan not realise that merely playing the notes is no way to make such a piece palatable?[5]

But how much rehearsal time had there been? The Matinée also featured Geo Monthy and Else Barther, Karajan's Count and Countess from *Figaro*, singing songs and arias by Mozart, accompanied by Karajan at the keyboard.

*

If the Mozart Trio was under-rehearsed, so was Karajan's next venture. Returning to Salzburg in time for his twenty-first birthday on 5 April 1929, he agreed to conduct a single performance of Richard Strauss's *Salome* which Walter Hofstötter was staging (it was the work's Salzburg première) in the Festspielhaus on 19 April. With players arriving from Vienna to augment the Mozarteum Orchestra, and a shoestring budget, orchestral rehearsals were limited to a single run-through. Sitting in the front row was Karajan's mother, desperate to know from a friendly musician whether Herbert was coping or not. She need not have worried. Reviewing the performance, the *Salzburger Volksblatt* was astounded, not so much by the production, as by the conductor's nerve.

Herbert Karajan mastered the score's difficulties with an astonishing air of superiority. Detail was clearly and compellingly placed within an intellectually cogent ground-plan; at the same time, he allowed this splendidly coloured night-piece to surge over us in a passionate glow.[6]

The orchestral players from Vienna, two of them from the Philharmonic, were equally astonished and would remember the event to Karajan's advantage in years to come.

Salome over, Karajan left for Vienna where the company of La Scala, Milan was to perform Donizetti's *Lucia di Lammermoor* and Verdi's *Falstaff* under Toscanini's direction. What a relief, and what a revelation those May evenings in the gallery of the Vienna Opera would have been after Ulm's *Die Hochzeit des Figaro* and Salzburg's *Salome*! Here were performances of supreme musical accomplishment that had been rehearsed to a fine tilth. Here, too, were Italian voices singing Italian music *in Italian*. What had the poet Heine said? Italian music is made for Italian throats as surely as Strasbourg pâtés are made for the throats of gourmets.

Though he was now Kapellmeister Herbert von Karajan, he continued to sit in the fourth gallery with his old friends from the claque, those vociferous denizens of the upper tiers who can make or break an artist or a performance. And it is as well that he did. With the Milanese singing unfamiliar repertory in an unfamiliar language, the members of the claque would have been at a loss had Karajan not been there to give their leader the necessary cues.

The La Scala *Falstaff*, with Mariano Stabile in the title role, had a great influence on Karajan theatrically as well as musically. He would later remember:

To be sure, Toscanini had employed a stage director; but basically the essential conception came from him. The agreement between the music and the stage performance was something totally inconceivable to us. Instead of people standing pointlessly around, here everything had its place and purpose.[7]

As for *Lucia di Lammermoor*:

Lucia was branded in Vienna as a hurdy-gurdy opera. When we heard that Toscanini wanted to conduct this in Vienna, I too honestly asked myself after playing through the vocal score, 'What can there be in this?' And it is astonishing that this music, which in a routine repertoire performance or in a piano play-through can sound truly banal, was made to sound not at all banal. It was simply another type of music. There are wonderful melodies, of course, even if they are not always immediately memorable; yet when one heard it under Toscanini, the music took on infinite significance.[8]

In 1956 Karajan would bring his own La Scala, Milan production of *Lucia di Lammermoor* to the Vienna State Opera with Maria Callas in the title role. Like Toscanini, he would ensure that music and stage movement were indissolubly linked. As Franco Zeffirelli recalled:

[Karajan] didn't even try to direct. He just arranged everything around [Callas]. She did the Mad Scene with a follow-spot like a ballerina against black. Nothing else. He let her be music, absolute music.[9]

During the early 1930s Karajan became something of a camp-follower of Toscanini. In May 1930 he again travelled to Vienna, this time to hear him conducting the New York Philharmonic. Two months later he was off on his motor-cycle to Bayreuth where Toscanini was making his début in Siegfried Wagner's long-awaited new production of *Tannhäuser* (to the fury of conductor Karl Muck and the 'Bayreuth for the Germans' lobby). Fewer journeys were needed when Toscanini began to make regular appearances at the Salzburg Festival between 1934 and 1937; as one of the festival's official répétiteurs, Karajan had almost unlimited access to Toscanini's rehearsals for *Falstaff, Fidelio, Die Meistersinger*, and *Die Zauberflöte*.

*

In the summer of 1929 it was back to a more workaday kind of reality. While preparing for the winter season in Ulm, Karajan took on work around Salzburg. In June he conducted the end-of-term production of Lortzing's *Der Waffenschmied* for Dr Gross's Opera School at the Mozarteum. In September, he conducted *Tosca* in the town cinema in nearby Berchtesgaden. This was another of Walter Hofstötter's shows; Paumgartner had conducted it in Salzburg, now Karajan took over the roadshow. It was *Tosca* with an orchestra of seventeen players plus piano and harmonium. The title role was sung by a girl called Helen Gahagan, a young American whose career would eventually take her via Broadway and Hollywood to a seat in the United States Congress.

For the 1929–30 Ulm season Karajan was entrusted with five operas: Verdi's *Rigoletto*, Flotow's *Martha*, Mascagni's *Cavalleria rusticana* (part of a double bill with Cornelius's *Der Barbier von Bagdad* conducted by the theatre répétiteur Max Kojetinsky), Mozart's *Don Giovanni*, and Weinberger's *Schwanda der Dudelsackpfeifer*.[10] Since the Ulm theatre also had to accommodate stage plays and operetta – for the 1930–1 season, the percentage share was opera 15.3 per cent, operetta 35.6 per cent, theatre 49.1 per cent – this was a substantial share of the operatic programme.

Such opera productions as there were used the *stagione* system whereby a production is given a single limited run of performances within a season rather than being retained in a permanently rotating repertory. Karajan rather liked the *stagione* system; as Director of the Vienna Opera in the late 1950s he took the house ever closer to it. In Ulm, the policy was dictated by economic necessity and a severe lack of storage space.

Karajan's salary at Ulm was modest even by Ulm's standards. Where a member of the Ulm theatre orchestra could expect to earn something in the region of RM 240 a month, Karajan's salary was RM 80. It kept him in board and lodging, such food as he bothered with, and fuel for his Harley Davidson. He lived frugally, spent little on clothes, and continued to send his washing home to his mother in Salzburg – at her insistence, no doubt. (The return parcels usually included such things as soap and toothpaste.) After moving lodgings in the autumn of 1933, he even got his beer cheaply; his new rooms were sublet to him by the director of a local brewery. In the fullness of time, and to satisfy his pride, he put in for a rise, helped by some generous lobbying from the orchestra. Dieterich was unimpressed: 'You must be joking! He's our apprentice. He should be paying us for everything he is learning here.'[11]

Dieterich was right. For the first – and certainly not for the last – time in his life Karajan was working on terms that were more or less of his own choosing. As second conductor in Ulm, he was a kind of sorcerer's apprentice, paid next to nothing but able to learn the trade of the opera conductor: not just conducting and chorus-training, but lighting, stage design, stage management, finance, administration, publicity and even a bit of acting thrown in by way of good measure. What Ulm provided was an all-expenses-paid postgraduate course tailored precisely to his needs.

General Manager Dieterich was exactly the right person to oversee such a programme, for he, too, was a man of many talents. He had come to Ulm from Stuttgart in 1925. During the late 1920s, in an all too short period of economic upswing, he had revitalised the Ulm theatre, bringing in new ideas, new repertory, even a certain amount of 'new' technology. A modern-dress *Faust*, operas by Janáček, back-projections: Ulm was aghast. But Dieterich also endeared himself to his audiences. As well as being a first-rate administrator and a skilful stage director, he was also a fine actor and an accomplished performer in musicals and operetta. His Danilo in *Die lustige Witwe*, his Eisenstein in *Die Fledermaus*, and his Adam, the eponymous bird-seller of Zeller's *Der Vogelhändler*, were all admired and enjoyed.

Karajan would have liked to get in on the operetta act, too; but, like many opera houses, Ulm employed its own *chef de cuisine* for operetta. The story goes that Karajan begged the operetta director Eugen Neff to let him conduct the overture at the première of a new production of *Die Fledermaus*. 'Provided I can conduct the Prelude at the première of your new production of *Lohengrin*,' Neff retorted, a quid pro quo Karajan brusquely declined.

*

Ulm's first Kapellmeister, Otto Schulmann, was the musically gifted son of a Munich banker. If Karajan's own testimony is to be believed, Schulmann was that rare but not unknown phenomenon, a Jew who was also an ardent supporter of the National Socialists. There was, however, a difference. Where groups like Dr Max Naumann's League of German Nationalist Jews praised Hitler's economic policies while at the same time hoping to establish some kind of *modus vivendi* with the National Socialists,[12] Schulmann seems to have been far more hard-headed, reconciled to the inevitability of his own exile. (He emigrated to the United States in 1933.) Tracked down in San Francisco many years later by Karajan biographer Robert C. Bachmann, Schulmann was unforthcoming:

The statement that Karajan and I were friends is the only one that is entirely correct [Bachmann does not reveal what other ideas he had placed before Schulmann] . . . the fantasies of later jealous and self-important people about an important man merit no attention from me.[13]

The division of duties between Schulmann and Karajan seems to have been made on a basis of mutual respect. Certainly, whenever Schulmann conducted, Karajan was usually either backstage, or on stage fully costumed cueing the chorus by a system of his own devising. Of the two conductors,

Karajan was the less experienced and the more assertive. When rehearsing a difficult passage or one requiring a special quality of sound or rhythmic articulation, he would insist on each musician playing it alone. The players were not especially enamoured of this, but they accepted it as being consistent with the house's diligent style. As one old double-bass player, Fritz Kaiser – no great fan of Karajan – later put it: 'There are two professions where you can't do without discipline: the military and the musical.'

Since the theatre itself was used for plays as well as operas, music rehearsals often took place in a large reception room in the Ship Hotel, no great distance on a motor-bike but a fair journey by handcart, the only available method of transporting the orchestral instruments. The orchestra itself was thirty-two strong, with a chorus of twelve that could be expanded to twenty, a tight fit on the theatre's tiny stage. If extra musicians were needed – usually brass or woodwind – Kaiser would cycle round Ulm trying to rustle up players from the local military bands. If they declined his request, Kaiser recalls, 'Karajan then swept round on his motor-bike like a maniac.' That usually did the trick. It is not true, however, that Karajan used the pit piano to supplement the orchestral sound. The piano was used only in emergencies, if a key player went sick or failed to appear. In such circumstances, it was a case of minimising the shortcomings and 'preserving the artistic impression' (Dieterich's phrase).

Karajan told his first biographer, Ernst Haeusserman, that the Ulm orchestra was dreadful, that he trained himself to listen to an imaginary ideal while the real orchestra was playing. He was similarly dismissive of the chorus: 'manual workers who could not even read music'.[14] When Haeusserman's book appeared in 1968, Karajan was accused by the local *Südwestpresse* of dragging the nursery of his talents through the mud. His remarks, the paper suggested, were at best ungentlemanly, at worst untrue.[15]

The remarks about the chorus certainly were ungentlemanly. These were amateurs mainly, honest burghers who gave freely of their time for precious little reward. As for the orchestra, here the paper trawled the curricula vitae of key players for evidence of future eminence; it also scoured the archives for evidence of praise disinterestedly conferred: to little effect in either case. In reality, the orchestra was probably better than Karajan suggested and less good than surviving players have claimed. Crucially, from the point of view of Karajan's own training, it was an orchestra that *needed* schooling. Where, nowadays, do young conductors learn the nuts and bolts of the trade at a time of greatly improved orchestral standards and rapid promotion to top jobs?

*

An opera with which Karajan was much associated and which he often talked about conducting in Ulm was Richard Strauss's *Der Rosenkavalier*. As he later recalled:

In a theatre like Ulm there were many fresh, unspoiled soprano voices. Many of the girls were what we call *verpflichtet*: they were contracted to sing so many performances, and they simply turned up and sang them. On the other hand, there was a great shortage of good young basses and baritones. When I did *Der Rosenkavalier*, the man down to sing Ochs came to me and said, 'I don't know this part.' So I said I would teach him. Then I discovered he couldn't read music. So I taught it him at the piano – we had over one hundred sessions. So even now if you wake me at three o'clock in the morning and sing me one bar of *Der Rosenkavalier* I will be able to carry on from where you start![16]

The review of that production in the *Ulmer Tagblatt* in March 1932 confirms those memories.

Walter Papst sees [Baron Ochs] from the humorous, 'good-natured' side. And whatever vocal solidity he does not get from this delicious figure, he replaces it by the quality of a thoroughly likeable interpretation.[17]

In other words, a nice fellow who acts better than he sings. As for the Marschallin:

With Frau [Leopoldine] Sunko-Saller, the result is the reverse. Her acting is as yet unable to convey the resigned, self-sacrificing woman which her marvellously expressive voice convincingly portrays.[18]

In other words, a nice girl who sings better than she acts.

The stage director was Erwin Dieterich himself, skilfully 'separating the realistic from the symphonic', says the reviewer, which seems to imply plenty of stage 'business' during the scenes of social mêlée but relative stasis and simple congruence with the music at other times. The chorus, we are told, laid aside its previously perceptible signs of fatigue to put its heart into the acting. As for the conducting:

In Herbert von Karajan [Dieterich] has a brilliant colleague at his disposal. What we heard from the young musician again yesterday evening is quite unsurpassable given the means at our disposal. An unbelievable vividness of sound grips the listener utterly. Faithfulness to the score, realised with fanatical musical [here the review lapses into verbal incoherence] ... Our orchestra appears no less involved, faithfully following the inexorable Karajan to the final bar with enthusiasm and skill.[19]

*

The inexorable Karajan: so inexorable that the previous December, during

53

a special Christmas performance of *Schwanda der Dudelsackpfeifer*, a member of the Ulm orchestra threatened to assassinate him.

The would-be assassin was the leader of the orchestra, the violinist Willy Döpke. Karajan had played chamber music with him, but now wanted Döpke demoted. He was not the only player Karajan had picked on. If the private recollections of former Ulm musicians are to be believed, Karajan often tried to demote older players and recruit new ones. He also tended to take it amiss if appointments were made by Dieterich or Schulmann without his approval. 'His Majesty,' as one player tartly recalls, 'disapproved of the appointment of Hans Peckatsch as leader. When I said to Karajan: "We all have to start sometime, even *you*," he was so offended he started plots against me too.'[20]

As for Döpke, he was found in Dieterich's office with a loaded Browning revolver, the safety-catch off. The fact that he was more or less openly touting the gun suggests that the episode was more a *cri de coeur* than a serious attempt on Karajan's life. A more determined assassin would have had little difficulty in executing the deed in the orchestra pit, or (as in a famous Hitchcock film) noiselessly from a box under the protection of a cymbal clash. In the event, the start of *Schwanda der Dudelsackpfeifer* was held up for half an hour while Döpke was disarmed, dismissed, and removed from the building.

Karajan said he found the Swabians unfriendly, keen supporters of the theatre but condescending to theatre-folk.

That hurt me a lot, and I said to myself that if things carry on in my life as I think they are going to, I shall do all I can to get this profession the status and dignity it deserves.[21]

Many great conductors end up as solipsists. After his début at the Henry Wood Promenade Concerts in London, Leonard Bernstein offered to 'tell the world' about the Proms, something the world had been well aware of for the best part of a century; and here is Karajan vowing single-handedly to bring status and dignity to a profession that *c.*1930 was palpably awash with it.

As for the citizens of Ulm, they saw it otherwise. Respected families regularly entertained musicians and actors, offered them rooms, and generally drew them into the circle of their acquaintance. Karajan, by contrast, was a difficult creature to pin down. He was a regular guest in the house of the music critic Ludwig Hepperle, where he fell under the spell of a newly published work that was to fascinate him for most of the rest of his life, Stravinsky's *Symphony of Psalms*. Musicians in general interested him, and music of virtually every type. The programme for Ulm's 1930 New Year's Eve theatre party lists him as accompanying a recitation in which he provides music improvised from the works of Mozart, accompanying his Don Pasquale in Neapolitan songs and his Musetta in Strauss's *Voices of Spring*, and joining Schulmann and Kojetinsky in 'jazz for three pianos', improvisations on 'St Louis Blues', 'Hallelujah!' and *The Blue Danube*.

Sport remained his other obsession. On a famous occasion in January 1932, he kept goal for the theatre's football team in a widely publicised game against the local press. Fritz Kaiser recalls:

> We lost 1–2 on that occasion, but only because our General Manager [Dieterich], who hadn't the least idea about football, fell over the ball when he was taking a penalty. If you look at our goalkeeper Karajan, with his cap on, you'll see he was a real sportsman. At that time he used to say he would rather be a racing driver than a conductor.[22]

Casual socialising held no interest for Karajan. His appearances at receptions given either by the orchestra or by the theatre management were, at best, fleeting. During the winter opera season, he seems to have lived like a student, eating intermittently, dosing himself with pills, draining his energies with long days and late nights, often working until three and four in the morning. The spring and summer months at his parents' home in Salzburg thus became periods of physical and mental recuperation and were to remain so for several years to come.

There was one blot on his copybook. He had taken to conducting without a score (trade mark of the myopic Toscanini) and had been comprehensively upended during a performance of *Cavalleria rusticana* when the tenor singing Turiddu had come in forty bars early. Nevertheless, Dieterich was happy to renew his contract at the end of the 1929–30 season.

*

Karajan again conducted *Cavalleria rusticana* in June 1930, for Dr Gross's Opera School in Salzburg; and that same summer he conducted publicly in Vienna for the first time, an open-air concert with the Vienna Symphony Orchestra. As for Salzburg, the 1930 Festival was dominated by Bruno Walter and the new director of the Vienna Opera, Clemens Krauss. Walter conducted Gluck's *Iphigenie in Aulis* and a revival of *Don Pasquale*, Krauss *Die Hochzeit des Figaro* and *Der Rosenkavalier* with Lotte Lehmann as the Marschallin and Richard Mayr as Baron Ochs. Krauss also repeated a popular novelty from the previous festival, a concert entirely given over to music of the Strauss family, precursor of the famous New Year's Day concerts in Vienna.

Though he was not yet forty, Krauss was already a dominant presence on the Austrian musical scene. A thoroughly modern man with a keen interest in contemporary music, he none the less contrived to rule the Vienna Opera like an old-fashioned Habsburg monarch. By birth, Krauss was indeed a scion of old Austria, an aristocrat, albeit a wrong-side-of-the-sheets one. As such, he must have been a potent role-model for the young Heribert Ritter von Karajan, who also aspired to marry a *ritterlich* inheritance with a sensibility that was thoroughly modern.

Though Karajan worked alongside Krauss, teaching conducting at Salzburg's summertime Orchestral Academy where Krauss gave what were no doubt extremely grand 'supplementary sessions in the practice of Conducting', the two were never close. Karajan, retiring at the best of times, kept his distance from a man who was famous for his disdain of the young.[23] As the years went by, he was less openly in awe of Krauss but his manner was never less than deferential. Commending a young Italian friend, Raffaello de Banfield Tripcovich, to him in the summer of 1941, Karajan wrote to Krauss:

> Grandi Alberghi Brioni
> 27 July 1941

Dear Professor,

May I introduce you to the bearer of this letter, a young Italian who is enthusiastic about art and whom I have advised to enrol in your [Salzburg summer] course in order to further his education as a conductor. I met him in the Maggio Musicale [in Florence], he listened to all the orchestral rehearsals, and I think he is a really keen and enthusiastic musician. Consequently, I am asking you to take some interest in him; you know how hard it is for Italians to get a thorough grounding in conducting at the moment. I am enjoying a few weeks' really wonderful and rather peaceful holiday in this wonderful country. Hearty greetings to you, and a devoted kiss on the hand of Frau Ursuleac [Krauss's wife].

Yours,

Herbert von Karajan [24]

The international summer school in Salzburg was a marvellous forum for Karajan the teacher. Born to music, he was also born to teaching, as his widely attested genius as a rehearser confirms. As early as the summer of 1929, only months after his own professional début, he was supervising classes for conductors and solo instrumentalists. While the great names wafted in and out of the Mozarteum – Krauss and Bruno Walter, Paumgartner and Cologne Opera's Meinhard von Zallinger – Karajan was often left to bear the brunt of the supervision. One of the students in 1930 was the 18-year-old Erich Leinsdorf:

I gained [the] impression ... of a perfectly well-prepared and enthusiastic young conductor whose personality and tastes *were already formed* [my emphasis]. I recall in particular his spirited discussion of Richard Strauss's *Tod und Verklärung*. Besides teaching classes, he also led rehearsals for Puccini's

Tosca at the local State Theatre. During those rehearsals he was coached by an older conductor, Meinhard von Zallinger. Of course, this will sound like the wisdom of hindsight, but it seems to me now that even in those days a gambler would happily have staked much money on the young Karajan.[25]

By all accounts, Karajan's methods were more inquisitorial than dogmatic. 'You do it that way? Why is that? Is there not perhaps another way?' The great teacher, someone once said, takes his pupil to the window; what he does not do is describe the view. Karajan was just such a teacher.

The teacher also learns. Working with students and alongside distinguished colleagues, Karajan was able to widen his repertory and begin to develop further his understanding of the problems of musical interpretation.

In Ulm, too, he was eager to expand his repertory. Initially, he took charge of many of the house's Italian and French operas. In 1930–1 he conducted Rossini's *Il barbiere di Siviglia* (directed by Dieterich), Donizetti's *Don Pasquale*, Bizet's *Carmen*, and Puccini's *La bohème*. The only German work was d'Albert's *Tiefland*. The following year he added to his repertory Puccini's *Madama Butterfly* and Verdi's *Il trovatore*, though he also conducted a single performance of *Die Meistersinger*, an orchestrally thrilling account of Beethoven's *Fidelio*, complete with the overture *Leonore No.3* before the final scene, and *Der Rosenkavalier*.

It was in this same season 1931–2 that Karajan organised his first concert appearance in Ulm. Money was short, schedules packed, the orchestra unfamiliar with non-operatic repertory. Finding a suitable venue was also a problem, until Karajan talked Dieterich into making a temporary apron for the tiny stage by placing iron girders across the orchestra pit. On this crudely improvised concert platform, Karajan gave his first Ulm concert. It began, as was often the custom in Germany in those days, with the principal work on the programme, Beethoven's *Eroica* Symphony. After the interval he conducted his old set-text from his student days in Vienna, Weber's overture *Euryanthe*. The concert ended with Strauss's *Tod und Verklärung*, the 60-strong band ably led by Karajan's friend and colleague Josef Schmalwieser. 'One listened and was astonished,' reported the *Schwäbischer Volksbote*.[26]

Karajan's next concert with the opera orchestra took place on 22 February 1933. After some weeks 'oiling my fingers again for public performance' and using his own cadenzas, he played and directed from the keyboard Mozart's D minor Concerto K466, before going on to conduct Debussy's *L'après-midi d'un faune* and Tchaikovsky's Sixth Symphony. The orchestra, he told his parents, played with 'unparalleled intensity'. As for the response: 'When it was all over, the audience sat as if dead for ten seconds; then they bawled their approval as if at a football match.'[27]

Later that same year, in honour of Richard Strauss's forthcoming seventieth birthday, Karajan conducted a vastly augmented theatre orchestra in an all-Strauss programme, ending with *Ein Heldenleben*. In another letter home to his parents, Karajan is aglow with news that Strauss himself might attend the concert; but there is no evidence that Strauss appeared. We would have heard about it if he had.

That was probably the highlight of Karajan's extra-operatic music-making in Ulm, along with what was by all accounts a daringly spectacular attempt on the Verdi *Requiem*.

Karajan began the 1932–3 season with Lortzing's *Undine*. It was an inauspicious start to what was to be an inauspicious season. From the very first scene, reported the critic of the *Schwäbischer Volksbote*, Karajan made things difficult. Tempi veered between those that were too slow and those that were too quick. Perhaps he wanted to 'do' something with the piece; in the event he merely burdened the singers and vexed the audience. Things improved with Nicolai's *Die lustigen Weiber von Windsor*, directed by Dieterich, and a production of *Tannhäuser* which Karajan openly admitted was given an added intensity by his having recently heard Toscanini conduct the opera in Bayreuth. Verdi's *La traviata* completed the season. It was politely received, but this was a work, like Schubert's Ninth Symphony, Karajan always had trouble with.

*

As the 1932–3 season drew to its close the people of Ulm had more on their minds than consumptive courtesans. After four years of government by presidential decree and in the midst of a continuing financial crisis, President Hindenburg attempted a democratic solution to Germany's problems. He invited the majority parties in the Reichstag, the National Socialists and their allies, to form a government.

So it came about that on 30 January 1933 Adolf Hitler was appointed Chancellor. In the eyes of the power brokers in Berlin he would be little more than a figurehead. They could not have been more wrong, of course. Within days of assuming office, Hitler was ruling by decree and special dispensation. On 27 February the Reichstag was set on fire; the following day, amid a whipped-up frenzy of public anxiety about an imminent Communist *putsch*, he was granted wide-ranging emergency powers, the draft version of the law – *Gesetz zur Behebung der Not von Volk und Reich* (Law for Removing the Distress of People and the Reich) – that was to be the legal base of the Nazi tyranny. And what was Karajan doing that day? He was in Ulm playing cabaret songs and a jazzed-up version of 'Life is a Carousel' during a 'Merry Evening' at the opera.

In the election that followed on 5 March 1933, the Nazis secured 43.9 per cent of the national vote. Technically, they still lacked an overall majority; in practice, with the Communist deputies proscribed, they could do what they liked. In Ulm/Württemberg the Nazis polled 42 per cent of the vote, a vast improvement on 26.2 per cent in November 1932. Against the national trend, Ulm had made an unusually large lurch to the Right.

Young voters in particular had been fired by the drive and *élan* of the Nazi campaign, with its promise of a new meritocracy and a break with the failures of the past. While the educated young argued the issues, street hooligans simply switched allegiance from Left to Right. Ten months after Hitler's coming to power, Patrick Leigh Fermor lodged one night in the attic of a young worker. The attic was a shrine of Hitleriana. The young man explained:

You should have seen it last year! You would have laughed! Then it was all red flags, stars, hammers and sickles, pictures of Lenin and Stalin and Workers of the World, Unite! I used to punch the heads of anyone singing the *Horst Wessel Lied* ... Then suddenly when Hitler came to power, I understood it was all nonsense and lies. I realised Adolf was the man for me. All of a sudden!' He snapped his fingers in the air. 'And here I am!' What about all his old pals, I asked. 'They changed too! – all those chaps in the bar. Every single one! They're all in the S.A. [*Sturmabteilung* = stormtroopers] now'.[28]

In the population at large, Leigh Fermor found a mood of bewildered acquiescence.

Occasionally it rose to fanaticism. Often when nobody was in earshot, it found utterance in pessimism, distrust, and foreboding, and sometimes in shame and fear, but only in private.[29]

As for the young stormtrooper's parents:

'*Mensch*! They don't understand anything. My father's old-fashioned: only thinks about the Kaiser and Bismarck and old Hindenburg – and now he's dead, too – anyway he helped the Führer to get where he is! And my mother, she knows nothing about politics. All she cares about is going to church. She's old-fashioned too.'[30]

*

One of the immediate results of the election of March 1933 was to throw Ulm's Stadttheater into disarray as its winter season drew to a close. The opera company was already enduring a hand-to-mouth existence amid the political uncertainty and falling subsidies theatre companies and opera houses had been living with since the Wall Street Crash in 1929. During the 1932–3 season, Dieterich had cut seat prices by 5 per cent in an attempt to hang on to an audience that was increasingly stretched financially. It was not for nothing that the critic of the *Ulmer Tagblatt* had finished his lengthy end-of-season review of *Der Rosenkavalier* in March 1932 with the words: 'Thus the final opera of the season was a dazzling justification of the Ulm audience's demands not to abandon this genre in future, if at all possible.'³¹

Would the new government make further cuts in subsidy? If not, what price would it exact for continued support?

Dieterich's contract as General Manager of the Stadttheater was with the city of Ulm; Schulmann's contract and Karajan's were with Dieterich himself,³² in his capacity as General Manager. For many years, the city's artistic life had been run by an essentially moderate coalition of political interests, led by the mayor Dr Emil Schwamberger, whose support for Dieterich had always been rock-solid.

Now this was all at an end. On 28 February, a Reich Commissar had been appointed to oversee the state of Württemberg. On 31 March Hitler issued a law dissolving all state parliaments. Five days later new state commissars were appointed, with sweeping powers that affected all aspects of local government. Ulm's new Staatskommissar was the 39-year-old Friedrich Foerster, a planning officer with the local electricity company and a Nazi Party (NSDAP) member since 1931. He would remain in office until 1945.

Schwamberger was immediately sidelined; and on 3 August 1933 he lost his position as mayor to Staatskommissar Foerster. Though Schulmann showed every intention of leaving Ulm of his own volition, Dieterich's own job was now on the line in a situation where it was increasingly a case of every man for himself.

Negotiations over Dieterich's future, and the orchestra's, would drag on well into the spring of 1933. As for the identity of Schulmann's successor as first conductor, that, too, was unclear. As early as March 1933, there were signs that Dieterich was unwilling – or unable – to offer Karajan the job. Worse, Dieterich seemed disinclined to offer Karajan *any* work for the 1933–4 season.

On 5 April 1933, the day after the NSDAP take-over in Ulm, Karajan celebrated – if that is quite the right word – his twenty-fifth birthday. As he kicked his heels back home in Salzburg in the first week of April 1933, there was a very real chance that he might soon be joining the vast congregation of German musicians – 23,889 as of January 1933 – officially listed as unemployed.

CHAPTER 8

Swastikas in the sky

So many waiting, how many waiting? what did it matter, on
  such a day?
Are they coming? No, not yet. You can see some eagles.
  And hear the trumpets.
Here they come. Is he coming?
                    T. S. Eliot, *Coriolan*, 'Triumphal March'

Within the Karajan family, old worries resurfaced. Was not the crisis in Ulm precisely the kind of thing Herbert's parents had warned him about when he decided to stake everything on a career in music? And what of the political situation itself? However starry-eyed Herbert and his contemporaries were about the prospect of an economic revival in Germany and the promise of cultural renewal within a larger, pan-German order, the fact remained – as the Karajans knew at first hand – the National Socialist movement harboured a peculiarly nasty virus within it.

In the winter of 1931–2 Ernst von Karajan had become embroiled in a controversy, stirred up by local Nazis, that received wide coverage in the local press, as well as in the national press in Austria and Germany. One of the pillars of the Salzburg Festival, the actor Alexander Moissi – Reinhardt's Everyman since the play's inception in 1920 – was attempting to write a novel, one of whose scenes involved a description of a woman giving birth. This being long before the time when such mysteries were widely available on film and television, Moissi asked the Senior Registrar of the local hospital Dr Ernst von Karajan if he might have permission to attend a birth. Dr von Karajan had no objections, though whether or not he agreed to the idea of the woman being paid by Moissi is not clear.

Local Nazis got hold of the story. Assuming, wrongly, that Moissi was a Jew (he was a Catholic from Trieste), they launched a noisy campaign on the streets of Salzburg and through the pages of their propaganda sheet *Eiserne Besen* denouncing this as a moral outrage and demanding that 'Moses Moissi' and others of his 'degenerate race' (i.e. Reinhardt) be banned for ever from the public stage. Unfortunately for Moissi and Ernst von Karajan, the Nazis were joined in their protest by a number of Catholic women's organisations. Under pressure from the Archbishop of Salzburg, the Festival authorities caved in. Moissi was barred from the 1932 Festival and never appeared in Salzburg again.

Though Herbert regarded the Nazi loudmouths who hounded his father with contempt ('Hottentots' was what he later called them[1]), he was not untouched by some of the ideas they peddled. As we have seen, there is his university enrolment entry 'German-Aryan'. Later, job-hunting in 1934, Karajan informed his parents that he would not be applying for a vacant post at the Vienna Volksoper. 'Until now,' he wrote, 'it has only been an out-of-the-way theatre, without reputation.' To which he added, 'Besides which, all of Palestine seems to gather there.'²

There is a distinction to be drawn, of course, between private prejudice and public action; there is a distinction, too, to be drawn between what it might be reasonable to write in a private letter before the Nazi genocide and what could be written after it.³ Public abuse by Nazi activists of Bolsheviks, Jews, homosexuals and those who associated with them was common enough in Salzburg in the 1920s. In the circle with which Karajan was most closely connected the abuse was aimed principally at Hofmannsthal *père*, Reinhardt, Bruno Walter, and the stage director Lothar Wallerstein, Clemens Krauss's theatrical *alter ego*.

It had little effect. Within the musical community there were intricate ties of friendship and trust the rats gnawed at in vain. The fact that Wallerstein was a Jew and Krauss a publicly committed National Socialist was irrelevant in the artistic milieu in which they operated. There were, of course, some aggrieved anti-Semites active within the musical community.⁴ In the main, however, it was jealousy, greed, and the pursuit of power – old toxins within the body politic – that were the greater irritants. Yet by the mid-1930s these old toxins had new breeding grounds, as a bewildering zigzag of Nazi policies slowly polarised international opinion, isolating the German-speaking musical community in a way the musicians themselves can barely have envisaged at the time.

Though the figures for the Nazi genocide are awesome, the size of the Jewish community in Germany in the 1930s was relatively small. At a little under half a million in the census of 1933, it represented less than one per cent of the total population. No doubt the extraordinary aggregation of Jewish talent in commerce, medicine, the arts, and the universities made it seem disproportionate. But outside Berlin itself, and to a lesser extent Hamburg, it was a scattered community. (In Ulm-Württemberg the figure was 0.4 per cent of the population.) At this time, anti-Semitism found little favour with the German people as a whole. (Hitler's call for an indefinite boycott of Jewish businesses as of 1 April 1933 collapsed within twenty-four hours.) When the first of the notorious Nuremberg race laws were passed in September 1935 – the new Law of Citizenship and the Law to Safeguard the Hereditary Health of the German People – the announcements were wrapped in language that was deliberately intended to obfuscate their criminal content. ('Slowly, slowly,' Goebbels confided to his diary at the time.)

Internationally, there were a number of vociferous denunciations of Nazi policy (by Toscanini, among others) as leading academics, doctors, and musicians began leaving Germany. But there was support and understanding, too. On 31 March 1933, the 30-year-old Rolf Gardiner, nephew of the English composer Henry Balfour Gardiner, wrote to *The Times* suggesting why the German – and Austrian – people had good cause to turn to Hitler. He offered the classic arguments: a cumulative protest against the humiliation of the Versailles Treaty, disenchantment with what he called the drab and flameless style of social-democrat republicanism, and a yearning for a renewed sense of 'community'.

Gardiner, whose maternal grandfather was Viennese, had first visited Austria as a teenager in 1920, assigned to youth projects whose task was to help rebuild war-damaged settlements. Later, he worked assiduously to develop cultural ties using similar lines of communication to those Ernst von Karajan had used to send his two boys to England for three months in the summer of 1924. Gardiner's view was both optimistic and uncompromising: the new German nationalism, he argued, was intensive and integrative, not extensive and expansive; if it became a menace to Europe, other people's failure to understand it would need to take a share of the blame.[5]

A number of foreign governments were less high-minded. They appeared to be more concerned with the threat of mass immigration than with the need to understand Austro-German susceptibilities.[6]

*

And what of the Nazi Party itself, to which Karajan was ineffectually recruited in Salzburg in 1933 – the application made on his behalf was later declared invalid – and which he formally joined in Aachen in 1935? The NSDAP is often written up as a monolithic entity. In practice, it had many departments and served numerous diverse functions at different points in its history. At the Nuremberg trials three Nazi organisations were declared criminal: the SS, the Gestapo, and the Reich's State Security Office (RSHA). Party membership as such – by 1940 there were eight million members – was never considered a criminal offence.

All political parties require mass-membership as a launch pad and operating base, and the National Socialists were no exception in the years leading up to 1933. Equally, nothing boosts party membership more than electoral success. This certainly happened in March 1933. *Märzgefallene*, the March Fallen, was the sarcastic title later used to describe the tens of thousands who signed up to the Nazi Party in March and April 1933.

For the Nazis themselves the flood of new members was far from welcome. Now that the Party was in power, the administration of a large general membership was a vastly cumbersome chore it could do without. On 1 May 1933 an embargo was imposed on new mass memberships, which was not lifted until 1937.

Why, then, did Karajan hand over a provisional joining fee of five Austrian Schillings (roughly £2 or $3) in Salzburg in April 1933? Since he was not by nature a follower, it is unlikely that he was merely caught up in post-election fever. The real cause almost certainly has to do with the abrupt destabilisation of his position, and that of the entire theatre administration in Ulm, in the final days of March 1933. A week, Harold Wilson once said, is a long time in politics. The first week of April 1933 saw the Nazis' assumption of power in Ulm. It also saw the enactment nationally of laws and proposals for administrative change that must have seemed like the destructive aftershocks of an already serious earthquake.

On 7 April two pieces of legislation were announced, both of which bore directly on the administrative hierarchy to which Karajan was answerable in Ulm: a law enacting the reorganisation of regional government and the Law for the Restoration of Tenure for the Civil Service. The latter edict had an immediate effect on the administration of state opera houses. Nor was it intended to rust unused. Within weeks of its announcement opera managers in Berlin, Breslau, Chemnitz, Cologne, Dresden, Frankfurt, Hamburg, Karlsruhe, Leipzig, Mannheim, and Stettin were sacked. Several principal conductors also found themselves in the dole queue. In the main, those who lost their jobs were Jewish, but not exclusively so.

*

What happened the very next day, 8 April 1933, is perhaps best described by an official report in Nazi Party files:

Party Member Herbert Klein, Salzburg, Sigmunds Haffnergasse 16, confirms that in April 1933 he recruited Herbert von Karajan in Salzburg as a member of the NSDAP, and received from him 5 Schillings as a recruitment fee, and also sent him the relevant certified registration form. Party Member Klein later handed in the registration form at the recruitment office in Salzburg, Schwarzstrasse 1. Shortly after the Party ban, Karajan left Salzburg and moved to the old Reich. Party Member Klein never heard anything more from him, and thinks it possible that Karajan did not pay any membership contributions in Austria.[7]

Did Karajan approach Klein (who, after the war, became Director of the Salzburg State Archive) or was he, as the letter states, recruited by Klein? Either way, Karajan did not follow up the application. Though the application form was handed in by Klein and eventually processed and allocated a provisional Party Number 1 607 525, the procedures required for full Party membership were never completed. At a later date (7 July 1939) the membership number 1 607 525 would be declared invalid.

The reasons for this are not difficult to discover. By April 1933 the Nazi Party membership machine had more or less ground to a halt. It is clear, for example, from documentation in the Federal Archive in Koblenz[8] that its Provincial Leadership in Austria had run out of numbers by early April. It was not until 16 April that a new tranche of membership numbers was issued – 1,600,001 to 1,630,00 – from which the number 1 607 525 was provisionally allocated to the Karajan-Klein application.

The Nazi Party was, in fact, doing everything in its power to stem the tide of applications. Its most effective weapon in this respect was the general ban on new memberships imposed as of 1 May 1933, a ban which was reinforced some weeks later by the announcement that all members recruited after 30 January 1933 would be subject to a two year probationary period. If Karajan was ever sent an official application form (stage two of the administrative process) he either never received it or failed to return it.

Nor did he, as has been widely alleged, make a second application to join the Party in Ulm on 1 May 1933. How this farrago of misinformation came to be assembled and generally believed is a story in itself which is set out in Appendix B of the present volume.[9] Suffice it to say, whatever else Karajan may have been doing on 1 May 1933, he was not filling out more registration forms for the NSDAP. When he did finally join the Party at the behest of the Nazi-controlled Aachen Administrative Authority in March 1935 he was allocated the number 3 430 914 ng (*nachgereicht* or retroactive) *back-dated* to 1 May 1933, the date of the temporary suspension of new applications for memberships.

Some time during the course of the political shake-out in Ulm in the spring of 1933, Karajan managed to sweet-talk Dieterich into giving him another season.[10] Did the provisional registration help Karajan's cause in any way? If it did, no one has recorded the fact. What we do know is that he was told that he would have to share the season with his junior colleague, the conductor and répétiteur at Ulm, the Viennese-born Max Kojetinsky. Unlike Karajan, Kojetinsky was already an established NSDAP Party member, and an outspoken supporter of the regime.

*

In the summer of 1933 Karajan made his official début at the Salzburg Festival, conducting the stage music for Reinhardt's long-awaited production of Goethe's *Faust*. This opportunity came in the middle of the worst crisis to affect the Salzburg Festival since the crises and cancellations of 1923–4. In the spring of 1933, Hitler's assumption of power in Germany had excited an extremist rump of Nazi agitators in Austria to a ferment of disruptive activity. If Hitler was in power, *Anschluss* could not be far behind.

This was not something which the majority of the Austrian people, or the Austrian government headed by Engelbert Dollfuss, viewed with equanimity. In June 1933, after a series of German terrorist outrages in the wine-growing Wachau region, Dollfuss moved against the Nazis, outlawing the Party in an attempt to distance Austria from the new German government. For the time being *Anschluss* was off even the Austrian Socialists' political agenda.

The German response was as swift as it was ill-considered: a tax – set prohibitively high at 1000 Marks – on any German citizen wishing to travel to Austria. The effect on Austria's tourist trade was catastrophic, with Salzburg, not for the first time, very much in the firing line.

One of the first things to be thrown into disarray was the administration of Salzburg's international summer school for musicians. Without tax waivers, few German students could afford to attend the course, a point that was brought to the attention of Goebbels's Ministry of Propaganda by a clearly agitated German consul in Salzburg. The Ministry was unsympathetic; unsurprisingly so, since it was already masterminding the withdrawal from the 1933 festival of such key 'German' artists as Hans Pfitzner and the Swedish-born contralto Sigrid Onegin.[11]

But worse was to follow. Clearly enraged by the prospect of Reinhardt's production of Goethe's *Faust*, a sacred 'German' text if ever there was one, and by the invitations extended by the festival authorities to such distinguished émigré Jewish musicians as the conductor Otto Klemperer, the Nazis subjected Salzburg to a barrage of propaganda. The Luftwaffe rained down leaflets from the air, loudspeakers blared at border crossings, firework displays etched red and white swastikas on to the black of the night sky. There were also bombings, primitive acts of urban terrorism, that brought police and army units on to the streets and turned the city at festival time into Fortress Salzburg.

Ticket sales plummeted. Operatically, the 1933 festival offered a staggering array of riches but it played to a mere 52 per cent capacity.[12] By contrast, *Faust* was a sell-out, though on the first night it was also a wash-out. Clemens Holzmeister's set, a cross-section of a small medieval town, was too elaborate to move; and the set's prohibitive cost had pushed still further into the future the possibility of the Felsenreitschule stage being roofed over.

Like many Salzburgers, Karajan feasted on the stories that emanated from Schloss Leopoldskron. He even had a few of them at first hand since he occasionally appeared at the castle to play the piano during some of the grander receptions. One of his favourite stories was of Franz Molnár gate-crashing a Reinhardt party shortly after having had a row with the great man. After casually engaging the head of Warner Brothers in conversation, Molnár told him that Reinhardt invariably peopled his receptions with suitably costumed actors whose job it was to add an extra note of grandeur to the occasion. And who, asked Jack Warner in horror, might these 'extras' be? To which Molnár responded by identifying several (genuine) princes, dukes, and bishops. Karajan thought that very amusing.

One person Karajan did meet at Schloss Leopoldskron was the actor, director, wit, and polymath Egon Friedell, whose two vast and immensely stimulating cultural histories *Kulturgeschichte der Neuzeit* and *Kulturgeschichte des Altertums* were then in the process of being published. They were volumes to which, even as an old man, Karajan would return for enlightenment and amusement.[13]

Reinhardt's personality, and the aura that seemed naturally to surround him, greatly impressed Karajan. Here was a man who lived at a certain social and physical distance from Salzburg but whose influence was all-pervasive; a personality whose presence one felt even when the man himself was not visible.[14] Karajan noted, and would later emulate, Reinhardt's meticulous advance planning, his detailed work with the leading players months ahead of the final rehearsal period; his skill in leaving ample time for a production and interpretation to 'settle' in the players' minds; and his habit of taking breaks away from the city during the festival to allow himself to restore perspectives and recuperate.

Karajan would tell Ernst Haeusserman:

What impressed me hugely about [Reinhardt] was his almost instinctive ability to cast roles correctly. He engaged an actor because he knew how the man would grow away from himself, given proper direction. He would then manage to get the actor exactly where he wanted him. The situation did not arise of someone arriving with an entirely different concept which Reinhardt would then have to wrestle with in order to impose his own view . . . It was wonderful to see them all growing together without actually knowing how it happened. That was Reinhardt's huge talent; it conserved his energies and protected him from disappointment.[15]

The idea of the director (stage director or conductor) being certain of his ground, rested, and psychologically at ease with himself ('protected from disappointment') is a typical Karajan concept.

Protecting himself from disappointment was, however, a skill Karajan would need to learn to acquire in the years that lay ahead.

CHAPTER 9

Nearly in the dust

Schon war ich nah' im Staube,
dem lauten Spott zum Raube,
dahin gestreckt zu sein.*
Beethoven, *Fidelio*

Karajan began the new season at Ulm with Lortzing's comic masterpiece *Der Wildschütz*. Lortzing's operas thrived in Germany in the 1930s largely due to a surge of interest in his two best-known comic operas *Zar und Zimmermann* and *Der Waffenschmied*. Other German-born composers fared rather less well. Indeed, it is a curious fact – not untypical of musical life at grass-roots level in Nazi Germany – that between 1933 and 1939 German opera houses gave fewer and fewer performances of the very repertory their political masters were keenest to promote. Wagner's operas suffered the steepest and steadiest decline, from a total of 1837 performances in 1932–3 to 1154 in 1939–40. Works like *Fidelio* and *Der Freischütz* also received fewer performances while operas by Verdi, Puccini, and Mozart flourished as never before.

The next opera conducted by Karajan was Handel's *Julius Cäsar* in a truncated and musically marmoreal performing edition by Oskar Hagen that had became hugely popular with audiences between the wars. Karajan revived the piece in Aachen in June 1935 and would later invite Leontyne Price to sing Cleopatra's ravishingly lovely aria 'V'adoro pupille' at a concert in Berlin in 1960.

Karajan had a great if somewhat eccentric fondness for Handel's music. In the late 1960s he recorded the Op.6 *Concerti grossi* in a thoroughly unabashed romantic style after the manner of Furtwängler.[1] Curiously, he never conducted *Messiah*, though the idea that he might perform it at the 1975 Salzburg Easter Festival had EMI pencilling in soloists for a possible recording: Elizabeth Harwood, Janet Baker or Anna Reynolds, Jon Vickers, and John Shirley-Quirk. In the end, Karajan dropped the idea on the grounds that it was better left to Colin Davis whose recording he greatly admired. In fact, left to his own devices, Karajan would have loved to record the camped-up edition (orchestrated by Goossens) Sir Thomas

---

* Once I was nearly in the dust,
  a prey to open mockery,
  to be laid low.

68

Beecham had used for his 1959 RCA recording. David Bell was asked by him to look out the parts, but they were nowhere to be found.

*

During January and February 1934 Karajan conducted *Lohengrin* and, more ambitiously, Richard Strauss's latest opera *Arabella*. Clemens Krauss had conducted the première in Dresden the previous July, and the first Viennese performances the previous October.

The Ulm *Arabella* was the high point of Karajan's work with Erwin Dieterich. Without their two abiding passions – Karajan's for Strauss, Dieterich's for musical comedy and for anything that was interesting and *à la mode* – it is unlikely that a house of Ulm's size would have considered staging such a show, especially in the depths of an economic recession. Dieterich himself directed. By now he was expert at cutting his suit to fit Ulm's meagre supply of theatrical cloth; on this occasion, he saved on costumes and pointed up the contemporary nature of the score by switching the opera's milieu from fashionable Vienna in the 1860s to fashionable Vienna in the 1920s. According to the critic of the *Schwäbischer Volksbote,* Karajan conducted with 'ease and elegance'.[2] The *Ulmer Tagblatt* noted a new airiness in his conducting, rich sounds complemented by a wonderfully fresh way with Strauss's contrapuntal texturing. And there was architectural reach, too.[3]

Did Karajan have a sense of being airborne at last? A company and an orchestra he had helped reshape performing a brand-new work by Germany's most admired living composer, and doing so with a daring and a flair that had the locals rubbing their eyes in disbelief at what their opera could achieve? Frustratingly, Karajan never returned to *Arabella*.

*

Though he must have known that his time in Ulm was almost up, Karajan continued to improve the orchestra, ferreting out fresh young instrumental talent from the music academies in Munich and elsewhere. This can hardly have endeared him to the existing players and gave added force to the argument that he had outgrown Ulm. There is usually a limit to what small-time institutions, however ambitious and status-conscious, can take from someone as talented and demanding as Karajan; it does not need much imagination to guess what was being said about him in the green-room and theatre corridors.

Evidence of a certain amount of back-biting emerges in a memorandum on Karajan drafted by the Information Services of the United States forces in Austria in 1946: 'He was unsuccessful [*sic*] there [Ulm] for reasons of character.'⁴ The memorandum was drafted by someone we shall hear more of in later chapters, the Austrian-born Otto de Pasetti. To whom, one wonders, had he been talking?

The local press saw things rather differently:

His achievements in our city are numerous. First of all, he has added young talented musicians to our orchestra and deliberately set about teaching them, so that in time a body of musicians was created that easily stood comparison in operatic and concert performance with the orchestras of far larger cities. This achievement gave the lie to the assertion in certain circles that one really had to go to Stuttgart or Munich to hear anything good.⁵

But there was to be no second reprieve. There were those in high places, as well as certain members of the orchestra, who wanted rid of him. And so, with a fine sense of the dramatic power of recapitulation, he bowed out on 31 March 1934 with a performance of the opera with which he had made his début in Ulm in March 1929, Mozart's *Le nozze di Figaro*: a new production in a new and uncredited German translation entitled simply *Figaros Hochzeit*.⁶

Whatever he felt inwardly, Karajan was putting a brave face on things. Like a smug schoolboy drafting his own end-of-term report, he wrote to his parents of the performance:

It was from beginning to end the purest joy; all concern with technical matters fell away; and I must say the result was not to be called conducting but, in the best sense of the word, creating music.⁷

Dieterich told Karajan that he had outgrown Ulm, a version of the story of his dismissal Karajan often used in later years. And yet a residue of bitterness remained: a feeling that he had been exploited, misled, and misunderstood. 'I was thrown out,' he told Franz Endler in 1987. 'There's no other way of looking at it.' One thing Dieterich is supposed to have said rankled especially deeply, so much so that you could be sure Karajan would quote it whenever he was in bleakly reminiscent mood: 'You'll either *go to the dogs* [Karajan's emphasis] or you'll make a career for yourself.'⁸ Karajan was not the first young man to be told that nor the last; as a schoolmaster of my acquaintance once wrote on an end-of-term report: 'Your son will go far; I hesitate to predict, however, in which *direction* he will go.'

How much Dieterich himself had to do with Karajan's dismissal is not clear. He himself was also shortly to lose his job, in May 1935. No doubt Dieterich was thought too liberal by the Nazis. The playwrights favoured by him – Shakespeare, Goldoni, Molière, Goethe, Gogol, Shaw, Brecht, Tennessee Williams – would not have disgraced a leading metropolitan company. An explicitly National Socialist drama *Der 18 Oktober* had been included in the programme in 1932, and two others followed: *Flieg roter Adler nach Tirol* (*Fly Red Eagle to the Tyrol*) and a piece about the front in the 1914–18 war *Die endlose Strasse* (*The Endless Road*). But this was not enough to convince the new Nazi authority that Dieterich was 'one of us'.

Karajan's temper cannot have been improved by an exceptionally flattering letter sent to him (unsigned) by Ulm's new National Socialist Mayor, Friedrich Foerster. If I am so remarkable a talent, he must have asked, why are my services being dispensed with? Dated 18 April 1934 and addressed to Herrn Reichsritter Herbert von Karajan, it suggests that Karajan's demand for more money – and an effective end to his 'apprentice' status – was one of the factors in the decision to release him. The letter reads:

To my great regret I was unable, as a result of official duties, to attend your farewell performance. Consequently I should not wish to fail to say goodbye to you in writing and, in doing so, express my fullest recognition to you for what you have done during your five-year period of office at the Municipal Theatre in Ulm for that institution and for artistic and musical life in Ulm, which enjoys an excellent and widespread reputation. You understood how to build the Municipal Theatre Orchestra, particularly by the introduction of young talent but above all by your untiring rehearsals, into a body of musicians which could bear comparison in both operatic and concert performance with the orchestras of far larger cities. Under your direction, our Opera has achieved results which were never considered possible in earlier times. I regret your departure especially deeply at this precise moment when we are striving to place the theatre at the very centre of our cultural life. I would have been able to find very fruitful tasks in the new season when operas and concerts will be placed first and foremost at the service of the N[ational] S[ocialist] community as part of "Strength through Joy". On the other hand, it is quite understandable that you should wish to look for another field of activity in the interests of your further artistic development, and particularly as well that you should seek to better yourself financially. In the name of the Municipal Authority, therefore, I again express my most hearty thanks and hope you will find a fruitful and busy sphere of activity corresponding to your exceptional capacities as a musician.

  Heil Hitler!
    On behalf of
      [initialled in his absence]
        Mayor[9]

The National Socialist power brokers were extremely adept at writing letters like this; in December 1934, Göring wrote in not dissimilar terms to Furtwängler on the occasion of his dismissal as Director of the Berlin State Opera.

It cannot have helped the situation that in the spring of 1934 Karajan had no Nazi Party credentials, unlike the No.3 in the Ulm hierarchy, his friend Max Kojetinsky, who was already a Party member. There is no evidence of Karajan being in any way active in National Socialist circles in Ulm in the winter of 1933–4, the very time when it might have been to his advantage to be so. Rather, it was Kojetinsky who made all the running, regularly reporting back on musical affairs to the local NSDAP office, gracing 'family' music evenings in the NSDAP branches, and assiduously promoting the work of so-called 'National Socialist' composers from his native Austria.[10]

*

If Karajan was largely uninterested in Party affairs in the winter of 1933–4, it was singularly remiss of him. During the summer and autumn of 1933, a power struggle was taking place within the German government that was to have a far-reaching effect on the administration of musical life in Nazi Germany. In essence, it was a struggle for the administrative control of the arts between the Estonian-born Nazi ideologue and survivor of the failed 1923 Munich *Putsch* Alfred Rosenberg and Hitler's propaganda chief Joseph Goebbels. Initially, there had been other players in the game, notably Hermann Göring who, as Prime Minister of Prussia, was determined to keep the Berlin State Opera firmly within his bailiwick. That done, he had retired to his lair, leaving the Führer to sort out the dog-fight between Rosenberg and Goebbels.

That Goebbels won was, in the circumstances, the lesser of two evils. Apart from Albert Speer, who was not yet part of the government, Goebbels was the most intelligent and best educated of Hitler's ministers. Unlike the crudely confrontational Rosenberg, who saw dissident musicians as a problem to be eradicated, Goebbels regarded the musical community as a resource to be husbanded. And he boxed clever, cajoling and outmanoeuvring dissidents while side-stepping many of the more preposterous demands which the Rosenberg faction continued to make right up to the end of the war in 1945.[11]

The first sign that Goebbels had outsmarted Rosenberg came in September 1933 with the announcement of the setting up of the Reichskulturkammer (RKK), a system of political and bureaucratic control over the media and the arts, with specially dedicated 'chambers' for each of the individual constituencies: press, radio, film, the fine arts, literature, theatre, and music (the Reichsmusikkammer or RMK). On 1 November 1933 an additional law was passed requiring anyone concerned with the 'production of cultural material' to be registered with the RKK, something Karajan initially omitted to do.

The Reichsmusikkammer, under whose aegis Karajan would spend the next eleven years either working or seeking work, had several administrative layers of its own within the larger structure of the RKK. At the top were the President and Vice-President (Richard Strauss and Furtwängler, initially) and an inner cabinet of advisers on musical, economic, and legal matters. At the bottom were the thirty-one regional officers. In the middle were the foot soldiers: composers, performers, concert agents, music publishers, music dealers, instrument manufacturers, plus a somewhat egregious group entitled 'Choral and Folk Music', made up of church musicians and various ethnically approved minstrels.

It would be churlish to deny the RMK its successes, particularly in cutting unemployment among musicians and extensively reforming their working conditions. It established a guaranteed minimum wage, limited working hours, and protected the position of freelance instrumentalists by making it illegal for salaried players in state-funded orchestras to accept additional work. Funding was provided for talented young artists, pensions and retirement provisions were improved, and, after 1939, legislation was put in place exempting unemployed musicians from forced labour that might damage their long-term ability to perform. On the other side of the coin, there was much that was racist and restrictive. Jewish musicians were further marginalised. From 7 March 1934 no member of the RMK could travel abroad without the express permission of the administration. Concert programmes had to be vetted in advance. It even became illegal for an artist to adopt a foreign-sounding pseudonym.

The restrictions on foreign travel were especially useful to the Nazis in their continuing war of attrition against Austria in general and the Salzburg Festival in particular. With Furtwängler, Toscanini, and Weingartner set to make their festival débuts, the 1934 festival promised to be one of the finest yet. Then, in May, the RMK struck. First Strauss withdrew, citing poor health; then Furtwängler, citing overwork. Neither excuse fooled anyone.

*

During the spring and early summer of 1934 Karajan was unemployed. It had been his usual practice to return home in April, but there was nothing for him in Salzburg; only an anxious mother and a concerned father. The Ulm newspapers, no doubt briefed by Karajan, had spoken of concerts in Berlin and the possibility of engagements in Florence. Instead, he went to Berlin, hub of the musical universe, not to conduct or appear as a solo pianist but to sign up with the city's largest theatrical agency Paritätischer Bühnennachweis as a répétiteur. It was menial work, but he reasoned it was as good a place to be as any. At least he would be on hand when the opera bosses rode into town for the annual round of close season auditions of aspiring young singers.

Though there were no opera directorships on offer, he travelled most weekends to out-of-the-way opera houses. He would leave Berlin on a Friday night, book into a Saturday-evening performance, try to cajole people into seeing him, and return to Berlin on Sunday. Shy and unsociable, he loathed the whole futile process. It was during this time that he developed a lifelong aversion to railways and railway stations. He later recalled:

I travelled back and forth many nights in order to introduce myself . . . There is an Italian film by De Sica *Bicycle Thieves* in which a man sees everything that happens to him in Rome from the point of view of a bicycle which has been stolen from him. I saw everything from the point of view, not of a bicycle, but an orchestra. For me, a town in which I arrived or through which I went at night was not a town but the seat of an orchestra. That was why the lights were on! And then one was flung out into the night again, unnoticed.[12]

Older members of the Berlin Philharmonic remember travelling through Germany with Karajan by train in the 1960s. As the train stopped at Oberhausen, Karajan, hunched in the corner of the carriage, muttered bitterly: 'Even they rejected me!' Refusing to let his boss's depressed state get him down, the tour manager Erich Berry quipped: 'Why not give them a ring; they'll probably make you an offer now.' Karajan cackled loudly at the suggestion and spent the rest of the journey in high good humour.

Karajan was neither as disadvantaged nor as humble a man as Antonio, the hapless father in De Sica's *Bicycle Thieves*. His identification with the film reflects the self-pitying, maudlin side to his character: pity for his own self-imposed loneliness. It is also possible to ask to what extent Karajan identified with Antonio's sense of personal disgrace. After days tramping the streets with his young son in search of the stolen bicycle, Antonio finally attempts to steal one. Lacking the true criminal instinct, he is caught in the act, and almost lynched. The man whose bike it is refuses to press charges but the jibe of a bystander inflicts a more terrible wound. 'A fine way to bring up your son,' he jeers, as Antonio, aghast at what he has done, shambles away, too shocked at first even to take the hand of the weeping boy.

Karajan, too, was to do things he would have preferred not to have done. He was no criminal, though circumstances would shortly bring him into contact with those who were. He also developed at this time a considerable interest in the criminal psyche. In later years he was much given to quoting a remark by Goethe: 'I would be able to commit all crimes in my life if I did not have the possibility to express them.' Conducting *Tosca*, steeping himself in the world of Baron Scarpia, was, Karajan often said, a kind of therapy. (His old sparring-partner Gottfried von Einem once said, 'He could express hatred well in music. His *Tosca* was fine.'[13]) Did this bright, musically focused, highly strung, politically naïve young man from Salzburg ever fully recover from the discovery in Berlin in the summer of 1934 that Scarpia and his henchmen were alive and well, and waiting to do business with him?

In his strangely shambolic way, Karajan made no contact at all with the Reichsmusikkammer. Perhaps he thought that as an Austrian citizen he need not register. If so, it was wishful thinking. Membership of the RMK was now a pre-condition of employment for musicians seeking permanent work in Germany.

Karajan eventually registered towards the end of May. On 1 June, replying to a request from home that he visit his ailing grandmother in Graz, he wrote of two days of 'terribly complicated formalities (I must become a member of the Reichsmusikkammer)'.[14]

Perhaps Dr Edgar Gross had told him to buck up his ideas, for it was around this time that Dr Gross, the recently appointed Intendant of the Aachen Opera, turned up in Berlin. Karajan remembered:

I hypnotised him, saying 'I won't let you go until you take me'. I had told myself that I had to get something out of this interview.[15]

It must have been a singular experience for Dr Gross, being confronted by this gaunt young man with his hyper-intense manner and matinée-idol looks and being 'hypnotised' by the laser-beam of those famously blue eyes. ('Hard, light eyes, like fissures in a block of ice,' as Walter Legge once described them.[16]) But, then, as Karajan later told his parents (paraphrasing Beethoven's Pizarro), 'So [was] I near the dust.'

Hypnotised or not, Dr Gross bowed to the young man's demands. He invited him to the auditions which were due to take place in Aachen on 8 June.

CHAPTER 10

'Tell me now: are you happy with me?'

And 'Gallop,' gasped Joris, 'for Aix is in sight'.
Robert Browning

Aachen, once the northern capital of the Holy Roman Empire, stands fifty miles west of Cologne on the Belgian–Dutch border, a short bicycle ride from Liège or Maastricht. Architecturally handsome, with a famous cathedral and an internationally renowned choir, it was the German Reich's distinguished western outpost.

In the early 1930s the Aachen Opera, once a moderately important provincial house, had fallen into a certain amount of disarray. At the start of the decade, a more than competent team was in place, headed by General Intendant Heinrich Strohm (an apparently inoffensive little man, an old school-friend of Goebbels) and the conductor Paul Pella.[1] Financially, though, the Opera was in poor shape. In 1932 there was a palace revolution. Pella was ignominiously sacked and Strohm left for Hamburg.[2] As a stop-gap, a former Aachen Intendant, Francesco Sioli, was re-engaged, alongside a man who since 1920 had been very much a driving force in Aachen musical life, the 60-year-old Liszt scholar, conductor, and academic Peter Raabe.

In the spring of 1934, the new National Socialist Mayor of Aachen Quirin Jansen sacked Sioli and vetoed the plan to engage the conductor Hans Swarowsky as Aachen's new Generalmusikdirektor. After much local manoeuvring, Jansen decided to plump for an outsider to replace Sioli. The job went to Dr Edgar Gross, a 47-year-old theatre producer and dramaturg who had previously run small opera houses in Weissenfels, Halberstadt, and Lübeck.

Gross had no National Socialist credentials whatsoever; he was, however, promptly required to join the NSDAP by the new Aachen authority. He was a mild-mannered, reserved, somewhat donnish man with a reputation for judiciousness and fair-mindedness in his treatment of his staff. To outward appearances, he was not a risk-taker; and since he had no doubt heard good reports of Karajan's work in Ulm, or read about them in such reasonably reliable publications as *Zeitschrift für Musik*, inviting him along to audition was not an especially remarkable thing to do.

That, however, was to overlook the character of the highly-strung young thoroughbred he was about to unleash on a largely unsuspecting Aachen orchestra.

Karajan's audition engraved itself on the memory of everyone who was there. One witness, an influential one as it turned out, was the music critic Dr Wilhelm Kemp, a writer who was rapidly to become one of Karajan's most ardent admirers:

Gross said he had one more applicant to introduce, someone he had 'discovered' in Ulm. So Karajan jumps up onto the rostrum, says a few words to the orchestra, conducts the *Oberon* overture with verve, and then carefully rehearses the first movement of the *Haffner* Symphony. The initially hostile orchestra begins to adapt to the young man up there, and finally plays with ease and flexibility, attentively following the precisely sprung beat. Finally the *Meistersinger* Prelude rings out. After that the representatives of the orchestra and various invited members of the press gather round Dr Gross to discuss the matter. The musicians say that he's too young and inexperienced, not mature enough to stand in front of such an orchestra. The press agrees – with one dissenting voice. I say to orchestral chairman Stanke: 'You played better under that young man than you have done for a long time, surely you must have heard that.'[3]

He probably had. But what Stanke and his men may also have recognised was that here was someone who would make their lives difficult: a taskmaster, a perfectionist. Willy Wesemann, a first violinist in the orchestra, later admitted as much, even though he himself had been tremendously taken with the fire of Karajan's conducting:

In the beginning it was very difficult playing under Karajan. He demanded so much. His working methods were more spontaneous and more intense than those of any of his predecessors. Quite simply, he was different. And what he eventually achieved was greater; it came closer to perfection.[4]

With the orchestra and most of the press lined up against his 'discovery from Ulm', Dr Gross had a problem. Karajan later claimed that there was a man at the audition who had worked with the Berlin Philharmonic and who spoke up for him. We know that the music critic Kemp did. The local NSDAP Cultural Officer Albert – 'fat Albert' – Hoff would also claim a share of the glory. In the end, though, it was Gross's decision, and he decided to offer Karajan the job.

No doubt other jobs would have come up. However 'near the dust' Karajan felt he was, it is difficult to believe that he would seriously have considered giving up music altogether. He was already too old to have any realistic chance of taking up a career as a professional racing driver. As for his ideas of replacing the petrol engine or designing turbines for the straits of Gibraltar to irrigate the Sahara desert, such thoughts by this stage were mere fantasy.

As jobs went, the Aachen post offered wonderful opportunities to a rising star. It gave him access to an opera orchestra of seventy players, easily augmented for big occasions, and two fine choirs. There was the cathedral choir directed by the Theodor Rehmann and an opera chorus that had recently been entrusted to the care of Wilhelm Pitz, a former Aachen Municipal Orchestra violinist who was destined to become one of the most celebrated chorus masters of the twentieth century. There was a fine 1000-seat opera house, a concert hall (Raabe's responsibility still), and a tradition of touring abroad.

There was also Aachen's recent unhappy history, making it a situation ripe for improvement.

*

In August 1934, shortly before taking up his position in Aachen, Karajan conducted the Vienna Philharmonic for the first time. It was a private occasion, a lavish musical party laid on during the 1934 Salzburg Festival by a wealthy American widow, Mrs Gertrude Moulton.

The evening began in the main hall of the Mozarteum with Debussy's neglected early *Fantaisie* for piano and orchestra, with the American Ralph Lawton as soloist. This was followed by Ravel's *La valse* (a piece Karajan later claimed to dislike but which he always conducted with a properly powerful sense of corruption and menace). After supper, the guests reassembled in the open-air theatre of the Mirabell Gardens where students from the ballet in Vienna danced Debussy's *Prélude à l'après-midi d'un faune*, a work Toscanini would conduct with the orchestra, as part of the official festival, nine days later. Willy Fränzl, the Vienna Opera's most gifted male dancer, danced the faun, Margarete Wallmann directed.[5]

In order to lead the music-making at Mrs Moulton's soirée, Karajan had been obliged to do a certain amount of ducking and weaving. Newly signed up to the Aachen Opera, he found himself in the bizarre situation of having to seek permission from the Reichsmusikkammer to conduct in his own native Salzburg. He was small fry in comparison with Richard Strauss or Furtwängler, who had had permission withheld earlier in the year. But by early August the war of attrition between Austria and Germany had turned into something far worse with the assassination on 25 July of the Austrian Chancellor Dollfuss.

Karajan framed a two-pronged excuse. First, Mrs Moulton's soirée was a private occasion; secondly, the evening was being used by him to test the efficacy of the Mirabell Gardens' open-air acoustic. The request ended up in the in-tray of the Reichstheaterkammer[6] and was eventually waved through. Wisely so. No doubt they saw through the story about acoustic tests, but to be seen to be interfering with the private entertainments of an

American citizen in a foreign country was precisely the kind of publicity Goebbels's ministry was keen to avoid.

*

Aachen audiences would later say of Karajan, half jokingly, half seriously, '*Er hat das "Heilige Feuer" in sich* [the "sacred flame" burns within him]'. The flame appears to have been lit immediately with a vividly conducted account of Beethoven's *Fidelio*. The audience loved it and even the initially somewhat sceptical press corps began to sing Karajan's praises. The performance's real centre of gravity, wrote one reviewer, was the orchestra: 'here the new Kapellmeister von Karajan created a sensation'. Another reviewer wrote:

Karajan has at his disposal everything that a conductor, especially an opera conductor, needs: a secure and clear stick technique, great judiciousness, and, it would seem, a very good memory that allows him to establish direct contact between stage and orchestra independently of the score in front of him . . . To those capabilities are added a good dose of verve and vitality, and – for one so young – a strongly developed creative will.[7]

'Every word of the text on his lips, every bar of the score in his head': the pundits were duly impressed.[8]

During the 1934–5 season, Karajan offered a shrewd mix of repertory that was both familiar to him and new. Alongside *Fidelio*, *Der Rosenkavalier*, *Tannhäuser*, and *Giulio Cesare* came *Die Zauberflöte* and his first foray into Wagner's *Ring*, with performances of *Die Walküre* and *Siegfried*.

In December 1934, Karajan conducted his first orchestral concert in Aachen. Peter Raabe had been invited at short notice to make a guest appearance in Berlin. It was unusual for the local Opernkapellmeister to conduct a symphony concert, but when it became clear that there were difficulties in finding a substitute for Raabe, Karajan put in his bid. The concert, which included Weber's overture *Euryanthe* and Tchaikovsky's Violin Concerto with Sigmund Bleier as soloist, was a sensation, culminating in a meticulously rehearsed and brilliantly played account of Brahms's First Symphony.

The success of the concert further called into question Peter Raabe's already somewhat semi-detached place in Aachen's musical life. The Nazis needed men like Raabe, respected musicologists who were sufficiently rooted in the ways of the 'old' German school to be naturally suspicious of anything vaguely Leftist or avant-garde. Raabe's period as co-chairman of the forward-looking Allgemeiner Deutscher Musikverein (ADMV) had been distinguished largely by its timidity. The ADMV had been founded by Liszt in 1861 to promote German music in all its aspects, in particular new music. Under Raabe, the organisation back-pedalled furiously, withdrawing important new works by Braunfels and Webern from the 1933 festival in Dortmund and substituting lesser pieces by Unger and Trapp.

Raabe's visit to Berlin in December 1934 coincided with the resignation of Furtwängler as Vice-President of the Reichsmusikkammer, one of several crises to beset the RMK in its earliest years. Raabe was not immediately approached by the RMK. However, when Richard Strauss was forced to resign the presidency in the summer of 1935, after making some extremely robust remarks about the job to Stefan Zweig in a private letter which the Gestapo intercepted, Raabe was appointed to succeed him.[9]

*

If Raabe were to leave Aachen, or simply retire, the way would be open for Karajan to assume control of both the opera and the Städtische Orchester. There would no doubt have been opposition to so hasty a promotion, but already pressures were building to keep Karajan in Aachen. He was enormously popular with the public, and the musicians, too, were beginning to warm to him. Years later, in 1977, former principal trumpeter Kurt Noack would recall:

When Karajan became Generalmusikdirektor in 1935, many colleagues thought he was just too young. Perhaps that was only an excuse, since he used to be very demanding. Karajan was a bit of a schoolmaster as well. He used to enjoy driving his car through town in order to hear if we were practising at home. I at any rate was enthusiastic about the new style of work. As orchestral representative I often had to see Karajan and I always found an understanding ear. And he was not unwelcoming in his relations with other colleagues either.[10]

Word of the Wunderkind was spreading fast. During the autumn of 1934, Karajan received an invitation to conduct a performance of Wagner's *Tannhäuser* in the elegant eighteenth-century southern German town of Karlsruhe. In its heyday, Karlsruhe had become one of music's most fashionable resorts, a Mecca for Wagnerians. In the 1880s and 1890s, during Felix Mottl's time as Music Director, it was known as 'the Little Bayreuth'. Karajan arrived there in January 1935 and thought little of it:

When I arrived, I was horrified. At that time, Karlsruhe was full of retired people, very petit bourgeois. The theatre was a typical old court theatre [the original court theatre had burned down; what Karajan saw was Heinrich Hübsch's theatre, opened in 1853] with a lot of exhausted singers. The orchestra was good, but also too old. When the General Manager wanted to give me a contract the next day, I said: 'Don't be angry with me, but I don't think I could live here.'[11]

It was a somewhat premature judgement. At the rehearsal later that same day, Karajan found everything sounding much better than he had anticipated. Before travelling back to Aachen, he agreed to return to Karlsruhe in five weeks' time to conduct a performance of Mozart's *Le nozze di Figaro*.

Back in Aachen, intrigue was afoot. Karlsruhe, it turned out, was not the only opera house interested in Karajan. Enquiries were also being made by Berlin's Deutsches Opernhaus. Pre-1933, this had been the city's prestigious second house, the Städtische Oper; it was here that Max Reinhardt's protégé Carl Ebert had made a name for himself. Now Goebbels was in control; charged with staging middlebrow repertory in 'accessible' productions at affordable prices, the house had become second-rate. Karajan never conducted there.

Nine months previously no one wanted Karajan; now he found himself at the centre of an auction. Dr Gross, having 'discovered' Karajan, was more than ever determined to hang on to him, as indeed was Mayor Jansen. And here the problem was not so much Raabe or Berlin as Karlsruhe, which was making strenuous efforts to engage Karajan through a series of private and public negotiations masterminded by a local political power broker, Minister Dr Wacker. In the ensuing war of words, Wacker was comprehensively outmanoeuvred by Jansen whose principal political weapon was Aachen's status as 'the Reich's westerly capital' and its role as a cultural shop window on Germany's western border. When the announcement came that Aachen had secured Karajan's services, the notice from the city's Press and Propaganda Office was largely given over to a blow-by-blow account of the mayor's negotiating skills; the paragraphs devoted to Karajan concentrated on his rather grand family pedigree.

Yet it is an ill wind that blows no one any good. When it became clear early in March 1935 that Aachen would not be releasing Karajan, the Karlsruhe post was offered to a talented young répétiteur from the town, Joseph Keilberth. Keilberth and Karajan were contemporaries almost to the day and were to become good friends, inasmuch as the solitary, bookish Keilberth or the shy, workaholic Karajan ever became friendly with anyone. When Keilberth died in Munich in June 1968, after collapsing during a performance of *Tristan* – 'In a *quiet* passage,' Karajan later told me, 'when the tension is all gathered within' – Karajan set up a medical research programme to determine the precise nature of the stresses a conductor undergoes. What made Keilberth's death so eerie was the fact that another ex-Karlsruhe music director, Felix Mottl, had also died in Munich during a performance of *Tristan*, in June 1911. 'And, you know,' said Karajan, still bewildered by the whole affair, 'that is the way Keilberth always said he wanted to die: "Like Mottl, conducting *Tristan*".'

The announcement that Karajan was to be Aachen's new Generalmusik-direktor was released to the press on 13 April 1935. He was twenty-seven, and the youngest music director in Germany. He wrote home to his parents:

My salary in the first year is 14,000 Marks; in the second year, 15,000; in the third 16,000. [Furtwängler's salary at the Berlin State Opera in 1934 was 32,000 Marks.] They're giving me a 3-year contract. So: I have attained all that one could hope for. When I consider that the first discussions, in December, had a salary of only 7,000 Marks . . . I am now chief of the music of the city of [Aachen], with a stipend that is greater than the Lord Mayor's. And so I see that I am a clever diplomat. The offers from Berlin, Karlsruhe, etc., have naturally raised my market value much higher. Therefore, I am very content, it has all gone relatively quickly, in a couple of months. When I think how things stood a year ago, when, like Pizarro in *Fidelio* I could literally sing, 'So am I near the dust' – the change is indeed gratifying. Let's just hope that it continues that way! The Director in Karlsruhe, who was unbelievably moved after my performance and shed bitter tears [at losing me] told me directly: In two years I should be one of the major conductors in Germany! . . . so tell me now: are you happy with me?[12]

What recriminations within the Karajan family circle lay behind that final sentence?

CHAPTER 11

Chess moves

In those troubled times, especially when one is young, it is very difficult to make choices ... It is unjust to judge people from errors which are explained by the atmosphere of the times.

François Mitterrand

If one had been able to predict what would have become of this Party ...

Herbert von Karajan, denazification hearing, 15 March 1946

It is a terrible thing for a man to find out suddenly that all his life he has been speaking nothing but the truth.

Oscar Wilde, *The Importance of Being Earnest*

Under the terms of his new three-year contract Karajan was given autonomy over the orchestra, the chorus, the hiring and firing of singers, and his budget. He would conduct six or seven operatic premières a season, the Aachen Orchestra's six subscription concerts and seven popular 'open' concerts. He was his own 'boss' as he liked to put it, using the American vernacular.

Or almost. His appointment was subject to confirmation both by the local municipal authority and by the Reichsmusikkammer in Berlin. Dr Gross had been required to register with the Nazi Party – the membership retroactive to 1 May 1933 – and the same request was now put to Karajan. As Karajan told Ernst Haeusserman:

Three days before my appointment, when the desired goal was just within reach, the town clerk came to me and said: 'Listen, there is' – and these were his words – 'there is one more formality to be carried out. You are not a Party member. According to the *Kreisleiter* [the NSDAP District leader], however, you cannot take up a post of this kind without being a Party member.' So I signed.[1]

He was twenty-seven. At the age of twenty-one, like many a young man talented and brimming with self-belief, he had backed his talent and put it to the test by taking up a risky career in difficult times against his parents' advice. Landing the job at Ulm had been a stroke of luck. He had seized the opportunity and capitalised brilliantly on it; yet it proved nothing. Dieterich had employed him because he was enthusiastic, talented, and cheap. After four years, Ulm had tried to dispense with his services; a year later it succeeded, forcing him, as he hung around in Berlin looking for work, to face the grim fact that his parents had probably been right all along. Now, he had power and success in his sights. And he signed.

Did he pause to reflect on what he had seen of Nazi activists in Salzburg or consider that – despite the German government's new-won economic success – certain warning signs were there? It would appear not. Though, again, one is bound to ask: warning signs of what and for whom? If the wider national and international community had, at worst, mixed feelings about the new German government and no clear sense of where its policies might eventually lead, what price the judgement of a 27-year-old musician? It is doubtful whether anyone in his right mind could have anticipated that the leaders of a democratically elected Western European government, however unsavoury, might one day enact a policy of industrialised genocide on an epic scale. In March 1946, Karajan told a denazification tribunal in Vienna:

Others were hoping to get the job, and the easiest lever was the political one. Today I completely accept the fact that I made an error, and I am prepared to suffer the consequences. In Germany in 1935 no importance was attributed to the matter . . . As it is at the moment here in Vienna, so it was in Aachen in 1935. Anyone who had a personal antipathy to someone else would exploit it. One didn't see the consequences clearly at the time – if one had been able to predict what would have become of this Party . . .[2]

Karajan's remark, 'In Germany in 1935 no importance was attributed to the matter' may seem banal. Yet, as J. P. Stern has argued in his book *Hitler: the Führer and the People*, an absence of strong feelings on matters of civil liberties or the promptings of individual conscience is one of the most marked (and least studied) features of life in Germany in the earliest years of Nazi rule:

Different social groups were attracted by the promise of full employment on the one hand and strict control of labour and low wages on the other, by the revanchist attitude to 'the crime of Versailles', economic autarky, or again the old dream of a 'Greater Germany' beyond the confines of Bismarck's Reich. But, however varied their ends, there was one thing which every social and political group that voted Hitler into power as well as some that opposed him, chief among them the Communists, were prepared to forgo, and that was political liberty under the law; one thing that every group (except the Jehovah's Witnesses) was ready to sacrifice, and that was freedom of individual conscience.[3]

By 1940 there were over eight million civilian members of the Nazi Party. Like trades unionists elsewhere in Europe where Communist- and socialist-led unions operated closed shops in key areas of national economies, members included ideologues, political activists and members of party faithful alongside large numbers of white- and blue-collar workers for whom non-membership would have been a direct bar to employment.

No analogy is ever wholly exact, of course; violinist Nathan Milstein would later say of Karajan's Nazi Party membership:

Membership *per se* in the party proves little. The brilliant Soviet violinists [David] Oistrakh and [Leonid] Kogan joined the Communist Party during Stalin's lifetime. Does that mean that they supported Stalin's crimes? No, they were just surviving, and in the West, as far as I know, no one ever condemned them for it.[4]

Political and ethical relativism is one of the reasons why Soviet artists who were Party members were never pursued in the Western media in the way that German artists were. Way back to the time when pioneering British socialists Sidney and Beatrice Webb excused the mass murder of the kulaks, the peasant landowners in Stalin's Russia, on grounds of a pressing need for greater agricultural efficiency in the Soviet Union, there has been a long history of toleration – even on occasion justification – of 'Uncle Joe' Stalin's acts of genocide that would be unthinkable in the case of Hitler's.[5]

Perspectives become blurred down the years. It is often forgotten how junior a figure Karajan was in the 1930s. Conductors later written up as Karajan's immediate contemporaries were in fact his seniors in calendar years and, exponentially, in maturity and influence, by some considerable distance. Men who would continue working in Germany, in Berlin in particular, throughout the war years included Schuricht (54 in 1935) Ansermet (51), Furtwängler (49), Rother (49), Knappertsbusch (47), Elmendorff (43), Clemens Krauss (42), and Böhm (40). Only Jochum (32) was more or less of Karajan's age and generation. All these men prospered in one way or another, benefiting from the government's highly ambivalent attitude to the place of musicians in the body politic.

In his pioneering study *The Rise and Fall of the Third Reich*, William L. Shirer would note:

Music fared best, if only because it was the least political of the arts and because the Germans had such a rich store of it from Bach through Beethoven and Mozart to Brahms ... the excellent musical fare did much to make people forget the degradation of the other arts and of so much life under the Nazis.[6]

When Gitta Sereny, Albert Speer's biographer, asked him how it came about that the vast majority of non-Jewish musicians stayed in Nazi Germany in the 1930s, he confirmed what was in fact the main thrust of the government's (principally Goebbels's) policy:

I really don't think people understand what it was like. People like Furtwängler, Wilhelm Kempff, Richard Strauss and others were considered to be, well, like national treasures. If they expressed disapproval or doubts, they would be argued with; if they remained unconvinced, they would be warned and put under open supervision. What would never have been allowed under any circumstances would be for them to leave – nothing so damaging to Germany's reputation abroad could have been permitted.[7]

During the denazification hearing into Karajan's case in March 1946, transcripts of which are published for the first time in the present volume, independent witnesses were called and affidavits deposited. One point that emerges from the testimonies is that few people who worked with Karajan during the years 1935–45 were aware that he *was* an NSDAP member.[8]

If Karajan had views, it would seem he kept them strictly to himself. No one beyond his immediate family circle recalls him discussing politics: except where politics impinged on music, when he could be extremely voluble. Certainly, there is nothing of politics or politicians in the few private letters we have from him during this period. Administrative letters and letters sent by him to government officials are signed with the obligatory 'Heil Hitler'. Privately, he uses no such greeting.

Within the Aachen Opera itself, the musicians largely ignored the saluting, heel-clicking etiquette of the new National Socialist culture. The sole memory anyone in Aachen had of Karajan acknowledging the existence of the Hitler salute dates from the summer of 1938. And that was part of a comic routine. Rendered temporarily voiceless after a minor operation to remove nodules from his vocal chords (the origins of the famously gravelly voice), he wrote out a number of cards, some serious, some not so serious. On one of them, he scrawled the words 'Heil Hitler!' According to Christa Ludwig's mother, who was a singer with the Aachen company at the time, Karajan's schoolboyish insistence on holding up the card whenever he entered a room occasioned a certain amount of mild amusement for a number of days.[9]

*

Setting aside the false though widely promoted theory that Karajan was lying about being asked to join the NSDAP in Aachen in 1935 (see Appendix B); and setting aside, too, what we shall come to later – the post-war testimonies of those who worked alongside Karajan in the years 1935–45 – what is the broad opinion of those who in subsequent years knew and worked with him? Yehudi Menuhin first met Karajan in Chile in 1949. He would later reflect:

[Karajan] joined [the NSDAP] because he was able to. He knew his worth musically but he knew his position was weak. In this respect, you can say he always knew very well how to guide his life. This decision wasn't essentially

86

different in attitude or method from any other decision he took. It was the correct chess move. That's all it amounted to. He always seemed to make the right career move. He knew how to do that.[10]

Though the facts of Karajan's early and middle years do not always bear out the assertion that he invariably made 'the correct chess move', many would agree with the broad thrust of Menuhin's judgement. Christopher Raeburn, for instance: one of the wisest and wariest of Karajan's post-war recording producers:

Joining the Party when he did – in 1935 or whenever – was a move that was very much of its time. What happened subsequently, when he became much better known by a far wider public, was that people began using him as a particular *example* of a certain type of opportunist. He certainly was an opportunist. I also suspect that when he was young he believed, if not in Nazism itself, then in quite a few of the ideals the Nazis espoused: efficiency, order, '*Tradition ist Schlamperei* [tradition is sloppiness]', that sort of thing. In that sense, he was not typically Austrian. I'm sure he saw a future in all this musically and that he was prepared to overlook most of what went with it.[11]

There was, in fact, an unusually wide split within Karajan's character and personality between the musical idealist (for he was certainly that) and the professional careerist.

As for his broad political beliefs and aspirations, they were similar to those of the majority of young men and women of his background and class in Germany in the early 1930s; aspirations that, in turn, are remarkably similar to those of the great majority of people from the 1950s onwards: a vision of material well-being that the war had merely postponed. (Karajan's rising status and huge selling power at the time of the coming of age of the so-called 'consumer society' was not, of course, wholly coincidental.) As an old man, Karajan would recall how Salzburgers watched the improvements Hitler was making just seven kilometres away across the border in Germany: how, with six million unemployed, he promised an elaborate and hitherto undreamed-of network of highways whose construction would bring employment and prosperity.

Of course, he was counting on the possibility of war. He knew from World War 1 the value of mobility. He promoted the Volkswagen factory and brought out the VW Beetle. You could take away the body and make a military car in no time. It was useful, cheap, reliable, and could move until the road was nearly non-existent . . . Hitler said every workman would have a car. We laughed. It couldn't be possible. Tractors were unknown and we always yearned for cars. A car – and I felt this myself – changed you. When I was in Ulm, I was too poor to have a car, but after three months in Aachen I had one.[12]

Driving to the opera house or concert hall in his own car, Karajan admitted, added to his sense of self-esteem, made him feel better about the job he was doing. 'Your own car, your own house,' he would recall. 'Work seems worthwhile when it brings you such benefits.'

If Karajan was thought by some not to be typically Austrian, there were those – Hitler among them – who would later question his 'Germanness' too. Certainly, there were substantial differences between the 27-year-old Karajan and his conducting peers in Germany at the time: not only in age but in attitude and cultural orientation. There was Furtwängler, greatest of German conductors, the late-nineteenth-century liberal idealist who was extremely active politically in a wayward and frenetic sort of way but who lost as many political chess games as he won. And Böhm, the shrewd lawyer with a peasant's instinct for survival, a fine musician, the fieriest of the *echt*-German conductors, a Party refusnik who was none the less raucous in his support of Hitler. (Asked to back Hitler's decision to hold a plebiscite on 10 April 1938 to 'ratify' the *Anschluss* with Austria, Böhm declared publicly: 'Anyone who does not say a big YES to our Führer's action and give it their hundred per cent support does not deserve to be called a German.'[13]) And there was the most profoundly German of all the great German conductors born in the last years of the nineteenth century, Hans Knappertsbusch: sceptical, anti-Hitler, anti most things. Knappertsbusch was rather like Orwell's Benjamin, the shrewd and cynical old donkey in *Animal Farm*: cynical enough, certainly, to conduct the Führer's birthday concerts in Berlin in 1943-4 when Furtwängler bowed out.

If Karajan resembled anyone from among the generation before his own, it was Clemens Krauss, the well-bred, well-connected autocrat, a born moderniser, expedient in the forging of alliances with other modernisers, but politically semi-detached; intelligent enough to stay onside with those who mattered but essentially distrustful of any power centre other than his own. Where the two men differed was in the circumstances of their careers. None of us has any control over when we are born. For the young Krauss, the musical world in the 1920s was more or less instantly his oyster; once that world had vanished, he never really regained a proper footing. The young Karajan, by contrast, had his bad times early. It was during these years that he taught himself patience. 'My time will come, I can wait' was his motto.

*

The Party was on display in all its glory on 29 June 1935. The city of Aachen was *en fête* for what was to become an annual event in these years, NSDAP Party Day. It was high summer and the government was somewhere near the zenith of its popularity. War reparations were a thing of the past, the economy was sound, unemployment had fallen from its 29.9 per cent peak in 1932 to a modest 10.3 per cent, defences were being rebuilt, Hitler's foreign adventurism was as yet a relatively minor affair. National pride had been restored.

The highlight of the day was a celebratory open-air concert in Aachen's historic Katschhof Square. The orchestra and the massed voices of 750 singers were conducted by Karajan, Pitz, and others in a programme almost exclusively given over to the kind of rowdy musical rodomontade the Nazis were now commissioning by the barrow load for showpiece rallies from 'loyal' composers. Richard Trunk's *Feier der neuen Front*, dedicated to Hitler, with a text by Baldur von Schirach, was the highlight of this particular occasion. It must have been just about the largest gathering of musicians Karajan ever conducted.[14]

Nor did his conducting go unnoticed by the powers-that-be. Here is a man, purred the Nazi-controlled *Westdeutscher Beobachter*, who can give 'a direction to the new organisation of our artistic life, a direction that National Socialism demands'.[15] The visiting Gauleiter from Cologne was no doubt well pleased, too. Seeing this keen young man at the head of a vast army of musicians must have made a refreshing change from arguing the toss with Furtwängler about whether or not Hermann Abendroth should be removed from his position as Director of the State High School for Music in Cologne. (He was; Furtwängler lost.)

In his denazification hearing in March 1946, Karajan said he never conducted for Party functions, though in his parallel written deposition he wrote, 'I successfully avoided political functions, unless they were purely musical.'[16] The fact is, as Aachen's General Music Director he had little option but to conduct on such occasions. Equally, it is difficult to imagine him not relishing this particular rally: the populace *en fête*, the looming cathedral, the swastika-draped Town Hall, the massed choirs. Did his long-standing fascination with Verdi's *Don Carlos* date back to all this? It is one thing to conduct *Don Carlos*, quite another to have been a bit-part player in a comparably sinister drama.

There was also the power such occasions bestowed. Musical power came with the job, of course. But the sociological use of power also interested Karajan. He liked to have his own way professionally, parrying opposition in all its forms, as the *Kreisleiter* in Aachen would shortly discover. In this workaday form, the sociological use of power could be said to have buttressed his career. Yet, underpinning this careful career management was something deeper, not so much *Macht* – power in its more usually accepted sense – but Nietzsche's 'will to power' as defined and redefined by writers like Martin Heidegger and Paul Tillich. In his book *Love, Power, and Justice* Tillich writes:

[It] is the drive of everything living to realise itself with increasing intensity and extensity. The will to power is not the will of man to attain power over men, but it is the self-affirmation of life in its self-transcending dynamics, overcoming internal and external resistance.[17]

However one regards Karajan as a man, and whatever view one takes of his success or otherwise in interpreting the works of individual composers, it is impossible to understand his inner motivation as a performing artist without reference to this idea in one form or another.

CHAPTER 12

General Music Director, Aachen

The happiest years of my life.
Herbert von Karajan, interview, Aachen, 1951

Even as a young man, Karajan fascinated and baffled in more or less equal measure. He was impatient and highly-strung. Impatient with words, his mind raced ahead of his speech. The effect was a curious kind of self-induced stammer. Victor Sheean would remember being with him during Toscanini's time in Salzburg:

Karajan especially, young and very eager (he stammered in those days, at least in English, although this has since disappeared), went to every Toscanini rehearsal and was incapable of getting a coherent word out, in spite of frantic struggles, after any of the supreme performances.[1]

This abrupt, elliptical manner of communicating was something he never entirely lost, making him appear brittle and aggressive to those who did not know him. With close friends such as Michel Glotz the natural impatience could readily be transformed into a well-honed comic routine:

KARAJAN [*dining*] Please, das Ding [the thing].
GLOTZ So, is this the bread, the water, the wine, or the vodka that you require?
KARAJAN You don't know the meaning of 'Ding'?
GLOTZ Yes, I know the meaning of 'Ding'.
KARAJAN Then you are an idiot. Pass me das Ding.
GLOTZ You are right, I am an idiot. On the other hand, you are not expressing yourself clearly.

Yet as a musician, paradoxically, Karajan was possessed of an extraordinary power of concentration and a capacity for creating and communicating a feeling of great inner calm. The distinguished German bass-baritone Hans Hotter, who was a year younger than Karajan, remembers singing Brahms's *German Requiem* under his direction in Aachen in 1937:

The thing I remember mostly from Aachen was the absolutely striking and fascinating control he had over his emotional behaviour – after all, he was only 29 years old and he conducted one of the most moving pieces I have come across in my whole life.[2]

When Karajan first arrived in Aachen, he rented a small house by a wood in countryside to the south of the city. It was surrounded by meadows and was only a short drive from the forests, fields, and woodland walks of the Eifel region. He bought his first car, but he also walked a lot, either alone or, after he met the singer Elmy Holgerloef, for hours on end with her: Herbert in front, in a scruffy old camel-hair coat, beltless but tied up with string, Elmy following behind.

He was also a good deal more sociable than he had been in Ulm, and more settled within himself. Magdalena Kemp, wife of the influential local critic, would recall, 'Karajan struck us as being a nice person: simple, hard-working, calm, though always a little distant.' A number of local families found him less distant. Tired of living like a student, he seems to have been more than happy to be welcomed into family homes. Open fires, home cooking, and the smell of freshly baked bread reasserted their claims. (Years later, when Gundula Janowitz told him that the cottage she had just bought had a bread-oven by the fireplace, he threatened to take up residence.) Which is not to say that he ceased working long, unsocial hours. After dinner, like some earnest young man in a Chekhov play, he would proffer his thanks and leave. 'I must work. It is a sad fact, but the Holy Spirit does not descend and do it for me,' he would remark.

The Erckens family – the father was a successful textile manufacturer in Aachen – were particular friends. Karajan would take the demure and lovely Marly Erckens, the 23-year-old daughter, bathing in the woods in the summer, sometimes alone, sometimes with other girls. There are photos of him bathing and punting with Marly, and of the two of them with one of Herbert's older female admirers, the 40-year-old Helene Merzenich, to whom Herbert was known as 'Fluffy'.

Interviewed about Karajan by the *Aachener Volkszeitung* in 1977, Marly would recall:

He paid many happy visits to us, and there were occasions, too, when his parents would come and visit us from Salzburg. They were happy times within our family circle and we all shared enthusiastically in Herbert's many artistic successes. It was clear even then that he had a great career in front of him. The really fascinating thing about him was his ability to separate his private life from his career as a musician. For instance, though he was very industrious, often working till four and five in the morning, he had no grand piano in his house. When I asked him why, he replied, 'A general does not have a field gun in his room either!'[3]

Richard Talbot, a neighbour in Aachen, remembered Karajan calling round one Christmas Eve:

My wife and I were busy decorating the Christmas tree. Herbert came in through the back garden, saw what we were doing, said 'I obviously can't be much use here', sat down at the piano, and started playing carols. Once he had started, he began transposing the carols into the styles of various composers, starting with Mozart and Beethoven and getting more and more modern until he was playing pure jazz. It was lovely! I tell you, no coffee-house jazz pianist could have done it better.[4]

Karajan lived frugally. When members of the company signed for their money at the end of the month, they often noticed that his salary was still uncollected from the previous month.⁵ On excursions to Cologne or Brussels he rarely ate in restaurants or cafés. Bread and cheese and a bottle of beer in some country spot on the running-board of his car was what seemed to please him best.

There were those who said – and more who would say it later – that he worked too hard, that he never had time to enjoy the material wealth which he slowly began to accumulate. This was always a mistaken view. Karajan's ability to separate out his affairs and concentrate absolutely on what he was doing at the time was crucial to his success, both as a man and a musician. Even in Aachen, as Marly Erckens's testimony proves, he was highly practised in the art of relaxation, dividing his private from his professional life. Churchill once defined a holiday as a period in your life when you need to think only of one thing at a time. This was something Karajan trained himself to do from quite an early age.

Artistically, no family was more important to him in Aachen than the Ludwigs. Anton Ludwig and his wife, the mezzo-soprano Eugenie Besalla, are best remembered as the parents of the illustrious Christa Ludwig. She was six when Karajan arrived in Aachen, eleven when the family moved to Hanau where her father had been appointed Intendant of the local opera in 1940. Like most members of the Aachen company, Frau Besalla found Karajan extraordinary yet likeable. The mordant wit helped. Recalcitrant singers trotting out familiar excuses such as 'I've always sung it like this' would be met with 'I didn't know you were that old'.

Anton Ludwig had worked in Aachen since the early 1920s and was clearly an influential figure there. A pupil of Bernhard Paumgartner's mother, he had begun his career as a baritone. From Europe he went to the United States where he once sang alongside Caruso in *Pagliacci*. Back in Germany, now a dramatic tenor, he sang a ferociously demanding repertory including Florestan, Canio, Parsifal, and Fritz in Schreker's *Der ferne Klang*. His third career was that of stage director, and it was mainly in this capacity that he worked with Karajan, though he still occasionally appeared in cameo roles in his own productions (Loge in *Das Rheingold* was a favourite part).

*

Ten days after conducting the massed ranks of the Party faithful in the city square in June 1935, Karajan conducted something very different, a *Rokoko-Abend* in Aachen's Couven-Museum: a triple bill made up of Mozart's youthful Singspiel *Bastien und Bastienne*, a short ballet *Ein*

Schäferspiel (*A Shepherd's Play*, music again drawn from Mozart), and, finally, a danced version of a work that was already of absorbing interest to Karajan, Debussy's *L'après-midi d'un faune*.

The programme for the *Rokoko-Abend* carried a reminder that booking for season tickets for the 1935–6 opera programme closed in five days' time. Demand, it seems, had been unusually heavy. Critic Wilhelm Kemp would later report:

The new General Music Director has built a reputation with his work at the Municipal Theatre which has triggered a curiosity even in those members of the public who would not normally frequent an opera house.[6]

Karajan's drawing power with audiences was evident even then.

A month later, Karajan published his aims and objectives for the new season.[7] It is an interesting article that reads rather like the corporate plan of a modern Chief Executive. (How much the article was Karajan's work and how much Gross's, it is difficult to say.) There is a reminder of the importance of Aachen's status as a showpiece border town, and there is a reference to a new 'youth' policy (a choral festival in 1937 and competitions for young singers) making a significant contribution to 'the creative power of the new Germany'. For the rest, the aims are specifically musical and typically Karajanesque. He writes of his desire for purity and beauty in music-making. Technical skills must be improved. There is a need for the orchestra to develop its sound, in particular, the weight of its sound. He talks of building an ensemble, not in the sense of recruiting a permanent roster of artists, but of learning how to draw soloists, chorus, and orchestra into a single musical orbit. He is also proud to announce the names of a number of internationally esteemed instrumentalists and singers who will be visiting Aachen.

For the Verdi *Requiem*, three soloists from the Berlin State Opera had been engaged: Viorica Ursuleac, Gertrud Rünger, and Helge Rosvaenge. Clearly, Karajan was determined to exploit the city's reputation as a home of fine choral singing. With Theodor Rehmann as the city's distinguished Director of Cathedral Music and the young Wilhelm Pitz as the theatre's chorus master, the barometer was set fair. If there were clouds on the horizon it was the threat to the repertory posed by the government's anti-Semitic policies. Rehmann, grumpily anti-Nazi, was impressed by Karajan's stand on this. Though he found Karajan a somewhat 'Mephistophelean' character, he admired his brinkmanship with party bureaucrats on the question of the right to perform, unaltered, the great choral works of the Judaeo-Christian tradition.[8]

*

The 1935–6 Aachen season proved to be something of a sensation. Karajan opened with *Die Meistersinger* and followed this with a production of Richard Strauss's fairy-tale epic *Die Frau ohne Schatten*. Walter Gieseking, then at the height of his powers and a much more leonine pianist than he often appeared to be in the post-war years, played Beethoven's Fifth Piano Concerto in an all-Beethoven concert, Georg Kulenkampff played the Brahms Violin Concerto in a concert that also included Debussy's *La mer* and Tchaikovsky's Sixth Symphony, and the great Spanish cellist Gaspar Cassadó came to play the Dvořák concerto.

The performance of the Verdi *Requiem* alone, crowed Dr Kemp, proved the wisdom of those who had recommended Karajan for the Aachen job in the first place:

[Von Karajan] belongs to that school of conducting which realises music through a peculiar kind of inner absorption whilst at the same time discreetly overseeing the business of the individual moment . . . [he] conducted [the Verdi *Requiem*] in a grand and superior way, attacked the score, yet remained flexible and buoyant. He accompanies singers yet allows each singer to evaluate what he or she may contribute at any given moment.[9]

If Kemp ventured a criticism of Aachen's new General Music Director, it was that fewer contemporary works were being programmed than would have been the case in Raabe's time. Karajan's aim, Kemp informs his readers, is to produce 'unique and exemplary performances of the most important classical and modern works'. This was to be a familiar Karajan battle-cry: why alienate audiences by performing 'difficult' new music badly?

In fact, Kemp's point was not entirely accurate. In January 1936, Karajan conducted a choral programme consisting of a Bach cantata, Kodály's *Psalmus hungaricus*, and the *Sinfonische Friedensmesse* written shortly after the end of the First World War by the distinguished organist and Bruckner follower Franz Philipp. Later, in May, he conducted on successive evenings separate concerts of contemporary music by Frommel, Pepping, the Swedish composer Atterberg, Georg Schumann, and Ravel. No wonder he was often up until five in the morning.

For the players in the Aachen orchestra, these were taxing times. If there was a consolation, it was that Karajan was working even harder than they were. Some older musicians grumbled. The younger ones generally admired Karajan, warming to his already precociously paternalistic way of running their affairs. A young string player from those days, Bernhard Stahl, would later recall:

He was a strong personality! Almost like a father-figure even then, and always very fair. After two and a half hours' rehearsal one felt one could do it all again. For us youngsters, it was a very instructive time. He dealt with orchestral difficulties better than many more famous conductors of my acquaintance. I have nothing but good things to say of those times.[10]

Karajan worked assiduously, teaching the players to listen to the music and to each other. Clarity of texture seems to have been a particular priority. The technical shortcomings of some of the strings players could be a source of irritation, not least because good alternatives were in increasingly short supply. 'The Jews have all left,' he was heard to mutter one day, 'and now you haven't the faintest idea how to play this.'[11]

Karajan was, however, greatly taken with the playing of the new leader of the orchestra, Detlev Grümmer, whose wife Elisabeth he would later catapult to fame as a singer. When Karajan visited Ulm in February 1936 to conduct a concert with his old orchestra, he invited Detlev Grümmer along as soloist in the G minor concerto of Bruch. Willi Hermann, the Aachen orchestra's principal flute, was also given solo billing in the 1935–6 season.

As winter turned to spring, the pace of work quickened further. Bach's B minor Mass was exhaustively and exhaustingly rehearsed for Eastertide performances in Aachen and a subsequent Belgian tour. There was radio work in Cologne (studio transmissions of *Carmen* and *Rigoletto*, and a concert with Backhaus) and in Aachen *Tiefland*, *Tosca*, and Karajan's début in a work that would have a crucial bearing on his entire career, Wagner's *Tristan und Isolde*.

Within the space of two seasons, Karajan had settled into a taxing but finely honed working routine. The 1936–7 season saw the start of his first *Ring* cycle, directed by Anton Ludwig. While *Das Rheingold* and *Götterdämmerung* were in rehearsal in the autumn of 1936, Karajan also conducted *Aida*, followed by a fiercely dramatic account of *Don Giovanni* (Karajan himself directing the recitatives from the piano) that appears to have been somewhat at odds with a blandly picturesque stage production.

A performance of Bruckner's Fourth Symphony, in Robert Haas's new performing edition, also took the critics by the ears. This was Raabe territory but Karajan instantly made an impact with his scrupulously clear unfolding of the newly revised text. Local critic Franz Achilles wrote of Karajan's inborn feeling for the natural splendours and cathedral-like spaces of the music, something he attributed in part at least to his Austrian roots and his familiarity with the cathedral architecture of Salzburg and St Florian. Had he known about it, he might have added Karajan's knowledge and love of the organ as another factor in his precociously complete understanding of the Bruckner idiom.

Distinguished instrumental soloists began coming to Aachen in yet greater numbers: the 1936–7 season included Cortot, Francescatti, and Edwin Fischer. There was even a chance for the audience to hear a concerto specially written by the composer Walter Rehberg for the eccentric and ill-fated 'Janko' piano with its radically revised keyboard layout.

Brahms's *German Requiem* was chosen for the spring tour of Belgium, with Hans Hotter as baritone soloist. Haydn's *The Creation* was also performed: two unexceptionably 'German' works strategically chosen by Karajan to clear the ground for the *St Matthew Passion*, which he was determined to perform at Eastertide. Party zealots grumbled, but Karajan got his way. He was helped in all this by the fact that in August 1936 he had accepted Raabe's request to succeed him as the Reichsmusikkammer's Aachen representative. The details bored him, and most of the work was delegated. It was the authority that Karajan valued: the added leverage it gave him in his disputes with the bureaucrats and the ideologues.

The Evangelist for these Eastertide performances of the *St Matthew Passion* was one of the most distinctive and distinguished of all interpreters of the role, Karl Erb. Now in his sixtieth year, Erb would be immortalised by Thomas Mann in his novel *Doctor Faustus* as the creator of the role of the narrator in Leverkühn's *Apocalypsis cum figuris*:

a tenor with an almost castrato-like high register, whose chilly crow – objective, reporterlike – stands in terrifying contrast to the content of his catastrophic announcements.[12]

Karajan had first heard Erb singing Lieder in Salzburg in 1925 with Schwarzkopf's teacher Maria Ivogün. It was a voice, like that of another great Evangelist, Peter Pears, once heard never forgotten.

*

Meanwhile, Vienna beckoned. It was the Salzburg-born Erwin Kerber, a key figure in the early years of the Salzburg Festival and now the resourceful and talented new Director of the Vienna State Opera, who invited Karajan to conduct a single performance of *Tristan und Isolde* there on 1 June 1937. Having got rid of Weingartner as music director in Vienna and secured Bruno Walter's services in his place, Kerber had lavish plans for the Opera. Engaging this able and charismatic young fellow Salzburger as a guest conductor was an interesting move; for as well as asking Karajan to conduct *Tristan und Isolde*, Kerber was also planning to offer him a job as one of the regular house conductors.

Karajan would eventually decline the offer. Fond as he was of Kerber, the idea of giving up Aachen to become a house conductor in Vienna did not really bear thinking about. Kerber was not ousted by the Nazis until 1942.

Talent, popularity with his staff, and enormous charm were his principal weapons, though it is said that from 1938 onwards he took the precaution of knocking on his own office door each morning just in case a successor was already sitting at his desk.

Karajan's début in Vienna appears to have roused Furtwängler's interest, the first intimation of troubles to come. Furtwängler's girlfriend and local sleuth (later his secretary) Fräulein von Tiedemann was seen in the audience on 1 June. In Vienna, where such things are noted and discussed, Karajan's stock rose accordingly.

The reviews for the *Tristan und Isolde* performance were good, though they reflect what Bruno Walter and, indeed, Karajan himself would later say of the performance. 'Unbridled and headstrong' were the words used by the influential critic of the *Neues Wiener Tagblatt* Heinrich Kralik. But better that, he argued, than 'cool, supercilious routine':

Even in outward appearance, [Karajan's] style of conducting has a theatrical effect. There is theatricality as the slight figure, crowned by a narrow head and an artist's flowing mane, trembles with passion, now standing erect, now bowing down again; there is the conductor's right hand, used with such emphatic effect to unloose storms from the orchestra, whilst the left hand, with its tautly stretched surface, calms the churned-up waves. In matters of tempo and dynamics the effect is wholly theatrical. Urgent, driving tempi and thundering, crashing discharges determine the character and colour of a performance that powerfully fans the flames of Wagner's symphony of love . . .[13]

It was this kind of performance, in Berlin a year later, that would cause people to talk of '*Das Wunder Karajan*'. If Kralik emphasised the passion of the conducting, others chose to dwell on its moments of dreamy introversion. The critic of the *Wiener Zeitung* noted Karajan's youthfulness ('a young man who looks even younger than he is') and the fact that, though he set lively tempi, he often muted the orchestra's fortissimo and was often to be seen 'lost in the dreamy sound-spell cast by Wagner's music'.[14] Even more interesting from the technical point of view is a short review tucked away among the small ads of the *Neue Freie Presse* which remarks on Karajan's unusual habit of pointing solo instrumentalists to the stage and a particular singer, as if to say 'Don't watch me, listen to her; listen and make music with her'.[15]

And all this, without a single rehearsal. In later years, Karajan tended to dine out on the story of his Vienna *Tristan* and the case of the vanishing rehearsals:

I had been promised three rehearsals, but when I arrived in Vienna I was met at the station by a functionary from the orchestra who said that a programme change had necessitated a reduction to just two rehearsals. I had three days of piano rehearsals – which is a story in itself. My Isolde [Anny Konetzni] was more interested in attending to her correspondence. Then another functionary appeared and said that the orchestra could now manage only one rehearsal. Naturally, as a young Kapellmeister from the provinces, I didn't want to make too much of a fuss, so I agreed. Finally, some players came to me and said, 'Look, there's nothing we can achieve in just one rehearsal. Give up that rehearsal and, we promise, we'll play for you on the night as though you were Mahler himself.'[16]

The orchestra was true to its word. Otto Strasser would later recall:

You know, that first performance really impressed us. He conducted it more or less by heart, even though he had the score lying in front of him. From the beginning he was *the* Karajan we would all come to know and admire. Incredible security and dynamism, and all without rehearsal![17]

In later years, when he was director of the Vienna Opera, Karajan would reduce orchestral rehearsals to a necessary minimum. He would also, ironically, come to be something of an advocate of the rehearsal-free debut. The first time Placido Domingo worked with Karajan, in Vienna in 1974, was on the soundtrack of the film of *Madama Butterfly*. The evening before the sessions, Karajan announced a ten o'clock start, promised a couple of hours of rehearsal, and estimated that actual recording would begin around midday. In fact, like a surgeon briefing a nervous patient, he was merely making reassuring noises. Domingo would later recall:

I arrived at 10 and took my place. All of a sudden I saw the red light next to [Karajan] go on. He began to conduct, and in fifty-five minutes we had finished recording the first act.
'Maestro,' I said, 'I thought we were going to rehearse.'
'Among musicians,' he replied, 'rehearsal is not necessary.'
I can confirm that we were indeed together on every note. In the afternoon we recorded the third act, and that was that . . . Never before had I worked with a conductor of that calibre without having a piano rehearsal – without even exchanging a word about the role. I appreciated the great compliment he was paying me.[18]

Not all the singers Karajan worked with were willing to be so trusted, but many who did will testify to its effectiveness. Not that it was a technique practised only by Karajan. Jon Vickers has recalled that all the great Wagner conductors he worked with – Knappertsbusch, Kempe, Karajan himself – operated on the basis of experience, intuition, and trust; music logically learned and studied, but *performed* by a process that has little to do with ratiocination, everything to do with the outflow of the music itself and the performers' own richly accumulated store of wisdom and experience.

Where there were problems with the unrehearsed Vienna *Tristan und Isolde*, they concerned the staging. If the reviews are to be believed, it was a shambles. Alexander Kipnis's King Marke appears to have been largely unbriefed as to where he should be at any given moment; both Konetzni and the Tristan Josef Kalenberg, poor actors at the best of times even by the standards of this histrionically undemanding age, were in indifferent form; while Anton Dermota, the Young Sailor, perched far aloft in the crow's-nest of the stage ship, had no visible means of contact with anyone.

Word travels fast in the musical world, and the success of Karajan's Vienna *Tristan und Isolde* was soon being noised abroad. Singers and instrumentalists who had appeared with him in Aachen were also taking travellers' tales to some of Europe's most important musical capitals: Stockholm, Amsterdam, and Berlin.

In the autumn of 1937, Karajan began an extraordinarily demanding pre-Christmas schedule in Aachen, conducting *Der fliegende Hollander*, *Così fan tutte*, his first complete *Ring* cycle, the *Missa Solemnis*, Bruckner's Eighth Symphony, and several orchestral concerts. At the same time, offers began to dribble in from outside: serious offers, from important people, with whom Karajan was happy to negotiate on his own terms from a base in Aachen that looked increasingly secure.

CHAPTER 13

1938: The promised land

It was the best of times, it was the worst of times, it was the age
of wisdom, it was the age of foolishness, it was the epoch of belief,
it was the epoch of incredulity, it was the season of Light, it was
the season of Darkness . . .

Charles Dickens, *A Tale of Two Cities*

1938 was a remarkable year for Karajan, and a fateful one. During its
course, he made a famously successful debut with the Berlin Philharmonic,
and a yet more sensational one with the Berlin State Opera. In Stockholm,
he conducted Sibelius's Sixth Symphony, thus discovering a composer
whose music was to become for him a lifelong source of fascination and
spiritual solace. He conducted the Amsterdam Concertgebouw Orchestra
for the first time. He made his first gramophone recording. And he got
married.

Yet what was an *annus mirabilis* for Karajan was, for others, an *annus
horribilis*. For 1938 was also the year of Hitler's annexation of Austria
and the start of his dismemberment of the fragile post-First World War
construct that was Czechoslovakia. It was the year of the ill-fated Munich
Agreement. And it was the year, too, of an event which signalled to a largely
unseeing world terrors that were to come: the anti-Jewish pogrom of the
night of 9–10 November 1938, dubbed '*Kristallnacht*'.

*

Elmy Holgerloef, the woman Karajan would marry in the summer of 1938,
was an operetta star. She has been described as 'flawless in appearance and
speech, with sparkling blue eyes, a refined bearing and nature whatever her
mood, clever, witty, charming, and lively in spirit'.[1] Did such a paragon
ever exist? On stage, apparently so. Elisabeth Grümmer would remark:

I have only the fondest memories of her. What a superb artist she was in her
repertoire, which was operetta. Very few have ever equalled her, for she had
grace, style, and musicality.[2]

Karajan first worked with Elmy on a 1935 New Year's Eve gala production of Strauss's *Die Fledermaus*. Elmy was starring as Rosalinde and, like a
lot of people who later came to know and like Karajan, she began by having

a row with him. Perhaps it was precisely because she was so vivacious and alluring, with her trim figure, sparkling eyes, and fashionable Marcel wave, that Karajan decided to be difficult. Physically attracted to her, he used the shy man's tactic of being more than usually distant.

'So what about giving me a chord?' she enquired, rather loudly, as Karajan sat drumming his fingers on the piano lid. Karajan recoiled like a startled animal. 'Well, at least I've thrown you off balance!' purred Elmy. For a time, things were rather grim, Karajan endlessly finding fault with her singing. By now she was less amused. 'If my voice doesn't suit you, then go out and hire one of your operatic cows.'

Karajan half apologised. 'Please, when one is as pretty as you are, one doesn't have to sing like an operatic cow.'³

The performance was a triumph, Elmy at her charming, volatile best. Nor was it long before the two of them were going on long country hikes together and sharing Elmy's house outside Aachen. She was older than he: ten years older, it was rumoured.⁴ At first, it seems, they were simply good friends. 'Love came later,' Elmy would recall, 'after marriage.' She knew that Karajan was passionate about music, that he worked 'like a man possessed'; but she quickly learned that he could shut out work completely when he was so minded.

The idyll was not to last. The war and Karajan's attempt to hold positions simultaneously in Aachen and Berlin broke the relationship asunder. Elmy eventually went back to singing full time. But the marriage, while it lasted, was blissfully happy:

We were in love and playful like children. I had married a joyful receptive man. Certainly, he was not a man who would do anything foolish for a woman; but he came out of his shell more and more, especially when we were in our little kingdom, our house in the meadows near the Belgium border.⁵

Elmy brought no wealth or grand connections to the marriage, but she provided one significant link with the turbulent world beyond their private kingdom in the meadows. Among her theatre friends was the actress Emmy Sonnemann, whom the most theatrically minded and spendthrift member of the Nazi High Command, Hermann Göring, had fallen for after seeing her on stage in Weimar in 1932. The affair had dragged until, more or less on Hitler's instructions, Göring had married her – in a style befitting one of the later Roman emperors – on 10 April 1935.

Outside politics, narcotics, the pleasures of the flesh, and the wearing of bizarre uniforms, nothing gave the boorish but intellectually gifted Göring more pleasure than his overlordship of the Berlin State Opera, the prestigious cultural heirloom he had wrested from Goebbels's grasp shortly after the Nazis came to power in 1933. Until 1 September 1939 – when, with war imminent, Göring signed over all responsibility for running the Opera to its *de facto* boss Heinz Tietjen – Göring treated the house on Berlin's Unter den Linden as a private club. Emmy, too, was very much at home there. Indeed, to Tietjen's fury, she went on playing Lady Bountiful to the stars (she was less concerned with the house's domestic staff) throughout the war.[6]

When, in the winter of 1937–8, the Berlin State Opera made its first tentative approaches to Karajan, the channels of communication may not have been exclusively musical ones.

*

In January 1938, after concerts with Wilhelm Backhaus and performances of Verdi's *Otello* in Aachen, Karajan travelled to Amsterdam for a concert with the Concertgebouw Orchestra. Mengelberg's orchestra since 1895, this was currently the nonpareil of European ensembles, its impeccable musical pedigree backed by a sovereign technique. Karajan knew its work well; often, of a winter's afternoon, he had threaded his way north by car to Amsterdam to hear them play.

Oddly, he never seems to have coveted the Concertgebouw Orchestra as he later would the Berlin Philharmonic. It was Dutch, of course, not German. But was not Karajan perhaps concerned that, after Mengelberg, so perfectly honed a musical instrument had nowhere to go but down? (Which is where Karajan later came to believe it did go after Mengelberg and Van Beinum.[7]) His programme in January 1938 ended with Brahms's First Symphony, a work he would record with the orchestra, to magnificent effect, in somewhat disputatious circumstances five years later in the autumn of 1943.[8]

The immediate consequence of Karajan's visit to Amsterdam was the issuing of an invitation to Mengelberg to conduct Karajan's own rather more modest band in Aachen. Mengelberg agreed and duly appeared for two concerts in February 1939. The programme he chose was characteristic: Berlioz's overture *Le carnaval romain*, the gaudily coloured *Ciaconna gotica* by Mengelberg's former deputy at the Concertgebouw Cornelis Dopper,[9] and Tchaikovsky's Sixth Symphony.

Before Mengelberg arrived, Karajan had briefed his players on the great man's familiar repertory of comic sallies.

'How many players are present?'

'108.'

'So I have to say everything 108 times . . .'

The players laughed politely. The joke safely out of the way, Mengelberg proceeded to savage a violinist who was playing with the neck of his instrument angled lazily towards the floor. 'And for whom are you playing, my friend? Please make your music in the proper direction.'

It was a story Karajan liked to repeat in later years. His own orchestras would always be trained to look well, to carry themselves with distinction. Karajan also noted Mengelberg's trick of using slightly quicker tempi in rehearsal so as to give his players the sense of having more time 'live' in concert.

After Amsterdam, Karajan's next stop was Stockholm.[10] The Head of Swedish Radio, Per Lindforsch, had invited him to conduct three contrasted programmes. The first was made up of assorted musical sweetmeats: the Prelude to *Die Meistersinger*, Smetana's 'Vltava', and Ravel's *La valse*. The second was given over to symphonies by Mozart and Dvořák. Finally, there was a concert of contemporary Scandinavian music: Sibelius's Sixth Symphony and the Piano Concerto (1935) by the Norwegian composer Marius Ulfrstad.

The Sibelius was a revelation to Karajan. It was also a challenge. Wandering around Stockholm he noticed a poster advertising a rival performance under the direction of the Finnish conductor and Sibelius specialist Simon Pergament-Parmet. Parmet's rivalry notwithstanding, Karajan had a considerable success with the Stockholm Radio Orchestra. He was invited back for more concerts the following year, and was sounded out about the possibility of accepting a permanent position there. He declined, though the memory of the Stockholm approach would return to haunt him in later years.

Karajan himself had somewhat surprisingly brought up the subject in conversation with me as we sat in his shed-cum-film-editing suite in the suburbs of Berlin one December morning in 1988.

'So why did you say no?' I asked.

'I was happy in Aachen. I had a house there. I had just got married.' He paused. 'And now I can't help thinking how much trouble it might have saved me later . . .'

*

By far the most important entry in Karajan's diary in the early months of 1938 was '8 April, Berlin'. During 1937, he had received an invitation from the management of the Berlin Philharmonic to conduct one of their non-subscription 'special concerts'. (Their 'speciality' being their relative cheapness: RM 1–6 per ticket as opposed to the more usual RM 2–11 for Furtwängler's concerts.) The programme Karajan had agreed with the orchestra had three items: Mozart's youthful chamber symphony in B flat K319, the Second Suite from Ravel's ballet *Daphnis et Chloé*, and Brahms's

Fourth Symphony. Not surprisingly, all three works appeared in Karajan's winter concert programmes. The Ravel and the Brahms were played with the Aachen orchestra; the Mozart was played in Stockholm, and again in early March with the Mozarteum Orchestra in Salzburg.

The Salzburg concert is an oddity in Karajan's 1938 spring schedules.[11] A report in the *Salzburger Volksblatt* on 26 February suggested that he was 'passing through' the city and that some kind of discussions were afoot. Was he being courted by the Salzburg power brokers? Even before Germany's annexation of Austria on 11 March 1938, the festival was in crisis. During the winter, Bruno Walter had angered Reinhardt by turning down his long-cherished plan to produce *Die Fledermaus*. In mid-February, Toscanini had resigned, sensing (correctly, as it turned out) that Chancellor Schuschnigg's willingness to meet Hitler in Berchtesgaden on 12 February was the beginning of the end for Austria, and for Salzburg.

It had been rumoured that if Walter would not conduct *Die Fledermaus*, Karajan might. Nothing came of the project. The *Anschluss* put paid to everything as far as Reinhardt was concerned. It also seems to have put paid to plans for Karajan to appear at the festival. With his mentor Bernard Paumgartner soon to be exiled by the Nazis, Karajan would be off the festival authorities' wish list until the end of the war in 1945.

His concert in the Mozarteum was lengthily and interestingly written up by Dr Otto Kunz in the *Salzburger Volksblatt*.[12] Though the review is in part a paean of praise to Karajan ('a great hope, one of the greatest of his generation'), it contains a number of pertinent observations. It is one of the first reviews of a Karajan concert to use a motoring metaphor. Karajan, argues Kunz, is not only a modernist after the manner of Clemens Krauss; he is also a child of the new age of motorisation. Kunz does not use the analogy perjoratively; Karajan's Mozart appeals, he argues, precisely because it is so deft and aerodynamic.

Kunz detects, too, a new functionalism underlying Karajan's powerful account of Brahms's First Symphony: the music-making more obviously calculated and systematically pre-planned than it might have been a generation earlier. Karajan is also reported to be experimenting with orchestral layouts. For the Mozart and Brahms symphonies his violins are divided antiphonally left and right; for Smetana's 'Vltava' the violins are seated on the left. Kunz does not approve of this latter arrangement. It may be common practice in 'romanisch' countries, he suggests, but to German ears it sounds literally 'one-sided'.

*

A month later, Karajan was conducting the Mozart symphony with a very different orchestra. One of Berlin's most experienced and exacting critics, Heinrich Strobel, began his review of Karajan's debut with the Berlin Philharmonic:

The season's end brings with it a surprise: Hubert [*sic*] v. Karajan. One has heard a great deal about this conductor from Aachen. Now he stands before the Philharmonic. After just twenty bars of the Mozart symphony, one knows: here is a remarkable conducting talent. With small gestures, with little more than a meaningful roll of the wrists, he leads the orchestra.[13]

It has sometimes been suggested that Karajan's successes in Berlin in the late 1930s were Nazi constructs, backed by a Nazi publicity machine that had effectively stamped out all forms of independent criticism. As far as Karajan's début with the Berlin Philharmonic is concerned, it is an argument that is largely denied by the facts. It is true that all journalists were required to be registered by the Reichsschrifttumskammer [RSK]; it is also the case that even the best writers – and there were few more distinguished than Strobel – had to watch their backs.[14]

Strobel's difficulties were certainly acute. A former editor of the banned magazine *Melos* and a fierce, albeit somewhat doctrinaire, promoter of new music, Strobel and his wife (who was Jewish) had contemplated leaving Germany in 1934. In fact, for a number of reasons (principally to do with the problem of securing suitable salaried work elsewhere) he stayed on, writing much as he ever did, until shortly after the outbreak of war, when his registration with the RSK was formally rescinded on racial grounds ('Dr Strobel is married to a Jew and his political reliability cannot therefore be guaranteed'[15]), at which point he went into semi-enforced exile in France. Though Strobel was proud of his German origins, and though, like all would-be survivors, he did his fair share of ducking and weaving with the authorities, his writings about Karajan are of a piece with his criticism as a whole. An articulate exponent of *Die neue Sachlichkeit* (the new functionalism or objectivity) he had always admired Kleiber more than Walter, Klemperer more than Furtwängler (with whom he was none the less allied in various causes, most notably the defence of Hindemith).

Nor was Strobel alone in his admiration of Karajan. Critics of the conservative right, such as Walter Abendroth, also acknowledged the effectiveness of the young man's début, though in rather blander terms. And there were other voices, too. A review by the Belgian-born composer and critic Robert Oboussier in the *Deutsche Allgemeine Zeitung* is more sensational in tone. Indeed, it is wholly sensational if it is read in the misleadingly abbreviated version which appears in the Berlin Philharmonic's (widely quoted) official three-volume history. Oboussier, another musician who left Germany in 1939, writes of Karajan taking the audience 'by storm', 'like the explosion of a bomb', his sharply etched musical personality expressing an 'elemental passion for the musical experience', 'a will to masculine power and spiritual concentration'.[16] Equally, there are things Oboussier does not like. He is far from convinced, for instance, by what he perceives to be Karajan's somewhat tense and airless reading of the first two movements of Brahms's Fourth Symphony. If politics were involved here, they were of a more narrowly musical nature. It is surely no coincidence that the following January Karajan began one of his Aachen concerts with Oboussier's *Suite in C for Small Orchestra*.

By his own admission, Karajan did not greatly endear himself to the grandees of the Berlin Philharmonic during his first rehearsal. His insistence on rehearsing music they claimed they knew caused a certain amount of difficulty; though this was as nothing to the offence that was given when he asked for separate rehearsals with individual sections of the orchestra. The players protested, but this time Karajan dug his heels in, mindful no doubt of his having all too easily given in to the blandishments of the Vienna Philharmonic over *Tristan und Isolde*.

Karajan would later give his version of the exchanges he had with the leader of the orchestra:

'We've never done that before.'
'I think you'll see I'm right after five minutes.'
'Yes, but we know this piece!'
With all the impudence of youth, I replied, 'Well, we'll see, shall we?' I then went straight to the hardest sections with the violas, and they couldn't manage them at all.[17]

All the reviews agree that the suite from Ravel's *Daphnis et Chloé* was the highlight of the concert. Not even Strobel, whose knowledge of the score was second to none, could recall hearing a more atmospheric, a more brilliantly coloured or a more dazzlingly exact reading than this. Like Kunz in Salzburg, Strobel also greatly admired the performance of the Mozart – the chamber-music textures, the finely sprung rhythms, the exemplary phrasing, the sense of the music walking on air[18] – and he thought better of the Brahms than Oboussier.

Strobel's review also made an interesting and, as things turned out, highly significant comparison between Karajan and another conductor much lionised in Berlin at the time:

He calls to mind de Sabata. Indeed, v. Karajan has a great deal in common with the great Italian conductor: the rhythmic inexorability, the incredible musical energy, and the intensity of the melodic shaping.[19]

After hearing Karajan conduct *Tristan und Isolde* in Berlin a few months later, De Sabata himself would remark to the young Gottfried von Einem, 'At last, we have in our midst another great conductor'.[20] Karajan and De

Sabata quickly became friends, opening the way to the Italian career that would play an increasingly important part in Karajan's musical life.

Karajan left Berlin having glimpsed the promised land. His first meeting with the Berlin Philharmonic may have been a classic example of what happens when a young Turk crosses the path of an élite congregation of somewhat older Turks. But no matter: he now knew where, in an ideal world, his future might lie.

*

Back in Aachen, the local *Gau* had instructed General Manager Gross to revise the opera house schedules to make way for a number of performances of Beethoven's *Fidelio* to mark the successful reabsorption of Austria into the German Reich. There is no record of what Karajan thought of the extraordinary charade that in a matter of weeks had turned Schuschnigg's Austria from being a half-hearted candidate for a state of semi-detached *Zusammenschluss* with Germany to being a fully integrated member of the Third Reich, backed by a 99.73 per cent vote in favour of *Anschluss* in a plebiscite that two months earlier might just as well have gone the other way. Given his pan-German leanings, Karajan would probably have endorsed Schuschnigg's position that the situation did not warrant the spilling of 'German [i.e. Austrian] blood'. In later years, Karajan made slighting remarks about Austrian Nazis in general and the Tyroleans in particular ('the fanaticism of converts', 'more "Nazi" than the Nazis'[21]). But at the time, he was probably rather relieved. Though he had always treated his Nazi Party membership as a formality, the fact remained that, as an Austrian citizen, albeit an Austrian citizen working in Germany, he had broken the spirit, if not the letter, of Austrian law by joining the Party in Aachen in 1935. Pre-*Anschluss*, he was an Austrian beyond the pale; now, at least, everyone was back behind the same fence.

During the spring and early summer of 1938 private negotiations began with the Berlin State Opera. In Aachen, Karajan was focusing his energies on the production of Richard Strauss's *Elektra*, which was to bring the 1937–8 season to a memorable close. Anton Ludwig directed, and his wife Eugenie Besalla sang the title role; but it was Karajan's conducting that caught the headlines.

Karajan had by now proposed to Elmy. 'We understand each other so well, why don't we stay together?' he asked.

She agreed and 26 July was chosen as the day of the civil wedding. Unfortunately, between the end of the run of *Elektra* performances and the wedding day itself, Karajan was admitted to hospital for a minor operation to remove nodules from his vocal chords. Since he was still unable to speak, he hung a card round his neck: 'I am unable to speak because of an operation. Yes, I take Elmy Holgerloef to be my wife.'[22]

The honeymoon was spent on the Chiemsee, the lake resort between Munich and Salzburg. Karajan had acquired his first yacht, the *Karajanides*, plus a brand-new BMW sports car. Whenever the weather was set fair, they sailed. When it turned nasty, Karajan took himself off on private motor rallies where he raced, in Elmy's phrase, 'like Caracciola'.[23]

CHAPTER 14

1938: *Das Wunder Karajan*

The only enemy of the good artist is the bad critic, and that
of the bad artist the good critic.
Wilhelm Furtwängler, *Notebooks*

O! beware, my lord, of jealousy
Shakespeare, *Othello*

Heinz Tietjen, Generalintendant of the Berlin State Opera, was short of
conductors; or, rather, was short of good house conductors. The loss the
previous year of his Jewish-born chief conductor, the 66-year-old Leo
Blech, had been particularly hard to stomach. Though the Berlin State
Opera remained to some extent a semi-autonomous state within a state,
even it was not immune from political interference.

Furtwängler's amanuensis, Bertha Geissmar, an early victim of Nazi race
laws who had been forced to resign all her positions in 1935, returned there
as Beecham's assistant in 1937:

The atmosphere of the only opera house of the Reich outside Goebbels'
orbit was much less stifled than in the theatres depending on the radical
and fanatical Minister of Propaganda. The old Prussian State Opera House
attendants officiated with the same dignity as they had done under the
Hohenzollerns. The staff at the administration was mostly of the old regime.
Whenever possible, the artists had remained unchanged. Tietjen himself was
of the old school, Preetorius and all the leading spirits were artists of the first
rank, and Goering, who held his protecting hand over this institution, was in
this instance not such a 'good Nazi' as he had been on June 30, 1934.[1]

With Blech gone,[2] Tietjen was left with a somewhat dreary trio of resident
State conductors: Robert Heger, a good musician but sober-suited, Karl
Elmendorff, ambitious but essentially second-rate, and Johannes Schüler
whose performances were euphemistically dubbed by the press 'ruhig
[calm]'.

Tietjen knew all about Karajan, about his successes in Aachen and the
brilliant effect he had made with his Berlin Philharmonic début in April.
This is not to say he necessarily wanted Karajan in his team. Managers
fear mavericks. Yet needs must when the devil drives and Tietjen was
secure enough in his own methods to regard an approach to Karajan in
the winter of 1937–8 as both prudent and timely.

*

Heinz Tietjen was one of opera's most remarkable administrators. Born of an English mother and German father in Tangier in 1881, he had been intended for the law and commerce before a chance meeting with the conductor Arthur Nikisch changed his life. By the age of twenty-three, he was running his own provincial opera house.

Musically, he was a competent conductor (competent enough to conduct at Bayreuth where he was Artistic Director for many years) but it was as an administrator, famously clear-headed and politically astute, that he made his name and built his power base. In the 1920s he worked with Bruno Walter, who never entirely trusted him. In the early 1930s he nursed and to some extent protected Klemperer's stormy genius. After the Second World War, he ran opera houses in Berlin and Hamburg every bit as expertly as he had run the State Theatres of Prussia in rather more perilous times.

Had Tietjen lived in medieval times, the compilers of bestiaries would have portrayed him as a fox and a chameleon. 'There has never been such a person as Heinz Tietjen,' musicians used to joke, referring to his legendary invisibility. 'Did Tietjen ever live?' others would ask. Privately, opinions of him varied. Dietrich Fischer-Dieskau, who knew him after the war, has written affectionately, even protectively, of him as a wise counsellor and an amusing man.[3] Bruno Walter's memories are rather more testy:

He was a man of medium height, with drooping eyelids, a constant sideways look of his bespectacled eyes, a narrow-lipped and tightly compressed mouth, and a nervously twitching face. Never a spirited or spontaneous – to say nothing of an interesting – word came from his lips. His speech, soft and well considered, was devoid of temperament. Suddenly, a friendly smile, and an unmistakably good-natured, intimate expression would break through his natural reserve. He would indulge in cordial conversation – ah, Tietjen was actually living, one thought – when, just as suddenly, the attack would disappear behind a mask of blankness.[4]

Tietjen's judgement and treatment of Karajan were to be key factors – *the* key factors, possibly – in the rise and partial eclipse of the young man's fortunes over the next five years. He would also be an important mentor to Karajan. Temperamentally, the two men had much in common, notably a passion for music (Tietjen was a surprisingly impulsive conductor) and a latent wit and affability which their inborn reserve all too readily masked. The most patient of men, Tietjen also taught Karajan patience, helping to foster in him a belief that if something is worth acquiring, it is worth waiting for. Bruno Walter would say of Tietjen what many would later say of Karajan:

... there dwelt behind this strange immovability and self-possession a certain obstinate tension, able to outlive a long and patiently borne period of waiting, and likely to manifest itself suddenly and at a cleverly chosen moment by well-ordered action. This quiet, long-term planning, combined with his faculty of being able to wait, was one of Tietjen's particularly characteristic traits. In that respect, he was the equal of men of great power in worldly affairs. The 'breath control' of his determination may to a large extent explain his surprising rise and the permanence of his success.[5]

*

Tietjen's immediate need had been to find a conductor capable of taking charge of a new opera by Rudolf Wagner-Régeny, *Die Bürger von Calais*, commissioned by the Berlin State Opera and promised for January 1939. This was offered to Karajan. He responded by asking for a number of engagements conducting repertory operas, so that he could familiarise himself with the house before tackling the Wagner-Régeny.

Initially, Tietjen delegated the negotiations to his trusted assistant, the courtly Dr Erich von Prittwitz-Gaffron.[6] Already wise to the ways of the world, Karajan retaliated by employing an intermediary of his own. Tietjen was amused by the young man's presumption, and by his refusal to accept offers of *Lohengrin* or a well-sold run of performances of *Carmen*. Karajan's nominated operas were *Fidelio*, *Tristan und Isolde*, and *Die Meistersinger*. When Tietjen himself eventually entered the fray, Karajan wrote a personal letter pointing out that his nomination of these operas had been a request, not a stipulation.

Part of Tietjen's genius as an administrator was that, in the short term at least, he did not allow pique to colour his judgements. Klemperer had played fast and loose with him, often abusing him verbally; yet Tietjen's letters and memorandums on him continued to be models of fair-minded good sense. It is not surprising, then, that after due consideration Tietjen replied to Karajan conceding both the argument and the operas.

'Bury the hatchet, but mark the spot' was his philosophy. In Karajan's case, it worked to perfection.

Given all that he had been told about Tietjen, Karajan was not much looking forward to meeting him. When, however, Tietjen did finally manifest himself (after a rehearsal of *Fidelio* in late September), Karajan was somewhat disarmed.

'So, you are the great shooting-star,' Tietjen wonderingly remarked. Karajan tried to stammer a reply, but Tietjen continued, 'Don't say anything. Go on conducting the way you have done until now. I heard the rehearsal. We no longer need to discuss these matters.'[7]

Shortly before making his début at the State Opera with *Fidelio* on 30 September, Karajan conducted a second concert with the Berlin Philharmonic. On this occasion, Haydn's D major Cello Concerto and Beethoven's

Fifth Symphony were prefaced by Sibelius's Sixth Symphony. Karajan's decision to play the Sibelius (it was virtually unknown in Berlin at the time), let alone start with it, took the audience by the ears, and the critics too. Heinrich Strobel again wondered at the clarity of Karajan's conducting, at the luminous, finely graded sound and his fine structural control. As for the Beethoven, here Strobel noted that Karajan seemed more interested in bringing out the music's rhythmic power and structural logic than exploring its 'poetic idea'. Was this an implied criticism of Furtwängler (who had just made for HMV what is, by any standards, an exceptionally fine recording of the symphony)?

Furtwängler always claimed that the laudatory reviews that had greeted Karajan's first concerts with the Berlin Philharmonic had in no way unnerved him. If this is true, it must have been Karajan's début at the Berlin State Opera, Furtwängler's own former stamping-ground, that first caused the red alert to sound within the all too penetrable confines of Furtwängler's mind. The headlines for *Fidelio* praised both Karajan and his Leonore, Gertrud Rünger. The electricity of Karajan's conducting was singled out, the feeling of his breathing new life into a tradition he evidently knew and respected.

'*Was soll man hier mehr bewundern*? [What should one most admire here?]' asked Heinrich Strobel, in a sentence which strangely anticipates the headline '*Das Wunder Karajan*', which would make so explosive an impact in a rival paper three weeks later. By now, even Strobel was using the language of conquest. Reporting the audience's wildly enthusiastic reception of *Fidelio*, he concluded his review, '[Karajan] has conquered Berlin with a single blow.'[8]

With this triumph ringing in his ears, Karajan returned to Aachen to conduct Verdi's *Il trovatore* and two orchestral concerts, before travelling back to Berlin to prepare for the performance of *Tristan und Isolde* on 21 October.

*

The Berlin *Tristan* was a sensation waiting to happen. Few music-lovers in the city can have been alerted to the fact, but all the evidence of Karajan's earlier performances of the opera in Vienna and Aachen pointed this way. And a sensation it proved to be. The audience, the press, and, most significantly of all perhaps, many fellow musicians declared it to be something of a red-letter day in the affairs of the Berlin State Opera.

But what of the reviews, and one review in particular? Some weeks earlier, Edwin von der Null, a deputy critic working for the paper *Berliner Zeitung am Mittag*, had written a hugely laudatory piece on Furtwängler subtitled 'The Rise and Life of a Great Man'.⁹ Now, reeling from the impact of Karajan's conducting of *Tristan und Isolde*, he sat up late into the night writing a not dissimilar piece on Karajan. His colleague Bernd Ruland, a sub-editor on the paper, was amused by the review's extravagantly effusive tone and suggested they give it a suitably grandiose layout: a four-column spread complete with a huge banner headline that Ruland himself would concoct.

The review, whose repercussions would go on sounding down the years, has rarely been reproduced in its entirety. It read as follows:

State Councillor Tietjen's great coup
In the State Opera: The Karajan Miracle
Ovations for the conductor of "Tristan"

Yesterday evening Herbert von Karajan, the 30-year-old General Music Director in Aachen, conducted his second performance as guest of the State Opera. He had a success with Wagner's demanding work "Tristan und Isolde" that sets him alongside Furtwängler and de Sabata, the greatest opera conductors in Germany at the present time.

This is the way it was. When Karajan appeared on the podium, there was no hint of applause, just as there had been none before his recent *Fidelio*. At the start of the second act, the applause whipped through the auditorium the moment he entered the pit. Before the third act there were shouts of 'Bravo!' from every corner of the house. At the end, the singers were acclaimed. The calls for Karajan grew louder. As soon as he appeared in front of the curtain, he was greeted with a series of ovations. The audience demonstrated even more clearly than it had after the recent *Fidelio*, Karajan's first performance in the State Theatre, that it knows the difference between good and bad.

That is the outward manifestation. It is hard to speak of the artistic aspect of the evening. In the haste of the early hours it is as yet impossible to assess the implications of the occasion. To put it bluntly: we are faced with a prodigy. This man is the century's most sensational conductor. No one aged thirty in our time has achieved so objective or personal a triumph at such a level.

The first word of thanks is due to the man who gave Karajan his big chance: Councillor of State and General Manager Heinz Tietjen. The energy with which this man has cleared every bureaucratic and administrative hurdle in order to allow Karajan to work is only too well known to the writer of these lines. Yesterday evening must have brought Tietjen the great artist and organiser double satisfaction.

1. He has found a congenial partner for his productions at the Lindenoper [Berlin State Opera]; 2. the long years of waiting, and the tenacity with which Tietjen has resisted obvious compromise solutions have been most marvellously rewarded.

Here is the man who already meets every demand one could make of a world-class conductor. After yesterday evening, there is no point in keeping quiet about it. Karajan has given two exceptional concerts with the [Berlin]

Philharmonic. Karajan exceeded this impression three weeks ago with his debut at the State Opera. What he revealed yesterday borders on the inconceivable.

A man of thirty achieves something our great men in their fifties might envy. He conducts a score such as *Tristan* by heart. He does it with an ease that is simply uncanny. He masters the complicated apparatus of an operatic performance in such a natural manner as if it were merely a question of singing a children's song.

It is impossible to classify him in the familiar categories. He does not specialise particularly either in rhythm or sound, and is neither typically operatic nor typically symphonic as a conductor: he is all these together. But one thing tells the initiate what is going on: truly amazing was the way he grasped and realised the psychologically conditioned diminuendo style of *Tristan* with its eternally unreached and unreachable climaxes.

Karajan is a godsend. I think he knows exactly what he is worth. The operatic centres of the world will soon be scrambling to get hold of him. Therefore I have a request and a very urgent one: *let him take care of himself and be taken care of.* Such precious property must be guarded. I was able to watch his face as he conducted *Fidelio* recently. It was a face which showed total dedication to the matter in hand, a face which expressed extreme concentration and artistic possession. *May he remain true to himself.*

Yesterday in this column, I wrote enthusiastic words about the brilliant French pianist Casadesus. Today I add to my enthusiasm: Karajan is one of ours, he comes from Salzburg, a place where music is at home. It is a great pleasure to know that this artist, a German artist, exists.

In the performance, Gertrud Rünger sang Isolde for the first time. As with her Fidelio, this is a highly dramatic characterisation of some stature. The sumptuous voice is enhanced by a stage performance that shows the influence of Tietjen's steady direction. Albert Seibert, a guest artist, sang Tristan: a very refined artist from General Manager Strohm's Hamburg school. Both were extremely well received by the public.[10]

Since critics are regularly accused of getting things wrong at the time, it seems slightly unfair that von der Null should have been hauled over the coals for what later proved to be so pertinent a piece of talent spotting. Nowadays a rant like that would be welcomed with open arms and run on the news pages.

What the article fails to do is to make any coherent report on why Karajan's conducting of *Tristan und Isolde* was so remarkable. Apart from the somewhat foggy reference to Karajan's sense of the opera as a perpetually postponed state of orgasm (von der Null using the phrase 'diminuendo style' to describe what is principally an harmonic phenomenon) there is nothing about the interpretation as such.

For more informed comment, we need to turn to other reviews. Here what was written by a number of analytically competent reviewers – Oboussier, Strobel, and others – is of interest, not least because the qualities of the interpretation singled out by them coincide to some extent with those qualities we can hear for ourselves in tapes of Karajan's remarkable 1952 Bayreuth performances of *Tristan und Isolde*.

First, it would seem to have been an intensely dramatic performance, yet lyrical too, with great clarity of contrapuntal texturing and a purity of orchestral sound (in Strobel's phrase '*kammermusikalisch erhellt* [a chamber music-like elucidation]' that was rare in German Wagner conducting at the time. Secondly, there appears to have been an especially sensitive rapport between stage and orchestra pit, Karajan showing great 'discretion' in his accompanying of the voices. If there was a 'miraculous' element – and here several critics were at one with von der Null – it was that the 30-year-old conductor was capable of achieving all this without so much as a glance at the printed score, which lay closed on the desk in front of him for the duration of the evening.[11]

As for von der Null's review, the consensus of opinion among those who knew him at the time is that he had been genuinely enthused by Karajan's earlier performances in Berlin and that the *Tristan und Isolde* had merely spun him into yet higher orbits of enthusiasm. But was it a set-up job, a political fix, a deliberate snub to those – including Furtwängler and Goebbels – who had reasons (different reasons, assuredly) for relishing the difficulties facing the Göring-Tietjen regime at the State Opera?

Like all critics who double as journalists, von der Null had contacts at or near the centres of power. In his case, the contacts were with Göring's state secretary Paul Körner with whom von der Null had enjoyed a nodding acquaintance since childhood. The *Tristan* review, with its self-consciously lavish praise of Tietjen and the administration of the Berlin State Opera, would certainly have pleased Körner and Göring. Here at last, the review suggests, is a possible solution to the conducting problems that had dogged the State Opera since Furtwängler's semi-enforced resignation in 1934 and Blech's subsequent exile.

Whether von der Null's response was set up by Körner on Göring's behalf, or whether von der Null was writing out of private enthusiasm, though with a particular constituency in mind, will never be known. What is clear are the consequences that flowed from the review. Goebbels, taking the bait, immediately fired off a warning to the editor of *B.Z. am Mittag*. So did Furtwängler.

Unfortunately, in doing so, Furtwängler opened a Pandora's box of intrigues and recriminations that would haunt him, and Karajan, for years to come.

*

To fathom the bizarre sequence of events that followed the review's publication, it is necessary to realise that Furtwängler was a passionate and thoughtful man who fancied himself misunderstood: quick to anger, and much given to fearful bouts of jealousy, both in sexual affairs and in anything that impinged on his work as a performing musician. In saying this, one is not denigrating Furtwängler. The passions and the private vulnerabilities were part and parcel of his greatness as an artist. His predisposition to jealousy was, however, a fact of his personality that determined many of his actions and coloured many of his opinions.

What specially riled Furtwängler was the sub-heading that placed Karajan in the same class as himself as an opera conductor, and the sentence in the review: 'A man of thirty achieves something our great men in their fifties might envy.'[12] It was a barbed remark, certainly, and may well have been written maliciously in the knowledge that Furtwängler would be stung by it. Furtwängler being Furtwängler, it continued to rankle. In 1940, using De Sabata's name as a private psychological decoy, he confided to his notebook:

If they discuss Staatskapellmeister X [i.e. Karajan] in just the same way as they discuss Sabata, they are doing no harm to Sabata. But they are betraying and damaging art and confusing the public. If they overrate material qualities such as the technique of conducting from memory, they are prizing hard work instead of artistic practice. They are aligning themselves with the stupid people who never seem to be in short supply, and who feel nostalgic for the circus when they are in the concert hall.[13]

Though von der Null himself was officially reprimanded for aspects of the review and warned to steer clear of anything to do with Furtwängler,[14] Furtwängler continued to pursue him; so much so, that when von der Null was drafted into the Army, word had it that Furtwängler was responsible. Whether this was a black joke or deliberate misinformation is impossible to ascertain. Having helped start the witch hunt, however, Furtwängler was obliged to live with the consequences.

Intrinsically absurd as the story of the drafting was, it became an issue at Furtwängler's denazification hearings in 1946. By then, von der Null was dead, killed near Potsdam in the final days of the war. In his absence, various witnesses squabbled among themselves.[15] The tribunal even summoned von der Null's wife (as she thought she still was, fondly believing her husband to be a prisoner of war) to give evidence in the case, a move that was as pointless as it was poignant.[16]

*

And what of Tietjen in all this? He made no secret of the fact that he did not like Furtwängler. Furtwängler had been a useful ally in 1933 when Tietjen was in serious danger of losing his job under the new political dispensations, but the two men never really saw eye to eye. Nor could Tietjen, either as stage director or would-be rival on the podium, ever bring himself fully to admire Furtwängler's work. In 1937, he would complain to Friedelind Wagner:

When he conducts Wagner he's like a woman with perfume – always adding touches. It is the last time in my life I ever try and produce Wagner with him; for ten years now I have been trying to make him stick faithfully to the work, but he's always turned it into an act of public hypnosis and then it appeared that Wagner was the idiot – and so we split![17]

Personal pique aside, the idea that Tietjen would stoop to rigging the review of a second-string critic on a Berlin paper has little credibility. Starchily old-fashioned, the Berlin State Opera tended to keep its distance from the press, even in this propaganda-hungry decade.

As it happens, evidence of Tietjen's own view of the von der Null affair exists in the form of a letter he wrote in Berlin on 11 December 1946 to his former deputy Prittwitz-Gaffron. As well as undergoing denazification hearings into his own case, Tietjen had been summoned to give evidence in the case of Furtwängler, with particular reference to the von der Null affair. Tietjen's response to the court was that he believed the '*Wunder Karajan*' review was unprompted. His letter to Prittwitz-Gaffron suggests that he believed the only way to clear his own name was to ensure that the facts were as he remembered them:

Dear Mr von Prittwitz,
Today saw the start of Dr Furtwängler's denazification hearing, for which I have made myself available as witness. The first step today was to hear preliminary evidence by putting individual questions to witnesses, in the course of which I was asked whether I could remember pressure being brought to bear from any official quarter on Mr von der Null to write his famous 'Wunder' review in autumn 1938 on the occasion of Karajan's trial guest appearance conducting *Tristan*. In accordance with Fräulein Graeger's [Tietjen's private secretary] recollections, I testified that we were not particularly enthusiastic at the time about the headline Das Wunder Karajan, and we told Mr von der Null so quite openly, since we were convinced that he was not doing any favours with his review, especially with its screaming title, either to the State Opera or to Mr von Karajan who first had to win his spurs in the hothouse of Berlin. I testified that Mr von der Null had replied spontaneously that the screaming title did not originate from him but that it had been given to his review by the editorial staff as a gigantic headline against his own wish.
It is now a question of preserving absolutely untainted our own honour, the Institute's, and ultimately that of Mr von der Null who is not available; and I therefore ask you, because the above-mentioned suspicion also affects you in

the end, since you were responsible at that time for liaison with the gentlemen of the press, to let me know whether the representations I made today to the denazification commission were correct as far as you can remember, and whether you can add to them.

I would be very grateful to you if you could let me have your views as soon as possible. In the meantime, I send you my best wishes.

Yrs

Tietjen

PS I was asked during the above hearing whether I had the impression that the 'Prodigy' review was influenced from any quarter. I said no, because I still recall the open honest way of von der Null, who would certainly not have allowed himself to be 'influenced', although critics did come under shameful pressure from [Goebbels's] Propaganda Ministry; I was under the impression at the time that v. d. Null was writing with honest enthusiasm about both guest performances, *Fidelio* and *Tristan*, and was certainly not influenced in any way.[18]

It is possible that even this (private) letter was a strategic act on Tietjen's part, an attempt to get an agreed version of events on paper ahead of the relaunch of his post-war career in Europe. The more likely explanation, however, is that Tietjen had been genuinely disconcerted by being required to give chapter and verse on an old occurrence.

A little over three weeks later, Tietjen received his reply:

Baden-Baden, 2 January 1947

Dear Mr Tietjen,

I confirm with many thanks the arrival here on 31 December of your letter of 11 December 1946 in which you inform me of Dr Furtwängler's denazification hearing and of the statements you have made about the so-called 'Prodigy' review.

As long-standing artistic adviser to the Berlin State Opera, I can confirm that the representations you have made to the denazification commission correspond completely with the facts. My impression of Dr von der Null's review was that, in his honest enthusiasm at the two guest performances, *Fidelio* and *Tristan*, he had seen in the highly gifted 28-year-old [*sic*] Aachen General Music Director Karajan an important acquisition for the Berlin State Opera in its endeavour to find a personality to take over responsibilities which had until 1936 fallen to Leo Blech. The leading circles in our Institute were just as united over Mr von Karajan's positive qualities as a conductor as they were 'horrified' at the screaming headline above the Null review, which considerably impeded the development of our work at the Institute under your direction.

Concerning the absolutely grotesque untruth from a witness, suggesting that you, or one of your representatives, may have bribed or otherwise coerced Mr von der Null, I may say that it was you who refused to reinstate the State Opera's own Press Office, precisely in order to avoid the development of any sort of influence over the media. Contact with the gentlemen of the press only occurred from time to time, mostly through me and then only so as to inform them about matters concerning the programme, first nights or first performances.

Some critics quite frequently complained that the Berlin State Opera, in contrast with the theatres under Dr Goebbels's control, held no press conferences and distanced itself from the politico-cultural line of official operatic policy.

Yours sincerely,

Dr Erich von Prittwitz-Gaffron[19]

*

'*Wunder Karajan*' or not, Karajan's appearances at the State Opera in September and October 1938 had convinced Tietjen that he had found his man: a conductor sufficiently out of the common run of things to bring a new freshness and excitement to the affairs of his institute.

Others were interested, too. At the beginning of November, the Vienna Philharmonic approached the authorities in Berlin about the possibility of their 'fellow countryman' making appearances with the orchestra in Vienna. The orchestra's new chairman, Wilhelm Jerger, had been in touch with Karajan and a correspondence had ensued during which Karajan had forwarded a batch of Berlin press cuttings to Jerger, including, inevitably, the von der Nüll review.[20] Jerger's request ran into difficulties on two fronts: Berlin was non-committal, and Furtwängler furious. As early as the winter of 1938–9, Furtwängler was prepared to play his trump card with the Vienna Philharmonic: invite Karajan and I withdraw.

In November, Karajan made a rare appearances with the orchestra of the national broadcasting station Deutschlandsender.[21] Again there was a tumultuous reception, or so it sounded on the radio; in reality, there were fewer than a hundred people in the studio. The concert was widely reviewed. Writing in the *B.Z. am Mittag*, the paper's chief critic Walter Steinhauer delivered a punning rebuke to his colleague von der Nüll. In a very short space of time, Steinhauer noted drily, Karajan has covered himself in glory: '*Kein Wunder, denn Karajan ist ein ausserordentliche Musiker* [No wonder, because Karajan is an extraordinary musician]'.[22]

Back, briefly, in Aachen, Karajan began work on a forthcoming production of Mozart's *Die Entführung aus dem Serail* and conducted a marathon concerto concert in which Elly Ney played Mozart's C major Concerto K467, Beethoven's Fifth Piano Concerto and the First Concerto of Liszt. He also became entangled with somewhat fraught negotiations. The Aachen authorities took a dim view of Berlin's interest in their prize musical asset; there was little, however, that they could do given the fact that the Aachen Opera was itself within the Göring-Tietjen dispensation.

By early November, Tietjen had moved to close a formal deal with Karajan. The immediate sweetener, apart from the title 'Staatskapellmeister' (officially conferred the following April as part of the Führer's Birthday Honours list), was the chance to conduct a new production of Mozart's *Die Zauberflöte* in December. This was in addition to Karajan's being contracted to conduct the world première of *Die Bürger von Calais* in Berlin in January 1939. It was also confirmed that he would conduct Wagner's *Die Meistersinger* in Berlin the following June.

The Aachen press release announcing Karajan's Berlin appointment is not a happy document. Bitterness and a sense of betrayal are palpable in every sentence:

When Intendant Dr Gross engaged von Karajan at Aachen and his stature emerged at the very first opera performances, the people of Aachen did not fail to show their cordial appreciation of the General Music Director's talents. Aachen possesses in its Opera – with its assured stage director and highly gifted set designer, its hard-working and unselfish orchestra ready to face up to any technical difficulty, and its municipal chorus distinguished by its richness of sound and readiness to rehearse – three elements well suited to help a gifted and ambitious conductor further his aims and reach for the heights.[23]

The press release goes on to remark that no one in Aachen was in the least surprised to learn that Karajan had taken Berlin by storm. Nor did they in any way resent it, even though they might now be looking on with a tear – a large tear – in their eyes. Aachen has grown used, the announcement wearily continues, to watching 'ungrudgingly' as talented young men and women move on to greater things elsewhere in Germany. Finally:

Fame carries its obligations. We are pleased to record that von Karajan himself has acknowledged the sincerity of the feelings towards him in the hearts of the people of Aachen. For that reason, he will work half the month in Berlin and half in Aachen, thus sparing us the necessity of a farewell. But those who know what huge expenditures of intellectual concentration are required in the conducting of an opera or a Bruckner symphony will warn against overexertion. We note with satisfaction von Karajan's expressions of goodwill, and hope that the future of our musical city will continue to be happy and full of promise.[24]

It was a timely warning, but Karajan, drawn to Berlin like a moth to flame, ignored it. Flattered by Tietjen's new offer, he had let his guard slip. As it turned out, there was nothing in his agreement with Berlin that guaranteed him any real range of repertory. He would add Strauss's *Elektra* in 1940, and a semi-staged version of Orff's *Carmina burana* in 1941. For the rest, it was a ceaseless round of performances of *Die Zauberflöte*, *Fidelio*, *Tristan und Isolde*, and *Die Meistersinger*. Worse, trying to ride two horses simultaneously would drain even Karajan's formidable energies, break his marriage, and eventually, after four hectic years, land his entire career in the mire.

*

Karajan conducted a second performance of *Tristan und Isolde* in Berlin on the evening of 9 November. Elsewhere that evening, a far more fearful drama was unfolding. On 7 November a German diplomat, Ernst von Rath, had been gunned down in Paris by Herschel Grynszpan, a 17-year-old unemployed vagrant of Polish-Jewish extraction. Initially, the event was played down in the German press, but on the afternoon of 9 November Rath died in a Paris hospital. As the news broke, what had been sporadic anti-Jewish demonstrations in Germany turned into a grim catalogue of rioting and fire-bombing. Hitler, in Munich for the anniversary of the 1923 *putsch*, appears to have given typically equivocal instructions to his lieutenants. The police should crack down on the rioters, but not too harshly. Goebbels, though, was out of control. Fearful of what such mayhem was doing to Germany's image abroad as a bastion of 'law and order', he panicked and in an extraordinary volte-face decided to make a virtue of necessity and unleash the SA on the Jewish community. By three o'clock on the morning of 10 November synagogues had been burned to the ground and thousands of Jewish shops and properties smashed and ransacked all over Germany.

It was one of the worst mistakes of Goebbels's career. Though the Jewish community was subsequently fined a billion marks, on the pretext that Rath's assassination had triggered the mayhem, most of the cost of repairs and rebuilding had to be borne by German insurance. Worse, from Goebbels's point of view, the violence was not only condemned abroad, it was also viewed with dismay by large sections of the German public at home, not least in Berlin where Goebbels faced the additional embarrassment of being bawled out by his old sparring partner Göring. 'What the *public* needs is a bit more *enlightenment*!' Göring is said to have thundered in cabinet next day, mocking Goebbels's official title 'Minister of Propaganda and Public Enlightenment'.

'The Night of the Broken Glass' taught the Nazi high command a lesson that had unimaginably tragic consequences. It confirmed the need to tread warily on the Jewish question, breeding new levels of secrecy and the further interiorisation and bureaucratisation of anti-Semitic policies. Himmler, whose men had quietly rounded up 20,000 Jews during the night of 9–10 November, and not Goebbels, would emerge as the new driving force, evolving bureaucratic systems that would render possible the implementation by stealth of genocide on a previously unimaginable scale.

*

The morning after this second Berlin *Tristan und Isolde* – the streets littered with broken glass, smoke still billowing from a handful of half-gutted buildings – Karajan left for Aachen. The reviews of his second Berlin *Tristan* were calmer than the first batch, though no less adulatory. Did he pause to read the rest of the news that morning in Berlin?

Back in Aachen he conducted performances of Haydn's *The Creation*, a new production of Mozart's *Die Entführung aus dem Serail*, and a concert in which he prefaced Franck's Symphony in D minor with a pair of works that always amused and beguiled him: Haydn's Symphony No.83, *The Hen*, and Brahms's *Liebeslieder* waltzes, Karajan himself playing one of the two piano parts.

By the beginning of December, he was getting his first taste of commuting. The reference in the Aachen press release to the 'huge expenditures of intellectual concentration required in the conducting of an opera or a Bruckner symphony' may have seemed vague, but it was a precisely aimed barb. Scheduled performances of Bruckner's Ninth Symphony and *Te Deum* in Aachen came plumb in the middle of rehearsals for a prestigious new Berlin *Die Zauberflöte*.

*

This 1938 Berlin production of *Die Zauberflöte* would rapidly assume legendary status. It was directed by the 39-year-old Gustaf Gründgens. One of the most talented actors of his generation, Gründgens had turned to directing – theatre and opera performances – while still in his twenties. Some of his most memorable work in the opera house had been done with Klemperer at Berlin's Kroll Opera, though a dispute over how best to stage Mozart's *Così fan tutte* – and Klemperer's general tactlessness – eventually put paid to the relationship.[25] Klemperer wanted simplicity in Mozart, Gründgens wanted elaboration in pursuit of specifically designated ends.

In *Die Zauberflöte* Gründgens began with Schikaneder's libretto: with the spirit of pantomime and the technical daring of the so-called 'machine-comedies' Schikaneder had developed at Vienna's experimental Theater an der Wieden. There were aeronautic stunts for the three boys in their flower-bedecked chariot. (Real boys, at Karajan's insistence, not women.) There was a vast mechanically operated boa constrictor and, for Sarastro's entrance, a huge white elephant. Yet the opera itself was not played as farce. Just as the lighting of Traugott Müller's solid yet fanciful Egyptian-style stage designs helped 'distance' and dematerialise the pantomime effects, so Gründgens's direction concentrated on the hieratic and human elements: on Sarastro and, crucially, on Papageno who was played as a Rousseauesque *enfant sauvage* (Fritz Krenn, sporting a broad Viennese accent).

What Karajan did, to near-miraculous effect if contemporary reports are to be believed, was to draw from the orchestra a deft, light-filled sound that perfectly complemented the stage pictures, the lighting, and the production's inner mood. The singers, too – the pick of the Berlin company: Lemnitz, Rosvaenge, Berger, Krenn – were lured by him into singing the opera with a lightness and *sotto voce* beauty that must have struck traditionalists in the audience as being decidedly newfangled and 'un-German'.[26]

As a memento of the production, Karajan and the State Opera orchestra recorded the *Zauberflöte* overture for Polydor. It was Karajan's first recording for the gramophone. Re-hearing the recording after more than half a century, it still sounds astonishingly 'modern'. Much as Karajan admired the complete recording of *Die Zauberflöte* released in July 1938, which Sir Thomas Beecham had made in Berlin with many of 'his' [Karajan's] singers, he made no attempt to copy it. Beecham's conducting of the overture is slower and more elastic than Karajan's, which is cleaner and quicker in a style that nowadays we would more nearly associate with the Mozart conducting of someone like John Eliot Gardiner.

Having tested the water with the recording of the Mozart overture, Polydor offered Karajan an altogether more prestigious project: the chance to record Tchaikovsky's Sixth Symphony with the Berlin Philharmonic the following April. This, too, was destined to worsen relations with Furtwängler since Polydor was clearly looking for a commercial challenge to the Electrola-HMV recording Furtwängler had recently made with the same orchestra.

If the younger man's performance proved to be more straightforward than Furtwängler's, less complex emotionally – the work in no sense 'recomposed' – it none the less revealed formidable skills. One of its most remarkable features is the very thing Hans Hotter remembered about Karajan's conducting of Brahms's *German Requiem*: the sense of calm command and artistic self-possession. Clearly, the young Karajan was not a man to tear a passion to tatters, keenly dramatic as much of the performance is. Rather, the ear is drawn time and again to the beauty and clarity of the orchestral sound and the long lines of the reading.

All of which tends to contradict a widely quoted judgement on Karajan's conducting Furtwängler himself made in a diary entry of 2 February 1939. According to Furtwängler's analysis, slow tempi are too slow, fast ones too fast, everything hysteria-laden and aimed merely at the 'here and now'. It is also said to be over-nuanced conducting; individual voices are over-emphasised; there is 'no total experience of harmonic-polyphonic orchestral sound'.[27] The entry is annotated 'Karajan, *Tristan*'. But since Furtwängler cannot possibly have heard Karajan conducting *Tristan* (he was in Hamburg on 21 October and in Dresden on 9 November) the conclusion must be that the judgements are those of Furtwängler's friends and paid assistants, rather than of Furtwängler himself.

Recording a long symphony in four-minute sections evidently held no terrors for the 31-year-old Karajan. He also benefited enormously from the fact that the sound he drew from the orchestra tended to record well. From the earliest days of the gramophone, it was evident that some artists were better suited to the medium than others. In the acoustic era, there were voices that charmed the recording horn and others that irritated it. Later, when electrical recording finally made it possible for orchestras to be recorded at full strength in normal concert hall layouts, the same thing applied: some conductors proved to be more phonogenic than others.

As early as 1926, Compton Mackenzie, founding editor of *The Gramophone*, claimed that conscientiousness was not enough, that the gramophone demanded conductors of fire and energy who could galvanise an orchestra. He suggested there were three such musicians: Toscanini, Albert Coates, and his friend Eugene Goossens, though the arrival that month of a recording conducted by Stokowski of Saint-Saëns's *Danse macabre* caused him to add his name to the list.[28]

In fact, Mackenzie was only partly right. What the gramophone really required was interpretations of temperament and character that recorded well (good tuning, clean lines, first-rate internal balances) and which were sufficiently unquirky to bear repetition. For this reason, Furtwängler was less obviously suited to the gramophone than conductors such as Toscanini, Koussevitzky, Beecham and, eventually, Karajan himself. Yet Furtwängler's own sense that this was some kind of shortcoming left him restless. The Vienna Philharmonic's Otto Strasser recalls being buttonholed by him during a recording session in the Musikverein in the late 1940s. Agitated to the point of high fury, Furtwängler demanded to know what was so special about Karajan's recordings that made them such a success with critics and the public:

At first, I was taken aback by the directness of the question. But I quickly thought it over and suggested that his [Furtwängler's] great strengths – the intensity of the feeling, the beauty of the sound, the tremendous build-ups – found only imperfect expression on record, whereas Karajan's attributes of brilliance and precision were reproduced one hundred per cent by the records.[29]

Furtwängler appeared satisfied with the reply, though Strasser could not help reflecting how difficult he was making life for himself; and for no very good reason, given the splendour of his own best recordings.

CHAPTER 15

Peace and war

The white dove had to die, though she bore an olive branch.
Caspar Neher, libretto for Rudolf Wagner-Régeny's
Die Bürger von Calais

Ever since that fateful day in July 1914 when, gazing out over the sea at Brioni, he had heard his uncle murmur 'Now there'll be a war', Karajan had harboured a private terror of war. It was a scar on his consciousness that later events would only serve to deepen. Yet it was something that he kept largely to himself. At the interstices of life and politics, Karajan either sublimated his feelings or gave vent to them through music. Once, on New Year's Day 1987, he broke silence by uttering to however many million people were listening and viewing the five words: '*Friede, Friede, und nochmals Friede* [Peace, peace, and again peace]'.

As 1939 dawned, the idea of 'peace in our time' remained a powerful placebo. Hoodwinked by a daily diet of headlines from the Goebbels-controlled press about Germany's 'peaceful' intentions in the face of foreign threats, the civilian population went about its business in the vague hope that the politicians and diplomats would come to some sort accommodation. Nor had the Nazis, with their internally inconsistent system of arts censorship, entirely suppressed a pacifist, anti-militarist strain in German writing. Two of the operas Karajan was scheduled to conduct in the early months of 1939 – Strauss's *Friedenstag* and Rudolf Wagner-Régeny's *Die Bürger von Calais* – were anti-war.

Die Bürger von Calais, which had its world première, conducted by Karajan, at the Berlin State Opera on the evening of Saturday, 28 January 1939, is arguably one of the most affecting and finely crafted anti-war pieces in the annals of opera. It could also be said to be one of the best operas Kurt Weill never wrote. Had it been written by Weill – or by Britten and Auden in their *Paul Bunyan* phase – it would almost certainly be known, recorded, and occasionally performed. Yet mention the opera or its composer nowadays, even in musical circles, and the response is likely be: 'Wagner – who?' The circumstances of the work's making would appear to have sealed its fate.

The year is 1347 and the English have laid siege to Calais. Unable to penetrate the marsh-girt fortress, the English are now starving the population into submission. (The landscape in the opera is starkly reminiscent of the ditches and waterlogged trenches of World War One.) The mood among the townsfolk is bleak and defeatist, and a failed embassy by the Wissant brothers, from which Josef Wissant has not returned, has further darkened it. The Burgomaster's wife determines to make a clandestine peace mission to the English Queen, but that fails, and she takes her own life. When Josef is discovered behind enemy lines, half dead from starvation, he is ejected by a genial posse of English soldiers. He re-enters Calais to urge compliance with the English demand that six Burghers be handed over, shackled and dressed as penitents, to die in atonement for the town's resistance: 'Six thousand live,' he cries, 'only six men need die.' One by one, the volunteers come forward as the townsfolk begin loading their wagons in hope of a safe passage into exile. In a moving coda to the opera, the men are reprieved.

The episode, a true story in certain particulars, had already inspired a celebrated sculpture by Rodin and a virulent anti-war drama *Die Bürger von Calais* (1914) by the expressionist playwright, banned by the Nazis, Georg Kaiser, whose masterpiece this is generally thought to be. In accepting the subject in a new adaptation by the left-of-centre team of Wagner-Régeny and the stage designer turned writer Caspar Neher, the Berlin State Opera was not exactly playing safe. True, Neher and Wagner-Régeny had previously collaborated on a work, *Der Günstling* (The Favourite), that had become a smash-hit in German opera houses in the mid-1930s; but even there, lurking just below the surface of a tale of amorous intrigue in Tudor England, is an exploration of the tensions that exist between a dissatisfied people and a system of unscrupulous political dictatorship.

Neher had grown up with Bertolt Brecht and had become one of his closest collaborators. As well as being a grey eminence of the Brechtian revolution and the librettist of Weill's *Die Bürgschaft* (Berlin, 1932), he had also worked closely with men like Zemlinsky, Klemperer, Reinhardt and Carl Ebert. Since he stood for just about everything the Nazi ideologues detested, how had he survived? Paradoxically, given his Communist sympathies, it was partly because Germany in the late 1930s was a somewhat easier place to work in than the Soviet Union would have been. Neher did make certain accommodations, notably in the area of stage design on which Nazi thinking on architecture had to some extent impinged; but this was an area where concessions were relatively easy to make. He also had the good fortune to find a shrewd and artistically successful protector with whom the authorities were reluctant to interfere. This was the Tietjen-like Hans Meissner, whose appointment in July 1933 saved the Frankfurt Opera from artistic and financial ruin.

The libretto for *Die Bürger von Calais* is not about dictatorship. Like Kaiser's play, it is about peace and 'community', something the guileful Neher would have hoped might appeal to ideologues of all parties. More especially, *Die Bürger von Calais* is about Neher's own times: about the degree to which the individual can influence, defy, or, indeed, be held responsible for the decisions of the many. As BBC producer Clive Bennett would later observe in his notes for the work's British première: 'Neher's ambivalent text suggests that squaring the individual conscience is neither easy nor uplifting.'[1]

Wagner-Régeny was more of a political chameleon than Neher; though as his post-war career in East Germany would demonstrate, he too was essentially a man of the Left. Born in German-speaking Transylvania in 1903,[2] he was more a skilled purloiner of the idioms of other composers – of Weill, and more peripherally Hindemith, Stravinsky, and the group of French composers known as 'Les six' – than an original creative force in his own right. Yet *Die Bürger von Calais* has a style and musical consistency that is peculiarly its own. The two outer acts, set within the besieged city, use a Weill-like orchestral palette, a pair of alto saxophones giving their own distinctive colour to the grieving mood. Time and again the music penetrates to the heart of the situation: to its pathos and, in the case of the Burgomaster's wife Cornelia, its tragedy.

Neher's libretto is not, as the plot summary might suggest, anti-English. For all his and Wagner-Régeny's stylish guying of the courtly airs of the Queen and her attendants in Act 2, the English are portrayed with wit and humanity. The gossiping washerwomen's not entirely sympathetic reception of the vagrant Josef – a beautifully crafted ensemble for tenor, women's sextet, and solo string quartet – is a masterly essay in musical bitter-sweet. The contrast between this and Cornelia's tragic Act 1 'Ricercar' confirms the score's range. And yet nothing is obtrusive; everything is of a piece with the whole.

The opera ran for six performances before certain 'bigwigs' (Wagner-Régeny's word) were alerted to the fact that the sight of a downtrodden and beleaguered people desperately suing for peace was not doing much for audience morale at a time when a real war might be imminent.

According to Wagner-Régeny, it was Göring's sister who first raised the alarm. This did not stop the opera being performed elsewhere in Germany; but by now ominous rumblings were also being heard from the Party machine in Berlin. The March issue of *NS-Monatshefte* carried an article suggesting that in future Wagner-Régeny would be well advised to find a librettist more in tune with the 'world view of the new Germany'.[3] The writer of the article was Dr Herbert Gerigk, co-author of the notorious *Lexikon der Juden in der Musik* and a member of the extremist Rosenberg faction, for whom he worked collecting and collating potentially incriminating information about artists and intellectuals. There can be little doubt that Neher and his various collaborators had been in Gerigk's sights for a number of years. Not that Neher or Wagner-Régeny took much notice. In their determinedly anti-Fascist opera *Johanna Balk* (Vienna, 1941) they openly reverted to the style of Weill's *The Threepenny Opera* for the satirical unmasking of the dictator in the final scene. Not long after that Wagner-Régeny was drafted into the army.

In his review of *Die Bürger von Calais* in the *Berliner Tageblatt*, Heinrich Strobel remarked on the characterfulness and 'composure' of the score and Karajan's beautifully considered conducting of it.[4] The Berlin State Opera's official history merely records the conducting as being 'fantastic'. The choral writing would have appealed to Karajan. It is also clear that jazz and cabaret music meant rather more to him than it did in later years, when he developed a barely disguised distaste for the art of the inter-war years.

Karajan never returned to the opera. During the war, he lost touch with Wagner-Régeny who later settled in East Germany. As for Neher, like Karajan, he had to undergo 'denazification'; after which, as he told Brecht in 1952, he took a personal vow to have done with local and national politics in all its forms. He went on working with Karajan until the late 1950s, though relations were often strained for reasons that will become apparent in later chapters. There is, however, a bitter-sweet coda to Karajan's connection with Wagner-Régeny. In the late 1950s, the Salzburg Festival, of which Karajan was now Artistic Director, commissioned a new opera from him based on Hugo von Hofmannsthal's play *Das Bergwerk zu Falun* (The Mine of Falun). Meeting Karajan again after so many years, Wagner-Régeny found him immensely charming and enthusiastic, yet at the same time cursory and bland as he talked of his fondness for *Der Günstling* and the possibility of reviving *Die Bürger von Calais*.[5] In the event, the new opera was a flop, its reception after the première on 16 August 1961 soured by Wagner-Régeny's refusal to condemn the Soviet decision, announced three days earlier, to seal the East German border and erect the Berlin Wall.

*

The second so-called 'peace' opera Karajan conducted in 1939 was Richard Strauss's *Friedenstag* (Day of Peace). The decision to schedule this in Aachen in May had little to do with politics, everything to do with Karajan's fanatical admiration of Strauss and his close interest in the work of Clemens Krauss who had conducted the work's première in Munich the previous autumn. The parallels between *Friedenstag* and *Die Bürger von Calais* are superficially striking. Both are historically based dramas set in beleaguered citadels, in Strauss's case a besieged town facing imminent extinction in the dying moments of the Thirty Years War. In both operas it is a woman who initiates the bid for peace. Both have a powerful choral element. And both found favour with Nazi opinion-formers until the penny dropped and it was realised that the message most opera-goers were taking away with them was a liberal-pacifist one.

To my mind, the Wagner-Régeny is the better piece: more consistent stylistically, emotionally more honest. (Compare the movingly muted sense of relief at the end of *Die Bürger von Calais* with the brash rodomontade of the end of *Friedenstag*.) Despite the best efforts of Strauss's two librettists, Stefan Zweig and Joseph Gregor, *Friedenstag* wears its war-wearied mood awkwardly. Like the Piedmontese youth who longs to flee the citadel and return to his native Italy, Strauss seems to care only for the music of the Commandant's peace-loving wife Maria, whose lyrical outpourings (largely pre-composed, independent of the libretto's original demands) dominate the opera's entire central movement.

The role of Maria was a superb vehicle for Clemens Krauss's wife Viorica Ursuleac. How Karajan must have cast envious glances towards Vienna where Krauss was preparing a special production of *Friedenstag* in honour of Strauss's seventy-fifth birthday starring Ursuleac, Hans Hotter, and Anton Dermota as the Piedmontese youth.[6] Still, the Aachen production was something of a triumph in its own right. Pitz's choir was praised to the skies, and Karajan was applauded both for scheduling the work and for his inspired conducting of it. One local critic, Franz Achilles, buttered him up by comparing his conducting to Strauss's own: the steady pacing, the beautifully judged tempi, the 'discretion' of the orchestra *vis-à-vis* the stage.

*

Aachen's late winter and spring season in 1939 was something of a golden period. Though Karajan was now dividing his time between Aachen and Berlin, he continued to honour the plans he had put in place prior to Tietjen's Berlin offer. He was already developing the trick of seeming to be in several places at the same time.

That winter, in addition to Mengelberg's appearance, there were several starrily splendid concerts led by Karajan himself. One of Strauss's favourite cellists, Enrico Mainardi, came for *Don Quixote*, Kulenkampff played the Tchaikovsky concerto, and there was first-rate home-grown talent on display when Karajan invited Detlev Grümmer and viola player Otto Petermann to join him in a performance of Mozart's *Sinfonia concertante* K364. There was more Sibelius, *En saga* and the First Symphony, a burgeoning love-affair with Brahms's Second Symphony, and a triptych of great choral works to keep the choirs busy.

Most interesting of all, perhaps, were the performances of Puccini's

Tosca Karajan conducted in Aachen shortly after Christmas, a powerful foil to the so-called 'peace' works he was currently studying. Aside from the sheer power of the performances (Karajan playing up the Scarpia factor), the readings were widely judged to be *orchestrally* revelatory. In Puccini's operas, melody is almost invariably born in the orchestra; it is also a trick of his that the orchestra lends colour to the singers, rarely vice versa. Karajan had an instinctive understanding of this. One of the greatest Puccini conductors there has ever been, his command of the orchestra was such that he could realise precisely Puccini's art of transforming a scene with the colour of a single chord. He understood, too, the thematically intricate, quasi-symphonic style of Puccini's writing.

It is a pity the two men never met. With their shared love of the peace and quiet of lakes and mountains and their antitheses – every conceivable form of modern gadgetry, high-speed motor-boats, and fast cars – they would probably have got on famously.

*

In Berlin, Karajan's career began to take a zigzag course. During February 1939, between further performances of *Die Bürger von Calais* and *Die Zauberflöte*, he made more recordings with the Staatskapelle for Deutsche Grammophon, including a phenomenally well-played account of the overture to Verdi's *La forza del destino*. Compare the Staatskapelle's playing here with that on other discs they were making at the time and Karajan does indeed seem to be some kind of miracle worker.

His concert with the Berlin Philharmonic on 14 April followed the form of his début the previous year. This time he offered Haydn's *Drum Roll* Symphony, Debussy's *La mer* and Tchaikovsky's *Pathétique* Symphony. Again, the concert was a sensation. Von der Nüll wrote another of his rave reviews, but the most detailed analysis of the concert came from Fred Hamel, critic of the *Deutsche Allgemeine Zeitung* (*DAZ*).[7] Discussing the performance of the Haydn, he drew attention to Karajan's consciously sparing use of string vibrato and a complete absence of romantic slurs and swells in the string playing. The following Sunday, in an article in the magazine *Deutsche Zukunft* entitled 'The Round Dance of the Generations: Richard Strauss and Herbert v. Karajan', Hamel explored the links between Karajan's conducting style and Strauss's, the man widely regarded to be the founding father of the new 'modern' school of conducting. Hamel noted the passion of Karajan's conducting:

He exhibits all the impulse of youth . . . yet this passion is not a manifestation of the exuberance of the Romantic, for it is overruled, re-channelled by the new Realism of the rising generation. There was clear proof of this in the Haydn:

in the absolute transparency of the sound, in the hair's breadth precision of the phrasing, and the precise 'terracing' of the tuttis.[8]

Nor was Karajan applying the 'new Realism' only to classical composers. His Wagner conducting was already exhibiting a vitality and clarity of contrapuntal detailing that was to some extent at odds with the methods of an older German school. Again, it is conducting that puts one in mind of the New Age authenticists of the 1980s.[9]

In June 1939, Karajan conducted two performances of *Die Meistersinger* at the Berlin Opera. The first of these, on 2 June, was a State Gala in honour of Prince Paul of Yugoslavia. Since it was an old production with a largely familiar cast (Bockelmann as Hans Sachs, Käthe Heidersbach as Eva)[10] the reviews concentrated mainly on Karajan's conducting. This was more or less universally praised for its clarity and youthful urgency; and for the degree of freedom Karajan accorded his singers. If there was a cautionary note, it came from Walter Steinhauer. Writing after the second performance, Steinhauer noted that Karajan's fresh and flexible approach did occasionally create difficulties for one or two older singers. Did this refer to Bockelmann? And, more specifically, to the confusion that had overcome the performance a week earlier when Bockelmann – allegedly rather the worse for wear from drink – made a mistake from which Karajan, conducting without a score, temporarily failed to recover?

These things happen, and the incident might have gone largely unremarked were it not for the fact that it was a State Gala and Adolf Hitler's first experience of 'the Karajan miracle'. Hitler was furious. A huge admirer of Bockelmann (the admiration was mutual), he railed against the incompetence of the '*Kerl*' Karajan and his 'pretentiousness' in not using a score.[11] He also decided that Karajan was a musical lightweight, insufficiently 'German' in his treatment of Wagner's music. (This was not a passing dislike. Towards the end of 1940, Goebbels confided to his diary, 'The Führer has a very low opinion of Karajan and his conducting.'[12])

The incident caused Karajan problems within the State Opera. According to Fritz Krenn, his Kothner in the Berlin Opera's 1941 Rome performance of *Die Meistersinger*, Bockelmann and others made life increasingly difficult for Karajan. During rehearsals for the Rome performance, as Karajan attempted to inject some humour into Eugen Fuchs's playing of Beckmesser, Fuchs turned on him and announced bluntly: 'My Führer does not wish me to change anything in this part.'[13]

*

A day or so after the gala *Meistersinger*, Karajan travelled to Athens, where he conducted a single concert with the well-regarded orchestra of the Athens

Conservatory. Was it here that he first met Dimitri Mitropoulos, friend and hero of Karajan's later years, recently returned from Minneapolis? It is possible, though there is no record of any meeting.

During the summer of 1939, Karajan spent some time in Bayreuth at Tietjen's invitation. For Karajan, the high point of the festival was *Tristan und Isolde* conducted by De Sabata, with Germaine Lubin as Isolde. He would later remember: 'She was gracious, noble, the most wonderful Isolde I have ever encountered, better than those endless German cannons who have sung the role.'[14] Interested to get to know her better, Karajan put his car at Lubin's disposal. Since artists were not allowed to leave the town without written permission of the festival management, it was quite a treat for Lubin. Karajan would recall:

I thought it would be a nice idea to show her some of the wonderful churches near Bayreuth. There are two in particular I thought she might like. She agreed to come and I took her first to the more brilliantly decorated one, not knowing that she was not only a very religious woman but also a girl who had been brought up in the strictest kind of convent – no heating, nothing for show. I can still remember proudly opening the door and seeing the look of complete horror on her face. 'This is not a church,' she said 'It is a boudoir!'[15]

During the summer of 1939, a new Intendant took over in Aachen. His name was Otto Kirchner, the successor to Edgar Gross who at the age of fifty-two was being moved to a somewhat less prestigious post in Eger and Aussig in the Sudetenland. Karajan was to forge a perfectly good working relationship with Kirchner but things would no longer be quite as they had been.

Nor was much else staying the same. Though the man in the street knew little other than what he was told him by the state-controlled media, Hitler's long-standing desire to seize Polish territory was about to be realised. The signing of a non-aggression treaty between the Soviet Union and Germany on 23 August made some kind of conflict more or less inevitable.

This time there were no cheering crowds on the streets of Berlin, as there had been in July 1914. CBS's William L. Shirer was in Berlin on 3 September 1939. He would later write in *The Rise and Fall of the Third Reich*:

I was standing in the Wilhelmstrasse before the Chancellery about noon when the loudspeakers suddenly announced that Great Britain had declared herself at war with Germany. Some 250 people – no more – were standing in the sun. They listened attentively to the announcement. When it was finished, there was not a murmur. They just stood there. Stunned. It was difficult for them to comprehend that Hitler had led them into a world war.[16]

And this was only the start. Hitler's greatest follies were yet to come.

CHAPTER 16

'More Diogenes than Alexander . . .'

No longer can guns be cancelled by love,
Or by rich paintings in galleries;
The music in the icy air cannot live,
The autumn has blown away the rose.
                              Roy Fuller, 'Autumn 1940'

Materially, not a great deal changed in Germany and Austria in the first year of the war. A coal shortage during the bitterly cold winter of 1939–40 caused hardship among some poorer people, but there was no serious rationing of food or consumer goods. The German Reich, with its annexed territories and those of its allies, was rich in human and mineral resources. It was also Hitler's intention that the civilian population should be protected for the duration of what it was thought would be a brief but glorious war.[1] Thus, as Britain put its domestic economy on a war footing and mobilised its entire labour force, including women, the German government allowed numerous exemptions from military service, with Hitler himself insisting that the best place for German womenfolk was in the home.

Karajan's life in Germany between 1939 and February 1945 was that of a reasonably well-to-do civilian, albeit one with a greater power of removal than most, skiing in the high Alps or on retreat at his shore-side hideaway in Thumersbach on Lake Zell in Austria. However, like many who survived the war, he began it in good health and ended it in poor shape mentally and physically as anxiety and deprivation took their toll.

Though there was an attempt to draft him into the Army in 1942, his war work was confined to a number of tours of duty as an air-raid warden in Aachen. Group 7 of Aachen's *Luftschutzwache*, as allocated by theatre manager Otto Kirchner, consisted of Manfred Steffen, Hans Schalla, the Italian tenor Alexander Remo (the Italian Tenor in Karajan's 1941 Aachen production of *Der Rosenkavalier*), and Karajan himself. It is not clear how often Karajan did this. Being on duty meant a week of night-shifts beginning each evening at seven o'clock and ending at six o'clock next morning. Group 7's look-out post was on the roof of the Konzerthaus (Aachen's Old Spa Rooms) whence the detail would go on orders from the monitoring group situated in the basement of the main Post Office. Blue-grey overalls were provided, straw mattresses, and a certain amount of rather rudimentary fire-beating equipment. Signor Remo also took with him his bicycle, a gift from his mother. The remuneration was RM 1.50 a night.

Fire-watching in Aachen was a far cry from Karajan's new-found status as pin-up boy to chic Berlin society. With his intense manner and matinée-idol good looks, predators of both sexes were to be found circling the camp fires at night. If the majority were kept at bay, it was more to do with Karajan's reticence and unapproachability than with anything as cheering as his loyalty to Elmy.

One person, though, did penetrate Karajan's defences: a charismatic and highly articulate girl bearing the name of one of Germany's best-known commercial dynasties. Anyone who possessed a sewing-machine – and there were few people then who did not – would be familiar with Gütermann's sewing silk and the ubiquitous advert for the company's products ('Gütermann's Nähseide'). Anna Maria Gütermann, or Anita as she was known to her friends, was twenty-one rising twenty-two when Karajan first met her in Berlin in 1939. He was, it seems, instantly smitten. A letter dated 29 January 1940 which eventually found its way into – of all places – the archives of the Gesellschaft der Musikfreunde in Vienna begins 'Geliebte Anita' [Beloved Anita] and goes on to reveal the lovelorn writer's obsession with 'your manner, your voice, your eye, and your figure – and that has nothing to do with the way you look at that moment, whether your hair is crimped or not . . .'[2]

It was in some respects a dangerous liaison. A Jewish grandparent made Anita 'eine Vierteljüdin', quarter Jewish. Love blinds, but Karajan must have known that there was a problem here. He had first-hand knowledge of the difficulties facing artists whose wives were Jewish; Fritz Krenn had poured out his troubles to him on more than one occasion. Anita's past also involved a failed marriage and, it is alleged, a child and a serious rift with her family. 'A kind of sensational black sheep' is how Franz Endler has described her.[3]

According to Anita, when she first met Karajan, she had no idea that he was married.[4] Nor, apparently, did Karajan admit to the fact. It was only some time later when he proposed to her one day in the Berlin U-Bahn that the truth came out. She was furious. Karajan later retaliated by telephoning her from the State Opera, shortly before going on stage to conduct a concert, to say that there was an audience waiting and he had no intention of starting the concert until she accepted his proposal. Anita was flattered by that.

She was taller than Karajan, but adept enough to disguise the fact in company. She was also far more extrovert. The actor, film director and mountaineer Luis Trenker, Leni Riefenstahl's co-star in *Mountain of Destiny* (1926) and *The White Hell of Piz Palu* (1929), and a great friend of Karajan in the war years, has left a graphic account of meeting Anita for the first time:

I was sitting in the third row of the stalls and was able to observe Karajan closely. Everything was under his spell. When he put down his baton, there was loud cheering and boundless enthusiasm from the audience.

So as not to have to queue at the cloakroom afterwards, I had taken my hat with me into the concert-hall. When everyone stood up clapping and cheering, I put it on the empty seat in front of me that had been occupied by a young lady. What I had not foreseen was that in her enthusiasm this young beauty was going to jump up on the seat and stomp around with both feet on my nice new 'Borsalino' hat. Now I had no choice but to wait for the cheering to die down and for her to get off the seat, and off my hat.

'What an ovation that was, *gnädiges Fräulein*. Wonderful. Nobody's stiletto heels have ever trampled on my nice hat with such spirit as yours!'

'Oh, yes – but you're Luis Trenker, aren't you? Please forgive me – but Herbert and I are engaged, you see – I'm still totally confused – was it wonderful?'

'Indeed it was! You're engaged to Karajan?'

'Yes, Anita Gütermann – didn't you know?'[5]

Anita was no musician, yet she appears to have possessed a kind of sixth sense where music was concerned. The veteran Viennese music critic Heinrich Kralik often sat opposite her during Karajan concerts in the Musikvereinssaal after the war. He would recall that if the orchestra wavered – for a split-second, in a way imperceptible to the audience at large – Anita's gaze would instantly swivel towards Karajan. She knew.

Self-centred, lonely, intolerant, incorruptible: those were some of the epithets Anita would later attach to the personality of the 'lovely man' she eventually married. It would be the best part of three years, however, before the marriage took place.

*

In February 1940, Karajan conducted a new production of Strauss's *Elektra* at the State Opera which Strauss himself attended. After years of patient waiting, Karajan finally got to meet his hero.

Despite the mix-up in *Die Meistersinger* the previous season, Karajan was once again conducting without a score. It was a phenomenon Tietjen would never forget. During a speech given in Bayreuth in 1963 as part of the sesquicentennial celebrations of Wagner's birth, his thoughts turned to the conductor whom, back in the 1940s, he had simply called 'the boy':

Well, one can say a great deal or nothing at all about Karajan: with people who are vastly talented, it is usually better to say nothing at all. Initially, this young man was something of a tearaway, towards the orchestra too. But things calmed down and – I have to say – he was an exceptional person. Richard Strauss was sitting with me in my box and suddenly nudged me. They were giving *Elektra*, with Karajan conducting: 'Look, look, the rascal!

[*Schauen S', schauen S' hin, der Lauser!*]' At first I had no idea what he meant. Well, the rascal was conducting by heart. OK, that's easy to say. But anyone who knows the score of *Elektra* – I couldn't do it myself, I can tell you that now, even though I've conducted it in my time. To conduct *Elektra* by heart is sheer impertinence as much as anything else. It's a work that's so insanely difficult that it is the easiest thing in the world to go wrong, which would be a catastrophe for the orchestra. They'd never get back into it again.[6]

Things did not go wrong, and afterwards Strauss told Karajan it was the best performance he had ever heard of *Elektra*; a nice piece of flattery to which Karajan responded by saying that he would rather know what was wrong with the performance. Strauss was either sufficiently impressed or sufficiently intrigued to invite the rascal to lunch. Karajan would recall:

He said, 'You have made the music very clear, the *fp* here, the accent there; but these are not at all important. Just wave your stick around a bit!' He made a gesture like stirring a pudding. But what he meant was, let the music flow naturally. And then he added something which made a deep impression on me. He said, 'I can see you have worked on this opera for many months and concentrated very hard. You conduct it without a score, which I couldn't do any more as I am far away from the work. So you are right and I am wrong! But' – and he laughed – 'don't forget that in five years' time you will have changed again.' The great wisdom of an old man![7]

It was typical advice from Strauss. He once complained during a rehearsal of *Ein Heldenleben* with Rome's fabled Augusteo Orchestra, 'Gentlemen, I can hear all the notes. Please, give me an *impression* of the music.'

Karajan learned a lot from Strauss about the craft of orchestral conducting. Strauss's example impressed upon him the need for an impeccable sense of rhythm that was in no sense metronomic, for an 'inner rhythm' that worked for entire movements and even, possibly, for an entire work. Karajan admired the keenness of Strauss's beat: the incisive upbeat and its equally vital continuation. And he admired the unostentatious manner of the conducting.

The emotion came through the music. He knew in each piece exactly where the real climaxes were and he avoided completely the kind of hurrying or dragging which ruins so many performances.[8]

Karajan also learned a lot about opera conducting from Strauss. He would recall a conversation with Hans Hotter about the occasion when Strauss told him to omit a difficult top E: 'Nobody will hear it, the orchestra's too loud. But don't forget to breathe in and open your mouth or else the audience will know you're not singing.' On the other hand, where beauty of vocal sound and the rhythmic accuracy of the declamation were concerned Strauss was an absolutist. He was an absolutist, too, in his detestation of unnecessary stage movement. 'Sing the music without moving,' he would insist. 'Express yourself through your voice, your bearing, your gesture, your eyes.' In all this, Karajan would prove to be one of Strauss's most steadfast disciples.

Which is not to say that by 1940 Karajan had mastered all the Straussian arts. In March, he recorded Dvořák's *New World* Symphony with the Berlin Philharmonic. It is a performance that tends to reduce the work to a series of separate episodes that are either very beautiful or very dramatic. What is missing is any larger sense of a fully thought through Dvořák style. A recording of Johann Strauss's waltz *Artists' Life* made with the same orchestra the previous month also reveals Karajan in nervy, wilful mood. Clearly, something was beginning to wind him up.

*

Karajan's concert programmes in Aachen during the first winter of the war continued to show considerable catholicity of taste. The season began with a concert celebrating the organ: a Bach transcription, a Handel concerto, and *Three Psalms for Chorus, Orchestra, and Organ* by Jules van Nuffel, a distinguished veteran of the Belgian organ and choral world whom Karajan knew and admired. The following week, Karajan conducted Beethoven's Ninth Symphony for the first time. In December he programmed Tchaikovsky's Fourth Symphony and Scriabin's *The Poem of Ecstasy*. There was also a fair smattering of contemporary works (placed first in the programme and often boycotted by the more conservative Aachen subscribers) including Boris Blacher's brilliant, jazz-inspired *Concertante Musik für Orchester*. And though the supply of top soloists appeared to be drying up, Wilhelm Kempff finally honoured a long-standing invitation to play Mozart's D minor Concerto with the orchestra.

How much, if any, of the repertory was politically driven it is difficult to say. The signing of the German-Soviet pact had caused Goebbels's Propaganda Ministry to encourage pro-Russian sentiments, but it did not need some cynically engineered pact between Hitler and Stalin to encourage Karajan to conduct Tchaikovsky or to try (unsuccessfully, as it turned out) to develop a taste for Scriabin. When the man who would eventually replace Karajan in Aachen, Paul van Kempen, made his début with the orchestra on 29 February, he began with a piece of Party rodomontade by the rising young German academic Philipp Mohler entitled *Wach auf, du deutsches Land*; but Karajan's only concession to the mood of the times came towards the end of the season with his programming of Pfitzner's cantata *Von deutscher Seele* (Of the German Soul). Like Wagner-Régeny's

Die Bürger von Calais, this has more to do with peace and inner searching than war or rampant nationalism. Pfitzner wrote the work immediately after the First World War in an attempt to come to terms with the idea of 'Germanness' in a period of moral and cultural crisis.

Karajan's Easter offerings to the people of Aachen in 1940 were the *St Matthew Passion* and a new production of Wagner's *Parsifal*, which has become famous in retrospect for the strange case of the fourth Flowermaiden: 'Elisabeth Grümmer as guest', the programme states. In his previous job in Meiningen, the leader of the Aachen orchestra, Detlev Grümmer, had fallen in love with a young actress called Elisabeth Schilz. They married and moved to Aachen where, giving up all thoughts of a stage career, Elisabeth settled into her new life as a wife and mother of two children. She did, however, continue taking singing lessons and often sang for friends after dinner.

One evening Karajan came to dinner and heard her sing. Since it was an intimate social occasion, she was a little surprised that he said absolutely nothing to her afterwards: not even a formal 'thank you'. Some weeks later, the phone rang. It was Karajan:

I naturally thought he wanted to speak to my husband, so after greeting him, I said I was sorry that he was out and that I would have him call him on his return. 'But it is to *you* I want to speak,' he said. 'I shall explain in a minute the favour you must do me. The first performance of *Parsifal* is on Good Friday' – as I can well remember since it was less than a week away – 'and I am very dissatisfied with one of the Flower Maidens. Will you oblige me, come right over, and take it on?'[9]

Grümmer was thunderstruck. She knew *Parsifal* and knew how tricky the Flowermaidens' music was, the frequent rapid entries all requiring split-second timing. If she refused, or messed it up, would not her husband take the blame or become a laughing-stock? In fact, Detlev was hugely amused by the idea, so Elisabeth accepted the challenge.

I must say that even in those early days, Karajan had a wonderful and easy beat. You must realise that I had never been on any operatic stage before and I was really being thrown to the wolves, floating around in those rather ridiculous veils. Somehow I lived through the experiment. The dissatisfaction of the maestro with that particular soprano entirely changed the course of my life, and the die was cast. Again, I don't recall Karajan complimenting me or even thanking me. But that is not his style.[10]

Nor would it ever be. It was not simply that Karajan was shy. Strategically, he reasoned that praise or blame casually uttered in corridors or dressing-rooms could store up a heap of trouble.

If that experience was a shock for Grümmer, it almost paled into insignificance beside what happened next. A call came from Karajan inviting her to appear the following season in three more operas: in *Tiefland*,[11] as Alice in a new production of *Falstaff* to be directed by Walter Felsenstein, and as Octavian in *Der Rosenkavalier*.

My husband was again highly amused and told me I could not refuse. Believe it or not, as I learned later, my being given Octavian was entirely due to my legs, because Karajan always had a great sense of the character looking just right, and he felt that my legs, in knee breeches, would fit correctly into the picture.[12]

Happily, Grümmer not only looked good, she also sang Octavian very well; Karajan's interest in the legs of androgynous young girls did not always guarantee a fine artistic effect.

In Grümmer, Karajan had discovered a pearl of great price, a singer who would grace the world's stages as one of the aristocrats of the vocal art for the next three decades. Sadly, it was a career that her husband would not live to share and enjoy. Detlev Grümmer, 'my beloved husband, our dear father' as the newspaper notice records, was killed in an air raid on Aachen on the night of 11 April 1944. He was forty-eight.

Another singer who began her career with Karajan in Aachen was Irmgard Seefried. Karajan did not exactly 'discover' her, though he engaged her, with her mother's connivance, when she was still below the legal age for employment. That was as the Priestess in *Aida*. She fidgeted terribly, and got a rocket from Karajan. In 1940, he offered her the role of Nuri in *Tiefland*. Then, out of the blue, came an offer to sing Donna Anna in *Don Giovanni*:

When he asked me if I knew the score, I was stunned. No, I replied; since I was a lyric soprano it had never occurred to me to learn it. 'I need a Donna Anna,' he said, with a total lack of concern, 'so you had better prepare it fast.' I was overcome with fear, for I knew that this was sheer madness and could be the rapid beginning of the end . . . But even then Karajan never thought of anything but the orchestra. Singers are there to be used, and from the early days he loved to experiment with them. None of this has changed; it's still very true today [c.1970]. I don't believe, as many persons claim, that he does not know voices. He simply employs them as though they were members of the orchestra. He is full of contradictions, for when you sing with him he is very considerate of your limitations; but then why does he so often cast performers in wrong roles?[13]

Seefried survived the ordeal, she claimed, because the theatre was of a modest size and because she opted to sing 'a totally lyrical Donna Anna – which of course was not right'.[14]

*

The experience of working with Gründgens on Mozart's *Die Zauberflöte* had unsettled Karajan. Collaborating with a first-rate director, who was also musically aware, made him even more conscious of the limitations of the system that for so many years had been the norm in German provincial theatres. Most of Karajan's stage productions between 1929 and 1939 had been the work of the director-managers themselves – Dieterich, Gross, and now Kirchner – though in Aachen Karajan had usually managed to secure the services of Anton Ludwig, a worthy enough figure, but no Gründgens.

In 1940 the Ludwig family left Aachen, and Karajan seized his opportunity to direct as well as conduct. With Kirchner's permission, he planned to open the 1940–41 Aachen season with his own production of *Die Meistersinger*. Musically, he knew the score inside out; as a répétiteur he groaned – half sang, half acted – every part from Eva to the Nightwatchman; and as an actor manqué he was without doubt a better stage performer than most of his singers.

Karajan was also looking to make radical changes in the way singers were recruited and cast. His ideal was a singer who looked well and sang beautifully; but someone who could also move well and gesture effectively. Not that this was a cue for theatrical licence. Overarching everything was the idea that the stage performance should be in step – literally so, if need be – with the musical one.

And indeed the new Aachen *Die Meistersinger* was, by all accounts, a highly disciplined affair. Writing in the *Aachener Anzeiger*, Franz Achilles exclaimed:

The Prelude is like a programmatic fanfare. One listens in astonishment, for even Karajan has not previously been heard to play it like this: so simply, so tightly, one might also say in such a Spartan manner.[15]

During the spring and early summer of 1940, countries had folded like dominoes before the well-ordered German advance: Denmark and Norway, Belgium and Holland, and, in June, France. For Hitler, the French surrender at Compiègne on 22 June was the sweetest victory; what it did, symbolically speaking, was wipe out the humiliation of the German capitulation on the same spot in 1918. As he stood glowering in the forest glade, his every look and gesture, according to Shirer, who was standing just fifty yards away with the foreign press corps, expressed anger, contempt, and a kind of triumphant hate. Most Germans were cock-a-hoop. As for Karajan's production of *Die Meistersinger*, it clearly had something of the mood of the time about it:

A steely sheen spreads across the piece, the bourgeois motif of the mastersingers takes on an heroic character which later wonderfully fits with Hans Sachs's final address, so that the Prelude and the address 'Verachtet mir die Meister nicht' join together as the first and last links in a chain.[16]

Steel, chains, and an heroic temper: it does not sound a very comfortable or joyous *Die Meistersinger*. As for Karajan's stage production, Achilles notes that this fits the music-making like a glove; though, once again, the language of the review suggests a form of imposed discipline:

There is no room here for dramatic exuberance. Economy of gesture and clarity of gesture are self-evident necessities, which the singers entirely acknowledge. The chorus, too, adapt the extent of their movements to the strict rhythm of the baton. For example, the commotion on stage during the Riot Scene is never allowed to overwhelm the gaudiness, the well-contrasted colours of the orchestra.[17]

There are signs here, as there are in the March 1940 recording of Dvořák's *New World* Symphony, of an element of wilfulness creeping in to Karajan's work. This was also the case personally. He was beginning to get a reputation as someone who was brilliant but difficult: unswerving in his artistic ideals but endlessly demanding; extraordinarily hard-working but increasingly aware of his financial worth.

He had always been headstrong and ambitious but his talent was beginning to make him vulnerable to the demands of his ego and the machinations of the power-brokers who judged him (for the time being) to be a commodity worth investing in. Aged thirty-two, in a country at war, seeing less and less of his wife and increasingly uneasy within himself, he was overworked and moving into one of those 'lonely' phases that would often coincide with crises or false moves in his career.

*

All this was meat and drink to Furtwängler as he continued lobbying against Karajan. Furtwängler could not stop the Berlin Philharmonic making the occasional gramophone record with Karajan; nor was it strategic to kick up a fuss over the concerts the orchestra occasionally gave for soldiers, the war-wounded, or Berlin armaments workers (many of whom were Jewish). What Furtwängler could and did do was bar Karajan from conducting the orchestra at concerts in Berlin's principal hall, the Philharmonie. Moreover, since the Berlin Philharmonic had exclusive access to the Philharmonie (the result of a lucrative rental deal the hall had concluded with the orchestra in 1937), Karajan could not conduct the Staatskapelle there either. In effect, Furtwängler had withdrawn to fortress Philharmonie and pulled up the drawbridge.

The only viable alternative, from Karajan's point of view, was the Berlin

State Opera. Though Tietjen was beginning to be wary of the combined demands of Karajan and his ruthlessly self-serving agent Rudolf Vedder, he agreed that for the 1940–41 season Karajan should have his own series of concerts with the Staatskapelle in the opera house itself; six programmes to be given monthly on Sunday and Monday evenings.

In his book on Furtwängler, *Trial of Strength*, Fred K. Prieberg makes no mention of Tietjen's part in all this, preferring to concentrate on Vedder. It was Vedder, he notes, who helped 'instigate' the Staatskapelle concerts. This is broadly true; it is, after all, what agents are paid to do. The point about Vedder, however – as Furtwängler himself rarely failed to point out – was that he was a crook. Karajan, who never disguised the fact that he got on with him, preferred to phrase it differently. The Vedders, he told Roger Vaughan in 1982, 'were sometimes rough people, but good businessmen'.[18]

Furtwängler had never succumbed to the Vedders' blandishments. When Rudolf Vedder first appeared on the Berlin scene in 1927, Furtwängler was well settled with Wolff und Sachs, the influential Berlin concert agency whose director Hermann Wolff had helped found the Berlin Philharmonic back in 1882. Others were not so lucky. By the late 1930s it was difficult to find leading German and Italian musicians who were *not* signed up to Vedder.

The rise and rise of Rudolf Vedder was extraordinary. He had first set up as an independent concert agent in 1927, after being sacked by Steinway for embezzling artists' fees. In July 1935 he had his permit withdrawn by the Nazis' newly established Reichskulturkammer, this time for attempting to blackmail artists who no longer wished to use him as their agent. Nothing deterred, he returned to private practice, where he worked with an astonishing array of artists, including Arrau, Edwin Fischer, Eugen Jochum, Paul van Kempen, Clemens Krauss, Kulenkampff, Mainardi, Mengelberg, the young Michelangeli, Elly Ney, Swarowsky, and Gioconda de Vito. In order to shore up his own position and counter threats to his artists from paid informers within orchestras and opera houses, he cultivated high-level contacts with the NSDAP (which he joined in 1940 at a time when the Party's credibility with the public was at an all time low) and with the Gestapo, whose responsibilities included the overseeing of foreign tours by musicians and theatre companies.

Karajan had first encountered the Vedders in Karlsruhe in 1935, where he had been sought out by Vedder's father. Karajan had declined to do business with him but not long afterwards he signed up to the agency. His day to day dealings were with Gertrud Weinsberg, who would eventually take over and close down the agency when Vedder's licence was withdrawn for a second time in July 1942; but it was Vedder himself who worked assiduously on

Karajan's behalf in 1940–42. For Vedder, Karajan was a most convenient milch-cow. As well as the fees from Karajan's own work, there were rich pickings to be had from the growing number of artists who wished to work with him. And there were radio fees from the prestigious Short-wave Transmitter of German Radio, which was heard all over Europe, including Great Britain, where the Sunday afternoon series 'Immortal Music of the German Masters' had a considerable following.[19]

The programme for Karajan's first Staatskapelle concert on 20 October 1940 was Cherubini's overture *Anacreon*, Strauss's *Also sprach Zarathustra*, and Brahms's First Symphony. It was broadcast. But the second concert on 10 November was not. Kulenkampff had been engaged to play the Dvořák Violin Concerto, but Vedder had overreached himself on the computation of the soloist's fee. A stiffly worded letter from the formidably well-run Short-wave section of German Radio to Tietjen's deputy Prittwitz-Gaffron explains:

In the course of our discussions about broadcasting the concerts of the Staatskapelle under Herbert von Karajan on the German Short-wave Transmitter, we declared ourselves ready to pay RM 1000 demanded by the General Management of the State Opera. Unfortunately, negotiations with the representative of Professor Kulenkampff, the soloist in the second concert, were unsuccessful. The [Berlin] Philharmonic, for example, divides the fee for the soloist into two instalments: one for the final rehearsal and one for the main performance. It is customary for the Radio to pay 25% of the fee for the broadcast concert; Mr Vedder, however, maintains that we must reimburse 25% of the fee for *both* performances.

Bearing in mind our interest in propaganda abroad, part of which is the broadcasting of such prestigious and artistically superior events as the Staatskapelle concerts, we very much regret that the broadcast of this concert has fallen through owing to Mr Vedder's unwarranted demands.[20]

The Staatskapelle concerts brought the hostility between Furtwängler and Karajan into the open. With the real war now moving into its second year, this somewhat childish 'conductors' war' had the merit of providing a certain amount of light relief among Berlin's concert-going classes. Karajan would later recall:

It got to be like a cockfight, with people betting on Furtwängler or me. There were personal notices in the newspapers: 'Seek Karajan concert – will trade two Furtwängler tickets' or 'I seek Karajan subscription will give five onions'. Goebbels didn't care what Furtwängler said about the Nazis. It was serious for Furtwängler, but not serious enough for Göring and Goebbels to get into an argument about it. But Tietjen used it, even when he saw that Goebbels would never replace Furtwängler.[21]

For the most part, audience loyalty was divided along the familiar lines of class and generation. Karajan had youth on his side: his own and that of his ever-widening circles of young admirers. He also seems to have made an early calculation that he had time on his side. The von Dohnányi family, which was towards the patrician end of the social scale, took the view that 'Karajan wasn't somebody you would really want to hear if you could hear Furtwängler'.[22] The 22-year-old Marie ('Missie') Vassiltchikov wrote in her *Berlin Diaries*, somewhat primly:

[Karajan] is very fashionable and some people tend to consider him better than Furtwängler, which is nonsense. He certainly has genius and much fire, but is not without conceit.[23]

A later entry on the subject is equally prim, though this time it is Furtwängler who is on the receiving end:

Dined tonight at Gottfried Bismarck's in Potsdam with Adam Trott, the Hassells and Furtwängler. The latter, who is terrified of the possible arrival of the Russians, disappointed me. From a musical genius I had somehow expected more 'class'.[24]

The press had a field day with the Furtwängler–Karajan *Krach*, until Goebbels became edgy and once again tried to put a damper on things. Karajan made wonderful copy, of course. The rapid advance towards the rostrum, the prayerful pause before the music was allowed to begin, the conducting with closed eyes. (An old Furtwängler trait, later abandoned by Furtwängler, and by Karajan himself when directing choral works and opera.) 'When does he start to fascinate . . . ?' a young man is said to have asked his girlfriend as Arthur Nikisch ascended the rostrum. It was an old story, even in 1940, but it is not surprising to find the critic of the *Berliner Zeitung* using it at the start of his review of one of Karajan's first concerts with the Staatskapelle.[25]

Already, Karajan was doing what he would continue to do throughout his entire career: giving a performance within a performance. There are great actors – Olivier was an obvious example – who have audiences doubly in their thrall: fascinating in their own right even as they hold the audience spellbound with the insights and truths of their interpretation. In Karajan's case the fascinating tended to be done before and after a performance rather than during it, though the beauty of his gestures and the concentration of his manner – the lower body absolutely still, the feet, once settled, never moving – also exerted their own particular spell.

Since Furtwängler was rapidly reaching the stage where he could not bear even to utter Karajan's name, any critic who had the temerity to compare the two conductors only further excited his fury. A review that is sometimes quoted in this respect is the one written in the *Frankfurter Zeitung* in December 1941 by Karl Holl. Fifty years on, it reads rather well. Listen to extant wartime recordings of Bruckner's Eighth Symphony by Furtwängler and Karajan, and Holl's comparison seems apt in most essentials:

Furtwängler is primarily a sculptor in sound, inspired by strong impulses and spiritual powers. Karajan is more a painter and designer, even though he also has a strong feeling for the organic whole, and for creating a three-dimensional quality in the music-making. Furtwängler's is a passionate temperament, Karajan's a gentler one. The former is a very expressive musician, the latter – and one not only hears this, one can also see it from the way he beats time – more reticent and introspective, though also capable of ecstasy. With Furtwängler one is immediately aware of the formative individual at work, while with Karajan one is aware of more of the finely strung and sensitive individual who feels himself above all to be a medium, but at the same time retains a visible distance from the work.[26]

That is shrewdly put. It is often said that music criticism was another of the war's cultural casualties. Journalists were chivvied and corralled, certainly, but good writing did not entirely disappear.

Karajan's first season of Staatskapelle concerts had a number of obvious highlights. The December concert included the Grieg Piano Concerto with the young Arturo Benedetti Michelangeli as soloist and Beethoven's Seventh Symphony in a sturdy but cumulatively exciting reading which Karajan and the Staatskapelle would record the following June.[27] In early May Karajan brought his first season to a magnificent close with a performance of Bruckner's Eighth Symphony prefaced by the overture to Gluck's opera *Alceste*.

*

Radio work and foreign tours were a significant feature in Karajan's 1940–41 season, work he would come increasingly to rely on as the war dragged on and his position became less and less secure. On Sunday, 1 December 1940 German Radio broadcast the fiftieth edition of the popular Forces' Request Concert. There were contributions from, among others, Toti dal Monte, Helge Rosvaenge, and Karajan, who conducted Johann Strauss's *Emperor* waltz with 'energy and zest'.[28] Goebbels masterminded the event with his usual flair. The Commander-in-Chief of the German Army, General Field Marshal von Brauchitsch, a pious and compliant professional of the old school, was summoned from his Berlin HQ to add weight to the occasion, though it was General Dietl, hero of the Norwegian campaign, who gave the broadcast address.

Later the same month, the Aachen choir and members of the orchestra travelled to Paris to give three Christmastide performances of Bach's B *minor Mass.* Two were public concerts, the third was for German troops stationed in France.

In 1940, after the signing of the armistice at Compiègne on 22 June, Paris enjoyed a kind of protected status: a cosmopolitan playground that was, on the surface at least, strongly pro-German. As the Vichy government's 'ambassador' to the German authority in Paris put it in April 1941:

All Frenchmen, who share the conviction that France can only participate in the New Order in Europe in collaboration with Germany, wish German arms a speedy success . . . The driving of the British from the Continent will contribute to the rapid conclusion of the war and save much suffering for France.[29]

Many years later, when Karajan was challenged by an American journalist on the rights and wrongs of conducting in Paris in 1940–1, he retorted that one of the first people he had been introduced to there was the United States *chargé-d'affaires* Mr Pinckney Tuck. Whom the French chose to do business with, Karajan claimed, was not his problem.

Abroad was also where Anita Gütermann liked to be: Paris, Rome, Florence, Milan. Between 1940 and 1942, these cities became the favourite trysting places of Karajan and his new love. Wherever Anita went, she made an impression. Even today there are those who remember her courting the fashionable White Russian community in Paris; or, slim, beautiful, and elegantly suited, strolling nonchalantly down Rome's via Veneto. Once met, never forgotten.

*

In Rome in March 1941, Karajan was fêted by the public and the press in an extraordinary way. While the Berlin papers were soberly proclaiming 'Italian jubilation over *Die Meistersinger*: magnificent conclusion to State Opera's Rome visit', the Italian press was running headlines such as '*Bravo, bis, bis, Karajan* [Bravo, encore, encore Karajan]'. He conducted one performance of *Die Meistersinger* and an extremely lavish concert which began with the Locatelli *Concerto Grosso* and ended with Beethoven's Seventh Symphony: a reminder, wrote one critic, that the palm of contemporary Beethoven interpretation had not yet been formally ceded to the Italians.[30] An aria from *Der Freischütz*, some Pfitzner songs, and Strauss's *Tod und Verklärung* provided the solidly German filling to the sandwich.

When the same concert was given in Florence ten days later, the critic of *La Nazione* Valentino Gucchi wrote:

A singular kind of conqueror, this Karajan. One cannot say that he has a fist of iron. Quite the reverse. The orchestra is not dominated; it is wholly free. Free, that is, to do what Karajan wants it to do. It is a graceful kind of conquest, more Diogenes than Alexander.[31]

In Florence, Karajan met Mario Labroca, the composer and theatre administrator who since 1936 had run Florence's Teatro Comunale and its prestigious spring festival the Maggio Musicale. Labroca was a remarkable man. Privately, a convinced Fascist, with a wardrobe full of the appropriate uniforms, he was regarded by fellow professionals (including Toscanini) as a man of unimpeachable integrity in the conduct of his public duties; a man who ascended professionally without ever lowering himself personally. He immediately engaged Karajan: for a concert at the 1941 Maggio Musicale and for a run of performances of Mozart's *Don Giovanni* the following year.

*

One young man who had been shouting '*Bravo, bis, bis, Karajan*' at the Rome concert was the 19-year-old Raffaello de Banfield Tripcovich. He was from Trieste, heir to a family whose maritime and industrial interests had brought them wealth and influence in the port and a residence of ambassadorial splendour on the wooded hillside above the city. His father, Baron de Banfield, was a fabled Austrian flying ace of World War One; his mother, a woman of great charm and culture whose counsel Karajan would later come to value, was the Countess Maria Tripcovich. Raffaello had been born in 1922 in England, in Newcastle-upon-Tyne where the family had shipbuilding interests. Music was his passion, one that his mother shared and was prepared to indulge.

Karajan was already something of an idol for him, and in the spring of 1941 he determined to hear him conduct. Getting permission from his academic tutors to take time off to travel to Rome had not been easy. Then, *en route* to Rome, he started running a temperature. Fearful of being sent straight home again, he attempted to lower his temperature by hanging out of the railway carriage window. This had the opposite effect; by the time he reached Rome he was running a fever. But he got to the concert.

Back in Trieste, he cut Karajan's photograph out of the programme, framed it, and put it on his desk. Next time, he vowed, he would get to meet him as well. The chance came three months later in Florence. During rehearsals for the Maggio Musicale, a friend introduced Banfield to Karajan who seems to have taken an instant liking to him. He was allowed into rehearsals, found tickets for concerts, and provided with a handsome letter of introduction to Clemens Krauss's conducting course in Salzburg.[32] At the age of thirty-three, Karajan had found a sort of protégé. Whenever Karajan visited Brioni, his old childhood holiday haunt off the Adriatic coast, Banfield would be there too. 'Were you in love with Herbert?' Eliette von Karajan would later ask Raffaello. (A question she put to quite a few people, usually in company and often over lunch.) Raffaello said not. In 1941, so he claimed, he was playing Cherubino to a rich baroness.

'She may be a baroness,' Karajan had advised. 'But, believe me, she's not worth the price of a manicure. Music is your life. Concentrate on that.'[33]

Karajan went further, steering Raffaello away from conducting towards composing. If, nowadays, one looks in vain in some musical dictionaries for an entry on Raffaello de Banfield it is more the compilers' fault than the music's. His three ballets *The Duel*, *Acostino*, and *Quator* enjoyed huge success in Europe and America in the 1950s, and his one-act opera based on Tennessee Williams's play *Lord Byron's Love Letter* (New Orleans, 1955, with Astrid Varnay in the leading role) is a small masterpiece, albeit a largely forgotten one.[34]

CHAPTER 17

Down, down I come

Down, down I come; like glistering Phaeton,
Wanting the manage of unruly jades.
Shakespeare, *Richard II*

It was while he was in Rome with the Berlin State Opera that Karajan learned that his contract in Aachen would not be renewed beyond the end of the 1941–2 season. Aachen needed more than a part-time General Music Director and to that end Otto Kirchner had invited the 47-year-old Dutch-born conductor of the Dresden Philharmonic, Paul van Kempen, to take Karajan's place.[1]

The decision cannot have come as a total surprise to Karajan. Many years later, he would say of it, 'It is mere weakness if one cannot give up something in which one is deeply involved but which no longer has meaning for one's future path.'[2] Yet, at the time, he was shocked. First in Ulm and now in Aachen, he had been removed from a position in circumstances which largely ignored his record of diligence and success.

After the Italian tour, Karajan had returned to Aachen to prepare for Eastertide performances of Wagner's *Parsifal*. It proved a safer place to be than Berlin. On the night of 9–10 April, the Berlin State Opera was destroyed in an Allied bombing raid. The house would be rebuilt with astonishing speed, but while this was going on the company was obliged to transfer its productions to the Kroll Opera and, for the Staatskapelle concerts, to the Philharmonie. With a little help from the Royal Air Force, Karajan had finally penetrated fortress Furtwängler.

Karajan's last year in Aachen showed a narrowing of the range of the orchestral repertory but a more than usually rich programme of choral and operatic works. New to the choral repertory was Carl Orff's *Carmina burana*, which Karajan would conduct again, to sensational effect, in Berlin later in 1941; as for opera, he conducted *Parsifal* and *Don Giovanni*, a new production of *Der Rosenkavalier* which he directed himself, and another of Verdi's *Falstaff* directed by Walter Felsenstein.

Aachen in 1941 was an odd place to find either *Falstaff* or Felsenstein, who worked in Germany only by special licence. (He had been excluded from the Reichstheaterkammer in 1936 on ideological grounds.) As for *Falstaff*, it is clear from some of the reviews that Nicolai's *Die lustigen Weiber von Windsor* would have been the more 'usual' choice for a German opera house intent on some kind of Falstaffian revel.

Karajan had no use for the 'usual'. For him, Verdi's last opera was the apogee of operatic comedy, a score that glittered all the more brilliantly for having been subjected to the bright beam of Toscanini's genius. In fact, none of the reviews mentioned Toscanini. The comparisons were all with Serafin, who had conducted *Falstaff* in Berlin and in Salzburg in 1939. And here the critics stumbled on a paradox: the Italian Serafin conducting with fervour, joy, and a certain Germanic *Schwung*, the 'German' Karajan conducting with what one writer called true 'südländischem Feuer [Latin fire]'.

Felsenstein's production of *Falstaff* is one of those historic stagings that has been largely lost to history. He seems to have based it on the premise of the work's closing ensemble, 'Tutto nel mondo è burla [All the world's a joke]'. Rather as Jean-Pierre Ponnelle's Rossini productions would later be, this was a pulsing, bustling affair, precisely choreographed to the rhythms of the music and played out in a series of simply designed but historically realistic theatrical 'spaces'.

By contrast, Karajan's production of *Der Rosenkavalier* some months later seems to have been more rooted in the music than impelled by it. Reviews that praise the vitality of Karajan's conducting – 'sparkling', 'lissom', fully alive to the music's 'humour' and 'irony' – tend, when discussing his staging, to revert to abstract theorising about such things as 'the interdependence of music and drama'.

*

During the spring and summer of 1941 Karajan undertook further tours with the Berlin Staatskapelle and the Berlin State Opera. In April the Staatskapelle played in Budapest. In May the State Opera's productions of Mozart's *Die Entführung aus dem Serail* and Wagner's *Tristan und Isolde* were seen in Paris, conducted by Schüler and Karajan respectively. The Wagner was superbly cast. Germaine Lubin sang Isolde, Max Lorenz was Tristan, Margarete Klose sang Brangäne, the Kurwenal was Jaro Prohaska. It was a production that would be remembered in Paris for many years by music-lovers on all sides of the political divide.

Karajan also conducted a concert at the Palais de Chaillot, a high-voltage, all-German programme: Mozart's *Haffner* Symphony, Strauss's *Tod und Verklärung*, and Beethoven's Seventh Symphony. The Prelude to *Die Meistersinger* was played as the encore. Here was the young superstar at his most histrionic, flailing his way through the music before swinging round to receive the audience's plaudits like a runner breasting the tape.

If the visit was a huge success artistically, it was also a well-orchestrated one politically. Winifred Wagner headed the guest list for the first night of *Tristan und Isolde*. Press coverage was extensive and mainly triumphalist in tone. The Nazi anthem, the *Horst Wessel Lied*, prefaced most events. Since

Karajan disliked national anthems in general and the habit of prefacing concerts with them in particular, it is difficult to imagine that he much cared for the intrusion. Nevertheless, when he died in 1989, London's *Daily Telegraph* headed its obituary notice:

He 'mesmerised' his players with a repertoire ranging from the Horst Wessel to Verdi[3]

a remarkable headline which suggests that whatever else the British press may have lost down the years, it has certainly not lost its mastery of the art of alliteration.

*

By the late autumn of 1941, Hitler's Russian offensive had stalled, mired in the rain and snow of a wet autumn and an early Russian winter. British air raids on German cities, such as the one that had destroyed the Berlin State Opera, were also increasing in number and effectiveness.

Life in Berlin – which had been pleasant enough since 1939, if not altogether as pleasant as life in Rome or Paris – was becoming grimmer and more difficult. On 1 September a decree was issued requiring the Jewish population to wear a yellow star. Since, for strategic and economic reasons, Berlin's remaining 70,000 Jews – principally armaments workers and their families – had been allowed to function at a basic level of normality, the shock to the community was fearsome. The United States embassy reported 'almost universal disapproval by the people of Berlin' and 'astonishing manifestations of sympathy with the Jews in public'. This was not surprising. Berliners had generally shown themselves to be tougher, more tolerant, more intellectually robust than many of their compatriots in the south.

Among those who went to ground as more and more Jews were rounded up and deported was Elsa Schiller, the woman who during the 1950s would steer Deutsche Grammophon back into the mainstream of international recording and lay the foundations of its formidably successful post-war artists and repertoire policy.

With the entry of the United States into the war in December 1941 and the mass exodus from Berlin of the Latin American diplomatic missions, Berlin's social life was further denuded. Not that Karajan would have noticed. Though every salon in Berlin was at his disposal, his dislike of small-talk and the 'smart' social life meant that he was almost as isolated there as he had been in Ulm. When he was not conducting, he was rehearsing, studying, spending time in private, or taking the train. Berlin never was, and never would be, his home.

Like many people in the early winter of 1941, Karajan was to some extent concerned with getting by:

Aachen
Städtisches Konzerthaus Couvenstrasse
25 November 1941

Dear Mama,

Forgive me for typing, but I am very short of time. Thank you so much again for sending the coupons, but I am always worried that you don't have enough yourselves. Please only send what you can really do without; I'm very grateful to you for them. Food is very short, travelling around like this. I'm in very good health. I hope with all my heart you will get better soon, too. Of course I am complying with your wish and sending you 650 Reichsmarks immediately. Don't worry about the 20 Reichsmarks, perhaps you will find an opportunity to send me something next month to cover them. Unfortunately, I don't have any chance to get mail privately to Italy, but it's best to send letters via a consulate. I arrived here this morning. Had the Mozart Festival Concert yesterday in Berlin.[4] Schuchter's playing here on 14 December; I'm very excited to see what it will be like. At Christmas I am conducting in Berlin, then returning here. I'll hardly have time for a holiday before March. But I feel very fresh and well, as work has got much, much quieter.[5] I would like to come to Zell with you for the festive season, but it's not possible now. I'm sure you'll soon be writing to tell me how you are and what Papa is doing. Don't be angry with me for writing a business letter, but I had to get on and answer all your questions, and I hope I have managed to do so to your satisfaction.

Much love to you both
Yours
Herbert von Karajan[6]

*

Shortly before Christmas 1941, plots began to be laid within the musical community over the question of who might succeed Karl Böhm at the Dresden Opera. It had been rumoured for some time that Böhm was being courted by the State Opera in Vienna. Returning from Italy in December 1941, the conductor Karl Elmendorff, the man who would eventually secure the Dresden position, received a call from Böhm advising him that, though contractual problems made it unlikely that the move would take place before the spring of 1943, Dresden was effectively up for grabs. 'The Führer knows about it,' Elmendorff wrote to the designer Gerdy Troost, widow of Hitler's first official architect, Paul Ludwig Troost, 'and it seems that he will no longer withhold his agreement to this severance.'[7] Elmendorff's letter continued:

Now the competition for Dresden is under way. Böhm, who is of the opinion that my artistic reputation sets me apart as far as Dresden is concerned, will recommend me accordingly to [Martin] Mutschmann [Gauleiter of Saxony]. But there are German conductors who have a more influential relationship with the Pro-Pa-Mi [Propaganda Ministry] than I do. It is a matter of winning the support of the Führer and Dr Goebbels. For the sooner authority is exercised on the matter from high up or from the very top, the quicker other plans can be made. I myself have no absolutely reliable direct contact with the minister. Do you, dear Madam, know anybody? Do you think it possible that Dr Goebbels would accord me an interview on your recommendation? Have you any contact with Mutschmann?[8]

By early January, Elmendorff had secured the backing of Heinz Drewes, Goebbels's music assistant. Drewes's backing was useful, despite the fact that his position within the ministry had been weakened by his attempted defence of the serious music budget at a time when Goebbels wanted more and more to exploit the mass appeal of popular music.

From Elmendorff's point of view, there was only one fly in the ointment: Karajan. Though *Time* magazine had once described Elmendorff as 'a man of mediocre talent who in past years has turned out stupid performances shoddily rehearsed',[9] he was, at fifty, one of Germany's best regarded Wagner conductors, and a safe pair of hands in other repertory too. But he was no star. Fearing that his present post in Mannheim might mark the boundary of his career, he again wrote imploringly to Gerdy Troost:

The most important thing is that [Erich] Gottschald [Permanent Secretary of the Saxon State Theatre] must find out as soon as possible that it is the Führer's overriding wish to see me in Dresden. Can and will you, dear Madam, inform him of this and perhaps even arrange for the Führer himself or the Imperial Chancellery to give instructions to Dresden? In that case, victory would of course be mine and Karajan's competition eliminated.[10]

In fact, Karajan's bid hardly amounted to much, whatever he himself or members of the musical community in Dresden might have thought. His musical qualifications were not to be questioned. What he lacked was a political power base. His principal backers were Tietjen, equivocal as ever, and Vedder who was about to lose his agent's licence after foolishly overreaching and eventually compromising himself in the case of the brilliantly gifted young co-leader of the Berlin Philharmonic, Gerhardt Taschner, a Furtwängler protégé whom Vedder had promised fame and fortune as a soloist working with – among others – Karajan and the Staatskapelle.[11]

It is widely believed that Hitler himself vetoed Karajan's application for the Dresden job, though as with many of Hitler's rulings it is impossible to say exactly when it was made and to whom it was communicated. (Karajan told the Austrian Denazification Tribunal in 1946 that the SS vetoed his application; a case, almost certainly, of the messenger being confused with the message.)

*

Karajan's final appearance in Aachen as General Music Director took place on 22 April 1942, the second of two Eastertide performances of the *St Matthew Passion*. Heinz Marten was the Evangelist, the young Josef Greindl sang Christus, with Aachen stalwart Arthur Bard (Karajan's Falstaff), playing the various villains of the piece. The young choir, whose wonderfully fresh-voiced singing had so impressed Berliners in the *Missa Solemnis* the previous January, surpassed itself. In later years, Karajan would dispense with the baton entirely when conducting choral works; on this occasion, he simply set it aside for long stretches of the performance.

Afterwards, he gathered everyone in the rehearsal room to give them heartfelt thanks for all they had contributed to the musical life of the city and for all they had done for him personally, and to wish them every success in the future. It had been a truly happy marriage. Little wonder that Karajan would later look back on this as one of the happiest periods of his life.

After Aachen, silence. For five months Karajan was on more or less permanent vacation. If it had not been for Labroca's promise of a new production of *Don Giovanni* at the Florence Maggio Musicale and a Beethoven Ninth there, he would have been wholly unemployed. In the event, the *Don Giovanni* was by no means a triumph, despite a cast that included Mariano Stabile in the title role, Tancredi Pasero (Leporello), Maria Caniglia (Donna Anna), Suzanne Danco (Donna Elvira), and Mafalda Favero (Zerlina). Karajan disliked the production, the orchestra was uncooperative, and there were communications problems; for though Banfield was on hand to help, Karajan was not yet as fluent an Italian speaker as he would later become.

*

With time on his hands, Karajan had more leisure for listening and study: in particular, the study of recordings. Someone he spent time with in Berlin was Ernst von Siemens, heir to the Siemens electrical empire. Far from robust physically and something of a recluse, Siemens had a love of music that, even by the standards of this music-loving family, was unusually intense. Those who feared (wrongly as it turned out) that he was too frail ever to take over as boss of Siemens had no doubt about the seriousness of his interest in the company's electro-acoustic operations. Between them,

Siemens and their rivals AEG effectively ran the German record industry. Until 1941, AEG owned Deutsche Grammophon, Siemens Telefunken. The two companies then exchanged responsibilities; Siemens sold Telefunken to AEG and acquired Deutsche Grammophon. It would prove to be an historic exchange.

Ernst von Siemens's record collection was huge and he and Karajan spent many hours listening together at Siemens's home in Berlinische Strasse, before the house was destroyed in an air raid in the autumn of 1943. He would later recall:

One day Karajan suddenly said to me, 'Do you perhaps have the Mendelssohn Violin Concerto?' 'Yes,' I replied. 'I have that.' 'Could we play it?' And there we were both blissfully happy listening to the Mendelssohn Violin Concerto. Kulenkampff, if I remember correctly. It was forbidden, of course. One wasn't even meant to own such a record, let alone play it.[12]

The risk may have seemed minimal, though from May 1942 onwards – following the serving of an order on his company prohibiting the pressing and publication of recordings by Jewish artists – Siemens's private and public activities were closely monitored by the authorities.

From the start, Siemens took an active interest in the artistic policies of Deutsche Grammophon. A chance meeting he had in Rome with the head of Cetra caused the Turin Radio Symphony Orchestra to be made available to Karajan for recording sessions in October 1942. For some time, Karajan had been asking to record Mozart symphonies for Deutsche Grammophon. The company was enthusiastic but suddenly – and this was typical of the situation now affecting Karajan – no Berlin orchestra could be found to undertake the sessions.

The Turin RSO was not a front-rank orchestra (Karajan later said, 'I heard in my inner ear what I wanted to hear and the rest – well, it went down!'[13]) though, equally, it was not the third-rate ensemble it has sometimes been made out to be. The *Haffner* Symphony, which by now had assumed the status of Karajan's personal visiting card, gets rather a good performance in the 1942 recording: the playing resilient and surprisingly exact, Karajan's reading songful, fiery, and intense. The recording of the G minor Symphony, moulded and lyrical in the Bruno Walter style, is also very recognisably a thing of substance and beauty. It is only really in the outer movements of the *Jupiter* Symphony that conductor and orchestra seem to be on opposite sides of some invisible musical divide.

The Turin sessions also included a recording of the overture to Rossini's *Semiramide*, behind which lies one of the earliest and most fascinating tales of Karajan's interest in the whole business of recording technology. During one of his listening sessions with Ernst von Siemens, Karajan came out with the assertion that Deutsche Grammophon recordings left a great deal to be desired technically. Siemens was somewhat taken aback by this ('sehr gekrankt [very hurt]', was how he later described it) and asked Karajan if he had a particular reason for making such an allegation. Karajan said he had. On his next visit, he brought with him Toscanini's 1936 HMV recording of the *Semiramide* overture.

Siemens acknowledged the excellence of the New York recording, though what it achieved technically was, he believed, well within the competence of the best German engineers. The question he preferred to ask was, is this the kind of sound we want? More particularly, was it wise, given the constraints of shellac pressings, to risk making recordings that flirted so dangerously with dynamic extremes?

After the theory, a practical experiment. It so happened that van Kempen and the Dresden Philharmonic were in Berlin recording in Deutsche Grammophon's studios in Alte Jacobstrasse.[14] During the sessions Siemens invited the company's executive head, Hugo Wünsch, van Kempen, and Karajan to lunch to discuss recording quality. Afterwards, the party returned to Alte Jacobstrasse to make some experimental test recordings of the *Semiramide* overture.

Van Kempen started the session and, after a while, Karajan took over. The first thing that Siemens noticed was that the sound of the orchestra changed the moment Karajan began conducting. This was significant, since it was evident to Siemens and Wünsch that the excellence of the 1936 New York Philharmonic recording was due in no small measure to the particular character and quality of the sound Toscanini himself drew from the orchestra. (Karajan knew that too. But for him, this was merely the starting point.)

Having mysteriously changed the orchestra's sound, Karajan asked the engineers to rig up on the conducting desk a series of peak programme meters so that he could make a running comparison between what he was hearing from the orchestra and what was being registered by the micro-phones and cutting lathes. Peak distortion and the interrelated problems of groove spacing and end-of-side distortion were not the only concerns here; the quietest playing needed to be judged in relation to the level of background noise generated by the rotation of the 78 rpm shellac disc. It is interesting in this context that Karajan had singled out the *Semiramide* overture as his proving ground. It begins with a pianissimo drum roll and reaches a searing fortissimo within forty bars.

The test recordings have been lost, but the commercial recording Karajan made shortly afterwards in Turin is certainly a great success technically.

*

It was on his return from Italy in October 1942 that Karajan learned officially that the position at the Dresden opera had gone to Elmendorff. The announcement coincided with the start of the new season of Staatskapelle concerts, an all-Beethoven programme in which the C minor concerto was played by that fine and nowadays too little remembered pianist, Eduard Erdmann. The concert series was secure for the time being, but it was just about the only thing that was secure in Karajan's musical life. Throughout 1942 one door after another had been not so much slammed in his face as found to be locked the next time he tried to open it. Why was this? Had his failed Dresden application finally alerted the higher echelons of the establishment to the fact that Karajan was *persona non grata* with the Führer? Was the gathering momentum of Furtwängler's campaign against Vedder and Karajan, and Vedder's sudden professional demise, a factor? And what about Karajan's own behaviour: the increasingly reckless mix of high-profile demands with acts of private defiance and withdrawal? All these things played their part; but there was more besides.

The first position mysteriously to vanish was that of house conductor at the Berlin State Opera. What proved to be Karajan's final appearance with the company had taken place on 19 February 1942. It was the eighth of the nine scheduled performances of a brilliantly successful semi-staging of Orff's *Carmina burana*. (The final performance on 23 March was also due to be conducted by Karajan; in the event, it was conducted by Orff's pupil, the composer Werner Egk.) There can be little doubt that relations between Tietjen and Karajan were already becoming strained, for all that the two men continued to be civil to one another. At around this time, Prittwitz-Gaffron wrote to Richard Strauss:

Mr von Karajan is not only, as you say, 'a young man from a distinguished family', but also tends to behave like a 'screen goddess' and is giving us problems which would be easy to overcome with goodwill.[15]

By the time Prittwitz-Gaffron wrote that, the rebuilt State Opera had opened with a gala production of *Die Meistersinger* (hitherto Karajan's patch) conducted by Furtwängler. Karajan had been skiing in the Italian Alps in the spring of 1942 when he was first alerted to the fact that Tietjen had invited Furtwängler to conduct the new production. According to Karajan, when he remonstrated with Tietjen over the decision, Tietjen told him, 'Do not try to understand. This is high politics. When Furtwängler returns to the house, you will leave by the back entrance.'[16]

Clearly, 'high politics' was at work. In a long, courteous, and characteristically business-like letter to Karajan in May 1943, Tietjen would guardedly recall the events of the previous year:

It is extraordinarily regrettable that you have not appeared on the podium of the State Opera during the current season; this has led to rumours circulating, which cannot be laid to your charge or mine.

In our preliminary discussions on opera in spring 1942 we spoke at length about a new production of *Don Giovanni* [to be produced by Gründgens], the reprise of *Die Zauberflöte*, a new production of *Rosenkavalier* with yourself as director as well, *Tristan* with Germaine Lubin, and *Capriccio*.

It is not of interest to the outside world why all these plans fell through; it merely observes the fact. As ever, I attach importance to your continued involvement with the State Opera and ask you to have a preliminary talk with Dr Prittwitz about works and dates. I stand by my commitment made last year that you should occasionally direct as well as conduct a new production.[17]

Since none of this came to pass, one is bound to ask again why 'all these plans fell through' and what it was that so decisively wrecked Karajan's career as an opera conductor in Nazi Germany. If there are half a dozen possible musical or musico-political causes, there is one extra-musical one: Karajan's decision to marry Anita Gütermann.

*

Karajan and Elmy had tried to remain friends. He would tell his biographer Ernst Haeusserman:

Elmy gave up her profession after the wedding. When I was conducting in Berlin, she sometimes came along, but basically she lived more in Aachen. Then we took a flat in Berlin, so she was alone there when I was in Aachen. And so we both became tense and alienated and the result was separation after a little less than three years' marriage.[18]

Did Elmy know about Anita? Whether she did or not, in 1941 she was offered a chance to restart her career as an operetta singer. It was the title role in Nico Dostal's *Manina*, scheduled for production in Berlin in 1942. Taking a leaf out of Karajan's book, Elmy decided to forget the past and look to the future. Her career briefly revived, but she never remarried. 'No one can follow Karajan,' she would later say, without rancour or regret. Nor would Karajan forget or neglect her. In her last years, she rather relished her role as unofficial aunt – 'funny Aunt Elmy [lustige Tante Elmy]' as she called herself – to his two young daughters Isabel and Arabel.

Karajan was deeply smitten with Anita. Yet was he so smitten as to be oblivious to the new and more ominous mood that was in the air? Hitherto in the Third Reich, a marriage between an Aryan and someone who was wholly or partly Jewish had not necessarily blighted the careers of talented and well-connected people. Karajan was not exactly that (talented and semi-connected would be a better description) but to what extent was he aware that those days were largely over?[19]

Anita's own formidable social skills merely complicated the problem. Never slow in coming forward, she made strenuous efforts to smooth the path to marriage. In early September, during a visit to Venice for the annual Film Festival, she sought out Goebbels to tell him that she and Karajan were hoping to marry. Since it was not in Goebbels's nature to reject the embassies of beautiful young women, whatever their racial origins or marital status, he heard her out and, it would seem, instructed his minister Hans Hinkel to write to Karajan informing him that the Reichskulturkammer had no objection to the marriage.

Karajan himself also met Goebbels some time in 1942, though when precisely is not clear, since Karajan's own accounts of the events of 1942 contain a number of factual inconsistencies.[20] What is reasonably certain is that in the spring of 1942 he received army call-up papers via the Intendant's office in Aachen. Somewhat taken aback, he asked Kirchner to make enquiries about the validity of the draft. Twenty-four hours later, Kirchner rang:

'I got a general drunk on your account. But I am now pretty sure that the draft has come via the Prussian State Ministry.'

Not wishing to become cannon-fodder on the Russian front, but desperately keen to fly, Karajan made an approach via Göring's office to the Air Ministry. There he was able to speak with – as he later put it – 'a well-known air commodore'. The 'commodore' in question was almost certainly Göring's Under-Secretary of State, the joint head of the *Luftwaffe*, Field Marshal Erhard Milch. Like his friend Albert Speer, with whom he shared a similar background, Milch was a keen observer of the musical scene. Printed guest lists confirm that he and Karajan occasionally coincided at musical functions in Berlin and, later in 1944, at St Florian. The ministry's advice was that at the age of thirty-four Karajan was too old to train as a fighter pilot but that he could be accepted for training as an air courier.

At this point, Karajan was sent for a series of medical and dental checks. If what he thought happened is true, this is how Goebbels got to hear of the draft. Karajan's dentist's daughter was private secretary to Goebbels's wife, the long-suffering Magda.

According to Karajan, he was summoned by Goebbels.

'Why the desire to fly?'

'The better to defend my country.'

'Why not defend it with your baton?'

'A baton is nice, but the stick of an aircraft is better.'

'When the war is over, you can fly. For now, please conduct.'

It is a rum old tale, and there are several loose ends. (Did Karajan *ask* his dentist to phone his daughter or did the dentist rush to the phone of his own volition?) Such credibility as the narrative possesses resides mainly in the supposition that if it is not true who would have seriously bothered to make it up?

There is no doubt that Karajan was drafted and there is at least circumstantial evidence that conversations took place with the *Luftwaffe*; but precisely why he was drafted, and why at this particular juncture, may never be known. Some put it down to bureaucratic incompetence. Salacious souls have speculated that it was all Goebbels's doing anyway; that he wanted unfettered access to Anita. Others have suggested that it was a threat, a shot across the young man's bows. What is certain is that drafting Karajan was hardly a practical possibility. Though he had, as yet, no great reputation outside occupied Europe, other than in Sweden, his reputation within Germany, Austria, France, and Italy was already sky-high. Dispatching him to the front in 1942 would have smacked of desperation. Whatever Goebbels thought of Karajan personally, he was too skilled a propagandist to walk into that particular trap.

At much the same time as Karajan was courting Anita, Furtwängler had fallen for Elisabeth Ackermann, the widowed half-sister of one of his former lovers, Maria Daelen. Furtwängler's love life had been infinitely more turbulent than Karajan's, but in Elisabeth Ackermann he found an ideal helpmate. Her husband, a lawyer who had joined the German army in 1940, had been killed in a shooting accident in Paris, leaving her with four young children. She never for a moment thought that Furtwängler would ask her to marry him, but he did. Both Karajan and Furtwängler were lucky in the personalities of the women they were about to marry.

Karajan and Anita were married on 22 October 1942; but within days of the wedding things started turning nasty. In November 1942 the Office of Dispensations of the Chancellery of the Führer of the NSDAP opened an enquiry into Karajan (or 'Carajan' as one document spells his name). What kind of enquiry was it? Was it an enquiry, as some have suggested, to establish Karajan's right to some form of exemption from the application of the NSDAP's racial edicts? Or was it, as Karajan himself claimed, a full-blown hearing during which he announced his resignation from the Party?

As we have seen, Karajan had become a Party member in Aachen in 1935 on demand and by career-led design. Like many of his class and background who had joined the Party in its heyday in the early and mid-1930s, Karajan had shown no interest in Party affairs. On the contrary, he had frequently opposed the pettifogging interventions of its officials. Was he rash enough, though, to try to face down the Party at a formal hearing in Berlin, and on a race issue?

No one knew more about the relationship between Karajan's career and the internal workings of the NSDAP than the late Gisela Tamsen. Her view of the matter was that a hearing certainly took place, that it concerned Karajan's marriage to a *Vierteljüdin*, that the questioning was, perforce, hostile to Karajan, and that he probably did tender his resignation from NSDAP, either as an act of compliance with NSDAP regulations or of defiance.

But if this was the case, why was Karajan's name not removed from NSDAP membership files? Inefficiency, she concluded, is not a reasonable explanation; nor is chaos in the postal services, badly disrupted as they often were by nightly air raids. If there was a malfunction at the bureaucratic level it may have been caused by Karajan's failure to submit his resignation in writing. It is possible that he omitted to do this, believing, incorrectly, that a statement in the presence of witnesses was sufficient.

The most likely explanation, however, is that the court was overruled. Goebbels could no more allow Karajan to resign from the NSDAP (or allow the NSDAP to evict him) than he could afford to have him drafted.[21] Karajan could, however, be punished, and the punishment that was meted out was both subtle and cruel. While kept firmly within the fold of Party and State, he was promised work but rarely given it. His fees were cut and his artistic demands ignored. What work he did get was insufficient to meet his own hunger for music. It was enough, however, to keep him in play on Goebbels's private chessboard: a spare knight that might occasionally be used to corner the king – or one of the bishops – of the conducting world.

Not that it was all one-sided. There were times in 1943 and 1944 when Karajan turned down work, even though he had no other to go to. Arrogance, wounded pride, a refusal to dance to other people's tunes: call it what you will, Karajan would always fight his corner. If he did not win, he would wait; if waiting served no strategic purpose, he would withdraw; banish him and, like Shakespeare's Coriolanus, he would banish you. In the post-war years these would become familiar Karajan tactics, but it was the war years that turned a predisposition into a game plan. The political aspect of Nazism may have meant little or nothing to him. There can be no doubt, however, that during the war years the high-grade ore of his personality was remixed and tempered into steel.

CHAPTER 18

City terrors and mountain vigils

Down there they are dubious and askance; there nobody thinks
   as I,
But mind-chains do not clank where one's next neighbour is the
   sky.
                                    Thomas Hardy, 'Wessex Heights'

He lived in a space and a world of his own.
   Herbert von Karajan on Anton Bruckner

In January 1943 Karajan conducted his first concert in the rebuilt Berlin
State Opera and immediately fired off a letter to Dr Prittwitz-Gaffron about
the acoustics:

                                          Berlin, 26 January 1943
Dear Herr Doktor!
I should like to repeat once more what I have already told you verbally, namely
that the present acoustic of the State Opera still shows serious shortcomings.
The sound is muffled in places, the echo equipment sounds more like disturbing
interference, the individual groups do not blend, the violins are toneless, and
the possibilities of achieving an increase in sound during big crescendi are very
slight. I ask you to report these shortcomings to the Generalintendant. There
are three weeks now in which possible ways of fundamentally improving these
matters can be found.
   The programme for the next concert is now: Strauss *Don Juan*, Mozart
Violin Concerto in D [K218], and Schumann Symphony No.4 in D minor.
Unfortunately, I have to have another operation after my return from Hungary,
but I hope it will go well.
   Cordial greetings,
      Herbert von Karajan[1]

Prittwitz-Gaffron annotated Karajan's letter: 'Decision of GI [Tietjen]: sees
no cause to undertake improvements for the 3 symphonic concerts still to
come.' He did, however, decide to consult Richard Strauss about Karajan's
letter. Strauss was fascinated by theatre acoustics and had turned himself
into something of an expert on the subject. A highly technical reply came
by return of post. In Strauss's opinion, the State Opera acoustic had
always been better suited to more lightly scored classical pieces than to
heavily orchestrated works like *Ein Heldenleben*, *Sinfonia Domestica* or
the Funeral March from *Götterdämmerung*, where the brass and drums
often sounded muffled. To this end, he recommended that the conductor

aim at producing 'a beautiful and moderate volume of sound' by reducing the volume of the brass and timpani in fortissimo passages. As to the new house, Strauss insisted that the whole orchestra be on the stage, with the backstage areas clear of all impedimenta and a second wooden baffle placed behind the players. Wood is the secret, he says: wooden walls, wooden ceiling, and precisely gauged spaces between those and the theatre's stone, brick, and plaster work. And remember, he adds sagely, the walls of the new building will still be damp. It will probably take eight to ten years for the mortar to dry out completely, so have patience, my friends![2]

Tietjen accepted Strauss's recommendations in full and in a letter to Karajan dated 7 May 1943 insisted that he comply with the new layouts and arrangements as a pre-condition of his being retained as director of the Berlin State Opera Orchestral Concerts in the winter of 1943–4. Karajan declined to agree:

I have checked the acoustic very conscientiously during the last four concerts and I was obliged to conclude that it is so constituted that a realisation of the kind of performance I am expected to produce is not possible.[3]

At the same time, he renewed his demand that the concerts be transferred to the Philharmonie: on acoustic grounds and because of enhanced public access. With 600 more seats than the opera house's auditorium, the Philharmonie could accommodate an additional '2000 people' per concert (i.e. the public dress rehearsal and two performances), 'a fact which is not being given enough weight at the present difficult time for the national community'.[4]

In making this last point, Karajan was drawing on the advice of Leopold Gutterer, the very able State Secretary in Goebbels's Propaganda Department. Gutterer, whose help Karajan had enlisted, was already privately convinced that Germany had lost the war.[5] An intensely practical man (when the Ministry building caught fire during an air raid, he saved it more or less single-handedly) he was more interested in maximising audiences for classical concerts than getting embroiled in tit-for-tat name-calling between conductors. Within the week, however, Furtwängler was writing to the Ministry advancing the somewhat tortuous argument that though it was 'desirable to cultivate as important a force as Herr von Karajan in the Berlin musical scene' a decision to move the Staatskapelle concerts to the Philharmonie would be an insult to its sister institution the Berlin State Opera.

In the short term, the Karajan–Gutterer view prevailed; Karajan began the 1943–4 winter season with a concert in the Philharmonie on 7 November. Shortly after that, however, the Allies launched a massive bombing offensive against Berlin that would continue for the next four months. With the city in total disarray and the outer fabric of the Philharmonie damaged, the Staatskapelle's December concerts were transferred to the Europahaus in Saarlandstrasse. Then, in January 1944, the Philharmonie itself was bombed and everyone – the Staatskapelle and the Berlin Philharmonic – ended up back in the new State Opera, which lead something of a charmed life until it too was destroyed in the most terrible of all onslaughts on central Berlin on the night of 3 February 1945.

Tietjen's other main stipulation – that 'in recognition of the exceptional difficulties brought about by total war', Karajan should refrain from asking for more than five rehearsals per concert – was more or less adhered to. In fact, where rehearsals were concerned, Karajan's position had been bolstered in February 1943 by the intervention of the conductor Obersturmführer Franz Schmidt, head of the SS's Staff Music Corps, which now had its own orchestra, its own soloists, and what it envisaged would eventually be its own élite cadre of Waffen SS conductors. These creatures – the musical equivalent of Napoleon's puppies in Orwell's *Animal Farm* – were being trained, in Schmidt's words, 'for special politico-cultural action'.[6] Meanwhile, they needed musical training, too, and to that end Schmidt had sought and gained Karajan's permission to allow a limited number of trainees access to rehearsals for Staatskapelle concerts. In a memorandum to Prittwitz-Gaffron, 'requesting' the State Opera's co-operation with the project, Schmidt writes:

It is noted that for participation in the relevant final rehearsals at most eight students should be assigned, and in principle only the most advanced, after thorough preparation, accompanied and supervised by the two music consultants of the SS HQ.[7]

At the bottom of the memorandum, Prittwitz-Gaffron has scrawled laconically, 'As far as I'm concerned, no problem.'

The fact that Karajan was in the habit of asking for more than five rehearsals per concert is interesting; but, then, his programme building was challengingly heterodox: popular crowd-pullers mixed in with works that were very much caviare to the general. In April 1943, Sibelius's Fourth Symphony began a concert ('What a peculiar work!' exclaimed Kurt Westphal in the *Berliner Börsen-Zeitung*[8]) that also included Haydn's Cello Concerto and the first two movements of Smetana's *Má vlast*. In another concert, dubbed 'Music of all epochs' by the *Berliner Börsen-Zeitung*, a brilliant, spare-textured performance of Bach's Brandenburg Concerto No.2 was followed by a grand, somewhat romanticised account of Haydn's *Drum Roll* Symphony, Reger's *Variations and Fugue on a Theme of Mozart* (the concert's highlight according to several reviewers) and an orchestrally resplendent account of the *Tannhäuser* overture. Sometimes the programme would have a narrower focus – the concert on 7 November 1943 consisted of Bach's Suite No.3 in D, Mozart's *Sinfonia concertante* in E flat K297b, and Beethoven's Fifth Symphony – only to open out into broader repertory again the following month.⁹

Looking at Karajan's last full season with the Staatskapelle, one notices how various it was. In March 1944, Mozart's Piano Concerto K488 was programmed alongside Bruckner's Ninth Symphony; the following month Schubert's Ninth Symphony (the slow movement, it was reported, especially bleak) was prefaced by something else that would quickly turn to dross in Karajan's hands, the première of Gottfried von Einem's *Concerto for Orchestra*.

The aristocratic von Einem, a composing pupil of Boris Blacher, would loom large in Karajan's later life. Karajan's junior by ten years, he was the pampered child of an illicit union between Baroness von Einem and the Hungarian Count László von Hunyady. It had been the baroness's custom to go on safari in Africa, taking with her a lover and an upright piano. After one such safari in the 1920s, she returned with the piano but minus the lover, who had been savaged to death by a wounded lioness. This gory fact, along with the true identity of his natural father, had been disclosed to the 20-year-old Gottfried by the Gestapo after they arrested him in the Adlon Hotel, Berlin on 28 September 1938. Throughout the war the family was under constant surveillance, which did not stop the dauntless baroness mingling with whom she pleased: 'good' Germans, 'bad' Germans, Jews, dissidents, and would-be assassins of the Führer.

Karajan, a Blacher fan, lurked somewhat uneasily on the edge of this circle and was instrumental in winning von Einem the commission for his *Concerto for Orchestra*. The work, which has more or less sunk without trace, is little more than a tarted-up concerto grosso, vaguely amusing in a Milhaudesque kind of way. It caused a certain amount of offence at the time; in retrospect, its only real offence is its head-in-the-sand fecklessness, its jaunty inconsequentiality.

Karajan's conducting of the première is reported to have been spirited. Yet harmless as the enterprise was, it opened up a whole new can of worms. In the audience for the first performance was the 34-year-old Werner Naumann, Goebbels's former bureau chief, who had recently taken over the duties of the increasingly sceptical and defeatist Leopold Gutterer. Naumann, who distrusted the von Einem family, found the piece baffling and lobbied Goebbels accordingly. Magda Goebbels, who was besotted with Naumann but who was also an acquaintance of the von Einems, sang a very different tune in her husband's ear.

Goebbels responded with a stick-and-carrot approach. First, Gottfried von Einem was given a formal dressing-down by music supremo Heinz

Drewes; then orders were given for new commissions to be placed in his way. Instructions were also given for a recording to be made of the work, though not with Karajan. The sessions, von Einem was officially informed, would be in Dresden with Karl Elmendorff conducting the Saxon State Orchestra.[10]

Karajan's final Staatskapelle concert of the season, in mid-May, was given in honour of Richard Strauss's eightieth birthday. It began with Strauss's *Divertimento for small orchestra*, a recent revision of his Couperin-inspired *Tanzsuite*. Karajan directed this from the harpsichord. Erna Berger sang two Strauss songs 'Die heiligen drei Könige aus Morgenland' and 'Allerseelen', and the concert ended with a grand and festive account of *Ein Heldenleben*. The *Divertimento* apart, it was a straight repeat of the programme Karajan had given in Ulm ten years earlier.

Since the 1943–4 season coincided with a series of massive air attacks on central Berlin – what the Allies called 'area bombing' and the Germans 'terror bombing' – it is a marvel that the series survived more or less intact. Only one concert was cancelled, on 2–3 January 1944. Notices placed in the press stated that Karajan and his soloist Wilhelm Kempff were both indisposed. For the rest, the show went on, albeit under a growing list of constraints. On 16 April 1944, Prittwitz-Gaffron wrote to the Foreign Bureau for Music in Berlin:

Because of the terror bombing of the Imperial Capital, unavoidable alterations have been made to the dates and programmes of the State Orchestra Symphony Concerts under Herbert von Karajan. Mr von Karajan was no longer able to perform the Sixth Symphony of Jean Sibelius. But even if this performance of Sibelius had taken place, the beautiful essay by Dr Toivo Haapanen of Helsinki could not have been printed, since by decree no more programmes may be printed. I therefore take the liberty of returning Dr Toivo Haapanen's essay to you with many thanks.[11]

*

'Commitments abroad' was the reason Karajan gave for politely declining to take up Tietjen's offer of 12 May 1943 inviting him to talk with Prittwitz-Gaffron about the possibility of operatic engagements in Berlin in 1943–4. Since Karajan had refused to deal with Tietjen through his deputy back in 1937, Tietjen must have known that he was even less likely to do so now, especially when it was clear from the manner of the offer that Karajan's services as an opera conductor were no longer required (or, rather, could no longer be countenanced) on a regular basis. Karajan did have 'commitments abroad' but they were few and far between.

During 1943 and early 1944, he was offered freelance engagements in Copenhagen, Milan, Amsterdam, Bucharest, and Paris. To secure the engagement in Copenhagen – where Furtwängler had conducted the previous year and where he would shortly return – Karajan offered to conduct without a fee. The concert, on 22 February 1943, was attended by the Crown Prince. According to Karajan, the prince's presence greatly improved the size of what threatened at one stage to be a very thin house. Karajan conducted three sure-fire show-stoppers from his repertory: Mozart's *Haffner* Symphony, Strauss's *Don Juan*, and Beethoven's Seventh Symphony. The concert was a huge success, but it would be many years before he went back to Copenhagen. In 1947, EMI's Danish branch, alone among the company's continental subsidiaries, refused to market his recordings.

In his dealings with Amsterdam, Karajan was at his haughtiest and most difficult. When the orchestra offered him a 'popular' concert rather than a place in the Concertgebouw's more prestigious subscription series, he rejected it out of hand. He did, however, manage to broker a deal with Siemens and Deutsche Grammophon allowing him to record with the orchestra. The sessions took place in September 1943, to generally glorious effect. The recording of Brahms's First Symphony is arguably the finest Karajan ever made of that work.[12]

In April 1944, he returned to Paris at the invitation of the Paris Radio Orchestra. Years later, Jacques Pernoo, a horn player in the orchestra, would recall:

He was, even at this time, an exceptional creature who astonished the French musicians with the absolute knowledge he had of their repertory, particularly the music of Debussy and Roussel which he conducted from memory. His interpretations were very precise, very calculated. He had a unique way of accommodating thematic elements with the most delicate modifications of tempo. Moreover, he was not the dictator one is given to believe, the very opposite of Furtwängler or Mengelberg.[13]

Karajan's travel plans, like those of other leading musicians, were closely monitored by the relevant department in Gestapo headquarters in Prinz Albrechtstrasse in Berlin. It was there, too, that other strategies were evolved. In a paper prepared for the Head of the SD dated 27 December 1943, the case for government-sponsored orchestral and operatic tours is re-examined in the light of current economic difficulties, and strongly reaffirmed. The success of the Berlin State Opera's visit to Paris in 1941 is singled out for special mention. It is clear from the document that Furtwängler and Karajan were regarded as being in a class apart when it came to drawing power and popular appeal. However, neither was available for the Berlin Philharmonic's proposed 1944 tour of the Balkans. Furtwängler was prepared to make no more than a provisional commitment to conduct in Ankara or Istanbul in March or April 1944; and even that was hedged round with provisos about 'health' and 'other engagements'. As for Karajan, though he had originally been pencilled in for the tour, he had now been ruled out because of financial demands and 'other difficulties'.[14]

Goebbels's ministry was also experiencing problems with the Berlin Philharmonic. Its propaganda film on the orchestra *Symphony and Love* (Paul Verhoeven, 1944) had to do without Furtwängler, who refused to take part, and Karajan, whom various unspecified 'difficulties' had also automatically excluded. Strauss, Böhm, Knappertsbusch, and Jochum duly appeared in the film, but its appeal was seriously undermined by the absence from the screen of Furtwängler and the Principal Pretender.

Left to his own devices, Karajan would have fled Berlin. As it was, he had no option for the time being but to return there, to the politicking and the bombing. Without permission from the authorities in Berlin he could not travel; the Staatskapelle concerts were a financial and musical necessity; and there were recording opportunities there too. As Germany's situation deteriorated and the squeeze on live entertainment became ever tighter, so radio transmissions and the gramophone were assuming a new and growing importance.

*

It was the mountains and, in summer, his lakeside retreat at Thumersbach that saved Karajan's sanity and general health at this time. In the winters of 1942–3 and 1943–4, he spent a good deal of time on the ski-slopes of Cervinia. There he met up again with Luis Trenker who must have caught in Karajan a glimpse of the character Trenker himself had played in his film *The Prodigal Son* (*Der verlorene Sohn*, 1934): the gifted mountain boy who makes a nightmarish visit to a soulless modern city (Trenker chose New York) before returning to the mountains where he renounces all interest in the world beyond the bounds of his native horizon.

Karajan and I often skied together down the big runs from the Rosa plateau into the valley. Karajan was very ambitious and always wanted Leo Gasperi, the top skier in Cervinia, to be available for him, and he would curse when Gasperi pulled away from him. I often asked the brilliant conductor how he managed to master great scores so fantastically accurately, with their thousands of notes and entries and rests: but he would always answer that he could manage the left-hand parallel turn better than the right. Back in the hotel in the evening, Anita and Herbert would tell me their woes, which were very real. What most depressed Karajan was that he had no orchestra suited to him: 'In Berlin, Furtwängler won't let me near the Philharmonic.' Karajan had conducted some concerts in Florence, and he complained bitterly about the behaviour of the orchestra, which he said persisted in passive resistance, incited by envious conductors. Yes, it was tough for Karajan in those days, and I can well understand how badly he suffered at that time under such hurtful treatment. Skiing on the magnificent runs at the foot of the Matterhorn helped both of them and myself through many worries.[15]

The mountain vigils would also continue to influence Karajan's thinking and music-making. In July 1944, he wrote to his mother from Bad Kissingen where – feeling 'old as the hills' – he was taking a cure for back and liver troubles:

What must be done here is to free ourselves from all those earthly things that weigh us down, and to return music to those spiritual heights from which they were born – that is what I am convinced of, and I wanted to share this with you. With this insight that has so powerfully impressed me, I now for the first time understand this music correctly.[16]

Karajan had started recording 'this music', Bruckner's Eighth Symphony, with the Staatskapelle for Berlin Radio the previous month. He was not the only musician who now found Bruckner's music speaking to him in a special way. At a time when the works of Beethoven must have seemed almost crassly optimistic[17] and those of Brahms too bourgeois and emotionally hesitant, it was left to Bruckner to articulate a sense of something at once grand and terrible, epic and *Angst*-ridden: the forces of darkness and death trampling, if not entirely obliterating, the old certainties of priest and peasant. What is astonishing about the Karajan Bruckner Eighth – in comparison with Bruckner recordings from this same year by conductors such as Furtwängler and Knappertsbusch – is the sense it conveys of a mood that is at once awesome and imperturbably calm;[18] a further manifestation of that almost other-worldly quality of self-possession Hans Hotter had noted in Karajan's pre-war performances of Brahms's *German Requiem*.

The background to the Bruckner Eighth recording is itself remarkable, revealing, as it does, Karajan's obsessive pursuit of what some would later dub 'perfection' but which was in reality a somewhat quixotic mix of distant ideals and short term preoccupations. The recording was begun in the latter days of June 1944, the month that marked the beginning of the end for Nazi Germany. Rome had fallen, the D-Day landings had taken place, and in the East the Russians were making fresh advances. An eerie calm had settled over the German high command. As Germany began to fall apart, Hitler lazed at the Berghof, where visitors came and went not knowing whether to be charmed or shocked by his mood. Albert Speer visited the Berghof, then travelled to Linz where a special 'Armaments Day' festival was being organised. Among the guests at a concert in the abbey church at St Florian on 24 June were Speer, Erhard Milch, the Karajans, and Karajan's parents. For Karajan the visit was a recce: he was due to conduct Bruckner's

Eighth Symphony in St Florian on 23 July. He was also deep in negotiations about the future of the recently refinanced and reorganised Reichs-Bruckner Orchestra in Linz.

Three days after his June visit to St Florian, Karajan was back in Berlin recording the Eighth Symphony with the Staatskapelle in Studio 1 of Broadcasting House. By the time a halt was temporarily called, three movements had been taped. The fourth would not be completed until late September, and that, astonishingly, would be in stereophonic sound.

The complete recording took an unbelievable thirty-two hours of studio time. And when it was all over, Karajan decided he wanted to start again from scratch. The reason he gave in support of this frankly incredible request was that the acoustic in Studio 1 was not right for Bruckner. Now that the radio engineers had sorted out the State Opera's acoustic, that was his preferred choice. As an argument this was both disingenuous and silly. When the whole thing finally came to a point of crisis in October 1944, the Head of Broadcasting in the Propaganda Ministry Hans Fritzsche – a languid *bon vivand* with a drawling 'educated' manner: a thoroughly evil man who knew nothing of music but who had perforce became involved in the controversy – gave a typically caustic response to Karajan's ally in the Ministry, Leopold Gutterer:

Yesterday [Karajan] expressed the opinion, partly to you and partly to Director Kult, that the acoustic in Studio 1 was not good enough. An expert of Mr von Karajan's stature could surely have made this remark at the start of the recordings which have cost us several tens of thousands of Reichsmarks. I have had these recordings checked by experts, and they declare them to be excellent.[19]

Gutterer tried to argue Karajan's corner, particularly with regard to his access to the Reichs-Bruckner Orchestra, but the radio executives were entirely at one with Fritzsche. A memo from German Radio to Fritzsche, written three days after Fritzsche's own broadside, concludes: 'Should Mr von Karajan in fact make such a demand [to re-record the symphony], I ask you to refuse it.'[20]

Karajan's reasons for wanting the re-recording are not difficult to fathom. First, having heard the finale in stereophonic sound, he now wanted the whole symphony to be recorded in that medium. Secondly, and more important, he was keen to re-record the work, not with the Staatskapelle, but with the Reichs-Bruckner Orchestra which he had good reason to believe was about to be further upgraded (with him, he fondly hoped, as its new chief conductor) and admitted to the select band of orchestras permitted to contribute to the prestigious Sunday evening radio series 'Immortal Music of the German Masters'.

The Reichs-Bruckner Orchestra was originally the brainchild of another radio executive, Heinrich Glasmeier, a Prussian aristocrat and former World War One cavalry officer with a taste for the good things in life: fine horses, fine houses, fine wines, fine women, and fine music in agreeable surroundings. Or, at least, that was what Karajan believed. He would tell his biographer Roger Vaughan:

He knew Hitler loved Bruckner. He knew of a convent twenty kilometres from Linz. It included a church and a great library. When the Nazis came it was secularised. So Glasmeier commandeered this convent, then went to see Hitler. He extolled the virtues of the convent, the beauty of the courtyard, the perfect set-up for the concerts that Furtwängler would conduct there, the pleasures of the Spanish Riding School in the moonlight. He was a salesman. He told Hitler the convent must be restored and made into a shrine for Bruckner.[21]

In practice, it was not quite like that, though Glasmeier was indeed the moving force behind the project as it finally came to be realised. Hitler, who had been brought up in Linz, had long harboured a plan to turn the city into a centre of musical excellence. His plan was that a music conservatory and symphony orchestra should be added to the existing opera house and that a foundation should be established in nearby St Florian to serve Bruckner, much as Bayreuth served Wagner. As early as 1939, Hitler had approved plans for the setting up of the orchestra, to be known as the Linz Bruckner Orchestra. It was a modest venture, based more or less exclusively on local talent. Standards were not high, though the appointment of the youngest of the Jochum brothers, Georg Ludwig Jochum, to the post of Music Director in 1941 did a certain amount to remedy that.

Then, in 1942, during a wholesale reorganisation of the German broadcasting network, it was decided to create a new national radio orchestra based in Linz. It would have the power to recruit the best players from all over Austro-Germany and it would be known officially as the Linz Reichs-Bruckner-Orchester des Grossdeutschen Rundfunks. Georg Ludwig Jochum was invited to oversee the orchestra for the 1943–4 season, with guest appearances by Kabasta, Keilberth, Knappertsbusch, and Schuricht. There is little doubt, though, that Glasmeier, who was by now very much master of the project, was looking for a more charismatic figure than Jochum to head the organisation in the longer term.

Glasmeier met Karajan in Berlin and immediately issued a personal invitation to him to conduct in St Florian. When Karajan visited St Florian he was both astonished and amused by Glasmeier's life-style. Here was a man straight out of the pages of Huysmans's *A rebours*:

Furnishings had been brought in from Paris. A coach and six matched horses was obtained – the coach was light blue damask inside. Glasmeier took a corner room for his office. From the windows he could look down the left cloister 120 metres; down the right cloister, 80 metres. There was an endless number of rooms, incredible space, all beautifully restored . . . He lived there, and how! He wore a monk's coat lined with sable and a mortarboard. He carried a silver cane. Each evening he dined with the old master of the convent.[22]

After the rehearsal for the Eighth Symphony, Glasmeier took Karajan down to the crypt where Bruckner's remains are preserved.

'You are beneath where the orchestra will play,' this man said. 'Bruckner never heard his Eighth Symphony [not true]. You have the opportunity to play for him. Now you will have ten minutes alone with him.' And he shut the door and left me there in the dark.[23]

The performance took place seventy-two hours after the attempted assassination of Hitler in the July bomb plot. Under stringent new censorship rules, only one review was permitted: a long, high-flown, and wholly admiring piece by critic Heinrich Hofer. It was widely syndicated, but it was printed in full only in the Berlin edition of the *Völkischer Beobachter*. Glasmeier was furious. He had hoped that the event would bring a welcome sheaf of publicity for the St Florian project; but St Florian was not even mentioned. For security reasons, the concert was simply said to have taken place in 'a South German Baroque church'.

None the less, Karajan's stock as a Bruckner conductor continued to rise with those whose opinions mattered in the musical world. In October 1944, shortly after Karajan had conducted three further performances of the Eighth Symphony with the Staatskapelle in Berlin, Prittwitz-Gaffron received a letter from that most distinguished of contemporary German musicological research organisations, Robert Haas's Bruckner Edition in Leipzig. The letter concerned the Staatskapelle's request for study scores of seven of the Bruckner symphonies. And it went on:

May we take this further opportunity to say that we place an extraordinarily high valuation on Herr von Karajan's Bruckner performances, which might at this time be judged exemplary. We had the good fortune to hear the Eighth in St Florian and are only sorry that we missed the most recent performances in Berlin.[24]

If merit was to be the determining factor, it is arguable that Glasmeier's instincts were correct: no one was better qualified to lead the Reichs-Bruckner Orchestra than Karajan. But as Karajan knew by now, merit had very little to do with it when it came to the handing down of official positions within the Reich. His best bet was Gutterer, and to that end he sent Gutterer what was in effect a formal job application, complete with the job reference number and all the appropriate Nazi greetings:

Sanatorium Dr von Dapper
Bad Kissingen 14 Aug. 44

Dear State Secretary,

Further to my suggestion with regard to Feldpost number 00080: I should like to request that the Reichsminister authorise the Reichs-Brucknerorchester to make recordings with me for the 'Immortal Music' series. I have conducted the orchestra recently and can vouch absolutely for its quality. My reasons: the increased possibility of the use of the orchestra and the reduced chance of recordings being threatened or endangered by air raids. I also believe it is in your interest to allow me to be involved in the recordings more than once during the run of broadcasts, which will soon have completed a year's duration. The orchestra still has dates free. If your decision is positive I shall get in touch immediately. With the very best regards to the Reichsminister and best wishes to yourself.

Heil Hitler
    Herbert Karajan[25]

It was the Dresden situation all over again: Karajan applying for a job that he felt his abilities merited but getting nowhere in the process. Both Glasmeier and Gutterer were rooting for him but the time was not right. Within a week of the attempt on Hitler's life in July 1944, a state of 'total war' had been declared at Goebbels's instigation. And it was Goebbels who was Germany's new *de facto* deputy leader, answerable to no one other than the palpably ailing Führer. In a desperate attempt to husband resources and release more men for active service, Goebbels shut everything down: theatres, opera houses, cabarets, circuses. Some orchestras were disbanded with immediate effect. In Linz, the orchestra stayed, but (despite protests from Glasmeier) the choir was disbanded and the foundation in St Florian shut down. Goebbels also closed whole departments in his own ministry, including the music department. Such decisions as had to be taken were taken, therefore, not by specialist advisers, who had been redeployed elsewhere, but by the broadcasting services' own slimmed-down inner cabinet. Administratively, the St Florian situation was down to Fritzsche.

With the opera houses closed and concert performances reduced to a bare minimum, radio was even more important. What Fritzsche had to decide was whether or not he should recommend to Goebbels that the Linz orchestra be added to the 'big five' broadcasting orchestras: the Berlin Philharmonic, the Vienna Philharmonic, the Berlin Staatskapelle, the Saxon State Orchestra, and the Bavarian State Orchestra. To Fritzsche the trained publicist, the orchestra's principal problem was that it had no reputation. Were it to be called 'The Führer's Orchestra' that problem might be partly addressed. But there were other issues. For example, raising the orchestra's status to this level – and here Fritzsche clearly had in mind Goebbels's obsession with manpower resources – would provide its members with a continuing excuse for exemption from military service.

During September and early October, Fritzsche put decisions on hold, pending further 'expert' opinion on the orchestra. In practice, it was a case of waiting for Furtwängler, who had agreed to conduct Bruckner's Ninth Symphony in St Florian on 11 October and report back. On 12 October, Fritzsche wrote to Gutterer confirming that Karajan would be considered as a conductor of the Reichs-Bruckner Orchestra 'within the context of overall planning'. However, he added, 'If he also wants Bruckner's Eighth Symphony to be the first work he conducts there, then I strongly urge you to refuse him this wish.'[26]

Glasmeier still wanted Karajan, but he could not have chosen a more inopportune moment to show his hand than the dinner he hosted in one of the grand salons in St Florian following the Furtwängler concert. Turning to Frau Georg Jochum, he announced: 'When your husband has done his military service, he'll reach the very peak of his artistic career. The call-up papers have just arrived.'[27] Glasmeier, who was himself about to be sent to Hungary,[28] had evidently secured Jochum's call-up in order to make way for the 'master conductor' of his choosing.

Word was soon out. A week later, Gerhart von Westerman, the Berlin Philharmonic's general manager, noted in a letter:

They say Jochum is going to join up . . . and now older conductors who have no orchestra are said to be coming. There is talk of Cl Krauss and Karajan, although he's only late twenties [sic]. So the good days under the ever friendly Jochum are over, too; they [the orchestra] are very down in the dumps.[29]

But Furtwängler had already moved to block Glasmeier's plan. When Frau Jochum told him of her husband's call-up, he replied:

There's no question of that. Jochum has done all the work building up the orchestra and he must carry on. It would be unfair if another person – and I have my suspicions – were allowed to nab the position. I'll ring up Dr Goebbels today to put a stop to it.[30]

In the end, Jochum stayed, though the orchestra never did broadcast in the 'Immortal Music of the German Masters' series.[31] Karajan's wish to record Bruckner's Eighth Symphony was quashed, and though a recording by him with the orchestra was scheduled for 21 January 1945, it was postponed, partly because of Berlin's insistence that Georg Ludwig Jochum, and not Karajan, should conduct the orchestra at its début in the 'Immortal Music' series. By the time alternative dates were offered, Karajan was in Italy. He did, however, conduct the orchestra – or members of it – on one further occasion. On 14 December 1944, he returned to Linz to conduct the players in a complete performance of Bach's *Art of Fugue*.[32]

*

Some indication of Karajan's state of mind in this final year of the war can be gauged from a letter he wrote to Richard Strauss shortly before leaving for St Florian to conduct Bruckner's Eighth Symphony. Strauss himself had described Karajan as 'a young man from a distinguished family'. And so he was: highly-strung but correct and courteous when he needed to be. Which is what makes this letter so extraordinary.

As a tribute to Strauss it is heartfelt in the extreme. As a revelation of Karajan's vision (no other word will do) of what he planned to make of his life it is both frank and revealing. Yet it is also a letter that is profoundly self-preoccupied and, oddly for Karajan, curiously discourteous in the way in which, in the opening paragraphs, it burdens the distinguished recipient with details of the well-wisher's medical and professional problems. In the original manuscript, the handwriting is neat and steady; the calligraphy as such gives no indication of illness, anxiety, stress or undue haste. (Such things are more in evidence in the job application to Gutterer, written a month later.) The letter is, however, poorly punctuated, an oddity which it is difficult to reproduce in English without obscuring unduly its larger impact:

Thumersbach bei Zell a. See 16.7.44

Hochverehrter Herr Doktor!

If this letter containing my best wishes reaches you only today, I beg you to forgive me. Since Christmas I have been coping with a serious liver complaint; time and again it keeps throwing me down, and this is one of the reasons for my delay.

It is with even greater cordiality that I would like to express my eternal thanks for those imperishable values you have bestowed upon us.

Because I was not granted the possibility of a position from which I would be able to organise an event worthy of you, I read of the week of festivities [in Vienna] with silent melancholy. It was a somewhat bitter experience to have to remain on the sidelines. Yet I did my last concert at the [Berlin] State Opera in the service of your works – and with the same programme with which, ten years ago, I celebrated your 70th birthday. How much has changed since! A small provincial orchestra [Ulm] translated into the prestigious State Opera Orchestra. I have personally had to pay for this promotion with a good measure – more than a good measure – of disappointments and difficulties; but <u>one</u> thing has remained and that is the eternal greatness of your works, something which obliges us and inspires us to be your totally devoted servants.

Furthermore, and this is something which must be the most beautiful gift for you personally, there is the feeling that you have created in your work a symbol of the relationship of our own time to future times – times that will demand the best of us in the service of pure Art.

And I know that one day I, too, shall have a circle of influence, something I most ardently desire, which will finally give me the opportunity to perform your operas as I imagine them to be.

And if to us young people your <u>works</u> are a matter of the heart, then we shall also take as our example your <u>personality</u> – and a life that through continuous advancement and creative power has been a <u>truly lived life.</u>

And now I beg you, in the name of all the many thousand musical hearts in the world, to take good care of your health and to give us in the future the things that we still await. And please accept again the best wishes of probably the most loyal of all your admirers.

With the greatest admiration,

Yours, Herbert von Karajan[33]

During the autumn, Karajan and Anita went to stay with Trenker and his wife in Kitzbühel. According to Trenker, Karajan was now in a deeply agitated state. It was clear that Hitler's Reich was on the point of complete collapse, yet there was no immediate prospect of escape. Anita worried about Herbert's future, worries Trenker brushed aside:

'You will conduct in New York, Buenos Aires, London and Berlin, and in Vienna. That's as sure as sure can be. There's no better conductor than you at present. Don't worry, one day audiences round the world will cheer you.'[34]

Was Trenker remembering that conversation with the benefit of hindsight?

'But how is one to survive the coming catastrophe,' [Karajan] cried. 'The Russians will kill me, they'll think I am a Nazi conductor, although I've nothing to do with these crazy people. The Bolsheviks will murder me! If I could at least show I am an Austrian, but they won't allow time for explanations. I suppose if I wore Austrian national dress – one of those smart Styrian suits with green lapels, damask and horn buttons – even the stupidest Russky would realise I am Austrian.'

'Oh, if that's all,' said my wife, 'we can sort that out quite easily. Luis has got a new Styrian suit from Miedler's that he doesn't like. Do you want to try it on, perhaps it will fit you?'

And it did fit! One hour later, Karajan left our house in Kitzbühel as a smart Alpine lad from Styria and travelled back to Thumersbach.[35]

Trenker claimed the magic suit did the trick, which is nonsense. Karajan was out of Berlin before the Russians arrived. In any case, Karajan's own original premise was badly flawed. To the Russian soldiery Austrians and Germans were all alike. Still, it would have been nice to have a photograph of Karajan in Styrian garb.

Trenker certainly knew what Karajan was going through. He had relations and property in Berlin and travelled there shortly after meeting the Karajans in Kitzbühel:

Down in the south there was scarcely any blackout, no howling of sirens with bomb craters and conflagrations, but here [in Berlin] were darkness distress and tired figures clearing up. Down there hardly any lack of food; here extreme shortage of everything . . . Once, staying with friends in Wannsee, the sirens went off at about ten o'clock in the evening. We drove anxiously towards the blazing city to check our home. Everywhere blue phosphorous flashes leapt up and even the angrily thundering sky above seemed to be burning. When we came to Dernburgstrasse, I saw a greenish light flickering from the dormer windows of our little house, with red flames in the midst of it.[36]

The flat the Karajans rented in Erbacherstrasse, at the city end of Berlin's Grunewald, was also destroyed in the bombing. (It had belonged to the parents of an acquaintance of Anita's, a Dutchman called Rommenhöller.) After that, whenever Karajan was required to return to Berlin during the final months of the war, he found temporary accommodation in the Hotel Esplanade or the Hotel Adlon. Neither was bomb-proof, but both had reliable air-raid shelters. (It was in the Adlon shelter that Marie Vassiltchikov said she saw him one night, barefoot, in a trench-coat, and with his hair standing on end.[37])

Karajan was back in Berlin at the start of November, conducting the scheduled Staatskapelle concert,[38] playing chamber music, and trying to plot his escape. On 11 November, he wrote to his mother in Salzburg:

We fly tomorrow to Milan, perhaps also Spain and Switzerland; do not worry about us. Here in Berlin it wasn't so bad, with the exception of a few air attacks, which we passed safely in the hotel's air-raid shelter. Last Sunday, I directed a concert where the people, for all their sorrows and troubles, were excited and devoted, showing the same passion for music as always. I hope to see you in the spring.[39]

The idea of the flight proved somewhat premature. Karajan had permission to travel to Milan to honour what he told the authorities was a long-standing invitation from the RAI orchestra in Milan. (The invitation had, indeed, been formally made but it was a put-up job between Karajan and a colleague in Milan.) Karajan calculated that though Milan was still in German hands it was beyond Germany's immediate borders. There were huge risks – notably from the Italian partisans in the event of a German retreat – but the Karajans believed they had enough contacts in Italy to see them through. In reality, the problem was getting a seat on a flight out of Berlin, most of which were reserved for the military.

Other matters must have intervened as well. November came and went. In December Karajan conducted the Staatskapelle in Mozart's *Trauermusik* from the *Masonic Funeral Music* and Beethoven's Sixth Symphony, an expression of grief, followed by a hope of spring. Briefly, he left Berlin but remained in touch for what was to be the last tussle – for the time being – with Furtwängler.

It concerned the recently completed Piano Concerto by the Swiss composer and Orff pupil Heinrich Sutermeister. The première had been given in Dresden under Elmendorff's direction with Adrian Aeschbacher as soloist. The problem was the Berlin première. The State Opera had acquired the rights from the publisher Schott, but the composer, it seems, had promised the Berlin première to Furtwängler. While trying to establish whether or not Furtwängler knew anything of this and, if so, whether he still wished to conduct the concerto in Berlin, Prittwitz-Gaffron also sounded out Tietjen and Karajan. Pencilled annotations to the correspondence reveal immovable positions. Tietjen's note reads:

We insist on our contract (v. Karajan). I will let Fu. know. T[ietjen] 9/1 [45]

Prittwitz-Gaffron's note reads, with double underlinings:

Karajan telephoned to say that he wants to conduct the concert at all costs.[40]

The concert never happened. Furtwängler left Berlin on the evening of 24 January on the night sleeper to Vienna. From there he went to Switzerland, where he stayed until the end of the war, shielded by, among others, officials in the German legation in Bern who were helpfully remiss in their handling of coded telegrams demanding Furtwängler's immediate return to Berlin, the suspension of his Swiss visa, and the withdrawal of his permission to conduct in Milan.

Karajan, meanwhile, was waiting for seats on any Milan-bound plane. On 3 February 3000 tons of high explosive were dropped on Berlin, starting a two-mile fire across the city centre. As Churchill, Roosevelt, and Stalin met at Yalta, the Soviet advance continued, helped on the night of 13 February by the destruction of the German communications centre in Dresden. It was an attack on a hitherto undamaged and now largely defenceless city in which half a million incendiary devices and hundreds of 4000 lb and 8000 lb bombs incinerated tens of thousands of civilians and all but obliterated one of the jewels of Europe's architectural heritage. Five days later, at 3.30 p.m. on 18 February, Karajan conducted his last concert in wartime Berlin in front of a packed audience in the Beethovensaal. Its mood was one of defiant optimism in the face of the surrounding devastation: Weber's *Freischütz* overture and Schumann's Fourth Symphony in the first half; Mozart's *Haffner* Symphony after the interval; and, to end with, Strauss's *Till Eulenspiegel*.

Shortly afterwards, a call came from the airport worker who some weeks earlier had agreed to keep an eye open for vacancies on flights to Italy. According to Karajan, he and Anita had half an hour to get to the airport. As they made their way through the rubble, another bombardment was just beginning.

CHAPTER 19

Flight to Italy

Like a beautiful middle-aged lady who is appreciated for her intelligence rather than for other virtues, it welcomes those who are attracted by its charm and detached gracefulness.

Official Guidebook to Trieste

Privately, Karajan used to say that lying low in Italy in the late winter and early spring of 1945 was the worst time of his life.[1] Publicly, he took a more positive line. He would recall the courage of the architect Aldo Pozzi who risked giving Anita and him shelter; remember the financial generosity of Edwin Fischer, at that time safe in Switzerland; and remember, too, the beauty of that particular Italian spring and the chance the months without music gave him properly to study and master the Italian language.[2]

After the war Karajan underwent a course of psychoanalysis which taught him the importance of reliving traumatic episodes to understand them emotionally rather than merely intellectually. And here we see another aspect of his changing personality: the private resolution of personal trauma transforming itself into an even more determinedly forward-looking resolve. The frequently stated accusation that Karajan did not care about the war years, never discussed them, and never apologised for them is a bizarre misrepresentation of the facts. What is true is that somewhere around his fiftieth birthday he decided to have done with discussing such things with journalists.

*

The Allied advance through Italy, a painstaking and troublesome affair, had stalled in November 1944. Bologna had yet to be taken and the Germans were proving tenacious in their defence of the Lombardy plain, the so-called Gothic Line. At the time of the Karajans' arrival in Milan, the situation was one of military stalemate, though a productive one in the longer term since negotiations were in hand that would eventually ensure the granting of PoW status to defeated Italian troops, something that helped minimise the risk of a bloody civil war between the troops and the partisans. Also being brokered, in defiance of orders from Berlin, was the possibility of a peaceful withdrawal of all German forces in northern Italy.

Initially, the Karajans were billeted in a hotel requisitioned by the German military authority in Milan. The problem was money. The Karajans had none. There was also the difficulty of the non-existent contract with the Milan Radio Orchestra. Several weeks passed, during which the Karajans moved to the boathouse of a villa on Lake Como.

By now Berlin was enquiring into Karajan's whereabouts. Losing one leading Berlin conductor might be accounted a misfortune; losing two was beginning to look like incompetence. Eventually, Karajan was summoned from his Lake Como retreat by the man he later identified to his biographer Ernst Haeusserman simply as 'General L'. It was, in fact, General Hans Leyers, Milan's Military Governor, who told Karajan he must return to Berlin. The General then looked at the schedules:

'The plane tomorrow is full, the one in four days is full, and the one in six days. Right then, you fly in eleven days' time. Get in touch again so that we can confirm that.' But I could see from his eyes that he had no intention of doing anything about it.[3]

General Leyers was himself in negotiation with the partisans, via Turin's Cardinal Fossati, putting out feelers about the possibility of a peaceful German withdrawal during which the partisans would guarantee not to attack the retreating Germans in return for a German agreement not to sabotage Italian industrial installations.

When the end came, in late April, it was mercifully swift, though not without unrest and bloodshed in Milan itself, where Mussolini's intemperate rejection of Allied, partisan, and finally German terms led to five hectic days during which he was seized, executed, and publicly hanged, and sporadic street fighting flared up between Fascist and German soldiers and the partisans. Though the main German army was now in retreat, getting on for a thousand German soldiers remained in Milan awaiting evacuation, 150 of them barricaded in the main Post Office, where they remained until they were given safe passage by the Allied Military Government.

The Karajans walked straight into these local difficulties. Returning to Milan to clear their belongings from the hotel room that had been provided by the now defunct German authority, Karajan encountered the music-loving architect Pozzi and was invited to lunch. During lunch, shooting broke out in the street. Afterwards, as they drove away, a car exploded in front of them. With hindsight, it is clear that these were minor incidents. When the Americans finally arrived in Milan on 30 April, all the main public services were working and the AMG's Italian appointee General Raffaele Cadorna had the situation broadly under control.

There was, however, a far more dangerous situation at hand. During the first few days of the liberation drumhead tribunals set up by the partisans led to the arrest and immediate execution of getting on for two thousand Fascist collaborators. The tribunals posed no threat to the Karajans. What was a threat, however, was the high level of random assassinations and revenge killings: forty-four on one night alone according to a British War Office memorandum.[4]

It was not until late May that the situation eased and Karajan was allocated secure if rudimentary accommodation in Milan by the newly formed Austrian Liberation Council. Social contacts also began to be renewed as restrictions were lifted and the threat of random killings diminished. During his time in Milan and Florence in 1942 and 1943, Karajan had made the acquaintance of a number of people in the wider artistic community, some of whom would now become very close friends indeed. One such was Vieri Freccia, Karajan's more or less exact contemporary, a person Karajan would later describe to Vieri's elder brother Massimo as 'the most intelligent man I have ever met'.[5]

Tall and fair-haired, with the kind of classic Florentine profile Andrea del Sarto would have enjoyed painting, Vieri was a painter by profession. Like Karajan's brother Wolfgang, he was also an inventor and lover of science, and disorderly and untameable in a not dissimilar way. Unlike Wolfgang, however, he was a highly social creature, a professional charmer and wit whose speculative interest in the arts, mathematics, science, and politics held his admirers (who were legion, and drawn from both sexes) spellbound.

Vieri had been brought up amid a certain amount of old-world splendour in pre-First World War Florence. Socially and professionally, his parents (his father was a solicitor) were not unlike Karajan's parents; the difference was that the Freccias were immensely wealthy. As a result of a ruling in the British House of Lords over a complex case of double intestacy in the 1870s, Vieri's grandfather had been declared sole heir to an estate which at the time was valued at over half a million pounds.

In 1945 Vieri was living in Venice. He lent Karajan money and tried to ameliorate his mood. Karajan needed the money; he also needed Vieri's ideas. When Karajan appeared in Italy in the late 1940s and early 1950s to conduct operas or choral music, Vieri would usually be on hand, charming and cajoling, and advising on things both within and beyond his competence. The 'staging' and lighting in Italian churches and basilicas of the great choral works Karajan was so passionate about was a particular speciality. Vieri would prove useful in other ways, too. His brother Massimo, who had recently taken up a conducting appointment in New Orleans, was a close friend of Toscanini.

After Milan and Venice, there was Salzburg to be faced. Returning there could be postponed, but not indefinitely so. As summer drew towards its close, Karajan effected one last postponement. He went to Trieste. And he got to conduct again.

Trieste, too, had been a dangerous city to be in during the late spring and early summer of 1945 as Tito and the Allies argued bitterly over its future status. Trieste was an Italian city with a Slovene hinterland. The port had been spared by the retreating Germans but many members of the Italian-speaking community had been rounded up and expelled during the Communists' forty-day tenure of power. On 12 June an agreement had been reached with the Allies by which Istria was ceded to Tito and the Communists, but Trieste remained within Italian borders pending the outcome of a yet-to-be-arranged international conference.[6]

In later years, Karajan would give those who enquired a brief and, it has to be said, improbable-sounding account of his Trieste visit and how he got from there to Salzburg. ('In Trieste I ran into an old friend, a colonel in the British Army . . .'[7]) There was nothing sinister about this; he was simply protecting the privacy of the Banfield Tripcovich family. There was an element of truth in what he said, since the British were closely involved in his stay there and his eventual return to Austria. However, it was the Banfields with whom he stayed, in their villa in the hills above the port.

According to Banfield, Karajan was 'in a terrible state', haunted by the idea that the partisans might still be pursuing him. The finest therapy the family could administer was rest, counsel, and the chance to make music. So it was that in late September Karajan was invited to conduct the orchestra of Trieste's Teatro Comunale Giuseppe Verdi in three symphony concerts. It was Banfield's mother who set the wheels in motion, consulting with the military authorities. Their principal concern was to ascertain whether Karajan would present a threat to public order. Did he have specific political affiliations; would activists on the Left or the Right be stirred into action at the mere mention of his name? Soundings were taken and permission was swiftly and – since the city needed its music – gratefully granted.

For a week, Karajan worked with the orchestra, itself regrouping after the traumas of recent months. He began the first programme with his favourite Haydn Symphony, No.104. After which it was death and transfiguration twice over: Strauss's *Tod und Verklärung* followed by Beethoven's Fifth Symphony. The second concert was unbearable in its intensity, both the programme and the performances: Tchaikovsky's Sixth Symphony, *Tod und Verklärung* and, as a rousing gesture of affirmation after an evening of soul-searching, Sibelius's *Finlandia*. Finally, on 6 and 7 October, a concert of abundance and grace: a Locatelli *Concerto grosso*, Wagner's *Siegfried Idyll*, and Brahms's First Symphony.

The concerts raised everyone's morale including Karajan's, but he still had to decide what to do next. It was Banfield's mother, for whom he had already formed a deep affection and respect, who finally pointed him in the right direction. Her argument was, in essence, a simple one: 'If you have

done things which are criminal – really criminal, not simply things that may
be interpreted as such by your enemies – then by all means stay here. There's
no point in running unnecessary risks. Things may blow over. On the other
hand, if there is nothing of a criminal nature, go back home immediately.
There will be problems. Deal with them, and then start again.'[8]

And so Karajan decided to go.

Transport for civilians was still a problem, however. In the end, he was
detailed to act as translator to a party of refugees who were travelling
north by train to Austria. The journey to Klagenfurt alone took twenty-
nine hours.

*

Karajan never forgot Maria Tripcovich's care and advice and they remained
friends until her death in 1976. At the time of her death, her son was
working on a concert piece for soprano and orchestra, *For Ophelia*, which
was shortly to have its première in London under the direction of Sir John
Pritchard, with Kiri Te Kanawa as the soloist.[9] In order to keep vigil by his
mother's bedside, he had moved his table and manuscripts into her room.
At two o'clock in the morning, he completed the fair copy of the score,
drew the final double bar, dated it and signed it. Ten minutes later his
mother died.

Next day, he rang Karajan.

'And shall I tell you something, Falli?' said Karajan. 'If you had finished
your score half an hour later, she would have waited.'

PART II
1945–1956

CHAPTER 20

Captain Epstein's dilemma

Trains crept over improvised bridges: only 650 out of 8000 miles of track were operating. You drove along roads where every few miles you met a sign, '*Umleitung*', and you were diverted down tracks and side-roads. The devastation of the bombed cities beggared description. Three out of four houses were destroyed, seven out of eight damaged and shattered. Calloused as our sensibility has become since . . . the memory of Germany in defeat has never faded from my mind.

Noel Annan, *Changing Enemies*

Back home in Salzburg there was palpable relief at Herbert's safe return, and few recriminations. His parents had, after all, been here before: respected, well-to-do Austrian citizens sitting out events in a defeated and bankrupt country newly subordinate to foreign rule. What the future held, no one knew; though Allied policy towards Germany and Austria in 1945 was to be radically different from the policies adopted in the wake of Germany's defeat in 1918. Between the summer of 1944 and the Berlin crisis of 1948, plans and policy objectives zigzagged back and forth. In the end, the American-led strategy that held sway was one of magnanimity born of enlightened self-interest.

Such retribution as there was would be handed down to individuals found guilty of specific crimes, after due process of law. No doubt a host of criminals and ne'er-do-wells got off scot-free, but it was a gamble the policy-makers in Washington and London were prepared to countenance. The alternative was to risk creating for the second time in a quarter of a century the kind of post-war economic and social swamp in which the Nazi beast had been spawned in the first place.

And there were other problems. 'I do not know the method of drawing up an indictment against an whole people,' observed Edmund Burke in 1775. And, indeed, how do you indict an entire nation? This, too, was acknowledged by the chief American prosecutor at Nuremberg, Justice Robert Jackson, when he observed:

We would also make clear that we have no purpose to incriminate the whole German people . . . If the German populace had willingly accepted the Nazi programme, no storm troopers would have been needed . . . The German no less than the non-German world has accounts to settle with these defendants.[1]

Many artists held this view too, none more tenaciously, in the face of inevitable dissent, than Yehudi Menuhin.

In the end it came down to a question of trust. If you trust a boy, a Head Master of Eton once remarked, he may let you down; if you don't, he will do you down. Germany's astonishingly rapid recovery – politically and economically – in the years following 1945 is ample testimony both to the good faith of the majority of the German people and to the wisdom of a policy that was based on trust, however erratically arrived at and implemented.

In all this, Karajan was very small fry indeed. Initially, he was a beneficiary of the softly-softly American policy at civilian level. Later, politics intervened: a heady brew of Austrian intrigue and Soviet intransigence, mixed with what can perhaps best be described as the principled pragmatism of the Americans and the British.

*

We all devise versions of our past. For the most part, it is idle fancy, the stuff of fireside yarns, a psychological balm that helps us keep our own private show on the road. But for tens of thousands of Austrians and Germans in the autumn of 1945 it was no idle game. It was a professional necessity.

Karajan's initial interrogation was undertaken by the Americans in Salzburg during the autumn of 1945, with a follow-up meeting in Vienna that December. It centred on his membership of the Nazi Party and on his wider relations with the power-brokers of the Third Reich. His responses tended to be as brusque as they were unelaborate. Yes, he had joined the NSDAP in 1935. No, he was not a Party activist. His reasons for joining, he insisted, had been purely professional. Far from being a Party sympathiser, he had openly defied the Party's racial edicts by marrying the quarter-Jewish Anita Gütermann in 1942. This, he claimed, had seriously damaged his career in wartime Germany and had led to his expulsion from the Party. It was a cleverly constructed argument, though he would later find it impossible to provide written evidence of an actual expulsion from the Party.

Karajan's case was the immediate responsibility of Theatre and Music Officer Otto de Pasetti, a not entirely reliable Austrian emigrant (and failed tenor) serving with the US Forces in Austria. It has been suggested that Pasetti and his colleagues were duped, that Karajan pulled the wool over the eyes of his interrogators by withholding facts and gambling on their being poorly briefed in the chaotic aftermath of war. This is a line of argument that attempts to square the circle between the 'facts' of Karajan's Nazi Party membership as they came to be presented in the press in the later years of Karajan's life and the seemingly 'lenient' action taken by the various denazification tribunals.

Karajan may have been economical with the truth at times (the 'Anita factor' has its grey areas) but he was not by nature a risk taker. Years later, when the Berlin Philharmonic's high-flying Intendant Peter Girth was proposing a confrontation with the orchestra that was, even by Girth's standards, enormously risky, Karajan begged him to reconsider. 'One of the guiding principles of my life,' he told Girth, 'has been never to begin something that I cannot see through [*durchhalten*].'[2]

As Karajan correctly surmised, American intelligence was neither gullible nor ill-informed. An extraordinary amount of documentation, including three lorry loads of files from the offices of Reich Culture Director Hans Hinkel, had been recovered from the Nazis. This was documentation which the Allies were well able to read and understand. If there was a problem, it was that there was too much information to process. Indeed, it was for this reason that independent witness statements were also taken from countless Austrians and Germans.

At first, Karajan was given a remarkably smooth ride. The Americans had no truck with the idea that he was an 'Austrian Nazi' – someone who had joined the Party illegally in breach of Austrian law. As a musician working in Germany, subject to German government controls, he was bound, it was accepted, to comply with such conditions and working practices as were required of him. The 'Anita factor' also worked strongly in his favour. Indeed, it was this that seems to have led to his clearance in November 1945, when it was decided to issue him with a permit to perform as of 15 December, 1945.

Pasetti's conclusions, released to the *Wiener Kurier* on 21 December, 1945 were as follows:

The Theatre and Music Division of the American news-monitoring service takes the view that von Karajan, by taking responsibility for his racially persecuted wife and shouldering the related consequences, compensated for his membership of the NSDAP.[3]

The announcement landed Pasetti in hot water. His office's rapid pronouncement on the Karajan case – with the cases of much bigger fish such as Furtwängler and Böhm (whom Pasetti personally disliked) nowhere near resolution – was considered over-hasty, and he received an official reprimand. What's more, not everyone was convinced that Karajan was 'clean'. The British, in particular, were suspicious both of him and his wife, whose enthusiasm for the Nazis was widely guessed to be far greater than was being officially conceded.

Pasetti's permission was not, however, rescinded and it was not long before the telephone lines were humming between Vienna and Salzburg. Fritz Sedlak, chairman of the Vienna Philharmonic, offered Karajan three concerts in Vienna in January 1946, with the possibility of further concerts the following March.

It was mid-winter. With Austria under military control, the railways unreliable, and fuel in short supply, the journey from Salzburg to Vienna could take anything up to twenty-four hours. Interminable delays at Russian-controlled crossing points only added to the misery. Nervous, irritable, and highly-strung, as hungry for work as he was for food, Karajan began schooling himself afresh in the art of patience.

*

The Vienna to which Karajan returned in January 1946 was a grey ruin of a place, a city under occupation and a hotbed of political and musical intrigue. Worse, with huge swathes of the housing stock destroyed and thousands of soldiers to be billeted, finding a room to bed down in was a virtual impossibility. Karajan ended up on the eighth floor of a block of flats sharing an unheated, unlit room with people he did not know, his privacy secured only by a curtain draped round his table and bed.

Musical life in Vienna had more or less ground to a halt in the autumn of 1944. The Opera had ceased giving performances under the terms of the Nazis' 'total war' edict but had remained open to members of the company for practice and rehearsals. At a time when heat and lighting were in increasingly short supply, the opera house was a congenial meeting place for those of its permanent company who had not yet been called up for military service; it was also a pretty good air-raid shelter. So rehearsals went on behind closed doors, the close-knit musical community whiling away the time restudying Mozart and Strauss operas with a couple of first-rate répétiteurs Karl Böhm had brought with him from Dresden.

In March 1945 an attempt had been made to stage Flotow's *Martha*, a bold move given the fact that the now largely defenceless city was being subjected to daytime air raids. Shortly after the start of a full orchestral rehearsal on the morning of 12 March, the sirens sounded and the company retreated to the shelters. A lively discussion ensued about how they might best use the theatre's various props to defend it against attack. The Valkyrie helmets were ruled out on the grounds that they were made of straw, but there was a set of fifty muzzle-loading rifles left over from the war against Prussia in 1866. 'Complete with bayonets,' added one optimist.

Within the hour, the local radio reported that the Allied bombers had left the city. Unfortunately, the radio was wrong. As musicians and stage hands began to assemble at the upper levels, the opera house took a series of direct hits. Scores of lives would have been lost had the shelters not been on the Ringstrasse side of the building, the only part not to suffer direct bombardment. Even so, there were lucky escapes. The 23-year-old Sena Jurinac, who had joined the company in August 1944 and who had yet to sing a note for the Opera in public, was only feet away from a heavy steel fire door when the blast blew it off its hinges.[4]

The Viennese had grown used to the bombing. The previous January, Jurinac had gone home at curfew time to find not only her flat but the entire street missing. But the loss of the Vienna Opera was something other. As news spread through the city, the Viennese assembled beside the smouldering building. With the cathedral damaged and the Opera destroyed it was almost as if Vienna itself had died.

Then the Russians arrived. For three weeks in April 1945, Russian soldiery ran amok in an orgy of pillage and rape, before Stalin finally called his forces to order. The damage they did, psychological as well as physical, was awesome. It was clear that they were working to an agenda that had little to do with the war that was almost over. Thousands of 'foreign' residents, whose papers declared them to be citizens of the pre-First World War Austro-Hungarian Empire, were rounded up and deported to Russia. Many were never heard of again.

While the Russians terrorised the Viennese, they also demanded to be entertained by them. Towards the end of April 1945, the hastily appointed commissary head of the Opera, Alfred Jerger, was instructed, at gunpoint, to stage a May Day performance of *Le nozze di Figaro* in the largely undamaged Volksoper.

'It is not possible,' stammered Jerger.

'Possible. Is,' replied the gun-touting official.

The performance duly took place.[5]

During the interval, a large amount of gilt rococo furniture mysteriously vanished from the stage, furniture that later turned up in the apartments of various Russian functionaries. Not to be made fools of a second time, Jerger and his men proposed that the next opera to be staged should be *La bohème*. There would be less to steal, they reasoned, from a production set in a student garret.

The conductor of the inaugural *Figaro* was the 43-year-old Josef Krips, a fine musician and an ebullient enthusiast of a man who had been born and brought up in Vienna.[6] By 1938 he had risen to a position of some influence in the Vienna Opera but he had been twice dismissed by the Nazis, first in Vienna, later in Belgrade. During the war he kept a low profile, working as a storekeeper in a factory that made sekt while doing clandestine work as a voice coach. Singers adored him; the Vienna Philharmonic was not so sure.

Alongside Krips were the newly appointed Director of the Vienna Opera, Franz Salmhofer, and Egon Hilbert, the new Head of the State Theatres

Administrative Office. Hilbert, a former cultural emissary who would later become locked in an infamous marriage of political convenience with Karajan, had spent most of the war in the concentration camp at Dachau. He was a great opera-lover and an even greater improviser; a man who is said to have used transport fatigues at Dachau to get to and from performances at the opera in Munich. In Dachau he had also conducted a ceaseless round of conversations with like-minded friends (among them, the ebullient peasant politician Leopold Figl, who would be Austria's first elected post-war Chancellor) about who would get what in Vienna when the war was over.

Breaking into this close-knit circle of friends and functionaries was no easy task. And for Karajan it would prove to be more than usually difficult. Hilbert himself was keen to offer instant contracts to as many top artists as he could for his new theatrical imperium. For him, the past was already a closed book. Others, though, were working to different agendas. There was, for example, no love lost between Krips and Furtwängler; they were, however, agreed on one thing: the need to keep the relentlessly ambitious 'K' as far from the Vienna Opera as was humanly possible.

The Vienna Philharmonic was a different matter. A self-governing body, it made its own arrangements. In the fullness of time, many of the old conductors would return. But Karajan's unexpected availability for concerts in January 1946 was an unlooked-for bonus.

'The demigod Karajan,' mused Elisabeth Schwarzkopf many years later, with more than a hint of irony.

'As early as 1946?' I asked.

'He was well on the way, even then.'[7]

Certainly, the name Herbert von Karajan would look well on the programme for the subscription concerts scheduled for 12, 13, and 19 January 1946.[8]

*

At which point, the Russians intervened. On Friday, 11 January an urgent message was sent to the Americans by the office of the Russian Censorship Officer, Captain Epstein. The Russians, it stated, knew nothing of the planned concerts and required a meeting to discuss Karajan's involvement in them.

The first in what was to be a series of meetings began in Captain Epstein's office in the Imperial Hotel at 9.15 on the morning of Saturday, 12 January, the day of the public *Generalprobe*. Despite American reservations about Pasetti's over-hasty clearance of Karajan, Pasetti was summoned from his headquarters in Salzburg to conduct the meeting. He was accompanied by

Miss Margot Pinter, the American music librarian in Vienna who took and typed the minutes of the meeting. Captain Epstein was accompanied by two women officers and an interpreter.

Epstein was a difficult man to deal with. During the war he is said to have seen the earth heaving over a mass grave into which the living and the dead had been indiscriminately pitched. He was fervently anti-Nazi. Yet he was no philistine. After the meetings were over, he talked at some length with Miss Pinter about music and musicians. He was, he said, a pianist and 'scientist of musical history'; he loved music and deeply regretted the enormous haemorrhage of Russian musical talent to the West, to the United States in particular, that had taken place between the two world wars.

It was not unusual in such confrontations for the Russians to say little, inviting their opposite numbers to make the running and thus reveal their hand. So it was on this occasion.

'What do you have to tell me?' was Epstein's opening gambit.

Pasetti responded with a semi-defensive lob. 'I was requested by Dr van Eerden to come to Vienna in order to deal with you about Herbert von Karajan. I am very anxious to know the reasons why you did not allow him to conduct.'

Clearly discomfited by this request to provide an explanation, Epstein launched into a lengthy tirade against Karajan, citing his successes under the Nazi regime, the numerous honours accorded him in Berlin, his joining the NSDAP in 1935, his status as an 'old' (i.e. long-standing) Party member. Pasetti countered with a brief summary of Karajan's education and background. Karajan was not, Pasetti suggested, a particularly sympathetic character. He was arrogant and ambitious, with a great force of will. Yet it was this very mentality, Pasetti argued, that made it virtually impossible to believe that he was a *follower* of the Nazis or even a sympathiser.

A letter from Bernhard Paumgartner was produced in Karajan's defence, Pasetti stressing Paumgartner's own anti-Nazi credentials. But Epstein knew nothing of Paumgartner and seems to have been far more interested in a note written on Karajan's behalf by the Deputy Officer Commanding the British Forces in Trieste. Clearly, what Epstein feared most was some kind of civil disturbance, possibly a pro-Nazi, anti-Communist demonstration outside the Musikverein. The fact that Karajan's appearances in the politically volatile city of Trieste had sparked no disorder was clearly of significance to Epstein. It was one thing for a man to have a musical following, quite another for him to be some kind of factional figurehead.

When Pasetti mentioned Karajan's marriage in 1942 to the quarter-Jewish Anita Gütermann, a woman officer in the Russian delegation intervened, stating that such a marriage could not possibly have taken place since the Nazis would have forbidden it. Pasetti replied by giving details of the problems Karajan encountered with the Nazis after his marriage to Anita.

The meeting was adjourned at 10.45 a.m. and resumed fifty-five minutes later. With time ticking away and Epstein clearly interested in postponing the concert, if not cancelling it outright, Pasetti spelled out the choices facing the denazification commission. Either they banned outright all artists who had performed under Nazi rule, thus depriving Austria and Germany of the services of many of its finest musicians, or they investigated the record of each artist in turn in order to establish whether he or she had denounced or in any way harmed non-Party members or opponents of the Hitler regime. He concluded:

As Austria is a liberated country and the Russians, as well as the Americans, the British and the French have to help the Austrian people to get again on their feet, we firmly believe that the last method is the right one. The experience we made so far is good. Karajan was investigated and thoroughly checked for two months by the commission and only after a careful recheck was he approved by us.[9]

Epstein requested a written report of the meeting. With the first public performance due to begin in under three hours' time, this was a further delaying tactic. Pasetti promised that Miss Pinter would have the report typed up within the hour.

Karajan and Fritz Sedlak, meanwhile, were kicking their heels in the Musikverein awaiting a ruling on the afternoon's performance; Sedlak wondering what on earth Karajan would do if he could no longer conduct, Karajan putting a brave face on things and saying that if the Russians did reimpose their ban on him at least he could go off and get something to eat, which he certainly wouldn't do if he had a concert to conduct.

To the end of his days, Karajan was convinced that what the occupying powers were really arguing over was gasoline rather than art; that cultural concerns were so much bric-à-brac in a far larger game of political barter. And it is probably true. Had Karajan failed as a musician in Germany in the 1930s and succeeded instead in implementing his fantasy of designing giant turbines for the irrigation of the Sahara Desert, there is every chance he would have been treated with more respect by the Russians. Left to their own devices, the Russians either liquidated former Nazis or, if they had proven scientific skills, shipped them back to the Soviet Union where, living relatively cosseted lives, they helped fashion the country's post-war strategic might.

At around 12.30 p.m. Sedlak was summoned to meet Epstein in the Imperial Hotel. Sedlak was the best possible advocate for Karajan and the orchestra. During the First World War he had spent five years on the Russian Front. He had learned to read and write Russian fluently and had eventually married a Russian girl. When the first Russian tanks rolled into Vienna in April 1945, it was Sedlak who had helped sweet-talk the tank commanders into temporarily sparing large swathes of the city.

If Epstein needed additional reassurance, Sedlak was the man to provide it. And he seems to have succeeded. At around one o'clock Epstein decided there was no need to speak to Karajan personally. He also phoned Pasetti to say that the Russians had no objection to Karajan conducting the Saturday and Sunday concerts but that the position would need to be reviewed the following Tuesday.

It was now getting on for two o'clock and Karajan's concert attire was still in his eighth-floor bed-sit. For the first, and probably for the last, time in his life he was obliged to do some hard running to make it to the podium on time.

*

For the concert the next day, the Golden Hall of the Musikverein was packed to overflowing, the audience coated and gloved against the winter cold. This was a time, so cold were the unheated war-damaged halls, when it was not unusual for choruses to disappear from view in a swirl of self-generated mist the moment they began to sing.

The audience, it has to be said, had come to hear the music, not to gaze on Karajan, though as a review by Roland Tenschert in *Die Furche* made plain, Karajan's physical presence was difficult to ignore:

A slim, delicate man steps up on to the podium. Youth and mature composure, unusually complementing one another, characterise the first impression of the artist's appearance. As soon as he wields the baton, his expression takes on a visionary quality and, eyes closed as if in a sleep-walker's reverie, he seems to convey his inner visions to the musicians like a medium of some higher power. He does not need the score to support his memory, nor the help of an understanding glance: his sinewy hands seem to shape the powerful sounds. His arm movements are generally measured, and only at particularly striking points is such restraint abandoned. But the expression is always intense and fascinating in its power. The decisive element in this conductor's achievement is intensity.[10]

The programme was the kind of thing Viennese audiences loved to hear: a Haydn symphony, No.104 in D, *London*; some orchestral pyrotechnics in the shape of Strauss's *Don Juan*; and, after the interval, one of the great symphonic masterworks of the Viennese repertory, the C minor Symphony of Brahms. It was also the kind of programme Karajan loved to conduct.

According to Pasetti, Karajan's reception at the start of the concert was desultory, a gentle smattering of applause from fewer than a hundred people. It was during the slow movement of the Haydn, recalls Vienna Philharmonic historian Erwin Mittag, that there appeared 'that stir of excitement among the audience which indicates that a pre-eminent artist is at work'.[11] After what Mittag describes as a 'fiery and crystal-clear' account of *Don Juan*, all hell broke loose.

Philharmonic violinist Otto Strasser had been suffering from flu that week and had been too ill to attend any rehearsals. By the afternoon of the concert, though, he felt well enough to go along to the Musikverein:

Straight away the playing of the Haydn symphony made a great impression on me, above all because the orchestra was in top form both in terms of its sound quality and the precision of its playing. Richard Strauss's *Don Juan* followed, a wonderful firework display of virtuosity and rhythmic *élan*. And it was here as the final pizzicato chord brings to an end the hero's philanderings that the most tremendous cheering broke out. Vienna had once more found an idol. The Brahms First Symphony which followed confirmed what the first half of the concert had promised.[12]

Yet for an audience (and in large measure an orchestra) that was seeing Karajan for the first time, what was most immediately striking was not so much what he did with the music, as the way he directed it. Like Dr Tenschert in *Die Furche*, the correspondent of the *Österreichische Musikzeitschrift* was as much struck by the manner of Karajan's conducting as by its interpretative matter:

The Austrian-born Karajan is a conductor of the modern school: *sui generis*, no stereotype. He does not beat time – he knows the work heart and soul, and barely indicates instrumental entries – rather his baton, his hands, his whole body mimic the rhythm's melodic overlay. On the podium he is in a trance. It is a hypnotist who conjures these wonderful sounds from our Philharmonic . . . [13]

*

Someone else who attended the concert and who was also hypnotised by it was the head of Pasetti's Vienna office, another Austrian emigrant, Lieutenant Henry Alter. Like any well brought-up Viennese child, Alter had begun attending concerts when he was barely out of swaddling clothes. This, though, was something else: a revelation, 'a seminal experience' as he later described it.

Alter had been present at Karajan's interrogation in Vienna shortly after Christmas. What had struck him then was Karajan's composure and the sense he displayed of a kind of absolute inner confidence. Now, as the audience drifted away from the Musikverein, Alter hung around waiting to go backstage. When he got there, Karajan was by himself. No, he had no one with him; yes, he would very much like a lift home. So it was that Alter, his mother, and a girlfriend found themselves squeezed into a rickety old jeep with Vienna's latest 'idol'.

Alter knew that Karajan would be in for more disappointments. Like Pasetti, Alter took the view that only those suspected of 'committing crimes against an orderly society' should be placed under a performing ban. (The Americans had 'black' lists and 'grey' lists; Karajan was on the latter.) At the same time, he realised that this was not how things were going to work out. In practice, Karajan and his new-found audience would be in for a bumpy ride and a long wait.

Karajan knew this, too. 'If you want me to stay for further interrogation,' he told Alter, 'first you must save me from starvation.'[14] Alter duly obliged by drawing extra rations, potatoes and suchlike, from Army stores.

The order banning Karajan's next concert, on 19 January 1946, came at midday, melodramatically reinforced by the ring-fencing of the Musikverein by the Russians. Captain Epstein had resolved his dilemma.

CHAPTER 21

Interrogation

Nazism was not so much a question of armbands as
a question of character.

Josef Krips

In February 1946, Vienna's occupying powers handed the entire denazification process over to the Austrian government. It was a sensible move.
Already overburdened with information, the Americans had begun to
lose their way amid a mountain of paperwork largely generated by their
decision to issue tens of thousands of potential suspects with a seven-page
questionnaire which, in the very nature of things, was widely abused.[1] Of
the four occupying powers, only the Russians were making much progress
on denazification, gathering information from the elaborate Communist-
run intelligence networks they already had in place on the ground within
Austria itself. Local intelligence was, indeed, what was needed; but local
intelligence that was being operated within the rule of law.

Karajan was summoned to appear before the Austrian government's new
legally constituted denazification tribunal at three o'clock on Friday, 15
March 1946. The meeting was chaired by a senior official from the Ministry
of Education, Dr Pernter, assisted by department head Dr Zellweker. The
chairman of the committee charged with overseeing the denazification
process, Dr Horak, assumed the role of the chief interrogating officer;
he placed special emphasis on Karajan's conduct as an Austrian citizen
working abroad in the years 1933–8. Also present at the hearing were the
department's legal adviser, Dr Lafite, a representative of the Musicians'
Union, Herr Sirowy, and a secretary. Three tribunal members sent their
apologies. One was sick, the other two – Stadtrat Dr Matejka and Egon
Hilbert – were otherwise engaged. By an agreed process of delegation,
Horak spoke for Matejka, Pernter for Hilbert.

The session began with a background briefing by Dr Lafite in which he
outlined details of the preliminary clearance that had been granted Karajan
by the Americans' Salzburg bureau in November 1945 as announced in the
Wiener Kurier on 21 December 1945. He also testified before the tribunal
that none of the witnesses called for cross-examination had been NSDAP
members.

What follows is a complete transcript of the tribunal's official minutes.[2]
These consisted of a verbatim report of what was said, linked by a number
of comments and paraphrases (printed below in italic) prepared in summary

form by the tribunal secretary. The testimony of the two orchestral players, Berger and Koller, is rather generalised and not particularly well informed; that of the singer Fritz Krenn is better informed. But it is the cross-examination of Karajan himself that clearly holds the greatest interest.

The first witness is [Vienna] *Philharmonic member Hans Berger.*

CHAIRMAN: You are called as witness in the case of General Music Director Karajan. What details do you know of his political past?

BERGER: I was at the State Opera in Berlin from 1928 until the end of the war. Karajan arrived in 1938 and was first engaged by the State Opera to conduct an opera which was a great success. He became, next to Furtwängler, the best known conductor in Germany. There were rumours that he was a Party member but I didn't believe them because he never declared himself to be one, never wore the Party badge, and never – even before the war – gave the so-called German salute.

ZELLWEKER: Why do you say 'Even before the war'?

BERGER: Because, after the war started, many people no longer said 'Heil Hitler!'

To the questions put by members of the commission as to whether Karajan had expressed political opinions, attended or spoken at works meetings, or conducted at Party functions, Berger replied in the negative each time.

CHAIRMAN: Did Karajan have any relationships with leading members of the National Socialist regime?

BERGER: Goering was in charge of theatre, but Karajan was never introduced to him. Tietjen made sure of that. Then Tietjen took over himself as Director of the Opera. Karajan's position there became more and more uncertain and then ceased altogether, although he continued to conduct the State Orchestra. Furtwängler conducted the opening performance of the rebuilt State Opera, although the rehearsals had been taken by Karajan.

Berger is dismissed and the second witness, Philharmonic member Josef Koller, is called before the commission.

CHAIRMAN: I must ask you to tell us what you know of Karajan's political past.

KOLLER: I had been working in Berlin since 1929, and Karajan arrived from Aachen in 1938. I can only tell you one thing, which is that there was never any talk of politics during concerts or operatic performances, nor was there any participation in political matters on Karajan's part. He never wore the Party badge, and never greeted anyone with 'Heil Hitler'.

ZELLWEKER: Did he have personal relationships with Nazi leaders?

KOLLER: No, only business ones.

CHAIRMAN: What was his position at the Opera?

KOLLER: He was installed by Tietjen as conductor of the Opera, as well as for concerts given by the State Orchestra. In any case, he worked as the principal conductor for concerts, but I don't think he had any managerial role.

CHAIRMAN: Do you know anything about the deterioration of his position and what lay behind it?

KOLLER: People say that he had some problem with Tietjen, but I can't add to that.

Koller is told to stand down. Kammersänger Fritz Krenn is now heard. The Chairman asks him for his statement since he was in Berlin at the same time as Karajan.

KRENN: I have known Karajan since 1938, when he came to Berlin to conduct *Die Zauberflöte.*
CHAIRMAN: What do you know about his political attitude?
KRENN: I never knew that he was a Party member at all. The first time I found out was when the Vienna Philharmonic concert [on 19 January 1946] was banned. I never saw him wearing a badge or using the Nazi greeting, even in rehearsals. I gathered from a few remarks that he was not in sympathy with the National Socialists. That was why I poured out my sorrow to him about my having to separate from my wife, who was Jewish. He was very warm and understanding about it. I told him because I felt he was an Austrian, not a Nazi.
CHAIRMAN: Did he clash with those in power?
KRENN: His work then suddenly stopped, and I assume it was for political reasons. I don't know if it was because of his marriage.
HORAK: Wasn't he held back by Tietjen?
KRENN: Yes, that was Tietjen's method. It struck me that singers who were known to be Nazis made disparaging remarks about Karajan. Like the baritone Fuchs, who said to Karajan during a rehearsal of *Die Meistersinger* in Italy: 'My Führer does not wish me to change anything in this part.' Bockelmann, who was very friendly with Hitler, put his oar in too. During a performance of *Die Meistersinger* Bockelmann 'boobed' and immediately blamed Karajan because he was conducting from memory. Hitler is supposed to have said: 'If that man continues to conduct, I shall not come to this opera house again.' So then Furtwängler conducted *Die Meistersinger* at the opening of the rebuilt State Opera House, although Karajan had rehearsed it. After that, I completely lost sight of Karajan. Goering is supposed to have said that he would never conduct in his opera house again. Perhaps this was in connection with the wife, probably in 1943, or later.
HORAK: Did he conduct abroad?
KRENN: I only performed with him in Rome. He conducted in Paris, and in Italy, even before the war.
ZELLWEKER: When were you with him in Italy?
KRENN: In March 1941.

That was the end of Krenn's questioning. Now Karajan was called before the commission.

CHAIRMAN: What was the position when you joined the Party in 1935?
KARAJAN: I remember my secretary telling me that the local Party boss was making my nomination, or the confirmation of my nomination, as General Music Director in Aachen dependent on my joining the Party – something which had already been proposed to me three times.

ZELLWEKER: If you had not joined the Party, what then?
KARAJAN: I would not have got the job.

According to Karajan's account, concerts in Aachen before 1933 had been directed by Raabe, the future President of the Reichsmusikkammer, while the opera had been under a certain Peller (?) [Paul Pella] who had to retire on racial grounds. Raabe had then taken provisional control of both concerts and opera for one year, but this became too much for him because of his age, and he asked to be pensioned off. This application was granted on condition that Raabe stay on and conduct concerts for a further year while a successor was sought for the opera. Karajan came in as guest conductor, and although Raabe liked him, he decided he wanted to keep control of both concerts and opera. But then Raabe retired, on the grounds of his original request and because his concerts were no longer crowd-pulling, and he went to live in Berlin [Weimar].

ZELLWEKER: Were you only provisionally employed in Aachen?
KARAJAN: I had a contract for just one year.
ZELLWEKER: I would like to investigate why you joined the Party.

The Chairman interjects that it was involved with Karajan's appointment as General Music Director.

KARAJAN: The man who was to appoint me was the Mayor, but in any case the [NSDAP] District Leader [*Kreisleiter*] had the right of veto.
ZELLWEKER: What happened then after that year? Your name was put forward as GMD?
KARAJAN: Yes, by the Mayor; then I was supposed to be appointed GMD. But the *Kreisleiter* was opposed to me and kept sniping at me. I was told that if I wanted to be left in peace, I had to join the Party.
ZELLWEKER: You became a member in order to turn this temporary arrangement into a permanent one.
KARAJAN: I wouldn't say that. I did it in order to put to an end the difficulties and attacks that I was repeatedly experiencing.
ZELLWEKER: If you had not become a member of the Party, do you believe you would not have become GMD?
KARAJAN: My motive was that I wanted to be allowed to work in peace.
ZELLWEKER: Were other conductors considered as well?
KARAJAN: Others were hoping to get the job, and the easiest lever was the political one. Today I completely accept the fact that I made an error, and I am prepared to suffer the consequences. In Germany in 1935 no importance was attributed to the matter.
ZELLWEKER: For you personally it simply didn't matter that people knew that this was a gang of murderers? There *was* talk about it at that stage; the 30th June [1934, the so-called 'Night of the Long Knives'] had already happened.
HORAK: Here [in Austria] we thought that would perhaps bring about the end of the Party.
KARAJAN: Politics wasn't of any importance to me.
SIROWY: Would you have been able to find work in Austria?
KARAJAN: I tried in Graz but it didn't work out. There was no opera in Salzburg, and it was still too soon for me in Vienna, though I did guest at the Vienna

Opera once in 1936 [1937] with *Tristan*. There were very difficult problems over demarcation there. I told Kerber [the Vienna Opera's Administrative Director, a fellow Salzburger] that it was still too early for me to take on the top job but that, equally, I was not accepting the third position.

The Chairman confirms that Karajan was invited at that time at [Kerber's] *wish, since he knew Karajan was an Austrian, and already had a good reputation.*

KARAJAN: I spoke to Kerber about it in Salzburg and said, 'Let's wait until I am worthy of being appointed as principal conductor.' When I went to Berlin in 1938, I was told that Bürckel would like me to come to Vienna, but I refused because I already had a contract with Berlin and wanted to fulfil it.

The Chairman returns to the subject of Karajan's membership of the Party and remarks: 'You wanted to liberate yourself from all the difficulties and attacks coming from the Kreisleiter?'

KARAJAN: I did, and I committed an error. The moment I saw that it went against my views, I took the logical step. I don't want to gloss over it. It would be unworthy of me not to admit this error openly and say that I made a mistake.

ZELLWEKER: Where did the mistake lie?

KARAJAN: In the fact that I joined the Party.

ZELLWEKER: You were unaware at that time what that Party meant

CHAIRMAN: You joined the Party as one joins a club.

KARAJAN: I would like to make the following analogy. As it is at the moment here in Vienna, so it was in Aachen in 1935. Anyone who had a personal antipathy to someone else would exploit it. One didn't see the consequences clearly at the time – if one had been able to predict what would have become of this Party . . .

HORAK: You didn't consider that it was high treason against Austria. You would have had to consider the situation from two points: ideologically, and then politically as an Austrian.

KARAJAN: I know those are the issues, and it's been hard enough for me to take. Particularly because I didn't do it out of conviction. One just blundered into it. I didn't want anything apart from the chance to make my music in peace. But on the other hand there's my resignation from the Party.

HORAK: Did you tell Tietjen about that?

KARAJAN: He couldn't raise any objection to it himself, because the marriage couldn't be refused by the registrar. When I got to know my future wife, one of those Gestapo people – Professor de Crinis – rang up my mother and said to her: 'You have to be clear about the fact that if your son marries this woman, his career in Germany is finished.'

ZELLWEKER: You had made up your mind to get married, so what did you do next? Go to the registry office, or to other places as well?

KARAJAN: I told Tietjen about the matter, then my wife met Goebbels in Venice and told him I wanted to marry her. Goebbels had always disapproved of me and reacted very badly to what she said. Then I asked Hinkel [Hans Hinkel, 1901–60, whose Department for Special Cultural tasks in Goebbels's

Propaganda Ministry involved the supervision of all Jews still active in German cultural life] to enquire of Goebbels whether the marriage as such was permitted, and I received notification – signed by Hinkel – that I could continue my work.

HORAK: Did you get a so-called special permit?

KARAJAN: No, this wasn't necessary. *As typical of the situation at that time, Karajan cites:* I was due to be called to Dresden, but when my marriage became known Obergruppenführer Woyrsch said that it was absolutely out of the question, and that if I had the courage to come to Dresden he would have my wife arrested. There was quite a noticeable fall-off in my work from 1942 onwards. My appointment to Berlin was actually a diplomatic initiative of Tietjen's to play me off against Furtwängler, which subsequently occurred. Then, when Goering lost ground and Goebbels got his hands on the State Theatre again, I fell out of favour and the usual problems came along, until finally the work dried up.

CHAIRMAN: I would like you to tell us again how the hearing went.

KARAJAN: I was summonsed. They said to me: 'You know your marriage is against the statutes.' I explained that I was fully aware of that, and would take the necessary action.

HORAK: Was that in front of the Supreme Chairman [Major Walther] Buch [former professional soldier and long-serving chairman of the NSDAP's Investigation and Arbitration Board USCHLA]?

KARAJAN: I don't know. It was the Berlin NSDAP Court.

CHAIRMAN: Did you tell the court you were resigning?

KARAJAN: That I do know, I announced my resignation.

CHAIRMAN: Did the court give you a verdict?

KARAJAN: My secretary must have had that. He was in Aachen and I was in Berlin and the post was unreliable even then. [No documentation has ever come to light.]

CHAIRMAN: Did you have German citizenship as well as Austrian?

KARAJAN: No, I would have needed a diploma for that. I always had great difficulties on leaving Germany because of my Austrian passport. The Austrian Consulate in Cologne was very inefficient, because passports were always sent to Vienna first. Then I got a German passport so that the formalities were easier when I left the country. I never fell beneath the 1000 Marks barrier [the punitive tax levied by the German Government between 1933–8 on anyone crossing into Austria]. In the time from Aachen on, I met Goebbels on only three occasions in the course of my job, and I did not know the other Party bosses at all. I was never invited by any of them.

SIROWY: Did you conduct at Party functions?

KARAJAN: No, I was never invited to them either. [In a separate deposition to the tribunal, Karajan wrote, 'I successfully avoided political functions, unless they were purely musical'. See Appendix C.]

ZELLWEKER: Since when had your relationship with your wife been public?

KARAJAN: Since 1940. People knew that I was meeting her abroad.

CHAIRMAN: How was it with your foreign journeys? Did you conduct in occupied countries as well?

KARAJAN: I conducted in Paris after the outbreak of war. The whole State Opera was invited by the French authorities. No propaganda or political demonstrations took place, it was a purely artistic event. [Karajan was, however, required to conduct the Horst Wessel Lied – as opposed to the official German anthem – before the curtain rose on *Tristan und Isolde*.] Then I was invited in 1943 by Radio Paris to do two broadcast concerts. A public concert with the Paris Radio Orchestra was later added to these. The second trip was to Denmark where I conducted a purely Danish orchestra. I offered to give my fee to the Danish State Orchestra if they invited me. The tickets went slowly at first, but when it became known that the Crown Prince had come to the rehearsal and would be present at the performance, it was very well attended in the end. It was a distinctively Danish event.

ZELLWEKER: Did the Crown Prince speak to you about political events?

KARAJAN: No, only about purely artistic matters, as among colleagues. The Prince himself was a practising musician. I did not conduct in other occupied countries. When I conducted abroad it was never of a political nature. I had to do it for economic reasons. All I had were the six concerts with the Berlin State Orchestra. For those my fee was heavily reduced. [By 50 per cent in 1944.] If you are a pet of the Party, they don't do that kind of thing to you.

HORAK: How often were you in Austria between 1933 and 1938?

KARAJAN: I once conducted a concert at the Mozarteum in Salzburg. Between 1933 and 1937 I was there occasionally as a member of the festival audience because I was an admirer of Toscanini. In 1933 and 1934 I taught alongside Paumgartner at the International Conducting School in Salzburg.

ZELLWEKER: Dollfuss was murdered in 1934. You must have heard various things about that here, even if politics did not interest you.

CHAIRMAN: Were you in Austria in summer 1934?

ZELLWEKER: Surely you must have had some thoughts about it, and then there you were in 1935 joining the Party.

KARAJAN: I'm prepared to admit that it was an error, but we artists live in another world, a self-contained one. Otherwise it would be impossible to play music properly, and music is the highest and only thing for me.

HORAK: The question is whether you were in touch with illegal cells, circles, and interests in those years.

KARAJAN: (*With great emphasis*) I am prepared to swear an oath that I have never undertaken even the slightest activity involving propaganda.

HORAK: The commission must arrive at the conviction that you never undertook any treasonable activity.

KARAJAN: I can solemnly swear that I did not. Nor was I in touch when abroad with expatriate German authorities, as was required. One either makes music or politics.

HORAK: I can't imagine today that even an artist can be completely unpolitical.

The commission concludes that Karajan was not involved in any illegal activity between 1933 and 1938.

End of hearing: 17.30.

CHAPTER 22

An Englishman abroad

Providence blew a stormy petrel into my office, with a cigarette
drooping from its mouth and waving a walking stick, a creature
of uncertain temper with a supreme indifference to the feelings of
those who sought to hinder its unerring flight.

Basil Dean, *The Theatre at War*

'How was your Swiss espionage? (I assume it was espionage). Did
you have to disguise yourself as a cuckoo-clock or a bunch of
Edelweiss or anything?'

Letter from Constant Lambert to Walter Legge

Two days after Karajan's concert with the Vienna Philharmonic, an
Englishman by the name of Walter Legge arrived in Vienna. He was in
Europe tracking down and signing a new post-war generation of artists for
his employer EMI, though as founder and managing director of London's
newest orchestra, the Philharmonia, he was also keeping a weather-eye
open for soloists and conductors with whom the Philharmonia might work
and record. Since Austria was still technically 'enemy territory', Legge was
forbidden to trade there; a trifling local difficulty which he circumvented
by getting a colleague then resident in Switzerland to arrange for him to
be seconded to the Swiss company Turicaphon, a firm in which EMI had
a substantial minority holding.

While in Switzerland, Legge signed the pianist Dinu Lipatti and renewed
his acquaintance with such formidable old-stagers as Backhaus and Edwin
Fischer. The question remained, how – even with Swiss credentials – to
get to Vienna, where lay the richest artistic quarry of all. In an episode
worthy of any 'B' movie of the period, Legge fell into conversation with
an American officer over a drink in an hotel bar. When Legge mentioned
his urgent need of essential papers and permits, the American obligingly
removed a sheaf of such documents from his pocket. Within the hour,
Legge had everything he needed (albeit in a variety of different names),
including a ticket for a first-class sleeper to Vienna.

*

Walter Legge was the son of Harry Legge, a west London tailor. Harry
Legge had taken up tailoring after a bout of polio had condemned him to
a sedentary life. He was a perfectionist in his trade, a devoted family man,

and a great lover of music. One of the family's most prized possessions was a handsome horn gramophone which would be lifted reverently on to the dining-room table each evening after the supper things had been cleared away.

Walter, the elder of the Legges' two children, was born on 1 June 1906. He was bright and extrovert but myopic and ill co-ordinated. He would have loved to conduct, or to play cricket after the manner of his schoolboy hero, the swashbuckling Percy Fender.[1] But it was not to be. Indeed, the myopia was so disabling that Legge left school at the age of sixteen, unable to cope with the pressures of the written exams that alone would have allowed him to capitalise on a potentially brilliant academic career. Like many a notable man before him, he ended up being largely self-taught. He taught himself to read music. By the age of twenty he was fluent in German.

Bumptious and opinionated and already, according to his sister, a born persuader, he was engaged by His Master's Voice record company, sacked for criticising the management, and, within the year, re-engaged. His first job had been as a 'music lecturer' charged with the task of promoting an interest in serious music and the gramophone as a means of disseminating it. Re-engaged, he became the sole member and *de facto* head of the company's newly created 'Literary Department'. Later, he began writing music criticism for what at the time was the most exactingly stylish of English newspapers, the *Manchester Guardian*, deputising for Neville Cardus whenever Cardus was away from London or abroad following the fortunes of the English cricket team.

At the age of twenty-four, with nothing to assist him beyond a ready wit, a pushy manner, and an insatiable love of music, Legge persuaded the directors of HMV to accept the idea of private subscription as a means of financing the making of great (Legge never thought of anything less) recordings of unrecorded repertory. 'The Hugo Wolf Society' was the first subscription list to be established in the summer of 1931 and the recordings that were made under the society's auspices remain to this day one of the glories of the gramophone.

Comparable splendours followed, some produced by Fred Gaisberg, others by Legge himself.[2] These included a six-volume Sibelius Society edition – including symphonies nos. 3–7 conducted by Kajanus, Beecham, Schnéevoigt, and Koussevitzky – that would become something of a *vade-mecum* for the young Herbert von Karajan. It was Legge, too, who had masterminded and produced Beecham's 1937 Berlin recording of *Die Zauberflöte*, another recording to which Karajan had already become addicted.

When war broke out, the 33-year-old Legge was declared unfit for

military service. His eyesight alone disqualified him. On Beecham's recommendation, he was taken on by the forces' entertainments service ENSA
as head of a newly created music department from which Legge was able
to mastermind an elaborate programme of concerts and concert parties for
troops and war workers in Britain and abroad; Basil Dean was the Director
General of ENSA, Legge his 'stormy petrel'. By the end of the war there was
barely a musician of quality working in Britain with whom Legge was not
personally acquainted.

It was against this background in the summer of 1944, as ENSA's work
began to wind down in the wake of the D-Day landings, that Legge made his
first moves towards realising the most astonishing of all his ideas, the launch
of a new London orchestra. Within a year, the Philharmonia Orchestra, or
at least an embryonic version of it, was in business, recording music by
J. C. Bach, Wolf, and Purcell for EMI in Abbey Road.

*

Did Karajan know anything of this highly consequential Englishman when
Legge telephoned him at lunch-time on 19 January 1946? Apparently not.
Legge's claim to have heard Karajan in Aachen before the war – and thus
to have 'discovered' him for Tietjen – was a typically elaborate piece
of embroidery on Legge's part. If he had heard Karajan in Germany
before the war, why was there so obvious a shock of discovery when he
slipped unannounced into one of Karajan's rehearsals in the Musikverein
in January 1946?

[Karajan] was due to give another [concert] on the following Saturday.
Although as usual with him the rehearsals were sealed, I managed to get in
and I was absolutely astonished at what the fellow could do. The enormous
energy and vitality he had was hair-raising.[3]

Some time during the morning of Saturday, 19 January, Legge learned that
the afternoon's concert was almost certainly going to be prohibited by the
Russians. At around one o'clock he managed to get a call through to the
apartment block where Karajan was living. Karajan said he was about to
have a rest, but that he would be willing to see him later that afternoon at
four o'clock.

So at four o'clock I went to the appointed address. I knew how difficult it was
to get anything in Vienna at that time so I took him a bottle of whiskey [sic], a
bottle of gin, and a bottle of sherry. Years after, he told me that after I had left
that evening he divided each of those bottles into thirty portions so that he had
one drink for each of the next ninety days but he did not touch them that day.
And he stuck to his rule. He had that sort of iron will.[4]

From the first, the two men got on famously, despite the fact that Legge wanted Karajan to sign a contract and Karajan merely wanted to talk. Karajan may have been the shyest of men, but where music was concerned he was a keen talker and an even more avid listener. Legge later remembered, 'It was one of those occasions when you meet someone and it as though you had spent all your lives together. There is an instant rapport.'

Though they had been brought up in different countries, and in vastly differing circumstances, there was already a considerable reservoir of shared experience between them; the new universalising medium of the gramophone saw to that. With his fluency and absorbing interest in all things German, Legge knew the work of artists Karajan must have been amazed to hear him enthusing over. A great stage performer, Legge had told actor Robert Donat in a letter in 1939, is someone who has the ability to create a personality, utterly unlike the actor's own, so vividly as to add significantly to the sum of the audience's experience. He cited Alexander Moissi as Faust and Hamlet, Emil Jannings as the professor in the film *The Blue Angel*, Lotte Lehmann's Marschallin, Hilde Konetzni's Chrysothemis, Rose Pauly's Elektra.

Karajan would have nodded agreement to all that. And there was another figure about whose genius Legge and Karajan were fervently at one: Toscanini.

*

Legge and Karajan met more or less daily during Legge's time in Vienna. Karajan also began attending Legge's EMI auditions, including that of a young woman he had pointed out one day in early March in the Musikverein.

'You see that blonde girl over there,' Karajan had said. 'She is one of the most promising singers in Central Europe. She will be one of our stars of the future.'

It was Elisabeth Schwarzkopf. The same evening Legge heard her sing Rosina in *Il barbiere di Siviglia* at the Theater an der Wien. After hearing her again, this time at a private concert party in Vienna, he offered her a contract which, being the proud and headstrong young person she was, she declined to accept without first being granted a full private audition with Legge. He asked her to sing Wolf's 'Wer rief Dich denn', during which he proceeded to spend the best part of an hour and a half making her experiment with different ways of colouring and shading the song's final phrase – the one in which the girl, incensed at her lover's indifference, sends him packing with what seems to be something suspiciously close to regret.

After an hour's work on the one phrase, Karajan (never a great lover of Wolf songs) muttered something about 'pure sadism', and left. Nowadays, Schwarzkopf says that Legge was right; that her voice was too 'white', too undeveloped to catch the song's emotional ambiguities. But there was more to it than that. In effect, she was auditioning Legge, a point that probably had not escaped Karajan's attention.

Though Legge tended rather to romanticise Karajan's stoicism at this time,

He was in no hurry to sign even though he had no money and no work – and no possibility of work – yet he had an inner sense of repose that I have never met in any man in similar circumstances.[5]

there is no doubt that, professionally, Karajan's position was almost as parlous as it had been in 1933–4 and 1942–5. If he was calm, it was probably because he had been here before. Yoga may have helped, too; it was around this time that he started practising hatha yoga.

By February, Legge was already briefing the EMI board in London:

After a good deal of discussion [Karajan] has agreed provisionally to a three year contract with us – 5% royalty, minimum of twelve double sided records a year, advance yet to be discussed. We discussed repertoire, – Karajan, as I think I have told you, has an admirable sense of the type of music that records effectively, – the following works are under discussion:
>> Beethoven's Third and Eighth Symphonies
>> Schubert's C major Symphony
>> Johann Strauss Waltzes and Overtures
>> Tchaikovsky's Fourth Symphony
>> Beethoven's *Fidelio* Overture

There is not a good modern recording of any of these works on Columbia. I shall see him again next week.[6]

It was a bullish briefing, and the terms were generous. A five per cent royalty on a two-sided twelve-inch 78 rpm disc was double what Rafael Kubelik was offered at the time. The advance also proved generous: 5000 Swiss francs, money the Karajans claimed they badly needed.

In addition to negotiating over recordings, Karajan was also, at long last, in negotiation with the Salzburg Festival. With his old friend and mentor Bernard Paumgartner now back in Salzburg after his seven-year exile in Italy, and with strong additional backing both from the veteran President of the Salzburg Festival, Baron Puthon, and from the ubiquitous Egon Hilbert, Karajan was offered no fewer than twelve festival appearances in 1946, including the chance to conduct *Le nozze di Figaro* and *Der Rosenkavalier*, and help prepare *Don Giovanni*.

*

During the spring and early summer of 1946, Karajan shuttled back and forth between Vienna and Salzburg: rehearsing singers in Vienna and supervising the stage preparations in Salzburg. He had advised the festival committee on casting and was assiduous in his work with the singers. And what singers! Maria Cebotari, Irmgard Seefried, and Erich Kunz starred in *Le nozze di Figaro*. Maud Cunitz took the title role in *Der Rosenkavalier*, with Fritz Krenn as Baron Ochs, and Hilde Konetzni (one of Legge's old flames, 'a broth of a girl' as he called her) as the Marschallin.

While in Salzburg, the Karajans lodged at Zistelalm high on the Gaisberg, the mountain to the east of the city from which the best views of the region are to be had. The house belonged to the Walderdorff family, owners of the Goldener Hirsch, the inn in Salzburg's Getreidegasse. This was one of the few hotels that had not been requisitioned by the American army and had already become a fashionable meeting place for festival folk. (It was here that the Baroness von Einem set up court.) The festival provided Karajan with a car, an old Steyr, complete with chauffeur, despite the fact he invariably drove himself.

The Walderdorff children thoroughly enjoyed having him around. He loved fast cars, swam, climbed, and played just about every game under the sun. (Their father was a professional tennis coach. 'Karajan? Oh yes, I know him well. He's a pupil of mine,' he would tell gullible guests at the Goldener Hirsch.) The children even came to relish the black mood that overtook Karajan whenever he was beaten at croquet.

The Russians continued to make life difficult for him in Vienna, but since they had no jurisdiction in Salzburg, these were difficulties he was prepared to live with. Trouble, however, was brewing elsewhere. In clearing Karajan afresh in March 1946, the Austrian denazification commission had filed a somewhat ambiguous ruling. Karajan could perform as a conductor 'but not in a leading capacity'.

The fact is, the more time passed, the more confused the denazification procedures became, as pragmatists tangled with hard-liners, and lawyers grew fat on the proceedings. It was a process that was beginning to take on a life of its own.

And there was another factor: the reappearance on the scene of a familiar and, for Karajan, baleful presence.

Furtwängler was back in town.

Legge imagined Furtwängler was still in Switzerland, but on his first night in Vienna he bumped into him, more or less literally, in a darkened street near the Hofburg. According to Legge, Furtwängler had a girl on either arm; Legge, by contrast, appears to have been content with a single companion, Mme Konetzni. Closing a deal with Furtwängler was another of Legge's top priorities and though the contract took even longer to negotiate than Karajan's (Karajan signed in mid-May, Furtwängler in July) the process at least started that evening with an amicable exchange of telephone numbers.

Meeting Furtwängler in Vienna might have been a happy chance for Legge, but it was bad news for Karajan, as a somewhat garbled memorandum for Pasetti's office on 23 February 1946 makes all too clear. Three days previously, the Americans had formally banned Furtwängler from conducting in public. It is clear, however, that in the run-up to the ban he had been doing some furious lobbying, enraged by Karajan's recent public appearance with the Vienna Philharmonic and irked by his all too palpable success:

> 2. Furtwängler tries with all means to put pressure on the Philharmonics [sic], that they give him already now a contract as the leading conductor of this orchestra. That means that he gets most of the concerts and consequently has to decide what other conductors can perform with the Philharmonics. He wants this contract, so he can show in Switzerland and also to the French and to the British, how much he is needed and welcomed in Vienna.
>
> 3. The Philharmonics plan a concert tour through Switzerland, France and England in the first half of April ... Von Karajan was suggested to be the conductor of this tour. When F. was informed of it he stated, that he would never forget [forgive?] the Philharmonics that another Austrian conductor would come with this Austrian orchestra in Switzerland ...
>
> 5. Reliable evidence was given to writer that F. started his intrigues against Karajan, which means that the same picture we could observe in Berlin where F. fought Karajan is now repeated in Vienna.[7]

Since the Austrian authorities were desperate to have Karajan available for the 1946 Salzburg Festival, and since he had strong backing from a number of well-placed Americans, it is difficult to see what harm Furtwängler could do him. But gradually, as winter gave way to spring, Karajan's position was more and more eroded at the highest levels.

On 2 March 1946, it was the Americans who vetoed his scheduled concert with the Vienna Philharmonic. Under a news report headed 'Another conductor is banned in Austria', the New York Times reported scenes of disarray outside the Musikverein as a frustrated crowd of Viennese concert-goers milled angrily around the hall. On 7 May, the paper reported that moves were afoot to reinstate both Furtwängler and Karajan on the grounds of local political convenience. On 31 May, Pasetti attempted to put pressure on the authorities to get a clear ruling, but he was in the process of being replaced by a man with ambitions of his own in post-war Austria.

*

Dr Ernst Lothar, Pasetti's successor, a lawyer by training, was a writer and theatre administrator. In the mid-1930s he had managed Max Reinhardt's Theater an der Josefstadt in Vienna. That was before the *Anschluss*, when Lothar and his family had been forced to escape to Switzerland with nothing more than the clothes they stood up in. In the fullness of time, Lothar would surrender his new-won American citizenship, and settle in Salzburg as the director of the festival's theatre programme.[8]

Lothar took a far tougher line with Karajan. While he was bowled over by Karajan's passionate concern for his work,

As is the case with many other creative and recreative artists, Mr K's love of music comes close to some sort of obsession. The intensity of his speech, his gestures, his emotional attitude add to the impression of a 100% musician.[9]

he did not share the view of the Austrian denazification commission that he was indispensable. Nor was Lothar prepared to believe that so intelligent a man could have been entirely ignorant of what had been going on around him in the years of Nazi rule.

Which raises the question, did Lothar have available to him – or did he simply discount – the testimony of those who had worked with Karajan in Aachen and Berlin?

Horrified to read in a local newspaper in January 1946 of the ban that had been imposed on Karajan, Theodor Rehmann, the Director of Cathedral Music at Aachen, and three members of the Aachen orchestra (all of them, like Rehmann, untainted by any form of Nazi affiliation) had submitted a voluntary sworn affidavit on the subject of Karajan to the American authorities. Rehmann's testimony read:

I used to be very close to Mr von Karajan during his Aachen years ... To anyone who knew Mr von Karajan's way of going about his business, the reproach that he made a career through the Nazis is absurd. On the contrary, I know for certain that high officials in the Aachen Party continually tried to undermine Mr von Karajan's career. I could list many statements that Mr von Karajan made, privately and in public, which others, less bold, would have been afraid to make.

I was present during a telephone conversation between Mr von Karajan and the Party's regional boss [*Kreisleiter*] during which Mr von Karajan explicitly, nay rudely, refused to remove from the schedules Bach's B minor Mass and *St Matthew Passion* and Beethoven's *Missa Solemnis* unless and until the *Kreisleiter* was able to suggest works of comparable greatness. What Mr von Karajan actually said was: 'The time when the budding composers of the Hitler Youth will be able to produce works of comparable rank is still some way off.'[10]

Did Karajan know that Rehmann had written this in January 1946? The evidence is that he did not; for it was not until May 1947, when the whole denazification procedure was finally coming to an end, that Karajan replied to a further communication from him:

St Anton/Arlberg, 17 May '47
Dear Mr Rehmann,
May I express my most cordial thanks to you for your letter. It has moved me deeply to feel that my old friends are thinking of me with continuing affection, and this feeling has been a source of constant strength to me in difficult times.

My problems are now at last moving towards a resolution, which will occur when I have proved that I had to leave the Party after my marriage at the end of 1942. The consequences which this step had for my career were starkly brought home to all music-lovers in Germany.

And now I hope that the sacrifices of that time and all the unpleasant treatment I have had to endure will finally cease, and that I shall be able again to do what I have yearned to do for so long, to bring harmony and beauty among human beings.

Again my thanks to you, Mr Rehmann, all my good wishes are with you and with your certainly very difficult task. Most cordial greetings from
  your old friend,
    Herbert v. Karajan[11]

In a memorandum of 15 June 1946, Lothar declared that Karajan should *not* be treated as a special case. This led to Karajan's being refused permission to conduct at the 1946 Salzburg Festival. However, the ruling of 21 June was so hedged round with qualifications that the festival authorities had little difficulty in driving a coach and horses through it. Karajan continued to work on *Figaro* and *Der Rosenkavalier*, with two hapless surrogates, Hans Swarowsky and Felix Prohaska, standing in for him in the pit. He also retained an element of control over *Don Giovanni*. Anton Dermota, the Don Ottavio in the production, would later recall:

Josef Krips then took over from Karajan the Salzburg production of *Don Giovanni* which was being sung for the first time in Italian. This caused difficulties because the Italian prompter had not yet arrived. We were put off rehearsal after rehearsal but still he did not come. Karajan, who appeared at every rehearsal and retired to some quiet corner to observe – which obviously annoyed Krips – saw our plight, came forward, and said: 'I'll do the prompting!' He then slipped nimbly into the prompter's box and helped out until the prompter arrived.[12]

Lothar, who had originally turned a blind eye to Karajan's continuing attendance at rehearsals, was furious. On the day of the opening of *Der Rosenkavalier*, he fired off another directive to Baron Puthon absolutely forbidding Karajan to show up 'in any capacity' in the festival. Ever the mischievous child, Karajan continued to direct proceedings from the cover of the prompt box.

The Americans did not know what to make of Karajan. Infuriated by his endless improvised acts of defiance, they seem none the less to have admired his tenacity and musical commitment. However, on 17 September steps were taken to place an absolute ban on his work as a conductor.

*

At which point, re-enter Walter Legge. Legge had spent most of August in Salzburg, staying with the Karajans at Zistelalm. Now, in mid-September, he returned to Vienna with an EMI recording crew in tow. Having convinced the EMI board that the bans on Karajan and Schwarzkopf applied only to their performing in public, Legge had been provided by the British Foreign Office with the necessary papers for himself and his crew. The British military authorities in Vienna were also briefed.

Unfortunately, when Legge pitched camp in the Musikverein with several tons of recording equipment, plus generators to supplement the wayward public electricity supply, all hell broke loose. The Russians were beside themselves; the Americans were outraged. Even the Vienna Philharmonic panicked, summoning Legge for an emergency meeting in their offices in the Musikverein. But Legge stood firm, as did the President of the Gesellschaft der Musikfreunde, Alexander Hryntschak. What went on in his hall, under his auspices, Hryntschak announced, was a matter for the committee of the Gesellschaft der Musikfreunde and no one else. Legge had also done his homework. These were private sessions, commissioned by a British company, backed by the Foreign Office. When an American spokesman intervened, he was invited to go and jump into the Danube.

As for Karajan, he was equanimity itself. During the first session, not a note was recorded. While the engineers busied themselves with technical matters, Karajan worked on Beethoven's Eighth Symphony as if he and the Vienna Philharmonic had all the time in the world. Legge was deeply gratified. 'We took an enormous time to get the first record out of him,' he would later recall, with more than a touch of pride.

The finished recording was released the following March in the UK, and in mainland Europe after special clearances had been obtained in Austria and Germany. Private soundings were also taken among EMI's distributors in adjacent territories. (Only the Danes refused to accept the discs.) Much hung on the reception accorded to the records in *The Gramophone*, the London-based monthly review which was already something of a record-collectors' bible in the English-speaking world and beyond. The review was written by one of the paper's senior contributors, W. R. Anderson. He managed to write over 500 words without once mentioning Karajan by name, but the notice itself was most enthusiastic. The opening sentence set the tone: 'An outstanding set, remarkable in depth, sonority, and a sense of Beethovenian power and humour that I greatly like.'[13]

Sonically, it was a huge advance on the raucous 1941 Toscanini recording of the Eighth, which Anderson had reviewed some years before. As for the music-making, Anderson thought it more than a match for the highly prized pre-war Vienna Philharmonic recordings of the Eighth:

We remember the magnificent Beethoven records of the Viennese, way back in pre-war days. Schalk did this with them late in 1930, and Weingartner in the Spring of 1937. Solidity with inward stir, a fresh wind always blowing, the fullest possible tone consistent with clarity: here is a breadth of sound and style that seems to measure itself in true terms of the master.[14]

Anderson thought sufficiently well of Karajan's reading of the symphony's delightfully droll second movement to suggest having 'this mid-side on several times'. If he had a criticism, it was that the sound itself was a shade 'dour'. He blamed the recording, or, more specifically, the hall: an unlikely culprit. If there is a dour feel to the performance it is in the finale, where Karajan has not entirely solved the problem of aligning the richly drawn harmonic argument with a free-flowing rhythmic motion. The first movement, by contrast, goes rather well, thanks largely to Karajan's nicely judged use of the old masters' trick of commuting between two tempos – one urgent, the other much more reflective – within a single commanding pulse.

In many respects, this performance of the Eighth confirms the 38-year-old Karajan to be an astute and mannerly disciple of the master conductors of the old school. The approach is respectful, conservative even. And yet there is one respect in which this is a more modern-sounding performance than either Schalk's or Weingartner's. Where Schalk allows the players to skimp many of the shorter notes – especially end-of-bar quavers and semiquavers when the music is in dotted rhythm: a common practice at the time – Karajan paints the music with a far fuller brush, every note sounded for its appointed duration. Anderson hints at this in his review ('any full brass chord is a delight') but does not go on to explore the nature of the revolution in playing styles that is being effected here. Many years later, Yehudi Menuhin would write of Karajan's Berlin Philharmonic:

There are orchestras, and artists, who have to be restrained, lacking the patience or the inner rhythm to hold a note or a pause. Not so the Berlin Philharmonic: it approaches a note with anticipation and leaves it with regret.[15]

This was a far cry from the kind of hurried, often sloppy playing Karajan heard so much of in his youth.

The Eighth Symphony took the best part of three days to record. By the end of the third day, Karajan and the orchestra were at work on Schubert's

Great C major Symphony. This was an odd choice of repertory: a long and interpretatively problematic work, difficult to record. Karajan had insisted on it, somewhat to Legge's dismay, during their preliminary discussions in January. Since no contract had yet been signed, Legge felt obliged to go along with the idea. Nor did he attempt to revoke the draft agreement when news reached EMI from the United States that Bruno Walter was about to record the symphony with the New York Philharmonic. The agreement should be honoured, Legge wrote in a memorandum, 'in view of the difficulty involved in signing up Karajan'.[16]

Why did Karajan wish to record the *Great* C major Symphony? The Vienna Philharmonic had played it under Toscanini at the 1936 Salzburg Festival, a performance Karajan heard and was deeply impressed by. The Vienna Philharmonic had also been impressed by Toscanini's illuminatingly 'straightforward' reading. This, though, was the art that disguises art, difficult to replicate. Karajan's 1946 recording is some way from being the 'bosh-shot' it was said to be in the influential *Record Guide*.[17] String slides are more or less consistently outlawed, tempi are more tightly regulated, note values more precisely attended to than in rival pre-war recordings under conductors such as Hamilton Harty, Boult, and Bruno Walter. Yet there is a good deal that is amiss, especially in the finale where rhythm and phrasing are often pernickety and over-nuanced.

Karajan knew what was wrong. After playing the test-pressings to a friend and being told the performance was not up to much, Karajan replied, 'You're dead right. I've too many ideas. What's on the records are my ideas, not Schubert's.'[18] The doubts also resurfaced in a letter to Walter Legge seeking advice about appropriate repertory for the 1948 Salzburg Festival. Beethoven's Eighth Symphony and the *Great* C major are both mooted: 'But do you think I am good enough with the Schubert?' Karajan asked. 'I doubt.'[19]

*

With the two symphonies safely recorded, Legge was potentially at a loose end. He had originally booked the orchestra and the hall for sessions with Furtwängler, as well as with Karajan and Krips. But not even Legge could circumvent the complexities surrounding the denazification of Furtwängler, the one German artist whose case was being treated by both Washington and London with a seriousness otherwise reserved only for members of the German high command.

So, while Furtwängler fumed and fretted, Legge and Karajan spent the available time recording a succession of commercially attractive musical lollipops. Karajan's performance of Mozart's *Figaro* overture suggests a rather fretful atmosphere in the Almaviva household; his *Eine kleine Nachtmusik* is the very reverse, measured and urbane; while the recording of the B flat Symphony K319 is a mixture of the two, a little hard-driven at times but for the most part agreeably witty and boisterous. There was also time to record the overture to Johann Strauss's *Der Zigeunerbaron* and two items that were not released until 1997: a superbly recorded *Pizzicato* Polka and a splendidly dashing account of the polka *Leichtes Blut*. Schwarzkopf also made her EMI début with a brilliant (and, by Karajan, dazzlingly accompanied) account of Constanze's showpiece aria from Mozart's *Die Entführung aus dem Serail* 'Martern aller Arten'.[20]

There was one piece recorded during this period, however, which was far from being an orchestral lollipop. Indeed, its musical qualities came as something of a revelation to the Vienna Philharmonic. It was Tchaikovsky's Fantasy Overture *Romeo and Juliet*, a six-sided set recorded in a couple of days right at the end of October 1946. The critic Hanslick had roundly abused the piece on the occasion of its Viennese première in 1876 and little had been done since then to restore its reputation. For Karajan, however, the work was a miracle of dramatic and atmospheric tone-painting.

If the Vienna Philharmonic owed Karajan a debt in the Tchaikovsky, it was the orchestra that gave the four Johann Strauss recordings their incomparable character. Three of them were remakes. Karajan had recorded the *Kaiserwalzer*, the waltz *Künstlerleben*, and the overture to *Der Zigeunerbaron* with the Berlin Philharmonic in 1940–2. However, these Berlin recordings (which the Czech Gramophone Company had seized at the end of the war and re-released into the European market) are cartoon cut-outs in comparison with the *echt*-Viennese EMI discs. What in Berlin is often heavy-handed and unidiomatic is in Vienna stylish and alluring. It is to Karajan's credit that the Vienna Philharmonic obviously loved playing for him. His vitality, his feel for the intrinsic nobility of the music, and his natural sense of its incipient melancholy were no doubt factors in the special chemistry that is clearly evident in these recordings.

The Strauss waltzes were all recorded on 30 October, the final day of the inaugural Legge–Karajan sessions. The sessions finished with *The Blue Danube*.[21] After that, for Karajan at least, silence was the order of the day. On 4 November the Austrian government ratified the Allied ban on his work as a conductor.

As for the Vienna Philharmonic, shortly before Christmas it was announced that thirteen players had been ordered to take early retirement. (Temporary early retirement as it proved to be in one or two cases.) It was a token number; many more players had been Party members. But on this occasion even the Russians appear to have been eager not to damage this finest of all Austrian cultural institutions.

CHAPTER 23

A capacity of taking trouble

In the mountains, there you feel free.
T. S. Eliot, *The Waste Land*

St Anton am Arlberg and its surrounding mountains lie seventy miles west of Innsbruck on the western edge of the Austrian Tyrol. Since the early 1900s it has been one of the great proving grounds of the art of Alpine skiing. In the winter of 1946–7 Karajan withdrew there to ski, read, relax, and rethink his life. He could ski the Arlberg's near-impossible runs alongside the finest sportsmen of the day. But it was not competitive skiing that interested him. Sometimes he would be away for days on end, going deep into the mountains with his ski instructor and guide, sleeping in the remote mountain huts, even doing a little shooting. (His instructor was a fanatical huntsman.)

It was not an environment for the faint-hearted. When Walter Legge stopped by for a few days, Karajan took him sledging, hurtling the famously unathletic recording supremo – his glasses frozen over with the cold – at unconscionable speeds across the snowfields. Legge was game for the occasional ride, but decided to call it a day when Karajan drove them at high speed across a railway line as the barrier descended and an Arlberg express rumbled into view.

Karajan would later describe his life in St Anton in a letter to his new-found ally in Vienna, Henry Alter:

Even though public appearances are not yet possible, I was able to do quite a number of recordings last autumn in Vienna, and they turned out extremely well, restoring my confidence in myself. Then, early this year, I secluded myself up here for a life of quiet, concentrated study and meditation, rediscovering myself in the vastness and solitude of the mountains. I feel wonderful inside and out. It has been the most productive period in ages, and one day I'll need my sound nerves more than ever. For the moment, let the others decimate themselves in the Viennese battle of all against all – my time is sure to come and I await it, calm and confident.[1]

While Karajan skied, and perused books on theology (genius, he believed, was God-given) and transcendental meditation, annotating them extensively in his strangely seismographic hand, others were fighting the good fight for him in the 'battle of all against all' in Vienna. Hilbert was the prime mover, desperately concerned to avoid another Salzburg Festival in which Krips would carry the main operatic burden while a roster of foreign conductors – Munch, Barbirolli, and Ansermet[2] – shored up the orchestral schedules. The composer Gottfried von Einem, a key member of Hilbert's new Salzburg team, also pitched in on 21 May with his statement to the Allied authorities defending Karajan's behaviour during the Third Reich.

Ernst Lothar, too, was coming round to the view that Salzburg needed Karajan. Indeed, by March 1947, it looked as though he would soon be free to work. As of 1 February 1947, artists, actors, and musicians who had been formally cleared by their own national tribunals were no longer subject to further confirmatory review by the American authorities.

At which point, the French intervened in Karajan's case. Though Pathé Marconi, EMI's French subsidiary, reported, at worst, a certain equivocation among the French public about Furtwängler and Karajan ('there are some people that like to remind us that [Karajan] was once a member of the Nazi Party'[3]), there was nothing comparable to the virulent criticisms that were being directed against certain French musicians: Germaine Lubin, or the pianist Alfred Cortot, the nature of whose collaboration with the Vichy regime certainly merited investigation. There were those in the French military, however, who were not prepared to forget Karajan's appearances with the Berlin Opera in Paris in May 1941; nor, perhaps, the lavish life-style Anita von Karajan was rumoured to have enjoyed during visits to Paris during the war.

Karajan was unmoved. Determined to have nothing more to do with what he saw was an increasingly politicised process, he mainly stayed put in St Anton, planning his autumn recordings.

*

As for Furtwängler, in December 1946, he had been taken by military train to Berlin to appear before an all-German 'Denazification Court of Creative Artists' on four specific charges: serving the Nazi regime, uttering an anti-Semitic slur against the conductor De Sabata, performing at official Nazi Party functions, and membership of the Prussian State Council. On 17 December, he was acquitted by the court only to find himself being retried in the media. On 29 December 1946 New York Times journalist Delbert Clark published a long and hostile report on the Berlin proceedings entitled 'Furtwängler's Standards on Trial in Berlin'. The article was clearly a put-up job, part of a relentless campaign against Furtwängler in the American media that had begun way back on 1 March 1936 when the businessman and former New York Philharmonic Board member Ira A. Hirschmann, a keen Klemperer supporter, launched a bitter press campaign against the Board's decision to nominate Furtwängler as Toscanini's successor as the New York Philharmonic's Music Director.

On 5 January 1947, the *New York Times* published a letter which attempted to refute aspects of Clark's article by drawing attention to the equally unsavoury behaviour of a young Austrian conductor called Herbert von Karajan; but though other, weightier testimony was provided in Furtwängler's defence, the paper saw fit to publish none of the letters. In the end, with the Allied authorities still dithering and speculation in the press mounting about the possibility of 'fresh evidence' emerging of Furtwängler's wartime activities, Furtwängler himself forced their hand by accepting an invitation to conduct a series of concerts in Italy in April 1947. The denazifiers had no jurisdiction over Italy and on 27 April they called it a day. It was an all-important breakthrough for Furtwängler, though it would not be the end of the affair.

*

At some point in the winter of 1946–7, Karajan had met Furtwängler. Hearing that Furtwängler was journeying to Zürich via the Arlberg, and desperate to make some kind of rapprochement – when all was said and done, were they not both dedicated to similar aims? – he persuaded Furtwängler to break his journey at St Anton. Like Karajan, Furtwängler loved the mountains (he had been an enthusiastic skier in his youth) and probably relished the break. The meeting, though, was predictably unproductive. Furtwängler's dislike of Karajan was too deep-seated to admit of any real cure.

Why, then, did Karajan go on trying? Partly, I suspect, out of a genuine respect for Furtwängler, partly because, deep down, Karajan was quite an emotional (not to say sentimental) man. He was also very courteous. 'Karajan had far better manners than Wilhelm,' Elisabeth Furtwängler told me. 'The problem with Wilhelm was his father. He had instilled into him the idea that art was all: that nothing should stand in the way of that. Wilhelm had an obstinate, angry [*zornig*] temperament which his father actively encouraged.'

So the Arlberg meeting was a flop. It also, according to Karajan, almost cost him his life. Having walked and talked with Furtwängler, and taken the train with him down the line as far as Stuben, Karajan got lost in a blizzard walking back over the Arlberg Pass. A search party found him shortly after he had regained the main road.

*

At much the same time as the French authorities were raising objections to Karajan's resuming work, an article appeared in the London *Daily Mail*, which gave Legge and Karajan a worrying hint of the public-relations minefields that lay ahead. It was written by a man who was both influential and well liked, the broadcaster and co-founder of *The Gramophone*, Christopher Stone.[4]

Stone's 'Off the Record' column on 28 March 1947 was subtitled 'Good music, bad policy'. It began with a rave review of Karajan's new recording of Beethoven's Eighth Symphony:

It's a smasher . . . It has got everything. It is so good that it may carry you away and make you think it the finest recording of the best playing of the best symphony that the finest composer in the world ever wrote.'

But there were caveats. First, was not the market already rather overstocked with Beethoven Eighths? True, the Toscanini set was not up to much, but what of Weingartner and the Vienna Philharmonic, Koussevitzky and the Boston Symphony or Boult and the BBC SO?

Secondly, one must assume that Columbia's enterprise received the blessing of our authorities at home and in Austria on spending money in an ex-enemy country instead of at home in order to help the famous orchestra in its difficulties and to polish up our appreciation of the Eighth Symphony. But did the blessing extend to covering the engagement of a conductor whom the Austrians themselves [*sic*] have rejected as a Nazi and the payment of his and the orchestra's fees in Swiss francs?[5]

It was not true that the Austrians – either the people or the denazification tribunal – had 'rejected' Karajan. None the less, the article struck home with considerable force. EMI considered drafting a letter to the *Daily Mail*, but thought better of it. Working on Dr Johnson's principle that 'few attacks of ridicule or invective make much noise but by the help of those they provoke' they decided to ignore the outburst.[6]

It would be idle to pretend that Karajan was not depressed by all this. In May 1947 he wrote to Legge – in slowly improving English, as was now his invariable habit:

My dear Walter,
Your letter was exactly what I expected it to be. The right word in the right moment and the understanding help of my best friend – Thank you! And I promise to pull myself together and try to forget about the whole mess.

Legge's original letter to Karajan has not survived, but it would appear that he had suggested that Karajan should follow Furtwängler's example and call the Allies' bluff by accepting a series of conducting engagements in Italy. Karajan's response is typically logical and self-aware:

Speaking of more practical things, of course it would be delightful to go to Italy but I fear at the moment I would not get the visa and on the other hand it is dangerous to come at the present moment in contact with this country [Italy] where everything is so easy and smooth. It might induce oneself of staying there and work and I feel it would not be the right place to restart a career. I am certain I will conduct here in the autumn but then I must start in the right place, possibly London. Do you still have in mind a Beethoven cycle which would be just the right thing?

The letter ended:

If you come to Vienna please bring with you some of the Turicaphon [EMI] test records. I need them badly for working.

My dear, don't overwork yourself. We need our nerves on important things. Look after yourself and thank you once more.

Always yours,
Herbert[7]

Legge's health is a persistent preoccupation in the letters Karajan wrote to him during the spring and summer of 1947, letters which are an engaging mishmash of gossip, jokes, and serious strategy-making. In one of them, Karajan hopes that Legge will 'have at least the same trouble reading this epistel [sic] as I had with the crossword puzzle that just arrived'; there is gossip from Salzburg, news of problems over the availability of Knappertsbusch, and news of Klemperer's erratic behaviour and general state of unpreparedness.

In early July, Karajan had travelled to Graz to hear Klemperer, a legendary figure in pre-1933 Berlin, conduct the Vienna Symphony Orchestra. Next day, he offered to drive him to Vienna, an offer Klemperer accepted. Though Klemperer did conduct one concert at the 1947 Salzburg Festival (Roy Harris's Third Symphony, Mahler's Fourth) he was forced to abandon plans to conduct the world première of Gottfried von Einem's *Dantons Tod*. Ferenc Fricsay took his place and became, more or less overnight, one of Europe's most admired conducting talents.

*

Apart from regular trips to Vienna to lay plans for the autumn and spy out the land, Karajan communicated with the outside world largely by letter and telephone. One by one, old friends resurfaced, old ties were re-established. In May he heard from Wilhelm Pitz in Aachen. A jaunty note of 1 June was followed on 1 September by a rather longer letter, written three weeks after news of Karajan's political clearance – the formal 'denazification' – had formally come through:

Anton 1 Sept [1947]

My dear Pitz,
Such a pity we missed each other, I was called to Vienna urgently at that

time. Now finally my case has been sorted out and I am completely free and guiltless according to Austrian law. It has moved me deeply to know that all my friends in Aachen have stood by me. Please tell them all from me that I will remember them as they have me, and when I can travel at all I will come to Aachen and give a few concerts. It is lovely to know that there is a circle of people who always retain their links with one. Please tell that to everyone!!! What pains me, however, is that we can no longer work together, but perhaps the opportunity will come again. It is possible that I shall be conducting in Hamburg in November. Yes, things are underway again. I have 8 concerts with the VPO and 3 with the Singverein, whose conductorship I am assuming. The chorus director is Grossmann. As an innovation I am doing William Walton's *Belshazzar's Feast*, the best choral music that's been written in the last 50 years. I strongly recommend it to you. The Singverein is under the patronage of the GdM in Vienna, and I have the function of joint musical adviser and conductor with Furtwängler. We recently had a long talk, and I hope we will work peacefully together. Then I'm on the [Salzburg] Festival Board and will be involved with operas and concerts next year; and there's abroad as well, Italy, Switzerland, a Beethoven cycle in London in April, and if there's time South America in May, and in between times preparation for Salzburg. So a great deal to do. Thank God, I'm in wonderful shape because of my 9 months stay here. So even that had its good side.

My dear fellow, do write once again. I so like hearing from there, everything interests me, and I'm pleased to hear that you and your wife are happy together. Warmest greetings to my beloved chorus, and to everyone else.

Best wishes to you and your wife,

Yours

Herbert Karajan[8]

Settling matters for the 1947–8 winter season with 'the crooks of the Philharmonic' (Karajan's phrase), had been a long and complex business. The problem was, the Vienna Philharmonic wanted both Karajan and Furtwängler; no other available conductors could be guaranteed to draw full houses on successive evenings for the same subscription programme. That was a problem in itself, added to which – as Karajan privately admitted – the orchestra also risked alienating a number of other conductors if they engaged him.

In the event, the Philharmonic gave the lion's share of the season to Karajan. And what a rich and musically varied season it was to be: sixteen concerts that would include Bruckner's Eighth Symphony and Beethoven's Ninth, Verdi's *Requiem*, the *St Matthew Passion*, Act 3 of *Parsifal* and orchestral music by Bartók, Prokofiev, and Vaughan Williams. Furtwängler was offered eight concerts plus a summer tour of Switzerland. His repertory was much more conservative: mostly Beethoven, Schubert, and Brahms, plus a couple of works by Mendelssohn.

The Philharmonic's decision to give Karajan the prestigious pre-Christmas performances of Beethoven's Ninth caused particular upset. The reasons, though, were largely practical and financial: the Vienna Philharmonic would be recording the Ninth with Karajan for EMI in the weeks immediately preceding the concert.

The choir for the recording of the Ninth Symphony was the Singverein der Gesellschaft der Musikfreunde, one of two distinguished Viennese choirs which had been founded in 1858. In 1950, the Singverein would confer on Karajan the unique honour of appointing him their Concert Director for life.[9] In May 1947, however, Karajan was nervously urging Legge to finalise his contract with it.

*

Beethoven's Ninth Symphony presents a peculiarly complex set of challenges to any conductor, let alone one not yet turned forty, however talented and well schooled. Writing from St Anton on 20 May 1947, Karajan provided Legge with an update on his preparations:

I was thinking very much of our forthcoming work in [the] autumn and especially of the Ninth Beethoven. We have to talk very much about it. I spent the last 3 weeks on this work and what I find now is the great difficulty of bringing the enormous conception of the work into the close and condense form in which it is written. It was a great experience with the 8th under your control to get the whole content into its really classical form. But what with the 9th? For instance, did you notice that in comparison with the Eighth nearly all the metronomes are too fast in the 1st and 3rd movements and too slow in the last to get out the enormous 'Steigerung [heightening and intensification]' which reaches to the stars. And all the right tempo modifications which are essential. In short, to get the fullest richdom [richness] of fantasy in the purest form. That needs an utmost degree of 'selbstzucht [self-discipline]'. In any case, it is very important to bring with you the best two existing recordings so that we get afterwards a close conception of what we want. I can work quietly in the summer on it. A long and serious task it is. I feel I must bring mein inneres Beethovenbild up to the present form in which I am feeling and thinking of music. The 9th is probably the key to the other sinfonies [sic] after the experience of the 8th and I need all your help for it.[10]

The 1947 recording of the Ninth goes some way to demonstrating what he meant by all this. The opening Allegro, ma non troppo, un poco maestoso is precisely that: a slowish, intensely concentrated but none the less vital and orchestrally transparent reading of what is by any reckoning one of the most difficult of all Beethoven's symphonic movements to pace and shape. Karajan does not modify the tempo as freely as Furtwängler; but, then, Furtwängler had lived longer with the piece, evolving and perfecting a visionary, essentially Romantic reading that traced its lineage back via the distinguished musicologist Heinrich Schenker (his influential monograph *Beethovens Neunte Symphonie*, 1912) to Wagner, and the man who is widely acknowledged to be the work's first genuinely successful interpreter, the French conductor Habeneck.

Karajan read Schenker, too. He may not have mentioned the fact; but he grew up at a time when musicians felt no compulsion to publish their reading lists or parade their learning. In the case of Schenker's *Neunte Symphonie*, Karajan would have been hard pressed to avoid it, since his teacher Bernard Paumgartner was a huge admirer of the book.[11]

Karajan did not agree with everything he read there. Where, in his letter to Walter Legge, he is understandably sceptical about many of the metronome markings in the Ninth, Schenker merely glosses over the problem by citing Beethoven's preference for 'a free manner of playing [rather than a] rigid one'.[12] On the other hand, there are things in Schenker which Furtwängler (the disciple and friend) jibbed at and which Karajan (the young Turk, progressive and open-minded) readily accepted. Surprising as it may seem to the self-styled authenticists of our own time, Karajan's 1947 Ninth is notable for its deployment of slimmed-down textures (no added horns in the *Scherzo*'s great flare-ups) and its radical 'back-to-the-score' treatment of such things as the finale's instrumental recitatives.

Legge's flair for assembling artists of the finest musical pedigree in skilfully matched teams shines through in his selection of the solo quartet: Schwarzkopf, Elisabeth Höngen, Julius Patzak, and Hans Hotter. This was not simply a matter of good casting. Legge had an ability, rare among musical laymen, to imagine in advance of a performance the precise sound he wanted. He also had a way with words which enabled him to communicate that sound-idea to the musicians and recording engineers with whom he was working. When Karajan writes of his need to realise his innermost vision of Beethoven's music and, more or less in the next sentence, adds 'and I need all your help for it' he reveals the degree to which their skills and insights were complementary.

Karajan did his homework, of course, even on matters that might more properly be thought of as Legge's responsibility or those of his recording engineer Douglas Larter. In another letter written before the 1947 sessions, Karajan reports back to Legge on 'the very interesting acoustic study' he has been making in the Great Hall of the Musikverein during a rehearsal of the Ninth Symphony under Krips's direction.

The sound on the finished recording of this 1947 EMI Ninth was certainly remarkable for its day. There is considerable depth of sonority yet there is great clarity too. Indeed, balances within the orchestra and between orchestra, choir, and soloists are as nicely judged as on any of Karajan's five studio recordings of the Ninth.

When it was released, the set won golden opinions. Unfortunately, the days of 78 rpm recordings were numbered. The set remained in favour only until the winter of 1952–3 when LP recordings by Kleiber and Toscanini swept it off the shelves.

*

The other large-scale recording planned by Legge and Karajan for the autumn of 1947 was an even more complex operation. The work was Brahms's *German Requiem*, a pillar of the choral repertory which, strange to relate, had never previously been recorded in its entirety. Legge was not the only person to notice this glaring omission from the record catalogues. Robert Shaw, a rising star among choral conductors in the United States, was also working on a recording for RCA at much the same time. What gave Karajan and his musicians a head start – and in this respect the recording has never been surpassed – is the sense we have of the enactment of a real requiem, a cry *de profundis* from a desolate people in a desolate city.

Elisabeth Schwarzkopf was the soloist in the fifth movement 'Ihr habt nun Traurigkeit'. ('So difficult to bring off,' she once remarked. 'The voice up in the ether, the feelings buried beneath.'[13]) She also sang in the chorus, helping the young sopranos of the Singverein negotiate difficult problems of pitch and helping them, too, with the delicately articulated word painting that is one of the performance's most distinctive features. She is distinctly audible in the remarkable passage towards the end of the second movement '*und Schmerz und Seufzen wird weg müssen* [and tears and sighing shall flee from them]'. She later recalled, 'It was very special. Certainly, we were remembering those whose lives had been lost.'[14]

The fact that the *Requiem* was being made for 78 rpm discs was an additional headache for Karajan. This was his first choral recording, and the prospect of dividing up the work into sixteen or seventeen four- to five-minute sections clearly preoccupied him, the more so as there were no extant recordings to use as yardsticks.

Karajan wrote at length to Legge on the subject. It is a letter that is worth quoting in its entirety. As Thomas Carlyle said of Frederick the Great, the first mark of genius is 'a transcendent capacity of taking trouble':

My dear Walter,
After three more days careful timing, I come to the conclusion that the only possible artistic way of dividing the 'Requiem' is in linking the numbers 1, 2, 3 and 5, 6, 7 together. I give you now the full details.
[Side] 1 to C, 2 to F, 3 to C of Number II, 4 to G, 5 to 8th bar after L, 6 to 176 bar after B in III, 7 to 6 bar before F, 8 to end of III.

The reasons are: one could with some hurrying come in the first part to 1 before D and with the second reach the end. But you lose the tranquillity which [it] is so important to establish right in the beginning. And, still more important, you must have the last big expansion in the end of I and – most dangerous – you get the final chord right at the inner end of the disc. As for No.II, my suggestion gives 'so seid nun geduldig' the opening of the disc, whereas if you have to divide No.II selbständig [as a separate entity] you have to cut this wonderful intermezzo in two pieces. Furthermore, you would have to cut right at the beginning of the fugue which would be very bad because the anticipation of the theme in 'Aber des Herrn Wort' must lead through in the fugue without stopping – which happens in my scheme. And more: I have plenty of time in the 'tranquillo' of the fugue which is so vital to bring this part to a peaceful end. Here too I avoid the final chord at the end of a disc. In number III I can reach quite comfortably the point 'Nun Herr' and get the whole following [unclear] in one piece, whereas with the normal cut you have to divide before 'Ich hoffe' which is terrible.

Now to the second half. [Side] 9 is number IV. 10 to D of V. 11 to A of VI. 12 to E. 13 to L. 14 to 6 before B of VII. 15 to two bars before Doppelstrich [double bar], and 16 to end. In a normal cutting, No.V would be divided in two shortish parts. Number VI would again cut right at the beginning of the fugue which would have to be played at an incredible speed, and the whole majesty of the piece would have gone. Number VII can't be played in two parts, so you have to cut in three – and if you would cut it so that the wonderful middle part 'Ja, der Geist' comes for itself, as it does in my scheme, the first part would be ridiculously short. Further, you will notice that in my propositions no great 'fortissimo' comes at the end of a disc with the exception of the end of III. But this is so timed that it comes to only about 4' so there is enough margin.

And chief thing of all, every idea is carried either to the end or, where it is part of a greater complex, this is introduced and established before the cut comes. Also in normal cutting you come to 17 parts instead of 16. And I know quite a lot of conductors who would vouch for the first because this gives them extra income without work.

But, seriously, think it over and you will agree with me that it is worth breaking with a tradition in this case for the benefit is a highly artistic thing. Because its timing is [such] that in the important parts I never need to be nervous whether I can reach my time because there is in every record a margin of about 10–15 seconds. And if this work sounds hurried, everything is spoiled.

Now think about it quietly and we talk in Vienna. The first choir rehearsal will be on 16 [October]. I am deadly frightened what will come out of this ensemble. Perhaps you can arrange to be there already.

Be sure to have petrol because the current frequency will be, according to the water shortage, terribly low.

Love

Yours, Herbert[15]

The letter is characteristic of Karajan. It is an intriguing mix of the far-sighted and the severely practical. Current exigencies – petrol supplies or the dynamic tolerances of 78 rpm records – sit cheek by jowl with an overarching concern for the work itself: with its organic integrity, and that mood of inner repose which can finally be achieved only when the performers themselves are, musically speaking, in a state of grace, calm and unflustered.

Such preoccupations take us close to the heart of Karajan's particular skills as a conductor and motivator. At the same time, the letter lays bare another Karajan characteristic: a desperate need to have his way. Not as a child in a tantrum might, nor as a power-hungry careerist, but as a man who cannot bear the idea of being overruled by someone less conscientious and less well informed than he considers himself to be.

In Legge he had the perfect partner, for he, too, was a perfectionist. Legge did not throw out Karajan's plans; he merely embellished them. When the recording was eventually released, it was royally treated by EMI. It was spread over twenty sides and handsomely packaged, its intrinsic merit trusted by EMI to give it a decisive edge over its cheaper American rival.

The sessions for the *German Requiem* had begun on 20–22 October and resumed five days later, sharing studio time, significantly enough, with sessions for the first recording of *Metamorphosen*, Richard Strauss's lament for the destruction of Germany:

I, too, am in a mood of despair! [Strauss wrote to Joseph Gregor in March 1945.] The Goethe house, the world's greatest sanctuary, destroyed! My beautiful Dresden, Weimar, Munich, all gone![16]

During the brief recess, Karajan rehearsed with the Vienna Philharmonic for the concert that would mark his official return to concert life. For this, he had chosen a single work, and a consciously Austrian one: Bruckner's Eighth Symphony.

Apart from the critic of the *Österreichische Zeitung*, Dr Dezsö Hajas, who wrote a review about the 'Heroen'-Kult of the conductor who raises himself above the music he conducts,[17] the Austrian press greeted the performance with acclaim. Writing in the *Österreichische Musikzeitschrift*, Heinrich Kralik expressed the view that Karajan's reading was at once grand and personal, an objective reading for an objective age, yet one that was also touched with magic.[18]

After the second of the two concerts, Karajan presented Walter Legge with his copy of the score, unannotated save for the dedication:

Meinem zweiten musikalischen Ich und lieben Freund zur Erinnerung an einen lang ersehnten Tag. Herbert von Karajan 26.X.47

[To my musical alter ego and dear friend in remembrance of a long-wished-for day.]

Shortly afterwards, the Bruckner Gesellschaft in Vienna sounded out

EMI in London about the possibility of their co-financing a cycle of Bruckner recordings with Karajan and the Vienna Philharmonic.[19] It was a nice idea, but premature.

*

Wonderful as the music-making was, the politicking went on. In October, Furtwängler, who was also about to resume work in Vienna, wrote a long and embittered letter to Legge accusing him of failing to honour the contract they had signed in July 1946. Once again, what rankled most was the fact that Karajan had been able to make records when he had not. Legge's reply was diplomatic:

You must forgive me if I say that we feel from your letter that you are attaching too much importance to the recordings by the Wiener and Berliner Orchestras by other conductors, and not appreciating the importance we attach to yours. The sun is not the less brilliant when the moon is visible by day.[20]

Legge and Furtwängler went on working together, says Elisabeth Furtwängler, because, in the final analysis, each respected the other's worth. It could never have been an easy relationship – no relationship with Furtwängler ever was – but now that Legge had so conspicuously thrown in his lot with Karajan it would often be a well-nigh impossible one.

Meanwhile, Karajan and Legge were using one another to make advances on a number of fronts. Plans were laid for Karajan to make his London début in the spring of 1948. Karajan also embarked on a bizarre plot to have Strauss's last opera Die Liebe der Danae staged at the 1948 Salzburg Festival. The festival committee had attempted to include the opera in the 1947 programme but had fallen foul of Strauss's refusal to contemplate any conductor other than the as yet undenazified Clemens Krauss who had helped him revise the original libretto.

Karajan's political touch was certainly wanting if he thought that there was the remotest chance of outmanoeuvring Krauss and persuading Strauss to let him – Karajan – conduct the official première. None the less, his cloak-and-dagger correspondence with Legge makes amusing reading:

The most difficult thing to settle will be to get Strauss' permission for the Danae and to avoid any interference from the other side. He must be convinced that next year the work must come off in the planned way. If you talk to him, make it clear to him, will you (but possibly after the Salome conductor has left London)?[21]

The Salome conductor was Clemens Krauss. Krauss would conduct Die Liebe der Danae's belated première in Salzburg in 1952, three years after Strauss's death.

A slightly more airworthy kite flown by Karajan in the same letter concerns the possibility of his being allowed to record a symphony by Sibelius. He personally favours the Seventh ('because the work is the one that comes nearest me') but wonders whether the Fifth might not *record* better, 'the instrumentation being more clear, whereas the 7th is rather thick and to compare with Brahms which generally does not so well record itself'.[22] Legge, or his repertoire committee, must have had doubts; it would be several years before EMI would allow Karajan to make any Sibelius recordings.

In the aftermath of the recordings of the *German Requiem* and Beethoven's Ninth Symphony, Karajan was obliged to mop up spare studio time with a strange array of musical odds and ends. There were two rather sombre Mozart pieces, his Adagio and Fugue in C minor and his *Masonic Funeral Music*. There was a ravishingly sung account of the Presentation of the Silver Rose from Act 2 of *Der Rosenkavalier* with Schwarzkopf as Sophie and Irmgard Seefried as Octavian, a set of discs that was originally issued without Karajan's name on the label. (There are several small lapses in the orchestral detailing to which he presumably took exception.) And a performance of the overture to Reznicek's opera *Donna Diana* of such breathtaking fire and charm that one almost forgives (nay, one begins actively to relish) the soured-cream-and-capers sound of the Vienna Philharmonic's first oboe.

*

1947 ended with a further triumph for Karajan, the much heralded live performances of Beethoven's Ninth Symphony that took place in the Golden Hall of the Musikverein shortly before Christmas. Both concerts were packed out and received with near-frenetic acclaim. The press notices were also enthusiastic, praising the performance's power and clarity. Not, however, Dezsö Hajas in the *Österreichische Zeitung*. Having set out his ideas about the *'Heroen'-Kult* of the conductor in his article of 29 October, in which, with strategic guile, he avoided all mention of Karajan's name, he now moved in for the kill:

Karajan's 'Ninth' is the victory of interpretation over the work and brilliant proof of the possibility of a new and 'timely' sense being provided by the conductor. For only through Karajan has this musical drama of humanity turned into a military parade ... the titanic inspiration of an enthusiastic love been transformed into cold 'demonism'.

The *Adagio*'s 'soulful singing', the review went on, had been lost in a general air of 'unemotional frivolity'. And there was more:

There is no doubt that in the interpretation of a conductor whose career began [*sic*] in the Third Reich, the spirit and taste of the Reich are involuntarily finding new expression: in the musical sphere, star-orientated individualism and superficial aesthetics become too integrated within the polish of cultural propaganda, in the service of a political ideology which has never been afraid of distorting even the most sacred cultural products for its own ends.[23]

It has to be said that those parts of Hajas's review which deal specifically with the musical interpretation are almost totally at odds with the interpretative 'facts' of the performance as we have them on the 1947 EMI recording. What makes the notice interesting, however, is its representative status as an early example of what was to be a long-term strategic assault in which hostile critics would try to present Karajan as though he had been some kind of standard-bearer for the Third Reich. It is reviewing by auto-suggestion, the critic-polemicist entering the concert hall with the jingle of spurs and the crash of jackboots already sounding in his ears.

One doubts whether Karajan was much upset by Hajas's review. Vienna had long been the home of poison-pen reviewing. As far as Karajan was concerned, the Vienna Philharmonic had surpassed themselves, a fact he communicated to them in a handwritten note sent from St Anton on Christmas Eve.

In St Anton, Karajan had a new-found acquaintance who was to become one of his closest friends, an Englishman by the name of Edge Leslie. Leslie was a diplomat based in Zürich, obsessed by music, though with no skills as a performer. The two men had met during the 1947 Salzburg Festival and since Leslie and his wife also had an apartment in St Anton they saw a good deal of the Karajans.

At Christmas, Anita did the cooking, Herbert took charge of the decorations. On Christmas Eve 1947 Leslie found Herbert alone in the house laying an elaborate trail of recording tape through the rooms. When Anita returned she was told that if she followed the tape-trail she would find her Christmas present. It was a fur coat. Things were looking up.

CHAPTER 24

New music: a tantrum and a tiff

It is generally better to deal by speech than by letter.
Francis Bacon, *Of Negotiating*

The new year is a time for toasts and libations, Strauss waltzes on the radio, and fresh resolutions. Karajan spent New Year's Eve 1947 in his St Anton hideaway writing a letter to Gottfried von Einem that even today is still rather shocking in its mixture of peremptoriness and passion.

At one level, the letter is what T. S. Eliot has called the vehement outpouring of the mild-mannered man safely entrenched behind his typewriter. More seriously, it is the outpouring of an angry idealist: a further indication of the toll the war and the protracted ban on conducting was taking of Karajan's nerves and temper.

Von Einem probably half expected the letter. The enormous success – politically as well as musically and theatrically – of his new opera *Dantons Tod* at the 1947 Salzburg Festival had won him worldwide critical acclaim. It had also secured for him, at the early age of twenty-nine, a place on the board of the Salzburg Festival. With Hilbert 'managing' the festival, Paumgartner and Lothar advising from the sidelines, and old Baron Puthon smiling benignly on, artistic decision making was now largely in the hands of three men: the formidable director-designer team of Oscar Fritz Schuh and Caspar Neher, and von Einem himself.

Schuh and Neher had in mind a balanced package of reforms, but it was von Einem who had come up with a raft of ideas more radical than any that would be seen in Salzburg until the arrival of Gérard Mortier in 1992.

'About Salzburg plans,' Karajan had written to Legge on 2 September 1947, 'please be very cautious about letting people know too much about the structure of the management.' But what structure, what management? How sensitive were Karajan's antennae to what was really going on in Salzburg? No one was in any doubt that it was his ambition to exercise 'a certain influence' over the festival. He had said as much to Paumgartner in 1946 and in a letter to Baron Puthon the following year. Von Einem also knew how strongly Karajan felt. The very last sentence of the defence of Karajan he had submitted to the denazification tribunal in May 1947 read:

But what hit Herbert von Karajan hardest [during the Third Reich] was the fact that, although he was a Salzburger, he was never invited to participate in Festivals there or in Vienna.[1]

However, if Karajan thought he could win the crown by buttering up Puthon and wheeler-dealing with Hilbert, he was wrong. In 1947, the question uppermost in the minds of most of Salzburg's power-brokers was not 'Who now?' but 'Where next?'

Not since the polemics and manifestos of 1929 had there been so acute a bout of introspection within the festival's body politic. It was Paumgartner's belief that the festival had lost its way with the waning of Reinhardt's star and the rise of Toscanini's. But now everything was being questioned, even the legacy of Reinhardt and Hofmannsthal. After the Nazi death camps, what price the medieval pieties of Hofmannsthal's *Jedermann*? After such knowledge, what forgiveness? *Dantons Tod*, with its vision of a revolution that (in von Einem's own phrase) had 'eaten its own children', seemed far more 'relevant', much closer to the mood of the times. In the event, *Jedermann* was spared, despite the best efforts of Ernst Lothar (who would later direct it for the festival) to commission a replacement. But the fact that the play's continuing suitability had been called into question must have alerted Karajan to the extent of the changes that were being contemplated.

Karajan identified himself with Salzburg's *ancien régime*: with Reinhardt, Hofmannsthal, Richard Strauss. Indeed, one of the cues for the New Year missive to von Einem seems to have been von Einem's attitude towards Strauss:

Dear Mr von Einem,
You are fully within your rights to seek out opinions whenever and wherever it suits you. That in doing so you seriously overstep the bounds of tact, I am prepared to attribute to your having spent too long in Germany. But what I really want to keep you from, is falling in your youth into an attitude of mind that you would associate with old Pfitzner: that is, the false idea that you are not sufficiently recognised. What do you actually want? You ought surely to be justifiably happy with your personal treatment in the recent past, and with plans that involve you in the future. The same treatment will be afforded to everyone who has something important to say for his times. But if you consider it important to remain in touch with me, then I demand from you an attitude towards the music of past generations which is dictated, if not by love, then at least by respect for it. I am convinced that if Richard Strauss was as well informed about your life as you are about his, he would at least be able to reproach you with the same lack of character. (If it was worth his trouble to do so.) But your personal attitude towards Strauss does not interest me in the slightest. I am only hurt by the dismissive way you speak of an artist who was the complete expression of the thought and sensibility of his own time. And may God bless you if you are able to do the same for your time.[2]

After this opening harangue, Karajan goes on to define the vision of the festival as he believed it to have been originally conceived:

I am quite clear about the task of the Salzburg Festival, much clearer than you can be, because you are looking at recent years while I have worked almost since the beginning on building it up and coping with its changing destiny. What you cannot or will not see, is that Salzburg has a really important task to fulfil: to re-establish a sense of harmony and beauty in artistic expression, regardless of whether it involves Gluck, Mozart, Beethoven or Blacher. That is its supreme principle, and the public must rediscover its faith in that, for then it will also find the capacity to understand and value the music of its own time.[3]

Once more the old vision is reasserted: the need for all artistic expression to be informed by a sense of harmony and beauty.

In his essay 'The Rehearsal', Karajan would spell out some of his thinking on the subject:

In the beginning [of the process of working with an orchestra], there may have been a struggle about the most elementary values in music: long, short, high, deep, loud, strong, until with time they all become a matter of course, and thereby are subjected only to a higher meaning. If one looks back from here to the beginning, the initial studying of the score, to the first elaboration of musical form as a spiritual concept, then it becomes almost painfully clear how much the dualism between mind and substance detains us in its claws.

One cannot hope to reach a state where lucidity of spirit is at the very heart of one's being before one has thrown off the shackles of material things. Man must of necessity transform what he physically encounters.[4]

Not for the first time in Karajan's utterances, there are echoes here of the thinking of Schopenhauer, a man whose writings had seeped into the very foundations of the late-nineteenth-century culture to which Karajan was heir. The aesthetic experience, Schopenhauer had argued, allows us to perceive what he calls 'the intrinsic and primary forms of inanimate nature'. By arresting the flux of everyday life and stripping away the veils of our subjective being, the aesthetic experience admits us into that purest and most desirable of all states, an entirely will-less state of being. In such a condition, we are no longer an individual standing in contrast to others but rather part of an impersonal and universal state of pure knowledge.

Whether or not Karajan had read a word of Schopenhauer is immaterial. What is interesting is that he appears to have possessed a similar inborn longing for the pure, the beautiful, the chaste, the timeless. As an interpreter gifted with an alchemist's command of the orchestra, it was a vision that bestowed rare powers on Karajan, which, in the years ahead, some would venerate, others revile.

It was also a vision – or psychological predisposition – that placed him in a curious position, and made him difficult to fathom. One of the central paradoxes of Karajan's career is that this seemingly most modern of men was, in some respects, very old-fashioned. How this manifested itself will become apparent as the story unfolds. The paradox is more than hinted at, however, in the New Year's Day letter to von Einem: Karajan the careerist, the rising star – a man already professionally devoted to avoiding anything remotely resembling a backward glance – holding to an aesthetic that is not so much old-fashioned as barely of this world at all.

Karajan had not, however, sat down to write von Einem a dissertation on aesthetics, though aesthetics came into it. Nor was the letter primarily about Richard Strauss, though criticisms von Einem appears to have made of Strauss were clearly a factor. What the letter is really about is new music: about the best way of performing it and doing so within the context of a festival that had not hitherto been regarded as a forum for the new.

Nowadays, premières of 'difficult' new works are often note-perfect first time round, such is the proficiency of late-twentieth-century instrumentalists. But it was not always so. As a student in Vienna, Karajan had watched Webern conduct his own music. People said it was cold. Not so, Karajan remembered. 'His commitment was immense. But the playing was . . . unbeschreiblich [unspeakable]!'

To some, this was part of the music's appeal: an earnest of its radicalism, its power to shock, music *pour épater les bourgeois*. (There were often riots during the concerts.) There were also those who saw commercial failure as a badge of success. 'From the middle of the nineteenth century,' wrote Theodor Adorno in the introduction to his *Philosophy of Modern Music* first published in 1948, 'good music has renounced commercialism altogether.'⁵

Marxism being as fashionable in musical circles in 1948 as it was in political ones, there were those who took Adorno's musical judgements seriously, despite the fact that the distaste he felt for composers he considered bourgeois and old-fashioned led him to dismiss some of the leading creative talents of the day, among them Elgar ('trumped up glory', 'a local phenomenon'), Shostakovich ('unjustly reprimanded as a cultural Bolshevist'), Britten ('triumphant meagreness'), Sibelius (his fame 'an exceptional case of critical ignorance'), and Stravinsky ('the only aspect of Stravinsky that can be publicly appreciated is his prestige').⁶

In comparison with Adorno, whose Marxism and distaste for technology is still occasionally used to beef up articles and postgraduate dissertations on the allegedly corrosive effects of the record industry on our musical culture, von Einem was a nice guy, an intellectual pussy-cat. To Karajan, though, he was in danger of underestimating the effect on listeners of ill-prepared performances of new music. The gifted listener, remarked Aaron Copland in his 1951 Harvard Lectures, is a key figure for all musicians, creators, and performers.⁷ Karajan would have said 'Amen' to that. And to the remark by philosopher Susanne Langer in her book *Feeling and Form*: '. . . the one support that every artist must have if he is to go on creating music is a world that listens.'[8] Alienating a potentially wider musical public, Karajan believed, only further postponed the day when the best of the new would be gratefully heard and absorbed by that public.

Later in his letter to von Einem, Karajan cites chapter and verse: a less than effective performance of Frank Martin's oratorio *Der Zaubertrank* (*Le vin herbé*) in Vienna the previous year. Martin was one of several contemporary composers to whom Karajan felt temperamentally drawn; the pale, dimly lit world of *Le vin herbé*, the subtleties and etiolated beauties of the Debussy-like score, clearly appealed to him. Not, though, in a German-language version as crudely rendered as this had been. And now, Karajan learned, *Der Zaubertrank* had been taken by the Salzburg Festival. One of von Einem's first ideas as a board member had been to pencil the work into the 1947 festival, not as an oratorio but as a mainstream operatic event. The experimental staging was to be by Schuh and Neher; Patzak and Cebotari would sing the Tristan and Isolde roles; Fricsay was to be the conductor. When it flopped, as it duly did – dubbed *Trauertrank* ('sad drink' rather than the 'magic drink') by the critics – Karajan was not surprised.

*

Apart from Raffaello de Banfield, whose successes with various ballet scores and his opera *Lord Byron's Love Letter* lay some way in the future, Karajan had formed no close ties with any living composer. This was partly a matter of temperament, an aspect of his shyness and insecurity, partly one of circumstance. Nazi Germany had not exactly been awash with front-rank creative talent, though Karajan had played a considerable amount of contemporary German and Austrian music during his years in Aachen.

Yehudi Menuhin believes that had Karajan first been employed anywhere other than on the Austro-German operatic circuit, he might have become a leading exponent of contemporary music, such was the natural quickness and brilliance of his mind. Others doubt this, believing that Karajan could have derived little satisfaction aesthetically from the kind of experimental music that was being written in mainland Europe in the immediate post-war years. This latter point is probably nearer to the truth, not simply because of the apparent 'ugliness' of much new music but because of *rhythmic* disjunction: a contradiction of our natural sense of pulse and motion, something he felt particularly acutely within himself.

As Tables A and B indicate, Karajan played less new music than he might have done but far more than he is often thought to have done. Though he would probably have agreed with Szell's quip 'I do not believe in the mass grave of an all-contemporary concert', he conducted more contemporary

Table A

Principal works conducted by Karajan 1936–68 which were no more than ten years old.

		1st pf	Karajan
Atterberg	*Älven*	1929	1936
Bartók	Concerto for Orchestra	1945	1951
Berger	*Legende von Prinzen Eugen*	1942	1943
	Homeric Symphony	1948	1948
	Concerto manuale	1951	1951
	Sinfonia parabolica	1956	1957
Blacher	Concertante Music for Orchestra	1937	1940
	Variations on a Theme of Niccolò Paganini	1947	1952
	Orchester-Fantasie	1955	1956
	Musica giocosa	1959	1959
Britten	*War Requiem*	1962	1964
Einem	Concerto for Orchestra	1944	1944
	Piano Concerto	1955	1957
Fortner	Impromptus	1957	1962
Frommel	Suite for small orchestra	1936	1936
Henze	*Sonata per archi*	1958	1959
Höller	Hymn for orch. on Gregorian Choral Melody	1934	1935
	Symphonic fantasy on theme of Frescobaldi	1935	1937
Honegger	Symphony No.3	1946	1955
Leimer	Piano Concerto for the left hand	1948	1953
Martin	Concerto for seven wind instruments	1949	1949
	Etudes	1956	1958
Messiaen	*Réveil des oiseaux*	1953	1959
Nono	*Incontri*	1955	1964
Orff	*Carmina burana*	1937	1941
	Catulli carmina	1943	1953
	Trionfo di Afrodite	1953	1953
Penderecki	*Polymorphia*	1961	1968
Pepping	Partita for orchestra	1934	1936
Pizzetti	*Assassinio nella cattedrale*	1958	1960
Prokofiev	Symphony No.7	1952	1961
	Sinfonia concertante	1952	1961
Ravel	Boléro	1928	1937
Shostakovich	Symphony No.10	1953	1959
R.Strauss	*Divertimento* (after Couperin)	1943	1944
	Friedenstag	1938	1939
	Metamorphosen	1945	1947
Stravinsky	*Canticum sacrum*	1955	1958
Thärichen	Piano Concerto	1961	1961
Trapp	Concerto for Orchestra	1935	1936
Viski	*Enigma*: symphonic poem	1939	1942
Voss	Variations for wind and timpani	1961	1961
Wagner-Régeny	*Die Bürger von Calais*	1939	1939

Table B			
Principal works conducted by Karajan 1936–68 which were no more than twenty years old.			

		1st pf	Karajan
Bartók	Music for Strings, Percussion and Celesta	1936	1948
Britten	Variations on a Theme of Frank Bridge	1937	1952
Casella	*Scarlattiana*	1926	1937
Hindemith	*Mathis der Maler* Symphony	1934	1949
Honegger	Symphony No.2	1941	1953
Kodály	*Psalmus hungaricus*	1923	1936
Matsudaira	Theme and Variations	1939	1954
Pfitzner	*Von deutscher Seele*	1921	1940
Philipp	*Friedensmesse*	1920	1936
Prokofiev	*Peter and the Wolf*	1936	1949
Respighi	*Pines of Rome*	1924	1938
Roussel	Symphony No.4	1935	1949
Sibelius	Symphony No.6	1923	1938
Stravinsky	*Jeu de cartes*	1937	1952
	Symphony in C	1940	1960
Tippett	*A Child of our Time*	1941	1953
Walton	*Belshazzar's Feast*	1931	1948
	Symphony No.1	1935	1954

music than either Szell or Ormandy, more than Böhm (whose experimental phase seems to have ended with Berg and Richard Strauss), more than his two near-contemporaries in Germany, Rudolf Kempe and Joseph Keilberth, and vastly more than Carlo Maria Giulini, whose honest admission that virtually no music written since 1945 held any interest for him has never seriously compromised his reputation as an outstanding exponent of music he does believe in.

Karajan often said that after the age of fifty the actual business of memorising new scores became increasingly difficult. Yet many of his most celebrated recordings of twentieth century music were made between 1965 and 1975 when he was in his late fifites and early sixties. This was partly a matter of lengthy gestation periods, themselves an aid to the learning process. Many of his most famous readings – Berg's *Three Orchestral Pieces*, Honegger's Third Symphony and Shostakovich's Tenth – had undergone quite long periods of gestation, both with the orchestra (the Berlin Philharmonic) and within Karajan's own mind.

But there was another factor that helped give the impression that Karajan was a late convert to twentieth-century music: the natural conservatism of record companies in the 1950s and early 1960s. This was a time when the rapidly expanding musical public was alienated from all but the most approachable new music, when mainstream repertory provided the principal challenges and excitements, and when the music business still exercised strict budgetary prudence.

EMI, and Legge, were remarkably prudent. Karajan frequently proposed repertory which he did not get to record until the heady days of the late 1960s when, in a changing musical climate, Deutsche Grammophon, their coffers awash with the proceeds of a growing number of Karajan best-sellers, could afford to take an intelligent interest in some of his more specialised demands.

Walter Legge did shift his ground in 1962 as part of a last gasp attempt to stop Karajan defecting lock, stock, and barrel to Deutsche Grammophon. Karajan, he reported, should be allowed to record *Le sacre du printemps* 'subject to his convincing himself after a few perform-ances that he can do the piece supremely well'.[9] As for Shostakovich's Eighth Symphony, another Karajan submission, this might be considered a commercial possibility on the ground of its being 'among the best of Shostakovich's later [*sic*] works'. Legge was also prepared to add to the list Prokofiev's Fifth Symphony, which Karajan had performed successfully with the Philharmonia Orchestra; though here it was Karajan who questioned the likely commercial success of such a recording. (An odd judgement. Was he perhaps saving the symphony for the Berliners?)

By the following September, however, the entire list had been thrown out by EMI. One highly placed executive questioned Karajan's suitability as a Shostakovich conductor; others rejected the Eighth Symphony itself as 'too esoteric'. What the repertoire committee really wanted Karajan to record was Rimsky-Korsakov's *Scheherazade*.[10]

After Karajan's death, Gottfried von Einem said of him: 'If he had weaknesses, they were an inclination to jealousy and the fact that he was hungry for power.'[11] I suspect that jealousy was, indeed, a factor in this extraordinary New Year's Eve outburst, though Karajan was less given to jealousy than many of his fellow conductors.

As for power, even as a child Karajan had always wanted to be his own boss. Now, though, he wanted it even more. The struggles in Ulm and Aachen, the setbacks of the later war years, the long drawn out denazification proceedings had all taken their toll. The need to have things his own way as a means of realising a private ideal is suddenly tinged with more than a hint of paranoia. The letter to von Einem ends:

And that is why I am here, because I take on the responsibility of deciding what is going to be played here and now. We will argue in three years' time about mistakes in the programming, whether there was too much consideration given to one side or the other. Their laughter in the press doesn't worry me; they too will sooner or later come to realise where I am going, and then they can feel free to condemn me. These reflections which you oblige me to express have shaped themselves over the past two and a half years. I have thought it over, and I am glad if you want to work with me to reach an ideal. If not, you must join the ranks of the stick-in-the-mud crowd of grousers who have always dogged my steps.

Think about it in the New Year.

Most warmly,

H. v. Karajan

Determination of that order of magnitude, coupled with a new and enhanced level of insecurity, had turned Karajan into a dangerous man to all but his most trusted associates.

*

Having delivered himself of this broadside about Salzburg, Karajan concentrated his attention on a busy round of winter season concerts in Vienna. The mood surrounding these was by now one of excitement bordering on hysteria. For the Vienna Philharmonic concerts on 10 and 11 January Karajan prefaced Tchaikovsky's Fifth Symphony with a concerto by Locatelli and Mozart's Symphony in B flat K319. In the Locatelli he caused something of a stir by choosing to direct from the harpsichord. A slimmed-down string section was used, with front-desk string players Schneiderhan, Sedlak, Morawec, and Brabec as the soloists. The concert caused the critic of *Neues Österreich* to ask the question Ariadne puts to Bacchus in Strauss's opera:

> *Wie schaffst du die Verwandlung? mit den Händen?*
> *Mit deinem Stab?*
> [How do you work the transformation? With your hands?
> With your wand?]

A month later, Brahms's Fourth Symphony was prefaced by two twentieth century works, Vaughan Williams's *Fantasia on a Theme by Thomas Tallis* and Prokofiev's *Classical* Symphony. This time the critic of *Neues Österreich* was hypnotised by Karajan's baton which, he claimed, frequently hung motionless in the air like Parsifal's spear. The review in the *Wiener Zeitung* was written by the doyen of Viennese critics, the composer Joseph Marx. He used the occasion to provide a progress report on Vienna's latest conducting phenomenon:

Herbert von Karajan is proving himself to be 'philharmonic' as well; which is indeed something with an orchestra of this stature. His profile announces his mastery: heightened, concentrated, and charged with all the energy of a strong will and passion which springs more from the head than the heart. It is a tension that is transmitted directly to the public. The result of such emissions of energy is success, if the orchestra wills it. And this orchestra trusts him as it trusts few men; for Karajan is gifted with the indefinable aura of a personality which is itself compelling, interesting, and of such a stature that one can, as it were, anticipate its achievements in advance. If further tangible advantages are added, the man is made. Karajan is also an excellent musician, possesses a superb memory, is a master pianist, and knows how to point up the formal instrumental coherence of a work.[12]

The concert also brought about an innovation; at Karajan's request, music students were admitted to the public *Generalprobe* free of charge.

On 21 February 1948, Karajan made his post-war début with the Vienna Symphony Orchestra, the Vienna Philharmonic's musically more adventurous state-subsidised rival. This was the only concert Karajan gave in Vienna that was not packed out. The programme: Reger's *Mozart Variations*, Sibelius's *Seventh Symphony*, and *Finlandia*. Programming Sibelius in Vienna in 1948 took courage, but promoting the music of Sibelius was just one part of the Karajan game-plan from which he had no intention of being deflected by 'grousers' and 'stick-in-the-muds'.

This was small beer, though, alongside the astonishing Lenten triptych of works Karajan had prepared for Viennese audiences. At the end of February, he conducted a brilliant, blazing account of the Verdi *Requiem* during which he took the unusual step of deploying two sopranos. Ljuba Welitsch sang the main body of the work, then the closing 'Requiem aeternam' was sung by Emmy Loose, radiant in a far-away gallery. (Was this one of Vieri Freccia's ideas?) This was followed three weeks later by a Palm Sunday performance with the Vienna Philharmonic of Act 3 of *Parsifal*; a long-breathed, luminously beautiful reading that was no doubt calculated to remind the management of the Vienna State Opera precisely what it was that they were missing by keeping Karajan at bay. Finally, on Good Friday and Easter Saturday came the season's *pièce de résistance*, Vienna's first complete performance since the time of Schalk of Bach's *St Matthew Passion*. The performance, in two parts, lasted well over four hours. Julius Patzak sang the Evangelist with a first-rate team of supporting soloists: Paul Schöffler (exchanging Amfortas for Christ), Irmgard Seefried, Elisabeth Höngen, Anton Dermota, and Ferdinand Frantz. To judge from a nearly contemporary (1950) off-air recording, Karajan's reading was both grand and dramatic. 'Michelangelesque in its monumentality' is how one American critic has described it, a reading that borders on the excessive but never quite crosses the line 'into the maudlin or the self-indulgent'.[13] A Viennese newspaper spoke of Karajan conjuring from the work a mood akin to 'the fervent mysticism of a Bruckner *Adagio*'.[14] Nowadays that would be a condemnation; then it was praise indeed.

CHAPTER 25

London

Mr Karajan favours the new German technique of marking the
strong beat by an upward movement, like a woman shooing
hens in a farmyard. But apart from these risky idiosyncrasies,
his interpretations are musical in a high degree of concentration.
The Times, London, 13 April 1948

London was a welcoming place. The luxury of fish and chips in Floral Street
was what Sena Jurinac remembered from her visit to Covent Garden with
the Vienna State Opera company in the autumn of 1947; that, and the
absence of road blocks and Russian soldiers on the streets. Karajan was
struck by how orderly the place looked in comparison with Vienna or the
bombed out lunar wastes of central Berlin.

He had come to London to conduct Walter Legge's Philharmonia Orchestra at a concert in the Royal Albert Hall: Strauss's *Don Juan*, the Schumann
Piano Concerto with Dinu Lipatti as soloist, and Beethoven's Fifth Symphony. There were also recording sessions for the Schumann Concerto in
EMI's Abbey Road studios on the two days immediately preceding the
concert on 11 April.

Recording first, concerts later: Karajan preferred it that way round.
Though he is often thought of as a recording animal, he used recordings
much as older conductors such as Klemperer did, as generously funded
rehearsals for live performances, for the 'real thing'. Where Karajan would
differ from his predecessors, turning an old-fashioned preference into a
newfangled game, was in the manner of his implementation of the strategy,
and the scale.

If London was welcoming, so was the orchestra and, in large measure,
the press. The leader of the Philharmonia, Leonard Hirsch, an ex-Hallé
player, Dublin-born, was telephoned by the *Jewish Chronicle* to ask if he
really intended to lead 'for that man'. The orchestra itself, though, showed
no obvious political animosity towards Karajan. 'Where he had been in the
war never really crossed our minds,' recalled flute-player Gareth Morris.

During these first sessions in 1948 Karajan was more grim-faced and
unbending than he would later be; but no one complained, largely because
here was no twopenny-halfpenny autocrat. Rather, the Philharmonia found
themselves in the presence of a courteous, quiet-spoken, quick-witted
musician whose command of English – a tendency to confuse 'fingerboard'
with 'fingerbowl' apart – was a considerable advance on that of many a

rival foreign maestro. Hugh Bean, who led the Philharmonia during the later years of Karajan's time with the orchestra, has said:

There is a very subtle aspect to the relationship between a conductor and an orchestra. We can tell if we are sitting as an assembled orchestra when a conductor takes one step towards us whether he is on the side of the players, whether he associates himself with us or not. We don't even need him to reach the podium and say 'Good morning'. We can tell. It's something in the manner. Beecham had this quality, supremely, as did Boult and Barbirolli. Sargent not at all. And Karajan's manner? Well, it was very pleasant. It's a stupid word, I know, but it's true. He was very pleasant. For all his celebrity and charisma, when he walked out, we felt he was one of us.[1]

A member of the Philharmonia Orchestra, a trombonist, remembers rehearsing Strauss's *Don Juan* under Karajan. It is an undated reminiscence and probably relates to a later concert, in 1952 or 1953.

I've always respected von Karajan, simply because he treated you man to man. The first time I played with him we were doing *Don Juan*. I was a new face in the orchestra, very inexperienced, I'd never played the piece, though I'd studied it and practised my part. Well, in the beginning the strings sweep up, then there are the basses and the bass trombone, which has the phrase on the beat, and it has to be there. Von Karajan made some loose, ethereal movement which the strings understood and the first fiddle led them up the sweep. But I couldn't feel or see a downbeat at all – he just had his arms in the air, he wasn't going to beat like a bandmaster – and I missed the entry. I think most conductors would have stopped and made a song and dance. Von Karajan simply looked over, as if to say, 'I know my job, I hope you know yours. I won't say anything now, but when we come to the recapitulation you'll know what I am doing, and we'll see what you do.' When the recapitulation came, of course, I was ready and played it. He just glanced over again, as if to say OK, but not a word was spoken. Von Karajan was fine. Well, he was a real man, a real general man, he drove fast cars and flew an aeroplane as well as being a fine musician. I could get on with a man like that.[2]

The players also liked Karajan because he did not waste their time. At the final rehearsal for the Royal Albert Hall concert, he spent just eight minutes on Beethoven's Fifth Symphony. He simply asked the orchestra to play the symphony's final climax with as much volume as they could muster consistent with a balanced and fully rounded tone. All he wanted to know was what to expect on the night, what the dynamic parameters would be.[3]

The Times did not mention the Fifth Symphony in its notice two days later. With newsprint still a scarce commodity, reviews were subject to more than usually savage treatment by hard-pressed sub-editors. The anonymous critic did, however, say that he considered the newcomer to be 'a conductor of distinction' and thought well of his technique, despite a near-calamitous lapse in *Don Juan* when a loose movement of the left hand brought the strings in while the winds were still waiting for the stick.

The reception accorded Karajan by *The Times* was in marked contrast to the savaging poor Furtwängler had been given after a concert with the London Philharmonic Orchestra the previous month. Criticism is as subject to fads and fashions as anything else, and London in the late 1940s was in hock to what might crudely be called the Toscanini school of performance. Furtwängler's concert on 14 March had ended with the *Tannhäuser* overture. *The Times* wrote:

It was quite a surprise to hear the pilgrims returning in the *Tannhäuser* Overture, for it seemed most unlikely when they set out that they would ever reach Rome. Perhaps they turned back half-way.[4]

Worse was to follow in the autumn when Furtwängler arrived in London to conduct a Beethoven cycle with the Vienna Philharmonic. For *The Times*, the cycle was very *déjà entendu*. Furtwängler's account of the Fifth Symphony, it alleged, lacked 'masculine grandeur' and that 'accumulation of power [that is] derived from an irresistible ground-rhythm'. True, the erratic beat was a kind of 'sporting curiosity', but would it not have been wiser, *The Times* asked, to have engaged Josef Krips for the tour rather than Furtwängler?[5] None of this helped Legge, or, indeed, Karajan.

If Karajan's reading of Beethoven's Fifth Symphony was thought to be fierier than Furtwängler's, then recorded evidence from the time would suggest that this was to some extent an illusion.[6] The Toscanini-ites did, however, have more reason to claim Karajan as one of their own in the case of the Schumann concerto.

Lipatti had first studied the work in 1945. He had been flattered by Legge's invitation to record it, and was gratified to learn that the conductor would be Karajan. At the same time, he was apprehensive. He loved the concerto, but did the concerto love him?[7] Was he ready to record it, let alone play it in public for the first time? The recording confirms that he was. Lipatti was surprised, however, by Karajan's contribution:

Alas! I did not count on an unexpected factor, a remarkable but superclassical conductor who, instead of helping my timid romantic *élans*, put a brake on my good intentions.[8]

Clearly, Lipatti wanted a little more room for expressive manoeuvrings, more time to drift and dream, as he does in his charmed yet vital account of the first-movement cadenza. Karajan's accompaniment is, indeed, very brilliant, and in the last two movements closely controlled rhythmically. Too brilliant, too closely controlled, thought *The Gramophone*'s Lionel Salter, 'What Clara Schumann would have thought, I shudder to think.'[9] Yet it is arguable that the sense we have of the concerto being played along a knife-edge is what helps give the performance its enduring freshness. It is was, however, a warning of things to come; over the years Karajan would have some famous tussles with pianists of all ages and persuasions.[10]

*

The day after the Royal Albert Hall concert, Legge and Karajan held an inquest on Legge's progress with the Philharmonia so far. According to Legge,[11] they concluded that the wind and percussion players were as fine as, in most cases finer than, any in Europe. The strings, by contrast, were thought to be too light-bodied, too anaemic-sounding. As a report, this does not ring entirely true. The famous array of solo winds Legge was eventually to recruit – Gareth Morris, Sidney Sutcliffe, Bernard Walton, Cecil James, Dennis Brain, Legge's so-called 'royal flush' – was not yet finally in place. In particular, there were problems with the first oboe, as the recording of the Schumann concerto readily reveals. Alec Whittaker was a wonderful player with a slender, plaintively beautiful tone not unlike the Vienna Philharmonic's preferred oboe sound. It was, however, based on procedures that were technically perilous. Whittaker rarely came to grief in the concert hall, but on an off day he could easily destabilise a recording session.

If Legge's memoirs are to be believed, he had no plans at the time to involve Karajan permanently with the Philharmonia. One of his criteria was that there should be no permanent conductor. The Philharmonia was to have *style*, not *a* style reflected through the personality of a single man. Yet it must have been apparent to him from Karajan's very first day with the orchestra that the two were supremely well suited, not only to one another, but to the whole business of recording. For Legge, clarity of sound and poise of utterance were primary requirements, not least because such playing is microphone-friendly. His aim was to create a concert and recording orchestra on a par with Beecham's pre-war London Philharmonic or the BBC Symphony Orchestra, which in its first flush of youth in the 1930s had made many memorable recordings under conductors as different as Elgar, Boult, Walter, and Toscanini. For this reason, there could be no 'passengers' among the players. Nothing muddies recorded sound more readily than poor intonation and imprecise ensemble.

But how practical was Legge's idea of developing the orchestra's 'style' via the good offices of a semi-permanent roster of leading conductors? Sir Thomas Beecham, who had conducted the Philharmonia's first public concert for the price of 'a decent cigar', thought nothing of the idea. He was currently engaged in setting up another new orchestra of his own, the

Royal Philharmonic; an orchestra, he told Legge, that would be launched under 'the most auspicious circumstances of glamour and *éclat*'.

Karajan was as keen a student of Beecham as Legge. He admired Beecham's musicianship, entrepreneurial flair, and caustic wit. (Even the famous remark about Karajan being 'a kind of musical Malcolm Sargent'; more a gibe at Sargent than a put-down of Karajan, though it was that, too). Above all, he envied Beecham his private means, which conferred artistic freedom, enabling him to pursue new projects with 'glamour and *éclat*'.

For the time being, Legge lacked the financial resources to tie Karajan more closely into his plans for the Philharmonia; yet there was a kind of *égotisme à deux* binding the two men together. With so many fields to be conquered, so many prizes to be won, where were the best moves to be made? There was Milan, not yet part of Legge's EMI territory, but already one of Karajan's stamping-grounds thanks to his friendship with De Sabata. Within a year or two Bayreuth would be reopening. There was even talk of Karajan appearing at the Royal Opera House, Covent Garden; though it was only talk. Having seen off Beecham in 1945 and declined to offer Legge the post of General Administrator, the Covent Garden board – on which Legge would later serve, intimidating administrator David Webster with peacock displays of wit and wisdom on all things operatic – was disinclined to allow a Trojan horse into the house. No doubt Legge made out a good case for Karajan, and for De Sabata whose name was also put forward at the time. But the board was conscious of music director Karl Rankl's 'sensitivity' to visiting stars and Karajan's nomination was particularly strenuously opposed by Sir Steuart Wilson, an influential and omnipresent figure in English musical life at the time, who expressed doubts about Karajan's 'standing' and 'ability'.[12]

There were also films to be considered, a medium in which Karajan was already taking a precocious interest. In April 1948 Egon Hilbert struck a deal with Sir Alexander Korda's London Film Production Ltd. There was talk of a film version of the Vienna–Salzburg production of Mozart's *Le nozze di Figaro*. Legge reported excitedly on the possibility of Karajan's involvement as conductor. Delay followed delay. Eventually, the devaluation of the pound in the autumn of 1949 put paid to the project, making it impractical financially.

By contrast, contacts Legge and Karajan had in Rome in the spring of 1948 with the Paramount-backed film director Franz Marischka did bear fruit. Marischka was proposing to make a film of Bach's *St Matthew Passion*. It was something he had promised his only daughter, who had recently died. It was to be his memorial to her. Marischka's plan was to use excerpts from Bach's music, a narrative spoken by the actor Raoul Aslan (one of Reinhardt's protégés), and a collage of images, often surrealistically juxtaposed, drawn from famous paintings of the Passion story. Karajan was asked to conduct the music. 'He is the greatest conductor in Central Europe today,' Marischka told actor and freelance film producer André von Mattoni. 'Please find him, negotiate with him, and bring me back a contract with his name on it.' Mattoni duly obliged. A deal was struck and work began in December 1948, with Karajan's old friend from Aachen, Walter Ludwig, singing the role of the Evangelist.

Karajan had been in Rome to conduct the Santa Cecilia Orchestra, the nominal successor of Rome's famous Augusteo Orchestra which Bernardino Molinari, a frock-coated disciplinarian of the old school, had turned into one of Europe's finest orchestras.[13] Leonard Bernstein also conducted the orchestra that year, on his way back from concerts in war-torn Israel. From Rome, Karajan travelled back to complete the 1947–8 season of concerts with the Vienna Philharmonic. The success of two concerts he had given in April with the young violinist Ginette Neveu – Karajan relishing the long lines of Neveu's performance of the Beethoven concerto – had been a further feather in his cap; and he had been praised, too, for the vital and romantically nuanced reading of Schumann's Fourth Symphony with which the concert had ended: 'dashing, chivalrous [ritterlich], and tender' as one writer put it.[14]

If Beethoven-with-Schumann was meat and drink to the Philharmonic subscribers, the combination of Bartók and Schubert certainly was not. Though Bartók's music had been tolerated by the Third Reich as a sop to the Hungarians, and though the Music for Strings, Percussion, and Celesta was in the repertory of a number of German orchestras, there were enough unreconstituted right-wingers in the Musikverein audience on 8 May for the concert to be interrupted by catcalls and fisticuffs. Still, it is an ill wind that blows no one any good. The rumpus in the Musikverein delighted the adventurous young manager of the Vienna Konzerthaus, Egon Seefehlner.

It is typical of post-war Vienna that Karajan and Seefehlner first met when Karajan heard that he was the man to go to if you needed under-the-counter rail tickets. Seefehlner's father was Generaldirektor of Austrian Railways. Unlike a lot of people, Seefehlner was quick to see that Karajan was shy rather than arrogant, hard-working rather than bumptious. He knew, as he put it, that they were never going to be 'chums'; but he fancied he could work with Karajan. It was a trust Karajan would repay handsomely down the years.

Hearing of the enormous success Bernstein had recently had in Budapest with the Bartók Music for Strings, Percussion, and Celesta, Seefehlner asked him to conduct the work in Vienna with the Vienna Symphony. It was an excellent idea, and a nice piece of gamesmanship setting these two stars-in-waiting alongside one another. Unfortunately, it did not work out. Bernstein, who had barely heard of the man he later noted down as 'Karryan', was less interested in Vienna's phoney conductors' wars than in the fact that the Vienna Symphony was dispirited and hostile. It was a bitter disappointment to both Seefehlner and Bernstein that Bernstein's typically bold plan to treat the Viennese to a first hearing of his *Jeremiah* Symphony had to be abandoned as well.

Seefehlner and Karajan had greater success with an all-contemporary concert on 12 and 13 June 1948. It consisted of a colourful new dance-symphony, the *Homeric*, by the Austrian composer Theodor Berger (one of Karajan's colleagues from his student days at the Hochschule für Musik), and the work Karajan had described in that earlier letter to Wilhelm Pitz as 'the best choral music that's been written in the last fifty years', William Walton's *Belshazzar's Feast*. To judge from the newspaper reviews, Karajan conducted it with unusual fire and ferocity.

Many years later, when the once amicable relationship between Walton and Karajan had fallen into disrepair, Walton railed against Karajan for his subsequent neglect of the piece, claiming the only reason he had conducted it in the first place was to impress the British army in Vienna. That was clearly not the case. Walter Legge probably hit upon the true explanation. His EMI colleague Suvi Raj Grubb remembers him remarking:

It was Karajan's view that even if he gave the finest imaginable performance of a piece of English music, the critics would say, 'Very good . . . BUT . . .'[15]

If that was indeed what Karajan believed, it was a somewhat defeatist position to adopt. In reality, nothing pleases the English more than the sight and sound of a leading foreign conductor taking up a greatly loved local masterwork, as Karajan himself discovered when Imogen Holst declared his 1961 Vienna Philharmonic recording of *The Planets* to be the finest account of her father's much-played masterpiece she had ever encountered.

CHAPTER 26

A tale of two Berlins

I cannot guarantee that even a firm and resolute course will ward off the dangers which now threaten us; but I am sure that such a course is not merely the best but the only chance of preventing a third war in which the most fearful agencies of destruction yet known to man will be used to the fullest extent.

Winston Churchill, 26 June 1948

On 24 June 1948 the Soviet Military Governor in Berlin Marshal Sokolovsky declared that Four-Power *Komendatura* in Berlin was 'to all intents and purposes' null and void. Road and rail traffic along the Berlin corridor into the city's western-controlled zones, which the Soviets had been disrupting since March, had finally been brought to a complete standstill a week earlier. The Soviets, it now seemed, were intent on enforcing a total blockade of the city, a *de facto* annexation. Allied currency reforms aimed at stamping out black-marketeers was the immediate pretext for the dispute, but the causes ran far deeper. Nor was the problem simply confined to Berlin. If Berlin fell it could only be a matter of time before Vienna, which was also under four-power control, followed. Political instability in Italy, France, and Yugoslavia only added to the dangers. For a time, it seemed as if the nightmare was about to begin all over again.

*

Karajan first met the distinguished British philosopher Isaiah Berlin in Salzburg a few weeks later, during the 1948 festival. Berlin had first visited the festival in 1929 while an undergraduate at Oxford and had returned regularly during that period before the *Anschluss* which legend would have us believe was Salzburg's true golden age.[1] A fellowship at All Souls, a university lectureship in philosophy, a book on Marx, and wartime service in New York on behalf of Britain's Ministry of Information had all helped add lustre to Berlin's name but none had brought him much material success. Had it not been for a welcome commission to write about the Salzburg Festival for London's most venerable Sunday newspaper *The Observer*, he would almost certainly not have been in Salzburg in 1948.

Not that it was all that wonderful a place to be. To anyone who remembered the pre-war festival, Salzburg seemed grey and jaded. The revival of confidence in German culture that would be so evident a feature of the reopening of the Bayreuth Festival in 1951 had yet to manifest itself. In 1948, the Americans ran Salzburg amid a mood of simmering resentment that the Allies had taken so long to regularise the affairs of those leading artists on whom the festival depended. Festival events were sparsely attended, there were few foreign visitors, and the pre-war mood of festive pizzazz was almost entirely absent. Confined to barracks by draconian foreign exchange controls, the British, too, were largely absent, though the egregious G. Ward Price, the *Daily Mail*'s monocle-wearing foreign correspondent whom Hitler had so admired, was still very much in evidence.

Isaiah Berlin reviewed two Karajan concerts, both, in their different ways, politically and emotionally charged. The concert on 18 August included Haydn's Symphony No.104, Richard Strauss's *Metamorphosen*, and Beethoven's Fifth Symphony. Four days later, Karajan led a Sunday-morning performance of Brahms's *German Requiem*, with Schwarzkopf and Paul Schöffler as the soloists.

Berlin also met the Karajans socially, Anita, pushy and vivacious as ever. Karajan he found 'not interesting in any way' as a conversationalist. But, then, the conversation appears to have been largely confined to immediate practicalities. He asked Karajan whether he intended to stay in Austria or move away and develop a career elsewhere in Europe.

'Neither,' retorted Karajan. 'I plan to go to South America.'

Now South America was not entirely beyond the pale musically. It boasted several front-rank opera houses and was occasionally visited by leading European orchestras. Furtwängler had only recently returned from a month's tour of Argentina.

Berlin was none the less baffled by Karajan's statement and pressed him further.

'It is quite simple,' said Karajan. 'There is going to be another war in Europe. And on this occasion I intend to be elsewhere.'

'Of course, he didn't go to South America,' Sir Isaiah told me, many years later, as we took tea in the Athenaeum.

'Well, with respect, he did,' I felt bound to interject. 'He went with Anita the following year. There had been talk of Legge taking the Philharmonia, of Karajan backing out, to Legge's predictable fury, and his trying to fix up a tour with the Vienna Philharmonic. In the end, he simply signed himself up for a series of concerts with local orchestras in Cuba, Argentina, and Chile. He didn't stay, of course. But he probably did genuinely think there was going to be another war.'

*

The review Isaiah Berlin wrote for *The Observer* is a masterpiece of conscious equivocation. There are aspects of it that make it almost as antagonistic as Hajas's account of the 1947 Beethoven Ninth. But Berlin was the subtler writer:

The most arresting and influential of the new personalities in Salzburg this year was without doubt the conductor of the Vienna Philharmonic, Herbert von Karajan. Greatly praised and hotly attacked, he has been hailed as a new Toscanini, as the greatest hope of Austrian art, and assailed as an irresistibly clever manipulator without heart or scruple, a cold self-infatuated monomaniac guilty of arresting the vital flow of the music with unexpected dams calculated to force a vulgar but spectacular artificial tension. At any rate, no critic has failed to react violently one way or another, which in itself is a sign of a powerful and disturbing new personality at work. And, indeed, there is something here to discuss: for Herr Karajan is clearly a man of prodigious gifts and may well cause a great stir in the musical world. An Austrian, he does not belong to the Viennese tradition, and is equally remote from the classical purity, the luminous refinement of Schalk, and from the tender lyrical melancholy, the poetry and elegiac sweetness of Walter.

Herbert von Karajan is a child of our time, a deliberate and ruthless planner with a very uncommon power of concentration, organisation and execution. He is in iron control of himself and his orchestra; imposes his personality on the players and the audience and in some degree hypnotises both. Since the Vienna Philharmonic is to-day the equal of any body of players in the world, it responds to Karajan's smooth, sharp, microscopically minute demands with astonishing precision and beauty.

Karajan seems to conceive music as a series of self-contained episodes, and these he articulates one by one with a clarity of detail and a strictly calculated imperious organisation of tempi and dynamics which moves with the remorseless accuracy of a dive-bomber intent upon its prey. His interpretations must inevitably shock and repel those who take for granted more traditional methods, but even those who feel lack of sympathy, or even indignation – as, for example, with his treatment of the slow movement of Beethoven's C minor Symphony as if it had been written by Mahler, or its opening movement as if the composer were Berlioz – cannot deny that a very formidable figure has appeared in the world of musical performance.

If Herr Karajan's style is at times over-rhetorical, it also rises to a vast and magnificent eloquence unattainable to the orthodox interpreters; his truest triumph was his performance of the Brahms Requiem: this is a work of considerable *longueurs* which needs a powerful hand if it is to be kept from sagging; Toscanini, for example, tends to desiccate it altogether. Under Karajan the Viennese played and sang with such noble dignity, and Mme Schwarzkopf sang with such purity and sweetness as to transfigure the work and give it, for the moment, new dimensions. After this triumph the greatest ovations accorded to this conductor in Vienna and Salzburg seemed justified; and yet he does not always remain upon this pedestal, his penchant for deliquescence, for the *pourriture ignoble* of bad Strauss is very strong – sometimes he seems to address the music as someone once said of Kerensky's speeches, not to the head nor to the heart but to the nerves. But be it addressed to what it may, the skill, the audacity, will-power and originality of Herr Karajan are most exceptional and make him the most interesting among the younger conductors of our time.[2]

Karajan was so thrilled by this review that he became a perfect pest, bombarding Berlin with invitations for years to come. The invitations were rarely taken up, though there were occasions when the offers were simply too tempting. 'For Lipatti's last concert in Lucerne,' Sir Isaiah recalled, 'Anita insisted on providing me with tickets. I was virtually on the stage.'[3]

Was Karajan impervious to even the most blatant ironies of the review, the image of the dive-bomber, for example, which Berlin had originally thought to name (a Messerschmitt or some such machine) but subsequently thought better of? Or was he simply flattered to be praised, albeit equivocally, by a British Jewish intellectual operating from beyond the bounds of run-of-the-mill music criticism?

Three months after the Salzburg performance, Karajan recorded the Fifth Symphony with the Vienna Philharmonic for EMI. There the slow movement is indeed unduly protracted and there is evidence in the finale of unnecessary tempo changes, what Berlin calls 'unexpected dams calculated to force a vulgar but spectacular artificial tension'. The first movement, by contrast, is about as perfectly judged a performance as you could wish to hear, not at all like Berlioz. At around this time, only Klemperer and Erich Kleiber would come up with performances of comparable quality on record.

*

It is inevitable that Isaiah Berlin had problems with Strauss's *Metamorphosen*. This musical lament for war-devastated Germany, played out in music of maudlin loveliness, struck many as being something close to an obscenity, though Strauss was doing no more than express what others had felt in similar circumstances.[4] Berlin himself had lost both his grandfathers, an uncle, an aunt, and three cousins to the Nazis in Riga in 1941. He had also experienced the curious and unexpected feeling of guilt by association, or rather disassociation: the guilt of the helpless bystander. He would tell the philosopher Ramin Jahanbegloo:

Even by 1943–4 I realized that the Nazis wanted to kill Jews even more than they wanted to win the war – the killing went on steadily when Germany was plainly heading for defeat in 1945. But, as I said before, I only discovered the full horror of the holocaust very late. I do not know why nobody ever told me – perhaps life in an embassy was too protected. Still, I met prominent American Jews from time to time, and nobody ever told me about this. I still feel some guilt about it, even though it was not really any fault of mine.[5]

But, then, nor was the Nazi genocide in any direct sense the fault of

Richard Strauss. A philosopher's guilt and a composer's despair are here joint manifestations of the wider evil of a world war that destroyed the lives of millions of innocent people of all ages, persuasions, nationalities, creeds, and colours.

By and large, time has looked kindly on *Metamorphosen*. The truth about its stature probably lies somewhere between Strauss scholar Norman Del Mar's belief that this is 'his true and greatest memorial work'[6] and Klemperer's sardonic 'basically quite nice'. Certainly, it could not have received a more deeply felt yet at the same time gracious and calmly collected performance than the one recorded by Karajan and the strings of the Vienna Philharmonic in October 1947.

*

Karajan conducted two operas at the 1948 festival, a new production of Gluck's *Orpheus und Eurydike* designed by Caspar Neher and produced by Oscar Fritz Schuh, and a revised version of Schuh's production of *Le nozze di Figaro* which Karajan had prepared and partly conducted in 1946 from his illicit hideaway in the prompt-box. This time he was in the pit; Schwarzkopf had taken over the role of the Countess, Giuseppe Taddei sang Figaro, Sena Jurinac was the new Cherubino.

It was, however, the production of *Orpheus und Eurydike* that made the deepest impression.[7] The influential local critic and politician Viktor Reimann declared it to be the most 'finished' production of the 1948 festival. It was also the most experimental, since this was the first time an opera had been staged in the Felsenreitschule, the theatre Reinhardt had used so effectively for some of his later stage productions.

Not all operas go well there, but Gluck's classical masterpiece was suited to it dramatically and musically. (With a little help from Berlioz; Karajan used a foreshortened version of the post-Berlioz Milan edition of 1889.) Former critic and Austrian Radio producer Gottfried Kraus has recalled:

It required only some minor adaptation of the arcades hewn in the rock to create the ideal setting for the timeless myth . . . No one who saw the production could resist the imaginative power exerted by the singing of Orpheus as he climbed down through the arcades to Hades, or the widening of the starry sky and the soft sound of Salzburg church bells as he arrived in the Elysian fields.[8]

The mood of the opera is predominantly slow and meditative, and it is this, its status as classical rite, on which Schuh, Neher, and Karajan appear to have concentrated. Film footage of the production shows Karajan as a slight, gaunt-faced figure wafting the music into life as though in a trance, the motions of the baton as gentle as the beat of a bird's wing.

And the chorus too, all in white, executes its own quiet wafting dance, much as choruses used to do in English revivals of Greek drama at the turn of the century and later, under Rutland Boughton's inspired direction, at the Glastonbury Festivals of the 1920s. If the 1948 Salzburg *Orpheus und Eurydike* was, in this sense, rather old-fashioned, it was also a reconsecration of old Salzburg vows.

Furtwängler appeared briefly at the 1948 festival, conducting a concert, and three performances of *Fidelio*. During the festival, Walter Legge tried to broker a peace between Karajan and Furtwängler by inviting the two men and their wives to a private dinner at the Hotel Kasererbräu where the Furtwänglers were staying. One has to ask whether Legge was the best person to undertake so delicate a mission; but it was a perfectly pleasant evening, helped along at the outset, Elisabeth Furtwängler recalls, by Karajan seeking the great man's advice on how best to determine the tempo for the slow movement of Beethoven's Seventh Symphony. Pure shop, but meat and drink to Furtwängler who seems to be have been strangely flattered by the idea that 'K' should want advice from him on anything.

Next day, according to Legge, the worm turned. Furtwängler summoned Hilbert 'and dictated a contract undertaking to conduct every year at Salzburg on the condition that Karajan should be excluded from Salzburg as long as Furtwängler lived'.[9]

Though Furtwängler did no doubt make some such demand, Karajan's exclusion from Salzburg during the final years of Furtwängler's life was not entirely of Furtwängler's making. During the summer and autumn of 1948 Karajan was already busily digging his own grave with the Salzburg management. Emboldened by his crowd-pulling power and his burgeoning reputation as a 'genius' (Reimann) and 'the most interesting among the younger conductors of our time' (Berlin), he began to bombard the management with sky-high demands which they could not begin to meet.

The dispute with von Einem over new operas at Salzburg became ever more acrimonious. Karajan threatened to boycott the 1949 festival if the proposed première of Carl Orff's *Antigone* went ahead in the Felsenreitschule; von Einem is said to have retaliated by filing adverse reviews of Karajan concerts with the festival directorate. Equally astonishing was Karajan's attempt to usurp Schuh as the stage director of the proposed new production of *Die Zauberflöte*. Karajan's work with Gründgens in Berlin before the war and his memories of the controversial Graf–Toscanini Salzburg *Zauberflöte* had clearly whetted his appetite for a show of his own. But Schuh was not to be moved; nor, indeed, was Furtwängler, who had put in his own bid to conduct the new production.

In the end, Karajan got nothing in 1949 except the two concerts he had already been promised. *Antigone* went ahead, as did the memorable Schuh–Furtwängler *Zauberflöte*. Josef Krips took over *Orpheus und Eurydike*, and George Szell was invited to make his Salzburg début conducting the other production Karajan had been eyeing, a revival of the old pre-war Wallerstein staging of *Der Rosenkavalier*.

At the time, Karajan barely knew who Szell was. 'A man from over the ocean,' he announced to Anita, somewhat airily.

CHAPTER 27

Furtwängler: showdown in Chicago

I have never encountered a more brazen attitude than that of three
or four ringleaders in the frantic and obvious efforts to exclude an
illustrious colleague from their happy hunting grounds.
Yehudi Menuhin, *New York Times*, 6 January 1949

'Over the ocean', as Karajan quaintly put it, another drama was unfolding
in the late summer of 1948, which lowered Furtwängler's morale and
intensified that mood of inner despair, brought on mainly by growing
deafness, which led to his unexpected death in 1954 at the relatively
early age of sixty-eight. The story is extensively documented in Daniel
Gillis's admirable monograph *Furtwängler in America*. The salient points
do, however, bear repetition because of the light they throw on Karajan's
own subsequent relationships with the American public, both privately and
as Furtwängler's successor as chief conductor of the Berlin Philharmonic.

On 10 August Furtwängler received a cable from Dr Eric Oldberg, Vice-
President of the Board of Directors of the Chicago Orchestral Association,
informing him that he was being considered for the position of General
Music Director of the Chicago Symphony Orchestra. Furtwängler ignored
the first cable but responded to a second, noting that his European schedules
for 1949–50 had yet to be settled and pointing out that, to the best of his
knowledge, there had been no diminution of 'the calumnies and difficulties
of a political nature' that had dogged his reputation in the United States
since the mid-1930s.

Though never the most decisive of men, Furtwängler's instinct was
to refuse the Chicago offer, which he did, despite a flurry of cabled
reassurances from Chicago and the personal appearance in Hamburg on
18 October 1948 of the board's special emissary George A. Kuyper.

Kuyper made no real headway; but when news of the negotiations
appeared in a brief report in the *Chicago Tribune*, the absence of hostile
public reaction emboldened him to continue the negotiation. 'I am more
than ever certain,' he wrote to Furtwängler on 10 November, 'that the
political campaign – about which you expressed some fears – will *never*
develop.'[1]

Furtwängler continued to set his face against accepting the position of
General Music Director but, against his better judgement, agreed by way of
compromise to an eight-week Chicago season at a time yet to be determined.
That was on 14 December 1948. The next communication Furtwängler
received from Chicago was a death threat:

Your appearance in the United States and particularly in Chicago is emphatically unwelcome. The climate in Chicago – a very famous city – would surely be intolerable to your health and would lead to fatal injury – against which Ryerson, Kuyper, Aaron etc. probably cannot give you guaranteed protection. Consider this warning carefully. It is the only one.[2]

A few days later, a further threat, signed by a certain Israel Stone, was sent to Furtwängler via the Vienna Philharmonic.

This, though, was small beer in comparison with the shock that was about to be administered by the Chicago Symphony Orchestra itself. Three important guest conductors had threatened to cancel if Furtwängler appeared with the orchestra. With this in mind, Kuyper cabled Furtwängler on 28 December, suggesting in a roundabout sort of way that their agreement was a mistake and should perhaps be quietly abandoned.

Furtwängler was flabbergasted. His reply was unflinching, though in its suggested solution, characteristically half-hearted and impractical:

Silent withdrawal on my part would be synonymous with confession of guilt before the whole public. Therefore withdrawal impossible for me if not first given sufficient opportunity to vindicate myself.[3]

By now, the whole sorry mess was turning into a national scandal. On 6 January 1949, the New York Times flagged the start of what was beginning to look suspiciously like a witch-hunt with a long article by Howard Taubman headed 'Musicians' ban on Furtwängler ends his Chicago contract for '49'. We now know that the campaign was masterminded by Furtwängler's old adversary from pre-war days Ira A. Hirschmann and the impresario Sol Hurok whose obsessive lobbying of Bruno Walter in the anti-Furtwängler cause eventually led Walter (no friend of Furtwängler) to sever all relations with Hurok. Also implicated was the all-powerful Toscanini lobby, raining down sniper fire from the moral high ground. Here, too, old scores were being settled, some of them by another long-standing Furtwängler antagonist, Toscanini's son-in-law Vladimir Horowitz.

Apart from Bruno Walter, only Yehudi Menuhin, among musicians of consequence, stood four-square in Furtwängler's defence. As a result, Menuhin, too, became the object of abuse. After a virulent attack late in 1949 in New York's Yiddish-language daily paper Der Tag, Menuhin's father Moshe advised the columnist in question 'to consult a good psychiatrist'. Quoting Old Testament scripture, he added: 'Oh, how shall I curse whom God hath not cursed?'

*

Lobbying and orderly public protest are a legitimate part of the democratic process. What was, and to some extent remains, so distressing about the attacks on Furtwängler – other than the lynch-mob atmosphere which they generated – is the way in which *ad hominem* criticisms were muddled up with a wider and deeper craving for some kind of retributive justice. Rabbi Morton Berman, President of the Chicago Division of the American Jewish Congress, characterised the problem with blunt honesty in a statement he issued on 14 January 1949:

With reference to Furtwängler's claim that he had helped individual Jews, it was my experience in Germany last summer, in listening to those who were being tried in Nuremberg, that every Nazi seeks to make the same claim. The token saving of a few Jewish lives does not excuse Mr Furtwängler from official, active participation in a regime which murdered six million Jews and millions of non-Jews. Furtwängler is a symbol of all those hateful things for the defeat of which the youth of our city and nation paid an ineffable price.[4]

Furtwängler was, indeed, being treated as 'a symbol of all those hateful things' Nazism embodied. Which is precisely where the injustice lay. To be described as the token living embodiment of one of the most evil tyrannies the world has ever known is not only manifestly unjust; it imposes on the chosen individual a burden of blame no man could reasonably be expected to bear.

The need to remember had become embroiled with the age-old instinct for revenge. 'If thou didst ever thy dear father love,' says the Ghost in *Hamlet*, 'Revenge his foul and most unnatural murder.' To which Hamlet replies:

> Haste me to know't, that I, with wings as swift
> As meditation or the thoughts of love,
> May sweep to my revenge.

It was the great American teacher Harold C. Goddard who noted: 'Wings, meditation, love: what inappropriate equipment for a deed of blood! As so often in Shakespeare, the metaphors undo the logic and tell the truth over its head.'[5] Goddard is right. Acts of remembrance which breed new terror is what the tragedy of *Hamlet* is all about.

By 1949, those who had masterminded the Nazis' genocidal policies, and a significant number of those who had implemented them, had been tried by due process of law at Nuremberg and executed. Others were in prison. Others would be hunted down and brought to justice. Furtwängler's case was not of this order. Inasmuch as he had transgressed politically, he had been interrogated, tried, and brought to book by the appropriate legally constituted body. That, publicly speaking, should have been the end of the matter. As Menuhin observed, 'It is not for us to question [that] judgement'.

*

In Chicago, a union official is said to have announced: 'Furtwängler will never come to Chicago. He wouldn't have an orchestra to lead'.[6] In the end, the Board backed away from the deal as honourably as it knew how. A lengthy defence of Furtwängler's character and record was drawn up and released to subscribers and the press. In addition, generous compensation was offered. This was refused by Furtwängler, though he was eventually persuaded to accept $900 in respect of cables and telephone charges.

The President of the Chicago board Edward Ryerson wrote:

I would like to add a word of personal comment as to my position in connection with the Furtwängler negotiations. I knew that this decision would create some opposition and controversy. I was confident, however, in my belief that all of us who have made great sacrifices to bring the war [with Germany] to a victorious conclusion had done so in the hope that our victory would above all else bring about a world attitude of tolerance . . . To find that this attitude of tolerance has not yet been realised and accepted by many people, including even some outstanding artists, is tragic evidence of the fact that our victory as yet has not been complete.[7]

In fact, the Chicago affair had partly lanced the boil. Though Furtwängler never did return to the United States, he would almost certainly have done so had he lived. Plans were well in hand at the time of his death in 1954 for visits with both the Berlin Philharmonic and the Vienna Philharmonic orchestras.

It was Karajan, of course, who went in his place. For would-be protesters, he was an even finer quarry, not so much a 'symbol' of Nazism, as a Nazi look-alike with a real-life Nazi past. Hollywood Central Casting could not have done better. And yet, as we shall later see, for all his understandable apprehension, Karajan's reception in the United States was a good deal more welcoming than has often been reported or supposed.

CHAPTER 28

Getting and spending

> Lou Witt had had her own way so long . . . she didn't know where
> she was. Having one's own way landed one completely at sea.
> D. H. Lawrence, *St Mawr*

Fearful of the Russians, spoilt for choice or merely adrift in a crowd of competing egos, Karajan began behaving oddly in the late summer and autumn of 1948. There was his idea of finding a bolthole in South America. There was his brinkmanship with the committee of the Salzburg Festival. And after only one concert was agreed for the 1948–9 season with the Vienna Philharmonic, there was a cooling relationship with them, too. Even Furtwängler was shocked by this decision,[1] more on the orchestra's account, perhaps, than on his own. With the packed houses Karajan or Furtwängler invariably drew, the orchestra could reckon on a small working surplus of around 20,000 Austrian Schillings per concert. With most other conductors they were lucky to break even.

The cause of this newest Viennese *Krach* appears to have been foreign tours. Since the orchestra's first excursion abroad, to France and Switzerland in 1947 during which the politically blameless French conductor Paul Paray had led the orchestra, Krips, Böhm, and Furtwängler had done the lion's share of the touring. There had been nothing for Karajan. True, Vienna had suggested – or, rather, Milan had requested – that he conduct two of the State Opera's performances of *Le nozze di Figaro* there in January 1949, but that was hardly ample recompense. Slowly but surely, he was being edged (or was edging himself) away from the Vienna Philharmonic towards the Vienna Symphony, away from the main arena back to the proving grounds. For a man who had just passed his fortieth birthday, it was an odd direction in which to be going.

During the winter of 1948–9 he led the Vienna Symphony in three concerts which featured the one Viennese group that was proving unwaveringly loyal, the Singverein. Karajan also conducted the orchestra in two purely orchestral concerts. One featured Debussy's *La mer* and Tchaikovsky's *Pathétique* Symphony, a work he was currently recording for Legge with the Vienna Philharmonic.

The concert performance of the *Pathétique* gave the Viennese critics a chance to compare Karajan's Tchaikovsky ('great power of will'), with Furtwängler's ('free and impulsive') and Erich Kleiber's ('classically shaped', 'rhythmically steadfast'). The Viennese-born Kleiber had spent the war years in Argentina. This did not commend him to the generality of opinion in Vienna, which was duly outraged by the red-carpet treatment accorded him by the government on his return to the city in 1948. Karajan's own scathing account of Kleiber's return was the only occasion I heard him speak ill of a distinguished fellow conductor. Much of this was due to envy: envy of a man who had upped sticks and left Germany in the mid-1930s; envy, too, of the praise that had recently been heaped on him in London, where his alert, logical style had been praised by critics as consistently as Furtwängler's very different style had been derided.

They were all there for Kleiber's first post-war concert in Vienna: Furtwängler, Krips, Karajan, Oscar Fritz Schuh and others. During the concert Furtwängler fidgeted and made semi-audible remarks about Kleiber's 'Napoleonic' demeanour.

'How does he do it: all that pointing and gesticulating at the woodwinds and brass?' he muttered. 'I have my hands full drawing the sound I want from the strings.'[2]

He called on Kleiber in his dressing-room after the concert, for old times' sake. Others merely lingered in the foyers, sniping. With so many influential enemies, Kleiber found it an uphill task getting work in post-war Austria.

Karajan's other concert with the Vienna Symphony took place early in the New Year. The first half was given over to a predictably fiery performance of Dvořák's *New World* Symphony, the second half to Prokofiev's *Peter and the Wolf* with Irmgard Seefried as narrator and a piece that was to feature a good deal in Karajan's future programmes, Ravel's *Boléro*.

'And now for the Wanja-Yoga-Music!' muttered one concert-goer. No one knew quite what to make of *Boléro* as a concert piece; but most agreed that, whatever it was, Karajan did it brilliantly.

They also began suggesting that when Karajan was conducting the Vienna Symphony you couldn't get a cigarette-card between the city's two leading orchestras in terms of quality.

*

Tchaikovsky's *Pathétique* took six days to record with the Vienna Philharmonic, Beethoven's Fifth four. The sessions were becoming more and more protracted. Nor was either recording especially well received. *The Gramophone*'s Basil Douglas had been bowled over by Karajan's 1948 London performance of Beethoven's Fifth. He later recalled:

It had a remarkable intensity of feeling, and the architecture was both clear and monumental . . . I came away impressed anew with the beauty and spaciousness of the music.[3]

Further exposure to Karajan's performances had, however, led him to a change of mind.

. . . more and more have I been made conscious of the conductor first, and of the music second. He is a remarkable conductor, but there is a quality of ruthlessness in his work that repels.[4]

Though Douglas was reviewing the Beethoven, what he writes could perhaps be better applied to the Tchaikovsky, where it is certainly possible to be repelled by a rather dangerous mix of deeply felt emotion and an iron but essentially unspontaneous control. When Karajan first recorded the *Pathétique* in 1939, he had Furtwängler's Berlin Philharmonic playing for him in the immediate aftermath of Furtwängler's own deeply affecting 1938 HMV recording.

Karajan's cooling relationship with the Vienna Philharmonic cannot have helped matters. Indeed, it is possible that the sudden stiffening of the orchestral sinews that is so marked a feature of several of the recordings he made with the Vienna Philharmonic in 1948–9 is a consequence of this. In a rather rawly recorded account of the overture to *Die Fledermaus*, also made in November 1948, the orchestra is in mulish mood, clearly reluctant to go along with Karajan's essentially dashing, debonair view of the music.

*

Those members of the orchestra who were engaged to work on the soundtrack of Marischka's film of the *St Matthew Passion* found that Karajan could be as mulish as they were. During negotiations with Marischka's intermediary André von Mattoni, Karajan had calculated that he needed twelve days to complete the project: choruses in the mornings, recitatives and arias in the afternoons when the singers would be in better voice. This was a tight schedule, the more so since none of the performers under contract to the Vienna Opera would be available for emergency evening sessions. Before the sessions started, Mattoni more or less went on bended knee to the entire company and crew. His plea: be prompt, come prepared, don't talk, remain one hundred per cent attentive at all times.

The recording took eleven days not twelve. 'And now,' said Karajan, turning to a much relieved Mattoni, 'you are my man. You close your film business and come to work for me.' What Karajan was offering Mattoni was a job for life.

It is generally agreed that it was an inspired appointment. Mattoni was the administrative rock on which Karajan's career would be built over the next twenty-five years. What else Karajan said to Mattoni when he appointed him can only be guessed at. Perhaps he said what he later said to Michel Glotz: 'Rough it will be. Boring, never.'

In his book on Karajan, Roger Vaughan provides a memorable verbal distillation of what might be termed essence of Mattoni. Vaughan had sought Mattoni out in Salzburg, a couple of years before his death in 1985. Though Mattoni had retired, he still had a house in Salzburg which he shared with his current companion 'a burly young fellow, involved in church work'. As for Mattoni himself:

He was perfectly groomed and aristocratic in black velvet slacks and Gucci loafers, a silver sliver of a man, an ageing trooper; the deep-set eyes still flashing a touch of lust, the voice steady – fragile as antique crystal.[5]

As for Mattoni's professional style, no one has left a more vivid description of this than Decca's John Culshaw:

Mattoni was an exceptionally handsome, perfectly groomed gentleman of aristocratic bearing. In the early days of the talkies he had played some minor roles in Hollywood, but there were dark rumours of some scandal that had driven him away from California. He was multi-lingual without the slightest hesitancy, and without accent. The English thought he was English, the French accepted him as French and the Italians assumed he was Italian by virtue of his name; in fact he was Viennese. With infinite politeness he kept undesirables away from Karajan, but smoothed the path for those who really needed or deserved an audience with The Master, as Mattoni always referred to him. If, as sometimes happened, The Master wished to wipe his feet on someone, Mattoni merely assumed a pained expression and became a doormat. He probably knew Karajan better than anyone else on earth, but his discretion was total. He was by no means averse to the latest bit of gossip about another conductor or singer, but where Karajan was concerned his lips were sealed.[6]

At one point during the crisis surrounding Karajan's resignation as Director of the Vienna State Opera in 1964, Culshaw found himself in Mattoni's office while Mattoni held the world's press at bay:

Karajan was in the very next office, but from the point of view of security he might just as well have been in Fort Knox: nobody was going to get past Mattoni, who threw all the balls back with his left hand while elegantly displaying one of his props – an inordinately long cigarette-holder – in his right. On such occasions he was in his element.[7]

Karajan once said self-deprecatingly that if he short-listed ten applicants for a job one of whom had an undisclosed criminal record, he would usually end up choosing the one with the criminal record. There is some truth in this. But despite rumours of naughtinesses in pre-war Hollywood, Mattoni proved to be one of his better appointments.

*

A Mattoni does not come cheap. Though he was nothing more that a touring actor ('André Mattoni brought a welcome injection of youthfulness to the production' the *Salzburger Nachrichten* reported in September 1945), he had style and knew his price. Since Karajan regularly pleaded poverty at this time, one wonders how he afforded him. In fact, like a lot of wealthy men who have known hard times, Karajan was both extremely frugal and extraordinarily acquisitive. He was not alone in this. Karl Böhm amassed money and trinkets with the fervour of Balzac's Monsieur Grandet. But though Karajan may have appeared to be destitute in the late 1940s (the patched tail-coat, the dress trousers for a London concert borrowed from an EMI chauffeur), he was beginning to earn a decent living from concerts and recording, albeit on a freelance basis and in financially precarious times.

In July 1948, he tried to set up a holding company in Liechtenstein but ran into trouble with the Swiss tax authorities. There were also problems over his EMI earnings. Finding the most effective way of paying British royalties in Swiss francs to an Austrian citizen of no fixed address without contravening the Bank of England's stringent guidelines on foreign exchange dealings was a persistent headache for the company. When sterling was devalued in September 1949, reducing Karajan's previous year's royalties at a stroke from £3747 to £2815, Karajan simply put pressure on EMI to come up with a solution to the problem.

Legge, meanwhile, had troubles of his own. In addition to trying to keep the Philharmonia afloat financially and its key players on board, all was not well at EMI, where his every move was being closely scrutinised by those who either disliked his methods or had been offended by him at some time or another. Legge was that awkward mix: a loyal 'company man' of flair and ability who was also a born outsider. All his professional life, there were those around him who were waiting for him to come a cropper.

The immediate problem in the spring of 1949 was keeping Furtwängler, and the Vienna Philharmonic, with EMI. The orchestra's two representatives, Rudolf Hanzl and Alfred Boskovsky, had indicated that 'for old friendship's sake' they wanted to make a recording with Hans Knappertsbusch, a Decca artist. Legge knew from Furtwängler that there was more to it than this: that Decca was eager to sign the Vienna Philharmonic on a more permanent basis. And as if this was not enough, there was the problem of Karajan's exclusive contract with EMI, which was due for renewal.

*

News that Karajan was taking himself off to Cuba, Argentina, and Chile in the spring and early summer of 1949 gave EMI breathing-space. Or so they imagined. What they had not thought to arrange were adequate supplies of Karajan recordings in Cuban, Argentinian, and Chilean record shops. The cables began arriving towards the end of March. Karajan had arrived in Cuba to prepare for two concerts with the Havana Philharmonic, one of which would feature Beethoven's Ninth Symphony. Not unnaturally, he was more than a little angry to find no copies of his prestigious new Vienna Ninth on sale; no window displays, no publicity leaflets, no newspaper advertisements tying the recording in to the concert.

In those days, Cuba was no Marxist backwater but an island awash with money and vibrant with music, local and European. During the war, the Havana Philharmonic had been taken in hand by Massimo Freccia. In addition, an Austrian refugee Paul Csonka had helped establish a Philharmonic chorus; so there was nothing novel about the Cubans hearing the Ninth Symphony. Karajan also took himself into the suburbs to hear local Cuban musicians playing:

People would normally arrive at the place around 12 o'clock with bloodshot eyes – they were clearly high on marijuana – and would sit down and make music for the next five hours. Within the space of around sixteen bars you could observe no more than a hundredth of a second's difference. Every musician was better than a metronome. Such a feeling for rhythm must be innate. During the carnival two-year-old children emerged from their houses dancing – and they already had the right rhythm. They'd never been taught it.[8]

Karajan was obsessed by rhythmic accuracy. He once told the Vienna Philharmonic that he was going to hear a concert by Louis Armstrong. 'Imagine!' he exclaimed. 'Two hours of music, and never once will it slow down or speed up by mistake.'

The frequency of the cables and their insistent manner started ringing alarm bells back in EMI's headquarters at Hayes, where it was already widely known that there were 'difficulties' over Karajan's new contract. Nor did it take Hayes long to discover that the situation Karajan had unearthed in Havana was likely to be repeated in Buenos Aires.

What happened next was an earnest of Karajan's ability, even then, to mesmerise and galvanise people and organisations. Though he was travelling alone, with Anita but with no famous orchestra in tow, and though his name was a relatively new one on EMI's immensely long and distinguished roster of artists, by late April EMI's Buenos Aires plant was pressing nothing but Karajan records, plus a few for the pianist

György Sándor, who was also touring South America. And while the factory worked round the clock pressing Karajan recordings, the local EMI representative was busy publicising Karajan's forthcoming concerts. The final bill for the promotional work was over £1000, an unheard-of sum in those parts at the time.

Perhaps because he knew he had the upper hand, Karajan swept into Buenos Aires with the air of a conquistador seeking out quisling chiefs. William Walton had advised the Karajans to avoid the Plaza Hotel, where the British Council had put him up the previous autumn, and enjoy instead the old-world elegance of the Alvear Palace. He also told Karajan to steer clear of Argentinian music; in Walton's opinion it was all rubbish apart from Ginastera's work and odds and ends by Juan José Castro. Those who met Karajan and Anita in Buenos Aires found them affable and courteous. But, already, there was the perception of Karajan as a man in a hurry. People snatched a word here, a word there; no one dared say too much, lest he or she upset the entire apple-cart.

The local press found his conducting fiery but well-balanced, demonstrating a fine 'equilibrium'. Uncharacteristically, though, he appears to have shown scant respect for the musicians of the excellent Teatro Colón orchestra. During rehearsals he sat in a low chair, legs stretched out, rather vaguely waggling his stick.[9] Perhaps he was trying to be as little like Furtwängler or the orchestra's former boss Erich Kleiber as possible; or maybe it was the money that was bugging him: he had demanded, and failed, to be paid in US dollars rather than in the local currency. Back in Vienna, his friend Gamsjäger received a postcard from him; on one side was a photograph of Buenos Aires's famous Avenida 9 de Julio, on the other side the words, 'Ein Negerdorf [A nigger village]. Dein Herbert.'[10]

From Brazil, Karajan moved on to Chile. And it was there, of all places, that Yehudi Menuhin first met him and heard him conduct. Menuhin recalls: 'He was already a marvellous conductor, absolutely superb, he got marvellous results.'[11] It was Menuhin's wife Diana who had rebelled, 'We come to all these lovely places and what do we see? We see the airport, the concert hall, the hotel – and the concierge's outstretched hand.'[12] So the Menuhins took off in small plane, and went trekking in the Andes.

This inspired Karajan, too, to cock a snook at the schedules. At the age of forty-one, he decided to learn to fly. He signed up with a local Chilean flying school and was soon dauntingly proficient.

*

Noting that the Russians had backed down over Berlin, Karajan readily returned to Europe in July 1949. Not that there was a great deal to return to. In Salzburg there were just two concerts. First, there was a Sunday morning performance of the Verdi *Requiem*, the music-making by turns demonic and exquisitely Italianate, after which Karajan was carried shoulder-high to lunch by a bevy of admirers. Three days later, he conducted Beethoven's Ninth. In the audience was the 20-year-old Bernard Haitink. He had heard so much about Karajan that he found the actual concert a bit of a let-down. 'So, what is all the noise about?' was his immediate reaction. He also wondered what he was doing at a performance of *Fidelio* conducted by Furtwängler: 'Until the Quartet. That was fantastic, and after that everything stayed that way.'[13]

Back in London, the future of Walter Legge's Philharmonia Orchestra was looking rosier thanks to the intervention of a wealthy young Indian. The Maharaja of Mysore had first become involved with Legge and EMI through his enthusiasm for the music of the émigré Russian composer Nikolay Medtner, recordings of which he wished to sponsor. The 'Medtner Society Edition' had begun in a modest way. Now Legge had been invited to India to discuss far more ambitious plans:

The visit to Mysore was a fantastic experience. The Maharajah was a young man, not yet thirty. In one of his palaces he had a record library containing every imaginable recording of serious music, a large range of loudspeakers, and several concert grand pianos. He had intended to be a concert pianist and had been accepted by Rachmaninoff as a pupil when both his father and his uncle died and he succeeded to the throne – which meant giving up all ideas of a musical career and returning home at once. In the weeks I stayed there, the Maharajah had not only agreed to paying for the recordings of the Medtner piano concertos, an album of his songs, and some of his chamber music; he also agreed to give me a subvention of £10,000 a year for three years to enable me to put both the Philharmonia Orchestra and the Philharmonia Concert Society on a firm basis.[14]

Thanks to what Legge describes as 'the malign interference of the late Krishna Menon', only a fraction of the promised largesse ever reached British shores. However, the first £10,000 was transmitted in full and proved sufficient to transform Legge's fortunes in 1949. He was able to engage Karajan for a short season of concerts in London in the late autumn. At the same time, he could begin to involve him more closely in the Philharmonia's recording plans at a period when it was clear that Karajan was less and less inclined to record with the Vienna Philharmonic.

The repertory the young Maharaja wished to sponsor was distinctly recherché, but Karajan balked at nothing; neither the Balakirev symphony nor Roussel's Fourth Symphony, both of which would eventually receive fine recordings under his direction, nor Busoni's *Indian Fantasy* which was never made but for which Egon Petri had been pencilled in as the solo pianist. More controversially, Karajan was even prepared to learn Ernest Bloch's *Israel* Symphony, a choral epic Bloch had laboured over during the years 1912–16.

Plans for the Bloch recording reached quite an advanced stage. At a meeting of the Columbia section of the EMI Artistes and Repertoire Committee it was decided that Karajan would conduct the Philharmonia Orchestra and an as yet unspecified chorus. The soloists would be Boris Christoff, Elisabeth Schwarzkopf, Irmgard Seefried, Elsa Cavelti, and Elisabeth Höngen. When Victor Carne, a committee member who had been absent on the day in question, read the minutes, he was flabbergasted. It was, he said, 'an incredibly stupid suggestion both morally and commercially'. Asking the committee to reconsider, he noted:

Without wishing to enter into political details, I think the choice of a musician [Karajan] who for the greater part of his career was associated with the Nazi Party in Germany and Austria to conduct an essentially Jewish work by one of the proudest and most racially conscious of all composers, Ernest Bloch, is an extreme example of miscasting.[15]

The idea was promptly dropped. How such a recording would have been received in Israel or the United States, the two territories where the *Israel* Symphony would have been most widely welcomed by collectors, is something one can only dispatch to the wilder shores of speculation.

Back in Vienna, he embarked on what were to be his last orchestral recordings with the Vienna Philharmonic for the foreseeable future. During these final sessions, which took place between 18 October and 10 November, he devoted many hours to recording Brahms's Second Symphony, a brooding, dramatic reading which finds him agreeing with that discriminating minority that believes this to be one of the darkest of all major-key symphonies; the light glimpsed 'from the heart of the forest'.[16]

What is also interesting is the way Karajan wove other music – Mozart's Symphony No.39 and dances by members of the Strauss family – in and around the Brahms sessions. On the first day, after a couple of rowdy warmers,[17] he settled to the Brahms and to a waltz for which both he and the Vienna Philharmonic had a particular affection, Josef Strauss's *Sphärenklänge*. The melancholy of Josef Strauss's music and its exquisite craftsmanship held a special fascination for Karajan. Nor was this the only music by Josef Strauss to be fitted around the Brahms and Mozart symphonies. The *Delirien* and *Transaktionen* waltzes were also recorded, the performances rich in insight. Of note, too, is the almost deliriously beautiful account of Johann Strauss's *Wiener Blut* recorded on 24 October and again at the end of the last session. The Mozart benefited, too, achieving a depth of utterance that goes beyond what Karajan had previously achieved in Mozart symphonies.

This strategy of working on several things at once was one which Karajan would develop and refine during his years as chief conductor of the Berlin Philharmonic. Many were the occasions when he would solve a problem, or intensify a mood, with one work by switching to another.

Karajan was always learning. During the Mozart sessions, he frequently referred to a recording Legge had produced in London in March 1940 with Sir Thomas Beecham and the London Philharmonic. Sir Simon Rattle once cheerfully admitted to me, 'All conducting is large-scale plagiarism.' Yet conductors caught listening to their colleagues' records have often been treated like schoolroom cheats. Constantin Silvestri was one such, a man, players mockingly claimed, whose scores were extensively annotated in different coloured inks for different conductors' interpretations. Because Karajan never wrote in scores, there were no annotations. But since he was never ashamed to learn, he was never ashamed to be seen learning and often took records into the studio with him.

*

As was to become his habit, Karajan did not renew his contract with EMI until the last possible moment. With the scheduled start of the Vienna sessions barely a month away, Legge wrote to him in St Anton on 29 September. Though the letter is clearly drafted with Company eyes in mind (not everyone in Hayes shared his enthusiasm for Karajan), it is none the less heartfelt for all that. Legge wrote:

But what are you worrying about? We as a Company, and I as its representative and your friend, have shown in three years of close association every willingness to help you solve your problems as they have arisen. Your earnings have exceeded your own, and my own, optimistic expectations. Our job together is to make records of ever-increasing excellence. The artistic experience and knowledge you have put into them, and the capital we invest in making and selling them, is a long term investment, the fruits of which you will gather for decades to come. None of us can foresee the possible alarms and changes of those years – but you may rest assured that as long as Columbia and Herbert von Karajan exist we shall do all in our power to see that you get a fair and just payment for the work we have done.[18]

On 9 October, Karajan flew to Northolt airport via Paris on his way back from Stockholm, where he had conducted Sibelius's Fifth Symphony.

Legge met him at the airport, but all casual talk of 'commerce' was strictly forbidden by Karajan. Contracts were not for chatting about in cars. Discussions did not begin until 10.30 in the evening. Not that matters ended there. The devaluation of the pound and Karajan's continuing paranoia about the possibility of his again losing everything, as he had done with his wartime Polydor agreements, took the negotiations deeper and deeper into legal and financial thickets where even Legge was temporarily at a loss.

When the Vienna sessions began on 20 October, there was still no contract. Then, on 1 November, during a break in the sessions, Legge was obliged to travel to Zürich for further discussions with 'the insatiable Karajan' (Legge's phrase) and his lawyers.

Dealing with Karajan's lawyers in Zürich was something record company executives would spend rather a lot of time doing over the next forty years.

CHAPTER 29

The hypnotist

'Ansermet finds it very good, I can't think why.'
Maurice Ravel on *Boléro*

Walter Legge began the New Year in a bad mood. The seemingly endless weeks spent haggling with Karajan over his new contract cannot have helped his temper; a fortnight's recording with Furtwängler and some problematic dealings with Igor Markevitch only made things worse. In a postscript to a letter written in Vienna on 28 January 1950, Legge bleakly apostrophised the entire conducting profession:

There is no form of occupation which has a worse effect on a man's character than that of conductor. In the practice of it a man has for six hours a day, five or six days a week, undisputed and dictatorial powers over a large body of experts in his own field and thinking. He has frequently similar powers over the most eminent soloists, instrumentalists, and singers. When it comes to a performance, it is he who culls the praise and the applause, not only for the orchestra's work, but for the creations of men whose boots he is, in the main, not fit to lick. Is it a wonder that the exercise of these dictatorial powers and the reaping of other men's harvests makes conductors impatient in normal relationships of the slightest opposition to their will?[1]

Legge had further reason to feel downcast after losing money on the first of the concerts he had been able to stage with the help of the Mysore subvention. The concert on 25 November 1949 had marked Karajan's return to London. It had been played in the ample arena of the Royal Albert Hall before an audience of no more than four hundred people. Poor planning was at the root of this financial misadventure; London audiences had already had their fill of Ninths that season. Yet, musically, the evening was something of triumph. Even today one comes across people who were there and who recall the small audience and the wonderful music-making.

As ever, Legge had assembled a remarkable solo quartet: Elisabeth Schwarzkopf, Jean Watson, Rudolph Schock, and Boris Christoff. Of those, only Jean Watson was not a household name; but then it was Legge's view that the function of the mezzo in the finale of the Ninth was to remain as inconspicuous as possible. As for Karajan, *The Times* critic noted an immediate bonding between conductor and orchestra. 'Coherent and convincing interpretation of this kind,' he wrote 'argues co-operation without stint.'

The Times review also attempted, within the prescribed limits of an overnight notice, to describe what it was about Karajan's conducting that helped give the attentive listener so clear an abstract of the music as music:

The ninth symphony is a breath-taking work and this was a breath-taking performance. Mr von Karajan achieved his effect by concentrating not on its dramatic or philosophical elements but on its musical power and lyric beauty . . . he showed that emphasis on the *espressivo*, primarily musical facets of the work strengthen the architectural outlines and give added force to the logical drive of Beethoven's argument. Thus the length, breadth, and height of the symphony's proportion, lyricism, intensity, and sonority were drawn together to display that fourth dimension, compact musical integrity.[2]

It is not possible to conduct the Ninth Symphony (and much else besides in the nineteenth- and early twentieth-century German repertory) without a proper command and understanding of a singing orchestral legato. Furtwängler had this in supreme measure and it was the one quality he freely and ungrudgingly commended in Karajan. 'K can do the most difficult thing of all,' he told his wife. 'He can command a true legato. And this he must have learned for himself. It cannot be taught.'[3] That Karajan sometimes overplayed the legato in later years cannot be doubted. Yet the obverse belief, the zealous rooting out of the *legato* style, has done great damage. In an age which favours prosily talkative Beethoven we are unlikely to hear the Ninth Symphony as memorably conducted as it was by Furtwängler or by Karajan in his middle years.

*

The second of Karajan's Mysore-sponsored Philharmonia concerts, on 2 December, was originally planned to include Roussel's Fourth Symphony, Bartók's Third Piano Concerto with Lipatti as soloist, and Tchaikovsky's *Pathétique*. Of these, only the *Pathétique* survived. Lipatti cancelled, and though the Roussel had been successfully recorded a few days earlier (a recording later hailed as being 'almost beyond criticism' by *The Gramophone*'s famously exacting Francophone critic Lionel Salter[4]), neither Legge nor Karajan felt it was worth risking the performance live in the concert hall. *Boléro* and *Till Eulenspiegel* were inserted as audience-grabbing substitutes.

Though Karajan disliked intensely Ravel's *La valse* (he preferred his Johann Strauss straight), *Boléro* held a special fascination for him. At one level, the fascination was rhythmic: the need to hold an orchestra *absolutely* in tempo for sixteen minutes of music through an extraordinary succession of changes of dynamics and colour. That was the technical challenge. Yet *Boléro* is also a sustained act of musical hypnosis.

The idea of the conductor-as-hypnotist is something Karajan clearly believed in. The word 'hypnotisch' crops up time and again in German and Austrian reviews of his pre- and post-war concerts. Nor is it surprising that many readers have chosen to see Elias Canetti's famous chapter 'The Orchestral Conductor' in his book *Crowds and Power* as being in some sense identified with Karajan.

He is inside the mind of every player. He knows not only what each *should* be doing, but also what he *is* doing. He is the living embodiment of law, both positive and negative. His hands decree and prohibit. His ears search out profanation.[5]

Karajan did, indeed, believe he could get inside people's minds. He has been quoted as saying: 'I can gauge the state of mind of a couple in a car instantly as they pass me on the road at sixty miles per hour.' And of conducting, he would say:

I have a tempo in my head long before I come to the passage in question. I know in advance, so to speak, what is going to happen. And the players react faultlessly, they don't need a gesture or glance from me. By contrast, I can also tell in advance when something is going to go wrong in the orchestra. I really can sense in advance if a player has problems with his breathing, and so I'll go faster for him. I sense in advance the fear that a player feels at a difficult entry, and I help him so that we get over the passage quickly together.

Certainly, Karajan was strongly interested in the power of hypnosis. Elisabeth Schwarzkopf remembers them spending several hours together at an airport in Spain waiting for Walter Legge to fly in from London. To alleviate the boredom, Karajan passed the time thinking up various bizarre ruses. At one point, his eyes lighted on an extremely attractive young woman who was sitting with her husband on a nearby bench. The couple had their backs to Karajan. 'I shall hypnotise that girl,' Karajan announced. Having established how many pesetas Schwarzkopf had in her purse, he bet her that within sixty seconds of his concentrating his gaze on the girl's back she would turn round and look at him. 'It took less than thirty seconds,' Schwarzkopf recalls. 'Herbert sat staring at the girl's back and she suddenly spun round and stared straight at him. He was so thrilled by this. He was like a little boy who'd performed some kind of conjuring trick.'

Even parapsychologists fight shy of explaining such occurrences, yet as Rupert Sheldrake has pointed out in his chapter 'The Sense of Being Stared At' in his book *Seven Experiments that Could Change the World*, it is a phenomenon which occurs in all societies and which many people admit to having encountered at first hand.[6]

*

For most conductors, eye-contact with players is all-important. Yet curiously Karajan was at his most hypnotic when his eyes were closed, which they invariably were during a concert performance of orchestral works. ('If the eyes open, it's dangerous!' horn-player Alan Civil once remarked.) This was not an affectation; it was an instinct he was born with. 'The constant shifting between seeing and hearing,' he once said, 'is impossible.'

Conducting with closed eyes was also an aid to concentration, and to realising what Karajan once called 'the sensed and thought-out sound [that is the key to] the idea which stands behind it'. Hugh Bean's wife would recall seeing Karajan coming off stage in Lucerne, the eyes having just opened: 'Brilliant blue, but not really seeing anything; it was a strange sensation seeing him in this state.'

During rehearsal, Karajan's eyes were open, as was the score, though he rarely seemed to need to consult it. In concert, by contrast, this keen-eyed and quick-witted beaver of a man turned into a kind of brooding eagle. Gareth Morris remembers the closed eyes as having a rather reptilian look to them; he also recollects Karajan's stillness, nowhere more so than in performances of *Boléro*:

He hardly moved. As you know, *Boléro* works by a simple additive process. With the eyes closed and the hands barely chest high, Karajan gave us the beat with a single finger, and even that barely moved. With each new addition, the hands moved fractionally higher. It was a form of hypnosis, I suppose. What we sensed was the power of the music within him, and that was bound to affect us. So with each slight lift of the hands the tension became even greater. By the end of the piece, the hands were above his head. And the power of that final climax was absolutely colossal.[7]

Though Ravel himself was famously rude about the piece – 'I've written only one masterpiece,' he told Arthur Honegger, '*Boléro*. Unfortunately, there's no music in it' – he suspected that the piece's popularity was not unconnected with an obsessive, destructive quality deep down in its being. Ravel's close friend Hélène Jourdan-Morhange suggested that the appeal of the piece was in some sense sexual.

Karajan may well have begun by seeing the work as a gigantic *étude* for conductor and orchestra, a vehicle for conductorial control and orchestral display. Yet as the writer Christopher Booker has argued in *The Neophiliacs*, *Boléro* is also to some extent a metaphor of our age, a work that symbolically re-enacts the rising spiral of an ultimately ungratifiable demand that has been a feature of Western social and economic life since the early 1920s.

'We had fed the heart on fantasies,/The heart's grown brutal from the fare', writes the poet Yeats.[8] The destructive power of fantasy, Booker argues, is what Boléro is all about:

... unlike such a mental pattern as, for instance, a Beethoven symphony, in which each ingredient plays its part in working for an organic and satisfactory resolution of the whole, a fantasy pattern based on a whole series of images that are themselves unresolved cannot by definition resolve everything that has gone before.[9]

In life, Booker argues, the 'fantasy cycle' has five clearly defined stages: anticipation, dream, frustration, nightmare, and death wish or 'explosion into reality'. Applying this to *Boléro*:

Here is a composition based nakedly on the rising spiral of sensations; the same tune, almost indefinitely repeated, rising louder and louder through a Dream Stage towards what? In what possible way could Ravel resolve this model fantasy pattern? If we examine the closing bars we can see that the momentum of his music left only one course open. Eventually, as the pursuit of the elusive climax becomes desperate, Ravel at last changes key (Frustration Stage). This only makes the music even more frantic and the piece accordingly falls into a series of raging discords (Nightmare Stage), culminating in the only possible way it could, by falling to pieces in cacophony and thus destroying itself.[10]

Much of what Karajan did operated at the level of pure musical intuition. He was never much given to intellectualising music, though he greatly admired anyone who could write intelligently and persuasively about it. Yet intuitions themselves grow out of deeper promptings and here there can be little doubt that from an early age Karajan was possessed by what Henry James once referred to as 'the imagination of disaster'. In later years Karajan would frequently list those works which left him emotionally drained for days to come: *Elektra*, Sibelius's Fourth Symphony, Mahler's Sixth, the *Three Orchestral Pieces* of Alban Berg, Honegger's *Liturgique*. Much of this is war music, music that concerns itself with the gratuitous desecration and destruction of human life and values. *Boléro* is too brief and too singular a piece to come into this category, but the frequency with which Karajan programmed it and the contexts in which he placed it[11] suggest that it held a significance for him that went beyond that of a mere orchestral *étude*.

CHAPTER 30

Hanging on to Karajan

If the men are wrong, nothing will be right.
Sir Ronald Edwards

Karajan's first solo recording sessions with the Philharmonia Orchestra in November 1949 proved to be more than simply a *succès d'estime*. True, the Roussel Fourth Symphony did not do especially well commercially, and Karajan would subsequently make an even finer recording of Bartók's *Music for Strings, Percussion, and Celesta* ('the very roots of music are touched on in this work'); but the thrilling account of the rarely heard Balakirev symphony was a triumph.

The Maharaja of Mysore, who had financed the recordings, was well pleased with the results. He was a diffident young man, though when asked by Legge to pass judgement on recent additions to the EMI catalogue his views were as trenchant as they were refreshingly unpredictable. He thrilled to Karajan's Vienna Philharmonic recording of Beethoven's Fifth Symphony ('as Beethoven wished it to be'), held Furtwängler's recording of the Fourth Symphony in high esteem (a recording belaboured by some critics for its rhythmic 'waywardness'), and was disappointed by Galliera's account of the Seventh Symphony which he would have preferred Karajan to record. Above all, he expressed serious doubts about Toscanini's latest recordings. 'The speed and energy are those of a demon,' he wrote to Legge, 'not an angel or superman as one would ardently hope for.' One of the reasons he so admired Furtwängler's Beethoven was that it was 'such a tonic after Toscanini's highly strung, vicious performances'.[1]

A further eighteen months would elapse before Karajan returned to London and the Philharmonia. It says much for the orchestra's quality, for Legge's powers of persuasion, and for Karajan's own peculiar mix of conservatism, loyalty, and commercial shrewdness that he returned at all; not for any want of personal rapport but because of the practical difficulties he was beginning to experience with EMI.

Some of these concerned marketing. Having fired a shot across the company's bows in the spring of 1949 about the availability of his recordings in South America, Karajan now turned his attention to Europe, where distribution was equally patchy, not least in Germany where EMI's Cologne-based parent-company Electrola seemed almost deliberately remiss in its promotion of Legge–Karajan recordings. It took EMI's London office some time to wake up to the fact that Karajan was employing an elaborate network of friends and acquaintances in mainland Europe to report back to him.[2] Even more serious were the technical shortcomings. Some of these were simple mishaps: the severe cold, for instance, which shattered a batch of wax masters in transit by air from Vienna to London in the winter of 1948–9 for which EMI had to offer abject apologies.[3]

Other problems were more deep-seated. When Karajan's 1949 Vienna Philharmonic recording of Mozart's Symphony No.39 was released by EMI in April 1951, it was on three 12" Columbia 78s. That very month, Karl Böhm's recording of the same symphony with the *Linz* orchestra was released by Decca in the new long-playing format.

Long-playing records had first appeared in the United States in 1948, pioneered and promoted by American Columbia (CBS). CBS favoured the 12" 33⅓ rpm format; but in February 1949, RCA countered with a 45 rpm 7" LP. While these two media giants attempted to outface one another, Decca seized the initiative by siding with CBS. The first Decca LPs were launched on the London label in the USA in the summer of 1949; Decca's UK launch followed a year later in June 1950. Meanwhile, EMI, who had important European licensing agreements with both CBS and RCA, stood nervously on the sidelines awaiting a resolution of the American impasse.

To Karajan, for whom practically all forms of technological advance had a mesmerising allure, magnetic tape and long-playing formats were of immense importance. 'These twin miracles' was how he described them to the press during a tour of Germany in January 1950. In an interview with the *Rheinische Post* in Duisburg that month, he reflected on the nightmare of recording lengthy masterworks in the 78 rpm format; spoke of the perfection 'in England' (*sic*) of the long-playing record; and for the first time mentioned the huge importance of the American market.[4] All this, and yet his own record company EMI would not make its all too obviously belated entry into the LP market until the autumn of 1952.[5]

Nor would that be the end of the story. While EMI settled back, tardily and somewhat complacently, to enjoy the longer playing times and 'silent surfaces' vinyl LPs afforded, its re-emergent German rival Deutsche Grammophon was developing pressing techniques and quality-control systems that would give their LPs a quietness and reliability few of their competitors would be able to match. Indeed, in the early 1950s Deutsche Grammophon invited Karajan to visit their new plant in Hanover, where side-by-side comparisons were made between their pressings and EMI's.

Karajan was duly impressed. Yet he was saddened, too. Like many Germans and Austrians brought up in the old pre-war order, he had an enormous respect for Britain. But things were changing. EMI, he told Legge in a letter in the summer of 1952, is beginning to seem old-fashioned, 'Like the motor-industry: in 1946 you had it all your own way, but now you are beginning to slip behind'.[6] His prediction that, if things did not improve, Britain would be without an indigenous motor industry within twenty years was strangely prescient. The time-scale was wrong but the essential judgement was correct.

*

EMI's tardiness in switching to LP resulted in a hiatus over the two Mozart opera sets Karajan recorded in Vienna in 1950. Originally released on 78s in Germany, they did not appear elsewhere until the autumn of 1952. The first was a brilliant, rather hard-driven *Le nozze di Figaro*, the second an altogether better-paced account of *Die Zauberflöte*, stylishly, often imaginatively conducted, and for the most part wonderfully well sung by a cast which showed the fabled post-war Vienna Mozart ensemble somewhere near its best. Reviewing the set in *Opera*, Lord Harewood thought it generally first-rate and a considerable improvement on 'the famous, but in many ways disappointing, Beecham-Berlin Staatsoper recording'.[7]

The *Zauberflöte* sessions had not gone especially well; or, rather, Karajan chose to represent them to Legge as not having gone especially well.[8] Games were being played, and for once Legge seems to have been unsure of who was doing what to whom. That Furtwängler was in a rage was widely known. Having removed the contract to conduct the new 1949 Salzburg Festival production of the opera from under Karajan's nose, Furtwängler was now beside himself at the news that Karajan would be conducting EMI's new recording. Threatening EMI with the non-renewal of his contract, Furtwängler wrote to David Bicknell on 3 January 1951:

What [Mr Legge] was able to say in explanation of his behaviour in the matter of *Die Zauberflöte* was not of a nature to throw a different light on his attitude. His one-sided partisanship for a particular Kapellmeister, in this instance against my direct interests, is moreover so well known throughout Europe ... that, as we say, 'the sparrows sing it from the roof-tops'. It also seems that he has 'shared out' in similar fashion the whole of the remaining great literature (operas of Mozart, Wagner, etc).[9]

Bicknell was by no means unsympathetic to Furtwängler's case, as subsequent arguments about who should record Wagner's *Tristan und Isolde* for EMI would make plain.

But Legge was worried, too. Karajan's complaints about poor orchestral discipline in the *Zauberflöte* sessions did not ring entirely true. As for his objection to different players attending different sessions (a standard procedure in Vienna because of the rota system at the Vienna Opera), this was clearly disingenuous. Now that Karajan was conductor for life of the Vienna Singverein, Legge feared that he might be about to do a deal with the Gesellschaft der Musikfreunde involving the choir, the Vienna Philharmonic, and the Musikverein hall which the Gesellschaft owned, managed, and hired out for recording projects. If so, Legge speculated, was a rival record company involved? Deutsche Grammophon, perhaps, 'who are waving a guaranteed royalty of DM60,000, paid in dollars in the USA, under his avaricious nose'?[10]

The rumour mills had been working overtime and Legge was clearly becoming paranoid. In fact, there was no plot. Outmanoeuvred by Furt-wängler, Karajan had, indeed, broken with the Vienna Philharmonic. He would not conduct them again until 1957. But the situation confronting Legge was real enough. And the dangers were compounded by the fact that not everyone in EMI was convinced that Karajan was a good investment, either personally or financially. When EMI's Milan office reported in the autumn of 1950 that he had been more applauded at a concert in Rome before the concert than after it, there were those who were happy to believe that it was not merely Italian antipathy to the programme – Beethoven's *Eroica* Symphony, Strauss's *Metamorphosen* and *Till Eulenspiegel* – that had caused the unwonted chill.[11]

Caught between a sceptical board in London and the more or less continuous fear that one day someone would make Karajan an offer which even he could not refuse, Legge continued to walk a tightrope as far as his most famous protégé was concerned.

CHAPTER 31

Wiener Symphoniker and return to Germany

Sixteen concerts – sixteen triumphs.
Wiener Tageszeitung

In Vienna, Karajan was rapidly assuming the status of a national asset. Concerts with the Philharmonic and the Vienna Symphony in December 1949 were written up with a lavishness matched only by the level of musical intrigue that surrounded them. Reviewing a concert consisting of Brahms's Violin Concerto and Tchaikovsky's Fourth Symphony, the pianist and critic Erik Werba commented:

The symbolic power of Herbert Karajan's gestures has already become a suitable subject for academic dissertations. The Symphoniker played in such a way as to make it hard for an expert unable to see the stage to decide which of Vienna's two great orchestras was on the platform.[1]

The following week, Karajan appeared with the Philharmonic in a concert which included Mozart's E flat Symphony K543, Ravel's second *Daphnis et Chloé* suite, and Brahms's Second Symphony. Having been bowled over by the 'ephebic charms' of the Mozart and the sensual power of the Ravel, Werba concluded his review:

Gentleness rules. Planning, economy, and logic make Karajan a great conductor. The person whom opponents like to accuse of egocentricity works like a man possessed. Physical self-sacrifice such as might sometimes fill us with concern in Karajan's case is the logical consequence of an intense concentration communicating itself to the virtuosos of the orchestra and the audience alike.[2]

Co-opting the audience and drawing it into the circle of his influence was a Karajan ploy which he would continue to develop and perfect.

His rivals, meanwhile, missed nothing. In a postscript to a letter to the Chairman of the Vienna Philharmonic dated 2 November 1949, Furtwängler noted:

I hear that recently K, during his 'Karajan Cycle', has been having the orchestra [Vienna Symphony] stand up before his entry, as we did on the Paris trip and in Switzerland. I would like, however, to urge you not to allow this at the Philharmonic concerts in Vienna, even if K were to propose it to you or demand it of you. In Vienna, where we are at home, and where people know us, we do not need such things. I hope that the orchestra is of one mind with me on this matter.[3]

Six days later Furtwängler was once more on the warpath, asking for the proposed dates of a Karayan (*sic*) concert to be changed to a time when Furtwängler himself would not be in Vienna. If this cannot be done, Furtwängler adds, it will show ill will on Karajan's part and a decidedly 'unaccommodating' attitude on behalf of the Philharmonic to Furtwängler himself.[4]

The problem was, Furtwängler was beginning to resent anyone offering Karajan work of any kind. It was a somewhat quixotic stance. His manoeuvring Karajan out of Salzburg and his successful blocking of his engagements with the Vienna Philharmonic merely encouraged others to shower Karajan with invitations. And they came flooding in: from La Scala, Milan, from the Venice Biennale, and (the crowning indignity from Furtwängler's point of view) from Bayreuth, where negotiations for Karajan's involvement in the first post-war festival were already at an advanced stage. 'This will send the old one [Furtwängler] sky high,' Legge wrote in an internal EMI memorandum in January 1950.[5]

*

The Vienna Symphony's tour of West Germany in January 1950 was of great importance to the orchestra, and to the Austrian government who sponsored it. It was not easy to arrange. Travel remained difficult and funds were in short supply. While audiences in provincial Germany complained about the high seat prices for the tour (a top price of DM15 as opposed to the more usual DM10), the Viennese press back home made much of the fact that the Vienna Symphony's subsidy was trifling in comparison with the sums that were already being lavished on orchestras in post-war Germany.

Many of the concerts took place in improvised venues. Some war-damaged concert halls had been renovated or rebuilt; most had not. In Aachen the orchestra played in a cinema, in Essen in an unheated circus tent. Karajan would later recall how salivating lions watched 'with terrible fascination' as he changed for the concert.

The tour was equally important for Karajan. It was the first big orchestral tour of his career; it also marked his official return to the country where he had made his name as a conductor. Asked by the German press about the tour's significance, he answered that it was twofold. First, there was an opportunity to explore music afresh after the dark events of recent years; secondly, music was an agent of reconciliation. The time had not yet come when he would be 'accused' of perfectionism. Yet he was already discussing it, arguing that seeking the very best was not a goal in itself but a means of ensuring that the musical experience was a truly potent force in the promotion of harmony and understanding between peoples.

Reading press reports of the tour, one sees the honing of a public persona that would later become so familiar. There is the sense of a man in a hurry, difficult to pin down, though generally courteous and relaxed on those occasions when he does condescend to talk to journalists. There are the increasingly familiar, often vaguely inaccurate accounts of his youth and early career. There is the preference for medicine to music as a topic of conversation. (On this occasion, the subject was rheumatic fever from which Karajan claimed to have been suffering in Rome the previous December.) The matinée-idol good looks are still assiduously cultivated. The slim figure, the swept-back lacquered dark hair, the slight 'lift' provided by the discreetly designed platform shoes: these all help to create an image of elegant athleticism. The off-stage gait, we are told, is unhurrying, casual even; in sharp contrast to the quick, elastic step with which he approaches the rostrum.

Comparisons are made in the press with another matinée idol, Sergiu Celibidache, the 37-year-old Romanian conductor who in the upside-down world of 1945 Berlin made the unprecedented leap from graduate music student to acting chief conductor of the Berlin Philharmonic. But where Celibidache had sprung from nowhere, Karajan was already something of a legend. The old headline '*Das Wunder Karajan*' was widely quoted during the tour; the words 'aura', 'myth', and 'legend' appear in numerous reviews and profiles. One paper, lapsing into English, describes Karajan as a 'Show-man' of the highest order. But, it also asks, is there substance behind the show? Is the man a charlatan or a true artist? The latter, comes the more or less instant reply. Where there is equivocation, it is often blurred by periphrasis or by resort to a somewhat convoluted use of metaphor, such as the *Süddeutsche Zeitung*'s 'a cool blazing flame behind asbestos'.[6] The same writer dubs Karajan the 'Savonarola of Music' while likening his rostrum manner to that of an oriental temple dancer.

Many Germans were seeing Karajan for the first time on this tour. They included the young Christoph von Dohnányi, whose initial impression had nothing to do with how Karajan interpreted the music, everything with his palpable power of command. 'Here was a man,' he remembers thinking, 'who has been born to conduct.'[7]

The programmes were traditional, made up of well-rehearsed Karajan favourites, the bias heavily in favour of classical and romantic Viennese symphonies.[8] There was just one contemporary work, Hindemith's *Mathis der Maler* symphony. Friedrich Gulda had played the Schumann concerto with Karajan and the orchestra in Vienna at an eve-of-tour concert, but there were no soloists on the tour itself; the budget did not run to it, a fact which allowed Karajan even more of the limelight.

The tour began and ended in Munich, extended as far north as Hamburg and Essen, and returned south via the Rhineland. Despite the evident logistical difficulties, it was generally without mishap. In Hamburg, Karajan threw a tantrum when a minor disturbance alerted him to the fact that some British national servicemen had slipped into a rehearsal; but he was given short shrift by a senior British official, who politely advised him that jurisdiction over the premises and facilities he and his orchestra were enjoying did not lie in his hands.

In Ulm, old acquaintances noticed that Karajan talked as rapidly as ever but that the Austrian accent, which had so amused people before the war, had more or less vanished. The concert was prefaced by a lengthy official welcome from the mayor; there was a rather greater stir, however, when word got round that Wieland Wagner was in the audience.

The Aachen visit was warmer and more elaborate. Karajan had been genuinely happy there ('the happiest seven years of my life', he told a local newspaper). He had also made an unusually large number of friends, many of whom had survived the war. Again, there was much speechifying and an extensive round of newspaper interviews. There was also an official visit to the Opel car works where a brand-new Opel Olympia Type 1950 was put at Karajan's disposal for the duration of his visit. 'A quick glance at the gears,' one paper reported, 'and he is off like a rally driver.' In fact he was away to call on friends in Grenzhof, and to visit his old boss Otto Kirchner who lay seriously ill in hospital.

Karajan and the orchestra returned to Vienna to widespread acclaim. 'Sixteen Concerts – Sixteen Triumphs' proclaimed a headline in the *Wiener Tageszeitung*.

*

After so triumphant a tour, it was bound to be asked what were the longer-term prospects for a developing relationship between Karajan and the Vienna Symphony. The orchestra's first post-war music director had been Hans Swarowsky. After a difficult first season, the orchestra opened negotiations with the pianist-turned-conductor Carlo Zecchi and the not yet denazified Clemens Krauss. Since the orchestra's constitution did not allow its music director any real autonomy over its day-to-day affairs, there was little chance of either of them accepting the offer; nor did they.

Karajan's availability, on a purely informal basis, early in 1948 turned out to be a happy chance for both parties. But it was never anything more than a marriage of convenience. Karajan held no official position with the orchestra. Such changes as he managed to bring about were achieved through force of personality and financial drawing power.

The roster of conductors appearing with the Vienna Symphony in the years 1948–51 was a quite exceptional one, but only Karajan could demand, and get, lavish extra rehearsal time for special projects, tours, or festival appearances. In the circumstances, growth, such as it was, was piecemeal rather than organic. It also meant that the orchestra's so-called 'parity' with the Vienna Philharmonic – much talked up by a gossipy press – was at worst a lie, at best an illusion. On a bad day, the Philharmonic could not hold a candle to Karajan's Vienna Symphony at its exciting best. But if the Symphony was capable of winning the occasional battle it never stood the slightest chance of winning a more protracted war. The Philharmonic's long tradition of independent music-making, rooted in an elaborate network of familial and teaching relationships and further nurtured by the players' unique training in the pit of the Vienna Opera, gave it advantages it has enjoyed more or less without challenge throughout the world these last 150 years.

In the summer of 1950 Rudolf Gamsjäger, the secretary of the Gesell-schaft der Musikfreunde, advised the Vienna Symphony that it needed as a matter of urgency to find a solution to the problem of how its artistic policy should be directed in the longer term. In other words, it needed to consider doing a deal with Karajan. The 1950–1 season underlined his point; but it did nothing to resolve it. A visit to Milan with the *B minor Mass* and *Missa Solemnis* in the summer of 1950 was followed by a highly successful autumn tour of Italy, beginning in Venice and moving south to L'Aquila and Perugia. Before the tour started, Karajan and the orchestra played Bruckner's Eighth Symphony in his mother's home town of Graz. It was his debut there, an event that was treated by the local press more like a Second Coming than a first appearance. The Italian tour over, Karajan launched a short winter season of concerts with the Vienna Symphony entitled 'Great Symphonies'.[9]

The high point of the 1950–1 season was not, however, a symphonic concert but a concert performance of an opera. To mark the fiftieth anniversary of Verdi's death, Karajan gave two performances of *Aida*, in Italian, in the Musikvereinssaal on 3 and 4 February 1951. The performances, which were sold out weeks in advance, created a sensation and led to further questions being asked about why he was being so pointedly excluded from the Vienna Opera. No doubt Karajan welcomed the questioning – it would be naïve to think that the *Aida* was not in some sense designed to provoke it – though not out of any desire on his part to be involved in the current set-up in Vienna. Not for the first time in his career, he was putting down markers for the longer term.

Nowadays it is often said that the 1951 *Aida* was not all it was cracked up to be;[10] and it is true, Karajan would perform and record a radically rethought and even more consummately played and sung *Aida* with the Vienna Philharmonic in Vienna in the late 1950s. Yet the 1951 performance is worth hearing for the blaze and theatricality of Karajan's conducting, for the extraordinary inwardness of the orchestral playing in the final scene, and for several fine solo performances.[11]

*

At Whitsuntide 1950 the orchestra enjoyed what was in effect a prestigious coda to the German tour. Wieland Wagner's appearance at the orchestra's concert in Ulm on 14 January had been no casual evening out. He was already talking seriously with Karajan about the reopening of the Bayreuth Festival, originally intended for 1950, but now rescheduled for 1951. An immediate problem was finance (the currency reform of 1948 had thrown Bayreuth's plans into disarray), to which end the 'Incorporated Association of the Friends of Bayreuth' had been established in September 1949. It was under the Friends' auspices that Karajan and the Vienna Symphony were invited to give a fund-raising concert in the festival theatre at Bayreuth on Whit Sunday 1950. After an opening address by Dr Moritz Klönne, Karajan conducted the Prelude to *Lohengrin* and Hans Hopf sang Lohengrin's Narration. After the interval, Karajan conducted Bruckner's Eighth Symphony.

The audience was ecstatic. As one player remarked, even by the standards of the ovations the orchestra had received on its January tour, this was something altogether special. The press, though, could not resist mischief-making. Under a banner headline 'Orchestral Sound of Spotless Beauty', Reinhold Scharnke of Coburg's *Neue Presse* reiterated the point about the Vienna Symphony being the Philharmonic's equal. As for Karajan, Scharnke went on to argue that he was well on the way to becoming 'Germany's first conductor'; only Knappertsbusch could be said to stand beside him.

Pitting Karajan against Knappertsbusch soon became a local Bavarian speciality, something which did Karajan no good at all. Unlike Furtwängler, Knappertsbusch was more than adept at looking after himself. A man who, when pressed to take up the cudgels against a particularly noisome local critic, dismissed the suggestion with the unforgettable neologism '*Kathedralehundpisser!*' (literally 'dog that pisses on the cathedral') was more than capable of winning any war of words the local Bavarian hacks might care to start.[12]

The Viennese press, by contrast, preferred to stoke the fires of older conflicts. By taking centre stage at Salzburg, Furtwängler had effectively ruled himself out of the Bayreuth Festival. How ironic, smirked Vienna's *Die Presse* when it was announced that Karajan would be conducting *Die Meistersinger* and the second *Ring* cycle at Bayreuth in 1951, that 'the great German conductor' should be working in Salzburg while the 'Salzburger Herbert von Karajan' should be so intimately connected with Bayreuth.

In fact, Furtwängler had been engaged to conduct the opening concert of the 1951 festival; but as the minutes of the Association of the Friends of Bayreuth record:

Wieland has again been negotiating with Furtwängler, who, after saying 'yes' three times and 'no' five times, has finally said 'yes' on condition that 1951 turns into Richard Wagner's Bayreuth, not a Herr von Karajan's Bayreuth.[13]

Furtwängler was right up to a point. Karajan, abetted by Legge, certainly had designs on Bayreuth. It did not need Wieland's less talented brother Wolfgang to discover that during the 1951 season Karajan had been using Bayreuth Festival notepaper and typing the word 'Management' at the top to work out the broad trajectory of Karajan's aims. But though genius respects genius, it can also repel as the similar poles of a magnet repel. The personal rapport that existed between Wieland Wagner and Karajan was contradicted by the need each of them had to go his own way.

Where Karajan left an indelible mark on post-war Bayreuth was in his persuading Wieland to accept his old Aachen colleague Wilhelm Pitz as Bayreuth's new chorus-master. It may not have been an entirely disinterested recommendation by Bayreuth's would-be music director, but it was an inspired one.[14]

*

The most emotionally taxing concert Karajan was involved in during the summer of 1950 was in Lucerne. The first half of the concert was given over to Roussel's Fourth Symphony and Mozart's C major Concerto K467. The soloist in the Mozart was Dinu Lipatti, now a dying man. Music, and faith in the cortisone he was taking, had sustained him through a summer of intermittent but ever rarer and more wonderful music-making. His wife Madeleine wrote of the occasion:

If you had been there you would have been as moved as I was by the reception of an enthusiastic, almost delirious, audience only a few days after he had been feeling so weak, and the nearness of this concert had only added to his sufferings.[15]

Artur Schnabel had agreed to play in Lipatti's place should he be too ill to go on. This was a gesture of some consequence, since there was no other circumstance in which Schnabel would have agreed to appear with Karajan.

Like Solomon and Artur Rubinstein (who dined out on stories of his various refusals to play with Karajan), Schnabel was not willing to perform with a former member of the Nazi Party. But there was another reason why he might have wished to avoid Karajan personally. Two years earlier, he had slipped into a rehearsal for a concert Karajan was giving with Backhaus and the Lucerne Festival Orchestra. Learning that Schnabel was present, and either ignorant of his views on former Nazis or oblivious to them, Karajan quickly finished the rehearsal and set off in search of the by now fugitive pianist. He eventually tracked him down to the gentlemen's lavatory, where Schnabel, summoning whatever vestiges of dignity are available to a man in such circumstances, refused to countenance any form of discussion or negotiation. Not to be gainsaid, Karajan began phoning the Schnabels' apartment. It was only when Schnabel's wife told Karajan that his best chance of winning over her husband was to leave him severely alone that he appears finally to have given up the chase.[16]

Shortly before the Lipatti concert, there was a curious parallel to this saga. Isaiah Berlin had travelled to Switzerland to visit Israel's President Weizmann, who had been undergoing specialist eye surgery. Anita von Karajan met Berlin in the street and declared herself deeply fascinated by his mission. There were few people she admired more, she said, than Chaim Weizmann. Doing his best to ignore this somewhat startling claim, Berlin talked of his frustration at not being able to get a ticket for the Lipatti concert.

'Herbert wouldn't dream of you missing the concert,' was Anita's prompt response.

Two tickets were duly provided – Berlin wanted only one – more or less on the stage.

'And how I should love to meet President Weizmann,' Anita sighed after the concert.[17]

CHAPTER 32

Bachfest

When Karajan did Bach, he shed all virtuoso glamour and made music, and what marvellous music-making it was! He was a part of the orchestra, rather like an eighteenth century Kapellmeister.

Anton Heiller

In February 1950 Karajan conducted a performance of Bruckner's Fifth Symphony with the Vienna Symphony.[1] His next appearance in Vienna was in June during the city's grand festival in honour of the two hundredth anniversary of Bach's death in Leipzig in 1750.

The *Bachfest* triggered another flare-up of Furtwängler's debilitating Karajan-complex. The Vienna Philharmonic's Otto Strasser would recall:

One will never know exactly what happened, but in 1950 the Gesellschaft der Musikfreunde, whose concert director Furtwängler had been, invited him to conduct the *St Matthew Passion* as part of the Bach Festival. At first, he rejected the idea. The Gesellschaft then turned to Karajan, who accepted, and made the now famous forty or fifty rehearsals with the choir. As the rehearsals drew to a close, Furtwängler reappeared and announced that he would now like to conduct the *St Matthew Passion* after all. The Gesellschaft felt they had no option but to remain loyal to the man who had done all the work. And so the crash came. From then on we were no longer able to use Karajan; if we had done so, we should have lost Furtwängler completely. He was, unfortunately, terribly jealous of the younger man.[2]

Conductors for the Vienna *Bachfest* were to have included not only Furtwängler, but Hindemith, Klemperer, Krips, and Mitropoulos. Of these, only Hindemith and Krips appeared. The principal choral works were directed either by Günther Ramin, the distinguished Kantor of the Thomaskirche, Leipzig, or by Karajan himself. Karajan conducted the *St Matthew Passion* and the *B minor Mass*, each meticulously rehearsed, as Strasser recounts, over several months. Kathleen Ferrier, who was Karajan's alto soloist in both works, wrote to an American friend Benita Cress, 'All these Viennese singers work themselves to a standstill. I just dawdle by comparison.'[3]

Karajan also conducted a Sunday morning performance of Mozart's *Coronation Mass* in St Stephen's Cathedral, and the festival's opening concert. This included *Brandenburg Concerto* No.2, the Concerto in D minor for Two Violins and Orchestra with Menuhin and Schneiderhan as the soloists, and the Cantata No.50 *Nun ist das Heil und die Kraft*, all directed by Karajan from the harpsichord. Menuhin would later recall:

Karajan was a very good accompanist, quite different from Toscanini who believed there was only one way with the music, which happened to be his way. I got on with Toscanini very well, but in this respect Karajan was not at all like him. My impression was that Karajan was closer to Bruno Walter, who was also a wonderful accompanist.[4]

Karajan's directing Bach from the harpsichord was no modish affectation, as some would believe it to be in later years when his presence at the harpsichord did, indeed, become something of a formality. Specialist musicians like Yella Pessl and Ralph Kirkpatrick, who taught alongside Karajan on Salzburg summer schools in the 1930s, knew that there was nothing dilettantish about Karajan's preparation of baroque music. After the war, the composer and organist Anton Heiller would tell H. C. Robbins Landon:

... even when he was modestly playing the continuo, you could see that the orchestra had been trained to a rare standard of perfection. I think that for a time Karajan flirted with the idea of becoming – and this apart from his work in the opera house – a sort of *collegium musicum* specialist.[5]

And, indeed, Robbins Landon himself vividly recalls that opening concert of the 1950 Vienna *Bachfest*:

It was a great vignette: Karajan conducting in the Musikverein from the *second* harpsichord and ending with 'Nun ist das Heil', which was simply outstanding.[6]

One should not underestimate the huge contribution these 1950 Bach performances made to Karajan's career. In the first place, he had personally trained the Vienna Singverein to a pitch of excellence that astonished and gratified those who heard it at the time. Toscanini, who heard Karajan direct the choir in the *Missa Solemnis* and *B minor Mass* in Milan in the summer of 1950, is said to have dubbed it 'the best choir in the world'; though it should be added that he admitted privately to being as bored by the performances as he had been by his own account of the Verdi *Requiem* some days earlier.[7]

As a Bach conductor, Karajan had a wonderful way with singers and some wonderful singers at his disposal: Walter Ludwig as the Evangelist, Irmgard Seefried, Ferrier, and Schwarzkopf, who at this time was a marvellously silver-voiced Bach interpreter. In some ways Karajan was, and was to remain, an old-fashioned Bach conductor. He revelled in the music's emotional power, and its quasi-operatic style; and he allowed trusted soloists to set their own pace. His view of the *St Matthew Passion* was unashamedly romantic: an intensely personal meditation rooted in deep quiet yet shot through with narrative incidents of startling power. His treatment of the *B minor Mass*, by contrast, was often daringly modern. His superfine control of orchestral dynamics and his skill in teaching singers new ways of breathing and articulation (how to breathe in very rapid music, for example, with finely tapered dynamics at phrase ends) made for a lightness, clarity, and buoyancy of utterance that startled and delighted those who heard it. In this respect, he was establishing a significant bridgehead between an older, highly coloured style of performance and something far closer to what we would now recognise as sparer, cleaner, supposedly more 'authentic' Bach.

The representative ground for examining Karajan's work as something of a modernist in Bach performance is his EMI recording of the B minor Mass made in Vienna and London in 1952–3 with Schwarzkopf, Marga Höffgen, Nicolai Gedda, Heinz Rehfuss, the Vienna Singverein and a small specialist group of players from the Philharmonia Orchestra. *The Gramophone*'s devout and worldly-wise Alec Robertson, described the recording as 'a landmark in the history of the gramophone'.[8] The *Record Guide* commented:

The Columbia performance moves under the impetus of consistent and high inspiration. The principal qualities of Karajan's reading are lightness, absolute clarity of sound and rhythmic buoyancy, all of them qualities that many performances miss. How often we have wished that the fugal voices could be distinguished, and how often missed the fiery trumpet runs; and how often have the 'Gloria' and 'Sanctus' thumped along with an accent on every beat! Karajan, and Columbia's engineers, allow us to hear all the vocal and instrumental parts. Another characteristic of the performance is the honeyed suavity with which many of the numbers are invested; the first 'Kyrie' fugue is a soft, gentle complaint in legato phrases that contrast strongly with the choral style to which we are accustomed. The 'Gloria' again is superbly exhilarating and airy, with much emphasis placed on lightly springing rhythm; here Karajan persuades his choir to articulate each semiquaver of the running countersubject in 'Et in terra pax', not quite to aspirate the runs, but to set the melodic shape in focus. The mode of articulation is applied later, with breathtaking effect, in the bass entry of 'Et iterum venturus est'. It may be objected that, in doing so, Karajan is applying a style foreign to that of the music; but the result so clarifies the texture and part-movement that only the die-hard choral traditionalist will complain for long.[9]

Not everyone approved of the long lines and the 'honeyed suavity' of some of the detailing. The Philharmonia's solo flautist Gareth Morris famously objected to Karajan's device of using a second player to 'cover' end-of-phrase breath-points.

The recording won widespread acclaim, in Europe and – important for Karajan – in the United States where the poise of the reading and its fresh, unshowy musicianship won it many admirers. The only thing that jarred for *High Fidelity* reviewer David Randolph was what was judged to be Karajan's over-hasty treatment of the 'Crucifixus'.[10]

For the most part, the studio recording offers a far 'purer' reading of Bach's score than the live performance Karajan conducted at Vienna's *Bachfest* in 1950.[11] The fact that this was a studio recording – made in the same intimate style Karajan and Legge favoured for some of their Mozart opera recordings – adds to one's sense of the performance's radical modernism. Karajan once remarked that he often felt as if he was freezing in the recording studio. The recording of the *B minor Mass* is not necessarily chillier than the live performance; what one does notice, however, is how much of the vestigial romantic detailing has been pared away.

Like Klemperer, whose Bach performances in Berlin in the 1920s were thought to be the last word in the new modern style, Karajan did not carry his reputation as a modernist into his later years. By the 1970s, his Bach had become a byword in some circles for how *not* to perform the music. This was unfair. His 1979 re-recording of the *Brandenburg Concertos*, with hand-picked members of the Berlin Philharmonic, is a model of stylish and urbane music-making, a latter-day addition to a distinguished discography that goes back via Britten and Menuhin to the famous pre-war recordings of Adolf Busch. Gundula Janowitz ranked the experience of performing the *St Matthew Passion* live in Salzburg at Eastertide under Karajan's direction as one of the high points of her musical life. Many in the audience would have concurred with the judgement, though Karajan's 1972 recording of this essentially studio-defying work is more a memento of the experience than the thing itself.

Where Karajan might be said to have gone awry in his later years was in the faith he continued to place in the Vienna Singverein. In 1950 it was essentially *his* choir, meticulously trained. As the years went by, and the training fell more and more into the hands of chorus-masters of varying degrees of competence, the Singverein sometimes resembled those rather foggy-toned pre-war choirs Karajan had done so much to reform. Ironically, it was the work of Karajan's old friend Wilhelm Pitz with Legge's newly created Philharmonia Chorus in the late 1950s that first cast a shadow over the Singverein's standing. Later, the rise of small professional choirs specialising in the performance of classical and pre-classical choral music would make its style seem even more *passé*.

Karajan remained the choir's director for life – though after 1964 he was rarely in Vienna itself – and its members always gave of their best for him personally. In 1974, at much the same time as Karajan made what he later judged to be a bitterly disappointing re-recording of the *B minor Mass* for Deutsche Grammophon, EMI was forced to abandon an entire recording project with the choir when the conductor, Giulini, refused to go on working with it.[12]

Yet Karajan remained stubbornly loyal, as he did to all those individuals and institutions who had stood by him in difficult times.

CHAPTER 33

Milan, Paris, and Bayreuth

Are you egotistic? I don't know. Vain? Certainly not: you are much
too intelligent to succumb to the pettiness of vanity. Headstrong?
Decidedly. Destiny for you is a cord which draws you with all
its strength towards a necessary end, and that is the only thing
that matters, isn't it? And besides, you possess attraction without
archness. You have hard muscles, a rugged profile, and the stern
heart of a conqueror. As I observe you, I am reconsidering the
sayings of a materfamilias: 'A dangerous maestro. Hell just round
the corner. Precipitate flight advised.' But we all know that in these
matters a human being is like a moth, unable to resist the flame
which burns.

Bernard Gavoty, Music Critic, *Le Figaro*

La Scala, Milan was not, strictly speaking, Legge territory as far as EMI was
concerned. Milan, however, was where Karajan was about to put down
roots as the newly appointed conductor of La Scala's German repertory.
During the denazification process in Austria, Karajan had firmly resisted
the idea of opting for an 'easy' restart of his career in Italy. But his work
with Labroca in Florence during the war, and his friendship with Victor
De Sabata, who had returned to La Scala in 1947, made it probable that
he would be involved, in one way or another, with Milan.

For Karajan, two factors weighed heavily in favour of La Scala. First,
there was the musical integrity and political disinterestedness of De Sabata
himself. Secondly, the house's musical and administrative structure was
based, not on the repertory system, but on a relatively short season of
meticulously prepared special events. The possibility of a month's rehearsal,
ten or twelve hours a day, much of it in the theatre itself, was artistic nirvana
to Karajan.

Fortunately, he established an instant rapport with Milan's newly
appointed *sovrintendente* Antonio Ghiringhelli. Ghiringhelli was a self-
made businessman of humble origins, a leather manufacturer who had made
a fortune during the war. Silver-haired, with a somewhat Karajanesque
profile, he had a passion for the theatre that was all-embracing, whether it
was opera or ballet, the smell of the grease-paint or the alluring fragrance
of the latest girl from the chorus or *corps de ballet* to grace his bed.
Ghiringhelli was capable of making huge mistakes. His initial hostility
to Callas has been widely chronicled. But he was tough, charming, and
gregarious; he was devoted to La Scala (he accepted no payment for his

work during his twenty-seven year rule), and he was superbly served by his staff.

In artistic matters he was a conservative who was open to new ideas that he all too rarely implemented. If it was suggested that La Scala might stage an opera by, say, Janáček, Ghiringhelli would immediately greet the idea with enthusiasm. Yet he would also find himself mentioning the proposal after dinner at the restaurant Biffi Scala to the woman on the cash desk.

'Janáček?' would come the inevitable reply. 'Never heard of him. What we need is a new *Tosca*.'

Thus persuaded, Ghiringhelli would return to the board of La Scala and utter the by now familiar mantra: 'Much as I approve the idea of the Janáček, *vox populi* demands . . .'

Whether *vox populi* had demanded Wagner's *Tannhäuser* or not, that is what Karajan had requested for the opening of the new season on 27 December 1950. The production was designed by one of the most highly regarded of all Bayreuth's pre-war designers, Emil Preetorius. The Austrian tenor Hans Beirer sang the title role; Schwarzkopf had been persuaded to sing Elisabeth.

It was not a happy event. Schwarzkopf must have rued the fact that she had not shown something of the young Lisa della Casa's pluck in turning down Karajan's urgent request that she should sing Venus. Della Casa would recall:

Karajan saw me as Marzelline [in *Fidelio* conducted by Furtwängler] and, if you can believe it, immediately asked me to sing in *Tannhäuser* with him. He told me I had just the right kind of sexiness to make a splendid goddess of love. 'But what about the voice?' I asked. 'We will manage,' he replied without any concern. Can you imagine my taking on Venus, which is sung by both dramatic sopranos and mezzos with an easy upper register? I had the good sense to refuse, but he held a grudge for some time. Eventually he got over it. I sang Marzelline and Sophie with him at La Scala in 1952. Those were the days![1]

Schwarzkopf was on safer ground a few weeks later when she sang Donna Elvira in La Scala's lavish new production of *Don Giovanni*, also conducted by Karajan. Again, his preparation was predictably meticulous. Schwarzkopf remembers him discussing long into the night with Walter Legge the gearing of the tempo at the point where the overture gives away to the opening scene, a musical hare Wagner had started running in his essay 'On Conducting' in 1869.

The Donna Anna was the gifted and intelligent young Spanish soprano Victoria de los Angeles. Karajan had heard her singing the title role in Strauss's *Ariadne auf Naxos* under Dobrowen's direction at La Scala the previous year. There was no question of de los Angeles being unable to sing Donna Anna; she sang the role with consummate ease. What she objected to was Karajan's draconian treatment of her when, as a practising Catholic, she declined to attend a rehearsal in Milan on 6 January, the Feast of the Epiphany. Having honoured one God, she eventually arrived in Milan to discover that she had seriously upset another. Whenever he could, Karajan made things difficult for her. She expected a piano rehearsal; none was forthcoming. At the first stage rehearsal she 'marked' her part, as is customary; Karajan demanded that she sing out. At this point, she took the attack to the enemy: she lapsed into total silence, merely opening and shutting her mouth in time to the music as she drifted noiselessly through the stage movements. In a desperate bid to have the final say, Karajan resorted to singing the part of Donna Anna himself.

The two never again worked together. De los Angeles, it has to be said, was playing with fire. In 1950 there still existed a number of 'old school' maestri who would have had her sacked on the spot. But then, paradoxically, Karajan was not an old school maestro. Though he had been born and brought up in the disciplines of pre-war Salzburg, he was in reality the first of a new breed of conductors, practical, efficient, forward-looking. Young singers – especially – were his passion, and were to remain so to the end of his days; gifted young singers, who looked well on stage, acted well, and had a talent that could be moulded.

A favourite story, which he never tired of telling, concerned a rehearsal in Milan which began with a member of the orchestra nervously informing him that 'the dancers have arrived, but no singers'. 'But those *are* the singers,' announced Karajan, casting an appreciative glance over the array of young lovelies assembled on stage.

*

A generally adulatory press in Austria and Germany, enthusiastic notices in Milan, seriously respectable ones in London: by the summer of 1951 Karajan must have begun to think that he could do no wrong. If so, he was in for a rude awakening.

On 24 May 1951, he set off for a two-week tour with the Vienna Symphony. A warning shot was fired in Stuttgart where the critic of the *Stuttgarter Zeitung* 'Dr W. B.' registered a vague sense of unease about Karajan's conducting. What was the cause, he asked? Was it too rational, too overtly dynamic, too obviously the work of a powerful poseur, or a combination of all three? Dr W. B. admitted to being baffled.[2]

Later in the tour, an anonymous Swiss critic would be less circumspect. In the course of an elegantly contrived collection of concert-goers' impressions of Karajan (whether actual or invented is not clear), a member of the audience observes:

And then the Brahms. Here it was not the soul or heart of a great composer that hovered over the concert hall but the peremptory 'me' [le 'moi' péremptoir] of the conductor himself.³

Other judgements culled by the anonymous critic were more flattering. Indeed, the critic himself conceded that he rather admired a man who did not throw himself about in climaxes or wave his baton under the noses of the first violins in passages of expressive beauty. Yet for all that, Karajan was for him little more than a 'salon' conductor: elegant, worldly, and rather boring.

Though Karajan was already a highly prized guest at the annual Lucerne Festival, Swiss reviews of his concerts in the late 1940s and early 1950s were often extremely hostile. Some of the criticisms were well founded; it was clearly a mistake, for instance, to agree to play one of the 1951 tour concerts in Lausanne cathedral. Perhaps Karajan imagined that the spacious cathedral acoustic would further intensify the benedictory mood of Brahms's Second Symphony. Lausanne's *La Nouvelle Revue* declared it 'a calamity'.⁴

*

Nor was the Parisian press as welcoming as it might have been. There were those in Paris who remembered the wartime performances of *Tristan und Isolde*: remembered them musically, that is. Ten years on, critic Emile Vuillermoz claimed to find a changed personality. Where the younger Karajan had appeared calm and collected, the revamped model had about him something of the air of a highly strung Arab stallion. Vuillermoz put it down to international success: the young master transformed into a precocious virtuoso, coquettishly addicted to strange tempi and superfine pianissimi.⁵

There was a bright splash of chauvinism in some of the notices. As the critic of *Le Figaro* Bernard Gavoty would later recall in an open letter to Karajan:

And also, you sometimes conducted second-rate orchestras. I can remember one session at the Palais de Chaillot with the Vienna Symphony Orchestra, which many people at that time confused with the Philharmonic. Three weeks earlier the same innocents, attracted by the name 'Mozarteum' . . . [applauded] to the echoes one of the most unpleasant orchestras in Europe. To be sure, I considered the Viennese orchestra the better, but by no means excellent, and I was intrigued by the repeated quacks of the Austrian horns in the trio of the *Eroica* Symphony [it was, in fact, the Seventh Symphony]. Perhaps I was wearing that evening what Sainte-Beuve called 'the enchanted smile of a critic who has detected a wrong note in the whole'. But what can you expect? The most phlegmatic man in the world would get annoyed in the end at hearing it so often repeated that our French orchestras fall far short of those of other countries. And I am certainly not the most phlegmatic man in the world![6]

Like rather a lot of people at the time, Gavoty did not greatly care for Karajan ('not my cup of tea') but he was spellbound by him none the less. Dodging in and out of concerts and rehearsals, he studied Karajan from every conceivable angle. Viewed from within the auditorium itself, he was strangely still:

In contrast with most conductors, who move their gaze from one group of instruments only in order to spy on another, and who in all circumstances show signs of feverish activity, you seemed strangely calm, buried in a brown study which was, as it were, disdainful and (for the spectator) rather irritating.[7]

The picture was complemented rather than confounded from backstage. Having abandoned the auditorium, Gavoty now peered intently at his quarry through a small tear in the backcloth that surrounded the orchestra:

If I may say so, the right side corresponded to the wrong. Thin as a rake, with slender legs, lips that frequently disclosed sharp incisors, foxy ears, bristling hair, immense consuming eyes in a bronzed face with strongly marked features – yes, before my eyes was a noble beast, and I had to resist a kind of fierce attraction which issued from you. I guessed you were distant and scornful, strained like a bow towards the position you had marked for yourself: I would place it – and so would you, no doubt – in the foremost rank.[8]

Writing about the June 1951 concerts in *Le Figaro* under his pseudonym 'Clarendon', Gavoty had produced one of those linguistically charged notices that often boded ill for Karajan. After placing the Vienna Symphony very firmly in the second rank of European orchestras and advising Furtwängler to sleep easy in his bed, he suggested that Karajan had injected into the radiant, light-filled blooms of Haydn (Symphony No.104) and Mozart (the Piano Concerto K482) a peculiar kind of poison.[9]

Later that week, in a much longer article written under his own name, Gavoty developed his ideas further in another of his open letters. Karajan's rivalry with Furtwängler, Gavoty suggested, was a trumped-up affair; if Karajan was jealous of anyone, it was surely of music's greatest snake-charmer Leopold Stokowski. He also discussed what he perceived to be the darkness and menace in Karajan's conducting. In the Mozart concerto, the baton had cast a spell that both entrapped the soloist and exhausted the music's energy. Warming to the idea, Gavoty embarks on a lengthy digression in which Karajan is cast in the role of the evil Golaud lurking in the castle vaults in *Pelléas et Mélisande*.[10]

Karajan was too intelligent entirely to discount such writing (he had met Gavoty and must have read him), just as he was too intelligent to set much store by the frenzied applause that greeted him in packed houses throughout this spring tour. It was, however, grist to the mill of his larger ambitions. A much longer and more important European tour was already being talked about for the following year, with Legge's Philharmonia Orchestra. The 1951 spring excursion had been a useful dress rehearsal.

The day after the Vienna Symphony's final concert in Zürich, Karajan was in London's Kingsway Hall involved in what must be accounted one of the shoddiest of all Legge's projects: the recording of five concertos in five days with Gieseking and the Philharmonia.[11] The finished recordings *sounded* as if they had been made in a hurry.

*

Before leaving for Milan the previous December, Karajan had made a pre-emptive strike on the casting of the forthcoming production of Wagner's *Die Meistersinger* in Bayreuth. Out of the blue, a young Austrian bass-baritone called Otto Edelmann had received a letter from Karajan inviting him to sing the role of Hans Sachs in the production. Edelmann was thirty-three, with a stop-start career behind him; he had served in the war and been taken prisoner by the Russians. Karajan had heard him sing Veit Pogner in *Die Meistersinger* and told him afterwards, 'You have the voice for Hans Sachs.' Edelmann would later recall:

I was totally confused. Only a singer can imagine what it means for a 34-year-old to sing Sachs in Bayreuth, on that holy ground! This task was a unique chance and the preconditions were ideal. The whole world was going to look on this *Meistersinger*. The more carefully I studied the role, the closer I came to Sachs's personality; and I loved the words I sang for him. Karajan worked with me on the role in between times in Vienna. God alone knows how much I owe him.[12]

Edelmann was right to be bemused. If the offer was genuine, why had it come from Karajan and not from Bayreuth itself? In a subsequent letter Karajan told Edelmann that Wieland Wagner had been alerted to the fact 'that I insist on your involvement [*da ich auf Ihrer Mitwirkung bestehe*]'. When a letter from Wieland did finally arrive, it began: 'At the request of Mr von Karajan and with the agreement of Professor Hartmann . . .'[13]

Karajan took Edelmann through the role line by line but never once allowed him to sing out. 'This is a role the voice must be used to living with,' he said. Not until the dress rehearsal was Edelmann allowed to use his full voice. The trick worked. 'At the end of the performance,' Edelmann recalls, 'my voice was in as good a shape as it had been at the outset.'[14]

What had not been achievable in the time available was real maturation, Sachs's music seeping into the very foundations of the voice as it had done over the years with Schorr and Bockelmann. But it is a fine performance none the less, cleanly sung and well articulated. The long hours spent working on the text with Karajan (and with the Italian prompter Karajan brought along with him to Bayreuth to train the singers in a more *parlando* style of delivery) paid handsome dividends in the theatre.

Edelmann was a well-liked artist. 'Kindly and exceptionally self-sacrificing' was how Karajan later described him. Schwarzkopf, who sang Eva to Edelmann's Sachs in the Bayreuth production, recalls his 'classic voice production' and the fact that he acted 'across the stage, not just to the public'.[15] Inevitably, there was a certain amount of critical carping about Bayreuth using so young a cast – Edelmann, Schwarzkopf, Hans Hopf as Walther von Stolzing, Erich Kunz as Beckmesser – and a great deal of Beckmesserish gloating when the records were released and it was found that on the night in question Edelmann had made a marginally late entry in the glow-worm section of the 'Wahn' soliloquy in Act 3.

Yet it is the very youthfulness and vitality of this 1951 Bayreuth *Meistersinger* that gives it its enduring appeal. From the start of the Prelude, which Karajan imbues with an almost reckless *joie de vivre*, there is a sense of new beginnings, of an uninhibited, rumbustious communal life spilling spontaneously over the footlights. Politically, this was important. Between the wars at Bayreuth, productions of *Die Meistersinger* had all too obviously played the nationalist card, the crowd scenes increasingly stylised, the individual made more and more to seem conterminous with the mass. (As, indeed, had been the case with Karajan's own production in Aachen in 1941.) Rudolf Hartmann's 1951 production did away with all that. Naturalistic and picturesque (with costumes borrowed from the theatre in Nuremberg), it let light and humanity back into the work.

Hartmann, who was adored by many of the singers who worked with him, was very much Karajan's type of director; a man who allowed the music and the text to determine the pattern of the stage action.[16] Karajan himself also spent a lot of time on stage, acting out the roles alongside the singers. One of the high points of the production as preserved on record is the first half of Act 3, dominated by the 'Wahn' soliloquy and a radiant account of the Quintet but rendered unforgettable by the scene in which the scurrying Beckmesser, bruised and battered, steals the Prize Song from Sachs's workshop. If Karajan and Erich Kunz had ever been out of work, they could probably have earned a decent living as a pair of stand-up comics. In rehearsal, they vied with one another in their attempts to invent new comic routines. (Of the two, Schwarzkopf recalls, Karajan was often the funnier.) In performance, conductor and singer-actor worked hand in glove.

For the 1951 festival, Karajan reseated the orchestra in Bayreuth's famous – and, for conductors, famously difficult[17] – pit. There was much hue and cry at the time, though digital remastering of the *Meistersinger* recording suggests that the woodwinds were not as disadvantaged by the changes as has sometimes been claimed. Rather more significant was the openness and textural clarity of Karajan's conducting. The critic of the *Wiener Zeitung* wrote:

'Applied Bach' is the best way of summarising Herbert Karajan's *Meistersinger* interpretation. He disentangles the textures, makes polyphony transparent in the midst of all the colour ... At times the effect is that of chamber music. The orchestra follows him in all this as though it had been trained by him for years.[18]

Karajan himself never cared for the term 'chamber music'. In 1972 he told a Spanish journalist:

I do not make it chamber music; I produce music in which the design is clearly identifiable. The complex structure of the Wagnerian *melos*, with four or five themes interwoven simultaneously, can only be perceived in that way.[19]

Later, he told me:

When we did *The Ring*, people said it was 'chamber music'; but I would deny that. It was the full Wagner orchestra, with full sonority, but played with real subtlety and the full range of dynamic levels.[20]

Christoph von Dohnányi has gone as far as to suggest that Karajan's Wagner conducting changed – and changed for the better – the way Wagner's orchestral writing was perceived by musicians in the post-war period.[21]

In 1951, Knappertsbusch directed the first *Ring* cycle, Karajan the second. Critical opinion was more divided over the *Ring* than over *Die Meistersinger*, though, once again, the more perceptive critics sensed a new direction – or, rather, a new aesthetic based on a renewed regard for some older masters. Just as Wieland Wagner's relatively abstract stage designs for the *Ring* and *Parsifal* drew directly on the work of Edward Gordon Craig (in particular on Craig's designs for Ibsen's play *The Vikings of Helgeland*[22]), so Karajan's conducting brought back into contention a style of Wagner conducting that owed more to the precedents set beyond the strict parameters of the old 'German style' by such inspired interlopers as Toscanini, Beecham, Walter, and Clemens Krauss.

Recordings exist of much of Karajan's 1951 Bayreuth *Ring*, but only Act 3 of *Die Walküre* was recorded officially, to the considerable annoyance of Wolfgang Wagner. He thought Legge and Karajan a baleful duo and feared Wieland was being ensnared by them:

The pair had joined forces in 1946, and from then on, just as Alberich obtained the ring and *Tarnhelm*, they combined art and business in a 'world-inheriting way' ... Legge employed devious means of making *The Ring* recordable or unrecordable with the aid of his exclusive seven-year contract ... Although an equal partner in law, I was not consulted about this piece of horse-trading. Having failed to nip it in the bud and prevent Wieland from consenting to an arrangement whose disastrous repercussions were lost on him, and not wishing to stab my brother in the back by disavowing him, I reluctantly let matters rest.[23]

Whatever the internal politics, this recording of Act 3 of *Die Walküre* still has the power to thrill. Varnay is a superb Brünnhilde ('la torche brûlante' was Régine Crespin's description of her), Sigurd Björling is a sterling, steady-voiced Wotan. In Act 3 we get only the briefest glimpse of the Sieglinde of the young Leonie Rysanek. What we do have, however – her Act 3 exit – is incandescent, vocally and orchestrally. Little wonder that Karajan wanted to show her off in concert performances of *Die Walküre* in Vienna the following autumn.

There were those who said that the greatest performances in Bayreuth in 1951–2 took place when Karajan rehearsed an opera and Knappertsbusch conducted it. Things rarely happened that way round, though Karajan and his old friend from Ulm Max Kojetinsky did play for Knappertsbusch during rehearsals. (Two pianos, four hands, was Karajan's favourite way of rehearsing.) After one rehearsal, as Karajan stood smiling by the piano waiting for a word of thanks from the great man, Knappertsbusch turned to him and said, 'If there's a coach's job going begging somewhere, I'll put in a word for you.'

Taking a rise out of Karajan was good sport, and Karajan gave plenty of cues for such diversions, whether it was his persistent demand for a separate lavatory in the Festspielhaus or his habit of commuting up and down the Green Hill on a moped rather than in the car with which he had been officially provided.

As always, things were uglier where Furtwängler was concerned. One of his first actions on arriving in Bayreuth was to have Karajan thrown out of his rehearsal. But Legge, too, was in wounding mood. Presenting himself in Furtwängler's dressing-room at the end of the dedicatory opening performance of Beethoven's Ninth Symphony, he announced, 'A good performance, but not as good as it might have been.'

It took Furtwängler the best part of forty-eight hours to recover from this well-aimed barb.[24]

CHAPTER 34

Working with the Philharmonia

'Sorry, Mr von Karajan, there's a fly walking across my music.'
'Don't worry, play him as well.'

A great conductor allows you to make music. Beecham had that quality in supreme measure, and so, according to many of the musicians who played in the Philharmonia in the 1950s, did Karajan. Violinist Hugh Bean would put it thus:

I think it's probably fair to say that, from an orchestral player's point of view, there are two things that mark out the great conductors from the not so great. First, under a great conductor you play better than you knew you could. Secondly, it is never boring; you never feel time hanging on your hands. Beecham could come in at ten o'clock on a wet November morning and it would be one o'clock before you'd had time to draw breath. Nowadays these qualities often seem in rather short supply. In fact, the problem with many latter-day conductors is that they *don't* allow you to play. Every note seems to have to be itemised, packaged, stamped with sealing wax, and filed away in some private cubby-hole. In the end, it is little more than advanced military bandsmanship.[1]

He went on:

I would hazard a guess – and I played under everyone who mattered, including Toscanini in 1952 – that Karajan made the Philharmonia play better than anyone ever has. In those days, he still had the ability to get a wonderfully singing, sustained, atmospheric sound from the orchestra but to balance that with precision and a certain astringency. The result – in those days – was never cloying.[2]

No out-and-out Karajan admirer, flautist Gareth Morris saw Karajan as a facilitator of rare accomplishment:

Karajan allowed us to be ourselves, to remain as individual musicians, with our own skills and our own way of doing things. He was a magnificently trained classical musician, of course; but what he personally was able to do was to mould individuals into an ensemble where players are not arguing with each other but, rather, conversing. As in a conversation where you say, 'Oh, I absolutely agree with you, though, if I may, I would like to put it slightly differently . . .' It is true that there were times when Karajan would seem to be wanting a longer line, a more legato style than I personally approved; and then we had to work things out between us. But this does not detract in any way from the ability he had to create this special kind of atmosphere. Quite how he did it is difficult to put into words. I suppose you could say he had an aura about him.³

One of Karajan's greatest skills was, indeed, his ability to make players listen to one another. He had developed the technique early: the review of the 1937 Vienna *Tristan* makes that plain. Now the Philharmonia was experiencing the technique in a non-theatrical context. In rehearsals and in recording sessions, he would point to a solo player. 'Listen,' the gesture meant. 'Listen to him.' When the playing of the rest of the orchestra complemented that of the solo, Karajan would give a thumbs-up and move on.

He intervened, of course; but he did so selectively, in specific areas. Philip Jones would remember a rehearsal of the finale of Sibelius's Fifth Symphony:

It was only then that I realised how contained the dynamics are – nothing much above *mf* until the last thirty or so bars. Karajan spent most of the rehearsal controlling the dynamic levels. Which is how it should be. Top orchestral players don't need to be told how to count, though for what it's worth Karajan had a superbly clear beat. What they do need, however, is to be schooled in phrasing, dynamics, and the finer points of ensemble playing.⁴

On the podium, he was the least corybantic of conductors. His feet, once set, never moved. The movement of his hands, arms, and upper body was, however, distinctive, unmistakable. Ronald Wilford, a close friend of many years' standing, has said:

Like everyone, Karajan moved in a particular way. In his case it was an extraordinarily compelling and attractive way. The problem is, it was *his* way of moving. The young conductors who worked with him and tried to copy him were ruined because you cannot appropriate the way someone else moves. This is a particular problem with conducting because conductors don't have an instrument that, as it were, neutralises their physical self. In this sense conducting is a highly personal thing. It demands an answer to the question, *How does this body move?*⁵

In the early 1950s, the physical charge of Karajan's conducting was phenomenal. One senses this in the 1951 recording of *Don Juan*, a performance of breathtaking sweep and sensual allure. Indeed, it was partly for this reason that old Philharmonia hands found it difficult to adjust to images of Karajan in his last years: the ageing master, physically stricken. In his mid-forties Karajan moved and conducted with the suppleness and wiry grace of an Olympic athlete in peak condition. Simply watching him vault lithely over the pews in Kingsway Hall seems to have given some of the more earthbound members of the orchestra a certain aesthetic thrill. Not everyone was affected by this. Oboist Sidney Sutcliffe found playing under Furtwängler more spiritually and physically exhilarating than under Karajan. But there is undoubtedly an electricity about many of the Philharmonia recordings that is as evident today as it was when the LPs first appeared.

When Karajan asked the Philharmonia wind players why their ensemble was so good, they replied: 'We sleep together!' This troupe of master musicians – Morris and Sutcliffe, Walton, Brain, and James – gave character to everything they touched. How Karajan got such fine sound from the Philharmonia strings remains something of a mystery. String playing is traditionally the Achilles' heel of even the best British orchestras. True, the Philharmonia never acquired the richness and weight of string sound of the Berlin Philharmonic; even under Furtwängler the Philharmonia strings seemed lighter-toned. But they had style and great virtuosity.

This is something Legge and Karajan worked on assiduously. It is significant that for the recording of Beethoven's Seventh Symphony it was the slow movement that took up most of the studio time. Recorded complete on 29 November 1951, the movement was partly revised the following evening, re-rehearsed on 26 April 1952, and completely re-recorded three days later. What we have on the finished recording is string playing that is numinous and wonderfully concentrated. The distinctions between piano and pianissimo are especially finely drawn, based not on withdrawal of sound but on different *weights* of sound, one of the hallmarks of the work of the great Italian masters: Toscanini, De Sabata, Serafin, Giulini.[6] ('Pianissimo but play it forte' was one of Karajan's own favourite instructions.)

Karajan became so enamoured of the Philharmonia strings, he made a number of recordings with them alone. In November 1953, an eloquent and affectionate recording of Vaughan Williams's *Fantasia on a Theme by Thomas Tallis* was followed next day by an astonishing account of Benjamin Britten's *Variations on a Theme of Frank Bridge*, the burnished virtuosity and tragic intensity of the playing making one regret that Karajan never added Britten's *Sinfonia da Requiem* to his pantheon of war-inspired masterworks.

That said, his fascination with Mozart's *Divertimento* No.15 in B flat K287 for two horns and solo strings, and his desire to record it after the manner of Toscanini with a full complement of orchestral strings, did cause a near-mutiny in the ranks. The leader Manoug Parikian told Legge that the task was beyond even the Philharmonia's capabilities. When Legge marched Parikian in to break the news to Karajan, all Karajan said was, 'A little modesty is welcome. We go on.' Having studied the Toscanini recording, he believed that the Philharmonia players were more than a match for their counterparts in the NBC Symphony.

Legge had his own boast about how Karajan achieved his results:

We worked together for years on the theory that no entrance must start without the string vibrating and the bow already moving, and when you get a moving bow touching an already vibrating string, you get a beautiful entry. But if either of those bodies is not alive and already moving, you get a click, and Karajan had already calculated all that.[7]

Hugh Bean, Parikian's successor as leader, would offer a slightly different explanation:

Karajan was not a string player himself, but he got a wonderful sound from us – second, perhaps, only to Ormandy who *was* a string player. I think in Karajan's case it was because his gestures were so sympathetic. The stick technique was so fluent. The stick itself never stopped moving, it simply flowed over us.[8]

It even flowed at the very start of works. At the beginning of Brahms's Fourth Symphony, for example, as Bean remembered well:

All we received was a kind of roll of the baton. 'Mr von Karajan, when exactly do you want us to play?' 'When you can stand it no longer!' He wanted the entry as late and as vague as possible. This wasn't at all the same as Furtwängler. He gave a kind of double beat which was extremely difficult to read if you didn't know him. Of course, if we came in earlier than Karajan hoped, he'd go with us.[9]

If it was an aesthetically pleasing experience playing under Karajan, it was also a generally agreeable one personally. The tyrant's trick of picking out players in rehearsal and humiliating them – Mahler's trick and Stokowski's occasionally, for which both men were widely loathed – was something Karajan had tried and rejected in Ulm. The discipline he exerted was rooted in self-discipline and a natural authority born of his own inborn confidence where music was concerned.

It was underwritten, however, by a vague undertow of menace. Jane Withers, Legge's former ENSA secretary whom he had drafted in to administer the Philharmonia Concert Society in March 1951, would later recall:

At first, one was rather awestruck by Karajan. The initial impression was of someone who was rather aloof and not especially friendly. But once you got to know him, he was really quite tame, quite human, and often very funny. At the purely personal level I liked him a great deal. He was certainly an extremely courteous man. On the other hand, it was never an especially easy relationship professionally, simply because you were always afraid that one day he might suddenly turn.[10]

Since Karajan never raised his voice much above a semi-audible mutter, rebukes, when they came, put the fear of God into players. The silence was so intense you could hear a mute drop two blocks away. By contrast, singers or orchestral players who threw tantrums were studiously ignored. No one in the Philharmonia ever really knew whether Karajan actually noticed cellist Raymond Clark's sudden theatrical departure ('That's it, I've had enough') from under his very nose near the end of a long and much interrupted rehearsal of the slow movement of Beethoven's Fifth Symphony.

Mistakes hardly worried him. He rarely made them himself (when he did, says Gareth Morris, he was a past master at covering up) and he was generally indulgent of routine lapses in rehearsal.

Humour was also a great solvent. During the sessions in Kingsway Hall for the 1951 recording of *Till Eulenspiegel*, a performance and recording which is every bit as thrilling as the *Don Juan* that accompanied it, Parikian ran into trouble with the glissando that runs from the top to the bottom of the violin's compass in the transition linking Till's mock-sermon to his exchange of courtesies with a bevy of beautiful girls. After several abortive takes, Parikian's intonation failed yet again on the high E flat:

There was an audible groan from the whole orchestra. Karajan remained silent for a moment, and then began to go through an elaborate pantomime of standing on a chair, looking for a suitable beam in the roof of the Kingsway Hall, throwing an imaginary rope over the beam and catching its end, tying a noose in it, and finally proffering it to Parikian *à la Eulenspiegel*, and with the blandest of smiles. The orchestra, which had been watching this ingenious dumb-show with growing interest – to the point where the occasion for its introduction had long since been forgotten – exploded in gales of laughter, the tension of the moment was released, and Parikian – who had been visibly annoyed with himself over his blemished E flat – once more returned to his studied self-composure.[11]

*

During his visits to London, Karajan stayed in the spare room of Walter Legge's house in Hampstead. Jane Withers and Legge's housekeeper (whom Legge himself usually ended up remunerating when Karajan left) looked after his numerous fads. On one visit it would be lemon tea, on another buttermilk, on yet another peanut butter. There were girls as well; Karajan was not particularly open about them, says Schwarzkopf, nor did he make any special effort to hide what was going on.

He socialised very little. During the day, he would take catnaps, forty-five minutes or so, after which he would wake up entirely refreshed for more work. In everything he did, he was extraordinarily single-minded. He had trained himself, he told Schwarzkopf, to concentrate only on the matter in hand, whether it was shaving, walking down stairs, or conducting a Bruckner symphony. He had even trained himself to relax. He would often lie on the floor playing with Legge's cats. (He was a bit like a cat himself, Schwarzkopf recalls, 'sleek and attractive but capable of suddenly lashing out'.[12]) In the evening, after a visit to Covent Garden or one of EMI's 7 to 10 p.m. recording sessions, he liked nothing better than a light supper and the chance to lie on the floor watching a Marx Brothers film.

Mostly he was alone on these visits, for Anita, now in her mid-thirties and still very much in her prime, was travelling with him less and less. No one believed that he and Anita would ever split up. Cynics said he needed her organisational powers and her money, overlooking the fact that he now had Mattoni and a burgeoning income of his own. Others saw them, quite simply, as soul mates, as natural partners. But what had happened to Karajan's first marriage was beginning to happen to the second.

Floosies came and went, and one or two more formidable rivals to Anita. However, one girl drifted on to the scene who was entirely out of the ordinary. She was Eliette Mouret from Nice, a shrewd, elegant, teenage beauty who, rather like one of Legge's Siamese kittens, strolled casually into Herbert's life, liked what she saw, and determined to stay.

CHAPTER 35

On recording

Once it had been resolved which form of the LP should be adopted, there began a recording activity that came upon us like an intoxication. It was the second, the great period of the gramophone.

Herbert von Karajan, 'On the Technical Reproduction of Music'

Considering for what a brief span the public concert has seemed predominant, the wonder is that pundits allowed it ever would be. To its perpetuation, however, a substantial managerial investment is currently committed ('For Rent: Complex of Six Acoustically Charming Auditoria. Apply J. Rockefeller.'), and we must realise that to reckon with its obsolescence is to defy the very body of the musical establishment.

Glenn Gould, 'The Prospects of Recording'

After the charade of the Gieseking sessions in London in June 1951, Karajan had returned to London's Kingsway Hall the following November to work on a series of recordings with the Philharmonia Orchestra which would prove to be a turning-point in his career as a recording artist. The sessions lasted a week, from 28 November to 4 December. Two recordings were completed then and there, Strauss's *Don Juan* and *Till Eulenspiegel*, EMI-Columbia's first LP. Beethoven's Seventh Symphony was also recorded, though Karajan remade the two inner movements the following April. An orchestrally brilliant account of Bartók's *Concerto for Orchestra* and the first of Karajan's four versions of Sibelius's Fifth Symphony were also begun in December and completed the following summer.

The only thing to be discarded from the December sessions was a series of trial takes for a selection of items from Handel's *Water Music* in Sir Hamilton Harty's sturdily Edwardian arrangement. Karajan had something of an obsession with this and drove everyone to distraction with it. The suite was eventually recorded to his satisfaction in July 1952, at the fourth attempt. The magically distant off-stage horns at the end of the 'Air' and the wonderfully purposeful on-stage horns in the opening movement are but two of the splendours in this somewhat Beechamesque enterprise.

*

What was it that gave Karajan's 1951 recordings of Beethoven, Bartók,

Strauss, and Sibelius their landmark status? Quite simply, it was the fact that they offered the first full manifestation of a capacity that would ultimately establish him as one of the most complete recording artists in the history of the gramophone; a capacity to enter a recording studio and secure, exactingly but with a minimum of fuss, superbly played performances of established and not-so-established masterworks, orchestral or operatic, grave or gay, grand and not-so-grand, in stylistically well-centred readings that would bear repeated hearing. It was a phenomenon which Yehudi Menuhin would later shrewdly anatomise:

Karajan worked his interpretations to a fine tilth, aiming at the minimum of sentimentality and the minimum of exaggeration. A recording does not bear hearing more than a few times if you can predict, not the note, but the interpreter's private twist or change or eccentricity. Karajan wanted a recording that could be heard repeatedly.[1]

Such an approach to interpretation has its own kind of truthfulness, though as Menuhin would add, equally shrewdly:

Such are the demands that are put upon us by the times in which we live, it is difficult to say, 'I do that because it is the way I feel.' Instead, you must say 'That's the way it is.' Perhaps such a criterion increases the authority of a performance; though, equally, it may decrease its justification.[2]

Karajan would probably have accepted that distinction, not least because his attitude towards the gramophone was characteristically ambivalent. Though he regarded its invention as one of the seven wonders of the musical world, he was never tempted to rule out concerts in the way that his brilliant young colleague Glenn Gould would eventually do. True, Karajan loved to mock the irritations of concert-going:

In front of the person to the left a lady flicks her bracelet, and to the right someone is trying to read the score (on the wrong page) whilst beating the (wrong) time with his programme. Behind sits someone who has not been able to find a parking spot and is still complaining about it to his neighbour . . .[3]

But he never denied the importance of the live concert:

What would our profession be and our relentless efforts for music, if we did not stand in direct contact with those who love music?[4]

Indeed, for Karajan the ideal performance – a time-girt experience, unrepeatable – could only take place in the concert hall. Once, in Berlin in the 1970s, he telephoned his old friend Raffaello de Banfield to invite him to a concert that evening. It was a rare thing for Karajan to do, even with friends; and it was a still rarer thing for him, on learning that Banfield was already spoken for, to plead with him to attend.

The work he specially wanted Banfield to hear was Stravinsky's *Symphony of Psalms*. Though not in the best of tempers after being denied an evening of good food and congenial company, Banfield went to the concert and conceded afterwards that it had indeed been a rare experience.

'For forty years I have loved this work,' Karajan told him. 'And now we have done it as I always imagined it should be done.'[5]

He never conducted it again.

And were a recording to exist of that performance, would Karajan have sanctioned its publication? Almost certainly not. Only once did he agree to such a strategy, in 1982, when a live performance of Mahler's Ninth Symphony was allowed to supersede the 1979-80 studio recording.

Like Gould, Karajan believed – or, rather, his finely honed intelligence led him to conclude – that the idea of 'recording' a concert (for anything other than sentimental or documentary reasons) contained an inherent contradiction. In his essay 'The Prospects of Recording', Gould wrote:

Claudio Arrau was recently quoted in the English journal *Records and Recording* to the effect that he would not authorise the release of records derived from a live performance since, in his opinion, public auditions provoke stratagems which, having been designed to fill acoustical and psychological requirements of the concert situation, are irritating and antiarchitectural when subjected to repeated playbacks.[6]

Gould's use of the word 'antiarchitectural' is interesting, since it implies that the well-produced gramophone record is designed to adduce an entirely different kind of listening experience from that encountered in the concert hall.

Though Karajan never managed to argue the case for the tape-splicer's art with anything like the charm or verbal incisiveness Gould summons in his essay 'The Grass Is Always Greener in the Outtakes',[7] what he did write in his posthumously published essay 'On the Technical Reproduction of Music' makes it abundantly clear that for him recordings serve special ends and make special demands. Faced with the lady's jangling bracelet or the asystolic tap of the time-beater's programme, the music-lover will yearn to effect his own withdrawal. 'In such circumstances,' wrote Karajan,

I praise the peace of my room where I am free of all disturbance, and where I am alone or in the presence of some like-minded friend, able to give myself to the pleasure of the music whenever I want and for as long as I want.[8]

In this sense, the gramophone, like the novel, is an essentially antisocial medium, cherished by those who are irked by the noisy commerce of the theatre, the concert hall or the opera house. But Karajan goes further. It is impossible, he argues, to appropriate a concert, to bundle it up into any form other than that of a rapidly fading memory:

A concert is simply a festive event. One dresses accordingly, and at the end of the concert one celebrates with one's friends; one exchanges impressions (complains about the conductor) and has the elevating feeling of having done something for one's culture.[9]

As an idea, this is not far removed from the thinking of Jacques Attali in his 1977 monograph *Noise: The Political Economy of Music*:

The concert remains operative in a repetitive [i.e. recording-dominated] society. But the spectacle is more and more in the hall itself, in the audience's power-relation with the work and the performer, not in its communion with them: today, a concert audience judges more than it enjoys; music has become a pretext for asserting one's cultivation, instead of a way of living it.[10]

What Karajan would – and did – vehemently deny was the charge, levelled by Attali and others, that in the age of magnetic tape the gramophone had become a chilly, manipulative medium best served by a new breed of Dalek-like musician described by Attali as 'a virtuoso of the short phrase capable of infinitely redoing takes that are perfectible with sound effects'.[11]

Karajan was equipped to play that particular game better than most – and on occasion he played it with relish – but it was never for him a serious proposition. Wearied to distraction by the Procrustean demands of the four-and-a-half-minute 78 rpm take, he openly revelled in the new, longer takes that tape allowed (like Beecham, he liked to have a tape running continuously throughout a session) while at the same time relishing the opportunities it afforded him to work his interpretations to that 'fine tilth', free of error and exaggeration.

He also offered a perspective on the subject that was provokingly different from Attali's. Working on the assumption that no one would acquire a record (except perhaps as a present from some well-intentioned relative) without first hearing it or checking out its credentials, Karajan comes up with the thought-provoking conclusion:

Once one has acquired the record, once it is one's own, one *aspires musically and spiritually to appropriate it* [my italics] by frequent listening. One is no longer critical but far more open-minded in order, first to comprehend the music and then to appreciate its beauty.[12]

Listening as an act of musical and spiritual appropriation! It is a nice idea. Little wonder that Karajan paid scant attention to criticism in its more narrowly judgemental mode.

Not that he was blind to the gramophone record's essential transience. With his acute feel for such things, he recognised that even the most perfectly judged recording is time's subject. It was not mere technology he was thinking of when he wrote:

Listening to one's old records is a mysterious thing. Behind the sounding music there is an almost tangible feeling of vanished time.[13]

*

The best of Karajan's Philharmonia recordings bring together readings of vitality and good sense with orchestral playing of great articulacy and musical 'finish'. They also show every sign of being made specifically for the gramophone. Despite NBC's ill-fated attempts in the late 1930s to create a specifically 'radio' sound for Toscanini in their notorious Studio 8-H, and Decca's far more successful experiment with full-range frequency *ffrr* sound in the 1940s, this was a relatively novel approach. To Glenn Gould, writing in 1966, Legge and Karajan had been ahead of their time:

A far more precise comparison can be found between the discs made by Herbert von Karajan with the Philharmonia Orchestra in London for EMI-Angel and the same maestro's recordings for DGG in Berlin. Any number of the latter . . . suggest a production crew determined to provide for the listener the evocation of a concert experience. The EMI recordings, on the other hand, provide Karajan with an acoustic which, while hardly chamberlike, at least subscribes to that philosophy of recording which admits the futility of emulating concert hall sonorities by a deliberate limitation of studio techniques.[14]

Most of Karajan's Philharmonia recordings were made in London's Kingsway Hall, a famously successful recording venue much loved by musicians, not least because the hall's acoustic provided them with a wonderfully clear and luminous impression of their own sound. 'It put air on the sound,' one player would recall. Nowadays, engineers put 'air on the sound' of inferior halls with the aid of computers. This may solve the problem for the listener but it is of no help to performers whose distorted sense of their own sound at the time of recording is hardly an encouragement to great music-making.

The Kingsway Hall was not without its problems, most notably the not infrequent changes to the acoustic brought about by England's famously changeable weather. Many is the time when a *Heldenleben*-size band was assembled, only for the engineers to pronounce the hall fit for nothing more strenuous than a Mozart divertimento. Philharmonia recordings, according to oboist Sidney Sutcliffe, tended to 'fructify on the spot'. The rule of thumb: if such and such won't work, try something else.

Here Karajan was in his element, the absolute master of what he was doing. He loved experimenting; added to which, he had the ability to keep the shape and pace of a recording clearly in mind over however many months (or years) it took to complete it.

Since Karajan rarely wasted time, merely guilefully reallocated it, Legge could afford to let him experiment. Members of the orchestra did not always see it that way and occasionally became restive: disgruntled foot soldiers whom the second-lieutenant has denied a sight of the map. But, then, the map was largely in Karajan's own mind. Even with Legge producing, Karajan's method of making recordings was already beginning to resemble the art of a tapestry-maker who alone is privy to the design he is creating. Equally, players warmed to his practical, no-nonsense approach. If a passage was refusing to come right, Karajan would leave it and return to it another day.

And this was possible. Since recordings were rarely tied in to concerts (tours apart, Karajan conducted relatively few concerts with the Philharmonia) recording sessions were designed to accommodate a certain amount of musical and technical experimentation. One of the orchestra's administrators, Mary Harrow, later Mrs Hugh Bean, thought the sessions more exciting than the concerts largely because of Karajan's inventive way of working in the studio.

Once, in order to secure the most trenchant yet finely weighted chords at the start of the *Eroica* Symphony, he invited the orchestra to play an unending procession of E flat chords in 3/4 time. When he heard two successive chords that he liked, he gave the thumbs up and the performance continued on its way. Afterwards, he was tickled pink by the idea of the unwanted tape being lopped off and discarded. (Since digital remastering would later reveal an audible edit at bar three of the recording, history cannot be said to have looked kindly on the ploy.)

The *Eroica* recording is, none the less, a fine example of what was being achieved by Karajan, Legge and the EMI engineers in Kingsway Hall. Suvi Raj Grubb, who oversaw the remastering of this Philharmonia Beethoven cycle in the mid-1970s, has cited the extraordinary 'intensity, presence, colour, and bloom' on the wind and string detailing in the recording of the *Eroica*'s first movement exposition. Writing in 1986, he stated, 'I know of no other recording in which the sense of perspective of these instruments is so vivid and natural.'[15]

But, then, Grubb had reason to remember just how vivid the recording was. Shortly after joining EMI in September 1960, he opened the door of a listening room only to find the company's redoubtable chairman Sir Joseph Lockwood listening to a recording of the *Eroica*. This was an extraordinary occurrence and a rather disturbing one, since Lockwood was notoriously antagonistic, not to classical music as such, but to the power the classical department enjoyed within the company. As Lockwood would later recall:

When I first came to EMI [in 1954], there was too much emphasis on serious music, which is bound to happen when you have a Board made up of rather distinguished gentlemen. They used to indulge their fancies, not always with regard to commercial considerations. They would say 'let's record *The Magic Flute*' and I would shock them by commenting, 'Is this a new pop group?' . . . Walter Legge was the Field Marshal and the pop managers were treated as Lance-Corporals who got no support from top management, or not enough anyway. I changed all that, and we became real leaders in the popular field.[16]

'Come in, Grubb,' said Lockwood, that fateful morning. 'You classical people are always demanding we spend vast amounts of company money on new recordings by maestro this or maestro that. They all sound the same to me. So, tell me now, who's conducting this particular recording?'

Faced with such a question, there are various stratagems to which a man might resort. The cheat will attempt to glimpse the label; but Grubb could see neither the label nor the sleeve. If it was an EMI recording, it would significantly narrow the field; Grubb guessed it was, but could not be sure. The sound of the orchestra would help; in those days there were marked differences between the great orchestras of the world. But who was conducting? With a jumble of impressions racing through his mind, Grubb focused on the playing. Who would take so solidly reasonable a tempo yet at the same time invest it with this strange nervous intensity? And who would achieve the extremely clever balance he was hearing: winds and strings being encouraged to project with great intensity, yet being directed in such a way as to produce such finely terraced dynamics and such splendidly 'open' perspectives?

'I would say it's Karajan,' said Grubb, with as much nonchalance as he could muster.

Sir Joseph's jaw dropped. EMI's classical department lived to fight another day.

*

The company's repertoire committee had not, in fact, been quite as soft a touch pre-1954 as Lockwood liked to suggest. During the earlier part of 1951, it had made strenuous efforts to stop Legge's proposed new Karajan recording of Beethoven's Seventh Symphony. Weingartner's 1936 'Light Blue' and Galliera's 'Dark Blue' Sevenths, it was argued, were still in the Columbia catalogue; and there was additional competition from the United States from Ormandy and Bruno Walter.

More than ever determined to follow his own nose, Legge brushed all such objections aside and was rewarded with yet another clutch of glowing reviews in *The Gramophone* and, later, in *The Record Guide*:

Karajan's Seventh is magnificent. He adopts, for the first three movements, tempi far more deliberate than [Erich] Kleiber's. Every detail is given due weight and emphasis; at the same time the symphony is most clearly shaped as a whole. In the finale there is a great unleashing of energy; and though the pitch of excitement is set high from the start, there is no flagging. Wagner's phrase 'the apotheosis of the dance' has never seemed to us to throw much light on this mighty symphony. There is no suggestion of the dance, even the dance deified, in the powerful drama which Karajan unfolds. The Philharmonia Orchestra responds nobly to his demands, and the sound they produce is superb.[17]

What had given Legge the necessary room for manoeuvre was his decision, in March 1951, to buy out the original Philharmonia Company and replace it with the commercially rather more independent Philharmonia Concert Society. Rule by committee – 'an animal with four back legs', as John le Carré famously put it – was not Legge's way, nor would it be Karajan's.

CHAPTER 36

Crossing the Rhine

Mr Karajan exacts the utmost tension from his
audience as from his orchestra.
The Times, London

During the winter of 1951–2 plans were finalised for an important spring
offensive: a three week European tour by Karajan and the Philharmonia.
Dubbed by Legge 'Getting Herbert into Berlin', the tour was treated with
something of the seriousness of a military campaign.

Inasmuch as 'getting Herbert to Berlin' was designed to strengthen
Karajan's claims on the Furtwängler succession, it must be regarded as
one of the most disinterested of all Legge's initiatives. But then, Legge was
a realist where Karajan was concerned. He knew that the Philharmonia
would not detain Karajan for ever; nor need it. During one of his many
battles with EMI management over his apparent 'indulgence' of Karajan,
he wrote:

The turning point in the Philharmonia's history was the moment he decided
to make his records and tour with us. From that day, other conductors have
competed to play with the Philharmonia.[1]

Berlin apart, the 1952 tour was designed as a showcase for the
Philharmonia in Europe where it was known only as a recording orchestra.
It was also a lure. Toscanini had been unable to conduct in London during
the celebrations marking the opening of the Royal Festival Hall in the
summer of 1951; he had promised, however, to conduct there as soon
as an opportunity presented itself. His promise had originally been made
to the management of the Royal Festival Hall and was assumed to involve
Toscanini's erstwhile favourite British orchestra, the BBC Symphony
Orchestra. Legge had other ideas.

*

Karajan had returned to Milan in December 1951 to prepare *Fidelio* and
a new production of *Der Rosenkavalier*. Legge was there, too, hatching
plots to record both works for EMI with the Milan casts under Karajan's
direction. With Furtwängler endlessly prevaricating over the recording of
Tristan und Isolde which he was due to make for HMV in London in the
summer of 1952, Legge returned hotfoot from Milan in mid-January with
a set of proposals that would trigger a new low in his already compromised
relationship with Furtwängler.

Legge's proposal was that *Tristan* should be postponed and *Fidelio* scheduled in its place. As in Milan, the cast would be headed by Martha Mödl and Wolfgang Windgassen. Karajan would conduct. If he declined (a disingenuous rider), Furtwängler, or 'some other suitable German conductor', should be offered the recording in his place.[2]

Not surprisingly, the plan was greeted with dismay by David Bicknell, Legge's opposite number at HMV, and by EMI's International Classical Manager Bernard Mittell who over the next few months would be in receipt of a series of ferocious epistolary scoldings from a predictably enraged Furtwängler.

Tristan und Isolde was duly recorded: on schedule, with Furtwängler conducting and Legge as producer. That it proved to be a classic of the gramophone, goes some way towards explaining why these two masters of their respective trades put up with one another for so long. At the end of the sessions, Furtwängler is said to have put his arm round Legge and said, 'My name will be remembered for this, but yours should be.' Which is not to say there had not been problems. Black moods frequently descended on Furtwängler during the recording; on one occasion he fled the studio and took refuge in Regent's Park.

The success of the *Tristan* sessions turned out, however, to be little more than ashes in Legge's mouth; as we shall see, he had landed himself in deep trouble with EMI – and with Karajan.

The Milan *Fidelio* passed off successfully enough, a virulent stomach bug notwithstanding. Florestan's cry *'Gott, welch' Dunkel hier'* was turned by a clearly discomfited Wolfgang Windgassen into *'Gott, welch' dunkles Bier'* as he headed for the lavatory at the end of the dungeon scene. 'You should have let me know,' said Karajan afterwards. 'I would have conducted faster.'

The new *Der Rosenkavalier* made the greater impression. Drawing inspiration from sketches made towards the end of his life by Alfred Roller, the work's original designer, the production was at once traditional and innovative: traditional in its use of singers schooled in the Viennese style (Schwarzkopf, Jurinac, della Casa, Edelmann, and Kunz), experimental in that the cast was a predominantly young one. Preparation was spread over several weeks. Karajan took all the piano rehearsals himself, miming and groaning his way through even the smallest roles.[3] Within the year, Legge had twisted a sufficient number of arms to allow the production to be recorded. EMI shipped equipment to Milan, only to be brought up short by the extortionate financial demands of the La Scala orchestra.

*

The Philharmonia's European tour was being undertaken without any form of external funding. Even EMI refused to underwrite it, though they eventually coughed up £250 after being persuaded that it was not beyond the bounds of possibility that the tour might boost the sales of some of their existing recordings. According to Legge,[4] Karajan conducted without fee. Certainly, his name ensured that many of the concerts were sold out weeks in advance, enabling agents who had been charged with administering them locally to transfer back to London welcome transfusions of cash to help sustain the Philharmonia's sagging reserves as money was ladled out on fares and hotel reservations. Even so, eighteen sold-out concerts in thirteen cities over a period of twenty-four days left Legge's company out of pocket to the then not inconsiderable sum of £3800.

Logistically, the tour was a nightmare. Seven years after the war's end, European infrastructure was still in some disarray. As for Legge, like Sir Ethelred, the Permanent Under-Secretary in Joseph Conrad's *The Secret Agent*, he was not a man to be burdened with niceties. Swiss railway timetables held no interest for him, the subject of coach hire in Linz was a closed book, and it is reasonable to believe that he went to his grave wholly ignorant of the Byzantine complexity of the 'grey card' system that operated in Vienna's Soviet zone. 'No details, pray. Spare me the details' was the Ethelredian line which Jane Withers was obliged to toe; and she, poor girl, was a novice traveller who had barely set foot outside England.

The repertoire for the tour consisted of works which Karajan and the orchestra had previously played together, such as Beethoven's Fifth, or works they had recently been preparing in the recording studio. These included Handel's *Water Music* suite, Strauss's *Don Juan*, Stravinsky's *Jeu de cartes*, and three symphonies: Beethoven's Seventh, Brahms's First, and Tchaikovsky's Fifth.

It was also planned to show off the orchestra's string and horn sections by playing one of Mozart's divertimenti for two horns and strings. Legge had opted for the Divertimento in D K334, which the orchestra had not previously played with Karajan, rather than the more taxing Divertimento in B flat K287, which they had glanced at some months earlier. In a letter from St Anton in April 1952 that touches on all manner of unrealised projects – plans for a concert with Horowitz, the possibility of involving Frederick Ashton and Margot Fonteyn in the new Orff triptych at La Scala – Karajan slips in a plea for the B flat Divertimento:

While I was studying the divertimento in D major I realised that parts of it are less good than the B major [*sic*] divertimento we once tried to record. The substance of the two outer movements is very weak in comparison with those of the other work, particularly where melodic invention is concerned; and also the enchanting violin solos in two of the movements of the B major divertimento [the end of the *Adagio* and the introduction to the finale] would give the orchestra better possibilities.[5]

To which Karajan, practical as ever, cheekily adds:

Since it is only a change of a number in the programme we are talking about (which if the programmes have already been printed could always be said to be a printing error!) I suggest we alter both the performance and the recording.[6]

The orchestra was decidedly uneasy about all this, and about *Jeu de cartes* which it had recorded with Karajan over a period of two days at the start of May. Though the recording itself was of demonstration quality, the performance had been more or less stitched together bar by bar. The live performance in the Royal Festival Hall on 9 May was consequently a somewhat nerve-racking experience. *The Times* rather liked this:

The strings were reduced and the orchestra became all prickly, producing the nervous irritation intended by the composer. Even so, Mr Karajan would have no blatancy: the rhythmic dislocation, in which even with this orchestra there was an occasional lapse of precision, and the edgy tone, were allowed to provide their own calculated discomforts.[7]

The leader of the orchestra Manoug Parikian put it rather differently:

I was slightly anxious because we'd never played the work through. Karajan said, 'Oh, no, it'll be perfectly all right', and of course things went wrong. Everyone was terribly nervous because they'd never played their part through; everyone was, as it were, stopping and starting. It was a very poor performance, I thought. The ice was very *thin* that night![8]

Whether a performance is well played or ill played is something that it should be possible to establish with a reasonable degree of objectivity. Whether or not one *likes* a performance is largely (if not wholly) a subjective matter. Neville Cardus, perhaps the greatest of all masters of the analytically subjective review, liked Karajan's treatment of Strauss's *Don Juan* rather better than the *Times* critic – who was utterly convinced by it 'until afterwards' – but was rather less happy with his account of the First Symphony of Brahms:

The interpretation of the symphony as a whole was impressive for its high seriousness. Mr Karajan is able to combine with a virtuoso concern for technical polish a true musician's feeling for content and substance. But his tempi do not convince us that the music is always unfolding from an inner cell but rather is being manipulated, sensitively enough, from the outside. This was a Brahms of arresting prose, with a few italics thrown in, a Brahms of culture and a good wardrobe.[9]

*

The tour began well enough. In Paris and in Switzerland Karajan was fêted by audiences as never before; and though a number of critics remained wary of the new Svengali, they were more inclined to praise the Philharmonia than they had been to praise the palpably inferior Vienna Symphony.

By the time the orchestra arrived in Turin, the travelling was beginning to takes its toll. Minutes before the concert was due to start, Legge burst into the back stage changing area to announce that Toscanini's daughter had telephoned him. The Maestro could not now attend the Milan concert; he would, however, be listening to the evening's live radio relay from Turin. Whether Legge was wise to impart this eleventh hour intelligence to the players is a moot point. Handel's *Water Music* suite, the dreaded *Jeu de cartes*, and Brahms's First Symphony were on the programme. Things went moderately well; but by the orchestra's usual standards the concert was decidedly below par.

In Milan, another message awaited Legge. Toscanini had invited him and Elisabeth Schwarzkopf to tea at his villa. Hour succeeded hour and afternoon tea merged with early-evening cocktails before the great man appeared. Dismissing the idea of taking on a new orchestra at so advanced an age, he insisted on playing Legge some of his latest recordings and appears to have been grateful for Legge's characteristically blunt assessment of them.

After the first of the two Milan concerts, Victor De Sabata hosted a lavish reception for the orchestra. Legge would later recall:

De Sabata took me aside and said: 'Your orchestra is the most wonderful English virgin. All she needs to achieve the ultimate perfection is to be raped by a hot-blooded Italian. I will do that for you.' (Unfortunately his ill-health deprived the orchestra of that enriching experience.)[10]

Behind the scenes, all was not well. Jane Withers was clearly ailing, so much so that Legge had asked Fred Gaisberg's niece Isabella Corbett (Isabella Wallich as she would shortly be) to join the tour to help oversee the arrangements. Arriving in Milan, she was confronted by a dire state of affairs. In the first of a series of letters to Aubrey Wallich, she reported:

Milan, American Hotel, 19 May
It has been a frantic day. I am quite exhausted. They are all muddlers and leave everything to poor Jane Withers who is ill. Tomorrow we leave Milano at 12.45 in the night for a twenty hour journey to Vienna without any sort of head man. They are a pretty poor lot and I don't know whether I shall stay with the orchestra after getting back home. To my mind Walter is a dreamer.[11]

Dreaming of Toscanini, no doubt, and the great kudos his association with the orchestra would bring.

Milan, 20 May

This tour is a nightmare of bad organisation. Maybe because Jane was so ill during the days of preparation. Walter is full of idealistic dreams about the future but leaves the handling of this very awkward tour to inexperienced incompetents. I was livid with Walter yesterday but won my battle by insisting that either he or K[arajan]'s manager Mattoni comes with me on the trip tonight. I refused to take sole responsibility.

You should have seen me last night in the orchestra room of La Scala, coping with the men of our crowd and the men of the La Scala orchestra who were there to hear gossip and give advice. Our librarian was stretched out on the floor in a faint, his assistant, the fat girl, having hysterics, Jane Withers looking like a ghost, the second trombone stretched out on a chair having hurt his leg, the second flute missing and von K shouting for the men to come on to the platform. In the meantime, when I peeped out to see the hall, Walter was seated comfortably in the front waiting for the concert to start.[12]

It was a crazy state of affairs, but the concert was a sensation. It also did the trick. As midnight approached and the orchestra was packing up to set out on the twenty-hour journey across the Alps to Vienna, Legge was again summoned to Toscanini's villa. This time Toscanini was waiting to greet him, along with a convocation of elders whom Legge immediately guessed were players from the golden age of Verdi's late years at La Scala.

'Good evening,' announced Toscanini. 'I will come to London. Now, what programmes shall I conduct?'

As the orchestra headed for Vienna, Dennis Brain drove Legge, Schwarzkopf, and Gareth Morris to Zürich over the Gotthard Pass. In their general state of elation, no one seems to have noticed that because of adverse weather conditions the pass had been officially closed to traffic.

The orchestra's journey was less eventful, but grimmer. Bleary-eyed after a night on the train, the players were greeted at the Austrian border by the unwelcome sight of armed Russian soldiers lining the platform. In Vienna, where the streets were again full of uniformed soldiers and war-wounded beggars, the hotel was so squalid Isabella Corbett had a mutiny on her hands, with the players demanding the right to find their own alternative accommodation, an impossible request given the need to have everyone immediately to hand most of the time.

Isabella had persuaded Mattoni to travel with them on the train to Vienna but her relations with Karajan himself were becoming strained.

Vienna, Pension Opernring, 22 May

We haven't had our sleepers confirmed between Munich and Hamburg. The orchestra will riot if we don't get them. They grumble a lot but are good sorts. I'm always chasing Walter or von K for information. No wonder [Karajan] seems to hate me.[13]

After the Milan triumph, Vienna was something of an anticlimax. The public was enthusiastic; but the Viennese press, piqued by Karajan's decision to appear in Vienna with a foreign orchestra, cast its collective eye over the Philharmonia with something of the air of a middle-aged roué with a taste for old-world glamour assessing the vital statistics of a teenage stripper. As Isabella Wallich would report, the Viennese authorities, and more predictably the Russians, were also depressingly hostile.

Vienna, 24 May
I am having the most frantic and hectic time. We have had fabulous artistic success but we have been treated like dirt by the Vienna Musikverein. Complete lack of co-operation, even to the point of our agent in Vienna refusing to speak to us. Elisabeth [Schwarzkopf] walks around in tears swearing vengeance on all Viennese musicians and critics. Jane Withers left yesterday. I have had a frightful time since trying to get the grey cards issued by the Russians; they control the zone we have to go through to get to Linz. Ever since we have been in Vienna I have been trying to get those cards from the agent. They arrived yesterday afternoon. I instantly went through them and, as I expected, five names were missing, including mine. Imagine my horror. Two first trombones, the harp, the tuba, and myself. I couldn't find anyone anywhere. No Walter, no Mattoni, no anyone. So at about 6 p.m. I phoned the British Ambassador. He was in his bath getting ready for the concert. I told Lady Caccia, his wife, 'to get him out'. She was awfully nice. He arranged to meet me at the concert. Well, after a terrific hoo-ha, he contacted the American Ambassador who agreed to arrange for the US Air Force to fly us to Linz the next morning. At the same time, the First Secretary is working on our 'friends' [the Russians] to get us our grey cards in time to go to Linz tomorrow.

Well, at midnight the Ambassador phoned to say that he had laid on the aircraft so we didn't need the grey cards after all. So I went to bed and slept in peace. To my horror, when I woke it was pouring with rain and the flying was off. Imagine my despair. So there I was waiting with my little group, the rest of the orchestra having left by the early train, to be rescued either by the US or by our Embassy getting the grey cards in time from the Russians for us to catch the last train in time for us to get to Linz for the concert. Well, we made it in the end by the skin of our teeth. Poor Embassy, they must have this all the time. I am sure the Russians did it to tease us. In addition, Peter Mountain's Stradivarius was stolen.[14]

All Legge said when informed of the loss of Mountain's Stradivarius was, 'It would be Peter Mountain's.' As for Karajan, his sole remark to Isabella when she finally arrived in Linz with the hapless stragglers was, 'Can't you organise anything?'

What would have cheered her up, if she had known about it, was an article that had appeared in a Linz newspaper when the Philharmonia's visit had first been announced the previous January.[15] After an earlier visit, Karajan had made an official complaint to the Linz municipal authority about the sound of a distant train whistle being audible in the concert hall. Amused by the preposterousness of the complaint, an anonymous writer had penned a diverting essay on the subject under the headline '*Die Symphonie mit dem Pfiff* [whistle or catcall]'. The article concluded with a spoof advertisement for the forthcoming concert:

Performers
The London Philharmonia, Herbert von Karajan and as Solo
Whistle-Blower on the locomotive an anonymous 'Führer'
(Locomotive-Führer, you understand!)

From Linz, the orchestra travelled by train to Munich, changing at Salzburg. At Salzburg station Karajan's recently widowed mother appeared on the platform to see Herbert. But chaos again reigned and she was more or less trampled underfoot.

In Munich the players themselves caused most of the trouble. A prank involving the 'loss' of yet another prized instrument was more time-consuming than it was amusing:

Munich, 25 May
Wonderful success. Crowds hanging around after the concert in the pouring rain to applaud the orchestra. The usual travel chaos ensued. There was practically a riot on the special train because some silly idiots had shut themselves in sleeping compartments hoping to be alone. Shouts, yells, and the arrival of a furious von K who was actually travelling with us for once. Terrible scene with me afterwards. I just walked away and went into the sleeper with someone. Next morning I was summoned to von K's compartment. He was attired in black satin pyjamas, all curled up in the corner. He invited me to come and sit beside him to take orders. I did not.[16]

Karajan knew he had gone too far. His irritation was not with Isabella but with the maladministration of the tour itself. Legge was the real culprit here. But Isabella – a mere functionary whom, initially at least, Karajan did not know personally – was a convenient butt for his anger.

Schwarzkopf says that Karajan had a bully's instinct for picking on small fry. Once, playing mini-golf with the Waltons during a visit to Ischia, Karajan found himself losing to Legge, whose myopia and general lack of physical co-ordination would have given him star ranking in any list of the world's worst golfers. Greatly amused, Schwarzkopf started whistling quietly to herself.

After bungling yet another shot, Karajan turned on the boy attendant. 'Stop that whistling!' he snapped.

'He knew perfectly well that it was me who was whistling,' said Schwarzkopf. 'But being Herbert he preferred to take it out on the boy.'[17]

Some might see this as a courtesy to Schwarzkopf. Having rows with friends is never the best of stratagems. In later years, Karajan's entourage would contain men whose function it was to be shouted at, expensively retained lightning-conductors who could be guaranteed to run high voltage flashes safely to earth.

And so the 1952 tour neared Berlin:

Hamburg, 27 May
Once again, fabulous success and utter chaos. Now the Russians have closed Berlin off completely and we are not allowed to enter by road or rail. We chartered two planes. The orchestra were all making their wills and bemoaning their fate. I didn't blame them too much. Coming into Tempelhof is not fun at the best of times, the weather was awful, and the planes battle-worn. Still, we arrived. All this I did on my own. How Walter, Elisabeth, and von K got there, I don't know.[18]

Berlin was agog. Furtwängler had given three concerts in the same hall with the Berlin Philharmonic the previous week with Yehudi Menuhin as soloist. Direct comparisons would have been fun. Furtwängler had included Beethoven's Seventh Symphony in two of his programmes. But it was not to be. Karajan and the Philharmonia were obliged to play Brahms and Tchaikovsky instead: Brahms's First symphony at the end of the first concert, and Karajan's trusty *cheval de bataille* Tchaikovsky's Fifth Symphony as the grandstand finale to the entire tour.

Berlin, 30 May
The concerts at the Titania Palast, the goal to which all this suffering aspired, has been achieved. The concerts were a triumph. The orchestra played like gods and von K was totally magnificent. Walter turned to me at the end of the concert and said, 'Well, it was all worth it, wasn't it?' I had to agree.[19]

Much ale was quaffed that night as players from the Philharmonia and the Berlin Philharmonic got together, as orchestral musicians are wont to do, for a booze-up and a gossip. A ritual rendering by the Berliners of the Huntsmen's Chorus from Weber's *Der Freischütz* brought the Philharmonia's Sidney Sutcliffe smartly to attention, a gesture that caused a certain amount of bewilderment until he explained that it was his old regimental march.

Karajan, meanwhile, was having face-to-face discussions with the management of the Berlin Philharmonic who had been in correspondence with him about possible concerts. The discussions were inconclusive, largely because Karajan, like Celibidache, was more interested in touring with the orchestra than merely conducting the occasional concert in Berlin. As to dates, he was willing to sacrifice future tours with the Vienna Symphony but not, it seems, engagements with the Philharmonia.

Karajan would undertake more tours with the Philharmonia, better organised than the first one. As for the 1952 tour, this was another chapter in his long and exhaustive musical education: a first class example, from the logistical point of view, of how *not* to do things. British phlegm and a touch of the Dunkirk spirit had seen the Philharmonia through the tour. But in Karajan's evolving game-plan only the private autonomy of a conductor-entrepreneur working with public funds lavishly topped up by the proceeds of sure-fire commercial successes could be guaranteed to secure his ideal of an orchestra of princes in which every prince lived like a king. For the time being, though, he was not his own boss; simply a journeyman conductor making do with the best that circumstances allowed.

So the 1952 tour ended, with the orchestra travelling back to England by boat via Hamburg and Karajan travelling to Bayreuth to prepare for the next important event in his life, Wieland Wagner's new production of *Tristan und Isolde* at the 1952 festival.

It was Wieland's elder sister, the rebellious, determinedly anti-Fascist, partly English-educated Friedelind who would later furnish Isabella Wallich with a characteristically sensational explanation of why Karajan had treated her so shabbily during the 1952 tour.

'He was jealous,' she insisted. 'He suspected there was some kind of relationship between you and Walter.'

Isabella, recently widowed and about to remarry, was not aware of any such 'relationship'. But Friedelind, whose own sexual orientation was far from straightforward, was not to be gainsaid.

'Karajan's homosexual,' she persisted. 'He's in love with Walter.'[20]

CHAPTER 37

The girl with the flaxen hair

It may be possible to do without dancing entirely.
Jane Austen, *Emma*

Precisely when Karajan first met Eliette Mouret is difficult to ascertain. According to her, she was seventeen. Unfortunately, like many very beautiful women, Eliette was seventeen for an awfully long time. Since it would be ungallant to suggest an excessively early date and misleading to suggest too late a one, let us settle for the purposes of biography on the year 1951.

Where they met is not in doubt. It was on a yacht owned by friends of the Karajans in St Tropez. The local girls had been invited aboard more for their decorative value than for their sea-faring abilities and Eliette had been feeling decidedly queasy. Karajan offered to escort her ashore and took her to the Bar Pamyre in the old town, just off the sea front. The Pamyre is still there, though nowadays it is a restaurant. In more recent times, Eliette has taken to escorting friends there, not to dine, but to view the handsome old mechanical piano which is still in a corner to the right of the doorway. There is even a yellowing list of the dance numbers the machine once played: foxtrots, a tango or two, the Charleston. Karajan, it turned out, could do none of these. When Eliette kicked off her shoes, ready to dance the night away, she found that the famous conductor was capable of little more than a vague arhythmic shuffle.

Tall, with blonde hair, and large almond-shaped eyes of an aquamarine hue, Eliette was more huntress than sea-borne nereid. Her family background was conventional without being in any way straightforward. The daughter of older parents, both teachers, she had a sister twenty years her senior and had lost her father when still a child. Though she had been born in the shadow of Mont Ventoux in the ancient Provençal hillside town of Mollans-sur-Ouvèze where her parents owned a holiday home, she grew up and went to school in Nice. At the age of seventeen – that year again – she visited Paris and was invited to model for Dior. Wedding dresses were a speciality. With her mother's reluctant consent, she would shortly embark on an international modelling career that would take her to Paris, Milan, Rome, and London; to some of the very places, in fact, where Karajan now most regularly worked.

From such choice vantage points, the huntress could track her quarry. She likes to relate how in Rome she confided to a young American admirer that the two people who fascinated her most in all the world were Albert

Schweitzer and Herbert von Karajan; and how a year later she found herself sitting alongside Karajan and the Legges (Legge and Schwarzkopf had married in 1953) as Schweitzer made a private audition of London's new Royal Festival Hall organ. Karajan the organ buff was absorbed in the sounds Schweitzer drew from the instrument. Afterwards he would remark:

Watching Schweitzer play with that mane of grey hair over his concentrated brow revealed to me how right the old Italian painters were to paint angels and saints with haloes.[1]

And Madonnas with long blonde hair, he might have added.

The Schweitzer episode took place in 1955 by which time Eliette had become something of a fixture on the English social scene. Her photograph appeared in the London *Evening Standard* and in advertisements for *haute couture* in Covent Garden and Edinburgh Festival programmes. Eligible bachelors, some with titles and estates to bestow, whirled her around London. She even impinged on the political world. Anthony Nutting, Secretary of State for Foreign Affairs, Eden's Number Two at the time of the Suez crisis, was, according to Eliette, a particular acquaintance.

The Legges appear to have encouraged Herbert's *affaire de coeur* with Eliette, without, it seems, believing that the marriage to the independent-minded Anita was being seriously threatened. The Waltons were drawn in too, particularly William, who was greatly taken with Eliette. As Lady Walton would later recall:

Another visitor to Ischia in those early days [the early 1950s] was Herbert von Karajan. He used to come for the radioactive cure which had made the island famous. Most conductors, he told us, suffered from bad backs. With his girl-friend, Eliette, they would scamper back and forth on their Vespa scooter, she seated side-saddle, her long blonde hair blowing in the wind. It was a strange courtship. The music world did not believe that he would ever divorce his wife, Anita, to marry this girl. When she used to ask me what it was like to be married to a musician, I would think, 'Poor thing, she will never find out.' But Eliette was immensely patient with Herbert, whose idea of a good holiday was to get up at five o'clock in the morning, go for a walk up to the summit of the extinct volcano Mount Epomeo, then sail round the island and have several hot mud cures, which would have exhausted most normal human beings, and all this before breakfast. We noticed that Eliette was always seasick when out on the boat, but she never complained.[2]

Karajan was not the first conductor with a bad back and an eye for the girls to holiday on Ischia and take the radioactive cure; at the turn of the century, Toscanini had been a regular visitor to the island for not dissimilar reasons.

Karajan did not stay with the Waltons, who in the days before the building of La Mortella lived a somewhat hand-to-mouth existence in a series of charming but semi-derelict Ischian properties. His primary purpose was to take the cure, and work. After his early-morning exertions, he would spend the main part of the day studying or telephoning. Social life held no interest for him. The formidable Frau von Stohrer, widow of Eberhard von Stohrer, the career diplomat who as German ambassador to Spain had become briefly involved in the Nazis' attempts to start negotiations with the Duke of Windsor in the summer of 1940, also lived on Ischia. She was a great admirer of Karajan, but he studiously avoided her.

Walton, who spoke excellent German, Legge, and Karajan made their own company, dining in a side room in Karajan's hotel (Karajan, who refused to wear a tie on holiday, was barred from the main dining room), gossiping and joking late into the night. It was an unholy trinity, for all three men were intensely ambitious and extremely adept at using people for their own ends. In the end, there was a falling out. Legge invited Karajan to record Walton's First Symphony; Karajan agreed, but asked Walton to revise the orchestration. ('He was a difficult creature!' mused Lady Walton.3) On another occasion, Karajan included the First Symphony in a broadcast concert in Rome but failed to inform Walton, who was predictably furious at missing the event.

Yet, as an old man, Karajan always spoke affectionately of Walton, relishing memories of his droll North Country humour. And Walton never lost his respect for Karajan's musicianship; Karajan's Deutsche Grammophon recording of *The Ring* was a particular favourite of his, not least for the wonderfully balanced sound Karajan always managed to draw from the Wagner orchestra.4

The affair with Eliette runs as a continuous flickering pulse during the years 1950–7 when Karajan, now at the very peak of his physical powers, was in exile from his own land, adrift from his moorings: hugely successful but oddly disorientated and, certainly, 'difficult'.

There had always been women in Karajan's life. Women he fell for, women he used, women, such as the wife of a celebrated Hungarian pianist, who relentlessly pursued him. In the late 1940s, he became involved with the actress Margot Hielscher, one of the stars of Germany's wartime Babelsberg studios. On his return from South America they attended flying school together. Karajan would turn up, Hielscher has alleged, with a rucksack containing his climbing boots and gramophone records which inevitably got scratched or broken. He gave her a signed copy of the score, difficult to get then, of one of her favourite pieces, Gershwin's *An American in Paris*. And he wrote her love letters. The letters – or, rather, those extracts Frau Hielscher chose to read out on Austrian television some years after Karajan's death – were full of tenderness and charm.⁵ But then, in affairs of the heart, the normally reticent Karajan was a man of sensibility, a smooth-tongued linguist skilled in the practices of love. Girls working in the Philharmonia office who took to eavesdropping on Karajan's telephone calls to Eliette found them 'extremely poetic'.⁶

There were women whom he idealised and desired to excite (taking them flying was a favourite ploy) but whom he had no desire to gratify physically. Isabella Wallich sensed that he enjoyed being *watched* at a distance by adoring nymphets. She also noticed that he could behave strangely in such circumstances.

The behind-the-scenes ritual before the entry on to the concert platform provided an appropriate setting for some of these manoeuvres. His usual practice was to approach the curtain and take the baton from the male attendant, while at the same time allowing the attendant to remove from his shoulders the casually draped chill-defying overcoat. On the one occasion during the 1952 Philharmonia tour when Isabella Wallich was obliged to delegate this unwelcome duty to herself, Karajan subtly altered his routine. As he approached her to take the proffered baton, he casually shrugged the coat to the floor in an exquisitely timed display of coquettish insolence. In such circumstances, it was tempting to give credence to Friedelind Wagner's deliberately barbed diagnosis of Karajan's sexual preferences.

But what were his preferences? Like many men of sensibility blessed with an eye for beauty and a love of youth, Karajan was undoubtedly as much gratified by male beauty as he was by its female equivalent. Many of his most intimate, long-standing relationships were with men who, matrimonially speaking, were celibate. A more or less permanent celibacy, in friends of either sex, could be said to have been a necessary precondition for working with Karajan. The qualities he sought in his closest associates were rare enough in the ranks of single men, let alone those with wives and children to care for. It was a lengthy menu on which competence, breeding, and good taste were merely the hors d'oeuvres to an entrée of genuine affection and a main course of total dedication and absolute discretion.

In Vienna, the gossip mills rarely ceased, so much so that decoding the multitude of Karajan stories and placing them in some kind of perspective requires a ready wit and a dispassionate gaze. Happily, someone so possessed did work there for a time. In the cast list of Decca's famous gala recording of *Die Fledermaus* there appears a supernumerary Englishman, a certain Lord Barrymore played by an actor rejoicing in the name of Omar Godknow. Godknow was in fact Christopher Raeburn, a member of the Decca recording team, so nicknamed because of his habit of greeting news of who was singing or conducting at the Vienna Opera that evening with the despairing cry, 'Oh my God, *no*!'

I once asked Raeburn for a view on Karajan's sexual predilections.

'Much like most of us, I would imagine,' he drawled in his best Lord Barrymore voice. 'A little bit of everything.'

CHAPTER 38

Tristan and Lucia

The meaning of Song goes deep. Who is there that, in logical words, can express the effect that music has on us? A kind of inarticulate unfathomable speech, which leads us to the edge of the Infinite, and lets us for moments gaze into that!

Thomas Carlyle, *On Heroes, Hero-Worship,*
and the Heroic in History

It is said that after conducting a particularly sensuous and alluring performance of Berlioz's *Roméo et Juliette* the conductor Pierre Monteux was asked by his wife, 'Pierre, were you thinking of me during that performance?' To which the great man replied, 'No, my dear, I was thinking of Eleanor Roosevelt.' History does not record whom Karajan was thinking of on the evening of 23 July 1952 when he conducted the opening night of Wieland Wagner's new production of *Tristan und Isolde* in Bayreuth. But it was, even by his standards, a supremely involving and well-directed account of the great score: ardent, lyrical, unerringly shaped from first note to last.

There had been a good deal of politicking in Bayreuth during the run up to the first night. Simmering in the background was the question of Karajan's future relationship with Bayreuth: his artistic relationship with Wieland and his personal relationship with Wolfgang, whose distrust of his brother was surpassed only by his doubts about Karajan. In the end, it would come down to fees and spheres of influence, and there would be no solution. 1952 would be Karajan's second season in Bayreuth, and his last.

There were also serious problems over recordings. Karajan was under the impression that the 1952 Bayreuth *Tristan und Isolde* was going to be recorded by EMI: live, in the theatre, as the 1951 *Die Meistersinger* had been. But EMI was already committed to the studio recording of *Tristan und Isolde* with Furtwängler. Legge did his best to ignore this. In a series of internal memoranda which – even by Legge's standards – were astonishingly cavalier, he claimed that EMI was big enough to countenance rival versions of the opera. With the arrival of LP, he argued, complete opera recordings were destined to become 'the very backbone of the classical business'. As for Karajan, 'his best years as a recording artist were still to come'. With his contract due for renewal in 1952, rival companies would be 'only too happy to snap him up'. Whenever

Karajan was in Bayreuth, Wieland Wagner had told Legge, representatives of Decca, Deutsche Grammophon, and Philips could be found 'hanging around the Festspielhaus, like dogs outside a house in which there is a bitch on heat'.

HMV's normally mild-mannered David Bicknell would have none of this. In a memorandum dated 10 July 1952, he stated:

. . . we can't and won't let [Karajan] do *Tristan*. As I said some months ago, I feel the point has been reached where we cannot continue to give concessions to Karajan and get nothing in return from him. We have, in the last three years or so, given him too many plums of the operatic and orchestral repertory.[1]

Five days before Bicknell's letter, Karajan had written to Legge about the whole question of recording in Bayreuth during the 1952 festival. The tone of his letter is amiable enough, but it is in German (unusual for a letter from Karajan to Legge) and had clearly been drafted after taking legal advice. It begins 'Lieber Walter', but 'Lieber Walter' rapidly becomes 'Columbia' and 'the company':

Many thanks for your letter. I must say straight away that your arguments about *The Ring* recording are mistaken. As far as I know, and this is confirmed by the Wagners, I never agreed to conduct *The Ring* this year. You know quite well that, at the time of the reopening of the Festival, *Tristan* was discussed and that I was of the opinion that I would need the whole of the rehearsal time at my disposal for that. If Columbia has an option to record *The Ring* on 5th August, this was done at your end, <u>hoping</u> I would be conducting; but there is no proof that this would be so, either in verbal agreements or in any written statement or plan signed by me. I am, therefore, completely uninvolved in this matter. However, Columbia has stated its wish to record *Tristan* in many discussions, and even in writing. You may care to recall the case not long ago of Mödl being unable to sing Brangäne in another recording and also perform Isolde here in Bayreuth; this proves that the company had a firm desire to record *Tristan*. I do not think that it is right to put me in the wrong if the company has now decided not to record this work, whether for economic or for personal reasons. I can fully understand your difficulties, and that the company wants to have one single existing recording, although I have always firmly counted on another recording and have always said so, verbally and in writing. I therefore believe, as things now stand, that Columbia will have no objection if I record this work with another company.[2]

With under three weeks to go to the first night, this was more a shot across Columbia's bows than a realistic threat. Karajan had no intention of burning his boats with EMI; and, indeed, in the same letter he confirms his continuing interest in recording *Der Rosenkavalier* in Milan as soon as dates can be agreed.

*

As late as the morning of the dress rehearsal of *Tristan und Isolde*, Karajan had been fighting a rearguard (and, as it turned out, losing) battle to have his way over a further experimental reseating of the Bayreuth orchestra. He was also having problems with his Tristan, the Chilean tenor Ramon Vinay. During one of the stage rehearsals with the orchestra Vinay had fled Karajan's 'baleful presence' (Wolfgang Wagner's phrase), scrambled through an open window, vaulted a fence, and gone into temporary hiding.[3]

Vinay had shot to international fame in 1947 at the age of thirty-five after singing in Toscanini's celebrated 1947 recording of Verdi's *Otello*. In 1950, he took on the role of Tristan for the first time, originally under Jonel Perlea in San Francisco, where Flagstad was his Isolde, and later under Fritz Reiner in New York where he played opposite Helen Traubel. Though Vinay spoke no German, he appears to have won over audiences by the beauty of his singing and the sheer force of his personality as a singing actor.

Karajan was less easily impressed and, finding Vinay a less than apt pupil, had frequently pressured him in rehearsal. If a widely circulated recording of the production is anything to go by, Vinay's problems were not so much verbal as rhythmic, something that may have been exacerbated by Karajan's occasionally going into a trance-like state while conducting.[4]

The twin glories of the 1952 Bayreuth performance were Martha Mödl's Isolde and Hans Hotter's Kurwenal. Mödl's first act (and a gloriously sung *Liebestod* in Act 3) and Hotter's third act are both classic examples of the singer-interpreter's art, aided and inspired by the conductor's own quick-witted responses and imaginative daring. Here it is not so much the letter of the score that is attended to – though both Mödl and Hotter are extremely accurate singers – as the emotional tides that swirl around it.

Wieland Wagner's production famously abolished naturalism. Set on a slanting oval platform with raised sides, the staging made no attempt to represent ship, garden, or castle courtyard. Sailors and courtiers remained off stage. In the Act 2 love duet, what the composer himself once called 'the most beautiful of all dreams', only the singers' heads and shoulders were visible in the enveloping dark. In such a context, the impact of the voices and the orchestra is greatly enhanced. The orchestra becomes even more a leading player: both a commentator on the action after the manner of the Chorus in Greek tragedy, and a purveyor of those dramatic and psychological subtexts which the poet-dramatist – a Sophocles or a Shakespeare – explores in rhythm and image.

Wieland's approach should have been meat and drink to Karajan. Speaking on German television in 1968, shortly after the launch of his Salzburg Easter Festival *Ring* cycle, Karajan talked of the state of near-paralysis that overcame him when his innermost musical promptings were openly contradicted by stage movement or stage design. This is unlikely to have been the case with *Tristan und Isolde* in 1952 where there was almost no scenery and where Karajan himself was closely involved with gesture, movement, and lighting.

Why, then, did Karajan repeatedly represent the break with Bayreuth as being artistic rather than financial and administrative: a sub-Wagnerian saga of money and power? In 1979 Karajan told *Der Spiegel*:

[Wieland Wagner] rejected everything that had been done before, the wound was very deep, and in the process he simply left out everything that actually belonged there.⁵

Was Karajan lying, trying to cover the tracks of his own uncertain advances as a stage director (the equivalent of Wieland avoiding mention of his debt to Craig)? Or had he been genuinely shocked by what Wieland was doing in 1952 – shocked yet enlightened, and in the end too jealous to concede that it was Wieland who had helped him to find his own solution to the problem of damaging misalignments between music and *mise-en-scène*?

*

In London in late September, Toscanini honoured his promise to Legge and conducted two Brahms concerts with the Philharmonia Orchestra. Karajan was not there for the performances, though he had helped prepare the orchestra and had offered advice on various matters, including the need to have the orchestra seated and tuned preparatory to Toscanini's arrival in rehearsal.

In the event, the superlative quality of the orchestra and the meticulous preparation of Legge and Karajan helped ensure a rehearsal period that was mercifully free from those volcanic eruptions for which Toscanini was widely feared. There exists a recording of him rehearsing part of the finale of Brahms's Second Symphony in which the pre-war BBC SO is subjected to screams, shouts, sundry invocations to God and the Blessed Virgin, all uttered in the kind of voice you might expect Otello to adopt shortly after hearing about the handkerchief. During the Philharmonia rehearsal of the Second Symphony, Toscanini did not once stop the orchestra. Karajan was inordinately proud of this and often spoke of it in later years. According to Massimo Freccia, Toscanini had been expecting to stop; there are at least two notorious black spots in the piece. But on both occasions the Philharmonia had steered itself faultlessly through the musical chicane.⁶

That said, Toscanini did not especially like the interpretation he was being offered. One can see why when one listens to a celebrated recording of the symphony Karajan made with the Philharmonia in May 1955. It is a more leisurely performance than Toscanini's, with none of Toscanini's fiery line. Karajan rather rations the excitement, preferring to wait patiently for each movement's climax.

*

Karajan's 1952 autumn tour of Belgium and Germany with the Vienna Symphony must have seemed rather small beer in comparison with events in London. The repertory included some interesting material: Boris Blacher's masterly *Orchestral Variations on a Theme of Niccolò Paganini* and Debussy's *La mer*. Surprised that Karajan should be interested in either work, startled provincial critics lavished superlatives on both performances.[7]

Once again, the orchestra itself was less politely received outside Germany than in it. After a concert in Antwerp, 'coarse' wind sonorities were remarked on by a critic who also felt that Karajan often seemed to bring out the worst in the music.[8] Why, the writer asked, was it necessary to make Mozart's exquisite A major Symphony K201 seem so gloomy? Elsewhere on tour, the performance of the Mozart was reported to be gracious and gay, a model of urbanity and elegance.

Such divergent judgements would make one despair of music criticism were it not for the fact that Karajan was more unpredictable in Mozart than in the music of any other composer. I recall performances of the A major Symphony which were, indeed, models of urbanity and elegance; equally, I remember at least one performance (with the Vienna Philharmonic in London in 1965) which was gloomy and overweight, the phrasing extruded like toothpaste from a tube.

Back in Vienna, Karajan and the orchestra launched a cycle of the nine Beethoven symphonies, a mini-Beethoven festival planned to reach its climax in concert performances of *Fidelio*. Karajan also agreed to record more Beethoven symphonies with the Philharmonia Orchestra in London. In the Karajan–Legge scheme of things, the Vienna Symphony was being reduced to the status of a rehearsal orchestra.

The Vienna Beethoven concerts were juxtaposed with a number of concerts of contemporary music. There was no financial risk in this. Such was Karajan's drawing power now, he could command a full house whether he was down to conduct Stockhausen's *Punkte* or 'Pop goes the Weasel'. In the first of the two concerts in the 'Music of Today' cycle he conducted the Blacher *Paganini* Variations, a *Concerto grosso* by Martinů, and Roussel's Third Symphony. Britten's *Variations on a Theme of Frank Bridge* featured in the second concert, alongside music by Françaix and Bartók.

Some time between the two concerts, Karajan had the misfortune to step on a rusty nail. The foot became so badly infected, it required hospital treatment. This did not stop him conducting the scheduled Beethoven concerts on 25–27 October. He would later tell gullible admirers that he conducted the concert lying down using just one finger and the tip of his nose. It was a pleasing exaggeration. He did, however, require the support of two sticks to reach the podium. '*Stock*' being the German word for 'stick', one wag called out from the audience: 'My God! It's not Karajan, it's Stock – owski!'

The soloist for that concert was the great Romanian pianist Clara Haskil, with whom Karajan had an extraordinary rapport; indeed, it would hardly be an exaggeration to say that he worshipped her. It was an unlikely pairing. The saintly Haskil, physically stricken (curvature of the spine, and a brain tumour contracted and cured during the Second World War, had left her in the frailest health) and the Karajan of popular imagination: the ruthless whiz-kid whose love of youth and beauty, it was claimed, was complemented by a loathing of ugliness in all its forms and a private distaste for all intimations of mortality.

When the Russian pianist Tatyana Nikolaieva first saw Haskil she was appalled: 'her body twisted, her grey hair dishevelled, and looking for all the world like a witch'. According to members of the Philharmonia Orchestra Haskil often had the pallor of death upon her. Indeed, it was for this reason that Furtwängler had always given her such a wide berth; he refused to perform with her because he seriously believed she might die in mid-performance.[9]

Karajan, by contrast, not only engaged her. He played piano duets with her, coaxed and cajoled her, and, according to Gareth Morris, treated her in front of the orchestra as though she was the most beautiful woman he had ever encountered. If Haskil looked like a witch, then the aptly named Heribert Ritter von Karajan was her medieval knight, the handsome young squire whose crimes are redeemed, and his life spared, as a result of his truly *gentil* treatment of the Loathly Lady.

Concert audiences can barely have guessed at Karajan's feelings for Haskil, since whenever he conducted for her he became totally self-effacing. Tatyana Nikolaieva had attended the concert in Salzburg in January 1956 to hear Karajan, 'the new Toscanini':

Once again, the orchestral introduction was very well conducted and very well played by the orchestra, but it was not particularly inspired. What happened next was wholly unexpected. When Clara Haskil placed her hands on the keyboard, tears poured down my cheeks. I had come to discover the new Toscanini and instead I had discovered the greatest Mozartian I have ever heard. Her force of persuasion was such, her magnetism so powerful, that when the orchestra re-entered, everything changed. The quality of the dialogue inaugurated by a woman of such unprepossessing appearance but whose style of playing was so fluent and natural had transformed the orchestra and its conductor as though by magic.[10]

Karajan and Haskil gave many concerts together. Sadly, the only one which has so far had limited circulation on CD – almost certainly the one Nikolaieva herself attended – does not show Haskil at her entire best.[11]

*

During Novemner 1952 Karajan continued his Beethoven cycle with the Vienna Symphony. Like most things Karajan did in Austria at this time, it raised questions about the motives of those who were deliberately keeping him away from the country's three main centres of excellence: the Vienna Philharmonic, the Vienna Opera, and the Salzburg Festival. 'Nemo est propheta in sua patria' lamented the influential Salzburg critic Viktor Reimann.[12]

Meanwhile, it was announced in the Viennese press that the Minister of Education, Dr Kolb, was recommending the appointment of Clemens Krauss as director-designate of the Vienna Opera in anticipation of its reopening in 1955. Given Krauss's fraught relationship with the Opera during his earlier period of office in the 1930s, his high-profile defection to Hitler's Berlin, and his often uneasy relationship with the post-war regime in Vienna, it was an odd move. Nor did it stick. In October 1953, tired to distraction by the querulousness and endless demands of the hyper-dynamic Egon Hilbert, Kolb decided to replace him as Head of the Administration of the State Theatres. Ernst Marboe was Hilbert's successor, and the following February it was officially announced that Karl Böhm would head the new State Opera.

While Reimann was lamenting the case of the lost prophet, Karajan was in London, involved in one of those ten-day hotchpotch recording sessions out of which he, Legge, and the Philharmonia conjured gold in one classic recording after another. The sessions ran as follows:

21–23 November	Beethoven Symphony No.3, Eroica
24 November	Tchaikovsky ballet suites Swan Lake and Sleeping Beauty
25 November	Mozart Symphony No.35, Haffner (start)
23, 28–30 November	Bach B minor Mass (arias only)
1 December	Further sessions for Beethoven and Tchaikovsky recordings; more work on the Haffner [continued 11/54 and 5/55]

As we have seen, the recording of the Bach *B minor Mass* was an influential one: a huge *succès d'estime* and a not inconsiderable commercial success. The recording of the *Eroica* also did very well. Once more conferring its coveted two-star rating on the recording, *The Record Guide* commented:

As a reading it stands up to Toscanini's, whilst as a recording it is decidedly superior ... Karajan's conduct of the work is nearer to Kleiber's than Toscanini's, but where Karajan seems to us chiefly to gain is in the lyrical feeling that suffuses the music from end to end of the symphony.[13]

The *Eroica* recording sold well. At the time of its release in July 1953, a sudden thinning of the market left it with just two extant rivals: the Kleiber and the Toscanini. Over the next four years 13,769 copies of the Karajan LP were sold in the UK; 16,494 in the United States. The arrival of stereo and a tenfold increase in the number of rival recordings put a damper on sales thereafter, though by June 1960 combined British and American sales had crept up to 36,349.

The success of Karajan's recordings in the United States, at a time when he had yet to appear there in public, is one interesting aspect of these figures; another is the relatively poor German sales achieved by EMI's Cologne-based subsidiary Electrola.[14] EMI's French and Italian subsidiaries outsold Electrola several times over.

It was, however, the disc of suites from *Swan Lake* and *The Sleeping Beauty* that was the real sensation and money-spinner. The performances combine playing of rare finish and beauty with an edge-of-the-seat spontaneity that even now takes the breath away. By December 1957, the mono LP had sold nearly 100,000 copies in Europe and the United States. By 1959, when EMI decided to invest in a stereo remake, the figure had risen to 121,544 copies, roughly twelve per cent of Karajan's million-plus LP sales during his Philharmonia years. Not that a stereo remake was really necessary. Douglas Larter's 1952 Kingsway Hall recording is a classic of its kind. Even now, it has few rivals for clarity of sound and acuteness of orchestral balance.

*

For the new season at La Scala, Milan Karajan had elected to conduct and direct a new production of Wagner's *Lohengrin*, plus an Orff triple bill that included the Italian première of *Catulli carmina* and the world première of *Trionfo d'Afrodite*.

Musically *Lohengrin* was first-rate, luminously played and thrillingly sung, but Karajan had greater success with the revival of his production of *Don Giovanni*. His finely geared pacing of the score was noticed with approval (the composer Virgil Thomson would later advise a young musicologist 'the best tempi are Karajan's in *Don Giovanni*'[15]) and the production itself was adjudged simple but lively, amusing at times, but never cheap.

A rising young star, the baritone Rolando Panerai, sang the important cameo role of the peasant Masetto. The role was coals to Newcastle for Panerai, since when he was not singing he ran his own farm. 'Actually worked the farm,' Karajan later told me. 'Drove the tractors. Everything. I think he is one of the most balanced human beings I have ever met.'

Like Kunz, Panerai was also extremely amusing. 'Karajan adored Panerai,' Schwarzkopf recalls. 'They spent hours together working on the role of Masetto.' And, indeed, *Opera* reported:

Rolando Panerai's Masetto was an absolute masterpiece of carefully thought-out humour which evidenced itself every time he appeared on stage.[16]

The role of Don Ottavio was shared by two outstanding young tenors: the Canadian Léopold Simoneau, who would later sing an incomparably stylish Ferrando in Karajan's 1954 recording of *Così fan tutte*, and the Swedish tenor Nicolai Gedda. Gedda was reported in *Opera* as being 'a new tenor discovery of Karajan's',[17] though it is doubtful whether Gedda would have much enjoyed being so described. The possessor of a voice of such liquid beauty as his then was needs no conductor to 'discover' him. Moreover, Gedda did not much like Karajan. The original Swedish edition of his autobiography reveals a near-paranoid loathing of him, prompted, it seems, by Karajan's frank disapproval of Gedda's shortcomings as an actor. In later years, Gedda's attitude seemed to mellow. In 1996, he would tell Charles Osborne:

I started with the greatest – Beecham, Karajan and Klemperer. You didn't have to look at Karajan at all. The beat, the movement, the flow of the music were so clear, so logical, so beautiful, that you were with him.[18]

After three performances of *Don Giovanni*, Gedda's great opportunity came in the second and third parts of the Orff triple bill that opened at La Scala on 14 February 1953. The triptych was semi-staged by Karajan himself, with designs by Fenneker, choreography by Tatiana Gsovsky.

For *Carmina burana*, which had been performed once before at La Scala in 1942, the chorus was placed in tiers on either side of the stage, with Schwarzkopf and Antonio Pirino, centre stage, as the two narrators. For *Catulli carmina*, Orff's unblushing tribute to Stravinsky's *Les noces*, Schwarzkopf, Gedda, and the chorus joined Karajan, four pianists and assorted percussionists in the orchestra pit, leaving actors and dancers to mime the action on stage. The piece, subtitled 'Scenic Games' in five scenes, draws on poems by Catullus that chart the progress of the poet's troubled passion for Lesbia.

It was this idea that Orff took up again – drawing on verses by Sappho and Euripides as well as Catullus – in *Trionfo di Afrodite,* his raunchy, tender, often witty, evocation of the wedding night of an unnamed bride and bridegroom. Here the debt to Stravinsky's *Les noces* (which Giulini would conduct at La Scala a few weeks later) appears even more obvious. In practice, it is a very different kind of piece. A substantial orchestra is used by Orff with subtlety and imagination; the vocal writing is also more various, more transparently beautiful than in *Carmina burana.* The bride's hauntingly melismatic music was written specially for Schwarzkopf. Indeed, with Schwarzkopf and Gedda in prime form, it must remain a source of bitter regret that no recording was made.[19] Did Karajan himself regret the omission? Though he studiously ignored invitations to record *Carmina burana*,[20] he was promptness itself when it came to recording Orff's last major work *De temporum fine comoedia* at the time of its world première in 1973.

In the middle of the La Scala run of the Orff triple bill, Karajan travelled to Turin to conduct Michael Tippett's *A Child of our Time* for Italian Radio. Though Tippett composed the oratorio in the early years of the Second World War, it has come to be regarded as one of the most universally affecting pieces written this century on the theme of man's inhumanity to man.

From the purely professional point of view, it was an odd thing for Karajan to have taken time out to conduct in the middle of what, even by his standards, was an extraordinarily demanding winter season. It was probably Legge's idea. He had struck up a passing acquaintance with Tippett through William Walton and harboured ideas of luring the impecunious Tippett into accepting the position of Chorus Master of the yet-to-be-formed Philharmonia Chorus. But Karajan would have had his own reasons, too. He may have been Legge's friend but by no stretch of the imagination was he his poodle. Expiation is one possible reason. Was this another of Karajan's unspoken attempts – genuine or merely expedient – at atonement for times past?

The choruses had been thoroughly prepared in advance of Karajan's arrival, but now he and Tippett found themselves saddled with a singer, Mario Petri, who could make neither head nor tail of the bass recitatives. Since these carry some of the work's most overtly political statements – 'The dark forces rise like a flood/Men's hearts are heavy: they cry for peace', or 'And a time came when in the continual persecution one race stood for all' – the recitatives could not be mangled or glossed over. Karajan being Karajan, he decided to enlist the help of a tape-recorder. Tippett played the recitatives, Petri attempted to sing them, and Karajan would then go through the tape with Petri trying to explain to him what he was doing wrong. But it was all to little avail.

When it came to the transmission, it was Karajan's turn to throw a spanner in the works. Arriving late – so late that the radio producer had already panicked and ordered up stand-by gramophone records – he asked Tippett: 'Would you mind, Michael, if I make an interval half-way through Part 2? I think it would be more effective.' Tippett said he minded very much indeed, but was powerless to stop him. Karajan duly made the break, to the surprise of the musicians and to the further consternation of the radio producer who had not been party to Karajan's somewhat perfunctory negotiation with Tippett.

Rumour has it that a telephone call to Eliette Mouret was the cause of Karajan's arbitrary instruction, a repetition of the impulse that had caused him to keep a Berlin audience waiting while he waited for Anita Gütermann's response to his offer of marriage.

As for Karajan and Tippett, their dealings did not quite end there. Some time later, Karajan agreed to give conducting lessons to Tippett's companion John Minchinton, a talented musician whose short-lived career disintegrated, according to Tippett, for financial reasons.

*

Back in Vienna, Karajan conducted more contemporary music, this time a concert with the Vienna Symphony that included Honegger's Second Symphony, the Piano Concerto for Left Hand by Kurt Leimer (1922–74) with the composer himself as soloist, and Florent Schmitt's turn-of-the-century setting of Psalm 47.

The Leimer concerto, written in 1948, is an interesting curiosity: partly because his music is now rarely performed,[21] partly because Karajan later recorded the Left Hand and C minor concertos with Leimer as soloist for EMI. The sessions took place in London in November 1954: Karajan and the Philharmonia busking their way through Leimer's colourful, slightly louche orchestral accompaniments with a certain jazzy *joie de vivre*.

The disc is rare: a German Columbia LP that was never issued in Britain or the United States.[22] Which raises the question, why was it made at all? A possible answer is the Gieseking connection. Gieseking's most influential teacher had been Karl Leimer (1858–1944), Kurt's great uncle. The other is Karajan's fascination with any kind of virtuoso piano-playing. Certainly, Leimer was a formidable technician. In 1953 he became Director of Piano

Master Classes at the Salzburg Mozarteum; and Stokowski thought well enough of his playing to invite him to perform his Fourth Piano Concerto in New York in 1956.

The music is an odd mix of grand gestures and neo-classical garrulousness; an eclectic musical cuisine (echoes of Rachmaninov, Strauss's *Burleske*, and a certain amount of minor Gershwin) that would seem extraordinarily bland were it not for piquant orchestral writing that occasionally takes on an almost Ibert-like irreverence.

In Vienna, the Concerto for Left Hand, one of Leimer's best pieces by virtue of being one of his most compact, was given a serious rollicking by a noisy group of hardline avant-gardeists in Karajan's concert on 18 March. The critic of the *Weltpresse Wien* did not mince his words either; he described it as an unspeakable mix of 'bar music and bogus Romanticism'.[23] For many Viennese, though, music like this was the acceptable face of modernism.

*

Karajan concluded his Vienna Beethoven cycle in early June with three concert performances of *Fidelio*. The casting was exceptionally strong. Mödl sang Leonore, Windgassen Florestan. When the road-show moved to Switzerland in late October as part of the Vienna Symphony's annual autumn tour, Schwarzkopf took over the role of Leonore, with Lorenz Fehenberger as Florestan.

These Swiss performances of *Fidelio* have excited a good deal of interest down the years. In the theatre, Schwarzkopf had hitherto confined herself to the role of Marzelline. Taking on Leonore, even in concert, was a bold decision and one that has led to a good deal of adverse comment by those who would have us believe that Legge and Karajan often misjudged Schwarzkopf's talents and occasionally brutally misused them. I asked Schwarzkopf whether Karajan had been satisfied with her performances. 'I presume so,' she said with a smile. 'If he hadn't been, he'd have had no hesitation in replacing me after the first performance.'

The first performance, in Basle, did attract a certain amount of muted criticism. One reviewer felt that the voice was slow to warm up; another concluded:

As Leonore, Elisabeth Schwarzkopf impressed with her vocal beauty and great mastery, and with her vivid shaping of the text. None the less, the wonderful voice did not seem as free and flexible as usual and also occasionally sounded curiously stifled.[24]

In his book on Schwarzkopf, Alan Jefferson quotes this latter review, adding that subsequent performances in Geneva and Zürich met 'with much the same response'.[25] This is simply not true. Reviews in Geneva and Zürich were more or less unstinting in their praise. Where doubts are entertained they are rapidly laid to rest, as in the review which speaks of a wonderfully intelligent reading of the role of Leonore delivered in radiant tones that were 'surprisingly secure'.[26] Others tell of great beauty, rare precision, and a most sympathetic characterisation of the role, purveyed both through the voice and through Schwarzkopf's face and hands. (The great Lieder singer, it would seem, equally the mistress of the technique of performing opera on the concert stage.) Schwarzkopf's 1954 recording of Leonore's 'Abscheulicher' largely confirms these reports; it is a beautifully articulated performance, and a virtuoso one, her voice and the Philharmonia horns led by Dennis Brain symbiotically at one in a thrilling account of the closing bars.

Karajan's conducting was also almost universally admired, with several Swiss critics freely admitting that the man they had previously reckoned in concert to be a charlatan and show-off ('*un admirable "faiseur"*') was, in fact, the real thing ('it is necessary on this occasion to pay homage to a true musician'[27]), a conductor capable of putting the music first.[28]

What the Swiss critics were responding to was the fact that Karajan the podium prima donna was rather a different animal from the real Karajan: a creature best studied professionally in the relative privacy of the opera pit, the rehearsal room, or the recording studio. One critic noted:

This use of gesture – except in certain moments of dramatic extremity – was in no way imperious. It was a simple invitation, a suggestion stripped of the power of command, that seemed to draw the music directly from the players ... The impression one is left with above all is one of suppleness. There is a suppleness of phrasing that with the minimum of fuss is instantly absorbed and replicated by the musicians, so much so that it seems to emanate from the music entirely naturally. There is suppleness of sound, suppleness of thought even.[29]

This suppleness of thought and movement is well illustrated in Karajan's lofty yet enchanting 1953 Philharmonia version of Beethoven's *Pastoral* Symphony, the finest of his five studio recordings.

Throughout 1953, Schwarzkopf and Karajan were barely out of one another's company. Between *Lohengrin* in Milan in January and a radio performance of *Die Zauberflöte* in Rome in December when she sang Pamina – in Italian – with rare beauty and allure, they gave over thirty performances together, in repertory ranging from Bach to Tippett.

In August, the La Scala production of *Don Giovanni* played for one night at the Munich Festival. For Schwarzkopf, this came in the middle of a run of Salzburg Festival performances of the opera under Furtwängler.

'So, my dear, whose performance are you going to give me? Mine or the man K's?' Furtwängler enquired.[30]

Furtwängler had also somewhat shyly offered his services to Schwarzkopf as her pianist for a Lieder recital marking the fiftieth anniversary of the death of Hugo Wolf. This took place in Salzburg on 12 August and, somewhat bizarrely, was echoed by a recital Karajan gave with Schwarzkopf in Tunis in mid-September. What Karajan and Schwarzkopf were doing in Tunis, and who was with them, has never been adequately explained. One acquaintance has suggested that the visit was to do with off-shore accounts; but according to Schwarzkopf it was simply one of Karajan's holiday jaunts with the recital thrown in as part of a complicated deal he had struck with the Tunisian authorities over mooring rights for his yacht.

Karajan certainly needed a holiday. Summers spent in Salzburg or Bayreuth had meant a stable base and familiar repertory. Footloose in Europe in 1952–3, he had been travelling a vast amount, working with a variety of orchestras, and playing a lot of music that was either new in itself or new to him. There were glamorous venues – Milan, Rome, Paris, London, Edinburgh, Berlin, Munich, Zürich and Lucerne (where he conducted a riveting performance of Stravinsky's *Oedipus rex*) – but there were less glamorous ones, too. Two nights with the Philharmonia in Ostend in mid-July would not be every conductor's idea of bliss, and the Vienna Symphony's autumn perambulations through Switzerland, France, Germany, and the Low Countries were becoming ever more eccentric in their choice of venues. True, he was lionised everywhere he went (in Aachen the police had to be called to help clear the audience and allow the caretaker to lock up the hall). But he must occasionally have wondered what he was doing at the age of forty-five conducting Beethoven in Bielefeld.

What he did set his face against, however, was the lure of conducting provincial orchestras for inflated fees, the kind of thing Jochum did, blighting his career with several top orchestras in the process, and Böhm, too, when the financial itch was upon him. Karajan also turned down work which was politically problematical or which threatened to circumvent his own powers of control. Much as he admired Leni Riefenstahl as a film-maker, actress, and barefoot mountaineer ('a great woman', he told Roger Vaughan[31]), his response to her invitation to conduct the music for her film of *Tiefland* was to demand a fee that not even MGM could have afforded.

In September 1953, however, Karajan was hustled into making his first post-war appearance with the Berlin Philharmonic – a highly signficant occasion for him – with limited rehearsal time, hard on the heels of three concerts with the Philharmonia at the Edinburgh Festival. True, the Berlin visit was primarily to do with remaking links with the Berlin

Philharmonic's recently reinstated Intendant Gerhart von Westerman; but the concert itself – Bartók's *Concerto for Orchestra* and Beethoven's *Eroica* Symphony – was not without its importance. Every note, every gesture was bound to be analysed by the players, the Berlin critics, and the Berlin audience.

The *Concerto for Orchestra* had also been included by Karajan in his Edinburgh Festival concert on 2 September, along with Handel's *Water Music* suite and the Beethoven Violin Concerto with Menuhin as soloist. The performance of the Beethoven was dedicated to the memory of the great French violinist Jacques Thibaud, who had been killed in an air crash the previous day. *The Times* commented on the performance's great purity and depth of feeling.

The knives were out, however, for Karajan's treatment of the *Water Music* suite. By using just about every adventitious rhetorical device in the book, Karajan was said to have turned the sturdily Anglo-Saxon Handel into a kind of musical Beau Brummel. Warming to his subject, the *Times* critic went on to draw wider conclusions about Karajan:

He is a conductor who plays on the orchestra as a violinist plays on a fiddle, with every strand of the score under his hand, giving vivid and musical performances but plainly uncertain in his taste and command of style.[32]

*

During 1953, Karajan spent more time than previously recording with the Philharmonia. Six weeks in all: time that had been partly freed up by his refusal to appear at Bayreuth that year. Taken together with the December 1952 sessions and those of the summer of 1954 when Karajan made celebrated recordings of Mozart's *Così fan tutte* and Strauss's *Ariadne auf Naxos*, they constitute a high-water mark in his years as a recording artist in London. Again, the speed, economy, and versatility of the enterprise were breathtaking.

27 June–2 July	Humperdinck *Hänsel und Gretel*
2–3 July	R. Strauss *Tod und Verklärung*
4 July	Tchaikovsky Symphony No.4 (start)
6–7 July	Sibelius Symphony No.4
8 July	Tchaikovsky Symphony No.4 (cont.)
9–10 July	Beethoven Symphony No.6, *Pastoral*
10 July	Tchaikovsky Symphony No.4 (cont.)
14–15 July	Sibelius *Tapiola*
16 July	Patching sessions for Humperdinck's *Hänsel und Gretel* and Tchaikovsky Symphony No.4. Ravel *Rapsodie espagnole* (start)

17 July   Ravel *Rapsodie espagnole* (concl.). Chabrier *España*
20 July   Debussy *La mer* (start)
21 July   Debussy *La mer* (cont.), Waldteufel *The Skaters' Waltz*,
                 Sousa marches *El capitan, The Stars and Stripes Forever*
22 July   Debussy *La mer* (concl.)

The Strauss recording remained unpublished until 1982 and the Sousa marches have yet to be released. The rest quickly became classics, *the* versions to have in the 1950s.

Despite this, and rather to the chagrin of old Philharmonia hands, he always maintained that the orchestra was wonderful: up to a point. What it lacked, he suggested, was the ability imaginatively to take wing of its own accord, a limitation (if it did truly exist) perhaps best explained by the orchestra's relative newness and the imbalance that existed in those years between its numerous recording commitments and its somewhat limited experience as a concert orchestra.

Not that the Berlin Philharmonic would have it all its own way in later years. There was much glee in London in 1965 when it was rumoured that during sessions for a Deutsche Grammophon recording of Tchaikovsky's Fifth Symphony Karajan had called a break only to be found closeted with his old Philharmonia LP of the piece. Nor did any of the Berlin recordings of Beethoven's *Pastoral* Symphony ever match Karajan's Philharmonia version for ease and naturalness of orchestral diction. As for the Philharmonia account of Tchaikovsky's Fourth Symphony, this was also spontaneously fine. 'Phenomenal . . . a record in a thousand' was the view of *The Gramophone*, a paper not normally given to hyperbole.[33]

The fact that the Tchaikovsky took the best part of four days to record, rather than two, was due to a protracted hunt for an optimum placing of the horns. Such delays can fray tempers, but here the reverse was true. Philharmonia chronicler Stephen J. Pettitt has recalled:

Finally, it was found that the sound Karajan wanted would be achieved only by placing [the horns] with their backs to him and the bells of their instruments facing towards the microphones instead of towards the back of the hall as normal. The orchestra's response was typical of the rapport that existed between them and Karajan. When Karajan returned from the control room after hearing the sixth or seventh play-back of the problem passage, he could not see the horns at all. Suddenly, into the expectant silence came the *fortissimo* strains of the opening – from the organ-gallery, where the players had hidden themselves. Amid general merriment, not least from Karajan himself, they climbed down to try yet another placing.[34]

The 'horns in the organ-loft' spirit also seems to have infected the sessions for Humperdinck's *Hänsel und Gretel*. Schwarzkopf remembers these as being a labour of love, an enchanted return to a favourite childhood story, but also a voyage of discovery through a score that in places was far from familiar.

Much of the recording was improvised. The account of the overture is the only one Karajan and the orchestra ever made: a test take with the tape running, that was adjudged so good it was decided to use it exactly as it was. Nor did Karajan rehearse a great deal with the singers. 'Like the rest of us,' Schwarzkopf recalls, 'he seemed endlessly surprised and delighted by details of the score as they cropped up in performance.'[35]

What makes this all doubly remarkable is the fact that *Hänsel und Gretel* is not an easy score, even to practised Wagnerians like Karajan, Legge, and his singers. Colin Welch, a political writer by trade, but a music-lover too, put it well in an essay he wrote for the Christmas issue of the London *Spectator* in 1984:

For children? Well, it did originate in a little party *Singspiel* for the children of Humperdinck's sister and librettist, Adelheid Wette. It was then developed into a full-scale opera. Much of it remains definitely for children – immediately accessible, the plot familiar but thrilling, the effects, when properly done, eye-opening, the forest terrifying, the witch half-comic, half-bloodcurdling. But much of the development is highly adult, with longish Wagnerian monologues laid on top of complex orchestration. The children's father, a bit sozzled, moans on about hunger being the best cook, fine when there's money in your purse, hell when there isn't, and then boasts at length about his success at market. These economic facts of life among the poor make many children fidget. So does some of the heavy orchestration and subtle harmonisation, a taste for which comes slowly, if at all, like so much else, with puberty and maturity. The *whole* opera is accessible only to grown-ups who remember their own childhood (and music of this sumptuous sort) and know by experience or imagination the anguish, joys and fears of parental love.[36]

With Karajan's recordings of *Hänsel und Gretel*, *Così fan tutte*, and *Ariadne auf Naxos*, Legge established the complete opera recording as a new and compelling medium in its own right: opera repositioning itself in what André Malraux has called the *musée imaginaire* of the gramophone.

The studio skills were formidable. 'The last and greatest art,' wrote Goethe, 'is to limit and isolate oneself.' No one used the 'limitations' of mono sound better than Legge and his colleagues at this time. Like HMV's 1956 recording of Rossini's *Le Comte Ory* (produced by Legge's colleague Lawrance Collingwood), this 1953 *Hänsel und Gretel* is a classic example of how a well produced mono recording can seem more stereophonic than many of its later stereophonic rivals. Impervious to time, fashion, or technological advance – but not to the needs of the listener hearing the opera in the privacy of his own home and imagination – it has proved to be one of the most consistently collected of all opera sets.

Amid all the praise for it, there was, however, one dissenting voice. Shortly after the LPs were released, Legge received a letter from Wieland Wagner, full of extravagant fury. How could his old friend have perpetrated such an abomination? Did he not know that *Hänsel und Gretel* was a *terrible* opera, profoundly second-rate? As for Legge's cast – Schwarzkopf, Grümmer, Karajan himself – did not this make things worse? Hearing so wretched a piece so wonderfully performed merely served to quadruple one's anger.

The letter, very much the kind of thing Legge relished, was the icing on the cake, a rousing endorsement of a wonderful venture.

*

A five-day stint of recordings in August 1953 went less well. Gieseking produced more disappointingly neutral-sounding readings, this time of the Schumann Piano Concerto and Mozart's C minor Concerto K491. Mozart's *Jupiter* Symphony was briefly worked on and abandoned, as was three days' work on Beethoven's Fifth Symphony.

In November, however, serious inroads were made into the final stages of Karajan's Beethoven cycle. The First Symphony was recorded in a single day, and the Fourth, which Karajan endlessly agonised over and always claimed was the most difficult of the nine to bring off, was completed in two days. Britten's *Variations on a Theme of Frank Bridge* and Vaughan Williams's *Fantasia on a Theme by Thomas Tallis* were also completed in a couple of days. Fine recordings both, they never sold in anything like the numbers EMI required.

The wind players, by contrast, were mining gold. On 12, 13 and 23 November Dennis Brain recorded Mozart's four horn concertos, a classic of the gramophone that has never been out of the catalogues. Brain was in dazzling form: everything from memory, of course. A music-stand had duly been provided, though when Karajan strolled over during one of the breaks to check some minor discrepancy in the parts all he found on it was a copy of *Autocar*.

Records of this quality were more than timely, since Legge had been closely involved in negotiating an important new commercial outlet for English Columbia in North America in the wake of the breakdown of the old RCA-EMI agreement. The deal was with Dario Soria, head of the Italian Cetra label (known in America as Cetra-Soria), who had recently sold out to Capitol Records. The new American label was to be called 'Angel' after the long-forgotten EMI trademark 'At the Sign of the Recording Angel'. Like everything in which Legge invested his time and reputation, it was to be a label of unimpeachable quality and accomplishment.

Soria brought with him high-level artistic contacts (among others, the young Maria Callas whom he had helped Legge win over to EMI) but he was also committed to making Angel a top-quality label technically and presentationally. Given the high price that was being asked for LPs in those years – £1.16s.5½d. for a 12-inch LP in the UK in 1953 at a time when the weekly pension for a single person was £1.12s.0d. and the average weekly wage £10.2s.0d. – Soria reasoned that the customer had every right to expect to receive the record in mint condition. To this end, he proposed to deny browsers and casual collectors the chance to sample (and damage) LPs in record shop listening booths by sealing all LP sleeves at the factory. Legge was delighted with the idea. On 16 November 1953, he cabled:

Suggested slogan for your factory-sealed records: 'Every Angel a Virgin'.[37]

With records of the quality of Callas's new EMI recording of Bellini's *I puritani* or the Brain-Karajan LP of the Mozart horn concertos, Angel was set fair to prosper. When the Mozart disc appeared on Angel, *High Fidelity* reviewer C. G. Burke wrote one of his charmingly idiosyncratic notices:

Here a recording of surpassing art blows its predecessors to the four winds ... Mr Brain, whose family all play horns, may have peers but it is hard to imagine his superior: he skips over the bland hurdles and around the delectable pitfalls contrived by Mozart with shining assurance, while Prof. von Karajan manoeuvres his skilful orchestra with ebullience and grace, inciting Messrs EMI, whose agent the Angel is, to capture the sound with a felicity uncommon for the king of wind instruments and a sweet insinuation equally rare for orchestral strings.[38]

Midway through the Mozart sessions, Dennis Brain joined Sidney Sutcliffe, Bernard Walton, and Cecil James for a recording of Mozart's *Sinfonia concertante* K297 with Karajan and the Philharmonia. According to Sutcliffe, all four soloists had recently played the *Sinfonia concertante* with Harry Blech and the London Mozart Players; performing the work with Karajan was not much different, except in the slow movement where Karajan set a rather slower tempo.

'Could it perhaps be a shade quicker?' Sutcliffe enquired, on behalf of the soloists.

'Certainly,' Karajan replied, courteous as ever. Whereupon he returned to the hall and set precisely the same tempo as before.

Karajan was right, of course. The movement is marked *Adagio*. And if that is not plain enough there are other cues too: the use of the work's principal key for the slow movement, and falling wind phrases after the opening unison statement of a shape and intensity we find elsewhere in Mozart only when he is at his most serious. But all's well that ends well. Sutcliffe, in particular, plays the music gloriously at Karajan's slower tempo.

*

During the Philharmonia's visit to Edinburgh, Legge and Karajan had driven south to the Scottish Borders to absorb the atmosphere of Walter Scott country, to study the architecture and the light, and to visit Sir Walter Scott's home, Abbotsford. The reason for this sudden access of high-quality tourism was the production of Donizetti's *Lucia di Lammermoor* Karajan was planning to stage in Milan, with Maria Callas in the title role.

Karajan had met Callas the previous year. Legge had taken her backstage at La Scala after a performance of *Der Rosenkavalier*. (Two minutes of mutual courtesies during which, according to Legge, Karajan was unable to take his eyes off a huge emerald Callas was wearing.) In the spring of 1953, mindful of Ghiringhelli's desire to tempt Karajan into conducting Italian repertory at La Scala, Legge had handed him a small spool of tape: the end of Act 2 of *Lucia di Lammermoor* copied from the complete recording Callas had just made for EMI in Florence with Tullio Serafin. Karajan pocketed the tape with ill grace, Legge thought. It was not long, however, before he was on the phone to the La Scala library asking them to deliver the full score to his hotel. Two things must have weighed heavily with him: his thrill at the phenomenon that was Callas and his memories of Toscanini and the La Scala company performing *Lucia di Lammermoor* in Vienna in 1930.

Legge warned: 'No kilts and sporrans for Callas.' But nothing could have been further from Karajan's mind. He had already decided to stage the opera with a minimum of reliance on conventional scenic effects and a maximum concentration on the use of atmospheric lighting, with Callas herself as its central focus. Such visual restraint was anathema to the great Nicola Benois, La Scala's principal designer, a 'painter' of the old school; so it was left to an underling, Gianni Ratto, to work out what Karajan needed. (Gauzes and a few rather dim back projections was the answer.)

Initially, Callas was not pleased. The show's all-pervading gloom (she was as blind as a bat without her glasses), its lack of visual allure, and dust from old gauzes all irritated her in one way or another. With people she knew, trusted, and respected she was easiness itself, the consummate professional. Karajan was not easy to know; nor did he always find it easy to explain in words his musical intuitions. But he was immensely patient with her, and he won her trust. From the outset, she had had faith in him musically; but she now also began to realise that here was a man who knew better than almost any of the stage directors she had worked with how she could best be left to be herself.

The opening night, 18 January 1954, was one of the most sensational Karajan had ever been involved in. 'La Scala in delirium' was the headline in Milan's *La Notte*. 'A rain of red carnations. Four minutes of applause after the Mad Scene'. On stage, Callas became Lucia in mind and spirit in a way that was not entirely possible in either of her two studio recordings. When she is shown the forged letter that is designed to undermine her faith in Edgardo's love for her, the shock is monstrous. We hear this in her enunciation of the words '*Me infelice! Ahi! La folgore piombò*' and in the *Larghetto* that follows, where she seems already to have passed beyond this world. The Mad Scene is not so much presaged at this moment: spiritually, this is where it begins.

To what extent was Karajan a factor in all this? Leading Callas biographers – Ardoin, Kesting, Scott – take what are often radically different views of the strengths and weaknesses of her performances of Lucia between 1953 and 1959. (Six are extant on record, in whole or part.[39]) What they are principally responding to – as, indeed, were the performers working with Callas – was the shifting character of the voice itself.

In June 1956, when Karajan and the La Scala company took the production to the Vienna Festival, Chicago critic Claudia Cassidy would note:

At one point in the pyrotechnics of the Mad Scene her voice just simply doesn't respond. From our high loge we can see Karajan's instant alertness, the almost pricking ears of the Scala orchestra. But Callas recovers instantly, and the extraordinary mournful beauty of that voice makes the scene a duet of oboe with the Scala's sensitive flute. You might not have noticed that hazardous moment at all. Just in case you did, a Callas curtain call touches a hand ever so delicately to her throat. The orchestra men are a buzz of amused admiration.[40]

By this time Callas, Karajan, and the La Scala players were functioning more or less as a single organism. The previous September, in Berlin, the local radio orchestra had been used, to less good effect. Callas biographer Michael Scott finds the playing of the RIAS orchestra 'obtrusive', 'unidiomatic' and 'unstylish'.[41] And so it is at times, particularly at the peripheries of the performance where Callas herself is not involved. At such points Karajan's conducting can seem to veer between the perfunctory and the melodramatic.

It is difficult, though, entirely to accept Scott's theory that Callas did not really need Karajan, that 'all Callas's Lucia needed was someone who could follow her and keep the rest of the company together'.[42] Shortly after singing Lucia in Naples under Molinari-Pradelli in March 1956, Callas wrote to Walter Legge:

Unfortunately Karajan was not directing and I simply can't hear the opera without him. Tell him I miss him and it is a shame we don't work more together – don't you think?[43]

Rhythm, phrasing, and the use of the breath was probably at the bottom of Karajan's deep rapport with her. Her own sense of rhythm was flawless. Karajan would tell me:

It was incredible. When she had the piece within her I said: 'Maria, you can turn away from me and sing because I know that you will never be one tiny part of a bar out'.[44]

It is a point that Jürgen Kesting writes about with great insight in his book on Callas:

It is not only Maria Callas who said that Karajan could 'go with the voice'. This does not just mean clever accompaniment, nor just breathing with the singer, which in itself is very important, but much more a sense of timing, dynamics, and phrasing which amount to more than the listing of specific technical details. However banal this may sound, it is a matter of *organising time through movements which tighten and then relax* [my emphasis].[45]

This is a particularly interesting observation, given the fact that walking, breathing and the heart's systolic pulse were of fundamental importance to Karajan's way of experiencing musical rhythm. 'He was obsessed with rhythm,' Peter Alward would later recall. 'With pulse and time and his own pulse *vis-à-vis* the music.'[46] As for opera, Karajan developed the practice early in his career of using the preliminary rehearsal or *Sitzprobe* to identify the breathing points of the individual singer. Singers who were not familiar with his methods often feared they were being tested or re-auditioned. In fact, Karajan was merely working out in advance how he could best time and grade the orchestral accompaniment.

Later in his book, Kesting returns to the idea of breathing, in a passage which directly addresses the question of the artistic status of Callas's *Lucia*:

A great performance? It is one of the grandest she gave. Yet at the same time it is diminished [by being a performance] in which the battle with her voice becomes evident. However, it is certainly a great performance, in the sense understood by Wagner, in which the singer *handles breath so beautifully* [my emphasis] that doubts about her voice become irrelevant.[47]

One thing Callas and Karajan did fall out over was an uncharacteristic concession on Karajan's part: his allowing an encore of the opera's famous Sextet in response to what, performance by performance, was an ever-growing public clamour. The Sextet is a difficult piece for the soprano. Worse, it precedes the Mad Scene. Callas was furious: so furious that at one performance she sang most of the Mad Scene with her back to Karajan.

The sequel to this contest took place in a Paris restaurant some years later. Michel Glotz had arranged a dinner party for Callas, Aristotle Onassis, and the Karajans at the Berkeley. Napkins had barely been unfurled or menus perused when Callas turned to Karajan. 'Now, tell me,' she asked. 'What was it you did when I was so bitchy and turned my back on you in the Mad Scene? I knew you were clever. But the accompaniment was so perfect, I decided you were not only a genius. You were also a witch.'

'It was very simple,' Karajan replied. 'I watched your shoulders. When they went up, I knew you were breathing in and that was my cue for attack.'[48]

Being a bit of a witch herself, Callas must have known that this was only half the answer.

CHAPTER 39

Brandy in Les Baux

It is said that Herbert von Karajan conducts only these orchestras:
the Vienna Philharmonic, La Scala, Milan, and the Philharmonia.
This is not true in the case of the Philharmonia. As he showed us
last night, he merely stands and listens with closed eyes to their
magical playing.

Sud-Ouest

After the banquet that was *Lucia di Lammermoor*, it was back to more
traditional fare for Karajan with a revival of his Milan production of
Mozart's *Le nozze di Figaro*. It was a problematic revival, not least because
of Karajan's decision to cast a girl in the role of Cherubino who looked every
inch the adolescent boy but who lacked any recognisable vocal talent. She
got as far as the dress rehearsal, but no further. Peter Dragadze reported:

The star of the performance was Sena Jurinac, called in at a few hours' notice
to sing Cherubino. Schwarzkopf looked beautiful as the Countess and sang
well, though she sounded tired before the end of the opera.[1]

According to Schwarzkopf, no two performances of *Figaro* were ever alike,
Karajan's tempi veering this way and that from evening to evening. But
there were compensations:

One thing we did learn from Karajan was how to interiorise the drama in
works by Mozart and Richard Strauss. At moments of intense quiet, he would
make us stand absolutely still and sing with an awed *sotto voce*. It was chamber
music of the soul, the expression of things one person cannot speak to another.
Most conductors wouldn't have dared ask for such quiet because their control
of the orchestra was insufficiently exact. But Karajan could do it.[2]

There was also Karajan's larger dynamic control. In February 1954, the
critic Cynthia Jolly filed a report from Rome where Karajan's La Scala
production of *Don Giovanni* had been seen to huge acclaim shortly before
Christmas:

Musically, the portentous climaxes are built up from a steady basis of orchestral
piano which is the natural playground of singers like Schwarzkopf and Nicolai
Gedda. This fine Swedish tenor excels in *mezzo piano* and *legato* phrasing (he
sang the two phrases of 'Dalla sua pace' in one breath). Schwarzkopf, fighting
a heavy cold, sang exquisitely.[3]

*

During the rehearsals for *Le nozze di Figaro* Karajan was called back to Salzburg. His mother had been ill for some time with cancer and was now dying. Much has been made of the fact – first revealed by Karajan's brother and sister-in-law – that on this final visit he declined to go into the sick room to see her. Dilemmas of this order never admit easy solutions. Whatever the reason for Karajan's reaction, it was an ambiguous and troubled end to a relationship with a mother who had doted on him, worried over him, driven him and encouraged him for the best part of forty-six years. This final stage of the illness would also leave him with a morbid fear of himself dying alone amid what he called 'the white sheets' of a hospital ward.

Robert C. Bachmann has said that, 'Throughout his life, Karajan avoided anything ill, damaged, frail or deformed.'[4] Tempting as it is to promote such a theory, tying it in with parallel theories about Karajan's preoccupation with youth and beauty, it is a thesis that is refuted by the facts. The times when Karajan advised on medical care are legion. Those he helped ranged from fellow artists he barely knew (Montserrat Caballé, for example[5]) to members of the Berlin Philharmonic, and such seemingly remote figures as the seriously ill son of one of the concierges of Berlin's Kempinski Hotel.

Some cases touched him rather more personally. During José Carreras's protracted and life-threatening illness, Karajan frequently telephoned him in hospital in Barcelona and Seattle to encourage him and assure him that he was being included in all his future plans. The chapter on Karajan in Carreras's autobiography, published two years after Karajan's death, ends with the italicised words: '*I wish to give here a sincere expression of my homage to him*', which must surely rank as one of the rarer tributes a singer has paid to a conductor.[6]

It has been said by another biographer that 'Karajan simply did not make hospital visits', that he would 'sooner sit soaking wet in front of a January draft'.[7] In an age less health-obsessed than our own, such evasiveness would be applauded, its converse judged merely morbid. Again, though, the facts are at odds with the reports. In 1984, Karajan visited his colleague and biographer Ernst Haeusserman who lay terminally ill in hospital in Salzburg. When he arrived at the hospital, Karajan was told that no visitors were permitted. 'My father founded this hospital,' he growled, limping determinedly by. Haeusserman was much cheered by the visit.

There was also the case of Magdalene Padberg, doyenne of the Deutsche Grammophon A&R team, a woman, neither rich, famous, nor beautiful for whom Karajan had a deep respect and affection. Sadly, her retirement from Deutsche Grammophon was short-lived. She died of cancer in 1985 at the relatively early age of sixty-five. Shortly before her death, Karajan visited her in her modest Hamburg flat. He had flown to Hamburg to see his elder daughter in a play by Schiller. At the airport, he asked the driver if he could make a detour to Padberg's apartment. He spent two hours with her. Antje Henneking, Padberg's successor, who spent the time waiting outside in the car, told me:

It took me completely by surprise. It's not the kind of thing I would ever have expected Karajan to do. I know how shaken he was by the visit and I know how wonderful he was with her. I must say, it completely changed my view of him as a human being.[8]

Many of these events took place in the 1980s. Had he changed? Had he become wiser and more compassionate with time, chastened by earlier omissions and his own recent brushes with death? There is reason to think that this might have been so.

*

In April 1954 Karajan made his first visit to Japan, a six-week tour which helped lay the foundations for a relationship with a country and an audience that was unique in his career. The Japanese broadcasting authority NHK had been putting out feelers to him for more than three years. The post-war period had inevitably been a difficult one for Japan; but by 1954 foreign artists were once more beginning to visit the country. Karajan's own visit more or less coincided with visits by Heifetz, Backhaus, and the distinguished Italian tenor Ferruccio Tagliavini. None the less, Karajan was the first conductor of any consequence to visit since Weingartner in the late 1930s.

He was received with courtesy and much ceremony. A reception was given in his honour by Mr Tetsuro Furukaki, the President of NHK, and his wife. Guests were served 'Osaka-style' sushi and entertained by music played on the *samisen*, the long-necked plucked lute widely used in the *bunraku* puppet theatres. The Japanese Deputy Prime Minister was present, as were the ambassadors of Austria and several other European countries. The ambassador to the United States was there, a point that would not have gone unnoticed by Karajan; the United Kingdom ambassador was otherwise engaged.

The NHK Symphony Orchestra, its personnel over ninety per cent Japanese, had at that time a fearsome reputation for lawlessness. Minor misconductors (Legge's phrase) were usually eaten alive for breakfast. Karajan survived until morning coffee and beyond. 'They behaved like lambs,' he told the *Nippon Times*. He did not pretend the orchestra was in the same league as the Berlin Philharmonic or the Philharmonia, but he praised its dedication and responsiveness. 'I have never seen a group which has such a quick spirit to grasp what I wanted.'[9]

He conducted eighteen concerts in all, and taught a number of master-classes, a dry run for the classes he was planning to direct at the Lucerne Festival the following year. He was bowled over by the attentiveness and enthusiasm of the Japanese audiences, not only in Tokyo itself but in Osaka, Kyoto, and Nagoya. There was also a radio audience estimated to be in the region of four million listeners.

The opening two concerts consisted of Brahms's First Symphony, Beethoven's G major Piano Concerto, with different Japanese soloists at each performance, and *Till Eulenspiegel*. But it was the seven concerts featuring Beethoven's Ninth Symphony – prefaced either by Beethoven's overture *Leonore* No.3 or the *Theme and Variations* by Karajan's contemporary, the Japanese composer Yoritsune Matsudaira – that made the greatest impact. They had been sold out for weeks.

The Ninth had been a cult work in Japan ever since its first perform-ance there in the Bandô prisoner-of-war camp in 1918. In 1940, Joseph Rosenstock, the NHK SO's chief conductor, inaugurated the tradition of playing the symphony as a kind of rite of passage each New Year's Eve. In 1982, in an essay entitled 'Why is Beethoven's Ninth so well loved in Japan?', the writer Junichi Yano would observe:

[When] the baritone bursts out 'Freude!' [joy] and the chorus echoes the word back, listeners in their seats are inwardly singing 'Freude!' as well. The conductor, instrumentalists, chorus members, soloists *and audience* [my emphasis] all participate equally in the performance. And therein lies, it seems to me, the secret of the intimacy and the harmony between the music of Beethoven and the spiritual life of the Japanese.[10]

'Joy through suffering' is the idea that is most often mooted in this connection: a phrase taken from a celebrated study of Beethoven by Romain Rolland, first published in Paris in 1903, that had become a best-seller in Japan in the 1920s. It is hardly necessary to spell out the impact made by Karajan's performances of Beethoven's Ninth Symphony: a master interpreter guiding musicians through a work that had acquired near-sacred status within the culture.

For the rest, Karajan's conducting was admired for its restraint and practicality. He was not, it was noted, a flamboyant conductor. Even though he did not know the players, nor they him, he stuck to his usual conducting style, steadfastly refusing to transform himself into the musical equivalent of a traffic policeman on rush-hour point duty.

Karajan's closeness to Japanese audiences and the Japanese record-buying public would be a feature of his subsequent career and would continue way beyond his death. This latter point is unusual. Records of even the greatest conductors often sell poorly once the man is dead. As someone in Deutsche Grammophon said of Karl Böhm: 'He died the day after his death.' Karajan's records have proved to be an exception to this rule. They continue to sell well world wide. In Japan in the 1990s sales actually increased, reaching new all-time highs.[11]

Karajan's interest in Japan was rooted in the enthusiastic receptions he always received there, his fascination with new technology, and his many friendships: most important, his long-standing friendship with the founder of Sony, Akio Morita, whom he had first met in Salzburg in 1953.

But there was more. The formality and, in the best sense of the term, the impersonality of oriental life clearly appealed to him.

*

It had been Walter Legge's hope that Karajan would conduct EMI's new La Scala, Milan recording of *Pagliacci* on his return from Japan. Di Stefano, Gobbi, and Callas had been engaged for the leading roles. In the event, a shoulder condition, actual or strategic, prevented him from doing so. His place was taken by Tullio Serafin. Had Karajan accepted *Pagliacci*, it would have landed him with the challenge of making three complete opera recordings in six weeks. As it is, he completed two in the space of three weeks: Strauss's *Ariadne auf Naxos* and Mozart's *Così fan tutte*.

The *Ariadne auf Naxos* is another of Legge's productions that many collectors still consider to be unsurpassed. Again, the genius is partly in the casting. Irmgard Seefried had sung the role of the Composer for Strauss himself on the occasion of his eightieth birthday in Vienna in June 1944. Strauss biographer Michael Kennedy has described her interpretation as being 'without question one of the paramount Strauss performances of all time'.[12] Rita Streich's Zerbinetta is hardly less authoritative. It is dazzlingly well sung and every bit as touching as Strauss intended it to be:

A moment is nothing, a glance is much. People think my heart's in the coquette I play on stage. But they don't know how lonely I really am.

Streich's teacher – and Schwarzkopf's, the Ariadne on the set – was Maria Ivogün whose Zerbinetta Strauss considered to be beyond compare. Legge's casting of the *comprimario* roles was also typically ingenious and daring. Hugues Cuénod, the famously amusing Swiss tenor-*comédien*, was engaged as the Dancing-Master and a virtually unknown young German baritone by the name of Hermann Prey was allocated the role of Arlekin. Prey had never so much as glanced at the role before he was summoned to London; at the playbacks he sat nervously scanning Karajan's face for the merest flicker of approval or disapprobation.

The cast had been rehearsed ahead of Karajan's arrival by Heinrich Schmidt, for many years Strauss's right-hand man in Munich; another example of Legge settling for nothing less than the best that was available. In the circumstances, it might be argued that Karajan merely had to turn up and conduct, but there was more to it than that. *Ariadne auf Naxos* is scored for a large chamber orchestra. Texturally, it is extremely elaborate, but the surety and sophistication of the Philharmonia's wind and string soloists show an orchestra that has really come of age. When the set appeared in the United States, *Opera* magazine's New York critic James Hinton Jnr observed:

. . . in the last analysis it is von Karajan's unifying, urging force that makes the whole performance what it is – a truly magical evocation of the tenderness, the longing, the archaism, the lyric flow of a work.[13]

The *Ariadne* recording was completed in just five and a half days. On the last day, 7 July 1954, Karajan and the orchestra began recording Berlioz's *Symphonie fantastique*. Less than a week later, many of the *Ariadne* instrumentalists and one or two of the same singers were back in Kingsway Hall for Mozart's *Così fan tutte*.

It proved to be a frustrating day. For once, this finest of all London recording venues did not seem 'right'. Legge wanted a very intimate acoustic for *Così*. Having quickly realised that Kingsway Hall was not the best option, he bundled the entire company into a fleet of taxis and headed back to EMI's studio in Abbey Road.

During the sessions, Reginald Goodall warmed up the orchestra for Karajan, an all too familiar misuse of one the operatic world's finest talents. Not that it was Legge's fault; nor did Goodall mind. He had sat in the pit in Bayreuth during Karajan's conducting of *Tristan und Isolde* and in later years, after Klemperer's death, would allow no conductor, apart from Carlos Kleiber, to be mentioned in the same breath as Karajan.[14]

The cast Legge had assembled was, again, beautifully judged as an ensemble for the *musée imaginaire* of the gramophone (*Così fan tutte*'s ideal home, according to Karajan, whose dislike of small auditoria caused him to whip up a strange confection of arguments as to why the opera should be heard but not staged). This new approach to opera recording had the effect of disorientating critical opinion. The editor of *Opera*, Harold Rosenthal, who liked the set, objected that Legge's cast was not really a *theatre* cast.[15]

Schwarzkopf was new to the role at the time of the Karajan recording. Subsequent performances, under Cantelli in Milan and Böhm in Legge's celebrated 1962 stereo remake for EMI, show greater ease and freedom of expression. But this is not to detract from the achievement of the 1954 set. Simoneau is a Ferrando of rare pedigree, Merriman a superb Dorabella ('there was a voice, and a musician and a technician!'

Schwarzkopf exclaimed when we were discussing the set). And there is Sesto Bruscantini, wonderfully urbane, drawing what is an essentially sympathetic portrait of Don Alfonso, the cynical old bachelor whose wager on the fragility of the girls' fidelity sets the drama in motion. This is another performance Schwarzkopf would recall with admiration:

Later, it became the fashion to turn Alfonso into a poisonous, embittered old man, someone who sees the worst in human nature. Now, that isn't in the music. Bruscantini played him without malice. Perhaps it needs an Italian to see this, to see that life is a game to be enjoyed.[16]

Karajan's conducting is stylish and spare-toned, fleet-footed but never hasty as his Vienna *Le nozze di Figaro* had occasionally been. Certainly, it has nothing of the 'whipped-cream blandness'[17] received opinion would nowadays have us believe was the hallmark of Karajan's Mozart. If gastronomic analogies are in order, it would be fairer to say that the playing on this 1954 recording of *Così* most nearly resembles a perfectly judged dry martini.

Così fan tutte took a week to record, after which it was back to Kingsway Hall for a three-day end-of-term party. Karajan had decided to record a disc of operatic intermezzi, mainly from the verismo school but with music by Verdi, Bizet, Massenet, Mussorgsky and Granados mixed in. Oboist Sidney Sutcliffe, a hard-headed Yorkshireman who respected Karajan but was rarely moved by him, would later recall:

It was a real eye-opener for me when he started recording these operatic bits and pieces. I had never felt Karajan was a particularly emotional conductor. There were none of those great surges of emotion you had when, say, Furtwängler was conducting. But on this occasion he was completely 'sent'. I don't think he'd have noticed if a bomb had gone off beside him.[18]

Two of the intermezzi were by Mascagni whom Karajan had heard conduct in La Scala during the war. Though ill and lame, Mascagni had hobbled on to the rostrum to conduct the intermezzo to *L'amico Fritz*. Karajan would later recall:

He finally got there and settled himself. He lifted his baton. And well – there was suddenly a great explosion of sound no one could possibly have anticipated. I shall never forget it. It was incredible.[19]

The *L'amico Fritz* intermezzo was included on Karajan's EMI LP, along with the rather more famous intermezzo from Mascagni's *Cavalleria rusticana*. For this, Karajan badgered Dennis Brain into playing the organ part.

*

It was also party-time in Provence where Karajan and the Philharmonia had been invited to give two concerts as part of the Aix-en-Provence Festival. Thoroughly exhausted by a month in the recording studio in high summer, the players decided to unwind. So did Karajan. It was sun and sangria time. For the concert amid the rocky eminencies of Les Baux, Manoug Parikian was asked to rehearse the orchestra while Karajan lounged at the back of the arena canoodling with 'a slender blonde' [Eliette] and Dennis Brain wandered around filming everything with his newfangled ciné-camera. Several players got sunstroke and had to repair to the first-aid tent where liberal supplies of restorative medicines were discovered, mainly of an alcoholic variety. To add to the pantomime, the mistral blew during the concert, fluttering the players' music and eventually whisking some of it away completely. The final pages of La mer were played largely from memory.

Karajan took it in good part, though it is said that the eyes did open briefly during an utterly shambolic start to the overture Leonore No.3. Not surprisingly, the French critics took a somewhat dusty view of the orchestra. Nor was the visit quickly forgotten. On a return tour several years later, it was discovered that the orchestra's drinks bill had still not been settled.

After Les Baux, Lucerne. A dispute between the Lucerne festival authorities and local Swiss musicians had led to the engagement of the Philharmonia as orchestra-in-residence for the 1954 festival. Karajan conducted the opening concert, followed by Kubelik, Fricsay (a high-speed Tchaikovsky Fifth, his début with the Philharmonia), Edwin Fischer, Furtwängler, and Cluytens.

Karajan, meanwhile, was allowing Dennis Brain to drive his new Mercedes and Dennis Brain was giving Karajan lessons on the alphorn. Karajan had been fascinated by the sound of this famously picturesque wooden trumpet ever since hearing a herdsman's call echoing across the waters of Lake Lucerne. He had mentioned the experience to the Festival Orchestra the following day, prompting one of the bassoonists, a notorious bore, to make a lengthy speech on the subject.

'Finally, you may be interested to know, Herr von Karajan,' he said, warming to his peroration, 'that the alphorn is still taught in all Swiss schools.'

'Very nice,' replied Karajan. 'And perhaps one day they'll consider adding the bassoon to the curriculum as well.'

From Lucerne, he travelled to Bavaria to conduct Bruckner's Eighth Symphony as part of a festival of Austrian and German music in the eighteenth-century basilica at Ottobeuren. The performance of the Bruckner was prefaced by Bach's Prelude and Fugue in E minor played by Alois Forer, who later joined Wolfgang and Hedy von Karajan for a late-evening performance of their three-organ version of *The Art of Fugue*.

This was the first time the brothers had met since their mother's funeral, and once more a certain gentle rivalry was in the air: Wolfgang talking of a tour of the United States with the Von Karajan Organ Ensemble, Herbert announcing that he would be making his North American debut in the autumn of 1955 with the Philharmonia Orchestra.

*

In Edinburgh, Eliette Mouret was more or less formally on show. Officially featured in the Edinburgh Festival programme, modelling expensive woollen sweaters, she was also a guest of the Legges. The fact that another of Eliette's well-to-do admirers was also on hand allowed for a certain amount of not entirely admirable fooling at Karajan's expense. During the second of the three concerts, the hapless admirer was persuaded to sit amid the second violins. It was a ruse that afforded a good deal of pleasure to those in the know and rather less inconvenience to Karajan (whose eyes were shut) than to the players, who had to make room for this cuckoo in the musical nest.

The 1954 festival coincided with the twenty-fifth anniversary of the death of the Russian impresario Diaghilev. Legge had proposed to Festival Director Ian Hunter that an exhibition be mounted in Diaghilev's honour. It proved to be one of the festival's outstanding features. Less gratifying, and extremely irksome from Hunter's point of view, was Karajan's refusal to conduct the national anthem before the Philharmonia's opening concert. As usual in such crises, Legge was nowhere to be found, so it was left to Jane Withers to tackle Karajan. In a singular flash of inspiration, she suggested to him that if he didn't conduct the anthem it would give the wrong signals to the British Council, who might well withdraw funding from the Philharmonia's proposed tour of the United States in 1955. Karajan made no response, leaving everyone guessing. When it came to the concert, he motioned the players to stand, then simply suspended his baton before them while they played the anthem. Karajan's explanation to Hunter was that he had had his fill of nationalism and was determined to have nothing more to do with it in any form, real or symbolic.

If this was another attempt to put clear water between himself and his past, it was ill-advised. To his Edinburgh hosts it merely seemed rude. The following year he would have no option but to conduct William Walton's flamboyant arrangements of the 'Star-spangled Banner' and 'God Save the Queen' during the Philharmonia's tour of the United States. Later, in 1972, he actually *recorded* the national anthems of all seventeen member states of the Council of Europe. But then, like many continental Europeans, he had come to see Europe-wide political and economic integration as a catch-all solution for the errors of the past.

The Edinburgh concerts, shared between Karajan and Cantelli ('there is room for both of us,' Karajan is reported to have told him[20]), found the orchestra back in prime form. 'There is a kind of insolence of virtuosity,' noted *The Scotsman*, 'about a concert that starts with the *Symphonie fantastique*.'[21] Karajan himself, though, received equivocal notices. His minimalist beat in the *Haffner* Symphony was admired more for the kind of charge it was intended to generate ('calculated to produce a psychological alertness from the orchestra and an acute nervous response to the conductor's requirements'[22]) than for the performance that flowed from it.

There can be little doubt that Karajan's erratic behaviour, both on and off the rostrum, was due in some measure to the tomfoolery surrounding Eliette. Nor was it just bystanders who got hurt. For the first of Karajan's three concerts, there was a soloist, Claudio Arrau. It was a somewhat strange pairing. Arrau was a great pianist but an idiosyncratic one, deeply suspicious of the logical positivism of the Toscanini–Cantelli–Kleiber school of conducting and much enamoured of the more intuitive music-making of conductors such as Furtwängler and Jochum. Stories differ as to what happened at the rehearsal of the Schumann concerto. According to one source, Karajan behaved impeccably, deferring throughout to Arrau's moderate tempi and his sophisticated use of rubato. According to another, Arrau, shaken by Karajan's aloofness, agreed to play the concert itself only after being persuaded to do so by Neville Cardus.

In those days, conductor and soloist were obliged to share the same rather stuffy back stage quarters in the Usher Hall. Arrau arrived extremely early (the concerto was not scheduled until after the interval), already dressed, and immaculately groomed as ever. Karajan arrived much later, in his day clothes. Having undressed himself and spent an inordinate amount of time prancing about the room stark naked (Arrau, challenged and embarrassed, obliged to gaze fixedly into the Schumann score), Karajan proceeded to dress himself extremely slowly in what appears to have been a rising state of nervous irritation.

As for the performance (adjudged by *The Scotsman* to be somewhat 'vehement'), it was worthy of inclusion in one of those occasional entertainments by the musical satirist Gerard Hoffnung. Gone was all vestige of whatever musicianly accord had existed during the rehearsal. From the outset, Karajan hurried Arrau, and fought his every inflexion. Arrau tried to hold back, but to no avail. In the finale, Karajan pressed ahead even more remorselessly and actually succeeded in reaching the end of the concerto before Arrau.[23]

Conductors occasionally do strange things. Toscanini stamped on gold watches, Giulini once threw a table at a Welsh tenor who had accused him of playing God. Szell resorted to biting sarcasm; and Klemperer, if the manic phase of his illness was upon him, would create havoc in the local brothels. Since Karajan never lost his temper with anyone, he was to all outward appearances an altogether calmer and more rational creature. Yet there lay just beneath the surface of his elegantly groomed persona a potentially explosive cocktail of forces. It was increasingly becoming what one observer would later call 'a personality of stark contrasts', one which could both bewitch people or persecute them; a *Jupiter tonans* or a charming and inspired Hermes, effortlessly serene.[24]

What Karajan craved above all was security: the security of an orchestra or an organisation he could call his own. He was about to acquire it, and he would do so, interestingly enough, in a manner strikingly reminiscent of the way he had landed the job in Aachen in 1934.

CHAPTER 40

Death and succession

I know my life's a pain and but a span,
I know my sense is mocked in everything;
And to conclude, I know myself a man,
Which is a proud, and yet a wretched thing.
Sir John Davies, 'Affliction', *c.*1600

Furtwängler had been ailing for some time. A serious bout of pneumonia in the summer of 1952 in the wake of the EMI *Tristan und Isolde* sessions had been particularly debilitating. Worse, drugs used to treat the illness appear to have hastened the onset of a disabling deafness. By 1954 he was still doing wonderful work. There survive from this period a witty and uproarious recording of Strauss's *Till Eulenspiegel*, a Brahms Third (a symphony he conducted better than anyone) lovingly painted in cool yellows and autumnal greys, and a live performance of Beethoven's Ninth, recorded in Lucerne with the Philharmonia Orchestra, that has some claim to being the most satisfactory of all Furtwängler's extant recordings of the work.[1]

But there were also mishaps, incidents that made it clear to the Berlin players that he was no longer hearing properly. Furtwängler fretted about this. He fretted, too, about the forthcoming North American tour with the Berlin Philharmonic. Air travel seriously exacerbated his hearing problems; what's more, he feared being made to look foolish in society. In a country like Japan, he could affect not to understand what people were saying to him; but in New York, he would be confronted with German émigrés, fluent in German and not necessarily sympathetic either to him or his visit.

To aid his hearing, microphones were placed in the orchestra during rehearsals, wired to a small loudspeaker which he wore on a girdle attached to his waist. By a cruel irony, it was his inability to hear the quiet bassoon line at the start of his own Second Symphony that finished things. After working on the symphony for a quarter of an hour, he turned to the orchestra with a resigned wave of the hand and said: 'Yes, thank you, gentlemen. That will be all. Goodbye.'

He knew it was the beginning of the end; so did the players. It was a terrible moment. Nine weeks later he was dead.

Furtwängler's last concert took place on 20 September. Karajan was in London recording Beethoven arias with Schwarzkopf and eavesdropping on sessions with Maria Callas, who was making her first recital discs for

EMI with Tullio Serafin. Three days later, Karajan conducted the Berliners for only the second time since the war.

The reviews were mixed. The critic of the *Berliner Morgenpost* Friedrich Herzfeld suggested that 'we are constantly interested but not actually gripped, since [Karajan] lacks the true tragic sense necessary for Brahms's First Symphony'. Nor did Herzfeld much like Karajan's manner. In a much-quoted put-down, he wrote:

He still prays like a saint while conducting, and smiles like a *conférencier* [compère] when taking his bow . . . He is not a priest but rather a magician, although one who is privy to a wonderful kind of magic.[2]

Herzfeld was a somewhat discredited figure. Part Jewish but ardently pro-Nazi, he had been commissioned by the Nazis in 1941 to write an 'official' biography of Furtwängler, a book he trickishly rewrote in denazified form once the war was over.

The orchestra itself was less interested in Karajan's platform manner (though his habit of conducting with closed eyes was initially disconcerting to some players), more interested in his working methods and the quality of his musicianship. Here he scored highly. He rehearsed with speed and economy. He also allowed the orchestra freedom to play, to express its own personality. Seen from the players' perspective he was well attuned to Furtwängler's way of doing things. His conducting of Brahms's First Symphony may not have pleased Herzfeld; but since it was finely geared to the players' own needs and expectations, the orchestra itself felt reassured.[3]

This was not something the Berliners felt to the same degree with Celibidache, whose stock had fallen significantly since the high noon of his relationship with the orchestra in the late 1940s. He could still make marvellous music with them, especially when there was an orchestral showpiece toward, and he remained on intimate terms – '*Du*' rather than '*Sie*' – with many of the players. But rehearsals were gruelling and long-drawn. He was hostile to recording, more so even than Furtwängler had been. And, fatally, he had let it be known that changes were needed in key areas of orchestral personnel.

Karajan knew this, too. How wretched the Berlin clarinets must have sounded after the rare mellifluence of the Philharmonia's Bernard Walton. But Karajan kept his counsel, just as he had done in Bayreuth in 1951. These were sensitive matters and needed time – time Karajan knew he would have if he succeeded in winning Berlin on his own terms.

*

Karajan was next due to conduct the Berlin Philharmonic in November.

Meanwhile, he returned to Vienna where he conducted two concert performances of Bizet's *Carmen* that caused an even greater stir than his concerts of *Aida* and *Fidelio*.

For the packed audiences in the old-gold gloom of the Musikverein on those late October evenings, it was like stepping out of a shuttered room into the sun's noonday stare. The Vienna Symphony played on the beat, not behind it; and their tone took on a cleanness and spareness the audience was unaccustomed to, even with Karajan on the rostrum. Again a cry went up in the press about Karajan's continuing exclusion from the Vienna Opera. One paper quoted Talleyrand on Napoleon's execution of the Duc d'Enghien: 'It is worse than a crime. It is a mistake.'[4]

Karl Böhm had now officially taken up his position as the head of the Vienna Opera in a situation that was already politically fraught. In May 1954, Joseph Wechsberg had filed a report to *Opera* in London:

Böhm's appointment was received with muted enthusiasm by Vienna's press and musical world. There is nothing to be said against him – he is a first-rate musician, able, thorough, and a man of good taste – but even his fiercest admirers admit that he is hardly likely to live up to the memory of his predecessors, among whom were Mahler, Weingartner, Schalk, and Strauss. Some call him a human metronome, others refer to him as a schoolmaster. Being the perfect *Beamte* [civil servant] he has been careful to say not too much about his plans in order not to antagonise Vienna's many fractions and factions.[5]

That same May, Clemens Krauss had died of a heart attack in Mexico City, aged sixty-one: died of disappointment at not getting the Vienna job, some said.

He is unlikely to have flourished under Böhm who was already more than happy to turn over huge swaths of the repertory to the house conductors: Moralt, Hollreiser, the young Berislav Klobucar and a talented young répétiteur by the name of Michael Gielen. Aside from a series of performances directed by guest conductor Rudolf Kempe, the 1954–5 Vienna season would prove to be one of the drabbest in living memory.

*

By the time of Karajan's return to Berlin in November, Furtwängler had been admitted to the Ebersteinburg clinic near Baden-Baden after the recurrence of a viral chest infection. The doctors saw no cause for serious concern, but Elisabeth Furtwängler knew that her husband was dying, and so did Furtwängler.

The programme for Karajan's Berlin concerts on 21 and 22 November had been planned months in advance. Yet it had the uncanny air of a requiem about it. To Furtwängler it must have seemed like a malediction. It consisted of just two works: Vaughan Williams's mystically beautiful *Fantasia on a Theme by Thomas Tallis*, a work Furtwängler himself had occasionally conducted, and Bruckner's Ninth Symphony whose fearful, unresolved journeyings and final nightmarish clamour in C sharp minor had been the very ground and inspiration of Furtwängler's own work as a symphonist. No symphony meant more to him than this. Hans Heinz Stuckenschmidt wrote of the concert:

Only a highly refined sense of sound can divine the furthest secrets of the *Tallis Fantasia*'s impressionistically ecstatic score. It is precisely this, however, which is Herbert von Karajan's great strength. His whole interpretation takes tonal quality as its starting-point, seeking first the perfection of the sound picture for which he reveals special sensibilities.[6]

Karajan himself often spoke of the need for the conductor first to prepare his palette before advancing further into the interpretation of a work. But if the ear is one thing, the breath is another. Turning to the performance of Bruckner's Ninth Symphony, Stuckenschmidt observed:

Nowadays Karajan has what might be termed great breath control. He knows how to pace a work, how to locate its moments of tension and release so that the need for large-scale forms becomes clear. Thus the *Adagio*'s Alpine massifs can be taken with a single sweeping glance.[7]

On 25 and 26 November, Celibidache led a performance of Brahms's *German Requiem*, another *memento mori*.

Furtwängler died on 30 November: wearied by political machinations, weakened by illness, and finally brought low by the humiliation of deafness. It was a tragic end. He had a young family and a splendid wife; he had his compositions to work on. But like Shakespeare's Othello 'his occupation was gone'. During his final days, he conceded that Karajan would be his successor.

*

Karajan was in Rome when he heard of Furtwängler's death.[8] Mattoni had slipped out of the hotel to buy an evening paper, and there on the front page was the news. Shortly afterwards, an anonymous telegram arrived from Vienna: '*Le roi est mort, vive le roi!*'

There was also a call from the United States. It was from André Mertens, vice-president of Columbia Artists, America's leading concert agency. Mertens had already brokered the idea of Karajan's touring the United

States with Legge's Philharmonia in the autumn of 1954. Now he was on the phone to say that the tour by the Berlin Philharmonic would be off unless Karajan was willing to lead it.

Karajan confirmed that he would be more than happy to lead the Berlin tour. There was, however, one all-important proviso. He wished to lead it, not as a front-running candidate for the Furtwängler succession, but as the Berlin Philharmonic's new chief conductor.

The German press, meanwhile, was awash with speculation, much of it ill-informed, some of it touting the line that the 'Age of the Great Conductor' was over. Berlin's *Der Abend* floated the question: '*Götterdämmerung der grossen Dirigenten?*'

Furtwängler and Clemens Krauss are dead. Toscanini has stepped down. Klemperer is a sick man. Stokowski, Bruno Walter, and Thomas Beecham belong to the older generation. Scherchen and Kleiber are no longer exactly young. Is this the twilight of the conducting gods?[9]

The paper then prepared its own short list of front-runners. Would it be Böhm ('Elegance and energy') or Keilberth ('Whole-hearted'), Celibidache ('A genius') or Karajan ('The secret: fascination')? There was no mention of Jochum who, it was later discovered, had already approached a Berlin estate agent with a view to buying a property in the city, nor of Barbirolli whom the Berliners themselves would subsequently take to their hearts as a kind of private laureate. Of Karajan, the paper wrote:

'Poseur' say some; 'genius' say others. Initiates know that when people speak like this, they are talking of Herbert von Karajan. Karajan was born in Salzburg in 1908. His father was a doctor, his grandfather a physicist [*sic*]. He learnt his trade in Ulm and became Germany's youngest Generalmusikdirektor at 27. In 1937, he was invited to Berlin. Since then, he has always been in the news. Such lasting success must have genuine underlying qualities . . . an enigmatic, ambiguous personality with an extraordinary power of fascination. The final word has not yet been spoken about 'the Karajan case', and perhaps never will be.[10]

If Karajan had a rival for the succession, it was Celibidache, a sitting tenant who, for all his foibles and temperamental shortcomings, probably understood the nature of Furtwängler's craft better than any living conductor. It was strange that the two principal contenders should both have conducted the orchestra in the days immediately preceding Furtwängler's death. Even stranger was Celibidache's decision – or was it perhaps an uncontrollable compulsion? – to have a blazing row with the orchestra during the rehearsals for Brahms's *German Requiem*. There was nothing new about this; but it cannot have helped Celibidache's cause. Looking back across the years on the events of those sombre days in the late autumn of

1954, cellist Peter Steiner would reflect: 'In the end, Karajan came out a little bit on top *as a musician*. I think that is why we chose him, much as we admired Celibidache.'[11]

On 13 December 1954 a statement was issued on behalf of the orchestra, whose views had been canvassed and co-ordinated by its two joint-presidents and its five-man ruling council:

... the members of the Berlin Philharmonic Orchestra believe that in Herbert von Karajan they see the artistic personality capable of carrying on the tradition of the Berlin Philharmonic. They therefore ask their Intendant Herr Dr von Westerman to begin negotiations with the aim of inviting Herbert von Karajan to conduct the major Philharmonic concerts and tours for a period of time as yet unspecified. This resolution was taken unanimously.[12]

The race was effectively over. The negotiations, though, had barely begun. The phrase 'for a period of time yet unspecified' gave a clear signal that tenure had already become an issue: a larger one, perhaps, than salary, the number of concerts to be conducted, or the exact nature of the chief conductor's sphere of influence.

Karajan was demanding a contract with the Berlin Philharmonic *for life*. It takes nerve to demand such a contract; and it takes courage to grant it. But such a demand also implies vision and invites trust. It craves stability and concedes constraint. It seeks power, but seeks it in the context of larger responsibilities. As has already been mentioned,[13] 'power' is a problematical concept where Karajan is concerned, since it has almost invariably been used in the sense of power-crazed. ('*Macht* possessor' as Schwarzkopf would put it in a famously ferocious outburst against Karajan to Furtwängler's biographer Sam H. Shirakawa.[14]) But power is real only in its actualisation; in its encounter with other bearers of power and in the ever-changing balance which is the result of these encounters.

Of particular complexity is the relationship between an individual's power of being and his power of being within a family or a group; or within the group-as-family as Karajan would later conceive the remade Berlin Philharmonic to be. As Tillich warns in *Love, Power, and Justice*:

The centre of power is only the centre of the whole as long as it does not degrade its own centrality by using it for particular purposes.[15]

As it turned out, questions about the 'degrading' of power centres (Karajan's or the orchestra's) would not arise in any serious form until conductor and orchestra had been together for more than a quarter of a century, by which time it was not 'tenure' that was the issue but 'spheres of influence'.

Karajan's original contract with the Berlin Philharmonic (never officially published) would not be signed until 25 April 1956, over a year after the start of the negotiations. Were the orchestra and the Berlin Senate outmanoeuvred by Karajan or did they outmanoeuvre him? A little of both, it would seem. For though Karajan mainly had his way, there was a significant emendation to the wording of the contract as Furtwängler would have known it.

This concerned the rights of the chief conductor in the matter of the appointment and the dismissal of the orchestra's General Manager or Intendant. Under the terms of Furtwängler's contract, no decision could be arrived at without the 'agreement' of the chief conductor. Karajan's, by contrast, merely required that the chief conductor be consulted. Were Karajan and his lawyers ignorant of the precise terms of Furtwängler's original contract, or was this seen as a peripheral detail, something to be traded during negotiations? Whatever the explanation, it was a clause that would cause serious trouble in the 1980s.

'I am not in the giving vein' says Shakespeare's Richard III; nor was Karajan during these negotiations. The question of the minimum number of concerts he was required to conduct in Berlin each year was the basis of one of his most surprising victories. With Nikisch and Furtwängler, it had been ten. With Karajan – who clearly saw the possibility of a second position opening up, in Salzburg and even, perhaps, in Vienna – it was reduced to six. In practice, he conducted many more than that. It was not until the mid-1980s, when infirmity and mutual ill-will cast their shadow over things, that the legally binding minimum of six concerts suddenly became a lifeline for Karajan.

*

In the winter of 1954–5, the main problem was the 'contract for life' issue. The power brokers in Berlin feared that unless they were willing to negotiate on Karajan's own clearly stated agenda, the new 'sun king of international musical life', as he was mockingly called, might walk away from the offer.

In this, they were mistaken. Karajan craved the job with a zealot's longing. At the same time, he feared he was being used. Preparing for the American tour would be an immense labour. Merely to contemplate it had involved a major diplomatic initiative in Milan, whence Mattoni had been dispatched to try to extricate Karajan from a commitment to conduct and produce a much previewed new staging of Wagner's *Die Walküre*. And to what end? If the American tour was a success musically and politically (and on neither front was this in any way a foregone conclusion), it would be all smiles and contracts. If not, it could well be: 'Thank you very much, Herr von Karajan, another time perhaps.'

What had virtually been a lifetime spent observing power play at or near the centre of musical life in Salzburg, Berlin, and Vienna had not so much armed Karajan for the fight as made him wary of it to the point of paranoia.

*

Karajan spent the greater part of January 1955 in Milan preparing and conducting the new production of *Carmen*, which had received its musically brilliant preview in Vienna the previous autumn. There had been talk of Picasso being invited to design the sets. 'And if the sketches do not please us, who is going to tell him?' Karajan is said to have asked.

The designs were eventually entrusted to the talented Russian-born designer Ita Maximowna. Recalling how Karajan had rehearsed Simionato (and a monkey), Maximowna declared Karajan to be the finest Carmen she had ever seen. 'It's just a pity he couldn't also sing the role,' she added.

By early February, Karajan was back in Berlin rehearsing the Philharmonic for a brief provincial tour that had been put in place as a warm-up for the all-important American tour. Christa Ludwig and her mother attended the concert in Hanover. Frau Ludwig had not seen Karajan since she had last sung with him in Aachen in 1939. How he had changed! He was so much calmer now and so very assured; and more of a showman, too, with his highly cultivated platform manner.[16]

A few days later, mistaking bureaucratic delay over his contract for something rather more sinister, Karajan requested a meeting with the Mayor of West Berlin, Ernst Reuter, during which he threatened to pull out of the American tour altogether. What was needed now was a diplomatic initiative acceptable to all parties. The man charged with bringing this about was the Minister of Education and the Arts, an economist by profession, Joachim Tiburtius, a smiling, affable man in his middle years who never did come clean on whether Karajan's final contract really was for life. (The nearest Tibertius ever came was the phrase 'more or less for life'.)

Nor was what he offered Karajan in public after a Berlin Philharmonic concert in Berlin on 22 February 1955 a significant advance, legally, on what the orchestra had stated in its press release on 13 December. What it was, however, was a *political* endorsement of Karajan's nomination, which could be placed officially before the Berlin Senate and the appropriate committee of the House of Representatives.

Every inch the politician, Tiburtius clearly relished the after-concert formalities on 22 February. His first task was to ask Karajan whether he desired his name to go forward.

'Senator,' Karajan replied, 'it would give me infinite pleasure. What more can I say?'

'That's wonderful,' beamed Tiburtius.

Karajan spoke about the past fortnight's work in rehearsal, of the 'indescribable harmony' that existed between himself and the players. When you have experienced that, said Karajan, there's no point in even trying to discuss it.

'Then let's not do so,' agreed the Senator. 'Let us, instead, make it as easy as we can for the Senate and House of Representatives and thank you from the bottom of our hearts.'

Clearly, though, Karajan was going to be have to sing for his supper that evening. Tiburtius turned to the audience. 'I am sure you would like Herr von Karajan to say a few more words – from the artistic point of view – about his plans for the tour. It is possible that not everyone here is familiar with them.'

Karajan took the microphone, rattled off details of the repertory, and then launched into a five-minute speech – partly planned, partly improvised – which touched on a number of his principal preoccupations. He talked about the 'Philharmonic spirit [*der philharmonische Geist*]'; about the Philharmonic as a 'family' and those players who had worked with him in earlier years in the Philharmonic, in the Berlin Staatskapelle, and at the Bayreuth Festival. He talked of teaching, and the young; of the need for a proper teaching of rhythm ('Everything else – forgive me for saying so – is probably unteachable') and how tradition must be simultaneously sustained and renewed. He also paid tribute to Furtwängler.

Since Karajan was a courteous man, a somewhat sentimental man, and also a guileful one, the remarks he made about Furtwängler can be judged in a number of different ways. He began by referring to a book he was planning on his own conducting heroes. Here there would be 'a very special chapter' on Furtwängler, 'because, I believe, none of the existing biographies has really said the essential thing about him'. What Karajan went on to say was neither very wide-ranging nor very precise, but the focus of its attention is interesting:

... he created a completely new expressive language in music [Karajan presumably means in 'music-making'], a language that was not imposed on the orchestra by the conductor but created in collaboration with them. Sometimes he even left decisions to them, as all of you here will know! These transitions, when the old is played out and the new is not yet begun. These magical transitions where the listener does not know whether the moment of change has been reached or not. The result was a language of expressive music-making with an orchestra of a kind that had not previously existed.[17]

Having played his part in this promotional pantomime, Karajan felt rather more assured. If everything went to plan, and if Tiburtius was true to his word, the Berlin Senate would be in a position to ratify his appointment the moment the orchestra returned from the United States in early April. Like it or not, though, he was still on probation. And the North American tour was going to be no picnic.

CHAPTER 41

American journey

So we beat on, boats against the current, borne back
ceaselessly into the past.
Scott Fitzgerald, *The Great Gatsby*

To the casual observer, the situation in the United States did not appear
promising. Even before Karajan and the orchestra had left Berlin's Tempelhof airport on two Pan-American Super Six Clippers, protests about the
tour had been lodged in the United States by musicians' union leaders,
battle-scarred veterans of the anti-Furtwängler campaigns in New York
in 1936 and Chicago in 1948.

In fact, circumstances were now rather different. In early March, Virgil
Thomson wrote to his friend Gottfried von Einem:

Karajan opens on Tuesday with the Berlin Philharmonic. The Veterans of
Foreign Wars are protesting and will probably picket Carnegie Hall, but I
don't think there will be any serious trouble. He has Washington support.[1]

The support was not so much for Karajan (though he had obviously
received official clearance by the Americans) as for the city of Berlin,
no longer the seat of government of a hated tyranny but a brave and
beleaguered frontier town caught up in the toils of the Cold War.

The reception given to the Berliners at the all-important opening concert
in Washington on 27 February was extremely warm. Members of the
orchestra were applauded as they came on to the stage, a commonplace
in later years, but practically unheard of in those days. Karajan, too, was
warmly received. At the end of the concert, reported the *Washington Post*,
conductor and orchestra were cheered to the rafters. Call followed call.
Eventually, four additional horns emerged from the wings and Karajan led
the orchestra in a performance of the overture to Wagner's *Tannhäuser*.

The Berliners' style of music-making was significantly different from
anything that was being heard in America at this time. The events of
the previous two decades had left the great German orchestras – Berlin,
Dresden, Leipzig – in a kind of time warp. For all that the United States
was richly peopled with European-born players and conductors, the vast
majority had been absorbed into what was a recognisably American way
of doing things. Toscanini is the obvious representative example here;
and, after him, Szell, Reiner, Ormandy and even, to a degree, Bruno
Walter. Those who could not, or would not, adapt – Beecham, Klemperer,

377

Barbirolli – came and went with varying degrees self-possession. Hans Knappertsbusch refused even to contemplate working in America.

The gulf between the American and the old-world-European way of doing things would have seemed wider still had Furtwängler led the 1955 tour. Karajan had already to some extent absorbed the influence of Toscanini, albeit pre-war Toscanini heard in a specifically European context. That said, there is little evidence from the widely circulated recording of the Berliners' first Washington concert of any real accommodation with the Toscanini style.[2] The performance of Mozart's *Haffner* Symphony is festive and songful; it is also brilliantly articulated, though no more than Furtwängler's Mozart invariably was. Much the same could be said of the performance of Strauss's *Till Eulenspiegel*.

The second half of the concert was given over to Brahms's First Symphony. Here Karajan stays very close to the Furtwängler style. In the first place, the performance is grounded in that rich, rounded sound, peculiarly Furtwängler's own, which Karajan inherited and so interestingly developed. Even more striking is the way the performance moves freely and naturally between a number of different tempi, while at the same time maintaining a larger rhythm, a longer line: a line that, for all its legato beauty, is never uniform in its articulation.

To American ears, this was all rather baffling, not at all the way Toscanini, Munch, or Reiner directed Brahms. Critic Paul Hume would write in the *Washington Post*:

The Brahms reminded us of Atlantis, who ran her race well but lost it because she could not resist slowing down to pick up the golden apples along the way.[3]

How Furtwängler would have relished the image but snorted at the judgement! Comparison between this live Washington performance and Karajan's 1952 recording of the symphony with the Philharmonia Orchestra suggests that in the slow movement the Berliners were still playing Furtwängler's performance. Where the Philharmonia-Karajan account of this *Andante sostenuto* is slow to the point of being comatose, the Berlin performance is grand and searching, hugely eloquent; a private salute, perhaps, to their former chief. It is also a wonderful example of the orchestra's ability to take wing in performance.

Washington, benign and courteous, was followed by Philadelphia where the air was chillier, the mood a good deal more reserved. At a reception given in honour of the visitors by the Philadelphia Orchestra, the orchestra's chief conductor Eugene Ormandy, an Hungarian *émigré* who had settled in the United States in 1921, refused to shake Karajan's hand. Since Ormandy had recently accepted an invitation to conduct the Vienna

Philharmonic in Salzburg, Karajan saw this less as a principled gesture, more as a discourteous snub. He never forgave Ormandy, whose first visit to Salzburg would also prove to be his last.

The orchestra arrived in New York on 1 March for the first of three concerts there and was greeted by pickets:

TONIGHT AT CARNEGIE HALL
THE MUSICAL DICTATORS OF THE NAZI REGIME

ran the headline on an ill-typed handout of the 'Citizen's Committee of 100'; but the concert itself was trouble-free. As in Washington, the players were applauded when they came on to the platform. Karajan himself was given a thunderous reception. The former Music Editor, now chief Music Critic of the *New York Times*, Howard Taubman, declared him to be – if not, as his admirers claimed, the best conductor in Europe – 'remarkably gifted':

Herr von Karajan conducts from memory with very little fuss or furbelows, with a craftsman's knowledge of his business and an artist's understanding of the music in hand.[4]

Someone who was fascinated by the effect of Karajan's conducting and yet mystified by how the effect was achieved, was the 27-year-old Ronald Wilford, a young concert agent destined to play a significant role in Karajan's career. Wilford had already more or less single-handedly helped revive Klemperer's career in New York in 1953; now he resolved to gain access to a Karajan rehearsal at the earliest opportunity.

The day after the first Carnegie Hall concert Karajan faced the New York press. Predictably, the questions were primarily political, mainly focused on Karajan's alleged Nazi past. This was a trifle rich coming from a press that in the summer of 1942 had tucked away well-informed reports of the Nazi genocide in brief paragraphs on inside pages.[5] Karajan did not say this; he merely froze the journalists out. Having begun the news conference in English, he lapsed into German, leaving André Mertens to crawl ahead through the political and linguistic minefield.

Security was tight. Karajan's accommodation was separate from that of the main party and had been reserved under the name of Mr Johnson. Mattoni was with him, Anita was not. Eliette was in Europe, so was Walter Legge. And so, unfortunately, was someone who might well have cheered Karajan up and shown him the sights, his new-found friend Leonard Bernstein. He was back in Milan; which is where the two men had first met in the winter of 1953–4.[6] In January 1954, Bernstein had written to his wife Felicia: '[I have become] real good friends with von Karajan, whom you would (and will) adore. My first Nazi.'[7]

The two men were never close. In later years there were too many squabbles and petty jealousies (mainly instigated by Karajan) and too many outrageous up-stagings (most of them masterminded by Bernstein, including, allegedly, a fling with Anita). But Bernstein always had a soft spot for 'the old Nazi' (his posthumous tributes were generous to a fault) and Karajan's respect for Bernstein's talents, strangely dissipated though they seemed to him to be, was rarely less than fulsome. His nickname for Bernstein, used without malice or irony, was 'Mr Music'.

In New York, Karajan met and became instantly infatuated with Mary Roblee, a journalist working for *Vogue*. From the letters he wrote to her during the American tour, and afterwards from Europe, it is clear she was more than just an object of adoration. She was a conduit for his feelings of loneliness and self-pity, a shoulder to cry on. When the letters were auctioned in London in 1990, there was an air of wonderment that a man 'commonly regarded as cold, autocratic and steely'[8] could write such letters. Of particular interest are Karajan's remarks about the pressures he was subjected to when young and the sense of isolation he experienced as a child.

The sale catalogue described the Karajan of the Roblée letters as an almost 'Byronic' figure. Faustian might have been a better epithet. Schuyler Chapin, who had the job of minding Karajan for Columbia Artists during the tour, remembers him staring into a shop window in Washington and saying, very quietly and passionately, apropos of nothing that was before his immediate gaze, that the Berlin Philharmonic had been the only thing he had ever really wanted.[9] Now he had it. Yet, at the age of forty-six, where was he personally?

A shade unreasonably, perhaps, he viewed his past as an exhausted boatman might view his storm-shattered skiff. He had made landfall, but at what cost? 'Until I was fifty,' Karajan would later tell Anna Tomowa-Sintow, 'I spent so much time just *thinking* about what it would be like to be a normal human being.'[10]

Walter Legge liked to quote a remark his assistant Walter Jellinek passed on to him at around this time. Karajan is alleged to have told Jellinek, 'I think any further development in my life has to come from within, and I am not certain there is anything within me any more.'[11] When telling the story, Legge usually added the proviso that since Karajan was a dissembler and Jellinek a congenital liar, the chances of the remark being wholly or even partly true were remote. On this occasion, it is possible to think that Legge's scepticism got the better of him.

It would be a mistake, however, to imagine that Karajan merely moped in his apartment during his time in New York. He undertook an exhaustive round of auditions in Carnegie Hall, aided by Nellie Walters, Columbia

Artists' indefatigable singing expert who had first met Karajan in pre-war Berlin. 'He was like a magician,' she would later recall. In the case of one young artist, 'It was as if he pulled the voice right out of her throat. She fairly squealed with delight.'[12] Another audition was of a 28-year-old black singer who had already made something of a name for herself singing Gershwin's Bess at the Ziegfeld Theatre. Karajan waved away her accompanist and played for her himself. 'You are an artist of the future,' he told her. Her name was Leontyne Price.

He also took the opportunity to do a good deal of flying. In New York he signed up for a couple of days of tough schooling in instrument flying at La Guardia Airport. He had also got permission to fly himself between engagements; which turned out to be another job for Schuyler Chapin. Chapin was an ex-World War Two transport pilot who had learned his flying in the school of hard knocks. He had kept up his licence as a commercial pilot and knew all about the perils of flying in America's crowded north-eastern corridor.

Karajan absorbed information at a terrifying rate. He had no problem actually flying the Apache twin. What he did not immediately adjust to was the need to keep a weather eye open for other aircraft. Despite constant chivvying from Chapin, he remained absorbed in the cockpit instrument panels. When, finally, a plane came within view at the kind of distance and trajectory a pilot would need to take note of, Chapin waited until the crucial moment, flung the stick forward and, having made the point, bawled Karajan out: 'I survived World War Two and I'm damned if I'm going to end up in a pile outside Baltimore.'

Karajan made a perfect landing but seemed pretty shaken. Chapin wondered whether he had overstepped the mark. As they parted in the hotel foyer, Karajan said, 'I am going upstairs to write out one hundred times "I will look around when flying".' That night before the concert, he handed Chapin an envelope containing the completed imposition. Chapin would later reflect, 'It was all worthwhile. He was a damn good pilot.'[13]

Baltimore was one of the cities on the tour where silent protest was used as a weapon by Jewish protesters. Either a direct boycott aimed at reducing ticket sales would be organised or tickets would be bought up and then not used. The latter ploy was the more spectacular, the former more financially damaging. At several concerts, seats were heavily discounted or filled up with members of local German communities, many of whom had never set foot in a concert hall in their lives.

Wherever he could, Karajan made a quick exit from halls and official receptions. He was happiest by himself, or dining privately with people who had no idea who he was. In Chicago, he was rescued by his old friend from post-war Vienna, Henry Alter. They went for a meal together:

Then I suggested to him that we might go to some very good friends of mine who would be delighted if he were to spend an evening with them. At that time, he was still very spontaneous with regard to his inclinations, and this appealed to him. He wanted to know just one thing: whether it would turn into a 'party', because the last thing he wanted was a party. I assured him faithfully there was no question of a party. With luck we might get a knackwurst and a small beer. So we drove across town in my old Plymouth and there were a couple and one other man as guests. As they sat down together, the man said to Karajan, 'What is your name, please?' I have never seen Karajan so unmistakably happy as he was then; from that moment the evening was a great pleasure. He turned very nicely to the man and answered him, 'My name is Karajan; I am a conductor.'[14]

In Baltimore, Karajan also dined with the Italian consul-general, Raffaele Canevaro. Among the guests was the conductor Massimo Freccia, who would later recall the meeting in that most elegantly crafted of conducting autobiographies *The Sounds of Memory*:

I found Karajan charming. He made you think that you were the only person in the world who mattered to him. The admiration he had for my brother was boundless – he called him the most intelligent man he had ever met. He also told me how much he appreciated all that my brother had done to help him after the war during the period when he was not allowed to conduct. (When my brother died, knowing how intimate he and Karajan had been, I wrote him a letter. He never answered.) His secretary, André von Mattoni, an ex-actor and a professional charmer, underlined every compliment with his own captivating remarks. We talked at length about music, and about the recent offer Karajan had received to become life conductor of the Berlin Philharmonic, which he still felt doubtful about accepting.[15]

If Karajan really did say that about the Berlin Philharmonic, he was indeed a great dissimulator. Freccia met Karajan on many subsequent occasions in Europe:

He was a good-looking man; his eyes in repose were gentle and warm, but they could change suddenly to become as hard as steel. His most obvious characteristic, I suppose, was his ruthlessness: he would hesitate at nothing to get what he wanted. He could detach himself from his work at the flick of a switch.[16]

By the time the orchestra got back to New York for the final three concerts of the tour, the protest groups were better organised and a good deal more strident, irked, possibly, by the marked lack of rancour in the reception Karajan and the orchestra had been accorded earlier in the month. Not all the protesters were antagonistic to the orchestra. Five hundred Jewish war veterans who held a vigil outside Carnegie Hall during the concert on 30 March were at pains to stress that they were protesting, not against the Berliners, but against the McCarran-Walter immigration act that was currently before Congress.[17]

The one group that was protesting against Karajan, Westerman, and the orchestra – and protesting violently – was a radical Zionist youth group called Brit Trumpeldor. In a handout bearing the scrawled heading 'Listen to your <u>conscience</u>', the group did what a number of lobbyists and journalists would attempt to do in later years: establish a direct connection in the public mind between the target of their protest, the musicians in general and Karajan in particular, and those *who actually carried out* the mass murders in the Third Reich. One section of the Brit Trumpeldor handout reads:

Can you forget Buchenwald, Dachau, Bergen-Belsen, Tremblinka [sic] and the other notorious concentration camps?
Can you forget those humans, tortured, buried alive, burned in crematoria, thrown into lime pits?
If you can face the murderer—
If there is no goodness or humanity left in you—
Then listen to the music of the masters of death and torture!

It was the distinguished military prosecutor Edward Russell, later Baron Russell of Liverpool, who pointed out that where such things as rape, child abuse and Nazi war crimes are concerned – issues on which people wish to prove beyond doubt their detestation of the crime – the risk of hysteria, false accusation, and further miscarriages of justice is concomitantly great.

To many ex-servicemen attending the Carnegie Hall concert, these youth protests were misguided. Vincent Sheean would recall:

My host let us out of his car in the midst of a bunch of hysterical boys and girls carrying banners which said: 'Nazis go home!' I found one of these objects being shaken in my face by a girl who was probably still playing with her dolls when Hitler blew himself up in his bunker: I who had, so to speak, fought, bled, and died on every battlefield from Spain to China for twenty years. This aroused in me that unreasoning fury to which we are so often prey when our deepest sincerities are twisted and turned against us . . . I was very nearly seized with the palsy and started shouting at the girl: 'Go home yourself! You don't even know what a Nazi is: Go Home!' She stared at me in consternation. I suppose she may have thought I was Hitler's ghost.[18]

Inside the hall, Brit Trumpeldor let loose three pigeons. Two were coaxed out of the auditorium by officials, the third took up station on the proscenium above the orchestra where it proved to be a model listener, attentive and unmoving throughout the larger part of Tchaikovsky's Fifth Symphony. Later, two more pigeons were found dead, suffocated in a briefcase that had been abandoned by Brit Trumpeldor in the Dress Circle. Alongside them was a card that read: 'Heil von Karajen [sic], the cleansed Nazi.'[19]

CHAPTER 42
Trouble at mill

At all turns, a man who will *do* faithfully, needs to believe firmly. If
he has to ask at every turn the world's suffrage; if he cannot dispense
with the world's suffrage, and make his own suffrage serve, he is a
poor servant; the work committed to him will be *mis*done.

Thomas Carlyle, *On Heroes*

We met in his room in the offices of the Gesellschaft der Musikfreunde after a rehearsal. Karajan was sitting in his usual working
clothes on the large sofa, and I presented my request to him.
Using all the arguments at my disposal, referring to Toscanini
and Furtwängler, I requested him to take over the [Vienna] Philharmonic concerts in their totality or, at any rate, in a greater
number than hitherto and to become our chief conductor. He
refused, and I remember his answer with the greatest clarity. 'With
your democracy,' he said, 'who is going to guarantee me that you
won't change your mind one day? Berlin,' and as he said this he
gave the wall behind the sofa a slap with his open hand, 'that's
the wall I can lean against!'

Otto Strasser, *Und dafür wird man noch bezahlt*

The outcome of the American tour was the formal ratification of Karajan's
appointment as Furtwängler's successor. There was still no contract, but
at the end of the second of the concerts given to celebrate the orchestra's
homecoming, an announcement was made by Senator Tiburtius on behalf
of the Berlin Senate. Karajan was also presented with a small replica of the
city's Liberty Bell. The date was 5 April 1955, his forty-seventh birthday.

The orchestra itself was reasonably happy with the decision. Some of the
players were still disconcerted by Karajan's habit of conducting concerts
with closed eyes and by his trick of throwing responsibility back on them
by virtually withdrawing the beat. But even the doubters conceded that
they were listening to one another with a new intensity.

Towards the end of April, Karajan returned to London to record Johann
Strauss's *Die Fledermaus*, another finely honed studio production with
another of Legge's hand-picked casts. Where operetta was concerned,
Legge was even more of a stickler over matters of style than he was in
more heavyweight repertory. As a critic in the 1930s he had deplored what
he called the 'Ruritanian' excesses of the Covent Garden production of
Die Fledermaus. 'Great conductors of Johann Strauss and the best Lehár,'
he opined, 'are rarer than men who can squeeze out the face-flannels of
Mahler's exhibitionistic self-pity.'

384

Schwarzkopf, the Rosalinde on this 1955 recording – a superbly sung performance, idiomatic, and exquisitely finished – would later recall what Legge and Karajan wanted from the performance:

It was the opposite of 'routine'. They wanted grit, dash, pep. Nothing vulgar or sleazy. Karajan wanted the merest hint of rubato – freedom, yes, but a freedom that was so subtle it was impossible to talk about. In a word, he wanted 'style'.[1]

Not all the critics appreciated this. *High Fidelity*'s James Hinton vastly enjoyed the set but missed Clemens Krauss's 'hair-breadth control of sentimental rubato'.[2] The key word here is 'sentimental'. Krauss's famous 1950 Vienna recording is certainly beguiling in an *echt-wienerisch* sort of way but it is generally slower than the Karajan and, in many places, rhythmically slacker. By opting for 'grit, dash, and pep' Karajan and Legge were trading cosy charm for something smarter and wittier, a *Die Fledermaus* Noël Coward might have enjoyed. When Governor Frank turns up to accompany the man he takes to be Rosalinde's husband to prison, his suggestion that Rosalinde should give her 'husband' a farewell kiss is treated by Schwarzkopf as an outrage. Such high seriousness – the comedy played absolutely straight – is a good deal funnier than Hilde Güden's rather mousy rejoinder on the Krauss set.

Legge's decision to cast Prince Orlofsky as a tenor was unconventional, but the rest of the casting is masterly: Nicolai Gedda as Gabriel von Eisenstein, Rita Streich as Adele, Erich Kunz as Falke, and Franz Böheim, an unbeatable comedy turn in the spoken role of the drunken jailer Frosch. Karajan's 1960 Vienna recording of the opera, bristling with atmosphere and vastly better known, lacks something this 1955 set's *élan* and absolute stylishness. It would be Carlos Kleiber, in a 1975 recording, who would again bring 'grit, dash, and pep' back to this much mistreated work.[3]

*

The day after finishing the *Fledermaus* sessions, Karajan and the Philharmonia gave one of their rare London concerts, an emotionally exhausting affair in which Mozart's *Haffner* Symphony landed the listener, not on the fairway, but in the briars and bunkers of the fourth symphonies of Sibelius and Tchaikovsky. The concert moved *The Times*'s critic on duty that evening to write a review of charming singularity:

A ZEALOUS SERVANT

In the days when householders could afford servants, there was once a zealous housemaid. She swept and dusted and dried crockery with such zeal that nothing, unless it was made of concrete, was safe from disaster. When the master of the house suggested that her services were more expensive than the household could support, his wife replied: 'No, my dear: she is a treasure, and treasures are known to be expensive. Other servants there may be who will not break our Crown Derby or our Sèvres, but they will not leave the house clean. This girl is not careless, she simply hates the sight of dust and dirt.'

Mr Herbert von Karajan may be likened to that housemaid, for he too is a servant, though of music. His zeal is such that he is inclined, on occasion, to damage the coherence or the style or the spirit of the music that he interprets. Last night be jostled the Andante of Mozart's Haffner Symphony along until its gentle breezes fled. He exaggerated the dynamic contrasts in Sibelius's fourth symphony until that barbaric enigma sounded almost euphonious. The brass that depicts fate, and the oboe who begins the middle section of the scherzo in Tchaikovsky's fourth symphony played alike with such incisive brilliance that their sounds were uncomfortably sharp, while the [glockenspiel] in Sibelius's finale was struck with such ferocity that the major third above its fundamental tone made a chord with the written note.

But Mr Karajan's performances are never, for a minute, dull; no speck of dust can be seen on the mantelpiece. The whole concert was intensely exciting: shattering bursts of sound lifted Tchaikovsky's symphony from the somnolent rut of popular classics; Sibelius was illuminated from within as well as without. The Haffner was less thrilling, but was beautifully played.[4]

There is no over-striking of the glockenspiel in Karajan's broodingly impressive Philharmonia recording of Sibelius's Fourth Symphony, made in July 1953. Of his three recordings of the Fourth, this is in some ways the darkest, the most Germanic, underlining Sibelius's debt to Wagner's *Tristan und Isolde* and stressing the baleful influence of Edgar Allan Poe's 'The Raven':

> Ghastly grim and ancient Raven wandering from the Nightly shore—
> Tell me what thy lordly name is on the Night's Plutonian shore!'
> Quoth the Raven, 'Nevermore.'

As we have seen, few pieces of music meant more to Karajan than this. He used to cite it – along with Strauss's *Elektra*, Mahler's Sixth Symphony, and Berg's *Three Orchestral Pieces* – as one of those works that left him emotionally exhausted for days afterwards. Other music he could – and indeed did – immediately clear from his mind with a scorchingly hot bath, a vodka, and a light supper with a chosen colleague: but not the Fourth Sibelius.

His approach to the work was intensely personal and would become more rarefied and searching with the passing of the years. By the time of Karajan's Philharmonia recording, Legge had already produced a celebrated account of the symphony with Beecham and the LPO in 1937. There exists an interesting correspondence between Legge and Sibelius on the subject of the tempo markings (Beecham's queries, evidently) to which

Karajan would presumably have had access. It is an interesting fact, none the less, that the new post-war generation of Sibelius interpreters, of whom Karajan can perhaps be seen as *primus inter pares*, explored moods and opened up vistas in Sibelius's music that are not necessarily to be found in the great pre-war Sibelius recordings of conductors such as Beecham, Schnéevoigt, and Koussevitzky.

Sibelius admired Karajan. Since he tended to say pleasant things about anyone who conducted his music, the admiration may not be all it seemed to be. Yet there is some evidence that his regard for Karajan was genuine. His daughter Eva Poloheimo told Robert Layton that of all the many recordings of her father's music, Beecham's 1947 recording of the Sixth Symphony was his absolute favourite; but that among conductors of a younger generation it was Karajan who had the greatest feeling for his music.

In the winter and early spring of 1954–5, Legge received not one, but two letters from Sibelius about the recordings he had recently sent him.

Järvenpää 15 September 1954

Dear Friend,
As you know, I have always been a great admirer of Mr v. Karajan, and his magnificent recording of my works has given me the keenest satisfaction. Especially in the Fourth Symphony, his great artistic line and the inner beauty of the interpretation have deeply impressed me. I beg you to present my grateful greetings to him.
    With all best wishes,
        Very sincerely yours,
        Jean Sibelius[5]

Either Sibelius had not heard the LP when he wrote this (unlikely, in view of his singling out the performance of the Fourth Symphony) or he had forgotten he had sent the letter. Eight months later, another arrived:

Helsinki 11 May 1955

Dear Friend,
You have perhaps wondered why I have not written to you before and thanked you for the excellent recordings of my Fourth and Fifth Symphony. I have now heard them many times and can only say that I am happy. Karajan is a great master. His interpretation is superb, technically and musically.
    With kindest regards and all good wishes,
        Yours always sincerely,
        Jean Sibelius[6]

In July 1955, Karajan recorded the Sixth and Seventh symphonies with the Philharmonia. The performance of the Seventh was much revered at the time. Such a task, remarked Malcolm Macdonald in *The Gramophone*, is not lightly undertaken, but here a great occasion is made of the work.[7]

The performance of the Sixth Symphony has many points in common with the 1947 Beecham recording. However, Karajan's account does not quite have the finish and charm of the Beecham, and there is an odd lapse of ensemble four bars from the end involving the drum and the divided violas.

The sessions following the 1 May concert were given over to a plausible but ill-starred re-recording of Tchaikovsky's Sixth Symphony[8] – and three recordings – Brahms's Second and Fourth symphonies and Schubert's *Unfinished* – that would win Karajan and the Philharmonia fresh laurels as the premier recording ensemble of the age.

Flying back to Vienna after the completion of the sessions on 27 May, Karajan was taken ill with a burst appendix. He was taken off the plane at Zürich and operated on immediately. As he was wheeled towards the operating theatre, he said to Mattoni, 'Call the Freccias and offer them my apologies.' Massimo Freccia was making his début at the Vienna Festival the next day and Karajan had promised to be there for him.

There were no complications. Indeed, by 25 June, Karajan was back at work in Vienna, conducting the thousandth performance of the Vienna Singverein, a performance of Beethoven's Ninth Symphony.

A month later the Philharmonia Orchestra travelled to Vienna to record the symphony with the Singverein in the Musikvereinssaal. It was not the happiest of ideas. Away from their beloved Kingsway Hall, the orchestra seemed scratchy and ill at ease. Karajan's own reading of the symphony was changing, too, in a Toscanini-wards direction that was not yet fully absorbed.

*

In August 1955, Karajan renewed his partnership with Maria Callas: a studio recording in La Scala, Milan of Puccini's *Madama Butterfly*. Callas had not yet sung the role on stage[9] and Karajan's own experience of the opera dated back to his years in Ulm; but, between them, they created something utterly special.

The supporting cast was a La Scala 'house' ensemble, perfectly adequate to a performance that draws everything inward towards Cio-Cio-San's own private tragedy. In an ideal world, Legge would have been able to cast Giuseppe di Stefano as the bounder Pinkerton and Tito Gobbi as Sharpless, the wise and sympathetic American consul; but both singers had already recorded the roles for EMI under Gavazzeni's direction.

Legge's decision to use Gedda as Pinkerton was widely criticised. 'Mr Gedda would not hurt a flea, let alone a butterfly,' mused Alec Robertson in *The Gramophone*.[10] This is unfair to Gedda. The characterisation may be somewhat pallid but the singing is stylish and secure, a not inconsiderable achievement given the extreme slowness of many of Karajan's tempi in Act 1. When Karajan re-recorded *Madama Butterfly* in 1974 for Decca (with Luciano Pavarotti as Pinkerton) and later that same year for Jean-Pierre Ponnelle's memorable film of the opera (with Placido Domingo), the tempi were equally slow but more buoyant, more subtly varied, the opening of Act 1 altogether wittier and more ravishingly coloured than on the 1955 set.

It is not for Act 1, however, that one turns to the Callas/Karajan recording of this work. Wilfrid Mellers has argued that *Madama Butterfly* is a great, not merely a good, opera because its sequence of love-scenes grows in depth as the lovers themselves cannot. Act 2 is the work's rich dramatic kernel. Here we are taken to the heart of the tragedy in a way that few rival recordings have managed or envisioned. Michael Tanner, in a memorable essay on Callas's Butterfly, has pointed to the confraternity of Act 2 of *Madama Butterfly* and Act 3 of Wagner's *Tristan und Isolde*; and, indeed, one wonders to what extent Karajan's radical and searching treatment of the music here is not, in some sense, a by-product of his deep and abiding fascination with *Tristan und Isolde*. The tempi, broad and finely sustained, can certainly be dubbed 'Wagnerian', as can Karajan's tendency to absorb the set-piece arias into the larger whole. ('Arias are fairly sparse in *Butterfly*,' observes Tanner, 'but Karajan almost manages to convince us that they don't exist at all.'[11]) But there is also his extreme punctiliousness over Puccini's dynamic markings. De Sabata was the same; so much so, that in his analytical writings on opera, the conductor Gianandrea Gavazzeni, shrewd and amusing, invariably refers to De Sabata–Karajan as though they were one and the same person, a single musical organism, sufficient unto itself.

The result of all this is a great gathering in of the inner musical content in the context of a reading which is as radical and simple-seeming as the score itself. It is also clear that the La Scala orchestra loved playing for Karajan; his fluency of gesture, his inner passion, his command of a true orchestral cantabile, coupled with his near-fluent Italian, made him one of their own.

Opera being opera, there has been a great deal of ink spilled on the question of whether Callas's talents suited the role of Cio-Cio-San. John Ardoin has, I think, 'placed' the characterisation as well as anyone:

[Callas's] Cio-Cio-San was a composite of previous dramatic factors: Amina's innocence and quiet devotion, Gilda's metamorphosis and betrayal, and Violetta's passion and sacrifice. Not only did these dramatic pieces form a new character mosaic, but vocal elements from each were employed as well. If there was one dominant source, it was Gilda, whose transition from maiden to woman in Callas's voice parallels the same transition in Butterfly. Yet the whole of Butterfly is strikingly different from its parts. The tragedy of Puccini's geisha is a private one; even the maid Suzuki is kept on its perimeter. Callas defined this dramatic premise in inward, concentrated terms, reaffirming her gift of acclimatising herself to specific theatrical terrain.[12]

Karajan's response to Callas's view of the role seems to have been one of absolute agreement, intuitively recognised. But, then, like Callas, Karajan never saw Cio-Cio-San simply as a sad little girl, the stuff of which teenage soap-operas are nowadays made. Old social codes caught in the toils of new freedoms, Butterfly as the victim of a past she distrusts: these were themes, in Karajan's mind, out of which the real dramas of his own and his parents' age had been fashioned.

*

From Milan, Karajan travelled to Lucerne to teach as well as to conduct. As we have seen, he was a born teacher. Yet his teaching of conducting had its own special slant. A teacher rather than an academic, he combined a high level of inborn musical talent with a severely practical streak that plainly derives from the fact that, as a conductor, he was more or less completely self-taught. It is not unusual, of course, for a conductor to be self-taught. What marked out Karajan was the extent and quality of the self-schooling.

It was his visit to Japan in 1954 that had helped reawaken his interest in teaching. A few months after his return, he would tell a Berlin audience:

I made a start last year in Japan and it gave me an immense feeling of satisfaction. I received two letters from people who had difficulties with their right arm. One of them was slow to bring his arm down, and I was able to rid him of this inhibition. I saw then that I had not yet grown too remote from these problems. By the time you are sixty-five, you've probably forgotten what it once was like. Today I can still remember that I struggled for ten years to find a conducting technique. And it is in this way, I believe, that you can help someone, if you really have the inclination to do so.[13]

Karajan loved the element of legerdemain that a good conducting technique involves. Walter Legge would recall talking to him before one such masterclass about the difficulty youngsters have in getting chords together:

And he said, 'Well, I will show you. I'll bet you five marks that I can get the wind in first, the brass in first, the strings in first, and then I will get them together'. They will know nothing at all, simply that by the upbeat I will throw them and then get them together. And, incredible as it may seem, he did it. I merely said which I wanted in first and he got them in first. Just by a hair's breadth, but it was not together. That shows that the man really knew what to do with his hands.[14]

Bernard Gavoty attended one of Karajan's Lucerne classes. He concluded that there are no secrets in the art of conducting, 'only a difficult technique, and mystery'. That morning, Karajan's advice had been sternly practical:

Give your commands accurately: don't expect staccato playing from your musicians when you yourself are beating the theme legato . . . Don't overdo it, don't get agitated: everything's going well, so leave it alone . . . Don't keep your baton rigid. On the contrary, allow it the maximum of agility, let it dance in the hand. It must be as mobile as the arm itself . . . Are you conducting from memory or not? Yes? Well, close your score.[15]

The symphony being rehearsed was Haydn's *London* Symphony, No.104, an old Karajan favourite. The finale starts with a low pedal-note on the horns:

This holding-note of the horns is always catastrophic. Don't be insistent: the more anxious the horns are, the worse their attack will be. What do you do? Nothing at all. The audience always chatters between movements, so get started without losing a second. The noise of their chatter will disguise a bad note . . . You don't think that is a serious attitude? There is nothing mathematical about conducting an orchestra. There is more psychology in it than algebra . . .[16]

*

There are some who saw Karajan's interest in the 'psychology' of an orchestra as being decidedly sinister, a baleful game. One such person was an engaging young Englishman who occasionally turned up to play the celeste and orchestral piano parts for the Philharmonia. His name was Raymond Leppard, a brilliantly gifted all-round musician, one of the *jeunesse dorée* of early 1950s Cambridge. Karajan seems to have taken a shine to Leppard (Leppard's phrase) and was more than happy to admit this amusing and decorative youth to his entourage, though it is possible that Mattoni (whom Leppard would later describe as 'a fat, gay person who tended to put his hands where he shouldn't put his hands'[17]) was the instigating agent. Leppard found Karajan charming: witty, friendly, physically attractive. Years later, he would be touched to receive an invitation from him to perform Monteverdi's *Orfeo* at the Salzburg Festival.[18] Yet Leppard's memories of Karajan the orchestral leader have the taste of wormwood about them:

Wonderful musician. Extraordinary. He played games and must have been one of the last examples of the old *Führer* type. His game with an orchestra was largely psychological. He used to do terrible things . . . He would call a rehearsal at 10.00 for the whole orchestra, and rehearse a Mozart divertimento for forty people, and insisted they all stay there until ten to one. Then he would do ten minutes of Respighi. He did that on purpose. Just to keep them there. Just to tell them who's boss. That was a disciplinary thing from his point of view, and he thought it necessary. The English hated that, and they finally revolted.[19]

The 'revolt' Leppard talks of (and later describes in his memoirs, with a tabloid mix of flair and swashbuckling inaccuracy) took place on the Philharmonia's North American tour in the autumn of 1955. Leppard was on the tour. So, disastrously as it turned out, was a supernumerary violinist, a former RAF fighter pilot, Peter Gibbs, who had been asked to travel with the orchestra in place of Kathleen Tierney who was seriously ill.

*

The Philharmonia Orchestra arrived in Washington on 22 October 1955 after a week's rehearsal and two concerts in London the previous week. Thirteen works were taken on tour,[20] along with a clutch of encores and arrangements of the British and American national anthems specially commissioned from William Walton. Walton had not held back. The *Belshazzar*-like thrust and brilliance of the horn parts rather startled some of the American audiences.

The orchestra's confidence was at such a peak that the Mozart Divertimento K287, which it had so feared and shunned on the 1952 European tour, now drew an awed response. *Washington Post* critic Paul Hume spoke of 'a kind of sound and playing whose parallel in this country we cannot name'. He went on:

The brightness of the slender-bored horns favoured by the discerning Englishmen matches the perfect sheen of the strings, who played the most dazzling passages, scales, arpeggios, and melting soulful adagios as Kreisler might once have done. It is Mozart playing with heart and soul, all music, and all living.[21]

The horns, led by Dennis Brain and Neill Sanders, also surpassed themselves in the suite from Handel's *Water Music* in the Hamilton Harty arrangement. Hume recalled having heard Harty himself conduct the suite some twenty years earlier:

Not since then from anyone has it had the combination of regal splendour and scintillating verve von Karajan gave it.[22]

During rehearsals for the first Washington concert, Karajan sprang from the rostrum and ricked his already suspect back. The following evening in Carnegie Hall, now in considerable pain, he limped gamely on to the platform. It was a premonition of things to come.

The players were more interested in the New York audience than in their temporarily incapacitated conductor. 'We couldn't take our eyes off them!' Hugh Bean would later recall.[23] Kreisler attended the rehearsal and the concert. Primrose and Piatigorsky were there, so was Benny Goodman, not to mention a host of old and not-so-old movie stars including Basil Rathbone and Mary Pickford.

Again, the reviews were highly laudatory. Paul Henry Lang declared the playing and conducting of the Mozart Divertimento a thing 'of unadulterated joy':

The sound was enchanting, the strings homogeneous and flexible, their staccatos light and clear and their legato smooth yet without a trace of sentimentality. The two horns must come from another planet. But above all the delights of the sheer beauty of sound and wonderful ensemble there stood the exceptional quality of the interpretation. Mr von Karajan moulded this little masterpiece with solicitous care and well-nigh infallible musicianship that filled everyone with admiration.[24]

Debussy's *La mer* and Berlioz's *Symphonie fantastique* followed. Here Lang noted what others would note during the tour, more or less approvingly: an element of calculation in the ensemble, the performance of *La mer* more symphonic than picturesque, the reading of the Berlioz surprisingly classical. Lang also commented on the orchestra's youthfulness, concluding that you did not need 'a venerable barn' (Carnegie Hall), an equally venerable board, an elderly conductor, and 'an orchestra whose original members watched Hendrik Hudson sail up the river' to make music in great style.

This was a gibe at the New York Philharmonic, which was currently lurching towards one of the most serious crises in its history. 'A matinée idol in danger of growing a paunch,' quipped *Time* magazine. The Philharmonia, by contrast, was a 'blazing prodigy'.[25] In a retrospective in the *New Yorker*, Winthrop Sargeant drew similar comparisons, this time with the Berliners and the Amsterdam Concertgebouw Orchestra, both of which had recently visited the United States. Weighing them in the scales against the Philharmonia, department by department, in some cases player by player, he found both wanting. In a passage that must have intrigued Karajan, he went on:

The Philharmonia is evidently the product of a highly fastidious process of selection, and whoever put it together – whether Mr von Karajan or Mr Walter Legge, or very likely both in collaboration – has, I think, matched his players as deftly as a jeweller might match the diamonds in a royal tiara.[26]

Selecting diamonds for the Berlin tiara, currently at the jeweller's awaiting restoration, was a task Karajan had barely begun to embark upon.

What amazed American audiences was the sheer virtuosity of the

Philharmonia playing. 'I had never thought of virtuoso orchestral playing as a typically English pursuit,' remarked Sargeant. He was right. Paradoxically, what made the Philharmonia so remarkable an ensemble was its training as a recording orchestra. A review by Glenna Syse in the *Chicago Sunday Times* touched interestingly on this debt:

A good recording machine has a flawless ear and pampers no shortcomings. Thus, perhaps, this is why the Philharmonia is constantly alert – its members are well accustomed to striving for perfection because they know well the ever watchful commands of the recorder. Even in the world of music, an audience must pay rightful homage to the machine, if, as we think is the case here, it is the instrument that encourages such splendor, verve and musical excellence.[27]

The precision of the tuning was a factor in all this. Poor tuning muddies recorded sound. Singing with the Philharmonia, and with Szell's Cleveland Orchestra, Schwarzkopf once told me, was like stepping out of the surgery after having one's ears syringed. The Philharmonia's playing, noted one American reviewer, was 'like a chime truly struck'.[28]

The question of the Philharmonia's essential 'Englishness' obsessed several reviewers; analogies were drawn with things as different as the British weather and, when it was learned that the players had no long-term contracts, the unwritten British Constitution. The orchestra, meanwhile, worked its socks off, took a modest interest in the praise that was being heaped upon it, and grumbled about this and that in the time-honoured manner of all true Britons.

They even began grumbling about Karajan. Musically, he was still close to the players. Every inch the old-fashioned Kapellmeister, he would call the strings together for last-minute rehearsal before any concert in which the Mozart *Divertimento* was being played. Socially, he was more distant, hedged around by tight security; though he did attend a party in New York's Lotus Club to celebrate the Philharmonia's tenth birthday. He even helped cut the cake. Left to his own devices, he would had flown between engagements but the risk was too great: 'You can be grounded by bad weather for days on end, and then where are you?'[29] Instead, he chartered a sports car, a Thunderbird: an even greater risk, one would have thought. Its road-holding qualities, Karajan told a possibly somewhat bemused Harold C. Schonberg, were not a patch on those of the Mercedes 300 he drove in Austria:

'My Mercedes holds the road on high speeds better than any other car. You have wonderful roads here. But what good are they? You can't go fast. After five minutes they've got you.'
Mr von Karajan looked fearfully over his shoulder, as if expecting a state trooper on a motorcycle to come bowling down the center aisle of Carnegie Hall.[30]

Karajan also talked about acoustics and the unease an orchestra feels in a strange hall. The orchestra's pleasure in Symphony Hall Boston or Philadelphia's Academy of Music was offset on the tour by less agreeable experiences: Woolsey Hall, New Haven with its sullen acoustic and a new hall in Columbus, Ohio where the echo of the heavy brass 'returned to the centre of the hall after about a third of a second'.[31]

There were no such problems in Chicago where the orchestra gave two concerts. This was a particular triumph for Karajan, since the city's own orchestra, now under Fritz Reiner's incomparable leadership, was currently as fine as any in the world. Karajan had already been invited to conduct the Chicago Symphony by Reiner, an invitation he had politely declined, mindful, perhaps, of the fate that had befallen Furtwängler there. Claudia Cassidy, the city's most influential music critic, mourned his loss but heaped superlatives on Karajan and the orchestra that had had 'the wisdom to choose [him] as its favourite conductor'.[32]

Away from the metropolitan centres, audiences varied. At Amherst, four thousand people attended the concert, many of them students from the University of Massachusetts; yet for the New Haven–Yale concert there were fewer than a hundred people present, an audience described by the local paper as 'sparse but vociferous'. No reason was given for the poor turnout. In Detroit, there was an official boycott of the concert by local Jews – the bulk of the Detroit concert-going public, the *Detroit Times* ruefully conceded. The Jewish Community Council of Metropolitan Detroit also delivered a formal protest to Washington, arguing that Karajan was not 'a desirable visitor' under the terms of United States immigration law.[33]

As the tour moved further west and north, as the temperatures dropped and winter finally began to take hold, so Karajan seems to have become less approachable: wary of political demonstrations, irked by the unpredictability of unfamiliar halls and occasionally disappointing audience numbers, and suffering still with his back. A certain coolness also appears to have sprung up between Karajan and the players. In less glamorous centres and before smaller audiences, it was claimed that Karajan was conducting much more quickly; that his bows were perfunctory, and his departures from halls ever more rapid. Over the years, the orchestra had come to value his courtesy, notably his habit of taking most of his bows from within the orchestra, leaning on the shoulders of the front desk fiddle players. What they could not understand was the new brusqueness and the seeming discourtesy to audiences whose enthusiasm for the orchestra (and for Karajan himself) was being rather casually received.

Sometimes the players resisted what they perceived to be Karajan's hastiness. In the slow movement of Beethoven's *Pastoral* Symphony flautist Gareth Morris deliberately held the music back at one point as the stream flowed busily along. Karajan's eyes opened momentarily, gazed in Morris's direction, then closed again.

'A minor victory,' I suggested to Morris when he related the story.

'Hardly. As soon as my solo ended, he moved the music on again.'

The critics, it has to be said, wrote admiringly of all the performances of the *Pastoral*, praising the ease and naturalness of the playing and the freshness and buoyancy of Karajan's reading. The review of that particular *Pastoral* is especially glowing.

That was the penultimate concert of the tour. After the *Pastoral* Symphony, Karajan is said to have walked off the platform without acknowledging the applause. No one knew why, though it would appear that he had noticed a microphone suspended above the orchestra, evidence of someone making a professional but illegal recording of the occasion.

Perhaps the orchestra was more conscious of Karajan's irritation than the audience. According to the *Portland Press Herald*, he had returned to conduct an encore that evening, which rather takes the gloss off the story that he simply walked off at the end of the concert and never came back.[34]

The final concert of the tour was in Boston. During the morning of 19 November there was a brief seating rehearsal in Symphony Hall. Quite a few of the Boston Symphony players were there, waiting to take their opposite numbers out to lunch. So was Charles Munch, the orchestra's music director, a man much admired by Karajan.[35]

To help the orchestra acclimatise, Karajan suggested they play a few bars. Between his making the suggestion and the music starting, the supernumerary second violinist Peter Gibbs stood up and confronted Karajan. The gist of what he said – in the imposingly clipped tones of an old-fashioned BBC announcer – was: 'Mr von Karajan, in view of your inexcusable behaviour and lack of courtesy to the audience last evening, I have to say I no longer feel I am able to play under your direction.'

Since no one knew why Karajan had behaved as he did, and since some would probably have reacted the same way even if they had been better informed, there was a certain amount of sympathetic stand-tapping. Gibbs may have been a hired hand, a late addition to the tour with little to lose, but there was evident sympathy within the orchestra for what he was saying.

Karajan tried to ignore him. But there was more. In the view of Gibbs the former RAF fighter pilot, Karajan – an Austrian parading at the head of a British orchestra – had behaved badly, and behaved badly, what's more, in the United States, Britain's most loyal ally. Reports vary as to what Gibbs said next, but it was something along the lines, 'I spent the most valuable five years of my life destroying the likes of you.'[36]

'Please resume your seat, Mr Gibbs,' boomed Legge.

Karajan affected to carry on as if nothing had happened. That was merely the public face, however. Privately, he was livid. As a condition for conducting the evening's concert, he demanded Gibbs's absence, plus a formal apology signed by every member of the orchestra. A group of senior players retaliated by stating that they would not play *without* Gibbs and that Karajan should issue a written apology to the orchestra for his discourteous behaviour the previous evening.

These things happen at the fag end of long tours when everyone is tired and far from home; and once again it was left to Jane Withers to pick up the pieces. There was not the slightest chance of getting the orchestra to sign an apology, nor would she have asked them to. Instead, she got her assistant to type out, as crudely as possible, a brusque apology to Karajan which was then handed to Mattoni. Gibbs did play in the concert, and Karajan conducted it, his entry delayed sufficiently long to scare the orchestra without leading the audience to suspect that anything was amiss.

The concert, that cold, snowy evening in Boston, was judged 'an occasion for superlatives' by the critic of the *Christian Science Monitor* Harold Rodgers.[37] Rudolph Ellie, writing in the *Boston Herald*, was not so sure. The Mozart was a miracle of fine music-making but the performances of the Sibelius and the Bartók struck him as being strangely subdued.[38] How right he was.

*

Like the Philharmonia's first European tour of 1952, this first American tour had ended in triumph; but it had also left a bitter taste. This was sad, not least because orchestra and conductor were such a wonderful team. Karajan had received many plaudits on the tour – none more flattering than Paul Hume's 'Von Karajan is a master conductor in the manner of men who made conducting an art'[39] – but it was the teamwork that was most noticed. A reviewer in Charleston wrote:

Von Karajan is businesslike in conducting, yet he works with such feeling and understanding that he becomes part of the orchestra, while remaining most decisively its leader.[40]

Another noted:

. . . the men played with freshness and a complete absence of routine. In a mood of controlled relaxation, they played with joy, simplicity, and love. Much of this was in response to the will of a young conductor who obviously conceives music as a profoundly communicative human experience. He used the simplest gestures as though conscious of a tremendous reserve of spiritual and musical energy.[41]

The reviews of this 1955 tour are as perceptive as any about Karajan's conducting at this time; they are perceptive, too, about the nature and character of his craft. The art of 'controlled relaxation' is precisely what Karajan had been attempting to teach on his course at Lucerne; and he did, indeed, believe in guiding an orchestra so that in performance it could drink of its own accord at the well of spiritual and musical energy.

As for his baton technique, his Lucerne students would have recognised the truth of a fine analysis of this by Jay S. Harrison in the *New York Herald Tribune*:

His is a beat that strikes the eye as though reflected in still water, and it is the message conveyed by this beat that accounts for much of the limpidity of his work. Indeed, this grace of hand, all precise and controlled, has a tendency to soothe, permits the orchestra to retain its poise and equilibrium, and jars them not for a moment. A nervous orchestra, rendered frantic by wild arm movements, cannot under any circumstances play legatos as shapely and as silken as those which recurrently emerged last night. Nor can an ensemble turn its thoughts to lyricism of phrase if it is constantly being swooped into hysteria by baton gestures that appear to simulate lance thrusts. Mr von Karajan, with a wondrous dignity and elegance, held his band in rein through every measure; but he did so with a suppleness and ease that allowed it to concentrate on the music and not every instant on him.[42]

Even the greatest talent, pushed a hair's breadth in the wrong direction can end up seeming like a parody of itself: the maniacal Toscanini, the blockish Klemperer, Gielgud crooning, Olivier ranting. Karajan's Achilles' heel would be a tendency to over-refinement and an excess of smoothness, the downside of his highly cultivated art. Harrison touches on this, too. His review continued:

This is a condition undoubtedly cultivated over many years by the Austrian maestro, since lyricism is his strong suit and there is no other legitimate way to obtain it. At any rate, Mr von Karajan is clearly a conductor who sees music as a series of curves, never as a collection of angles. His phrases are all rounded, polished, honed to a point of such refinement that an occasional abrasive moment might serve to set off, as a desirable relief, the bulk of his work. Even cadential Mozartian chords, normally hammered out like a chain of tonic thuds, were, under his command, delicate and airborne. Certainly Mr von Karajan is a man of aristocratic sense and sensibility. Of his breed there are all too few in our time.[43]

*

The Boston flare-up had left the Philharmonia in limbo, uncertain as to whether Karajan would honour his obligation to conduct the Mozart bicentenary tour to Salzburg, Munich, Berne, Zürich, and Paris, planned for January 1956. It was not until Christmas Eve that news came that 'the maestro would be there'.

In later years, there were those who would blame Peter Gibbs for the sudden sharp reduction in Karajan's work with the orchestra. This is unfair. It would have happened anyway; Karajan's recent appointment in Berlin would have seen to that. Added to which, larger dramas were beginning to unfold in Vienna and Salzburg. The newly built Vienna Opera had reopened while Karajan and the Philharmonia were in the United States but Böhm's days as its director were already numbered. (His fate sealed, ironically, by his insistence on concluding a lucrative freelance deal with the Chicago Symphony Orchestra.)

As for Salzburg, negotiations had begun more or less the moment Furtwängler died. Predictably, Karajan had shown no interest in a scattering of short term engagements. As a consequence, the board was unable to engage him for the 1955 festival; and negotiations over the 1956 festival also broke down.

However, when the Philharmonia arrived in Salzburg for their Mozart bicentenary concert on the evening of Saturday, 28 January 1956, the place was awash with rumour and speculation about the imminence of Karajan's 'Festspiel-Inthronisation [festival enthronement]'. The following Monday the *Salzburger Nachrichten* carried an enthusiastic review of the concert, plus a lively and mischievous piece about the lavish reception that had been thrown afterwards in the Mozarteum. All Salzburg's leading power-brokers were there: Puthon and Paumgartner, Lothar and von Einem, Hurdes (who had presided over Karajan's denazification hearing and who was now a leading member of the Austrian government) and Salzburg's influential Provincial Governor Josef Klaus. The only person who was not there (to the frustration of a vociferous gaggle of autograph-hunting Spanish music students) was Karajan, who had made his excuses and slipped away early.

In fact, his draft plans for the 1957–60 festivals were already with Baron Puthon. The battle lines had been drawn. Merely socialising with those who, over the next few weeks, would decide his fate would have served no useful purpose.

In all this, the Philharmonia was something of an irrelevance, though Karajan would continue conducting and recording with it for another four years, a fact that is often forgotten nowadays.

As for Peter Gibbs, he had said what he felt he needed to say and one can only admire him for that. A sensitive man and a good musician, he had served his country and suffered much in the aftermath of that service. Raymond Leppard would remember:

Even later on, after the Philharmonia, when leader at Covent Garden, there was something unresolved, unsettled in him, perhaps due to the war. Finally it seems he could cope no longer and flew his own small plane out alone above the North Sea and never came back.[44]

Karajan, you might say, survived his war; Peter Gibbs was not so lucky.

CHAPTER 43

A resignation and three recordings

Karajan walked in, no rehearsal, no attention to the microphone. 'Good morning, let's begin – ready?' He played it straight through down to Octavian's first words and then said, 'Let's listen to it.' I said, 'Do you think the horns are loud enough – you see what Strauss has written? Let's really get them to do what he meant.' He said, 'All right, if you want to do it again, we'll do it, but I'm satisfied.' And by ten past ten, we'd done the first four minutes of *Rosenkavalier* without a splice!

Walter Legge, *On and Off the Record*

In making his pitch for the directorship of the Salzburg Festival, Karajan did not repeat the mistake of trusting to his talent alone. His experiences of Tietjen's Berlin and the political mazes of post-war Vienna had forced upon him the recognition that real power lies ultimately with the politicians. In Salzburg this meant the local politicians and festival elders. If von Einem, Schuh, and Neher had the talent, it was Baron Puthon, Cultural Counsellor Josef Kaut and Provincial Governor Josef Klaus who had the power to hire and fire. The conservatively minded Josef Klaus, later to be Austria's Chancellor, was neither as long-serving nor as influential a figure in Salzburg affairs as his predecessor Franz Rehrl had been in the 1920s and 1930s. In the mid-1950s, however, it was Klaus who made the big decisions. And it was he with whom Karajan was now privately negotiating.

Klaus's first important decision had been to forge ahead with plans to build a new festival theatre. A committee had been set up in 1953, to which the distinguished stage director Herbert Graf had been invited to submit proposals.

Graf's plan, jointly prepared with Salzburg's senior theatre architect, Clemens Holzmeister, was that a new theatre should be built on the site of the old court stables adjacent to the existing Festspielhaus. The plan was immediately opposed by von Einem, Kaut and others. Traffic congestion in the city centre and the huge cost of excavating 58,000 cubic metres of rock from the Mönchsberg (the entire mountain might collapse, some said) were the practical reasons given for the opposition. After two years of in-fighting, Klaus's committee quashed the von Einem lobby and gave the go-ahead for excavations to begin in November 1956.

For some reason, it has come to be assumed that it was Karajan who commissioned the theatre and determined its proportions. He certainly lobbied for it; and, after Furtwängler's death in November 1954, his was the voice that was most closely listened to. Yet, like all Salzburg's festival theatres, it was a collaborative venture.[1] The original Festspielhaus had been designed in 1924–5 by Eduard Hütter in consultation with Max Reinhardt and stage designer Alfred Roller, remodelled by Holzmeister the following year, and further remodelled by him in 1937–8, largely at Toscanini's instigation. Its newer neighbour has gone through fewer convulsions, but its genesis was no less complex: Graf's scheme, Holzmeister's design, acoustic planning by the team who built the new Vienna State Opera, and – during the period 1956–9 – a great deal of input from Karajan himself on the equipping and fine tuning of the project.

According to Günther Schneider-Siemssen, it was Karajan who had challenged Holzmeister on one particularly important aspect of the design:

Karajan said to Holzmeister, 'It isn't deep enough. It's impossible for back-projections.' Holzmeister said, 'What are back-projections?' Some of us would say that the trouble with the stage is that it is not *high* enough. But it's typical of Karajan that he was already way ahead of most people, looking to a new kind of stage design – and this was especially important with Wagner – that would 'paint with light'. I think it was Karajan who actually called the explosives people to see if it was feasible to blow up the mountain. 'What, that little hillock?' the man said. 'I can blow that up in no time!'[2]

By the mid-1950s, the building of the new festival hall had become a key factor in Klaus's bid to lure Karajan back to Salzburg as the festival's artistic director. By late 1955 this goal had been achieved. In January 1956, Karajan delivered to Baron Puthon his paper 'Proposals for Salzburg Festival, 1957–60'. From the point of view of repertory, these were very much in line with the festival's tradition as it had evolved over the past thirty years.[3] However, some of Karajan's other ideas were contentious. He proposed ending the Vienna Philharmonic's absolute monopoly of Salzburg's concert programmes. He also suggested that the festival increase the fees paid to artists: a pre-emptive strike in what he saw as the imminent war over singers between festivals and opera houses in the new age of jet travel.

He also wanted to restore, by subscription if necessary, the kind of artistically discriminating 'core public' the festival had attracted – or fancied it had attracted – in the heydays of Reinhardt and Toscanini. This was less welcome to Klaus. The proposed cost of the new Festspielhaus had already caused him severe political embarrassment, and the idea that taxpayers' money was going to be spent on an operatic pleasure-garden for a new international 'élite' was unacceptable. If Reinhardt had been damaged by the élitist charge in the 1930s, how much worse would the situation be in post-war Europe?

This was an issue, however, on which Karajan would prove to be pretty well immovable. By inclination and upbringing he was disinclined to settle for second-best. (He once said to me, 'I am not an élitist, I am a super-élitist.') His understanding of the new economic and social order that was being shaped by high-speed travel and new technologies told him that things were about to change irrevocably. Not all the change would be for the worse. New technologies brought with them levels of access to the arts that were beyond the dreams of any of the old cultural élites. Karajan approved of this. (There were few who did not.) Yet at the same time he was acutely aware of the need to secure the artistic and financial base that was needed to generate the *quality* of music-making the public was becoming increasingly used to through the medium of the gramophone.

*

In Vienna, meanwhile, a crisis was looming. The desultory nature of Böhm's leadership of the State Opera had again been evident in the weeks following the gala opening of the new house in November 1955. Shortly before Christmas, Böhm left Vienna for the Mozart bicentenary in Salzburg and conducting engagements in Chicago. In principle, this should not have been a problem; unfortunately, many of the leading singers had also taken off for what local critic Joseph Wechsberg called 'greener dollar pastures'. Böhm had left no strategy in place to deal with this. Indeed, such instructions as he had left only made matters worse: his refusal, for instance, to allow any other conductor near *Wozzeck*, for which a first-rate cast was standing by ready to sing. The press was aghast, the noisy denizens of the *Galeriestehplätze* furious.

Böhm flew back from Chicago on 28 February and gave a press briefing of startling ineptness: 'I have no intention,' he said 'of sacrificing my career to the Vienna Opera.'[4]

Two days later, he appeared in the pit of the Opera to such a clamour of booing and derision it was some time before the performance of *Fidelio* could begin. (The longer Böhm waited, the worse the booing became. His administrative assistant Deputy Director Egon Seefehlner was shouting 'Begin! Begin!' from his stage box, but he could not be heard above the racket.) Later that evening, after a superb account of the overture *Leonore* No.3, Böhm was cheered to the rafters. What the Viennese were saying was: 'We love your conducting, Dr Böhm, but we sure as hell don't want you as director of our Opera.' He resigned next morning.

Karajan was the inevitable choice as successor. Böhm later claimed the whole thing was a conspiracy, that the man who had appointed him, Ernst Marboe, had wanted Karajan all along. This is not true. Whatever the coffee-house gossips at their reserved tables were saying, back in 1954 it had been a straight choice between Böhm and Clemens

Krauss. What Marboe – an extremely able and charming man – did hope was that, *in the fullness of time*, Karajan would come to Vienna as Böhm's successor.

If Karajan had any doubts about accepting the job at this particular juncture, he quickly suppressed them. Schwarzkopf recalls Walter Legge reeling off reason after reason why it was a job to be avoided at all costs: a state-funded, state-run bureaucracy, with a salaried ensemble of artists many of whom were past their prime, hostile unions, a fickle press, and public whose interest in the house was proprietorial in a way that was unknown in any other city.

'How, Herbert, do even *you* propose to deal with all that?'

According to Schwarzkopf, Karajan looked at him with his ice-blue eyes, closed both fists, placed one above the other, and began making the kind of twisting motion one uses when working a pepper grinder.

'If anyone stands in my way, I shall simply . . .'[5]

Karajan's negotiations with Marboe were easier than those at Salzburg had been. Again, Karajan had a series of radical proposals which he did not so much offer as insist upon; the difference was that Marboe agreed with most of them. In the first place, the time had clearly come to bring to an end the Vienna Opera's tradition of performing everything in German. This, in turn, meant competing in the open market for top international artists. Where the Italian repertory was concerned, Karajan proposed a series of co-productions with La Scala, Milan. In an increasingly competitive world, it made sense, he argued, to share costs.

The problem with the Milan deal was that unsalaried Italian artists cost more to engage than salaried Austrian ones, raising the Vienna Opera's costs rather than lowering them. But then, Karajan was frank about this. 'I warn you,' he told Finance Minister Reinhardt Kamitz, 'I am going to cost you an awful lot of money!'

Karajan did not propose the abandonment of the repertory system, nor would Marboe have permitted it; but the La Scala proposal brought elements of the Italian continuous limited run (*stagione*) system into Viennese operatic life. In the autumn, and in the early summer, the repertory system would be, to some extent, in abeyance; mid-winter, the period in which Böhm had come to grief, would be a time, Karajan somewhat airily suggested, for introducing promising young artists under the umbrella of the repertory system.

Since Karajan had no intention of leaving Berlin and since his existing engagements could only slowly be disentangled, there remained the key problem that had bedevilled Böhm's tenure: the question of the Artistic Director's own time and availability. This, too, was deftly dealt with. If Karajan had learned anything from Furtwängler's behaviour, it was the futility of trying to keep one's so-called 'rivals' at bay. Mahler had tried to do it during his time in Vienna and worn himself out in the process. Böhm had been highly protective of his position. Karajan, by contrast, wanted the best singers in Vienna *and* the best conductors. His initial wish list included Böhm, Cluytens, Giulini, Keilberth, Knappertsbusch, Krips, Mitropoulos, Rossi, Serafin, and Szell. Of these, only Giulini failed to materialise. There would also be a strong 'B' team: men like de Fabritiis, Ferencsik, von Matačić, Prêtre, and Votto.

Legge was right, of course. The directorship of the Vienna Opera is a Bermuda Triangle of a job, and, experienced helmsman that he was, Karajan must have had his qualms. He did, however, have up-to-date charts, seemingly limitless energy, and a good crew. Mattoni was a key player in all this, smoothing ruffled egos and keeping the press at bay. Marboe's support would also be crucial. Alas, Karajan had barely taken over when, on 28 September 1957, Marboe died of a heart attack. He was forty-eight. It was the first blow in Karajan's seven-year tenure, and probably the most grievous.

The negotiations with Karajan had been conducted in great secrecy. Even Marcel Prawy, at the time dramaturg at the Volksoper, was completely in the dark. Having talked Marboe into allowing the Volksoper to play its first ever American musical *Kiss me, Kate!* as a season rather than in repertory, Prawy was given the curious stipulation that it must not finish a day later than 11 June.[6] Eventually, all became clear. On 12 June, the La Scala company was to give the first of three performances of *Lucia di Lammermoor* at the State Opera under Karajan's direction, with Callas in the title role. It was Vienna's first *Lucia di Lammermoor* since Toscanini's La Scala visit in 1929. It was also Karajan's own post-war début at the Vienna Opera.

Some of the critics were sniffy about the state of Callas's voice, but the evening was a sensation. On the morning of the second performance, the news of Karajan's appointment was released to the press. He would take up his duties as Artistic Director on 1 September and make his conducting debut as director in April 1957. Seefehlner, who had always got on very well with Karajan, remained in post, as did the veteran head of artist management Ernst August Schneider.[7]

For the Viennese it was going to be a long wait, but Karajan had no room for manoeuvre. Important recording sessions loomed in London and Milan, and from September through to November, he had commitments with the Berlin Philharmonic culminating in a six-week tour of the United States and Canada.

*

Between June and December 1956 Karajan and Legge made three classic opera recordings. It was an extraordinary achievement: Verdi's *Falstaff* in London in June; *Il trovatore* in Milan a month later; and finally *Der Rosenkavalier* in London in December. As always the preparation was meticulous and the casting excellent, despite the fact that Legge's first choices for a number of key roles were unavailable to him. Richard Tucker, pencilled in for Manrico in *Il trovatore*, declined to work with Karajan for political reasons, and things were even more problematic in the case of *Der Rosenkavalier*. Karajan wanted Irmgard Seefried as Octavian, but Legge vetoed the idea.[8] With Jurinac unavailable for contractual reasons, it was agreed to use the young Christa Ludwig.[9] Teresa Stich-Randall was also a second choice, brought in when Rita Streich dropped out. There were no problems, however, with the leading players in the three operas: Gobbi, Callas, and Schwarzkopf.

The *Falstaff* was closely modelled on Toscanini's 1950 Carnegie Hall recording, though player for player Karajan's was better cast. Where Valdengo is good, Gobbi is incomparable, where Herva Nelli is diligent and pale-toned, Schwarzkopf is witty and vocally lustrous. Nan Merriman, who sings Meg on both sets, is funnier in the Legge–Karajan production. Of Toscanini's cast, only Cloe Elmo, the Mistress Quickly, is obviously superior to EMI's rather hammy Fedora Barbieri. As for Karajan's conducting, it matches Toscanini's in everything except the earthiness and elementalism of its humour. Schwarzkopf has recalled how assiduously Karajan and Gobbi worked on the comedy, on the score's myriad half-lights. There was nothing in any way 'English' or 'Shakespearian' about all this, she said; it was all done through the music.[10]

Again, one is drawn back to Karajan's all-absorbing interest in music as music. It is an interesting fact of his career that while he never wholly believed in *La traviata* (whose plot he claimed to find implausible), he was a devoted and masterly interpreter of *Il trovatore*, a work which has been persistently maligned by the literary intelligentsia. George Bernard Shaw spoke both for the musical and the literary tendency when he wrote:

It has tragic power, poignant melancholy, impetuous vigour, and a sweet and intense pathos that never loses its dignity. It is swift in action, and perfectly homogeneous in atmosphere and feeling. It is absolutely void of intellectual interest: the appeal is to the instincts and the senses all through.[11]

Though Karajan would have endorsed Shaw's view of the music, he would have regarded the distinction he draws between musical and intellectual pleasure as at best baffling, at worst specious. Karajan himself has said of the work:

My conception of *Il trovatore* is that here are what Jung calls archetypes – fear, hate, love. This fascinates me. And, you know, there is not one dull moment in the entire opera![12]

That is certainly the case in this 1956 recording. As Roland Graeme observes in the Metropolitan Opera's *Guide to Recorded Opera*:

Some other versions are just as exciting; a few just as beautifully executed. The difference is that Karajan's is a beautiful, exciting *performance* – it is all of a piece. The reading combines musical logic with Italianate fire: it is disciplined *and* impulsive, elegiac *and* intensely dramatic. The La Scala orchestra plays as though it knows exactly how good Karajan is making it sound.[13]

Though Azucena is the opera's most significant character, the Karajan–Legge recording is built round Callas's portrayal of Leonora. Callas's personality gave her insights into the role that earlier generations of interpreters had not really begun to explore; and Karajan backed her to the hilt. This is one of the first recordings in which his accompaniment so attaches itself to the singer – like chewing-gum to the heel, as Schwarzkopf once graphically put it – as to provide the listener with something akin to a form of physical pleasure in its own right.

*

That summer, Karajan holidayed with Eliette in Ischia before returning to Berlin by yacht, car, and plane via Portofino, Genoa, and Zürich. It was a useful vacation before the stresses and strains promised by the months ahead, and Karajan extended it by sailing to New York on the *Queen Mary* rather than flying from Berlin with the orchestra.

The Berliners' second visit to the United States in eighteen months was calmer and more relaxed than the previous one. The repertoire was mainly traditional, built round such old Karajan favourites as the *Haffner* Symphony and *Don Juan*, the *Eroica*, Brahms's Second Symphony, and the orchestral version of the Prelude and *Liebestod* from *Tristan und Isolde*. One piece did, however, ruffle critical feathers. Almost as if to say, '*This* was what we went through in the war and what we yearn for most,' Karajan had included in the programme Honegger's Third Symphony, *Liturgique*, 'a drama in three acts, a formless prayer articulated in a world in turmoil' completed in the winter of 1945–6.

Of all contemporary pieces, it was this, Karajan felt, that spoke most eloquently of the traumas of war and the hope for peace. It was his conducting of the symphony (it had been quietly maturing in his repertory for a number of years now) that had caused the scales to fall from the eyes of the French critic Bernard Gavoty, a personal friend of Honegger. After describing the symphony and its concluding *dona nobis pacem*,

The city is dead and the stones smoke, but the day breaks and the innocent bird pipes joyously above the ruins. The little flute practises its exercise, and then all is silent, because all is said.[14]

Gavoty turns to Karajan himself, remarking that even Honegger 'addressing humanity from the pinnacle of his genius' needs an interpreter apt to that genius:

You played your part like the great tragedian you are. Not that you were dissimulating unfelt emotions: you were merely their translator, and you transcended those emotions, imparting to them that furnace heat which makes a work of genius give off light if it is brought to the desired temperature. Even as you were ordering the march of your troops you made some of those sudden discoveries which throw more light than a painstaking analysis. In the finale, as the whole orchestra was pronouncing the triple supplication 'Do-na-no-bis-pa-cem', all at once a wonderful gesture escaped you: you plunged your left fist deep down as if you were setting the torch to the side of a funeral pyre. Immediately the whole orchestra burst into flame. From my seat I could see your profile. And truly it was no longer, as I had once thought, a matter of a star courting success by adopting the affectations of a prima donna, but of a man who has given himself up to a trance. You were a medium, in the full force of the word, maintaining the subtle link between the musical work and the audience.[15]

Since the Berliners were famous for their Brahms rather than for their Honegger, the American reaction to the symphony revealed a certain amount of impatience with the fact that it was being programmed at all.

Back in Berlin, a Philharmonic concert of music by Blacher and Tchaikovsky also included 'Es gibt ein Reich' from Strauss's *Ariadne auf Naxos* sung by Schwarzkopf: a warm-up for the *Rosenkavalier* sessions which were about to begin in London. It was not often that Karajan and Schwarzkopf appeared together in concert, something that had been remarked upon by *The Times* the previous June, when they performed Strauss's *Four Last Songs* at the Royal Festival Hall. Here, observed *The Times*:

[Karajan] realised to a nicety the penetrating lightness of the music . . . and Mme Schwarzkopf floated the long, flowing melodic lines with glowing tone, and still found time to mark and communicate the words.[16]

Much of the early preparation for *Der Rosenkavalier* had been done in Milan in 1952 after Karajan had persuaded Schwarzkopf that the time was ripe for her to take on the role of the Marschallin. 'You are the type, my dear, you have the mind for it, and you have the vocal inflections of a true Lieder singer.' Legge agreed, not least because in Karajan he had a conductor who could, as he put it, 'keep the orchestra so far down that even a light voice can get those inflections through'.

Now the reading was at its subtle, settled best. To this day, the 1956 recording is regarded by fellow professionals as being little short of miraculous. The conductor Jeffrey Tate, a distinguished Straussian in his own right, has recalled:

Things like the *Ariadne* and the *Rosenkavalier* were extraordinarily beautiful. *So* perfect, but perfect in the right sort of way. After all, *Rosenkavalier* can take a certain sort of perfection and there's no doubt Legge and Karajan achieved that. At the entry of the full strings in the Marschallin's monologue at the words 'Und in dem "Wie" da liegt der ganze Unterschied' ['And in the "how", there lies the whole difference'], the sound is so breathtaking one wonders how on earth did he do it? In fact, Carlos Kleiber told me he actually went and asked Karajan: what did he actually *do* to get that particular sound. It hardly enters: unbelievable! He could do that. Mind you, it was terrifying to watch because you didn't really know where to play. People would just creep in. But the effect, when it came, was unbelievable.[17]

The rest of the cast acquitted themselves well: Edelmann as Baron Ochs, the young Christa Ludwig learning minute by minute about breathing, phrasing, and tone-colouring, yet giving a marvellous performance as Octavian, and Theresa Stich-Randall sounding *echt*-Viennese, for all that she was born and brought up in the United States. At the time, Schwarzkopf thought Stich-Randall a trifle 'stiff' in her phrasing. What was remarkable, though, Schwarzkopf would generously add, was the beauty of the sound she produced and the extent of her breath control: 'She was a gifted sportswoman and great underwater swimmer!'[18]

Der Rosenkavalier was Karajan's last operatic collaboration with Legge and the Philharmonia. They had recorded six operas together – *Hänsel und Gretel*, *Ariadne auf Naxos*, *Così fan tutte*, *Die Fledermaus*, *Falstaff*, and *Der Rosenkavalier* – all of which can lay claim, in one way or another, to classic status. It was, however, the end of an era during which the art of monophonic electrical recording had been brought a pitch of perfection by engineers whose experience, in Douglas Larter's case, stretched back thirty years to the halcyon age of Sir Edward Elgar's early electrical recordings for EMI.

It would be two years before Karajan recorded another opera: a recording which would be conceived, unequivocally, for the stereophonic age.[19] It, too, would be made by a British company, with British engineers. It would not, however, be made with Legge, and it would not be for EMI.

PART III
1957–1964

CHAPTER 44

Riding high

It was a new era in Vienna, a new style: black sweaters, jeans, and svelte moccasin footwear.

Christa Ludwig

In a tight finish, a strong jockey may seem to be doing nothing in the saddle except throwing his hands forward – that's all you'll see, but the horse is going flat out, and still going straight. In the same finish a 'weaker' jockey will be throwing himself about in the saddle, and his horse will be rolling about off balance.

Lester Piggott, *The Observer*, 7 June 1970

The Vienna Philharmonic turned up to Karajan's first rehearsal as Artistic Director of the Opera with a more than usually keen sense of anticipation. Chairman Hermann Obermeyer made a short speech of welcome, to which Karajan replied, 'Well then, we've finally made it [*Na also, nun wären wir endlich so weit*]' and raised his baton to begin the rehearsal. Who 'we' were was not entirely clear.

The production, which opened on 2 April 1957, was of Wagner's *Die Walküre*, the start of a new *Ring* cycle staged and lit by Karajan himself, with designs by the 73-year-old Emil Preetorius.[1] Grafting Preetorius's pre-war Bayreuth style on to the new Bayreuth style which he and Karajan had to some extent absorbed from Wieland Wagner was not without its problems, but it was a cycle, imaginatively if occasionally rather too broodingly lit, which would change and develop during Karajan's time in Vienna. Being a conductor-director – for Ingmar Bergman, a Karajan admirer in these years, the operatic 'ideal'[2] – had its advantages.

In rehearsal, the Vienna Philharmonic was reminded how intelligently and economically Karajan worked, moving through the score in what seemed to be an almost random way: touching on this passage, waving aside that ('Das nehme ich Ihnen ab ['That I relieve you of']') and always homing in on the difficult corners, the awkward transitions, the false climaxes and the real ones. Older players were reminded of Toscanini: both the method and, to some extent, the gestures.

The second new production a fortnight later was Verdi's *Otello*. Two days before the opening, Karajan announced that since he knew the score and the players knew the score, the orchestra would not be required for the dress rehearsal, a piano would suffice.[3] The orchestra was flattered but the singers and technicians were not so certain. On the opening night, Karajan's pre-recorded storm in the opening scene largely eclipsed Verdi's own.

There were other problems. Karajan insisted on *Otello* being sung in Italian, which came as a shock both to the Viennese audience and to those members of the company who found themselves without a part. The only Viennese singer among the principals was the Desdemona, Leonie Rysanek. When she discovered that the Emilia, a guest from Italy, was being paid three times as much as she was, she confronted Karajan, though to no avail. Singers, he said, had to adapt to the new dispensation; members of the company could not necessarily expect parity with unsalaried freelance guests. He then rubbed salt into the wound by telling Rysanek she was not a big enough star to be asking for extra money. (A somewhat gratuitous rebuff. As Callas would shortly discover, Karajan was not prepared to be held to ransom by 'star' singers either.)

What upset the Viennese most, however, was Karajan's decision to give the role of Iago to Anselmo Colzani, a middle-ranking baritone from Bologna, rather than to their own local favourite Paul Schöffler. It upset the orchestra, too; the more so when it developed, in typical Karajan fashion, into an eleventh-hour crisis over the renewal of Schöffler's contract.

Schöffler was rehearsing Strauss's *Capriccio* when a call eventually came instructing Mattoni to sign the contract on Karajan's behalf. When he reached La Roche's line 'Was wisst ihr Knaben von meinen Sorgen?' ['What do you boys know of my cares?'] he strode down to the footlights and sang the line to the Vienna Philharmonic with a particularly marked emphasis. They loved it. As the Philharmonic's resident poetaster Camillo Öhlberger puts it in his poem 'Herr Kunibald plays *Capriccio*':

> The scene goes on and we detect
> In Schöffler's voice there lingers yet
> A sense of what he's fought and done
> Whilst a hundred hearts rejoice as one.[4]

A good general knows when to withdraw. When Karajan revived *Otello* for the Vienna Festival two months later, Schöffler was his Iago.

What the singers most feared was unemployment. In fact, Karajan dismissed – or was able to dismiss – very few and persisted with some he had not much liked in the first place, even though they were now getting on in years. Anton Dermota was one such singer. Dermota rather doted on Karajan, though as he admits in his memoirs, 'I was never Karajan's favourite tenor.' The poor man was certainly accident-prone where Karajan was concerned. Recording Tamino for him in Vienna in 1950, he got his dates mixed up and had to run panting to the microphone. Years later, Karajan booked him to sing the tenor role in Mahler's *Das Lied von der*

Erde but on this occasion Karajan himself failed to turn up to rehearsal (his first daughter had just been born) and the performance had to be done without rehearsal.

The worst incident took place in 1961. Shortly after Dermota had been cast in what was possibly Karajan's most famous production in Vienna, Debussy's *Pelléas et Mélisande*, Dermota spotted his daughter in the centre of Vienna, wondered why she was not in college, ran across the road to talk to her, and was hit by a tram. Karajan sent him flowers but the role of Pelléas went elsewhere.

By the early 1960s, Dermota's voice had become vulnerable to the slightest infection. There was a particularly desperate performance of *Don Giovanni* after he had taken over the role of Don Ottavio from Fritz Wunderlich. Graziella Sciutti would remember the occasion all too vividly:

Dermota was obviously not well, even before he got to 'Il mio tesoro'. When the aria started – well, he was in real difficulty. We were all standing there on the stage absolutely frigid with fear for him. We knew Karajan didn't much like him and was only keeping him on for old times' sake. He could have sunk him there and then. In fact, Karajan completely reshaped the aria. Where there was a sustained note in the voice or a long phrase to negotiate he moved the tempo on. Every time there was a break in the phrasing, he made space for Dermota to breathe as fully as possible. I can tell you, Dermota wouldn't have finished the aria with any other conductor. It was a miracle of conducting, not least because if you hadn't known what was going on you probably wouldn't have noticed that anything was wrong.[5]

Dermota alludes to the incident in his memoirs; a cautionary tale, he says, about the need to know when to cancel and when to soldier on. Afterwards, he apologised to Karajan who simply said, 'But we are all only human'.[6]

'Human' was the last epithet some would have thought of applying to Karajan in the Vienna years as the packed schedules began to take their toll. His assistant Peter Busse remembers a time of increasing frenzy, of respect mingled with fear. Word that 'the boss is back, Karajan is here' would 'pass along the hallways of the opera house like an ice-cold wind'.[7] Perhaps that is what Vienna needed. Mahler, who presided over the century's first 'golden age' in Vienna was even more of a despot, though it is doubtful whether he – or anyone – was ever so dauntingly active a director as Karajan. Winthrop Sargeant would report in an article worthy of the pen of Stendhal:

Dressed in his slacks and sweater, he looks more like a choreographer than like a conductor. He walks up and down the aisles, nervously appraising the action from different parts of the house. He vaults over the orchestra-rail like a twenty-year-old to seat himself momentarily at the piano, where he thumps out a passage while the regular rehearsal pianist stands deferentially aside.

Leaving the piano, he bounds over the footlights on to the stage to correct a flaw in the action; he perches on top of one prop or another to scrutinise the stage; he prowls around the leading soprano while she sings, studying her from as near as six inches and sometimes stopping the performance to pantomime her role so that she will understand it better; and he assumes the role of one singer so that he may get the response he wants from another, grunting out lines in a typical conductor's voice and putting on a demonstration of acting that shows him to be a better practitioner of this craft than most singers are.

Karajan's father, one recalls, had wanted to be an actor, before medicine was put in his way.

During the whole spectacle, von Karajan preserves the aspect of a restless athlete. His slim body is always in motion. When he is not actually taking part in the action, or correcting a misplaced smile or frown or wave of a hand or movement of a torso, he is stretching himself restlessly, or leaping from one place to another, or clasping and unclasping his hands, or waving them in front of his chest – behaving generally like a healthy caged animal.

And there were the clothes:

The sweaters change with every rehearsal; he has scores of them, turtle-neck and open-neck, in all sorts of designs and colours. For dress rehearsals, he puts on a lily-white turtleneck, which, in its informal way, is the last word in sartorial splendour. The sweaters strike a note of violent contrast in a scene where every man is wearing an ordinary suit, and with them he usually wears loud plaid sport socks and moccasins, which along with his deeply-tanned face and hands, enhance the out-of-doors, man-of-action effect. This effect is somewhat theatrical, but then von Karajan is as much a man of the theatre as any actor . . .[8]

There was, however, a price to be paid for this incessant activity. There were times during the Vienna years when Karajan took himself close to the edge physically and psychologically. Music remained his profession and – along with skiing, sailing, flying and hatha yoga – his therapy too. But stress is an insidious thing and it did not take much to activate the old neuroses: the insecurity, the bitter resentment at what he considered to be past slights and unrighted wrongs. Once, in the foyer of the Vienna Opera, he walked straight past his old boss Heinz Tietjen. Egon Seefehlner, who had greeted Tietjen, assumed Karajan had not seen him.

'Herr von Karajan, that was Tietjen.'

'I know,' grunted Karajan. 'There's no way that I'm going to talk to that man.'[9]

Karajan's home when he was in Vienna was a farmhouse at Mauerbach. It was a splendid retreat with its paddocks, pools, woodlands, and abundance of wildlife. Deer would occasionally startle visitors by peering through the windows. But even this space was not sacrosanct. The Viennese wanted to know whose house it was, who paid for it, and what status it had with the tax authorities. Nor was it in all respects an idyllic place for Karajan himself. According to one insider, it was a place to which he would retire every so often for 'a great explosion of the nerves'. For a time, drink was a problem. 'He felt himself going,' says another close observer. But Karajan being Karajan, he never did quite 'go'. Nor did he overreact. He continued to drink wine (usually in a glass slightly larger than everyone else's), vodka, and whisky in moderation until the end of his life.

His relations with the Vienna Philharmonic at this period seem to have been workmanlike and productive, though occasionally tinged with unease. Lie-abeds resented his fondness for early morning rehearsals; others relished the freedom to be free by eleven o'clock. Early rehearsals after late-running performances the night before could be wearing, of course. Tired players and a stressed-out director trapped in the State Opera's noisy and airless sixth floor rehearsal room was not the best recipe for trouble-free music-making. On one occasion Karajan snapped at the double-basses over a passage in *Götterdämmerung*. Ludwig Streicher, a great bass player, had read Karajan's mood and was waiting for him like a coiled snake.

'Herr Karajan, if you would care to give us a clear upbeat, we will be happy to show you what we can really do.'

Karajan muttered something under his breath, gave an exceptionally clear upbeat, and the basses responded with the utmost eloquence. After the rehearsal, Streicher said to Karajan: 'You know, we don't really need an upbeat there.' Walter Weller, who tells the story, said that Karajan enjoyed that. He understood the game. It shook him out of his bad mood.

Weller respected Karajan 'a thousand per cent' but never entirely fathomed his tactics. Up, at the age of twenty-one, for the post of leader of the Vienna Philharmonic, he was auditioned by Karajan:

He asked me to play the solos from *Ein Heldenleben*. He played the piano. At one point he jumped three bars. To this day, I don't know whether it was deliberate. I never had the courage to ask! But I could see from the expression on his face that he was thinking, 'This is my man'.[10]

Weller's impression was that Karajan had a limited knowledge of the techniques of string playing:

He would occasionally make suggestions which where physically impossible to carry out. But it didn't matter. We knew exactly what he wanted, so we gave it him. But he also taught us things: for instance, how to prepare and play the perfect pizzicato. It was all to do with listening and timing. 'Prepare yourself and listen for a moment,' he would say, 'and then you don't need me at all.'[11]

As always, Karajan's habit of conducting concerts with closed eyes bothered players until they got used to it and re-learned the art of listening to one another. In the opera house it was different. There the eyes were open all the time. But the players still had to listen and stay awake. Karajan never beat rests. He also frequently grabbed the telephone in mid-performance to give instructions to the stage crew. This was not a conductor, recalls Otto Strasser, with whom one sat 'uncaring at one's desk'.

Unlike many conductors, including Toscanini and Furtwängler, Karajan never reacted to players' mistakes. To do so, he reasoned, would be to increase the tension and risk further upset. He was also, says Strasser, unsparing of his own energies:

In the actual performance, especially in operas, an unbelievable power and tension radiated from him. I always saw him from very close at hand: the muscles of his conducting arm were often as tense as they could be. He suffered sometimes from painful cramps in the hand, which he overcame with great difficulty. He never spared himself when standing on the rostrum; indeed, I often heard him make highly critical remarks about conductors who sat to conduct.[12]

The shrewdness of Strasser's mind and the sheer length of his service (1922–67) enabled him to 'place' conductors in some kind of proper musical and historical perspective. His memoirs also help correct misapprehensions. He denies, for instance, that Karajan was unreceptive to the emotional values in the music he conducted. Karajan's first concert with the Vienna Philharmonic in 1957 was given over, not surprisingly, to Bruckner's Eighth Symphony. Strasser recalls a rehearsal full of explanatory asides: 'The upbeat here, please, especially arduous' or 'The beauty of this passage must be heard to lie in its sense of resignation.'[13]

*

The 1957 June Festwochen brought Karajan's debut season in Vienna to a more spectacular close than many had been predicting. The German repertory looked safe and occasionally exciting, and the Italian was a good deal more than that. Hearing *Don Giovanni* and *Aida* in Italian after so many years in German translation, wrote *Opera*'s Christopher Raeburn, 'had the effect of a hazy lantern slide being jogged into focus'.[14] Karajan conducted a brilliant *Carmen* with the principals singing in French and the chorus in German. There were some interesting collisions en route ('Toreador' sounding against 'Stolz in der Brust') but it was a *Carmen* which revealed how by merely appearing in the pit Karajan could banish routine and transform a potentially drab evening into an arresting one.

He came a cropper, however, over *La traviata*. This was a production, borrowed in part from La Scala, Milan, which should have starred Callas in the title role. Stories of the refusal of the State Opera to pay Callas's fee took the local and international press by the ears and became, in Jürgen Kesting's phrase, 'embellished like a baroque aria'. One newspaper gave a graphic account of an enraged Karajan tearing up Callas's contract in his office. In fact, no such contract ever existed. In the heady aftermath of the Vienna performances of *Lucia di Lammermoor*, Karajan had floated the idea of bringing the La Scala *La traviata* to Vienna. Callas had agreed (verbally) but others were not so sure. Visconti, whose staging this originally was, was furious that Giulini was not being invited to conduct the production he had helped create. In a long letter to Callas's husband, Meneghini, he railed against Karajan, talking melodramatically about a return to 'the spirit of 1848' when the Austrians governed Milan. Meanwhile, Meneghini, whose life was now largely given over to dreaming of dollar bills, had decided to up his wife's fee from $1600 a performance to $2100, a hike of thirty per cent over and above the top rate paid by Vienna to La Scala artists. No one, from the Finance Minister downwards, was going to wear that. In the end, Karajan went ahead without Callas, using the La Scala sets, a stand-in producer, and a cast led by Virginia Zeani, Gianni Raimondi, and Rolando Panerai. The result was an unmitigated disaster. Faced with an inadequate cast, a disembowelled production, and a drama he did not care for anyway, Karajan turned a tragedy into a tournament.

*

From Vienna, Karajan travelled to Salzburg for his first festival as Artistic Director. It offered a richly varied programme with a dazzling roster of artists in the traditional Salzburg style. The programme had Karajan's fingerprints all over it; but, then, how else does one run a festival? The best of the great international festivals have always been private parties masquerading as public events. The conductors included Böhm, Kubelik, Mitropoulos, Keilberth, Szell, and van Beinum, all men, in one way or another, whom Karajan admired. Klemperer, too: Karajan had done him the singular honour of asking him to conduct the opening concert. In the event, he was too ill to travel, and Karajan was forced to deputise. There were other tributes to old friends and revered colleagues. The chamber groups included the Dennis Brain Wind Ensemble and the Lucerne Festival Strings. There were instrumental recitals by Mainardi, Milstein, and Clara Haskil; *Liederabende* by Seefried, Schwarzkopf, Dermota, della Casa, and Fischer-Dieskau.

Because of Klemperer's cancellation, Karajan had found himself conducting the Vienna Philharmonic and the Berlin Philharmonic on successive evenings: the Vienna Philharmonic in Bruckner in the Festspielhaus, the

Berlin Philharmonic in Mozart in the Mozarteum. For the press, it was a rare opportunity to compare the two. Both orchestras, noted the critic of Vienna's *Die Presse*, are horses of the finest pedigree; and Karajan, the expert jockey, rides both with equal skill. In the case of the Vienna Philharmonic, his direction is calm and unostentatious. He does not push the orchestra; he knows that it prefers an easy pace and a relaxed manner. The Berliners, by contrast, play from the very edge of their seats. Within moments of Karajan's arrival on stage the orchestra is poised like a runner waiting for the starting gun. And Karajan's direction, for all its comradely involvement, is emphatic and intense.[15]

The best of Karajan's concerts was judged to be the second of the two he gave in the Mozarteum with the Berlin Philharmonic. It was one of a pair of concerts (Mitropoulos conducted the other) given over to contemporary music. It featured the world première of Theodor Berger's *Sinfonia parabolica*, von Einem's Piano Concerto, and Honegger's Third Symphony, *Liturgique*. 'Distance' and 'refinement', noted Karl Löbl in Vienna's *Bild-Telegraf*, had become features of Karajan's conducting in recent times, but here was 'fantastic intensity, utter dedication, and an extraordinary dramatic élan'.[16]

Karajan's operatic contributions to the festival were not, perhaps, among the most distinguished. The festival opened with Beethoven's *Fidelio* produced by him in the Felsenreitschule. It was well received by the German press but to others there was something depressingly formal and triumphalist about the production and about the conducting.[17] The casting, too, was strange. Karajan's Leonore was the shrill-voiced Christel Goltz, with the Italian Giuseppe Zampieri as Florestan. The *Falstaff* was hugely liked by the public, some of whom talked nostalgically of the pre-war Toscanini production. But this was the occasion that prompted Friedrich Torberg's famous jibe, 'A conductor of Karajan's quality needs a better producer than Karajan.' Once again, he lit the production himself, creating some marvellous chiaroscuro effects. But it was a nightmare for the singers, hopping in and out of narrow bands and pools of light in such fast-moving music.[18]

After Salzburg, *Falstaff* transferred to Vienna as part of Karajan's new-look 'autumn festival' at the State Opera. *Otello* and *Carmen* were also revived. Then Karajan was off to Japan with the Berlin Philharmonic, though not before he had made a flying visit to London to hear Klemperer conduct the *Eroica* Symphony with the Philharmonia. It was a visit which led to a famous encounter in Klemperer's dressing-room after the concert:

KLEMPERER: Herr von Karajan, what are you doing here?
KARAJAN: I have simply come to thank you and to say that I hope I shall live to conduct the Funeral March as well as you have done it. Good night.[19]

The tour of Japan was a triumph for Karajan and the Berliners. The programme was more or less identical with the one Karajan had taken to the United States in 1956. There was, however, one omission: Honegger's *Liturgique* was dropped. 'The city is dead and stones smoke, but day breaks and the innocent bird pipes joyously above the ruins . . .'. It was a sensible omission. No birds sang in the ruins of Hiroshima and Nagasaki.

Back in Vienna, Karajan added *Siegfried* to his evolving *Ring* cycle and ended the year with a performance on the stage of the Vienna Opera of Palestrina's *Missa Papae Marcelli*. This was an astonishing event that drew together a number of Karajan's private and not-so-private preoccupations: his interest in the sound and the vague spiritual allure of the music of the High Renaissance, his passion for choirs, and his fascination with 'dark' lighting that was more cinematic than theatrical.

The singers, hand-picked from the Concert Association of the Chorus of the Vienna Opera, were placed in groups at some distance from one another on the stage. Since they were dressed in black and only half lit, they appeared as distant shadowy presences. Karajan, too, was in the dark. Only his hands were lit. (Half an hour was spent on this alone at the dress rehearsal.) Michael Gielen, who witnessed the event, says it was like something from a Fellini film.[20] As for the music-making, it was by all accounts extremely beautiful: Palestrina's Mass beckoned lovingly into Isolde's realm of eternal night.

CHAPTER 45

Incessant traffic

Whether in a period of incessant traffic in concerts and opera houses, his gifts will mature to some philosophical vintage and depth is for Karajan himself to decide.

Neville Cardus, *Manchester Guardian*

During the late 1950s, some wag came up with the Karajan taxi joke:

'Where to, Herr Karajan?'

'Wherever you like. I'm in demand everywhere.'

January 1958 was not untypical. First, there were concerts and recording sessions in Berlin. (There was work on a disagreeably Teutonic account of Dvořák's *New World* Symphony, and sessions for a recording of Reger's *Mozart Variations* which, alas, was never completed.) After that, there were recording sessions in London and a somewhat hit-and-miss concert with the Philharmonia in which a grievously out of sorts Second *Brandenburg Concerto* was compensated for by a very fine Prokofiev Fifth. Back in Vienna, Karajan conducted Bruckner's Ninth Symphony (twice) with the Vienna Symphony, and two performances of *Le nozze di Figaro* in honour of the Mozart bicentenary. During the sessions in London, Erich Auerbach photographed Karajan – now sporting an American-style crew cut – in the middle of an enormous yawn. Legge said it was boredom with Tchaikovsky's *1812* Overture. Tiredness is a more likely explanation.

This was the fag-end of Karajan's hastily extended five-year contract with EMI and show-pieces and collections of orchestral lollipops were the order of the day, music that could be recorded without too much ado and which would be certain to sell reasonably quickly. A thrillingly played and spectacularly engineered 1956 recording of the Mussorgsky-Ravel *Pictures at an Exhibition* had pointed the way, and the January 1958 recording of Respighi's *The Pines of Rome* was every bit as fine. It was coupled with Berlioz's overture *Le carnaval romain* and a powerful but mercifully uninflated account of Liszt's *Les Préludes*. EMI managed to release the disc fairly promptly. *The Gramophone*, lapsing into colloquial mode, thought it 'smashing'.[1]

Equally 'smashing' was a brilliantly played selection of numbers from the Offenbach-inspired ballet *Gaîté parisienne*. This marked Hugh Bean's début as leader of the Philharmonia. He would recall: 'Karajan shook me by the hand, then ignored me for two days, which was just about perfect. He let me play myself in.'[2]

Vienna, meanwhile, had been enjoying its best pre- and post-Christmas season for many a long year. As well as conducting and directing a musically splendid account of *Siegfried*, Karajan demonstrated his good faith by taking over a number of repertory performances with the company: the *Figaro* (previously Böhm's preserve), *Fidelio* (with Birgit Nilsson as Leonore), and two performances of *Madama Butterfly*, a new production, directed by Josef Gielen and designed by Tsugouhara Foujita, which Dimitri Mitropoulos had so rivetingly launched the previous autumn. Sena Jurinac sang the title role and was as fine a Cio-Cio-San as anyone in Vienna could remember. ('Butterfly, would you believe!' she later exclaimed. 'I was not young. I was tall. It was extremely courageous of him.'³) Karajan's urging this fine singer to explore the Italian repertory was one of the early inspirations of his directorship.

In April, he celebrated his fiftieth birthday with a performance of *Otello* starring Tebaldi and Gobbi, with the Argentinean tenor Carlos Guichandut in the title role.⁴ In May, the entire Vienna company visited the World Fair in Brussels. There were performances of Mozart's *Coronation Mass* and Beethoven's Ninth Symphony, an evening of music by the Strauss family, and a staging of *Le nozze di Figaro*. Again, everything was done on the hoof. Christa Ludwig would recall:

Walter Legge had turned up with some pages of vocal ornamentation for Cherubino of the kind used in Mozart's time. Karajan knew about this but as we hadn't met beforehand I had no idea whether we were performing the arias with or without the ornaments. As we approached the first aria, I raised my eyebrows, and Karajan nodded, which I took to mean 'with'! He then simply opened the whole thing out for me there and then. It was magical. There was a real sense of improvisation about it.⁵

After a brief visit to Berlin, 'Karajan Worldwide Musical Activities, Inc.' (Joseph Wechsberg's phrase) returned to Vienna for what would prove to be a spectacularly successful Vienna Festival. A rejuvenated Karl Böhm conducted a tolerably good *Don Giovanni*, a flawless *Così fan tutte*, a superb *Die Frau ohne Schatten*, a predictably fine *Wozzeck*, and an electrifying *Elektra*. Karajan conducted *Die Walküre* and *Siegfried*, took over a seriously tatty house production of *Aida* and turned it into vocal and orchestral gold (with the young Leontyne Price in the title role), and conducted two more performances of *Tosca*, the first with Brouwenstijn and Gobbi, the second, even finer, with Rysanek and George London.

He also conducted the first night of a new staging by Schuh and Neher of Stravinsky's *Oedipus rex*. For this, Karajan had lured the work's librettist Jean Cocteau to Vienna to talk about his life and times. Cocteau, in turn, had trapped Karajan into acting as his public interlocutor. This was Karajan's début in the somewhat improbable role of multilingual chat-show host. To his surprise, he rather enjoyed it.

Later in the year, Stravinsky himself arrived to conduct a single performance of *Oedipus rex* at the State Opera. Though Karajan had rehearsed the work until, in one player's phrase, 'the fingers burned', the orchestra was faced with the old problem of having to cope with Stravinsky's fallible conducting technique. Karajan was in the middle of a Berlin Philharmonic tour at the time, but he stopped over in Vienna to hear Stravinsky's rehearsal. It was just as well. Some of the players were decidedly at sea, including 'Herr Kunibald', the poet-bassoonist Camillo Öhlberger. Having successfully negotiated a solo and several runs, he was busy trying to work out whether Stravinksy was beating in two or in four, when disaster struck. He missed an entry:

> Stravinsky curses: 'Where's the bassoon?'
> For Herr Kunibald – wretched loon! –
> Th'embarrassment's too hard to bear.
> Now Karajan, with gen'rous care,
>
> Gives him a sign the second time
> So Kunibald, with speed sublime,
> Sounds the C and then plays on.
> In later years, he'll dine upon
>
> The tale of this sad scandal:
> Stravinsky flying off the handle,
> And Karajan's great charity
> In prompting him to play that C.[6]

Stravinsky was presumably unaware of Karajan's 'kapellmeisterisch' intervention from the stalls. Aeroplane schedules, international tax laws, and hair-styling, he would later asseverate, are more the modern maestro's cup of tea than anything so mundane as solidly *musical* disciplines.[7] On the other hand, Stravinsky appears to have been genuinely impressed by the choral work in Vienna. 'E peste', he said, was sounded as though the singers really did have the plague.[8]

Caspar Neher was also involved in Karajan's next major project, the 1958 Salzburg Festival production of Verdi's *Don Carlos*. The producer, another of Karajan's collaborators from his days at the Berlin State Opera, was Gustaf Gründgens. Sadly, even Gründgens was foxed by the Felsenreitschule which was fine for opera-oratorio but no friend of late-nineteenth-century Grand Opera. The cast was good, but not that good. Again, it was Jurinac who stole the show with her portrait of Elisabeth of Valois.[9]

Karajan also used the Felsenreitschule for a curiously presented performance of the Verdi Requiem. Vieri Freccia, in one of his wilder moments, had suggested that the *Requiem* could be ritually performed after the manner of a Greek tragedy. Karajan took up the idea but then – typically – did something completely different: he turned the work into a species of *son et lumière*. It was not an idea that bore repetition.

In 1958 Salzburg staged the European première of Samuel Barber's *Vanessa*. It had flopped in New York (when Stravinsky told Auden he was hoping to see a show Auden was involved in, Auden replied: 'You'll never get in. *Vanessa* is on at the Met that night'[10]) but if any new opera was going to be a success in conservative Salzburg, this should have been it. There is a turn-of-the-century setting in a grand house in some unnamed 'northern country', a tragic tale of amorous entanglement, and music that is colourful, bitter-sweet, and – above all – tonal. But, no: the audience sat on its hands.

No expense had been spared. Choreography was by Willy Fränzl, designs and costumes by Cecil Beaton. There were successes for the singers: Eleanor Steber, who had taken over the title role from Jurinac at short notice, Rosalind Elias as the niece, and Giorgio Tozzi as the Old Doctor. But it was a huge disappointment to Barber, his librettist Gian Carlo Menotti, and the conductor Dimitri Mitropoulos. Afterwards, they dined alone in a Salzburg café. And Karajan? There was no sign of him: an extraordinary omission by the Artistic Director of the festival. His claim that he had a personal aversion to the style and manners of the period in which the opera was set was but the thinnest of excuses.

The failure of *Vanessa*, and Karajan's conscious distancing of himself from it, further dented the cause of 'new' opera at the festival and inspired a fresh bout of introspection in the press, 'Whither Salzburg?' The influential critic of the *Süddeutsche Zeitung* K. H. Ruppel put the question to Karajan in Latin: '*Quo vadis, illustrissime?*' Others were more down to earth, notably the writer Kurt Klinger who argued that talk of Salzburg's 'traditions' and 'responsibilities' was all so much hot air. In the end, the festival needed an audience and in a changing world there were not that many options left as to how to get one.

Klinger was right. Like a great restaurateur, Reinhardt had created a particular cuisine in a particular place for a particular clientele. Though frequently threatened with bankruptcy (*haute cuisine* never comes cheap), the festival had survived and flourished. The cuisine could be adapted, but the critics were fooling themselves if they believed that Salzburg could be radically changed and still claim to be 'the Salzburg Festival' the world had come to know. In practice, change – radical change – was never on the agenda whilst Karajan was alive. For better or worse, Salzburg had found its second Reinhardt.

*

After Ruppel's '*Quo vadis?*', an outspoken attack on Karajan's running of the Vienna Opera was launched by the Cologne-based critic Manfred Vogel. He dubbed Karajan 'Rex Liquidator'. Vogel's principal allegation was that Karajan had 'liquidated' the old repertory system in Vienna. But he went further. He accused Mattoni of abusing his position as Karajan's manager by earning commission from singers he managed to 'place' in Viennese productions. Karajan and Mattoni sued Vogel in a joint action, and won.

The two questions raised by Vogel were not unrelated. In an old-fashioned company, a 'second cast' would usually be in place and understudies available. The closer Karajan moved towards the *stagione* system, the more problems there were in covering indispositions and sudden cancellations. As he later said, 'If I have to engage a singer overnight, I cannot wait six weeks for an official decision on the matter.' Karajan never had any problem with his advisers doubling as artists' agents, though after the Vogel affair he took the precaution of redefining Mattoni's role. Mattoni now became consultant to the Artistic Director, a move that formalised his function as Karajan's eyes and ears in the operatic world at large.

Vogel was not the only journalist who was on the war-path about the *stagione*. The heat having gone out of the debate about opera in the original language, attention now turned to the large number of Italian works in the Vienna repertory. According to one disgruntled critic, during the first three weeks of the 1958–9 season there had been fourteen performances in Italian, one in French, and only six in German. What he failed to mention was that if Vienna wanted the best Italian singers it was obliged to book them for the autumn and early summer, either side of the La Scala season.

Karajan's contribution to this further outburst of Italianism was a single performance of *Aida* with Nilsson in the title role and two lavishly praised performances of *Falstaff*. Klemperer heard one of them and later declared it to be 'really excellent'. But, then, like Falstaff, Klemperer was himself in something of an amorous frenzy. After conducting the Philharmonia in Lucerne, he had followed the orchestra to Vienna in pursuit of the orchestra's flame-haired lady cellist.

Legge had brought the Philharmonia to Vienna to record Beethoven's *Missa Solemnis* with Karajan and the Vienna Singverein. For Schwarzkopf, this meant gruelling recording sessions overlapping with *Falstaff* at the State Opera. Karajan promised that she would have time to rest before the opera, but when the time came he refused to let her go. He also pressed on ruthlessly in the sessions themselves. He knew exactly what he wanted and was determined to get it as quickly as possible. The problem was, there were occasions when neither Legge nor the engineers had the time they needed to patch and adjust. The performers, too, became stressed.[11]

Still, all was not gloom and doom. Klemperer's pursuit of the flame-haired cellist provided a certain amount of comic relief. Though Karajan had tried to turn the Musikverein into a fortress during the sessions, Klemperer had managed to effect an entry. Unfortunately, he got lost. The Philharmonia librarian Clem Relf eventually found him sitting in the dark in a room in the basement. 'Stick 'em up!' shouted Klemperer (in English), flashing his cigarette lighter in the gloom, and nearly setting himself on fire in the process. After that, he went and sat on the platform alongside the leader Hugh Bean. It was the ideal vantage point both for eyeing the flame-haired cellist and keeping up a running commentary on Karajan's conducting

After his somewhat summary treatment of the *Missa Solemnis*, Karajan seems to have been in a better mood. With sessions to spare, he recorded Mozart's *Prague* Symphony, a performance of great exhilaration and sensuous allure in which he seems to have been more in touch with his real self. The trouble was, EMI had nothing to couple it with. It, too, had became a victim of Karajan's inadvertence.[12]

Back in London, it was Legge who had to take the rap for the poor quality of the stereo tapes of the *Missa Solemnis*. When the recording eventually appeared in the autumn of 1959 it was in mono only, an acute embarrassment to EMI at a time when Decca was about to release Karajan's spectacular multi-studio stereophonic recording of *Aida*. Worse, the set was commercially uncompetitive, an also-ran in a field that already included electrifying mono recordings conducted by Klemperer and Toscanini.[13]

*

For their 1958 autumn tour, the Berlin Philharmonic travelled south through Germany to Basle, Zürich, Milan, and Rome before doubling back to Paris (where Bernstein and his wife were in the audience) and London, where Karajan had not previously conducted the orchestra. If he was beginning to see himself as Europe's new musical imperator, it would soon be apparent that London was one city which was not yet ready to run up the white flag. Though audiences were enthusiastic, a number of London's most gifted writers voiced their doubts.

There were two concerts. The first was an all-Beethoven programme. The second was a slightly tired concoction of Karajan stand-bys: Mozart's *Haffner* Symphony, the Prelude and *Liebestod* from *Tristan und Isolde*, and Brahms's First Symphony. Since its long-standing animosity towards Furtwängler had not yet been laid to rest, it was *The Times* which seemed best pleased with Karajan's efforts. Here, at least, it was argued, was a conductor with a decent beat, with none of that 'fivefold dithering of stick and shirt-cuff with which Dr Furtwängler used to encourage his men'.[14] Neville Cardus, writing in the *Manchester Guardian*, took a different view of the beat:

The Berlin Philharmonic Orchestra is still magnificent, if not quite as easefully sonorous as in the Furtwängler days. In the climaxes during the *Eroica* Symphony the texture hardened, and even the lithe and round-toned strings tended to sharpen under the sometimes stressful, urgent beat of Karajan.[15]

This was as nothing, however, to the bravura attack on Karajan by the 32-year-old critic of *The Spectator* David Cairns:

Karajan, master of half Europe, has conquered London. At the Berlin Philharmonic concerts last week he drove his glittering war chariot over the outstretched necks of the multitude and they loved it. After the Brahms C minor Symphony such a deep-throated roar went up as can rarely have been heard in a concert hall. You felt that anyone daring to dissent would be thrown to the horns. Through the tumult the heavy brass and percussion moved up and the conqueror, who smiled with his lips while his level gaze took us in dispassionately, celebrated his triumph with a performance of the *Tannhäuser* overture so ruthlessly insensitive that, as I stared at those spidery arms feeling at the controls and the faceless trombones, their yelling bells raised to the roof, images of Attila and Frankenstein went feverishly through my brain. It was superb, irresistible, and terrifying. I was glad to get out into the air.[16]

It had taken Cairns, the sceptical Wykehamist passionate about music, to catch an aspect of Karajan's current mood. Nor was Cairns's review merely a tirade. Point followed musical point with unerring aim. Karajan was formidable, Cairns argued, precisely because 'what may be politely called his limitations as an interpreter are indissolubly linked with an exceptional sensitivity in training an orchestra'. How easy it is to be wrong-footed by him when 'there is so much beauty on the surface and so little music below it'.[17] Cardus had made a similar point when he noted that so gracious a reading of the *Pastoral* Symphony had precluded any communion with the 'sleeping grandeur' of the work's landscape; that beneath 'the finely spun musical surface' there was little sense of Beethoven's religious feel for nature.

Cardus also felt that the reading of the *Eroica* had lacked spontaneity. Cairns sensed this too, but saw it primarily as a failure of articulation and organic growth:

To dignify this bread and circuses technique by talking of classical restraint and mastery of form, as some have done, ignores the fact that classical form is a matter of organic growth, unity of opposites, resolution of tension; that a symphony is a drama, and truth arrived at by argument. Karajan, the Supermac [Harold Macmillan] of the musical establishment, does not like argument and sees to it that awkward facts (explosive sforzatos, unpredicted modulations, extreme disparity of dynamics) are safely smoothed over. There is usually very little inner tension about a Karajan performance. Take away the vote-catching codas and the most striking thing is the lack of incident.[18]

Such judgements, trenchantly and intelligently put, were in some measure just. I well recall other similarly polished and tensionless Beethoven performances – complete with what Cairns calls 'the crafty blaze of sound he rarely fails to summon at the end'[19] – on tour in later years.

Yet what was being defined here was not so much Karajan's style, as what happened to it when important constituent elements became worn or disengaged. Cardus recognised this at the very end of his notice:

Karajan is still young as conductors go (50 years). He has gifts and possibilities seldom shared. At present he is an interesting mingling of virtuoso and serious musician, brilliant and occasionally and paradoxically even pedantic . . . His command and personal power are obvious and potent. Whether in a period of incessant traffic in concerts and opera houses his gifts will mature to some philosophical vintage and depth is for Karajan himself to decide.[20]

The next thirty years would offer a somewhat zigzag response to Cardus's all too pertinent question.

*

After the London concert, Karajan took himself off to New York to conduct the New York Philharmonic. Ever the consummate actor, he slipped out of his conqueror's garb, and chose instead to present the hard-bitten professionals of the New York Philharmonic with a Bruno Walterish air of old-world affability. Webern's *Five Pieces* Op.5, reported the *New York Times*, were played with an 'intense if muted romanticism'. His Mozart was relaxed, his Strauss glowing and easy-paced.

Power being as great an aphrodisiac to the press as it is to the people who actually wield it, there was much fevered talk of Karajan as Europe's new Generalmusikdirektor. Howard Taubman wondered that rival European conductors did not sue Karajan for 'a combination in restraint of trade'. But the New York critics liked the Toscanini-like cut of Karajan's Beethoven style. The performances of the Ninth Symphony, Taubman suggested, were 'brimming with vitality and compassion', combining 'an awareness of tradition with a strong feeling of passionate involvement'. Yet his notice carried a fascinating rider:

One suspects that [Karajan] could approach Beethoven in different ways and fashion convincing interpretations in several styles.[21]

That, indeed, was part of the problem.

Shortly after the start of the finale of the Ninth Symphony a number of well-to-do New York matrons began leaving the hall, their farewells to their friends as protracted as they were audible. Karajan took no notice. That evening, America's most inveterate party-giver, the influential society columnist Elsa Maxwell, threw a lavish dinner party in his honour. Everyone who was anyone was there, including Maria Callas. Perhaps some of the early departures from the Ninth Symphony were heading that way too.

The invitation to conduct the New York Philharmonic had come from Bernstein. Karajan was far from amused, however, when he discovered that Bernstein was making a TV programme about Beethoven's Ninth Symphony on the back of Karajan's run of rehearsals and performances. So peeved was he, he refused to receive Bernstein in his dressing-room after the concert. The breach was papered over during the New York Philharmonic's visit to Salzburg in August 1959, Dimitri Mitropoulos appearing with a musical 'son' on either arm, but for years afterwards the musical world was abuzz with rumours of hostility between the two men.

Back in Vienna, some of the staff were finding Karajan less than fatherly. House conductor Michael Gielen tried to solicit Karajan's opinion on his work, but all Karajan would say, putting on his best Richard Strauss manner, was: 'Splendid conducting!' Then Mitropoulos came to conduct Verdi's *Un ballo in maschera*. Gielen was scheduled to take over the work in repertory, with instructions to stay as close as possible to Mitropoulos's reading. (A tall order given the fact that Mitropoulos was both a genius and a law unto himself.) Karajan heard one of Gielen's performances and summoned him to his office: 'Listen, the Trio. It's far too fast.'

Gielen protested, claiming that was how Mitropoulos had conducted it.

'Mitropoulos is wrong,' Karajan persisted. 'Look at the metronome.'

He then asked Gielen whether he knew Toscanini's recording of *Un ballo in maschera*. Gielen said he knew the *Otello* and the *Falstaff* recordings but not that.

'You must listen to it,' he said. 'It caused me to change my entire view of how Verdi is conducted.'

Karajan's theory was that Verdi's music often sounded glib and superficial in German opera houses because German conductors starved the rhythms. The most obvious way they did this was by cutting short the final beat of a 4/4 bar.

Gielen was enjoined to go away and study the matter.

CHAPTER 46

Three courtships and a marriage

KARAJAN: Why do you have an exclusive contract?
SINGER: Because it suits me. You get better looked after. Cars at
the airport, that sort of thing.
KARAJAN: Wouldn't it be better to pay for your own car and retain
your independence?

In the winter of 1958–9, the real business between Karajan and the record
companies was taking place outside the recording studios. For EMI, Karl
Böhm's precipitate departure from the Vienna State Opera and Karajan's
appointment as his successor could not have come at a worse time.
Since 1950, Vienna, once the grandest of EMI preserves, had been Decca
territory, removed from under the old lady's nose by the Swiss entrepreneur
Maurice Rosengarten. To make matters worse, Karajan's existing five-year
contract with EMI had expired on 31 August 1957, with a negligible chance
of him renewing it on an exclusive basis.

There were limits to what EMI were prepared to offer Karajan, contractually and financially. He, in turn, had good reason to be dissatisfied with
them: with their poor marketing, lax distribution, and a less than first-rate
service from the pressing plants. Nor was Vienna the only problem for
EMI. If Decca now had a legitimate interest in Karajan, so did Deutsche
Grammophon, whose courtship of him during the 1950s had been both
persistent and decorous.

The courtship had mainly been conducted by one of the post-war record
industry's most remarkable figures, Elsa Schiller. Physically tiny (when she
stood up she was often lower than she had been when seated) with striking
eyes, a large nose, and an Hungarian lilt to her voice, Schiller had been
born near Vienna on 18 October 1897. She had settled in Berlin where she
taught the piano at the Stern Academy. By origins an Hungarian Jew, she
had gone to ground in Berlin in 1941–2 and survived in hiding, until the
bombing and the threat she posed to her friends and female lovers caused
her to give herself up to the authorities. From Berlin she was transported
to Theresienstadt where she survived until the liberation in 1945. After the
war, she joined RIAS Berlin as the station's Head of Music, from where
Ernst von Siemens recruited her to steer Deutsche Grammophon back into
the mainstream of international classical recording.

Her appointment sent shock waves through the company's senior management. From the start, male executives tried to oppose or outflank her.

Lengthy pre-meeting anti-Schiller strategy sessions would be held, during which stacks of briefing papers would be conscientiously assembled. But she would have none of it. She herself took nothing into meetings except a handbag, empty of everything save the lipstick with which she would occasionally daub her strikingly thin lips. Time and again, men would leave meetings muttering, 'This time, perhaps. But never again!'

One of Elsa Schiller's key working relationships, first at RIAS and later at Deutsche Grammophon, was with the conductor Ferenc Fricsay, a partnership as close and in many ways as successful as Legge's with Karajan. Fricsay made many fine recordings for Deutsche Grammophon in the 1950s. Unfortunately, he was not an international 'name', nor was he ever likely to be. Awkward as it was for her relationship with Fricsay, Schiller knew that as long as Deutsche Grammophon had the Berlin Philharmonic under contract, but not Karajan, the company would remain compromised: an international player unable to call the shots in its own backyard.

Schiller's principal strength in dealing with Karajan was a singular one. She understood him. One is reminded here of the old Confucian saying, 'The way out is via the door, how is it no one will use this method?'

What Schiller instantly identified in Karajan was his shyness and inner reserve and the dangers these qualities posed to anyone who might try to move too quickly or get too close. She knew he was talented and demanding and capable of swift acts of aggression, like a cat, jealous of its territory or fearful of hurt, which will always get its strike in first. Equally, she knew how loyal he was to those he trusted and to those who trusted him. She recognised that he was worth investing in, not just commercially, but personally. And since the real Karajan was a human being, and not the alien construct we sometimes read about, this was not a bad ploy either. As Schiller's colleague Pali Meller Marcovicz would later put it, 'You had to learn to love Karajan. It took a lot of training, and a great deal of rehearsal, but in the end it was worth it.'[1]

In the early 1950s, Schiller was working in a highly protected environment. Deutsche Grammophon's earliest LPs were virtually bespoke products: elegantly designed with gatefold sleeves individually sewn by ladies working treadles on old-fashioned sewing-machines. Inside the sleeves were LPs whose surfaces were famously silent. Karajan had visited the factory in Hanover on several occasions in order to meet Schiller and talk with the company's Technical Director, Hans-Werner Steinhausen. He would bring his own LPs, play them, question Steinhausen, then sample some of Deutsche Grammophon's latest offerings. He did the same with Ernst von Siemens and declared their pressings to be 'light-years ahead' of those of rival companies.[2]

The LPs were expensive: DM32 initially, the equivalent of the monthly salary of a young trainee.[3] Nor were the most prestigious releases required to generate large sales or huge sums of money. Lifetime sales of around 2000 copies were judged adequate recompense for the privilege of recording a Bruckner symphony. In the longer term, the economics of this policy were unsustainable. But this was not a manufacturing and sales strategy, it was a research and development one by a company which regarded its gramophone operations more as a culturally improving 'hobby' than a mainline business venture.

It was also a case of *reculer pour mieux sauter*. By investigating quality and investing in it, Siemens was laying foundations which in the heady days of economic expansion in the 1960s would give Deutsche Grammophon a position second to none as purveyors of quality recordings to the international classical market. Karajan was well equipped to contribute to this strategy. By 1958, it was simply a question of when and how the final pieces of the strategy would be assembled.

*

Legge was less worried about Deutsche Grammophon, however, than he was about Decca. In the weeks and months following Karajan's Vienna appointment, his advance planning, once so precise, took on a somewhat frenetic air. Though EMI no longer had a big enough annual quota of sessions in Vienna to contemplate making large-scale opera recordings, Legge talked wildly about recording *Fidelio* there (despite the fact that he had already promised the opera to Klemperer),[4] as well as *Elektra*, and *The Ring*. The recordings would follow the stage productions. Later, as the dust settled and *Der Rosenkavalier* began selling well, Legge changed his tack. Sales of 9000 copies in two months was proof positive, he wrote, that an opera set does not need the name of a prestigious opera house on it to do well in the shops.[5]

The more immediate problem, however, was getting Karajan to renew his EMI contract at all. Karajan's instinct, in a complex and rapidly moving situation, was to play for time: delay the renewal, contemplate a temporary extension. Matters were further complicated by the fact that Legge's own contract was due for renewal. This was itself a potentially explosive situation, since there were those in EMI who would dearly have liked to see the back of him. The fact that he was, in the view of many people, rude, autocratic, and in no sense 'a team player' was not in those days sufficient reason for dismissing him; nor, since EMI itself was party to the arrangement, was there any mileage in pursuing the charge that as an employee of EMI there was an element of illicit double-dealing in his selling back to the company the services of his own orchestra.[6] Where Legge was vulnerable – technically at least – was on the question of promoting the work of his wife, Elisabeth Schwarzkopf, and his orchestra, the Philharmonia, during company time when not on company business.

Legge used the situation surrounding Karajan's contract renewal to try to shore up his own position. He told David Bicknell, now Manager of EMI's International Artists Department and Legge's immediate boss, that Karajan had made it a 'condition *sine qua non*' of his contract renewal that he, and he alone, should continue to supervise Karajan's EMI recordings. Bicknell's reply was robust:

The Company has never accepted the stipulation that an artist's contract should be dependent on the availability of one of its servants and we are not prepared to accept this as a condition of the contract.[7]

Legge and Bicknell were as different as chalk and cheese. Legge, the bright grammar-school boy and self-made entrepreneur, up against Bicknell, the public-school-educated gent of the old school, a 'company man' to the very roots of his being, intellectually complacent and politically robust. A healthy organisation needs both, and it is to EMI's credit that until Legge's resignation in 1963 – an event greeted by Bicknell with the remark, 'Work? What work? I fear he will write his memoirs' – it retained both.

EMI was none the less in something of a bind over Karajan. At least, the London office was. In Paris, things were slightly different. Pathé Marconi, EMI's French wing, had often taken a more enterprising line with artists London considered 'important' but 'difficult'. Beecham and Callas had both benefited from its ministrations. During the time the fur was flying over Karajan in London in 1957, Pathé Marconi's boss Peter de Jongh dispatched his recently appointed young assistant Michel Glotz to St Tropez to help sort out the listening equipment in the bay-side holiday home Karajan had recently acquired there.

Glotz, who had spent a portion of his teenage years as a student of the great French pianist Marguerite Long, had already won his spurs in musical management by successfully arranging Nicolai Gedda's first North American tour. With Karajan now setting a course that threatened to take him deep into foreign waters, was de Jongh thinking that this personable young man might at least help get a line aboard before it was too late? There is no evidence that de Jongh had any such intention, other than the fact that the mission was rather an odd one. Karajan was extremely demanding where company equipment was concerned,[8] yet, as de Jongh must have known, what Glotz knew about woofers, tweeters, turntables, and pre-amps could have been written down on the back of a cigarette carton.

Glotz duly delivered the equipment and that – for the time being – was that.

*

During the winter of 1957–8, Karajan's contractual position with EMI lay unresolved. In January 1958 further quakes and aftershocks were felt within the industry, this time from the United States. Abandoning their historic ties with EMI, RCA had signed a deal with Decca. This elaborate game of musical chairs bore heavily on the Karajan situation. In terms of scale of operation in the United States, EMI-Angel and Decca-London were much of a muchness; Decca-RCA, by contrast, was an altogether bigger fish.

In February, Legge let fly an internal memo on Karajan that shows the gall rising:

Now proudly conscious of his unique eminence, and of having more power and authority than any conductor ever had, [Karajan] is out for his last ounce of flesh, both in conditions and for the satisfaction of his ego.[9]

Within the month, however, Legge was redirecting his fire back at Bicknell. Karajan, who enjoyed collecting star pianists rather as the rest of us enjoy collecting stamps or exotic moths, had expressed a desire to make records with the young Hungarian virtuoso György Cziffra, newly settled in Paris after fleeing the 1956 Soviet invasion of Hungary. Bicknell had signed Cziffra, but for HMV, not for Columbia for whom Karajan recorded. In another blistering memorandum, Legge took Bicknell to task for keeping EMI's various labels – 'your ridiculous play-pen' – entirely distinct.[10]

On 18 June 1958, Karajan agreed to a provisional extension of his contract until 31 January 1959. Legge, meanwhile, was becoming more and more edgy. On 4 July he complained that EMI's advertising department, not content with printing Barbieri's name above Callas's in a Covent Garden programme, had now had the temerity to place an advert in *The Gramophone* which bracketed Karajan 'with a second-rate routine conductor whose average sale per coupling is about 25 per cent of Karajan's'.[11] A full-page advert for Giulini was also criticised by Legge: 'a superb conductor with a great future' but still 'five years away from a fame comparable with Karajan's'.[12] To what extent this was Legge's objections and to what extent Karajan's is not clear.

Towards the end of July, Karajan formally entered into negotiations with Deutsche Grammophon at a meeting in Munich, which he asked Legge to attend. This may seem odd, but Karajan had the Berlin Philharmonic to think of. Under the terms of an eight-year agreement signed in 1956,

Deutsche Grammophon had an exclusive contract with the orchestra that included a subset agreement guaranteeing EMI-Electrola a maximum of thirty sessions per year.[13] There were also strong historical ties linking the three organisations; EMI and Deutsche Grammophon had a shared ancestry in the Gramophone Company, for whom the Berlin Philharmonic had made its first recording (Beethoven's Fifth under Nikisch) in November 1913. Karajan was neither ignorant of such matters nor, at bottom, careless of their significance. As subsequent events would prove, EMI and Deutsche Grammophon were to him home and family in a way that Rosengarten's Decca and RCA, its partner across the ocean, could never be.

Legge was not party to the exact terms of the five-year contract Karajan agreed with Deutsche Grammophon in October 1958. What he did know, however, was that the sums would be spectacular. If Fricsay's royalty earnings were as high as they were rumoured to be, Karajan's would be even higher. And so it was. In today's terms, the contract was worth something in the region of £1m spread over five years.

*

There was, however, a complication. In October 1958, Karajan remarried. Ever since he had first met Eliette Mouret in 1950, he had been deeply taken by her, and she by him. Close friends – the Legges, the Waltons – knew of the relationship, others no doubt suspected. (Though not the Italian customs officer who apologised to Eliette for keeping 'her father' waiting while he checked the equipment stowed in the boot of Karajan's Mercedes.) For several years now, Mattoni had been working overtime secretly spiriting Eliette around Europe.

There are conflicting stories about Anita's response. Edge Leslie claimed that Anita had to some extent encouraged the liaison in the fond belief that she was indispensable to Karajan. Karajan, on the other hand, wanted children and reasoned that, in any case, it was better ('more moral') to marry Eliette and have Anita as his best friend. None of Karajan's immediate acquaintances believed he would divorce Anita; nor did Anita who, according to Eliette, had tried to warn her off by alleging that Karajan was homosexual and that he would never go through with the idea of marriage and children.[14]

If Anita did indeed believe this, she was profoundly mistaken. Certainly, Karajan had wanted nothing to do with family and children when he married her in 1942. But the desires of a rising young star of thirty-four can be very different from the needs of a man of fifty whose career is substantially made. This is doubly so in the case of a man who was as susceptible as Karajan was to the influence of those he most admired and trusted. Dimitri Mitropoulos was one such and Mitropoulos had often spoken to him about the price he had been obliged to pay for his own priest-like dedication to music. Karajan would hear Mitropoulos's words keening in his ears: 'I don't have a family. I have missed too much. I tell young people: don't go down this path.'

What was also too little recognised at the time was that Eliette had been astonishingly patient. She had been prepared to wait. Moreover, once married, she was prepared to do what neither Elmy nor Anita had really been willing to do: she was prepared to go on waiting through the long days and nights when Karajan, actually or imaginatively, was elsewhere.

As for Karajan, he was true to his word: Eliette became his wife and Anita remained his best friend. For the rest of his life there were, in effect, two Mrs Herbert von Karajans. Those in the know always thrilled to the spectacle of Karajan bowing to one wife at the conclusion of the first half of a concert in the Musikverein in Vienna and to the other at the conclusion of the second half.

The marriage itself was a somewhat precipitate affair. Mattoni would tell Ernst Haeusserman:

My dear, you've no idea what it was like. Suddenly the phone rang at my home in Rome. The boss was on the line. 'Come at once to Mégève, I'm getting married tomorrow!' I leapt into my car, and was in Geneva next morning. Then I had another call from Karajan. Would I also get a ring – the size was unimportant – and a wedding bouquet. The boss had naturally forgotten to get either. I was a witness, along with two of Eliette's ski instructors. That was 6 October.[15]

Like Karajan's two earlier marriages, it was a civil ceremony, though in 1964 there was a formal blessing in the small country church near Kitzbühel. Thus the marriage would be drawn within the church's sphere of influence; and there it would stay, despite various vicissitudes, until Karajan's death in 1989.

The divorce settlement with Anita was complicated. Having known what it was to be without money, Karajan did not readily give it away; thus, though he eventually provided her with a house and income, there was a good deal of evasive action in the area of recording royalties. It was not by chance that the 1958 contract with Deutsche Grammophon mixed in flat fees with royalties.

The contract was framed to unfold slowly over the five-year period, culminating in its most important element, the first integrally recorded stereophonic cycle of the nine Beethoven symphonies. And here was what would later prove to be the nub of the problem. The costs involved in recording the Beethoven cycle were astronomical (they seriously worried the Siemens board) but so, in the end, were the sales. Ten years after the

LPs were first released in February 1963, nearly a million sets had been sold: around seven million discs. By negotiating a flat fee, albeit a high one, Karajan had cost himself millions of Deutschmarks. Or would have done had he not had the gall and the commercial clout to demand (and eventually get) a retrospective renegotiation of the 1958 contract.

*

Karajan made his post-war début with Deutsche Grammophon in March 1958 with Strauss's *Ein Heldenleben*, a classic recording that, as things turned out, sold rather poorly. In September, he followed that with a selection of Brahms's *Hungarian* and Dvořák's *Slavonic* Dances that quickly became a runaway best-seller. The LP sold 55,000 copies in its first year and like the Brain-Karajan disc of Mozart's Four Horn Concertos would never leave the LP catalogue where it sold in large numbers at premium price for several decades.

The two records make an interesting contrast. The Brahms-Dvořák disc is astonishingly vital and free-spirited. Karajan takes liberties with the music in ways that border on the vulgar: swooning 'singing' string-playing and fiercely contrasted tempi. (*The Gramophone*'s Edward Greenfield cannot be the only collector to have thought that he was playing the first of the Brahms dances at 45 rather than 33 rpm.[16]) Four years into Karajan's reign, the Berlin Philharmonic sounds younger, leaner-toned and fitter, the playing witty and urbane in a way it had occasionally been under Furtwängler, though never with quite this degree of coquetry and Gallic refinement.

The performance of *Ein Heldenleben* also stands apart from what had gone before, but in a different way. The reading, particularly the portrait of Strauss's wife Pauline, is brilliantly detailed. In 1957, Karajan had won for the orchestra a leader he had long coveted, the Polish-born Michel Schwalbé. Karajan had known him from his early years in Lucerne and had begged Westerman to sign him. Schwalbé had to audition, of course; the orchestra's constitution permitted no other way of appointment:

I had to play the first movement of the Brahms concerto and also Paganini's twenty-fourth *Caprice*. I still remember playing the infamous pizzicato passage in the Paganini particularly fast and, instead of using my bow and left hand, I played it with both hands and without a bow. When I'd finished the variation, I suddenly heard someone laughing. I turned round and saw Herr von Karajan with his arms raised heavenward. He said: 'What more do you want? Enough, enough. Don't go on.'[17]

If Schwalbé is one of the stars of the 1959 *Ein Heldenleben*, so are the hall, the superb engineering, the orchestra, and Karajan himself whose performance has a fire and sweeping breadth which results, as Deryck Cooke observed in *The Gramophone*

... surprisingly, not in bombast but in true nobility. In this case, one might say he penetrates through the superficial vulgarity of the work to its underlying greatness ... The bitter-sweet, long-drawn, quiet coda has always sounded sentimental because it has invariably been played passionately, and [Clemens] Krauss's rendering is no exception, but von Karajan, by delivering it with restraint, in a hushed undertone, reveals it as the lofty summing-up that Strauss intended it to be.[18]

Hearing this performance of *Ein Heldenleben* in the knowledge of the letter Karajan had written to Strauss in 1944, one cannot but see it as an act of homage. Here, at last, was that 'circle of influence' Karajan had 'so burningly desired'.

Nor was *Ein Heldenleben* Karajan's only recorded homage to Strauss in March 1959. Between initialling the agreement with Deutsche Grammophon in October 1958 and the *Heldenleben* sessions in Berlin the following March, Karajan had signed an agreement with Decca-RCA to record operas and orchestral music in Vienna. According to John Culshaw, 'the news struck the recording world like a meteor':

I met [Karajan] for the first time on February 3rd to discuss his programme, but most of my energy was devoted to calming the other conductors in the Decca stable, who, to a man, considered they had been betrayed. The fact that Karajan's name would strengthen the name of the label did not strike them as a convincing argument, for they had convinced themselves that his object was to deprive them of their recorded specialities. It therefore came as more than a surprise when they learned that the first work he wanted to record was Strauss's *Also sprach Zarathustra*, which none of them had ever suggested. For the time being at least an uneasy peace was restored, and the Vienna Philharmonic was jubilant.[19]

Decca's Maurice Rosengarten was sceptical, curiously so given the fact that he had masterminded the whole deal. 'You're going to be disappointed in him,' he told Culshaw.[20] Though *Also sprach Zarathustra* was not a patch on the Berlin *Ein Heldenleben* – the Viennese playing and the Decca recording both disappointingly soft-centred – this did not prove to be the case, at least not where the opera recordings were concerned.

Ironically, if anyone was going to be disappointed, it was Rosengarten, since it was Karajan's lawyers who eventually uncovered the scam he was operating over artists' royalties.

CHAPTER 47

Vienna and London 1959–60

The class war is obsolete.
Harold Macmillan, 9 October 1959

Gordon Parry was waiting to meet Karajan at the door of the Sofiensaal, Decca's recording hall in Vienna, to show him through to the conductor's room. As he arrived, Karajan handed Parry his coat. Parry ignored the gesture. Young England was clearly going to have no truck with Imperial Austria.

As it turned out, Karajan had no problem with that. He had his Imperial Austrian persona and he had his contemporary persona. The art lay in combining the two. Where Decca's chairman Sir Edward Lewis, a truly old-fashioned autocrat, shook with paroxysms of rage when the 34-year-old Culshaw made claims on behalf of what he called his 'team', Karajan, most unusually for the time, insisted that he, Culshaw, and the Decca 'team' should be on Christian name terms.

John Culshaw had joined Decca in 1946 after service in the Fleet Air Arm hunting E-boats in an open biplane. His background was Liverpool and working-class, the very reverse of Karajan's. Like Karajan, though, he was a meticulous and somewhat lonely person, jealously guarding that feeling of personal integrity a precocious interest in music had helped form and deepen. He shared, too, something of Karajan's insecurity and his mistrust of institutionalised power. One of Culshaw's first heroes was Henry Gribble, manager of the Midland Bank in New Scotland Road, Liverpool. Mr Gribble ended his days in a gas-filled room, a pitiful image, says Culshaw, of what it is to be 'a marked man in a large organisation'.[1] Notwithstanding Culshaw's own feeling of being a marked man within Decca, he was, after only ten years in the company, the head of a brilliant team of engineers and producers: young, hard-working, inventive, unencumbered by personal ties, respectful of musical expertise but unimpressed by the outsize egos of many of its more eminent practitioners. By 1959, Decca's recordings of *Das Rheingold* and Britten's *Peter Grimes* had already changed the way opera was perceived in the stereo age.

Karajan's début for Decca, *Also sprach Zarathustra*, cost Culshaw and his men a vast amount of time and effort. (When Karajan saw the huge bell Decca had imported into the Sofiensaal, he asked: 'And when do you bring in the rest of St Stephen's Cathedral?') Things went rather more smoothly with Beethoven's Seventh Symphony and Brahms's First: too smoothly, in fact. Over-rich playing and a certain artificial cosiness in the orchestra–conductor relationship gives the readings a curiously bland feel.[2] If there is a winner in this first batch of Decca-RCA recordings it is a wonderfully urbane account of Haydn's *London* Symphony No.104, a work of which Karajan and the Vienna Philharmonic never seemed to tire.

March 1959 was another month in which Karajan found himself facing desperately overcrowded schedules as old commitments danced attendance on the new in Berlin, London, and Vienna. In Vienna, he conducted two Eastertide performance of his beloved *St Matthew Passion* with the Singverein and Vienna Symphony, and performances of *Otello* and *Das Rheingold*. He also conducted *Die Walküre*, with a new young phenomenon, Jon Vickers, as Siegmund.

Three years earlier, Vickers had come close to abandoning his career as a professional singer in his native Canada. An offer from the Royal Opera House in London had saved the situation, after which word of a prodigious new talent quickly spread through European opera houses. The invitation from Karajan duly came, though he kept Vickers waiting in Vienna for several days, with no word as to when the audition would be. On the third day, Vickers – not a man to be trifled with – informed Karajan's office that he was about to leave. The ultimatum had the desired effect. At the audition itself, Vickers was motioned to go centre stage. Since the piano was in the wings, he went and stood by the piano. What Karajan made of all this is not recorded. He listened to Vickers for all of ten seconds, after which he offered him the role of Tristan. Vickers, not unnaturally, declined it.

One might imagine from this that Vickers and Karajan were destined not to get on. The reverse was true. What Vickers had experienced was the ramshackle nature of a system of personnel management that tried (and frequently failed) to serve the whims of a man who seriously believed that he could make good practical use of every second of every working day. What ultimately bound Vickers to Karajan was the quality of the music-making; the trust Karajan placed in his singers, and the level of support he could give them. In Vickers's experience, this would prove to be a far cry from the methods of some of Karajan's immediate rivals.[3]

In May in Berlin, Karajan conducted Hans Werner Henze's new two movement *Sonata per archi*. Like Strauss's *Metamorphosen*, this was a Paul Sacher commission which Karajan had again requested to play with a larger body of strings than that originally prescribed by the composer. Henze agreed but years later recalled the event with ill-disguised disdain:

Herr von Karajan had asked me to sit next to him at each rehearsal, or rather a bit lower down, between him and the leader of the orchestra, so that I could follow his extremely careful work. He rehearsed every single part of the score for hours on end, until every detail of phrasing, intonation, and tempo conformed to his – or rather my – wishes, for he continually asked me questions like: 'Is that right?', 'Is it loud/soft enough?', 'Do you want more crescendo here?', 'Where does the crescendo stop?', and so on.[4]

During the lunch break, Henze was invited to walk with Karajan and Mattoni in nearby Grunewald. A car followed at a discreet distance. After lunch, the rehearsal resumed.

Now each voice, each line, each instrumental group practised its part, while the others listened and studied their tonal and contrapuntal relationship to what was being played before they were allowed to join in. At the end, there stood a serious piece of music, the first part roaring vehemently along, and the second, with its thirty-two short and diverse variations, sounding like a single rapturous choral hymn to Bacchus, over which the conductor had stretched a great bow.[5]

There are composers who would have been grateful to have such care lavished on their newest offering. The problem, so Henze claimed, was that there was no 'magic' in the playing: merely a deep-seated professionalism and a capacity to read and realise structures without leaving anything further to be desired.

Henze also said that he felt oddly bereft as though 'this *Sonata* by young Henze' had been 'assimilated into the work of the great Kapellmeister and his orchestra'.[6] This is an odd rebuke for a creative artist to offer a journeyman interpreter. Once completed and in the public domain, no work, in anything except the narrowly legal sense, is the property of its creator. Still, relations did not immediately cool. In 1960 Karajan conducted Henze's *Antifone* in Berlin (and was booed for his pains), though Karajan is on record as saying that there were times when what he called 'the musical line' was lost in the exotic texturing of the scoring for flutes, saxophones, trumpets, trombones, and timpani.[7]

*

In July 1959, Karajan flew to Los Angeles to conduct at the Hollywood Bowl. 'I like people,' he told the *Los Angeles Times*, slipping effortlessly into Hollywood-speak. 'A conductor who hates cannot make beautiful music.'[8] The programme was guilefully chosen and made a splendid opening to the thirty-eighth summer season: Wagner's *Meistersinger* Prelude, Ives's *The Unanswered Question*, Mozart's *Haffner* Symphony, and Strauss's *Ein Heldenleben*. Again, Karajan was in mellow mood. The *Los Angeles Times* reported that in rehearsal his hands 'moved with the gentleness of a leaf caught up on a soft summer wind'.[9] Workmen, the paper added, laid aside their tools to listen. This was Karajan in Bruno Walterish mood, which is not without significance given the fact that Walter, now a resident of Beverly Hills, was the local conducting deity.[10]

*

The 1959 Salzburg Festival, the last before the opening of the new Grosses Festspielhaus, was a very odd affair indeed. The French National Radio Orchestra was the orchestra in residence and with visits from the New York Philharmonic and Jerome Robbins's 'Ballets: USA' the whole thing had an oddly deracinated feel. There was another poorly received new opera[11] and the dullness of the Vienna Philharmonic programmes was relieved only by a performance under Mitropoulos's direction of Franz Schmidt's *Das Buch mit sieben Siegeln*. As for Karajan, he confined himself to a revival of the 1948 production of Gluck's *Orpheus und Eurydike* and a single performance of Beethoven's *Missa Solemnis*.

Eleven years on, the Gluck was even more powerful and alluringly beautiful than it had been in 1948. Simionato sang Orpheus, gloriously, imposingly, and Jurinac sang Eurydike: as touching an assumption of the role as you could want to hear. The new Eros was to have been Anna Moffo, but she cancelled and Karajan brought in Graziella Sciutti, who quickly found herself embroiled in a religious controversy.

Looking down into the Felsenreitschule from a path above the theatre a monk had spied the young Signorina *showing her legs*. An objection was lodged with the festival authorities and Eros – whose costume had hitherto been confined to a blonde wig, a gold breastplate, and tights – was duly provided with a floor-length tulle skirt. Karajan knew nothing of this until he saw Sciutti shortly before the show. She explained the problem. Karajan grunted and disappeared.

'Now,' he said, returning with a large pair of scissors and rapidly slitting the front of the skirt from floor to crotch, 'work with that.' Sciutti duly obliged, pushing a leg out here, a leg out there. In the end, the performance was more erotically suggestive than it had been before.

That evening, Sciutti remembers, Karajan conducted Eros's scenes with a look of benign amusement on his face. He must have been happy, too, that this would be the last time he would be using the Felsenreitschule. In a wet August, the place was intolerably cold and damp. It was also noisy. The sound of the rain beating down on the canvas cover all but wrecked the dress rehearsal.

At the end of the Salzburg Festival, Karajan joined the Philharmonia Orchestra in Lucerne for a concert in which, most unusually, he had two soloists: Glenn Gould in Bach's D minor Concerto, and Pierre Fournier in Strauss's *Don Quixote*. Since the concert started with the suite from Handel's *Water Music* (Karajan arriving across the lake in a high-speed police launch) he was in seventh heaven.

The next day he was called to Vienna to conduct *Die Meistersinger* in place of Keilberth who had cried off at the eleventh hour. Few front-of-curtain announcement have been greeted with more acclaim than Mattoni's was that evening. Karajan had not conducted the opera for eight years, but a few minor mishaps apart it was a relaxed evening rich in improvised musical delights.

Off-stage, interest focused on the preparations Decca were making to record *Aida* in the Sofiensaal. It was not by chance that *Aida* had been chosen by Culshaw and Karajan. No opera of Verdi's mature years had been more regularly bungled on stage or traduced in the orchestra pit than this; by 1959, it had about it something of the air of damaged goods. It was also politically suspect. In the aftermath of the Second World War, the opera was thought by liberal opinion to have a taint of Fascism about it, a view that conveniently ignored (or perhaps failed to notice) that it is in part a requiem for a classical culture which militarism has brutalised and destroyed. Karajan knew all about the opera's problems in the theatre (Vienna's own production was a representative case) and he was fascinated to re-imagine it in the context of the gramophone.

It proved to be a performance of great dignity and power, but one illuminated above all by Karajan's feel for the audacious delicacy of the orchestral writing in those scenes which are preoccupied with love, death, and vanished dreams. (The scene in the tomb is a particular example of his peculiarly searching way with music that is death-haunted and dematerialised.) In all this, he would be superbly served by the Vienna Philharmonic, the strings in particular, and by Culshaw's production which used multi-studio techniques (Karajan was occasionally obliged to conduct with headphones on) to catch the opera's strange and original mix of remoteness, mystery, and ceremonial splendour in a way that could never be achieved in the theatre.

Decca had assembled a strong cast, though Culshaw had been obliged to fight a fierce rearguard action against Rosengarten over the casting of Radames. Rosengarten wanted Mario del Monaco on the grounds that he was a 'name' who would 'sell'. Culshaw wanted Carlo Bergonzi, as did Karajan. The old-fashioned view that Radames should be an heroic figure sung by a *tenore robusto* was not one, unsurprisingly, with which either Culshaw or Karajan was prepared to go along. After much wrangling, the part was given to Bergonzi; but Rosengarten and his American backers had their way over the casting of Cornell MacNeil as Amonasro. Karajan, who had recently had Gobbi as his Amonasro in the theatre, was less than

444

impressed. 'Who engaged that cowboy?' he asked Culshaw during one of the sessions, a stricture that did not stop MacNeil getting headline billing on the cover of the American box.

Though Karajan was not involved in any way in the technical production of the recording, he was enthralled by what was going on. Wartime radio engineers and people at EMI had always got rather hot under the collar when Karajan started parading his interest in technical matters. Culshaw was more patient. Karajan, he concluded, did not know as much as he thought he knew; but he and Benjamin Britten, another great technomane, knew more between them than the rest of the conducting profession put together.

One or two things did go spectacularly wrong during the sessions, most of them in the triumphal scene. This was an immensely complex operation involving multi-studio techniques and the physical movement of singers and instrumentalists. The whole thing was meticulously planned. But you cannot plan for human inadvertence. Towards the end of a superb take of the second half of the scene, the *Aida*-trumpets failed to come in. Where they were is not clear. ('In another room, playing cards' was one suggestion.[12]) When Karajan, ashen-faced, arrived back in the control room, Culshaw asked him what they should do. 'They shall not be paid,' was Karajan's not altogether helpful reply.

The *Aida* sessions finished in time for him to fly to Berlin to prepare two programmes with the Berlin Philharmonic for a series of concerts beginning on 20 September. The first of the programmes included the Berlin première of Rolf Liebermann's *Capriccio* for soprano (Irmgard Seefried), violin, winds, percussion, and double bass; the second, Messiaen's *Réveil des oiseaux* with Yvonne Loriod.

By the time Karajan returned to Vienna in early October, Decca had completed the editing of *Aida* and had test pressings waiting for his approval. It was a formidable achievement, much of the work done by Culshaw and his men out of hours for no extra money. From the commercial point of view, this more or less guaranteed that the records would be in the shops in Europe and the United States well before Christmas. Not that Culshaw got any thanks from Decca's chairman, who chose instead to carpet him for daring to kick up a stink about an appallingly inept red plastic folder which was being proposed for the 3-LP set by a new cheapskate designer Lewis had recently appointed.

Karajan was not involved in this particular charade. Had he been, he would have realised that where senior management was concerned Decca could be every bit as blinkered as EMI. Karajan's eyes were finally opened to Decca's problems some years later, after Stanley Kubrick had sought permission to use his 1959 Decca recording of *Also sprach Zarathustra* on the soundtrack of the film *2001*. Unbeknown to Karajan, Decca had licensed the tape to MGM on the strict understanding that no mention should be made in the film's credits of Decca, Karajan, or the Vienna Philharmonic.

*

On 17 October 1959, two KLM airliners flew Karajan, Eliette, the Vienna Philharmonic, and three tons of luggage to India for the start of a tour of the Far East and America that would take in seventeen cities, twenty-six concerts, and over a hundred hours' flying-time in everything from luxury clippers to – for the journey across the Pacific to Honolulu – a battered old transport plane leased from the US government by Japanese Airlines.

Tours are often troublesome affairs, but this seems to have been an unusually happy trip for everyone, even for Eliette who was three months pregnant and suffered from terrible air-sickness. She stuck it out bravely until Los Angeles where she took a flight home to Switzerland.

Karajan, a more expert tourist now than he had been with Legge in the early 1950s, got on famously with the Viennese players and they with him. They particularly relished his improvisatory skills and impish sense of fun, more Eulenspiegel than Alexander. During a beer- and cognac-fuelled in-flight *Heurigen* session, Eliette attempted to play a posthorn and Karajan – no dancer, usually – performed a perfectly executed Schuhplattler. At Hong Kong airport, a local band struck up with 'O du mein Österreich'. Karajan listened respectfully, had a brief conference with the bandmaster (who, it turned out, came from Graz) and then, to the delight of the Vienna Philharmonic, conducted the band in a rousing performance of the *Radetzky March*. 'Without fee,' noted one wag. At a reception in Tokyo, a group of players formed a Viennese Schrammel Quartet. For the 'Fiakerlied', Karajan joined them on the piano.

In Japan, where the orchestra gave ten concerts, the television audience was estimated at fifty-five million viewers. It was the Vienna Philharmonic's first real taste of the power – including the earning power – of this newly influential mass medium. There was nothing on this scale in the Philippines or in Hawaii, which must be the most exotic location Karajan (richly garlanded with flowers) ever conducted in but the audiences were vast and enthusiastic. 'Hearing *The Blue Danube* played like this,' observed the *Honolulu Star Bulletin* with pardonable exaggeration, 'was like watching the Ten Commandments being brought down from Mount Sinai.'[13]

The halls were unpredictable, to say the least, but no one seemed to mind. In Honolulu a noisy air-conditioning system had been turned on for the concert itself: 'Everything fortissimo', said Karajan as he made his way to the podium. 'What do they think we are,' he asked, viewing a 7000-seat baseball hall in Salt Lake City, 'a circus troupe?'

The opening concert in New Delhi had been attended by the Indian Prime Minister Pandit Nehru, whose memories of the orchestra went back to the time of a visit to Vienna in 1910. In Los Angeles, a group of players visited Bruno Walter at his home in Beverly Hills. Though visibly ailing, he said he hoped to conduct the orchestra during the Mahler centenary celebrations in Vienna the following June. During this American leg of the tour, the orchestra was in especially fine form; and nowhere more so than in Cleveland where its old friend George Szell was on hand to receive the players. Karajan was so moved by the orchestra's playing during the Cleveland concert that he stood by the exit and thanked each musician personally as he came off stage.

After the final concert in Montreal he again thanked them, though this time he added a warning: 'Now I am your friend. But remember, tomorrow I am your boss again.'

*

The tour was skilfully exploited by Decca and RCA. They had fewer than half a dozen LPs to sell but they gave them maximum exposure. In the United States alone, advance orders for *Aida* were rumoured to stand at 35,000 sets. In a memorandum to EMI chairman Joseph Lockwood on 7 December 1959, Walter Legge ruefully remarked that this was roughly the same number of sets EMI had managed to sell of the celebrated Callas–De Sabata recording of *Tosca* in six years. He also noted that where Decca was taking three months to get Karajan recordings into the shops, EMI had taken the best part of two years to market the stereo versions of such obvious best-sellers as his LP of *Gaîté Parisienne*.[14]

Nor was that all. RCA had sold 5000 sets[15] of the four-disc edition of recent Karajan–Vienna Philharmonic recordings through the mail order 'RCA Club'. This alone had grossed £6400 in quarterly royalties at a time when Karajan's EMI royalties on a back catalogue of more than seventy orchestral and operatic LPs was down from £7888 in May–July 1958 to £3268 in May–July 1959. Not for the first time, Legge went on, Karajan had noted how little publicity his EMI recordings were being given in the United States; or, indeed, in Vienna where (according to Karajan) EMI's own shop near the State Opera stocked virtually none of his recordings.

Legge's attempt to stir Lockwood into action was doomed to failure. Lockwood was coming to regard Karajan as more trouble than he was worth. His reaction was to check Legge's figures (he even rang up Rosengarten) rather than bawl out the sales force. Bicknell had no time for Legge's lobbying either, but, unlike Lockwood, he thought it would be foolish to let Karajan go. It was for this reason that in February 1959 he successfully argued the case for a two-year extension to Karajan's existing contract.

And yet having retained Karajan's services, no one at EMI seems to have had any real idea about what to do with them. Re-recording existing repertory in stereo appears to have been the principal preoccupation. Two of the three proposals forwarded to the repertory committee in December 1959 – Sibelius's Second and Fifth symphonies[16] – were turned down on grounds of cost. Copyright fees, it was argued, and a thirteen per cent royalty (Karajan's plus the Philharmonia's) made the proposal financially unrealistic. A remake of Tchaikovsky's Fourth Symphony was sanctioned on the grounds that this was a popular, non-copyright work which would be recorded in Berlin where the royalty element in the orchestra's fee was much lower. In fact, all three works were recorded the following year: the Tchaikovsky in Berlin, and the Sibelius symphonies with the Philharmonia in London. They are all, to some extent, readings in transition, destined to be replaced by versions which collectors would later rank among the finest of all recordings of these particular works.[17]

Legge, however, was still thinking positively. In February 1960 he submitted a proposal that Karajan should record *La traviata* with Callas, Taddei, and Alfredo Kraus in the principal roles. With the benefit of hindsight, it is possible to wonder whether this was ever a realistic proposal; yet at the time none of the artists demurred. Legge's principal problem was with the company itself. Bicknell queried the proposed terms of Karajan's contract and went on to question Legge's assertion that the Callas–Karajan team had a unique drawing power. The 1954 HMV recording of *Madama Butterfly*, Bicknell pointed out, had sold nearly twice as well as Legge's much vaunted 1955 Callas-Karajan version. This proved nothing, of course. The HMV set – a fine recording, too little remembered these days, with de los Angeles in the title role – had simply pre-empted the market. Bicknell also threw in for good measure the fact that the excellent conductor of the HMV set Gianandrea Gavazzeni had undertaken the work 'for a modest sum'.[18]

Possibly because he believed the thing would never happen, Bicknell gave Legge the go-ahead, albeit on an amber light. But now it was Karajan who began to have doubts. What, he wanted to know, would be the contractual situation if Callas cried off at the eleventh hour or even in mid-session? Karajan's doubts were as nothing, however, to the problems Legge was having with Alfredo Kraus. After issuing a complex string of demands, including his right to hear any case for breach of contract in a London court, Kraus had handed the whole thing over to his manager. Since this strangely elusive figure could never be contacted when he was needed, the deal eventually fell through. As did the entire project. In September, Callas re-recorded *Norma* with Serafin in Milan and Karajan ended up recording orchestral lollipops in London.

*

While Legge and Bicknell were arguing over *La traviata*, Karajan was in Vienna supervising the German-language première of an opera his close acquaintance of some years' standing, Ildebrando Pizzetti, had derived from T.S. Eliot's *Murder in the Cathedral*. The *prima* had taken place in Milan two years previously, with Nicola Rossi-Lemeni as Thomas Becket. Handsomely designed by Piero Zuffi and finely directed by Karajan's old ally Margarete Wallmann, the opera had been extremely well received. Now in his late seventies and a lone survivor from Italy's so-called '1880 Generation', Pizzetti was felt to have rediscovered his musical roots. As a young man in revolt against the new verismo school of operatic composition with its low-life libretti, he had cast himself in the role of religious ascetic. Palestrina, Monteverdi, and the seventeenth century Florentine monodists were the influences he most freely acknowledged, though the famously flexible 'Pizzettian declamation' also owes something to *Tristan und Isolde* and *Pelléas et Mélisande*. Where declamation and arioso failed or became too protracted, there was always the choral writing to fall back on. Here, too, Pizzetti was formidably gifted.

Outside Italy, the temptation has been to play the opera in translation. Karajan decided this was necessary in Vienna in 1960, as did London's Sadler's Wells company in 1962 when, with Eliot's permission, Geoffrey Dunn undertook the daunting task of translating the Italian text back into English.[19] Unfortunately, the opera only really works in Italian. Inspired by the eloquence of Monsignor Alberto Castelli's justly admired Italian version of the play, Pizzetti had lavished great care on the integration of text and music. Translating it into another language – Vienna's *Mord in der Kathedrale* was a particularly ungrateful affair – undermined the lyricism and 'inspired discourse'[20] of the score.

Karajan had no problems casting the opera. Indeed, it was the availability of Hans Hotter, whose Becket promised to be every bit as fine as his Cardinal Borromeo in Pfitzner's *Palestrina*, that partly decided him to bring it into the Vienna repertory. He had dispatched Hotter to Milan to make his own judgement of the work. After hearing it and witnessing Rossi-Lemeni's deeply impressive playing of the role of Becket, Hotter had agreed with alacrity.[21]

In Vienna, the opera was no more than a *succès d'estime*. Yet, the translation apart, the production was well-nigh flawless. Joseph Wechsberg reported in *Opera*:

One had the satisfying feeling that this work just couldn't have been done in any other way. Karajan conducted with great devotion and obvious warmth for the beautiful, lyrical score, and the Philharmoniker played the music with especially mellow sound. The centre of the whole performance and perhaps its sole *raison d'être* was Hotter's Archbishop Thomas Becket . . . The part is made to order for his powerful personality. How he strides without seeming to move his legs, how he spreads out his arms, how he gets up from his chair and moves around. All that has to be seen to understand the tormented soul of Thomas Becket.[22]

*

During a break in the run of performances of *L'assassinio nella Cattedrale*, Karajan flew to London for recording sessions and a concert. Though no one knew it at the time, the concert on 1 April would be his last with the Philharmonia. The programme consisted of Bach's Suite No.2 in B minor, with Gareth Morris as the solo flautist, Strauss's *Tod und Verklärung*, and Schumann's Fourth Symphony. Publicly, it was a triumph, but the reviews were mixed.

Legge, who was worried about losing Karajan completely and who even now was beginning seriously to worry about the future viability of the Philharmonia itself, lashed out at the 'offending' critics. He cancelled their press tickets for the Philharmonia Concert Society's concert on 10 April, explaining his action in a lengthy essay in the programme book. Critics, he argued, were his guests every bit as much as the artists; and he had no intention of letting one guest gratuitously insult another without 'an occasional word of protest or correction in the pages of these programmes'.

Odd as it may appear in this context, Legge had a high regard for the English musical press. He revered its strengths, literary, musical and musicological, and valued the role it played in disseminating interest and educating taste. The *Daily Telegraph*'s weekly Saturday essay was a particular joy to him. On one occasion, he wrote to Peter Stadlen:

If the public that goes to concerts and buys records had a regular diet of one essay a week like that for five years – London would have an audience worth making music for![23]

Nor did Legge expect unconditional praise. When Neville Cardus savaged Klemperer's conducting of Mahler's *Das Lied von der Erde* (his British début in Mahler) at the 1957 Edinburgh Festival, he kept his counsel in trying circumstances: for the time being.[24] Cardus presented a difficult case for Legge. The two men had known each other since their days on the *Manchester Guardian*. Both were intimates of Sir Thomas Beecham. Each knew the other's worth. And though Cardus was as wary of Legge as the next man, there is no doubt that on a good day he vastly enjoyed his company. That said, Cardus's continuing coolness towards Klemperer posed a problem for Legge; as did Cardus's evident dislike of Karajan the man, if not, in all respects, Karajan the musician.

Cardus's review of Karajan's concert on 1 April had begun with a lengthy first paragraph, almost certainly written ahead of the performance, on the Karajan 'phenomenon'. It started:

The Festival Hall was crowded on Friday night for the visit of Herbert von Karajan, the most fashionable conductor of the present day, and indeed a symbol of the present day's approach to the art of music. All over the world people go in herds to see and hear him. He is undoubtedly a master of the orchestra, and he has some hypnotic power, though often he conducts with closed eyes: and sometimes it is advisable for us to attend to him with closed eyes, now and again perhaps with closed ears.

After describing in some detail Karajan's physical prowess on the rostrum, Cardus ended his introduction:

His physical agility is remarkable, spectacular, and fairly inexhaustible. No doubt it all keeps him fit for skiing.[25]

That concluding note of comic bathos was not lost on Legge, nor was the use of the word 'herds' to describe those who attended Karajan concerts with such enthusiasm. Drawing on the full might of the Oxford Dictionary, Legge noted that the word meant 'A company of domestic animals of one kind . . . Said also contemptuously of men'.

Like most of his colleagues, Cardus thought the Bach dull, though he exempted Gareth Morris from his criticism, adding pointedly 'his playing provided just about the only music, real music, we were to hear all the exciting evening'. This, too, touched on a sore point. During the rehearsals for the Bach, Morris had suggested that Karajan was hurrying. Whether this was true or not, it cast a pall over the proceedings. There were few things Karajan guarded more jealousy than his ability to maintain an internally consistent pulse. Legge was furious, Karajan discomfited; so much so that next morning he pulled the old trick of appearing not to turn up by arriving ten minutes late.

The performance of Strauss's *Tod und Verklärung* presented Karajan's critics with a rather different target. Writing in the *News Chronicle*, Charles Reid, never one of Legge's favourite writers, described it as 'the worst performance I have ever heard of Strauss's least worthy tone-poem'. For Legge, this offered a relatively easy target:

I envy Mr Reid his sheltered past, but is such innocence the ideal background for the music critic of an influential national newspaper? Such phrases as 'twilight loafings' and 'Karajan crawl' lack elegance. From his closing paragraph, I have the impression that this critic has left the hall a broken Reid.[26]

Peter Heyworth, whose brief review in *The Observer* was cited by Legge as a model of its kind, described the performance of *Tod und Verklärung* as 'opulent and orgiastic', 'good, unclean fun'.[27] Cardus's reaction was rather more analytic and heavy with distaste. In this 'Technicolor performance' the hero 'died a thousand deaths'; the strings 'oozed out prayerful Schmaltz', the brass were 'compelled to gigantic and resounding rhetoric'. He continued:

I have been told that in Vienna Karajan conducts *Tristan und Isolde* so sensitively that it sounds like chamber music. In this frenetic performance of *Tod und Verklärung* we were given chamber of horrors music.[28]

Of the performance of the Schumann, Cardus enquired, how does one connect the 'intense and masterful showman' who by the end had 'rushed poor Schumann – what was left of him – out of all recognition and countenance' to the artist who has so 'beautifully interpreted Bruckner's Eighth Symphony and whose entirely musical *Die Meistersinger* counts among a lifetime's memories'? The *Daily Telegraph*'s Martin Cooper, a critical heavyweight Legge could also ill afford to ignore, was even more disapproving:

Swooning ritardandos, earth-shaking timpani and trombones and a final coda whipped up to a seemingly impossible speed completely destroyed the work's character, though it brought the conductor an ovation.[29]

Only Peter Heyworth disagreed. For him, Karajan's 'supercharged' performance underlined Schumann's stature as a symphonist and his importance as a bridge between the worlds of Beethoven and Brahms.

It was from such divergent reviews that T. E. Bean, the Manager of the Royal Festival Hall, drew material for his entertaining digest of contradictory opinions, the 'Meat and Poison' department, which appeared on the back of the Royal Festival Hall's monthly calendar. For Legge, though, it was not a game, or a spat about how to play Schumann. It was an argument about the danger of top talent being run out of town.

CHAPTER 48

Salzburg shenanigans

> Will people in the cheaper seats clap your hands?
> All the rest of you, just rattle your jewellery.
>
> John Lennon

Salzburg was *en fête* in the summer of 1960. It was a double celebration marking the festival's fortieth anniversary and the opening of the new £3 million Grosses Festspielhaus (or 'Karajanenburg', as Legge instantly dubbed it). On 25 July a lavish reception and fireworks display was held at the elegant eighteenth century Schloss Klessheim, the very place, ironically, near where the von Einem lobby would have preferred the new theatre to be built.

Next morning, Mass was celebrated in Salzburg Cathedral to the accompaniment of Mozart's *Coronation* Mass. Then, at eleven o'clock, the new hall was formally opened. The music would again be by Mozart: the 'Gloria' from the C minor Mass, Karajan's particular choice. But, first, there were speeches to be heard: or, rather, endured if the look on Karajan's face was anything to go by. He was not in the best of moods that morning. Nor would his mood improve as the days went by. Within a month of the opening of the new hall, he had resigned from the festival directorate.

Two of the speeches were of more than passing interest. The Minister of Trade and Reconstruction, Dr Fritz Bock, chose to defend the building itself. It was a modern theatre, he said, which expressed the sensibility and creative impulse of the twentieth century without indulging in the kind of experimentation for which – in Austria, certainly – there was as yet neither the appetite nor the understanding. The Education Minister, Dr Drimmel, addressed the rather more pressing question of the growing competition between international opera companies for a finite amount of talent, as well as another, rather different question: the dangers posed by what he sensed were changing attitudes towards the arts in the economically emancipated democracies of the post-war world. The new consumerism, coupled with the ever-present threat of nuclear extinction (fears about nuclear war were currently at their height) was, he argued, breeding a new desire for instant gratification in the arts. All the more reason, therefore, for institutions such as the Salzburg Festival to help people sustain 'a natural scale of values' and find their way towards the experiencing of 'more than minute-long joys'.[1]

The Provincial Governor and the Austrian State President Adolf Schärf also spoke. The moment the speeches were over, Karajan sprang to his feet, turned batonless towards the Singverein and released from them a shattering cry of 'Gloria!' It was a public rebuke to the wordy world of politics, a blunt assertion of music's power to wash away speech.

The soprano soloist was Leontyne Price, a black American: another of Karajan's rebukes, this time to provincial prejudice. Nothing was said publicly (though a stone was thrown through Price's hotel window) but there was a good deal of discussion in Salzburg's bars and cafés about Karajan's 'judgement' in such matters.

The Grosses Festspielhaus itself was instantly declared an acoustic success; a touch dry, perhaps, but as agreeable for the singers as it was for the audience. The problem was the size of the stage. By rights, the new hall should have opened with a Mozart opera, but the festival committee could find no producer willing to grapple with Holzmeister's CinemaScope space. So the lot fell on *Der Rosenkavalier*, a famous production as it turned out, directed by Rudolf Hartmann and designed by Teo Otto. Even this, though, was not devoid of controversy.

The first row had blown up when Karajan decided he wanted Lisa della Casa as the Marschallin and not Schwarzkopf. Since della Casa did not greatly care for the Marschallin ('depressing and – just between you and me – almost a bore'²), it was a double blow to Schwarzkopf whose singing of the role under Solti's direction at Covent Garden the previous December had been accorded what might best be described as a 'mixed' reception in the British press. The bonds between Schwarzkopf and Karajan were not severed, merely stretched and loosened. Having threatened to pull out of the 1960 festival altogether – she was due to sing Donna Elvira for Karajan and Fiordiligi for Böhm – Schwarzkopf succeeded in ring-fencing the agreement she already had to appear as the Marschallin in the film of *Der Rosenkavalier* conducted by Karajan and directed by Paul Czinner.³

But the film, too, was drawn into controversy when Karajan refused Austrian Television permission to broadcast the first night of *Der Rosenkavalier* live from the new hall. The refusal caused huge ill will, not least among Austrian taxpayers who had contributed massively to the cost of the new theatre. Karajan's refusal – he later admitted that the protesters had 'a good case' – was based on the premise that television could not yet cope with opera. Diminutive black-and-white images and execrable sound, he argued, served neither the composer, the performers, nor the public.⁴

It was not often that Karajan was lined up with the Luddite tendency, but it would be many years before he came round to accepting the idea of televised opera. As for Czinner's film, it was in colour and in half-decent sound. Like his 1954 film of the Graf-Furtwängler production of *Don Giovanni*, it was an essentially conservative affair: a stage performance shot with just three cameras and very few retakes. According to Schwarzkopf, the only retakes Karajan permitted were his own, in the preludes to Acts 1 and 3.[5]

*

For the 1960 festival, the 88-year-old Baron Puthon had been succeeded as festival president by the 72-year-old Bernhard Paumgartner. To outward appearances, Karajan was in clover. Who better to do his bidding than his old mentor? In fact, things did not quite work out like that. Karajan was an unruly adoptive son and Paumgartner, too, could be stubborn. In a strategically timed aside, Paumgartner told an interviewer:

It was I who launched him on his career as a conductor. I knew that was the job for him. Even as a student, he was a born commander. He had a strong sense of his own importance, he was arrogant towards his inferiors, he had a way of keeping others at a distance, and he was also very clever about treating the right people in the right way.[6]

This was very much the man Paumgartner was now having to deal with: power-conscious, condescending, coolly manipulative. Behind the scenes, the two men agreed about very little: the problems and potential of the new hall a principal bone of contention. One thing they did agree on, however, was the need to face down the press on the actual details of their disagreements. Though Karajan resigned from the festival board on 24 August, neither he nor Paumgartner gave much away.

The press speculated wildly – there was fevered talk of Karajan decamping to Bayreuth or the Metropolitan Opera in New York[7] – but neither he nor Paumgartner was in the business of burning bridges. For the next three years, Karajan remained affiliated to the festival as 'a conductor and producer'. Then, in 1964, after resigning his position at the Vienna State Opera, he drove through a deal with Paumgartner which would lay the basis for his twenty-five-year reign in Salzburg.

If the 1960 festival was a disaster politically, it was first-rate musically. Older players in the Vienna Philharmonic could not readily recall an orchestrally finer *Der Rosenkavalier*. And the *Don Giovanni* was judged at the time to be masterly. Since the producer Oscar Fritz Schuh declined to stage it in the new hall, it was consigned to the old one. But Karajan's choice of opera was interesting. Spike Hughes once said that if Toscanini had had his way, he would have opened the Bayreuth Festival with *Falstaff*. Left to his own devices, Karajan would probably have opened the Salzburg Festival with *Tristan und Isolde*. In the circumstances, *Don Giovanni* was a more than adequate substitute. Joseph Wechsberg reported in *Opera*:

Musically, Karajan's *Don Giovanni* ranks with his *Tristan* and the best moments of his *Ring*. This was a great, genuine Mozart experience from beginning to end: everything was in there, the drama and the conflicts, the terror and the moments of fun, the enormous emotional scale of Mozart's supreme operatic score.[8]

Teo Otto's sets and Georges Wakhevitch's costumes cast the opera in a twilight zone of red, blacks, and golds, the backgrounds spare and jagged in the El Greco style. No wonder Karajan wanted Leontyne Price as his Donna Anna, ideally fitted, Wechsberg noted, to 'the weirdly baroque night-scene' and singing with lustre and warmth.[9]

Disagreeable as much of the festival had been off stage, there was at least one happy extra-curricular event, the baptism of the Karajans' first child, Isabel, who had been born on 25 June. The ceremony took place during the festival in a small country church at Oberndorf between St Johann and Kitzbühel.[10] The Vienna Philharmonic, which Karajan had invited to be one of the child's godparents, was represented by clarinettist Alfred Prinz and members of the Vienna Philharmonic Quartet. Otto Strasser signed the baptismal register on the orchestra's behalf. The slow movement of Mozart's Clarinet Quintet was played during the service and Elisabeth Schwarzkopf sang the Bach–Gounod *Ave Maria*, accompanied on the church harmonium by the proud father.

CHAPTER 49

Controlling interests

Naturally, my dear, we control, *everything*.
André von Mattoni as Herr Cariconi in
Karajan's recording of *Die Fledermaus*

1960 was very much a Wagner year at the Vienna Opera. A new production
of *Götterdämmerung* completed the Karajan–Preetorius *Ring* and cycles
were performed during the Vienna Festival and again in the autumn. There
was also a memorable run of performances of *Tristan und Isolde* with
Nilsson and Windgassen. Karajan's conducting of *Tristan* always seemed
to take audiences by the ears; it had happened in Vienna in 1937, in Berlin
in 1938 ('*Das Wunder Karajan*'), and at Bayreuth in 1952; now it was
Vienna's turn again. In a portrait of Karajan published in *The Gramophone*
in 1964, H. C. Robbins Landon would recall:

The great breakthrough was surely his production of *Tristan* for the Vienna
State Opera ... His concept owes something to Wolfgang and Wieland
Wagner; but the end of the opera, in which darkness swarms over the stage
to obliterate everything except the loving Isolde, is very much Karajan's own.
Apart from the staging, Karajan's reading of this music was, for me and many
others, one of the great experiences of our lives: it ranged from the delicate,
gossamer-fine accompaniment to the lovers in Act 2 to the terrifying timpani
crash which presages the entrance of Marke and his followers – and the end
was unspeakably beautiful.[1]

Fellow professionals thought so too. In an academic treatise written some
years later, the conductor Gianandrea Gavazzeni described the revolution
that Karajan's clear, intimate yet at the same time sensuous and powerfully
expressive Wagner style had ushered in.[2] This 'anti-heroic lyricism' (Peter
Conrad's phrase) left its mark, too, on a younger generation of Wagner
interpreters. Quite how the ideas were transmitted is difficult to pin down.
Though there are recordings to study, Karajan left no annotated scores
and much of what he did was, literally, inexplicable: unclear even to the
instrumentalists themselves. ('Free-bowing', or 'staggered bowing' as some
called it,[3] a technique Karajan adapted from Stokowski, is one element, but
that affected only the strings whose playing was also strongly influenced
by Karajan's use of gesture.) Bernard Haitink has recalled discussing the
so-called 'art of Karajan' with Carlos Kleiber. 'That is the strange thing,'
replied Kleiber, 'he does not appear to "interpret" the music. He simply
plays the notes. It is a kind of black magic.'[4]

Because Karajan was his own stage director, and because his interest in staging and lighting technology was all-absorbing, his Wagner productions were constantly changing and evolving. Writing in the autumn of 1960, Joseph Wechsberg noted:

There was also a performance of *Tristan und Isolde* [on 11 September] that should be remembered for a long time. I was reminded of the great *Tristan* performances of the twenties when Richard Strauss gave incandescence to this score . . . Vienna's scenic changes continue, as in all Karajan productions . . . The silly trap-door in the first act has disappeared, the ship's bow has been moved forward, and the whole act is more intimate and emotional. There are new and beautiful lights in the second act, and the disappearance of Marke and Brangäne at the end of the third is less noticeable. Another year and we will have a perfect *Tristan*!5

During one of the piano rehearsals for *Tristan und Isolde*, Birgit Nilsson's necklace snapped, scattering pearls over the rehearsal room floor.

'Tell me,' asked Karajan, scrambling around on his hands and knees, 'is this stage jewellery or are they real pearls, bought with the phenomenal fees La Scala Milan pays you?'

'No, they are very cheap and ordinary,' replied Nilsson. 'I bought them with your Vienna fees.'

It is well known that Nilsson and Karajan did not get on. Christa Ludwig would later suggest:

Here was the great shining Wagner voice of the age. The fact that Birgit tended to sing sharp when in full flood worried Karajan less than the fact that it wasn't an especially moulded sound, or a very human one. The phrasing was splendid but simple, which was not really Karajan's tipple. Add to that the fact that she had quite a mouth on her, and it was never going to be a marriage made in heaven.6

Nilsson and Karajan seem to have rather enjoyed their verbal joustings, in a grim kind of way. Karajan made some outrageous statements about her in public

I think Birgit Nilsson is a better singer than Kirsten Flagstad ever was. And who made Nilsson what she is today? We, at the Vienna Opera! Before she came to Vienna she was nobody!7

and some grimly comic ones in private. (Of these, the remark about Nilsson being able to play Scarpia 'without make-up' is either the funniest or the nastiest, depending on whose side you are on.) Nilsson could be equally withering. In 1995, after Karajan's mortal remains had been safely stowed in Anif churchyard, she gave an interview to *Der Spiegel*:

NILSSON: He tried to kill me many times.

DER SPIEGEL: Sorry?

NILSSON: With the orchestra! Singers who were in disfavour with the maestro were rushed through their roles at enormous speeds. He allowed you no time to produce a beautiful tone. When I was sitting in the dressing-room listening to the performance over the loudspeakers, I could hear immediately whom he particularly hated or cherished. I swear it.

DER SPIEGEL: What made Karajan angry?

NILSSON: Resistance.[8]

On an earlier occasion, Nilsson had said, 'I loved to sing with him when he was concentrating on the music.' It was the power play and Karajan's preoccupation with 'black lighting' – 'he liked the stage to be as dark as a mine'[9] – that irked her beyond measure.

*

While Nilsson, Windgassen, Karajan and the Vienna Philharmonic were giving their wondrous account of *Tristan und Isolde* at the State Opera, Decca was desperately trying to record it with Solti and an ill-assorted cast in which Nilsson was pitted against the woefully inadequate Tristan of Fritz Uhl. It was never the smartest of plans to record *Tristan* under Karajan's nose, in his own house, with a rival conductor; and, true to form, he indulged in some not-so-gentle sabotage by demanding (and getting) recording sessions of his own with the Vienna Philharmonic during the sessions for *Tristan*. Karajan would have a prime-time morning session, *Tristan* would come in after lunch, a schedule that involved endless disassembling and re-rigging of the studio. This exhausted the technical staff. Whether it affected the *Tristan* performance, it is difficult to say.[10]

Frustrating as it was to be denied *Tristan und Isolde*, Karajan made several fine recordings for Decca during the summer and autumn of 1960. An LP of Richard Strauss's *Till Eulenspiegel*, *Tod und Verklärung*, and Salome's Dance was genuinely memorable. *The Gramophone*'s Edward Greenfield declared it to be technically one of the most breathtaking Strauss records he had ever heard, a welcome advance on earlier Decca–Karajan recordings which he had found 'rather cold and over-refined'. And he made a further observation:

Karajan always seems to react to the type of recording given him – I tend to think of him as a quite different conductor, Karajan–Columbia, Karajan–Deutsche Grammophon or Karajan–Decca, depending on the label – and I suspect that his listening to the 'takes' as the performance is built up affects the final result.[11]

What Greenfield omitted to say was that the three categories could equally well be represented as Karajan–Philharmonia, Karajan–Berlin

Philharmonic, Karajan–Vienna Philharmonic. Still, the point is an interesting one. It was not in Karajan's nature as a musician to work against the grain of an orchestra's individual sound. If, in addition to that, this most pragmatic and aurally sensitive of conductors was also responding to what he was hearing in playback, there is little wonder that his recordings at this time were often markedly different one from another.

In fact, the very complexity of his recording activity was beginning to unsettle his own attitude towards the medium. As he would tell American journalist Herbert Pendergast:

Recordings have accomplished some remarkable things . . . [but] nothing for me is so exhausting as making records. I may rehearse with the orchestra six hours for a concert before stopping and I am not greatly fatigued. But in a recording you must stop and start continuously. In a way, I always feel as if I am freezing when I record, whereas in the concert hall I am warm.[12]

This sense of discomfiture would lead Karajan to develop new and surprising strategies for studio recording in later years.

*

In September 1960, Karajan spent five days in London's Kingsway Hall during which he re-recorded Sibelius's Fifth Symphony. For the orchestra, it was an object lesson in how to shape a great symphony through the most scrupulous observance of the composer's own dynamic restraint. Karajan, too, was still learning. Trumpeter Philip Jones would recall watching him studying his own arm: experimenting with the precise relationship between the movement of arm, hand, and baton; assessing the quality of the attack, the dynamic response, he was drawing from the orchestra.

He also made a superb selection of 'Ballet Music from the Operas' during the sessions, and a disc of musical lollipops 'Philharmonia Promenade Concert' which is one of the most joyous and stylish things he and the Philharmonia did together. They had always got on well in the recording studio; now the atmosphere was even more free and easy. Though Karajan took immense trouble over the Sibelius, everything else was recorded in a slightly crazy end-of-term holiday mood. Legge produced as rigorously as ever. Suvi Raj Grubb remembers the instructions being rapped out: 'Horn crack, 10 bars before letter C.' 'Oboe intonation doubtful 3 after D.' 'Ensemble is suspect for three bars after G.' 'Take 5 is the master up to letter K – cover the horn crack with take 4.' But these were not normal retakes. Karajan and the orchestra were repeating things such as the Polka from *Schwanda the Bagpiper* and Chabrier's *España* for the sheer hell of it. (Never did trumpets croon and shimmer under Karajan's direction as they do here in the final climax of *España*.) Sometimes he would start the piece off and then monitor things from the control room, sitting alongside Legge and recording engineer Douglas Larter. (The recordings are spectacularly good.)

It has been said that this was rather a 'tame' ending to what had been a richly productive partnership.[13] But that is to take too lofty a view of the ground on which greatness can reveal itself. If all Sir John Barbirolli's recordings were lost except that of Lehár's *Gold and Silver* Waltz, there would be reason enough to say, 'Now, *there* was a conductor!' And here, in item after item, there is reason to exclaim, 'What an orchestra! And what a conductor!'

This is the Philharmonia at the very peak of its powers, corporately and individually. The ensemble is extraordinary, whether it is in this dazzling, sunlit account of *España* (in a different league from the lumpy Vienna Philharmonic playing on Karajan's 1947 recording of the piece) or the brilliant mimicry of strings and winds in what must be the most gossipy of all recordings of the *Tritsch-Tratsch* Polka. For sheer dazzlement of sound, the polka from *Schwanda the Bagpiper* is unforgettable. Yet the sound – the string sound in particular – changes from track to track, sumptuous in Suppé, chastely beautiful in Waldteufel. And there are the individual voices, too: the exquisitely shaped violin solo of Hugh Bean in the overture to *Orpheus in the Underworld*, the gamy interventions of bassoonist Cecil James in the two Chabrier pieces, and the wonderful playing of Dennis Brain's successor Alan Civil in the preamble to Waldteufel's *Skaters' Waltz*.

Suvi Raj Grubb remembers marvelling at the Waldteufel, Karajan at his elegant, stylish best: the Viennese waltz rechannelled through a specifically French sensibility. It tells us much about Karajan's instincts and predilections; it also illustrates to perfection what Legge meant when he said he wanted his orchestra to have not 'a style' but 'style'.

But what did Legge think, seeing his protégé in party mood? The players themselves had long since been aware that Karajan was slipping the leash, and not simply because of the jokes he occasionally made at Legge's expense. (Summoning Legge from the control room with a wolf whistle or, when stopped in mid-take, dangling the telephone in front of the orchestra and announcing 'His Master's Voice'.) Grubb would later observe:

Karajan listened courteously to Legge's comments on the performance but stiffened noticeably when he tried to influence the interpretation. In a mixture of German and English he would say '*Ja, ja* – of course – *natürlich*', without paying any real attention to what Legge said.[14]

There can be little doubt that by 1960 Karajan had wearied of playing Eliza Doolittle to Legge's Professor Higgins.

*

461

Two months later, EMI began seriously to confront the question of their future relationship with Karajan. A decision needed to be taken by February 1961 as to whether or not the company was willing to sign a further three-year non-exclusive contract to run from 1961 to 1964. Bicknell's briefing paper makes baffling reading. It shows a total paucity of imagination on the key question of repertory – he seriously wonders what they might 'do' with Karajan – yet it is immensely shrewd on the strategic reasons for keeping Karajan on their books:

These appointments [Vienna, Salzburg Festival, Berlin] give him an immense power of patronage as the engagement of soloists, both vocal and instrumental, in connection with these institutions is in his hands and, in common with all leading conductors who have held such appointments, it is at his discretion to channel established and particularly rising artistes to the gramophone company with whom he is principally associated. Moreover, he is a most enterprising record-maker and has proved his mastery of this field by the long line of records he has made for us and his recent recordings of *Aida* and *Die Fledermaus* for Decca.[15]

Bicknell also made another important observation:

He is the only conductor in his fifties of international stature. There is no young conductor approaching his eminence and he is at least twenty years younger than older conductors of equal eminence.[16]

On this latter point, Legge absolutely assented. Returning from Berlin where he had been recording Bartók's *Music for Strings, Percussion, and Celesta* with Karajan,[17] he drafted a memorandum, copied to Bicknell, in which he noted:

Even since we met two weeks ago, the conductor situation has changed considerably. Mitropoulos has died. Reiner has had a heart attack, and since he has resigned from the Chicago Symphony Orchestra it may well be that he will not conduct or record again. I would not myself count on Klemperer for much work after the 1961–62 season: from occasional recent remarks I suspect that he is considering retiring. It cannot be long before Monteux, Stokowski, Knappertsbusch, Walter – and three or four others – will die and leave Karajan as the most popular and successful conductor in the world. His [Berlin Philharmonic] tour of Germany, Switzerland and Milan, which finished last week, was such a success that most of the concerts could have been sold out three times over. We shall never forgive ourselves if we fail to keep him for a substantial amount of work in the next two years, with a long-term view of getting him back exclusively.[18]

Stokowski and Klemperer proved to have more staying power than Legge anticipated, but his diagnosis was broadly correct. As for Karajan's near contemporaries, Keilberth and Wand were virtually unknown outside

Germany, Solti's career had been slow to ignite, neither Giulini nor Kempe appeared to have had any real desire to run large musical institutions, Fricsay was mortally ill, and Cantelli was dead.

Unfortunately for Legge, no deal with Karajan was closed, despite Legge's own best efforts. Part of the trouble was the United States. Karajan blamed EMI for their poor market penetration there, while EMI in London was up against an A&R department at Capitol Records which refused to accept that Karajan was in the same league as the 'great masters': Toscanini, Klemperer, Furtwängler and the like.[19]

Between 1961 and 1963, when Karajan finally signed a five-year exclusive contract with Deutsche Grammophon, numerous proposals were aired. Some were accepted by EMI's classical repertory committee but turned down by Karajan (Orff's *Carmina burana* and *Catulli carmina* and Rimsky-Korsakov's *Scheherazade*), some remained in limbo, others were rejected by the committee. There was a particular reluctance to let Karajan record twentieth century repertory. *Oedipus rex* was proposed but given instead to Colin Davis and all the Shostakovich suggestions – the Fifth, Eighth, and Tenth symphonies – were turned down. John Whittle, Manager of the UK Classical Division, stated that he 'did not see Karajan as a Shostakovich conductor'.[20]

'Too esoteric' was the term used by the committee to sum up its view of many of the Legge–Karajan submissions. Legge countered with an idea which curiously anticipates Deutsche Grammophon's 1994 anthology *Adagio*, a disc to be called *Moments of Enchantment*. It was never made. Nor was a shrewdly planned disc of orchestral Scherzi. These sops to the populists apart, Legge's plans were full of pith and interest. In addition to pushing the Shostakovich idea, he proposed a number of relatively unfamiliar works for which he knew Karajan had a great affection, including Dohnányi's Suite in F sharp minor and Rachmaninov's Second Symphony. In April 1962, he also proposed making what would have been the first stereophonic studio recording of *Die Meistersinger*, with Fischer-Dieskau as Sachs, Schwarzkopf as Eva, either Gedda or Vickers as Walther von Stolzing, and Geraint Evans as Beckmesser. *Die Zauberflöte*, too, was mooted, a recording that was eventually conducted, to marvellous effect, by Klemperer.

The problem was that Karajan was over-committed. Privately, he proposed keeping the EMI contract alive on a disc-by-disc basis, but here it was Legge who was dubious. Each proposal, he forecast, would lead to an auction, with Ernst von Siemens outbidding EMI for the greater glory of Deutsche Grammophon.

*

Decca's most important Karajan recording of the year, a follow-up to the hugely successful *Aida* project, was *Die Fledermaus*. It was a set which would be remembered for its famous Act 2 'Gala', star singers turning up at Orlofsky's party to perform all manner of improbable things.[21] It was a stunt that had been dreamed up by Terry McEwen, a larger-than-life Canadian who had worked for a number of years in Decca's Public Relations department in London. Karajan seemed perfectly happy with the idea and with a whole string of topical rewrites of the dialogue, including one which gave the normally ultra-discreet André von Mattoni a walk-on part. The cast was very much the Vienna State Opera's own: Güden and Waechter, Kmentt and Kunz, Erika Köth and – a brilliant piece of casting – the house tenor Giuseppe Zampieri as Alfred, the amorous singing teacher. Culshaw's production was predictably elaborate, groaning with 'atmosphere' and special effects, the very reverse of Legge's deliberately restrained direction on Karajan's earlier recording. And, again, Karajan adapted, conducting a performance that is less stylised and a good deal more rumbustious than his 1955 EMI set.

What comes across is a sense of the febrile, raffish, louche, rather bitchy side of Viennese musical life. After all, Vienna *c.*1960 was as rich in intrigue and scandal as it had been *c.*1860. How, for example, might you connect the case of a lover escaping through a garden at dawn, a twisted ankle, and a short paragraph in a local paper with the apparently unrelated case of the soubrette and the unhelpful conductor? Or, put more directly: why, during the recording of *Die Fledermaus*, did Karajan cut the orchestra from under his cheeky, spirited, hard-as-nails Adele, Erika Köth, every time she went for the top note at the end of her Act 2 aria? He did it six times in a row without a word of explanation. Onlookers were mystified. Only the orchestra was smiling.

Cutting the orchestra from under a singer – a favourite trick of Karajan's if he needed to crack the whip – happened a good deal during the sessions for the Decca recording of *Otello* in May 1961. Though the end result was generally superb, the sessions cost Culshaw's team, and Karajan, an inordinate amount of trouble. Ettore Bastianini failed to learn the role of Iago and had to be replaced by Aldo Protti. The Vienna Philharmonic double-basses got into all sorts of trouble in the famous passage in Act 4 where Otello enters the bedchamber, and ended up being put through the musical wringer in a gruelling two-hour late-night session with Karajan. The cannon shots in the opening scene kept going off at the wrong time because the Italian répétiteur in charge of the tape loop could not count, and there were problems with the subterranean organ pedal in that same scene. (It was eventually recorded in Liverpool Cathedral. Karajan later borrowed the tape for the Vienna Opera and inadvertently blew all the speakers.)

When it came to the actual recording of the opening scene, the Otello, Mario del Monaco, was nowhere to be found. Karajan started without him. When del Monaco finally showed up, Karajan willed him into singing the '*Esultate!*' of his life, after which he affected to make a succession of retakes during which he cut the orchestra from under him every time he reached the G sharp on '*L'orgoglio*'. It was the musical equivalent of six of the best. Tebaldi also found herself suspended orchestraless in mid-air during the recording of Act 3. This was for what is known in the trade as 'schlepping': slowing up before a high note.

Vienna lived and breathed Karajan during these years, his every move noted and commented on. Within the musical profession, though, he was not so much the showbiz celebrity as the super-talented teacher with the fast life-style – the kind of teacher colleagues abhor and students revere.

*

Karajan had been Director of the Vienna Opera now for the best part of five years. For all his evident administrative shortcomings, he had breathed new life into the place. He had revolutionised the Italian repertory, directed and conducted a new *Ring* cycle, and made small but appreciable inroads into reducing the number of evenings when what went on at the Vienna Opera was frankly routine and third-rate.

But now a strange quiet seemed to be settling on the place. In March 1961 he directed and conducted a new production of Wagner's *Parsifal*. Despite the all-encompassing gloom, and an ill-fated experiment with the casting of the Venus-and-Mary role of Kundry – Karajan used two singers instead of one[22] – it was quickly judged to be a musical event to set alongside his Vienna *Tristan und Isolde*. And yet neither administrators nor singers could get a great deal of sense out of Karajan about *future* plans. Something, clearly, was afoot that went beyond his evidently deepening commitment to the Berlin Philharmonic.

Crises sensitise human antennae, and Culshaw – who had yet to be given the go-ahead by Decca for a complete *Ring* cycle and who had been further thrown into confusion by Solti's appointment as Music Director at Covent Garden – began to suspect that Karajan was already thinking beyond Vienna. Was he planning his own recorded *Ring* cycle, Culshaw wondered, away from Vienna?

Karajan himself always gave 1965 as the year in which he conceived the idea of the Salzburg Easter Festival and a *Ring* cycle there. But who is to say what was swirling around in the recesses of his mind and what signals were being picked up by Culshaw, whose quick intelligence and high musical ambition were stimulated, like Karajan's own, by a drip-feed of deep personal insecurity?

In fact, Karajan was brooding on something else. And while he brooded, the music-making went on at new levels of intensity. Otto Strasser would recall a performance of *Parsifal*:

We were about halfway through the Prelude and I said to myself, 'My word, this is something special'. As Karajan came off at the end of the first act, he said, 'That was extraordinary. And now they are giving me a new orchestra!' This was the arrangement we had whereby we brought in a completely new set of players for Acts 2 and 3. Well, next day we had some routine business meeting with Karajan, and the first thing he said was, 'You won't believe this, but Acts 2 and 3 were even better!'[23]

Players on stage and in the pit also recall an extraordinary performance of *Aida* during the Vienna Festival that year: Price, Simionato, Vickers, and Karajan striking sparks off one another in ways that had the orchestra marvelling at the sheer cheek, daring, and eloquence of it all. None of these things were known, of course, to those who never encountered Karajan's work in the theatre.

The 1961 festival coincided with a summit meeting in Vienna between Khrushchev and Kennedy. Neither leader attended the special concert in the Musikverein; Khrushchev sent his wife, Kennedy his mother. But Karajan had the thrill of working for the first time with one of the Russian visitors, David Oistrakh, whose playing he had revered ever since Walter Legge had turned up in the late 1940s with a pirate pressing from Eastern Europe of the Khachaturian Violin Concerto. On this occasion, Oistrakh played the Brahms Violin Concerto which Karajan had chosen to preface with Anton Webern's Symphony, Op.21. The Webern caused a minor riot: the Viennese public, as ever, in the radical rearguard of musical thought. Karajan was not much bothered, but Mme Khrushchev – who was clearly unfamiliar with the phenomenon of civil unrest in the concert hall – was reported to have been visibly nervous.

With *Parsifal* in production, Karajan was already deeply involved with plans and preparations for his next new production *Pelléas et Mélisande*, the work with which he had chosen to mark the Debussy centenary in 1962. The man he chose as designer was the 35-year-old chief designer of the State Theatre in Bremen, Günther Schneider-Siemssen. That Schneider-Siemssen was a Mattoni discovery is another typically bizarre fact of Karajan's biography, since Schneider-Siemssen and his family had been under Karajan's nose for the best part of a quarter of a century. His father had relatives in Aachen with whom Karajan had dined handsomely during his years as Music Director there. (Karajan later developed a comic fantasy – he and Schneider-Siemssen quickly became bosom pals – about

Schneider-Siemssen being as food-obsessed as the rest of his family.) As a boy, he had wanted to conduct; but it was Clemens Krauss who, after seeing some of his paintings and drawings, steered him towards design. 'Conductors are ten a penny,' he announced. 'What we desperately need are designers *who can interpret the music.*'

After a period of study in Munich, working alongside men like Preetorius, Hartmann, and Ludwig Sievert, Schneider-Siemssen began a long association with Salzburg's celebrated Marionetten-Theater.[24] 'It took fifteen years for me to get from there to the Festspielhaus,' he would later remark with rueful good humour, 'which is very frustrating when you think that the walk takes a little under four minutes.'[25]

The naturalness and 'rightness' of Schneider-Siemssen's puppets had always been much admired. But it was 'rightness' of a wholly different order which Karajan required for *Pelléas et Mélisande*. What Karajan wanted was transparency of image and truth of colour: 'a transparent prison for the souls of Pelléas, Mélisande, and Golaud'.[26] As he would later tell Ernst Haeusserman, 'I saw quite definite colours in the music, and if I had not been able to realise them on stage, the music would have lost its sense for me.'[27] Karajan's fear of being physically unable to conduct a production which disconcerted him visually was integral to his quest for a designer he could trust, a quest which effectively ended with his discovery of Schneider-Siemssen.

Pelléas et Mélisande was not, however, Schneider-Siemssen's first commission for the Vienna State Opera. Scanning the arts page of a German newspaper, he read that he was doing the designs for a new ballet in Vienna: *Jahreszeiten* by Theodor Berger. This was news to him! It was a typical Mattoni–Karajan administrative air-shot; they had decided on Schneider-Siemssen but had not got round to telling him. None the less, he was on the first train to Vienna to thrash the whole thing out. It was a visit that did him no harm at all. Karajan hated sceptics, but he had no time for yes-men either.

Karajan took his responsibilities towards the Vienna State Opera Ballet moderately seriously. One of the several losses he suffered in the early months of his directorship was the death at the age of fifty-two of Erika Hanka, the woman who had put ballet on the Viennese musical map in the post-war years. Her policies had been surprisingly radical, and Karajan encouraged the continuation of that tradition. Leading contemporary dance groups were invited to Vienna and a good deal of new (or newish) music was performed. Eventually, the Hungarian dancer and choreographer Aurel von Milloss was appointed as Hanka's successor.

Karajan would have liked to conduct Stravinsky's *Le sacre du printemps* in the theatre with Balanchine as choreographer but plans fell through; then

Milloss himself backed away from the project when he discovered how decided (and restrictive) Karajan's ideas were about the choreography.

The only ballet Karajan conducted in Vienna was Holst's *The Planets*, choreographed by the Wuppertal ballet-master Erich Walter. This was in November 1961. By way of preparation, Karajan recorded *The Planets* for Decca, along with a disc of music from a particular favourite of the Vienna ballet-going public in the 1950s, Adam's *Giselle*. The Adam record, which Decca had commissioned at New York's behest, quickly became a popular best-seller, though, the claim on the sleeve – 'This recording, made from Adam's own orchestration, gives some idea of how the ballet must have sounded at its first performance' – is hooey. The parts arrived from Paris in no sort of order and Karajan promptly set about busking his way delightedly through whichever dog-eared sheaf of papers happened to be at hand.

The recording of *The Planets* was quite a different matter. The Vienna players were not unfamiliar with the music; billed as the 'Vienna State Opera Orchestra', they had recorded the work in March 1959 under Sir Adrian Boult. But the playing there had been wretched beyond belief.[28] Now there were troubles with Karajan, whose beat was never entirely clear in the 5/4 rhythms of 'Mars' and 'Neptune'. There were numerous breakdowns and retakes, notably in 'Mars' where the orchestra seemed as much as sea as it sometimes was in Stravinsky's *Le sacre du printemps*.[29] These things happen. Yet when Karajan and his players finally got their act together, the results were remarkable. Karajan's genius for realising orchestral sound found an apt proving ground in this astonishing score, nowhere more so than in 'Mercury, the Winged Messenger' with its gossamer textures and slip-stream sonorities.

But Karajan's response to *The Planets* was not driven by sonority alone. Having brilliantly exploited the orchestra, Holst ends by renouncing it altogether as female voices, soughing like an Arctic wind, waft us into oblivion. Like many works that particularly engaged Karajan's mind and imagination, this is music that concerns itself with war, dissolution, and last things; it is another of the great representative works – a musical metaphor, in fact – of the century he had grown up in and come grimly to know. And whatever the problems in rehearsal, this Vienna performance of 'Mars' was without parallel in the annals of the gramophone, remorseless and weighty as never before. The end is especially extraordinary.

It is said that during the Battle of the Somme, the barrage of the twenty-ton Krupp-designed field guns could be heard as far away as London. Had Karajan read about that or was he simply hearing again the thudding mayhem of the Berlin blitz?

1 Ernst von Karajan 2 Martha von Karajan
3 Martha von Karajan *(left)*, 1925 4 Wolfgang and Heribert, with governess, 1915

5 Bernhard Paumgartner

6 Ulm Stadttheater *v.* the local press, January 1932, Karajan as goalkeeper. General Manager Erwin Dieterich *(back row, third from left)* fell over while taking a penalty. The team lost 2-1.

Franz Schmidt,
rector of Vienna's
Hochschule für
Musik during
Karajan's time there.
'A man who knew
all music.'

8 Max Reinhardt

9 With the Ulm Stadttheater orchestra.

10 Touring with Edi von der Mauer and friends, 1931.

11 Conducting in Aachen.

12 Edwin von der Nüll's review of Karajan's 1938 Berlin State Opera performance of *Tristan und Isolde*. Bernd Ruland's head line competes with the story of row over fees for actors' voice-overs in Walt Disney's *Snow White and the Seven Dwarfs*.

.253 Zweites Beiblatt   *B·Z am Mittag*   Sonnabend, 22. Oktober 1938

aatsrat Tietjens großer Griff

der Staatsoper: Das Wunder Karajan

Ovationen für den Dirigenten des „Tristan"

Gestern Abend dirigierte Herbert von Karajan, der dreißigjährige Aachener Generalmusikdirektor, seine zweite Aufführung als Gast der Staatsoper. Er hatte mit Wagners schwerstem Werk „Tristan und Isolde" einen Erfolg, der ihn in eine Reihe stellt mit Furtwängler und de Sabata, den größten Operndirigenten, die zur Zeit in Deutschland zu hören sind.

war es. Als Karajan am Pult erschien, te sich, genau wie neulich beim „Fidelio", Hand. Zu Beginn des zweiten Aktes zuckte Beifall wie ein Peitschenschlag durch das in dem Augenblick, wo Karajan den Or- erraum betrat. Vor der dritten Akt tönte aus allen Ecken „Bravo!". Am Schluß wurden Sänger gefeiert. Die Rufe nach Karajan mehr- sich. Sobald er vor den Vorhang erschien, tete man ihn eine Serie von Ovationen. tele man ihn eine Serie von Ovationen, die deutlicher als kürzlich beim „Fidelio", wo- man zum erstenmal den Staatstheater- stum trat, gab das Haus zu erkennen, daß ut und böse zu unterscheiden versteht.

as ist der äußere Rahmen. Vom künstleri- Gesicht des Abends zu sprechen, fällt schwer. einer frühen Morgenstunde noch gar nicht haben. Rund heraus gesagt: wir stehen vor Wunder. Dieser Mann ist die größte Diri- entsensation des Jahrhunderts. Mit 30 Jahren es keinem, der unsere Jahrzehnte kreuzte, Tragweite dieses Ereignisses läßt sich in der

as erste Wort des Dankes gilt dem, der rajan die große Chance gegeben hat: atsrat Generalintendant Heinz Tietjens. welchem Elan er diesen Mann über alle bü- tischen und verwaltungstechnischen Bedenken eggesetzt hat, um Karajan an die Arbeit zu m, ist dem Schreiber dieser Zeilen nur zu gut nnt. Der geistige Abend dürfte dem Dirigen- es keinem, der unsere Jahrzehnte kreuzte, stler und Organisator Tietjens eine doppelte agnung gebracht haben.

hat er einen kongenialen Partner für seine inerungen an der Lindenoper gefunden; hat sich die jahrelange Wartezeit, die Aus- ., mit der Tietjens naheliegenden Kompro- lösungen widerstand, auf das Herrlichste be- t.

as ist der Mann, der heute schon alle Wünsche diegt, die man an einen Dirigenten von

Weltrang stellen muß. Es hat noch den geistigen Abend keinen Sinn mehr, damit länger hinter dem Berg zu halten. Karajan hat zwei außer- gewöhnliche Konzerte mit den Philharmonikern absolviert. Karajan hat diesen Eindruck mit seinem Debut in der Staatsoper vor drei Wochen noch realisiert. Was er gestern zeigte, grenzt ans Unbegreifliche.

Ein Mensch von dreißig Jahren stellt eine Leistung hin, um die ihn unsere großen Fünf- zigjährigen mit Recht beneiden dürfen. Er dirigiert die Partitur wie den „Tristan" aus- wendig. Er tut das mit einer Souveränität, die einfach unheimlich ist. Den komplizierten Appa- rat einer Opernaufführung meistert er so selbst- verständlich, als ob es sich nur darum handelte, ein Kinderlied zu singen.

Nicht möglich, ihn in geläufige Vorstellungen einzuordnen. Er ist weder Rhythmiker, noch auf Klang spezialisiert, weder typischer Operndirigent noch Sinfoniker: er ist alles in einem. Allein das eine sagt dem Wissenden, was los ist; wie er den psychologisch bedingten Decrescendostil des „Tristan", dieses ewig unerfüllte und unerfüllbare Sich-Aufbäumen erfaßte und durchführte, das brachte einen aus dem Staunen nicht heraus.

Karajan ist im Geächtel. Ich glaube, er weiß genau, was er wert ist. Um ihn werden sich in Kürze die Opern-Metropolen der Welt reißen. Darum eine Bitte, eine ganz dringende: er

schone sich, man schone ihn. Solch kost- bares Gut muß gehütet werden. Ich habe ihm ins Gesicht sehen können, wie er neulich den „Fidelio" dirigierte. Es war ein Gesicht, von dem der heilige Ernst für die Sache ausging, ein Gesicht, das äußerste Konzentration und be- sessenes Künstlertum ausdrückte. Er bleibe sich selber treu.

Gestern habe ich in diesen Spalten begeisterte Worte über den genialen französischen Pianisten Calabeus geschrieben. Heute verbinde ich mit der Begeisterung mehr: Karajan ist einer der Linsersten, er stammt aus dem Salzburgischen, daher, wo die Musik zu Hause ist. Es ist eine große Freude, zu wissen, daß dieser Künstler, ein deutscher Künst- ler, da ist.

*

In der Aufführung sang Gertrud Rünger zum erstenmal die Isolde. Auch das ist, wie ihr Fidelio, eine hochdramatische Figur von Format. Die sonbare Stimme gewinnt noch durch ein Spiel, dem man die ordnende Hand Tietjens an- merkt. Tristan war Albert Seibert als Gast: ein sehr gepflegter Darsteller aus der Hamburger Schule von Generalintendant Strohm. Beide haben dem Publikum außerordentlich gefallen.

— Edwin v. d. Nüll

Um sie gab es Krach

Walt Disney, der — wie aus Hollywood gemeldet wird — einen neuen großen Farben-Zeichenfilm mit den Abenteuern Don Quichottes plant, bereitet sein (sonst so erfolgreicher) Schneewittchenfilm Sorgen: wie die „B. Z." gestern meldete, verlangen die „Stimmen" des Schneewittchens und des Prinzen Schadenersatz, weil Walt Disney ihre gesprochenen Worte angeblich vertragswidrig „mißbraucht" habe   Presse-Photo

Filmvorstellung zu Hause

Kulturfilme auf neuen Wegen

Die Zahl der Besitzer von Schmalfilm-Vorführ- geräten ist ständig im Wachsen. Aber das Film- material, das die Amateure selbst herstellen, ist meist nicht abwechslungsreich genug. Die Foto- händler werden oft gefragt, ob man nicht inter- essante Schmalfilme entleihen könnte. Da greift nun die Degeto-Kulturfilm G. m. b. H. ein. Sie hat soeben — wie Dr. Johannes Eckhardt in einer Pressebesprechung mit- teilte, einen Kulturfilmverleih gegründet. Alle Arten von Kulturfilmen und

Im Krankenstuhl...
zum Ritter geschlagen!
Frankreich ehrte Invaliden
des großen Krieges: In
feierlichem Zeremoniell
wurden sie zu Rittern
der Ehrenlegion ernannt.
Presse-Photo

✳

Fliegerhauptmann
Bruno Mussolini
heiratete.
Der zweite Sohn des Duce,
der sich als Kampfflieger
in Abessinien und als Re-
kordflieger ausgezeichnet
hat, vermählte sich mit
Gina Ruberti, einer Nichte
des ersten faschistischen
Finanzministers.
Weltbild

In München: Kronprinz Umberto von Italien als Trauzeuge.
Der italienische Thronfolger (links in Uniform) bei der Hochzeit der Prinzessin
Lucia von Bourbon-Sizilien mit Prinz Eugen von Savoyen, Herzog von Ancona.
Presse-Bild-Zentrale

Der Musik-Winter hat begonnen:
Wilh. Furtwängler,
der erste deutsche Mu-
siker, der geistigste und
innigste Dirigent der
symphonischen Musik,
feiert seine ersten Tri-
umphe in der Saison.
Keßler, Hubmann

Herbert von Karajan
der erst dreißigjährige Aac...
Generalmusikdirektor, eine ...
hörte opern-dramatische Begal...
ist die große Entdeckung des Ber...
Musikwinters. Ministerpräs...
Generalfeldmarschall Göring ...
ihn an die Berliner Staats...

13 *Berliner Illustrierte Zeitung*, autumn 1938. A French war veteran is honoured,
the wedding of Bruno Mussolini, the wedding of the Duke of Ancona, and promise
of an exciting winter of music-making in Berlin with Wilhelm Furtwängler
('Germany's first musician') and the 'incredibly gifted' Herbert von Karajan.

14 With Richard Strauss and Heinz Tietjen, 1941

15 Polydor advertisement   16 Elmy Holgerloef

17 With Luis Trenker in the Italian Alps, 1943.
18 Countess Maria Tripcovich   19 Raffaello de Banfield Tripcovich

With Wieland
Wagner and
Anita von Karajan,
Bayreuth, 1951

With Elisabeth
Schwarzkopf

22 With Maria Callas

23 With Victor De Sabata

24 Antonio Ghiringhelli greets Karajan after a performance of *Salome* at La Scala, Milan, with Tamara Toumanova, dancer of the 'Seven Veils' sequence, and Nicola Zaccaria.

25 Elsa Schiller   26 John Culshaw
27 EMI recording session with Walter Legge and the leader
of the Philharmonia Orchestra, Hugh Bean.

28 Eliette Mouret models
a Dior wedding-dress.

29 Church blessing

30 With Eliette and daughters Isabel and Arabel at Mauerbach.

31 Henri-Georges Clouzot with Herbert von Karajan
and *(below)* cameraman Armand Thirard.

32 Berlin Philharmonie
33 With Wolfgang Stresemann, André von Mattoni looking on.   34 Hans Scharoun

35 Guru with two acolytes: Karajan and Leonard Bernstein with
Dimitri Mitropoulos, Salzburg, 1959.

36 Eliette von Karajan plays the posthorn at 30,000 feet during the Vienna
Philharmonic's 1959 world tour. Otto Strasser dozes through the hubbub.

37 With Egon Hilbert, press conference, Vienna, 1963.

38 Vienna, 1964. The Crisis. The psychiatrist said: 'Tell me the whole story from the beginning.' And Herbert von Karajan began . . . 'Well, in the beginning I created Heaven and Earth . . .'

19 Günther Schneider-Siemssen, design for *Lohengrin*, Salzburg, 1976.

20 Best man at the wedding of Günther and Eva Schneider-Siemssen.

21 Playing Sieglinde to the Siegmund of Jon Vickers. Salzburg, Easter, 1967.

42 Michel Glotz

43 A payment of five
Deutschmarks was d
after every session in
which Karajan had
behaved and conduc
especially well. Günt
Breest observes the ri

44 'Rough it may be
Boring, never.'

Oxford, 1978,
ith David Smith
nd Ingegerd
stman-Smith.

46 With Joy Bryer, Anne-Sophie Mutter, and Edward Heath at the European
    Community Youth Orchestra's retreat in Courcheval.

47 Berlin Philharmonie, 1984. Edgar Wisniewski, architect, chamber music hall;
Wolfgang Stresemann; Volker Hassemer, Culture Minister; Peter Girth; Eberhard Diepgen
Mayor of West Berlin; Klaus Franke, Public Works Minister.

48 Uli Märkle   49 Sabine Meyer

50 At the helm of *Helisara VI* off St Tropez.
(Photograph by Emil Perauer)

51 'It seems to me that the music is coming from another world.' And he said,
'You are right. It *is* coming from another world. It is coming from eternity.'
(Photograph by Emil Perauer)

CHAPTER 50

Vienna: the phoney war

The colour of my soul is iron-grey and sad bats
wheel about the steeple of my dreams.
                              Claude Debussy

During the late autumn of 1961, as preparations continued for the opening
night of *Pelléas et Mélisande* the following January, the Vienna Opera's
stage crew threatened to go on strike. The strike threat was not directed
against Karajan himself, though the increasing sophistication and complexity of his productions was the prime cause of the growing workloads
on lighting technicians, stage-hands, and the transport teams who ferried
sets and equipment back and forth between the opera house and the
out-of-town workshops and scenery stores. Karajan sympathised with
the crews but had no immediate power to intervene. The government
controlled the State Opera budget; civil servants administered it.

With the crews working to rule, it was a baptism of fire for Schneider-
Siemssen. In November, Karajan called him in and asked for simplifications
to the set. Not that Karajan was backing down. The simplifications,
he pointed out, would need to be offset by an even more radical and
creative use of lighting. Since the lighting resources themselves could not
be expanded in any way, this required additional ingenuity, imagination,
and planning. Schneider-Siemssen would later reflect:

Looking back, it became clear to me that one does not need vast expenditure
to create lively and exciting music theatre. One must provide a unity of light
and space in which the conductor [*sic*] can make decisions. So that 'less can
be more'.[1]

Karajan found himself experimenting in other ways too. Denied rehearsal
time in the theatre with the orchestra present, he pre-recorded parts of the
opera and rehearsed with the tapes. It is an interesting fact that within five
years of this enforced experiment, he would be preparing all his theatre
productions with the aid of recordings: commercial recordings made ahead
of time by whichever record company was prepared to foot the bill.

Karajan's reading of *Pelléas et Mélisande*, which is preserved for us in the
recording he made in Berlin in 1978, is controversial in one crucial respect.
Is it too *human* a reading? As the composer and Debussy specialist Robin
Holloway has asked: 'Does this explicit warmth of expression move you to
pity for God's poor creatures, or do you think it goes against the French
virtues of decorum and reserve?'[2]

Joseph Wechsberg reported from Vienna for *Opera*:

For the first time in my experience I was shaken by the power of Debussy's music; previously I had been only moved by its beauty. This is a lyrical *and* a dramatic interpretation and, when the inexorable climax comes towards the end, one sits spellbound. At the same time Karajan opens the delicate texture of the score, lovingly displaying its beauty, making everything clear and transparent . . . and always painting, painting with music.[3]

Even after the house lights went up, many of the audience did, indeed, remain in their seats, reluctant to leave the theatre and so break the spell.

One visitor from abroad was Neville Cardus, making a rare return to a city which had provided him with some of his most cherished musical memories. He travelled, he confessed, with depressed expectations:

For isn't Karajan a man of our modern world, a musical apotheosis of it, with a flair for glamour, closed eyed in his personal appeal, master of the spectacular, and a sort of Svengali brought up to date, an exhibitionist *au fond*? What is Karajan to *Pelléas* or *Pelléas* to Karajan?[4]

His own 'astonished' answer was that *Pelléas* was everything to Karajan and he to it. The charm of Cardus's review lies, however, not in the praise he heaped on the performance but in the effect the performance had in drawing from him so expert and movingly written an evaluation of the opera itself:

Pelléas et Mélisande is a drama of the inner, the really 'real' world, a drama of implications, of psychological conflicts too secret to concentrate into the obvious attitudes of life, exhibitory and active . . . Arkel is old age poignantly particularised. The music by which Debussy gives him grief and wisdom is bowed in its sombre-moving phrases and harmonies, so pathetically in contrast to the golden-throated lyricism of Pelléas; the innocent youngness – but older in her self than she knows – of Mélisande; and the simple manliness of Golaud, that unfortunate horseman.

All these people are pulsatingly themselves, but we see them from a distance: they move in a permanent timeless dimension. It is ourselves, watching and overhearing from *our* clock-measured, active, merely phenomenal world, who are unreal. Debussy does not describe, he evokes. His orchestra, unlike Wagner's, does not *point*. It covers everything, a veiled unheard, yet heard, presence – omnipresent.

And returning to the performance:

I can make no better compliment to Karajan, the Vienna State Opera Orchestra, and the singers than to say that all these intrinsic qualities of the work, not generally understood, were brought home. I confess that more than once I came near to tears, eyes as misted as the beautiful stage settings of Günther Schneider-Siemssen. The opening forest scene was an endless world of high trees, alluring and mysterious. The fountain in the park was an enchantment all seen in reflection from afar. What magic of tone-chemistry is here! Different but in perfect harmony was the grotto scene, dark, and the darkness more revealed when a glow of the outer night entered.[5]

Important eras in the affairs of great theatres and opera houses have their defining moments. The 1961 revivals of *Tristan und Isolde* and the 1962 production of *Pelléas et Mélisande* were to Karajan's years in Vienna what *Tristan und Isolde* and Gluck's *Iphigénie en Aulide* had been to the Mahler–Roller era fifty years before. Yet a peak can also abut a precipice. Though the new *Pelléas et Mélisande* had been as much enhanced by the stage crew's go-slow as hindered by it, the dispute itself remained unresolved.

During January and early February, Karajan was shuttling back and forth between Vienna and Berlin. With the dispute still not resolved, the government made a formal approach to him, enlisting his help – something of a calculated risk given the fact that he had unresolved demands of his own where the Opera was concerned.

What happened next could only have occurred in Vienna. On 1 February, the Minister warned that if the dispute was not settled promptly, the Opera Ball would have to be cancelled. This was serious stuff. The Opera Ball, which takes place in the State Opera each February, is the climax of the Viennese winter season, a court ceremony in a democratic age. The event is shown live on television and for a modest sum ordinary Viennese can acquire tickets for the galleries and upper tiers from where they can watch the rich, the famous, and the fashionable young partying the night away.

Within hours of the threat being made, negotiations began in earnest between the government and the unions. Karajan, who was not in Vienna on 1 February and who, in any case, regarded the Opera Ball as a bore and an irrelevance, knew nothing of this. The Opera House was informed of developments on 3 February; but by the time Karajan arrived back in Vienna on 5 February an agreement had been reached between the government and the unions. Realising that he had either been ignored by the bureaucrats or deliberately outmanoeuvred by them, Karajan briefly took stock, then resigned his position as Artistic Director.

So as to avoid immediate personal confrontation – in disputes of this nature, Karajan preferred to confront his opponents by edict, and at a distance – he arranged for Mattoni to deliver his resignation letter only after he himself had left Vienna for an 'unidentified' destination. The letter concluded:

The fact that a compromise was agreed with the deliberate exclusion of the Artistic Director and his staff represents such a serious attack on the competence of the Artistic Director that his function becomes meaningless

471

under such circumstances, and makes it impossible for him to justify in future the confidence you have placed in him for many years. Therefore I find myself obliged to return the artistic direction of the State Opera into your hands with effect from today.[6]

Uproar followed. There were demonstrations and sit-ins and a vast amount of editorialising in the public prints. Since the bulk of public and critical opinion was rallying to the Karajan flag – Vienna's senior music critic Heinrich Kralik described the government's handling of the situation as 'a world disgrace for Austria' – Education Minister Drimmel decided to go for broke by making public details of proposals Karajan had put before him for the future development of the Vienna Opera.

In his Salzburg address in July 1960, Drimmel himself had spoken of the problems facing opera houses in a changing cultural and economic environment, but the proposal Karajan had now come up with – what we would nowadays term the partial 'privatisation' of the Vienna Opera – had left him flabbergasted. Drimmel told a press conference on 10 February:

I say today what I have always said: full freedom of artistic creation for the Artistic Director of the State Opera. For anyone, even for Karajan, if he were to return. But the liberation of the State Opera for a completely new existence, perhaps in some world-wide conglomerate – No! No minister and no government can take it upon themselves to make the Vienna State Opera a branch of a world-wide combine.[7]

Karajan moved swiftly to counter the more sensational aspects of Drimmel's claim. At a press conference in Zürich, he denied that he had proposed a transfer of ownership of the State Opera. The idea he had recently put to the Minister – an extension of the planned collaborations that were already taking place between Vienna and Milan – was that the foundations should be laid for a world-wide operatic 'co-operative' in which Vienna would be a leading player. Karajan would later tell an American journalist:

The idea of the operatic ensemble is dead. It is a mark of our times that everybody – opera directors, singers, the man in the audience – wants everything. The man in the audience has heard the great singers on TV and records and he feels that he is entitled to hear them also in his opera house . . . As for opera house managers, they compete against each other as if at an auction by offering the singers more and more money to keep them a few weeks longer. My solution was a proposal to pool the first-rate talent in every field of opera production so that the same singers, conductors, and scenery for a given opera could first be properly integrated and then shifted from one great opera house to the next, ensuring audiences the best possible performances. My God, the cry that was raised over this in some quarters! I wanted to be Generalmusikdirektor of the World. I wanted to control a world-wide cartel on opera production. Finally, I had to give up this idea. It cannot be done.[8]

That was the problem. Outlandish though the plan was when viewed in its totality, it had within it a kernel of good sense. The difficulty was, Karajan was entirely the wrong person to propose it. The fact that he wielded less power – less direct power – than many people suggested, or supposed, was an irrelevance in the face of widely held beliefs to the contrary.

This crisis in Vienna demonstrated the limits of that power. Yet, ironically, its resolution only served to enhance Karajan's reputation as an unstoppable force within the body politic. Having misread the significance of Drimmel's manoeuvrings over the Opera Ball and having been forced into a resignation he had neither planned nor desired, Karajan now launched his own counter-offensive. Ideas about the 'internationalisation' of the Vienna Opera were instantly set aside; arguments about the rights and wrongs of the recent settlement with the unions were also sidelined. Instead, he concentrated on redefining the terms of his directorship, while at the same time demanding significant changes to the way the government administered the budgets of the state-run theatres.

Backed by a powerful – albeit temporary – coalition of interests and pressure groups, Karajan eventually won major concessions from the government. 'Völlige Dispositionsfreiheit' or 'Full Independent Budgeting' was introduced. From now on, provided the state theatres stayed within budget, they would not be required to account to civil servants for every individual budgetary decision.

As always in such disputes, heads eventually rolled. Karl Haertl, the music-loving junior minister who had brokered the deal between the government and the unions, was moved to another job and was later removed from the board of directors of the Salzburg Festival at Karajan's behest. Meanwhile, Karajan finally got round to revitalising his own management team which had been seriously weakened by the departure the previous year of Egon Seefehlner to a post with West Berlin's Deutsche Oper. Karajan's choice of administrative co-director was Walter Erich Schäfer, Intendant of the Württemberg State Theatre, a cultured and erudite man much admired by Karajan not least for his abundant repertory of *risqué* jokes.

So the crisis was over: for the time being, at least. On 16 March, Karajan assembled the staff of the State Opera to thank them for their support and three days later he was given a hero's welcome when he returned to the conductor's desk to conduct Verdi's *Aida*. Then, he was gone again, this time on a short tour with the Vienna Philharmonic which took them to Moscow, Leningrad, Oslo, Stockholm, Copenhagen, Hamburg, and London where he conducted Mozart's *Jupiter* Symphony, the Seventh Symphony of Bruckner, and the Prelude to *Die Meistersinger* before a 'packed, raving' (Cardus's epithets) audience in the Royal Festival Hall.

But the strain was beginning to take its toll. On his return to Austria, Karajan was laid low with a kidney infection and was thus prevented from conducting the new production of *Pelléas et Mélisande* in Milan. By the end of the year, he would have suffered another, rather more serious, collapse of a 'circulatory' nature.

Meanwhile, in Vienna itself, coalitions were dissolving, old factions regrouping. Amid the general rejoicing over Karajan's victory, the journalist Hans Weigel gazed wearily out over the recently vacated battlefield and penned a melancholy piece about Karajan's failure to distinguish between tactics and strategy, between a single battle and the larger war.

A pity about Karajan, he mused. They'll have him in the end. And sooner, perhaps, than most of you imagine.

CHAPTER 51

Karajan's Circus

Can it be an accident that wherever improvised music is heard people tend to gather round performers in a circle? The psychological basis of this natural process seems self-evident to all; it had only to be transposed into a concert hall.

Hans Scharoun

Towards the end of 1956, a decision was taken to build a new Berlin Philharmonie. The orchestra was about to celebrate its seventy-fifth birthday, yet ten years after the war's end this most famous of German orchestras was still camping out in temporary accommodation in a converted theatre-cum-cinema known as the Titania Palast.

An architectural competition was announced, and a steering committee set up consisting of Tiburtius, Westerman, the composer Boris Blacher, Stuckenschmidt, and Karajan. It is a matter of record that the competition was intense, the debate heated, the outcome spectacular. In the end it was Karajan and Stuckenschmidt who carried the day in the face of a complex mix of indecision and fiercely reasoned opposition.

The man who submitted the winning design was Hans Scharoun, one of the great German architects of the century but a man who in 1957 was virtually unheard of abroad and little regarded in his own country beyond an immediate circle of pupils and fellow professionals. Nowadays, those who venerate Scharoun's work single out different achievements,[1] but it is the Philharmonie which is generally thought to be his masterpiece.

Born in 1893, Scharoun was forty when Hitler came to power. He considered emigrating. But he spoke no English and feared that his particular brand of modernism – its mingling of Mies van der Rohe with an interest in landscape, scale, and location that owed something to the English Arts and Crafts movement – might prove untranslatable. Like many Left-leaning Germans, he also wondered how long the Nazis would be in power. When it eventually became clear that they might be there for some time, he withdrew into a self-styled internal exile and concentrated on interior design and commissions for private houses and suburban cottages.

When the Russians arrived in Berlin in 1945, he was appointed Berlin City Architect, charged with redesigning the bombed-out city, only to find himself removed from office the following year by the newly elected West Berlin city council. With the conservative Right now looking to employ main-line traditionalists, including a number of architects who had worked for Speer during the Third Reich, and with a virulent form of anti-modernism being drip-fed into the East Berlin planning system by Moscow, Scharoun abandoned any hope of pioneering a new post-war style of organically evolved 'social' building and concentrated instead on teaching (he held a professorship at Berlin's Technical University) and the establishment of his own private office, out of which came a string of prize-winning competition submissions, many of which were never built. Happily, the Philharmonie was an exception; and in this Karajan played a decisive role.

Karajan's submission to the competition judges, a document which has not previously been reproduced outside the specialist architectural press, is of particular interest. He wrote:

Of all the designs submitted, one seems to stand out above the others; which is founded on the principle that the performers should be in the middle (its number I forget, but the model is white with gold seats). This project seems fortunate on several grounds: the deployment of the walls certainly makes good sense acoustically, but the most impressive of all is the complete concentration of the listener on the musical event. I know of no existing hall in which the seating question is so well resolved as in this project. It seems to me and to my assistant Winckel that this arrangement with the orchestra centrally placed will be better suited than any known hall to the musical style of the Berlin Philharmonic, *whose main characteristics are the long distant outswing and the special breath in beginning and ending a musical phrase* [my italics], and that it will accommodate performances and rehearsals in an ideal manner.[2]

There is no doubt that there is a visionary quality to Scharoun's concept of the Philharmonie which lay deep within him and which can be traced back many years. The hall's exterior and interior forms are to some extent prefigured in a striking series of water-colours he completed in 1922–3 entitled 'Kino II', 'Music Hall', and 'Theatre'. His writings at that time, though absurdly high-flown, also speak of something far removed from architecture as mere function:

The human being should be the centre, with our aspirations forming a lofty vault over us like the firmament.[3]

Or,

People facing one another, lined up in circles in a powerfully curving arc around a sweeping crystal pyramid. Room of blue and black, rolling through a thousand sprays of colour; rising upwards to a yellow and silver star; in arches, ribs, projections, and cavities, groping from dark mass to living purity, sweeping up to crown the expectant masses below.[4]

The ship-like shapes also relate back to Scharoun's formative years. He was brought up in Bremerhaven where he developed a passion for sailing-ships and ocean liners.[5]

The idea, fundamental to Scharoun's design, of an encircled and encircling *community* of musicians and music-lovers did, however, present problems to the acousticians. The sound of individual instruments, including the human voice itself, travels in different ways and at different levels of intensity. In the past, a modified rectangle had proved to be acoustically as safe a bet as any, though even this is not without its problems, and the 'them-and-us' relationship which the rectangular form established between players and listeners was anathema to Scharoun. His plan – the sunken playing area acting as a kind of 'landscape valley', the audience surrounding it on a series of 'steeply banked vineyards' – opened up new acoustical possibilities and new problems. Fortunately, Scharoun had at his disposal Lothar Cremer, one of the great pioneering acousticians of the age, with whom he got on famously. Though Scharoun refused to deviate in any way from the basic idea, in all other respects he was flexibility itself. 'Virgin territory,' he later wrote 'was discovered, explored, and conquered.'[6] Not everything worked at once. The acoustic only finally came good in the 1970s when a wooden platform, originally used for filming, was retained in the well of the hall.

One of the earliest critics of the hall's acoustic was George Szell; yet he loved the building and had no doubt that solutions would be found. Knappertsbusch and Jochum berated the whole concept, as did a large number of journalists. Ignoring Scharoun entirely, they gave vent to the idea that the hall had been personally ordered up by Karajan for his own private exhibition and glory. It was left to fellow creative artists to sing Scharoun's praises. Luciano Berio called the Philharmonie 'a milestone in musical architecture' and Pierre Boulez declared the hall to be the first successful attempt to break out of the strait-jacket of that old-fashioned form of concert hall design in which 'the frame is not right, the disposition of the audience is not right, everything is wrong'.[7] In later years, a number of the world's finest new halls would be directly inspired by the Philharmonie,[8] though as Peter Blundell Jones observes in his book on Scharoun, 'the fact that none of them quite lives up to the original only emphasises the originality of Scharoun's conception'.[9]

As for the Berliners themselves, they dubbed the hall 'Zirkus Karajani', 'Karajan's Circus', a pun – not entirely unaffectionate – on the name of the popular Zirkus Sarasani.

*

The Berlin Philharmonic had marked its seventy-fifth anniversary in April 1957 with Beethoven's Ninth Symphony. Afterwards, Karajan found himself being addressed by a gentleman he barely knew. Did the gentleman entirely disguise the fact that, hitherto, he had been no great fan of Karajan? No matter. On this occasion, he had been bowled over by the music-making; and he told Karajan so. Told him, too, how the performance had put him in mind of a glorious account of the Ninth he had heard Bruno Walter conduct in New York, a performance that had cost Walter and the orchestra much effort in rehearsal, not least where the opening pages were concerned.

Talk after a performance always irritated Karajan. On this occasion, though, there was no escape and he had been obliged to listen to these courteously phrased expressions of appreciation. Yet at the mention of Walter's name, his face clouded over, and talk of the 'difficulty' of the Ninth Symphony's opening had been met with a somewhat impatient glance. (When Michel Schwalbé learned of the encounter, he said: 'The problem is, we never even looked at the opening. Karajan knew we would have no trouble with it.')

The meeting would have been of little consequence had it not been for the fact that the Berlin Philharmonic's Intendant, Dr Westerman, now no longer in the best of health, was nearing the end of his time with the orchestra. A successor had to be found. What was required was a man who was both a musician and a diplomat. In Westerman's view, no one was better suited to the task than the person who had spoken to Karajan that April evening in 1957, the General Manager of the Berlin Radio Symphony Orchestra, Wolfgang Stresemann.

*

The name Stresemann has a noble yet forlorn ring. If anyone could have diverted the course of events between the two world wars – anyone, that is, other than the man who so tragically did – it was Wolfgang's father Gustav Stresemann. A monarchist and, during the First World War, an ardent nationalist, Gustav Stresemann's position after Versailles was not significantly different from that of other German politicians: one of anger and resentment. His position did differ, however, inasmuch as he believed that the revival of German power by peaceful means would lead to the wholesale dismantling of the treaty, where others, including the Nazis, saw the treaty itself as the insuperable barrier to progress. Although Stresemann briefly became German Chancellor, at the nadir of the Weimar Republic's fortunes in 1923, it was during his time as Foreign Minister between 1923 and 1929 that he did his finest work, for which he was awarded the Nobel Peace Prize. It is often said that his death in 1929 at the early age of fifty-one deprived Germany of its wisest statesman since Bismarck. What it undoubtedly did was throw national politics into disarray, badly weakening Hermann Müller's 'grand coalition' at a time when support was already beginning to leach away to the Nazis.

Wolfgang was twenty-five when his father died. He had studied the piano, composition, and conducting in Dresden but had made little headway with his career. In 1939, he emigrated to the United States, but things did not greatly improve there. When he finally returned to Germany after the war, it was not as a musician but as a musical manager. It was a job which was destined to bring him closer to his father's world of diplomacy and politics than anyone might have imagined.

Over a year elapsed between Stresemann's first meeting with Karajan and Stresemann's being formally sounded out about the possibility of taking over as Intendant of the Berlin Philharmonic. Their next meeting took place in Karajan's room during the interval of a concert. Glenn Gould had just played Bach's D minor Concerto, a performance Stresemann had thought utterly remarkable. (As had Gould, though in Gould's case it was Karajan's accompaniment that had intrigued him.[10]) Karajan's response to Stresemann was again oddly muted, something Stresemann put down at the time to the fact that he was about to go on to conduct again. (Beethoven's Fifth Symphony, hardly unfamiliar territory.)

After the meeting, Karajan asked Westerman to widen the field. It must have been as obvious to Karajan as it was to Westerman that Stresemann was ideally equipped to do the job. Clearly, though, doubts were swirling around at the back of Karajan's mind.

Though it was rarely openly stated, there remained a strong residual dislike in post-war Germany of those who had jumped ship in the 1930s only to return after the war to help 'put things right'. Where a man like Scharoun had stayed, bound by his profession and his cultural allegiances, Stresemann had not. And there was more. Where Karajan had partly defied his parents, taken up music, fought his way through the profession like a ferret in a sack, made personal and political misjudgements and, in spite of everything, become a huge success, Stresemann had turned his back on his father's world, taken up music, made all the 'right' decisions politically, and palpably failed in his immediate ambition.

There was no reason to think less of Stresemann as a result; where music is concerned many are called and few are chosen. But jealousy, however repressed, will always be a barrier to real amity and trust. The unease that characterised Karajan's first meetings with Stresemann, and Stresemann's own ambivalent feelings towards Karajan, ensured that any relationship they would later enjoy would be fed more by respect and natural courtesy than by anything resembling real human warmth.

In the end, says Stresemann, it was Mattoni who tipped the scales in his favour. In 1959 there was a further brief meeting with Karajan at the

Savoy Hotel in Berlin, followed by dinner at the Ritz. Improbable as it might seem, Karajan wanted to make sure that Gustav Stresemann's son could cope with the social side of things.

As for Stresemann, at his inaugural meeting with the orchestra he promised that his principal concern would be to 'lavish care and attention [hegen und zu pflegen]' on its relationship with Karajan.[11]

CHAPTER 52

Berlin Philharmonic

I see you stand like greyhounds in the slips,
Straining upon the start.
Shakespeare, *Henry V*

The Berlin sound, it is like the English lawn which has to be cut
and watered twice daily – and for three hundred years.
Herbert von Karajan

Stresemann's first meeting with Karajan as the orchestra's new Intendant lasted the best part of an hour. Thereafter, ten minutes would be the norm. 'This is a man,' wrote Stresemann to the Cleveland Orchestra's Beverly Barksdale, 'who works twenty hours a day and is besieged by too many people everywhere.'[1] What Stresemann and Karajan were locked into was what the French call political 'cohabitation'. It worked well for the most part, though Stresemann would never entirely rid himself of the memory of a phrase his father had used about his relations with President Hindenburg. 'Hindenburg looked on me,' Gustav Stresemann would recall, 'with benevolent distrust.'[2]

Coping with the Berlin politicians was less of a problem for Stresemann, though the city's post-war status – imperilled fortress and symbol of Western freedom – made its sober-suited citizens sensitive to the variety of roles the Berlin Philharmonic was expected to play. As Berlin's most prized cultural asset, the orchestra was in receipt of lavish public funding; the question was, to what extent should it be allowed to develop an independent commercial life of its own?

The building of the Berlin Wall in 1961 raised the stakes for the orchestra. It was given additional players and funding to try to lure players to a city which young West Germans now tended to see as a social cul-de-sac. However, a suggestion by Senator Tiburtius that Karajan might consider conducting more than his stipulated six concerts a year in Berlin itself was met with an angry refusal.

How to free up this potentially awkward situation was one of Stresemann's earliest diplomatic challenges. What emerged was a kind of 'gentleman's agreement' that additional concerts might be scheduled during Karajan's now increasingly frequent visits to Berlin for recording sessions. Karajan insisted, however, that the concerts should be non-subscription. He was coming to dislike the 'old' Berlin public – was it their fondness for harking back to past glories that so irked him? – and insisted that tickets should go to 'genuine music-lovers' on a first come first served basis, with special concessions for young people and students.

He also used the negotiation with Stresemann to help break the log-jam on the subsidy versus private profit argument. The fact that the promised concerts arose out of an accelerating programme of recording made it even more urgent that a solution be found. In 1959, the orchestra had offered to pay a ten per cent levy to the Senate on its private earnings, but the offer had been rejected. Karajan, who had already helped renegotiate the Berlin Philharmonic's salary scales,[3] now went further, throwing his full weight behind the players' request that they should be able to benefit collectively and personally from the increasing demand for the orchestra's services.

Karajan's argument was simple. Recording, TV, and film work were part and parcel of the orchestra's activities: they brought extra rehearsal time, enabled the players constantly to monitor their work, raised standards, fostered closer ties between himself and the orchestra, and helped further enhance the Berliners' reputation abroad. It was a compelling case, which the politicians and eventually even Karajan's detractors in Berlin came to accept. As Stresemann himself later reflected, it was the spur Karajan and the orchestra needed at this point. Karajan began to look more and more like a 'permanent conductor'; the music-making flourished; the musicians' private earnings grew, and for two glorious and largely untroubled decades Berlin basked in the glow.[4]

The more serious battles were internal ones, over appointments to the orchestra. These were few and far between but they always brought with them the risk of more permanent scarring. For Karajan, with his vast experience and his long-term vision of what he wanted to achieve, such disputes were of a strictly musical nature. For the orchestra, they tended to be constitutional as well.

During the late 1950s and early 1960s, a string of brilliant appointments had been made, none more so than that of the orchestra's new first oboe, Lothar Koch. After a concert in London in January 1964, *The Times* Music Critic William Mann wrote:

Unhappy the vainglorious soloist who plays Brahms's Violin Concerto with the Berlin Philharmonic Orchestra, for the solo oboe-playing in this orchestra attains a standard of artistry that is almost bound to make the melody of the *Adagio* the musical high point of the work . . . [5]

Schwalbé, Brandis, Spierer, Borwitzky, Zepperitz, Zöller, Koch, Leister, the trombonist Duse-Utesch: these were just some of the outstanding appointments that were made in these years.

There was, however, no settled decision on the horn section. Karajan had known the late Dennis Brain, though whether, had Brain still been alive, he would have been thought right – sufficiently 'German' in his sound for the Berlin Philharmonic – shows how tricky these decisions can be. For a time, a young Swedish player, Bengt Belfrage, was accepted on probation. Karajan liked his playing, especially in the French and Russian repertory. But the orchestra noticed that he was inclined to 'wobble' on the big occasions: at the start of Bruckner's Fourth Symphony, for example.

At the end of the probationary year, it was clear that the players were about to vote him down. Stresemann advised them to delay their vote until Karajan was back in Berlin so that he could be told personally of their doubts. The orchestra declined Stresemann's advice and presented Karajan with a *fait accompli* by letter to the Vienna State Opera. Not surprisingly, he was furious and, as was his habit in such circumstances, he went straight for the jugular. He threatened to withdraw from a Brahms cycle the Berlin Philharmonic was scheduled to give in Paris the following April: a high-profile visit which had already drawn in its wake plans for a meeting between the French government and the Mayor of West Berlin Willy Brandt. Two targets for the price of one.

Werner Thärichen, a member of the orchestra's board, was dispatched to Vienna. Karajan kept him waiting for two days, argued the toss with him for two hours, and then, out of the blue, conceded the orchestra its point. The orchestra was amazed that Thärichen had been able to 'change Karajan's mind'. But Thärichen knew he had changed nothing; the players had been remiss and Karajan had managed both to reprimand them and to outmanoeuvre them.

The job eventually went to Gerd Seifert, a genius and a maverick, whom the elderly Karajan would describe as the greatest horn player he had ever known.[6]

*

What Karajan was seeking in this all-important process of rebuilding and renewal has been well described by Denis Stevens: 'a wonderfully responsive, infinitely flexible instrument which represented the sound ideal that had coursed through his veins for decades'.[7] But just as Legge had wanted 'style' rather than 'a style', so Karajan wanted a varied palette of sounds out of which individual performances could be developed.

Nothing could be further from the truth than the often stated view that there was 'a Karajan sound' – generally characterised as being full, rich, and smooth – as opposed to a uniquely effective palette of sounds *available* to Karajan and the Berliners for the exploration and delineation of works from widely differing musical styles.

All great orchestra-conductor combinations develop some such sound culture. Listen to tapes of rehearsals by Evgeni Mravinsky, Karajan's distinguished contemporary in Leningrad, and you will hear him asking time and again for 'beautiful and meaningful sound'. Whenever Mravinsky uttered the baleful phrase 'There is carrion in your sound' the players looked to their jobs. Mariss Jansons, who studied with Mravinsky and later with Karajan, has suggested:

Before any rehearsal a conductor must have within his imagination his 'sound model' which is then compared with that of the orchestra. Mravinsky had that awareness in the highest degree, as did Karajan. Often in rehearsal Karajan didn't conduct. The art was to make the orchestra listen to itself. Critics sniped but, for musicians, what he did bordered on the miraculous.[8]

The argument over sound is a matter of aesthetics though, like the parallel issue of 'perfectionism', it is all too rarely pursued with any real philosophical rigour. Phrases such as 'the cult of the beautiful' or the 'cult of perfection' have tended to be used, in Karajan's case, simply as terms of disapprobation. The fact is, any form of aesthetic purism tends to upset those who prefer the artistic experience to be rooted in graspable reality. The founder of the Tallis Scholars, Peter Phillips, a musician who has himself occasionally been accused of 'perfectionist' tendencies, addressed the issue in an essay prompted by an exhibition of paintings by Whistler:

In recent years musicians have often been criticised for making a sound which is simply too beautiful, as if such a thing must offend a modern sense of social responsibility. The Berlin Philharmonic, especially under Karajan, was often sneeringly referred to as having a Rolls Royce sound, the prime feature of which was a smoothness, deriving from superlative technique, which to some listeners was incapable of expressing the nastier turns in programmatic music. This objection loses its force if music is heard to be a succession of unspecific emotions, ebbing and flowing, carrying its audience to another world where to apply labels (like devotion, love, pity and patriotism, for example) is to trap and reduce it. There was never any problem with the basic sound of the Berlin Philharmonic, it has been one of the most consistently emotive sounds in Western musical culture; but it is a strictly musical experience, offering little to those who declare that music by itself, on its own terms, is not enough.[9]

The visceral power – what Phillips calls the 'emotive' quality – of the Berlin Philharmonic sound is something that can be traced back, through Furtwängler, to Nikisch's time. Karajan inherited the sound, much as a son might inherit acres of prime arable land. He also inherited a state of mind, a temperamental predisposition deep within the orchestra's collective unconscious. As the critics had noticed in Salzburg in 1957, the Berlin style is full-bodied, fiery, and physically intense. Film footage reveals how the renewals of the early 1960s had made this an even more marked feature of the style. Neville Cardus would describe it thus:

The playing throughout the evening was truly superb, every instrumentalist bowing and blowing and thumping as though for dear life. The violins waved and swayed like cornstalks in the wind. The drummer, white haired, might have been a conjuror drawing rabbits from his instrument's interior. One cello player, at least, swept his bow with so much passion that he seemed likely to roll off the platform. Every note had vitality, yet every note was joined to all the others. There were no tonal lacunae, not a hiatus all night. We could hear things in the score which usually we are obliged to seek out by eyes reading the score. Phrase ran beautifully into phrase, viola took on from violin, cello from viola without an obvious 'join'. The double-basses were magnificent and capable of quite delicate shading. Woodwind choired, perfectly blended. The violins were alternately warm and brilliant.[10]

There is a story which Berlin players like to tell of a dispute over the design of the back-rests for new orchestral chairs in the Philharmonie. 'And since when,' demanded one player, 'did a Philharmoniker need a back-rest?' I was told the story by Fergus McWilliam, a horn player who joined the Berlin Philharmonic in 1984. He and his wife had first heard the orchestra at the 1972 Edinburgh Festival: Stravinsky's *Apollo* and Brahms's Second Symphony. The tickets had been a wedding present from the bride's family:

After the Stravinsky, we wanted to leave. It was so beautiful, we couldn't comprehend that we would want to listen to the Brahms. Staying was going to leave us with too cluttered an experience; we wanted to keep the memory of the Stravinsky pure and perfect in its own right. We stayed, of course; our family would never have forgiven us if we'd left in the interval! But that was the first time I had come across an intensity of music-making which had such an effect. In a sense, it attracted and it also repelled. There was a limit to how close you come to it, like a fire which is giving out unbearable amounts of heat and light. After an experience like this, you can see why the Berlin style of music-making is too much for some people to take.[11]

Acquiring repertory, Karajan once said, had two aspects. First, the orchestra must learn the piece; secondly, it must build 'its performance culture'.[12] Here time was a crucial factor. Time to study a work, time to go away from it so as to allow it to 'rest in the mind', time to return to it and start the real work of final preparation and performance. The process was important to Karajan, too. Though he had a huge repertory from his days in Aachen, Berlin, and post-war Vienna, he was not – once past his fiftieth year – a quick study. He, too, needed time to absorb the music into his system. He remembered music not photographically (the idea of remembering music visually was anathema to him) but sequentially and as sound.[13]

By the early 1960s, critics found themselves writing about a new quality and style of music-making. In February 1964, the London *Times* would describe a Berlin Philharmonic Brahms concert:

There were a number of occasions last night when we thought that our best players can put up a technical performance of a similar quality of excellence. But where the Berliners perhaps put their best foot forward is in the integration of the various instrumental groups into a perfectly rounded whole. They are like a body of chamber musicians, minutely listening to one another and adjusting their volume of sound and degree of dynamic accentuation to a nicety.[14]

Karajan believed that the mark of a great – as opposed to good – orchestra lay in its ability to take wing in performance, to move and change direction, independent of the conductor: like a flock of birds working on its own internal radar. It is a distinction that, as far as I know, no other conductor has made in quite the same way. Though Karajan's methods were grounded in the best practice of the old masters, there were elements in his thinking and approach which owed much to his quasi-mystical belief that music inhabits a realm apart, born of the real world but ultimately detached from it.

It is an approach that involves risks. There can be little doubt that by responding to these deeply felt intuitions, Karajan alienated himself from those listeners and critics who look for a simpler kind of cut-and-thrust in the music-making. (Something any half decent conductor can provide on a good day and which Karajan himself provided in ample measure in the early and middle part of his career.) James Galway, who played under Karajan's direction for six years between 1969 and 1975, would make the provocative observation, 'Unquestionably, [Karajan] learned much from men like Toscanini, but whereas Toscanini was a driver, Karajan [had] the soul of music in him.'[15] Pianist and conductor Vladimir Ashkenazy considered Karajan to be 'a great intuitive musician who communicates as well as anyone could imagine', but he added the interesting rider, 'If he has one fault, it's that he has a habit of placing too much trust in the orchestra.'[16]

So deep did the trust (at the artistic level) eventually become between Karajan and the Berlin Philharmonic, that as the years went by the question of what he 'did' on the rostrum became an ever deeper mystery to listeners and professional observers alike. It was less of a mystery to the Berlin players; and not simply because of their long and intimate contact with him. What Karajan was responding to – and he had been doing this on and off since 1938 – was a culture within the orchestra. When Fergus McWilliam joined in 1984, it was fathoms deep:

It's very interesting that his beating hand, his right hand, was very often held still. The stick held firmly but almost never moving – except occasionally when a kind of swinging, shovelling motion was used to impart a certain *Schwung* to a passage. And the left hand, the one for expression, had a kind of kneading motion – kneading the dough – and again not much physical

486

action. The impression one had was that he was experiencing the music as a kind of tactile sensation. And that's all we needed; we knew he was on our wavelength. I don't mean that in a condescending way. There was a sense of leadership but, paradoxically, it was the kind of leadership that does not lead.[17]

In this sense, Karajan was more the Great Co-operator than the Great Dictator of popular legend.

Twenty years earlier he had been outwardly more insistent, far more physically active, the very opposite of that pain-racked and partly immobilised old man. Yet the signs were already there of his wanting to achieve his own musical quietus. Even in the 1960s, in the music of certain composers – Wagner, Bruckner – he would become lost in reveries that risked leaving players and singers temporarily becalmed. Cardus noticed this in a performance of Bruckner's Seventh Symphony Karajan gave with the Vienna Philharmonic in London in 1962:

Karajan has his recurrent moments of quite heavy and slackening tension and tempo. But soon the first movement and the symphony as a whole opened out into a spacious far-flung tone pageant, and the *Adagio* – one of the most majestic and eloquent of any – was truly *feierlich*, the coda, lamenting the passing of Wagner, a noble echo of Walhall.[18]

Two years later, when Bernard Haitink heard Karajan conduct the same symphony in Amsterdam, this time with the Berlin Philharmonic, he was surprised by the number of times he found his attention wandering:

'Is this so good?' I asked myself. Then he had us back again. He was a devil! He knew exactly where the real points of tension come.[19]

Karajan's skill was that he could cast an eighty-minute Bruckner symphony as a single piece. His ability to sustain and where necessary re-engage a basic pulse was second to none.

On tempo itself, he was a fanatic for accuracy. Peter Girth remembers a game that, even as an old man, Karajan liked to play on long flights. With someone timing him, Karajan would mentally play through a section of a piece of music. He would then do it again: the trick being to get the thing identical next time round to the nearest millisecond. This was not an end in itself. It was simply something Karajan believed a proficient musician should be able to do.

In the final analysis, though, Karajan was driven by a feeling for something deeper. In his profile of Karajan in the *New Yorker*, Winthrop Sargeant would note a larger concern:

It involves the rhythms of nature, from the human heartbeat to the waves of the sea; it involves a theory about the advantages of exerting force while in a state of relaxation; and it also involves the achievement of results by carefully economised effort, the co-ordination of physical effort with the exigencies of physical nature, and the perfecting of the mental and physical resources of the human organism to attain maximum efficiency in whatever field it enters.[20]

'Do you realise,' Karajan once remarked, 'that every seventh wave is the powerful one?' Feeling the pulse of the sea, judging the power and contour of that seventh wave and setting the helm accordingly was, he said, 'very, very satisfying – a real adventure in rhythm'.

When Karajan made remarks like this people never quite knew whether it was the schoolboy talking or some latter-day Leonardo da Vinci. In any case, what did it matter? Sailing, skiing, flying: what were they to music or music to them? In Karajan's case, it mattered a very great deal, since his inner and outer lives were of a piece and tended to one end: a preoccupation with achieving a sense of harmony with the pulses of nature itself. As an old man he would recall:

I remember once, I was rehearsing a piece of Bach – I forget which piece it was – and I suddenly felt in a state of absolute harmony. So much so that I stopped the rehearsal at that point.[21]

Professional sailors do not mock at Karajan's remarks. Helmsmanship is, indeed, all about rhythm; about watching and listening, about threading the boat through the waves to the sea's pulse.[22] And when the analogies switch to flying (the 'flock of birds' image) or horsemanship (the ability to 'place' the orchestra as a rider places his horse before the fence), the professionals again listen and nod agreement, and express interest in the fact that a musician should understand so precisely such fundamental issues.

Karajan had sailed, of course, since he was six, learning to judge in those early days, not the pulse of the waves but the shifting patterns of the thermal breezes as they flowed down from the mountains to duck and weave their way over the surface of the Grundlsee. No wonder he understood Debussy's *La mer* so well. No wonder, too, given the pedigree of the orchestral playing, that his 1964 Berlin recording of *La mer* is now one of the classics of the gramophone.[23] And no wonder that he often felt empowered by nature. 'When you return from ten days in the mountains,' he once said, 'you can overwhelm them [fellow musicians] with energy, simply overwhelm them.'[24]

*

Karajan was not the first conductor, nor would he be the last, to work out that performing the music of one composer can help sharpen, illuminate and refine an orchestra's playing of another. But because he had the Berliners 'for life', he was able to work the system in an extraordinary way. In the years 1960–5, he complemented the preparation, playing, and recording of complete cycles of the Beethoven and Brahms symphonies with a great deal of work on early twentieth-century repertory: in particular, music by Strauss, Debussy, Stravinsky, and Ravel. Paris, London, and New York were treated to complete Beethoven and Brahms cycles, while the prestigious festivals – Edinburgh, Lucerne, Salzburg, and a new favourite, Athens – were plied with more exotic combinations. In November 1961, when the Berliners were accorded the unique honour of playing their Cleveland, Ohio concert in Severance Hall,[25] Karajan conducted a programme of Bach, Stravinsky, and Richard Strauss. Herbert Elwell, critic of Cleveland's most venerable newspaper *The Plain Dealer*, wrote:

The program was one of contrasts, almost antitheses. Who could stand farther apart than Igor Stravinsky, in his Symphony in C, and Richard Strauss in his tone poem *Thus Spake Zarathustra*? The latter lingers over the past like an elegy for a dying world, while the former peeks through the lattices of tradition to find escape in new realities. The Stravinsky was clean and effortless, powerful and trenchant. The Strauss was a somber song, growing into a gigantic monument of eloquent nostalgia.[26]

Karajan concerts in Berlin usually took place at the New Year and in the late summer, during the Berlin Festival. Here there were a number of gestures and experiments that would bear fruit only in the longer term; and there were some musical dead-ends too. These included performances of music by Henze and the less obviously talented Werner Thärichen. The first Thärichen work Karajan agreed to conduct was the Piano Concerto which Thärichen had talked the 29-year-old Alfred Brendel into playing after hearing Brendel play a concerto by Krenek at the Salzburg Festival. Brendel had accepted, sight unseen, on the premise that it afforded him a chance to play with Karajan in Berlin. He would later recall: 'It was the only time we worked together, and one of the very few occasions in my life when I played a piece with which I could not identify.'[27]

Ahead of the Mahler centenary in July 1960, Karajan tried conclusions with *Das Lied von der Erde*. But the orchestra was not ready for Mahler and Rössl-Majdan made heavy weather of the mezzo-soprano part. Serious work was also begun on *Le sacre du printemps*, though only after Karajan had breached the orchestra's anti-Stravinsky defences with months of high intensity work on the Symphony in C.

Spurred on by his friend Stuckenschmidt, Karajan also began preparing Schoenberg's *Variations for Orchestra*, the work in which the twelve-tone method finally bursts into full flower. The Berliners had given the *Variations* its première, under Furtwängler's direction, in December 1928; but they had never taken it into their larger repertory. Getting them to play it with the eloquence and accuracy they would naturally accord to the music of Brahms or Debussy would take Karajan the best part of twelve years to achieve.[28]

Shortly before Easter 1964, Karajan gave two performances of Britten's *War Requiem* in Berlin, with Wilma Lipp, John van Kesteren, and Dietrich Fischer-Dieskau, who had sung at the work's première in the rebuilt Coventry Cathedral in May 1962. The Berlin Philharmonic had played during that same Coventry Festival, without Karajan. Although the Nazi question had not yet re-emerged in any real way, he evidently feared opening old wounds.[29]

*

In November 1962, Karajan and the Berliners completed their recording of the nine Beethoven symphonies for Deutsche Grammophon. For the first time in the history of the gramophone, the recordings were planned as an integral cycle and released as an 8-LP subscription set, handsomely boxed and annotated. This caused something of a sensation, for though the price (£14.8s.od.–$40) was merely a multiplication by eight of the cost of a premium price LP, the idea of having to buy all nine symphonies at the same time was seen by some as an affront to choice, by others as a lure to insolvency.[30]

Watching from the sidelines, EMI's David Bicknell predicted that Deutsche Grammophon was heading for 'a colossal financial catastrophe'. To recoup the estimated investment of nearly one and a half million Deutschmarks, over 100,000 boxes would need to be sold. Other analysts were equally sceptical, and the Siemens board remained nervous.

Ernst von Siemens had attended several of the recording sessions, though more as an interested music-lover than as an anxious chairman. His confidence in the project, and Elsa Schiller's, proved well founded. When the set arrived in the shops in February 1963, it rapidly attained the status of a phenomenon.

That the cycle would be something remarkable had been flagged in advance by the live concert cycles in Berlin, Paris, London, and New York. 'Karajan presented the symphonies plus high fidelity,' Cardus had written in his London review.[31] The set was not merely an offshoot of the age of high fidelity; Karajan's musical roots went deeper than that. It had, however, been extremely carefully positioned from the interpretative point of view. As Howard Taubman had speculated in the *New York Times* in 1958, Karajan was probably capable of fashioning convincing interpretations of Beethoven's music in a number of different performing styles.[32]

This was almost certainly true. As we have seen, he was a skilled actor, and, as an interpreter, something of a chameleon. He was also an intensely practical man. In November 1962, William Mann had flown to Berlin to report on the sessions for *The Gramophone*:

I came to understand, before long, that for Karajan this recorded performance was like a new enterprise, in that the transitory factors – these singers, these players, in this church, with this recording staff – created new circumstances that had to be taken into account. Karajan is, in the best possible sense, a practical musician: his musicianship automatically connects the score with the circumstances. At any given moment, his conception of how the work should go may collide with what happens, and at once his mind visibly poses musical equations and solves them. You can see him thinking 'That doesn't work here'. And instead of compromising his ideal to fit the circumstances, he works out the best way of adapting the available conditions so that they serve the conception.[33]

Yet the conception itself had, to some extent, been modified. Where Karajan's 1950s Philharmonia Beethoven cycle still had elements in it that owed a certain amount to the old German school of Beethoven interpretation, the new-found virtuosity of the Berliners allowed him to approach more nearly the fierce beauty and lean-toned fiery manner of Toscanini's Beethoven style as he had first encountered it in its halcyon age in the mid-1930s. Nothing demonstrates this better than the 1962 recording of the Fourth Symphony, the fieriest and most radiant of Karajan's five studio recordings of the work.

The old shibboleth that the even-numbered symphonies are less dramatic than the odd-numbered meant nothing to Karajan. His accounts of the Second, Fourth, Sixth, and Eighth symphonies were every bit as intense as their allegedly sturdier neighbours. Only in the Seventh Symphony's third movement *Trio* and the *Menuetto* of the Eighth Symphony – where he continued to follow Wagner's idea of this as an essentially stately dance, a kind of surrogate slow movement[34] – did he deviate significantly from the Toscanini model. And it worked. True, the first two movements of the *Pastoral* Symphony emerged somewhat tense and airless (the recording was made in February 1962 at the height of the 'resignation' crisis in Vienna) but this was the only real lapse.

Where such an enterprise was concerned, the reviews mattered hugely, though in 1963 there was little of the proselytising, lobbying, and arm-twisting within the record industry that would go on in later years over new sets of the nine. When the reviews came in, they were mostly enthusiastic. The playing dazzled, as did the recordings: clean and clear, and daringly (occasionally too daringly) 'lit' with a bright shimmer of reverberation. The engineer was a young man called Günter Hermanns whose début with Karajan this was and who would remain with him to the end.

Above all, the critical predispositions of the age were well served. It was Klemperer who said of Karajan, in 1969, 'He's just the conductor for 1969.' Yet the prejudice – and it is a prejudice – in favour of an 'objective' Beethoven style was not the preserve of the 1960s, or of Karajan. All the commercially successful gramophone cycles of the nine – Toscanini's, Klemperer's, Karajan's in 1962 and again in 1976, and those of the best period performers in the 1980s and early 1990s – have their roots in the *neue Sachlichkeit* (the 'new objectivity') of which Klemperer himself had been so influential an exponent back in the 1920s.

Walter Legge, who was about to quit EMI, looked on from the sidelines: admiringly, and a little jealously. He adjudged Edward Greenfield's review in *The Gramophone* 'a touch over-enthusiastic', which was hardly fair, given the fact that the review, for all its enthusiasm, was riddled with caveats.[35] What so enthused Greenfield – and the record-buying public at large – was the urgency of the music-making, its vitality and, ultimately, a fierce sense of joy that had its natural point of culmination in a thrillingly played and eloquently sung account of the finale of the Ninth.

Not everyone, needless to say, approved of all this athleticism and hypertension. Cardus had suggested that Karajan's account of the Seventh Symphony might confidently be entered for the next Olympic Games; around this time, too, Klemperer stumped out of a performance of the Ninth Symphony, outraged by Karajan's over-quick tempo in the Scherzo.

In later years, less pressured, Karajan would readjust; but not before he had conducted a similarly quick and tense account of the Ninth Symphony for the opening of Scharoun's Berlin Philharmonie in October 1963. Among the guests was Elisabeth Furtwängler. Like Klemperer, though for different reasons, she was not impressed.

CHAPTER 53

A strange marriage

An two men ride of an horse, one must ride behind.
Shakespeare, *Much Ado About Nothing*

During the summer and early autumn of 1962 an eerie stillness had descended on the Austrian musical scene, as on some hot August afternoon when heat-haze shrouds the distant hills and the sound of thunder is far away and someone else's concern.

Artists fretted, they always do, but Karajan's manner was now both detached and endlessly reassuring. 'Trust me,' he told an anxious Christa Ludwig shortly before a performance, marking her forehead with the sign of the cross; though when Geraint Evans, a new Karajan favourite but a great worrier, begged for a clear upbeat at the start of Figaro's 'Se vuol ballare', Karajan dismissed his concern with a benign wave of the hand. That summer, the renovated Theater an der Wien had reopened with a new production of *Die Zauberflöte*. Schneider-Siemssen wanted the Queen of the Night to emerge from the back of the stage, as if from the underworld, in a moving star. The producer Rudolf Hartmann said Karajan would never accept the idea. 'Provided it looks good,' said Karajan, 'I am happy. Leave me to sort out the music.'

In September he recorded Tchaikovsky's First Piano Concerto with Sviatoslav Richter and the Vienna Symphony Orchestra. Richter gave a performance of astonishing intimacy and refinement, which Karajan, appreciating to the nth degree what his soloist was about, wrapped round with an accompaniment that both served the interpretation and set it off with a ferocity and exhibitionist dash of its own. If, orchestrally, the results are a touch brazen, it was a risk Karajan was prepared to take.[1]

That same autumn, he also recorded *Tosca* for Decca-RCA with a cast that included Leontyne Price, Giuseppe Taddei, and Giuseppe di Stefano. John Culshaw, who produced, would later judge it to be a performance

... which, from the musical point of view, remains second only to the great Columbia set with Maria Callas conducted by Victor De Sabata. When so much has been written about Karajan's arrogance, it says much for the other side of him that he knew the rival set very well indeed, and often asked us to play parts of it to him. One exceptionally tricky passage for the conductor is the entry of Tosca in Act 3, where Puccini's tempo directions can best be described as elastic. Karajan listened to De Sabata several times over during that passage and then said, 'No, he's right but I can't do it. That's *his* secret.'

Nobody can sensibly fault Karajan at that point, and what he does in his own way is every bit as faithful to Puccini as is De Sabata: when it comes to that sort of fine point there are no rules.[2]

The firing squad in Act 3 posed a problem for the recording. It sounded absurd indoors, and in those days it was not possible to decamp to some distant field, play in the music on one machine, fire the rifles, and re-record the whole effect on a second machine. In the end, it was decided to use the open-air courtyard at the side of the Sofiensaal and to schedule the session for a Sunday afternoon when traffic noise would be at a minimum.

It was not a good idea. A practice fusillade roused local residents who were sleeping off their Sunday lunch. Within minutes the place was surrounded by police. Fortunately, the police saw the funny side of it. Having checked the rifles to make sure real bullets were not being used, they helped pacify the residents. Not that it took very long:

At the mere mention of Herbert von Karajan's name there was, as it were, a wave of comprehension: if *he* wanted such things to disturb the peace of a summer Sunday, then it would only be an extension of the wishes of the Almighty.[3]

In October, Karajan conducted the same cast in a revival of *Tosca* at the Vienna Opera. For the rest, he was seen in Vienna on just three occasions that autumn. The fact is, games were now being played. The promised 'reform' of the opera's funding regime was being stalled within the vast apparatus of the State Theatre Administration by bureaucrats who were every bit as expert in the art of 'masterful inactivity' as their predecessors had been in the time of Karajan's great-grandfather. That Austria was temporarily without a government also helped their cause. Now that Drimmel was no longer Minister of Education, merely the 'acting' minister, he and his aides could distance themselves from all talk of 'crisis'.

But Karajan, too, was playing his own delaying games. A new production of *Tannhäuser*, due to open at Christmas, was postponed until the new year, ostensibly because of the indisposition of Wolfgang Windgassen. (He had been ill but was now perfectly well.) The truth was, Karajan wanted more time to rehearse and light the production.

When it did finally open on 2 January, Windgassen was genuinely unavailable. Hans Beirer took his place and sang so wretchedly there was surprise among members of the cast that his career was not ended then and there. Vocally, there was little else to celebrate. Waechter and Gottlob Frick were hamstrung by Karajan's slow tempi and Gré Brouwenstijn was a none too certain Elisabeth. Gundula Janowitz's Young Shepherd was a ray of light in the encircling gloom, but a production of *Tannhäuser* is not redeemed by its shepherd.

The performance sounded well orchestrally, it looked superb, though it is remembered now mainly for the hunting scene in which Karajan used real hounds and falcons. (A rehearsal shot of him handling one of these handsome birds of prey reveals a deep mutual fascination between him and the falcon and a more than passing physical resemblance. He once said that he would like to return to earth as a falcon.)

It did not help the situation in Vienna that this dismal Wagner première more or less coincided with the opening, in Milan, of one of the great landmark successes of Karajan's career: the new La Scala production of Puccini's *La bohème*, directed by Franco Zeffirelli. To Italian critics, the production was a milestone in the opera's stage history, comparable to Toscanini's 1923 La Scala revival of Puccini's *Manon Lescaut*. It would tour as far afield as Moscow and Montreal, and was for Karajan a representative example of how quality productions can thrive in a commercially competitive world. It had been cast from within the La Scala company; and though Zeffirelli's staging was expensive to mount, the costs were defrayed through co-production, touring agreements, and film and television rights. Nowadays such strategies are commonplace; yet when Karajan and a handful of like-minded folk first staked out the route, they were treated with great suspicion.

In March spirits were lifted by an unexpected triumph for the Vienna Opera: a new production of Monteverdi's *L'incoronazione di Poppea* which Karajan himself conducted in a new realisation by the German musicologist and self-styled *Klangregisseur* ('sound producer') Erich Kraack. This was a new approach to Monteverdi;[4] it was also near the start of the so-called 'Swinging Sixties', when Monteverdi's celebration of amorality and sexual libertarianism chimed sweetly with the mood of the times.

The stage director was Günther Rennert, a Felsenstein pupil whom Karajan had known in Berlin in the early 1940s and who was currently joint artistic director of the Glyndebourne Festival Opera, where he had produced *Poppea*, in Raymond Leppard's performing edition, the previous summer. 'Intense' and 'luminously beautiful' were the words most often used in reviews of the Vienna *Poppea*. Some thought Karajan's heart was not in it, musically or scenically. Others, including Sena Jurinac who sang the role of Poppea, ranked it among his finest achievements as Artistic Director. According to her, the Viennese were all against the idea at first, as were the scholars; but those who saw the production never forgot it.

Though some of the musical preparation had been by Hans Swarowsky and though Karajan and Rennert had had a spectacular falling out over the opera's comic elements, the rapport between stage and pit was remarkably close. It is also clear from Jurinac's memories that Karajan had fed into the production ideas from his own experimental staging of Palestrina's *Missa Papae Marcelli*:

I remember the duet with Nerone and Poppea. A bare stage, with a white rug, Poppea in red, everything else dark. And then as this wonderfully quiet music slowly grew in intensity, the two hands coming gradually together. It was utterly simple, and absolutely spellbinding.[5]

*

On 13 May 1963 a not-so-trivial lapse occurred at the State Opera which can be seen, with hindsight, as being the beginning of the end of Karajan's period of rule.

Twenty minutes after the curtain was due to rise on *Die Meistersinger*, the audience was informed that because of the 'indisposition' of Wolfgang Windgassen the performance could not now take place. In fact, Windgassen was perfectly well; the problem was, he did not know he was meant to be singing in Vienna that evening.

Whose fault this was is not clear. Excuses flew back and forth, and the press had a field day. Karajan was on holiday in St Tropez, and Schäfer was in hospital recovering from a heart attack. General Secretary Moser and Ernst August Schneider both offered to carry the can, but too many people remembered Karajan's claim at a press conference that an opera house can be run perfectly well from the other end of a telephone.

With Schäfer now unlikely to return to his old post, the Vienna Opera was once again in crisis. It was yet another endgame; and numerous people, well-meaning and not-so-well-meaning, now got caught up in it.

The man widely expected to succeed Schäfer was former Volksoper Director Hermann Juch. Juch's period at the Volksoper had ushered in a new golden age; but his love of grand opera left him hankering after something more substantial than the directorship of 'the Bayreuth of operetta'. With Juch all set to transfer to the State Opera and the contract of his successor at the Volksoper, Heinrich Reif-Gintl, already in an advanced state of readiness, two bombshells landed in quick succession. Albert Moser, it was announced, was to be the new head of the Volksoper. As for the State Opera, the new co-director would be that zealot of operatic zealots – and a long-standing foe of Karajan – Egon Hilbert.

After his removal as Head of the Administration of State Theatres in 1954, and a brief period as a diplomat in Italy, Hilbert had clambered back on to the Viennese bandwagon via the Vienna Festival, which he was now running every bit as busily and as successfully as he had run the Viennese theatres in the years 1945–54. He did not disguise his glee at being back in post at 'his' opera. 'I am madly happy,' he told the assembled journalists at his first press conference.

The man who talked Karajan into taking Hilbert on was the administrator and stage director Paul Hager, one of the least distinguished members of the State Opera production team but an intimate of both men. On paper, it seemed an ideal solution. Karajan's executive musical talents and Hilbert's administrative ones were exactly what the State Opera needed. It also pleased the press, which had always harboured within it a small but vociferous pro-Hilbert faction.

The problem was that the accord was based on the idea that Karajan and Hilbert would run the opera jointly, consulting closely with one another on a week-to-week basis. This might have worked in any normal circumstance, but by no stretch of the imagination could Hilbert or Karajan be considered normal. Marcel Prawy knew both of them well:

Hilbert talked a lot, wrote a lot, was given to interminable memoranda and a great deal of fuss; without an atmosphere of excitement, he could not exist. Karajan, on the other hand, disliked putting things in writing and was a man of few, but crisp, words. If people started to shout, he would leave the room.[6]

Like Gérard Mortier, Karajan's successor in Salzburg in the 1990s, Hilbert lacked specific artistic skills but more than made up for that with his intellectual quick-wittedness, his stanchless energy, and his huge passion for anything and everything to do with opera or theatre. Prawy would also write:

Hilbert was a daemonic military commander who unfortunately knew very little about strategy . . . He was quite incapable of listening to what the other person was saying, yet suggestions one had put to him often cropped up later as his own. He hardly ever attended auditions or listened to a new work being played over; but when he did, he often hit the nail on the head in a matter of seconds. His reactions were instantaneous. If he wanted to speak to someone he would manage to get hold of him by hook or by crook, even if the victim was on a sleigh-tour of the Arctic.[7]

To his dying day, Karajan was as enigmatic as the Sphinx on the question of why he agreed the deal. The nearest he ever came to an explanation of what happened was that, having accepted the proposal in principle, he had spent a fortnight walking, talking, and dining with Hilbert who, once in office, promptly went back on everything he had said.

Mattoni told journalists at the time, 'My dears, it will all be wonderful. Hilbert will do exactly what we ask him to do.' No one swallowed that. At this remove of time, it is possible to believe that, in his heart of hearts, Karajan knew that the game was up; that the Vienna Opera was unmanageable; and that the shrewdest thing to do was to summon into partnership the one man who hubristically claimed to know all the answers.

As with his dismission from Aachen, he may have thought, 'It's just weakness if one cannot break away from something to which one is still attached but whose importance in one's own life has disappeared.'[8]

*

Two sets of minutes exist of meetings between Karajan and Hilbert, one dated Vienna-Mauerbach, 16 June 1963, the other dated Zürich, 12 January 1964. The one charts the setting up of the power-sharing structure, the other chronicles its descent into acrimony. From the outset, Hilbert was obsessed, first with defining his position, then with setting down on paper his status as Karajan's absolute co-equal. There was another point, too, with which Hilbert (a lawyer by training) was particularly concerned. He wished to establish the right to be freed from his contract in the event of Karajan himself resigning. Karajan agreed to this as a self-evidently reasonable request. What he omitted to do was to bind Hilbert securely into the arrangement by insisting that if he went, Hilbert went too. When the crunch came and Karajan resigned, Hilbert sat tight. All Hilbert's *written* contract stated was that in the event of Karajan's resignation, Hilbert himself had the *option* to resign as well.

Though Karajan was fairly good at running his own life, his Achilles' heel was a casualness over paperwork and, by devolution, a vulnerability to the machinations of lesser men, friends and foes alike, for whom power play was a way of life, an end in itself. Hilbert was not one of these. For all his oddity, he had been a star achiever. But he knew how to rile Karajan (persistent physical nearness was usually enough to do the trick) and how to entrap him legally.

Artistically, the Karajan-Hilbert cohabitation – 'Die unheimliche Ehe [Sinister marriage]' as one wit punningly put it[9] – got off to a reasonably good start. During the Salzburg Festival it was announced that Böhm would be returning to the Vienna Opera (Karajan and he were said to be bosom pals again), as would Hilbert's old friend Josef Krips. In early September Karajan formally introduced his new 'co-director' to the State Opera company before flying off with the Vienna Philharmonic to give three concerts at the Athens Festival, a visit which gave Karajan and the orchestra an opportunity to pay homage to Dimitri Mitropoulos, who had died in November 1960. A short service was held at the graveside and wreaths were laid in the orchestra's name and Karajan's.

Back in Vienna, Karajan conducted performances of *Don Giovanni*, *Otello*, *Aida*, and *Pelléas et Mélisande*, and brought his Salzburg production of *Il trovatore* to the State Opera.

On 3 November, the La Scala production of *La bohème* was due to arrive in Vienna, an event that promised to turn a memorable autumn into an unforgettable one. But it was not to be: at least, not immediately. When the unions discovered that Karajan had engaged not only the La Scala cast, but their prompter (their *maestro suggeritore*, more a fully-fledged assistant conductor) the unions threatened an all-out strike. Months later, when the dispute was over but not forgotten, the Austrian courts ruled that the unions had acted unreasonably,[10] but that did not help now.

The commotion was immense, as Marcel Prawy would recall:

The episode split little Austria into two irreconcilably hostile factions. My grocer, who had never been to the Opera in her life, regarded it as uncivilised to deny Karajan his 'maestro zutscherritohre'. My bootmaker, on the other hand, who had also never been to the Opera in his life, regarded it as an impertinence that this Karajan should squander the taxpayers' money on a 'mestro dschuzerridoore'.[11]

When Gundula Janowitz, strap-hanging on a crowded Viennese tram, tried to bring a few facts to bear on the debate that was raging all about her, she was almost lynched by the anti-Karajan tendency and had to get off at the next stop.

Though industrial action had been threatened, no one knew when it would happen. It came just fifty seconds before the start of the performance. Hilbert himself had led the Italian prompter to his place beneath the stage; the Austrian President was in the state box; Karajan was about to enter the pit. And then the strike order came.

It caused total confusion. After twenty minutes, Karajan and Hilbert appeared in front of the curtain, Karajan in tails, Hilbert in a dinner jacket. Hilbert read out a statement about the dispute, announced that there would be no performance that evening, affirmed his loyalty to Karajan, and as an earnest of that loyalty sealed his affirmation with a kiss. It is said that no one who saw the look on Karajan's face as Hilbert planted the kiss will ever forget it.

Three days later, Karajan went ahead without a prompter of any kind. In the highly charged atmosphere that now surrounded the already famous production, it was an occasion the like of which even the Viennese had rarely experienced. By the time everyone finally went home, Karajan and the cast had taken thirty-eight curtain calls.

The Vienna correspondent of the London *Times* wrote of the score 'glowing to vibration point'. A recording exists of the performance on 30 November which does, indeed, confirm the astonishing vibrancy, intensity and, in the final moments, tragic power of the music-making. There are those who swear by the studio recording of *La bohème* Karajan made in Berlin in 1972 with Freni and Pavarotti in the leading roles, preferring it even to the classic Beecham set. It is finely done but it is a sterile artefact alongside the live theatre performance. Somewhere deep within Karajan there lurked the spirit of Pagliaccio. Yet there was spirituality, too, which is why this live Vienna *La bohème* was so soaring an experience and so gut-wrenching a one.

Ironically, the production also demonstrated the virtues of the system of ensemble theatre which Karajan himself had declared dead and buried. With the Vienna Philharmonic in the pit and a group of mainly Italian singers, several of whom Karajan had worked with for years, the genius of the performance resided in no small measure in the fact that this *was* an ensemble. Such 'stars' as there were in the cast – Taddei, Panerai – took the comprimario student roles. Gianni Raimondi, the Rodolfo, was in reality no more than talented house tenor (Karajan had refused to have di Stefano), and though Mirella Freni became a star with this production, she too was young and still relatively unknown.[12]

During November, Karajan somehow found time to record *Carmen* for Decca-RCA with Leontyne Price as his cajoling, lustrous-voiced, sexually alluring Carmen. It is a performance driven by two imperatives: the character of Carmen, and Fate. Culshaw, who produced, has recalled how Karajan balanced a series of apparently simple string chords in the fateful Card Scene with a care that amounted to a kind of genius. He claimed that no critic noticed this, which is not strictly true. Philip Hope-Wallace, who like most critics did not much care for the set (he thought it lacked 'ebullience and shimmer'), singled out the Card Scene for special praise;[13] and, years later, another writer described (or, rather, accused) the performance of suggesting a kind of 'intergalactic doom' at this point.[14]

It was, indeed, a doom-afflicted set. On 22 November President Kennedy was assassinated. The crew's first thought that evening – and, to his eternal credit, that of the Don José, Franco Corelli – was for the one member of the cast who was American, black, and deeply committed to the Kennedy cause: Leontyne Price. Culshaw offered to postpone the sessions for a day or two, but Price insisted on going on. Just about the next thing they recorded was the Card Scene. No wonder it sounds as it does.

*

After a month of non-stop work and unremitting crises of one kind or another, Karajan left Vienna for Munich to conduct a new production of *Fidelio* as part of the inaugural celebrations of Munich's rebuilt National Theatre. His Leonore was Christa Ludwig who, for all her manifest success with the role, never felt comfortable in it. Karajan was aware of this and adapted his speeds accordingly. One or two critics savaged his pacing of the opera, as Ludwig warned him they would, but that did not bother him. He read the papers as avidly as the next man; but he also knew when to ignore them.

While Karajan was in Munich, Hilbert was busying himself as usual: sitting at his desk in the State Opera plotting, planning, and issuing reams of directives which he knew Karajan had neither the time nor the inclination to read. Claiming that Mattoni was blocking the channels of communication between himself and Karajan, he was now demanding Mattoni's removal from the State Opera management. He was also beginning to interfere in artistic policy.

The morning after the first night of *Fidelio*, Karajan held a meeting with Hilbert in Munich. Next day, he flew back to Vienna to attend a State Opera press conference, during which he sat silent and motionless alongside Hilbert, apparently oblivious of everything including the photographers' flash-bulbs to which he normally took such strenuous exception. After the press conference, he returned to Munich, where he conducted a second performance of *Fidelio*.

Shortly after the performance, he suffered a sudden physical collapse and was rushed to hospital.

The collapse was attributed to 'a circulatory disorder'. It was not heart trouble but physical and nervous exhaustion brought on by overwork, stress, and the possibly unwise use of alcohol as a balm to shattered nerves. (Liver-related illnesses had dogged Karajan since the 1930s.) Perhaps it is as well that the collapse happened when it did. After Munich, he had been scheduled to return to Vienna to conduct and direct a new production of *Elektra*, a work which, by his own admission, took more out of him than almost any other.

While Karajan was still in hospital in Munich, the director of the ballet in Vienna Aurel von Milloss submitted his resignation. Once again Hilbert travelled to Munich, this time to discuss the resignation and to remonstrate further with Karajan over what he perceived to be failures of communication by Mattoni and Karajan's Swiss lawyer, Dr Steffan.

By Christmas, Karajan was out of hospital and recuperating in St Moritz, where Eliette was about to give birth to their second child, Arabel, born there on 2 January 1964. It was not, however, the season of peace and goodwill. Hilbert was now beside himself with fury and frustration over a whole range of issues.

At New Year, oblivious of Karajan's health and immediate family concerns, he demanded a further top-level meeting. Karajan had cancelled all conducting engagements until the end of January, but he agreed to see Hilbert in Zürich on 12 January, along with Dr Steffan, and the latest addition to the Karajan entourage, the new General Manager of the Vienna

Opera, the Swiss-born agent Emil Jucker. The purpose of the meeting was
to clarify matters arising from the minutes of previous meetings, and to
agree schedules preliminary to finalising contracts for the period 1964–6.
So acrimonious was the encounter, the second part of the agenda was never
reached.

The meeting began with Karajan objecting to Hilbert's use of the title
'Staatsoperndirektor'. It implied, he argued, that there was only one Director at the State Opera; as opposed to 'Direktor der Staatsoper' which, he
suggested, carried no such implication. Hilbert acknowledged the distinction but denied responsibility for adopting the title.

Karajan then taxed him over the question of costume hire. Why had
he not been informed that for the new *Fidelio* in Munich Christa Ludwig
would be wearing a costume from the Vienna State Opera wardrobe?
Hilbert suggested that costume hire was a matter for the federal theatre
administration, not the artistic director. Karajan disagreed: a somewhat
quixotic stand, except for the fact that the oddest things interested him.
He had, for instance, a huge admiration for the head carpenter at the State
Opera, a man, he said, who always knew exactly how much wood and
how many nails were still in stock: 'A good housekeeper can smell when
treachery's afoot,' he would later remark. 'This man knew instinctively
whenever something had been stolen from his workshop.'[15]

It was now Hilbert's turn to go on the offensive by insisting that all
written communications between himself and Karajan should be sent
directly from office to office and not via a third party (i.e. Mattoni).
This argument was eventually halted by Dr Steffan who suggested that
the discussion was losing itself in detail and was in danger of undermining
the basis of the relationship.

The warning was of little avail. Eventually, Steffan intervened again,
asking that 'Dr Hilbert try to trust his colleagues a little more and not to
overestimate the significance of minor issues'. Unimpressed by Steffan's
scholarly circumlocutions, Karajan put it more crudely: it was impossible,
he announced, to have a rational discussion with a man who 'believes that
all human beings are his enemies'. If Hilbert considered this rather rich
coming from Karajan, he managed (for the moment) to hold his tongue.

Jucker now tried to address the question of artist contracts for 1964–6; but
Hilbert had had enough. How could they discuss contracts, he demanded,
when the meeting had clearly failed to establish a proper basis of trust
between Karajan and himself?

It had been a truly childish tiff, and it ended in an appropriately childish
manner, with Hilbert announcing that he would be returning to Vienna to
'report' Karajan to the Minister. As a parting shot, Hilbert demanded that
conclusions of the meeting should appear promptly 'in writing'. This was

not a wish, the minutes record, 'from which Herr von Karajan wished to dissociate himself'.

Fondly thinking he had had the better of the spat, Karajan passed the minutes on to his biographer Ernst Haeusserman who later published them in full.[16]

CHAPTER 54

Pet savage

Stravinsky's music used to be original. Now it is aboriginal.
Ernest Newman, *The Musical Times*

Karajan's first concerts after his illness were in London, a Brahms cycle with the Berlin Philharmonic with soloists Géza Anda and Christian Ferras. Once again, the D minor Piano Concerto was conspicuous by its absence. No one knows why Karajan avoided the work; whenever the matter was raised, he always changed the subject, as though the piece was jinxed.

The Berliners played gloriously and won lavish praise in the press. If a note of qualification was struck, it was occasioned by the fact that on the Sunday evening, between the Berliners' second and third concerts, the Philharmonia Orchestra played Bruckner's Eighth Symphony under Klemperer. In those days, Bruckner concerts were something of a rarity in London. To some, it seemed the more significant event.

Did Legge have Karajan on standby should Klemperer cancel, as he had done in Salzburg in 1957? More important, did he give any indication that all was not well with the Philharmonia? Legge had resigned from EMI in June 1963, an unenforced but ultimately inevitable parting of the ways. Now, a little over six months later, he was contemplating suspending the Philharmonia on the grounds that it was no longer possible to maintain the orchestra in the first division – alongside Karajan's Berliners and Szell's Cleveland Orchestra – where Legge naturally wished it to be.[1] With Karajan in deep trouble in Vienna, it was a bad time all round for these two former comrades-in-arms.

With Legge's resignation, EMI effectively lost its direct contact with Karajan. He had, however, offered to continue working for EMI – with Michel Glotz as his intermediary. Since Glotz had first met Karajan in St Tropez in 1957, his career in the recording business had gone from strength to strength. He had worked with Beecham and was now Maria Callas's personal recording producer. At a meeting with Glotz in the Lancaster Hotel in Paris, Karajan clarified his ideas. EMI was informed, and a further meeting was arranged with Glotz in Zürich to finalise the legal details.

Over lunch in Zürich, Karajan went through the broad outline of the agreement – he clearly intended using Glotz in some capacity – then gave him the bad news. That morning, he had received a letter from David Bicknell in London blocking the entire deal. Bicknell's warning had been as blunt as it was final: 'Michel Glotz is a minor employee of a subsidiary company and therefore has no authority to discuss, let alone sign, a contract on behalf of EMI.'

'I don't know whether this is intended as a slap in the face for you or a slap in the face for me,' Karajan told Glotz, 'but either way, you can forget EMI.'[2] A somewhat premature threat, as it turned out.

As for the Philharmonia – the New Philharmonia as it became in the wake of Legge's withdrawal – there was a strange little codetta to Karajan's time with the orchestra. In 1973, Hugh Bean was in Salzburg with the London Symphony Orchestra. Karajan was around, lurking in the auditorium, spying out the land as he was wont to do. Suddenly the two men came face to face. Bean thanked him for the wonderful years he had given the Philharmonia. Karajan smiled, shook hands, and patted his arm. Bean hoped for more but all Karajan said was 'Ja, ja'.

It was a warm response that signalled agreement. Yet there was also a sense of Karajan – in Bean's phrase – 'putting a shock-absorber' into his reply.

For Mary Bean, this came as no surprise:

'He was always absolutely devoted to the matter in hand. Yet when he had finished something, that was it. He was not a man who carried any baggage.'[3]

*

After the London Brahms cycle, there was an intensive round of recording sessions. These produced one superb LP (Debussy's *La mer* and *L'après-midi d'un faune* and the second suite from Ravel's *Daphnis et Chloé*), one near miss (Karajan's, and the orchestra's, first recording of Stravinsky's *Le sacre du printemps*) and some oddly routine re-makes of popular classics.[4]

The 1964 recording of *Le sacre* became something of a *cause célèbre*. Stravinsky himself used the LP's release that autumn as a cue to write the first of two comparative reviews (the second was written in 1970) of recordings of *Le sacre*.[5] This was inspired mischief-making by Stravinsky, a burst of critical grapeshot that managed to pepper a number of choice targets, including critics ('the useless generalities of most record reviewing') and conductors (Boulez, Zubin Mehta, and Robert Craft also suffered ritual abduction).

Some people got very hot under the collar about Stravinsky's conductor-baiting, especially since his own conducting left a certain amount to be desired. Ingmar Bergman has a particularly blistering paragraph on the subject in his autobiography *The Magic Lantern*, in which he excoriates, not so much Stravinsky, as the mediocrities who were witless enough to take him seriously.[6] This was an exaggerated response. Karajan, no mediocrity, took much of what Stravinsky had to say very seriously indeed.

Stravinsky famously dubbed the 1964 Berlin *Le sacre* 'a pet savage rather than a real one', blaming the tradition from which the performance came (German and unduly sostenuto) more than the performance itself for its obvious shortcomings. Not everyone agreed with this. While admitting that Stravinsky's own 'rhythmic propulsiveness, melodic cynicism, and shyness about rubato took one directly to the heart of the music', Glenn Gould was concerned that other interpretative options might be shut out by the hegemony of Stravinsky's Stravinsky. To Gould, kite-flying as usual, Karajan's account of *Le sacre* was 'the most imaginative and, in a purely compartmentalised sense, "inspired" realisation' there had yet been on record.[7]

Stravinsky's own judgement, however, was one that Karajan greatly valued. It was Karajan, after all, who had said to Richard Strauss, 'Don't tell me what's right about my conducting of *Elektra*, tell me what's wrong with it.' The jokes in Stravinsky's review and the largely otiose remarks about (correctable) details of orchestral balance were neither here nor there; but his remarks about the orchestra's *culture* were telling and useful. They helped Karajan set fresh targets.

After 1964, he let *Le sacre* rest for a while. Then, in the early 1970s, he returned to it with a renewed intensity and an even better orchestra: better horns, better support in the subsidiary wind sections, and an even more finely schooled string section. There were also many more live performances.[8]

By the time the work went back into the recording studio in November 1975, it was a performance of astonishing intensity. What is on the finished record is an uninterrupted final take of a reading that no longer cloys the appetite it feeds.

CHAPTER 55

Farewell, Vienna

Not every Director is a Karajan, and not every
Karajan is a Director.
Erich Kunz, ad lib in *Die Fledermaus*

In the spring of 1964, Austria had a new government, with the former
Provincial Governor of Salzburg, Karajan's old ally Josef Klaus, as the
new Federal Chancellor. Within days of Klaus taking office, Karajan
began lobbying him, threatening resignation if Hilbert was not brought
to heel.

Relations with Hilbert had reached a new low the previous month when
he had screamed down the telephone at Karajan, then slammed down the
receiver while he was in mid-sentence. Since then, Karajan had refused to
communicate except by letter.

On 2 April, the long-serving Dr Drimmel was replaced as Minister
of Education by a political worthy from rural Styria, the fantastically
named Theodor Piffl-Perčević. No country bumpkin, but a classical scholar
well grounded in the strange ways of city people and the practices of
ancient tyrants (he counted the *Orations* of Demosthenes among his
favourite reading), Piffl-Perčević had barely had time to unpack when
disaster struck.

In what was clearly a deliberate act of provocation, Hilbert had scheduled
a revival of Karajan's own production of *Tannhäuser* for 17 May, the
same evening Karajan was due to conduct the first of three concerts
with the Berlin Philharmonic as part of the Vienna Festival. Hilbert had
not consulted Karajan about this and it was some time before Karajan
realised what was afoot. When he did, he asked that the *Tannhäuser* date
be altered; but Hilbert, who had already engaged Oscar Danon to conduct
the performance, refused.

On 7 May, the Danon performance was confirmed in a State Opera press
release. The following day, Karajan resigned.

On the matter of his remaining in post as Artistic Director of the Opera,
Karajan's letter to Piffl-Perčević was final. The letter did, however, make
it clear that he was willing to continue as a conductor and producer at the
Opera if required to do so by the new Director or Directors. In saying this,
Karajan was assuming that Hilbert would also be required to resign. Yet,
search as he might, Piffl-Perčević could find no document which said that
if Karajan went, Hilbert must go too. Even more bizarre was his discovery

that Karajan himself currently had no formal contract with the Austrian government, merely an unauthorised, unsigned draft document that made no mention of Hilbert.

Piffl-Perčević did his best to find a way through the mess, but it was a thankless task. The public wanted Karajan to stay; so, not surprisingly, did Chancellor Klaus. But Hilbert refused to alter any of his plans. He was, in effect, running the Opera as though he alone now commanded its destiny. As part of his initial response to Karajan, Piffl-Perčević had requested that he and Hilbert should honour their obligations until the end of the season. Karajan agreed to this but, on 8 June, wrote to Piffl-Perčević giving him a list of Hilbert's blatant contraventions of the terms of the transitional arrangements.

Inevitably, Karajan took against Piffl-Perčević, preferring to see him as a purblind politician rather than a man of principle on the horns of a dilemma. Piffl-Perčević took all this in his stride. The Viennese, his memoirs suggest, are a people apart.[1] As for Karajan: was it, he wonders, quite 'the done thing' to summon a government minister to a meeting in a public reception room in the Imperial Hotel?

When news broke of Karajan's resignation, the hope was that he would stay in Vienna in some capacity or another. A headline in *Die Presse* over a piece by veteran critic Heinrich Kralik stated:

THE SEARCH FOR THE RIGHT MAN
The next Director of the Vienna Opera will have to succeed in
bringing Karajan back

For a time it was thought that Oscar Fritz Schuh might be that man. But he knew the state of play, even before receiving a typically frank background briefing on the situation from the overly conscientious Piffl-Perčević. In his article, Kralik praised Karajan – 'this complex and far-sighted man' – for his achievements at the Opera: for the many necessary reforms he had instituted, for the pioneering agreement with La Scala, for the bold experiments in trying to reintegrate the musical, dramaturgical, and scenic elements of operatic production. He also reminded his readers that

The Vienna Opera owes its individuality, and indeed its superior rank, to the fact that it is not a manager's opera house but is dominated by its artists and conductors. During the last hundred years, the men who have guided the destinies of the Opera from the Director's office have been, with a few awkward exceptions, great artistic personalities.[2]

It goes without saying that the Danon *Tannhäuser* was loudly heckled. Four days later, when Karajan entered the pit to conduct *Fidelio*, the place went wild. He appears to have been much moved by this. For the first time in anyone's recollection he conducted a performance of Beethoven's opera that was genuinely uplifting. But there were interruptions here, too. When Florestan enquired of Rocco, 'Who is the Governor of this prison?', a well orchestrated cry of 'Hilbert!' came from the gallery.

Three days later, *Parsifal* was heard in total silence. At the end no one even attempted to applaud. Joseph Wechsberg reported in *Opera*: 'One had the feeling that, having made his decision, Karajan was now experiencing an acute sense of loss. Never before has he conducted this work with such depth of feeling.'3

*

The row dragged on through the Vienna Festival which culminated in two performances of a new staging of Strauss's *Die Frau ohne Schatten*, a production, designed by Schneider-Siemssen, which would stay in the Vienna repertory for many years. Had Karajan remained in Vienna it would almost certainly have undergone further modification, though whether he would have restored the cuts and minor re-orderings he imposed (in a vain attempt further to 'clarify' the action) it is impossible to say.

The first night was glorious: with sumptuous orchestral playing, a superb Empress from Leonie Rysanek, and Christa Ludwig giving one of the finest performances of her career as the Dyer's Wife. For the second performance on 17 June, the American soprano Gladys Kuchta sang the Dyer's Wife, to less good effect, and Karajan's young protégée Gundula Janowitz took over the role of the Empress.

'Why do you sing the Empress with such heart?' Karajan had asked Rysanek. 'The Empress should be cool.'

'I don't see her that way. She's the one who gives up the Emperor for the human race.'4

The critics were happier with Rysanek than with Janowitz, who was thought *too* cool. But the music staff was impressed. Michael Gielen would later recall: 'Janowitz sang brilliantly. He got her through. With any other conductor she would have been destroyed by the role.'5

In the final weeks, the situation in Vienna had become impossible. It was the politics of the madhouse, and the Opera itself was the principal victim. The horn-player Volker Altmann, who joined the Vienna Philharmonic shortly after Karajan's departure, remembers being auditioned by him as he walked down a corridor. Karajan rejected him out of hand.6

Karajan's farewell came on 21 June when he conducted Strauss's *Don Quixote* and *Also sprach Zarathustra* at a Strauss centenary concert in the Musikverein. It was an eerily apt note on which to end an era: man and nature, B major and C major, pitted irreconcilably the one against the other in *Zarathustra*'s closing bars.

'Karajan must stay!' the students noisily chanted; but things were so bad now there was no chance of him staying with the Vienna Opera in any capacity. Worse, he was threatening to leave Austria altogether.[7] It was the cry of a desperate Coriolanus, 'I banish you.'

*

Karajan's reign at the Vienna Opera had lasted twenty-one days fewer than Mahler's, which it had resembled in all manner of ways, alternately distressing and wonderful.

With Karajan gone, Hilbert took over. His contract ran to 1968 and, despite deteriorating health, he was determined to see it through. In the autumn of 1964, the government gave a massive boost to the funding of the State Opera. Joseph Wechsberg reported:

The State Opera just announced that it is to receive an increase of 20 million Schillings (over £250,000) in its subsidy. The increased subsidy is said to be necessary because of the higher cost of living. You do not have to stay long in Vienna to realise that everything is getting more expensive, but it is curious to see some of the people who violently opposed Karajan's budgetary policies now defending the higher budget of the present management.[8]

Whether this staggering rise in subsidy was a vote of confidence in Hilbert, a snub to Karajan, conscience money, a wise and disinterested investment, or a combination of all these things, is neither here nor there. Hilbert was one of the world's big spenders and in the years following Karajan's departure he made some spectacular investments and some spectacular blunders. When agent Robbie Lantz told Bernstein how much Hilbert was offering him to conduct a new production of *Falstaff* in Vienna in 1966, Lennie blenched: 'That's not possible. That much money no one pays a conductor.'[9]

As Prawy would later observe, in comparison with what happened *after* Karajan left, the Karajan era in Vienna was a time of relative financial prudence. This is not what one reads nowadays. It has been alleged that Karajan virtually drained the Vienna Opera dry of funds before going on to undermine (more than any other single individual) the probity of musical affairs and the delicate balance of musical economics in the world-wide music business at large.[10] Attributing to a particular individual or group blame for the economic and moral decline of an entire culture or economic system is, at best, a doubtful strategy. If, indeed, there is a case to be answered (which in this case there probably is) the facts need to be weighed, messy, awkward, and contradictory as they will often prove to be.

Whether or not Bernstein was worth what Hilbert paid him, his visits were immensely cheering to a city which had been laid low by Karajan's departure. The music-making was rumbustious and alive, and the buzz of intrigue was never far away. That, too, was music to Viennese ears.

A red rose placed anonymously on the conducting desk before each performance of *Falstaff* caused a riot of speculation, which Bernstein fomented by taking the rose, bowing to the box in which Anita von Karajan was sitting, and giving the orchestra its downbeat, Karajan-style, in a single sweeping gesture.

'There *is* a conductor!' Anita was heard to murmur.

It was in her house in Grinzing that Bernstein often held court during his Vienna years.

*

In 1967, Hilbert, his health now failing rapidly, succeeded in having his contract extended for a further two years. His last act as Director of the Vienna Opera was to ensure that his third wife, whom he had married before managing to annul his previous marriage, should receive in full after his death the salary from the unexpired part of his contract. It was a typically eccentric deal to which the government agreed in exchange for a written guarantee that Hilbert would stand down on 1 February 1968.

Hilbert signed the agreement, stepped into his chauffeur-driven car, and fell back dead.

It really was the end of an era.

PART IV

1964–1975

CHAPTER 56

Fresh woods and pastures new

The first of earthly blessings, independence.
Edward Gibbon, *Autobiography*

And so Karajan returned to the country, to the relative tranquillity of Salzburg, his readopted home, from where he would see out the remainder of his career. Did he reflect, as he conducted Strauss's *Don Quixote* in the Festspielhaus on the final Sunday morning of the 1964 festival, that, like Quixote at the hands of Sampson Carrasco, he had suffered a bloody but possibly benign defeat?

It was thirty-five years since Heribert Ritter von Karajan had ridden out from Salzburg to confront the operatic world. He had enjoyed some notable victories and suffered some humiliating set-backs. He had always wanted to be 'his own boss'. That was now a possibility. And there were his other preoccupations: a loathing of cities, a desire for quiet, a desire, paradoxically, to be 'settled'. His childhood apart, the happiest years of his life had been in Aachen, where he had enjoyed companionship, a house in the meadows, and his own show to run. If such things could be replicated in Salzburg, the return to the place of his birth could be both a development and an act of recapitulation.

At fifty-six, Karajan was married, with two young children; he had an orchestra to command in Berlin and a festival in Austria he could partly call his own; he was famous and relatively rich. I say 'relatively rich', since Karajan was neither an industrial tycoon nor a gold-disc-touting pop star. A snapshot of top royalty earnings for EMI in the first quarter of 1964 helps put things into some kind of general perspective:[1]

The Beatles	£46,982 10s. 4d.
Cliff Richard	£18,847 15s. 9d.
The Dave Clark Five	£13,535 16s. 10d.
Herbert von Karajan	£10,903 7s. 8d.
Maria Callas	£10,022 9s. 9d.
The Shadows	£ 7,760 3s. 6d.
Dietrich Fischer-Dieskau	£ 7,165 17s. 3d.
Otto Klemperer	£ 6,234 7s. 5d.

Karajan needed the money he earned if he was to reinvest in his own future. He also needed new places to live; with a wife and young family to care for, it was no longer an option to exist in hotels and rented properties. A new home was already being built in the fashionable Suvretta district of

St Moritz; another would be built in a meadow outside Salzburg in the late 1960s. There was an aircraft to maintain, a yacht, and a succession of state-of-the-art motor cars, as well as a substantial personal staff. None of this came cheap.[2] Most important, Karajan was beginning to turn over in his mind where he might best continue his theatre work, and most effectively make his entry into the production of high-quality music films.

The self-reliant conductor-entrepreneur was not unknown. Beecham and Koussevitzky had been pioneers; but Beecham had inherited wealth, and Koussevitzky had married into it. Karajan, by contrast, was a grafter, a self-made millionaire, and like many such men was inclined to be 'careful' with money. In this respect, Legge's entrepreneurship had been instructive: a glorious initiative that had ended up as a cautionary tale.

As for filming, the trick here, as Stokowski and Bernstein had shown, was to get the media moguls to pick up the tab.

*

During the 1964 Salzburg Festival Karajan devoted himself exclusively to the music of Richard Strauss. He repeated centenary programmes he had conducted in Berlin and Vienna,[3] there was a revival of the 1960 staging of *Der Rosenkavalier*, and a new production of *Elektra*.

Few operas affected Karajan more deeply than *Elektra*. A key work in his early career, it had become a troublesome dream whose unexpected return could never be wholly discounted. Strangely, he never recorded the opera, which is why radio tapes of the 1964 Salzburg production are of particular interest and value.[4]

Yet even this *Elektra* was a chance affair. Karajan had originally turned down the idea of a new Salzburg production because of casting difficulties, whereupon the project had been handed to Karl Böhm. When Böhm's plans foundered (a minor saga in itself[5]), the project came back full circle to Karajan who accepted the idea of producing *Elektra* as a joint Vienna–Salzburg collaboration. The Vienna cast was to have been led by Amy Shuard and Regina Resnik,[6] but Karajan's illness intervened. Now he turned to two singers who had worked with him in Bayreuth in 1951–2: Astrid Varnay and Martha Mödl. The surprise reconciliation with Varnay – who had formally complained about Karajan's conducting to the Wagner brothers in 1952 – was brought about by Legge, who thought her incomparable among contemporary exponents of the role of Elektra. He told Karajan so, and set about brokering a rapprochement.

Teo Otto's designs, sparingly lit by Karajan himself, caught the mood of barbarism and moral degradation in the Mycenaean court. From the first, Karajan had wanted to re-explore the opera's Greek roots, rather than its *fin de siècle* Austro-German ones, a point that Varnay herself particularly approved. Karajan's staging, one of his finest yet, concentrated everything inwards, banishing generalised frenzy in favour of what *The Observer*'s Peter Heyworth aptly described as 'sustained and pointful tension'.[7] To this end, the production often defied the letter of Hofmannsthal's stage directions, removing Aegisthus's appearance at the window and omitting Chrysothemis's final return, their cries of desperation heard but not seen. Such details as were added were all the more effective: the palace after the murder of Clytemnestra suddenly seething with light and noise like some vast anthill that has been disturbed.

Mödl's Clytemnestra was magnificent by dint of superb diction and sheer force of personality, grand and dissolute. Varnay was not dissimilar. She had been bothered in stage rehearsals by Karajan's insistence on the use of a pre-recorded tape; she would rather have 'marked' the part herself, especially when what she was hearing from the tape was another singer's performance. In all other respects, however, it was a most productive collaboration, with Karajan clearly determined to heal the breach between them. On the day of the dress rehearsal a huge bunch of red roses arrived in her dressing-room with an envelope attached. It was Varnay's practice never to read messages before a performance, but her dresser indicated that she might like to make an exception in this case. The roses were from Karajan; in the envelope was a signed contract for the following year. She had not yet sung a note of the 1964 *Elektra* and here was a contract for 1965. She was, to put it mildly, flattered and moved.[8]

In the production itself, there were times when she would have liked a wilder, more virulent emphasis than Karajan would allow but she respected the symphonic integrity of his reading and drew sustenance from the extraordinary rapport that now existed between pit and stage.

Critics heard in Karajan's conducting remarkable virtuosity but also great inner expressiveness and poetic delicacy. Legge himself would write of the performance:

The transparency of texture on the stage and in the orchestra was a miracle unlike any I have ever heard. Not only did every voice ride over the orchestra but also every word was clearly audible. Until this performance I had always felt – even when Strauss himself conducted it – that his inspiration flagged in Elektra's triumphant dance scene, but Karajan filled these closing pages with a crazed dionysiac ecstasy which, to borrow Hugo Wolf's metaphor, would shatter the nervous system of a block of marble.[9]

I remember the performance's cumulative power, and the transfigured calm of the recognition scene. I also recall a man standing at the front of the stalls clapping for several minutes with his hands held high above his head (it was George Szell) and the Austrian critics making unflattering comparisons with Mitropoulos's performances in Salzburg in 1957, where anger and unbridled frenzy had been the order of the day.

*

During August, Karajan instituted a new initiative with the Berlin Philharmonic; he invited members of the orchestra to St Moritz for a week's holidaying and music-making. A recording venue had been found in the town's Queen Victoria Concert Room which was suitably intimate and quiet, with a clean, lively acoustic. It was perfect for music of the baroque and early classical periods, though, in later years, the venue would be switched to the small whitewashed French Protestant church in Bad St Moritz.

Every summer, for nine blissful years, Karajan and his players (the whole orchestra on a jealously guarded rota system) would repair to St Moritz. Daytime was given over to outdoor pursuits, unless the weather closed in, in which case there might be an improvised afternoon recording session. Most evenings the music-making began at six o'clock and finished in time for supper and a visit to the skittle alley. This was an event in itself. One year Glotz, to whom all forms of sport were a profound mystery, knocked over all nine pins with a single bowl. This so shocked Karajan, he too fell over, laughing. In later years, when relations between conductor and orchestra were under strain, older players would look back nostalgically to the easy camaraderie of these summers in St Moritz: Bach amid the beer and the skittles.

In 1964, it was all Bach: wonderful Bach, joyous and strong. For Karajan, it was clearly an act of ritual cleansing after *Elektra* and the troublesome *démarche* in Vienna. The sessions yielded up recordings of five of the six *Brandenburg* Concertos, plus the Second and Third Orchestral Suites, recordings which had a significant public following in the 1960s and which still give pleasure today.[10]

*

In October, Karajan flew to Moscow to join the company of La Scala, Milan on its Russian tour. He conducted two performances of *La bohème* and two of the Verdi *Requiem*, to predictable acclaim. It would be five years before political tensions had eased sufficiently to allow the Berliners to visit Moscow, but Karajan was already taking a predatory interest in what was self-evidently one of the richest and best preserved of all musical cultures.

Back in Milan, the new La Scala season opened in the middle of a strike of opera house administrative staff. This delayed by several days a new production of *La traviata*, the sequel to the Zeffirelli–Karajan *La bohème*. It was nearly ten years since La Scala had mounted what was possibly the most celebrated of all post-war productions of *La traviata*; the production whose tattered remnant Karajan had conducted in Vienna in 1957 without Callas and with the curses of Visconti raining down on his head. Now he and Zeffirelli were attempting to replace that.

It is a matter of history that they failed spectacularly. Karajan blamed the Milanese claque, but he too must carry part of the blame. Determined to find a 'new' Violetta for the post-Callas age, he talked Mirella Freni into accepting a role for which she was demonstrably not ready. Nine times out of ten when he did this, Karajan could cover for the deficiency. If he wanted a fresher, younger, more lyrical reading of a role, he had the resources to nurse the singer through; but where *La traviata* was concerned, he himself was partly at sea. The reading – amended Toscanini – was rooted in no particular view of the piece. What's more, Karajan knew this was the case. In the early of hours of the morning of the dress rehearsal, he called Raffaello de Banfield in Trieste and begged him to come to Milan immediately. 'I need you to listen to my tempi,' was his all too evidently desperate plea. (Later, puffing up his feathers, he explained to Banfield that he would not have dreamt of waking him at four o'clock in the morning to consult him about a *German* opera.)

Banfield duly turned up in Milan, but there was little he could do other than watch the vessel founder. Freni, in particular, was excoriated by the claque. Afterwards Karajan dined at his usual table near the door in Biffi Scala. As the opera-goers drifted in, arguing and joking, their faces fell the moment they saw him, like sunshine strollers suddenly glimpsing a funeral cortège.[11]

At the second performance, Anna Moffo sang Violetta. She had been engaged to sing the role when the production moved to Vienna and clearly thought she should have been singing in Milan as well. According to Banfield, she was seen on the first night parading in front of La Scala in her furs 'like a street-walker', a splendidly theatrical gesture for which she paid dearly on the second night. Karajan did not exactly destroy her musically (a recording is extant) but there is a terrible dispassionate chill about the orchestral playing which sets Moffo's reading in an alien context, draining it of meaning.

All this was in stark contrast to the Salzburg production of *Il trovatore* which Karajan was now hawking around German opera houses in what was a clear attempt to find fresh points of reference within the operatic world. In West Berlin, where it was rumoured he was about to do a deal with the Deutsche Oper, his old friend H. H. Stuckenschmidt reviewed the performance, welcoming its old-world values:

Karajan makes the singers of aria or duet face the front, and collects groups of halberdiers and standard-bearers for group portraits. When the power of melody arrests all movement, this aesthetic of opera has reached its climax. This is great singing theatre, completely ruled by the score, in which even the orchestra constitutes only a background.[12]

Wonderful as all this clearly was, could any contemporary German house seriously consider addressing such a style?

Karajan directs all this musical entertainment as a passionate omnipresent arranger and organiser. One feels the stream of his ideas when suddenly a background makes itself felt and an army appears; or when a trumpet passage, which is dramatically important, is played by four costumed wind players on the stage. One can hear his ultra-refined aural sense, his love for a precise rhythm, in the orchestral sound. And yet his whole achievement is put behind the singers: his rapid adaptation, his fluctuating beat – softening of the strong beats and accents – are all theirs.[13]

Strangely, the Salzburg *Il trovatore* was also staged at the Hamburg Opera, Germany's leading 'modernist' house at the time, an institution which was famously rubbished by Pierre Boulez in a celebrated interview in *Der Spiegel* in 1967.[14]

Boulez's jeremiad on the state of opera in the western world was uttered at a critical moment, when all that was effectively left was a museum culture on the one hand (what Boulez dubbed 'musty old wardrobes') and a certain amount of bogus experimentalism on the other. The situation was saved – in the short term, at least – by turning the musty old wardrobe into a lavishly funded outpost of the avant-garde theatre movement. Since few musicians have any real power of removal, the majority of singers and conductors went along with this. There were, however, some famous abstentions. It was at about this time that Giulini turned his back on opera in the opera house, a startling decision by one of the leading opera conductors of the age.[15] Karajan did not do that, but as he smelled the air around him he must have realised that if he was to continue working with the art form he had known and grown up with he would need to find a well-appointed wardrobe of his own.

*

As if unsettled by his recent uprooting, Karajan once again became an impatient tourist. In January 1965, he took the Berlin Philharmonic to New York for a long-awaited Beethoven cycle. Several writers noted an air of desperation in the conducting. Karajan had been seen in the United States as a remarkably *calm* musician, exciting but calm; now, as the *New*

York Times reported, there were rather a lot of 'wide-swinging frenetic gestures'.[16]

In March he returned to Vienna to honour the completion of his recording contract with Decca-RCA, after which he joined a somewhat disgruntled Vienna Philharmonic for two concerts at the Royal Festival Hall in London. They were disgruntled because Karajan's new five-year deal with Deutsche Grammophon effectively excluded them from recording with him for the foreseeable future.

The first movement of Mozart's Symphony No.29 emerged sultry and lush, the phrasing squeezed unctuously out. It was difficult to tell whether this was Karajan's doing or the Vienna strings deliberately parodying his legato style. The *Minuet* lumbered, the Finale raced charmlessly on. It was a horrible performance whose sole merit was its brevity; Karajan had omitted every single repeat. But worse was to come. As the audience rose for the interval, an announcement came over the Tannoy that Mr von Karajan had cancelled the interval. Bruckner's Eighth Symphony would begin immediately. None of the reviews mentioned this bizarre edict, but the spirit of the evening was more than adequately caught by *The Times*:

> The work's colour and character were hardly at all conveyed: even the Scherzo seemed bland and empty of personality. It was thus inevitable that the performance gave an impression of strong bones without flesh, heart, or soul – or, perhaps more aptly, of the shell of a great cathedral without an altar or cross.[17]

Was it boredom, arrogance, or a kind of sterile anger that was causing Karajan to do this kind of thing? The concert two nights later was utterly different: an account of Haydn's Symphony No.104 that was incomparably done, a surging fiery *Don Juan*, and a performance of Dvořák's Eighth Symphony that had at its heart a slow movement that was almost unbearably poignant.

It was all very odd; yet it can been seen, in retrospect, as an earnest of things to come. The more Karajan concentrated his live music-making within a narrow geographical sphere, the greater the clamour in the world at large to attend concerts which would be either bland or breathtaking. One never knew which. The maestro's mood was all.

CHAPTER 57

Pilgrimage to Järvenpää

> Whereas most contemporary composers are engaged in manu-
> facturing cocktails of every hue and description, I offer the public
> pure cold water.
>
> Jan Sibelius

If the concerts in New York and London suggested that for the time being
Karajan had conducted his fill of Beethoven cycles and Bruckner Eighths,
there was one composer whose music was bringing him to new levels of
interpretative intensity: Sibelius. In February 1965, he recorded Sibelius's
Fifth Symphony with the Berlin Philharmonic for Deutsche Grammophon,
a wonderfully paced and proportioned performance that even today could
be said to overtop all rivals.

That is to state a preference, of course; and as Glenn Gould suggests,
in a famous disquisition on Karajan's Sibelius Fifth, aesthetic judgements
are not necessarily helpful in such circumstances:

I [had] absolutely no idea as to the 'aesthetic' merits of Karajan's Sibelius Fifth
when I encountered it on that memorable occasion [Berlin, May 1957]. In fact,
the beauty of the occasion was that, although I was aware of being witness
to an intensely moving experience, I had no idea as to whether it was or was
not a 'good' performance. My aesthetic judgments were simply placed in cold
storage – which is where I should like them to remain, at least when assessing
the work of others.[1]

To Gould, Sibelius was the great chronicler of isolation and Karajan his
most expert exponent:

... even though some Sibelius discographers quibble about the quasi-
impressionistic textural refinements favoured by that maestro, it strikes me
as the ideal realisation of Sibelius as a passionate but antisensual composer.[2]

The 1965 recording of the Fifth Symphony was later incorporated by Gould
into his pioneering radio documentary *The Idea of North*,[3] a rare example
of a recorded interpretation feeding a new creative initiative.

The cue for the Berlin recording of the Fifth Symphony had been
the Sibelius centenary which had brought Karajan and the Berliners an
invitation to give a concert of his music in Helsinki. It was an invitation
that meant a great deal to Karajan. On 15 May he visited Sibelius's villa
at Järvenpää, twenty miles north of Helsinki. Sibelius had purchased the
land for the villa on a wooded slope by the eastern shore of Lake Tusby in

1903. 'In Helsinki,' he said, 'all melody died within me. My art demanded a different environment.'

As Sibelius's biographer Erik Tawaststjerna relates, the villa was designed by the distinguished Finnish architect Lars Sonck:

[It] seems to grow out of the surrounding countryside, and comprises two log storeys. With its sharp sloping roof, it recalls a Swiss chalet, though the windows in the library constitute a Karelian element. In the basement there were originally four rooms, while, in 1911, an attic was converted into a study cum bedroom. Sonck's architectural skill can be seen even in the interior and layout. The rooms are beautifully proportioned.[4]

Karajan was deeply taken with the house, and the setting. Here was somewhere he himself would have been happy to be. Indeed, the house bears an uncanny resemblance to the one Karajan would shortly have built on church land in a meadow outside Salzburg looking out towards the Untersberg.[5]

At Järvenpää, he met members of the Sibelius family and laid a wreath on Sibelius's grave in a clearing beside the house. It was a bright spring day, with a dusting of snow on the ground, the trees barely in bud.

The music for the Helsinki concert was readily chosen. In the first half, the Fourth Symphony, in the second the Fifth, with *Finlandia* as an encore. As Karajan came off the platform after conducting the Fourth Symphony, Stresemann heard him say, 'It can't be played more beautifully than that!' It was a startling moment, not because of what Karajan said, but because it was the only time Stresemann heard him pass comment on a performance the moment it was over.

Afterwards, there was a dinner at which, unusually for him, Karajan made a speech. It was a heartfelt affair, though it was not without its characteristic emphases. In particular, he dwelt on the *rejection* of Sibelius's music in the 1930s and 1940s – Sibelius the great Outsider – and his own determination to help right the wrong.

The recording of the Fourth Symphony was made in Berlin the following October. It is, as Karajan remarked, a very 'beautiful' performance, almost perfect. Yet is it *too* beautiful, a further daunting example of that aesthetic purism which so disturbs some listeners? Since it is rare, where Karajan is concerned, to find this important question addressed in anything other than a negative way, I remember being especially struck by comments Sibelius scholar Robert Layton made in a BBC interview some years ago:

I think it is true that the kind of cultured, perfectly tuned and perfectly blended aural image that Karajan was capable of producing could excite a negative response in some people. Greatness isolates. (It also, I'm sorry to say, excites the envy and malice of the second-rate.) Often when people are confronted with something that is too beautiful, they react against it. That has never been a problem for me, though I confess that when I first heard the 1965 version of Sibelius's *Fourth* Symphony I reacted to it in exactly that way. It was like the Finnish landscape perceived through the windows of a limousine; there was a feeling of being insulated from experience. And yet when I went back to the performance in later years, I didn't feel that. What I recognised later was great depth of feeling. That sense of something coming *between* the music and the listener had completely disappeared.[6]

Layton would come to regard this 1965 Berlin account of the Fourth Symphony as being among the finest of all Sibelius recordings, a judgement that would appear to be endorsed by another distinguished Sibelian. Looking one day through a shelf of books in the sitting-room of Karajan's house in Anif, I came across a copy of the German version of Tawaststjerna's biography of Sibelius, placed, with charming incongruity, between a book on the paranormal and a paperback copy of Kenneth Grahame's *The Wind in the Willows*. Inscribed on the flyleaf were the words: 'To Herbert von Karajan. The only conductor who understands the Fourth Symphony. Eric Tawaststjerna'.

CHAPTER 58

Towards the Easter Festival

Thanne longen folk to goon on pilgrimages.
Chaucer, *The Canterbury Tales*

To find the origin of the idea of the Salzburg Easter Festival, it is necessary to trace Karajan's career back almost to source. He had always kept Easter as a special time, honouring it whenever he was able with performances of the sacred music of Bach or Wagner's *Parsifal*. Christmas was to him a 'dead' season, often empty and socially problematic, but Easter was a time of renewal. Walter Legge's blasphemous quip in a letter to Hilde Konetzni in February 1967 that he was looking forward to the imminent 'crucifixion, burial, and resurrection of Heiliger Herbert in Salzburg' was not without its point.

Karajan told his earliest biographer Ernst Haeusserman:

The Salzburg Easter Festival actually arose out of my need for further involvement with the works of Wagner. Indeed, this artistic involvement had already been my principal concern during my time in Vienna. With the exception of *Lohengrin* [scheduled for 1965] and *Dutchman*, I put on new productions of all Wagner's principal operas in Vienna. By 1964, the shortcomings of the production of *Die Walküre*, which was already six years old, were such that I knew I must start again. Because of the events of 1964, this never happened.[1]

In 1963, Schneider-Siemssen had said to him: 'Salzburg has a great Wagner theatre. It's too big for Mozart, but for Wagner, it would be wonderful.'[2] But Karajan appeared to take no notice, just as he appeared to have taken no notice of a suggestion put to him by the young Christoph von Dohnányi:

I remember attending a three-day course in the Salzburg Mozarteum which Karajan addressed. He taught brilliantly, sharing his experiences, and speaking about the demands and responsibilities of the conducting profession. I was so impressed by this, I said to him, why don't you start a festival here that would be perhaps a little bit like Tanglewood in the United States? He seemed really intrigued with the idea, and the next thing I heard, he was starting an Easter Festival devoted to the music of Wagner![3]

Karajan may have appeared to take no notice, but he had a habit of fermenting ideas. Just as Dohnányi's remark can be seen as anticipating the setting up of the Karajan Foundation, with its musical and medical research programmes, its conducting competition and its festival of world youth orchestras, so Schneider-Siemssen's remark may have fallen on more fertile ground than he imagined at the time.

None the less, in the spring of 1965 Karajan was still searching for a formula and a venue. Ironically, the man he first turned to for help over his embryonic 'Wagner project' was Herbert Graf, who had originally helped shape plans for the new Salzburg theatre. Graf was in the process of moving from Zürich to Geneva, where he had been appointed Artistic Director of the Grand Théâtre, a lavishly funded house that had been expensively restored and re-equipped during an eleven-year closure following a fire in 1951. The Grand Théâtre was attractive to Karajan for a number of reasons. First, the restored stage area had been specifically designed to take existing productions from larger houses; secondly, though the Orchestre de la Suisse Romande was the house orchestra, a visiting production would be expected to bring its own instrumentalists. In Karajan's case, this would be the Berlin Philharmonic.

When Karajan first raised the idea with Stresemann in Berlin, Stresemann was somewhat taken aback. The Berlin Philharmonic as a *pit* band? Wagner in Calvinist Geneva? It all seemed rather improbable. And what would the political ramifications be? How would the Berlin city fathers feel about their orchestra playing opera in some minor European capital? Graf, however, jumped at the idea. Like Karajan, he was convinced that ensemble theatre was a thing of the past, that the future lay in the creation of houses capable of providing first-rate productions in the context of some kind of festival *en permanence*.

There was also cheer from across the Atlantic. For some time now, Rudolf Bing, the General Manager of New York's Metropolitan Opera, had been trying to lure Karajan there. An offer to him to conduct Zeffirelli's production of *Falstaff* had been refused, as had proposals for new productions of *Il trovatore* and *La bohème*. Bing was baffled. There seemed to be no real way of knowing *what* Karajan would accept: until now and news from Geneva that he was seriously interested in re-staging *The Ring*.

In March 1965, Bing once again cast his fly over the water. In a letter that was as cautious as it was canny, he suggested to Karajan that the Met might be interested in his conducting and producing Wagner there, though not *The Ring*: unless, of course, Karajan was interested in presenting *all four* operas over a period of time.

*

With the 'Easter' project quietly on the simmer, Karajan returned from the Sibelius Festival in Helsinki to film the Zeffirelli production of *La bohème* in Milan and to prepare for his new Salzburg production of Mussorgsky's *Boris Godunov*.

La bohème was being made by Karajan's newest venture Cosmotel, a film and distribution company owned on a fifty-fifty basis by Karajan and Beta Films, a subsidiary of Leo Kirch's Munich-based conglomerate Unitel. For Kirch, this was something in the nature of a minority interest 'art' film. He had made his fortune acquiring German television rights for foreign films, Hollywood films in particular, where at one time he had more or less exclusive control of the market.

The film of *La bohème* was a studio mock-up of the La Scala stage production. Karajan himself undertook the 'artistic supervision', though, in practice, he had given himself a watching brief: looking and learning while a crew of top professionals got on with the relatively straightforward task of filming and recording.

The Salzburg *Boris Godunov*, by contrast, was a Hollywood-style epic. Numerous people had compared the stage of the new Festspielhaus to a CinemaScope screen, and now Karajan took them at their word, putting on a show that even Reinhardt might have blenched at. The stage crew called it *The Tsar and I*; others dubbed it *My Fair Boris*. It was *Boris Godunov* performed by a cast of hundreds in a cut and reordered version of Rimsky-Korsakov's sumptuously orchestrated edition. Scenically, it was a triumph. Andrew Porter reported in the *Financial Times*:

The frontier inn, complete except for its fourth wall, was built to life scale, with the road winding past it, an outbuilding, and land stretching all around . . . Boris's study was realistic and so was the huge moonlit garden of Sandomir, with palace wings stretching down both sides, and paths and terraces and bridges so broad there was no need to free any special dancing area. The Kromy clearing, however, was a bare stage, with cunning entrances on many levels that allowed a surging mob to fill or leave it in a few moments.[4]

The problem was, the scenery was the lure, not the production. The chorus, Porter suggested, 'was used for pageantry, for mass effects of splendour and power'. It was, he said, the 'work of a pageant-master, rather than an interpretative producer'; 'wonderful – except that the heart of the music is not there'.[5] Walter Legge, who would later review the production in *Musical America*, was doubtful about other things too:

The opera was sung in Russian by one German, two or three Austrians, a large contingent of Yugoslavs, Bulgarians, and Romanians – and one Russian, who sang and acted the Idiot with extraordinary and genuine pathos. This preponderance of miscellaneous Balkanese was presumably due to a misconception that Russian is the *lingua franca* behind the Iron Curtain.[6]

As for Boris's death, this

. . . was simply overproduced. Before the poor man was dead, there emerged from each side of the stage a procession of nuns or monks in pairs each holding a tall white candle, implying that they were on day and night duty in case the Czar should die. For one anxious moment I feared that the heavens would open and reveal the murdered Dimitri safe in the arms of the Roger Wagner Chorale singing an 'Ave Maria' to the tune of the Volga Boatman's song. They didn't.[7]

Ghiaurov sang Boris, and Jurinac Marina, though when Decca came to record the opera in Vienna in 1970 Karajan gave the role of Marina to Rostropovich's wife Galina Vishnevskaya. Jurinac had no problems with that, though she did think that after all they had done together Karajan might at least have had the courtesy to phone her, if only to say 'goodbye'.[8]

Karajan always claimed that it was in a pause between scenes in *Boris Godunov* that he suddenly said to himself, 'You fool! *This* is the place to do your festival. Here, in this theatre.' According to his own version of events, he went home after the performance, walked around in the dark in the pouring rain for two hours, and worked out the entire strategy. Some have questioned the story, but I suspect it is roughly what happened: a series of speculative and hitherto inchoate thoughts suddenly gathered up into a single idea rather as a magnet gathers up iron filings.

Financially and logistically it was a formidable undertaking. Legge would later dub it 'a masterpiece of ruseful planning, a paramilitary operation in organisation and co-ordination'. First, Karajan had to hire the state-owned, state-subsidised Grosses Festspielhaus on terms that would be acceptable to the government in Vienna (who owned the building) and the local authority in Salzburg (who ran and maintained it). Karajan offered to acquire it for the period of the festival at cost: running costs plus whatever charges would normally be incurred maintaining the building during a comparable period.

According to him, the idea was agreed to without demur.

'They said they didn't imagine I was planning to put on a strip-tease show, so there was no problem.'[9]

This is not strictly true. Numerous high-level meetings were held with the mayor and provincial governor who, in turn, were answerable to the minister – the ubiquitous Piffl-Perčević – whose agreement was vital. As in the 1920s, it was a case of 'Salzburg proposes, Vienna disposes'. Piffl-Perčević came, listened, sought clarification on the legal and financial probity of the deal, gave his agreement, and left.

The bigger problem for Karajan was paying for the productions. There would be a subscription list, and the income from subsidiary ticket sales; and he knew that, initially at least, he would have to put his own money into the project. But that would not be enough. Sponsorship was out of the question because he wished to be beholden to as few people as possible.

Since Bing's letter in March, there was the possibility that the productions might go to New York, but that had yet to be negotiated and might well exacerbate the financial problem rather than help solve it.

The masterstroke, financially, was the involvement of Deutsche Grammophon in recording *The Ring* and recording it *in advance* of each new production. The company was not keen on this, any more than it was keen on getting involved in Karajan's film initiatives. But they wanted a Karajan *Ring* cycle and had little option but to comply.

It was a daring initiative that showed how Karajan used his record companies financially to further his musical ambitions while at the same time keeping his distance from them in other areas.

This applied with particular force to such things as *per diem* expenses: flights, hotels, meals and suchlike. Many international artists lived off these perks, getting fat on expenses for which the companies paid.[10] Karajan never accepted a penny in expenses from Deutsche Grammophon[11] and very little from EMI. Once – furious at being called to Paris to sort out some editing problems with a recording of *Don Carlos* – he billed EMI for hotel expenses and aviation fuel, a gesture that caused the company's accounts departure to suffer a collective seizure. But this was the exception rather than the rule.

*

Karajan's resignation from the Vienna Opera had allowed his schedules to open up in new and interesting ways. In the late summer of 1965 he took the Berlin Philharmonic to Lucerne, Venice, Athens, Epidaurus, and Milan before returning to Berlin for the Berlin Festival. In the autumn, he made a short provincial tour of Germany, recorded *Cavalleria rusticana* and *Pagliacci* in Milan (an astonishing set that would cause the Italians to divide the works' interpretative histories into two ages: 'pre-Karajan and post-Karajan'[12]), flew to New York to negotiate the *Ring* proposal with Bing, and returned to Europe to make the first in a series of pioneering music films with the French film director Henri-Georges Clouzot.

The visit to the Athens Festival included a pilgrimage to the ancient Greek theatre near Epidaurus, where Karajan conducted the Verdi *Requiem* on the evening of 12 September. The 14,000 seat theatre, built in the fourth century BC and restored to full working order in the mid-1950s, is the Western world's most charismatic acting space. There is so much history there, the setting is breathtaking, the acoustic near-perfect. It is rare for the Greek government to grant permission to anyone other than their own professional theatre companies to perform in the theatre. Mitropoulos had conducted there, and in 1960 Maria Callas performed Bellini's Norma there; but they were both Greek. The invitation to Karajan and the Berliners was thus all the more extraordinary.[13]

Before the building of the magnificent road that now runs south along the coast from Corinth, it was not easy to get to Epidaurus. The journey from Athens was either a four-hour drive inland via doom-laden Mycenae and the charming port of Nauplion, or by sea, skirting the islands of Salamis and Aigina. Karajan arrived by sea on the cruise-boat *Aphrodite* along with members of the Berlin Philharmonic and the Vienna Singverein. *The Times*'s Special Correspondent reported:

Suddenly there was clapping on the quayside near the white and blue chapel perched on the rock: that slight figure in the polo neck sweater stepping out of a launch was none other than the maestro himself, with his own small personal group: their waiting car had to break through a swarm of dogs, perambulators, villagers and visitors before gaining the tobacco, olive and lemon-tree flanked road up to the theatre away in the mountains.[14]

As a general rule, Karajan disliked performing al fresco, the pitfalls of which are well known. *The Times*'s essayist agreed:

Of course, there are valid arguments for not performing great music in the open air. Bored children cannot always resist the temptation to crack open pistachio nuts, cicadas never cease their electronic-sounding bleats from the outer space of the surrounding pine trees. And even in a theatre with the acoustic of Epidaurus, musical sound is liable to disintegrate and dissolve. Yet even Verdi himself might have ranked Sunday night's performance of his *Requiem* as one of the great experiences of a lifetime. By 8 pm the sky was like black velvet and there was not a breath of wind: as soon as Karajan (now more conventionally dressed) lifted one finger (he spurned a baton on this occasion) for the first whispered entry of 'requiem aeternam' it was clear that the timelessness of Aegean history and the beauty of the nightfall together could not but give the performance a sense of wonder, indeed of dedication, rarely achieved in the concert hall.[15]

If Christa Ludwig gave the performance its human dimension, Renata Scotto and Carlo Bergonzi spun vocal lines of otherworldly beauty. Ludwig recalls how Bergonzi lingered over phrase after phrase, with Karajan and the Berliners holding the instrumental line like a thread of unbroken gossamer. And afterwards:

The moon was up by the end of the performance: down in the harbour lights glistened from every boat, with the *Aphrodite*, biggest and brightest of all, anchored out to sea waiting for a host of little benzinas to bring its musicians back aboard. Soon the bows of our boat were throwing up white furrows of foam as she cut her way through the glassy sea, following the silvered path of the moon through ghostly islands. And behind the mountains of Epidaurus, black and once more silent.[16]

Night, death, and the timeless Aegean: it had been, in every respect, a very Karajanesque excursion.

*

Whilst Karajan was in New York discussing the Metropolitan Opera *Ring* project, he called on RCA's George Marek. As he arrived at Marek's office, he came face to face with Michel Glotz who was just leaving.

Glotz was in New York to explore further the idea of setting up his own artists' agency in Paris. He felt his days at EMI were numbered; things were not well between himself and the company, and he had recently made matters worse by an ill-judged intervention in a meeting that had been called to discuss whom the company might best promote as their new 'Karajan'.[17]

'What are you doing here?' Karajan demanded, surprised.

'I'm job hunting,' replied Glotz.

'Don't make any decision before speaking to me first,' rasped Karajan, switching into French, while greeting Marek in English. 'I am at Essex House on Central Park South. Call me this evening at eight o'clock.'

Glotz duly called, and was invited to dinner. Karajan's proposal was as simple as it was astonishing. He was inviting Glotz to become his collaborator, his right-hand man, his artistic factotum. The proposal was that he would help co-ordinate all Karajan's musical activities: conducting and touring, stage direction, recordings, films, TV, and, in particular, the Easter Festival.[18] Glotz gazed out over Central Park, moved and flabbergasted.[19]

The offer of work cannot have come as a complete surprise; nor can there be much doubt that Glotz's time with Callas had some bearing on Karajan's decision. Glotz had proved himself to be a shrewd record producer[20] and a loyal confidant to Callas at a time when her relationship with Onassis was deteriorating and other so-called friends were nowhere to be seen. It is Glotz's speculation that Karajan may also have heard that Onassis was considering employing him in some capacity. This would both have impressed Karajan, and irked him.

The position Karajan was creating was unique, carefully tailored to the fact that recordings would now be one of the main engines driving forward his plans for opera production and film. It would be years before people fathomed the full significance of Glotz's appointment, and even now there are few outside a magic circle of chosen performers who understand how, precisely, it worked.

There was resentment, of course, not least from the record companies, who would increasingly come to see Glotz as a cuckoo in the nest. This was especially the case at EMI, Glotz's old company, some of whose employees would wage a war of attrition against him, logging every blip and false edit on the recordings he supervised. But, then, Karajan had warned him over dinner at Essex House: 'Rough it may be. Boring, never.'

Glotz, who was thirty-four at the time of the appointment, had been brought up in Paris. His father was Jewish. During the early part of the war, the family was on the run before settling in the so-called Free Zone. One brother joined the Resistance, another ended up as a prisoner of war. Music had been a great driving force in those early years, and remained so.

As for Glotz's plans to found his own Paris-based artists' agency, these were placed fairly and squarely before Karajan, who encouraged him to go ahead. It was important, he believed, for him to retain some measure of independence. Being wholly beholden to one person for one's living, Karajan argued, is never sensible and serves no one's interests in the long run. His only stipulation was that he be kept informed of the roster of Glotz's artists.

There is no doubt that the Karajan connection would later prove a huge boost to Glotz's agency, Musicaglotz. Down the years, industry insiders would gossip and grumble. ('Not ideal,' remarked one British executive, 'but it's the way of the world.') Yet few questioned Glotz's fundamental integrity, or his ability to do what he had been appointed to do extremely well.

Some saw his job as simply keeping Karajan happy: Schwarzkopf referred to him as 'an ointment'; a rival record producer likened him to a court jester. These are bizarre simplifications. Peter Alward, who first worked with Glotz on EMI recording projects in the 1970s, would recall how ferociously Glotz would argue with Karajan: 'Some of the things he said to Karajan were very near the knuckle.'[21]

Getting Karajan to do retakes was a recurring problem.

'*Später*, *später*!' he would insist.

'You may not like listening to your records,' Glotz would retort, 'but the public is paying for this.'

Once, Glotz threatened to have the retakes done by an assistant. Karajan objected: 'That would not be honest.'

'So I might do it anyway – behind your back.' This was a threat not even Karajan could afford to ignore.

Working with Karajan on a day-to-day basis was tough. He became particularly difficult when major decisions were imminent. Glotz kept the most important plans and documents in a green file ('Green for hope!'). These, however, were the problems of the daylight hours. Come the evening, Karajan and Glotz would dine together: a civilised dinner, when all talk of business and the day's music-making was absolutely forbidden. Glotz would recall:

The evening always brought serenity. I do not recall a single evening – however terrible things had been during the day – when Karajan was not in a benign mood.

Dinner was for him a form of ritual. He never dined before nine o'clock. When he was ready, he would collect a vodka from the mini-bar in his room and come downstairs to the restaurant. He would order bouillon, and the vodka would be stood in it until it was fresh but no longer absolutely frozen. It would then be drunk straight from the bottle, and dinner would begin.

In the evening, he would eat quite a light meal: pasta or veal or fish and a salad, never a dessert, though if he had guests he would ensure that they had everything they wanted. He was a wonderful host. At lunch, he would tend to eat more, and then take a nap, which is why he found recording in Vienna, with its afternoon session at 3.30, such a trial. 'C'est brutal!' he would exclaim.

At around midnight he would retire. I think it was often his habit to have a small whisky alone, and a cigarette perhaps, though at the very end of his life he gave up cigarettes altogether. He liked to sit and review the day, and focus on what had to be done tomorrow.[22]

Karajan respected Glotz's privacy. If Glotz was delayed or unaccountably absent, Karajan would enquire by indirection rather than do anything that might be construed as intrusive. This was partly a matter of old-fashioned discretion, partly an example of his shyness and fear of rebuff.

The change that had overtaken social behaviour in the 1960s – the new informality – was something Karajan found it easier to adjust to in practice than in principle, as Glotz would quickly realise:

On Sundays when I was in Paris I would usually give a supper party for members of my family and a few close friends. It was an informal occasion, and entirely private. One Sunday, Karajan called me at lunch-time. 'What are you doing tonight, can I invite you for dinner at the Plaza?'

'I'm sorry,' I said, 'I already have something arranged for this evening.'

Almost the moment I put the phone down, I felt horrible. I knew it would have taken an enormous effort for him to ring me, simply because it might seem intrusive, and I might well say no. So I called him back, and explained the situation: the informal supper, the fact that we had no one to serve us, and my doubts about whether he would want to spend the evening with friends of mine he did not know.

He said, 'Well, first, am I not one of your friends? And, second, if you want someone to help you serve, I am happy to do that for you.'

So he came. All my guests were petrified, with the exception of my mother who knew him very well and whom he liked. Yet within minutes it was if they'd known him for twenty years.[23]

Like all Karajan's employees, Glotz had to get used to being flown by Karajan and, like several others, he had a phobia of flying in small planes.

Schneider-Siemssen recalls Mattoni arriving for a meeting beaming from ear to ear. 'The boss's plane is grounded, we're going to have to drive to Munich.' Whereupon it turned out that Karajan had hired another plane: a single-propeller job.

When Mattoni objected, Karajan retorted, 'I can land you in any field you like with a one-prop plane.'

'With all due respect,' replied Mattoni, with a languid wave of his cigarette, 'I have no desire to land in a field with you, or anyone else.'

Glotz's particular nightmare was flying into St Moritz where there is a relatively easy route and a wing-tips-brushing-the-mountains one. For reasons best known to himself, Karajan usually opted for the latter route whenever Glotz was aboard.

CHAPTER 59

Henri-Georges Clouzot

Switch it off. I don't like music.
Señor Jo in *Le salaire de la peur*

'Let's try to hold the long shot on camera two, Ole baby. Sir Joshua's perspiring again.' That, as far as Glenn Gould was concerned, was what classical music on TV came down to in America in the mid-1960s; the classical concert (inviolable form) filmed in long-shot with the occasional close-up of the (preferably unperspiring) maestro. There was Bernstein, of course, but Bernstein was a pedagogue not a film-maker:

. . . the typical Bernstein television effort is a straightforward 'This is your life, Ludwig Spohr' sort of show – taped before a live audience in Philharmonic Hall, Lincoln Center, with all the sound liabilities thereunto pertaining and with coy cutaways to some cute little kids in the balcony specially imported for the occasion from the Westchester Home for Insufferable Prodigies.[1]

American TV networks were also desperate to prove, Gould noted, that classical musicians were plain decent folk, the kind of regular guys you wouldn't mind living on the same street as you.

In Europe, where, as everyone knows, musicians aren't plain folk, Herbert von Karajan is as deeply engrossed in filmmaking for TV as Bernstein in America . . . The repertoire is conventional enough – Verdi *Requiem*, Tchaikovsky No.1 (Weissenberg), Dvořák *New World* – but the directorial approach, while by no means uniform, has been contrived as an affront to the conventions of the concert hall.[2]

Affronting the concert hall was an admirable thing, in Gould's judgement. These films were not, he said, the last word in TV film-making, but 'every other attempt at orchestral shooting pales by comparison with the Karajan approach'.[3]

What Gould called 'the Karajan approach' was, in fact, an experimental collaboration between three men: Karajan, the French film director Henri-Georges Clouzot, and Clouzot's director of photography Armand Thirard. They made five films together, films that in a far-sighted world should have effected an immediate revolution in the way orchestral music was seen on TV. It was not to be.

Henri-Georges Clouzot (1907–77) was a year older than Karajan and had had his career similarly skewed by war and politics. Though French, he had gone to work in Berlin in the early 1930s as a scriptwriter and

535

assistant director. His first film as a director was *Le corbeau* (*The Raven*, 1943), a baleful tale of life in a French provincial town that is riven by petty hatreds and further devastated by the activities of a writer of poison-pen letters. Clouzot made the film for the company Continental, a joint venture involving French production teams and German finance, set up by the Vichy government in 1940. After the Liberation in 1944, the company was outlawed and many of those who had worked for it suspended from film making. Like Karajan in not wholly dissimilar circumstances, Clouzot had declared his genius and lost his job. It was not until 1947 that he was able to resume his career, the same year Karajan was officially cleared to work again.

Clouzot was of no party, save perhaps the cynics' party. The French hated *Le corbeau* because they thought it showed French provincial life as narrow-minded, bitter, and morally twisted; the Germans banned it because of its 'negative' and 'offensive' manner. In later years, after he had created his two great masterpieces of suspense, *Le salaire de la peur* (*The Wages of Fear*, 1952) and *Les diaboliques* (*The Fiends*, 1954), Clouzot was accused of being other things, too: anti-women, anti-coloureds, and anti-capitalist. This was profoundly unfair to him. He was anti everything, the cinema's greatest misanthrope. At the start of *The Wages of Fear* a half-naked Negro boy (the film is set in a shanty town in a putative Venezuela) is seen with a stick-and-string contraption snaring flies in the dirt. It is an image that sums up Clouzot's vision of humanity.

The film, one of the bleakest odysseys in cinema history,[4] became something of a cult movie, helped along by reviews that were every bit as disapproving as those the Nazis and the French had passed on *Le corbeau*. (An anonymous critic in *Time* magazine called it 'the most evil film ever made'.) Yet, for all this, Clouzot's popularity was short-lived. Isolated within his own culture, he was sidelined by the Truffaut-led 'New Wave' school of French film-making which favoured an altogether freer and more informal style of scripting and editing. The criticism most frequently levelled at Clouzot by younger contemporaries – and here there is another parallel with Karajan – was that he was a 'perfectionist'. Writers in the influential French paper *Cahiers du cinéma* sneered at him for belonging to a so-called 'tradition of quality'. (As Robert McKee later remarked, 'Why this was a criticism, I've never quite understood; I've always had a weakness for quality.'[5])

For Clouzot, life had one redeeming feature: unlike Señor Jo in *The Wages of Fear*, he had a passion for music. Where he first met Karajan is not clear, though they evidently knew each other long before they began working together. Cinema people have paid scant attention to the work they did together; the general view being that after *La vérité* (1960), a chilly courtroom drama starring Brigitte Bardot, Clouzot became a recluse, and his talent withered on the vine.[6] This is not strictly true. His music films can been seen both as a private excursion from his obsession with evil and the pointlessness of the human condition, and a chance to experiment with the more informal techniques of the New Wave directors.

From the first, it is clear is that he and Karajan were absolutely agreed as to what a music film should try to do. Gould had talked of the need to confront the concert hall. In a discussion that preceded one of the TV screenings of their films, Karajan and Clouzot were saying exactly that:

KARAJAN: Nowadays, there's a widely used phrase – an English phrase – 'I want to sit in the cockpit' – which roughly translated [the Karajan–Clouzot conversation was in French] means: I want to see the thing from another perspective.

CLOUZOT: But, you know, that is exactly the definition of what a production is: it is placing the spectator in a privileged position whilst you tell him your story.

KARAJAN: Exactly. And in addition to that there is the sense – not just of a report on a concert but a visual interpretation that will give the public an added sense of the greatness of the music we are playing.[7]

*

The first sessions took place in Vienna in November 1965 in the spacious studios of Vienna Films. There were two contrasted projects: a film of Mozart's Fifth Violin Concerto with Yehudi Menuhin as soloist, and an hour-long filmed rehearsal of Schumann's Fourth Symphony.

Clouzot's filming of the Schumann Fourth Symphony was very 'New Wave'. Like all his films, it is shot in black and white. The players (the Vienna Symphony) are in casual clothes. Karajan himself is in black slacks and a dark sports shirt, with the collar turned up. (A seeming affectation. In fact, like a number of conductors, he suffered from a chronic bursa-related stiffening and inflammation of the neck and shoulder muscles.)

The setting is an ordinary recording studio with the microphones and lights plainly visible; they, too, are players in the drama. The film begins with a close-up of the conductor's hand putting down the studio intercom, followed by the red light's peremptory signal. During the performance itself, a panning shot of the orchestra veers suddenly upwards to frame a single microphone suspended from the ceiling: a sardonic reminder by Clouzot that the performance is being heard, not by us, but on our behalf.

As a visual exploration of the inner stuff of an orchestral performance – the labour of music-making and physical craft of conducting – the film is a masterpiece of the medium. It is also a very well told account of Schumann's symphonic story. As the cameras scan the performance, so they catch and calibrate the rhythms and sudden wayward impulses of what Glenn Gould calls Schumann's 'deceptively straightforward but logistically perilous' music.

There is relatively little trick photography: none at all in the symphonically driven outer movements, and only one effect in the slow movement which dims to blackout at the start, before oboe and cello intone their lonely songs. Aptly, it is in the Scherzo that Clouzot plays his tricks; in the Trio the image of a musically entranced Karajan is superimposed on the orchestra, whirled round as if on some heavenly carousel.

Elsewhere in the film, the conductor is studied from every possible angle and distance. Yet though Karajan is evidently controlling proceedings, he is never – such is the skill of Clouzot's editing – allowed to be seen as the *fons et origo* of the event, as he would later appear to be in many of his own films of the 1980s. Sometimes Clouzot's camera squats at a distance, looking dispassionately on like a bored back-desk fiddle player; at other times, we have the same shot, but closer and lower, the camera now gazing admiringly *up* at Karajan. The stick and hands are examined, but fleetingly, in ways that help intensify the musical moment.

Clouzot is also fascinated by Karajan's stance: the feet, about fifteen inches apart and turned slightly outwards, never shifting, even under the most extreme stress. This could be glimpsed in the concert hall; but by clearing the rear sight-lines and placing the camera at a convenient distance, Clouzot is able to open up a direct ground-level back view of what turns out to be the posture of an expert skier. With the feet set, the movement comes entirely from the knees and the hips. In moments of fierce acceleration, the arms, too, take on a thrusting forwards and backwards motion as if manipulating ski sticks. (It was around this time that Karajan, now in his fifty-seventh year, skied down Mont Blanc in a record-breaking twenty-seven minutes.[8])

As for the filming of the orchestra, here touches of Clouzot's misanthropy creep in. 'Their diversity,' Elias Canetti had written in *Crowds and Power*, 'stands for the diversity of mankind; an orchestra is like an assemblage of different types of men.'[9] Clouzot's film reproduces Canetti's point. Drawing on the unkempt, occasionally sullen look of the Vienna Symphony players, Clouzot presents us, not so much with a disciplined team, as with a bunch of professional navvies.

Tiny details help reinforce the impression. In the finale, a panoramic view of the orchestra is disturbed by the conductor's baton (longer than the one Karajan normally used and here seemingly moving of its own volition) dancing sadistically in the top right hand corner of the screen. In the rehearsal film, which Clouzot made to go alongside the performance itself, there are posed cutaway shots in which groups of non-participating players look blankly on as Karajan talks. That sense of involuntary imprisonment, which is so strong a feature of the opening scenes of *The Wages of Fear*, is also being hinted at here. Interestingly, Canetti's next point, that 'The willingness of its members to obey [the conductor] makes it possible for the conductor to transform them into a unit', is better illustrated in the Berlin Beethoven and Dvořák films where Clouzot's cameras seem actively to celebrate the corporate togetherness of the Berlin Philharmonic playing.

The Schumann rehearsal film, crucial to the TV project *Die Kunst des Dirigierens* (*The Art of Conducting*) for which these films were originally commissioned, is a unique document, since it is the only visual record we have of Karajan rehearsing an entire work in detail from end to end.

Originally, he tried to get out of doing this, on the grounds that Clouzot was turning him into an actor: Karajan playing Karajan. As we have seen, he was a good amateur actor and a first-rate mimic; but without professional training it was difficult to keep self-consciousness at bay. Clouzot, who was well known for his dislike of professional actors and claimed he could get a good film performance out of anyone, talked Karajan round. The results are fascinating, not only musically, but as a revelation of the wafer-thin divide that existed between Karajan the serious performing musician and Karajan the poseur. His friend of many years standing, Ronald Wilford, would later remark:

He was the least egotistical conductor I knew in those years because everything he did in music was intensely practical. His persona may have been vain, but what he did in music was totally practical.[10]

Clouzot might have spared Karajan the rather arch introduction in which he is obliged to tell the players (for the benefit of the TV audience) what it is they are going to be doing for the next hour. That ordeal over – and with it some awkward pauses and verbal fumbles – the rehearsal gets under way in earnest. And it is, indeed, 'totally practical', rooted, as always with Karajan, in a great deal of very specific work on rhythm, colour, dynamics, and modes of attack.

What is particularly interesting about his preparation of the Schumann is the way virtually everything he asks for relates to a view of the symphony – musical, historical, psychological – that has clearly been built up by him over many years of study and practice. The manner is pedagogic but the learning is lightly worn. Lying behind much of what Karajan is seeking is a desire to register and delineate the relationships between critical rhythmic and melodic elements: to bring the symphony to life as a fully functioning organism. The background preparation has clearly been Schenker-like in its rigour.

There is also a clear preoccupation with the music's obsessional and manic-depressive elements. Yet none of this is talked about for its own sake. The rehearsal is, first and foremost, a forum for practical music-making. At the transition to the *Allegro* in the first movement, Karajan addresses the violins and violas with a request that manages to combine functional analysis, psychopathology, and down-to-earth advice in a single swiftly uttered aside.

You see what we're trying to get at. When you start the subject for the first time now, it's only a hint, so leave it completely uncertain. Don't scan it precisely. It's just a first suggestion. Then it begins to grow and grow, more and more. When you [second violins, violas] enter in the last bar before the *Allegro*, the central idea of the symphony must already be there. The feeling here must be of clinging to a thought to the point of madness [waves hand] You know what happened . . . [referring to Schumann's madness and attempted suicide] Please. [Bar] Twenty.[11]

The Mozart film, which was made in Vienna at the same time, makes an interesting contrast to the Schumann. For this, Clouzot transformed the studio into an elegant rococo salon. The musicians are in modern evening attire but everything else is of the period: rococo furnishings, mirrors, and candelabra with real candles, not electrically simulated ones.

At the time, Menuhin found the whole thing a delight. Karajan clearly knew exactly what he was doing, and provided a sympathetic accompaniment; Clouzot was 'natural, warm-hearted, and direct'.[12] That was not the crew's view, however. Fritz Buttenstedt, Unitel's executive producer, found Clouzot impossible to deal with:

He was a terrible man. Far worse than Karajan ever was. He would arrive very early and spend a great deal of time smoking his pipe, staring silently at the empty studio walls, like Leonardo staring at that wall in Milan before he painted *The Last Supper*. The night before the shooting of the Schumann rehearsal, he told me that the entire studio needed to be painted grey to reduce glare. He said that if it wasn't done by 7 o'clock next morning, he would leave. It was a completely impossible demand, of course. After a sleepless night I got to the studio before him. When he arrived I said, 'I'm sorry. It wasn't possible. You'll have to go.' He didn't, of course. He never had any intention of going. It was simply a try-on. The only consolation in all this was that Armand Thirard [Clouzot's cameraman] was as nice as he was difficult.[13]

For Karajan, the Mozart film was his least happy experience with Clouzot. Again, the problem was Clouzot's insistence on his 'acting out' his role as conductor. The 'playback' system was used: that is, most of the actual filming was done while the musicians mimed to a pre-recorded tape. When Menuhin was re-shown part of the film during the making of Bruno Monsaingeon's biographical portrait *Yehudi Menuhin: The Violin of the Century* (1996), he commented: 'It's interesting to see how a very great conductor plays the music straight through, but the music does not live, does it?'

As Menuhin watches the film, he is amused by Karajan's poses, his affected demeanour. Lighting on a brilliant analogy, he describes him as prancing like one of the beautiful Austrian horses from the stables of the Spanish Riding school.[14] Ironically, this was the very thing Karajan was convinced would happen once Clouzot had had his way and persuaded Herbert von Karajan to play the role of Herbert von Karajan. Posing about after a performance was one thing, but *during* a performance: that was not something he cared to do.

Karajan was certainly camera-shy. He also continued to be shy off camera. When Yehudi and Diana Menuhin arrived at the studios during the making of the film, they were greeted by Clouzot, but not by Karajan, who stayed sitting quietly in the corner of the room.

'Herbert,' demanded Diana, 'Say good morning to us.'

Karajan looked extremely sheepish and there were 'good mornings' and warm embraces all round. He needed to be got at occasionally. The trouble was, most people were too scared to do what Diana Menuhin had done. The incident put Menuhin in mind of his friend Pandit Nehru, another shy man who needed to be roused to sociability.[15]

The incident with Diana Menuhin had an amusing sequel. She was chatting to Irmgard Seefried after a concert in the Musikverein when Karajan came into the room. Wary of another rebuff, he greeted her as effusively as he knew how.

'Diana, has anyone told you how beautiful you are?'

'Dozens of people,' was the swift reply. 'Now go away, Herbert. We're discussing obstetrics.'

In January 1966, Karajan and Clouzot moved to Berlin to film Beethoven's Fifth Symphony and Dvořák's *New World* Symphony, with the Berlin Philharmonic. These films would be every bit as exciting as the Schumann, but with smoother, more admiring camera work, and playing of incomparable precision and verve. Gould talks about the 'atmosphere of rehearsal-like spontaneity' in the Dvořák, 'a rehearsal which might conceivably be brought to an end at any moment but which in this case apparently succeeded so well that it simply grew into a performace'.[16] It is, without doubt, the best of all Karajan's recordings of the symphony.[17]

Since Karajan did not fancy trying to turn himself into an Austrian Bernstein for the series *Die Kunst des Dirigierens*, he settled for workshop sessions with students and prepared conversation pieces with guest writers and musicologists. For the Dvořák, he held a German-language discussion with Joachim Kaiser, during which he revealed himself to be very well briefed on Dvořák's love affair with Longfellow's *Song of Hiawatha*, and he also set up an English-language version, for which he was joined by the English musicologist Denis Stevens, at the time Professor of Musicology at Columbia University. Stevens was amused that Karajan was so keen to talk about folklore when his performance – vivid though it was – was not in the least folkloric. During the discussion, Stevens mentioned Dvořák's interest in trains and railways. Karajan was riveted.

*

Karajan's last collaboration with Clouzot was on Verdi's *Requiem*, filmed in La Scala, Milan in January 1967. Of all the Clouzot–Karajan films, this is the best known simply because the performance itself has come to be recognised (somewhat tardily, it has to be said) as a classic in its own right.[18] It was not, however, an easy film to organise. Logistically, it was a nightmare; indeed, by the end of 1966 financial troubles were threatening to destabilise the entire Cosmotel enterprise.

The problems were largely to do with the record companies, who controlled many of the artists' recording activities and whose engineering skills Karajan needed. Even at this early stage in his film-making career, he was looking to tie in films with records of the same performance. Yet he had gone about it in a surprisingly piecemeal way. Many of the artists he worked with were under contract to different record companies (for example, Menuhin to EMI when Karajan himself was contracted to Deutsche Grammophon). Worse, the record companies clearly resented being frog-marched into involvement with a medium which was unfamiliar, expensive, and commercially unproven. Deutsche Grammophon was being particularly guarded. Though Karajan was under exclusive contract to them, and though they were prepared to hire him technical staff at preferential rates, they were reluctant to buy and distribute his films. The offer of the rights to *La bohème* for £75,000 – judged by industry insiders to be a pretty steep asking price – had already been rejected.

At a meeting between Deutsche Grammophon and EMI in Amsterdam on 4 January 1966, the 'Karajan problem' floated to the top of the agenda. Unbeknown to Deutsche Grammophon's Kurt Kinkele, Head of Marketing and A&R, Karajan had been sounding out EMI about the possibility of their recording the Verdi *Requiem* for him. EMI's tariff for a recording crew was DM30,000 (Deutsche Grammophon's quote was lower, DM25,000) but it was not a crew Karajan was after. What he had asked for was a joint film and LP deal. Clearly, games were being played. As Kinkele pointed out, Karajan had every right to shop around for technicians, especially if he had sunk some of his own money into the film; but his exclusive contract with Deutsche Grammophon almost certainly precluded a film-cum-record deal with EMI, even on a one-off basis.

In fact, the EMI team was more interested in Karajan's longer-term plans than in the Milan *Requiem*. They no more liked the idea of a joint film and LP recording than Deutsche Grammophon; and they liked it even less when Kinkele outlined details of the problems Karajan was having with the project.

Because the gala performance on 16 January had been arranged to mark the tenth anniversary of the death of Toscanini, La Scala had forbidden the use of film lighting during the performance, or at the second performance on 17 January. Karajan was therefore obliged to complete the filming in just two days in an empty auditorium on 14 and 15 January. There was also trouble with the singers: Price, Cossotto, and Ghiaurov were available on those dates, Bergonzi was not. 'It seems,' crowed Kinkele, 'that he's ended up with a completely unknown tenor.' So he had. His name was Luciano Pavarotti, and he sang like a god. (Years later, after Karajan's death, Pavarotti would recall the event, the orchestra 'playing very, very precisely, with soul'.[19])

Both Deutsche Grammophon and EMI were quickly put out of their misery. While the Amsterdam meeting was actually taking place, a call was received from Cosmotel saying that Herr von Karajan was very happy to accept Deutsche Grammophon's offer of technical assistance at the offered rate of DM25,000.

Karajan's proposed 'deal' with EMI had merely been a device with which to rattle Deutsche Grammophon's cage. None the less, back in London EMI began to put in place a long-term strategy for film and television projects: opera films, workshops, profiles of young artists, and the like. There was speculation, too, that when Karajan's current contract with Deutsche Grammophon expired in 1968, the chances of either party wishing to renew on an exclusive basis were receding by the minute.

Unbeknown to the record companies, the Milan *Requiem* was also proving to be a logistical nightmare for Unitel. Clouzot had demanded the use of no fewer than fifteen Arriflex cameras, huge machines with built-on monitors. Having scoured Germany for them, the team had to get them to Milan by road in the depths of winters. At the same time, Clouzot had assembled a team of top cinema technicians to make the trip to Milan by air. Either way, the Unitel management gloomily reflected, a huge slice of the material and human resources of the continental European film industry was in imminent danger of being written off.

In the circumstances, all Clouzot could do with this mass of equipment and expert technical help was to film the performance as a piece of finely crafted musical reportage.

One of the problems with music on film is that the eye is less tolerant of repetition than the ear. Which is why, even here, Clouzot never quite lets the eye settle. For all the seeming conventionality of the filming, its respectfulness and its musicality, Clouzot does things no TV-station director ever would have dared do: sudden jerks and swivels of the camera, for instance. There are other minor naughtinesses, too, such as the lingering shot on two players desperately trying to turn the page. These tricks should offend, but somehow they don't. Rather, they place the performance in a human context. While the musicians contemplate Last Things, Clouzot's cameras remind us of the minor irritations of the here and now.

The ordeal over, Karajan wrote a letter to Clouzot thanking him 'a thousand times from the bottom of my heart' for his work on the project and for his success in once more putting the medium of film at the service of music as the two men had always hoped it could be. The letter goes on:

I take my hat off to a man who is not a professional musician who can grasp a score like the *Requiem* within ten days of his arrival when ten years might be a more appropriate period! I must also thank you greatly for the way you have helped free me of all my complexes: not just about working in 'playback' but in all our work. You have freed me of fear, and for that I shall remain in your debt for the rest of my days. Have a good rest.

I embrace you with all my heart.

Herbert [20]

The thought of the director of *Le salaire de la peur* freeing a man from fear is an irony even Clouzot might have smiled at.

CHAPTER 60

The Easter Festival

Karajan's wonderful Easter egg.
Walter Legge, letter to Maria Callas

Shortly after Karajan returned to Europe in November 1965, to film with Clouzot and undertake a busy round of recordings in Berlin,[1] the Metropolitan Opera received a letter from Birgit Nilsson. As far as Rudolf Bing was concerned, Nilsson's participation was a *sine qua non* of any new *Ring* cycle in New York. Without her, he had told Karajan, the project was impossible. Nilsson wrote:

Finally, let me say a word about the great maestro, who gave me the honour of his visit here in my hotel, last week ... As you know, I have recorded *Walküre* (Brünnhilde) last month [for Decca], and so I cannot do it again at the moment. I have therefore suggested to sing Sieglinde on the record, and Brünnhilde at the Met and in Salzburg. However, this idea fell on negative ground with him – he hardly seemed to believe that I could sing the part at all. There are two other reasons that make me believe you will have to count on another Brünnhilde:
(1) He is not willing to accept me to be part of the recording, which is my condition if I am to participate in the other two parts of his project.
(2) Before he spoke to me in Vienna, he has asked other singers to sing Brünnhilde, which shows that he is not really keen to have me.[2]

Bing thought Nilsson was being unreasonable, and told her so in the politest possible way. It was not Karajan's fault, he explained, that she was unavailable to record Brünnhilde, nor could Karajan be expected to deny his stage Sieglinde, Gundula Janowitz, the chance to record the role. As for Karajan talking to other Brünnhildes, this too was a self-evident necessity; indeed, the Met itself would require two Brünnhildes, one as a cover for Nilsson.

Since the Easter Festival would be based on two subscription cycles, Karajan himself was all in favour of having two casts available. He explained in a letter to Bing:

First and foremost, the competition that exists between two casts is always raising them to a higher artistic level. Secondly, the feeling of safety in having two casts adds much to the tranquillity of the whole enterprise. This is, on another level, why I prefer a twin-engine aeroplane. And although you refer in your letter to the Metropolitan Opera as a repertory theatre, you will doubtless agree with me when I tell you that when and wherever I conduct, my approach to my work is based on a standard of a festival *en permanence*.[3]

In the end, Nilsson agreed to sing Brünnhilde at the Met but not in Salzburg.

*

In April 1966, Karajan took the Berlin Philharmonic on a three-week tour of Japan. After a Beethoven cycle in Tokyo, the orchestra went on a twelve-day tour of provincial centres, before returning to Tokyo for concerts of music by Bruckner, Mozart, and Richard Strauss. The television coverage was again massive. By 3 May, it is doubtful whether there was a man, woman or child in Japan who did not know who Karajan was. He would later recall how in one of the smaller towns he slipped out of his hotel to buy a pair of socks (an improbable story, except that he was notorious for wearing odd or worn-out socks). Sensing he was being watched, he turned round and saw a huge crowd of people silently staring at him through the window from the street outside. By the end of his life, the only place he was safe from this kind of thing was China. A snap Uli Märkle took of him walking, unrecognised, through a crowded street in Peking in 1979 gave him particular pleasure.

The Japanese visit further deepened Karajan's contacts with the country's electronics industry and served to intensify his growing obsession with film and television. He would later tell the *New York Times*:

The role of the Medici will now go to television. The European television company that is obliged to cover everything *must* take a high stand on culture. It must do at least one opera a month.[4]

To this end, Karajan had already taken the precaution of buying the film rights to a number of operas. The problem lay in realising the asset.

In August 1966, he and Eliette joined Maria Callas on Onassis's yacht *Christina*. It was not a social visit. Well-advanced plans for a Warner Brothers film of *La traviata*, directed by Zeffirelli with Callas as Violetta, had fallen apart and the pressure was now on to get Callas to agree to the *Tosca* project. In theory, Karajan had everything in place: he owned the film rights to *Tosca* and had clearance to use the soundtrack of Callas's 1964 Paris recording conducted by Prêtre. But it was not enough. The usual explanation for the project's collapse is Callas's anger at Zeffirelli's desire to milk Onassis of huge sums of money. The real problem, however, was Callas herself. As Karajan later told me, 'She was afraid. She had left the thing [*Tosca*] and felt out of it.'[5]

*

The Berlin Philharmonic's schedules leading up to its inaugural sessions as a Wagner theatre orchestra reveal the care with which Karajan plotted the orchestra's musical evolution. A certain amount of Bruckner had crept back into the repertory;[6] but so, significantly, had music by Bach, Webern, Honegger, and Ravel.[7]

In November 1966, Karajan conducted and recorded Shostakovich's Tenth Symphony, a benchmark performance of what was, for him, another great representative work of the age. That the symphony was in some sense 'about' Stalin no doubt interested Karajan.[8] Certainly, the Stalinoid *Scherzo* is played with a virulence and scuttering anger which turns bare notes into a state of mind. But there are other reasons why Karajan was drawn to the Tenth. Of all Shostakovich's symphonies it is arguably the best crafted in a slightly old-fashioned way. It is also one of his most personal, his initials DSCH monogrammed into the third movement. To a conductor who would like to have *been* Shostakovich, these things mattered.[9]

In January 1967, there were recordings of Beethoven concertos[10] and (as a sop to the exchequer) Rimsky-Korsakov's *Scheherazade*, after which Karajan returned to weightier matters. To everyone's astonishment, he prepared and conducted two performances of Schoenberg's epic *Gurrelieder*, a Janus-like work which simultaneously salutes *Tristan und Isolde* and looks beyond it.[11] With Bruckner's Fifth Symphony brought into the repertory five days later, no one could say that the Berliners were not being well schooled for the great *Wagnerfest* that was shortly to come.

*

Karajan had chosen to launch the Salzburg Easter Festival, not with *Das Rheingold*, the shortest and most esoteric of the *Ring* operas, but with *Die Walküre*. The recordings for this took place ahead of the stage production in Berlin in the autumn of 1966.

He had assembled a superb cast of singers, the voices often in marked contrast to the 'old Wagner cannons' (his phrase) most people were used to. Karajan had a reputation for wanting singers to sing like instrumentalists and instrumentalists to play like singers; but he also had a preoccupation with vivid declamation of the text. Jon Vickers has recalled how he had no use for singers who simply made beautiful sounds. Those who lapsed into generalised warbling were usually drowned out and then banished.[12] The beauty of Vickers's *mezza voce* singing in parts of Act 1 of *Die Walküre* was something to wonder at. But the words told, too: extraordinarily so.

It was the same with Karajan's Sieglinde, Gundula Janowitz. She has said that Karajan looked for three things in a singer: a beautiful sound (in particular an ability to prepare and sustain a long line, without strain or rush), an individual way with words, and a loyalty to Karajan personally.[13]

There was some surprise expressed at her being cast as Sieglinde, but Karajan wanted just such a voice as hers: young, fresh, and lyrical. Similarly, in casting Régine Crespin as Brünnhilde, Karajan believed he had found a worthy successor to the great French soprano Germaine Lubin: a singer of impeccable vocal pedigree who could bring real humanity to the role.

In *Die Walküre* he succeeded. Crespin brings warmth and femininity to the part, even a certain sly wit. Alas, she lacked the resources to tackle *Siegfried* or *Götterdämmerung*. There was no falling out between her and Karajan:

People think he's difficult. He is! Distant, secretive, proud. Yet for myself I knew there a charming man: refined, extremely cultured, full of humour, with whom I spoke of books, Paris, yoga, Bayreuth. With him, it was always 'delightful, calm, and warm'.[14]

It was simply a case of mission impossible.

Singers not used to Karajan's methods found the recording rather an odd experience. Josephine Veasey, Covent Garden's distinguished Fricka, had a brief piano rehearsal with him but then spent the best part of ten days in Berlin waiting to be called to record. The call came on the tenth day at 10.30 in the morning. There was an immediate take of her scene, and that was that. She suggested a couple of passages she thought needed attending to but was told there were to be no retakes. Karajan had said it was OK. The thing was finished.

'I'd rather scrub floors than work with that man again,' she later exclaimed, angry at the *de haut en bas* manner of Karajan and his organisation.[15] Yet the music-making was exceptional:

At the piano rehearsal, he said to me, 'Very good. But I can hear your bar lines'. No conductor had ever said that to me before. I think they like to hear the bar lines for the sake of accuracy. What Karajan's remark did was give me freedom, wonderful freedom.[16]

And that connected directly to Veasey's sense of what it is that marks out a great opera conductor from a merely good one:

The really great ones don't impose. A chord at the end of the phrase isn't regimented; it will complement the phrase. You knew with Karajan that he would pick up the colour and emotion of the phrase. He could reflect that in the orchestra. That is very stimulating to a singer.[17]

*

As the opening of the Easter Festival drew ever nearer, Karajan became increasingly nervous. The budget, which he and Glotz had worked out during a flight to Stockholm, looked sound. But if it proved to be out of kilter, there would be no bureaucrats to blame, no government to pick up the tab:

For the first time in my life, I started worrying about myself. If I fell ill or had an accident, the whole thing would founder. I sometimes caught myself driving the Ferrari at 60 mph in second gear. It was sheer anxiety.[18]

Lloyds of London were anxious, too. As part of a package for insuring the festival for ten million Austrian Schillings, Karajan was told he could not ski, nor was he permitted to use a private aeroplane between 1 March 1967 and the end of the festival on 28 March.

Such mishaps as there were, were relatively minor. During rehearsals, Janowitz fell on stage and had to be taken to hospital. She was not badly hurt. Indeed, she came away smiling. Two old ladies, she claimed, had been sitting in out-patients:

FIRST LADY: Do you remember Karajan, the famous consultant? He treated me here.
SECOND LADY: He's been dead donkey's years. (*Long pause*) They say the two boys are still alive.
FIRST LADY: (*Even longer pause*) Didn't one of them go into the music business?[19]

Before the first performance of *Die Walküre* Jon Vickers misjudged his early afternoon nap and woke up later than he would have liked. Panic gave way to confidence when he realised that he knew the part inside out. The performance went very well. Or so he thought.

Next day Karajan asked, 'Jon, what was wrong last night?'

'Nothing, maestro, I felt fine. Why do you ask?'

'Because you sang the role about twenty per cent slower than usual!'

Vickers later told me that he must have known – subconsciously – that he had not gone into the performance precisely as he liked, and had overcompensated. Karajan had adjusted, effortlessly; he always did. But he was curious to know the cause.[20]

Being in the music business involves being nice to journalists, something Karajan was capable of if it suited his purposes. For the launch of the Easter Festival he invited 150 of them to Salzburg. The *Tagesanzeiger* would report:

Karajan arrives fifteen minutes late, followed by his wife Eliette. He is wearing a dark blue suit of Italian cut and billowing blue tie with white spots; she looks as elegant as ever despite her quite plain red dress . . . With his hands in his jacket pockets, he gives a short speech of welcome, speaking of the eighteen months of preparatory work and of the last three weeks in which he has experienced the most harmonious working climate of his life, with two hundred people coming together in a united effort to realise a great idea. He is in dazzling form, joking as he describes a break-in at the press office that morning, which he denies having stage-managed and which has not, as first feared, involved the theft of the press tickets. Nor had the burglars had any joy out of the festival till, for as expected receipts and expenditure were in balance, apart from a small excess of three hundred Schillings [£5] which he was hoping to pocket as his personal fee.[21]

For three-quarters of an hour, Karajan mingled, chatted, and shook hands. He even allowed photographers unlimited access, an unusual concession from a man who had once boxed a press photographer's ears.

Even more important were the subscribers, who had flocked from Europe, America, and Japan to be in Salzburg. The audience was dubbed 'jet-set' by the press, a term that always infuriated Karajan. When CBC's Robert Chesterman asked him – guardedly, for Chesterman was a shrewd and civilised interviewer – about Salzburg's 'élite public', Karajan turned the question back at him:

'What would *you* call an élite public?'

'A public which is so wealthy that it can afford to attend everything, to experience everything in life . . .'

Karajan interrupted. 'I call an "élite public" something *completely* different. It is a public that has *trained* itself to be the best public in the world. It has the knowledge, it has experience . . . nothing to do with dress, or arriving in a Rolls, or jewels . . .'[22]

Indeed, so: I have a not so distant memory of travelling to the Easter Festival by ferry and second-class couchette from Ostend, followed, as Karajan rightly surmised, by several hours in my Salzburg pension boning up on the libretti of *Das Rheingold* and *Die Walküre*. In fact, the bulk of the subscribers to the Easter Festival came from Austria and Southern Germany. Among visitors from abroad, the vast majority were dedicated music lovers drawn mainly from the professional classes: academics, doctors, lawyers, and the like. Successful, but not exactly 'jet-set'.

Among subscribers' perks were a signed copy of the recording of *Die Walküre* and access to an open rehearsal. At the very first rehearsal in 1967, Karajan addressed the audience which had made the enterprise possible.

'I am most grateful to you all, ladies and gentleman,' he said.

'No, Herr von Karajan, it is *we* who are grateful to *you*,' piped up an old lady in the front row.

This rather threw Karajan. He grinned boyishly and did what he always did when life got the better of him: took refuge in the music.

The *Die Walküre* was received with enthusiasm by the press, and remembered with affection in years to come. Writing in the *New Yorker* in 1972, Andrew Porter would recall:

The performances had so strong a character that, despite the year that elapsed between instalments and despite changes of cast in the principal roles, one entered the Festspielhaus and was caught up almost at once in the powerful, particular *Ring* world, unlike any other, that Karajan had created.[23]

Nor was he in any doubt about the ordering of Karajan's priorities:

Above all, it was distinguished by the most beautiful orchestral playing of our day. To the magnificent Berlin orchestra everything else was subordinate. It did not drown the singers, for Karajan held much of its playing to a chamber-music finesse. Rather, he accompanied his instrumentalists with voices that were, in the main, far lighter and less imposing than those of the heroic singers traditionally associated with *The Ring*.[24]

Schneider-Siemssen's sets, based on a huge cosmic ellipse, glowingly lit, remain among the most beautiful and effective of all *Ring* designs. 'They seemed to have been planned,' wrote Porter, 'solely as illustrations to a drama that was unfolding in the pit.' Karajan would have approved that last remark. As he explained on German television at around this time:

Music, in the last resort, is the art which gives expression to our psychic roots. In opera there is also the visual dimension, which is more than mere 'illumination'. The deeper psychological truth must be there, too. If this is not to the fore, I cannot conduct.[25]

On another occasion, he said: 'When I see lighting and staging that is right, the music runs out of my hand without effort.'[26]

The stagy acting worried some critics. 'Old-fashioned gestures that put one in mind of the acting of the stars of the silent film era,' was how an otherwise admiring Joseph Wechsberg put it.[27] There was also a certain distancing tendency in the production. 'Simple response to the singers was inhibited,' recalled Porter, though he added that things were improved in New York, post-Karajan, by virtue of the lights being higher. ('How important it is to be able to read the libretto from the singers' lips.'[28])

It would have been interesting to know what Wieland Wagner would have made of the Salzburg *Walküre*. He had died the previous autumn aged forty-nine. Winifred Wagner took upon herself a watching brief for Bayreuth. After her visit, she wrote:

My dear Herr von Karajan,
First of all may I thank you most warmly for allowing me to attend the dress rehearsal of *Die Walküre*. Then I must ask your permission to tell you how greatly I enjoyed the performance which was so inspired from first note to last. You conducted the work with your life-blood and endowed all the participants with the capacity to interpret their parts quite superbly and enchantingly – and with exemplary pronunciation and diction! My particular compliments are due to the orchestra, which mastered its task superbly – and accompanied the singers and from which you drew an ideal

sound, producing all the climaxes and making the lyrical parts sound so wonderful! The climaxes for me were the shaping of the winter storms, the Fricka scene, Wotan's story, and his departure. For this rendition my enthusiastic thanks!

With most cordial greetings,
Yours Winifred Wagner[29]

*

By the end of the festival, Karajan's affairs were in serious disarray. No one had been able to get access to him with other business, not even Mattoni who was gliding around with a look of world-weary despair. 'My dear, it's *ten* times worse than the summer festival; and you know how difficult *that* is.'

Karajan did have time, however, for more personal matters. Work on *The Ring* had further deepened his relationship with Schneider-Siemssen whose first marriage was currently drifting towards break-up. Karajan, whom Schneider-Siemssen would later describe as 'the truest of all my friends', tried to help; he spoke to the wife and spent many hours with Schneider-Siemssen himself. But it was to no avail.

Two years later, Schneider-Siemssen married an American girl. The ceremony took place in Salzburg, with Karajan and Haeusserman as his witnesses. Karajan carried the bride's train. She would later recall:

He was so simple, so nice. I didn't know a word of German but at the dinner afterwards he sat beside me translating everything. He also warned me about Vienna where we were going to live. 'Never trust the Viennese,' he said. 'They will be sweet, but they'll stab you in the back. Take everything there with a pinch of salt.'[30]

During the ceremony, Schneider-Siemssen turned to Karajan and said, 'For once it's nice to have you behind me,' a reference to the fact that at rehearsals in the Festspielhaus he always sat behind Karajan and a little to the side of him. (The two men's ironic backchat was occasionally reported in the press, mischievously, out of context.[31])

What most amused Schneider-Siemssen was the signing of the register. Haeusserman gave his profession as something rather grand: 'Hochschul-professor' or some such thing. Karajan merely signed himself: 'Herbert von Karajan, Kapellmeister'.

'Why not Dirigent?' asked Schneider-Siemssen.

Karajan grunted. 'Because Kapellmeister is a trade that you learn. Dirigent is merely the exercise of power.'[32]

CHAPTER 61

Carmen and Pagliacci

It is as though he were the embodiment of some
ancient prophetic cry.
David Cairns on Jon Vickers

How did Karajan see himself in the wake of the brilliantly successful first
Salzburg Easter Festival? 'A heavy burden' was the phrase he used in a
meeting with EMI's Peter Andry in London on 12 May 1967. The two
men were talking about Karajan's contract with Deutsche Grammophon
which was due to expire in eighteen months' time. Since the signing of the
contract in 1963, film work and the Easter Festival had greatly complicated
Karajan's already complicated media commitments.

Karajan was in London with the Berlin Philharmonic midway through a
short European tour.[1] In Paris the Berliners played two concerts. The first
consisted of a pair of oddly contrasted Karajan favourites, the devilishly
tricky Mozart Divertimento K287 and Shostakovich's Tenth Symphony.
The second was even more odd: Schumann's Fourth Symphony before the
interval, Ravel's *Pavane pour une infante défunte* and *Boléro* after it.

This was an extremely short programme, less than an hour's music.[2] But
it was a pointer to things to come. In the last years of his life Karajan would
often conduct short programmes. This was not laziness; rather, it was based
on a sub-Gouldian theory about what audiences could and could not attend
to at eight o'clock in the evening after a day at the office. As in other areas of
musical life, Karajan was quietly rewriting the rule book, helped by the fact
that by 1967 he and the Berliners could have played more or less anything
and still sold out the hall at three guineas a seat.

Restraint and display were the order of the day in the Schumann-Ravel
concert, Karajan 'now kissing his hand in ecstasy, now fingering his phrases
like a potter fashioning his wheel'.[3] In the *Symphonie fantastique*, which the
London audience heard in place of the Shostakovich, Karajan's conducting
was judged by Robert Henderson to be 'so articulate that even if there
was no orchestra one would still know exactly what kind of effect he
wanted'.[4] Yet in concerts in Florence the following week the playing
was all over the place, the conducting casual and brash. A truly dreadful
performance of Brahms's *St Antoni* Variations suggested misappropriated
Toscanini, as though Karajan was giving the Italians what he imagined they
hoped to hear. It was Brahms recast in the image of a harassed business
executive.[5]

It was the harassed business executive to whom Peter Andry had been making his overtures in London on 12 May. Though Karajan was convinced that Deutsche Grammophon would opt for a further period of exclusivity when his contract expired in November 1968, it was clear that the company could not cope with all his repertory interests. They had, for example, declined to commission new recordings of the Fourth, Fifth, and Seventh symphonies of Bruckner. Existing Jochum versions were thought to be more than adequate. Nor, given their commitment to the Karajan *Ring*, could they contemplate funding a new *Meistersinger*, despite the fact that no one had yet made a stereophonic recording of the opera.

The overriding problem, however, was Karajan's involvement with films. He knew that he was way ahead of the field as a promoter and experimenter. Frankly, though, he was at a loss as to what to do next; commercially, he had found himself chasing up one cul-de-sac after another.

During the meeting with Andry, he enquired about the possible release for film of his 1956 recording of *Il trovatore* with Callas, di Stefano, and Panerai; this, despite the fact that Callas had already reneged on *Tosca*. Andry mentioned the Paris Opéra production of Gounod's *Faust*. Karajan liked the idea but said it was Prêtre's show and it was his rule never to impinge on another conductor's territory.

In the end, he had to go it alone. He settled on *Carmen*, to be filmed *in situ* in Salzburg during the summer.

*

With *Carmen*, the Grosses Festspielhaus came of age as a film studio. In the theatre, Karajan's production had something of the air of '*Carmen* the musical' about it: lavish sets rich in local colour, huge milling crowds ('Anything Zeffirelli can do . . .'), and very much orchestra-led. On film, the production emerges as an acutely observed piece of operatic verismo, vividly shot in close-up, character-led, with an orchestra that is no more than a telling accompanist.

The Carmen was Grace Bumbry, a wonderful exponent of a role of which she was extremely wary, vocally ('very demanding on the middle voice') and theatrically:

All the other characters have marvellous show-stopping arias . . . but Carmen has none. She is basically a character part, a series of close-ups, as Callas used to say. And if a singer is not a strong character, or is feeling vocally below par, then it's going to be Micaëla's evening, especially if you have a Micaëla like Mirella Freni![6]

One wonders why Bumbry was so concerned. The film is, indeed, a performance of close-ups, superbly acted and sung. (And technically adroit: Bumbry's command of lip-synch is exceptional.) Perhaps Freni got the better of her some nights on stage in the Festspielhaus, but on film it is Bumbry who rivets sense. As does Jon Vickers: his Don José pathologically intense, a homicide waiting to happen.

Interestingly, Karajan chose to set *Carmen* near the sea. Act 3, the fateful nocturne that lies at the heart of the work, took place in his production on a beach strewn with abandoned skiffs and ruined hulks.[7] His reasoning was that in land-locked Salzburg geographical freedom meant the sea, not narrow mountain passes. But there was more to it than that. Though the designs were by Teo Otto, the bay's dark and vasty sweep has cosmic connotations not unlike like those of the swirling horseshoe of the Schneider-Siemssen *Ring*. As Peter Conrad would observe, '[Karajan's] sets have always been orchestrations of the drama';[8] and it was always Karajan who dictated the concept.

The directors of photography were François Reichenbach and a young man called Ernst Wild, who had arrived on the scene as part of a substitute crew when Paul Czinner's company went into liquidation. Wild would stay with Karajan as his director of photography for the next twenty-three years helping him consolidate, and in the last years conserve, his craft. In 1969, however, experimentation was still the watchword. The filming of the orchestral preludes and entr'actes makes radical use of close-ups and whir-ring shifts of perspective that even Clouzot might not have dared risk.

Karajan had now taken to appearing in his own films, fleeting glimpses, Hitchcock-style. In *Pagliacci*, he is an appreciative onlooker at the play; less of a distraction than in *Carmen*, where he gives an embarrassingly intrusive performance as a gypsy lookout, nodding and winking and rolling his eyes in defiance of every rule of the art of playing to the camera in close-up.

As for Karajan the conductor, he appears in formal evening attire, eyes closed (unusual for him when he was conducting opera), hair elaborately coiffured. Gone is the crew-cut of the early 1960s. In its place is a complex ensemble of quiffs and Mercurial wings, a nightmare from the continuity point of view, however strongly lacquered into place. During the filming of one of the entr'actes, Karajan stopped the orchestra and summoned his personal stylist Josef Kaiser. The Vienna Philharmonic was dumbstruck: not by the need for the barbering but by Karajan's imperviousness to embarrassment. Hitherto, 'the hair' had been a wholly private affair. 'My dear fellow,' Mattoni would drawl, 'you certainly can't disturb the chief at the moment, Kaiser Josef is with him.'

*

Karajan made two other films in the latter half of 1967. Both were experimental, marking the extreme limits of what he was prepared to try to do with the medium. One is an interesting *jeu d'esprit*; the other resembles a bad dream.

The *jeu d'esprit* is a performance of Tchaikovsky's First Piano Concerto, with Alexis Weissenberg as soloist, recorded in the Berlin Philharmonie in what looks like a late-night jam session: the hall empty with virtually no peripheral lighting. The director was Åke Falck. Rather than reverencing the music-making, Falck prowls around it and cheekily anatomises it. With the orchestra on the floor of the hall, Karajan above them on a box that seems to have been borrowed from the set for *Fantasia*, and the piano on yet a third level, the layouts wittily mimic the interior design of the hall itself, with its banks of adjacent 'vineyards'. Close-up shots use techniques which nowadays we would associate with natural-history films; far from cosying up to the orchestral instruments, and blithely assuming a knowledge of their function and character, Falck's cameras inspect them anatomically from strange angles.

The keyboard shots are equally absorbing. At the very start of the concerto, all we see is the prow of the instrument. With neither pianist nor keyboard visible, it appears to be playing itself. At other times, bits of the piano appear to be missing, allowing us an uninterrupted view of Weissenberg's fingers and the attendant mechanisms. Weissenberg himself is caught in a number of poses that seem discreetly to parody the 'Hollywood Concerto' style (changing coloured backgrounds and some fetchingly reflective attitudes). His playing is breathtakingly efficient, as is Karajan's direction, the stick and hands filmed in a way that presents the conductor as a co-equal in the virtuoso revel.

By contrast, the film of Beethoven's *Pastoral* Symphony, 'conceived and directed' by Hugo Niebeling, could be said to be an offence against music. With the orchestra stranded on its own private atoll and a cyclorama that is variously black, orange, and putrid green, Niebeling films the performance in a mess of uncoordinated trickery, including swivel-shots, soft focus, the use of distorting mirrors, and worse. Why Karajan agreed to the film's release is a mystery. Perhaps there were contractual constraints; maybe he was flattered by Niebeling's attentive camera-work. Yet watching Karajan, eyes closed, archly prayerful, in the symphony's final hymn-like utterance is to be reminded how little the film has to do with Beethoven's imaginative and spiritual purpose.

'With Niebeling,' Fritz Buttenstedt would allege, 'it was usually a case of one film, plus one legal action.' Niebeling's forte was industrial films: his masterpiece a documentary on Brasília, the high tech, jerry-built road to nowhere, hailed by avant-garde architects at the time as the 'City of the Future'.

In fact, Karajan entrusted two more films to Niebeling which turned out to be very different – and rather good. His 1971 film of Beethoven's Seventh Symphony is one of the most exciting films of an orchestral performance ever made for television.

*

In November 1967 the Easter Festival production of *Die Walküre* was staged in New York. It was the beginning of a fresh flirtation by Karajan with the American scene which would be rudely ended by two unforeseen events: the strike that brought the Met to its knees (and with it the Salzburg project) in the autumn of 1969, and an approach to Karajan by the Chicago Symphony Orchestra, which was almost as ill-judged as the orchestra's approach to Furtwängler in 1948.

As a prelude to the American visit, Karajan had welcomed Szell and the Cleveland Orchestra to the 1967 Salzburg Festival. Karajan conducted the last of the orchestra's three concerts. This was given over to Mozart's Concerto for Three Pianos and Orchestra K242, with Demus, Eschenbach, and Karajan himself as the soloists, and Prokofiev's Fifth Symphony.

Karajan always looked back fondly on this concert, and its repeat a fortnight later in Lucerne, not least because of Szell's own care and comradeship. Between the Mozart and the Prokofiev, Szell took the Cleveland cellos off to practise a tricky passage in the finale. Karajan was stunned by that ('in the interval of *my* concert . . . now there is *real* dedication and real generosity'[9]) though it may not be quite the pleasing story Karajan assumed it to be. A significant minority of the Cleveland players was disconcerted by Karajan's conducting technique: the closed eyes, the absence of precise cues, problems exacerbated by the fact that Karajan's reading of the Prokofiev was markedly different from Szell's. In the Salzburg concert, a passage in the third movement came perilously close to breakdown. That said, the Fifth Symphony was something of a Karajan speciality and the fresh pairing of conductor and orchestra made for an electrifying effect.[10]

Back in America, Szell wrote Karajan a gracious letter of thanks, to which he sent a heartfelt reply:

Dear Mr Szell,
I thank you a thousand times for your charming letter. I think it is about the first recognition I have had from a colleague for about 20 years, and I was deeply gladdened by it . . . See you soon. Most cordial greetings.
 Your,
  Herbert von Karajan [11]

Szell had found Karajan altogether easier to deal with than a number of his colleagues. (When he invited Reiner to conduct the Cleveland Orchestra, Reiner replied, 'I only guest conduct for two reasons: a good fee, and reputation. You are offering neither.') Szell died in 1970, and there was talk of Karajan succeeding him in Cleveland. It was never a realistic possibility. Maazel got the job, and when he left in 1982 it went to Christoph von Dohnányi who would recall:

When I was appointed, the first telegram of congratulations I received was from Karajan. He said, 'This is the only orchestra I have guest conducted where I didn't have something to say after three rehearsals.'[12]

In October 1967 Karajan flew to North America to conduct *La bohème* in Montreal as part of Expo 67, and the Verdi *Requiem* in New York, both with the La Scala company. EMI's New York office reported: 'He will never rest until he is deified in the United States.' But the knives were already out. The *New York Times* considered his conducting of the *Requiem* more calculating than natural, and Toscanini's daughter Wanda was heard loudly proclaiming her disapproval.

Karajan was more concerned with the transfer of *Die Walküre* to the narrower and more modestly equipped stage of the Metropolitan Opera. He had yielded on the size of the tree in Act 1 but on questions of lighting – the production's imaginative epicentre – he was adamant. The Met's technical chief Rudy Kuntner had visited Salzburg during the Easter Festival and thought the Met's 5kW lamps, the largest the house had, would be able to cope – at a pinch – with the back projections. Karajan had his doubts and asked Kuntner to make tests in New York with a light meter. The readings were, indeed, too low. To Bing's dismay thousands of dollars had to be spent re-equipping his new theatre with 10kW lamps bought in from abroad. When they finally arrived, he discovered, to his further dismay, that they were being shone through slides that were virtually opaque. Kuntner conceded it was odd, but the results, he said, were fascinating: Karajan knew what he was doing.

Bing was like a cat on hot bricks during Karajan's visit. Shyness was a complicating factor, and fear. He once said, 'Callas and Karajan were the two people who frightened me most and the two, unfortunately, I most respected.' The house had a special buzz about it the moment Karajan walked through the door but how, Bing worried, would the unions respond to his peremptory demands? What of the Met's less-than-first-rate orchestra? And what of Mme Nilsson?

Nilsson and Karajan rubbed along much as they always did. She donned a miner's lamp as a protest against the darkness of parts of the production; he played tapes of Crespin's Brünnhilde during stage rehearsals. ('He was malicious, with the charm of a cat,' recalls Crespin in her autobiography.)

Nilsson badmouthed Karajan in the press; Karajan demanded a formal apology. When he did not get it, he airily declared Nilsson to be beyond the circle of his 'artistic world'.

With the house orchestra – in those days one of the rougher bands on the international circuit – Karajan was patience itself. Privately, he complained bitterly. ('How did they choose these people?' he asked Ronald Wilford. 'In Berlin these players would not even get an audition. It's like my seven-year-old asking, "Daddy, can I study calculus?" She's not up to doing calculus.') When Mahler had come to New York, he publicly humiliated incompetent players and forced them out. Karajan simply got down to the task of training them to listen. It was more a seminar in the art of orchestral playing than a rehearsal of Die Walküre. Karajan did not go over passages again and again until they were theoretically (and temporarily) 'right'. Instead, he taught the players to draw musical sustenance from the singers. 'You must hear the harp here. All of you.' Or again, to the strings at the end of the first long rehearsal: 'All these phrasings that look so complicated: if you play for the woodwinds and the woodwinds play for the singer, it all becomes perfectly easy . . .'

As the work progressed, so the various bits of the jigsaw began to fit into place. The players warmed to this, and marvelled at the acuteness of Karajan's ear. Bing also appreciated what he was doing. It was, he ruefully notes in his memoirs, the experience of Ulm and Aachen shining through, something which many of the rising young conducting stars of the 1960s all too conspicuously lacked.

Karajan did not get many plaudits from the critics: at least, not in 1967. To those innocent of the revolution Wieland Wagner had effected in Europe in the 1950s, the production of Die Walküre was too abstract, too abstruse. Nor did the intimate, 'chamber-music' style of Wagner performance go down well with a public used to big voices and an altogether heftier orchestral manner. While Karajan was in New York, someone put it to him that his recording of Die Walküre was closer in spirit to Weber than to Wagner. Karajan looked puzzled at first, then said:

It is there, of course. Weber was the first composer with a sense of living nature which goes through all Wagner's work. If you do not carry this sense of the identity of music and nature you are not telling the truth to the audience. What is the Ring in the end but a parable of violated nature? That and the father-and-son complex – the elder who has the knowledge and admires the younger for his greater impact and instinctive force. Wagner identified with both.[13]

By the time of Das Rheingold the following year, the style had been absorbed, and most of the critics were out of denial. Having rubbished

Die Walküre in 1967, Herbert Weinstock conceded that the 1968 production of *Das Rheingold* was 'one of the true genuinely great Wagnerian performances of a lifetime'.[14]

*

In the winter of 1967–8 Karajan fell ill. This time it was flu coupled with a bout of double pneumonia and a severe attack of neuritis. Yet even as his nerve-ends were painfully flaring, so were some of his old ambitions. News of Hilbert's death reawakened a desire to conduct again in Vienna where Böhm and Bernstein were currently making hay. And Chicago loomed.

In 1968, the Chicago Symphony Orchestra was in the process of showing the door to Jean Martinon, Reiner's successor. 'If men could learn from history,' the poet Coleridge once remarked, 'what lessons it might teach us!' Despite the fact that the Chicago board had helped damage Furtwängler's post-war career and had also shown scant respect to Reiner at the end of his epoch-making rule (said one board member, 'We got that son of a bitch out of Chicago without even giving him a farewell party'), Karajan did not say 'no' when Michel Glotz and Ronald Wilford turned up in Milan with an offer from Chicago Chairman Louis Sudler that promised megabucks for doing rather little. Karajan was, however, extremely circumspect.

The moment news of a possible link between Karajan and Chicago broke within the music business, record companies started beating a path back there. But, as with Furtwängler in 1949, all was not what it seemed. Though the offer to Karajan had appeared to come jointly from Sudler and the orchestra's new General Manager John Edwards, it later became clear that Edwards was conducting a private negotiation of his own with Covent Garden's Music Director Georg Solti. Later, word was put about that Chicago had been trying for a world-beating triumvirate: Karajan as chief conductor, Solti and Giulini as the principal guest conductors.[15] In fact, the moment Wilford rumbled the Edwards–Solti negotiation he called Karajan to advise him that Chicago was 'not a place one wants to be'.

Perhaps it was a case of all's well that end's well. In Solti, the Chicago Symphony got a music director who in the fullness of time would devote a large part of his life to the orchestra; and Karajan was spared – for the time being, at least – further complications to his schedules and a further unwelcome revival of interest in his Nazi affiliations.[16]

*

While Karajan was in New York, he heard the young Montserrat Caballé sing Violetta. He immediately signed her as Donna Elvira for his forth-coming film and stage production of *Don Giovanni*. Caballé was delighted, though rather less thrilled when the contract arrived stipulating that she must lose thirty-three pounds in the interim.[17] The film ran into financial trouble and was never made.

Money was found, however, to film the La Scala productions of *Cavalleria rusticana* and *Pagliacci*. These were shot in June 1968 in a Milan ice-rink (drained), a great warehouse of a building in which the sets for the two operas were built back to back. Apart from conducting it, Karajan had relatively little to do with *Cavalleria rusticana*. This was Giorgio Strehler's stage production and, frankly, it worked better in the theatre. Luciano Damiani's sets look strangely drab on film and the outdoor location photography by Åke Falck is often bizarre.

Pagliacci, however, is masterly. Karajan directed this himself, catching well the colour and bustle of Calabrian town life *c.*1870 and using close-ups to superb effect at the great determining moments. The role of Tonio – the prologue sung powerfully, straight to camera – was taken by a young English baritone new to Karajan, Peter Glossop. Karajan was fascinated by Glossop's pale blue eyes, the gaze penetrating yet sad. It is a wonderful performance, panic and anger not far below the surface of Tonio's would-be affability.[18]

Jon Vickers is Canio, a towering characterisation, the clown's predica-ment brought searingly within the tragic ambit, backed by orchestral playing of phenomenal spaciousness and intensity. Nowhere is this more apparent than in an overwhelmingly powerful performance of 'Vesti la giubba', Canio gazing poignantly into a make-up mirror he has just crazed with his fist.[19]

During the filming, Karajan conducted a number of performances of the double bill at La Scala itself, though when Vickers fell ill, he cancelled *Pagliacci* and a ballet was played instead. The audience was given to believe that there was no suitable last-minute substitute for Vickers. This was not true. It was simply that Karajan refused to accept one. Worried that a distinguished colleague, who was available, would get wind of this, Vickers protested to Karajan.

'Jon,' said Karajan. 'The fact that I drive a Rolls-Royce does not mean that I despise a Mercedes.'

It was a tactful response. But he was adamant. For him, Vickers *was* Canio. A singer cannot expect a higher accolade than that; nor can one imagine it being more sincerely given.

CHAPTER 62

An urge to educate

And gladly wolde he lerne and gladly teche.
Chaucer, *The Canterbury Tales*

As his sixtieth birthday approached, Karajan boasted how much time – for all his seeming ubiquity – he spent *not* conducting:

I think I'm one of the few conductors who takes at least as much, if not more, time over preparation as over actual conducting. If one is conducting, producing or making a film, one cannot simultaneously think of making other arrangements. It simply does not work. I'm a person who cannot live in a town at all. I can only live in the country, in the mountains or by the sea. Then I can be myself. And for this time, which I find so vital, I now take between 180 and 200 days a year.[1]

This was one of the reasons why he never took a house in Berlin during his years as Chief Conductor of the Berlin Philharmonic. For many years, his Berlin home was the charmingly old-fashioned Savoy Hotel tucked away near the eastern end of the Kurfürstendamm. With its pre-war ambience and leafy inner courtyard it had style and a measure of quiet. Eventually, he was talked into taking a suite in the Kempinski, Berlin's glitziest hotel built in 1952, smart and soulless. But it was a struggle. There was a tree outside his room at the Savoy which he had watched grow from a sapling. Beethoven once said, 'I love a tree more than a man'; Karajan, too, was deeply reluctant to leave his tree.[2]

The illnesses that preceded his sixtieth birthday reinforced his belief in the need for a balanced regime of work and leisure. With Isabel rising eight and Arabel a lively and enquiring four-year-old, he was also beginning to take his responsibilities as a father seriously. Not the least of these duties was keeping the press at bay which is why, during the sixtieth-birthday year, when the demand for interviews and photo opportunities reached a new pitch of intensity, he and Eliette allowed picture journalists a limited number of carefully regulated assignments in their homes in St Tropez and St Moritz.

There are shots of the girls being swung in the garden by their mother and being given piggybacks in the swimming pool by their father. There are posed family groups in the library and under a palm tree in the St Tropez garden; photos of the girls out in the bay in a dinghy, Arabel sitting in the middle while her father and elder sister do the paddling. Karajan himself remained as difficult as ever about being photographed while working but there was easier access to his leisure pursuits. His yachting activities, in particular, were much photographed, supplementing the already familiar shots of Karajan the aviator and Karajan the racing driver. A new sixtieth birthday toy was a 250cc Yamaha motor-cycle.

The two daughters were brought up in a way that nowadays would be considered extremely old-fashioned. They were taught manners, schooled to sit and listen at table, and trained to value simple pleasures and pursuits. There would be problems later: over Arabel's search for a vocation and over Isabel's determined and eventually successful pursuit of an acting career, the very career, paradoxically, which her paternal grandfather had so wanted to pursue. Such time as Karajan was able to give his daughters was thought through and typically concentrated. And it paid dividends. As the girls came to maturity it would be remarked by those who knew them how serious they were, and how little affected by the trappings of fame and fortune. In this they were very much the daughters of their father, a tribute to his will and sagacity.

The girls were not put to music compulsorily. Like most people who are in the profession, Karajan knew well enough its pitfalls and had no intention of encouraging his children to entertain dreams they could not realise. But music was taught, teachers engaged, and sometimes dismissed. What most infuriated Karajan was hearing a piano lesson proceeding in a nearby room and breaking down over and over again at the same point. 'If you are not curious enough to know *why* things always break down at this point,' he told the hapless pedagogue, 'you are not really interested in music and should not be teaching.' At times, Eliette thought he was being too harsh. Karajan would recall:

The first time Isabel played me something, she came to a difficult passage and suddenly slowed down. I said: 'Child, what are you doing?' 'Well, I can't get my fingers round it.' 'All right, then, play it slowly, but keep in time.' My wife was horrified. She said I'd give the child a complex. Certainly not, I said, she's an extremely intelligent child. I spoke to her for three quarters of an hour. She took it extremely seriously and said: 'Daddy, I still can't play it exactly in time, but now I'll play it slowly'.[3]

Karajan himself had been teaching, on and off, since 1929. Wherever he went – Lucerne, Tokyo, Moscow, New York – he would talk with students and give informal master-classes. In Berlin in 1958 a somewhat curious article had appeared in *Der Tag* under the byline of a certain Rudolf Nestler. Karajan, it said, was giving lessons to young conductors, free of charge and in a manner that was wholly undogmatic:

Each of the lessons lasts two and a half hours and in the course of it each of the six to eight candidates is taken gently in hand . . . A considerable number of the conductors came from the school for conductors at the Berlin City Conservatory, whose director Herbert Ahlendorf was asked by Karajan to select and prepare the applicants.[4]

Rudolf Nestler, it later turned out, was none other than Ahlendorf himself.

Frustrated by his inability to advance and co-ordinate his interests in education, and in medicine, Karajan decided to mark his sixtieth-birthday year by setting up the Herbert von Karajan Foundation, an organisation that still functions in modified form in a number of areas. Its aims were 'to encourage young artists, support scientific research, and foster international understanding in the field of music'. It would be best known for the biennial International Conductors' Competition, administered by Ahlendorf, which ran from 1969 to the mid-1980s, and for the postgraduate orchestral academy which Karajan established in Berlin. Yet it is possible to think that the scientific and medical research grants, unquantifiable though their results are, might have the greater impact in the longer term.

By nominating scientific research as one of the Foundation's aims, Karajan knew he was doing no more than throwing a few pebbles into the mighty ocean of twentieth-century scientific enquiry. At the press conference in Berlin on 1 October 1968 at which he announced the Foundation's approval by the Berlin Senate and the granting of its legal articles, Karajan was frank about the apparently unspecific nature of the research agenda. Particular projects would be funded in response to particular issues and events. It is clear in retrospect, however, that Karajan was personally interested in a number of fields: stress in relation to music-making (even as the Foundation was being set up, Karajan's old friend Joseph Keilberth had died of a heart attack while conducting *Tristan und Isolde* in Munich), the therapeutic use of music, and neuroscientific research into degenerative diseases of the brain.

The Foundation's discussion forum would be the academic symposia which took place each year during the Easter Festival. Overseen by Karajan's personal physician Dr Walther Simon, the subjects alternated between science and the philosophy of music. The quality varied. Some papers were merely cranky, others had real substance. At best – as in the 1983 forum 'Time in Music' – papers on physics and neurobiology would sit happily alongside one on continuity of pulse in the Brahms symphonies.[5]

Karajan's preoccupation with rhythm and pulse drew together several apparently disparate projects. The immediate consequence of Keilberth's death was the setting up of an elaborate series of tests during the dress rehearsal for the Easter Festival production of Wagner's *Siegfried*. Karajan was wired like an astronaut in a test capsule and readings taken and analysed during the so-called 'Siegfried Idyll' section of Act 3. Shortly before the music began, Karajan's heartbeat shot up from 67 beats per minute to 148, then dropped back again the moment the music got underway. The next stress point came as the Brünnhilde approached what was (for her, and therefore for Karajan) a crucial top C. Curiously, when Karajan was then asked to lie down and hear the entire sequence played back on tape, the readings were more or less identical, even though the session was over and the music was, as it were, 'in the bag'; proof, Karajan concluded, that these things are mostly beyond the control of will-power or reason.[6]

Heartbeat came up, too, in a discussion he instituted about the use of music in paediatric practice:

Our susceptibility or receptivity to a particular rhythm stays with us throughout the whole of our lives. I don't know whether you're aware of an experiment that was carried out recently, in which a mother's heartbeat was recorded before the birth of her child. After the child was born – it was a difficult child and cried a lot – it became completely calm when its mother's heartbeat was played back to it. Heartbeats were then played to it involving very slight variations of their frequency, and the child remained completely without reaction. This single heartbeat shows the importance of the pulse with which the child was so long associated.[7]

The Foundation would give Karajan the cue he needed, and the legal and financial infrastructure, to undertake a whole range of significant small initiatives in the years to come.

In May 1981, three years after receiving an honorary degree from the University of Oxford, he endowed a Neuroscience Research Trust within the university. Research into diseases of the nervous system had advanced significantly since the late 1940s when his own father was stricken with Alzheimer's disease, but cures for this, and for Parkinson's disease, were still a distant dream. The aim of the Neuroscience Research Trust was to help tide over gifted researchers whose work might otherwise have to be abandoned because of a lack of transitional funding. It is impossible to assess what impact the Trust has had, even in the medium term, though the work of the very first beneficiary has already received widespread international recognition.[8]

*

In September 1968, Karajan and the Berlin Philharmonic played in two unfamiliar venues, the ancient city of Dubrovnik in Yugoslavia and Baalbek in the Lebanon. Using Baalbek's magnificent complex of Roman ruins, the Baalbek Festival offered a promiscuous mix of musical and theatrical events in the 1960s: a string quartet one night, Ella Fitzgerald the next, the Bolshoi Ballet or the great Arab vocalist Ibrahim Um Kalthum, who once famously held four thousand people spellbound throughout her entire four hour recital.

Since Eliette had been ill with tonsillitis, Karajan travelled with his old friend Raffaello de Banfield. Karajan hated air-conditioning. Having spied from the air a handsome hotel in the hills, he checked out of the Baalbek accommodation that had been booked by Stresemann and headed for it. When he and Banfield got there, they found it had already closed for the winter. For the owner, this was no problem: '*Pour Monsieur von Karajan, ça ne me dérange pas du tout!*' And so, for the best part of a week, Karajan and Banfield rested, read, swam, walked ('How we walked!' Banfield would later recall) and dined like princes in their own five-star retreat.

Karajan returned, refreshed, to Berlin to record Prokofiev's Fifth Symphony, to do additional work on Haydn's *The Creation* which had been all but completed in 1966 at the time of Fritz Wunderlich's sudden death,[9] and to record for the first time with Rostropovich, a classic recording of Dvořák's Cello Concerto (the Berlin winds at their ravishing best), paired with a deft and stylish account of Tchaikovsky's *Variations on a Rococo Theme*.

The loan of Rostropovich to a West German record company was an indication of improved relations between Moscow and Bonn. The success of the sessions, and Karajan's long-standing admiration for David Oistrakh and Sviatoslav Richter, now led to talk of a very high-profile collaboration indeed: a recording of Beethoven's Triple Concerto involving all four artists. The question was: if political approval was given, who would record it?

Karajan's five-year exclusive contract with Deutsche Grammophon ended in November 1968, opening up a fresh and potentially rather ugly round of negotiations between the interested parties. One card that was bound to be played was the Berlin Philharmonic, which was contracted to Deutsche Grammophon until 1971, with an option to renew for a further two years. It was a card Deutsche Grammophon was ready to play, with the tacit agreement of the orchestra, whose management was looking for ways of curbing a number of Karajan's demands, in particular, his long-standing insistence that all the players be available for every recording session irrespective of whether or not they were to be used.

Karajan, predictably, was infuriated by these stratagems. He sensed a conspiracy. In such circumstances his instinct was to lay waste the opposing forces or, failing that, lay siege to them.

In November 1968 a siege weapon came to hand in the shape of the

Orchestre de Paris. The orchestra had been founded the previous year, with Charles Munch as its principal conductor. On 6 November 1968, Munch died while on tour with them in the United States. In Paris, thoughts instantly turned to the question of a successor. Karajan's name headed the list, but, according to EMI sources, Glotz had informed Jessier, the orchestra manager, that Karajan was not interested.[10] This might have been a reasonable assumption on another occasion but it was not entirely the case now. To compound the problem, Jessier had begun a private negotiation with, of all people, the victor of the battle of Chicago – Georg Solti. Karajan got wind of this while in New York for the November run of *Ring* performances and immediately sounded out Ronald Wilford.

A call by Wilford to the Paris-based impresario Albert Safardi and one by Safardi to culture minister André Malraux established that the government in Paris knew nothing of the Jessier–Solti negotiation (Jessier was later sacked) and that it was, indeed, interested in Karajan. Because of Karajan's former Nazi Party membership, it was required that the matter be placed before President de Gaulle. Was de Gaulle's policy of *rapprochement* towards Germany a determining factor, or was he interested in acquiring for Paris a certain reflected *gloire*? Whatever the reason, he not only approved the idea of Karajan's appointment, he actively supported it.

Karajan showed no special enthusiasm for the proposition but agreed to accept the position of 'Adviser' to the orchestra, should Malraux formally offer it to him, which he duly did through Marcel Landowski, Director of Music in the Ministry of Culture. There is no doubt that Wilford was right in his conjecture that the factor that weighed most heavily with Karajan was his belief that the move would unnerve Deutsche Grammophon, the Berlin Philharmonic, and the Berlin Senate. There were other attractions, too; not least the chance the appointment gave him to spend time in the one city he enjoyed being in. But there were obvious problems. Even with Serge Baudo as his able deputy, a single concert or a single LP with this relatively new and inexperienced orchestra was going to require huge amounts of rehearsal.

And how much time did Karajan have? His contract stipulated ten weeks per annum. Yet, within months of coming to power, the new French president Georges Pompidou (a previous resident of Karajan's house in St Tropez) was questioning Landowski about the situation. In the summer of 1971, after a series of concerts in Paris and the provinces, Karajan was informed that he was spending too little time with the orchestra and was asked to stand down. He was succeeded by Solti: an interregnum that was as brief as it was ill-tempered.

In later years, there were those in Paris who rued the loss of Karajan. The Mayor of Paris, Jacques Chirac, said as much in Landowski's presence, when he made a presentation to Karajan on behalf of the city in 1986. Landowski looked decidedly sheepish but Karajan greeted him with all due cordiality: 'I would probably have died in the attempt to be in Berlin, Salzburg, and Paris. God made me very loyal, and since I love Paris as no other city, I would never have left.'[11]

*

In January 1969, the flautist James Galway first encountered the Berlin Philharmonic. Auditions for the position of solo flute were being held in Munich during the orchestra's tour of Germany. Galway himself has recalled, with great good humour, both the terrifying arrogance of the organisation and its breathtaking administrative inefficiency.[12] The general view is that it is conductors who are arrogant, not orchestras. What is revealing about Galway's story is that the saga of altered schedules, unsent telegrams, and high-handed ultimata was largely Stresemann's doing.

When Galway was eventually offered the job, he said he would think about it. Stresemann was appalled: 'In Germany, you are required by law to accept a position for which you have successfully auditioned.'

'And who's German round here?' was Galway's impeccably Irish retort.

In the end, he accepted, and had a wonderful time, despite some spectacular run-ins with 'Herbie', as he liked to call him, and occasional problems with some of the work-obsessed perfectionists who were his colleagues in the wind section in those years. Beards and the Irishman's dress-sense apart, there was a bond of mutual admiration between Galway and Karajan that survived until 'Jimmy' tendered his resignation in August 1974, thus putting himself beyond the pale of the maestro's 'family' of loyal musicians.

In February 1969, Karajan flew to New York to conduct further performances of *Das Rheingold* and *Die Walküre*. The February performances were seen by Lord Harewood, who was more receptive than most of the American critics had been to Karajan's painting in music and light:

That this example of total theatre as conceived by two men (Wagner and Karajan) is a major achievement for any opera house, I have no doubt at all ... The production was logical, simple and often beautiful to look at (lighter too than last year). I didn't care for the pantomime-devil red spot on the sword in Act 1, but there were discreet scene changes in Act 2, a most convincing fight (Siegmund's sword broke on a spear manifested overwhelmingly as a vast shaft of light) and a moving piece of lighting in Act 3 when Wotan, singing 'so küsst er die Gottheit von dir', moves his hand slowly over Brünnhilde's head and with a gesture extinguishes the light on her.[13]

But he, too, had caveats to enter:

Paradoxically, the chamber scale of the accompaniment made the huge voices sound smaller than usual and, while the rest of the music was restrained and even slow, anything like a set-piece ... was contrastingly allowed to flow which had the effect somehow of highlighting the highlights.[14]

Later that same year the Met was crippled by one of the most damaging labour disputes in its history. The dispute had been brewing for several years, a witches' cauldron of union militancy and management profligacy in the face of soaraway fees. The move to the new Lincoln Center in 1966 had intensified the crisis. Advised by labour lawyer Herman Gray, the orchestra had threatened an all-out strike. The musicians having got what they wanted, and more besides, the technical staff signed up with Gray, setting the scene for the even more debilitating dispute of 1969.

Because of the strike, the Salzburg *Siegfried* was put on hold. For Karajan, it was the end of the affair. The Salzburg stagings were later seen in New York, but Karajan was no longer the conductor. There are those who say that the strike was providential, that Karajan was so dissatisfied with the Met orchestra that he was looking for a way out anyway. There is probably some truth in this.

Karajan and Bing remained on good terms; Karajan even offered to appear at his farewell gala. Their final meeting took place in London in 1987 in the interval of a concert Karajan was giving with the Berlin Philharmonic. Two stricken old men: Karajan with all manner of physical ailments, Bing with Alzheimer's disease and the tabloid press snapping at his heels over an affair he was alleged to be having with a fortune-hunting beauty.[15]

*

After New York, Moscow. Karajan's suggestion that the Berlin Philharmonic should be allowed to visit Moscow and Leningrad had caused outrage in East Berlin. The Russian cultural attaché there had flounced into his office at the Philharmonie and told him so to his face. But Karajan had a friend in high places in Moscow, the culture minister Jekaterina Furzewa, whom he had first met in Vienna in 1962. To everyone's surprise (and to the fury of the East Berlin regime) the visit was agreed, with the proviso that the orchestra travelled via Prague where a concert must also be given.

In Moscow, the demand for tickets was phenomenal. To get over the shortage, the authorities issued hundreds of passes for standing places. The hall was packed solid, and even then there was a disturbance midway through Beethoven's *Pastoral* Symphony as more young people tried to break down a door. Shostakovich would recall:

It was like a siege, tickets were impossible to obtain. Police, mounted and on foot, surrounded the theatre. [Maria] Yudina [the pianist] sat down in front of the theatre and spread out her skirts. Naturally, a policeman came over to her. 'You're disturbing the peace, citizeness, what's the problem?' And Yudina said, 'I'm not getting up until I get into the concert.'[16]

Yudina was the woman who upon receiving a fee for a recording she had made at Stalin's behest had written a letter of thanks in which she said: 'I thank you, Josif Vissarionovich, for your aid. I will pray for you day and night and ask the Lord to forgive your great sins before the people and the country.'[17] No one knows why Stalin omitted to have her punished for this, but if anyone had a right to hear the Tenth Symphony, other than the composer himself, it was she!

The second concert was devoted to Bach's *Brandenburg* Concerto No. 1 and Shostakovich's Tenth Symphony. The orchestra's commitment was astonishing. Mariss Jansons would recall: 'They played at two hundred per cent capacity. It was unbelievable.' Shostakovich joined Karajan and the orchestra on stage afterwards, obviously moved by the performance and the reception he received. For Karajan, it was possibly the proudest moment of his life.

The Kremlin did its best to annoy its guests, but Karajan, too, was stubborn. The programme leaflets billed the orchestra as 'Symphony Orchestra [West Berlin]'. At the start of the second concert, Karajan sat down at the harpsichord and rather pointedly waited. Eventually a lady came on stage and announced that the concert was being given by the 'Berlin Philharmonic Orchestra'.

The authorities also tried to prevent the West German embassy holding a party for the players on the grounds that Berlin was not part of West Germany. First, they insisted that the orchestra fly to Leningrad a day early (fog was forecast, they said). Then, when the embassy brought forward the reception by a day, there was a vain attempt to cut off the catering supply. There was no fog at Leningrad, though when the plane landed, Karajan refused to disembark. 'It's too dangerous,' he told a bemused official. 'What if I get lost in the fog?'

The Leningrad concerts were almost as packed out as the Moscow ones. The 17-year-old Semyon Bychkov, whom years later Karajan would mention in connection with the succession in Berlin, clambered over a roof, eased himself in through the ladies lavatory, and was promptly arrested.

It was young musicians such as Bychkov, Mariss Jansons, and Dmitri Kitaienko whom Karajan was most interested to meet in Leningrad, though the authorities had done their best to stop this. A letter Karajan had sent to Mrs Furzewa proposing that he give an (unpaid) master-class in Leningrad had never reached her desk. While he tried to nose out talent, the Soviets feared defections to the West. It would remain a problem throughout Karajan's life. Russian prize-winners of the Karajan International Conductors' Competition frequently had their access to the West, and therefore to Karajan himself, severely restricted in the wake of the competition.[18]

*

During the summer and autumn of 1969 the difficult and complex negotiations between Karajan, the Berlin Philharmonic, and their various record companies moved slowly and uneasily forward. On matters of repertory, Deutsche Grammophon knew they would have more than enough and were prepared to concede anything except – as Hans Hirsch would later reveal – the Beethoven symphonies. As for EMI, they played their cards well. With the state of the market in 'great' conductors even more parlous in 1969 than it had been in 1959, David Bicknell no longer harboured any doubts about the need to win Karajan back, even if it was going to involve large advances and an unprecedented ten per cent royalty on the orchestral recordings. In fact, receipts and royalties from Karajan's older EMI recordings had held up well in the 1960s thanks to improved marketing. Andry and Bicknell were also prepared to be sympathetic to Karajan's film interests.

The British company was better placed, too, to negotiate with a number of the Russian artists in whom Karajan was interested. Indeed, EMI's first major breakthrough was the securing of the rights to record the Beethoven Triple Concerto with Richter, Oistrakh, and Rostropovich. Though it cost a great deal of money to make[19] and was budgeted for as a loss-leader (estimated lifetime sale 95,000 copies, break-even sale 125,000 copies) it proved to be a huge money-spinner. By 1977, the LP had already sold 457,980 copies.

The sessions for the Triple Concerto were generally amicable, though Oistrakh would have liked a quicker tempo in the slow movement. Rostropovich was delegated to talk to Karajan about this. Karajan agreed to the suggestion, then returned to the hall and set an even slower tempo.

Rostropovich had a great admiration for Karajan, though he disliked intensely his approach to concert-giving – arriving at the hall at the very last minute and refusing to receive guests afterwards – and he feared his driving. Once, as they hurtled down some narrow mountain road, he held up his hands in despair: 'Herbert, I don't mind dying. But please give the morticians a chance to sort out our bones. Yours need to go to Anif and mine need to go back to Russia. At this speed, they'll never know which are which.'

*

During the 1969 St Moritz summer vacation Karajan and the Berlin Philharmonic made recordings of some of the more intimate masterworks of the twentieth century repertory: Honegger's Second Symphony, Strauss's *Metamorphosen*, and Stravinsky's *Apollo* and Concerto in D. There were also some musical sweetmeats from the baroque era: recordings of the Pachelbel Canon and Albinoni's *Adagio* for strings and organ that would keep Deutsche Grammophon in funds for years to come.[20]

That summer, Karajan met Joy Bryer. An international festival of youth orchestras was taking place in St Moritz at the same time as the Berlin Philharmonic's annual vacation; Mrs Bryer was running it and Karajan invited her for talks to explore the possibility of her becoming involved with the festival of youth orchestras he was arranging in Berlin in September 1970. The meetings were productive and extremely amicable, but Joy Bryer said no. She saw Karajan's time as being limited. There would be delegation to aides and compromises to be made with his administrators. Karajan understood. He backed off but would later give her unstinting support when her dream came true and she was able to found the European Community Youth Orchestra.

Karajan's grand strategy was to run a conducting competition and an International Meeting of Youth Orchestras in tandem in alternate years in Berlin each September. Of the two, the convention of youth orchestras was the trickier to fund and sustain, though it ran, more or less successfully, until 1978.[21]

The International Conductors' Competition was inaugurated in September 1969 and got off to an auspicious start. For this, Karajan had broken a lifetime's rule and invited sponsorship from business and industry. He also pestered the record companies for contributions. EMI received a note saying that instead of sending expensive flowers to his hotel suite, they should give the money to the Foundation. He was right; huge sums were routinely wasted in this way. (The London office of Deutsche Grammophon always put a bottle of Perrier-Jouët champagne in his dressing-room. What he actually wanted was Perrier *water*.) The costs of the conducting competition were formidable. There were applications from over four hundred would-be contestants of whom some sixty or so were invited to participate. Though the Berlin Symphony Orchestra would later become involved, in 1969 the Berlin Radio Symphony Orchestra played the preliminary and intermediate rounds, the semifinals, and the closed final in which the order of the winners was arrived at. The Berlin Philharmonic was used only for the ceremonial 'closing concert'.

The stated aim of the competition was 'to further the development of gifted young conductors'. (Or, as Karajan occasionally preferred to put it, 'my revenge on the profession for not helping me when I was young'.)

Ahlendorf ran it with surprisingly little interference. Karajan had made just one stipulation. At a press conference held shortly before the closing concert on 28 September, he told his audience:

Right at the start, I advised the gentlemen of the jury that it wasn't a question of filling a second conductor's post but of finding an explosive new talent. Whether that talent is already fully formed or not is completely irrelevant. We wanted to find someone who has a genuine feeling for music and a genuine feel for communication.[22]

Stresemann chaired the jury, which was made up as much from his own and Ahlendorf's circle of professional acquaintance as from Karajan's. The first committee included conductors Sir John Barbirolli, Franco Ferrara, and Lovro von Matačić, two distinguished composer-teachers Wolfgang Fortner and Karl Höller, the critic H. H. Stuckenschmidt, and Karajan's two recording gurus Walter Legge and Elsa Schiller. Juries do not always agree among themselves but to judge from an abject letter of apology Karajan wrote to Legge after the event (he had omitted to mention Legge's name in his closing speech of thanks) all had been sweetness and light: on this occasion, at least.

The years varied and sometimes Karajan was more involved than others. If time permitted, he might appear unexpectedly at one of the preliminary rounds and offer some impromptu advice: to the delight both of the contestants and the battle-weary Berlin Symphony Orchestra which turned from a charmless caterpillar into a strangely beautiful butterfly the moment he picked up the baton.[23]

In general, Karajan left the jurors to make up their own minds, bitterly as he occasionally disagreed with their verdicts. Raffaello de Banfield would recall Karajan and Legge arguing over a conductor Karajan had not liked. 'Still, I bet you couldn't conduct as well as that when you were his age,' concluded Legge triumphantly. That angered Karajan, but he took it on the chin. Legge was useful in that respect, Banfield said. Joshing Karajan in front of others was not something many people risked doing.

Legge's views on the contestants often bordered on the unprintable. In 1975, he asserted that none of the sixty-five contestants was capable of conducting Haydn's *London* Symphony, while continuing to fulminate against the machinations of that 'recently deceased Valzacchi [the intriguer in *Der Rosenkavalier*]' Hans Swarowsky who, four years earlier, had lobbied for his pupil Gabriel Chmura in what was a flagrant breach of the spirit of Rule 11 of the Competition which stated that 'Jurors are excluded from judging and voting on those participants who are or have been their students'. Chmura won, ahead of Mariss Jansons, whom the wider musical world would judge to be the greater talent.

Perhaps it is in the nature of committees that they will end by choosing more good 'second conductors', as Karajan called them, rather than the 'explosive new talent' he had urged them to identify. The three prize-winners in 1969 – the 23-year-old self-taught Finn Okko Kamu who won the competition, the Belgian François Huybrechts, and Dmitri Kitaienko – all made careers but it was not until Jansons in 1971 and Gergiev and Kasprzyk in 1977 that genuinely explosive talent blazed through. And talent of that order of magnitude, many will say, would have blazed through anyway.

There were occasional grouses that Karajan was not entirely disinterested, that he favoured conductors from Russia and the Eastern European countries, and that he was too obviously protective of certain Jewish musicians. There may have been some truth in this. No doubt many young aspirants went away with their tails between their legs. As timpanist and sometime juror Werner Thärichen would observe, conducting is a profession in which self-doubt spells death. Yet failure to advance in the competition did not necessarily blight a man's career. Among those who fell by the wayside in the early rounds in 1969 was the Czech conductor Jiří Bělohlávek.

The strength of the competition was that it was demanding, formidably well run, and palpably, thanks to Karajan's presence, 'a great occasion'. It spawned a number of rivals and several important satellite competitions whose prize-winners would be forwarded to the larger competition in Berlin. For most of the contestants it was at worst useful, at best unforgettable.[24]

CHAPTER 63

Mr Andry plays his ace

The presence of death makes itself felt in the sadness of beauty.
Hanns Sachs, *The Creative Unconscious*

Karajan ended 1969 with the most extraordinary of all his New Year's
Eve concerts in Berlin. It began with the primeval yelp of Penderecki's
De Natura Sonoris I, continued with Beethoven's *Grosse Fuge*, and ended
with Strauss's *Also sprach Zarathustra*. Conservative tastes were appeased
a few days later by a New Year's concert of music by Mozart and
Tchaikovsky.

Meanwhile, his negotiations with Deutsche Grammophon were close
to stalemate. The principal sticking-point was the flat fee element (EMI
believed it to be fifty per cent of all his royalty earnings[1]) in the earlier
agreement which he had insisted on to avoid a significant proportion of
his income leaching away to Anita under the terms of the 1958 divorce
settlement. By Karajan's own estimation, the deal had cost him six million
Deutschmarks in lost royalty earnings, money that Deutsche Grammophon
had been able to retain as profit. Karajan's demand was that the company
should now pay royalties on all his recordings, including a retrospective
royalty on recordings made under the flat-fee agreement.

To Deutsche Grammophon the claim was neither legal nor logical but
they were willing to deal if Karajan himself was prepared to sign a further
exclusive contract with them. This he refused to do. Repertory was becoming a problem, as was the casting of big operatic projects. The recordings of
Siegfried and *Götterdämmerung* had been undercast; and with artists like
Freni, Vickers, and Pavarotti exclusive to rival companies there was little
chance of Karajan being able to make with Deutsche Grammophon the
kind of first-rate opera recordings he had made with Legge and Culshaw.

Karajan had one card to play in the negotiation: the stockpile of recordings he had completed since the formal expiry of his contract in November
1968. These had been made in good faith by both parties, pending later
agreement. They included such things as Honegger's Second and Third symphonies and a disc of Suppé overtures, all currently embargoed. Karajan's
own preferred option, and the one that was eventually settled upon, was
an interim joint agreement with Deutsche Grammophon (two-thirds share)
and EMI (one-third share), renegotiable in 1973, at which point, so he now
threatened, he would sign exclusively with EMI if no significant progress
had been made with Deutsche Grammophon on the royalties issue.

This was not an idle threat, since it was clear from the parallel negotiation both companies were having with the Berlin Philharmonic that the orchestra's own position was intimately tied up with Karajan's. Put simply, the orchestra was insisting on making as high a proportion of its records with him as was practically possible, largely because the royalties they earned from Karajan recordings far outstripped those they made with any other conductor. EMI hoped to record with Karajan in Paris and Cleveland, as well as Berlin. Deutsche Grammophon was also looking to record with him away from Berlin. Yet despite his strategic flirtation with the Orchestra de Paris, both he and the Berlin Philharmonic were hostile to these moves. Karajan was particularly infuriated by Deutsche Grammophon's decision to pour huge sums of money into a long-term deal with the Boston Symphony, an orchestra he ranked no higher than fourth or fifth in the American league, well to the rear of Cleveland, Chicago, and Philadelphia.[2] He was also keeping a wary eye on Deutsche Grammophon's activities in Vienna, where plans for integral recordings of the Beethoven and Brahms symphonies with Böhm and the Philharmonic were being mooted.

The style of the Berlin Philharmonic's own negotiations, led by violinist Eduard Drolc, was firm but gentlemanly, entirely different in tone and temper from the high-handed wheeler-dealing that would land Karajan and the orchestra in the mire a decade or so later. c. 1970, the orchestra had not yet been infected by the belief that it and it alone was what the public was paying to hear.

The long-running battle between the orchestra and the Berlin Senate on the balance between private earnings and public subsidy rumbled on (Karajan still tacitly backing the players) but the negotiation on recording fees was conducted in a reasoned and sensible manner. No one doubted that after seven years without change the basic rate of DM40 per hour was in need of some kind of increase. The problem was that the Berlin Philharmonic was already, by a narrow margin, the most expensive of the European recording orchestras.[3] At the new asking price of DM65 per hour, the cost per LP would be raised from £5265 to £8234, overtopping Chicago and Cleveland. This may have been good for prestige but it was a serious disincentive to record companies who could hire a crack ensemble such as the London Symphony for as little as £3500 per LP.

Finally, on 18 September, Deutsche Grammophon signed a two-year extension to their existing exclusive contract with the orchestra, agreeing to a forty per cent increase in rates to DM56 per hour with effect from 1 May 1971. EMI was allowed access under the terms of the deal, but there was a sting in the tail: the orchestra demanded that EMI pay the new hourly rate immediately.

On the same day, Karajan signed a new two-year joint agreement with

Deutsche Grammophon and EMI. For EMI, and for Peter Andry who had masterminded the negotiation, the return of Karajan was a red-letter day in the company's affairs. Without Karajan, its profile in the United States, Japan, and mainland Europe would have been considerably compromised, something which, in turn, would have seriously damaged the company's ability to attract and fund other leading talent during the 1970s.

There was, of course, a high initial price to be paid, both to the Berlin Philharmonic and to Karajan, who was now guaranteed an advance of DM100,000 per record on non-copyright works and a royalty of ten per cent dropping by degrees on partially protected and copyright works to four per cent on copyright opera recordings. No other classical artist commanded this level of remuneration, nor did anyone else enjoy such beneficial accounting terms as were agreed on Karajan's behalf.

Yet the deal was justified by the returns. None of the recordings made under the new contract did as well commercially as the 1969 recording of the Triple Concerto, but the figures suggest that the overall budget had been shrewdly pitched. Estimated lifetime sales for a central tranche of the recordings made under the 1969–70 contract were 2,783,000. By 1977 the actual sales were 2,861,929. By 1978, profits to EMI on the contract were put at £652,719, with an additional contribution to fixed overheads of £965,512.[4] The Triple Concerto made a significant contribution to bringing the account into balance as did best-selling sets of Mozart Wind Concertos, the last six Mozart symphonies, Tchaikovsky's symphonies nos. 4–6, and the Dresden recording of *Die Meistersinger*. What is interesting is that, of these, only the Mozart symphonies and *Die Meistersinger* won anything approaching widespread critical endorsement.

*

The 1970 Easter Festival brought the Salzburg *Ring* cycle to its appointed end with three performances of *Götterdämmerung*, supremely well played, beautifully staged, and decently albeit somewhat unevenly sung. Some of the stage effects were unforgettable, such as the aftermath of the murder of Siegfried, the scene darkening and indescribably sad. Joseph Wechsberg would report:

Karajan and his technicians have probably created the most astonishing stage effect in our generation: as Siegfried's body is carried away, the twilight becomes almost three-dimensional – a supreme moment of poetry and beauty.[5]

As part of his preparation for the *Ring*, Karajan had provided the players with individual vocal scores of all four operas. In *Götterdämmerung* he also went to the trouble and expense of giving them a private show of the visual effects in the final scenes, thus ensuring there would be no craning of necks in the pit in the denouement.

A revival of *Götterdämmerung* was announced for the 1972 festival, a plan that fell by the wayside the moment Jon Vickers informed Karajan that he was now ready to sing Tristan for him. But the greater frustration had come the previous year, after *Siegfried*, when Karajan announced that it was logistically impossible for him to contemplate bringing all four *Ring* operas together within a single Easter Festival. In this sense, the enterprise had been flawed from the outset. The recordings survived, both the studio-made previews and various live radio transmissions; and remnants of the production would live on, reassembled by other hands, in New York. But the European audience was denied the chance of experiencing Karajan's last *Ring* cycle in the way in which it would have been most effective: as an organic entity entire unto itself.[6]

*

In June 1970, Karajan returned to Vienna to conduct a Beethoven cycle with the Berlin Philharmonic. For this, he dressed himself in conqueror's garb, the performances ruthlessly exciting, designed to set the Viennese baying for more.

In August a new production of Verdi's *Otello* opened in Salzburg with Vickers, Glossop, and Freni in the leading roles, Karajan himself producing in the Zeffirelli style. It would spawn an eccentrically balanced and musically cumbersome EMI recording, made in the Berlin Philharmonie in 1973, and a 1974 film, based on the recording, that also manages sadly to misrepresent a production that in the theatre married scenic splendour with tragic power.

The key was, again, Vickers. It was a stagily acted performance but a peerless one musically and dramatically. '[Otello's] final farewell to the unhappy woman,' says the original 1887 production book, describing Otello's address to the woman whose life he has just extinguished, 'is said [sic] with a very sweet voice, in which love and compassion are united with the most ineffable sadness.'[7] Vickers was able to catch that, and more. As he twice intoned the name 'Desdemona', the voice took on a quality utterly unlike anything we had heard before. This was a man who no longer knew himself: a man literally beside himself with grief in an ecstasy of suffering.

In all this, Vickers was symbiotically at one with Karajan whose own art could beggar belief at such moments. The entrance of Otello into the bedchamber before the murder was such an instance. Otello's first utterance in reply to the '*Chi è la? Otello?*' of the half-waking Desdemona is '*Sì* [Yes]'. Though it is often blankly uttered, the word can be sounded in half a dozen different ways, any one of which will instantly convey Otello's state of mind. After that there is an orchestral postscript: pianissimo staccato semiquavers in the violas and cellos, and eerily sustained chords on cornets, trumpets, and trombones. Vickers would often have to explain the moment's significance to conductors, in particular the fact that that single '*Sì*' can carry a different weight and emphasis from performance to performance. With Karajan there was no need for explanations. He knew. What's more (and here is the miracle of the thing), he had the capacity to pick up Vickers's particular colour or emphasis each time and reflect it instantaneously in the orchestra.[8]

Vickers would smile when people alleged – disapprovingly – that Karajan was interested only in 'beauty' of sound. The preoccupation was there, sure enough. How else could Vickers and Karajan have realised the visionary loveliness of the end of the Act 1 love duet ('The burning Pleiades already sink into the sea . . . Come, Venus shines on high') in a way that catches both the beauty of the moment and the sense, as W. B. Yeats puts it in another context, of 'a soul sick with desire and fastened to a dying animal'? Yet when Vickers frowningly announced to Karajan that his voice might well crack in the great animal outbursts in Act 3, so ferocious was the orchestral attack, Karajan replied: 'Wonderful. I hope it shatters completely!'

During the run of performances there was a shattering of another kind. Vickers was involved in a car crash near Salzburg, a fearsome side impact that put him out of action for ten days and might have been more serious had it not been for the robustness of the family camper van and the formidable strength of Vickers's own shoulder and neck muscles. When he returned to the production, Karajan was at his most solicitous. What a nice man, thought Vickers, until Karajan revealed to him that the doctors had advised him that the patient might suddenly lose concentration or start uttering meaningless babble. Little wonder, that evening, that Karajan had the look of a man carrying a tray of eggs across a tightrope.

*

Karajan's reversion to non-exclusivity in September 1970 landed him with a sudden rush of recording commitments, mainly for EMI, but also with Decca who were keen to record his grandiose sables-and-diamonds reading of the Rimskified *Boris Godunov*.[9] Sessions for this took place in Vienna in the late autumn. In Berlin, Karajan recorded the last six Mozart symphonies and *Fidelio* with Vickers and Dernesch, both for EMI.[10]

Already, though, concerns were being expressed within EMI about recording values in Berlin, with Michel Glotz named as the guilty party. A memorandum from John Whittle claimed that the sound on the Berlin Triple Concerto was palpably inferior to that on Sargent's 1958 Columbia version, made at Abbey Road. This may well have been the case, but it had little to do with Glotz. Even in Legge's day, EMI had often been at sea when it came to recording classical repertory with Karajan and the Berliners in the dangerously reverberant spaces of the church in Berlin-Dahlem. What was needed was a new engineering concept, plus fresh ways of working with a conductor who in twenty years of LP recording had swung 180 degrees from being fascinated by the possibilities of tape editing to seeing it as something to be avoided wherever possible.

This latter problem was in some ways the most acute, since it made 'production' in the usual sense of the term, if not impossible, then extremely difficult. Karajan's methods would discomfit Decca's Christopher Raeburn and lead eventually to the removal of Deutsche Grammophon's Hans Weber, a gifted and scrupulous young producer who had successfully overseen virtually all Karajan's recording ever since the day in the mid-1960s when Otto Gerdes – a producer with ambitions as a conductor – had returned from a conducting engagement and addressed Karajan as 'My dear colleague'.

The only person who could really cope with all this was Glotz. Yet since he was now perceived to be the producer-cum-recording supervisor a great many memoranda were generated down the years attributing to him 'mistakes' that were in reality either Karajan's responsibility or those of the recording team.

The situation was further complicated by the fact that EMI's crew, headed by Electrola's Wolfgang Gülich – greatly gifted and much beloved of Karajan – was rather more accident-prone than some might have liked. In Paris in 1973 during the making of Strauss's *Sinfonia Domestica*, cross-over from the studio talk-back found its way on to the actual recording. Then, in January 1975, the whole of the first movement of Schubert's *Unfinished* Symphony was lost because of interference on one microphone and technical failure on another, none of which appears to have been noted at the time.

In 1973, Andry contemplated setting up a joint initiative in which EMI and Deutsche Grammophon would present Karajan with an ultimatum on the production issue. But since this would have meant asking for the removal of Glotz, Andry soon dropped the idea. 'The retribution,' he noted 'could be terrible.' The costly failures over the *Unfinished* Symphony did, however, bring something resembling an ultimatum, issued by Andry via EMI-Electrola's office in Cologne on 14 November 1975.

One of the points raised was poor woodwind balances in some recent Karajan recordings. This may have been caused in part by unfamiliarity with the Berlin Philharmonie. In 1973 the Philharmonic's recording activities had been transferred there from the church in Berlin-Dahlem. Yet in 1970 the woodwind balances on the Karajan/Gülich set of the late Mozart symphonies had been singled out for special praise by Trevor Harvey in *The Gramophone*:

Here [in the *Haffner* Symphony] I noted at once the excellent wind balance – a good mark to the recording engineers no doubt, as well as to Karajan. You can easily hear the bassoons running along with the string bass (I/35 etc.) and clarinets, then flutes, running up delightfully with the first violins (I/58 and 164). This is a feature throughout the series. Conductors (and recording engineers) are nowadays usually well aware of the importance of Haydn's and Mozart's woodwind when they have something special to do: but when they are doubling string lines, especially first violins, they are too often treated as though have been added merely to give the players something to do, instead of adding their colour to the strings.[11]

Mozart's use of instrumental colour fired Karajan's imagination much as it had done Bruno Walter's before him. Indeed, these are somewhat Walter-like performances, full-bodied and robust, free of unnecessary point-making yet, as Trevor Harvey noted, 'anything but the faceless kind of stuff that all too often passes as Mozart interpretation'.[12]

Yet facelessness had its followers in the early 1970s. In Madrid in 1972, a Spanish journalist taxed Karajan over the question of his 'Bruno Walter style' Mozart. Was not a more chamber-like approach more appropriate to our times? Karajan's response was unequivocal:

The misconception about Mozart persists! He is seen as an idler, a sort of playboy who roamed from palace to palace with his music. In fact, Mozart was with all his heart and soul a man of his times. He was always in a state of emotional exaltation. The mistake about him tends to reduce the stature of his personality, which is all the more unacceptable in the case of the Mozart of the later symphonies and the *Requiem* where the full orchestra is needed, although not an orchestra that is over-forceful.[13]

Karajan went on to quote, more or less accurately, the letter Mozart wrote to his father in April 1781:

I forgot to tell you the other day that at the concert the symphony [possibly the *Paris* Symphony] went magnificently and had the greatest success. There were forty violins, the wind instruments were all doubled, there were ten violas, ten double basses, eight violincellos and six bassoons.[14]

Even allowing for the relative discretion of the instruments of the period, this is a formidable ensemble. The letter is often pooh-poohed by authenticists, and certainly, taken in isolation, it proves very little. But as Charles Rosen notes in *The Classical Style*:

Mozart did not often get an orchestra of such size, but there is no reason today to perpetuate those conditions of eighteenth-century performance which obtained only when there was not enough money to do the thing properly.[15]

To mark Karajan's formal return to EMI, Glotz had suggested that the Mozart symphonies should be accompanied by a free rehearsal record. Karajan was indignant: 'You don't ask your hostess for her recipe, nor do you ask to inspect the kitchens as your meal is being cooked.'[16] But he gave in, and Glotz contrived an edit that pleased him well enough.

Among the most interesting sequences on the rehearsal disc is the work on the slow movement of the *Jupiter* Symphony. First, Karajan asks the violins to sustain and colour the very first note, a muted F. At bar 5 he takes enormous trouble over the phrasing and timing of the dotted quaver and triplet on the second beat. At bar 11, after the lower strings have played one of the most heavenly six-note phrases in all Mozart with a clipped, formal descent on the two falling demisemiquavers, he intervenes:

No, gentlemen, no – you get that on every single recording! [He sings what they have just played.] It's fine as an exercise in precision but it's horrible ['*Scheisse*', literally 'crap'] . . . Please now [as the orchestra plays] ardent and profound . . . that's it . . . a great veil over it . . . [17]

At bar 75, which is both a cadence and a transition and where Mozart once again writes a complex mix of triplet figures, slurs and staccatos for the flutes, bassoons and first violins, Karajan asks, 'Now, who has the artistry to phrase this freely, almost adding a ritardando and still keeping in tempo?' Moments later, as he enjoins the players to maintain the singing line, he asks for the staccato spaces to 'the finest hundredths of a second'. In the movement's coda, the skirl of demisemiquavers for flutes and bassoons are said to be too 'automatic'. It must be 'like a flurry of tiny wavelets on a smooth sheet of water'.

Such hair's-breadth judgements and snail-horn perceptions would be beyond the ken of most musicians, but the Berliners' response is palpable enough. It becomes a miracle of collaborative music-making.

What makes the rehearsal of the slow movement doubly interesting is the fact that the awkward little transitions on which Karajan chooses to concentrate are also things of exquisite beauty in their own right. In *Mozart: A Life*, published in 1995, Maynard Solomon writes:

Such moments wait to be discovered: they are transitional, passing references to pure beauty, captured for an instant before they sink back into the relative quotidian.[18]

Karajan would have been fascinated by the chapter 'Fearful Symmetries', in which Solomon explores the phenomenon of a uniquely Mozartean kind of beauty.

Karajan held writers about music – writers like Solomon, that is, not newspaper critics – in the highest regard. (He told Pali Meller Marcovicz that if he had the gift to write about music he would willingly give up conducting.[19]) When Solomon writes of 'a special kind of musical beauty, one that thenceforth came to exemplify the idea of superlative beauty itself'; or 'In the post-Paris works, a specifically Mozartean array of beauties emerges – death-tinged, melancholy, painful, containing a mixture of resignation and affirmation'; or when he follows an elaborate and partly Freud-inspired argument about music as 'a bulwark against extinction': in such moments he is putting into words the very concepts that in a mixture of words, gesture, and sheer force of telepathic communication Karajan himself is concerned to conjure forth from the slow movement of the *Jupiter* Symphony.[20]

It is clear, too, that these ideals were part of Karajan's imaginative make-up from an early age. The horns in his 1942 Turin recording may not be able to manage the astonishing pianissimo achieved by the Berlin horns in the pulsing low triplet Es in the movement's penultimate bar but the reading itself is every bit as rapt as the 1970 version. It is the 1976 Berlin remake for Deutsche Grammophon, paradoxically, which is a good deal cooler, the colours now those of a half-vanished rainbow. But, then, the 1976 performances generally have leaner textures and fiercer lines in the 'modern' style.

Mention has been made before in these pages of the inconsistency of Karajan's Mozart conducting. In fact, that very inconsistency is itself a source of fascination. Most conductors have a single Mozart style; Karajan had half a dozen. His Mozart is perhaps most revealing when he is the deeply engaged connoisseur of sensual beauty. But he could also play the *galant*, and he could be callous where Mozart is concerned, openly defying the universally held assumption that Mozart is someone we are bound to cherish at each new encounter. In this sense, Karajan was prepared to be bored by Mozart and publicly baffled by him, painfully aware of the music's ambivalence and instability.

'I fend off Mozart's music because I have difficulty determining where it ends and I begin,' wrote Nicholas Spice in a review of Solomon's book. 'I distrust my assumptions about it. My access to it seems too easy.'[21] I doubt whether Karajan could ever have afforded to be that honest, but I suspect it is what he often felt.

*

Extraordinary beauty of sound would also characterise Karajan's next important orchestral project for EMI, a three-LP set of Bruckner's Fourth and Seventh symphonies. Neither work had previously been recorded by him, despite the fact that the Fourth had been in his repertory since 1936, the Seventh since 1941. The Fourth emerges as a glowing essay in the pastoral style; the Seventh is quite simply the most purely beautiful account of the symphony there has ever been on record. Other readings – Furtwängler's or Knappertsbusch's – had surged and carolled more than this, but none has captured so intense a sense of spiritual longing within the context of a calm yet unerring articulation of the symphonic structure.

But again there were problems in production. To the barely disguised glee of Abbey Road engineers, a faulty edit in the Fourth Symphony got through to the first published pressings. While Suvi Raj Grubb was sorting it out, Lorin Maazel appeared in the editing suite. 'A mistake on a *Karajan* recording!' he exclaimed. Little did he know.

To help publicise Karajan's return to the EMI fold, the company had called in journalist Paul Moor to write a report on the Mozart sessions for general release to the press. The edited typescript is in the EMI archives and is full of interesting *aperçus*. Gülich describes himself as being 'downright excited' by Karajan's working methods: the *Haffner* Symphony, recorded in a single take without correction. Yet where corrections were needed, Glotz ran into difficulties:

About ten minutes before the end of one afternoon session, Glotz picked up the phone, listened to Karajan, and then repeated, '*Vous en avez marre?* [You've had enough?]' He covered the mouthpiece and informed the engineers, 'He's tired of it.' Then he glanced at his watch and said evenly into the telephone, '*Mais donnez-moi quand même* [But give it me none the less]' and proceeded to instruct Karajan as to just what passage he wanted him to do once more.[22]

During one playback, Karajan was angered by the fact that – not for the first time, it seems – a particular phrase sounded slower on playback than it did when he was conducting it. Mystified, he dispatched a minion to get hold of recordings of the work by Böhm and Klemperer.

Moor also reveals Karajan's enthusiasm for the Moscow Conservatoire String Players, currently in Berlin for the Karajan Foundation's international competition of youth orchestras. He urges the orchestra to hear them if they have time:

'Who knows,' he said letting the vowels soar out and dangle for an instant, 'perhaps we all might just learn something from them.'[23]

On another occasion, he makes casual reference to the fact that he has been approached to succeed George Szell in Cleveland and that he has declined the offer. His experience with the Orchestre de Paris has taught him, he claims, that he is no Mohammedan: 'I cannot share myself between two wives.' The orchestra had heard the analogy before. In moments of dissimulation, the old clichés are not necessarily the best ones.

*

The real prize in the autumn sessions as far as Peter Andry was concerned was Karajan's Dresden *Die Meistersinger*. Plans for a new Karajan recording of the opera had been on the table since Legge's draft proposal of April 1962.

Andry has told hair-raising tales of Karajan's delays and prevarications over the project, even at the last minute, when the venue, the orchestra, and most of the cast were in place. 'So, if you can't do it, we shall have to ask Böhm,' said Andry, playing his ace. Karajan promptly capitulated. It is an entertaining story and no doubt a true one, but one cannot help thinking that Andry was either very clever or very fortunate to have got the *Meistersinger* recording so promptly. With the ink barely dry on Karajan's new contract and with him already committed to recording the late Mozart symphonies, *Fidelio*, and *Boris Godunov* in the autumn, it is an earnest of his professionalism that he was able to be in Dresden on 24 November to begin the *Meistersinger* sessions.

What makes the whole episode doubly remarkable is that, once started, the opera was recorded in two-thirds of the time EMI had set aside for it, thirteen sessions instead of twenty-one. This was partly due to the fact that the Dresden Staatskapelle, Wagner's own favourite orchestra, was wonderfully well prepared. The players knew the score intimately and had taken the additional precaution of playing it in the theatre in Dresden shortly before the sessions began. But Karajan himself also worked with great speed and intensity. EMI producer Ronald Kinloch Anderson would later explain in a memorandum to Andry why only thirteen sessions were needed:

This was made possible by two factors: Karajan's present method of recording in very long stretches (sometimes up to 20 minutes) and his virtual refusal to do any re-makes unless something was grossly wrong with the first take. There are therefore small inaccuracies, mainly in ensemble, occasionally a mistake in the text (but only in concerted passages where it is hardly noticeable), perhaps a few slight studio noises which might not be found in other recordings. I personally do not think they are of any significance or will detract from the overall quality of the performance which of course also gains something in continuity from Karajan's method.[24]

Kinloch Anderson was less happy with Karajan's habit of barely giving singers time to find their place in the score, though he conceded that this was almost certainly a deliberate strategy on Karajan's part to deter them from using the score during takes:

On one occasion Karajan refused to continue recording with René Kollo until he had learnt the part from memory (he had never sung the role before). Otherwise there were few difficulties with singers: like everyone else, they come under the curious spell of Karajan and do exactly what he says with no questions asked.[25]

There had been doubts about Karajan's determination to have genuinely *young* singers for Eva and Walther von Stolzing. Helen Donath herself, Karajan's choice as Eva, had accepted the part only at the eleventh hour. 'Would you be very angry with me if I don't do it?' she had asked Karajan. He looked at her with his ice-blue eyes. 'I won't be angry, but I assure you I never make a mistake.'[26]

Kinloch Anderson had also been among the doubters. Now he reported:

Karajan's decision to use Donath and Kollo proved to be absolutely right. For the first time in my experience of the opera (going back 40 years) Eva and Walther sound really young and make thereby a splendid contrast to the heavier side of the cast – Sachs, Pogner, and the other masters.[27]

Some of the writers who reviewed the set were not so sure. 'Very nice – but . . .' was the tenor of many of the reviews of Donath's singing, and Kollo's.

The Sachs was the Dresden-born Theo Adam. Karajan had not been wildly enthusiastic when the East Germans put his name forward to Andry, but he had worked with Adam and thought sufficiently well of him not to veto the suggestion.[28] Over the Beckmesser, Geraint Evans, it was the other way round. Kinloch Anderson worried about his German and Evans worried about the fact that he was better on stage than on record. But Karajan would have none of it. He had promised Evans the role back in 1962 and he saw no reason to change his mind now.

Though the recording was a co-production between EMI and the East German VEB Deutsche Schallplatten, the EMI team quickly discovered that it was the East Germans, producer Dieter Worm and his sound engineer Klaus Strüben, who were in charge. They, and Karajan:

At certain times, mostly in regard to crowd scenes, [Karajan] took a very active part in deciding, indeed virtually dictating, what was to be done. Thus in several scenes he directed that the chorus was to be divided up into four parts – one in each of the side galleries, one on the stage and one in the back gallery of the church.[29]

Kinloch Anderson did not like the idea but added that 'arguing with Karajan is impossible'. In the event, the work of the chorus and its theatrical dispensations were lavishly praised. Desmond Shawe-Taylor would write in his quarterly column for *The Gramophone*:

I don't think I have ever heard, even at Bayreuth, such fresh, youthful, natural-sounding Apprentices or such brilliant clarity in the street riot at the end of Act 2. The determination that everything shall sound as clear and as beautiful as possible is characteristic of Karajan's approach.[30]

Much of the credit for this was due to the chorus master, Horst Neumann, but even he was ready to prostrate himself before Karajan's expertise: 'What he can get out of them in half an hour is more than I can do in weeks.'[31]

In *The Gramophone* Andrew Porter wrote a review of the set that amounted to a song of thanksgiving for the work and for the Dresden performance. The review anticipated many of the reservations Shawe-Taylor and others would have about aspects of the singing (down the years only Ridderbusch's Pogner and Kurt Moll's Nightwatchman have gone entirely unscathed); but Porter's larger judgement – that the set was 'a joy, a profound and moving experience', 'noble and heart-stirring' – was based on a sense of the spirit of the entire enterprise rather than on this or that particular detail.

Making music in Dresden clearly moved and affected Karajan. At the end of the sessions he made a touching speech of thanks to the company and, above all, to the orchestra:

My agent in Berlin once said to me, 'Wait until you stand in front of the Dresden Staatskapelle. Their playing shines like old gold.' A great deal of the city has been destroyed but you have remained a living monument to Dresden's tradition and culture.[32]

A good many tears were shed during this impromptu oration. Since the engineers had left the tape running, René Kollo suggested that copies of the speech be made as a memento. At which point a mysterious character who had been present throughout the recording stepped forward and announced that this would not be possible. Inasmuch as he had been noticed at all, people had assumed he was a caretaker or technician. In fact, he belonged to Stasi, the East German internal security service. The next day, Geraint Evans was delayed for two hours at the border while security guards conducted a minute search of his belongings. He was convinced that they were looking for the tape.[33]

*

The success of the Dresden *Die Meistersinger* was a good omen for the next Wagner project, the *Tristan und Isolde* which EMI was commissioned to record ahead of the 1972 Easter Festival. Yet the *Tristan* recording would be a troubled affair. The stage production offered a mix of abstraction and realism, with, as always when Karajan and Schneider-Siemssen were involved, the visionary elements winning through. Andrew Porter would report in the *Financial Times*:

Visually this *Tristan* is memorable above all for the moments when sea, land, and sky fade into one vast infinity in which the lovers are lost, when 'the surging swell, the resounding sound, the World-Breath's engulfing All', something that Wagner found it hard to find words (though not music) for, takes shape before us.[34]

Orchestrally, it was magnificent:

Karajan and Reginald Goodall are perhaps the last two Wagnerian conductors who understand how to paragraph the great scores, to 'hold back', infinitesimally, a change of harmony so that its effect can be really appreciated, never just to push ahead through the marvels of the music. Karajan pays specific tribute [in the programme book] to Furtwängler as the man who taught him and his Berlin orchestra 'the typical way of playing Wagner, with heavy basses, the succulent strings, the powerful breath, and the great patience for the development of tone – a great expansion and exhalation of sound' ... Karajan's reading was broad, unhurried, fiery when it needed to be, limpid (in so far as internal balance was concerned); and it spanned a huge range of colour and dynamics.[35]

Alas, in most of the performances the Isolde, Helga Dernesch, sank beneath the billows in the *Liebestod* and a good deal else besides. Karajan was held to blame for a major misjudgement in casting. But things were not quite as simple as that. Dernesch had already sung a great deal of Wagner, both at Bayreuth and with the Scottish Opera. In December 1971 she had been due to sing Brünnhilde in the Scottish Opera's *Ring* cycle but had cancelled because of illness. The *Tristan* sessions followed shortly afterwards. Dernesch convinced herself that she had recovered and Karajan believed her, but it rapidly became clear to Glotz that she was not at all well:

I tried to stop him in the studio, but he went on. Things got worse and I did what he always absolutely hated, I called him on the phone during an actual take. He was furious: 'Please, leave me alone!' But he stopped. He knew. He said to Dernesch, 'Please, Helga, go to the doctor. Michel says you must go to the doctor.'[36]

Perhaps because Karajan knew *Tristan und Isolde* so intimately and was so absorbed in it, he became well-nigh impossible to handle during the sessions. '*Hör' ich nur diese Weise* [Do I alone hear this melody?]' Isolde asks in the *Liebestod*. There were times when Glotz feared Karajan was similarly lost to reality:

I would ask for corrections in Act 1 and he would start correcting Act 3. We were all in the dark: me, the orchestra, the singers. After days of torture of this kind, I realised that he was making a huge tapestry, like a fifteenth-century artisan: an enormous puzzle made up out of four hours of music. For him, the fact that I was asking for a correction in Act 1 was reminding him that that same leitmotif in Act 3 was not the way he wanted it, and he didn't want to forget. To him it was an extremely intricate structure, yet to us at the time these things had no meaning whatsoever. To us, it seemed like complete disorder. But to him it was complete harmony.[37]

The strange and often internally inconsistent recorded balances that were so distracting a feature of the original LP set were no doubt a by-product of all this.

Like Knappertsbusch, Karajan barely bothered to rehearse with a singer he trusted. He went through the whole of Act 3 with Vickers, but changed nothing.[38] The previous year, at the end of an *Otello* rehearsal, Vickers had asked him about a notoriously difficult passage in Act 3 where Tristan's music moves forward with the time signatures shifting bar by bar.

'Forget the bar lines,' said Karajan. 'There is a pulse running through this passage. [He sang the words, beating out the underlying pulse.] Once you have that, it doesn't matter what beat I give you.' In the end, it became a bit of a game, Karajan beating the passage differently every time they performed the work together.[39]

Vickers and Karajan disagreed on the degree of sympathy Tristan should show King Marke at the end of Act 2. ('No pity for Marke!' Karajan had insisted.) But Karajan had not engaged Vickers to argue with him. As he would insist shortly after the Salzburg stage performances:

It is not enough to say that Vickers is a great actor; he is the very embodiment of the character. In addition to the intense musicality of his phrasing, he has such a great understanding of the role that nobody could say he is merely 'acting' it. Acting is a profession, but this is a complete artistic impersonation, an interpretation in which the singer becomes Tristan.[40]

Some critics have never reconciled themselves to the manner of Vickers's singing, 'the oscillations between cooing pianissimos and violent hysteria' as one writer more recently put it. This has always struck me as being a variation on the age-old evasion, 'I have no objection to what you are saying; what I object to is the *way* you are saying it.' This and such remarks as 'A great Tristan, no doubt, but with vowel sounds, open high notes, and so forth, that I now find I don't want to hear' are little more than the confessions of slippered old age. If Vickers's terrifying portrayal of Tristan is to be excoriated, let it at least be done with a proper passion, as it is by composer Robin Holloway:

For urgency and intensity [Vickers's] third act is without rival. It is absolutely authentic and extremely painful – the ravings of a stricken beast, what Melchior would be if he were not so irrepressibly cheerful. There is no doubt whatsoever about the stature of this unique *tour de force*, but it remains an extreme – something unique as if the story were, just this once, literally true. I can pay no higher tribute; but I never want to hear it again.[41]

CHAPTER 64

Brave new worlds

Our apparatniks will continue making
the usual squalid mess called History:
all we can pray for is that artists,
chefs and saints may still appear to blithe it.
W. H. Auden, 'Moon Landing'

At a press conference in Tokyo in May 1970 jointly hosted by Karajan and
Sony's Akio Morita, Karajan talked about an invention which he claimed
was 'a revolutionary achievement in the progress of mankind'. It was a
newfangled device called a video cassette, developed by Sony and due to
go into production to internationally agreed specifications in 1971–2. Up
until now Karajan had been making his opera films for the cinema and his
experimental orchestral films for television, neither of them commercially
viable. Video cassette looked set to change all that.

At the press conference, Karajan looked forward to the time when the
'several kinds of video devices now being produced' would be 'unified
into one device', a reference to the rival systems that were competing or
imminent in 1970.[1] What Karajan could not foresee was that the very
simplicity and practicality of the video cassette would all but obviate
the need for further improvement. What he saw and heard when he
inspected the prototypes on Sony's laboratory benches was good pictures
and indifferent sound. Unfortunately, that is how the video cassette would
remain during his lifetime and beyond.

He also made the rather more bizarre prediction that one day the video
cassette would replace 'all phonographic records'. It was a curious position
for a musician to take, and it was not one which was shared by classical
music's media establishment. One of Karajan's principal opponents in the
matter was John Culshaw, who had left Decca in 1967 to become Head
of Music Programmes with BBC Television. In a long article in *The
Gramophone* 'The Outlook for Video Music', published shortly after the
Karajan-Morita press conference, Culshaw launched a scathing attack on
certain 'companies on the Continent' who had tried to 're-stage' symphonic
performances for the camera. It was an oddly negative view for a television
executive to take, but Culshaw was a record man through and through.[2]

At the heart of his *Gramophone* article was an analysis of the tensions that existed between music and the medium in which he was now
working:

The law of diminishing returns applies quite severely when you are working with vision: the eye is a more powerful organ than the ear. It has, so to speak, a much better memory, which means that it gets bored far more quickly . . . Now it also happens to be true that the ear can memorise a particular gramophone performance after sufficient repetition: the difference is that where music is somehow mysteriously self-renewing even in the same performance, a series of visual images is generally not.[3]

Culshaw went on to cite the techniques used in the theatre productions of the late Wieland Wagner as a possible way forward:

What [Wieland] Wagner did was to provide an experience which was difficult, if not impossible, to memorise in terms of continuity. Individual moments, yes: they remained in the memory like a series of beautiful still photographs. But the *continuity* of the images and the movements was so subtle, and so lacking in the devices of the slick, knock-'em-between-the-eyes type of producer, that overall memory was defeated.[4]

Perhaps Karajan's period as an experimental film-maker in the orchestral field would have come to an end of its own volition. What the arrival of the domestic video cassette did was to turn him back towards a more conservative style of film-making, albeit one that incorporated many of the ideas that he and his new director of photography, Ernst Wild, had gleaned from Clouzot and Niebeling.

The last of the 'experimental' films had been made in 1971 when Niebeling and Karajan collaborated on recordings of Beethoven's Third and Seventh symphonies. In both films the orchestra is seated in three steeply raked inverted triangles. Seen in long shot in the broodingly lit *Eroica* film, they look like three large coffins propped up against a wall. The violins sit in the left-hand file, winds and timpani in the centre, lower strings on the right. Karajan himself is placed out front in his own circular space. It is possible that the inspiration behind the layouts was the Ancient Greek theatre at Epidaurus which has seven such inverted triangles, or files of seats, rising steeply up the hillside from the circular orchestra below. If so, it is a nice visual conceit: the *Eroica* played out in a space suggestive of Greek tragedy, the Dionysiac Seventh played out in an arena devoted to the cult of Dionysus. Unfortunately, to the innocent eye, it looks more German than Greek.

In the *Eroica*, Niebeling uses at least one visual metaphor that seems to owe a debt to the films of Leni Riefenstahl. As the first movement development section reaches its climax, the brass blazing out their baleful discords, Niebeling cuts away from Karajan to a shot of three trumpet bells lit from behind by a fierce blaze of light. It was this sequence that was used in the 1993 BBC television documentary *Everything You Wanted to Know about Conductors but Were Afraid to Ask*, where images of

Karajan conducting and the final blaze of the trumpets were intercut at four-second intervals with shots of swastikas, a Nuremberg rally, waving banners, and Hitler saluting. It was character assassination by film-editing. Yet reprehensible as the sequence was, it was the original film that had provided the all too tempting cue.[5]

Karajan and Wild went on alone to film more Beethoven symphonies in a manner that can best be described as workmanlike.[6] A set of live performances of the Brahms symphonies made in 1973 shows the team at its most predictable and a film of Strauss's *Don Quixote* made with Rostropovich in 1975 is extremely dull. Yet films of Tchaikovsky's Fourth and Fifth symphonies are intensely exciting, as is a beautifully filmed account of Rachmaninov's Second Piano Concerto with soloist Alexis Weissenberg.

Here Karajan had as a reference point Åke Falck's cinematic excursion around the Tchaikovsky concerto. Filming the Rachmaninov live in concert, Karajan now drew on the best of Falck's ideas, while at the same time systematically disposing of the jokey irreverence. It is a film that chronicles Karajan's passion for the music of Rachmaninov. He conducts from memory, drawing from the Berliners playing that puts one in mind of the famous pre-war recordings (much treasured by Karajan) Rachmaninov himself made with the Philadelphia Orchestra.

*

Where opera was concerned, Karajan remained fixated on the idea of making bespoke productions for the commercial cinema. In 1972, EMI raised with impresario Bernard Delfont the possibility of a collaboration between Karajan and the director Ken Russell on a film of *Tosca*. This unlikely idea was not the product of some daring leap of the executive imagination, merely a hard-nosed recognition of the fact that Karajan held the rights to an opera Russell was interested to film.

Like Karajan, Russell was a Puccini addict, but it is doubtful that the project would ever have come to fruition. Russell's Puccini was probably closer – imaginatively and psychologically – to Karajan's than Karajan would ever have dared admit; but theatrically the two men were worlds apart.[7] It is none the less curious that various top executives seriously believed that Russell and Karajan might work together:

Karajan's main worry is that Ken Russell may distort the musical intention of the composer . . . furthermore, Karajan does not like the idea of working with any straight actors who would not, in fact, be singing in the opera. Ken Russell in turn would not be interested in a straight operatic performance, but is not at all dogmatic about the use of the actual performers . . . Thus it seems

593

there is room to reconcile both sides to what might be an artistically satisfying compromise.[8]

Where Puccini was concerned, Karajan preferred the more orderly, less apocalyptic imagination of director Jean-Pierre Ponnelle. While memoranda about the *Tosca* project were being pushed back and forth in London, he teamed up with Ponnelle to make what would prove to be an outstandingly successful film of *Madama Butterfly*.

Resisting the temptation to reposition the opera either post-Hiroshima or post-Vietnam, Ponnelle set it in period, shortly before the First World War. 'Tragedy in Three Acts' announces the opening credit. By the time we reach the end, with the celebrated freeze-frame of a distraught Pinkerton leaping through the wall of Cio-Cio-San's house, the use of the word tragedy seems apt. What is interesting about the film is its emotional completeness. Cio-Cio-San's tragic odyssey from vulnerable teenage bride to mother, jilted wife, and sacrificial victim is movingly effected by Mirella Freni, whose film performance seems at once deeper and more intense than it is on the Decca LP recording made at much the same time.[9] Similarly, Robert Kerns, bland on record, plays the role of the American consul with a pathos and compassionate seriousness that Chekhov might have approved. As for Karajan's conducting, it offers a synthesis of all that is best in a reading that was always touched with greatness. Act 1 is lither and wittier than on either of his earlier sound recordings, yet the final two acts are as finely sustained, as tragically intense as on the 1955 Callas set.

*

In 1972 the orchestral academy of the Karajan Foundation came into being after Jürgen Ponto, the head of Germany's second largest bank the Dresdner Bank, pledged an annual subvention of DM250,000.[10] The Academy's ostensible aim was the establishing a degree of continuity in the recruitment of new players to the Berlin Philharmonic. I say 'ostensible' because this could not be its primary function. Admission to the Berlin Philharmonic was by audition, not by diploma, a point that the statutes of the Academy explicitly acknowledge. In practice, it was simply a postgraduate teaching institution whose primary aim was the cultivation of best practice in orchestral playing.

None the less, it was firmly centred on the Berlin Philharmonic. Students studied with members of the orchestra and were permitted in certain circumstances to play alongside their teachers in concert. ('Like pilot and co-pilot,' Karajan announced, resorting to another of his flying analogies.)

This idea was not entirely new. Members of the Berlin Philharmonic had always taught in the city's leading institutions, and it was not unknown for pupils to play in the orchestra on an *ad hoc* basis. Karajan's initiative formalised the idea, establishing it on a firmer footing and a grander scale.

The press, as ever, was sceptical. The players, it was alleged, found the teaching burdensome. (The reverse was true, for the most part.) In later years it was pointed out that the Academy had a poor track record as recruiting officer for the Berlin Philharmonic. This was true. But the teaching was not wasted. Other orchestras were the beneficiaries.

Students attending the International Meeting of Youth Orchestras were encouraged to audition for the Academy, though this rarely happened. Indeed, by 1972 there were stirrings of hostility towards Karajan from those students who clearly expected him to be on show throughout the week of the competition. In an interview at the end of the 1972 Berlin festival, Karajan harangued journalist Klaus Lang on the subject:

I've not only conducted three concerts but been working six hours a day, every day with my orchestra . . . my rehearsals with the Philharmonic were open to all the [youth] orchestras and, I have to say, practically no one came. I don't think it's up to me to go running after people. Don't forget that I cycled all the way from Salzburg to Bayreuth in order to hear Toscanini rehearsing. And here it's only five minutes on foot or by car to the Philharmonie. The fact that the participants didn't bother seems to me to show a certain lack of interest on their part.[11]

That said, Karajan was giving less time to the competition. In 1974, a reference in his closing speech to the pleasure he had experienced in meeting the young musicians was greeted with a loud guffaw. Karajan paused, like a headmaster addressing a sceptical assembly. 'I'm afraid I don't find that funny,' he snapped. An embarrassed silence followed, broken by a further catcall.

*

As if he was not busy enough, in June 1973 Karajan launched the Salzburg Whitsun festival. Mindful of the sacred nature of the Whitsun season, he devoted the first festival to the music of Bruckner. Since the 150th anniversary of Bruckner's birth was due the following year, the anti-Karajan brigade saw this as a calculated gesture, a pre-emptive strike. There were also rumblings within the Berlin Philharmonic when it was discovered that the Berlin state authority had declined to register the Whitsun Festival as a 'private' engagement on the same terms as the Easter Festival.

The first festival had an air of improvisation about it. Four concerts in three days – including Bruckner's Fourth, Fifth, and Eighth symphonies and the Mozart Requiem – had everyone on their mettle. No bad thing, notes Stresemann, in a wry aside in his memoirs. Seeing the Berliners flying by the seat of the pants had a certain novelty value.

In terms of the frequency of their appearances together, the early 1970s were a high-water mark in the history of Karajan's work with the Berlin Philharmonic. In the 1973–4 season, he conducted more than seventy concerts, twenty of them in Berlin itself. It was a time of immense productivity and, of course, great commercial success. When, in the not too distant future, Karajan would no longer be able to sustain such a workload there were those in the orchestra who would remember the years of plenty and be sorely aggrieved.

The contracts Karajan had signed with Deutsche Grammophon and EMI in 1970 were the principal stimulus here and were proving to be severe taskmasters. No autumn or New Year at this time passed without a busy round of concerts, recording, and filming. The results, though, were decidedly mixed. The Deutsche Grammophon recordings, the last before Karajan's watershed illness in 1975, are particularly uneven. Karajan himself was deeply disappointed with his 1973 remake of the Bach *B minor Mass*; happier with the inspired, romantically monumental *St Matthew Passion* of 1972. The recording of Lehár's *Die lustige Witwe*, with Elizabeth Harwood whom he adored, was a pleasing idea but no match for famous EMI sets conducted by Ackermann and von Matačić.

Yet a remake of Manuel Rosenthal's Offenbach extravaganza *Gaîté parisienne* was as scintillating and (in the final 'Barcarolle') as moving as ever. In 1927 the Viennese satirist Karl Kraus wrote of the 'inimitable double-edged nature of Offenbach's music' of 'the idyll that yields to parody, of mockery yielding to lyricism'. Rarely have the waltzes sounded as sumptuous and at the same time as dangerous as they do in this 1971 Karajan recording, nor has any conductor suggested quite so obviously the aristocratic allure of music which is both a salute to the Second Empire and a requiem for it. It is also interesting to note that within weeks of the *Gaîté parisienne* sessions, Karajan recorded a darkly ruminative account of Ravel's *La valse* – another waltz-requiem for a vanished age – the sessions with the Orchestre de Paris improvised out of thin air when a strike of technicians forced him to cancel film sessions in Paris.[12]

Some of the best recordings from this period were semi-improvised, among them cycles of the Schumann and Mendelssohn symphonies.[13] The celebrated recording of Strauss's *Four Last Songs*, with Gundula Janowitz, was certainly half improvised. Such rehearsal as there was became, in Karajan's hands, a kind of courtly charade: he the deferential squire, Janowitz the free-spirited maiden who finally yields to the squire's charms. The game-playing over, the songs were recorded, in complete takes, in two sessions. Only 'Beim Schlafengehen' was redone, at the request of the leader, Michel Schwalbé.

Strauss was never a problem for Karajan, and there are, indeed, several fine Strauss records from this period.[14] But he was now looking to Mahler, and to those seminal works of the Second Viennese School which he had often played but never recorded.

It was a performance of Mahler's *Das Lied von der Erde*, with Christa Ludwig as one of the soloists in December 1970, that seems to have determined him to look afresh at a composer whom expert advocacy by Bernstein, Solti, Haitink and others had turned into something of a cult figure in the 1960s.[15] Getting his head round the idea of Mahler as a contemporary cultural icon was less of a problem for Karajan than the fact that Mahler was the product of a culture that was in some ways foreign to him. 'Why,' I remember asking Christa Ludwig, 'is your *Lied von der Erde* with Klemperer rather more successful than the one with Karajan?' 'Because Klemperer was Jewish,' came the blunt reply. Ludwig also tossed the Berlin Philharmonic into the debate. She had once broached the subject of the orchestra's unease over Mahler with Schwalbé, who was Jewish. 'Tell me about it!' said Schwalbé, with a resigned shrug of the shoulders.

Mahler's Jewishness, and the degree to which this directly shaped and coloured his music, has long been a source of controversy.[16] Karajan's judgement – which for a host of reasons took years to form itself into anything remotely resembling a strategic action plan – was that Mahler's music was Jewish up to a point. Yet so complex was the mix that is Mahler, he remained uncertain about which works to engage and which to leave to others better versed in the music's idiom.[17] In the end, it was the classical Sixth Symphony, the Ninth Symphony, and the impossible-not-to-love Fourth Symphony under whose spell he most obviously fell.

Karajan was too young to have heard Mahler conduct but he had gleaned a good deal from those who had. From Paumgartner, he heard the story of Mahler throwing a party after he finally got the New York Philharmonic to play the opening of Beethoven's Fifth with proper *weight* of tone (a preoccupation Karajan shared), as well as tales of the première in Munich of the mighty Eighth Symphony when Mahler lit the performance himself, brought in the stage designer Roller to plan the visual layout of the choirs, and even demanded that the bells on the city trams be silenced for the duration of the event. Some thought Mahler was a megalomaniac; others put it down to his incurable perfectionism. Karajan, it goes without saying, opted for the latter explanation.

As Karajan pondered where best to begin his journey towards Mahler, Stresemann suggested he should tackle the Second Symphony or the Ninth. Karajan nodded agreement, then surprised everyone by beginning work on the Fifth. The reason for this unexpected decision was not far to seek: the release of Visconti's film *Death in Venice*. The film fascinated Karajan. What also fascinated him was the fact that the use of the Fifth Symphony's *Adagietto* as the film's musical leitmotif had turned the work into a prime commercial property.

Unfortunately, Karajan recorded it too soon. For all his talk of 'creating a palette of colours', of allowing works to 'rest in the mind', he knew that the discs needed to be in the shops sooner rather than later. It was not a good performance. I remember hearing him conduct the work one Sunday morning in Berlin in December 1977 with an eloquence and intensity – not to mention a technical command – which one listens for in vain on the LPs.

*

In February 1975, the four-LP set of music from the Second Viennese School was finally released after two years of intensive work. It caused a critical sensation and sold extremely well. Karajan later claimed that if all the LP and cassette boxes were stacked one on top of the other, they would reach the top of the Eiffel Tower.[18] Since he had invested some of his own money in the project, this must have been particularly gratifying. Yet the set has never enjoyed quite the same esteem with Karajan's professional colleagues. Some of this may have been sour grapes but Karajan's approach to one or two of the pieces is undeniably controversial.

Questions have most often been asked about Karajan's shaping of the work he himself found so emotionally shattering: the terrifyingly prophetic, war-racked *Three Orchestral Pieces* completed by Alban Berg in 1914–15. For some, Karajan's reading is more a free paraphrase of the music than a realisation of what Berg actually wrote, phrases elided, inner detail selectively used. That the reading was always a fiercely emotional one – more Furtwängler than Boulez – there is no doubt, Karajan consciously trading vision for accuracy.

Underlying all this was his long-standing belief – fiercely debated with Gottfried von Einem all those years ago – that the music of the Second Viennese School was not, of itself, ugly or unapproachable. Poor technique and inadequate rehearsal time, he still believed, had been the real barriers to a proper appreciation. Now he went as far as to say so publicly, commandeering Deutsche Grammophon's advertising space and using it to make a clear statement of his interpretative aesthetic:

At our many rehearsals, I repeated this again and again: 'Gentleman, a dissonance is a tension and a consonance is therefore the necessary and corresponding relaxation. But neither of them, tension or relaxation, can be ugly, because then they no longer constitute music any more.' I have in mind this nonsense, which one is always hearing, that I want to 'smooth off the rough edges'. One can only smooth off rough edges where the roughness consists of a note being played unprofessionally, i.e. when it is unclean, untidy, and unattractive. In our work together we have often rehearsed the intonation for hours on end. The tension too should be a thing of beauty. The musical content must be clean and pure.[19]

In his 'Ode on a Grecian Urn', Keats asserts

> Beauty is truth, truth beauty, that is all
> Ye know on earth, and all ye need to know.

Karajan's position – that a work of art, though it can express ugly emotions, cannot itself be ugly – is certainly tenable. Yet there will always be those who feel the need to run their hand across the surface of the music and sense its being rough to the touch.

In the case of early Schoenberg, there were fewer problems. In *Verklärte Nacht* the late-romantic string-writing becomes, in Karajan's expert vinification, as pungent as a late-gathered Gewürztraminer; yet the psychodynamics of the piece are powerfully suggested, the girl, who is carrying another man's child, and her lover feeding and dousing their passions in the moonlit wood. Karajan also understood from within the orchestral psychodrama *Pelleas und Melisande*, not least because of his abiding fascination with Debussy's opera on the same subject.

The Webern recordings were widely acknowledged to be very fine, more exact (necessarily so) than those of the music by Berg. Music that appears dry on the page, wrote Jeremy Noble in *The Gramophone*, emerges here as 'the glowing crystalline structure that Webern himself must have imagined'.[20]

Webern's brief two-movement Symphony held a special fascination for Karajan. Deciphering its tonal and thematic relations can test to destruction what Karajan once called 'the true music-lover's gift for listening'. But abstraction alone held no interest for him, intrigued though he was by the music's advanced mathematical formulas. What truly fascinated him about the Webern Symphony is that this is music which, in his own words, 'offers no development'; music which turns the flux of being into 'a condition which remains constant'.[21] To that side of Karajan's being that longed for a state of nirvana, the Webern Symphony was a kind of musical heaven.

After he had recorded Schoenberg's *Variations for Orchestra*, reseating the players for each variation,[22] Karajan dropped it from his concert schedules. This caused instant dismay. The work had been advertised as part of an all-Schoenberg programme at the 1974 Berlin Festival. The audience (which had come from far and wide to hear the programme) found that a Mozart piano concerto had been substituted for the *Variations*.[23] Karajan was booed when he came on to the platform and there were grumbles in the press.

Stresemann was furious: a victory of 'technology' over live music-making, he said. Glenn Gould might have put it differently: a defeat for the concert hall by music that did not necessarily belong there in the first place.

*

At the age of sixty-five, Karajan's days of playing premieres seemed long gone. Then, in 1973, it was announced that he would record and conduct the world premiere of a new work by Carl Orff, his 'stage play in three parts' *De temporum fine comoedia (Play of the End of Time)*.

This would be Orff's last large-scale work, a staged oratorio inspired by the Sibylline Oracles. In Part 1 the coming of the Messiah is prophesied but also the end of life and the cosmos when the godless and the wicked will be damned. Part 2 chronicles preparations for the end of time by early Christian ascetics. The Greek hermit Origen believes that then guilt will be forgotten; an idea, some have suggested, that had a particular resonance for Orff, given the ambiguity of his position in the war years. Part 3 takes place after the destruction of the cosmos. Still the damned grieve. 'Make an end!' they plead. Lucifer appears, abases himself before God and is reprieved. Light floods the stage (in the Salzburg production, another of Schneider-Siemssen's 'cosmic biospheres'), the choir sings '*Ta panta nus* [All is spirit]', and the work ends with a meditation by a quartet of violas, a four-part canon based on the melody of Bach's last work, the chorale 'Vor deinen Thron tret ich hiermit'.[24]

The work cut little ice with the press, for whom Orff was a discredited figure, nor could the audience, in an age before surtitles, readily follow the text – part spoken, part declaimed, part sung – with its mixture of languages, including Latin and Ancient Greek.

The orchestral interventions (for that is what they are, fiercely declamatory) are scored for woodwind and brass, keyboard, and an elaborate array of percussion including Japanese temple bells. Karajan's direction of all this was impeccable, very exciting, and in the final pages utterly simple. The Cologne Radio Symphony Orchestra played for the recording and at the Salzburg première where, unusually for him, Karajan had the orchestra pit set at its lowest pitch so as to give the cosmic scene absolute precedence.

CHAPTER 65

A question of image

Primitive man simply didn't know *what* he was: he was always half in the dark. But we have learned to see, and each of us has a complete Kodak idea of himself.

D. H. Lawrence, *Art and Morality*

A photograph is a quotation taken out of context.

Herbert von Karajan

All who seek you tempt you, and as soon as they find you, bind you to an image and a posture.

Rainer Maria Rilke

In 1972 EMI was in search of new images of Karajan. The huge archive of portraits and working photographs of him by Siegfried Lauterwasser, the most expert and trusted of the Karajan court photographers, was very much Deutsche Grammophon's preserve. EMI wanted something of its own.

It was Peter Andry who came up with the idea of using Christian Steiner, a photographer who specialised in portraits of classical musicians. Born in Berlin, the son of an orchestral player at the Deutsche Oper, Steiner had two brothers in the Berlin Philharmonic. 'Steiner is an excellent fellow,' wrote Andry in a memorandum. 'Karajan will not mind being photographed by him at all.' Since Karajan loathed and in some measure feared the camera, this was more than a little misleading. In Karajan's book, being a photographer and being an 'excellent fellow' were mutually exclusive concepts.

Steiner was told that he could have a limited number of sessions, none of which was to last more that twenty minutes. In order to get these, he was required to be on permanent stand-by during working hours. When Karajan did eventually appear, nattily clad in slacks and a polo neck, hair immaculately groomed, the shoot took place in complete silence. Tired of the silences and the hair, Steiner began one session by going over to Karajan and casually rumpling his quiff. It was not the most tactful of ploys but Karajan remained in place, gloweringly acquiescent.

To judge from the published results,[1] Steiner had decided to capitalise on Karajan's evident unease. The portraits record a mood of barely contained impatience and, in one shot, something close to anger as Karajan stares threateningly into the camera with the look of a hunted animal. When Eliette turned up, Karajan introduced his tormentor to her: 'The brother of my Steiners,' he said, revealing that he knew perfectly well who Steiner was, even though he had never admitted as much to Steiner himself.

EMI liked the portraits and so, it seemed, did Karajan. Two years later, Steiner was asked back. It was during this second shoot that a photograph was taken of Karajan in a black leather jacket (fashionable at the time) and red turtle-neck, with thin lasers of light from within the semi-darkened Philharmonie playing about his figure. A charitable view of this portrait would be that it makes him look like a superannuated biker, albeit an extremely well preserved one. But that was not the analogy which most immediately came to mind when the photograph appeared on the cover of Karajan's new EMI recording of Strauss's *Ein Heldenleben*. The Leni Riefenstahl lighting effects, the black-on-red colour scheme, the leather jacket, the decidedly Prussian pose, all contrived to give Karajan the look of a Nazi military commander. The only thing that was missing was his tank.

It is strange that no one thought to point out to Karajan the folly of the thing, as Deutsche Grammophon had done only months before when he had come up with an unworkable idea for the cover of his splendidly enjoyable set of Prussian and Austrian marches with the wind section of the Berlin Philharmonic.

Karajan had argued that, rousing as the marches were, we could no longer hear them as being anything other than part of a longer and more sinister march towards the carnage of World War One and the conflagrations that finally consumed the German Reich in 1945. To this end, he suggested the sleeve design should show an empty desert in whose sands were imprinted the footsteps of an army leading to a distant horizon where a marble swastika could be glimpsed engulfed in flame.

When the idea landed on the desk of Deutsche Grammophon's Head of Design, Pali Meller Marcovicz, he was both resigned and appalled. Resigned, because Karajan was always coming up with ideas that were better suited to film than to static design; appalled, because, whatever the thinking behind the idea, it was inconceivable that Deutsche Grammophon could release a record with a swastika on the cover. 'Worse,' added Marcovicz, 'a *marble* swastika. Marble doesn't burn. What would some of Karajan's more imaginative critics have made of that? An heroic image of the Nazi ideal's imperviousness to time and the elements? It didn't bear thinking about.'[2]

In the end, a studio in Hamburg came up with a rather limp design in which banners and swords in mailed hands were seen against a background of leaping flames. (Karajan had insisted on retaining the idea of conflagration.) It was effective and politely inoffensive, the kind of thing you might expect to find on the cover of a children's book.

*

When Leonard Bernstein was asked what the difference was between himself and Karajan, he replied, 'I'm ten years younger and five centimetres taller.' Karajan did, indeed, suffer from that familiar if medically unproven condition known as 'small man's complex'; but what he and Bernstein lacked in inches they more than made up for with striking faces and profiles. Matinée idols in their twenties, lean athletes of the rostrum in their thirties and forties, both men kept their hair and their looks long enough to enter their final decades as well-weathered sages. Bernstein's face may have had a more lived-in look but Karajan's had weathered naturally on ski slopes and the high seas.

Why, then, was Karajan so reluctant to be photographed in his professional role as orchestral conductor? There were a number of reasons: a desire for control, a fear of intrusion, and a need, in performance, for absolute concentration. To the best of my knowledge, Karajan never stopped a concert, as Sir Malcolm Sargent once did when a flash-bulb went off during a Promenade Concert performance of Beethoven's Ninth Symphony ('I can't concentrate with you fiddling about like that. Will you please go'[3]) but staff at the Berlin Philharmonie did have orders to hunt down illicit snappers and confiscate their film. On tour, restarts were sometimes delayed if Karajan had heard or seen a camera during a performance. I remember him saying, 'I used to tell my brother, you are an inventor. Please, invent something that I can wear round my head – a kind of miner's lamp – that destroys the film of people who come to my concerts and point flashlights at me.'

Yet Karajan was extremely adept at using the camera. When a photographer was legitimately at work, as Lauterwasser frequently was, he had a sixth sense as to where the photographer was and how he could best appear to him. Even in formal photo calls, such as the ones with Steiner, he was never less than practised and quick. His daughter Arabel thinks he learned a lot from Eliette in her modelling days: how a professional model conducts herself, and the speed and accuracy with which she works to camera.

What the record companies principally wanted on their LP covers was an image of Karajan himself; like a royal profile on an imperial coin, it validated the product. Yet, contrary to popular supposition, it was not what Karajan himself wanted in later years.

In the early 1940s, Polydor's Grammophon 'Meisterklasse' 78s carried his photograph on the record label. Later, in the 1950s, Legge was entirely unsqueamish about selling Columbia LPs with Karajan's photograph on the sleeve and his name in rather larger letters than that of the composer or the orchestra. Such marketing devices, which persist to this very day, have always outraged the purists;[4] nor can there be any doubt that Karajan was very happy to be established visually in the 1950s and 1960s.

It was in the early 1960s that he was at his most obviously narcissistic, working with Menuhin and Clouzot on the Mozart film or posing for the moodily suggestive black-and-white photograph of himself and Christoph von Eschenbach on the cover of their recording of Beethoven's First Piano Concerto; Karajan chastely studying Eschenbach's hands, while Eschenbach, dressed in a Karajan-style black polo-neck, turns his winning gaze back to the maestro himself.

Yet from the mid-1960s onwards, Karajan's record companies were subject to endless directives from him which stipulated that his image should *not* appear on record sleeves. And the directives were enforced. A Deutsche Grammophon catalogue of Karajan recordings issued in 1973 reproduces thirty-three sleeves, only five of which carry a picture of Karajan and only one of which (the box for the complete *Ring* cycle) has his name in larger type than that of the composer.

Deutsche Grammophon's famous yellow cartouche,[5] with its standardised title designs, meant that Karajan's name was almost never given precedence over that of the composer or the orchestra.[6] But it was the visual layouts that caused the company the greater problem. 'Historical' sleeves annoyed Karajan even more than those with his own image on them. The occasional undistinguished oil painting did slip through (Count Egmont on the scaffold, for example) but Karajan preferred modern artwork that was original and eye-catching: images that did not 'colour' or 'date' the music or prejudice its appeal to the audience at large.

During the 1970s, he was more and more inclined to suggest cosmic images, and designs or photographs drawn directly from nature. Photographs from the NASA space probes were a particular source of fascination to him. It was a NASA photograph that appeared in 1974, the same year as the EMI *Ein Heldenleben*, on the cover of his new Deutsche Grammophon recording of *Also sprach Zarathustra*: a sliver of the moon's rim picked out of the blackness by the beam of a shrunken, distant-seeming sun.

Karajan's favourite designer in these years was Holger Matthies, a designer-photographer of the radical Left who knew nothing about music but who was able to produce the images he wanted. It was Matthies who produced the rainbow motif which was used in different colours and densities on all Karajan's Mahler recordings in the 1970s. It was he who tracked down the bird's wing, a bas-relief from an ancient temple carving, that was used on the set of the nine Bruckner symphonies recorded between 1975 and 1981. For Karajan, these were models of what a good record sleeve should be: stylish, timeless, but also distinctive in its own right. They tell us a good deal about Karajan the musician, as opposed to the media megastar of popular imagination.[7]

Sometimes Karajan drove Matthies to impossible lengths to achieve what he wanted. In the case of the box for the 1980 recording of *Die Zauberflöte*, he asked for images of fire, wind, and water. Models were made and photographed: elaborate structures involving a flute and a water cascade hung round with gauzes on to which images of fire were projected. None of this was really capable of being caught on camera; at least, none of the stills was approved by Karajan. Eventually time ran out. This was meant to be the first digital recording of *Die Zauberflöte* and rival sets were imminent. In the end, a flute was draped with chiffon and photographed against a blue-grey backdrop: something of an anticlimax, it has to be said. Not that the work on Matthies's models went to waste. One of the images was later used for the cover of the LP of Bernstein's recording of Stravinsky's *Firebird* Suite, where it worked very well. Bernstein's manager, Harry Kraut, rang Deutsche Grammophon to congratulate the company on providing a sleeve that had been tailor-made for the music. No one dared tell him that it had been made for another project altogether by a musically illiterate designer.

In 1983 Deutsche Grammophon decided to mark Karajan's seventy-fifth birthday with a photograph album *Herbert von Karajan: a tribute in pictures*. Since it could not be published without Karajan's agreement, Marcovicz had sought numerous meetings and received the usual string of postponements. Eventually, he managed to get access to Karajan while he was cabined in a sanatorium on the Swiss border. The discussion was lengthy. There was the usual quota of acceptances and rejections, plus a good deal of banter about the possible addition of speech bubbles to some of the photos. Finally, Karajan looked at Marcovicz. 'The truth is, you've already printed the book. Am I not right?' Marcovicz admitted that this was indeed the case. Because of the imminence of the birthday, the book was already in production. Karajan acquiesced. He did not much care for the volume but he had been greatly diverted by Marcovicz's visit.

Karajan's own favourite portrait of himself was taken by Lauterwasser in 1967. A study in contemplation, it shows Karajan seated on a rehearsal chair in the Philharmonie with two harps looming behind him like a pair of angel's wings. With the baton held half aloft in the right hand and the left arm resting on the chair's back, the left hand rather limply draped, he gazes down as if in a waking trance. 'Heard melodies are sweet,' the look seems to say, 'but those unheard are sweeter.' It would not be everyone's idea of a representative Karajan portrait. In the Vienna Philharmonic's official history it is mockingly juxtaposed with a black-and-white action shot of Leonard Bernstein. But it is, as Karajan once put it, 'The man I remember when I think of myself.'[8]

CHAPTER 66

Disc trouble

slipped disc an intervertebral disc that has become displaced or prolapsed and can cause pain, weakness, or paralysis by pressure on nerves or the spinal chord. *videodisc*: see VIDEO a. & n.
The New Shorter Oxford English Dictionary

Since 1967, Karajan had personally signed the operatic albums which Easter Festival subscribers received each year. With over a thousand subscribers, it was a considerable labour. In 1974 he announced that his right hand should be reserved for the more important and congenial business of conducting.

The opera for the 1974 festival was *Die Meistersinger*, with Karl Ridderbusch as Sachs, René Kollo as Walther, and Gundula Janowitz as Eva. Since *Die Meistersinger* offers no cues for cosmic imaginings, Karajan and Schneider-Siemssen concentrated on historical authenticity and old-fashioned naturalism. The riot was just that (Karajan had called in professional tumblers to fall from attic windows and plunge into water troughs) and the final scene in the meadow was as rich and glowing a pageant as one could wish to see. Elements of 'dark' lighting did remain, sixteenth-century Nuremberg evoked in colours Rembrandt might have wondered at. As for the performance, it was lyrical and relaxed, glowing with what one writer described as 'a rare and delicate poetry'.[1]

Not everyone liked it. The editor of *Opera*, Harold Rosenthal, making his first visit to the festival, expressed reservations about the conducting, the singing, the staging, the age and nationality of the audience ('mostly German and French, few English can afford those prices') and the audience's dress code ('I thought it faintly ridiculous for most of them to dress themselves up to the nines at four o'clock on Good Friday afternoon for a performance of Bach's *B minor Mass* which was over by seven').[2]

What Rosenthal's jeremiad revealed was not so much a cultural clash as a political and economic one. Arriving in Salzburg from Britain, where by 1974 an out-of-date state-run command economy was in increasing disarray, was a trying experience. It was easy to feel a bit like a tramp on a catwalk.

Another visitor to the 1974 Easter Festival was Edward Heath who in February 1974 had called, and lost, a General Election on the issue 'Who governs Britain, the elected government or the trade unions?' For Heath, the visit to Salzburg must have been a welcome balm. In his book *Music: A Joy for Life*, published two years later, he describes this Salzburg *Meistersinger* as 'the greatest opera *performance* I have ever seen'.[3]

Heath and Karajan had struck up an acquaintance some years previously through their mutual love of music and sailing. Heath was keen to advance his fledgling career as a part-time orchestral conductor; Karajan was eager to glean what he could from the world's most famous amateur sailor.[4] They had less in common politically. It was Margaret Thatcher whom Karajan would later watch with awe as years of union domination in Britain were finally overturned and, for the first time in his adult life, the Soviet threat was peaceably yet decisively challenged.

What Karajan did share with Heath was a profoundly held belief in Europe's future as a confederation of nation states economically and politically interdependent within the EEC. (For Karajan this was, if nothing else, a bulwark against war.) On 4 January 1973, three days after Britain joined the EEC, Karajan had conducted an all-Beethoven programme with the Berlin Philharmonic at a BBC Winter Prom in the Royal Albert Hall as part of the festival 'Fanfare for Europe' masterminded by Heath.

*

Karajan had spent most of his life watching the play of the powerful, in music and in politics, much of it from a ringside seat. In 1973 an armchair version of the game arrived in Salzburg in the shape of Giorgio Strehler's adaptation of Shakespeare's *Henry VI* trilogy, translated into German and renamed *Das Spiel der Mächtigen*. Strehler had become an important presence on the theatre scene in Salzburg in the 1960s. His silhouetted *commedia dell'arte* production of *Die Entführung aus dem Serail* remains to this day one of the most famous of all Salzburg's Mozart productions. It ran for nine seasons, during which time Strehler looked as if he might assume an influence over Salzburg's theatrical affairs as great as that of any stage director since Reinhardt.

Reinhardt's widow, Helene Thimig, was one of his most influential backers and the Karajan-dominated Festival Direktorium also wanted him on board. In 1971 Strehler signed a consultancy agreement with the festival and in 1973 produced *Das Spiel der Mächtigen* in the Felsenreitschule, a two-part epic after the manner of Reinhardt's shows of the 1920s and 1930s, lavishly staged, vastly time-consuming, and hugely expensive. Unfortunately, it was also under-rehearsed and something of an organisational shambles.

Things were better in 1974, but this was also the year in which the first of the show-piece collaborations between Strehler and Karajan came badly unstuck. The opera was *Die Zauberflöte*. Luciano Damiani's designs were schematic and drab, Strehler's direction stiff and, in the judgement of many who saw it, lacking in humanity. Karajan loathed the production and did nothing to redeem it musically. After the scheduled six performances, it was axed, and Strehler with it.

In the autumn of 1974, Karajan took the Berlin Philharmonic to the United States. It was his first visit with the Berliners for nearly ten years, a hiatus that had alarmed Ronald Wilford who feared that, for whatever reason, they were being snubbed.

Karajan, who was now suffering from something rather more serious in the lumbar region than the ricked back which had made him so out of sorts during the Philharmonia tour of 1955, was at his least co-operative during the visit. The weather was unseasonably warm for November but in Washington he refused to allow officials at the Kennedy Center to turn on the air-conditioning. His susceptibility to draughts was cited. So he kept warm while thousands sweltered.

EMI also found itself in trouble, landed with a huge car-hire bill which turned out to be for private visits Karajan had been making to a doctor in New York and for journeys to and from the airport, where he was taking more flying lessons. His contract was up for renewal once again and, illness aside, he was up to all his old tricks, testing and threatening, and generally making people's lives as difficult as possible.

The concerts themselves were well received. 'Karajan Returns, a Great Legend Intact' ran a headline in the *New York Times* over a review by Harold Schonberg. Schonberg thought the performances of Brahms's Fourth and Second symphonies too carefully planned but was prepared to concede that they were mercifully free from the affectations of what he called 'interpretation in capital letters'.[5] After hearing Karajan conduct Bruckner's Eighth Symphony the following evening, Schonberg's colleague John Rockwell wrote a notice that was chidingly different. It was not sound alone that gave the performance its appeal, Rockwell argued; long and profound acquaintance with the music played its part too. Nor, on the evidence of this performance, was a thought-through interpretation necessarily a cold or 'inhumanly exact' one.[6]

Back in Berlin, Karajan was beginning to re-record his Bruckner interpretations with a view to making a complete set of the nine symphonies. With the move to the Philharmonie in 1973, recording such works had become easier. Whatever the virtues of the Dahlem church, it had the singular disadvantage of being on one of the axes of West Berlin's Tempelhof airfield.[7]

Throughout 1975, work continued to crowd in. For the summer festival Karajan revived Verdi's *Don Carlos* in a broodingly splendid new production with Cappuccilli, Domingo, Ghiaurov, and Freni in the leading roles.

Christa Ludwig fell foul of the role of Eboli after one performance and was replaced by Eva Randová who sang and acted very well though she received none of the plaudits from the pit that were forthcoming for Freni or Cappuccilli. In the autumn, Karajan embarked on an extensive round of audio and film recordings in Berlin,[8] flew with the Berlin Philharmonic to Iran for the opening of the Shah's new concert hall in Teheran, and then returned to Berlin to record *Le sacre du printemps*, Tchaikovsky's First Piano Concerto with Lazar Berman as soloist, and the remake of Schubert's *Unfinished* Symphony, which microphone failure had ruined the previous January.

The new performance of the *Unfinished* seems to have been conceived *sub specie aeternitatis*. Had Karajan died a few weeks later it could have been played as his requiem. What he and the Berliners give us here, the orchestral colours glowering like old gold, is a Schubert canvas in the manner of a late painting by Tintoretto. The lead across the double bar in the first movement is a glimpse into purgatory, the slow movement relentless in its grief-stricken mood.

In early December work started on a new recording of *Lohengrin*, ahead of the 1976 Easter Festival production. The earliest sessions were used for orchestral rehearsals and a limited amount of work with the principals, including the Lohengrin, René Kollo, none of whose material was usable. Shortly after these sessions, Karajan was taken ill. Having somehow managed to grind his way through performances of Bruckner's Eighth Symphony in Berlin on 6 and 7 December, he travelled to St Moritz in excruciating pain. His personal physician Walther Simon advised an immediate operation. Karajan objected. He wanted to spend Christmas quietly with his family. But the delay in acting on Simon's advice nearly cost him his life. A disc had slipped and had done so in such a way as to be digging into his spinal chord. It had trapped the nerves and compressed two-thirds of the marrow:

My surgeon was on the way to the airport with his family for a holiday in the Middle East. The moment he heard of my condition, he turned round and came back. He later told me that I was within four days of complete paralysis. The team took five hours to get the disc out. There was a man in the next room who was not so lucky. He suffered paralysis and died soon after.[9]

Karajan survived, but things would never be the same again.

PART V
1976–1989

CHAPTER 67

Easter 1976

Minnesingers travelled from town to town. They didn't really sing
too good, which is the main reason they kept moving.
　　　Art Linkletter, *A Child's Garden of Misinformation*

For the first time since its inauguration, the Salzburg Easter Festival
appeared to be imperilled. It was estimated that it would be at least six
months before Karajan would be recovered from his back operation. He,
however, had other ideas:

From the beginning I thought of only one thing – that I had to get out of
there as quickly as possible. On the third day after the operation I began to
do gymnastic exercises in bed so that I wouldn't go into a complete decline.
By the fourth day I was able to read and move. But I was in constant pain.
Apart from the pain from the operation scars, there was the pain from seven
kidney stones. The last of these held out until after my release from hospital. I
thought a great deal about myself and my way of working during those weeks.
I felt myself undergoing a process of change, though it is not something I can
put into words.[1]

　　He said that in the autumn of 1977, by which time it was clear that he had,
indeed, undergone some kind of change. The focus of his music-making was
more consistently sharp, the orchestra less likely than it had been of late to
be flying on automatic pilot. There was a sense of inessentials having been
stripped away, of a new incisiveness of rhythm and tone.

　　The cause is not difficult to determine. As Karajan himself put it, 'After an
experience like that, each new day you are granted has a fresh meaning.'[2] Or
again, in more poetic vein: 'A piece of bread, sunshine, a quiet stroll – each
is a gift, an adventure.'[3] He had experienced a similar sense of renewal in
1947.[4] Unfortunately, in 1976, all was not quite such plain sailing.

　　When Karajan made a startlingly early return to work in Berlin on 3
March 1976, he was received with genuine warmth and affection by the
orchestra. Yet to what extent were the players prepared for the arrival
on the scene of a new super-intense Karajan? By the mid-1970s, he had
brought the Berlin Philharmonic to a rare peak of musical sophistication.
Like the flock of birds he liked to speak of, the orchestra could indeed fly
of its own volition. There had been dangers in this. If Karajan's conducting
of the standard repertory in the early 1970s sometimes seemed predictable
and bland, it was partly because he had become too indulgent a taskmaster.
All this now began to change.

Devolving musical responsibility within the orchestra is one thing; wresting it back is quite another. While audiences and record collectors welcomed a new rigour in Karajan's conducting, seeds of discontent were being sown within the orchestra which would bear poisoned fruit.

Karajan's illness had changed things in various ways. While he was in hospital in Zürich, his concerts had been taken over by other conductors.[5] For the first time since 1955, the question of who might succeed him at the Berlin Philharmonic was now being openly discussed.

*

The 1976 Salzburg Easter Festival provided a grim preview of some of the problems that lay ahead. The *Lohengrin* recording sessions resumed in Berlin on 3 March, but René Kollo, who was still in poor voice, felt a throat infection coming on. There were hurried switches of schedule to try to record some of the more vocally exposed moments before the voice was further compromised.

One such was Lohengrin's '*Heil dir, Elsa!*' at the end of Act 2. Unfortunately, no organist had been engaged for these dates. Glotz suggested David Bell, one of EMI's assistant producers. Karajan agreed, but Kollo went sick next morning and nothing was done about it. Three days later Karajan suddenly said, 'OK, let's do the organ bit.' The mobile console of the Philharmonie's four-manual, 86-stop Schuke organ was wheeled into place behind the Berlin Philharmonic strings, the red light went on and Bell started playing for '*Heil dir, Elsa!*'

I had assumed we were simply laying down a track of '*Heil dir, Elsa!*' for Kollo's voice to be dubbed on later. But after a while it suddenly dawned on me that Karajan was going right through to the end of Act 2, a long crescendo in which everything – chorus, organ, and orchestra – ends up *tutta forza* in a blazing C major climax. I came in with the 32s flying and all four manuals coupled together. What a tumult! Karajan heard the playback, voiced his approval, and promptly invited me to play in Salzburg.[6]

Karajan's 'appointment' of a new organist got into the press, a bit like an entry in a Hapsburg Court Circular. Bell stayed with him until the end, though he always felt he would have been dropped without ceremony had Karajan found someone better.

For all Bell's heroics and Glotz's ingenious jugglings of the schedules, little was salvaged from the March sessions in Berlin, apart from some rough 'rehearsal' tapes for use on stage in Salzburg. With singers falling like flies, it was decided to use some of the free time to record Brahms's Violin Concerto.[7] EMI had spent £120,000 of their £136,000 *Lohengrin* budget and had nothing to show for it. (It would be May 1981 before the recording was finally completed.)

Meanwhile, arguments developed over who was responsible for paying the Berlin Philharmonic for the studio sessions. Since they had been simultaneously recording the opera and preparing it for Salzburg, apportioning costs was a problem. In the end, the Easter Festival agreed to reimburse the orchestra for a limited amount of rehearsal time but not for any of the losses directly connected with the recording.

The set designs for *Lohengrin* had been planned many months in advance and so were the one thing that had not been compromised by Karajan's illness. The concept was Karajan's, based on one of the greatest of all medieval illuminated manuscripts, the *Grosse Heidelberger Liederhandschrift*, an illustrated collection of poems by twelfth-century Minnesingers, commissioned in the late thirteenth century by a celebrated patron of the arts in Zürich, Rüdeger Manesse.

The designs, realised by Schneider-Siemssen, must rank among the most beautiful ever seen in an opera house. Murray Leslie would write in *Opera*:

Entering the Festspielhaus one saw a softly-lit triple-spread of this manuscript taking up the vast stage and its covers thrown back flanking the orchestra pit and extending into the auditorium. Except for the central section, the Manuscript was divided into sections by slender pillars, bridged by trellised Gothic arches. Behind this delicate structure the opera was enacted in a series of scenes which gave the impression of illustrations from an early medieval manuscript of the legend of Lohengrin. These illustrations were exquisitely beautiful in design and colour, enhanced by lighting effects which, on occasions, silhouetted the figures on the stage against a background sky.[8]

That was only part of the story. The sky was no ordinary sky. Karajan had asked for a particular blue, luminous yet intense, which he had seen in the opthalmological torches used by opticians to conduct eye examinations. And there was the peopling of the stage. The final scene of Act 2 looked like a Fra Angelico fresco: the courtly figures, dressed in greys, blues, white and gold, framed in the cloisters and arches. It was a scene, as one chronicler of Wagnerian stage performances has put it, of 'grave and remote beauty'.[9]

It was, however, a very static production, a beautifully staged oratorio rather than a living music-drama. Karl Ridderbusch, who sang the King, was one of the first to object, and he went public on his objections. He also announced that he would not be appearing at the 1977 Easter Festival, though this latter threat appears to have been provoked by a row with one of Karajan's staff rather than with Karajan himself. Karajan was angry, of course, but unfazed. Ridderbusch – in his early forties but an unreconstructed German of the old school, a right-winger with a taste for Nazi memorabilia[10] – was even more of a conservative on matters of staging than Karajan was. For Karajan, it must have seemed like a rerun of Rome in 1941 when the German 'traditionalists' (Bockelmann and others) refused to co-operate with his staging of *Die Meistersinger* on the grounds that 'my Führer would not wish it'.

Kollo presented a different kind of problem. He struggled through the first night, received some bad reviews, and, citing continuing ill health, withdrew from the second performance only hours before he was due on stage. Unfortunately, he, too, went public. The local evening paper quoted him as saying that he was sick and tired of being pushed into the background by 'star producer-conductors'. He was also quoted as saying that whereas there were only five tenors in the world who could sing Lohengrin, there were at least 5000 conductors who could conduct it.

Karajan whistled up Karl-Walter Böhm to take Kollo's place.[11] Meanwhile, the *Salzburger Volksblatt* was weighing in with its own thoughts on the crisis:

Herbert von Karajan does not make things easy for himself. He threw himself back into his work, which he regards as a duty, after a serious operation without the full agreement of his doctors. His physical performance is admirable, his commitment enormous. But Herbert von Karajan also demands unconditional commitment from his colleagues. No concessions are made to anyone, not even to people who think themselves stars. Rehearsals under Karajan are very tough, not to say merciless . . . To rehearse with singers who want to be spared is difficult. Who decides the extent of the protection?[12]

There were rumours, too, that the national and provincial governments were unhappy with the rising levels of subsidy the Easter Festival was beginning to suck in. As a *quid pro quo* they wanted the Vienna Philharmonic to be involved. Why, it was being asked, should an Austrian festival be providing private bounty for a foreign orchestra? It was an old gripe and, with Karajan's affairs in evident disarray, what better time to resurrect it?

Karajan had originally intended to perform Mahler's Sixth Symphony at the 1976 Easter Festival, as well as a concert of music by Berg and Webern. The choral work was Verdi's *Requiem*. Critics who had been looking forward to this festival of death complained bitterly when the Mahler and the Berg were replaced by repertory pieces by Mozart, Schumann, and Richard Strauss. 'The excuse,' wrote Arthur Jacobs in the London *Sunday Telegraph*, 'was an operation for a slipped disc.'[13] The Verdi *Requiem* was none the less deemed to be a special event. Montserrat Caballé's breath control amazed even Karajan, and there was wonderful singing from Cossotto, Carreras and van Dam.

This was Carreras's début with Karajan. He had been flattered to be engaged by the great man without an audition; what he had not reckoned with was the fact that Karajan liked to rehearse in the morning, something that was entirely alien to Carreras's routines and sleep-patterns. Extremely nervous, he slept fitfully and rose at six in the morning to start warming his voice. By the time he got to the rehearsal he was in a state of near catalepsy. And then the worst imaginable thing happened. He opened his mouth to sing the first phrase of the 'Kyrie' and nothing came out:

'That's it, I'm through,' I told myself, although Karajan did not so much as blink an eye to show what he thought about his new tenor. I was fully aware how important this rehearsal was to my future as I had already been informed earlier that Karajan was probably going to give me the role of Don Carlos the following summer. All through my voiceless *Requiem* rehearsal I felt I could kiss the project goodbye.

After the rehearsal, the Maestro said a few encouraging words to me, but nothing that would substantially change my deep dejection. I didn't even dare ask what would happen to me now. It was only later that I heard about my immediate future in Salzburg. A woman from the costume department called. She wanted to take my measurements for the Don Carlos costume.[14]

Karajan's famed taciturnity had its advantages. Long years in the business had taught him that there is a time to speak and a time to keep silence. According to Carreras, Karajan would often telephone him to discuss problems Karajan could only have known about telepathically. Or was it simply that forty years of working with singers had given him a kind of anticipatory sixth sense?

CHAPTER 68

Close encounters

Can I do you now, sir?
Mrs Mop in *ITMA*

When news filtered through in the autumn of 1975 that Karajan was about to embark on a further recording of the nine Beethoven symphonies, eyebrows were raised. There was no doubt the set would sell; but was it strictly necessary? In fact, necessity had never been an issue. The project had been brought about by a chapter of accidents.

EMI was desperate to have a stereophonic Karajan Beethoven cycle to replace the 1950s mono recordings he had made with Legge. Deutsche Grammophon already had such a set, but was determined not to have it trumped by a newer rival, not least because of the huge sums of money that were being set aside to cover the retrospective royalties Karajan was still demanding.

Deutsche Grammophon would have been content to do nothing, but a new factor had intruded: the arrival of the latest gismo from the world of high fidelity, Quadrophony. Since Karajan was incapable of resisting the lure of new technology, it was clear he would want to be first in the field with a Quadrophonic set of the Nine. As things turned out, his enthusiasm for Quadrophony was short-lived; but the genie was out of the bottle. In order to see off EMI, Deutsche Grammophon was obliged to offer Karajan a new cycle.

Work had begun in the autumn of 1975 but had been put on hold when Karajan fell ill. This was a blessing in disguise. When he resumed recording in the autumn of 1976, he was a changed person. Even without Quadrophony, there was a possibility that the set would be something other than a carbon copy of its predecessor.

Not that some members of the orchestra saw it that way. In his book *Paukenschläge*, Werner Thärichen expresses surprise that the set was made at all. If Karajan had any new thoughts, says Thärichen, he certainly did not communicate them to the orchestra; he conducted the symphonies just as he had always done.[1]

This is not a view that is confirmed by the records. Some of the changes are startling, as fascinating as they are self-contradictory. Where the printed metronome marks are good (or, at least, plausible) they are now much more likely to be followed. On the other hand, there is evidence of Karajan beginning to turn back to his and his orchestra's roots within the Austro-German tradition. The First Symphony's difficult opening movement has a strangely autumnal feel to it after the manner of Klemperer or late Furtwängler. This is not a success. By contrast, the Fourth Symphony is back within the fold of the German Beethoven style and sounds very well. As for the Ninth, this is arguably the best of all Karajan's studio recordings, closer to the style of his 1947 Vienna Philharmonic recording than to the 1962 Berlin version, where Toscanini's influence is too much in the ascendant in the first movement.

Back in Hamburg, Deutsche Grammophon remained nervous about the set's reception. Since it was not now going to be a 'Quadrophonic' first, other excuses had to be dreamed up for its release. Pali Meller Marcovicz was asked by the company's literary editor Ursula von Rauchhaupt to sound Karajan out about the possibility of his *writing* about Beethoven in the presentation booklet. Karajan turned the proposal down. The idea (commonplace nowadays) of a conductor 'explaining' his interpretations was anathema to him. Not even Weingartner, he later told me, had done that: interesting as Weingartner's book on Beethoven was, no one would dream of listening to Weingartner's own recordings book in hand.[2]

Karajan did, however, agree to do a series of interviews. Irving Kolodin, music critic of New York's *Saturday Review*, an exact contemporary of Karajan and an acquaintance of some years' standing, was flown over to interview him at home in Anif. It was also decided that there should be two short filmed interviews, one in German, the other in English, and that these soundtracks should be published on a bonus LP as part of a signed de luxe limited edition of the recordings.

*

The first I heard of this was when I got a call from Deutsche Grammophon asking if I would do the English interview. My answer was a qualified 'yes'. Qualified, because what was being sought was a twenty-minute filmed interview to be done ad lib to no clear brief with someone I had never previously met.

Shortly afterwards, I got a call from my former editor on *Records & Recording*, Robert Leslie, who was now working as a freelance consultant to Deutsche Grammophon. It says much for the company at this period that so sober-suited an organisation should have thought to employ someone as mischievous as Leslie. First-rate intuitive judgement and a deep distrust of the executive mind were the principal assets of this extremely funny man whose career had already embraced dance, editing, and a spell as personal assistant to the Ealing comedy star Terry-Thomas.

Robert's calls were always conspiratorial in tone, and this one was more than usually so.

'Dear boy,' the familiar Scotch brogue came rolling down the wire, 'I trust you said no.'

I conceded that I had said yes.

He tried to talk me out of it. 'If anyone can get a good interview out of Herbert, it is you. But this is not the time. It's just some cheap publicity stunt Uli has dreamed up.'

'Uli' was Uli Märkle, who at that time was working in Deutsche Grammophon's A&R department in Hamburg with particular responsibility for minding Karajan's schedules.³ Uli and Robert did not get on. Uli referred to Robert as 'this crazy man', Robert referred to Uli as 'Herr Dr Sidecar', a name derived from an elaborate fantasy he had of Karajan driving a high-speed motor-bike with the bag-carrying Märkle crouching nervously in the sidecar while Herbert (as Robert always called him) deliberately bounced the machine off walls and hedges.⁴

For some reason – vanity, I suppose – I declined Robert's advice and went ahead.

Salzburg in late May was strangely deserted. I checked into the Österreichischer Hof and, finding no instructions of any kind, went in search of the Deutsche Grammophon office. It was closed. During dinner I fancied I heard the waiters muttering my name. Since they could not possibly know who I was, I saw no reason to interrupt my enjoyment of a stunningly devised dish of Kaiserschmarren.

In fact, they had, indeed, been looking for me. At a quarter past nine I found a note from Märkle. He was having dinner at the Goldener Hirsch and would be there until nine o'clock. He should have rung earlier, I thought, legging it over the Makartsteg. I found him in the restaurant closeted with the film crew, two Bavarians and a genial Australian director, Peter Ording. As they had not even started dinner, I was invited to join them, so becoming one of the few people in history to have eaten a three-course dinner in the Österreichischer Hof *and* the Goldener Hirsch within the space of two hours.

Karajan, it was reported, was 'very relaxed' about the interviews. As someone who always arrives early, I promised that I would be at the Festspielhaus at about 11.15 ready for filming at noon. 'Noon,' exploded Märkle. 'We start at nine!' It was only years later, when I read James Galway's account of his audition in Munich with the Berlin Philharmonic, that I realised that the trick of inviting foreigners to turn up at midday for a 9 a.m. appointment is an old German custom.

When Karajan and his entourage swept into the first-floor bar of the Festspielhaus next morning at 9 a.m. (prompt), Karajan looked far from relaxed. He was wearing a grey-blue polo-neck, with an extremely stylish matching blue-and-grey-check sports jacket which he draped elegantly over his lap during the filming. Since there were to be two films, each of twenty minutes, forty minutes had been set aside. (An orchestral rehearsal was scheduled for 9.45.) As a plan, this struck me as being stronger on arithmetic than common sense.

I stood and watched the German interview. With a somewhat grim-faced Karajan and an already perspiring Joachim Kaiser seated at either end of a plain wooden bench – a kind of non-operative seesaw – Kaiser launched into what proved to be a very long first question. Karajan had just begun to answer when there was a terrific clattering noise. A door opened just behind where I was standing and a cleaning lady entered with a zinc bucket and a mop. It was at this point that I realised how blue Karajan's eyes were and how powerful their laser-like gaze. I fancy the cleaning woman beat a slow grumbling retreat, though I still imagine her being zapped by the laser and reduced to a pile of smouldering rags beside her bucket.

No one had told Karajan that there was only ten minutes of film in each cassette, so there was a further unannounced break while the camera was reloaded. By the time the interview finished it was 9.40.

'Your interview will now be at noon,' announced Uli, impervious to the irony of the fact that this was when it was meant to have been anyway. 'But first you must meet Mr von Karajan and give him your questions.'

It was obvious from Karajan's demeanour that the moment was not opportune. He was being badgered by hangers-on and was clearly impatient to get downstairs to his rehearsal. I objected, but was frog-marched into the presence.

I forget now what, precisely, the questions were. They were different from Kaiser's but not that different. What I do remember is that Karajan said no to the first three, approved the fourth (a question about advances in recorded technology since 1962), and became extremely irritated with the fifth question, during the course of which I happened to mention the name Weingartner.

I sympathised with him. He was late, and was clearly more interested in getting his early morning Strauss fix (*Also sprach Zarathustra* was down for rehearsal) than talking to an English journalist who was asking questions above his station.

But I also thought he was being rather stupid.

'I'm sorry you don't like the questions,' I weighed in, 'but they are very much the kind of thing Beethoven collectors in Britain and the USA would be fascinated to hear your answers to.'

'They are the wrong questions.'

'I'm sorry. I wasn't briefed. If that's what you feel, why don't you dictate some questions of your own?'

He stared and walked out, the entourage in nervous pursuit. When

Märkle returned he said that I had insulted 'the maestro'. I said that the whole thing was a farce, and threatened to leave. It was, indeed, a farce. (Robert Leslie had predicted it would be.) After tempers had cooled it was decided to draft three questions – in German, there being some curious notion that Karajan had not understood my English – which Märkle would then show to Karajan during the rehearsal break. One of his staff, a delightfully no-nonsense Scots girl, was called in to help.

When Karajan came back at noon, he appeared to be in a rather better mood after his mid-morning Strauss session. It was everyone else who was now on edge, with the notable exception of Peter Ording, who clearly thought that the locals were several tinnies short of a lagerfest. God bless Australia, I thought as the interview started.

I had been given instructions to ask no more than the three agreed questions. Karajan knocked off the first question – about the experience of returning to Beethoven after a significant gap in time – in about thirty seconds, and was threatening to be equally brief with the second. Eighteen minutes to go, I calculated, and one question left. It was at this point that I decided to go off script. I remembered Legge's story about Karajan's final rehearsal for Beethoven's Fifth at the Royal Albert Hall in 1948. Karajan remembered it, too. Out of the wreckage of the previous three hours, a conversation began to grow.

As a discussion it was pretty awful, fractured and superficial. Karajan said quite a lot of interesting things, but there was nothing he had not said before or which he would not say much better in less fraught circumstances when I interviewed him in Berlin the following December.[5] He ended with a long disquisition on the privilege of music-making in the modern world and the music-maker as social therapist. Then he was gone, sweeping off the set (Uli in hot pursuit) even before I had finished a mumbled *envoi*.

Peter Ording said something about Karajan being perfectly OK when people 'cut the crap and just talked to him'. And then Uli was back, all smiles. Karajan was very pleased with the interview, so much better than Kaiser's, he said, as Kaiser hovered within earshot. It wasn't, but no matter.

'And now we should all have a nice lunch. Some fresh strawberries perhaps, some champagne . . .'

I found myself warming to Uli.

After champagne and strawberries it was siesta time. 'But as you will not be here for the concert tomorrow,' Uli announced, 'Mr von Karajan invites you to attend the rehearsal at four o'clock.'

So I skipped the siesta and turned up at the Festspielhaus.

The hall was more or less completely deserted except for Karajan, the Berlin Philharmonic, and me. They played *Ein Heldenleben*, the whole thing, right through at full throttle. He stopped them just once. I had read about Ludwig of Bavaria being given private performances in his theatre in Munich. It was an indulgence, I decided, to which one could become addicted.

After *Ein Heldenleben*, the place suddenly came to life. Half the orchestra left, the remaining players regrouped, Karajan got down off his high stool, and a gaggle of people filed into the auditorium, settling themselves in remote corners. Eventually, a 13-year-old girl appeared on stage. She was wearing jeans and carrying a violin. Her name was Anne-Sophie Mutter and she was about to make her first appearance with Karajan and the orchestra. The moment the Mozart concerto started, the years seemed to fall away from Karajan. Standing now, no longer perched aloft, his conducting was exact, vibrant, intense. Tracking his new young soloist was a bit like trying to tail a pretty young girl in a fast sports car down an unfamiliar winding country road. He and the orchestra were loving every minute of it.

*

Mutter, who was only a few months older than Karajan's younger daughter Arabel, had been talked about since she was six. Karajan had first heard of her in Lucerne in 1976 and had invited her to audition in Berlin the following December. She was meant to play before the morning rehearsal, but once again Karajan's schedules were in disarray. He was there after the rehearsal, full of apologies, anxious that the wait had not made her even more nervous than she probably already was. He said he had time to hear a little Bach, part of the D minor Chaconne perhaps. He heard it all, and two movements of Mozart's Third Violin Concerto. The invitation to Salzburg followed immediately.

Once Karajan had done it, every international maestro wanted a teenage protégé of his own; but none made the mark that Mutter did, nor was any as expertly tutored. Karajan's care was exemplary. He taught her, protected her, helped her choose her first Stradivarius (a long session in the Philharmonie testing the various instruments for tone and carrying power), and eventually nudged her gently out of the nest at exactly the right moment. (As Mutter would later admit. She did not think so at the time.)

Mutter, in turn, was the ideal protégée. Hugely talented, she was a perfectionist who, even as a teenager, instinctively understood Karajan:

I saw him dedicate so much time and passion to things I know he had already lived with for fifty years. He truly was a genius who never stopped seeking for more expression, for what he felt was the ideal.[6]

Like other violinists, she soon realised that Karajan knew nothing about the instrument – and everything. As she would tell Reinhard Beuth in an interview for *Encounter* in 1988:

Things like fingering and bow changes he's not interested in at all, couldn't care less about them – which allows him to take a more detached approach technically as well. The result is that he has ideas about phrasing that you might have as a singer, say, but not as a violinist because you are too close to the material, too wrapped up in technique. It has nothing to do with technical problems, bow changes, or some leap or other, but simply with things like a gear-change, as it were – things that you can't surmount technically and that are getting in the way of your musical development.[7]

Mutter also inherited some of Karajan's extra-musical preoccupations, including an interest in yoga and fast cars:

Karajan always arrived two minutes before a concert, so I would arrive two minutes before. He drove a Porsche, so I bought one – except that his was turbo-charged, mine was ordinary.[8]

At the time Anne-Sophie Mutter bought her first Porsche, she was not yet old enough to drive it. That amused Karajan no end.

CHAPTER 69

The man with the golden jug

I am a man; I count nothing alien to me.
Terence, *The Self-tormentor*

In May 1977, Karajan returned to the Vienna Opera amid as great a hullabaloo as any in the institution's history. It had been thirteen years since he had resigned the artistic directorship and swept out, vowing never to set foot in Vienna again; thirteen years in which a residue of anger and self-pity had continued to gnaw at his mind. Ever since Hilbert's death in 1968, he had been imagining how he might return, not as artistic director, but as a kind of laureate superstar. When his old friend and former assistant Egon Seefehlner took over as Director of the Opera in the autumn of 1976, the way was suddenly clear.

Karajan had wanted to take his Salzburg productions of *Lohengrin* and *Die Meistersinger* to Vienna and had asked Schneider-Siemssen to look into the practicalities of transferring the sets to the Vienna stage. 'Herr von Karajan,' Schneider-Siemssen gloomily replied, 'you are a pilot. Tell me, can you get a jumbo jet into your garage?'

In the end, three operas were settled on, all in productions of varying degrees of venerability: *Il trovatore*, *Le nozze di Figaro*, and *La bohème*.[1] The casts were a spectacular blend of the new and the old. The Manrico was Luciano Pavarotti, the Rodolfo José Carreras. Leontyne Price was once again the Leonora, the voice now cosseted by Karajan as never before; Mirella Freni, no longer the *ingénue*, sang Mimi with fresh point and dramatic flair.

As the opening night on 8 May approached, the city was agog, the opera house under siege. Joseph Wechsberg reported in *Opera*:

. . . there were red roses on his stand, special floodlights and television cameras, and the house went absolutely crazy. I leave it to scientists to decide whether it was just hysteria or 'an historical event', as one famous singer called it. Nor would it be true to claim that it was only the standees, the operatic *aficionados*, who had hoped for his return all these years. It was the whole house. Dignified, overdressed ladies and elegant men shouted like children for minutes until the Maestro, who seemed pleased but also somewhat bewildered by this demonstration of public allegiance . . . began conducting the music. Perhaps he knew that nothing is as transitory and elusive as glory in Vienna.[2]

He did, indeed. When Stresemann congratulated him on his triumphant return, Karajan grimaced: 'You see, Mr Stresemann, I know the Viennese . . .'

Not everyone joined in the adulation. Fritz Herrmann, a political adviser to the Ministry of Education, penned some scabrous verses:[3]

> Every bum note that his ear reaches
> Causes Karajan to shit his breeches;
> He douses his arse from a golden jug
> It makes you anal, this cultural bug.

Startling stuff from a civil servant, the more so as the poetaster's publisher turned out to be Peter Kreisky, son of the Austrian Chancellor. The Viennese had not enjoyed themselves so much since the departure of the Russians in 1955. But Karajan was not amused. He demanded (and got) a broadcast apology from the Minister of Education Fred Sinowatz.

At the end of the final performance of *La bohème* on 20 May, the ovations lasted forty-five minutes. The stage crew tried lowering the fire curtain but had to raise it again as the tumult continued. Chancellor Kreisky – the 'Sun King' as the Austrians mockingly called him – remained in his box to the very end.

*

It had been a triumphant fortnight for Karajan, but though he took a certain grim satisfaction in being accorded so spectacular a welcome, his real aim in closing a deal with Vienna was a desire to secure an entrée into the rapidly expanding market for live television transmissions from leading operatic centres. Artistically, this was something of a volte-face, a turning away from the bespoke cinema productions he had been expensively involved with over the past twelve years.

Karajan covered whatever potential embarrassment he might have felt by arguing that, given adequate rehearsal time, opera on television was now a perfectly viable medium. To an extent, this was true. Though the Vienna *Il trovatore* was a dull affair, a gloomy production unimaginatively filmed, Karajan was already doing a great deal to make Outside Broadcast units work to the kind of standards a professional film studio might expect.

When Humphrey Burton arrived in Berlin later in 1977 to direct a live television performance of Beethoven's Ninth Symphony – an exceptionally fine performance, as it turned out[4] – he found a superb set-up. There was proper rehearsal time for lighting and camera-work, just as Karajan had said there should be: two complete days, with a student orchestra as stand-in.[5]

Burton had written his own shooting script, refreshingly different from some of Karajan's own. Karajan liked it, but still went through it in close detail. In particular, he wanted to ensure that the camera-work was at one with the rhythm and line of the music, doubly important given the fact that Karajan's reading was now more lyrical and long-breathed than it had been a decade earlier. 'Here you come back to the conductor and then immediately cut away,' Karajan noted. 'Having established the shot, please stay with it. Keep with the line of the music.'

'There was no taint of egocentricity here,' says Burton. 'Karajan's only concern was the music. That was the sole imperative.'[6]

Where the Vienna television experiment started to founder was in the area of singers' contracts and in the swamps and jungles of media business interests. Karajan himself had started the war of attrition when he took out an injunction to stop a live television transmission of Verdi's *Don Carlos* from La Scala on the grounds that the broadcast breached agreements several of the singers had with the Karajan–Kirch Cosmotel–Unitel group. 'The *Don Carlos* dispute makes him even more unpopular here,' noted EMI's Milan office, 'but he has as many lives as a cat.'[7]

In April 1978, Karajan ran into trouble in his own backyard, when the tenor Franco Bonisolli walked out of the dress rehearsal for a revival of *Il trovatore* due to be televised live from the Vienna Opera. Bonisolli did not so much throw in the towel as the sword, hurling it into the pit at the start of Manrico's 'Ah sì, ben mio'. Karajan did not miss a beat; he kept the orchestra playing – without the tenor – right through to the end of 'Di quella pira'.[8]

No one is irreplaceable. Though the television schedules were thrown into temporary disarray, the production was televised, on a different date, with Placido Domingo as Manrico.[9]

The real showdown over televised opera came in May 1980 when Karajan's Europe-wide transmission of *Don Carlos* was called off after – according to him – it was discovered that the Vienna Opera had failed to secure properly signed contracts for several of the singers. There was clearly more to it than that.[10] What made this 1980 episode more than just another storm in a teacup was the opprobrium that was now heaped on Karajan's head in the media. The *Frankfurter Allgemeine Zeitung*, West Germany's most respected daily broadsheet, wrote:

The private economic interests and the exaggerated monopolistic ideas of an artist, however important he may be, are coming into increasing conflict with the task of publicly subsidised culture, and thus leave Karajan's idealistic and humanist messages looking threadbare.[11]

The idea of a private empire being built up with the help of public subsidy was a charge that would be levelled against Karajan in the European media throughout the 1980s. Yet the *Frankfurter Allgemeine Zeitung*'s case begged a number of questions, not least: How *should* private initiatives mesh with 'the task of publicly subsidised culture'? The agreements Karajan had with the Austrian authorities concerning the use of Salzburg theatres and the televising of productions live from Vienna may have been unusual but they were legal and above-board, government-approved and subject to government supervision and review.

Karajan was certainly a poor media strategist. A public figure tangles with television and its web of related interests at his peril. His Viennese adventures in the years 1977–81 brought him distinctly limited artistic success. What they did attract was a set of powerful new enemies in the media.

*

The afternoon following Karajan's triumphant return to Vienna on 8 May 1977, sessions began there for what would be a less ephemeral success, a recording of Richard Strauss's *Salome*.

Shortly after leaving hospital in the winter of 1976, Karajan had gone to Düsseldorf to hear a singer, a late starter in her profession, who even as she neared her fortieth year was beginning to cause a stir in the musical world. Her name was Hildegard Behrens and on the occasion of his visit she was rehearsing *Wozzeck*. ('Marking' the part until she heard that Karajan was in the house.) He briefly introduced himself. Nothing of substance was said, but Behrens sensed that something rather wonderful was about to happen, so she went home and washed her hair.

Shortly afterwards, the phone rang. It was Karajan's henchman, Jucker. The maestro had been most impressed. Was there any particular role Miss Behrens had a mind to sing in the near future? Indeed there was, she said: Salome. 'Salome!' exclaimed Jucker. 'The maestro has been looking for a Salome for as long as I have known him.' That's nice, thought Behrens, and awaited developments.

Towards the end of the year, Karajan summoned her to Berlin to make a test recording of the opera's closing scene. And that was it: she would record *Salome* with him in Vienna for EMI and sing (though not dance) the title role in the production he was now preparing for the 1977 Salzburg Festival.

Strauss had described his ideal Salome as 'a 16-year-old princess with the voice of Isolde'. He had even tried to tempt Elisabeth Schumann into singing the role (more the 16-year-old princess than the voice of Isolde) though Karajan always said that Strauss's ideal in his later years was Maria Cebotari.

Karajan believed that Salome should be simple, childlike, 'as chaste as the moon', and unthinkingly ruthless. Behrens saw her this way, too:

We both felt she should be sung with the utmost beauty and the innocence of a very young girl who is completely natural, young, and unscrupulous, and who finds it perfectly normal that any obstacle to her desires should be crushed. It would therefore be wrong to portray her as a viper or demon or perverted vamp or even as *consciously* sexy, out to seduce the Baptist into submission. I don't think she is really aware of what she's doing or of 'turning it on'. She just wants something obsessively, with all the 'innocence' of a very young but very intelligent girl with sensitive and sure instincts.[12]

Karajan knew what he was looking for. Elements of this particular Salome – the intelligent spoilt child, the ruthless aesthete – lurked within his own psyche. Loyal to the precept he claimed he learned from Max Reinhardt

... the situation did not arise of someone arriving with an entirely different concept which Reinhardt would then have to wrestle with ... when Reinhardt arrived he was already on familiar territory ...[13]

Karajan did not need to cajole Behrens into accepting another view of the character. She was already the Salome he wanted. In rehearsal, she was simply encouraged to grow into the part, while Karajan concerned himself with the purely musical aspect, advising her where she needed to sing through the orchestra or where a diminished orchestral presence allowed her to refine her sound or point the text even more tellingly.

The results were remarkable. As always, though, there were reservations about aspects of Karajan's staging. Where a director like Joachim Herz revelled in the chance to conjure up a sense of debauchery in Herod's court, Karajan left it to the music and the stage settings to make their impact. At one point the *Daily Telegraph*'s Peter Stadlen fancied he saw a slave girl giving Herodias (Agnes Baltsa, alluringly young) a discreet lesbian caress. But that was about it. Peter Alward observed, 'There wasn't an ounce of eroticism in the staging. It was safe sex, just as his *Tristan* had been.'

It was not so much an avoidance of sex, as its sublimation. Peter Conrad would write of the recording, and the staging:

The drama, thanks to Karajan's control of musical dynamics, is virtually silenced. Salome and Narraboth whisper surreptitiously to each other about the rhetorician Jokanaan, an alien who has the temerity, among all these softened voices, to rail and rant. Herod mutters to himself on his entrance about the ill omen of spilled blood, and the guard informs him of Narraboth's suicide [barely visible in Karajan's staging] in a confidential aside. Herodias, no hectoring shrew, contradicts her husband by lowering her voice at him. Salome sullenly hisses her refusal to eat or drink, and is reduced to toneless panting as she awaits the execution. The expression denied to the voices is claimed by Karajan's orchestra, which is Salome's thought-stream.[14]

Strauss had said that one should play *Salome* 'as if it were Mendelssohn-fairy music'. Karajan took him at his word in the opening scenes, the sense of evil purveyed through sonorities of elfin subtlety and allure; yet he also built the drama slowly, remorselessly to a series of earth-shaking climaxes.[15]

Salome was a good example of Karajan's gift for casting well in depth. José van Dam proved to be a memorable Jokanaan, Karl-Walter Böhm is as fine a Herod as any on record, and the casting of Agnes Baltsa as Herodias was another stroke of imagination. ('I don't want another lump of old flesh,' Karajan is said to have remarked.) Baltsa had first sung for Karajan in Berlin in 1974, a performance of Beethoven's *Missa Solemnis* for which she arrived in almost as great a state of vocal disarray as Carreras for the Salzburg Verdi *Requiem*. With Baltsa, however, Karajan knew instantly he was dealing with a maverick.

'Maestro, I am so nervous and flustered,' announced the firebrand from Lefkas.

'You are neither nervous *nor* flustered,' retorted Karajan. 'You merely *wish* to be.'[16]

It was the start of a highly productive, if at times tempestuous, relationship.

*

During the years that the Vienna *Karajanfest* was up and running, he used the occasion each May to record an opera with the Vienna Philharmonic: *Salome* (1977), *Le nozze di Figaro* (1978), *Aida* (1979), *Falstaff* (1980), and *Turandot* (1981). Of these, the Decca *Figaro* is the obvious disappointment: a wonderful cast but a curiously grim-faced performance. 'I don't know why,' recalls Frederica von Stade, who sang Cherubino, 'but Karajan was in a mood. We felt a bit like children waiting to sit an oral exam!'[17] Christopher Raeburn produced, and found Karajan even more distant than usual. This despite the fact that he was using – and knew he was using – an ordering of the opera's third act which had first been suggested by Raeburn and his co-author R. B. Moberly in an article in *Music and Letters* in 1963.[18]

Quite why *Le nozze di Figaro* eluded Karajan on so many occasions is difficult to determine. Raeburn greatly admired him in the Italian repertory; admired, too, his Beecham-like skill in making a good deal of second-division music appear to be absolutely first-rate. 'He had a conjuror's talent and great wizardry where the work can take it. But a Mozart opera has its own inbuilt wizardry and that, in a way, is far harder to conduct.'[19]

Perhaps it was simply that *Figaro* sometimes brought out the automaton in Karajan. Robert Tear has recalled being auditioned by him:

There he was, sitting far at the back behind a console of NASA-like proportions, like the Mekon waiting to destroy Dan Dare. A voice croaked through the PA system.

'Could you sing a little of Basilio, Herr Tear? Begin with the first recit.'

I began: 'Susanna, il ciel vi salvi.'

I was stopped.

'Thank you, Herr Tear, that was excellent.'[20]

Whatever the explanation, in 1981 Decca assembled an equally starry cast in London, Solti conducting. It worked like a dream.

Karajan's Berlin recordings in the immediate aftermath of the crisis of 1975–6 have a quality and character all of their own. Some of the music-making is deeply, almost quirkily, personal. Having recorded a fascinatingly unheroic account of Beethoven's Fifth Piano Concerto with Alexis Weissenberg in 1974 (shades of E. M. Forster's remark, 'If I had to choose between betraying my country and betraying my friend, I hope I should have the guts to betray my country'), Karajan and Weissenberg now completed the cycle. The set has never been much noticed critically, which is how it should be, for this is music-making that is oblivious of the world's show, music-making among friends on terms of their own devising. Karajan's re-recording of Bach's *Brandenburg Concertos* is similarly personal, a hand-picked ensemble of players making music (and such music) in a stylish, relaxed, joyous way within as easy-breathing a pulse as anyone could hope to encounter.

There were bigger projects, too – complete cycles of symphonies by Schubert, Brahms, and Bruckner[21] – and some striking new initiatives. In September 1977, after several postponements, Karajan recorded Mahler's Sixth Symphony.

It seems that he harboured doubts about parts of the work's finale (he even contemplated making cuts[22]), but the symphony as a whole touched him profoundly at several levels. With its marching and counter-marching, its major triad souring on the instant into the minor, it is a work that predicts war: that strange, unsettling word the young Heribert von Karajan heard his uncle mention that fateful day in July 1914 as the funeral convoy of the assassinated Archduke passed by the island of Brioni. Ezra Pound once said that a great artist is like the member of the tribe who smells the forest fire long before anyone else. Mahler's Sixth, written in 1903–4, certainly does that.

And there is more. It is a symphony in which the hero is struck down by three hammer-blows of fate. It depicts married love, and its obverse: isolation and total solitude. The first movement development section is remote mountain music. Schoenberg marvelled at the scoring here, its icy purity and the quiet clunk and jostle of cowbells, the last terrestrial sound, said Mahler, to penetrate the solitude of the mountain peaks.

There can be little wonder that Karajan felt drawn to all this. What is surprising is that he did not feel threatened by it. He was a superstitious man with a weakness for astrology. Having been struck by one hammer-blow (the life-threatening spinal condition), he was about to be struck by a second. But the music drove him on. In the months before the recording in September 1977, he conducted the symphony in Berlin, Salzburg, London, Paris, and Lucerne. The following year he included it at the Salzburg Whitsun Festival, after which would come more serious illness. By rights that should have been that; but he went back to the work, in Tokyo in 1979 and in Berlin in the autumn of 1982 when, astonishingly, he conducted the Sixth and Ninth symphonies within days of one another.

'Last things' seemed to be preoccupying Karajan in the winter of 1978–9. The highlight of the 1979 Easter Festival was a performance of Brahms's *German Requiem*, his own private farewell to Gundula Janowitz, with whom he had worked so often and so memorably. In May in Vienna, he conducted Bruckner's Ninth Symphony and *Te Deum* with the Vienna Philharmonic. The performances were filmed with self-consciously subdued lighting, Bruckner seen, as it were, through a glass darkly.[23]

*

In the early summer of 1978, between an evening concert in Basle and a rehearsal in Paris the following afternoon, Karajan flew to Oxford. The previous autumn, he had been nominated for an Honorary Degree of Doctor of Music.[24] This was not the first honorary degree he had been offered but it was the one that touched him most. His old friend Edge Leslie had been asked to sound him out. Once Karajan ascertained that he would not have to make a speech, he accepted with alacrity.

There was, however, a problem over the conferral. In 1978, Encaenia fell on 21 June, bang in the middle of the Berlin Philharmonic's short summer tour. After much toing and froing it was decided that Karajan would fly from Switzerland to RAF Brize Norton early on the morning of the twenty-first, then on to Paris immediately the ceremony was over. The plan involved his missing the formal luncheon. When news of this got out, there were stories in the press about a 'snub' to the university; it was even suggested (and no doubt believed) that the reason why Karajan had declined the luncheon invitation was that he never allowed himself to be seen eating in public.

Edward Heath was on hand to receive him at a pre-Encaenia drinks party in Lincoln College, where former Cabinet Secretary Burke Trend was Rector; but apart from Heath, no one at the drinks party appears to have made any effort to speak to Karajan. It was something of a relief, therefore, when the official proceedings got under way.

For the procession down Broad Street to the Sheldonian Theatre, Karajan was paired with Dietrich Fischer-Dieskau, who was also receiving the degree of Doctor of Music *honoris causa*. Fischer-Dieskau was amused to note that even here he was not free from conductorial interference. 'Don't walk in time with the music!' ordered Karajan as, organ blazing and trumpets sounding, the procession entered the Sheldonian.

Karajan was welcomed by the Public Orator as a *'mesochorus consummatus* [a consummate conductor]', a man who in musical matters *'nihil a se alienum putat* [deems nothing alien to himself]'. Of Fischer-Dieskau it was said, *'In re musica Proteus est, non homo* [In music, he is Proteus personified, no mere mortal]'.[25] Other recipients of honorary degrees that day included the film director Satyajit Ray. But it was a Hungarian professor of neuroanatomy, János Szentágothai, whom Karajan was most interested to meet. He would later invite him to Salzburg to address the Karajan Foundation.

After the ceremony, it was back to Brize Norton. But Karajan promised he would return to Oxford to give a concert as a token of his thanks.

*

In his address to Encaenia, the Oxford Professor of Poetry, John Wain, had talked of the repairing and reworking of the Chancellor's ancient ceremonial robes by the present-day seamstresses of Oxford; a case, he said, of 'originality grounded in tradition, vitality continually renewed'. It was a phrase that stuck in Karajan's mind, as well it might. The need for renewal was back on the agenda in Berlin.

Wolfgang Stresemann, now in his nineteenth year as General Manager, was approaching his seventy-fourth birthday. Karajan had been heard to say that Stresemann could stay until he was eighty as far as he was concerned, but the Berlin Senate was not so minded. It was time, the politicians insisted, for a younger man to take over. This was easier said than done. With Karajan disinclined to accept change for change's sake, agreeing a short list of possible replacements was well-nigh impossible. An impasse was reached and the appointment put on hold. Stresemann would complete twenty years in the job, and retire at seventy-five.

But now a new factor intervened. A suspicion had been growing in Karajan's mind that Stresemann was working behind the scenes to groom Daniel Barenboim for the succession. Jucker was aware of Karajan's disquiet and had warned Stresemann to keep his distance. But it was to no avail. The volcano continued to rumble and an eruption duly occurred.

As Stresemann fondly contemplated a twentieth season in the job, it was announced that a new General Manager had been found. He was the 36-year-old Peter Girth, and he would be taking up his duties on 1 September 1978. The suggestion had come via Emil Maas, leader of the second violins since 1961, and one of the orchestra's two-man management committee. Karajan had approved the nomination (though his approval had no legal significance) and had agreed to interview Girth.

Brilliantly gifted in a number of disciplines, Girth had trained as a cellist. In 1965 at the age of twenty-three, he had suddenly and unaccountably switched to law. His friends were flabbergasted. Was he seriously contemplating giving up a potentially lucrative career as a cellist in order to go back to school? Desperate for some kind of alibi, Girth joked that he was not giving up music; once he had made it as a lawyer, he would go back to music: as General Manager of the Berlin Philharmonic. He did not seriously believe this, nor did any of his friends – until they opened their newspapers one day in 1978 and saw that his prophecy had indeed come to pass. A friend telephoned him: 'Well, it's nice to know, Peter, that there are one or two people left who can make their childhood dreams come true!'

In fact, Girth did not really want the job. A leading expert on copyright law, he was now working as the manager and legal representative of the Association of German Orchestras, the orchestral trade union. Going from that to the position of General Manager of the Berlin Philharmonic would be a case of poacher turning gamekeeper. Girth also had other ambitions. Writing, broadcasting, and the wider field of arts administration were all in his sights in 1978.[26]

But Karajan would not take no for an answer. The interview itself was bizarre. Since Karajan clearly knew in advance everything he needed to know, he was merely concerned to flatter Girth and cajole him: 'Dr Girth, please turn your head towards the window. You know, it is quite uncanny, the resemblance between your face and Gustav Mahler's.'[27]

The politicians were delighted with the appointment but the orchestra was less certain. Girth was clever, but was he wise? Would he be shrewd enough to see that in order to be even-handed, he needed, in some measure, to be on the orchestra's side *against* Karajan? And would he start *doing* things, taking initiatives, rather than simply holding the fort and running the orchestra on a month-to-month basis as Stresemann had done?

*

What would be a troubled time in office got off to a troubled start. Girth had been in the job just three weeks when Karajan had a stroke.

No one, apart from Karajan's doctors and members of his innermost circle, knew that it was a stroke, though several days previously Michel Glotz had sensed that all was not well with him, either mentally or physically. EMI had been recording *Don Carlos* in Berlin. As the sessions drew towards their close Glotz had noticed that Karajan appeared to be quite abnormally nervous and irritable. This bothered him, but the work progressed and was finished on schedule. It was only after Glotz had flown out of Berlin that he heard about Karajan's 'fall'. He suspected it was more than just a fall, and blamed himself for not summoning Dr Simon earlier.

What appeared to happen was simple enough. Karajan lost his balance during a rehearsal. He was working with the orchestra on Strauss's *Sinfonia Domestica* and, not for the first time, let go of the baton. Perched casually on his high rehearsal seat, he tried to catch it, toppled over, fell heavily, and was unable to get up. The double-bass player Rainer Zepperitz helped him to his feet and out of the hall. An ambulance took Karajan to the Urban Hospital in Berlin. whence he was airlifted to a private clinic in Munich. From there he travelled to Zürich for a period of recuperation in a private sanatorium.

Girth went to see him in hospital in Munich to arrange cover for his concerts. When he arrived, Karajan was inert and ashen-faced. He looked as though he was at death's door. Girth assured him that the manager of the Berlin Festival had everything under control; Daniel Barenboim had agreed to take over some of Karajan's concerts.

'Barenboim!' croaked Karajan, stirring suddenly into life. He did not actually take up his bed and walk, but it was clear to Girth that the word had effected a miraculous change in his boss's state of health.

Within two months, Karajan was back conducting.[28] On New Year's Eve, he even went so far as to shake his fist at Fate by adding Verdi's overture *La forza del destino* to the programme.

Audiences noticed that he now had a slight limp; further damage to the already damaged spine, it was assumed. But there was a slightly different look about the eyes and anyone who dined regularly with Karajan would have noticed that he now lifted his wine-glass with his left hand.

CHAPTER 70

Phoenix

> He was like the Phoenix, always coming back
> in better and better shape.
>
> Michel Glotz

As Karajan recuperated in Switzerland, he pondered his next great task, the recording of Debussy's *Pelléas et Mélisande* he was scheduled to make for EMI in Berlin. This would be no ordinary recording but another of Karajan's trysts with what he saw as his musical destiny.

Had his feelings about the work altered since he conducted the great Vienna production of 1962? Almost certainly. His own brushes with death must have intensified his sense of Maeterlinck's death-haunted libretto. 'One greatly needs beauty when death is so close,' sings the old king at one point.

A fine cast had been assembled, not of native French artists but of mainly first-rate French speakers over whom that most expert of coaches Janine Reiss tirelessly presided. 'Janine, this is *your* recording,' said Karajan at the end of a long and exhausting run of sessions. It wasn't, but everyone knew what he meant.

Though the orchestra had been rehearsed ahead of Karajan's arrival by Serge Baudo (a fine *Pelléas* conductor in his own right) and though Stilwell, von Stade and van Dam knew their roles intimately, Karajan spent an inordinate amount of time on the recording. Peter Andry eventually telephoned Peter Alward from London to tell him enough was enough; the recording must be brought to a conclusion with immediate effect. Karajan was with Alward when the call came. He took the receiver.

'Hallo, Peter. Is there a problem?'

'Not at all, maestro,' Andry replied. 'I was just asking how everything was.'[1]

There was no keener observer of what was really going on than the Mélisande, Frederica von Stade.

In a recording session, you tend to think 'It's not me' and start looking at your next passage. But what Karajan was doing was so fascinating, I thought 'If you don't pay attention to this you're a complete fool.' I only had the vocal score, so I couldn't see everything Karajan was trying to do but it was easy to get the gist of it. In the control room they were going berserk. The session was almost over and we hadn't recorded a note. It was the love scene in Act 4. After Pelléas's 'Je t'aime' and Mélisande's reply 'Je t'aime aussi', Pelléas has the line

'*On a brisé la glace avec des fers rougis!* [The ice has been broken with red-hot irons!]' and there is an amazing sound high in the violins. Well, the strings just couldn't get the right sound, and Karajan went over it again and again: the sound, the rhythm, everything. And then the strings got exactly what he wanted and it was just extraordinary – like seeing your child take his first step without falling over. Karajan had been all concentration. All the normal things you associate with recording – time, money, the worries you have – had simply vanished. The music was so important to him, the real world seemed to fall away. I guess I may have exaggerated this feeling over the years but I know that I saw and heard something utterly extraordinary.[2]

Like a lot of people who came into contact with Karajan, von Stade felt that she never really fathomed him. That he was some kind of genius, she had no doubt. Some are irked by the demands genius makes; she was fascinated and amused – 'all those nice little nastinesses', as she put it. (Böhm, she told me, was just as terrifying and just as funny. He once came into the room, muttered 'Von Stade, von Karajan . . . von Böhm' and walked out again.[3])

Karajan's approach to *Pelléas et Mélisande* was very different from that of those who see it as a score to be X-rayed and coolly dissected. In his book on the composer, Edward Lockspeiser writes of Debussy's orchestration and the subtlety of its relationship to the words of Maeterlinck's text:

Throughout, the orchestration is a model of delicacy, transparency and discretion, and it is such that if the singers enunciate clearly not a word is missed. *Like a mirage of the drama* [my emphasis], it rises behind their lines, giving perspective to the words of the moment.[4]

That is the Debussy Karajan knew and realised. One thinks of the end of Act 3 as the child Yniold pleads with Golaud to be lowered from the window where he is spying on Pelléas and Mélisande. Or the extraordinary sense of liberation as the sound world of the castle vaults gives way to the scene on the terrace: 'It is midday,' sings Pelléas, 'I can hear the clocks chiming and the children are going down to the beach to swim.' One of Eliette von Karajan's most enduring memories of her husband was of the moment shortly after midday during holidays in St Tropez when Karajan would appear at the window of his study-bedroom overlooking the garden and the bay beyond. 'If the breeze was stirring and an afternoon's sailing was in prospect, you could see it in his eyes, which looked even more intensely blue than usual.'[5]

There are those who think of *Pelléas et Mélisande* as a remote and unwordly opera, lacking dramatic thrust. But Karajan always paced it superbly, the text payed out on rhythms that neither hurried nor flagged; the climaxes, which in this opera arrive at every dynamic level from *ff* to *pp*, timed and driven home with the instincts of a true man of the theatre.

There can be little doubt that Karajan was fascinated by Golaud's character. José van Dam was his Golaud.[6] He would later explain:

At heart Golaud is a good man but primitive, and he can't master his primitiveness. So when he realises there is something between Pelléas and Mélisande, he follows his instincts, without really questioning or reasoning ... He's the only one in the whole opera who works. He's the man responsible for the castle, and that makes him a bit mixed up. He's not as strong as we think, or as he thinks. It comes to a point where it's all too much for him.[7]

Some years after Karajan's death, I talked with his former record producer Günther Breest about some of the grimmer events of Karajan's last years, in particular the long-running dispute with the Berlin Philharmonic in the 1980s. The portrait Breest painted had its Golaud-like aspects:

Karajan could not cope with betrayal. What went wrong is a complex matter but the tragedy for Karajan was that inability to come to terms with the fact that he had, in some sense, been betrayed. He was a man of very deep emotion and I think there was always a problem of controlling these emotions within a personality that was shy, often rather sentimental, and more than a little paranoid. On the job, he was great. A great musician, a perfectionist, immensely hard-working. But when things went wrong outside the music-making, it could be terrible.[8]

When the EMI recording was released it was widely acclaimed, not least in France, and by leading Francophones elsewhere.[9]

*

Still in a state of heightened sensibility after the *Pelléas* sessions, Karajan and the Berliners went on to record Tchaikovsky's three early symphonies, the performance of the First Symphony *Winter Dreams* achingly intense but also remarkably spruce and light on its feet.[10]

Meanwhile, rather more rational discussions about the orchestra's future were taking place. In an interview in *Der Spiegel* Karajan conceded that plans were being drawn up to give possible successors a chance to work with the Berlin Philharmonic for longer periods of time.[11] Three conductors were mentioned by Karajan: Mehta, Ozawa, and Tennstedt.

Of these it was Karajan's newest acquaintance, Klaus Tennstedt, who most interested him.[12] He had been fascinated by Tennstedt's 1978 recording of Mahler's First Symphony with the London Philharmonic Orchestra and had asked to meet him, an invitation which so thrilled and alarmed Tennstedt he was half drunk when he arrived. This did not bother Karajan. The two men got on famously and Tennstedt was immediately invited to record with the Berlin Philharmonic.[13]

In March 1979, Walter Legge died, only a fortnight after Schwarzkopf's farewell recital in London and three days after the one in Zürich where – to Walter's dismay – she hoped to settle after her retirement. The serious heart trouble that had flared up in 1967 at the time of Gerald Moore's farewell recital had finally caught up with him, exacerbated by the strains and tensions involved in trying to devise yet another perfect farewell.

Karajan was one of the first people Schwarzkopf telephoned. It upset him a good deal, understandably so.[14] He had never lost touch with his old mentor.[15] Perhaps, after 1964, Legge had hoped for something more from Karajan than continuing friendship and occasional spells of jury service on conducting competitions in Berlin. But that is not the way the world works. The first of the Salzburg Whitsun Festival concerts ended with a devastating performance of Beethoven's Seventh Symphony. Afterwards, Karajan told Schwarzkopf, 'I played it for Walter.'

Karajan, too, was far from well. After a concert of music by Bach and Bruckner, he rounded off the short Whitsun festival with Debussy's *La mer* and *L'après-midi d'un faune* and *Boléro*, a programme he had recently filmed in Berlin.[16] The following day he travelled to the abbey church at St Florian for a live television performance of Bruckner's Eighth Symphony with the Vienna Philharmonic.[17] Peter Alward remembers tracking him down to a local inn where he was resting before the concert. He was lying flat on his back, evidently in severe pain.

Throughout the summer, preparations were in hand for a new production of *Aida* at the 1979 Salzburg Festival. 'The shortcomings of this opera,' I remember Karajan joking, 'are the processions, when people come in with two left feet.'[18] That is one way of putting it; another is that the opera is exceptionally difficult to stage in a way that is effective both scenically and dramatically. Now, however, Karajan and Schneider-Siemssen brought off something that, even by their standards, was extraordinary. Using the entire width, depth, and height of the Salzburg stage, including the side aprons, they created images of the temples and palaces, the public and private places of Ancient Egypt which were as solid as they were beautiful.

And yet, as Charles Osborne would observe in *Opera*, the production was not merely grand. It was intimate, too, in all manner of revealing ways:

The consecration scene in the temple was extraordinary in that it looked both vast *and* claustrophobic. The triumphal scene had a central doorway of immense height, through which the processions advanced, flanked by two huge pyramids on which stood the chorus . . . The Nile scene captured the vastness of the desert vista of sand and sky, with the river flowing by in one of Schneider-Siemssen's most poetic stage pictures of the evening. When Aida turned upstage to gaze out over it towards the south and Ethiopia, at 'O patria mia', the effect was extremely moving. The other piece of sheer poetry came at the end of the opera, which I have never seen more effectively or more beautifully staged, with the lovers' tomb slowly sinking while they sing their *Liebestod*, 'O terra, addio'.[19]

There was much telling musical detail, things many conductors do not bother with. Critic Kenneth Loveland thrilled to the moment near the start of the opera when a messenger enters bringing tidings of war:

It was only two or three bars, but you suddenly felt the blood of battle and the heat of the desert. For me, that showed what a great conductor Karajan is, far more than any of the bigger things.[20]

There were disagreements about Karajan's casting, both in the theatre, and for the recording which EMI had made in the Musikvereinssaal in Vienna the previous May. '*Aida* cast like *La bohème*' was one judgement, a reference to Karajan's decision to cast Freni in the title role and Carreras as Radames.[21] It is true, neither singer is a match for Tebaldi or Bergonzi on Karajan's famous old Decca recording, nor, for all the added tautness and ferocity of Karajan's conducting, is the later recording better played or more imaginatively staged.

The only real misadventure, however, was the casting of Marilyn Horne as Amneris for the Salzburg stage performances. It was not the ideal role for her, but she reckoned any singer worth her salt ought to get to sing with Karajan at some point in her career; what's more, with Freni and Carreras in the cast, it looked as if it was going to be a lyrical, intimate *Aida*. What she had not reckoned with was the size of the Salzburg stage and Karajan's rehearsal method, which was to work with tapes from his EMI recording. Since she had not sung on the recording, her introduction to working with Karajan – live, on stage – was the dress rehearsal. By that time she also had a cold. It was a disaster. When the going got tough, Karajan simply turned up the volume and drowned her out.

Horne chalked it up to experience.

'Salzburg's a tough place. I guess it's easier to enjoy yourself here when you're a success.' She laughed. 'How's that for dipomacy?'[22]

Karajan never pretended to be Mr Nice Guy, but on occasions like this the dark side of his personality and experience showed through: the shy, frustrated, highly-strung child making common cause with the hardened professional.

Karajan played *Aida* more or less continuously. A single interval between Acts 2 and 3 was all he allowed. And that, on one occasion, he spent listening to unaccompanied Bach.

Though he was now recording violin repertory with Anne-Sophie Mutter, Karajan had long admired the playing of Itzhak Perlman. Contacts had been made through EMI, something that had faced the Israeli-born Perlman with a dilemma: should he make music with a former member of the Nazi Party? Suvi Raj Grubb, Perlman's producer at EMI, was aware of the problems; also that Perlman had eventually said no.

A year or so after the refusal had been given, Grubb attended a Perlman Bach recital in Salzburg's Kleines Festspielhaus. For some reason, he felt impelled to turn round during the playing of the D minor Partita. There, at the back of the hall, head and arms bowed over a rail, was Karajan. But wasn't he meant to be conducting *Aida* that evening, thought Grubb? So he was. It was simply that he had chosen to spend the interval listening to Perlman playing Bach.[23]

*

One of Karajan's stranger commitments in 1979 had been to conduct the Berlin Philharmonic at the opening ceremony on 2 April of West Berlin's newest show-piece, the monstrous twin-auditorium 5000-seat International Congress Centre. Only at the last minute, the press claimed, had the city fathers discovered that the Berlin Philharmonic was due to be rehearsing in Salzburg on the day of the opening ceremony. As a precaution, Böhm and the Vienna Philharmonic had been booked to appear the following day, an arrangement, it was now being said, that had been sufficient to provoke Karajan and the orchestra into making a flying return visit to Berlin.[24]

This was balderdash, certainly as far as Karajan was concerned. Months previously, he had contacted organist David Bell. He and the orchestra, he told Bell, would be flying back from Salzburg to play the *Festliches Praeludium* for Organ and Orchestra by Richard Strauss – all twelve minutes of it – at the start of the opening ceremony. Did Bell know of an organ that would be big enough for the hall and the piece?

The only organ Bell could think of was an Allen electronic organ currently parked in London's Alexandra Palace. It had been built as a touring instrument for Carlo Curley and partly paid for by the widow of the founder of the Coca-Cola Corporation. It had 4 manuals, 162 stops, and over 200 loudspeakers housed in 80 cabinets. 'Just the job,' said Karajan, his eyes lighting up in anticipation. 'Let's hire that.' It was duly hired.[25]

*

In the autumn of 1979, Karajan got caught up in one of Girth's bright new ideas: an evening of music-making in the Philharmonie in honour of West Germany's music-loving Chancellor Helmut Schmidt. It was Schmidt's first encounter with Karajan (he would later stay with the Karajans in St Tropez and do a little gentle sailing with the maestro) and he had suggested that the evening might be lightened up with some Gershwin. Karajan was not keen, but agreed to do the *Rhapsody in Blue* with Alexis Weissenberg as soloist. It was not a success. Karajan could conduct most music half decently, but he was at a loss with Gershwin.

The following month, the Berlin Philharmonic flew to the Far East for nine concerts in Tokyo, followed by three in Peking. For all but one member of the orchestra – violinist Hellmut Stern, who had spent the war years in China and who helped mastermind the tour – the Peking visit was an historic first. It was not, however, without its problems. A number of players were injured leaving their aircraft when a mobile stairway collapsed. Those most seriously hurt players were flown back to Germany, accompanied by Karajan's own doctor.

If the Chinese authorities were minded to see this as a snub to their medical facilities, Karajan provided the perfect diplomatic redress by requesting to sit in on a number of consultations and treatments where non-Western methods of medicine were being pursued. These were not wholly disinterested visits. Now suffering from continual bouts of severe back pain, Karajan was in search of analgesic treatments that were not drug-dependent as those in the West invariably are.[26]

What he also wanted – even more than pain relief – was permission from the Chinese Government to film Puccini's *Turandot* in the Forbidden City.[27] The Chinese did not say no, but later they backed out: or, rather, switched horses. The Forbidden City *was* made available to a Western film company, but not to Karajan's. Bertolucci's *The Last Emperor* proved to be the greater lure.

CHAPTER 71

Carpe diem

But at my back I always hear
Time's wingèd chariot hurrying near
Andrew Marvell, 'To his Coy Mistress'

'He takes advice only from Akio Morita,' complained a frustrated record executive in January 1980. To which Karajan might have retorted, there never came ill of good advisement. He was wise enough to take advice, and shrewd enough to know where it might best be found.

What Morita had been advising him was that a revolution was imminent: a way of recording and reproducing music by digital rather than analogue technology, which would eliminate the degradation of the sound image both at source and during playback in the listener's home. By 1979, equipment for recording digitally was already in production. What was taking rather longer to develop in commercially viable form was the revolutionary new carrier: the laser-read compact disc and its player. If this was accepted by the record-buying public, it would bring about the biggest change in the industry's affairs since the introduction of the LP in 1950.

Karajan was convinced by what he heard. From now on, he announced, all his recordings would be made digitally. In saying this, was he putting a gun to the head of the record companies? Deutsche Grammophon needed no persuading; the digital initiative was a joint venture between Sony and Deutsche Grammophon's sister company Philips. EMI was already developing its own digital recording system, though top executives were sceptical about compact disc – this, only months before the (admittedly premature) demonstration of the new disc by Morita and Karajan at the 1981 Salzburg Easter Festival.[1]

EMI was having other problems, too. The contracts the company had made with Karajan in the 1970s were showing a healthy profit but, not for the first time, asking prices were beginning to soar. In 1979, plans to record *Tosca* with Karajan were abandoned when costs started spiralling out of control. The project was immediately snapped up by Deutsche Grammophon's Günther Breest, a brilliant young producer whose flair for executive wheeler-dealing was already turning him into one of the record business's most formidable gatherers of exclusive talent. He was cock-a-hoop, but would later recall:

When EMI withdrew, I rushed in. The entire contract had to be renegotiated.

The fees the singers were asking – some of them Glotz's own artists – were ferociously high. But I pulled it off. I was the hero of the hour. Or, at least, I thought I was. I soon learned that the world I was operating in was an extremely dangerous one.[2]

As hero of the hour, Breest was invited to Karajan's home outside Vienna where he was rehearsing his new Scarpia, Ruggero Raimondi. It was a startling experience, recalls Breest, watching Karajan play Scarpia in his own drawing-room.

Raimondi had just finished working with director Joseph Losey on *Don Giovanni*, a film that Karajan would later love to hate. When the records of *Tosca* were released, Peter Conrad noted:

There are fascinating connections with Raimondi's Don Giovanni in the Losey film: this Scarpia, like Raimondi's Giovanni, is a suave brute, as elegant as he is violent, liable to switch in an instant from an undertone of sexy innuendo to the blaring might of his full voice.[3]

It was a distinctly different Scarpia from Giuseppe Taddei's on Karajan's 1962 recording. Did Karajan have anyone particular in mind? Heinrich Glasmeier, perhaps, living in decadent splendour in St Florian in 1944? Or was it a conflation of several characters from that time? Theatrically, the new *Tosca* was sumptuous and terrifying, every nuance of the drama tellingly painted on the orchestra.

Tosca was an analogue recording. Karajan completed his first digital recording in Berlin in the spring of 1980. The work was Mozart's *Die Zauberflöte* and it emerged, not fat and scant of breath as the Decca *Figaro* had been, but lean and airy. William Mann wrote in *The Times*:

The tempi are perfectly steady, seldom rushed; rhythm and pulse, the dance, are brought out as the essence of this music, together with legato singing, superbly exemplified in José van Dam's honeyed yet firm accounts of Sarastro's arias.[4]

Van Dam apart, it was not a set to delight connoisseurs of fine singing as Karajan's 1950 Vienna recording had been. It was a mainly young cast, consciously short on big names. There was nothing surprising about this. Karajan often used young singers in leading roles. What was unusual was the degree to which freshness of response appeared to be given priority over cultured sound and polished phrasing.

This cleaner, clearer, more urgent style of music-making had been a feature of Karajan's work since the crisis of the winter of 1975–6. Yet, welcome as this was, it came at a price. If Karajan's performances were suddenly leaner, fitter, and more intense, so was his way of recording, despite the fact that, in many people's judgement, the time he allowed in sessions had already been pared to the bone. Jeffrey Tate, who was principal répétiteur for *Die Zauberflöte*, would recall:

The Three Ladies actually met *at* the session. They and I rapidly ran through their music in a separate room while he was doing the first part of a session. And then they were taken into the hall where both Quintets were recorded, without any retakes, in the second half of the session. It was utterly terrifying![5]

Perhaps Karajan wanted it to be terrifying. Urging the Three Ladies to convey even more powerfully the sense of their being in the presence of a powerful demon, he called out, 'Think of me!'

There are, however, errors and untidinesses in this *Zauberflöte*, not to mention moments of unpleasing vocal rawness that take the edge off one's pleasure in an otherwise distinguished performance.[6] The freshness and spontaneity pleased the critics (or most of them), but what was the point of that if, on repeated hearings, numerous small failings began to irk the loyal collector? With Karajan it had usually been the other way round: flawless recordings, indifferently received, slowly acquiring classic status.

*

There was a more pressing reason for Karajan's haste in the studio. He clearly sensed that time was no longer on his side. His old motto, 'I have time, I can wait', had ceased to apply. As *Salome*, *Pelléas et Mélisande* and *Parsifal* indicated, he was still involved in making first-time recordings of some of his core repertory. At the same time, he continued to take on new material – symphonies by Haydn, Mahler and Nielsen – astonishing for a man of seventy-two.[7] (There was even talk of his recording Berlioz's *Harold in Italy* and Dvořák's Seventh Symphony, further Shostakovich, and more English music.[8])

His productivity in the years 1979–82 was astonishing. Though the results were mixed, there were few out-and-out failures.[9] (Most problematic were concerto recordings where there were some famous tussles.[10]) The intensity of the music-making, coupled with the inflexibility of the studio routines, had about them more than a hint of the style of the elderly Toscanini. Like Toscanini, Karajan seemed to be more and more obsessed with music-making that was down-to-earth, direct, and (problematic concept) 'as the composer intended it to be'.

Robert Layton has recalled visiting Berlin in the winter of 1980–1. Karajan was recording Sibelius's First Symphony, a work he had conducted on only one previous occasion, in Aachen in March 1939. The Scherzo was being recorded:

There had been no want of virtuosity on the part of the Berlin Philharmonic, nor was there any lack of fire or excitement in the insistent pounding of the lower strings. But, as [Karajan] rightly said, it was not up to speed – it did not represent the *truth*! A second take produced much more headlong, wilder playing even at a loss of some of the superbly controlled momentum of the earlier take. I was almost reminded of Beecham's pre-war *Lemminkäinen's Homeward Journey*, composed only three years earlier, such was the excitement generated.[11]

When Karajan heard the playback, he remarked that Sibelius's metronome was, perhaps, a fraction too fast.

Yet the very act of striving after the letter of the truth enabled him to capture the spirit. The recording team had been more than happy with the first take, as indeed they might well be for it was undeniably impressive, but the very pursuit of Sibelius's metronome marking, impossible though it really is, ensured the right character.[12]

What some might perceive to be 'the right character' proved to be rather more problematic in the case of Nielsen's Fourth Symphony which Karajan recorded in February 1981. This, too, was an intensely compelling performance, much lauded in the press, though not in Denmark where the playing – the wind playing, in particular – was thought to be insufficiently earthy. 'Like a peasant dressed in his Sunday best,' as one Danish listener put it.[13] Interpretative niceties apart (and few twentieth century symphonies are more littered with potential pitfalls than this[14]), the power of the performance derives almost exclusively from Karajan's own fierce response to a work which the composer himself described as embodying 'what music alone is capable of expressing to the full: the elementary will to live'.

When the recording was released, the cry went up, 'More Nielsen, please.' Of this there was no prospect. Karajan had chosen to record the Fourth precisely because it dramatised that 'elementary will to live' and because it touched on another of his most powerful private preoccupations, the First World War and its fearful legacy. Nielsen wrote the symphony in 1914–16. 'National feeling,' he wrote at the time, 'which up to now has been taken as something high and beautiful, has become a kind of spiritual syphilis, which has eaten up the brain and grins out through the empty eye sockets in crazed hate.'[15]

Nor was it a coincidence that Karajan chose to tie in the Nielsen sessions with re-recordings of works that share its world: Holst's *The Planets* and Shostakovich's Tenth Symphony, *The Planets* now bleaker and, in the war music, even more devastating than in his 1961 Vienna version.

There was other fare, too, Karajan lightening the war-stricken mood with Strauss waltzes and an intriguing disc that looked back – wryly, nostalgically – to a more gracious-seeming age. Grieg's *Holberg* Suite and Prokofiev's *Classical* Symphony were the principal works, the playing stylish and urbane, to which was added a wonderfully crisp and playful account of Mozart's *Eine kleine Nachtmusik*, the alternation of legato–staccato accentuation – the very thing Karajan's performances were often said to smooth over – a model of its kind.

The ability to command rehearsals and order studio time in a way that made such juxtapositions possible was, as Michael Tilson Thomas has remarked, a particular feature of Karajan's career, the badge of his commercial success. It is not something that will readily be repeated.

*

Towering over this profusion of new and reconsidered recordings were two that were self-evidently special. In November 1979, Karajan made his first (studio) recording of Mahler's Ninth Symphony. The following month he began work on his long-awaited recording of *Parsifal*.

Again, the two projects were not unrelated. The *Parsifal* sound-world – 'its play of light and shade, its sense of floating weightlessness, its substance constantly on the point of dissolution into atmosphere, its enveloping mystical energy'[16] – is also, in part, Mahler's sound-world in the Ninth Symphony. And just as *Parsifal* mixes specifically Christian elements with Schopenhauer-inspired, quasi-Buddhist ideas about the renunciation of the will and the purification of the soul through suffering, so Mahler's Ninth Symphony, with its fires and purgatorial chills, its lyricism and pantheistic longing, is similarly inspired.

Mahler was a Catholic convert; Karajan was a 'believing Catholic' (Stresemann's phrase) though a non-practising one, save through the medium of music. A conductor's religious beliefs are of little importance unless, as here, some current of feeling feeds the very texture of the music-making. The Bohemian-born critic Ferdinand Pfohl once asked:

Did Mahler really believe, in the deepest religious sense? I would have to say he did. Heaven, God's realm, was more to him than a beautiful dream. It was an essential need. The scepticism and pain that gnawed at him and gave him no rest are drowned in that need. Music, above all his own music, was simultaneously a narcotic, a trance, and an act of asceticism.[17]

The idea of music as a spiritual salve – as 'a narcotic, a trance, an act of asceticism' – was not foreign to Karajan either. Finding Mahler's Ninth Symphony lying by the wayside as he neared his journey's end must have been an extraordinary thing.

While the Mahler was being recorded, *Parsifal* was being rehearsed for the Salzburg Easter Festival. Karajan had conducted the opera in Aachen

647

in 1940, and again, in his own staging, in Vienna in 1961. This third and final production was an entirely predictable affair inasmuch as it was conventionally directed, occasionally rather too quietly sung for the size of the theatre, and memorably designed and lit. The reviews were mostly hostile. Salzburg regular Peter Cossé spoke of 'the work's descent into a visual panorama with few conflicts, a consecrating play with dancing'.[18] Others wrote in a similar vein.

Why was Karajan so reluctant to make fresh play with character and characterisation? One reason was his pathological fear that new 'readings' of the story would subvert the music. In this respect, *Parsifal* was particularly dangerous territory. By 1980, it had become a battlefield for Wagnerians and anti-Wagnerians of just about every religious and political persuasion.

On record, none of this matters. Nor does extreme intimacy of response. A singer may whisper Gurnemanz's awed utterance of the Grail's message '*Durch Mitleid wissend/der reine Tor*' and still be heard. Which partly explains why a production which was so execrated in the theatre was widely, even lavishly, praised when it appeared on record. 'Never in my experience,' wrote one old Wagner hand, 'has the score seared and glowed with so much anguish, poetry, beauty.'[19]

There was another thing, too. The introduction of the new technology had slowed down the planning and scheduling of the recording. As a result, it was not completed until *after* the run of stage performances at the 1980 Easter Festival. This clearly helped a number of members of the cast; in particular, the Parsifal, Peter Hofmann, and the Croatian-born Dunja Vejzovic, the fascinatingly feral Kundry with whom Karajan had already been working for well over a year. Kurt Moll – a towering Gurnemanz and one of the set's principal glories – may have benefited as well, though Karajan's shaping of Gurnemanz's music, and Amfortas's, tended to be theatrical rather as Bach's *St Matthew Passion* is theatrical.

The spatial perspectives which were so impressive a part of Schneider-Siemssen's stage designs were mirrored in the Deutsche Grammophon recording which was not only digital but multi-track. (A 32-track digital machine was specially leased from 3M in Minnesota.) When a computer expert from Linz, Hubert Bognermayr, told Karajan he knew how to produce electronically a perfect sound replica of the bells specified by Wagner in the score, he too was signed up. Yet, as David Murray would observe in the *Financial Times*:

... the technology has *not* supplanted practical imagination and sensitive ears. Karajan and his engineers have produced a *Parsifal* with vistas of breathtaking depth, miraculously detailed, subtly distanced ... Both the apparitions of the Grail are hypnotically staged for the ear; the new precision of the sound reproduction makes possible a quite hallucinatory range of distance and focus.[20]

As a performance, it was not, of course, the last word on *Parsifal*. William Mann wrote in *Gramophone*:

Solti, a greyhound to Karajan's Siamese, chases the innards of the music to expose them, takes risks, but has the spirit of the score always in his blood, where Karajan perhaps looks for its transcendental spirit. Whether either of them is a practising Christian means nothing; who understands the whole contents of *Parsifal*, and projects it all?[21]

Karajan's recordings of *Parsifal* and Mahler's Ninth won a number of top awards,[22] something of a novelty for a conductor who had rather come to value the distinction of being systematically ignored by awards conventions in Britain, the United States, and Germany.[23]

CHAPTER 72

Pleasant diversions

> The ceiling [of the Sheldonian Theatre] is painted with allegorical figures. The galleries are ornamented with carving enriched with gold. It was filled to excess. We were most WARMLY and ENTHUSIASTICALLY received.
>
> Princess Victoria, diary entry, 8 November 1832

Karajan's health continued to be a cause for concern. In January 1980, coming on stage in Berlin to conduct Berg's *Lyric Suite*, he stumbled and fell. There was a loud gasp from the audience. Nor would things be any easier until after further risky spinal surgery in June 1983. As Karajan later confided, 'Every step I have taken these last four years has been an adventure, planned and executed.'[1]

On 5 April 1980 he celebrated both his own seventy-second birthday and the silver jubilee of his appointment as Chief Conductor of the Berlin Philharmonic. Since the orchestra was in Salzburg, there were no civic formalities, no speeches. Beethoven's Violin Concerto, with Anne-Sophie Mutter as soloist, was followed by Tchaikovsky's Fourth Symphony, and that was that.

Parsifal and the Easter Festival over, Karajan flew to the French Alpine resort of Courchevel for a spell of work with the European Community Youth Orchestra, which Joy Bryer had now successfully established. The European Commission had ratified the setting-up of the orchestra in 1976, with Edward Heath as its President and Claudio Abbado as its Music Director. After a successful début tour in 1978, it had been invited by Karajan to play at the 1979 Salzburg Festival.[2] Now he had invited it again, this time to give a concert under his own direction.

He flew in for the preparatory sessions in Courchevel entirely alone; there were no minders, no advisers, no hangers-on. True, he had rung up the mayor of Courchevel to ask if the local airport runway could be extended to take his jet. But that was the only Karajanism. (The answer was no, and he hired something smaller.) Once there, he had his own room on the campus, took all his meals with the students, held a number of informal seminars, and went walking with Joy Bryer despite the fact (she could not help noticing) that walking was no longer exactly easy.

Edward Heath was there, as was Anne-Sophie Mutter, and one of Karajan's concertmasters from Berlin, Thomas Brandis. Brandis had briefed the students beforehand. His advice was simple: 'Don't chatter in rehearsal, listen carefully; this is a man who talks quietly and doesn't always finish sentences. The good thing is: he speaks most of your languages fluently.' Brandis concluded: 'When you meet him, you'll find he's very simple and straightforward. He's not much different from anyone else – except that he happens to be rather a good conductor.'

At the first rehearsal, Karajan said who he was (simple good manners, though his ingrained shyness meant that he never *expected* anyone to know who he was), complimented the orchestra on its wonderful Salzburg concert under Abbado, and began work. It was not all sweetness and light. There was hostility to him from a small contingent of Dutch students, though such coolness as there was vanished fairly quickly.

Most of the serious work was done in Courchevel. In Salzburg in August Karajan was back to being Karajan with a capital K. Access was impeded, his time severely rationed. There was more rehearsal, but it was less detailed than before. When it came to the concert, he did at least keep his eyes open; but the restraint of his conducting in something like the slow movement of the *Jupiter* Symphony baffled one or two of the youngsters who were clearly used to a more involved and interventionist style of direction.

It was, none the less, something of a red-letter day in the orchestra's affairs. Of all the big-name conductors who worked with the ECYO in the 1980s none, says Joy Bryer, brought more conviction to the task than Karajan or communicated a greater practical concern for the future: how and where these young musicians would find work, and in what conditions.[3] And all this without a penny being asked by way of remuneration. Karajan paid his bills in Courchevel and conducted without a fee in Salzburg.

He could afford it, of course; but, then, so could various other maestri with whom the ECYO longed to work but who could be engaged only when the coffers were full enough to meet their financial 'requirements'.[4]

*

The Berlin civic authorities had not forgotten about the long-postponed twenty-fifth anniversary jamboree. It was eventually held as part of the New Year's Eve celebrations in December 1980. The Mayor of Berlin, Dietrich Stobbe, made a fulsome speech in Karajan's honour and presented him with a portrait of Richard Strauss by Max Liebermann. Karajan began his reply with a disquisition on time:

There is a passage in *Der Rosenkavalier* which runs: 'Time is a strange thing.' And in many cases it can't be measured, it's something you have to feel. Or it simply doesn't exist.[5]

This was typical Karajan, plunging excitedly into an issue of profound concern to himself and his music-making – *khronos* versus *kairos*, clock time versus moments in time – before an audience that was presumably expecting only back-slapping and balloons. He went on:

Twenty-five years is a long time, but it's suddenly become compressed in my imagination to a single second. I've never had the ability to look backwards. I was always at the prow of the ship. And now that it's all behind us – the countless problems, the work, the pleasure in work, the pleasure in contact with the orchestra, and the fact that we've travelled all round the world together – it suddenly shrinks to a single second and all that remains is the awareness that the future is before us.[6]

He thanked the Berlin public, then turned to thank his orchestra. 'Above all, I am grateful . . .' But his voice gave way, choked with emotion. The audience knew what he meant. There was thunderous applause, Karajan recovered his composure, and he continued with as generous and heartfelt a tribute to the Berlin Philharmonic as anyone could have wished to hear:

Something has been acquired here which can happen only over many, many years with the same steady outpouring of – there's only one word for it – love. We've become a family, not merely people responding to a baton, but a family that does all it can to bring about as much good music as possible, through willing self-sacrifice, untiring commitment, and – it goes without saying – human contact.[7]

Talk of 'family' was not, however, something with which certain members of the orchestra necessarily went along. The knives were already out for Girth, and they were being sharpened for Karajan, too.

Karajan had long had opponents in the orchestra, of course; what conductor of worth and seniority does not? But the ringleaders – Thärichen, Stern and others – now had newer, younger potential allies, rising stars of the orchestra like oboist Hansjörg Schellenberger ('a gift from Heaven', Karajan had said) who were eager – some would say culpably over-eager – to secure the future against the day when (in Charles Rodier's elegant phrase) this 'superhuman but none the less mortal septuagenarian'[8] was no more.

The music for the anniversary concert had been chosen to match the Liebermann portrait: an all-Strauss evening given over to two of Karajan's favourite works, the *Four Last Songs* and *Don Quixote*. During the evening there was a great deal of kissing. At the end of the songs, Karajan kissed Tomowa-Sintow's hands and she, possibly without precedent, kissed his. At the end of *Don Quixote*, Rostropovich kissed Karajan on both cheeks and then went round to the Sancho Panza, the Berlin Philharmonic's Wolfram Christ, to do the same to him. Both kissed Rostropovich back. For one wild moment, noted *The Times*'s Berlin correspondent, people began wondering whether, amid this carnival frenzy, Christ would kiss his boss. Alas, he didn't.[9]

As for the Berlin press – Klaus Geitel apart, the orchestra's increasingly loyal ally – it was desperate to know who had drafted Mayor Stobbe's paean of praise to Karajan. No sooner were the bloodhounds loosed, however, than Stobbe was implicated in a financial scandal involving building contracts. By mid-January he had resigned his mayoral office and the search for the speech-writer was called off.

*

Karajan, meanwhile, had not forgotten the promise he had made to conduct a concert in Oxford. Sceptics had judged the promise to be no more than a polite gesture, a trumped-up story to allay disquiet at his having missed the formal luncheon on the day of the degree ceremony in 1978. This was not so. In May 1981, he and the Berliners were due to give two concerts in London before going on to perform Act 3 of *Parsifal* at the Paris Opéra. When London's Royal Festival Hall somewhat reluctantly accepted the first of Karajan's programmes, a concert given over exclusively to Bruckner's Fifth Symphony, but declined to accept the second because it clashed with existing schedules, he lost no time in having the engagement switched to Oxford.

The size of the small, circular Sheldonian Theatre – Sir Christopher Wren's early masterpiece of 1663 – allows for the deployment of only relatively modest orchestral forces. Since Karajan had already been in the theatre, there was no need to spell that out to him; but it was thought useful to provide him with the names of some earlier recipients of Oxford's honorary Doctor of Music. Prominent among these was Joseph Haydn. As Karajan was due to conduct a number of Haydn symphonies at the 1981 Salzburg Whitsun Festival, the Haydn idea seemed particularly timely.

But no: according to David Smith, it was clear that Karajan had already dreamed up his ideal programme; had done so, in all probability, back in 1978 as he sat in the theatre listening to the sound of organ and trumpets, sizing up the building and studying its acoustic. He nominated three works: Bach's *Brandenburg Concerto* No.2, Mozart's G major Violin Concerto, with Anne-Sophie Mutter as soloist, and *Metamorphosen* by Richard Strauss, D. Mus. hon. causa, Oxon. 1914.

The arrangements were simplicity itself. A Karajan adviser queried the use of a locally made Goble harpsichord: would the keys be too slender for Dr von Karajan's fingers? But when Karajan heard of the objection, he brushed it aside. (His days as a serious harpsichordist were long gone. He directed from the keyboard but Phillip Moll was the principal continuo player.) There were also worries about backstage facilities, the poky artists' room and a lavatory that was shared with the general public. Again, Karajan seemed unconcerned.

The concert was memorable above all for a searchingly beautiful account of the slow movement of the Mozart and an unforgettable performance of *Metamorphosen*. 'Here was supreme intensity of feeling,' Bryan Magee would later recall. 'All those strings: it took the top of one's head off.'[10] (None of the studio recordings was ever as intense as this.) Starting with the Second *Brandenburg Concerto* was not, however, a good idea. The solo trumpeter Konradin Groth, so deft and expert on the 1978 studio recording, had a wretched time of it.

The BBC broadcast the concert live on Radio 4, leaving Radio 3 to broadcast a repeat, minus the Bach, in what was one of the corporation's first ever digital recordings. Both Karajan and Mutter played without fee. There was also generous sponsorship from various businesses and Oxford colleges, and from Robert Maxwell's Pergamon Press. Even the BBC chipped in; having offered a derisory by-the-book fee for the broadcast rights, they were eventually persuaded to double it. The proceeds from the concert went to the Neuroscience Research Trust the Karajan Foundation was establishing in Oxford, and to two local charities: the Oxford and Mid Counties Society for Autistic Children and the Oxford Children's Heart Circle.

Next day, Karajan flew on to Paris. The Smiths had ferried him around southern England in the family Volvo, but at the start of the trip back to the airfield the car refused to budge. While David Smith was desperately trying to think what to do next, Karajan, who was sitting in the front passenger seat, reached down with a smile and let off the hand-brake. (This, mind you, from the man who, according to Roger Vaughan, burned his way down the Kehlstein Mountain near Berchtesgaden in his 500 SEL Mercedes sedan with the hand-brake on.[11])

*

The summer of 1981 was actively and happily spent. Though every footfall was 'an adventure in staying upright', Karajan was getting more pleasure than ever from sailing. His new high performance seventy-seven-foot racing sloop *Helisara VI* had been designed for him by top race-boat architect German Frers. It was a formidable competitor in the international maxi boat league, and it looked it, too, with its three distinctive red stripes sweeping along the grey hull. ('The object', said Karajan, 'is to make the boat look even bigger and more fearsome than it already is.')

Since he could not keep top international crews and advisers on permanent stand-by, he hired them as and when needed. And they were the best that a superb boat, money, and a famous name can buy: men such as America's Cup winner Dennis Connor and his strategist Gary Jobson. In July 1981, Karajan spent a great deal of time with Jobson putting *Helisara* through its paces, seeing what it could do, and whether – as Karajan liked to put it – he was 'worthy' of it. This was similar to an imperative that drove his music-making: the desire to master difficulty, to banish the rough edges of process, so as *to render the thing itself* absolutely complete and beautiful.

And there was the competitive streak, too. If Karajan was not vying with himself or Jobson in mastering the latest complex manoeuvre, he would be pursuing some hapless fifty-foot cruiser that was quietly minding its own business off the St Tropez shoreline ('it was like a Ferrari taking on a Ford,' says Roger Vaughan, 'but Karajan got satisfaction from it'[12]) or settling down for the real races, such as the epic day-and-night struggles of the 250-mile Giraglia.

Karajan also took his pleasures that summer in the opera house, re-staging Verdi's *Falstaff* at Salzburg for his own private joy and delectation. There were those who revelled in this as much as they revelled in the recording Karajan had made in Vienna the previous year. Peter Stadlen judged the stage production to be the most 'happy-making' performance he had attended since Toscanini conducted the work in an adjacent hall in 1937.[13] Yet for William Mann it was the reverse: a 'glum, oiled-wheels production'.[14] (It is on film, so one can judge for oneself.[15]) Karajan's reading was as attentive as ever to the myriad joys of Verdi's incomparable score but some of the wit and dazzlement had gone, without the compensation of those freshly garnered autumnal colours which were so marked a feature of Giulini's conducting of the opera at this time.

*

During the festival, Karl Böhm died. Karajan made an emotional and not entirely coherent speech immediately before his concert with the Vienna Philharmonic on 16 August and led the orchestra in a performance of Mozart's *Masonic Funeral Music*, the playing sounding truly grief-stricken.

In due course, various bits of Salzburg came to bear Böhm's name. Alive, he had been greatly exercised by the fact that the cart-track which ran past Karajan's house near Anif was called Herbert v. Karajan-Strasse. Karajan explained that it was a gesture by the parish council, nothing to do with Salzburg. To be officially honoured by the city, he pointed out, you had to be dead. He even offered Böhm part of the cart-track. Nowadays, Böhm has a hall named after him inside the Festspielhaus, while Karajan has the large square outside. That upset one or two people, and one imagines Böhm's shade is none too happy either.

1981 ended in bizarre fashion in Berlin, when the Christmas edition of *Stern* carried what was judged to be an extremely scurrilous feature on the Berlin Philharmonic and its conductors.

Karajan himself had inadvertently started the whole thing by suggesting that the orchestra's work should be chronicled in photographs. As a result, *Stern* photographer Dieter Blum and reporter Emanuel Eckardt had been following the orchestra around Europe and Japan, taking photographs and gossiping with the players. Since Eckardt was mainly interested in newsworthy titbits and punchy one-line put-downs, the members of the world's most famous orchestra emerged from the feature sounding like a bunch of disaffected school kids: Bernstein 'wept buckets', Solti was 'the most overrated conductor of all', Tennstedt was a 'hot-air merchant', Jochum was 'finicky', and Muti 'a tyrant'. As for Karajan, they would do anything he asked, they said, but only because they feared what would happen if they didn't.

Blum's photographs were a different matter: amusing, revealing, brilliantly varied. A shot of the Okura Hotel in Tokyo at night shows half the rooms darkened, the rest lit and uncurtained with a Philharmoniker seen practising by each window. The photograph was dreamed up by Blum after tennis star Björn Borg had called the hotel's night porter with the words, 'Stop that f****** horn player!' A photograph of five violinists and their five violin cases, marching in line and in step across a zebra-crossing in Tokyo, wittily parodies the famous shot of the Beatles on the crossing outside EMI's Abbey Road studios. There is an amusing photograph of a solitary violinist in blue jeans and donkey jacket slipping into the Sheldonian Theatre in Oxford under the baleful gaze of the massive bearded stone busts that somewhat improbably top the rail posts outside.

However, it was the image of Karajan lounging on an old leather bench in a slightly shabby-looking rest-room, Seiji Ozawa crouched at his feet, that was judged to be the true 'sensation'.

It is, in fact, a very funny photograph, as Karajan himself – gazing quizzically towards the camera's lens – seems to acknowledge. The pose is one thing. The room itself is another: a gloomy *chambre séparée* that has seen better days, the old leather bench, on which Karajan is sitting, framed by grand but rather faded red 'stage' curtains. What really puts Blum's portrait in the Cartier-Bresson class, however, is the fact that the real focus of interest is not Karajan or Ozawa but a Marlboro cigarette poster that has been slung over the top of the leather bench like an old-fashioned antimacassar.[16]

The hullabaloo that surrounded the publication of Blum's portfolio suggested that humour, best of solvents, would be at a premium should the going ever get really rough in Berlin Philharmonic affairs. The *Stern* feature did, however, contain a genuine bombshell. Peter Girth was quoted as saying:

The orchestra is a dreadful collective. Many of them don't know how lucky they are to have Karajan. There's poverty, unemployment, and war in the world but this orchestra is blind to all that. They've no sense of proportion. They're remote from the real world. But they know how to count.[17]

There was some truth in what Girth said, but he was the last person on earth who should have said it. Nor was it the best of curtain-raisers to 1982, the orchestra's centenary year.

CHAPTER 73

1982: Anniversary

But now, in the division of the kingdom, it appears not
which of the Dukes he values most.
Shakespeare, *King Lear*

Karajan ushered in the centenary year with a magnificent New Year's Eve
performance of Strauss's *Alpine* Symphony. In January, he conducted
Mahler's Ninth Symphony in Berlin; in February, there was a starrily
cast concert performance of *Tosca*. Deutsche Grammophon used this
latter occasion to launch its special hundredth-anniversary edition of
Berlin Philharmonic recordings. Journalists and record dealers were flown
in from all over Europe, yet another sign that the company was prepared
to pay whatever it was going to cost to keep Karajan within the fold during
the final phase of his career.

Masterminding Deutsche Grammophon's initiative was Günther Breest.
Initially, Karajan had been wary of Breest with his bullish manner, his jokes,
and his slightly unkempt appearance. Such things upset expectation. The
grave demeanour of Breest's predecessor, Hans Hirsch, had appealed to the
imperial Austrian side of Karajan's nature; it allowed him to condescend to
Hirsch in much the same way as a visiting monarch might to a high-ranking
civil servant. Breest neither looked nor behaved like a civil servant. And
this, for the ageing Austrian maestro, took some getting used to.

Breest's principal problem in the winter of 1981–2 was the Berlin Philharmonic, whose media representatives were playing a high-risk double-game.
On the one hand, they were conducting complex negotiations with Ronald
Wilford over the orchestra's involvement with the new film company
Karajan was proposing to set up; on the other, they were endeavouring
to break the Karajan–DG–EMI axis by making a unilateral deal of their
own with CBS.

For the time being, Deutsche Grammophon held all the cards. When
the orchestra asked to be released from its current contract in order to
make a Gershwin disc for CBS with Michael Tilson Thomas – hardly
a tactful choice of repertory given Karajan's recent unhappy experience
over *Rhapsody in Blue* – the request was immediately refused. The film
deal, by contrast, went through. It was Ronald Wilford who had finally
convinced Karajan of the need to break with Unitel and set up his own
film-making operation. It was a sensible proposal. It had been clear to
insiders for a number of years that Leo Kirch's patience and pocket were

both nearing exhaustion where Karajan was concerned. If he did not leave by the back door, there was every prospect of his being publicly evicted via the front.[1]

Wilford's argument was simple enough. 'The German TV companies have all the equipment you need. Pay them to shoot the films. You conduct and direct the films, and you retain the international copyrights.' The big problem was the orchestra. Without the Berlin Philharmonic's involvement, the project was a non-starter. A deal needed to be struck and, in Wilford's view, it needed to be an exclusive deal: a guarantee of a minimum of two or three productions a year for five years with the Berlin Philharmonic exclusive to Karajan for all television transmissions.

The plan made Karajan nervous, largely because he thought it would be impossible to negotiate. But Wilford pulled it off. After taking advice, Karajan had handed the entire negotiation over to him. Wilford would later observe:

He was a very practical man, and a very intelligent one. If I gave him an idea, it was not difficult to bring it into effect. You didn't have to argue with him, stroke him, flatter him. There was simply an enormous ability to function which most people in this business simply don't have. He knew exactly what he knew, and he knew just as precisely what he didn't know. Along with Judson [the founder of CAMI], he was the most intelligent man I ever met. I miss him terribly.[2]

The terms on which the new company, Télémondial, would operate were agreed and in place by the spring of 1982. The European operation would be based in Munich, with the commercial strategy co-ordinated from New York by one of Wilford's right-hand men in CAMI, Peter Gelb. Karajan also began looking for someone to run the European end of the operation, a senior aide who would report directly to him. EMI's Peter Alward, a fluent German speaker – his mother was German, his father half Austrian – was offered the position, but turned it down. Alward had become close to Karajan personally but that closeness had left him in no doubt as to how the system operated. Being bound formally into an old-fashioned imperial hierarchy in which everyone knows his place was not something that greatly appealed to him. Besides, he knew very little about film-making. The job went to the other principal contender, Uli Märkle.

As things turned out, it was a more important position than it might have appeared at the time. With so much of Karajan's work now centred on film-making, the influence of the on-the-spot film manager was considerable. Indeed, it was not long before tensions opened up between the Télémondial office and Karajan's own official office in Salzburg, further complicating already complicated situations with artists, record companies, and the press.

Karajan's sphere of operations had grown so large there was now a burden of commitments which even the combined diplomatic and organisational talents of Anita von Karajan and André von Mattoni might have been hard-pressed to advise on. After a year spent following Karajan in 1982–3, Roger Vaughan wrote:

If Karajan, or Lore Salzburger [head of Karajan's Salzburg office], or perhaps Märkle, doesn't think of something, it doesn't happen. So there is no public relations, no real organisation to keep things smooth . . . [There are] complex rehearsal and performance schedules, recording dates, programme planning, casting of soloists and singers, the logistics of four houses and staff, a twin-engine jet aircraft, ten or a dozen automobiles, a 77-foot million-dollar racing yacht that demands a full-time captain and four crew; and constant demands from the press, visitors, and people in business.[3]

And that was for starters. The Easter Festival, the various musical, educational, and scientific branches of the Karajan Foundation, and now, to top it all, the new film company, all required Karajan's personal attention. At the time, Lore Salzburger was probably the world's busiest secretary:

How she keeps the appointments straight, the plane in the air, the boat in the water, her hair in place, and her office immaculate – all at the same time and in four languages – is beyond comprehension. In ten days preceding Karajan's seventy-fifth birthday (April 5, 1983), she answered 850 pieces of mail in addition to her other duties.[4]

Yet it was not so much the logistics of the operation that was the problem as the private lines of communication. With Mattoni retired, only Glotz, among Karajan's long-standing advisers, had the knowledge, the access and – it is probably fair to say – the wisdom that was required. But even his role was circumscribed: by the demands of his job as Karajan's recording overseer and by the need Karajan himself had urged on him many years earlier to maintain an independent professional life of his own.

So lines of communication became blurred. Karajan was assumed to have seen people he had not, or, worse, to have refused to speak to people he had no idea were wanting to see him. There was, for example, a long and bitter stand-off during the 1980s between Karajan and Domingo, something, it was later discovered, neither man had either instigated or desired.

The authors of such misadventures have been variously identified down the years, but, in the end, the fault was Karajan's: an old man doing too much, operating a policy of divide and rule, while at the same time single-handedly trying to run an operation that had now assumed the proportions of a small Roman province.

*

The 1982 Salzburg Easter Festival featured a Karajan rarity: a new production of Wagner's *Der fliegende Holländer*. He had conducted this
storm-tossed drama of demonism and damnation once before in the theatre,
in Aachen in 1937, but had refused to perform it again until he had the
experience and the facilities to realise to the letter Wagner's all-important
stage directions.

During rehearsals, he reminisced bitchily about productions he had seen
in the past. Several had dispensed with the sea entirely, despite the fact
that it is one of the work's central images. (In the opening scene, Wagner
directs that the sea should occupy most of the stage.) Another production
was played on so small a stage (was this a memory of Ulm, perhaps?) that
when the Steersman raised his telescope to spy on the Dutchman, he only
narrowly missed hitting the Dutchman in the eye.

In Karajan's production the sea was there all right. It was there in the
Overture – terrifying and *cold*, Wagner's orchestra, as Karajan imagined
it, exposing the Salzburg audience to a form of musical hypothermia. And
it was there, as Wagner demands, on stage, rocking and billowing in its
sheltered cove. Daland's boat and the menacing hull of the Dutchman's
ship were grandly, broodingly realised by Karajan and Schneider-Siemssen:
the docking, the dousing of the sails, the paying out of the anchor all judged
to a nicety after hours of patient rehearsal. Nor were the rehearsals arranged
simply because Karajan, the professional sailor, wanted things right. It went
deeper than that. Wagner, Karajan averred, knew precisely what he wanted:
the flux of the sea, which carries with it ideas of death and dissolution, pitted
against the reassuring solidity of the land (the anchor's fall, in Karajan's
production, conjured a startling sonority in its own right[5]) and the domestic
'certainties' that lie beyond.

In casting José van Dam as the Dutchman, Karajan took the idea of
dissolution one stage further, setting before us, not some hardy blasphemer,
but a solitary, sensitive man in whom pride has mellowed to patient regret.
Thomas Mann spoke of the Dutchman's 'painful and sombre solitude' and
it was a measure of van Dam's and Karajan's powers of concentration
that his presence was felt on stage even when he was merely the isolated
observer.[6]

The rest of Karajan's cast ranged from the good (Kurt Moll as Daland
and Reiner Goldberg as Erik) to the more than acceptable (his Senta,
Catarina Ligendza). He had no such luck with the EMI recording, begun
in December 1981 and not completed until November 1983. This had a
substantially different cast and was almost as big a financial and planning
disaster as the *Lohengrin*. 'Will [Peter] Hofmann *ever* sing the cavatina
properly?' Karajan was heard plaintively to enquire.[7] The real problem,
though – the albatross Karajan had personally hung about his own neck

– was the vocally inadequate Senta of Dunja Vejzovic. The result was a sadly compromised set: a peerless performance of *Der fliegende Holländer* as orchestral tone-poem but an inadequate memento of the Salzburg production of the music-drama.

*

A performance of Mahler's Ninth Symphony at the 1982 Easter Festival left the audience shocked and drained, not so much reluctant to applaud as more or less incapable of doing so. Stuckenschmidt, who had had his disagreements with Karajan, described it as the greatest performance of a piece of music he had ever heard; a striking accolade from a man whose career as a writer had begun in Germany in 1920. Restaurants that evening remained strangely deserted. Tables reserved for 8.30 or 9 p.m. (the Mahler had finished a little after 8) remained unoccupied until 9.30 or 10 as concert-goers, braving the chill of the April air, wandered by the Salzach or through the city's labyrinth of streets and squares.

Karajan also brought to the festival Strauss's *Alpine* Symphony. It is a festive work that needs a festive setting. The orchestral requirements – re-doubled woodwind, twenty horns, organ, and thunder and wind machines – are those of the Wagnerian opera house rather than the conventional concert hall. Strauss had even asked for wind players to be supplied with 'Samuel's Aerophon', a form of breathing apparatus that pumped oxygen into the mouths of players who found the long-held pedal notes difficult to sustain. Not that the Berliners needed any such device; years of playing under Karajan had given them the breathing capacity of long-distance underwater swimmers.

Since he had spent the greater part of his life either conducting orchestras or tackling mountains, Karajan was peculiarly suited to understand the *Alpine* Symphony. As with *La mer* or *Der fliegende Holländer*, he knew it in all manner of intimate, practical ways ('On the glacier' is one sub-title, 'Precarious moments' is another), but he also knew it spiritually. The revelatory moments in Karajan's performance came where the music was at its most numinous: the apparition in the waterfall (the Alpine Witch of Romantic folklore), the oboe's strangely desolate hymn of wonder after the awed arrival at the summit, and the long, slow winding down of the epilogue as the sun sets and the mists begin to rise: 'Twilight and evening bell/And after that the dark!', as Tennyson puts it in another context.

And there was a further dimension. These were landscapes Karajan could admire but no longer engage. Nothing frustrated him more in his last years than the recognition that he would never ski again, that his mountaineering days were over.

And what of his days as a conductor? In 1983, he filmed the *Alpine Symphony* in concert. It is a fine performance but an agonising spectacle, Karajan – in poor shape physically after further spinal surgery – often flailing like a stricken animal.[8]

*

Mozart's *Jupiter* Symphony, Beethoven's *Eroica*,[9] and Mahler's Ninth Symphony were the works chosen for the Berlin Philharmonic's official centenary concerts in Berlin on 30 April and 1 May 1982. Karajan had been ill for some weeks with a virus – influenza probably, though the press reported a bout of malaria – but he soldiered on with what one journalist called 'a truly Prussian sense of duty'.[10]

The day after the Berlin concerts, Karajan and the orchestra flew to Vienna where they played Mahler's Ninth and (with Karajan now visibly running a fever) Beethoven's Ninth. News of the Télémondial deal had already reached the city. Some members of the Vienna Philharmonic began guessing at the extent of their rivals' new-found wealth, but older and wiser Berlin-watchers wondered where it all would end.

'You see,' the veteran Otto Strasser would tell me many years later, 'the Berlin Philharmonic never really understood Karajan in the way we did.'

'Is that not a somewhat biased view?' I asked.

'Not at all. You see, Karajan's roots were in opera. That's where his real genius lay. And that was a repertory they did not have.'

'Did he not teach it them?'

'Yes, and very well; he had that genius, too. But they never knew the music – or him – as we knew them.'[11]

Plans had been laid to record *Der Rosenkavalier* in Vienna but the recording was postponed pending an improvement in Karajan's health. So the spring and summer were surprisingly quiet. In September he recorded *Carmen* in Berlin, conducted Mahler's Sixth Symphony and the now celebrated performance of Mahler's Ninth Symphony which, breaking all precedents, he asked to be released on CD in preference to his recently made studio recording.

'Coming to the end of this symphony,' Karajan later told me, 'is one of the hardest tasks in all conducting.'[12]

Stresemann had been so moved by the performance, he wrote to Karajan and received an immediate and warm reply, something he had often looked for in vain during their years working together. It was Stresemann's belief that Karajan seriously considered retiring after these performances but that 'the restlessness that had characterised him throughout his life' had overruled the intuition.

The Berlin Mahler Ninth would certainly have made the perfect dying fall to Karajan's career. But it was not to be.

Worse, the sound of thunder was already ominously close: dry, sterile thunder that would bring succour to no one.

CHAPTER 74

Pressing matters

What is asserted by critics becomes, through repetition, an orthodoxy; and that orthodoxy is then treated as objectivity, the baseline
from which further criticism can be developed.

Noel Malcolm, *Daily Telegraph*

Karajan had been lionised in the opera house and the concert hall for most
of his working life. He both inspired applause and artfully provoked it.
Most conductors have their platform manner pretty well worked out; but
Karajan had long since turned old-fashioned platform etiquette into an art
form all of its own.

It was a manner that was rooted in a certain innate shyness but there
was egotism and vanity too, and an actor's gift for timing and gesture. The
routine of taking bows from within the orchestra, hands propped on the
shoulders of the front-desk first and second violins was genuine enough, yet
it was done in the certain knowledge that the solo bows from the podium
would be the more effective. In the opera house, he used the stage curtain
as a prop, much as Marlene Dietrich used to do. He was also one of the
few conductors – Bernstein was another – who could come back on stage
after the orchestra had left; though where Bernstein usually bounded on
centre-stage, Karajan would hang back with an air of mock diffidence, the
overcoat which was always draped protectively over his shoulders off-stage
now worn as a signal of final leave-taking.

It is difficult to see any harm in most of this. Musicians are performers
and the sense of occasion was never less than palpable. In any case, the
music-making often took one in very different directions; after the Mahler
Ninth in Salzburg or the *Alpine* Symphony, one's thoughts were not so
much of Karajan or even of the composer, but of the sense of having been
temporarily in touch with something beyond personality.[1]

Away from the concert hall and opera house, it was rather different.
My own impression is that few of the people who bought, and continue
to buy, Karajan recordings in their tens of millions were ever furiously *for*
him in any personal sense.[2] The musically inclined sociologist will see this
as a facet of consumerism: an essentially disinterested public buying an
extremely reliable 'product'. Equally, it is possible to think that the appeal
of the music-making lay partly in the fact that it did, indeed, go some way
beyond personality.

*

To that other important opinion former, the press, Karajan was always something of an enigma. In Germany in the late 1930s, he had become an 'issue' long before he had been accurately anatomised either as a person or as a musician; and the events of those years – both musical and political – ensured that he would remain an issue at the war's end. Later, when interest in the Nazi period revived and began to grow at almost exponential rates, the Karajan 'case' was again dramatically reactivated.

The problem of dealing with political atrocities is a complex one.[3] Some memories recede, others are actively renewed: and not merely by the victims. In Germany in the mid-1960s, it was the radical young who were partly responsible for a renewed interest in the nature of Nazism and the mind-numbing horror of the phenomenon that has come to be known as the Holocaust.[4] At the Auschwitz trial in Frankfurt in 1965, it was members of this new, highly politicised yet essentially unincriminated generation who largely packed the public galleries, aghast at what they were hearing.

Thus, far from going away, the past became ever more present as the old taboos were discarded and the new generation of the Sixties-educated young moved into positions of influence within the government, the universities, the media, and – since it was not isolated from society at large – the Berlin Philharmonic itself. By the 1980s, a quarrel had erupted in German universities – the so-called 'Quarrel of the Historians' [*Historikerstreit*] – between those who believed that a country can recover a crime-free national identity and thus become 'normal' again, and those who wished to demonstrate that it was just such a state of seeming 'normality' that had tolerated and perhaps in some sense fostered the rise of Nazism in the first place.

Little of this had any direct bearing on Karajan's career. It is true that, since the 1950s, journalists had been on the lookout for evidence of culpable wrongdoing by him during the Nazi years; yet, though scores of people had known him and hundreds more had first-hand knowledge of his life-style and whereabouts (a conductor's life is not, after all, a very private one), nothing of real significance had come to light.

Within the musical profession itself, the idea that he had been actively or ideologically 'a Nazi' was widely discounted. Even the allegations of the so-called 'double membership' of the NSDAP, first made in 1957, seemed to have been forgotten about. Then suddenly it all started up again. In 1982 Fred K. Prieberg published his book *Musik im NS-Staat*. Though only three of the book's 423 pages were devoted to Karajan, it was enough. The rehearsing of two or three apparently 'representative' events from the years 1935–43,[5] and the reiteration by a reputable scholar of the 'double membership' theory,[6] was enough in the prevailing atmosphere of the early 1980s to put Karajan back in the dock both as a token Nazi and, in some people's estimation, a 'real' one.[7]

There was in all this a bizarre echo of what had happened to Furtwängler in 1948–9 when, having been lengthily investigated by the competent and legally constituted authority, he found himself back on trial in the American media.[8] To Karajan's opponents and their allies in the press, Prieberg's so-called 'revelations' were a godsend and Karajan's final years would be blighted by them much as Furtwängler's had been. Karajan considered going to law but his lawyers told him what he already knew: that such a course of action would be expensive, time-consuming, and, in the end, self-defeating.

But a Pandora's box had been opened. During the years 1982 to 1989, when relations with the Berlin Philharmonic began to deteriorate almost as alarmingly as Karajan's health, references in the media to Karajan's Nazi past became routine and ever more extreme. It was a process that would reach its bizarre apotheosis a few months after his death, in a programme broadcast on the Public Radio network in the United States.

Entitled *The Karajan Case*, the hour-long feature by *Record Shelf* presenter Jim Svejda was an unctuously delivered denunciation of a man Svejda openly admitted he detested. At one point in the programme, as Johann Strauss's waltz *Artists' Life* played in the background, Svejda informed his no doubt suitably appalled American audience:

Nor was Karajan a casual National Socialist. [*Pause, fade up music.*] When he discovered that his second wife was partly Jewish [*Pause, fade up music*], he promptly divorced her [*Pause*] in 1942.[9]

What this astonishing inversion of the facts reveals is the degree to which allegation can transform itself into 'fact' which, in turn, can breed new 'facts' which themselves stand truth on its head.[10]

*

Outside Germany, there were different factors at work. In Britain, where union power had all but crippled large swathes of the newspaper industry, the sale of *The Times* to Rupert Murdoch both saved the broadsheet press and set in train its tabloidisation.

Karajan's name first appears in *The Times Index* in 1948, the year of his début with the Philharmonia. Between 1948 and 1979 there are frequent references to him: mainly London concert reviews and reviews of festival performances abroad. There are also reports of appointments and resignations filed by the paper's special correspondents in Vienna and Berlin, and the occasional news flash (the collapse in Munich in 1963) taken from Reuters or Associated Press.

In 1981 all this changed. Though the reviews and the foreign news reports remained in place, there was a sudden proliferation of casual news stories and so-called 'diary' entries. Eliette von Karajan, unmentioned in the paper pre-1981, began to feature. Since her gilded life-style had long been a source of fascination to the continental European press, her début in *The Times* was not unexpected. Not that the 'jet-set' angle was at all productive where Karajan himself was concerned. As one friend put it, 'While Eliette was out gadding with her friends, Herbert was usually back at home in his dressing-gown.'

The *Times* 'Diary' started pushing the Nazi angle. When Schwarzkopf's memoir of Walter Legge *On and Off the Record* was imminent, it singled out for preview the trouble Legge allegedly had with the two 'so-called Nazis', Furtwängler and Karajan. A few weeks later, when John Culshaw's memoir *Putting the Record Straight* made its posthumous appearance, a photograph of Karajan, captioned 'Von Karajan: ruthless and unpredictable', appeared alongside a story in the diary based on the 'revelation' that in his book Culshaw had compared Karajan to Hitler. What Culshaw had written was: 'Unwittingly, he had filled the void left by the death of Hitler in that part of the German psyche which craves for a leader.'[11]

In the press as a whole, hard-nosed commercialism began driving concert and opera reviews more and more to the margins. Space was cut, fewer events were covered. The musical 'essay' more or less died overnight. In its place, came 'hard news' stories, new forms of investigative journalism, and a great deal of commercially driven puffery. It was a decade that changed fundamentally the way classical music is covered by the press and, by devolution, perceived by large sections of the general public. It was also a decade in which Karajan's own controversial past and increasingly troubled present itself became a rich source of forage.

*

The release of Karajan's new recording of *Carmen* in 1983 polarised opinion dramatically: a further manifestation of how things were changing. As late as 1996 one leading guide was continuing to list the recording as the best of the many available.[12] Yet, another guide would conclude:

With all its grandiosity, the set made me yearn for the hopelessly anachronistic but lively Emmy Destinn performance in German, recorded in 1908 in what sounds like a broom closet.[13]

In fact, the set contained some really rather fiery conducting, Agnes Baltsa's angry, earthy, cynical bitch of a Carmen, a fine José (José Carreras) and an exceptional Escamillo (José van Dam). It had also been put together with immense care. There was a first-rate performing edition, the use of a French chorus and (like it or not) French-speaking actors to play the dialogue.[14] The technical quality was excellent, and the orchestral playing had an elegance and polish – noted Alan Blyth in a review in *Gramophone* that *was* balanced – comparable to that of the famous old Beecham recording.[15]

For sure, it was a controversial set; even those who made it felt that. The producer Michel Glotz later told me: 'I don't think that *Carmen* was one of the best pieces for Mr von Karajan. He had a deep understanding of French music but somehow the spirit of Bizet always seemed to elude him.'[16] Agnes Baltsa, whose career as an alluring, smoulderingly contemptuous Carmen was rudely interrupted when Karajan slung her out of the dress rehearsal of his 1986 Salzburg stage revival for dissent, took a slightly different view:

I felt as if someone had amputated both my legs but failed to provide me with crutches, either. He just had no specific conception to suggest. The whole production seemed like a hole, a backdrop for some folkloric scenery, complete with imported flamenco dancers.[17]

But went on:

To have performed Carmen in a production directed by Ponnelle and conducted by Karajan would have been nirvana.[18]

It was a complex case. Yet the hype and the groans, the lavish praise and the sniggering abuse, which attended the release of the recording suggested that critical opinion about Karajan was becoming ever more polarised between those who favoured his work – or who were at least prepared to listen disinterestedly to it – and those for whom he could do no good.

In one important respect, however, the press in its new antagonistic mood served a useful function. There were, by 1982, questions that merited an airing. Was Karajan too influential? Had he been around too long for his own, and other people's, good? Certainly, the prospect of a fourth – digital – Karajan Beethoven cycle, draining away custom at the very time when performers and scholars were inviting us to reappraise the way Beethoven's music is heard and played, was not the most enticing of prospects. As D. H. Lawrence remarks in *Etruscan Places*:

Give us things that are alive and flexible, which won't last too long and become an obstruction and a weariness. Even Michelangelo becomes at last a lump and a burden and a bore. It is so hard to see past him.[19]

CHAPTER 75

1982: Divisions in the kingdom

The personnel list in the Carnegie program included famous names but was manifestly incomplete. Who was the remarkable first clarinet at the opening concert? I hardly believe she is called Karl, Peter, Herbert, or Manfred.

Andrew Porter, *The New Yorker*

Since 1980, one of the two solo clarinet positions in the Berlin Philharmonic had remained unfilled, though at an audition in January 1981 a 21-year-old girl from the Bavarian Radio Symphony Orchestra had caused something of a stir. She was called Sabine Meyer, and it was evident that her refined and sensitive playing had touched Karajan's imagination. 'This one or no other,' he murmured to Peter Girth after hearing her play barely a dozen bars of a particularly taxing piece.[1] Though it was agreed that she should be engaged as an occasional freelance deputy, the orchestra's own solo wind players were not so sure. Did she have the right weight and 'blend' of sound for them to work with?

Situations like this were not unusual. When James Galway left the orchestra in 1975, his post had remained unfilled for want of suitable applicants.[2] Then as now, Karajan had approved a candidate – a girl whose playing of a piece by Berio had seemed to him to possess a rare lightness and purity of tone – and again the issue of weight and blend of sound had been raised. The first oboe, Lothar Koch, had talked the matter through with Karajan and the girl had not been put up for election.

In such situations goodwill was needed on both sides. One thing the orchestra's founding fathers had not provided back in 1882 was an enduringly workable definition of the role of the 'permanent conductor' in the audition and appointments procedures. According to the constitution, the 'permanent conductor' was required to attend all auditions. Yet he had no vote; nor did he have any formal say in the first stage of the procedure, the compulsory probationary year, for which applicants needed to win the backing of fifty per cent of the permanent ensemble. The conductor was, however, required to approve all non-probationary appointments and sanction all dismissals.

It was not, if followed literally, the most sensible of arrangements. Great conductors fashion orchestras according to the promptings of their own will and imagination, a process in which the appointment of personnel is crucial. During the years 1955–64, Karajan had refashioned the Berlin sound so as to give it greater lightness, sheen, and flexibility. This was not at the expense of the orchestra's traditionally weightier manner, but a refinement of it. And having reached one plateau of excellence, he had gone on to another, reclaiming some of the weightiness and lustre of the Furtwängler era, while retaining much of the new-won clarity and manoeuvrability. The end-product was a richness, concentration, intensity and *balance* of sound that was unique, as a glass of Château d'Yquem is unique.

In the early 1980s, there was much talk of the orchestra needing to assert its 'sovereignty'. Some of this was to do with Karajan's occasional high-handedness off the rostrum, but it was also to do with a changing political climate. Back in 1969, timpanist Werner Thärichen had taught a course at the Musikhochschule in Berlin in which he had tried to work out with his students a new 'democratic', 'anti-authoritarian' model for the 'interaction of conductor and orchestra'. In his book *Paukenschläge*, he describes the exchanges as 'fruitful',³ though even his own description makes the course sound like so much hot air.

And slightly stale hot air. Karajan's own rehearsal methods, developed in Aachen and finely honed after the war with the Philharmonia in London, were generally considered to be models of modern good sense, practical and quick-witted, and as democratic as any genuinely successful teaching method can ever hope to be.

*

By the middle of 1982, no vote had yet been taken on Sabine Meyer, though the orchestra had effectively fended off charges of sexual discrimination by electing a young Swiss violinist, Madeleine Carruzzo, to a probationary post beginning on 1 September. Meyer, meanwhile, had been invited by Karajan to play at concerts in Salzburg and Lucerne. When it became clear that clarinettist Karl Leister would not be fit for the important visit to New York in the autumn of 1982, Karajan had no hesitation in inviting her to join the tour under the terms of the existing arrangements.

*

Shortly after his arrival in New York, Karajan told the *New York Times*: 'What I exert over the Berlin Philharmonic is not control. It is influence.'⁴ Whatever was happening off-stage, his influence on-stage seemed largely benign. Reviewing the concerts in *The New Yorker*, Andrew Porter would observe:

After the Berlin Philharmonic's last New York visits in 1974 and 1976, I tried to define the baffling mixture of admiration and reservations which Karajan inspired. I'm older now, and perhaps mellower, less critical, readier to be grateful for glorious sound and flawless execution. And Karajan is certainly mellower. The October concerts reached a new summit. Two of them, at least – the first [*Apollo* and *Alpine* Symphony] and third [Brahms's Third and First symphonies] – seemed to me 'never-to-be-forgotten' events, to be recalled with, if not ranked beside, a Furtwängler Beethoven cycle that in student years changed my life.⁵

There were reservations: about Karajan's playing down of the brutalities of the *Scherzo* of Mahler's Ninth Symphony, and about what was perhaps too smooth a ride in Brahms's Fourth. Writing about the performance of the Brahms in the *New York Times*, Tim Page addressed a similar issue – the view of Karajan as 'the brilliant craftsman whose erections are simply inhuman' – but could not find anything here to substantiate the charge. What he heard was 'a deep strain of melancholy', the finale grave in a way that was almost Elgarian.⁶

It was Karajan's performance of Brahms's Third Symphony, a work which had often eluded him in the past but whose mixture of aspiration and regret now more closely reflected his own inner mood, that most caught Porter's imagination:

The third concert, of Brahms's Third and First Symphonies, revealed the new Karajan at his most lovable, for these were natural, emotional, and – let the word escape at last – profound interpretations: voyages of discovery; loving traversals of familiar, exciting ground with a fresh eye and mind, in the company of someone prepared to linger here, exclaim there; summations toward which many of his earlier, less intimate performances had led.⁷

It was a review to die for, and possibly to die to as well. For here, in the serene closing pages of the Third Symphony, was music of dissolution and farewell. Michel Glotz would recall a parallel occasion earlier that year:

After the Mahler Ninth, I said to him. 'It seems to me that the music is coming from another world.' And he said, 'You are right. It *is* coming from another world – it is coming from eternity.' And at that point I knew that in a strange way he too was somehow 'gone'.⁸

*

Karajan was, indeed, becoming more lovable and yet – ever the paradox – he was also becoming more difficult, an ageing autocrat harassed by pain. This worried the orchestra. Physically and emotionally drained by the demands recent concerts had been making on them, their feelings about Karajan veered between pride and apprehension. Michel Glotz noted:

There was a father–son, love–hate relationship between Karajan and the orchestra. He was very much a family personality, a father-like figure. He was careful of the individual musicians, always paying attention to their problems: marital problems, illnesses, illnesses of their children. And yet somewhere the orchestra was a little bit jealous of his glory. However careful he was to praise them, to ensure they had more prominent billings than himself, and so on, there were those within the orchestra who believed that the glory he was basking in was really their own.[9]

Such feelings generally remained hidden beneath the surface. Known antagonists, such as Thärichen and Stern, paraded their views in public, but the majority of players, if they complained at all, were inclined to do so privately. And, in any case, there was always the American factor to draw comfort from. It was felt that whenever Karajan was in the United States he was on the defensive, unsure as to the kind of reception he was going to receive. This was good for morale; it showed that he was vulnerable, that his powers of command were not limitless.

Then came 1982, and Carnegie Hall. The *New York Times* reported:

... the reception was probably more vociferous than at certain times in the past. Mr von Karajan, it would seem, has passed into the saintly sphere that leading conductors seem to inhabit by rights as they reach elderhood.[10]

Michel Glotz was standing with the audience:

As the members of the orchestra came on stage they were warmly applauded. But when Karajan came on stage the whole audience rose and gave him a ten-minute standing ovation – an ovation that was clearly addressed *to him personally*. At that moment, I saw in the faces of certain members of the orchestra a look which told me that the jealousy which had previously lain largely dormant was no longer so. It was as if they were thinking, 'Now there is no check. Even here they worship him.'[11]

In the weeks and months after Glotz made this observation to me, I tested it out on others who were close to Karajan and the orchestra at this time. Some were surprised, others intrigued. Yet no one was willing seriously to discount it. What Glotz witnessed was, indeed, some kind of defining moment.

*

Back in Berlin, after film sessions for Beethoven's Fifth and Sixth symphonies,[12] the orchestra took a vote on whether or not Sabine Meyer should be formally engaged for a probationary year. It turned her down. It also, for good measure, passed a vote of no confidence in Peter Girth, announcing that his contract would not be renewed when it expired in 1985.

Had Karajan been expecting this? After the concert in Berlin on 30 September, Stresemann had overheard him say to the Mayor of Berlin,

Richard von Weizsäcker, words to the effect, 'I'll show them', as though some kind of confrontation was already being contemplated.

Be that as it may, the formal rejection of Sabine Meyer was too much for Karajan to stomach. On 3 December 1982, he sent a letter to Girth which he asked should be read out to the orchestra; a request which was vetoed by Rainer Zepperitz, the most recently elected member of the orchestra's two-man ruling council. In the letter, Karajan announced that in view of the orchestra's refusal to grant Mrs Meyer a probationary year he was 'adjourning [*sistieren*]' all activity with the orchestra beyond the six double concerts a year he was obliged by statute to conduct. There would be no tours, no engagements with him in Salzburg or Lucerne, no film or television work, and no gramophone recordings.

It has been said since that he should have continued talking to the orchestra. But, in reality, there was no more to say. As Stresemann himself had frequently pointed out, that part of the orchestra's constitution which formally excluded the permanent conductor from the probationary appointments procedure was a crisis waiting to happen.

Karajan took the rejection of Meyer as a vote of no confidence in his musical judgement. As he said in his letter:

It is your right, contractually, to decide upon either a positive or negative recommendation vis-à-vis a candidate. In this instance, however, I find that my judgment and that of the orchestra are diametrically opposed.[13]

Sir Thomas Beecham might have put it more colourfully. As he indicated in January 1945, when contemplating setting up the Royal Philharmonic Orchestra: 'I have no intention of once more viewing the melancholy spectacle of my labours being vitiated continually by the butchering hand of oaf or clown.'[14] But Karajan did not have Beecham's freedom of manoeuvre. This was Germany and a publicly owned institution; there were political and legal ramifications, and an orchestra that was now talking openly of its artistic 'sovereignty'. There was an orchestra, too, which, having delivered a hurt, had now been hurt in return. Yehudi Menuhin would later reflect:

When you conduct an orchestra, it is a very great training in human relationships. You have to look after them, which Karajan did to a remarkable degree. Yet, to the very end, he was accustomed to exercising authority, perhaps without sufficient compassion. I don't know to what extent he was a compassionate man.[15]

*

The first consequence of the rift was the cancellation of the filming of the New Year's Eve Johann Strauss concert. The *Four Last Songs* and the *Alpine* Symphony were played instead, without cameras present. The financial loss was substantial and the orchestra retaliated on 4 January 1983 with an announcement confirming its refusal to grant Meyer a probationary year. Other people were also dragged in. On 12 January Karajan asked EMI (and, through them, Riccardo Muti) to withdraw from recording sessions planned for February. Muti refused to become involved. 'What if Karajan settles?' he asked Peter Andry. 'Where would that leave me and my relations with the orchestra?' It was a wise response.

Behind-the-scenes advice, from the government minister Wilhelm Kewenig and from Ronald Wilford in New York, was that the situation had got badly out of hand; that the players had mismanaged the Meyer affair from the outset, and that a compromise should be found by which, though unelected, she should continue to play in the orchestra as and when Karajan wished. Girth listened to this advice, but then decided he had a better solution. If the orchestra was going to play things by the letter of its constitution, so would he. He would, as was his legal right, make the appointment himself.

When he advised Karajan what he was proposing to do, Karajan was somewhat taken aback. He did not try to talk Girth out of the decision, but he did question him closely about its feasibility. Was it practicable? Was he sure that he could see the thing through (Karajan used the verb '*durchhalten*') to a successful conclusion? All his life, Karajan told Girth, he had applied that test. Never start something you can't be sure of seeing through to the bitter end.[16] Girth assured him he could, and on 16 January issued Meyer with a one-year probationer's contract.

While all this was going on, the press, desperate to stir the pot, was kept well away from the kitchen. Key documents were slow to appear and most news reports were several days in arrears of the events themselves. Girth's move on 16 January effectively caused Karajan to suspend his boycott of the orchestra, though for the next week stories continued to be filed in the national and international press suggesting irreparable damage. When a violinist died of a heart attack, his death was linked directly to the dispute. Karajan's absence from the man's funeral (not an event he would normally have been expected to attend) was also widely discussed. On 25 January the London *Times* ran a front-page story stating that a permanent break between Karajan and the Berliners was now inevitable. Karajan, the paper reported, had withdrawn to St Moritz. The end was nigh.

In fact, the orchestra – having balled out Girth and publicly called for his immediate dismissal – had accepted Karajan's offer of a return to the *status quo ante*.

On 27 January, Karajan began a rehearsal of Saint-Saëns's *Organ* Symphony with the words, 'OK, let's make great music together.'

CHAPTER 76

The Erlking

Happy families are all alike; every unhappy family
is unhappy in its own way.
Leo Tolstoy, *Anna Karenin*

Not that things were wholly back to normal. How could they be now that
the delicate balance of power between orchestra, permanent conductor,
and general manager had been so rudely upset? As far as the orchestra
was concerned, Girth had sold out to Karajan.

In March, Karajan made a short visit to Bulgaria during which he
conducted the opening concert in Sofia's new Palace of Culture. The tour
had originally been planned with the Berlin Philharmonic, but the Vienna
Philharmonic went instead. From Sofia, Karajan sent a telex to Girth who
was about to give a press conference in Berlin announcing the 1983-4
programme. The telex ended with the words, 'You have my continuing
trust.' Unwisely, Girth read the telex out at the press conference. This was
too much for the 82-year-old Hans Heinz Stuckenschmidt who stood up
and announced: 'Herr Girth, you have destroyed the unity between Karajan
and the Berlin Philharmonic.'[1]

Rumours persisted that Karajan was looking for an alternative to the
Berlin Philharmonic for the 1983 Easter and Whitsun festivals. This was
true, but the move was as much defensive as aggressive, an attempt
to guard against humiliating and costly cancellations should the Berlin
Philharmonic raise the stakes further. Karajan was also discussing with
Girth the possibility of making his stipulated six double concerts in Berlin
non-subscription. Given the fact that Karajan lacked established social and
political roots in Berlin, there was a need to think about how best to exploit
his most powerful asset, the huge following he still enjoyed among the wider
musical public.

Another concern was the proliferation of small and not so small chamber
groups within the Berlin Philharmonic. The 'Twelve Cellists of the Berlin
Philharmonic' had already made a name for themselves, and there were
other groups, drawing players away from regular commitments.[2] Paradoxically, it had been Karajan's own generosity that had helped create the
situation in the first place. In the 1960s, during the summer sojourns in
St Moritz, he had openly encouraged the formation of informal chamber-
music groups. He had even wondered aloud (to the great consternation of
Stresemann) about the possibility of the Berlin Philharmonic setting up its
own specialist Bach Chamber Orchestra.

Amid a muddle of conflicts about money, the future, and players' rights, it was not surprising that the matter had surfaced again, and in more serious form, with plans for a fully-fledged chamber orchestra involving upwards of forty players. After taking soundings from various people (including Stresemann), the new Senator for Cultural Affairs, Dr Volker Hassemer, ruled in Karajan's favour. Chamber music groups of no more than thirteen players would be allowed to continue, provided they abided by the existing regulations concerning leave of absence.

*

While Berlin was arguing over the present, Aachen was remembering the past. In February 1983, a bronze bust of Karajan was unveiled in the foyer of the new State Theatre. Two months later, during the night of 17 April, Karajan's first wife Elmy Karajan-Holgerloef died of heart failure in the town's Luisenhospital. His Salzburg office issued a statement to the *Aachener Nachrichten* saying that he was 'very shocked, affected, and deeply upset by the news. He had never forgotten her; she had been a part of his life.'3 After he heard the news, Karajan cancelled all his engagements for the day. He did not, however, attend the funeral in Aachen the following Monday. A large wreath of white roses was sent. The card read simply '*Dein Herbert*'.

The reason given was a filming engagement. As an excuse, it was bizarrely apt. His projected 'legacy for home video' had already taken on the character of his own hedge against mortality. Fearful of losing even a day's work on the project, he now allowed nothing to interfere with the schedules, a decision that was beginning to petrify his diary for months – even years – ahead.

But there was a further reason why Elmy's death so disorientated him. He himself was again far from well. It was becoming clearer by the day that further spinal surgery was going to be needed if he was not going to end up in a wheelchair. Karajan knew this but, as in 1975, he prevaricated, fearful that surgery might not work, that he might not survive the operation.

In early May, gnawed by pain and barely able to walk, he travelled to Vienna to conduct the Berlin Philharmonic in the four Brahms symphonies, part of the sesquicentennial celebrations of the composer's birth. He also led the Vienna Singverein and Vienna Philharmonic in a recording and filmed concert performances of the *German Requiem*.4 The sessions for the *Requiem* were a particular trial both to Karajan – who clearly feared he might be conducting his own requiem – and to those around him. Word had got out that he was about to be readmitted to hospital, with one record company employee giving confidential briefings to friends and colleagues –

'Strictly *entre nous*, dear boy' – that Karajan might well be suffering from cancer of the spine.

It was nothing of the sort. During the Brahms sessions in the Musikverein, Karajan told Roger Vaughan:

'What I have is like a stunt-man's disease, from taking falls. There is a spur this size' – he held up the last section of his little finger – 'in between the vertebrae in my neck. It must be removed. That's why my legs are like this.' He slapped his thigh as he spoke. 'Please don't tell anyone about this.'[5]

Glotz knew, of course, and was expert as ever in his handling of Karajan. When Karajan made what was clearly a desperate request for him to leave his hotel and come and keep him company in Mauerbach, Glotz turned the visit into a comic diversion, treating the prospect of a night in rural Mauerbach as a perilous excursion into the *Urwald* requiring special clothing and emergency rations.

Back in the hall, Karajan played the *German Requiem* movingly through. Glotz would later tell Vaughan:

'I sensed [afterwards] that I could go to him, kiss him, and he would burst into tears. It was best to laugh. The moment could go either way. So I said, "Cancel the concerts, we have all we need." Karajan laughed. He was relieved that there was no big sentiment.'[6]

Back home, Karajan agreed to travel to Hanover for an exploratory check on his condition. It was a fine May morning when he left Anif, and he seemed in good spirits, with a new interest to divert him. At the age of seventy-five, he was learning to fly helicopters. He could have returned to flying propeller-driven aircraft when he reached the upper age limit for flying jets, but that would have bored him. Mastering the new, very different, and decidedly tricky task of flying helicopters was just the kind of challenge he needed.

He flew the helicopter to Salzburg Airport, where he filed his flight plan, and on to Munich where he caught a scheduled flight to Hanover. Roger Vaughan went along as far as Munich, marvelling at the well-nigh perfect way this lame and ill 75-year-old with only six hours' experience of flying helicopters was managing. The instructor was watching him like a hawk, his hand permanently near the stick during take off and landing, but Karajan's handling of the machine was flawless.[7]

In Hanover, the diagnosis was that an operation was necessary, but again Karajan delayed. By now, those around him were in a state of near panic as his condition visibly deteriorated. Eventually, he was taken back to Hanover as an emergency case. A call was sent to his surgeon, Professor Madjid Samii, who was lecturing in New York, and the three-and-a-half-hour operation was performed on the morning of 6 June. A bulletin issued by Professor Samii announced that the operation (which Karajan had insisted should be videotaped) had been carried out to correct 'a progressive compression of the cervical spinal chord'. The patient had been in a critical condition at the time of admission ('any further postponement would have been catastrophic') but

Mr von Karajan recovered from his foot drop the very next day, and his gait improved rapidly and considerably. He also feels very well in his upper limbs. I must admit that his neurological recovery is as yet incomplete since it is being affected by elements of unresolved spasticity . . . the final results will depend on the degree of permanent damage suffered by the sensitive spinal chord.[8]

*

Karajan returned to St Tropez to recuperate. He was feeling extremely well. The pain had largely vanished and with it the drained look in the eyes and face. He was walking better; the ground was no longer the cockeyed skating-rink it had progressively seemed to be.

Within the month, he was back in Salzburg, working on a new production of *Der Rosenkavalier* scheduled to open on 26 July. The production turned out to be a slow-moving, sumptuous affair re-staged by Karajan in an expensively refurbished version of the designs Teo Otto and Erni Kniepert had provided for him in 1960. It was staging in a scenic time-warp, Karajan apparently impervious to the fact that even in so moribund a discipline as costume drama, design concepts do evolve. But, then, this was another in a slow-moving procession of death-haunted farewells from him, a strangely uneventful production (for all the admirable fooling in rehearsal) that took its cue from the Marschallin's Act 1 monologue:

> I hear time flowing –
> Staunchlessly.
> Often I rise in the middle of the night
> and stop all, all the clocks.

Karajan's new Marschallin was Anna Tomowa-Sintow, casting that itself turned back the clock to an almost vanished age. Karajan had described his former *Rosenkavalier* cast (Schwarzkopf, Jurinac, Edelmann, Rothenberger et al.) as 'gaslight', a remark that had rather upset Schwarzkopf. But when I spoke to her, she was generous in her remarks about her successor and interesting in her analysis of what it was Karajan had been looking for:

What Karajan discovered in Anna was a kind of vocal beauty that is now almost extinct, but which could still occasionally be found in unspoiled young singers from Eastern Europe where Anna herself came from. It is to do with the almost vanished art of pianissimo singing, with the ability to create that special 'hanging [*schwebend*]' tone which a singer like Milanov had such a genius for. I should also say that Karajan was not the only musician who mourned the loss of these skills. Henze once asked me where he could find 'real' singers, real vocal beauty.[9]

Never was Karajan's ability to bewitch singers – to imbue them with his own sense of inner patience, to hold them as though on the end of an invisible thread – more apparent than it was now. Jeffrey Tate conducted Tomowa-Sintow in *Der Rosenkavalier* shortly after the Salzburg performances and found that she was still under Karajan's spell:

She had been taken over, bless her heart, by this very patient, very sensuous approach to the music. By now, I had rather come to think this was not the way to conduct the opera, that there was too much else going on. But Karajan's ability to bewitch a singer was an enormous gift. It is something which, if we are honest, any conductor would envy.[10]

The orchestral contribution astonished some people, repulsed others. Seiji Ozawa linked the Salzburg *Der Rosenkavalier* with the Mahler Ninth he had heard in New York the previous autumn:

Both times he seemed to stop conducting because he had created a single, deep line, a unity with his players and performers which took music-making beyond anything I have ever heard.[11]

Daniel Barenboim said the orchestral playing was so emotionally explicit, the singers were more or less *de trop*.[12] Ingmar Bergman, on the other hand, recalled 'a wave of devastating, repellent beauty'.[13]

Bergman was in Salzburg directing Molière's *Don Juan*. During the festival, Karajan arranged a meeting with Bergman to discuss the possibility of their filming *Turandot* together. Having been left in the lurch by the Chinese authorities, Karajan was trying another tack.

Bergman has left a striking account of the meeting with Karajan in his autobiography *The Magic Lantern*, a spellbinding memoir ('You mean the novel Ingmar wrote about his life?' said one of his former actors) but a dangerous book to be in since Bergman's charm here is as spectacular as the demons that so evidently possessed him. No one suffers more than Karajan's eminent contemporary Laurence Olivier, who had invited Bergman to direct Ibsen's *Hedda Gabler* at London's National Theatre.[14] 'You cannot have two Napoleons in the same room,' sighed one writer, after reading the chapter in question. The same applied to Karajan, whom Olivier resembled in a number of ways.[15]

Karajan was prepared to flatter Bergman. He told him how much he had admired his production of Strindberg's *A Dream Play*: 'You direct as if you were a musician. You have a feeling for rhythm, the musicality, pitch.' Yet he objected to Bergman's film of *Die Zauberflöte*. Scenes had been switched in the second act. 'You cannot do that with Mozart,' Karajan announced. 'Everything is organic.'[16]

In other circumstances, Bergman might have rallied to his own defence. Yet he describes himself as being wholly transfixed by this slender, lame old man with his large head and penetrating gaze. The conversation turned to *Turandot*:

[Karajan] stared at me with his pale cold eyes. (I usually think *Turandot* an unpleasant, cumbersome, perverted mess, a child of its time.) I was totally absorbed by this little man's hypnotically pale gaze, and heard myself saying that this was a great honour, that I had always been fascinated by *Turandot*, that the music was puzzling but overpowering and I could think of nothing more stimulating than to be allowed to collaborate with Herbert von Karajan.[17]

Strangely, the production was being planned, not for 1985 or 1986, but for six years hence. Bergman marvelled:

In 1989 an eighty-one-year-old conductor and a seventy-one-year-old director would together breathe life into this mummified oddity! The grotesqueness of the project never occurred to me, I was helplessly fascinated.[18]

The audience over, Bergman quickly recovered his wits as the corridors of the Grosses Festspielhaus filled up with a cavalcade of characters you might find in a Bergman film:

As we slowly moved forward, we were transformed into an imperial procession of assistants, helpers, opera singers of all sexes, obsequious critics, bowing journalists, and a shattered daughter.[19]

Several years later, Karajan again approached Bergman, this time on Carlos Kleiber's behalf. It was Kleiber's belief that Bergman was the only man capable of bringing off Weber's *Der Freischütz* on stage. If he was to do it at Salzburg, Kleiber said, he needed two things: Bergman as stage director and (a nice whimsy) somewhere to park his car during the festival mêlée. The festival cabled Bergman and Karajan himself sent a card to Kleiber. A substantial correspondence exists between Kleiber and Karajan, mostly on postcards signed respectively 'Carlos Kleiber, Kapellmeister, Munich' and 'Herbert von Karajan, Kapellmeister, Salzburg'. On this occasion, Karajan said that parking was no problem ('You have my space. I will go on foot') but since Bergman was in Japan that might take a little longer. Alas, Bergman declined.[20]

*

The 1983 festival had been a private triumph for Karajan. He was relieved to be alive. Not that merely being alive was ever enough. He needed to be active and in command, physically in touch with music. That, too, had been achieved.

Yet the disability, the lengthy operations, the frequent exposure to general anaesthetic, were beginning to take their toll. After his first major operation in 1975, Karajan had come back physically renewed, spiritually invigorated. In 1983 there were the first real signs of the onset of a kind of musical sclerosis. For a while, until he agreed to sit (or perch) to conduct, the strain of standing drained him of energy, impairing the movement of his upper limbs. Films shot around 1984–5 reveal the gestures of a frustrated athlete. The beat, for a while, takes on a lurching, uncertain quality.

And there was another problem, too. 'The single, deep line' Ozawa talked of in relation to Karajan's Mahler and Strauss performances was not something to which all listeners readily related. The writer Duncan Fallowell quoted Somerset Maugham in this context: 'Have you not noticed that the tightrope walker skips now and then in order to rest his audience from a feat too exactly done?'[21]

*

During 1983, in both Salzburg and Vienna, there had been a great gathering of the clans as Karajan first ailed then recovered. Anita was much in evidence; and Karajan's old friend from post-war Vienna, Henry Alter, flew in from the United States. Alter had helped get the eighteen-year-old Arabel into the Parsons School in New York,[22] though he had been somewhat taken aback to be thanked, not by Eliette, but by Anita who repeatedly referred to Arabel as 'Herbert's and my little girl'.[23]

One province Karajan was not prepared to cede while there was breath in his body was Salzburg. In 1983 the cost of the festival was once again up for public scrutiny; it was also the year in which festival president Josef Kaut died. He was seventy-nine, a Salzburger by birth, and a man who had been involved with the festival most of his working life. For the would-be reformers, this was too good a chance to miss. The name of the composer and administrator Rolf Liebermann was mentioned (a bizarre choice, given Liebermann's personal dislike of Karajan[24]); others suggested Karajan's old friend, the Director of the Vienna Opera, Egon Seefehlner. But Karajan was not in a mood to brook interference. Albert Moser, an experienced and trusted colleague of many years' standing, was summoned from Vienna to see the festival through the dying fall of the Karajan era.

*

In the winter of 1983–4 Karajan resumed filming and recording the Beethoven symphonies.[25] In January, he returned to Vienna to complete the Deutsche Grammophon recording of *Der Rosenkavalier*, patching here and there but also playing through long sections of the opera for which perfectly good takes already existed. This was pure indulgence, like a child in a sweet shop who refuses to leave.

During the visit, he conducted and filmed Tchaikovsky's Sixth Symphony.[26] The first of the rehearsals had been a relaxed and intimate affair in the Musikverein at 4.30 one January afternoon. There were no cameras or microphones, no recording crews or record executives; simply Karajan and the Vienna Philharmonic, and the occasional guest tucked away in remote corners of the half-lit hall. It was not so much a rehearsal as a private seminar. Occasionally, Karajan would break the spell with a droll reminiscence in the Beecham manner; but for the most part he worked patiently and quietly on the symphony, taking scrupulous care over the ostinato rhythms in the opening paragraphs and the gradations into and out of silence which Tchaikovsky's writing so dauntingly requires.

As I watched in the twilit gloom, I recalled Lawrence's description in *Women in Love* of a class of young schoolchildren at work as evening approached. 'The work went on as a peaceful tide that is at flood, hushed to retire.' Certainly, Karajan was absorbed in what Lawrence calls 'the passion of instruction'.

What I did not realise at the time was how different the atmosphere here was from that in Berlin; which is why the scene now comes back to me across the years with an atmosphere even more richly endowed.

Things were not so cosy when Karajan returned to Vienna in March with the young Ivo Pogorelich in tow. Pogorelich was the talented, temperamental, preeningly handsome *Wunderkind* whose exclusion from the final rounds of the 1980 International Chopin Competition in Warsaw had caused Martha Argerich to resign from the judging panel. He had played at the 1983 Salzburg Festival (a late replacement for Claudio Arrau). Karajan had heard him there: had been seen in the Grosses Festspielhaus during a rehearsal slumped admiringly over the prow of the Steinway.

An engagement to play the Tchaikovsky concerto with Karajan was every young pianist's dream. It was, however, a terrible risk. Karajan collected star pianists as Duke Bluebeard collected wives. In Pogorelich's case, the union was never consummated. During a rehearsal in the Musikverein, Karajan uncharacteristically ran out of patience. There were heated exchanges. Karajan got off the rostrum and hammered out the rhythm on the piano lid. At the end of the rehearsal, he announced: 'Tomorrow evening we play Tchaikovsky Symphony No.6.' Decoded, this meant, 'The concerto is cancelled.'

A statement was released announcing that Pogorelich had sustained an injury to his arm. It was not true. But the following evening when Karajan came on to conduct, there, seated in the hall, was Ivo Pogorelich, his arm elaborately swathed in several feet of white bandage. Even Karajan was amused.

*

The following morning, negotiations resumed over a project which had already caused a good deal of trouble. In 1982, Anne-Sophie Mutter had signed a four-year 'contract of first option exclusivity' with EMI. Personally overseen by Mutter's agent Michel Glotz, it was an expensive deal from which EMI needed at least one money-spinning blockbuster to help defray costs.

Now there is one work in the classical repertoire which will always deliver a tidy profit, whoever records it: Vivaldi's *Four Seasons*. Record it on a shoestring budget with Divina Dervish and the Derby Philharmonic and you will sell 10,000 copies within the year; record it with Anne-Sophie Mutter, the Berlin Philharmonic and Herbert von Karajan and you will sell 10,000 copies within the week.

Long before Mutter signed with EMI, Deutsche Grammophon had been hungry for such a deal. Karajan's recording with Schwalbé had been a huge best-seller and the new record promised even greater returns; so much so that Deutsche Grammophon had continued to agitate for a deal even after Mutter signed with EMI. Glotz was flabbergasted. On 20 January 1982, he wrote to Karajan in Berlin:

Mon cher Maître et Ami,
Je suis *absolument stupéfait* [my emphasis] d'apprendre que la question des *Quatre Saisons* de Vivaldi et de Mademoiselle Mutter ne vous semble pas encore claire, après toutes les explications que j'ai pu vous donner.[27]

Having had the situation put to him with what Glotz, later in the letter, describes as '*une clarté absolument totale*', Karajan went quiet on the subject, though he certainly wanted to film the *Four Seasons* with Mutter at some stage.

What brought the project back on to the agenda was a somewhat despairing plea from EMI's Peter Alward. Karajan kept promising EMI recordings, but nothing ever materialised. The ill-fated *Lohengrin* had eaten up huge sums of money, as had *Der fliegende Holländer*. There was also the problem of the large unearned balances Karajan had built up with both EMI and Deutsche Grammophon as a result of the ruinously high advances they had been prepared to pay to keep him on board in the late 1970s and early 1980s. Alward reported back to Peter Andry:

I pointed out [to Karajan] that no artist had yet ever got wind of the fact that his advance is probably five times that of any of his colleagues. He had the grace to blush![28]

Karajan's response was to offer Alward the *Four Seasons* project. This was tremendous news for EMI but when it came to tying Karajan down financially things got very complicated indeed as figures were traded back and forth on royalties, advances, and the further option of a flat fee buy-out.

Karajan had always been difficult over money; now he was becoming well-nigh impossible. The large sums he was sinking into Télémondial were partly to blame. Having become used to making films on a no-expense-spared basis, creaming off such profits as there were and leaving Leo Kirch to pick up the tab for the losses, he was now having to finance his own obsession.

And it was an obsession. He was shooting approximately 60,000 feet of film per forty-minute symphony, a staggering 12–1 ratio of raw to edited footage, running up costs (at 1982 prices) of roughly £200,000 per film. With approximately forty-five films planned, the initial outlay, on a project Karajan did not expect to release commercially until the early 1990s, was in excess of £9 million. Karajan had the money, but the successful entrepreneur does not live off capital; he prefers to generate fresh profits with which to fund new investments.

That was one explanation; the other was an old man's pride. Despite Mutter's presence on the recording, Karajan was clearly intent on treating the *Four Seasons* as a non-copyright orchestral recording for which he would be paid a ten per cent royalty plus a hefty advance based on expected lifetime sales of getting on for a million copies.

In the midst of all this, there was a surprise. On 22 March 1984, Peter Alward reported back to London:

Another project which Karajan proposed was the Bach *Art of Fugue*, for which he proposes to create a historic meeting on record between himself and his brother, Wolfgang, who, as you know, runs an organ ensemble. Karajan, almost with tears in his eyes, described how marvellous it would be to have both brothers appearing together for the very first time. I made my excuses and left.[29]

It took a further two months to complete the negotiations over the *Four Seasons*. A date was eventually set for the recording to take place in Vienna in the Hofburg in June 1984. Anne-Sophie Mutter turned up in a slinky black number, the Vienna Philharmonic appeared in tails, and Karajan showed up in ... trainers and a track suit. Here was a million-dollar project and no one had thought to tell the artists that there would be no cameras that day. The film, based on EMI's soundtrack, was due – it now turned out – to be made on another occasion, in even more salubrious surroundings than the Habsburgs' winter palace.

In fact, it was never made. Télémondial eventually filmed the *Four Seasons* 'live' on the occasion of the opening of the new Chamber Music Hall of the Berlin Philharmonie in October 1987. It is a wonderful film, an elegantly photographed record of a famous occasion during which it is difficult to know what to admire most: the dazzlingly elegant playing of the Berlin Philharmonic strings, the visionary beauty of Anne-Sophie Mutter's playing of the work's meditative interludes, or Karajan's ear for Vivaldian onomatopoeia and the sly kick he gives to the rhythms when the music is at its earthiest:

> No wonder of it: shéer plód makes plough down sillion
> Shine . . .

as the poet Hopkins once put it.

The Vienna LP was not quite in this class. None the less, it was a prestigious project, handsomely treated.

Lord Snowdon was engaged to 'create' the images for the LP cover. Since a gatefold sleeve was planned, two complementary images were needed. Snowdon took Karajan and Mutter into the Vienna Woods by Mauerbach. On the finished portrait, Mutter sits at the foot of a tree in the sun-dappled glade, violin in lap. The slinky black number is now worn off the right shoulder; Karajan's red sweater is draped provocatively over her left shoulder. Karajan's portrait is altogether stranger. The wood is darker now. Propped half smiling against the tree, he has the look of the Erlking about him.

'Death and the Maiden' is what one wag dubbed this sylvan diptych. That might have amused Karajan; he loathed the portrait, and all the others Snowdon took featuring the famous red sweater, though he did not stop EMI using them.

*

In the first three months of 1984, Karajan gave just one concert with the Berlin Philharmonic; the rest was an intensive round of film work and recording, including a sensitively shot film of the Beethoven Violin Concerto, lyrical and slow-drawn, in which the rapport between Karajan and Anne-Sophie Mutter – and in the slow movement between the two of them and the solo clarinettist Sabine Meyer – is fathoms deep.

Not only was Karajan conducting fewer concerts, his repertory was now static. At the age of seventy-five, after fifty-three years during which he had prepared a wider range of works than any of his distinguished predecessors would have dared contemplate, he had decided to call it a day.

There were even signs of a reversion, conscious or otherwise, to past practices. In February 1984, he made a Wagner record with the Berliners that took him and them back to the age of the 'bleeding chunk'. The programme was sombre, reflective, and dangerously charged: the *Tannhäuser* Overture and Venusberg music, the contemplative Prelude to Act 3 of *Die Meistersinger*, and the Prelude and *Liebestod* from *Tristan und Isolde*. It was a terrific record in both senses of the word: torrentially splendid but terrifying in the scale and intensity of the playing. Barenboim's remark about the Salzburg *Rosenkavalier* not really needing singers is not so much confirmed here as redefined. No stage performance of *Tristan und Isolde* could survive an account of the Prelude as overwhelming as this.

But whom was Karajan attempting to overwhelm: the listener or the orchestra? 'When you return from ten days in the mountains,' he had once remarked, 'you can overwhelm them with energy, simply overwhelm them!' That may have been benignly meant, but Karajan's feelings were no longer benign. The Berlin Philharmonic 'family' which he had once been so proud to head was rapidly coming to resemble the House of Atreus.

With a vote on Sabine Meyer imminent, the atmosphere at the 1984 Salzburg Easter Festival was grim beyond belief. On 2 May, Peter Alward filed a report to Peter Andry in London:

In the nine years that I have worked in Salzburg, I have never experienced a more unpleasant atmosphere and, for the first time, the music suffered as well. It is likely that both Meyer and Girth will go, the former after a secret vote scheduled for the end of May, the latter at the end of his contract in July 1985. Karajan has threatened to reduce his activities to the contractual minimum (six double concerts per season) and cancel all recording and filming activities should this occur. Whatever happens, his relationship with the orchestra is irreparably damaged and the new regime of Schellenberger and Gellermann are busily looking to the future.[30]

Later in the memorandum, Alward spelled out the musical disappointments:

The Beethoven Ninth sounded under-rehearsed and the Wiener Singverein were their usual appalling selves. Tchaikovsky 6 was loud and fast. The Brahms Double Concerto had ill-matched soloists with Mutter dominating and Meneses (a warm, rich sound) far too reserved and chamber-like. Eschenbach and Frantz played the Mozart Double very beautifully, possibly because Karajan did not conduct. Only *Zarathustra* was of truly festival standard. As for *Lohengrin*, the singers were mostly drowned by Karajan . . . The [Act 1] Prelude came to a grinding halt when Karajan beat a false entry – rather embarrassing![31]

Things were even worse backstage. Ten minutes before the start of *Lohengrin*, Peter Girth found Sabine Meyer in tears, in no fit state to play.

He was in no doubt she was being subjected to all manner of taunts and acts of exclusion. Girth was not renowned for his tact, but on this occasion he kept his counsel. It was only later, when things were past repair, that he told Karajan of the incident. Karajan said he was not surprised: 'This is no longer my orchestra.'[32]

The festival over, Sabine Meyer and her advisers sought help. The vote on her future was set to take place on 23 May. Should she allow her name to go forward or should she – despite Karajan's own continuing support and encouragement – throw in the towel?

At some point, the further question was put: 'What would Stresemann advise?' He was approached on Meyer's behalf. Shrewdly, he did not proffer a solution; instead, he asked a question. If Miss Meyer's appointment was to be ratified, did she see herself making a long-term career with the Berlin Philharmonic? The answer was that she did not. 'In that case,' concluded Stresemann, 'she should withdraw her name.'

Which she did. The orchestral board breathed a collective sigh of relief and wrote her a conciliatory letter in which they held out the possibility of her appearing with them as soloist on some future occasion. Karajan later described the letter as 'hypocritical', 'quite despicable'.

After their poor showing in Salzburg, Karajan and the Berliners at least got their music-making back on an even keel in early May during a short tour of Frankfurt, Mannheim, and Stuttgart; but, on 12 May, Sabine Meyer formally resigned, throwing Karajan into a silent fury.

With relations tinder-dry, it needed the merest spark to start a conflagration. This duly came in the shape of a report that during the orchestra's autumn tour of the United States a concert would be given in New York's Avery Fisher Hall by a thirty-four-strong Berlin-based chamber orchestra. Works would include Mozart's *Eine kleine Nachtmusik*, Grieg's *Holberg Suite*, and a Haydn symphony. (All works Karajan himself had recently recorded with the orchestra.) The players would not be in breach of the Senate's ruling on chamber groups since only thirteen players would be involved. The remaining twenty-one players were being recruited locally.

Had a fully functioning General Manager been in place, he would have advised the players of the folly of such a proposal at such a time. But there was no one to call them to heel. The checks and balances within the orchestra's constitution were no longer functioning as they were intended to function. By the end of the month the parties were once again at war.

CHAPTER 77

War and peace

Musical discussions are conducted in Berlin with more heat and
animosity than elsewhere.
Charles Burney, *Present State of Music in Germany*, 1773

The declaration of war came in the form of a change to the schedule of
the Salzburg Whitsun Festival where the Berlin Philharmonic was about to
give three concerts under the direction of Ozawa, Maazel, and Karajan.
Karajan's concert, it was announced, would now be played by the Vienna
Philharmonic whom he would be flying to Salzburg at his own expense.
He had effectively sacked his own orchestra.

Future historians might ask how, in an age of workers' rights and
workers' solidarity, the Vienna Philharmonic was so readily bought. One
reason is that the two orchestras were commercial competitors. If – as had
recently happened – the Berlin Philharmonic wished to hold Karajan to the
letter of his contract over film sessions by demanding the full DM200,000
fee for recording the *Four Seasons* even though only twenty-four players
were needed, why should the Vienna Philharmonic not go into solemn
session and emerge with the news that they might well be able to provide
twenty-four professors rather more cheaply on a strictly pro rata basis?

And there was another, deeper reason than this: territory. Ever since the
spring of 1925, when Erwin Kerber beat down the Vienna Philharmonic's
asking price as the Salzburg Festival's orchestra in residence by threatening
to open negotiations with Berlin, the Berliners' claims on Salzburg had
been a sore point, not only with Salzburgers, but with the government in
Vienna.

Karajan, meanwhile, was asking why he should be required to make
music with individuals who spent a significant part of their lives plotting
against him. 'The Vienna Philharmonic, they love me,' he told Girth. And
he them. After the concert in Salzburg on 11 June, he showered them
with roses.

Not everyone there loved Karajan. When he came on stage, he was both
cheered and booed. The atmosphere was electric. Bach's E major Violin
Concerto came first, played by Anne-Sophie Mutter with Karajan directing
from the harpsichord, then a tumultuous account of the C minor Symphony
of Brahms, which left no one in any doubt as to the power of the feelings
that were now being stirred.[1]

*

The Berlin Philharmonic's response to their dismission was to invite Karajan to 'review his attitude to the position of artistic director'. In other words, they asked him to resign. Even Rudolf Weinsheimer, the more moderate of the two board members and generally thought to be sympathetic to Karajan, had been appalled by his switch to the Vienna Philharmonic. 'Nothing like this has happened in a hundred years,' he said.

But Karajan had no intention of resigning. On 5 June he wrote to the new Mayor of West Berlin, Eberhard Diepgen:

Could I ask you personally to ascertain and specify the artistic director's rights and duties, and let me know to what extent the observation of these rights and duties can be reconciled with the orchestra's conduct during the last two years.[2]

Diepgen was not a regular concert-goer, which may have helped him to see more clearly than some why the city of Berlin could no more tolerate Karajan's humiliation than it could the orchestra's. Not a man to risk communication by letter, Diepgen determined to visit Salzburg to talk to Karajan face to face. Before leaving, he consulted Stresemann, who observed:

Karajan is like the weather. Both are subjects for conversation; yet there is nothing one can do to change either of them. Both are hard to predict.[3]

The meeting on 9 June was courteous and business-like; but it was a case of one step forwards, two steps backwards. It was clear from what Diepgen told Karajan that the Senate was about to send Girth on extended leave, pending agreement over the terms of his dismissal. For Karajan, this opened up another old wound – the idea that he had been double-crossed back in 1955 when the orchestra and the Senate had surreptitiously removed the Permanent Conductor's right actively to approve the appointment of the General Manager.

And there was worse to come. No sooner was Diepgen back in Berlin, edging matters forward and asking an intermediary to sound out Stresemann about the possibility of returning as caretaker General Manager, than the orchestra raised the stakes on 13 June by voting to terminate with immediate effect their film and recording contract with Karajan. With his films of the nine Beethoven symphonies in a state of fragmentary incompleteness, it was a blow Karajan could ill afford to sustain and he immediately began legal proceedings against the orchestra.[4]

On 17 June, he sent a telex to Berlin requesting action in four areas: (i) the reinstatement of the Permanent Conductor's rights over the appointment of the General Manager, (ii) the redrafting of provisions for probationary appointments, (iii) new rules on leave of absence, (iv) restrictions on the right of players to comment publicly on matters of artistic policy.

Stresemann, meanwhile, had not needed much persuading to make a come back. Three days after Karajan sent his telex, the handover was completed at a meeting between Stresemann, Girth, and Senate Director Lutz von Pufendorf. The orchestra was also called in. Girth made a dignified speech of farewell in which he conceded that he had perhaps taken on the job at too young an age. He was heard in silence and received no applause. Stresemann, who was greeted with applause and a nosegay, immediately hopped on to the diplomatic high wire. His task, he said, was to restore and defend the infringed rights of the orchestra; at the same time, he was bound to point out that Karajan had received a life contract from the Berlin Senate, an agreement which also needed treating with the utmost respect.

*

It was late June and the season was drawing to its close. This should have provided a breathing-space, but emotions were still running high, especially among those members of the orchestra who were now implacably opposed to Karajan. It was also the start of the press's annual silly season, when political stories are thin on the ground and a first-rate scandal is a welcome source of copy. Stresemann's policy, conscientiously backed by von Pufendorf and Cultural Affairs Minister Volker Hassemer, was softly, softly, steady as she goes. But even Stresemann was hard-pressed to restrain some of the hotheads.

Other people, too, were working behind the scenes trying to get the show back on the road. CAMI's boss in New York, Ronald Wilford, was under no illusions about the long-term seriousness of the crisis. He would later reflect:

The break, in my view, was totally commercial. Karajan could no longer do twenty-five LPs a year. The father could no longer feed the family in the way the family had come to expect. It had been the largest recording commitment ever made. Karajan's contract was for just six concerts a year in Berlin. And yet there he was for the best part of quarter of a century conducting the orchestra in Berlin and Salzburg, touring Europe, Japan and the United States and – tied in with all this – devoting eighteen weeks a year to recording.[5]

The pity of it was, Karajan was a great orchestral trainer and an untiring servant of the craft of orchestral playing:

What makes a great orchestra is rehearsing, performing, rehearsing, performing. Work with the symphonic repertory, work on opera, work on the chamber repertory. And all the time rehearsing, performing, rehearsing, performing. Karajan had a genius for that. When he physically couldn't do it any more, they turned against him.[6]

Wilford's approach was to try to hatch strategy with Stresemann and Glotz, then leave the orchestra to Stresemann, Karajan to Glotz. With Karajan's agreement, Glotz also talked to the orchestra or, rather, to its two influential media representatives Schellenberger and Gellermann. He would later recall:

It was a nice evening but it came to a dead-end. They did not deny for a moment Karajan's genius, his importance to the orchestra, and what he had done for it. But when I talked about 'entity', they talked about 'sovereignty'. This was their *idée fixe*. I said, don't go down the legal route. Remember that you are dealing with an old man whose upbringing was in an age very different from our own; who finds it difficult to unbend, but who retains a great feeling for the orchestra. In the end, I had to ask: 'Do you really want to get rid of Karajan? And, if so, do you think there is the remotest chance of the Senate agreeing to this? While he is alive, no one can replace him.' Their response was, 'Karajan cannot replace *us*.' The words 'Vienna Philharmonic' came into my mind, but I said nothing.[7]

Ever since the start of the disputes, the orchestra had been attempting to chip away at agreements freely entered into down the years with Karajan, with Deutsche Grammophon and with EMI: bedrock agreements that were now seen, by some strange logic, to be too inhibiting. CBS was the company that had been keenest to talk to the orchestra, but, according to Günther Breest, Schellenberger and Gellermann had even more ambitious plans: they believed they could recruit Deutsche Grammophon to the anti-Karajan cause. At a private meeting convened by Schellenberger, Gellermann and Hellmut Stern,[8] Breest was invited to examine a plan that was designed to drive Karajan firmly into a corner. He would recall:

I was appalled by what I was hearing. Apart from the sheer ineptitude of the strategy – Karajan at that time accounted for twenty-five per cent of all Deutsche Grammophon's sales, from which the orchestra itself was receiving massive royalties – the whole thing was grossly disloyal. I didn't even stay to hear the details of the proposal. After the meeting, I was frosted out for fifteen months until the orchestra got itself a hard-line new lawyer who eventually rang me and said, 'Now we talk.'[9]

There was an element of hubris in the orchestra's behaviour. Pali Meller Marcovicz, Head of Design in the 1980s, told me:

In 1987, the orchestra came up with their own design concept: a logo, standardised 'Berlin Philharmonic' CD covers, everything. (All quite dull, but that is by the way!) They tried to impose this on Deutsche Grammophon. They wanted to ditch the famous yellow cartouche and minimise Karajan's impact. Commercially, it would have been disastrous. The overwhelming majority of non-specialist collectors buy from browser racks. They look for the cartouche and they look for successful artists and combinations of artists, of which 'Berlin Philharmonic : Herbert von Karajan' was perhaps the most successful of all.

The plan was based on a false premise which – for me – sums up the problem of the orchestra's relations with Karajan at that time. They had come to believe that *they* were the primary selling point. When I asked, 'And how do you expect me to sell this idea to Mr von Karajan?' they replied, 'We will pressure him.' Such arrogance![10]

Marcovicz was not alone in thinking this. Insiders whose concerns were practical and personal (less to do with abstract issues of sovereignty) tended to be, if not openly pro-Karajan, decidedly wary of the orchestra's aims and tactics.

Few of these doubts found their way into the press. The record industry had nothing to gain, and much to lose, from briefing against the orchestra. As for the press, their stories were personality-led. Such issues as were discussed tended, not unnaturally, to centre on questions of democracy and players' rights.

*

On 20 July, Stresemann celebrated his eightieth birthday. Among the many cards and telegrams was one from Karajan congratulating him and wishing him all the best. Four days later Volker Hassemer met Karajan in Salzburg for a discussion that was described at the time as 'serious and thorough', though Hassemer later reported that Karajan seemed strangely unaware of the storm he had unleashed in Berlin or of the psychological state of the orchestra.

The next day Karajan sent a telex to the players confirming their scheduled Salzburg Festival engagements:

Sehr geehrte Herren [*sic*]
Looking forward to our concerts together in Salzburg and to a heartfelt welcome for you here.[11]

It was not enough. The orchestra rejected the invitation out of hand and Stresemann set about the melancholy task of informing the festival authorities in Salzburg and Lucerne that the Berlin Philharmonic would not now be honouring its commitments. It was a risky move, as it was a clear breach of contract; but in human terms the engagements were now an impossibility. Naturally, Stresemann offered the possibility of the Berliners appearing with a conductor other than Karajan, but Salzburg could not accept that, and Lucerne was far from happy. In the end, the Vienna Philharmonic played all four concerts, Karajan conducting.

If the orchestra was digging in its heels – 'We decided that the only way to get Karajan back', Schellenberger later told me, 'was to show him how strong we were' – Karajan appeared to be weakening.

Had he foreseen, when he embarked on his precipitate action, that Girth would have to go, and that Stresemann would replace him? Stresemann's return had certainly altered the political chemistry. It had restored to full working order the old tripartite power structure of orchestra–manager–conductor, and it had also effected subtler changes. With an octogenarian as general manager, Karajan found it less easy to play the role of the 'wronged elder', the wise old man abused by feckless youth.

In early August, towards the end of a short holiday in Italy, Stresemann received a telephone call from Karajan. Would he and his wife care to visit him in Anif on the way home?

The Stresemanns arrived early; the Karajans arrived late, after a morning concert conducted by Karajan's newest enthusiasm, Riccardo Chailly. During lunch, Stresemann steered the conversation round to the subject of monarchy. A strong personality, his father had always argued, could achieve great things even if his legally constituted powers were limited. The role of Edward VII in forging the Anglo-French alliance prior to the First World War was a case in point. Karajan appeared uninterested in this; which is not to say that he was anything other than extremely attentive to Stresemann's line of attack.

Later, after Karajan had retired for a nap, it became clear to the Stresemanns how upset Eliette and Karajan's two daughters were about his reluctance to mend fences with the orchestra. But a private meeting Stresemann had with him later in the afternoon was far from easy. Outwardly, it was a rant by Karajan, a rehearsal of all his old grievances; and yet Stresemann sensed that, in the midst of all this, he was looking for a formula to end the dispute. Every inch the practised diplomat, he now persuaded Karajan to let him scribble down an outline peace deal: the basis of a letter which, suitably embellished and emended, Karajan might see his way clear to forwarding to the orchestra in the fullness of time.

It had been a difficult day but a not unsuccessful one. Its reward was a harmonious alfresco supper enjoyed by flower-strewn meadows in the lee of the Untersberg on a flawless summer's evening.

*

If Stresemann had been disappointed by Karajan's apparent lack of interest in his thoughts on monarchy, power, and the political acumen of King Edward VII, he would no doubt have been intrigued to be in Anif a few days later when Margaret Thatcher came to lunch. 'Thatcher to see Von Karajan', London's *Daily Telegraph* announced, preferring this to news of plans for an informal meeting between the British Prime Minister and the Austrian Chancellor. 'Thatcher to see Sinowats' did not have quite the same ring to it.

The cue for the visit was a holiday the Thatchers were taking near Salzburg with an old family friend, Lady Glover, widow of the Tory MP Sir Douglas Glover. At the time, Mrs Thatcher was approaching the peak of her fame and influence: twice elected Prime Minister, victor of the Falklands campaign (which Karajan had followed with absorbed interest), scourge of the trade unions, and implacable critic of the Soviets, who had unwittingly given her one of the greatest of all her propaganda triumphs by dubbing her 'The Iron Lady'.

Like Karajan, she currently had an insurrection on her hands, the long anticipated show-down between the government and the National Union of Mineworkers. Unlike Karajan, in his dispute with the Berlin Philharmonic, she and her ministers had spent years devising a battle plan. It was the miners' leaders who had acted precipitately, calling a strike at the start of the summer against a background of record coal stocks and declining demand; and it was the miners who – rightly or wrongly – were perceived to be the dinosaurs.

Mrs Thatcher began by doing most of the talking, not lecturing, but questioning. How, she asked, does a conductor create a sense of ensemble when the players are in different relationships to one another and at different distances? How do you best control an orchestra: is it by force of will or by persuasion? Is a conductor *necessary*?

Karajan was fascinated, not only by the lady herself, but by the clarity of her questions and the wider issues they raised. He hated small-talk, verbal flannel, and what the French call *la langue du bois*, official-speak. What he loved was a conversationalist with the ability to get to the heart of the matter. Margaret Thatcher fitted that prescription perfectly.

Luncheon was drawing to a close, and the guests were thinking of their next move. Karajan was not, however, willing to yield up so fine a conversational quarry – or so promising a source of advice: 'You have asked me a great many questions about my profession and I have answered them very directly. Now it is my turn to ask you about your profession.'

In a sense, they were similar questions, concerning the exercise of power and the nature of authority; and they were answered, by all accounts, every bit as rigorously by Mrs Thatcher as the previous questions had been answered by Karajan. It had been an absorbing encounter and, from Karajan's point of view, a highly instructive one.[12]

*

The breathing space the summer had provided eventually bore fruit. On

23 August, Stresemann was called by Karajan's office in Salzburg and told that he had sent the orchestra 'a really very beautiful letter'. Stresemann had been sent a copy and it would be with him shortly. The letter read:

The international music world and our public expect that we make music together in Bach's B minor Mass during this year's Berlin Festival. This is exactly the work, imbued as it is with humanity and Christianity, that should make it easier for us to draw a line under recent events in a spirit of reconciliation, and reclaim our mutual heritage.

Over a long period of thirty years, which embraces almost my entire professional life and that of many members of the orchestra, we were able to achieve together such great and lasting performances only because we were at one with the music and respected each other. Recent unhappy chances, all-too-human failures of communication, and errors made in earlier times, cannot and must not be allowed to darken the effect of a musical triumph and uninterrupted progress esteemed throughout the world.

I therefore propose to you that in September 1984 during the Berlin Festival, with which I have been associated as a conductor of the Berlin Philharmonic since 1953, we resume our work together as musicians. In such a context we shall find the peace, the objectivity, the relaxation, and the calm with which to find better solutions to our outstanding problems.

With heartfelt greetings,
    Herbert von Karajan[13]

The letter was mocked by the press, and by one or two people in the orchestra. The reference to a humane and Christian spirit was taken particularly amiss, though since what Karajan was referring to was not his own humane and Christian spirit but a context in which solutions to their mutual problems might best be sought, it is difficult to see why. (And was he not right? If music can instil in performers and listeners alike a sense of harmonious well-being is not Bach's as fine as any?)

The Mayor and Senate did not underestimate the letter, nor, naturally, did Stresemann; though he took the precaution, before discussing it with the orchestral board, of underpinning it with a guarantee of his own that he would be requiring Karajan to negotiate with them face to face.

On 31 August, a meeting of the full orchestra was convened, during which it heard separate submissions in closed session from Stresemann and from the orchestra's legal representative on media affairs, Dr Meyer-Wölden. Both men urged a qualified acceptance of Karajan's offer. Some players remained unhappy – even going so far as to accuse Stresemann and Meyer-Wölden of colluding in what they said – but the vote in favour of playing the two Bach performances was unanimous. It was, however, made clear that any further co-operation would be dependent on the successful outcome of direct negotiations with Karajan.

When Karajan arrived in Berlin to rehearse the Bach he was tense and apprehensive. He declined to be met at the airport, kept himself to himself, and got the first rehearsal off to a thoroughly bad start by simply saying 'Good morning' and indicating which part of the Mass he wanted to rehearse.

His every move was being closely monitored. The first crisis came when he asked for the concertmaster to be changed. The orchestra had put up the young Toru Yasunaga but – for Bach – Karajan wanted Leon Spierer. He was perfectly within his rights to specify which concertmaster he wanted for which performance, and he had gone out of his way to talk to Yasunaga about the change. But the board was persuaded to write Karajan an aggressively phrased letter charging him with a breach of the orchestra's administrative statutes. Fortunately, it never reached him. Uli Märkle intercepted it and took it straight to Stresemann. This was not something, Märkle suggested, Karajan ought to be confronted with at this particular moment. Stresemann agreed.

It had been assumed that the formal meeting with Karajan would take place after the Bach performances, in what he had predicted would be a new spirit of 'peace, objectivity, relaxation, and calm'. But when it came to it, he could not wait. A free morning was spotted on the day of the first performance, and the meeting was called for 10 a.m. in Karajan's own office at the Philharmonie. (There was barely space there for nearly twenty people but Karajan refused to use the conference room. It would, he said, convey to him the impression that he was on trial.)

The meeting was attended by Karajan, Stresemann, Märkle, Cultural Senator Hassemer, his Secretary of State and civil servants, the orchestra's board and 'Council of Five', and its two media representatives Schellenberger and Gellermann.

Hassemer welcomed everyone and invited the newly elected board member, 55-year-old Klaus Häussler, to address the meeting on behalf of the orchestra. He avoided all mention of Girth, Sabine Meyer, or the Whitsun Festival, choosing instead to speak forcefully about the feeling of alienation that had grown up between the players and their chief conductor. Karajan looked hurt, but said nothing. When his turn came, he spoke about his long years of intensive work with the orchestra and the 'sense of belonging' this had brought.

As an opening exchange it had gone better than anyone (anyone, that is, who was looking for a *rapprochement*) dared hope. After that, it was a matter of winning agreement on specific issues. This, too, went surprisingly well. The current pay scale and administrative statutes were approved without discussion. Auditions policy looked trickier, both in principle and in practice. Fourteen posts currently required filling. Would Karajan be able to attend all fourteen auditions and, if not, might the orchestra proceed without him? Karajan said yes. He even offered to abandon his right, *de facto* if not *de jure*, to veto a candidate before the probationary year.

Was he, at the age of seventy-six, no longer concerned to build for the future? Was this a case of what Thomas Carlyle once called 'The foul sluggard's comfort: "It will last my time"'? Or was it simply that after the traumas of the Sabine Meyer affair he had decided there was nothing to be gained now from brawling with the orchestra over the appointment of players at the probationary stage? Whatever the reason, it was a gesture Stresemann could have done without. The rules governing the probationary appointments were already a cause for concern; this gesture weakened them still further.

The final possible stumbling-block concerned tours within Germany. Karajan had an elephantine memory for places where there had been poor acoustics, empty seats, or personal unpleasantnesses. If he refused to return to such venues, would he allow someone else to take the orchestra in his place? Again, the answer was yes. Provided he approved the conductor, there was no problem.

A further demand was that Karajan should meet the orchestra's board on a more regular basis than previously. Once more, he agreed, though he now put a crucial question of his own: Do you genuinely want me back?

The two board members and 'gang of five' withdrew, slightly bemused, to assess the progress the meeting had made. Shortly afterwards, they returned, still looking bemused, to announce that there was nothing further to negotiate. They did want Karajan back; a 'Peace Treaty' could be signed.

The press conference given by Volker Hassemer at four o'clock that Saturday afternoon was something of an anticlimax. 'They're only interested in bad news,' observed Schellenberger. There was clear disappointment that there had been no final break; or, failing that, an announcement that Karajan had agreed to accept some kind of laureate status. Either way, there would have been a rich crop of stories to come as Berlin set about electing its new musical Pope.

*

In fact, Karajan had become a kind of laureate conductor, albeit an uniquely powerful one. Two things had determined his strategy: first, a refusal to be beaten into submission by a faction within the orchestra ('Even if they spit on me, I'm staying,' he told Uli Märkle); secondly, the years of achievement with the orchestra and the sense of belonging they had created.

A few months after Karajan's death, I asked Hansjörg Schellenberger whether the relationship really was re-established in the wake of the Meyer affair. He replied: 'Certainly. It was absolutely re-established.'

At the musical level, this is probably true. The evidence was not in Bach but in Strauss, in a lovingly played and deeply affecting performance of *Ein Heldenleben* which was filmed and recorded a few months later, in February 1985.[14] Karajan's touch with the piece was as sure as ever, the lambency of the sound astonishing even by the standards of this orchestra. Yet there was more to it than this. Of the dozens of performances of *Ein Heldenleben* Karajan and the orchestra had given together, this was perhaps the most revealing. That fact that *Ein Heldenleben* was, in some sense, apt to the moment cannot have been lost on Karajan or the players: the hero striding manfully forth, the hero confronting his critics (and being strangely disappointed in them), the hero in love and at war, his retreat to the countryside, remembrance of things past, retirement and renunciation. *Ein Heldenleben* can seem a trumpery piece, vainglorious even, but not in this performance. The meditative passages in particular have a depth of feeling that seem at times to bring Karajan – on camera – close to tears.

What is also interesting about the film is how generous it is to the orchestra, with a more than usually complete array of solo portraits, including several of Karl Leister, whose clarinet playing is beyond compare. If any performance redeems the promise Karajan made to Richard Strauss in the letter he wrote to him on the occasion of his eightieth birthday in 1944, it is this.

Which is not to say that the politicking stopped. Karajan signed the 'Peace Treaty' without reading it, would occasionally have to be reminded of its contents, and did not, as we shall see, die in harness. Stern and his allies neither forgot nor forgave, and continued the war of attrition by other means.

Meanwhile, a rush of younger players joined the orchestra. These raw recruits gazed with awe on the sacred monster who appeared before them, and felt the force of his and the orchestra's personality, whilst having little understanding of how it had all been created in the first place.

CHAPTER 78

Soldiering on

Shame on the soul, to falter on the road of life
while the body still perseveres.
            Marcus Aurelius, *Meditations*

So the show was back on the road. In October, Karajan flew with the orchestra to Japan, and this time Eliette went along to keep an eye on her husband. She hated touring and rarely travelled with him outside Europe, which was a pity. She was rather a good tour hostess; her wowing of the Vienna Philharmonic during the 1959 world tour had proved that.

The widely publicised *Krach* between orchestra and conductor had driven interest to new heights. Wherever Karajan and the Berliners appeared over the next four years, tickets changed hands at exorbitant prices; touts grew fat on the pickings. Underlying all this was the feeling that time was running out, that every visit was likely to be Karajan's last. People who had studiously ignored his work now began attending his concerts to 'see him before he went'. What they saw, however, was not so much a conductor at work as a phenomenon chronically on show. Karajan never became quite as sparing of gesture as Karl Böhm did in his last years, but he ran him close. A brush of the hand, a change in the look of the eyes (usually open now) was enough to communicate to the Berlin or Vienna players an encyclopaedia of meaning.

The critic Christopher Breunig described the phenomenon well on the occasion of Karajan's final visit to London in October 1988.

Karajan listens to, anticipates and adjusts the sound. His gestures are limited: more like *reminders* of how he used to direct those players ... Above all, one felt he was still perfecting readings: as if in a workshop. Playing not for the present but in preparation for some other, future time.[1]

On that occasion it was *Verklärte Nacht* and Brahms's C minor Symphony, the Schoenberg played as a haunted half-remembered memory, the Brahms more unremittingly anguished than it had ever been.[2]

And Breunig was right, Karajan did seem to be contemplating 'some other, future time'. Late one evening in February 1985, Michel Glotz had called him to report that the editing of the new Beethoven cycle had been completed. Next day Glotz was off to Florida for a winter break.

'You can't wait to get your arse in warm water!' Karajan rumbled down the phone. 'And what about the Brahms?'

'The Brahms?' queried Glotz

'Yes, the Brahms.'

'I don't know what you're talking about.'

'A German composer,' replied Karajan, adopting a tone of mock exasperation. 'Born in Hamburg in 1833. He wrote four symphonies. But I was forgetting: you are French – it is possible you have never heard of this man . . . Michel, the Brahms symphonies which we have also recorded.'

'Which we will *start* recording in the autumn.'

There was a pause at the other end of the line. 'You know, I thought they were already done. In my mind, they are prepared . . . and now I am already thinking of other things.'[3]

Old men forget. But Karajan was not senile; the gods chastised his body but he was spared the indignity of his father's Alzheimer's-ridden end. My friend, the composer Christopher Headington, was not at all surprised by the story. Work that is fully and finally imagined, he said, is work that is finished; the execution is of little account.[4]

Karajan's work was done in the mind. He read scores but never annotated them; he merely absorbed and pondered them. On the last occasion I saw him, he was preoccupied with the image of a great bridge, its massy piers reaching down into the water beneath; he was trying to fix in his imagination the final bars of Sibelius's Fifth Symphony as he hoped one day to be able to conduct it.

*

Not everyone thought the old man's music-making either enjoyable or edifying. John Eliot Gardiner would recall:

I got the impression from the concerts I attended towards the end of his life that there was something almost evil in the way he exerted the power, and that that was to the detriment of the music. There were *no* surprises, no moments of joy. One felt it was to a formula; everything was self-regarding, everything came back to himself.[5]

One wonders what he heard. The playing of Bach and Vivaldi concertos, Dvořák's Eighth Symphony and Prokofiev's First remained joyful enough.[6]

If 'moments of joy' were generally in short supply, it was as much to do with a choice of repertory that could be dauntingly bleak in these last years. The programme Karajan devised for the traditional All Souls' Day concert after the orchestra's return from Japan in November 1984 was not unrepresentative: Brahms's Fourth Symphony, *Tod und Verklärung*, and *Metamorphosen*.[7] Not much joy there. Three weeks later, the programme consisted of Honegger's Third Symphony and Brahms's First.

But it is the word 'evil' that sticks out in Gardiner's retrospective assessment. Sir Isaiah Berlin once told me that he thought Karajan an 'ignoble' conductor. But one has to go back to Dr Hajas and his fulminations against Karajan in the columns of the *Österreichische Zeitung* in 1947 to encounter a judgement of this order of severity.

Gardiner's fusillades (there were others) came as a reminder that people who took against Karajan had always tended to do so with an almost missionary zeal. But Gardiner's persistent sniping was also rather odd. Ground clearance is one thing, hacking out dead wood in order to open up new vistas. But why should so prodigiously gifted an Englishman appear to be so bothered by a dead Austrian maestro?[8]

If Gardiner has appeared bothered by Karajan, driven occasionally to leap out of the bushes and stamp on his shadow, Carlos Kleiber would be the reverse. For him, Karajan was an inhibition, a constraint, and an excuse. Kleiber never disguised his enormous admiration for Karajan or his intense dislike of a profession to which he had been bound both by his genius and his father. 'I conduct only when I'm hungry,' he told Karajan, who turned the remark into an amusing yarn about Kleiber only accepting conducting engagements when he needed to fill up his deep-freeze.

In 1988, Kleiber was invited to conduct a benefit concert for UNICEF with the Berlin Philharmonic. He accepted, only to find that he and President Richard von Weizsächer had become embroiled in a plot by the Berlin Karajan-baiters to bypass Karajan's own plans for the occasion. When Karajan wrote to him, surprised and sad, Kleiber replied:

Whenever I feel that people might perhaps be causing you trouble, I'd like to strangle them with my own hands. I have no ambitions as a conductor. I prefer to listen to you. So if you tell those bandits ['Hiesln', a reference to the Berlin Philharmonic], 'It's not on', the matter will be closed and everything will be fine again. I am – this perhaps sounds very conceited – one of those few people who have the pleasure of really knowing what endless miracles of conducting you have achieved. I remain your unworthy pupil and, if I may, your friend.[9]

*

In 1985, readers of the French periodical *Diapason* voted Karajan the most popular contemporary classical performer, ahead of Montserrat Caballé and Mstislav Rostropovich. Caballé was thrilled to be in such distinguished company, despite the fact that 'I am evidently not thin enough to be allowed to make music with one of them'.[10] Later, in a series in the London *Observer* entitled *The Experts' Expert*, Karajan was voted 'The conductors' conductor'. Among those who mentioned his name were two of the finest Kapellmeisters of the age (the trade, happily, is not quite extinct), Sir Andrew Davis and Sir Charles Mackerras.[11]

Though Karajan was now old and ill – and though Eliette was occasionally heard to ask why he battled on, dragging himself before the public like some awful old cripple – he kept going, moved to do so by those things that had always driven him: a craving for esteem and a compulsion, a more or less *physical* compulsion, to be in touch with music.[12]

At the 1985 Salzburg Easter Festival, Karajan staged *Carmen* and conducted a concert of music by Debussy and Ravel; Klaus Tennstedt took care of the remainder of the programme. From now on help would be invited each Easter: Chailly in 1986, Giulini in 1987, Masur in 1988, Solti in 1989. Not that Karajan was quite ready for the knacker's yard. In June, Peter Alward reported from the Whitsun Festival:

Karajan's concert consisted of Mozart's *Divertimento* K334 and Strauss's *Zarathustra*. Any doubts as to his state of health can be dispelled if one realises that he did this concert also on two rehearsals – one of them between 6 p.m. and 9 p.m. having conducted the Brahms *Requiem* in Vienna with the VPO in the morning, flown himself to Salzburg and had a two-hour directorate meeting leading straight into the rehearsal![13]

Alward was still hoping to get him to record Sibelius's Third Symphony, the only Sibelius symphony Karajan had never performed or recorded. Orff's *Carmina burana* was also being touted for, but this, it now turned out, had been promised to Deutsche Grammophon as part of Karajan's latest (and last) contract with them. The Orff recording was never made; nor would there be anything further for EMI. The relationship which had begun in Vienna in September 1946 with Beethoven's Eighth Symphony had effectively ended in 1984 in the same city with Vivaldi's *Four Seasons*.

*

After a draining three months, Karajan retired to the country to prepare for the most important event of 1985, a performance of Mozart's *Coronation Mass*, which was to take place in St Peter's, Rome as part of High Mass celebrated by Pope John Paul II.

It is probably true to say that the Papacy was the only temporal authority for which Karajan had any real respect. Nation states preened themselves, fought wars, and fell prey to outlandish ideologies. Chancellors, presidents and prime ministers came and went. After 1945, two figures briefly held him in thrall, Charles de Gaulle and Margaret Thatcher, both leaders whose political achievements were in large measure fashioned against the grain of established expectation. But they were one-offs. If, as St Paul says, 'Here is no continuing city,' the Vatican was for Karajan the next best thing: a state within a state, conservative, hierarchical, in no way self-effacing, confident in its powers.

Michel Glotz would describe the elderly Karajan as a cross between 'a child and a very wise old Chinese man'. The very wise old Chinese man would speculate endlessly on reincarnation, not necessarily in human form; the child, by contrast, yearned for the secure embrace of old-fashioned Catholic ritual.

29 June was, unsurprisingly, a day of sweltering heat in Rome. Even away from the sun's glare, within the cooler confines of St Peter's, it was stifling. The Mass was a lengthy affair. The service and the Mozart – treated functionally, with nothing of the 'concert' about it – sorely taxed Karajan's powers to remain upright for so long. His conducting of the slimmed down Vienna Philharmonic and the Vienna Singverein was none the less powerful and robust, almost Klemperer-like in its trenchancy, forward-moving and exact. Yet the most telling moment was a lyrical one: the 'Agnus Dei' between the Eucharistic prayer and the Communion, exquisitely sung by Kathleen Battle.[14]

Karajan and his family received communion from the Pope, who spoke with him after the service. Those close by saw Karajan awed and still, like a boy at confirmation.

*

The next significant event in his life would be well over a year away. Greatly to the exasperation of Stresemann, the Berlin Philharmonic, and the Berlin Senate he had accepted an invitation to conduct the New Year's Day Concert in Vienna on 1 January 1987. Tradition had it that Karajan was in Berlin on New Year's Eve. But it was a tradition with shallow roots, going back to the early 1960s when Vienna's New Year's Day Concert was the preserve of Willi Boskovsky. Things were different now and it was not unnatural that Karajan should wish to make at least one appearance on this most famous of Austrian musical occasions.

Fortunately, relations with the Berlin Philharmonic were in reasonably good shape. Board members Häussler and Wedow were assiduous in maintaining contact with him and he, too, was making an effort. He resumed going to the parties the orchestra held in Salzburg each summer and at the end of the year in Berlin. True, he would get angry about small matters, but where bigger things were concerned he was as he had always been. When he heard that a member of the cello section was in need of a heart bypass operation, it was fixed within a matter of hours.

Occasionally small tremors set off larger shocks. In November 1985, during a recording session that was already in disarray because of an unseasonable blizzard, Karajan had a run-in with Gerd Seifert, whose horn solos were crucial to the extracts from Richard Strauss's *Capriccio* which were being recorded. After ignoring a summons to Karajan's room, Seifert was carpeted by the orchestra's management, and – when the situation further spiralled out of control – dismissed. (He was later reinstated after successfully taking legal action against the orchestra for wrongful dismissal.)

In January 1986, Karajan filmed and recorded Strauss's *Don Quixote* with the young Brazilian cellist Antonio Meneses and Wolfram Christ as the soloists.[15] Twenty years on, Karajan's view of Quixote was not so much that of Quixote the Holy Fool, the visionary martyred by his own imagination, but of a sweet, misguided adventurer, a man whose lofty ideals and crazy exploits have left him vulnerable and alone. *Don Quixote* was also one of the works chosen by Karajan for the concert in January 1986 marking the centenary of Furtwängler's birth. Afterwards, Elisabeth Furtwängler thanked him. The performance of the Strauss had been even more beautiful, she thought, than the ones Karajan had given in earlier years with Fournier.

'It would be impossible for anything bad to happen now,' replied Karajan.

Elisabeth Furtwängler was rather taken aback by this. It suggested a belief in the perfectibility of musical performance which her late husband would never have subscribed to. Having paid her respects, she made to go, but Karajan begged her to stay and talk. He seemed very lonely.[16]

In February 1986, Stresemann retired for a second time. At a concert in the Philharmonie, he formally handed over his job to Hans Georg Schäfer. For reasons best known to themselves, Stresemann and Schäfer had decided to enact the handover in mid-concert. Karajan had not been invited to speak, but he had been asked when the interval would be: something of a teaser in a programme consisting of Haydn's Symphony No.104, Ravel's *Pavane pour une infante défunte* and Mussorgsky's *Pictures at an Exhibition*. Having been told that the interval would be 'after the *Pavane*', they plumped for the gap between the Haydn and it.

Stresemann was rapturously received and made an affecting short speech ending with the words: 'I hope that things will work out harmoniously here, for harmony is the most important thing in music, if only we know how to interpret it correctly.'[17]

Karajan could not have had a better cue to launch into Ravel's wistful and harmonious *Pavane*; but he had sat stony-faced throughout the speeches, much as he had used to do during Egon Hilbert's press conferences in Vienna in the early 1960s. After the applause had died down, he struggled to his feet, waited for absolute quiet, then fired into the microphone three words: '*Jetzt ist Pause* [The interval's now]'. Whether this was a musical whim, a decision to play the *Pavane* when the orchestra was resettled after the interval or (as many suspected) a calculated snub to Stresemann, it is difficult to say.[18]

In the winter of 1985–6, there was further speculation about Karajan's health. When rumours began circulating that he had flown to the United States for emergency medical checks, obituary editors went on to red alert. He was, indeed, ill; this time with prostate trouble. In early April, shortly after the end of the Salzburg Easter Festival, it was announced that he had been admitted to the University Clinic in Essen for tests and surgery.

The 1986 Easter Festival had been a sombre affair, with Verdi's *Don Carlos* and Bruckner's Ninth Symphony as its two dark peaks. Karajan had revived his 1975 production of the Verdi in order to film it. The duologues, shot in a Rembrandt-like chiaroscuro, gain an added intensity on film, but television shrinks and demeans the public scenes. Karajan's casting had also gone awry. Bringing the 35-year-old Ferruccio Furlanetto in to play the King was almost as bad an idea as retaining Cappuccilli, now in his mid-fifties, portly and baggy-eyed, as the Marquis de Posa. In fact, the *real* King – the true image of Schiller's humanly frail old despot – was not on stage but in the pit, now awed by the music, now angrily shushing the strings into submission.

The anthology of death-haunted works continued in Vienna in May when Karajan recorded the Mozart *Requiem* for film and CD. As was often the case after surgery, he looked remarkably well; happy to have seen the Grim Reaper turned away at the gate yet again. It is a strong, trenchant performance such as his old Salzburg enemy Joseph Messner might have approved and admired in the 1920s.

*

During the summer and early autumn of 1986, Karajan conducted relatively little. He also began to talk rather more openly about how long was left to him. He told critic Klaus Geitel:

I'm seventy-eight, I might be struck down tomorrow or something else might happen, and it'll be impossible to stop someone else being pressed into the job [the Berlin Philharmonic] for totally obscure reasons, someone who's ultimately not up to it.[19]

Though Karajan seemed well enough in May, his moods and general health were unpredictable. No one quite knew what would happen next. During preparations for the Salzburg Festival, he sacked his too argumentative Carmen, Agnes Baltsa, and replaced her with Helga Müller Molinari. 'The result,' wrote Bryan Magee in *Opera*, 'was a *Carmen* with two Micaëlas.'[20] In Berlin in September, he conducted and filmed a performance of Beethoven's Ninth Symphony of rare eloquence, despite the fact that he was seriously ill with a 'mystery' virus.

This was eventually diagnosed as Lyme Disease, a chronic condition – first identified in Connecticut in 1977 – in which humans are infected by ticks or horseflies which have been in contact with wild deer. The symptoms are a general malaise and inflammation of the joints; the only treatment is high doses of intravenously given penicillin. Karajan's infection appears to have been caught in time; the progress of the disease to the spinal chord, the general nervous system, and the brain can be remorseless and ultimately fatal. Even so, he may already have suffered collateral damage to his heart. For weeks, he felt as rough as he had ever felt, tired, depressed, unable to sleep.

One day, Solti phoned. 'How are you?'

'Terrible. Absolutely terrible!' was the bleak reply. But the old spirit was still there. In early October, he wrote to Peter Alward:

Dear Peter,
Thank you so much for your nice letter of October 6th. Your thoughts on my illness are very comforting, but you can bet that I won't give up.
    With every good wish,
        Yours Herbert[21]

David Smith wrote from Oxford, sending his wife's best wishes and mentioning how well she was doing as a newly appointed consultant paediatric cardiologist. 'How could it be otherwise?' Karajan promptly and charmingly replied. The Smiths also had a telegram thanking them for sending him Oliver Sacks's *The Man who Mistook his Wife for a Hat*.

The main spur to his penicillin-induced recovery was preparation for the New Year's Day concert in Vienna. A year or so after the event, Karajan would tell me:

It was a really hard time. When I got the invitation, I said, 'Well, gladly I will accept.' For three weeks I had nothing to do and I sat down and decided . . . to see if there was something more behind the music. And suddenly I was changed in myself. When I came before the orchestra, I had nothing to explain. It was just there. And from this time I knew I had to give up so many things – my sailing and so on – but the music came back to me a hundred times better.[22]

'Seldom', says Dr Johnson, 'is any splendid story wholly true.' This one certainly wasn't. What Karajan was recalling was a trauma with a happy ending. The nearer the three concerts came the more anxious he seemed to be; and the more anxious he became, the more anxious everyone else was, not least ORF, whose radio and television coverage was due to be heard and seen by an estimated 700 million people.

On 29 December, the evening before the first of the three concerts, Karajan told Glotz he simply did not have the physical capacity to go through with it. Glotz stood firm:

It seemed to me that the problem was not so much physical as psychological. I *never* pushed him. But on this occasion I said: 'You can do it, you have to do it. I even think you *feel* like doing it. But there is – somehow, somewhere – an obstacle in your psyche which you must overcome.' Later that evening, he called me: 'I'll do it.' After that, it was four days of total happiness. No one who knew him had seem him happier on the podium for years.²³

His family knew just how depressed he had been in the weeks before the concert. But it was the old thing with Karajan: put him before an orchestra and the moment the music sounded he was a changed man. His daughter Arabel would recall:

He looked in terrible shape in the dressing-room beforehand. But once he was on the podium I looked at his face and it was as though a mask had been peeled away. He seemed completely changed.²⁴

The film of the concerts confirms Glotz's point about Karajan enjoying himself.²⁵ There are more smiles here than on the whole of the rest of his film legacy. When a confetti cannon explodes at the end of the *Thunder and Lightning* Polka, Karajan feigns sudden death as expertly as a veteran of a dozen spaghetti westerns. (It is difficult to imagine him doing this in Berlin; a Berlin cannon might have had more than confetti in it.) Karajan was even ready to laugh at the amnesiac fit which overcame him on New Year's Day itself when he cued *The Blue Danube*, forgetting that Josef Strauss's *Ohne Sorgen* was due next.

He took a close interest in the television presentation, in particular the on-screen ballet sequences choreographed by Gerlinde Dill. It was his idea to involve the famous white stallions of Vienna's Spanish Riding School. Johann Strauss's *Annen-Polka* was chosen to accompany the sequence and great care was taken to ascertain the exact tempo at which the horses most easily moved. With or without them, it was a performance of incomparable grace and nobility, tinged, as was the entire concert, with a profound sense of sadness and longing.

Karajan's other idea for the concert was the introduction of a vocalist. At Clemens Krauss's very first Strauss family concert in Salzburg in August in 1929, Adele Kern had sung a version of the waltz *Voices of Spring*. Karajan now repeated the idea, with Kathleen Battle, in a rhododendron-red dress, as his bewitching, note-perfect soloist. Battle intrigued him. 'She's a complete bitch,' he would laugh, 'but, my God, what a voice!'

One of the traditions of the New Year's Day Concert is the conductor's New Year greeting to the world: music's equivalent of the Papal *'urbi et orbi*'. Murphy's law ensured that this, of all concerts, should be afflicted by microphone failure at the critical moment. To make matters worse, a huge fan bearing the words '*Prosit Neujahr*' came lumbering into view bang in the middle of Karajan's electronically compromised address.

By the time he repeated his greeting in English, the microphone was working again:

All over the world we all wish one thing. Our dearest wish is peace, peace, and [the voice breaking with emotion] once more peace.[26]

The 1987 New Year's Day Concert, and the concerts conducted in 1989 and 1992 by Carlos Kleiber, proved to be high-water marks in a series that has never quite been the same since the halcyon age of Clemens Krauss and Willi Boskovsky. Why the Karajan concert was so special, to Austrians in particular, was well explained by Franz Welser-Möst:

His New Year's Day Concert was one of the most beautiful I have ever heard. Carlos Kleiber's was the most exciting – there's always fire on the roof when he conducts – but I don't think it necessarily caught the whole spectrum and expression of meaning in that music. Very often I miss the melancholy in it, almost a lethargy which Karajan did in an incredible way. It has to be on the racy side, this music, and on the other it's almost depressed. That's typically Austrian. If you look at Schubert, Johann Strauss, Mahler or even Alban Berg, there's always depression somewhere.[27]

The conductor Walter Weller – one of the leaders of the Vienna Philharmonic in the Boskovsky era – would tell me:

When Karajan conducted Josef Strauss's waltz *Music of the Spheres* at that concert in 1987, it was just that – music of the spheres. I play the recording whenever I'm tired or depressed or in need of inspiration. Why it was so wonderful is impossible to put into words; but, then, I think it is good that in life we have these wonderful experiences which *are* utterly mysterious.[28]

Non-Viennese opinion was rather more divided. The director of the Tallis Scholars Peter Phillips, who saw the concert on black-and-white television in an hotel room in Vienna,[29] wrote a piece in the *Spectator* gently deriding the Austrian habit of treating the music of the Strauss family *à la* Bruckner. He did not quote Ira Gershwin – 'Oh, give me the free 'n' easy/Waltz that is Viennesey' – but that is what he appeared to be hankering after. His ideal, he said, was Erich Leinsdorf, the conducting wistful and gay.[30]

CHAPTER 79

Trouble over Taiwan

Even the best-intentioned of great men need
a few scoundrels around them.
La Bruyère, *Characters*

Lawyers continued to grow fat on Karajan's many activities. In January 1987, negotiations resumed with EMI over the back-catalogue of Karajan recordings which had not yet been transferred to CD. With his eightieth birthday looming, a deal needed to be struck; further delay, it was argued, could be construed as 'a dereliction of duty and damaging to Karajan's market impact and income'.[1]

Karajan himself also continued to wage a somewhat quixotic battle against pirate record labels. In 1984 he had won a case in the Hamburg Higher Regional Court forbidding the sale in West Germany of an Italian pirate of a live recording of *Die Zauberflöte* made in Vienna in 1962. The case was not without its funny side. The LP box had as its cover illustration a phallic totem: a huge, gold penis pointing skywards. Among the legal procedures that had to be gone through was a submission to the court that the plaintiff was not suing for indecency or the misrepresentation of his person.

Less amusing was the paternity suit which was issued against Karajan in 1987 by a 43-year-old German-born housewife living in the north-east of England. Medical evidence, taken in 1989 shortly before Karajan's death, proved there was no case to answer, but the story itself was widely reported in the tabloid press in the spring of 1987. The *Daily Mail* (owned by Eliette's friend Lord Rothermere) was particularly insistent. 'Von Karajan is my father' bawled the headline. A sub-heading added: 'He was a German soldier in the war. My mother was a munitions worker. Now he is the most famous conductor in the world.'

The mother of the love-child was alleged to have met Karajan in a restaurant in the small town Treuenbrietzen forty miles south-west of Berlin in 1943:

She remembered that the other soldiers treated him with great respect. He was in uniform, using the last name Hoffner – the same name on the soldiers' identification book he showed her – and he played the guitar [*sic*] and sang [*sic*].[2]

The article, a soupily written piece by 'Femail' reporter Anthea Gerrie, repeated the old journalistic canard about Karajan's movements in the years 1942–5 being a complete mystery.

*

In 1987 the Salzburg Easter and Summer festivals shared a new production of *Don Giovanni*, conducted by Karajan, with staging and design by Michael Hampe and Mauro Pagano.[3] What most people remember about this production is the end, a vast cyclorama revealing an ice-blue galaxy of stars and planets. As the Commendatore's statue trundled forward to carry Giovanni off to hell, the galaxy glowed red. Rarely can the music have been so powerfully complemented by a stage picture in which heaven, hell, and the cosmos itself seemed to become one. It was a triumph of imaginative design

For the rest, the production, lit in various shades of midnight blue, had a forbiddingly classical feel to it, the characters not so much 'played' as marmoreally embodied. Orchestral dynamics ranged from *Tristan*-like fortissimi to pianissimi that had the hush of death on them.

The highlight of the summer festival was a concert as momentous, in its way, as Karajan's New Year's Day Concert had been eight months earlier. The Feast of the Assumption is a public holiday in Austria and the Assumption Day concert has long had a place of honour in the festival programme. In 1987, Karajan made it the more special by conducting an all-Wagner concert – something of a rarity in Salzburg – with Jessye Norman as soloist.

The programme, the last of Karajan's Wagner projects,[4] was a digest: the overture to *Tannhäuser* from the early years, the *Siegfried Idyll* representing *The Ring*, and the Prelude and *Liebestod* from *Tristan und Isolde*. The spell was broken on the day itself (though not on the subsequent CD) by an intrusive interval after the *Idyll*; but even that could not lessen the mesmeric power of the *Liebestod* in this context, the human voice entering at the very end of the morning – 'mild und leise [gently, quietly]' – like an annunciation. So placed, the *Liebestod* became both an annunciation and an assumption, Isolde received bodily into the realm of eternal night just as, on the Feast of the Assumption, the earthly body of the Blessed Virgin is received into heaven.

This was another of Karajan's guilefully devised dying falls. As the final chord faded into silence, his face registered tension, regret, and, finally, a kind of resigned calm. After his death, the theatre director August Everding would recall:

He was no pacifier or reconciler; the orchestra pit was the command post from which he organised his company. But sometimes I refused to look, because the bliss on his face moved me . . . He heard blissful sounds and gazed into eternity. Creation was still perfect in that world.[5]

'It's over,' Karajan had murmured to Eliette as they were driven from Anif to the Festspielhaus that August Saturday morning. His career was not quite over, but there was a growing sense of an era coming to a close. Which conductor nowadays would dare make his distinguished soloist spend an entire rehearsal simply *listening* to the orchestra? Jessye Norman was more amused than annoyed. Never before, she told the crew filming the eightieth-birthday documentary *Karajan in Salzburg*, had she realised how many piano and pianissimo markings there were in Wagner, more than thirty in the *Liebestod* alone. 'Singing with a conductor like this,' she said, 'makes the role possible.'[6]

*

In early November, Karajan's brother died. Karajan would tell me:

I don't think it need have happened when it did. He refused to go near a doctor. He had some minor heart ailment, and then a kidney problem which could probably have been treated. But he was always a law unto himself. He would go off into the mountains for days on end. No one would know where he was.[7]

For all their seeming differences, the brothers were alike in that respect: solitary, independent, mountain men. They had long ceased to be close socially, partly because Herbert had an intense dislike of his sister-in-law. Wolfgang would very occasionally visit Anif for a private supper. On such occasions, the years would slip away and they would be boys again, for there is a sense in which neither of them ever fully grew up. I remember Karajan telling me how Wolfgang never bothered washing anything up; he would simply lick the plate clean and put it back on the shelf. There was no malice in the tale, simply a kind of fraternal amusement. But he regretted that his brother had not done more with his life, had not really harnessed his gift for electrical engineering:

He made a radio receiver when we were children and set it up on the main bridge over the Salzach. So many people wanted to see it, the police had to be called to disperse the crowd and take the equipment away.[8]

Karajan was on a tour in Germany with the Berlin Philharmonic when he received the news. Halfway through the tour, he went down with a minor stomach ailment. The press had a field day. Ignorant of the bereavement and brushing aside the food-poisoning story (remnants of a meal and an empty champagne bottle had been spied in Karajan's hotel suite in Frankfurt), the reports concentrated on rumours of fresh feuding between Karajan and the orchestra.

Karajan was, indeed, ill; but not so ill as to have to suffer the indignity of being upstaged. Having said he could not conduct the Frankfurt concert, he rapidly changed his mind when he discovered that Zubin Mehta was on pre-arranged stand-by. The next evening in Stuttgart (when Mehta was due to conduct in Munich and no longer available) Karajan did cancel.

The incident illustrates the kind of scrapes he was now getting into by obstinately soldiering on. Gossip about the Stuttgart cancellation was as nothing, however, to a larger storm that was brewing over plans for a tour which was scheduled to start shortly after his eightieth birthday in April 1988.

The itinerary had been planned to take Karajan and the Berliners to Osaka, Tokyo, Moscow, and Leningrad, but the Soviet leg of the trip had been cancelled on instructions from the government in Bonn. With dates going begging, Hellmut Stern, who had successfully masterminded the Berlin Philharmonic's visit to China in 1979, suggested that Taiwan might be a possible alternative venue. The Taiwanese were keen to entertain the orchestra, there was a brand-new cultural centre to perform in, and the necessary funding.

The idea was approved by the orchestra and taken to Uli Märkle for further discussion with Karajan, who did not disapprove. As long as the visit was organised by Columbia Artists Management, which was already handling the Japanese leg of the tour, he was happy. CAMI's Peter Gelb, who had recently finished shooting *Karajan in Salzburg*, was now brought into the discussions, first with Märkle, later with the Berlin Philharmonic manager Walter Erich Schäfer, who authorised Gelb to make a formal approach to Taiwan. The offer was sent by Gelb on 7 October. The telex began:

I have been advised by Mr Stern of the Berlin Philharmonic Orchestra that you are interested in presenting the Berlin Philharmonic in your new concert facilities in Taiwan. On behalf of Mr von Karajan and the Berlin Philharmonic, I have been asked to explore this possibility with you.

Though it was, indeed, the case that Gelb had the orchestra's approval for the approach, the terms which were now presented to the Taiwanese had little to do with the Berlin Philharmonic – travelling on an official assignment for which it received no fee – or with Karajan's position as its principal conductor. The offer went on:

You would provide all-inclusive fees for von Karajan and the Orchestra, totaling [*sic*] 600,000 DM[£200,000] for a total of 2 concerts. In addition, you would be required to purchase the Taiwan broadcasting rights for 10 previously produced television programs of von Karajan and the Berlin Philharmonic or the Vienna Philharmonic at the price of 35,000 US dollars [£22,000] per program, hence totalling 350,000 US dollars [£220,000] for all ten programmes. You would be required to purchase the 10 programs before the tour takes place. You would also be required to present us with an unconditional letter of credit for all the above fees no later than Nov. 1, 1987.[9]

These were steepling terms, which the Taiwanese rejected with the words 'another time, perhaps'.

Hellmut Stern, meanwhile, was baffled as to why his idea had run into the sands. When a copy of Gelb's telex was sent him by friends in Taiwan, he was flabbergasted. Gelb later claimed that neither Karajan nor CAMI was seriously interested in taking up the idea, which is why the asking price had been pitched so high. No one believed this. The Taiwan leg of the trip showed every indication of being a nice little earner for CAMI, and was too good a chance for Télémondial to pass up. With Europe still lukewarm about music on film, and with Laserdisc already floundering in Europe and the United States, the Far East would be crucial to the commercial fortunes of Karajan's 'Legacy for Home Video'.

Business managers have to think of these things. What defied belief was the idea that these disparate artistic and commercial interests could be so glibly packaged together – Stresemann later described the deal as 'immoral, unethical, impossible to imagine'[10] – and packaged together, what's more, on the back of an idea from as eagle-eyed and keen a critic of Karajan's methods as Hellmut Stern.

Throughout the winter, a damage limitation exercise was put in place by the West Berlin government. Gelb's story that the offer had merely been a try-on was backed – initially, at least – by Secretary of State Pufendorf.[11] This, despite the fact that, if it was a try-on, it was singularly inept, since it had demonstrated to the Taiwanese, and thus to the world at large, the nature of the game that was currently being played in Berlin.

Karajan said nothing in public. Ronald Wilford told me:

He pretended an interest in finance – pretended an interest – and, indeed, *had* an interest in knowing certain things about it. But it was not something he was actually interested in pursuing. Among his priorities it was very much a subsidiary element. As for actually negotiating – no, never. What interested him was function. How to fly an aeroplane, how to sail a boat: things that had to do with precision and timing and function.[12]

None the less, Karajan must have known what was going on. A more scrupulous – some might say, a less effective – man would have apologised to the Berlin Senate and required a number of his advisers to consider their positions. But that was not his way. Whatever was said in private to malfunctioning functionaries, Karajan's public demeanour was one of growing irritation with opponents who continued to scavenge among the entrails.

In the circumstances, no one had any claim to the moral high ground. Karajan, Télémondial, and CAMI were all exploiting the orchestra, but so – in the guise of its commercial *alter ego* the Berliner Philharmoniker – was the orchestra itself, whose own highly lucrative film deal with Télémondial had been negotiated through CAMI.

*

The 1988 Easter Festival ended on the eve of Karajan's eightieth birthday. It had been a somewhat stodgy affair: a grandiose new production of *Tosca* with a second-rank cast, Brahms's *German Requiem*, and the *Alpine Symphony*.

The principal birthday events took place off-stage. There was Gelb's film *Karajan in Salzburg* and Peter Csobádi's comprehensive and lavishly illustrated 300-page anthology of homage and reminiscence *Karajan oder die kontrollierte Ekstase*. Karajan approved of neither. The film showed him as he was, not as he had been or imagined himself still to be; the book contained criticisms. As a Karajan lawyer had once advised, 'the maestro does not greatly care to be confronted with information which puts him at a disadvantage to himself'.[13]

Perhaps Karajan had a right to be aggrieved about some of the coverage he was receiving. There is time enough, in a long life, to settle old scores; an eightieth birthday is not one of them. I remember him saying how he envied the way Bernstein was treated on the occasion of his seventieth birthday later that same year. Loath to point out that Bernstein's was, perhaps, an easier life to celebrate, I mentioned the generous greeting Bernstein had sent that April

. . . let me thank you for the best *Don Carlo* I have ever heard, the best *Salome*, and the best *Prague* Symphony, among others. May you go from strength to strength.[14]

Karajan conceded that he had been touched by that.

EMI reissued a significant proportion of their Karajan archive for the eightieth birthday. Deutsche Grammophon did that, and more: they asked Karajan if they could reissue the complete archive of recordings he made for Polydor between 1938 and 1943. To their surprise, he said yes. He, in turn, secured from them a special jubilee edition of twenty-five CDs, each 'embellished' (his word) with one of Eliette's paintings.

Most of the paintings that were used suggested the landscapes of Eliette's native Provence as they had been painted by Cézanne eighty years earlier.

Yet it was far from being a negligible body of work; she had talent, and some distinguished teachers: Herbert Breiter in Salzburg, Antonio Clavé in the south of France. Karajan had encouraged her to paint, partly as an antidote to loneliness. He also enjoyed having a creator in the house. Having so conspicuously bucked the creative challenge during his time as a music student in Vienna, he now drew sustenance from watching work in progress. Eliette would recall:

He liked to fall asleep contemplating my latest canvas, imagining what it was about. If the paint was still wet, which it often was, the chemical stench was decidedly unpleasant. But he was undeterred![15]

Eliette also gave a round of interviews for the eightieth birthday, bravura performances in their own right. Interviewed for the women's page of the *Daily Telegraph*, she treated the photographer to every trick of the mannequin's trade. She even offered to lop off the collar of her Valentino suit if that improved the shot. 'That', said reporter Catherine Stott, 'is to be very rich indeed.'[16] As for her octogenarian husband:

[Eliette] raised her wine glass to an imaginary audience of women: 'I wish for my daughters and for all women that they should have the possibility of having such a husband in their lives. Where *are* these men these days?[17]

It was a fickle, sportive Cleopatra toasting her wounded Antony.

And he was wounded. The anti-Karajan lobby had held its fire over the Taiwan affair until the eightieth birthday. A week before the birthday, *Der Spiegel* ran the story in full. Karajan appeared on the front cover over the legend '*Der Finanz-Magier* [The Finance Wizard]'. Inside, was a seventeen-page article headed '*Sie zahlen für Herrn von Karajan . . .* [You pay for Herr von Karajan . . .]'. The article was as arid as its headline; but it was a stunning piece of journalism, a real hatchet job. During April, newspapers throughout Europe, America, and the Far East picked up the story, turning the tour into front-page news even before it had begun.

In Berlin, meanwhile, things were going from bad to worse. In the absence of detailed explanations from CAMI or Karajan about the charges which were now being laid in the press, Cultural Senator Hassemer revoked CAMI's contract to organise a projected tour of the United States by Karajan and the orchestra. Furious, Karajan made a late withdrawal – more 'gastric flu' – from a concert that had been arranged to mark Berlin's year as 'European City of Culture'. The Federal President, Richard von Weizsächer, who had been due to confer on Karajan the highest order of the Federal Cross of Merit, was not amused.

Next day, Karajan flew himself to Düsseldorf, where he joined the Lufthansa flight to Japan. It would be his last visit there. The German press agency reported 'an audience fascinated to the point of losing its self-control'. *Der Spiegel* offered another angle:

For three days and three nights students were queuing up for standing-room costing DM260 [£90] per person. A 21-year-old Tokyo girl publicly protested that she had preserved her innocence for the last ten years for the sole purpose of offering it to Karajan; now that there was evidently no opportunity of making this sacrifice, the virgin was prepared to go to bed with anyone who would take her to one of the concerts.[18]

There were five concerts, and they brought full circle Karajan's thirty-four-year reign in Japan as Europe's most sought-after conductor. His opening concert in April 1954 had begun with Brahms's First Symphony; now he was bowing out with the self-same work.

While he was still in Tokyo, the crisis in Berlin deepened. With Gelb in Japan and Wilford en route to Berlin to talk turkey with Hassemer, Karajan fired off a lengthy telex of his own to Hassemer. In it, he rehearsed all the old grievances about his Berlin contract, made new demands, and issued new threats. Among these, interestingly, was a threat to *stay*.

*

Though the planned tour to the United States was not reinstated, the parties brokered a peace; the show remained on the road. The orchestra appeared with Karajan in Salzburg at Whitsuntide, and at the summer festival, where they played more performances of Brahms's *German Requiem*. Evidently ailing, Karajan conducted only three of his six scheduled performances of *Don Giovanni*. There were even awkwardnesses with Anne-Sophie Mutter; the performance of Tchaikovsky's Violin Concerto, part of the Assumption Day concert, was not a success.

During the festival, it was announced that Karajan was standing down as a member of the festival Direktorium. If this seemed uncharacteristic, it should be borne in mind that plans were already in place as far ahead as 1991, the bicentenary of Mozart's death.[19] Karajan had also secured Verdi's *Un ballo in maschera* (from under Abbado's nose) as his own special festival project for the years 1989–91. Beyond that, he did not care to look.

In October 1988, he made a short tour with the Berlin Philharmonic; it included a concert in Vienna and one apiece in London and Paris, his final appearance in either place.[20] In November, he filmed and recorded Bruckner's Eighth Symphony with the Vienna Philharmonic, after which he returned to Berlin for further film editing and two concerts in which he took an almost malicious pleasure in encoring the decidedly tricky finale of Prokofiev's *Classical* Symphony.

I met him in Berlin and found him much preoccupied with the racial disturbances in Azerbaijan and what he considered to be Mikhail Gorbachev's tenuous hold on power in the Soviet Union. Karajan admired Gorbachev; yet, like an animal picking up the vibrations of an imminent earthquake, he sensed that something momentous was about to happen in the East. What he feared was a violent implosion which would engulf the whole of continental Europe; what he hoped for was what actually came about in Berlin in the autumn of 1989 and the Soviet Union in August 1991.

*

On New Year's Eve 1988, Karajan conducted what would be his final concert in Berlin. His soloist was the 17-year-old Evgeni Kissin, the last great prodigy of the piano (so history would later decree) to emerge from the Soviet Union. Minded by a bevy of mainly female relations, teachers, and Soviet sleuths, Kissin was so cocooned as to be virtually inaccessible, even to Karajan who had to battle for the one-to-one rehearsal he eventually secured. Yet, on the morning of the recording, as Klaus Geitel would recall:

[Kissin], the protagonist . . . stood around without anyone seeming to take any notice of him. At times, he tried to make his way surreptitiously towards the grand piano, to prepare further, to acclimatise himself, but repeatedly – before he had even reached the instrument – he was scared away by one or other of the recording managers. Everyone there probably had one thought: this demonic youngster is indeed a fantastic pianist. At that precise moment, however, he was nothing more than a diabolical disturbance.[21]

Karajan conducted the first movement of Tchaikovsky's First Piano Concerto extremely spaciously. It was a slow mountain ascent of a performance, with Kissin – stiff as a marionette and pale-faced beneath his circular shock of black hair – following, bravely but wary-eyed, in the old man's tracks.

It was a long haul for Karajan, too. Before he went on, a cocktail of pain-killing and life-sustaining drugs was injected in his hindquarters by his doctor, Walther Simon. (Always an alarming spectacle. Since Simon had only one arm, he would adjust his balance and then, as it were, launch the hypodermic into the patient.) As he shuffled towards the entrance, Karajan announced: 'Now you can watch a man die on the podium.'

CHAPTER 80

Resignation

'Tis better playing with a lion's whelp
Than with an old one dying.
Shakespeare, *Antony and Cleopatra*

Karajan's strength was failing. There were days when moving around his own home was becoming a Sisyphean task. In early January, he drafted a letter to Cultural Senator Hassemer requesting a renegotiation of his Berlin contract. This was neither a demand nor a threat; it was a plea. He could no longer manage the six double concerts per annum in Berlin itself to which his existing life-contract bound him.

Hassemer was sympathetic to the request but did not remain in office long enough to act upon it. After January's city elections in West Berlin and protracted behind-the-scenes negotiations, a new majority coalition had emerged of socialists and Green Party members. Later that month, as artists and managers gathered in Vienna to record *Un ballo in maschera* with Karajan, I noticed long faces and a somewhat muted atmosphere. 'We are worried for Karajan,' Antje Henneking told me. 'For the first time he is faced with politicians who are openly hostile to him.'

The recording had begun well but four days into the sessions, at ten o'clock on Tuesday morning, consternation. With musicians and industry insiders crowding the boxes of the Musikverein like pigeons in St Mark's, word got out that Karajan had asked for the layouts to be altered. He now wanted the orchestra on the floor of the hall, the soloists on stage. 'It will work perfectly well,' remarked old Vienna hand Christopher Raeburn. 'The problem is, they're now short of time. They've only got until Friday and they won't be able use anything from those earlier sessions. I'm sure Karajan has done it deliberately.'

The project had been a battle of wills from the outset. Karajan had cast the opera in his imagination long before he spoke to Glotz or Deutsche Grammophon. The King would be Domingo; Amelia, the blighted heroine, would be Josephine Barstow, a singer-actress Karajan had first seen in Penderecki's *Die schwarze Maske* in Salzburg in 1986. Barstow was no discovery for London audiences or, indeed, for opera-goers elsewhere; her portrayal of Shostakovich's Katerina Izmaylova was revered even in Russia. Unfortunately, she was not a gramophone 'name'. Deutsche Grammophon was furious. What was Karajan doing casting an 'unknown' singer in so important a project? The pressure on him to change had been relentless.

At the end of the Tuesday morning session, Karajan – frail, shrunken, and white-faced – called for his Oscar, the young Korean singer Sumi Jo. The Golden Hall was emptied of people; the great double doors closed and secured.

'That was mighty impressive,' I said to her later. 'An imperial summons! What on earth did he want to say?' The conversation, she revealed, had hardly been to do with the recording: a couple of points, no more. What Karajan had wanted to talk about was *her*; what she had done, what she was planning to do:

He didn't want my career to be destroyed singing 'on the road'. The *real* surprise was that he was saying it all. Perhaps I've been unlucky, but I'd come to the conclusion that conductors were people who simply ordered you about: 'Do this. Do that. Do it *my* way, or else!' Karajan is the first conductor who's ever asked me about my life.[1]

Domingo also had surprises awaiting. The long stand-off between his camp and Karajan's had blurred his memory of Karajan's methods:

I was surprised and impressed that what mattered to him was not precision but expression: the flow of the music, the expression of inner feeling. He simply let you sing and interfered only when you needed help. I learned so much from watching him during those sessions. That it was happening so late in both our careers has always been for me a source of deep regret.[2]

Had Karajan lived, the occasionally lack-lustre account of Act 1 would probably have been remade after the run of live theatre performances in Salzburg in August. The rest, however, could barely have been bettered. For this is a performance – utterly unlike Toscanini's, so much admired by Karajan – which goes by stealth to the very heart of the tragedy. The music in the gallows scene in Act 2 is where Karajan begins to weave his spell: the declaration of love, with its *Tristan* cellos, bathing the potentially raucous cabaletta in a strangely quiet afterglow. Thereafter, the orchestra, Verdi's loyal courier, draws the characters lovingly into death's demesne, the shrewdness of Karajan's casting now shining through. This is an opera of protracted farewells and Karajan knew precisely how he wished those farewells to sound: the terrible emotional claustrophobia of Amelia's 'Morrò, ma prima in grazia', the sense of a strong man reduced to pity in the flute-girt farewell to a lost Eden in Renato's 'Eri tu', the majesty of Riccardo's renunciation of love in 'Ma se m'è forza perderti'. Here, Domingo's singing is grand, free, and endlessly subtle, the soaring phrases challenged but not overthrown by the emotion within.

All four principals were daunted by Karajan's method of recording: long takes mixed in with sudden, unexplained switches of scene. Josephine Barstow would recall:

Often there was barely time to work out where we were meant to be. Yet the way the very first chord – the Vienna Philharmonic seemed to know instantly where he was! – would give you the scene's atmosphere in an unforgettable way. Yes, it was frightening at times, but the seriousness and concentration of it all was something that nowadays is rare. I had been in the profession a long time, but it was worth the wait. Music-making on this level was what I had come into the profession for.[3]

The recording of *Un ballo in maschera*, an opera where even the humour is black-edged, further darkening the tragedy, was another of Karajan's trysts with death. Yet it was an apt opera for him to have ended with in other ways as well. Some years after the work's premiere in 1859, the critic Filippo Filippi wrote:

Do you want ideals, gracefulness, distinction of character? Do you want banality banished and in its place the new and the elegant? Do you want the orchestra and the stage to be like a single statue? And a kind of aesthetic pantheism to prevail everywhere? Help yourselves; there is plenty for all your needs.[4]

*

Towards the end of February, Karajan flew by Concorde to New York for three concerts with the Vienna Philharmonic, two devoted to Schubert's *Unfinished* Symphony and music by members of the Strauss family flanking a concert devoted solely to Bruckner's Eighth Symphony.

They were non-subscription: Karajan's way of rebutting what he called 'musical mink'. (He had not forgotten the stampede of rich widows towards the exit at the start of the finale of Beethoven's Ninth back in 1958.) Which is not to say that these were not star-studded audiences. Sinatra was there. He had been as fascinated by Karajan as Karajan had been by him. Yet when they met they had nothing to say to one another. A look and a murmured greeting, over in less than half a minute.

The concerts caused a sensation; 'the type of concert to tell your grandchildren about', wrote John Rockwell in the *New York Times*.[5] Carnegie Hall had recently experienced a questing, adrenaline-rich performance of Bruckner's Eighth by the Philadelphia Orchestra under Klaus Tennstedt. Karajan's performance was very different, lofty and sublime. The critics debated the differences intelligently, honestly. For some, the loftiness was all, for others it marked a limitation. 'Some conductors make a journey,' observed Will Crutchfield, but Karajan, for all the wonder of his beginnings, 'often seems to end up where he began'.[6]

Could Karajan have made so deep an impression with the Berliners? Certainly not in the slow, sad, bitter-sweet playing of the Strauss waltzes

– *'valses d'adieu'* as Klaus Geitel described them.[7] And possibly not in the Schubert or the Bruckner. Mentally, Karajan remained a Titan but he needed the orchestra – *this* orchestra – as never before. And he admitted as much. Sitting, drained and physically diminished, after the Bruckner – 'Please, do you have a comb?' he begged an aide, in a small, broken voice – he marvelled at what he had heard. 'That was not me,' he told Ronald Wilford. 'I don't know who or *what* it was, but it was not me.'

Writer and critic Tim Page would recall the concert in an obituary notice some months later:

The beginning of Schubert's *Unfinished* Symphony summoned to mind a poem by Stefan George that Arnold Schoenberg appropriated for a text: 'I breathe the air of other planets.' Here the lower strings played with a smoothness and repose that was all but unearthly; the music seemed to emanate from the walls. At intermission, when the last notes of the Schubert symphony had died away and Karajan was enjoying his second standing ovation of the evening, I turned to a music student friend of mine and said: 'Never forget what you have heard here tonight. Never forget that an orchestra can play with such unity, such subtlety, such luxuriance of tone. You may never again hear such playing, but now you know that it can be done. We will remember. And Karajan set the standard.[8]

They were momentous concerts which would leave an aftershock no one can have known about at the time and which few have guessed at since. The tour over, Michel Glotz was due to fly on to Florida. On the morning of the last concert, Karajan called him to ask if he was free that evening. He wasn't, but he made himself so; Karajan's tone was troubled. Whatever it was he had on his mind was serious:

Immediately after the concert, we returned to his suite for dinner. We were entirely alone. He came straight to the point. 'I have only one question for you.' He was looking me directly in the eye. 'Do you think that at my age I need to continue making music *against* people when I have the privilege and possibility of making music *with* people?' I took a deep breath. 'Herbert, of course, you have to make music *with* people. Therefore, be happy. You don't need, at your age, to continue making music against people. Nevertheless, my considered advice – although I am younger than you are – is that you cannot abandon thirty-four years of your life simply with a resignation. I would give them [the Berlin Philharmonic] one more chance. You will soon be in Salzburg with them for the Easter Festival. If something can be repaired during the festival, maybe we can have another discussion, with another view of the situation.' He said, 'Fine, I'll do that.'[9]

*

Easter 1989 was early, the weather in Salzburg glorious; while late winter snows lay thick on the Alpine slopes, holiday-makers sunned themselves on the banks of the Salzach. The festival promised well. *Tosca* had been recast with Josephine Barstow in the title role, Pavarotti as Cavaradossi. Solti was conducting the additional orchestral concerts; Karajan was down for the Verdi *Requiem* and a rerun of the New Year's Eve concert with Kissin.

Prominent among the guests was Edward Heath. He gave the prodigious Kissin a wintry nod of approval ('I hope he will not take the tumultuous reception too seriously'[10]) and voiced an old gripe among subscribers that Karajan's open 'rehearsal' was merely a fireside chat and a play-through of some *morceau de concert* not otherwise on the programme.

When Glotz arrived in Salzburg for what he knew would be a make-or-break festival where the Berliners were concerned, he was quickly summoned by Karajan, who told him:

The situation, Michel, is simple. I can explain it to you in very few words. I arrived in Salzburg, remembering what you said to me, in good humour, wanting to play the game honestly. I hadn't seen the orchestra since January. As I arrived at rehearsal, they were talking, and they went on talking, even after the point where it must have been clear that we were ready to start. Eventually, Borwitzky [the orchestra's principal cellist] stood up and asked for silence. I said, 'Good morning, gentlemen,' to which there were maybe fifteen or twenty answers. At that moment, I knew it was finished.[11]

If it was the finish, Karajan said nothing publicly, though Eliette must have known something was afoot. During the festival, she had a fearful bust-up in the early hours of the morning in the dining-room of the Goldener Hirsch with Hansjörg Schellenberger. Günther Breest, who was there with his wife, would recall:

She really blasted Schelly. Did they not realise the pain Herbert was in? Did they not know what they had done to him down the years: how grasping and ungrateful they had been after all he had given them? But there was more than just recrimination. She was convinced that events were destroying him, that his death was imminent.[12]

Karajan had talked with Schellenberger in Berlin the previous December, not about the orchestra, but about personal matters. (He had sensed a change in Schellenberger, but only now learned that his marriage had broken up.) During the Easter Festival, Schellenberger had asked to see Karajan but got no further than Uli Märkle who (in the nicest possible way, says Schellenberger) refused him access. After Karajan's death, Schellenberger told me: 'I shall always regret the fact that I didn't simply walk through the door.'

*

On 23 April, a few weeks into his eighty-second year, Karajan conducted in public for the last time, It was a Sunday morning concert with the Vienna Philharmonic: the work, Bruckner's Seventh Symphony. He also recorded it with an artlessness, an unaffected plainness – even, at times, a certain roguish coarseness, apt to Bruckner – which was light years away from what 'a Karajan performance' was by now usually thought to be.

Thinking back to this last concert the day Karajan died, the Viennese critic Wilhelm Sinkowicz smiled at its fractures and edges, its unvarnished honesty. Had Karajan deliberately been making a monkey of his critics? He went on:

You cannot obtain the respect, let alone the love, of the public for decades with mere polish and glitter. What distinguished Karajan from all others was his ability to push the expressive elements within the music to excess. The eloquence of the sounds he drew from an orchestra told us more things than most performances, and different things, too. It was because of this that musicians who played for him would always excel themselves. Brilliant educator that he was, he never simply asked for a fortissimo; as he famously said during a rehearsal of *Elektra* in Salzburg, stopping at a chord that needed to be sharper, more angular, more brutal: 'It must sound as if someone is kicking you in the chest with hob-nailed boots' – a saying that may perhaps shock an outsider.[13]

For me, none of Karajan's recordings brings back more vividly than this Bruckner Seventh the man I knew in those last years: simple, without taint of vanity or 'side', impressive without in any way wishing to impress. Since Karajan was also the construct that was 'Karajan', I have no doubt he was also the reverse of all these things. But that was not the aspect I encountered. One speaks as one finds.

*

Berlin's 'Red–Green' coalition had taken an age to get its affairs in order. Now, finally, a new Cultural Senator was in place, Frau Anke Martiny. The day after Karajan's Vienna concert, she set out for Salzburg to discuss the issues raised by Karajan in the letter he had written to her predecessor in early January. Since Karajan had also written to her, asking for clarification of the terms of his contract, she must have been expecting a negotiation. However, when she arrived, he simply handed her a letter:

Dear Frau Senator,
  I beg to inform you that as of today I am resigning my position as artistic director and permanent conductor of the Berlin Philharmonic Orchestra.

The results of the medical examinations which have now been proceeding for weeks render me incapable of fulfilling my professional obligations as I see them.

Furthermore, I must point out that for many years now I have been requesting your predecessor in the Senate to get down to establishing a fundamental specification of my duties and rights. Although this has been promised repeatedly, to this day nothing has happened. I even asked you personally last week for written clarification before our meeting in Salzburg since these important definitions are not included in my contract. Once again I have received no answer!

With kind regards,
    Herbert von Karajan[14]

The letter had been typed, not by Karajan's secretary Lore Salzburger, but by Uli Märkle. Karajan had signed it, but so slowly and effortfully that he had felt obliged to go back over the signature so as to give it a more decisive look. The fact that Märkle typed the letter has led to speculation that he played some part in Karajan's decision to write it: possibly as a ploy, not thinking the resignation would be accepted. The normally circumspect Wolfgang Stresemann is among those who have advanced this theory. However, the evidence of the conversations Karajan had in New York and Salzburg with Michel Glotz would seem to put paid to this idea. Karajan may have been in two minds at the eleventh hour – abandoning one's life's work cannot be easy – but, in essence, the die had been cast weeks earlier.

Whether the resignation was genuinely meant or not, Frau Martiny accepted it, to the delight of party colleagues back in Berlin.[15] Karajan later told me:

I thought Frau Martiny was going to have a heart attack when I gave her my resignation. She obviously didn't expect it. I must say, she was very charming, and very capable. I liked her very much. I think she hoped there might be a possibility of some talks, but I had to say that I had made up my mind. The thing was over.[16]

The resignation threw the orchestra into disarray. A petition was drawn up, but proved to be self-defeating since a third of the players refused to sign it. Two of the orchestra's most loyal and long-serving players, Peter Steiner and Gerhard Stempnik, were dispatched to Salzburg to try to talk to Karajan, but he refused to see them. Steiner, who had joined the orchestra in 1948, later told me: 'We were disappointed. But one remembers the happy times. I am glad to have worked with him.'

'Were you upset by his death?'

'Yes, very much. I loved him to the very end.'

CHAPTER 81

A necessary end

A man of action rarely keeps a journal; it is always later on and
in a period of prolonged inactivity, that he does his recollecting,
makes his notations, and, very often, has cause to wonder at the
course his life has taken.

Marguerite Yourcenar, *Memoirs of Hadrian*

In early June, I visited Karajan in Anif to discuss the typescript of *Conversations with Karajan*, which Oxford University Press was planning to publish in the autumn. For a man who for most of his eighty-one years had steadfastly refused to look back, his absorbed, almost childlike interest in the text was strangely touching. He had evidently read it in close detail. He had a good deal to say and a few things to add – principally about Eliette – but he asked for only one change: the removal of what he took to be an implied criticism of Sir George Solti in one of the questions.

That same week he had also begun a correspondence with Gisela Tamsen. For years, he had pushed aside her questions and the sheaves of primary documentation she had been sending about his early career. Now he seemed to be taking an interest.

There may, however, have been a reason for this. Karajan's artistic canonisation during the Carnegie Hall concerts in February appears to have dismayed a number of influential Americans who, even at this late hour, felt the need to stop him in his tracks and rake over his past. One way of going about this would be to seek a ban on his entering the United States. Such a move would win widespread publicity, put a check on his conducting activities, and hinder any promotional work he might be considering.

The idea of implementing a ban under United States immigration law would have seemed bizarre were it not for the fact that in April 1987 another famous Austrian with an essentially unremarkable but none the less controversial war record had been so excluded. In 1986, Kurt Waldheim, the former Secretary-General of the United Nations, had been elected President of Austria. Ten months into his term of office, he found himself placed on the 'Watch List' of the US Department of Justice, after intense lobbying by the World Jewish Congress. It was a move which gave him the status of 'undesirable alien', and it effectively barred him from entry into the United States.[1] As the journalist and historian Gordon Brook-Shepherd has explained:

The process had the great convenience that it could be implemented without the need to produce documentary proof of any misdeeds. Under the so-called

Holtzman Amendment of 1978 to the [United States] Immigration Act, all that was needed was a *prima facie* case. It was a bizarre interpretation of justice; the amendment amounted to a charter for denunciation.[2]

Karajan was certainly vulnerable to such a process, and in the summer of 1989 an enquiry was set in train under the terms of the Holtzman Amendment. Karajan's death caused its abandonment, but the abandonment itself was widely reported, fuelling speculation that the United States government possessed further incriminating information about his Nazi affiliations. In fact, as the Department of Justice would have confirmed had anyone asked, there was no new material, nothing that was not already in the public domain.[3]

*

Though we talked about the Berlin Philharmonic during my visit to Anif, Karajan would permit none of the discussion to go into the *Conversations* book. Was he still keeping his options open? There are differing views on whether there might have been some kind of formal farewell. One of the more interesting features of Karajan's resignation letter was that it had said nothing at all about the orchestra. It had offered neither praise nor blame.

During our conversations, I mentioned a remark Riccardo Muti had made to me many years ago: that no conductor in his right mind would turn down the Berlin Philharmonic, but that Karajan's immediate successor was almost certainly bound to fail, financially or artistically, and possibly both.

Karajan disagreed. 'Look what happened when Toscanini left the New York Philharmonic,' he countered, somewhat enigmatically.

'Precisely my point,' I replied.

'But what did happen?' he persisted.

'Barbirolli took over, was given a roasting by all and sundry, and left.'

'But it *went on*,' Karajan triumphantly concluded. 'And it is the same in Berlin. It will go on.'[4]

My visit to Anif coincided with the protest in Beijing's Tiananmen Square which was cruelly and bloodily suppressed by the government. Karajan was much exercised by this and quite angry; not with the government of Deng Xiaoping but with the student demonstrators, and the Western media. 'They should heed the wisdom of an old man,' he announced.

I was too perplexed to respond, though, some years later, I would hear respected political analysts rehearsing the very arguments Karajan had advanced that morning in Anif. Were memories so short, he asked, that no one in the West remembered the so-called 'Cultural Revolution', when the Party lost control, and, encouraged by Mao, teenage mobsters murdered and terrorised millions of people, laying waste to an entire cultural heritage? China was not a democracy and never could be, which is not to say, Karajan argued, that its people could not thrive and prosper under a stable government which was prepared to give the merchant and entrepreneurial classes their head in economic matters. Deng himself could probably not have put it better: a case of one conservative, autocratic, octogenarian pragmatist effectively reading the mind of another.

Eliette appeared on the last morning of my visit and seemed strangely nervous. After Karajan had shuffled off to be driven into Salzburg, we went out to the paddock to see the celebrated Karajan menagerie: 'Bourbon' the sheep, 'Folie' the donkey, the goat, and the llama. Eliette paced up and down the lawn, plucked a rose or two, and talked about her fear of losing Herbert.

In late June, he travelled to Leukerbad in Switzerland to bathe in the hot sulphur baths, rest, and take the cure. His long-serving physician Dr Simon may not have been the most conventional doctor in the world, but he was sufficiently rich and well connected to know exactly when and where to send Karajan to be treated for whatever ailment he fancied he had at the time. Karajan himself, alas, always tended to overdo things. If he was meant to spend fifteen minutes a day in the sulphur baths, he would spend an hour. By the time he returned to Anif, he seemed a good deal more tired than when he had left.

Rehearsals for *Un ballo in maschera* had already begun. Like Karajan's new *Tosca*, this had been planned as a visual extravaganza, the Swedish court and famous Drottningholm Theatre brought all but bodily to the Festspielhaus stage. The director was John Schlesinger, whose work in the opera house had revealed him to be shy neither of architectural excess nor (Karajan would have noted with approval) of the need for the occasional set-piece 'big sing'.

At rehearsal, Karajan was as active and interfering as ever, but he felt tired within himself. One evening, towards the middle of the month, as he sat watching a televised concert from Marseilles featuring Jessye Norman, he turned to Eliette and said, '*Ich kann nicht mehr* [I can't go on].'

Next day, Saturday 15 July, he talked at length on the telephone to Uli Märkle in Monaco about a meeting scheduled to take place at Anif next morning during which Karajan's old friend and commercial confidant, Sony President Norio Ohga, was expected to make a substantial bid for the rights to the 'Legacy for Home Video'.

Towards the end of the call, Karajan remarked that he did not feel particularly well. Since he had not felt well for years – his tombstone, he once said, should contain just three words: 'He died painfully' – it was a remark that hardly seemed significant at the time. During a rehearsal with the Vienna Philharmonic, he complained of chest pains. He was given a brief medical examination and advised to rest. He was assured that there was absolutely nothing wrong with his heart, an assurance somewhat compromised, one would have thought, by the fact an electrocardiograph test was suggested for the following morning.[5]

*

Montaigne once observed that no man is fully mature until he is reconciled to the fact of his own death. Whether Karajan was so reconciled I would not presume to know. He was, however, much fascinated by death. Friends such as Michel Glotz, whose squeamishness about death bordered on the pathological, were often treated to long disquisitions on the subject, liberally spiced with quotations from Verdi's *Don Carlos* and other works.

One of the reasons why Karajan got on so well with Schneider-Siemssen was their shared delight in graveyard humour. Towards the end, Schneider-Siemssen would recall, Karajan talked about death a great deal. He was much troubled by the fact that Schneider-Siemssen had been told by the village priest that his local churchyard was full; that reserving a plot there was not possible.

'Buy one in Anif,' was Karajan's response.

'But we don't live there.'

'I will speak with the priest.'

'That's very kind of you. But does it mean that we're going to go on chattering and arguing through all eternity?'

'Certainly not. I shall insist you are at least thirty metres away so I can get some peace at last.'

That was Schneider-Siemssen's version of the story.

Karajan's version had a codicil. 'He said that, as a German in Austrian soil, he was more than happy to be buried standing up, if it would save space.' He laughed. 'Typical Schneider-Siemssen!'[6]

Karajan believed that we have different lives, possibly in metamorphosis. As far as the here and now was concerned, however, he was a Catholic; and had requested a Catholic burial. Years previously, he had purchased a modest burial plot in Anif churchyard. Raffaello de Banfield would remember being taken to see it, a serious journey, seriously meant. (This after a family luncheon during which Banfield had been asked by Karajan to explain to his two daughters the concept of the Holy Trinity.)

*

The Sony team of Norio Ohga and the chief executive of the Sony Corporation in America, Michael Schulhof – a pilot and a doctor, very much Karajan's kind of man – flew into Salzburg on the morning of Sunday, 16 July and were immediately summoned to Anif. Karajan was in bed, Eliette out cycling.

The early talk was all of flying. A doctor arrived with the electrocardiograph. Karajan sent him away. 'I have the most important of all my friends here today and not even the King of China will be allowed to disturb us.' Lunch was ordered, Karajan issuing instructions in Italian to his butler Francesco in a rapid *parlando* that left neither of the guests any the wiser as to what it was they would be eating.

Some time around one o'clock Eliette returned home. She would have still been out cycling had she not met someone from the Goldener Hirsch out jogging. They had gossiped so long, she had decided to abandon her usual route.

She was not in the room, however, when, to Ohga's and Schulhof's consternation, Karajan suddenly stopped talking and asked for water. Schulhof reached for a bottle of mineral water. Karajan took a sip, said he felt better, then slumped sideways, snorting. Schulhof knew instantly what was happening. But it was too late. Karajan had suffered a heart attack, and was dead.

*

Eliette sat cradling her husband in her arms for more than an hour until the doctor arrived. Later that same afternoon, Karajan's llama dropped dead in the paddock.

Karajan's death-mask was taken; family and officials were informed. Michel Glotz heard the news through a third party:

I don't know why, but I didn't believe it. I didn't even try to ring Salzburg. I looked at my watch, and it was four o'clock. I said, 'No, he is sleeping. It is the time of his afternoon nap.' Unfortunately, he was sleeping for eternity.[7]

As newspapers and TV stations rushed to judgement,[8] Leonard Bernstein interrupted a concert in Paris, bidding the audience stand for a minute's silence in honour of '*la mémoire d'un collègue, le grand maître Herbert von Karajan*'. That, as much as anything, would have moved and gratified Karajan.

It is generally agreed that in the hours and days that followed, Eliette behaved magnificently, well schooled, no doubt, by Karajan himself on how the obsequies should be handled.

The principal need was to outwit the media or, as one observer waspishly put it, 'to stop Uli [Märkle] charging admission to the funeral and flying in the Pope to deliver the benediction'. Secrecy and speed were Eliette's principal weapons. Like most countries, Austria has laws governing the period of time which must elapse between death and interment; but these were now circumvented by judicial and ecclesiastical dispensations, privately agreed. Fewer than a dozen people knew of the arrangements for the funeral, which was set to take place the following evening in the village church in Anif.

In fact, the service was delayed for a number of hours. As the gravediggers set to work, they found immediately beneath the surface of the soil a stone plinth, the remains of an old monument razed to earth long ago. A local farmer had to be called in with a tractor and heavy lifting gear to remove it.

So it was past nightfall when Karajan's body was finally laid to rest.

Herbert von Karajan
The Rehearsal*

Were one to ask a conductor what purpose a rehearsal serves, he would answer: 'To explain one's understanding of a piece of music to an orchestra.' Without fail, an orchestra would answer the same question: 'During a rehearsal, a conductor gets to know the full score through us.' And a concert promoter would say: 'So that they do not simply go for a stroll, but rather work for my money.' Who is right? Probably all three of them. Why? An answer to this question calls, first, for a definition of the term 'rehearsal'.

The word [*Probe*] is not an easy one. Its meaning derives from the Latin verb *probare*, meaning 'to test, to inspect, to examine, to judge'. In German the word has lost much of its original meaning such as we have it in a word like '*Weinprobe* [wine-tasting]' (to judge quality through taste) or as in the idiom '*die Probe aufs Exempel machen* [to prove]'.

Our old piano teachers would always ask children, who were repeating the same mistake, to '*try* it again', as if anything could be achieved through meaningless repetition. That is not what a conductor defines as a rehearsal. Rather, to rehearse means to render a piece of music performable while working efficiently and systematically at its form, at its content, and, above all, at its musical and technical structure.

A rehearsal begins when a composer seeks (tries!) to translate his inner experiences into notes.

As I have often sought to explain, apart from the choice of pitch, our system of notation merely gives us hints and directions. Thus, as the composer tries to express the meaning behind the notes, so the conductor has to try to understand the real sound and life of the score. As for the musicians, after having rehearsed their instruments and mastered their technical difficulties, they will subsequently concentrate on ensemble playing. An orchestral musician cannot possibly have the complete overview of the conductor; the conductor has all the voices of the score in front of him, where the musician sees only his own. Yet it is precisely out of this feeling

---

* 'Die Probe'. From Karajan's unfinished book on conductors and conducting. Original German text first published in Franz Endler, *Karajan: eine Biographie* (Hamburg, 1992), p.267.

of dependence that there grows the feeling of belonging to a whole, a feeling that is at the very root of the common musical experience.

What, in reality, happens during a rehearsal? Probably the most difficult example of a rehearsal is the one where a piece of music is being performed for the first time. Everything is new, and there are moments when the conductor hears an entirely different sound from the one he had imagined when studying the score. In that case, he must decide whether or not to correct his ideas according to the new sound, or vice versa. It has often happened that even a composer has sometimes been uncertain what to do.

The first thing that happens during such rehearsals is what is commonly known as 'reading through the score'. The piece is played through as well as possible in order to get a vague idea of the character of the music and of the tempo.

Here begins the task of the conductor. By means of graphic explanations, he must establish an initial approach to the music. There should be no long speeches which every orchestra hates. One word, one comparison, can be the key to understanding; it can awaken interest and stimulate pleasure in the approaching task.

And so begins the systematic work. In many cases, one must work on each bar. When dealing with technically difficult passages in the string sections, one has to rehearse in a very slow tempo. This requires infinite patience. Above all, it is important to motivate an individual or a group of musicians: mistakes must be explained, and every new attempt must lead to something better.

Nothing is worse than to make musicians repeat a passage five or six times, topped off by an impatient or even irritated exclamation, 'Again!'

If one explains a mistake clearly *and* calmly to a musician, so that he fully grasps the problem, then he will most definitely play better the next time. What's more, since the musician is pleased with the improvement, a trust in the conductor is established and an increased interest in the work. It is best if the conductor refrains from all shows of emotion during this period. He ought, literally, to be '*ganz Ohr* [all ear]', in order to detect unerringly any mistakes, or even the merest hint of a mistake.

Once this period has come to an end and the orchestra has achieved technical independence in the music in question, then the fascinating part of one's work begins: ensemble-playing.

Every musician must play his part, but he is also beginning to perceive what others are playing: where two groups hang together, where he needs to suppress his voice, where he needs to come forward as a soloist, and where he must lose himself in the mass. The changes of tempi, the accelerandi and ritardandi, the well-applied crescendo or diminuendo, are no longer beaten by the conductor as if he was controlling a horse but are developed out of a feeling of mass belonging. It is not the conductor who conjures these changes with his magic gestures; rather, the inner tension of the music must be so great that the crescendo comes as a necessary discharge which can be controlled by the conductor only during its physical outflow.

Thus each musician feels content, feels he has contributed creatively to the entire process, and is not merely an insignificant part in a scheme of things that is directed by someone else.

Once the conductor is freed from the technical aspect of the performance, he may – indeed, he must – liberate himself. He must let himself be carried away by what has been achieved, in order to work out the expressive fluidity and dynamics of the inner experience.

Now there also exists another type of rehearsal. When a guest conductor stands before a new, alien orchestra and is to perform a great Classical or Romantic piece of music that is familiar to both participants, then it is clear that an orchestra which works regularly with its own permanent conductor has certain preconceived ideas about what (for instance, a Beethoven symphony) ought to sound like. Suddenly the orchestra is confronted with a completely new, or even opposed, interpretation. On such an occasion, it takes the conductor an immense amount of tact, discretion, and power of conviction to achieve a good result.

It would be totally wrong to dismiss the existing ideas of the orchestra as wrong, or – worse – to ridicule them. Though, as was mentioned earlier, every note, every dynamic, every agogic allows for certain liberties that are inherent in the nature of musical notation.

This is where the real work begins. And in spite of all respect for the values maintained in the notes, there are still possibilities of forming a new sound which derives from the conductor's own inner imagination.

Some years ago, the conductor George Szell came with his Cleveland Orchestra as guests of the Salzburg Festival. The previous year, he had asked me to conduct one of the concerts. As we were discussing the programme, he kept mentioning the Fifth Symphony of Prokofiev. Initially, he was totally open to other suggestions from me, but he returned with a particular insistence to the symphony in question until I finally agreed. What I did not know at the time was that he wanted to show his orchestra at its best. Their performance of the Prokofiev symphony was considered to be the Clevelanders' *pièce de résistance*. They knew the work by heart.

On the day of the first rehearsal, I was introduced to the orchestra and began to rehearse with great pleasure what has always been to me a fascinating work. I felt after only one minute that the orchestra was prepared to take new suggestions and reshape them imaginatively. During a break in the rehearsal, Szell approached me in a state of high excitement and said how shocked he had been when he realised at the very outset that our views of the work were diametrically opposed. He had feared a catastrophe; but then was thrilled by the orchestra's split-second adaptation and their ability to play a new interpretation so naturally, as if that had always been their way. I had not realised any of this; I had been far too enchanted by the encounter. And the concert remains printed on my memory.

But what influence a conductor's personality really has – without his having to utter a single word – became clear to me in Bayreuth in 1951. The unforgettable Hans Knappertsbusch was conducting *Der Ring*; I was doing *Die Meistersinger*. For the stage rehearsals, I brought with me my own personal répétiteur with whom I had developed the cherished habit of playing for the rehearsals with two pianos, four hands. Sometimes he played the upper voices and I the middle and bass; at other times, one of us would play the winds, the other the strings. Suddenly, Hans Knappertsbusch was standing behind us. 'You're hired,' he said. Continuing the game with him, we asked: 'When?' And he replied: 'This afternoon, piano rehearsal *Götterdämmerung*.' The two pianos were brought into the orchestra pit, Knappertsbusch was sitting high on the podium, and we began.

Now, it was no secret that he and I differed considerably when it came to tempi. During that afternoon, I learned my most precious lesson about what it is to have the power of persuasion. From the very beginning, it was clear that there could be only one opinion; yet neither my partner nor I had actually perceived anything, so natural, so self-evident was the process of what we were doing. I then understood what I had always been asking myself: How is it that an orchestra can express so many fundamentally different ideas? It is the art of identifying and embodying another opinion. The vital prerequisite is that the person holding the differing view should be in no doubt about it. He must be convinced – self-evidently so – that this is how it ought to be. In that way, one can move mountains. It is the old story of the horse and the horseman.

However, the loveliest rehearsals are those when one plays well-known works with one's own orchestra, either as part of the preparation for a tour or in the process of taking up a piece which has been too long out of the repertory and which is 'due' again. Let us assume that we are dealing with a symphony that has been played down the years forty to sixty times. One or more gramophone recordings may have been made, even perhaps a film for television.

Here the starting-point is totally different. Both parties know the piece from the experience of many concerts. They have possibly played it in all the great concert halls of the world with constantly changing acoustics – acoustics that, on tour, are often adjusted to only during the evening's performance. They know the music intimately after many rehearsals.

There is an unbelievable wealth of experience, ups and downs, pressed together, clinging to the piece. The musicians have read their own impressions into the score; the notes are no longer dead characters, but lively, living symbols.

It is self-evident here why musicians prefer to play, not from newly printed music, but from the badly printed copies they have been using for years. At this stage, they need the printed notes only as support. In reality, they are playing what is written between the lines. It is easy to see why such rehearsals are different from the ones mentioned above.

It is like taking a loved one around a picture gallery. One has been there often and believes one knows every picture; but through the newly shared experience fresh points of view may suddenly arise. For decades one has passed by a picture, but suddenly a new point may gain decisive importance.

The wealth of experience that is hidden in a great masterpiece is inconceivable. Who can assume, or be so arrogant as to think that he can ever fully exhaust it? But through the years one can try to unite opposing impressions in one form so as to achieve a feeling full of meaning – the Tao*. This is why the procedure of rehearsing with one's own orchestra is so entirely different.

Musicians have a very fine memory for musical happenings that may lie far back in the past. This is the point where one needs to start. For instance, one chooses the passage that did not work last time. One of those wonderful moments that appear in almost every symphony where something dies down and disappears and gives way to something new. And this presentiment needs to be felt even before it occurs. The orchestra must have it on its lips, so to speak, even before it can express it.

Why at the earlier time did the passage fail? There can be many reasons for this. A small inaccuracy or insecurity in the musical moment, a diminuendo that was taken up too late and needs correcting, and already the atmosphere is disturbed.

Or one was too tense as a conductor to let the piece flow rightly. In this, one needs to be totally self-critical without any fear of the consequences.

Or another example. A grand-scale intensification of tempo with a simultaneous crescendo to a climax. How often may such a passage have gone wrong: a crescendo that starts too late and thereby can never reach its climax, or gets there too early and uses up all the force, leaving nothing for the climax.

Through many years, it is possible to have experienced all that together. Now, in the rehearsal, one will talk about it and attempt, first of all, to improve the technical aspect. In such a case, the orchestra must itself

---

* The way. In Taoism, the principle underlying the universe, ultimate reality.

bring out the crescendo without having to be told by the conductor. It is a wonderful feeling to be carried away as if by a wave that towers higher and higher, and suddenly collapses with crushing force.

But it takes years of work before all that is possible. It is also utterly impossible to try to rehearse a piece once and for all. Nor is this a question affecting only the orchestra. It goes hand in hand with inner dynamic tensions that derive from decades of effort, work, and love. It is *always* a mirror of the soul's state *and* its impact on other human beings.

However, in the struggle of the representation of the musical form there arises a significant problem. The second question at the beginning of the chapter indicates that problem: Can – or must – a conductor learn from the orchestra?

The famous pianist Walter Gieseking had a particular talent. His memory was so well developed that on a trip from Hanover to Berlin he learned by heart a piece of new music and publicly performed it that same evening. Later on, he said that learning the piece had been the easiest part; in his subconscious his hands had already chosen the right fingering. The difficulty was transposing that into reality. The fingers that had, so to speak, moved in his mind were hindered by the actual physical contact with the keyboard. Thus was the whole process thrown out of balance. It is the eternal confrontation in the mind of the artist between spirit and substance. Michelangelo is said to have seen in the marble itself an enemy that worked against his artistic will.

How much greater than the pianist's problem is the problem for the conductor who has in front of him human beings who, in turn, can express themselves only through their instruments.

It would be an unmitigated conceit for a conductor to think that he could mentally appropriate a piece of music and then immediately realise its harmonious interpretation. Yet – let us be honest – did we not all do that in our youth? Life, however, quickly taught us better.

We conductors need an orchestra for the maturing process of a musical work as much as the orchestra needs us. That's why rehearsals with one's own orchestra are so beautiful. It may be that one has lived very intensively with a piece for a long time and has worked on it. And then there might be a period when the same piece may have gone further away, lying dormant, stored in the subconscious. Then suddenly, like a compulsion, it comes to the surface, and during rehearsals one realises one has changed. It is as if one looks in a mirror, and the orchestra feels it, too. Sometimes the whole thing may sound entirely different from before.

In the right place, a sudden exclamation may help more than any number of useless phrases when an orchestra is familiar with a piece from earlier occasions. '*Es klang so alt und war doch so neu*'*, Wagner lets Hans Sachs exclaim.

Those passages in a piece where the mood fundamentally changes take the longest time to mature: Crescendi – Decrescendi – Accelerandi – Ritardandi. In all possible combinations, of course.

The first few times one tries to work out a piece, it is impossible to predict where such changes will occur. There is, for example, a passage in Sibelius's Fifth Symphony where a change from a very slow tempo to a prestissimo lasts approximately two minutes. Each bar must be played a little faster than the preceding one. This demands the acqusition of a clear overview. In fact, one needs to be able to feel both tempi simultaneously.

In rehearsals with one's own orchestra, one also adjusts the degree of intensity with which notes will be played. With an orchestra which one is conducting for the first time, one can never be certain with what degree of intensity a particular passage will be played. One frequently experiences how a conductor's dynamics can become distorted. The problem is, gesture – however encouraging or soothing – only takes effect *after* the passage in question. The mistake has been made, the gesture is futile. With one's own orchestra, both parties know from common experience with what degree of intensity they should play. A single word can remove the source of a mistake.

The conductor should – and must – demand that the sounds determined in rehearsal recur in performance of their own accord. Only then can the conductor concentrate on his real task without suffering the constant fear that something will not sound as he hoped it would. This is a fundamental requirement of any interpretation.

The work that now begins, once one is freed from the chains of technique, takes place on a level of give and take. It is an exchange of what one has lived through and suffered together, and the consequences of such experiences. It is an attempt to perceive oneself in the course of time and translate that perception into reality.

One ought not to forget, however, that it will have taken decades to achieve this. At the outset, there may have been struggles over the most elementary musical values: long, short, high, deep, loud, strong, until with time they all become a matter of course and are thereby subjected to a higher meaning and purpose. If one looks back from here to the beginning of the process – the initial studying of the score, the first elaboration of musical form as a spiritual concept – then it becomes almost painfully clear how much the dualism between mind and substance has us in its claws.

One cannot hope to reach a state where lucidity of spirit is at the very

---

* 'It sounded so old, and yet was so new.' *Die Meistersinger*, II, iii.

heart of one's being until one has thrown off the shackles of material things. Man must of necessity transform what he physically encounters.

Heisenberg* once said that if I want to examine a snowflake that has fallen on my hand, it is no longer a snowflake, for through the heat of my skin it has already been transformed into water.

Similarly, if I want to realise my spiritual concept through an orchestra, the concept has already been transformed by contact with that orchestra. Yet through continuously evolving changes and refinements, the perceptions and experiences of the mind are similarly changed and refined.

From this point of view, one also needs to respond affirmatively to the second question posed at the beginning of this chapter. In fact, it needs to be answered a thousand times more affirmatively than the question suggests. The answer to the question derives from a recognition that the conductor and orchestra are inextricably bound to each other.

What does an orchestral manager answer to the question, why must the conductor rehearse with an orchestra? 'So that they do not simply go for a stroll, but rather work for my money.'

With this response, he touches upon the eternal question about human idleness, and man's fear of the strains and the efforts he knows are necessary but which he would quite like to avoid.

A Yogi must practise before every meditation session both the Asana *and* the Pranayama† for at least an hour in order to exert his mind. No professional sportsman would dare enter a competition without having stretched his muscles before. The hour of preparation on the bar is self-evident to any dancer.

The conviction that musical rehearsals are necessary – rehearsals that strain both one's spiritual *and* physical strength – was accepted relatively late. The orchestras after the First World War were of the entirely unjustified opinion that rehearsals were humiliating; there was no trust in rehearsing. The motto was *'Auf d'Nacht, Herr Direktor'*.‡ This meant that during rehearsal they would merely indicate difficult passages. During the evening, if you were lucky, they might make a half-decent effort at such moments. In an opera house in central Germany, a world-famous conductor was invited to conduct *Tristan* for the orchestra's Pensioners' List (without fee). He confirmed, and demanded three rehearsals. The orchestra refused the request on the grounds that they had already 'cracked it', which is the jargon they used for knowing and mastering a piece.

No Intendant of a Repertory Opera today would offer a guest conductor

---

* Werner Heisenberg (1901–76). German physicist noted for his theory of quantum mechanics and the Uncertainty Principle. Nobel Prize, 1932.
† Positions and breathing exercises in Yoga.
‡ 'For tonight, Herr Direktor!'

fewer than three rehearsals. In the case of a new production, ten to twelve sessions are the norm.

The change of attitude coincided with the development of the gramophone, when long-playing records conquered the world. Suddenly conductors had to learn to listen to their mistakes and those of the orchestra. Inexorably high standards were set and those who were not prepared to take – or were incapable of taking – their fellow musicians to the limits were left hopelessly behind.

And slowly but surely the conviction took root that a merciless commitment of all one's available forces was a precondition of successful artistic direction.

To overcome one's idleness and take pleasure in necessary exertion has always lent wings to the intuition of the spirit.

APPENDIX B

Karajan's membership of the Nazi Party and the trail of misinformation

The facts as to when Karajan joined the Nazi Party, and why, could be adequately stated on the back of a postcard. In practice, we have had rather more than a postcard's worth of comment on the subject down the years, largely due to the extraordinary trail of misinformation that was laid in the post-war period. Most of this was inadvertent: investigative journalists foraging among the papers of the Nazi Party membership system, an over-elaborate and at times poorly administered bureaucracy, without the means of adequately reading documents which Allied and Austrian denazification commissions had rather better understood in 1946. Karajan's own attempts to distance himself from the issue in later years did not help; nor was he well advised during the period when misinformation began to harden into received opinion.

The true situation, as we can now be said definitively to know it, is this. Karajan, 27, joined the Nazi Party [NSDAP] in Aachen in April 1935 in response to a formal request from the head of Aachen's NS-controlled municipal authority under whose aegis the musical life of the city was organised.

The request was not unusual. Dr Edgar Gross, the 47-year-old Head of Aachen's Stadttheater who appointed Karajan, had been similarly enlisted the previous year. Whatever his private views of the effectiveness or otherwise of the new National Socialist government in its early days in power, Gross had no previous record of any kind of active involvement with NSDAP politics; nor had Karajan, despite the fact of his having been 'recruited' by Salzburg party activist Herbert Klein in April 1933. (Klein received a joining fee of five Austrian Schillings from Karajan enabling Klein to prepare the paperwork for provisional membership. In the event, no further dues were paid and the bureaucracy subsequently lost track of Karajan. The application was later declared invalid.)

The freshly researched 'facts' about Karajan's NSDAP membership that were widely promulgated from the late 1950s onwards were quite other. They stated that he joined the party officially in Salzburg on 8 April 1933; that he joined again three weeks later in Ulm on 1 May 1933, and that his account of the Aachen membership was, at best doubtful, at worst a lie. How, then, did this extraordinary farrago of misinformation come about?

In 1957, a little time after Karajan's appointment to the chief conductorship of the Berlin Philharmonic and shortly after his appointment as
Artistic Director of the Vienna State Opera, the American magazine *High
Fidelity* commissioned an article on Karajan from Paul Moor, a highly
respected journalist who lived and worked in Berlin between 1956 and
1981 as a correspondent for Time-Life International and CBS. The article
'The Operator', appeared in October 1957, a trenchant, well-written piece
which, though by no means complimentary to Karajan, was certainly
not written in a spirit of animosity. (In the years that followed, Moor
continued to write about Karajan, interviewed him, and was even admitted
to recording sessions. If Karajan read 'The Operator', he appears to have
borne Moor no ill will.)

Being a good journalist, Moor asked for documentation and was given
access to what he called 'the master file' on Karajan in the Berlin Document Centre. The crucial document here is Karajan's heavily annotated
membership card. (See Bachmann p.351 for a trimmed and slightly foggy
black-and-white photocopy of the card. The original has annotations in
several different coloured inks and can be reliably read only *in situ* or in
a high quality colour print.)

At first glance, most of it – the salient details – are easy to read.

Karajan's name is there and his date of birth. There is an address, difficult
to decipher and not, in fact, Karajan's own but that of an NSDAP recruiting
booth in Salzburg. Beneath the address, neatly crossed out with three ruled
lines are the provisional membership number 1 607 525 (a number issued
to Salzburg, we now know, some time after 16 April 1933) and the date of
the Klein recruitment and registration 8.4.33. Beneath that in large letters in
the centre of the card is the actual membership number 3 430 914, preceded
by the date 1.5.33. The five has a tick over it.

Looking at all this, Moor concluded: 'He paid his due for that month, but
before the end of April, he left to return to Germany, which caused a small
administrative snarl, because he did not actually pick up his membership
card. However, back in Ulm, he got this straightened out on May 1, 1933,
and received another card, # 3 430 914.'

Neither Paul Moor, nor any of the writers who subsequently recycled
his conclusions, appeared to ask how the number managed to jump from
1 607 525 to 3 430 914 in the space of twenty-two days. The Nazis were
popular in April 1933 but not so popular as to be recruiting at the rate
of 600,000 a week. (And if they were recruiting at that rate, how could
an application possibly have been processed so quickly?) Did the NSDAP
possibly have some complex, private numbering system?

Had that question been asked, the truth might have begun to emerge
since it is relatively easy to track down the dates between which tranches

of membership numbers were issued to individual NSDAP districts. (They can be found in the files of the Berlin Document Centre and were later published in Radomir Luza's *Austro-German Relations in the Anschluss Era*, Princeton, 1975, pp.374–5.)

The lower part of the membership document contains more crucial information; though it is possible that someone unfamiliar with the nature of the information might overlook this, not least because the lower part of the card has three diagonal red lines across it, suggesting material that has been deleted.

Below the membership number 3 430 914 there is a repetition of the date 1.5.33, this time with *ng* (*nachgereicht*, retroactive) added. In other words, this membership is being *backdated* to 1.5.1933. What is more, for administrative neatness the place of registration is given as that of the member's residence on 1 May 1933, which in Karajan's case was Ulm. Beneath the line Ulm Wrtbg (Württemberg) is the all-important date 3.35. Along the line from that is 35/33 *ng*.

Though this makes no sense to the untrained eye, it is all absolutely consistent with Karajan's actual NSDAP number which is, indeed, from a batch of numbers which were issued during the years 1933–5, *backdated* (*ng = Aufnahmegruppe der 1933er, nachgereichte*) to 1.5.33, the date when a temporary halt was called to the recruiting of new Party members.

Though there is no doubt that Karajan was thus officially registered with the Party in March/April 1935, it appears that Karajan (or his secretary who handled all such matters) had misplaced the card. Shortly before Karajan's wedding to Elmy Holgerloef on 26 July 1938 an application was made to the Cologne-Aachen Gauleitung for a new card. It was at this point that the NSDAP membership office started a year-long enquiry into whether or not Karajan was a member of the Party.

In a letter of 5 January 1939, the raw facts of Karajan's membership(s) are set out in summary form. This letter, too, is open to misconstruction if taken at face value, since it merely reproduces the information in the form in which it appears on the file card, i.e: '8.4.1933 – joined with Party number 1 607 525 in Salzburg, Austria, address: Salzburg, Schwarzstr.1. 1.5.33 – without interim cancellation, joined once more with Party number 3 430 914 in Ortgruppe Ulm (Gau Württemberg), address: Ulm, Stadttheater.'

Working with this outline summary, the enquiry continued for a further six months. Finally, on 7 July 1939 the Cologne-Aachen office received from the NSDAP membership office in Munich the following clarification: (1) The application of 8.4.1933 in Salzburg was invalid and the membership number 1 607 525 is thus declared null and void. (2) The membership number 3 430 914, taken out on 1.5.1933 (*sic*) in Cologne-Aachen, is valid.

Not that the matter ended there. As late as the summer of 1944, the Reichsmusikkammer, which by now was itself in some confusion about Karajan's 'status' within the Third Reich, was asking the NSDAP's membership office for confirmation of the validity of Karajan's NSDAP membership. By now the system was in total disarray. In their reply of 25 May 1944 the Munich membership office stated that according to their records, Karajan was registered with the Aachen district (he left Aachen in 1942) and that he joined in Salzburg [sic] with the number 3 430 914.

Clearly, their records were both inaccurate and badly out of date. The matter was further complicated for the Munich office by the fact that the action which we now know to have been taken against Karajan after his marriage to the quarter-Jewish Anita Gütermann in 1942 was both politically sensitive and non-specific (i.e. unofficial). As such, it had nothing to do with the membership bureaucracy in Munich and was not communicated to them.

Faced with this tangle of information, one is reminded of Henry James's remark to Elgar after missing him at a reception: 'It was a confused and scattered scene and one wasn't one's master.' No wonder Paul Moor got a wrong steer on the facts back in 1957.

Unfortunately, Moor's version of the story was repeated by other journalists and by a number of Karajan's later biographers, most of whom cited each other in their lists of 'research' sources. Anyone who did not toe the revised line was accused of being involved in a cover-up.

Some time during 1982, Roger Vaughan confronted Karajan with a black-and-white photocopy of the NSDAP membership document while working on his book *Herbert von Karajan: a biographical portrait*. Vaughan's sources were Moor and Fred K. Prieberg who had confirmed Moor's findings in his own book *Musik im NS-Staat* (Frankfurt, 1982). Prieberg's confirmation of Moor's conclusions was less easy to fathom since he was a respected historian of the period with access to primary source materials. Perhaps he too was misled by a too cursory reading of the letter of 5 January 1939. He must have looked at the Karajan documents. Yet in a footnote on pp.359–60 of his book *Trial of Strength: Wilhelm Furtwängler and the Third Reich* (Wiesbaden, 1986/London, 1991), he calls Karajan a liar and cites *inter alia* Moor's article as an original, and it would seem definitive, refutation of Karajan's claim to have joined the Party under political pressure in Aachen in March 1935.

Vaughan's confronting Karajan with the documents had unfortunate repercussions. Whatever else can be said about Karajan's relations with the Third Reich, he was always clear in his own mind about the fact of his having agreed to join the Party at the specific request of the Aachen authorities in April 1935. Angered by Vaughan's (and Prieberg's) presumption to know more about this than he did, he declared the documents to be forgeries. They were not; they had simply been misinterpreted. In the heat of the moment, Karajan also made a remark about Prieberg (quoted by Vaughan) which was almost certainly libellous.

In 1983, in his book *Karajan: notes on a career* Robert C. Bachmann, a former Karajan pupil and admirer who had turned into one of his most virulent critics, made even more extensive use of the researches of Moor (whom Bachmann describes as a 'musicologist') and Prieberg, from whom Bachmann acquired Moor's article.

Having told us what the weather was like in Ulm on 1 May 1933 (it was raining, apparently), Bachmann goes on to denounce those biographers (or 'Karajan court reporters' as he prefers to call them) who have helped perpetuate what Bachmann considers to be the 'entirely false' story of Karajan joining the Party in 1935. In some ways, Bachmann's performance is the oddest of all since, as we have seen, he actually reproduces the disputed membership card on p.351 of his book; though having done so he fails properly to decipher, interpret, or explain it. A crucial piece of documentary evidence is thus turned into an illustration, a piece of Nazi memorabilia, rather than used as a source to be read.

The clearest and most authoritative reading of the document was eventually provided by the Swedish writer and scholar Gisela Tamsen in summary form in John Hunt's concert and opera register of Karajan's career *Philharmonic Autocrat* (London, 1993, pp.17–20). Miss Tamsen, who had spent more than a decade researching from primary sources the whole vast and intricate question of how the Nazi Party administered its membership system, takes us through the document line by line and explains the background situation with admirable clarity. Nor was she content to leave the matter there. Letters found among her papers at the time of her death in 1995 suggest that she was still checking and re-checking the facts.

One late letter is of especial interest. On 3 June 1993, the Director of the Berlin Document Centre, Dr David G. Marwell, wrote to Tamsen, stating:

According to the survey 'monthly highest membership numbers', of which I enclose a photocopy, it must be assumed that the number 3 430 914 was allocated in April 1935.

Still, however, the juggernaut runs on. A recent variation on the Moor-derived story appears in Professor Michael H. Kater's *The Twisted Muse: Musicians and their Music in the Third Reich* (New York, 1997). Kater, whose inability to get right even basic facts about Karajan's career hardly inspires confidence, resurrects the theory that Karajan hoodwinked the Allies in 1946 and goes on to assert that the membership number allegedly allocated in Ulm was simply transferred directly to Aachen. Since, as Luza states and Marwell confirms, the number 3 430 914 belongs to a tranche of numbers first issued in the spring of 1935, this cannot be the case.

Tamsen also continued digging for information on what was a potentially far more serious matter: suggestions of Karajan's possible involvement with the SD or *Sicherheitsdienst*, the internal security branch of the SS. Since the suggestions are largely American in origin, it has to be assumed that the Americans recovered a document or documents that establish some kind of *prima facie* link between Karajan and the SD.

It would, however, be surprising if such documents did *not* exist. Department VI, the Foreign Intelligence Service of the German SD, held cards on all persons who travelled abroad on official or semi-official business. On their return, travellers would be asked about their impressions, though not always by someone whom the interviewee would necessarily associate with the SD. Digests of all such 'debriefings' would then be entered on the person's SD file card. (After the war, the security system of the communist-run German Democratic Republic operated in exactly the same way.) An SD card would certainly have existed in Karajan's name in Berlin; there may also have been a duplicate card taken out by a sub-section of the SD in Aachen. The question of whether Karajan was in touch with 'illegal cells, circles, and interests' was raised at his denazification hearing in 1946. He vehemently denied this, adding for good measure that he was never 'in touch when abroad' with expatriate German groups.

Ironically, it was not until shortly before his death that Karajan himself showed any interest in Tamsen's researches into his Nazi Party membership. (See Chapter 81.) Whether he would have pursued the matter, it is impossible to say. Tired more or less to death by a controversy which had turned into a witch-hunt, and settled in his own belief that the matter had been definitively dealt with by the competent, legally constituted Allied and Austrian investigating authorities in 1945–7, he had long ago decided he wanted nothing more to do with it. As he had known all along, people will believe what they want to believe.

Karajan's deposition to the Austrian denazification examining board, 18 March 1946

This document begins with an astonishing error concerning Karajan's age and birthday ('Ich Herbert Karajan bin in Salzburg am 4 Mai 1918 ... geboren'). There are other minor errors and some (in the circumstances, no doubt predictable) glossing over of the facts – for example, on the subject of when and why Karajan accepted engagements outside Germany in the years 1941–44. The original German text is generally well expressed, the tone coolly 'factual'. After some biographical preliminaries, the deposition proceeds immediately to the subject of Karajan's NSDAP membership.

In Ulm pressure had already been put on me to join the Party. In Aachen, I could no longer refuse this request. I was admitted, as far as I can remember, without any waiting period. The Party card remained in the possession of my private secretary Nellessen, who also took care of all the formalities and especially the regular subscriptions. For this reason, I do not recall my card number and date of admission. Neither up to this point, nor thereafter, was I active on behalf of the Party. I did not accept any appeals or requests to attend rallies, and I successfully avoided political functions unless they were purely musical. This involved me in continual conflict with the Aachen *Kreisleiter*. He repeatedly reproached me for my lack of National Socialist thought and action, and took offence at the fact that I conducted exclusively spiritual works in the three annual choral concerts. I can still remember a clash with him in 1936. When the *Kreisleiter* wanted to cancel my projected *Matthew Passion* because of the section in it which dealt with a rabbi, I only just managed – I went as far as threatening my resignation – to get my way. My time in Aachen also contained a considerable amount of activity abroad (Sweden, Holland, Belgium). Although as an Austrian I was in possession of an Austrian passport, I received a German passport as well to facilitate journeys abroad. During this time I appeared on one occasion as guest conductor at the Viennese Opera. The opportunity arose through the good offices of Mr Kerber, whom I knew from Salzburg, and on that occasion I conducted *Tristan* without a rehearsal. In 1938 I accepted an invitation from the Berlin Philharmonic Orchestra to conduct a concert there. The success that this concert had with the public led to further concerts and finally to my appointment as one of the conductors of the State Orchestra.

In 1940 [1939] on Hitler's birthday, as was customary, I was invested with the title of *Staatskapellmeister*. Despite the increasing success I was known to be enjoying with the Berlin public from that time on, I was not in favour with the National Socialist regime. This was attributable to two factors:

1.) Hitler's personal aversion to me

2.) my marriage

Re. 1.): In 1939 I conducted *Die Meistersinger* in the Berlin State Opera. On the occasion of the State Visit to Berlin of the Yugoslavian Prince Regent, Hitler attended the performance with the Prince Regent. Afterwards Hitler spoke disparagingly of me and said he would never attend another performance with myself as conductor; I was not a representative 'German conductor'. Subsequently, Hitler made this declaration come true.

Goebbels said, when someone praised me: 'Stop talking about this passing fashion [*Saisongrösse*]! The Führer doesn't like him. In a year's time all this fuss will be over and done with.' It was Goebbels too who banned the filming of Mozart's *Don Giovanni* when I was due to conduct it. Secretary of State Esser said that the Führer saw red whenever he heard the name Karajan.

When my performances were received in the papers with words of the highest praise, instructions came from on high that my performances were to be reviewed only in purely descriptive terms, and two editors were removed from office on this account. Numerous witnesses could be called to testify to all these circumstances, which should however perhaps prove superfluous because so far nobody has undertaken to assert that I overreached myself in pursuing my career.

Re. 2.): When I first met my present wife in 1940, my first brief marriage to a singer in the Aachen Municipal Theatre was dissolved. Before I entered upon the second marriage, warnings came from sections of the SS that there were racial reservations concerning my fiancée, and I was threatened with the termination of my career in Germany. These threats were so serious, and the particular direction they were coming from was so dangerous that my future wife made up her mind to seize an opportunity to meet Goebbels, which presented itself to her in Italy; on meeting him, she explained that she wanted to marry me, although a subsequent question from my future wife obliged him to admit that he had never met me. The conversation did, however, result in our receiving a letter from Hinkel, the Director of the Reichskulturkammer, stating that there were no objections to my marriage. So we were married in October 1942 which none the less led to my being summonsed to appear before the Party Court and, in order to avoid further consequences, to my resignation from the Party.

Hitler's dislike for me, and my marriage, brought me, among other things, the following disadvantages:

a) A lasting impediment to my work as an operatic conductor, which finally caused me to discontinue my work at the Opera from 1942.

b) The Saxon State Orchestra's proposal to transfer the leadership of the Dresden Opera to me as Böhm's successor was turned down at the instigation of the SS and the Party.

c) From now on I was banned from conducting in neutral foreign countries (Switzerland and Sweden). In the first case, the ban was justified by claiming that it was inappropriate for a German to conduct in Switzerland. In fact, however, it was a German who conducted the concert in question. Obviously, Hitler's generally circulated pronouncement that I was not 'a representative German conductor' played a part in this.

d) Obstacles were repeatedly put in the way of my appearances in centres of German music such as Bayreuth, and especially Salzburg and Vienna.

e) My fee as Director of Philharmonic Concerts was reduced by half in 1944.

f) In contrast to all my colleagues, I was never invited to receptions or banquets, and I never received the otherwise customary tax relief, villas, cars, etc.

For the sake of completeness, I further note that, with one single exception (Paris in 1941) and in the face of repeated invitations, I never conducted in countries occupied by German forces. (The Danish State Orchestra's invitation to Denmark, which I once accepted, cannot really be counted among them, because Denmark kept its old government and head of state.)

To sum up, I may say that I cannot be taxed with any reproach other than that of having joined the Party in Aachen in 1935. As a result of Hitler's animosity and my marriage I was not popular in the Party or with the government, and my career was not promoted in any way since I supposedly did not embody the 'typical German conductor'.

Vienna, on 18 March 1946

ACKNOWLEDGEMENTS

'Ah, you publishing scoundrel!' exclaims the elderly Juliana at the end of Henry James's *The Aspern Papers*. Rereading a novella by Henry James before starting work on a biography of Herbert von Karajan may seem a strange priority; but the prospect of raking over the facts of a life so recently ended – a life already subject to so many tales and strange narrative manipulations – seemed as good a cue as any to reflect on the business of biography.

After Karajan's death in July 1989 and the publication later that same year of my book of conversations with him, I had no great desire to pursue the subject further. Though I was fascinated by his personality and musicianship, the spell he exerted was no greater than that cast by other historically important conductors – Beecham and Furtwängler, for example – who, even now, lack what I would consider to be properly worked biographies.

While Peter Conrad was urging me to write 'the definitive psycho-biography' of Karajan, other voices were urging caution. 'Attempt to write about Karajan,' announced Lord Weidenfeld on the only occasion I met him, 'and you will have nothing but trouble.' Weidenfeld had published Roger Vaughan's *Herbert von Karajan: A Biographical Portrait* but there had been a falling out with Karajan over Vaughan's treatment of the Nazi issue. I remember Karajan somewhat ruefully informing me that 'Lord Weidenfeld is not a gentleman', a feeling which may have been mutual.

There was, however, a rather larger problem standing in my way. Nothing less than a properly researched biography of Karajan would 'do'; but to what extent is the life of a recreative artist a suitable subject for a full-dress biography? Most biographies of performing musicians omit the two elements that make the life interesting: the childhood and the music-making, the former, as Thomas Mann remarks in *Dr Faustus*, a necessary element since

no biography, no depiction of the growth and development of an intellectual life, could properly be written without taking its subject back to the pupil stage, to the period of his beginnings in life and art, when he listened, learned, divined, gazed and ranged, now afar, now close at hand.*

---

* Mann, op. cit., p. 172.

751

To remove either from a life of Karajan would be fatally to compromise it; yet to include both would be to risk working on a scale more usually reserved for a major political figure (which, in some respects, Karajan was) or a creative artist. My first act of indebtedness is therefore to my old friend Jerrold Northrop Moore, wisest of counsellors, to whom such matters are meat and drink.

The book owes its origin, however, to Penelope Hoare who seems to have been determined to have a Karajan biography from me for longer that either of us probably cares to remember. Of rival publishers, only Stuart Proffitt at HarperCollins showed a similar interest and grasp of what was involved (his instant recall of the bibliography of Sir Isaiah Berlin led me to the famous profile of Karajan Sir Isaiah wrote for *The Observer* in 1948) but it was Penelope Hoare who eventually acquired the book for Sinclair-Stevenson in 1992. A bewildering series of changes of ownership and management in the publishing world intervened, none of which, happily, unseated either of us. Her reading of the final manuscript was trenchant, enlivening, and wonderfully helpful.

The draft manuscript was also read by Robert Henderson and Roy Westbrook to whom I am grateful, not only for their interest, but for their comments on the book's balance and tone. I should add that it is Roy Westbrook's submission that the book is too *short*. (As with Albert Grivault's finest Meursault, he observed, sufficient is rarely enough.)

The biography was begun with as clean a slate as I could muster. True, I already knew a good deal about Karajan and had known him personally, though not so well as to pass Dr Johnson's test of a biographer being qualified to write *A Life* only when he has 'eat and drunk and lived in social intercourse' with his subject. My intention was to examine written archives and talk to a representative cross-section of people who had either worked with Karajan professionally or, indeed, 'lived in social intercourse' with him. Since I had no idea what I would find, the material would, in some measure, shape itself.

The book was not commissioned by the Karajan Estate, nor has it been approved by it. However, my task would have been infinitely more difficult if, for whatever reason, the Estate had wished to influence or obstruct the book. It did neither. I am grateful to Dr Werner Kupper, the Estate's legal representative, for the permissions he has granted and the help he has given. Among those members of Karajan's immediate family I approached, only his second wife, Anita, failed to respond in any shape or form. I am grateful to Arabel von Karajan for the interview she gave in Salzburg and to Eliette von Karajan for her hospitality in Salzburg and in St Tropez.

*

No one, in the post-Legge era, knew Karajan better – either professionally or personally – than Michel Glotz, yet glance through the indexes of extant biographies of Karajan and you will find that he, like Legge, has no more than a walk-on part. I first interviewed him in Paris in 1990 for the BBC, and it was clear then that here was a witness of rare worth. He was one of the first people I approached after signing the contract for the present volume and the nine hours of conversation we had in Paris in the autumn of 1993 were of absorbing interest. Researching a biography is a bit like being a detective on a case: one ends up with a greater weight of factual information than any of one's interviewees. This can be alarming when the information one finds oneself being given does not quite 'add up'. Michel Glotz's conversations added up handsomely, however they were computed. A biographer is fortunate to find such a source: reliable, yet attuned to what I can only call 'the heart of the matter'.

Someone else who 'eat and drunk and lived in social intercourse' with Karajan – in the war years and for at least three decades thereafter – was Raffaello de Banfield Tripcovich. My visit to Trieste was among the happiest of the whole enterprise. It is not absolutely necessary to stand where one's subject stood at some great turning-point in his life; it was curious, none the less, how the years seemed to fall away as I stood on the terrace of the Villa Tripcovich looking over the same woodland and maritime scene Karajan looked out over in the autumn of 1945.

*

Another great prize, comparable to the memories of Glotz and Banfield, lay here in England: a huge file of documents in the EMI archive at Hayes. Karajan was involved with EMI more or less continuously from January 1946 to his death in 1989; yet for all that has been written about him in the last thirty years, this vast archive had lain entirely unexamined. I am grateful to Charles Rodier, EMI's Director of Contracts and Business Affairs, for his granting me permission to examine it and for his great personal interest in the project. I am also grateful to EMI's senior archivist, Ruth Edge, for all her help. There is no gramophone archive quite like this; it is a national and international treasure which I hope will be guarded as zealously in the next hundred years as it has been in its first hundred.

Though Walter Legge died in 1979, I am fortunate in having been able to talk at length with others who worked with Karajan at EMI, in particular: Suvi Raj Grubb, Peter Andry, David Bell, and Peter Alward. Their help has been of inestimable value.

Karajan's other principal record company Deutsche Grammophon has no comparable archive yet here the list of those people to whom I am indebted is even longer. Christoph Schmökel, Charles Rodier's opposite number and until recently Executive Vice-President of Deutsche Grammophon, gave my project a warm and properly circumspect welcome, and his office provided much valuable statistical information. In England for many years, Deutsche Grammophon *was* Peter Russell. Dubbed 'Black Cloud' by one of his more anarchic deputies, he presided over an age of affluence in the affairs of the gramophone companies in general and Deutsche Grammophon in particular, the like of which we are unlikely to see again. I have found Peter a shrewd adviser and generous host down the years, and he has had some wonderful helpers, including Robert Leslie, Mary Jo Little, and Bill Holland, all of whom provided a first-rate service to the press while at the same time managing to ply Peter with a life-sustaining diet of bad news. Tim Harrold, a former Executive Vice President of the company, also offered me considerable help during the later stages of writing.

Of Deutsche Grammophon's staff in Hamburg, I am indebted to Antje Henneking who organised my many press assignments in Salzburg, Vienna, and Berlin, in particular the all-important interview I did with Karajan in Berlin in December 1977. I am also indebted to Deutsche Grammophon's famously meticulous and civilised editorial department, in particular to Richard Evidon and David Butchart.

A number of my more most significant debts are to former Deutsche Grammophon executives: Andreas Holschneider, who was kind enough to let me have a sight of the interviews he conducted with the late Ernst von Siemens, Hans Hirsch and Günther Breest who, in their different ways, gave me interviews of great frankness and interest, and Uli Märkle. During the 1980s, after he left Deutsche Grammophon to join Télémondial, Dr Märkle took on the role of Karajan's expensively retained fall-guy, since when it has been fashionable to heap opprobrium on his head. The tensions and rivalries within the various Karajan camps never held much interest for me. All I can say is that he has been immensely helpful: generous and prompt in all his dealings. His interest in Karajan remains as strong as ever; a more cynical man might have shut up shop long ago.

My last and most delighted debt in this category is to Pali Meller Marcovicz whose memories of Deutsche Grammophon go back to the 1950s. His reminiscences have proved priceless, the more so for the wisdom which lay behind them and the wit with which they were invariably delivered.

*

The first musician I interviewed was Josephine Veasey whose memories of Karajan were generally so unhappy that she nearly declined my invitation. That she ended up saying all manner of positive things about him was an early indication that interviewees can be generous almost to a fault when a biographer is present. The second musician I met was Lord Menuhin, who interviewed himself. I had my questions, but his were infinitely more probing. These two encounters made for an instructive start to my work.

I would like to thank a number of artists who gave me interviews of unusual length and interest. The list of singers includes Josephine Barstow, Gundula Janowitz, Sena Jurinac, Anna Tomowa-Sintow, Graziella Sciutti, and Frederica von Stade. Among conductors, I would wish to mention Riccardo Chailly, Christoph von Dohnányi, Bernard Haitink, Mariss Jansons, Mstislav Rostropovich, Jeffrey Tate, Walter Weller, and Franz Welser-Möst. I am also grateful to Sir Simon Rattle for letting slip some amusing anecdotes and warily delivered judgements in the wake of a BBC interview he gave about one of his real heroes, Carlo Maria Giulini.

Sometimes it was necessary to travel long distances. Flying to Bermuda might seem to be no great deprivation, but I was unprepared for the reception I would receive there from Jon Vickers. Interviewing him about Karajan was a case of talking to one legend about another. I am grateful to him and his wife Judy for their wonderful hospitality and to Ken Vickers for the further help he gave me on his father's behalf.

There is a sense in which this is a book about Legge and Furtwängler, as well as Karajan. Here I am deeply indebted to Walter Legge's sister, Mrs John Tobin, to Elisabeth Furtwängler, and to Dame Elisabeth Legge-Schwarzkopf. The impression that relations between Schwarzkopf and Karajan had become strained in later years opened up the possibility that an interview might not be forthcoming; had that been the case, there would have been a significant hole at or near the centre of the book. In the event – thanks, in part, to the good offices of Charles Rodier and Alan Sanders – Dame Elisabeth was particularly generous with her time, in London and, later, at her home near Zürich. Like Jon Vickers, she is an artist blessed with high intelligence and a strong personality. She made a bracing interviewee, robust and fair-minded.

*

I had the good fortune to be able to work on a number of BBC documentary series which had a direct bearing on this book. Shortly after Karajan's death, the Controller of Radio 3, John Drummond, asked for a seven-programme retrospective on his career. Nick Morgan produced the series and it was during our visit to Berlin that I was able to interview Peter Steiner, Hansjörg Schellenberger, Fergus McWilliam, and Klaus Geitel. In England, there were important interviews with Gareth Morris, Robert Layton, and Christopher Raeburn. I am also grateful to Nick Morgan for ideas and information gathered from his many excellent *Vintage Years* programmes. In 1992, I compiled a twelve-part documentary on the 150th anniversary of the Vienna Philharmonic, produced by John Evans: Clemens Hellsberg, Helmut Weis, and Volker Altmann were kind enough give us interviews. There was also material to be gleaned from a series of programmes on Giulini on which I worked with Jeremy Hayes in Birmingham. A series, produced by Peter Tanner, about the post-war Vienna Opera, *Singing in the Ruins*, produced a trip to Augsburg and a long interview with Sena Jurinac. Finally, as the book was being rounded off, yet more material was forthcoming from a six-part series, *Celebrating Salzburg*, produced by David Gallagher, whose genius for hunting down archive sources was as gratifying as it was occasionally alarming. During this series, I had the pleasure of talking to Gérard Mortier, Hans Landesmann, archivist Gisela Prossnitz, and Gottfried Krauss, the moving spirit behind the historically invaluable series of CDs drawn from the Salzburg Festival-Austrian Radio archive.

The BBC Gramophone Library, the BBC Sound Archive, and the BBC Music Library, have all provided invaluable help. As access to these has become more complex because of technological and managerial changes of a near-Kafkaesque complexity, I was greatly helped in the later stages of my work by *Record Review*'s Jenny Pitt, a nonpareil among PAs.

An institution which is just one year younger than the BBC is *The Gramophone*. I would like to thank members of the Pollard family, the owners of *Gramophone*, for their many acts of help and consideration; Quita Chavez for inspiration and kindnesses over a period of more than thirty years too numerous to mention; my two editors, Malcolm Walker and James Jolly; and the small army of people who keep the contributors to this most distinguished of gramophone journals fed, watered, and up to the mark. I have also had help and advice from past and present fellow contributors, among whom must be numbered Julian Budden, Edward Greenfield, Stephen Johnson, Michael Kennedy, Robert Layton, Edward Seckerson, and, most particularly, Alan Blyth, who has provided me with a steady stream of articles and recordings which he fancied might be of interest.

*

There are other special debts to be acknowledged. Among the most prominent of these is to Isabella Wallich who generously agreed to allow me to read and publish the diary she kept of the Philharmonia Orchestra's 1952 European tour. Karajan's Philharmonia years are still remembered by those who were involved as vividly as if it was yesterday. I am grateful for interviews and information I have received from Mr and Mrs Hugh Bean, Professor and Mrs Philip Jones, Sidney Sutcliffe, and Jane Withers. I must also mention Stewart Brown of Testament Records; no one is doing more to keep that period alive by mining the archives for recordings other companies are unwilling to reissue.

I am grateful to Schuyler Chapin for his memories of Karajan in America in the 1950s, to Ronald Wilford whose agreement to be interviewed was a good deal more prompt than his reputation might allow, to Jeannie Williams who kept me abreast of Karajan's visits to New York in the 1980s, to Carol Jacobs of the Cleveland Orchestra's archive, and Friede Rothe.

Sir Isaiah Berlin gave me tea at the Athenaeum and later, for the Salzburg series, a long and immensely entertaining interview at his home in Oxford. He had profound misgivings about Karajan but, characteristically, that was no bar to his wishing to talk about him as pointedly and entertainingly as he talked about greater men and weightier matters.

Conversations I had with the conductor Adrian Brown, Joy Bryer of the European Community Youth Orchestra, Humphrey Burton, Peter Diamand, Mr and Mrs Massimo Freccia, Professor David Smith and Dr Ingegerd Östman-Smith, Jonathan Steinberg, Denis Stevens, and Lady Walton all provided rich quarries of material; as did discussions I had further afield with Fritz Buttenstedt of Unitel, Franz Endler, Peter Girth, Roland Latzko, Günther and Eva Schneider-Siemssen, and that indomitable nonagenarian Otto Strasser.

Denis Hall and Robin Cherry gave me useful advice on the kind of player-pianos Karajan would have encountered during his childhood. I must also acknowledge help, incidental and otherwise, from Helen Anderson, Thomas Angyan, Tony Cheevers, Didier de Cottignies, Peter Csobádi, Anneliese Eggebrecht, Sir Ian Hunter, Kate Kay, Patrick Lambert, Klaus Neumann of WDR, Cologne, H. C. Robbins Landon, Simon Maguire, Ray Minshull, Bruce Phillips, Costa Pilavachi, Clive Portbury, Crispin Read Wilson, Ken Russell, and Trevor Russell-Cobb.

*

During the writing, three books have been permanently on my desk: the *Chambers English Dictionary*, the *Collins German Dictionary*, and John Hunt's concert register and discography *Philharmonic Autocrat*. One of the most comprehensive of John Hunt's many publications, it has saved me many hours of additional work.

As for other books on Karajan: of the existing biographies only Ernst Haeusserman's *Herbert von Karajan* contains a significant amount of original source material. An underrated study (assumed to be a hagiography, it was never translated into English), it contains much valuable and reliable information about Karajan's early years. Roger Vaughan's stylishly written biographical portrait and Wolfgang Stresemann's *Erinnerungen an Herbert von Karajan* both contain useful source material, mainly, though not exclusively, concerning the later years of Karajan's career, as does Klaus Lang's *The Karajan Dossier*.

*

After Rossini, Karajan: next time I will choose a subject with the sources in English. Meanwhile, I must thank Olga Geralounos for providing me with a draft translation of Karajan's chapter 'On Rehearsal' (Appendix A) and my friend and former colleague David Barnes who for nothing more than a case of Wine Society beers each Christmas (and that unlooked for) has undertaken a huge burden of translation of primary texts and materials from the German.

The art of copy-editing, I am happy to report, is not yet dead. Ilsa Yardley read the entire text, twice, corrected it, annotated it with scrupulous care, and made a number of recommendations, both technical and editorial, which I was happy to accept. Having a Viennese-born, English-educated copy-editor, someone who knew Karajan's world at first hand, was a particularly happy chance. Judy Collins read the proofs. Any mistakes that persist are mine.

The book has been designed by Simon Rendall, a distinguished printer of the younger generation schooled in the old ways of doing things. Karajan would have approved of that. Things that were unstylish, sloppy, and second-rate were anathema to him.

*

I often turned for advice while writing this book to my friend, the composer, pianist, and writer Christopher Headington, a man of immense erudition, lightly worn and generously shared. His death in a skiing accident in 1997 was both a shock and a loss. He was the one musician I knew who understood Karajan's passion for flying and fast locomotion; indeed, it was Karajan's example that caused Christopher himself to take up flying at the relatively late age of forty-five.

It is a considerable sadness to me that my mother did not live to see the book's completion; she would have declared it a masterpiece, and I would have been pleased to believe her. My five-year-old son, Harry, recently asked, 'Daddy, how is your book getting on?' and promptly reported back to my wife, 'Yes, Daddy says I can have the extra éclair.' He should go far.

As for my wife, shortly after our marriage she asked, 'What are you like when you're actually *writing* a book?' I said I didn't know. I still don't. She, unhappily, almost certainly does.

*

I must thank Laurence Pollinger Ltd and the Estate of Frieda Lawrence Ravagli for permission to quote from the works of D. H. Lawrence. Quotations from T.S. Eliot's *Collected Poems 1909–1962* appear by permission of Faber & Faber. Lines from Roy Fuller's 'Autumn 1940' from *New and Collected Poems 1934–84* are quoted with the permission of the Estate of Roy Fuller. All quotations from *The Times* and *Sunday Times* are © Times Newspapers Limited. All quotations from the *Manchester Guardian* are © The Guardian. All quotations from the letters and writings of Herbert von Karajan are copyright. They can be reproduced, distributed, and communicated to the public only with the written consent of the copyright owner, the Karajan Estate.

The author and publishers have made every effort to trace the owners of copyright. They much regret if any inadvertent omissions have been made, but these can be rectified in future editions.

Notes

Sigla

BA	Bundesarchiv, Koblenz
BDC	Berlin Document Centre
BPhO	Berlin Philharmonic Archive
CO	Archives of the Musical Arts Association/The Cleveland Orchestra
DGG	Archive of Deutsche Grammophon Gesellschaft, Hamburg
EMI	EMI Archive, Hayes
GdMV	Gesellschaft der Musikfreunde Archiv, Vienna
GStA	Geheimes Staatsarchiv, Berlin
KTC	Karajan Centre, Vienna, Gisela Tamsen collection
LA	Landesarchiv, Berlin
NA	National Archives, Washington
ÖStaA	Österreichisches Staatsarchiv, Vienna
PAA	Politisches Archiv des Auswärtigen Amtes, Bonn
PRO	Public Records Office, Kew
RSA	Richard Strauss Archiv, Garmisch
UStA	Stadt Archiv, Ulm
VPhO	Vienna Philharmonic Archive

Bachmann	Robert C. Bachmann, *Karajan: notes on a career* (London, 1990)
Conversations	Richard Osborne, *Conversations with Karajan* (Oxford, 1989)
Csobádi	Peter Csobádi, *Karajan oder Die kontrollierte Ekstase* (Vienna, 1988)
Endler	Franz Endler, *Karajan: eine Biographie* (Hamburg, 1992)
H1	Ernst Haeusserman, *Herbert von Karajan* (first edition, Gütersloh, 1968)
Haeusserman	Ernst Haeusserman, *Herbert von Karajan* (revised edition, Vienna, 1978)
Karajan	*Herbert von Karajan: my autobiography*, as told to Franz Endler (London, 1989)
Lang	Klaus Lang, *The Karajan Dossier* (London, 1992)
Legge	*On and Off the Record: a memoir of Walter Legge*, edited by Elisabeth Schwarzkopf, with an introduction by Herbert von Karajan (London, 1982)
ORF	*Karajan* von und mit Marcel Prawy. Three-part documentary (Austrian Television, 1992)
Strasser	Otto Strasser, *Und dafür wird man noch bezahlt* (Vienna, 1974/R1993)
Stresemann	Wolfgang Stresemann, *'Ein seltsamer Mann . . .' Erinnerungen an Herbert von Karajan* (Frankfurt, 1991)
Vaughan	Roger Vaughan, *Herbert von Karajan: a biographical portrait* (London, 1986)

CHAPTER 1
An atmosphere of war
pp. 3–6

1 The island of Brioni was a fashionable resort, both before and after the First World War, much frequented by writers and musicians. Richard Strauss was a regular visitor; it was on Brioni that he met, among others, G. B. Shaw.
2 Haeusserman, 22.
3 Shakespeare, *The Winter's Tale*, I. ii. 63.
4 Bachmann, 39.
5 One of Karajan's favourite recordings in his later years was the 1971 RCA set of Rachmaninov's *Preludes* made by his friend and colleague Alexis Weissenberg.

CHAPTER 2
Sunday's child
pp. 7–16

1 Haeusserman, 21.
2 Vaughan, 210. Karajan never wrote in scores and often varied the editions he used so as to stop himself memorising the music visually.
3 Conversations, 100.
4 Karajan later argued that since the title had originally been granted in Saxony, it is a German title not an Austrian one.
5 Haeusserman, 25.
6 T. G. von Karajan, *Joseph Haydn in London, 1791 und 1792* (Vienna, 1861/R1975).
7 T. G. von Karajan, *Aus Metastasios Hofleben* (Vienna, 1861).
8 Conversation, Christa Ludwig.
9 Conversation, Herbert von Karajan.
10 Haeusserman, 21.
11 Ibid., 28.
12 Vaughan, 99.
13 Conversation, Bernard Haitink.
14 Conversation, Johannes, Graf von Walderdorff. The story relates to the visit his father Graf von Walderdorff made to Ernst von Karajan.
15 'We know that how the brain develops is partly determined by the external stimuli to which it is exposed. It would not surprise me to learn that exposure to music with a reasonably complicated structure facilitates the establishment of neural networks which improve cerebral function.' Anthony Storr, *Music and the Mind* (London, 1992), 48.
16 Conversation, Josephine Veasey.

CHAPTER 3
Teachers' boy
pp. 17–25

Epigraph Thomas Mann, *Doctor Faustus*, translated by H. T. Lowe-Porter (Martin Secker & Warburg, 1949/R1968), 63.
1 Bachmann, 46.
2 *Omnibus*, BBC 2 Television, March 1995.
3 Quoted Haeusserman, 27.
4 Sauer's last appearance at the Salzburg Festival was in 1962.
5 Conversation, David Bell.
6 David Bell, 'Bell and Karajan', draft manuscript, subsequently published in revised form as 'Organist to Karajan: Working with a Great Conductor', *The American Organist*, January 1997, 58–62.
7 'There were many powerful moments in the Bruckner at his request. I was able to bring on the full organ nine bars from the end. Karajan requested: "When the chorus sings their top C, *everything* from you, please." The three-stave organ part is liberally sprinkled with *fff* markings, but the two points of real climax – the aforementioned top C and the organ entry at the words "In aeternum" – had to dominate. At this point, the sopranos soar to a high B flat, and during rehearsal Karajan turned to me and, with eyebrows raised, jabbed down his finger (indicating more weight on the pedal). We rehearsed the passage again, and once more he indicated extra bass, even though I was already using both flue and reed 32s as written. So I doubled the part an octave lower as soon as I could, and this time he looked over and nodded. He omitted the organ unisons in "Aeterna fac" but requested at the first rehearsal that I double the brass

at the "Sanctus Dominus" (where the organ is normally *tacet*). It was fortuitous that I was playing from the full score!' David Bell, draft manuscript 'Bell and Karajan'.

8 Sauer played the organ in the performances of the *German Requiem* Karajan gave in Salzburg on 22 and 23 August 1957, the year of Karajan's return to the festival.

9 Conversation, David Bell.

10 David Bell, 'Organist to Karajan: Working with a Great Conductor', op. cit., 62.

11 Always a memorable occasion in its way. The music's curious mixture of the grave and the florid is reflected in St Peter's own architecture with its fantastically rich rococo shell-work and the colourful paintings that cover just about every available surface. Paumgartner's performances tend to play up the musical contrasts in a way that would have been considered eccentric in any other church or hall. It was an approach very different from the superlatively stylish performance of the C minor Mass Karajan himself recorded for Deutsche Grammophon in 1981, one of the finest of all his Mozart recordings.

12 Henry-Louis de La Grange, *Gustav Mahler: Vienna, The Years of Challenge (1897–1904)* (Oxford, 1995), 164.

13 Haeusserman, 25.

14 Hugo von Hofmannsthal, 'Die Salzburger Festspiele', *Gesammelte Werke*, ed. Herbert Steiner (Frankfurt, 1945–55), vi, 88–94. See also Michael P. Steinberg, *The Meaning of the Salzburg Festival: Austria as Theater and Ideology, 1890–1938* (New York, 1990), 1–36.

15 Edda Fuhrich and Gisela Prossnitz, *Max Reinhardt: The Magician's Dreams*, translated by Sophie Kidd and Peter Waugh (Salzburg, 1993), 105.

CHAPTER 4
A Salzburg education
pp. 26–32

1 Haeusserman, 30.
2 Haeusserman, 25.
3 Stefan Zweig, *The World of Yesterday* (New York, 1943), 295.
4 Many years later, when Karajan's daughter Arabel was sent to stay with friends in Oxford, she too seems to have been similarly strapped for cash.
5 Haeusserman, 30.
6 Vaughan, 95.
7 An adaptation by Hofmannsthal of a seventeenth-century morality play, *The Great World Theatre*, by the Spanish dramatist Calderón.
8 Legge died in 1979 before the musico-political mayhem of Karajan's final years.
9 Quoted in Christopher Brookes, *His Own Man: the Life of Neville Cardus* (London, 1986), 151.
10 Not to be confused with the legendary Polish-American pianist Josef Hofmann.
11 They played the sonata again in Ulm in November 1932.

CHAPTER 5
Vienna
pp. 33–39

1 Bachmann, 46.
2 Wolfgang von Karajan, conversation with Walter Weller.
3 Karajan, 17.
4 Massimo Freccia, *The Sounds of Memory* (Salisbury, 1990), 72–3.
5 Conversation, Herbert von Karajan.
6 Strasser, 67.
7 Herbert von Karajan, letter to Martha von Karajan, 3 November 1927, photocopy in KTC.
8 Conversation, Christoph von Dohnányi.
9 Harold Truscott, *The Music of Franz Schmidt. 1: Orchestral Music* (London, 1984), 7.
10 ORF, 1, *Der unbekannte Karajan*.
11 Karajan, 16–17. His 1971 Berlin recording of the overture is worth seeking out. It is a performance of great sensitivity and brilliance.

CHAPTER 6
A leader of suggestive power
pp. 40–44

1 Modris Eksteins, *Rites of Spring: the Great War and the Birth of the Modern Age* (New York, 1989), 251.
2 It is perhaps not entirely coincidental that Reinhardt later turned his production of *A Midsummer Night's Dream* into a Hollywood movie (1935).
3 Quoted in Stephen Gallup, *A History of the Salzburg Festival* (London, 1987), 54.
4 Joseph Schröcksnadel, *Salzburgs musikalische Botschafter: Das Mozarteum-Orchester* (Salzburg, 1984), 98.
5 The *Coronation Mass* originally appeared on Christschall 80–3, the *Requiem* on Christschall 74–9. Both recordings subsequently appeared on LP on the Eurodisc label. In 1995 Orfeo issued the *Requiem* on CD along with 1952 Salzburg Festival recordings by Messner of Mozart's Church Sonata for Organ and Strings, K67 and his *Grabmusik*, K42. There is also a 1948 recording of the *Coronation Mass* conducted by Messner, originally issued on Festival FLP 100.
6 Originally on Nixa PLP 534.
7 ORF, 1, *Der unbekannte Karajan*.
8 Like Karajan, Yella Pessl studied with Wunderer and Schmidt. She emigrated to the United States in 1931, founded the New York Bach Circle, recorded a good deal, and eventually ended up teaching at Columbia University. As a harpsichordist, she made numerous recordings in the 1930s and 1940s. Composers whose music she recorded include: C. P. E. Bach, J. S. Bach, Handel, Purcell, and Domenico Scarlatti. Recordings which were issued in Europe as well as the USA include J. S. Bach's Concerto in A minor for Flute, Violin, and Harpsichord BWV1044 and a six-record collection of Scarlatti sonatas. Her *The Art of the Suite* was published in New York in 1947.

9 *Salzburger Volksblatt*, 23 January 1929; Haeusserman, 42–3.
10 Louis de Bernières, *Captain Corelli's Mandolin* (London, 1995), 268.
11 Haeusserman, 24.
12 As even the most cursory examination of Ulm theatre and newspaper archives reveals, the name is Dieterich and not Dietrich as printed in books on Karajan by Haeusserman, Bachmann, Vaughan, Endler, and others.

CHAPTER 7
A young bandmaster from Ulm
pp. 45–60

1 Karajan, 19. In 1954, after Furtwängler's death, he similarly declined to allow the Berlin Philharmonic's forthcoming tour of the United States to be used as a probationary trial of his suitability for the position of chief conductor.
2 Patrick Leigh Fermor, *A Time of Gifts* (John Murray (Publishers) Ltd., 1977/R1979), 91–2.
3 *Opera*, February 1953, 105.
4 *Donauwacht*, 4 March 1929.
5 *Swäbischer Volksbote*, 18 March 1929.
6 *Salzburger Volksblatt*, 21 April 1929.
7 Haeusserman, 104.
8 Ibid.
9 Quoted in John Ardoin and Gerald Fitzgerald, *Callas* (London, 1974), 24.
10 The opera's colourful Act 1 polka was a great favourite with Karajan. He recorded it twice during his time with the Philharmonia Orchestra in London: in 1954 and again in 1960.
11 Fritz Kaiser, letter to Gisela Tamsen, 11 February 1983, KTA.
12 See 'The Jew as German Chauvinist' in Donald L. Niewyk, *The Jews in Weimar Germany* (Manchester, 1981), 165–177.
13 Bachmann, 82–3. Bachmann adds: 'Schulmann's refusal, whatever his reasons, to help us clarify matters might remind us that there is also a psychological phenomenon of solidarity between victims and criminals.' It would appear that to refuse to co-operate with Bachmann's speculations

about the 'criminal' Karajan is to expose oneself to a charge of being psychologically damaged.

14 Haeusserman, 47.

15 'Die Lehrstätte in den Schmutz gezogen', Südwestpresse, 15 March 1968.

16 Conversations, 45–6.

17 Ulmer Tagblatt, 16 March 1932.

18 Ibid.

19 Ibid.

20 Ludwig Meyer, former viola player in the Ulm orchestra, letter to Fritz Kaiser, 30 March 1968, KTA.

21 Haeusserman, 49.

22 Fritz Kaiser, letter to Gisela Tamsen, 11 February 1983, KTA.

23 However brilliant a young singer's audition was with Krauss, the question would inevitably come: 'Now tell me, how old are you?' Sena Jurinac recalls how she decided to lie about her age. Twenty-one at the time, and thinking to render herself as old as Methuselah, she said she was twenty-three. 'Too young,' replied Krauss. Then, removing his cigar, he added, 'But I can assure you, it is a problem that will improve as the years go by.' Conversation, Sena Jurinac.

24 Letter, Herbert von Karajan to Clemens Krauss, 27 July 1941, Barone Raffaello de Banfield Tripcovich, private archive.

25 Erich Leinsdorf, On Music (Portland, 1997), 216.

26 Schwäbischer Volksbote, 11 November 1931.

27 Letter, Herbert von Karajan to Martha von Karajan, 1 March 1933, photocopy in KTC.

28 Leigh Fermor, op. cit., 130.

29 Ibid., 129.

30 Ibid., 131.

31 Ulmer Tagblatt, 16 March 1932.

32 Officially, not, as some sources have suggested, privately.

CHAPTER 8
Swastikas in the sky
pp. 61–71

1 Conversation, Herbert von Karajan.

2 Letter, Herbert von Karajan to Martha von Karajan, 1 June 1934,

photocopy in KTC.

3 During the 1925 Salzburg Festival, Lady Diana Manners, Duff Cooper's wife, appeared as Madonna in Max Reinhardt's festival revival of Das Mirakel. Off-stage, she found herself playing Marschallin to the Octavian of the 18-year-old son of the poet Hofmannsthal. 'I don't much like the sound of Mr Hofmannsthal,' wrote Duff Cooper, who would later resign from the British government over the Munich agreement of 1938. 'It is uncanny the fascination German Jews seem to possess for you. But there's no accounting for taste.' (Philip Ziegler, Diana Cooper, London, 1981, 145.) It is unlikely that Duff Cooper would have written such a thing in similar circumstances after the war, even in a private letter.

4 Max von Schillings, who pitched in as an adviser on Nazi music policy a month before his death in July 1933, never seems to have forgiven the Hungarian-born Jew Leo Kestenberg for the part he played in removing him from his position as Intendant of the Berlin Staatsoper in 1925.

5 The Times, 31 March 1933. The elder son of Sir Alan Gardiner, the British Egyptologist, and Hedvig von Rosen, Rolf Gardiner was born on 5 November 1902. He was educated at Winchester, Rugby, Bedales, and St John's College, Cambridge. As a young man he was given land by his uncle Balfour Gardiner and would later become an internationally respected authority on afforestation and landscape husbandry. His sympathies and ideals were recalled in an obituary note in The Times on 7 December 1971 which suggested that Gardiner belonged as much to Germany as to England; that his aim was to interpret one nation to the other and to recall each country to a closer heritage and purpose. His powerfully pro-Austrian, pro-Anschluss sentiments were made public after the assassination of Chancellor Dollfuss in a further letter to The Times on 20 August

1934. While regretting the methods used, Gardiner argued that Austria was as German as Hanover or Schleswig-Holstein and that the present impasse was a direct result of the Allies' refusal in 1918 to allow Austria to become part of Greater Germany. Gardiner blamed the Austrian press (partly owned, he noted, by Czechs and Jews) and various financial, clerical, and political cabals for standing in the way of *Anschluss*. See also: *Rolf Gardiner of Springhead, Fontmell Magna: A Chronology of his Life and a Harvest Thanksgiving Sermon, Cerne Abbas Church, 6th October 1968* (The Springhead Trust, 1982).

6 The decree of 6 October 1936 requiring all Jews' passports to be stamped with the letter J was worked out in collaboration with the governments of Sweden and Switzerland.

7 Ortsgruppe V, Neustadt/Salzburg letter to *Gau* Treasurer of NSDAP, Salzburg, 15 May 1939, BA.

8 Letter, NSDAP Admissions Office, Munich, to Provincial Leadership, Austria, Linz, 19 April 1933, BA.

9 See pp. 742–7.

10 Karajan claimed that he persuaded Dieterich during a journey to Vienna to recruit singers.

11 In the event, the Foreign Ministry in Berlin was given limited discretionary powers over tax waivers for students, a typical Nazi fudge at a time when public opinion still mattered and when policy was being made on the hoof.

12 Clemens Krauss conducted three operas by Strauss – *Die Frau ohne Schatten, Der Rosenkavalier*, and the première of the revision of *Die ägyptische Helena* – as well as two by Mozart. Strauss himself conducted *Fidelio*. Bruno Walter conducted operas by Gluck, Mozart, and Weber – plus what was by all accounts a highly emotive account of Wagner's *Tristan und Isolde*. This was a further irritant to the Germans. Though the production had been planned some time in advance, it was seen as a snub to Bayreuth, which had been plunged into crisis in June 1933 by Toscanini's resignation over Nazi race policies.

13 Egon Friedell (1878–1938), *Kulturgeschichte der Neuzeit* (3 vols, 1927–32) and *Kulturgeschichte des Altertums* (2 vols, 1936–49). Friedell, who was a Jew, committed suicide after the occupation of Austria in 1938.

14 Karajan would acquire this, too, in later years. Rudolf Bing recalls Karajan's time at the Metropolitan Opera in New York: 'The level of tension rose in the house the moment it was known he had entered the door. Everyone worked his best because he was working for Karajan, and it was known that Karajan paid attention to everything.' Rudolf Bing, *5000 Nights at the Opera* (London, 1972), 266.

15 Haeusserman, 29.

CHAPTER 9
Nearly in the dust
pp. 68–75

1 One critic wrote of Karajan's late 1960s Berlin Philharmonic recordings of Handel's *Concerti Grossi*, Op.6: 'a fabulous set and the most eloquent argument against making any style of music the sole preserve of specialists'. Quoted in John Hunt, *Philharmonic Autocrat* (London, 1993), 9. Writing in *The Gramophone* in April 1967, Edward Greenfield observed, '[The performances] represent an unashamed return to "big Handel", and try as I did to put on my scholar's vinegar face while listening to them, I must confess the sumptuousness of the sound . . . had me capitulating very quickly.'

2 *Schwäbischer Volksbote*, 10 February 1934.

3 *Ulmer Tagblatt*, 10 February 1934.

4 Otto de Pasetti to Headquarters, US Forces, Austria, NA.

5 *Ulmer Tagblatt*, 31 March 1934.

6 In 1929, in common with most other German opera houses, Ulm used the familiar Hermann Levi

translations of the Da Ponte operas. By 1934 these had been outlawed on racial grounds by the powerful Rosenberg faction within the Nazi Party. *Figaros Hochzeit* was in fact the work of the talented scholar and translator Siegfried Anheisser, a first-rate craftsman who would later be drawn into the anti-Semitic lobby. His interesting and in all other respects politically unexceptionable study *Für den deutschen Mozart* (Emsdetten, 1938) includes a section entitled 'The Position of Judaism with regard to Mozart and Wagner' in which he attacks both Da Ponte and Hermann Levi, accusing Levi of masterminding a Jewish take-over of Mozart's musical legacy.

7 Letter, Herbert von Karajan to Martha von Karajan, April 1934, photocopy in KTC.

8 Karajan, 31.

9 Letter, Friedrich Foerster to Herbert von Karajan, 18 April 1934, UStA.

10 See Oliver Rathkolb, *Führertreu und gottbegnadet* (Vienna, 1991), 206–7.

11 As late as 1944, the Rosenberg faction was demanding the outlawing of the use of cadenzas by Joachim and Kreisler (both Jews) in performances of the Beethoven Violin Concerto, a demand ignored by Goebbels's Ministry. See Erik Levi *Music in the Third Reich* (London, 1994), 81.

12 Haeusserman, 51.

13 Gottfried von Einem, ORF, 3, *Verklärung und Tod*.

14 Letter, Herbert von Karajan to Martha von Karajan, 1 June 1934, photocopy in KTC.

15 Karajan, 33.

16 Draft obituary, *The Times*, unpublished.

CHAPTER 10
'Tell me now: are you happy with me?'
pp. 76–82

1 The production of Alban Berg's *Wozzeck* which Pella mounted to coincide with an international musical congress in the nearby town of Lüttich

in 1929 had been particularly admired.

2 Strohm later moved – on Goebbels's recommendation – to the Vienna State Opera where he developed a fit of megalomania, went barking mad, and in 1941 disappeared into a lunatic asylum.

3 Haeusserman, 55.

4 Willy Wesemann, '*Acht Jahre habe ich zu ihm aufgeschaut*', *Fono Forum*, No. 4, 1978, 368.

5 Both Fränzl and Wallmann worked for Karajan during his time as Director of the Vienna State Opera in the late 1950s. By then Wallmann had developed a none too flattering reputation as a producer of rather gaudy shows, though that was not the case with her staging of the world première of Poulenc's *Les dialogues des Carmelites* (Milan, 1957), a production of great sensitivity and power which Karajan brought to Vienna in 1959.

6 Letter, President of Reichstheater-kammer to Ministry of Propaganda, 9 August 1934, BA.

7 Unidentified review, H1, 49.

8 *Die Musik*, XXVIII, 12 September 1936, 905.

9 Raabe's willingness to serve as president of the RMK has done little to enhance his posthumous reputation, yet it is a position to which he brought a good deal of dedication and dignity. Like Strauss before him, he seems to have been primarily concerned to improve the lot of working musicians, while keeping to a minimum the problems and misunderstandings Nazi policies inevitably engendered. When the fanatic Hans Ziegler staged his *Entartete Musik* (Degenerate Music) Exhibition in 1938, Raabe refused to have anything to do with it: either privately, or publicly in his role as President of the RMK.

10 '*Auf den Spuren Herbert von Karajans*' by Klaus Schulte and Peter Sardoc, *Aachener Volkszeitung*, 10 December 1977.

11 Haeusserman, 58.

12 Letter, Herbert von Karajan to

Martha von Karajan, undated, photocopy in KTC.

CHAPTER 11
Chess moves
pp. 83–90

1 Haeusserman, 79.
2 Copy of Protokoll der Sitzung der Begutachtungskommission, Vienna, 15 March 1946, NA/KTC. For complete transcript see Chapter 21.
3 J. P. Stern, *Hitler: The Führer and the People* (London, 1975/R1990), 83–4.
4 Nathan Milstein and Solomon Volkov, *From Russia to the West* (London, 1990), 151.
5 For a perceptive discussion of the issue see Anne Applebaum, 'The lesser of two evils?', *Spectator*, 12 February 1994, 9–12.
6 William L. Shirer, *The Rise and Fall of the Third Reich* (New York, 1959/R Folio Society, London, 1995), I, 264.
7 Gitta Sereny, *Albert Speer: His Battle With Truth* (London, 1995), 172.
8 See Chapter 21.
9 Conversation, Christa Ludwig. Her mother also remembered Karajan's Party badge lying on his desk amid a jumble of pens, pencils, rubbers, and ink bottles.
10 Conversation, Lord Menuhin.
11 Conversation, Christopher Raeburn.
12 Vaughan, 113.
13 'Musiker bekennen sich zur Heimkehr ins Reich', Dokumentations-archiv des Österreichischen Widerstandes, Vienna/KTC.
14 Karajan had contemplated conducting Mahler's Eighth Symphony, the so-called 'Symphony of a Thousand'. He dropped the idea after hearing a performance in London conducted by Lorin Maazel. 'If only I were twenty years younger . . .' he is reported to have said at the time.
15 *Westdeutscher Beobachter*, 1 July 1935.
16 See Appendix C.
17 Paul Tillich, *Love, Power, and Justice* (London, 1954/R1960), 36–7.

CHAPTER 12
General Music Director, Aachen
pp. 91–100

1 Vincent Sheean, *First and Last Love* (London, 1956), 196.
2 Letter, Hans Hotter. Hotter recorded the *German Requiem* with Karajan in Vienna in 1947.
3 Interview by Klaus Schulte and Peter Sardoc, *Aachener Volkszeitung*, 10 December 1977.
4 Ibid.
5 Conversation, Christa Ludwig.
6 *Kölnische Zeitung*, 1 December 1935.
7 Various newspapers in the Aachen-Cologne area, 7 September 1935.
8 For Rehmann's testimony on behalf of Karajan to the Allied denazification commission, see Chapter 22.
9 *Kölnische Zeitung*, 1 December 1935.
10 Bernhard Stahl, interviewed in *Aachener Volkszeitung*, 10 December 1977.
11 Reminiscence, ORF, 1, *Der unbekannte Karajan*.
12 Mann, op. cit., 363.
13 *Neues Wiener Tagblatt*, 3 June 1937. One can glimpse the fiery – nay, frenetic – young Karajan in a snippet of film of him conducting the Prelude to *Die Meistersinger* with the Berlin Staatskapelle in Paris in May 1941.
14 *Wiener Zeitung*, 3 June 1937.
15 *Neue Freie Presse*, 3 June 1937.
16 Conversation, Herbert von Karajan.
17 Conversation, Otto Strasser.
18 Placido Domingo, *My First Forty Years* (London, 1983), 108–9.

CHAPTER 13
1938: The promised land
pp. 101–109

1 H1, 62.
2 Lanfranco Rasponi, *The Last Prima Donnas* (London, 1984), 111.
3 *Hörzu*, December 1977.
4 1898 and 1903 have both been given as Elmy Holgerloef's year of birth. In 1977, she gave her age as seventy-one, which adds 1906 to the list of possibilities.
5 *Hörzu*, December 1977.

6 Clara Graeger, personal secretary to Heinz Tietjen 1927–45, letter to denazification court, 1946, BDC.

7 It was Karajan's belief that after the death of Eduard Van Beinum in 1959 the orchestra itself neither desired nor received the kind of systematic, day-by-day training that even the finest ensembles need.

8 See Chapter 18.

9 The work was one of Mengelberg's favourite orchestral showpieces. Riccardo Chailly, who has examined Mengelberg's conducting score, told me it is so heavily annotated it is virtually impossible to see the printed text.

10 This was not Karajan's first visit to Scandinavia; he had conducted two concerts in Gothenburg the previous February. On that occasion, he had chosen mainly German repertory.

11 The other oddity was two performances of d'Albert's *Tiefland* with the Utrecht Opera.

12 *Salzburger Volksblatt*, 5 March 1938.

13 *Berliner Tageblatt*, 10 April 1938.

14 For a detailed résumé of Strobel's jockeying with the Nazi authorities, see Fred K. Prieberg, *Musik im NS-Staat* (Frankfurt, 1982), 310–17.

15 Letter from the NSDAP Gauleitung, Berlin, to the President of the Reichsschriftumskammer, 16 October 1939, BDC.

16 *Deutsche Allgemeine Zeitung*, 9 April 1938.

17 Haeusserman, 63.

18 It is curious that Karajan did not play and record the Mozart symphony more often in later years. He programmed it infrequently and recorded it just twice, once for EMI with the VPO in October 1946 and once for DG with the BPO on vacation in St Moritz in August 1965. The latter performance with the BPO is charming.

19 *Berliner Tageblatt*, 10 April 1938.

20 Remark quoted by Gottfried von Einem in his deposition to Karajan's denazification hearing dated 21 May 1947, Gottfried von Einem Archive, GdMV.

21 Vaughan, 114.

22 *Hörzu*, December 1977.

23 Elmy Holgerloef's phrase. Rudolf ('Rudi') Caracciola, the finest German motor-racing driver of his generation, was European Champion in 1938.

CHAPTER 14

1938: *Das Wunder Karajan*

pp. 110–125

1 A reference to the so-called 'Night of the Long Knives', which Göring partly masterminded.

2 Blech temporarily ended up in political no-man's-land. Having survived the Nazis until 1937, he found himself barred from the United States by the same radical Jewish lobby that had successfully kept Furtwängler at bay.

3 Dietrich Fischer-Dieskau, *Echoes of a Lifetime* (London, 1989), 92–101.

4 Bruno Walter, *Theme and Variations*, translated by James A. Galston (London, 1947), 298.

5 Ibid., 299.

6 The family Prittwitz und Gaffron was well known in military and court circles in Germany pre-1914. The Falstaffian Lieutenant-General Maximilian von Prittwitz und Gaffron (1848–1917), obese, raffish and self-important, was a particular favourite with Kaiser Wilhelm II. His inert and inexpert command of the German Eighth Army on the Russian front in August 1914 led to his prompt removal to less demanding duties.

7 Haeusserman, 69.

8 *Berliner Tageblatt*, 1 October 1938.

9 '*Wilhelm Furtwängler: Aufstieg und Leben eines grossen Mannes*', *Der Stern*, 4 October 1938.

10 *B.Z. am Mittag*, 22 October 1938.

11 Robert Oboussier, *DAZ*, 23 October 1938; Heinrich Strobel, *Berliner Tageblatt*, 10 November 1938; Karl Westermeyer, *Berliner Tageblatt*, 23 October 1938.

12 In his original page layout Ruland had illustrated the sub-heading

by including photographs of Furtwängler and De Sabata, though these were later dropped to make way for a drawing of Snow White and the Seven Dwarfs and a story that Walt Disney was being sued for breach of contract by the actor and actress who had recorded the voices of the Prince and Snow White for the soundtrack.

13 Wilhelm Furtwängler, *Notebooks 1924–1954*, translated by Shaun Whiteside, edited with an introduction by Michael Tanner (London, 1989), 130.

14 A number of people complained to von der Nüll's editor and to von der Nüll himself about the tone and content of the review. Von der Nüll's senior colleague, Wilhelm Matthes, later wrote an editorial calling for restraint in the writing of criticism, while fellow critic Walther Steinhauer, another Karajan admirer but a calmer one, reviewed Karajan's performance of *Tristan und Isolde* on 10 November in more consciously measured tones. Von der Nüll was not, however, barred from writing about Karajan, which he continued to do with more or less unabated enthusiasm.

15 One of the witnesses was *B.Z. am Mittag* music critic Annaliese Theiler (née Wiener). In a lengthy written submission to the commission, she suggested that von der Nüll openly boasted about his pro-Karajan, anti-Furtwängler stance and his contacts with the Göring ministry. In fact, Theiler did not join the music staff until shortly after the publication of the '*Wunder Karajan*' review by which time the somewhat discredited von der Nüll may well have decided that he had little to lose and much to gain by becoming the cheer-leader of a pro-Karajan lobby. For an English-language translation of Theiler's testimony see Daniel Gillis, *Furtwängler and America* (New York, 1970), 76–8.

16 Arguments over the review and the 'drafting' of von der Nüll followed Furtwängler to the grave, and

beyond. Largely ignorant of the primary source materials, journalist quoted journalist, and critic quoted critic. In 1995 the case was revisited – powerfully, for it is the stuff of which drama is made – in Ronald Harwood's play *Taking Sides*.

17 Letter, Heinz Tietjen to Friedelind Wagner, 16 November 1937, Wilhelm-Furtwängler Archives, Zürich.

18 Letter, Heinz Tietjen to Dr Erich von Prittwitz-Gaffron, 11 December 1946, BDC.

19 Letter, Dr Erich von Prittwitz-Gaffron to Heinz Tietjen, 2 January 1947, BDC.

20 Letter, Wilhelm Jerger to Hermann Göring, 4 November 1936, VPhO.

21 The programme for the broadcast was: Mozart Symphony No. 35, *Haffner*, Beethoven Piano Concerto No. 5, soloist Willy Stech, and R. Strauss's *Tod und Verklärung*.

22 *B.Z. am Mittag*, 2 November 1938.

23 Press release, Aachen Opera, 5 November 1938, KTC.

24 Ibid.

25 Sunk in gloom after seeing a particularly poor production of *Der Rosenkavalier*, the two men were walking through Berlin's Tiergarten bemoaning the problems of the operatic world when – according to Gründgens – Klemperer remarked, 'And the worst of it, Gründgens, is that one never finds a decent producer.'

26 Among those who later took a serious dislike to the production was the somewhat conservative-minded Wolfgang Wagner who joined the State Opera in 1940 as a 21-year-old trainee. 'Truly frightful and vastly expensive' is how he would later describe the production in his memoirs, adding, somewhat naïvely, that seeing it from on stage was a very different experience from seeing it from the auditorium. See Wolfgang Wagner, *Acts* (London, 1994), 59.

27 Wilhelm Furtwängler, Notes, 1939-I, p.23 of unpublished MS, quoted by Fred K. Prieberg, *Trial of Strength: Wilhelm Furtwängler and the Third*

Reich, translated by Christopher Dolan (London, 1991), 246.

28 *The Gramophone*, November 1926. Mackenzie returned to the subject in *My Record of Music* (London, 1955), 158–60.

29 Strasser, 254.

CHAPTER 15
Peace and war
pp. 126–133

1 Clive Bennett, BBC Radio continuity script, 15 June 1987, BBC, London. The production of *Die Bürger von Calais*, produced by Clive Bennett in a specially commissioned English version by Elizabeth Forbes, was broadcast by BBC Radio 3 on 21 June 1987. Simon Joly conducted the BBC Singers, the Glyndebourne Festival Chorus, and the BBC Concert Orchestra. The cast included: Marie Slorach (Burgomaster's wife), Jane Eaglen (Queen of England), David Johnston (Joseph Wissant), John Graham-Hall (Peter Wissant), John Connell (Burgomaster), and Nigel Douglas (English Officer).

2 In Szász-Régen, from which Wagner-Régeny took the distinguishing addition to his name.

3 Herbert Gerigk, *NS-Monatshefte*, X/108, March 1939, 278.

4 *Berliner Tageblatt*, 30 January 1939.

5 This was not the kind of repertory the record companies, or Karajan, were looking at *c*.1960. There was also the additional problem of the hullabaloo a decision by him to record an obscure 'Nazi' opera would almost certainly have caused.

6 The performance of 10 June 1939 was recorded and has since appeared on CD as Vol.15 of Koch Schwann's historic series *Vienna State Opera*. The sound is dreadful, though Ursuleac's vocal pyrotechnics manage to penetrate the sonic gloom.

7 *DAZ*, 15 April 1939. Music criticism in the *Deutsche Allgemeine Zeitung* was notably independent-minded, even in the later stages of the war, provided one was prepared to do a certain amount of reading between the lines. It was *DAZ* that had published Furtwängler's defence of Hindemith, 'Der Fall Hindemith', in November 1934. Shortly after that, Goebbels screamed at a *DAZ* journalist, Alfred Detig: 'Do you know why we allow *DAZ* to keep publishing? It's because if you've got a plague of rats you always leave one or two holes open to see which rats peep out. That way you can trash them better.'

8 *Deutsche Zukunft*, 23 April 1939. Fred Hamel also occasionally wrote under the pseudonym Hans Lyck [=Hanslick].

9 When Sir Roger Norrington recorded the Prelude to *Die Meistersinger* with the period instrumentalists of the London Classical Players in 1994 he made much of the fact that Wagner himself had mentioned a playing time of a few seconds over eight minutes. The modern norm, he pointed out, was nearer nine or ten: readings strong on bourgeois respectability but short on comic energy or the urgings of young love. Analysing the discrepancy, Norrington attributed this progressive slowing to larger orchestras and an increasing use of string vibrato. His own reading came in at 8′19″, tantalisingly close to Wagner's estimate. And Karajan's crisp, unhurrying, vibrato-light 1939 recording with the Berlin Staatskapelle: how quick is that? Interestingly, it is virtually the same: 8′24″.

10 The one relative newcomer was the Walther von Stolzing, Set Svanholm. With his open-mindedness and intelligence, and his scrupulous care for note values, he was a valuable ally for Karajan.

11 Hitler's reaction is chronicled in Nicolaus von Below, *Als Hitlers Adjutant 1937–45* (Mainz, 1980), 166. Tietjen subsequently instructed Karajan to have the score in front of him during performances of *Die Meistersinger*: '... because the score, ultimately, is a form of visual help. It takes some of the burden away from

your brain, and it's important not to have constantly to rummage around in your memory but to be able to concentrate entirely on the work.'

12 Joseph Goebbels, diary entry, 2 November 1940.

13 Fritz Krenn, evidence to Austrian Denazification Tribunal, 15 March 1946. See Chapter 21.

14 Conversations,72–3.

15 Ibid., 73.

16 Shirer, op. cit., I, 676.

CHAPTER 16
'More Diogenes than Alexander . . .'
pp. 134–149

1 'Protection' meant the prompt and ruthless institutionalisation of Hitler's own fetish for secrecy in '*Grundsätzlicher Befehl Nr.1* [General Order No.1]', 11 January 1940. This ordered that no member of any government or military agency should be informed *or should seek to discover* (my emphasis) more about secret matters than was strictly necessary for the enactment of his or her duties.

2 Endler, 97.

3 Ibid.

4 Anita Gütermann, ORF, 2, *Auf neuen Wegen.*

5 Luis Trenker, *Alles gut gegangen: Geschichten aus meinem Leben* (Munich, 1972), 417.

6 Quoted in Lang, 21.

7 Conversations, 112.

8 Ibid.

9 Rasponi, op. cit., 110.

10 Ibid., 111.

11 Grümmer states that the opera was Lortzing's *Der Wildschütz.* The work was in Karajan's repertory, but there is no evidence of his having conducted it in Aachen. *Tiefland* was given in November 1940, with performances conducted by both Karajan and Pitz.

12 Rasponi, op. cit., 111.

13 Ibid., 495.

14 Ibid.

15 *Aachener Anzeiger*, 13 October 1940.

16 Ibid.

17 Ibid.

18 Vaughan, 125.

19 In August 1947, following a reader's plea the previous June for more recordings by 'the brilliant young conductor Herbert Von [*sic*] Karajan', *The Gramophone* received a letter from a reader in Aberdeenshire, Mr E. K. Borthwick, concerning a broadcast of Beethoven's *Eroica* Symphony by Karajan and the Prussian State Orchestra: 'I heard this in the summer of 1944 on the German wireless . . . and have never heard a more impressive performance. It may have been recorded for broadcasting purposes only, but I am hopeful that it may have been generally issued.' See Chapter 18 n.17.

20 Letter, Reichs-Rundfunk GmbH, Deutscher Kurzwellensender to Dr Erich von Prittwitz-Gaffron, 11 November 1940.

21 Vaughan, 126.

22 Conversation, Christoph von Dohnányi.

23 Marie 'Missie' Vassiltchikov, *The Berlin Diaries 1940–1945*, edited with a foreword by George Vassiltchikov and with an introduction by Christabel Bielenberg (London, 1985/R1991), 33.

24 Ibid., 95.

25 *Berliner Zeitung*, 12 November 1940.

26 *Frankfurter Zeitung*, 16 December 1941.

27 In January, Karajan included in the programme the César Franck Symphony, Haydn's Symphony No.95 in C minor, and Respighi's *The Pines of Rome*; in February a *Concerto Grosso* by Locatelli, which he directed from the harpsichord, Mozart's Divertimento K287, Rachmaninov's Second Piano Concerto with Gieseking as soloist, and Strauss's *Tod und Verklärung.*

28 *DAZ*, 3 December 1940.

29 M. de Brinon, news report, *Keesing's Contemporary Archives*, 1940–43, 4579.

30 To Toscanini and De Sabata.

31 *La Nazione*, 18 March 1940. Diogenes was the independent-minded Greek philosopher who,

when asked by Alexander the Great if he might oblige him in any way, retorted drily, 'Yes, by standing out of my sunshine.' Alexander is said to have remarked afterwards, 'If I were not Alexander, I would wish to be Diogenes.'

32 See p. 56.

33 Conversation, Barone Raffaello de Banfield Tripcovich.

34 *Lord Byron's Love Letters* had its première in New Orleans in 1955. In November 1955 it was performed at the Lyric Opera, Chicago, conducted by Nicola Rescigno with Astrid Varnay and Gertrude Ribla in the leading roles; these artists recorded the opera shortly afterwards for RCA Victor (LM 2258). A second recording was made in 1991 in the Teatro Rossini, Lugo, conducted by Gianfranco Masini for the Ermitage label.

CHAPTER 17
Down, down I come
pp. 150–162

1 Paul van Kempen (1893–1955) had been a violinist in Mengelberg's Concertgebouw Orchestra before turning to conducting. In 1934 he became chief conductor of the Dresden Philharmonic. His successes with the Dresden orchestra and choir had greatly enhanced his reputation in Germany.

2 Quoted in *Aachener Volkszeitung*, 10 December 1977.

3 *Daily Telegraph*, 17 July 1989. Karajan's obituary was treated by the paper as a news story.

4 Staatskapelle, Berlin, with Edwin Fischer as soloist. The programme, scheduled to mark the 150th anniversary of Mozart's death, consisted of Symphony No.40 in G minor K550, Piano Concerto No.20 in D minor K466, and Symphony No.41 in C K551.

5 Things were, indeed, getting quieter, though, Karajan's Christmas schedule was hectic enough. In Berlin, he conducted *Carmina burana* on 20, 22 December and a Christmas Day performance of *Die*

Zauberflöte. Having returned to Aachen, he conducted a New Year's Day performance of *Don Giovanni*, but then returned to Berlin the following day to conduct a further performance of *Carmina burana*. On 19 January, the Aachen choir joined Karajan in Berlin for two highly acclaimed performances of Beethoven's *Missa Solemnis*.

6 Letter, Herbert von Karajan to Martha von Karajan, 25 November 1941, photocopy in KTC.

7 Letter, Karl Elmendorff to Gerdy Troost, 21 December 1941, BA/KTC. Paul Ludwig Troost was one of the most distinguished German architects of the pre-Nazi era. Albert Speer first came to Hitler's notice while working for Troost and effectively inherited Troost's mantle as the Führer's chief architect after Troost's death in January 1934.

8 Ibid.

9 *Time*, 19 June 1933.

10 Letter, Karl Elmendorff to Gerdy Troost, 13 January 1942, BA/KTC.

11 Like Josef Wolfsthal, the enormously talented young violinist who was the leader of the Staatskapelle from 1929 until his death in a flu epidemic in Berlin in 1931, Taschner showed promise as an orchestral player, as a chamber musician, and as a solo player, the manner fiery and expressive in the Furtwängler style. (Recordings exist of him playing Bruch's G minor Concerto with Abendroth and the Berlin Philharmonic in December 1944, and the Fortner Violin Concerto with Furtwängler and the Berlin Philharmonic in December 1949.) Vedder discovered Taschner's salary with the Berlin Philharmonic and attempted to lure him away with promise of higher fees working with Karajan's Staatskapelle and as a soloist. Vedder's claim that 'the future lay with Karajan' certainly showed prescience; but by attempting to promote the Staatskapelle's interests at the expense of those

of the Berlin Philharmonic, he was (as Furtwängler was quick to point out) interfering with the carefully balanced power structures established by the Reichskulturkammer itself. Vedder's agent's licence was formally withdrawn by the RKK on 30 July 1942.

12 Interview, Dr Andreas Holschneider with Dr Ernst von Siemens, Munich 1988. Unpublished typescript.

13 Conversations, 55.

14 They included Weber's *Jubel* Overture with the tune of the English National Anthem 'God Save the King' snipped out.

15 Letter, Dr Erich von Prittwitz-Gaffron to Richard Strauss, 31 January 1943, GStA.

16 Vaughan, 126–7.

17 Letter, Heinz Tietjen to Herbert von Karajan, 7 May 1943, GStA.

18 H1, 63. For some reason, this passage is omitted from the revised edition of the biography.

19 In 1934, Göring had offered reassurances to Furtwängler's Jewish secretary, Berta Geissmar, with the words, 'It is for me to decide who is a Jew.' Berta Geissmar later commented: 'This may have been his opinion then. But it must not be forgotten that in the Totalitarian State the Leaders control the development of events far less than some of the small party agitators.' Berta Geissmar, *The Baton and the Jackboot* (London, 1944), 138.

20 Karajan told the Austrian Denazification Tribunal that, prior to Anita's meeting with Goebbels in September 1942, he himself had never met Goebbels. However, if, as he claimed, he went to see Goebbels about his being drafted into the armed forces, that meeting would almost certainly have preceded Anita's Venetian encounter.

21 To judge from a letter written on 23 June 1943 by Goebbels, who clearly wished to draw a line under the matter, NSDAP zealots had continued enquiring into Anita von Karajan's racial origins even

after the Party hearing (cf. n.19 above).

CHAPTER 18
City terrors and mountain vigils
pp. 163–180

1 Letter, Herbert von Karajan to Dr Erich von Prittwitz-Gaffron, 26 January 1943, GStA.

2 Letter, Richard Strauss to Dr Erich von Prittwitz-Gaffron, 27 January 1943, GStA.

3 Letter, Herbert von Karajan to Heinz Tietjen, 12 May 1943, GStA.

4 Ibid.

5 When Gutterer proposed, the following March, that the government should find a political settlement before the Reich was destroyed, Goebbels had no option but to have him removed to other duties within the ministry.

6 Memorandum, Obersturmführer Schmidt to Generalintendanz Staatsoper Berlin, 6 February 1943, GStA.

7 Ibid.

8 *Berliner Börsen-Zeitung*, 21 April 1943.

9 In December 1943 the concert consisted of Haydn Symphony No.93, the Prelude and *Liebestod* from *Tristan und Isolde*, Bruch's G minor Violin Concerto, with the orchestra's leader Siegfried Borries as soloist, and Weber's *Oberon* Overture.

10 Grammophon 68186–8. The idiom seems foreign to the Dresden players, but the performance chugs along nicely enough.

11 Memorandum, Dr Erich von Prittwitz-Gaffron to Dr Kapp, Foreign Bureau for Music, Berlin, 16 April 1944, KTC.

12 The recording was reissued on CD by Deutsche Grammophon in 1988. For comment on this and other classic recordings of the symphony – including recordings by the Concertgebouw Orchestra under Mengelberg and Van Beinum – see *Diapason: Dictionnaire des disques et des compacts* (1993 Edition), 201–2. During the same sessions

Karajan also made memorable recordings of Richard Strauss's *Don Juan*, the 'Dance of the Seven Veils' from *Salome*, and Weber's overture *Der Freischütz*.

13 Jacques Pernoo, Honorary Director of the Bordeaux Conservatoire, *Sud Ouest*, 17 July 1989.

14 SD report, '*Stellungnahme zur Frage des Einsatzes der deutschen Musik im Ausland*', 27 December 1943 (incorrectly typed '1934'), BDC.

15 Trenker, op. cit., 417–8.

16 Letter, Herbert von Karajan to Martha von Karajan, 28 July 1944. Photocopy in KTC.

17 Though not the *Eroica* which Karajan also recorded at this time, in May 1944. It is a performance in which the Funeral March, in particular, is powerfully realised. The recording, part of the vast Reichs-Rundfunk-Gesellschaft tape archive seized by the Soviet Army in 1945 and not made available to the West until 1990, has been reissued on CD on Koch Schwann.

18 Reissued on CD on Koch Schwann. Three movements only. The tapes of the first movement have not been located.

19 Letter, Director of Broadcasting (Hans Fritzsche) to State Secretary (Leopold Gutterer), 12 October 1944. GStA.

20 Memorandum, (Reichs-Rundfunk) to Ministerialdirektor Fritzsche, 16 October 1944, GStA.

21 Vaughan, 129.

22 Ibid.

23 Ibid., 130.

24 Letter, Bruckner-Verlag, Leipzig to Dr Erich von Prittwitz-Gaffron, 13 October 1944, GStA.

25 Letter, Herbert von Karajan to State Secretary Leopold Gutterer, 14 August 1944, BA. The subscription 'Heil Hitler!' was a formality in such communications. Like most people, Karajan, or his secretary, used it where appropriate. Karajan never used it in private correspondence. It was also frequently omitted in correspondence within the Berlin State Opera: e.g. between Karajan and Tietjen or Prittwitz-Gaffron. Where it is used, it invariably indicates a degree of formality in the exchange.

26 Letter, Hans Fritzsche to Leopold Gutterer, 12 October 1944, GStA.

27 Conversation, Hanns Kreczi and Frau Georg Jochum, quoted in Hanns Kreczi, *Das Bruckner-Stift St Florian und das Linzer Reichs-Bruckner Orchester (1942–1945)* (Graz, 1986), 230.

28 Glasmeier was called back to St Florian, on Hitler's personal orders, on 16 December 1944.

29 Quoted in Kreczi, op. cit., 231.

30 Ibid., 230.

31 Recordings exist of Georg Ludwig Jochum conducting Bruckner's Second and Fifth symphonies with the Reichs-Bruckner Orchestra. They have appeared on CD on the Tahra label.

32 The recording has been lost. Performances of *Art of Fugue* later became a speciality of the organ ensemble which Karajan's brother Wolfgang played in and directed. There is no reason, however, for thinking that the Linz performance was directed by him.

33 Letter, Herbert von Karajan to Richard Strauss, dated '10.6 *heu.* [today] 16.7.44', RSA. Strauss's eightieth birthday was on 11 June 1944.

34 Trenker, op. cit., 418.

35 Ibid., 418–9.

36 Ibid., 419.

37 Vassiltchikov, op. cit., 193–4.

38 Weber's overture *Euryanthe*, Schumann's Piano Concerto with Walter Gieseking as soloist, and Brahms's Fourth Symphony.

39 Letter, Herbert von Karajan to Martha von Karajan, 11 November 1944, photocopy in KTC.

40 Memorandum, Dr Erich von Prittwitz-Gaffron, Berlin State Opera, 8 January 1945, GStA.

CHAPTER 19
Flight to Italy
pp. 181–185

1 Conversation, Eliette von Karajan.
2 The Pozzi episode is somewhat muddied in Vaughan's biography where he reports that Karajan said that Pozzi had been shot for harbouring Anita and himself. The truth of the matter is most likely what Karajan told Haeusserman and also told Vaughan on a subsequent occasion: that Pozzi was taking a risk; that he *could have been* shot for harbouring the Karajans.
3 Haeusserman, 76.
4 WO 106/3965A, PRO. Quoted in Richard Lamb, *War in Italy 1943–1945: A Brutal Story* (London, 1993/R1995), 239.
5 Freccia, op. cit., 160.
6 Trieste was formally handed back to Italy by the British and American governments on 26 October 1954. The border with Yugoslavia is within the city suburbs.
7 See Vaughan p.132 for a representative version of this story.
8 Conversation, Barone Raffaello de Banfield Tripcovich.
9 Raffaello de Banfield's *For Ophelia* had its première with Kiri Te Kanawa and the London Philharmonic Orchestra conducted by John Pritchard at the Royal Festival Hall, London, on 15 March 1977.

CHAPTER 20
Captain Epstein's dilemma
pp. 189–199

Epigraph Noel Annan, *Changing Enemies* (HarperCollins Publishers Ltd, London, 1995), 48.
1 *Trial of the Major War Criminals* (Nuremberg, 1948), II, 98.
2 Conversation, Dr Peter Girth.
3 Memorandum, November 1945, NA.
4 Conversation, Sena Jurinac.
5 Conversation, Sena Jurinac.
6 According to Otto Strasser, Anton Paulik conducted on 1 May, with Krips taking on later performances.
7 Conversation, Dame Elisabeth Legge-Schwarzkopf.

8 Different sources give different dates for Karajan's concert with the VPO in January 1946. Karajan biographers from Haeusserman to Vaughan give the date as 18 January, which is clearly wrong. An announcement on p.8 of the *Wiener Kurier* on 8 January 1946 gives the dates as Sunday, 13 and Saturday, 19 January, with a *Generalprobe* [public dress rehearsal] on 12 January. Thus the *Generalprobe* took place on 12 January, shortly after the conclusion of the Pasetti–Epstein meeting, with the concert itself next day. This is confirmed by Otto Strasser in his autobiography, where 13 January is given as the date of the concert. The concert scheduled for 19 January was cancelled, after a further review of the situation by the Russians.
9 Memorandum, 12 January 1946, NA.
10 *Die Furche*, 26 January 1946.
11 Erwin Mittag, *The Vienna Philharmonic*, translated by G. R. L. Orange and G. Morice (Vienna, 1950), 113–4.
12 Strasser, 228.
13 *Österreichische Musikzeitschrift*, January 1946, 43.
14 'At its worst, the official food ration in Vienna was a bare 600 calories a day, less than many a concentration camp level. Thanks mainly to emergency deliveries of flour and other supplies from American army reserves, it rose, during the winter of 1945–6, to a more sustaining 1550 calories a day, only to be cut back again in the spring to 1200.' Gordon Brook-Shepherd, *The Austrians: a Thousand-Year Odyssey*, (London, 1996), 386.

CHAPTER 21
Interrogation
pp. 200–206

1 Much has been made of the fact that Elisabeth Schwarzkopf made false entries on her questionnaires. If she did, she was not alone. The British, who used the questionnaire system rather more reluctantly than the Americans, set little store by the answers they received.

2 ÖStaA, copy KTC.

CHAPTER 22
An Englishman abroad
pp. 207–219

1 Percy Fender was the scorer of the fastest ever first-class hundred. A photograph exists in the *Daily Mail* archive of him signing the 13-year-old Legge's autograph album.

2 There were fifteen volumes of the Beethoven Piano Sonatas played by Artur Schnabel, the Beethoven Violin Sonatas from Kreisler and Franz Rupp, several volumes of Bach's keyboard music played by Wanda Landowska, Albert Schweitzer, and Edwin Fischer, and Mozart operas from the newly founded Glyndebourne Festival company.

3 Legge, 222

4 Ibid.

5 Ibid.

6 Walter Legge, memorandum, February 1946, EMI.

7 Memorandum, 23 February 1946, NA.

8 Lothar's successor as director of festival theatre productions was his son-in-law Ernst Haeusserman, Karajan's first biographer.

9 Memorandum, 15 June 1946, NA.

10 Th. B. Rehmann, letter to Theater-und Musikabteilung des Amerikanisches Nachrichtendienstes in Österreich, 10 April 1946, NA.

11 Herbert von Karajan, letter to Theodor B. Rehmann, 17 May 1947, KTC.

12 Dermota, op. cit., 237–8.

13 *The Gramophone*, March 1947, 149.

14 Ibid.

15 Yehudi Menuhin, *Unfinished Journey* (London, 1976), 351.

16 Walter Legge, memorandum, 31 March 1946, EMI.

17 Edward Sackville-West and Desmond Shawe-Taylor, with Andrew Porter, *The Record Year*: 2 (London, 1953), 256.

18 Edge Leslie, quoted Vaughan, 150.

19 EMI, undated. Karajan rarely played the symphony in public in later years, and when he did – in Vienna in May 1948 and Berlin in January 1969 – he invariably prefaced it with a piece of contemporary music, just as he had done in Berlin 1944. Bartók's *Music for Strings, Percussion and Celesta* and Ligeti's *Atmosphères* were both paired with it. As to his recordings of the symphony, his 1977 Berlin recording, part of a complete cycle of the Schubert symphonies for EMI, is a sudden and unexpected delight: a carefree musical excursion played with great elegance and verve. Even here, though, Karajan's refusal to point up the music's autochthonous Austrian moods suggests a certain distaste for the lederhosen and green loden jacket side of Schubert's make-up.

20 Schwarzkopf told me that Moralt was the conductor here, but there is no doubt that it is Karajan. EMI's archives confirm the fact. The brilliance of the accompaniment and the virtuoso realisation of the concertante wind and string parts are also entirely typical of the kind of playing Karajan was capable of drawing from the Vienna Philharmonic at this time. Schwarzkopf had sung the opera under Moralt's direction the previous evening at the Theater an der Wien.

21 A performance praised more for its 'warmth and dignity' than for its gaiety in *The Gramophone*, November 1948, 90.

CHAPTER 23
A capacity of taking trouble
pp. 220–233

1 Herbert von Karajan, letter to Henry Alter, 1 June 1947.

2 Ansermet's involvement was a particular bone of contention locally; he had made his Salzburg début in 1942 at the height of the Nazi hegemony, despite ample opportunities for work in Switzerland and elsewhere.

3 Memorandum from Pathé Marconi, Paris, 24 February 1948, EMI.

4 Co-founder is perhaps something of an exaggeration since when Stone's old Oxford friend and brother-in-law

Compton Mackenzie dreamed up the idea of starting the magazine Stone poo-pooed it, declining to stump up the £1000 Mackenzie originally asked for and declaring that the gramophone, like the wireless, would soon be obsolete. Within the year, however, Stone had invested £300 in the project and had become the paper's London editor. Later, when the BBC, with its characteristic imperviousness to private circumstances, invited Mackenzie – who lived in the Channel Islands – to make a weekly visit to London to present a programme about gramophone records, Stone's name was suggested instead. He was an instant success and rapidly became one of the best-loved voices on British radio.

5 *Daily Mail*, 27 March 1947.

6 In June 1947, however, a letter appeared in the correspondence columns of *The Gramophone*. Though it did not mention Stone's article, it was almost certainly a rejoinder to it. The letter began: 'I should like to congratulate Columbia on bringing back into the domestic lists the Vienna Philharmonic under their brilliant young conductor Herbert Von [*sic*] Karajan. Though his name is scarcely known here, he has an enviable reputation on the continent, and his recordings, most of which can still be bought in the British zone of Germany, show him to be a conductor of the front rank.' The letter ended, pointedly: 'It is pleasant to note in conclusion that Columbia have shown themselves to be considerably more broadminded than the present administration in Austria which for a long time forbade Karajan to conduct for political reasons.' *The Gramophone*, June 1947, 14.

7 Herbert von Karajan, letter to Walter Legge, 20 May 1947, EMI.

8 Herbert von Karajan, letter to Wilhelm Pitz, 1 September 1947, KTC.

9 Not 1947 as is stated in most biographies and biographical profiles of Karajan. From 1938 to 1950,

Furtwängler was the Singverein's Concert Director.

10 Herbert von Karajan, letter to Walter Legge, 20 May 1947, EMI.

11 See Paumgartner's letter to Schenker of 6 March 1915 in Hellmut Federhofer, *Heinrich Schenker* (Hildesheim, Zürich, and New York, 1986), 183.

12 Heinrich Schenker, *Neunte Symphonie,* translated and edited by John Rothgeb (New Haven and London, 1992), 40–1.

13 Conversation, Dame Elisabeth Legge-Schwarzkopf.

14 Conversation, Dame Elisabeth Legge-Schwarzkopf.

15 Herbert von Karajan, letter to Walter Legge, 20 September 1947, EMI.

16 Richard Strauss, letter to Joseph Gregor, 2 March 1945.

17 *Österreichische Zeitung*, 29 October 1947.

18 *Österreichische Musikzeitschrift*, November–December 1947.

19 Memorandum, 3 February 1948, EMI.

20 Walter Legge, letter to Wilhelm Furtwängler, 10 October 1947, EMI.

21 Herbert von Karajan, letter to Walter Legge, 9 September 1947, EMI.

22 Ibid.

23 *Österreichische Zeitung*, 24 December 1947.

CHAPTER 24
New music: a tantrum and a tiff
pp. 234–243

1 Declaration upon oath, Gottfried von Einem, to Allied Denazification Commission, 21 May 1947, NA/Gottfried von Einem Archive, Gesellschaft der Musikfreunde, Vienna (unsigned copy).

2 Herbert von Karajan, letter to Gottfried von Einem, 31 December 1947, Gottfried von Einem Archive, Gesellschaft der Musikfreunde, Vienna.

3 Ibid.

4 Herbert von Karajan, *The Rehearsal.* See Appendix A.

5 Theodor W. Adorno, *Philosophy of Modern Music*, translated by Anne

G. Mitchell and Wesley V. Bloomster (London, 1973), 8.

6 Ibid., 7–8, 211.

7 Aaron Copland, *Music and Imagination* (Harvard, 1952), 9.

8 Susanne K. Langer, *Feeling and Form* (London, 1953), 148.

9 Memorandum, 5 December 1962, EMI.

10 Memorandum, 9 September 1963, EMI.

11 ORF, 3, *Verklärung und Tod*.

12 *Wiener Zeitung*, 22 February 1948.

13 Teri Noel Towe, *Choral Music on Record*, ed. Alan Blyth (Cambridge, 1991), 37.

14 *Wiener Kurier*, 27 March 1948.

CHAPTER 25

London

pp. 244–250

1 Conversation, Hugh Bean. Cf. the remark of Richard Strauss's father, the horn player Franz Strauss: 'When a new man faces the orchestra – from the way he walks up the steps to the podium and opens his score – before he even picks up his baton – we know whether he is the master or we.'

2 André Previn (ed.), *Orchestra* (London, 1979), 161–2.

3 Karajan repeated the exercise in the same hall in January 1973 when Prime Minister Edward Heath invited the Berlin Philharmonic to take part in the celebrations marking Britain's entry into the EEC. It was, in every sense of the word, a flying visit. Once again, he simply played the end of the symphony.

4 *The Times*, 15 March 1948.

5 *The Times*, 29 September 1948.

6 See the recording of the Fifth Symphony Karajan made with the Vienna Philharmonic for EMI in November 1948. An interesting comparison with this version is the dramatic and imaginative 1937 studio recording which Furtwängler made with the Berlin Philharmonic for HMV.

7 Letter, Dinu Lipatti to Florica Musisescu, 1 January 1946, quoted in Dragos Tanasescu and Grigore Bargauanu, *Lipatti*, translated by

Carola Grindea and Anne Goosens (London, 1988), 119–20.

8 Letter, Dinu Lipatti to Florica Musisescu, 16 May 1948, ibid., 155.

9 *The Gramophone*, November 1948, 96.

10 Compare Karajan's accompaniment for Lipatti in 1948, with the strangely erratic, often glutinous accompaniment he provides for Krystian Zimerman on their 1981 Berlin recording for Deutsche Grammophon. Legge was thrilled with the sessions and subsequently laid plans for a follow-up recording by Lipatti and Karajan of Tchaikovsky's B flat minor Concerto: 'a record that should be on the best-seller list for ten years', he noted in an internal EMI memo. Whether Lipatti would have gone along with this plan, we shall never know. Already ill at the time of the Schumann recording, he died a little over two years later.

11 Legge, 95.

12 Minutes of the meeting of the Covent Garden Opera Trust, 22 December 1947. Sir Steuart Wilson (1889–1966) was a distinguished tenor in his day. During the Second World War, he taught at the Curtis Institute, Philadelphia. In 1945, he was appointed Music Director of the newly formed Arts Council of Great Britain and in 1948 Head of Music at the BBC. For an account of his wretched treatment of Sir Adrian Boult, whose wife had previously been married to Wilson, see Michael Kennedy, *Adrian Boult* (London, 1987), 161–3, 215–19.

13 The orchestra was obliged to change its name after 1936, when Mussolini decreed that the acoustically splendid Augusteum be razed to the ground as part of a search for imperial remains.

14 *Wiener Kurier*, 20 April 1948.

15 Conversation, Suvi Raj Grubb.

CHAPTER 26
A tale of two Berlins
pp. 251–257

1 See Victor Gollancz, *Journey Towards Music* (London, 1964), 173–190.
2 Isaiah Berlin, 'Karajan: A Study', *The Observer*, 19 September 1948.
3 See p. 289.
4 After the bombardment of Rheims Cathedral in September 1914, Henry James wrote to Edith Wharton: 'Rheims is the most unspeakable and immeasurable horror and infamy . . . no words fill the abyss of it – nor touch it, nor relieve one's heart nor light by a spark the blackness . . .' *The Letters of Henry James*, selected and edited by Percy Lubbock (London, 1920), II, 420.
5 Ramin Jahanbegloo, *Conversations with Isaiah Berlin* (Oxford, 1992), 20.
6 Norman Del Mar, *Richard Strauss: a critical commentary on his life and works*, Vol.3 (London, 1972/R1978), 425.
7 A recording of one of the 1959 performances appeared on the Orfeo label in 1993. In an essay on recordings of the opera – a postscript to his fine chapter on *Orfeo ed Euridice* in *Opera on Record*, ed. Alan Blyth (London, 1979, 25–41) – Max Loppert has remarked: 'Karajan's conception of the opera I find utterly riveting: not for every day, and never to be copied, but coherent, "personal", and monumental.' *Gramophone*, September 1997, 32.
8 Gottfried Kraus, 'The Return of the Salzburg Orpheus' (CD booklet essay, Deutsche Grammophon 439 101–2), 12. (2-CD set of *Orfeo ed Euridice*, conducted by Karajan, recorded live in the Felsenreitschule, Salzburg, 5 August 1959.)
9 Legge, 228.

CHAPTER 27
Furtwängler: showdown in Chicago
pp. 258–261

1 Daniel Gillis, *Furtwängler in America* (New York, 1970), 99.

2 Ibid., 100–101.
3 Ibid., 101.
4 Ibid., 115.
5 Harold C. Goddard, *The Meaning of Shakespeare* (Chicago, 1951/R1960), Vol.1, 349.
6 Gillis, op. cit., 22.
7 Ibid., 122.

CHAPTER 28
Getting and spending
pp. 262–272

1 Walter Legge, memorandum, 30 September 1948, EMI.
2 Conversation, Elisabeth Furtwängler.
3 Basil Deane, *The Gramophone*, December 1950, 140.
4 Ibid.
5 Vaughan, 52.
6 John Culshaw, *Putting the Record Straight* (London, 1981), 201–2.
7 Ibid., 202.
8 Herbert von Karajan, Berlin College of Music, January 1972. Quoted in Lang, 72.
9 Letter, Michael Gielen.
10 Ibid. It would be wrong to conclude from this that Karajan was anti-black. As someone once remarked, 'The man who can cast Leontyne Price as Donna Anna *in Vienna* can hardly be said to be a racist.'
11 Conversation, Lord Menuhin.
12 Menuhin, op. cit., 235–6.
13 Conversation, Bernard Haitink.
14 Legge, 95.
15 Memorandum, 4 March 1949, EMI.
16 Malcolm MacDonald, *Brahms*, (London, 1990), 253.
17 *Tritsch-Tratsch* Polka and a violent and rawly recorded account of the polka *Unter Donner und Blitz*. Karajan made far finer recordings of both pieces with the Philharmonia Orchestra in London in September 1960.
18 Walter Legge, letter to Herbert von Karajan, 23 September 1949, EMI.

CHAPTER 29
The hypnotist
pp. 273–277

1 Walter Legge, letter, 28 January 1950, EMI.

2 *The Times*, 26 November 1949.

3 Conversation, Elisabeth Furtwängler.

4 *The Gramophone*, January 1951, 173–4.

5 Elias Canetti, *Crowds and Power* (London, 1962/R1973), 460.

6 Rupert Sheldrake, *Seven Experiments that Could Change the World* (London, 1994), 99–116. The idea of the eye casting a spell occurs in negative form in the concept of the 'evil eye'. The sense of being stared at, something which many people have experienced personally, is also a literary commonplace in most societies. It has been noted, too, in the animal world – for example, the vixen who simply raises her head and turns her gaze in the direction of a cub who has strayed too far.

7 Conversation, Gareth Morris.

8 W. B. Yeats, 'Meditations in Time of Civil War', *W. B. Yeats: The Poems*, ed. Richard J. Finneran (London, 1983), 205.

9 Christopher Booker, *The Neophiliacs* (London, 1969), 71.

10 Ibid., 74.

11 Karajan often placed *Boléro* after Debussy's *L'après-midi d'un faune* to make up the second half of a concert programme.

CHAPTER 30
Hanging on to Karajan
pp. 278–281

1 Maharaja of Mysore, letter to Walter Legge, 30 December 1950, EMI.

2 Memorandum, 11 January 1951, EMI.

3 Memorandum, 18 January 1949, EMI.

4 *Rheinische Post*, 24 January 1950.

5 One of EMI's last releases in the old format was the Karajan's 1951 Bayreuth recording of *Die Meistersinger*. Though recorded on tape, it was first released on sixty-eight 78 rpm sides.

6 Herbert von Karajan, letter to Walter Legge, 1 July 1952, EMI.

7 *Opera*, February 1953, 106–7. The cast included Anton Dermota, Irmgard Seefried, Erich Kunz, Wilma Lipp, Ludwig Weber, George London, Sena

Jurinac, and Emmy Loose.

8 Karajan memorandum to Walter Legge, 11 December 1950, EMI.

9 Wilhelm Furtwängler, letter to David Bicknell, 3 January 1951, EMI. David Bicknell (1906–88) joined The Gramophone Company in 1927 as Fred Gaisberg's assistant. After the Second World War, he returned to EMI to manage the HMV label. Between 1957 and 1971 he was Manager of EMI's International Artists Department.

10 Walter Legge internal memorandum, undated, EMI.

11 Memorandum from EMI Milan, October 1950, EMI.

CHAPTER 31
Wiener Symphoniker and return to Germany
pp. 282–289

1 *Wiener Tageszeitung*, 16 December 1949.

2 Ibid., 21 December 1949.

3 Letter, Wilhelm Furtwängler to Rudolf Hanzl, 2 November 1949, VPhO.

4 Letter, Wilhelm Furtwängler to Rudolf Hanzl, 8 November 1949, VPhO. This was an absurd demand. Karajan had no proposed concert dates with the Vienna Philharmonic in the latter part of January 1950. While Furtwängler was giving concerts and recording with the Philharmonic, Karajan and the Vienna Symphony were on a fourteen-day tour of West Germany that had been arranged months previously.

5 Walter Legge, memorandum, 28 January 1950, EMI.

6 'Savonarola der Musik', *Süddeutscher Zeitung*, 27 January 1950.

7 Conversation, Christoph von Dohnányi.

8 Haydn Symphony No.104, *Till Eulenspiegel*, and Brahms's Symphony No.1; Mozart's *Haffner* Symphony, Hindemith's *Mathis der Maler*, and Beethoven's Symphony No.5; Weber's overture to *Der Freischütz*, Schumann's Symphony No.4, and Tchaikovsky's Symphony No.4.

9 The season began with Bruckner's Eighth, continued with Berlioz's *Symphonie fantastique* and ended with

a concert that included Beethoven's Second Symphony and Sibelius's Fifth. The invincibly conservative Joseph Marx took issue with the title of the series. The Beethoven might, he said, be dubbed 'a great symphony', but the Sibelius? 'The undeveloped thoughts of a lonely Finn snug in his remote Nordic peasant dwelling?' Marx was not convinced, though he had nothing but praise for Karajan's advocacy of music, which he had conducted 'by heart and from the heart'. *Wiener Zeitung*, 19 November 1950.

10 See Ernst Kobau, *Die Wiener Symphoniker: eine sozialgeschichtliche Studie* (Vienna, 1991), 164.

11 The performance has made a number of unofficial appearances on LP and CD. The Radames is Lorenz Fehenberger. He is no Bergonzi, but one can hear why Karajan chose him and how finely he supports him; Nell Rankin is a superb Amneris, and the little-known Yugoslav soprano Dragica Martinis is a striking and distinctive Aida. Furtwängler would use her later that same year as Desdemona in his Salzburg Festival performances of *Otello*.

12 This memorable Knappertsbusch story was told me by Jon Vickers.

13 Wolfgang Wagner, op. cit., 106.

14 Hans Knappertsbusch later dubbed Pitz 'Hugo', a reference to the legendary Bayreuth Chorus master Hugo Rüdel.

15 *Lipatti*, op. cit., 131. The performance was recorded and released on LP on EMI Columbia 33C 1064, and later on CD.

16 Conversation, Peter Diamand.

17 Conversation, Sir Isaiah Berlin.

CHAPTER 32
Bachfest
pp. 290–294

1 A work over which both Karajan and the players appear to have had an as yet imperfect grasp. This judgement is based on the evidence of a 1954 broadcast performance of the symphony which was subsequently released on CD by Orfeo.

2 Conversation, Otto Strasser.

3 Maurice Leonard, *Kathleen: the life of Kathleen Ferrier 1912–1953* (London, 1988), 165.

4 Conversation, Lord Menuhin.

5 H. C. Robbins Landon, 'Portrait of the Conductor as Celebrity', *The Gramophone*, March 1964, 410.

6 Letter, H. C. Robbins Landon.

7 Harvey Sachs, *Toscanini* (London 1978/R1993), 298.

8 *The Gramophone*, February 1954, 348.

9 Edward Sackville-West and Desmond Shawe-Taylor, with Andrew Porter and William Mann, *The Record Guide* (London, 1955), 54–5.

10 David Randolph, *High Fidelity Record Annual*, ed. Roland Gelatt (Great Barrington, 1955), 23–4.

11 There have been CD reissues on Foyer, Hunt, and Verona.

12 A Schubert Mass. Giulini and the Vienna Symphony recorded instead a memorable account of Bruckner's (at the time) rarely heard Second Symphony.

CHAPTER 33
Milan, Paris, and Bayreuth
pp. 295–303

1 Rasponi, op. cit., 333.

2 *Stuttgarter Zeitung*, 28 May 1951.

3 *Feuille d'Avis de Lausanne*, 5 June 1951.

4 *La Nouvelle Revue*, 5 June 1951.

5 *Paris-presse-l'intransigeant*, 2 June 1951.

6 Bernard Gavoty, *Herbert von Karajan*, translated by F. E. Richardson, (Geneva, 1956), 8.

7 Ibid., 6.

8 Ibid.

9 *Le Figaro*, 3 June 1951.

10 *Opéra*, 6 June 1951.

11 The works in question were Grieg's Piano Concerto, Franck's *Symphonic Variations*, Beethoven's Fourth and Fifth piano concertos, and Mozart's Concerto in A, K488.

12 Steffi-Maria Schlinke, *Otto Edelmann: Ein Meistersinger aus Wien* (Vienna, 1987), 84–5.

13 Wieland Wagner, letter to Otto Edelmann, 5 February 1951.

14 Schlinke, op. cit., 95.
15 Conversation, Dame Elisabeth Legge-Schwarzkopf.
16 Lisa della Casa recalls: 'The only stage directors I really respected were Rudolf Hartmann and Herbert Graf. They knew how to deal with personalities and did not try to annihilate them, which is the system today. I remember in Munich when I was having some difficulties with *Ariadne*, Hartmann was so sensitive and sensible. The heroine's problem is that she must sing with a lot of expression but move very little. He used to say, "Do what you think is right. If you do too much, I will tell you, and if you do not do enough, I will warn you of that too."' Rasponi, op. cit., 336.
17 The problem for the conductor in the covered pit is the sizeable time-lag that requires him continually to anticipate the singers. Sir George Solti reportedly said of Bayreuth: 'If anybody had told me when I was at music school that I would one day be in a pit where I couldn't hear anything or see all the players, I would have become a doctor.'
18 *Wiener Zeitung*, 8 August 1951.
19 Translation of Spanish press briefings, May 1972, EMI.
20 Conversations, 50.
21 Conversation, Christoph von Dohnányi.
22 It is a little noted fact that Wieland Wagner's 1951 design for Act 1 of *Parsifal* closely resembles Craig's 1903 design for Act 2 of *The Vikings at Helgeland* and that the designs for his 1951 *Ring* cycle are also closely modelled on Craig (cf. Act 3 of *Siegfried* Act 3 and Craig's design for Act 2 of *The Vikings at Helgeland*).
23 Wolfgang Wagner, op. cit., 110–11.
24 Conversation, Elisabeth Furtwängler.

CHAPTER 34
Working with the Philharmonia
pp. 304–309

1 Conversation, Hugh Bean.
2 Ibid.
3 Conversation, Gareth Morris.
4 Conversation, Philip Jones.

5 Conversation, Ronald Wilford.
6 Toscanini recalled a rehearsal for the first performance of Verdi's *Otello* during which the cellos were playing at a hushed mezzo piano. '*Play* it!' shouted Verdi from the stalls. Conversation, Carlo Maria Giulini.
7 Legge, 226.
8 Conversation, Hugh Bean.
9 Conversation, Hugh Bean. The secret, says Gareth Morris, was to watch Furtwängler's eyes and follow 'his beautiful rhythm'; however, this would not necessarily help at the start of a piece.
10 Conversation, Jane Withers.
11 David Wooldridge, *Conductor's World* (London, 1970), 257–8.
12 Conversation, Dame Elisabeth Legge-Schwarzkopf.

CHAPTER 35
On recording
pp. 310–317

1 Conversation, Lord Menuhin.
2 Ibid.
3 Herbert von Karajan, '*Technische Musikwiedergabe* [On the Technical Reproduction of Music]', draft chapter for uncompleted book, reproduced in Endler, 280–99, 294.
4 Ibid., 297.
5 Conversation, Barone Raffaello de Banfield Tripcovich.
6 Glenn Gould, 'The Prospects of Recording', *High Fidelity*, April 1966; reprinted in Glenn Gould, ed. Tim Page, *The Glenn Gould Reader* (London, 1987), 337–8.
7 Glenn Gould, 'The Grass is Always Greener in the Outtakes', *High Fidelity*, August 1975; reprinted in Gould, op. cit., 357–68.
8 Karajan, '*Technische Musikwiedergabe*', Endler, 294.
9 Ibid., 297.
10 Jacques Attali, *Bruits: essai sur l'économie politique de la musique* (Paris, 1977); translated by Brian Massumi (Minneapolis, 1985), 118.
11 Ibid., 106.
12 Karajan, '*Technische Musikwiedergabe*', Endler, 295.
13 Ibid., 296.
14 Gould, op. cit., 334.

15 Suvi Raj Grubb, *Music Makers on Record* (London, 1986), 116.
16 Sir Joseph Lockwood, interview with Alan Blyth, *Gramophone*, November 1974, 859.
17 *The Record Guide* (London, 1955), 83.

CHAPTER 36
Crossing the Rhine
pp. 318–327

1 Walter Legge, memorandum, 14 April 1954, EMI.
2 Walter Legge, memorandum, 16 January 1952, EMI.
3 Despite the horseplay, it was Karajan's aim, said Legge, to play *Der Rosenkavalier* as 'an aristocratic comedy freed for the first time from the accumulated vulgarities, overstatements, and underlinings that have weighed it down'. Walter Legge, 'Elisabeth Schwarzkopf', *Opera*, July 1953, 401.
4 Walter Legge, letter to Wilhelm Furtwängler, 6 May 1953. EMI. After the success of the 1952 tour, Furtwängler made representations to Legge about the possibility of his leading a Philharmonia tour. Legge declined, pointing out that a tour could be financed only if it (a) played to full houses (b) was based on works that had already been rehearsed for recording and (c) was able to maximise the sales of those recordings. Though Furtwängler would undoubtedly draw full houses, there was no likelihood, let alone guarantee, that he would make the necessary recordings.
5 Herbert von Karajan, letter to Walter Legge, 12 April 1952, EMI.
6 Ibid. Karajan had no doubt that K287 – tarnished, alas, by scholarly evidence of a significant debt to a string quintet by Michael Haydn – is the tauter, wittier, more dramatic work. To judge from his three extant recordings, he relished every moment of it. By contrast, all his recordings of K334 have passages in them that seem strangely disengaged. On the Philharmonia's European tour, K334 was played six times, K287 only once.

7 *The Times*, 10 May 1952.
8 Manoug Parikian, in conversation with John Amis, BBC Sound Archive.
9 Neville Cardus, 'With the Philharmonia', *Manchester Guardian*, 12 May 1952.
10 Legge, 96.
11 Isabella Corbett, letter to Aubrey Wallich. Correspondence made available to the author by Isabella Wallich from her private archive.
12 Ibid.
13 Ibid.
14 Ibid.
15 *Oberösterreichische Nachrichten*, 2 January 1952.
16 Wallich archive.
17 Conversation, Dame Elisabeth Legge-Schwarzkopf.
18 Wallich archive.
19 Ibid.
20 Conversation, Isabella Wallich.

CHAPTER 37
The girl with the flaxen hair
pp. 328–332

1 Legge, 59.
2 Susana Walton, *William Walton: Behind the Façade* (Oxford, 1988), 116–7.
3 Conversation, Lady Walton.
4 Lady Walton, interview, *BBC Music Magazine*, June 1996.
5 ORF, 3, *Verklärung und Tod*.
6 Conversation, Mrs Philip Jones.

CHAPTER 38
Tristan and Lucia
pp. 333–355

1 David Bicknell, memorandum to Walter Legge, 12 July 1952, EMI.
2 Herbert von Karajan, letter to Walter Legge, 5 July 1952, EMI.
3 Wolfgang Wagner, op. cit., 119.
4 Variously reissued on Cetra (LP), Hunt (CD), and other labels. See Alan Blyth's review, *Gramophone*, September 1978, 550, and Robin Holloway's comments on the performance in *Opera on Record*, ed. Alan Blyth (London, 1979), 365–6. Astrid Varnay would also complain – in writing to the Wagner brothers – about the difficulties she experienced

with Karajan's beat in some of the music's more introspective moments.

5 Herbert von Karajan, *Der Spiegel*, No.23, 1979.

6 Conversation, Massimo Freccia.

7 The full tour repertory was: Mozart Symphony No.29, Beethoven symphonies nos. 1 and 3, Brahms Symphony No.2, Tchaikovsky Symphony No.5, R. Strauss *Till Eulenspiegel*, Debussy *La Mer*, Blacher *Paganini* Variations.

8 Paul Vaucaire, *La Soirée*, Anvers, 15 October 1952.

9 Conversation, Elisabeth Furtwängler.

10 Quoted by Alain Lompech in his essay 'Touching on Musical Truth' in the CD booklet for Vol.1 of *Clara Haskil: the legacy*, Philips 442 625-2. Nikolaieva was in Salzburg for the start of the Mozart bicentenary celebrations during which she played Mozart's E flat Piano Concerto K482 with Carl Schuricht and the Vienna Philharmonic.

11 Mozart Piano Concerto No.20 in D minor K466. Philharmonia Orchestra, Salzburg, 28 January 1956. Internationale Stiftung Mozarteum Salzburg, ISM 56/4.

12 'Die letzten Karajan-Konzerte', *Neue Front*, Salzburg, 29 November 1952.

13 *The Record Guide* (London, 1955), 80.

14 The figures originally supplied by Electrola to EMI in London underestimated the sales, something which exacerbated an already difficult situation. However, even the revised figures were disappointingly low, something that has subsequently been attributed to a deliberate unwillingness by Electrola managers to promote Legge/Karajan recordings in Germany.

15 Virgil Thomson, letter to Wye Jamison Allanbrook, 10 February 1975, *Selected Letters of Virgil Thomson*, eds Tim Page and Vanessa Weeks Page (New York, 1988), 345.

16 *Opera*, April 1953, 230.

17 *Opera*, May 1953, 296.

18 *Opera*, March 1996, 267.

19 Legge was clearly not keen. 'After

the *Hauptprobe* of *Trionfo di Aphrodite* [*sic*] I gently suggested [Orff] cut some of his repeated verses. He replied, "I know the effect of my rubber stamp music."' Legge, 86.

20 *Pace* the claim of Norman Lebrecht, 'Releases by Herbert von Karajan and André Previn were big sellers in the Sixties and Seventies', *Daily Telegraph*, 26 November 1994. It is a touching aspect of Lebrecht's view of Karajan as a died-in-the-wool Nazi with an eye for making huge amounts of money out of prime commercial properties that he should have imagined (a) the existence of a Karajan recording of *Carmina burana*, and (b) its being a runaway best-seller.

21 He has an entry, not entirely accurate as to dates, in *Baker's Biographical Dictionary of Musicians* but *The New Grove Dictionary of Music and Musicians* ignores him.

22 German Columbia WCX 1508; Electrola SME 91793.

23 *Weltpresse Wien*, 20 March 1953.

24 *Basler Nachrichten*, 29 October 1953.

25 Alan Jefferson, *Elisabeth Schwarzkopf* (London, 1996), 132.

26 NZN, 3 November 1953.

27 *Voix Ouvrière*, Geneva, 2 November 1953.

28 *La Suisse*, Geneva, 30 October 1953.

29 *Journal de Genève*, 30 October 1953.

30 Conversation, Dame Elisabeth Legge-Schwarzkopf.

31 Vaughan, 222.

32 *The Times*, 3 September 1953.

33 *The Gramophone*, June 1956, 12.

34 Stephen J. Pettitt, *Philharmonia Orchestra: a record of achievement 1945-1985* (London, 1985), 65.

35 Conversation, Dame Elisabeth Legge-Schwarzkopf.

36 Colin Welch, 'My sentiments exactly', *The Spectator*, 22 September 1984, 35.

37 Legge, 8.

38 C. G. Burke, *High Fidelity Record Annual*, ed. Roland Gelatt (Great Barrington, 1955), 168.

39 There are two studio recordings both on EMI, both conducted by Serafin. Of these the 1953 Florence version is generally preferred to the 1959 London remake. Live recordings: Milan, 18 January 1954, cond. Karajan (extracts); Berlin, 29 September 1955 (EMI); Naples, 22 March 1956, cond. Molinari Pradelli; Rome 26 June 1957, cond. Serafin (radio recording of concert performance).

40 *Chicago Tribune*, 9 July 1956.

41 Michael Scott, *Maria Meneghini Callas* (London, 1991), 159–60.

42 Michael Scott, 'A Connoisseur's Callas', *Opera News*, September 1987.

43 Maria Callas, letter to Walter Legge, undated [filed April 1956], EMI.

44 Conversations, 75.

45 Jürgen Kesting, *Maria Callas* (London, 1992), 143.

46 Conversation, Peter Alward.

47 Kesting, op. cit., 319.

48 Conversation, Michel Glotz.

CHAPTER 39
Brandy in Les Baux
pp. 356–366

1 *Opera*, April 1954, 233.

2 Conversation, Dame Elisabeth Legge-Schwarzkopf.

3 *Opera*, February 1954, 107–8.

4 Bachmann, 268.

5 In 1985, Montserrat Caballé was found to have a serious condition of the cerebro-spinal hypothalamus gland, a condition further complicated by the presence of a tumour. Had she been operated on, as her Spanish doctors planned to do, her upper jaw and nasal septum would have been drilled through; metal bolts and plates may have had to be inserted. Recalling stories of Karajan's lengthy battle with spinal degeneration, Caballé's brother Carlos telephoned him at his home in Anif. Karajan immediately put him in touch with Dr Yasserghyl at Zürich's Kantonal Hospital. Yasserghyl's advice, which proved to be well-founded, was preventative medicine, not surgery. See Robert Pullen and Stephen Taylor, *Montserrat Caballé: Casta diva* (London, 1994), 284–6.

6 José Carreras, *Singing for the Soul* (Seattle, 1991), 136.

7 Vaughan, 172.

8 Conversation, Antje Henneking.

9 *Nippon Times*, 11 May 1954.

10 Junichi Yano, 'Why is Beethoven's Ninth so well loved in Japan?', *Japan Quarterly*, 12, 1982, 477.

11 In 1996, *Karajan Adagio* was officially credited with being Japan's biggest-selling classical release ever.

12 Michael Kennedy discussing *Ariadne auf Naxos* in 'Building a Library', BBC Radio 3, 30 November 1993.

13 *High Fidelity Record Annual* (1956), 243–6.

14 John Lucas, *Reggie: The Life of Reginald Goodall* (London, 1993), 209. Karajan's 1964 Berlin recording of Debussy's *L'après-midi d'un faune* was chosen by Goodall when he appeared on *Desert Island Discs* on BBC Radio 4 on 5 January 1980. Asked why he chose this, he replied: 'Because I think the Berlin Philharmonic with von Karajan get the coldness and the heat of this work, and [because of] the way it's interpreted: icy cold and yet with the heat of the hot, burning Grecian sun.'

15 *Opera*, November 1955, 716–7. Since three members the cast – Schwarzkopf, Merriman, and Panerai – were soon to take part in a brilliantly successful run of performances under Guido Cantelli's direction in Milan (albeit in the smaller Piccola Scala) it is a judgement that hardly rings true.

16 Conversation, Dame Elisabeth Legge-Schwarzkopf.

17 'Cleansing Bach and Beethoven', *The Economist*, 10 August 1996, 75–6.

18 Conversation, Sidney Sutcliffe.

19 Conversations, 105–6.

20 Pettitt, op. cit., 72.

21 *The Scotsman*, 7 September 1954.

22 *The Scotsman*, 9 September 1954. Raymond Leppard has described a similar effect used by Karajan when conducting Mozart's D minor Piano Concerto K466. The

beat was, he recalls, 'mystifyingly unclear'. 'No one could tell where the point of the beat would occur. A mere parting of the hands . . . and there followed what seemed an interminable, electrifying silence. With lesser players nothing would have happened, or, alternatively, it would have resulted in chaos. With the Philharmonia . . . experience, responsibility to the music and sheer nerve meant that the first desk of cellos and basses eventually began the triplet semiquavers which followed, like magnetic dominoes, by the rest of the section a fraction later. The opening sounded like a magic wave breaking on a D minor shore – Mozart would never have recognised it – and audiences marvelled. But it was cold calculation on his part and a terrible expenditure of nervous energy on the part of the orchestra.' T. P. Lewis (ed.), *Raymond Leppard on Music: An Anthology of Critical and Personal Writings* (New York, 1993), 378.

23 Joseph Horowitz refers to Cardus's intervention in *Conversations with Arrau* (London, 1982), 69. Arrau, whom I knew in later years, never spoke of the incident. This version was told me by his long-serving personal manager Friede Rothe.

24 Stresemann, 29–30.

CHAPTER 40
Death and succession
pp. 367–376

1 *Till Eulenspiegel* (3 March 1954, VPO, EMI); Brahms Symphony No.3 (27 April 1954, BPO, DG); Beethoven Symphony No.9 (22 August 1954, Philharmonia, Tahra).

2 *Berliner Morgenpost*, 25 September 1954.

3 See Klaus Lang, interview with Berlin PO flautist Aurèle Nicolet, '*Celibidache will das Orchester "brechen"*', in Klaus Lang, *"Lieber Herr Celibidache . . .": Wilhelm Furtwängler und sein Statthalter – Ein philharmonischer Konflikt in*

der Berliner Nachkriegszeit (Zürich, 1988), 198–202.

4 *Neues Österreich, Wien*, 12 October 1954.

5 *Opera*, May 1954, 284. The following May, seizing on a factual error in one of Wechsberg's reports about the size of the new Vienna Opera, Böhm fired off a brief letter to the editor, stating: 'The ensemble will be so built up, that first-class casts will be possible at *all* times.' *Opera*, May 1955, 333.

6 *Neue Zeitung*, 24 November 1954. An apostle of new music, Stuckenschmidt had been blacklisted by the Nazis and exiled to Prague during the war, before being conscripted and put to work as a military interpreter. He wrote as he found. In the late 1940s, he had been highly critical of Celibidache's rostrum antics; latterly, he had written of a new integrity in his music-making.

7 Ibid.

8 Karajan was there to conduct the now regular pre-Christmas season of concerts with the Rome Radio Orchestra and to prepare broadcasts of *Hänsel und Gretel* and Debussy's *Pélleas et Mélisande*. This was in French – to Toscanini's consternation, so Karajan claimed. He met Toscanini once, in Milan during the Philharmonia tour in the October of 1954. The following January, Toscanini is said to have left a Karajan *Carmen* rehearsal at La Scala in high fury. Why is not clear.

9 *Der Abend*, 3 December 1954. Earlier in the year, Walter Legge had written a memorandum on the subject for EMI. In it, he pointed out the long-term importance to the company of Karajan and Cantelli, in Europe and in the United States, at a time when 'Toscanini is failing in concert, Furtwängler is ill and has badly impaired hearing, Klemperer is unlikely ever to return to the United States, Monteux is approaching 80 and Clemens Krauss is ill and, in any case, never an exportable commodity'.

10 Ibid.

11 Conversation, Peter Steiner.

12 BPO, Vol.2, 272.

13 See p. 88–90.
14 Sam H. Shirakawa, op. cit., 381.
Schwarzkopf later told me that she
regretted some of the things she
said to Shirakawa, though I have no
evidence that the use of the idea of
Karajan as '*Macht* possessor' was
one of these.
15 Tillich, op. cit., 45.
16 Conversation, Christa Ludwig.
17 Lang, 12.

CHAPTER 41
American journey
pp. 377–383

1 Virgil Thomson, letter to Gottfried
von Einem, 3 March 1954, op.
cit., 286.
2 Originally on LP on Cetra LO
506 (2), later on CD on Classical
Collection CDCLC 6000.
3 *Washington Post*, 28 February 1955.
4 *New York Times*, 2 March 1955.
5 In May 1942, verified reports of
the extermination programme were
received by the Polish National
Committee in London from the Polish
Jewish Labour Bund. These included
reports of gas vans at Chelmno and
the murder of 700,000 Jews. On 26
June 1942, the *Boston Globe* ran
a headline 'Mass Murders of Jews
in Poland Pass 700,000 Mark' but
relegated the report to p.12. The
following day, the *New York Times*
allocated two column inches to what
it described as 'probably the greatest
slaughter in history'. A further,
rather fuller report, was published on
2 July 1942.
6 Bernstein had been commuting
between Rome, where he had a long-
standing conducting engagement,
and Milan where he had been asked
by La Scala to conduct Cherubini's
Medea, with Maria Callas in the title
role, in place of the indisposed Victor
De Sabata. Karajan had also been
in Rome, conducting *Don Giovanni*,
before travelling to Milan to work
on his new production of *Lucia di
Lammermoor*, also with Callas.
7 Leonard Bernstein, letter to
Felicia Bernstein, 7 January 1954.
Quoted in Humphrey Burton,

Leonard Bernstein (London,
1994), 235.
8 Sotheby's catalogue, Fine Printed
and Manuscript Music, Lot No.137,
17 May 1990. '19 pages . . . on the
headed notepaper of Hampshire
House, New York, Megève, and
London, undated, postmarked
1955.' The letters were bought by a
Japanese collector.
9 Schuyler Chapin, *Musical Chairs*
(New York, 1977), 404.
10 Conversation, Anna Tomowa-
Sintow.
11 Conversation, Suvi Raj Grubb.
12 Vaughan, 25.
13 Letter, Schuyler Chapin, 18 March
1993. Later, when Karajan moved
on to jet aircraft (first, a Lear
and after that a Dessault Aviation
Falcon) he was rebuked for being
too adventurous. 'Don't try to be
cleverer than M. Dessault!' said one
of his instructors. He still managed
to qualify with a 93/100 rating,
only four marks short of that of his
instructor.
14 H1, 101–2.
15 Freccia, op. cit., 60.
16 Ibid.
17 Spokesman, quoted in *New York
Times*, 31 March 1955.
18 Vincent Sheean, op. cit., 257.
19 *New York Times*, 31 March 1955.

CHAPTER 42
Trouble at mill
pp. 384–400

1 Conversation, Dame Elisabeth
Legge-Schwarzkopf.
2 *High Fidelity Annual* (1956), 239.
3 A 1975 recording, made in Munich,
for Deutsche Grammophon.
4 *The Times*, 2 May 1955. William
Mann is the probable author of the
review.
5 Jean Sibelius, letter to Walter Legge,
15 September 1954, EMI.
6 Jean Sibelius, letter to Walter Legge,
11 May 1955, EMI.
7 *The Gramophone*, April 1956, 419.
'The strings have found muscle and
determination enough to sound fierce
and intense for the duration of the
piece, which means under recording

conditions that their task was protracted and arduous; and their efforts of those and other players have been integrated by Karajan into an overwhelming performance of the masterpiece.'

8 The recording was tidied up a year later, in June 1956, but not issued until April 1959, by which time its mono-only status rendered it largely uncompetitive.

9 She would sing three performances in Chicago in the autumn of 1955.

10 *The Gramophone*, December 1955, 280–1. Robertson did, however, greatly admire the 'gallantry' of Gedda's singing and its evident musicianly qualities.

11 Michael Tanner, 'Callas's Butterfly', *International Opera Collector*, Autumn 1996, 14.

12 John Ardoin and Gerald Fitzgerald, *Callas* (London, 1974), 20–1.

13 Lang, 14.

14 Walter Legge in conversation with John Amis, BBC Radio interview, published in transcript *Gramophone*, October 1989, 614–15.

15 Gavoty, op. cit., 18–19.

16 Gavoty, op. cit., 19.

17 Leppard, op. cit., 328.

18 A memorandum in the EMI archives reveals that Karajan could remember Leppard but not his name. The idea was not followed through.

19 Leppard, op. cit., 328.

20 Bartók *Concerto for Orchestra*, Beethoven Symphony No.6, Berlioz *Symphonie fantastique*, Brahms *St Antoni Variations*, Britten *Variations on a Theme of Frank Bridge*, Debussy *La mer*, Handel *Water Music* Suite, Mozart Divertimento in B flat K287, Mozart Symphony No.39, Ravel *Rapsodie espagnole*, Sibelius Symphony No.5, Tchaikovsky Symphony No.4, Vaughan Williams *Fantasia on a Theme of Thomas Tallis*. Encores included Sibelius's *Finlandia*, Sousa marches, and Verdi's overture *La forza del destino*.

21 *Washington Post*, 24 October 1955.

22 *Washington Post*, 30 October 1955.

23 Conversation, Hugh Bean.

24 *New York Herald Tribune*, 26 October 1955.

25 *Time*, 7 November 1955.

26 *New Yorker*, 4 November 1955.

27 *Chicago Sunday Times*, 6 November 1955.

28 *Saturday Review of Literature*, 12 November 1955.

29 *Philadelphia Inquirer*, 13 November 1955.

30 Ibid.

31 *Columbus Citizen*, 3 November 1955.

32 *Chicago Tribune*, 6 and 8 November 1955.

33 *Detroit Michigan Times*, 11 November 1955.

34 *Portland Press Herald*, 19 November 1955.

35 Charles Munch's sister used to tell stories of Anita von Karajan cavorting with high-ranking Nazis in wartime Paris. But Anita was not in Boston, nor is there any evidence of animosity towards Karajan on Munch's part.

36 Conversation, Hugh Bean; Pettitt, op. cit., 81–2.

37 *Christian Science Monitor*, 21 November 1955.

38 *Boston Herald*, 20 November 1955.

39 *Washington Post*, 30 October 1955.

40 *Charleston Mail*, 2 November 1955.

41 *Huntingdon Dispatch*, 1 November 1955.

42 *New York Herald Tribune*, 27 October 1955.

43 Ibid.

44 Leppard, op. cit., 379.

CHAPTER 43

A resignation and three recordings

pp. 401–409

1 Herbert Graf, a Viennese Jew who had become a naturalised American in 1934, was what might be called an informed outsider. He subscribed to no particular Salzburg lobby. His work there with Toscanini before the war and with Furtwängler on productions of *Otello* and *Don Giovanni* after the war had given him immense prestige.

2 Conversation, Günther Schneider-Siemssen. Karajan knew Holzmeister from pre-war Salzburg and through his friendship with Luis Trenker. Holzmeister and Trenker first met as architectural students. After the First World War they travelled together vainly looking for work in the northern and southern Tyrol. Mountaineering was their passion. In 1967, recalling a hair-raising climb in the Dolomites in their youth when Holzmeister had fallen and been left dangling on his climbing rope, Trenker mused: 'That was a fateful day.' 'Why fateful?' asked Holzmeister. 'Just think, dear friend, how many Austrian Schillings I would have saved the province of Salzburg if I had let go of the rope when you were dangling out there!' Trenker, op. cit., 491.

3 The proposed [and actual] programme for 1957 was as follows. *Falstaff* and *Der Rosenkavalier* [*Don Carlos*] (Karajan); *Le nozze di Figaro* [also *Così fan tutte*] (Böhm); *Don Giovanni* [*Elektra*] (Mitropoulos); *Orfeo ed Euridice* [the German première of Rolf Liebermann's *Die Schule der Frauen*] (Szell). Those with a less certain grasp of Salzburg's history than Karajan's own were shocked, however, to find more Verdi (*La traviata*) and an opera by Donizetti (*Lucia di Lammermoor*) included in the plans for the 1958 and 1959 seasons. Eyebrows were also raised at Karajan's plan to stage Honegger's *Jeanne d'Arc au bûcher* in the cathedral square, an idea that, sadly, he did not pursue.

4 In his memoirs, Böhm attributes his blunder to exhaustion after a long flight and press entrapment. (Böhm, op. cit., 128–30.) In fact, several senior critics pleaded with him to take a more conciliatory line.

5 Conversation, Dame Elisabeth Legge-Schwarzkopf.

6 Marcel Prawy, *The Vienna Opera* (New York, 1970), 189.

7 Schneider had briefly been Director of the Vienna State Opera in 1942–3 before Böhm arrived from Dresden to replace him.

8 Conversation, Christa Ludwig.

9 Jurinac had recently recorded the role for Decca under the direction of Erich Kleiber.

10 Conversation, Dame Elisabeth Legge-Schwarzkopf.

11 G. B. Shaw, *London Music 1888–9* (London, 1937), 379.

12 Conversations, 76.

13 Paul Gruber (ed.), *The Metropolitan Opera: Guide to Recorded Opera* (London, 1993), 598–9.

14 Gavoty, op. cit., 13.

15 Ibid., 13–15.

16 *The Times*, 20 June 1956. EMI later reissued the performance on CD.

17 Conversation, Jeffrey Tate.

18 Conversation, Dame Elisabeth Legge-Schwarzkopf.

19 The EMI *Der Rosenkavalier* was planned and recorded in mono by Legge and Douglas Larter, with Christopher Parker working in a separate studio to try to balance the stereo version which EMI also required. (Stereo recording remained a closet activity in the industry at large until 1957–8, largely because companies feared artists would make additional financial demands.) The results seemed acceptable enough at the time. However, in 1970, when Suvi Raj Grubb started work on a remastering of the set – a pre-emptive strike by EMI against Bernstein's new CBS recording produced in Vienna by John Culshaw – he found that the stereo tapes for side one were not the originals. When the curtain rises on Act, the Marschallin is in bed, having just made love to Octavian who is now kneeling beside the bed. Legge, it appears, had calculated that if the stereo spread were to be computed in terms of an actual stage performance the bed would be approximately thirty feet wide. This somewhat absurd piece of pedantry – an attempt, presumably, to discomfit the stereophonic tendency – had led to the set's first side being dubbed off using a narrower stereo spread. (See Grubb, op. cit., 114–15, for a slightly more guarded account

of events.) In 1996, Schwarzkopf herself personally oversaw the reissue on CD of the original mono version of the recording.

CHAPTER 44
Riding high
pp. 413–421

1 *Die Walküre* received a characteristically lyrical performance from Karajan, with his Sieglinde, Leonie Rysanek, very much the star of the show. There was also casting in depth, with Hans Hotter and Birgit Nilsson, Ludwig Suthaus, Gottlob Frick, and, as Fricka, the charismatic American contralto Jean Madeira.
2 Bengt Janzon, 'Bergman on Opera', *Opera*, October 1962, 652.
3 'Really? Smart.' Conversation, Sir Simon Rattle.
4 Camillo Öhlberger, *Neue philharmonische Capriolen* (Vienna, 1993), 170–2. My verse rendering.
5 Conversation, Graziella Sciutti.
6 Dermota, op. cit., 237–42.
7 Vaughan, 161.
8 Winthrop Sargeant, 'Space-Age Maestro', *New Yorker*, 7 January 1961, 48.
9 Egon Seefehlner, *Die Musik meines Lebens* (Vienna, 1986), 70.
10 Conversation, Walter Weller.
11 Conversation, Walter Weller.
12 Strasser, 279–80.
13 Ibid., 283.
14 *Opera*, August 1957, 499.
15 *Die Presse*, 29 August 1957.
16 *Bild-Telegraf*, 15 August 1957.
17 See Andrew Porter's review, *Opera*, October 1957, 624–5.
18 Conversation, Dame Elisabeth Legge-Schwarzkopf.
19 Legge, 181.
20 Michael Gielen, interview in *Il Maestro: die Karajan-Bilderbiographie*, ed. Stefan Siegert (Hamburg, 1991), 99.

CHAPTER 45
Incessant traffic
pp. 422–430

1 Trevor Harvey, *The Gramophone*, October 1958, 196. Playing *Les Préludes* under Karajan, Hugh Bean recalls, was 'a bit like playing some undiscovered Beethoven symphony. He treated it with enormous care.'
2 Conversation, Hugh Bean.
3 Conversation, Sena Jurinac.
4 Guichandut, a baritone turned heroic tenor, had appeared with Callas in *Norma* in Florence in 1953. He recorded Otello for Cetra in 1954, and sang the role at Verona the following year. Post-Vinay and pre-Vickers, he was employed more out of necessity than choice. When Karajan recorded the opera for Decca in 1961 Mario del Monaco sang the title role.
5 Conversation, Christa Ludwig. See also Csobádi, 157.
6 Camillo Öhlberger, *Philharmonische Capriolen* (Vienna, 1992), 40–1. I am grateful to David Barnes for this verse rendering.
7 See Igor Stravinsky, *Themes and Conclusions* (London, 1972), 131.
8 Igor Stravinsky and Robert Craft, *Dialogues and a Diary* (London, 1968), 25.
9 Though Karajan was using the four-act Italian version, with cuts, he opened up a number of cuts in Elisabeth's music.
10 Igor Stravinsky and Robert Craft, op. cit., 184.
11 John Steane, in an essay on recordings of the *Missa Solemnis*, notes 'something very like exhaustion settling upon the company'. *Choral Music on Record*, ed. Alan Blyth (Cambridge, 1991), 147.
12 The recording finally appeared in August 1960, coupled with a stylish – though, CD transfers now reveal, rather too resonantly recorded – account of Mozart's Symphony No.29 with the Berlin Philharmonic.
13 The stereo version was eventually released through EMI's subsidiary World Records. In 1998, Testament Records reissued the recording as a 2-CD set, along with reminiscences of the occasion by Elisabeth Schwarzkopf, and a number of rehearsal sequences.
14 *The Times*, 6 November 1958.

15 Donald Wright (ed.), *Cardus on Music* (London, 1988), 307–8; reprinted from *Manchester Guardian*, 7 November 1958.
16 David Cairns, *Responses* (London, 1973), 165–7; reprinted from *The Spectator*, 15 November 1958.
17 Ibid.
18 Ibid.
19 Ibid.
20 Cardus, op. cit.
21 *New York Times*, 21 November 1958.

CHAPTER 46
Three courtships and a marriage
pp. 431–439

1 Conversation, Pali Meller Marcovicz.
2 Interview, Dr Andreas Holschneider with Dr Ernst von Siemens, Munich, 1988. Unpublished typescript.
3 DM32 was the equivalent of £2 13s. 6d. at a time when one of Karajan's EMI LPs retailed in the UK at £1 16s. 5½d. DGG eventually dropped the price to DM29 – a 'red letter day for German record collectors', recalls Pali Meller Marcovicz – before reducing it further to DM24 [£2, approximately £20 at today's prices], where it remained for many years, at rough parity with UK record prices.
4 Legge confirmed this in a memorandum to David Bicknell on 26 November 1957. When it was clear that Karajan was not going to record *Fidelio* for EMI, Legge revived the idea of a Klemperer recording, which is just as well since it is one of the glories of the gramophone.
5 Memorandum, 5 February 1958, EMI.
6 In his book *When the Music Stops* (London, 1996), 304, Norman Lebrecht observes: 'One cause of [Legge's] resignation [in June 1963], never revealed before, is that EMI awoke to Legge's double-dealings. The chairman, Sir Joseph Lockwood, took legal advice and was told that Legge was doing nothing criminal [*sic*] in hiring his own orchestra to EMI . . .' It is difficult to see how the arrangement could have begun to be judged illegal (let alone 'criminal') when for more than twenty years EMI itself had been party to the arrangement.
7 Memorandum, 13 September 1957, EMI.
8 Karajan's contract with EMI gave him the right to vet the quality of pressings in all territories. On more than one occasion, he took issue with the company over breaches of procedure on this. He frequently asked for state-of-the-art equipment to be shipped to wherever he was at the time. In November 1955 EMI's Milan office was amazed when he asked for a portable record player. Previously, the office reported, he had 'never been satisfied with less than forty cubic feet of equipment'. Memorandum, 23 November 1955, EMI.
9 Memorandum, 5 February 1958, EMI.
10 Memorandum, 7 March 1958, EMI.
11 History has not looked kindly on this particular outburst. The record being promoted alongside Karajan's Berlioz-Liszt-Respighi collection was Paul Kletzki's recording of Mahler's Fourth Symphony, a famous recording that would sell strongly for many years to come.
12 Memorandum, 4 July 1958, EMI.
13 Legge had drawn on these to make EMI's first recordings with Karajan in Berlin. A disc of orchestral extracts from Wagner, Schumann's Fourth Symphony, and Karajan's celebrated 1957 recording of Bruckner's Eighth Symphony had already been recorded, though at the time of the meeting only the Wagner LP had been released.
14 Conversation, Eliette von Karajan.
15 Haeusserman, 119.
16 *The Gramophone*, November 1960, 271.
17 Lang, 93.
18 *The Gramophone*, December 1959, 288–9.
19 Culshaw, op. cit., 197.
20 Ibid.

CHAPTER 47
Vienna and London: 1959–60
pp. 440–452

1 Culshaw, op. cit., 13–14.
2 A good example of this is the playing of the *Allegretto* of Beethoven's Seventh Symphony: rather quick and very legato.
3 Having sung Siegmund successfully under Karajan, Knappertsbusch, Kempe, and Böhm, Vickers – famously – failed to get on with Solti. Solti attempted to 'teach' him 'Winterstürme' at a piano rehearsal by whistling the melody and giving him a blow-by-blow account of what was going on in the orchestra. Vickers would recall: 'I told Solti I was well aware of what was going on in the orchestra. I also pointed out that whistling is not singing; that there is a *text* here, a text rich in poetic and alliterative effects which Wagner probably lay awake at nights revising and refining. I then made my excuses and left.' Conversation, Jon Vickers.
4 Csobádi, 158–9.
5 Ibid.
6 Ibid.
7 *Saturday Review*, 26 October 1962; *Music and Musicians*, March 1964, 14.
8 *Los Angeles Times*, 2 July 1959.
9 *Los Angeles Times*, 3 July 1959.
10 There is a photograph taken during the Hollywood Bowl rehearsals in which Karajan looks uncannily like Bruno Walter, smiling and gently gesturing. EMI later used the photograph on the cover of the LP of German Romantic overtures Karajan recorded in Berlin in 1960.
11 *Julietta* by the 35-year-old Heimo Erbse, a composition pupil of Boris Blacher.
12 Conversation, Christopher Raeburn.
13 Alexander Witeschnik, *Seid umschlungen Millionen: Mit den Wiener Philharmoniker unter Herbert von Karajan um die Welt* (Vienna, 1960), 62.
14 Memorandum, Walter Legge to Joseph Lockwood, 7 December 1959, EMI.

15 Legge's memorandum says '200,000 records of the set of the four discs'. This is clearly a typing error. Karajan's royalty earnings for the quarter were £6400. Since Karajan received a royalty of nine cents per record distributed (in 1959 £1 = $2.80), that is 20,000 records or 5000 sets.
16 The existing mono recording of Symphony No.2 had been conducted by Kletzki. Karajan had recorded symphonies nos. 4–7.
17 Sibelius Symphony No.5, 1965, Deutsche Grammophon; Tchaikovsky Symphony No. 4, 1975; Deutsche Grammophon; Sibelius Symphony No.2, 1980, EMI.
18 Memorandum, J. D. Bicknell to Walter Legge, 4 March 1960, EMI.
19 The English première took place on 12 June 1962 in Coventry, as part of the festival marking the opening of the newly built Cathedral. Don Garrard played Becket, Colin Davis conducted.
20 Claudio Sartori, *Opera*, May 1958, 308–9.
21 Letter, Hans Hotter, 17 October 1994.
22 *Opera*, June 1960, 412–13.
23 Letter, Walter Legge to Peter Stadlen, 29 November 1966.
24 Writing in the *Manchester Guardian* on 31 August 1957, Cardus declared it 'a surprising and grievous disappointment', the work seen from the outside rather than from within, with (a phrase Legge never forgot) violin tremolos sounding 'like barbed wire'. Klemperer himself had been dissatisfied with the performance, frustrated at not being able to feel his way back into the work; but that did not lessen the hurt the reviews inflicted. The problem was, Klemperer was not Bruno Walter, whose 1947 account of *Das Lied von der Erde* with Kathleen Ferrier and the Vienna Philharmonic had become a sacred memory within the festival's communal consciousness. If Legge kept quiet at the time, he became incandescent with rage when, in an amnesiac moment,

Cardus later suggested that 'Mr
Legge should invite Klemperer to
conduct *Das Lied von der Erde*'. It
was Legge's fury over this, combined
with his anger at Cardus's review
of the Karajan concert of 1 April
1960, that prompted his programme
book article.

25 *Manchester Guardian*, 2 April 1960.
26 Philharmonia Concert Society
programme, 10 April 1960, EMI.
27 *The Observer*, 3 April 1960.
28 *Manchester Guardian*, 2 April 1960.
29 *Daily Telegraph*, 2 April 1960.

CHAPTER 48
Salzburg shenanigans
pp. 453–456

1 Report, *The Times*, 27 July 1960.
2 Rasponi, op. cit., 335.
3 By way of preparation, Schwarzkopf
replaced Lisa della Casa for the third
performance of the run on 6 August.
4 Ironically, the man who had overseen
the preliminary planning of the
Grosses Festspielhaus was Herbert
Graf, one of the world's leading
proponents of televised opera. What's
more, in 1956 the Salzburg Festival
had hosted the most high-powered
conference to date on the subject
of opera on film and television.
See Dennis Arundell, 'The Salzburg
Conference in Radio, Television and
Films', *Opera*, November 1956, 670.
5 Conversation, Dame Elisabeth
Legge-Schwarzkopf.
6 Quoted by Winthrop Sargeant in his
article in the *New Yorker*, 7 January
1961, 35.
7 Articles of representative interest
can be found in *Wiener Zeitung*, 24
August 1960; ibid. 25 August 1960;
Kronenzeitung, 24 August 1960;
Wochenpresse, 3 September 1960.
8 *Opera*, Summer Festivals Number,
Autumn 1960, 47–50.
9 Though the cast was mainly
German-speaking – Waechter as the
Don, Walter Berry as Leporello, and
Schwarzkopf as Elvira – Karajan had
managed to cast Italian singers in the
roles of Zerlina (Graziella Sciutti) and
Masetto (Rolando Panerai). Sciutti
has recalled the intense flurry of

excitement Karajan liked to arouse
at Zerlina's entrance ('Giovinette,
che fate all' amore') when there was
an Italian singer on hand capable of
releasing the vowel and consonant
clusters at lightening speed.
10 Strasser, op. cit., 303. Vaughan
states that the baptism took
place in the Salzburg home of the
Karajans' close friend, the Austrian
industrialist Herbert Kloiber. This
bizarre suggestion is repeated by
Alan Jefferson in his biography of
Schwarzkopf.

CHAPTER 49
Controlling interests
pp. 457–468

1 *The Gramophone*, March 1964, 411.
2 Gianandrea Gavazzeni, *La bacchetta
spezzata* (Pisa, 1987), 53. Gavazzeni
dubbed Karajan's Wagner style
'neo-decadentismo'.
3 Stravinsky noted with admiration
the way Stokowski would get his
cello section to stagger its bowing
in the *Tristan* Prelude for a smooth
and consistent crescendo. See Igor
Stravinsky, *Themes and Conclusions*
(London, 1972), 230.
4 Conversation, Bernard Haitink.
5 *Opera*, November 1960, 760.
6 Conversation, Christa Ludwig.
7 *New Yorker*, 7 January 1961, 35.
8 *Der Spiegel*, 4 December 1995, 222.
9 Ibid.
10 Though the set was received with
near delirium at the time, notably
in the pages of *The Gramophone*,
subsequent judgements have not
been so kind. In particular, Solti's
conducting has come to be seen by
a number of writers as sonically
crude and rhythmically garbled.
See Robin Holloway, 'Tristan und
Isolde', *Opera on Record*, ed. Alan
Blyth (London, 1979), 368; David
Hamilton, 'Tristan und Isolde',
*The Metropolitan Opera: Guide
to Recorded Opera* (London,
1993), 696.
11 *The Gramophone*, April 1961, 533.
12 *Saturday Review*, 26 October
1963; *Music and Musicians*, March
1964, 14.

13 Pettitt, op. cit., 103.

14 Grubb, op. cit., 10.

15 Memorandum, J. D. Bicknell, 3 November 1960, EMI.

16 Ibid.

17 Legge's last recording with Karajan. This intense, richly coloured recording of Bartók's score suggests that EMI's engineers were beginning to get the hang of the Jesus Christus Kirche acoustic. Most of Karajan's EMI-Berlin recordings 1957–60 give the impression of the orchestra being at one end of the building and the microphones at the other. Exceptions are the recording of Bruckner's Eighth Symphony and a collection of German Romantic overtures which includes superbly atmospheric accounts of Mendelssohn's *Hebrides* Overture and the overture to Wagner's *The Flying Dutchman*.

18 Memorandum, Walter Legge, 14 November 1960, EMI.

19 Memorandum, F. M. Scott to EMI, 7 October 1960.

20 In 1965, Whittle reported 'little public interest' in the Karajan back catalogue. His suggestion that it could be sold off was not acted on.

21 The Gala included, among others, Birgit Nilsson singing 'I could have danced all night' from *My Fair Lady*, Leontyne Price singing 'Summertime' from *Porgy and Bess*, Jussi Björling singing 'Dein ist mein ganzes Herz' from *Das Land des Lächelns*, and Giulietta Simionato and Ettore Bastianini singing 'Anything you can do' from *Annie Get Your Gun*.

22 Elisabeth Höngen sang Acts 1 and 3, Christa Ludwig sang Act 2. Joseph Wechsberg commented: 'What is today perhaps understood as the psycho-analytical complexity of the figure (John Warrack a few months ago referred to Kundry as serving "the Venus-cult *and* the Mary-cult") became a mere stage trick, in a futile effort of vocal cosmetics.' *Opera*, June 1961, 393.

23 Conversation, Otto Strasser.

24 In the eighteenth century it was not unusual for leading designers to work with both marionettes and singers (Pietro Travaglia at Eszterháza is the most famous example). 'The *rightness* of these figures,' noted Andrew Porter after seeing the Schneider-Siemssen's *Die Zauberflöte* at the Marionetten-Theater one wet Salzburg afternoon in 1966, 'specially in these days of quirky interpretations, is very striking. So cunningly are these Salzburg marionettes conceived, and built, and moved, that in bearing and range of movement they can present us with the essential Tamino, Pamina, Queen of the Night or Sarastro.' *Financial Times*, 24 August 1966.

25 Conversation, Günther Schneider-Siemssen.

26 Csobádi, 206.

27 Haeusserman, 144.

28 *The Planets*, Vienna State Opera Orchestra, Vienna Academy Choir, conductor Sir Adrian Boult, Westminster.

29 Karajan conducted two performances of *Le sacre du printemps* with the Vienna Philharmonic in December 1962. During one of these, the orchestra lost its way and had to regroup. Conversation, Walter Weller.

CHAPTER 50
Vienna: the phoney war
pp. 469–474

1 Conversation, Günther Schneider-Siemssen.

2 Robin Holloway, 'Building a Library', *Record Review*, BBC Radio 3, 25 April 1992. Holloway was illustrating the scene in Act 2 in which Golaud, bedridden after a hunting accident, is troubled by Mélisande's sunless, closed-in mood. Holloway's monograph *Wagner and Debussy* (London, 1979) offers illuminating insights into the tradition within which Karajan himself was working.

3 *Opera*, March 1962, 172.

4 *Manchester Guardian*, 15 January 1962; reprinted in Donald Wright (ed.), *Cardus on Music*, 309–11.

5 Ibid.

6 Haeusserman, 146.

7 Ibid., 147–9.
8 *Saturday Review*, 26 October 1963; *Music and Musicians*, March 1964, 16.

CHAPTER 51
Karajan's circus
pp. 475–480

1 Outstanding among Scharoun's early work are the flats he designed for the Siemens Town project of 1929–31, one of Berlin's great pre-war 'social housing' projects (Scharoun himself lived there until 1960); the private houses he designed during his years of 'internal exile' in Germany during the Nazi years; and after the war, the influential Geschwister Scholl school in Lünen, which is more or less contemporary with the Berlin Philharmonie. These and other projects are discussed in detail in Peter Blundell Jones's authoritative study *Hans Scharoun* (London, 1995).
2 Peter Pfankuch (ed.) *Hans Scharoun: Bauten, Entwürfe, Texte* (Berlin, 1974/R1993), 279; quoted in translation in Blundell Jones, op. cit., 177.
3 Quoted in Ulrich Conrads and Hans G. Sperlich, *Fantastic Architecture* (London, 1963), 142.
4 Pfankuch, op. cit., 20.
5 Scharoun's last commission, and last masterpiece, appropriately, was the new German Maritime Museum in Bremerhaven (1969–75).
6 Publicity leaflet, Thormann & Goetsch, Berlin 1963.
7 Luciano Berio, Scharoun Symposium, Harvard University, 4 December 1993; Pierre Boulez, BBC Radio interview *c*.1970. Quoted in Blundell Jones, op. cit., 221.
8 Blundell Jones cites Böttcher Hall, Denver (1971), Concert Hall of Sydney Opera House (1973), Tonhalle, Düsseldorf (1978), Vredenburg Music Centre, Utrecht (1979), Leipzig Gewandhaus (1981), St David's Hall, Cardiff (1982), Thompson Hall, Toronto (1982), Royal Concert Hall, Nottingham (1982), the Suntory Hall, Tokyo (1987).
9 Blundell Jones, op. cit., 222.

10 Gould would later recall looking up to see precisely what it was that Karajan was doing during a passage which always caused problems but which was being played to perfection by the Berliners. To his astonishment, Karajan was absolutely still. A wonderful example, said Gould, of a conductor knowing when *not* to conduct.
11 Stresemann, 39.

CHAPTER 52
Berlin Philharmonic
pp. 481–492

1 Letter, Wolfgang Stresemann to A. Beverly Barksdale, 11 October 1961, CO.
2 '*Mit wohlwollendem Misstrauen*'. Stresemann, 110.
3 In the post-war years, Berlin Philharmonic salaries had lagged behind those of musicians in West Germany's principal radio orchestras. By using 'quality at entry' as a measure, Karajan was able to insist that on a Civil Service scale of 1–5 no player should come into the orchestra below level 3.
4 Stresemann, 64.
5 *The Times*, 4 February 1964.
6 Conversations, 86. Karajan had originally invited the Philharmonia Orchestra's Alan Civil to join the Berlin Philharmonic. Civil played with the orchestra on a number of occasions but decided against uprooting himself and his family. Karajan's emphatic endorsement of Seifert in a conversation I had with him in 1989 was no doubt sincere; none the less, it was something of an embarrassment to the Berlin Philharmonic, who had expelled Seifert but been obliged to reinstate him after he successfully sued the orchestra for wrongful dismissal.
7 Conversation, Professor Denis Stevens. Stevens, who was briefly a string-player in Legge's Philharmonia Orchestra in the pre-Karajan era, worked with Karajan in Paris in 1966 as interviewer for the programme on Dvořák's *New World Symphony* in the TV film series *Die*

Kunst des Dirigierens directed by Henri-Georges Clouzot. A perceptive obituary essay on Karajan by Professor Stevens appeared in the American periodical *Stereophile*.

8 Conversation, Mariss Jansons.

9 *Spectator*, 26 November 1994, 59–62.

10 Neville Cardus reviewing Karajan's London Beethoven cycle, *Manchester Guardian*, 17 April 1961.

11 Conversation, Fergus McWilliam.

12 From 'Ideas about the art of conducting', originally prepared by Karajan for his conducting course in Lucerne, reproduced in Haeusserman, 86–90.

13 So decided was Karajan's dislike of the printed page, Menuhin was surprised he did not try to get the orchestra to play certain works by heart. But though Karajan liked choirs to sing from memory, he never seriously entertained the idea for the orchestra itself. The nearest he ever came to this was asking the orchestra to play certain passages by heart: the opening bars of Beethoven's *Eroica* Symphony, for example.

14 *The Times*, 1 February 1964.

15 James Galway, *An Autobiography* (London, 1978), 159.

16 Vladimir Ashkenazy, 'The Experts' Expert', *The Observer*, 24 July 1988.

17 Conversation, Fergus McWilliam.

18 *Manchester Guardian*, 7 April 1962.

19 Conversation, Bernard Haitink.

20 *New Yorker*, 7 January 1961, 50.

21 Conversations, 144.

22 I am grateful to international helmsman and former world champion yachtsman Crispin Read Wilson for his responses to Karajan's various statements on the subject.

23 'How do you do this *La mer* justice in short summary? Effortless and limitless but never showy virtuosity; a largely faultless balance; some of the most sheerly beautiful orchestral sound ever recorded; and perhaps most significant of all, a *La mer* with a properly mobile pacing that connects like a symphony while doing proud all its maritime mystery and majesty.' Jonathan Swain,

'Building a Library', *Record Review*, BBC Radio 3, 23 November 1996.

24 *New Yorker*, 7 January 1961, 50.

25 Cleveland's only acoustically viable hall was barred by statute to all profit-making organisations other than the Cleveland Orchestra itself. In November 1960, George Szell wrote to Karajan in Vienna: 'I am most happy to inform you that I have been successful in convincing the Board of Trustees of the Cleveland Orchestra of the desirability to depart from established precedent and to sponsor the concert of the Berlin Philharmonic Orchestra under your direction on November 1, 1961. This will make it possible for your great orchestra to be heard in Cleveland in the only place whose acoustics are worthy of the occasion. As you perhaps know, the charter of Severance Hall contains a number of very severe stipulations and forbids expressly the renting of the hall to managers or to any profit-making organisation. By acting as a sponsor of your concert, the Trustees of the Musical Arts Association, which own Severance Hall and operates the Cleveland Orchestra, have found a way round these limitations for the first time since the existence of Severance Hall, and I am very proud of it.' Letter, George Szell to Herbert von Karajan, 5 November 1960, CO.

26 *Plain Dealer*, 2 November 1961.

27 Letter, Alfred Brendel. Brendel went on: 'I remember Thärichen as a most amiable man and excellent timpanist. As for Karajan, I always greatly admired his performances of Italian opera while, in the German symphonic repertory, there were other conductors who impressed me more.'

28 Karajan and the Berlin Philharmonic finally recorded the *Variations* in the winter of 1973–4. The earliest performances in Berlin in October 1962 were met with rapture by a devoted band of die-hard modernists, but with coolness elsewhere. (Eliette von Karajan found the music so

repulsive, she took herself off to the cinema during the repeat performances.) For Karajan, the work became something of an obsession, causing him to send players off in the middle of concert tours and recording engagements to work privately on individual variations.

29 In December 1962, Karajan included in Berlin's end-of-year concert a work he greatly liked, Bloch's Hebraic rhapsody for cello and orchestra *Schelomo*. It was, however, slipped it in at the eleventh hour. The soloist, Ottomar Borwitzky, had been expecting to play one of the Shostakovich concertos. Ottomar Borwitzky, *Die Weltwoche*, 20 July 1989.

30 In the UK at the time, £14 8s. 0d. was a little over half the average weekly wage.

31 *Manchester Guardian*, 17 April 1961.

32 *New York Times*, 21 November 1958.

33 'Was die Mauer frech geteilt', *The Gramophone*, December 1962, 283–5. Compare Sir George Solti's remark: 'He did what he thought he could do best under the best possible circumstances.' Interview with Hugh Canning, *Sunday Times*, 9 December 1990.

34 Richard Wagner, 'On Conducting', ed. Robert L. Jacobs, *Three Wagner Essays* (London, 1979), 60–2.

35 *The Gramophone*, February 1963, 382–4.

CHAPTER 53
A strange marriage
pp. 493–503

1 At the time, there were writers who thought the whole performance too cultivated and refined, academic even. See Joachim Kaiser, *Great Pianists of our Time* (London, 1971), 116.

2 Culshaw, op. cit., 301.

3 Ibid., 303–4.

4 For several decades, *L'incoronazione di Poppea* had hovered on the distant borders of the repertory in adaptations by composers – d'Indy,

Malipiero, Krenek, Ghedini – who, despairing of writing an original masterpiece of their own, had taken refuge in adapting a 'lost' masterpiece by someone else. By the early 1960s, a new generation of musicologically informed 'authenticists' was taking over.

5 Conversation, Sena Jurinac.

6 Prawy, op. cit., 193.

7 Ibid., 202.

8 See Chapter 17 n.2.

9 A play on the German title of Cimaroso's opera *Il matrimonio segreto*, *Die heimliche Ehe*. In German, '*heimlich*' and '*unheimlich*' are not antonyms. The former means 'secret', the latter 'sinister' or 'eerie'.

10 The court ruled that it was unreasonable for a largely Italian cast to work with an Austrian prompter. As for the high fee that the prompter had been offered, this was ruled to be in order in view of the fact that the Italian *maestro suggeritore* is a fully-fledged assistant conductor whose job it is to cue the singers, pitch their entries, and even mime their movements.

11 Prawy, op. cit., 194.

12 Prior to 1962, Freni had been learning her trade in the relative seclusion of such places as the Netherlands Opera, Glyndebourne, and Wexford.

13 *Opera*, December 1964, 824–5.

14 London Green, 'Carmen', *The Metropolitan Opera: Guide to Recorded Opera*, ed. Paul Gruber (London, 1993), 53.

15 Karajan, 90.

16 Haeusserman, 282–6.

CHAPTER 54
Pet savage
pp. 504–506

1 Legge suspended the orchestra's activities 'for an indefinite period' on 10 March 1964. See Pettitt, op. cit., 120.

2 Conversation, Michel Glotz.

3 Conversation, Hugh Bean.

4 Tchaikovsky's Sixth Symphony and a sadly unidiomatic recording (the

third such to date) of Dvořák's *New World* Symphony.

5 The first review was written for *Hi-Fi Stereo*, New York in October 1964 and reprinted in Igor Stravinsky and Robert Craft *Dialogues and a Diary* (London, 1968), 82–90; the second was written in June 1970 and appeared in Igor Stravinsky, *Themes and Conclusions* (London, 1972), 234–41.

6 Ingmar Bergman, *The Magic Lantern*, translated by Joan Tate (London, 1988), 35.

7 'The Prospects of Recording', *High Fidelity*, April 1966; Gould (ed. Page), op. cit., 344.

8 In his comment on the Boulez recording in his 1964 review, Stravinsky noted that the work's huge dynamic range tended to be reduced to what he called 'a standard recording mezzo forte'. The ubiquity of such recordings, he suggested, explains why a live performance of *Le sacre* is, even now, a shock to anyone who has learned the work from records.

CHAPTER 55
Farewell, Vienna
pp. 567–511

1 Theodor Piffl-Perčević, *Zuspruch und Widerspruch* (Graz, 1977).

2 *Die Presse*, 13 May 1964.

3 *Opera*, July 1964, 462.

4 Alan Blyth, 'Leonie Rysanek', *Opera*, January 1994, 21.

5 Siegert, op. cit., 105.

6 Conversation, Volker Altmann.

7 The threat had originally been made, with a measure of decorum, on 8 June in a covering letter Karajan sent to the Federal Chancellor Josef Klaus to whom he was forwarding his complaint about Hilbert's non-cooperation with the transitional arrangements. The relevant paragraph reads: 'If this present week brings no satisfactory solution, I must, to my regret, assume that the requirements of my artistic work cannot be provided in Austria, and that I am forced to draw the appropriate conclusions.' Haeusserman, 287.

8 *Opera*, November 1964, 746.

9 Humphrey Burton, *Leonard Bernstein* (London, 1994), 352–3.

10 Norman Lebrecht, *When the Music Stops* (London, 1996), 168–9. The economics of music-making have been a law unto themselves since Renaissance times. As for the gramophone, it was held to ransom at birth. The artists who 'made' the medium in the early years of the century – Caruso, Melba, Chaliapin – were paid sky-high fees, expensively cosseted and cajoled, and granted numerous concessions over scheduling and presentation.

CHAPTER 56
Fresh woods and pastures new
pp. 515–521

1 EMI. I am grateful to Ruth Edge, Chief Archivist, EMI, who originally compiled this information.

2 Karajan used to joke that Eliette was not much enamoured of the new villa in St Moritz – she preferred the brilliant social life in the Palace Hotel itself – until her near neighbours the Agnellis expressed their admiration and offered to buy it. After that, she became very fond of it indeed. Not all Karajan's cars were top of the range luxury or sports models. He owned (and crashed) a Mini and was much taken with Peter Alward's Citroën 2 CV.

3 The Berlin Philharmonic concert consisted of the Oboe Concerto (Lothar Koch), the *Four Last Songs* (Elisabeth Schwarzkopf), and *Ein Heldenleben*; the Vienna Philharmonic of *Don Quixote* (Pierre Fournier) and *Also sprach Zarathustra*.

4 Issued on CD in 1992 on Orfeo. The opera was on Walter Legge's wish list in the early 1960s but circumstances and a shortage of available, recordable singers in key roles conspired against him. Karl Böhm had conducted the first commercial studio recording in Dresden in 1960. Six years later, Solti recorded the opera for Decca in Vienna with Birgit Nilsson and Regina Resnik in leading roles, a set that effectively wrapped up the LP market

for the next fifteen years. Karajan would have liked to record the opera with Hildegard Behrens in the title role but by the time Behrens agreed to sing it (Paris, 1987) it was too late for him.

5 Böhm had asked Wieland Wagner to direct (his 1962 Stuttgart production had caused a minor sensation). When that plan all too predictably foundered, Böhm, impervious to bathos, suggested his son Karlheinz as replacement, an idea the festival direktorium instantly rejected.

6 Shuard, an Eva Turner pupil, and Resnik would later appear in a famous Covent Garden revival of *Elektra* in March 1965, conducted by Rudolf Kempe.

7 Peter Heyworth, *The Observer*, 16 August 1964.

8 For Astrid Varnay's own account of the production see her autobiography *Hab mir's gelobt: 55 Jahre in fünf Akten* (Berlin, 1997), 294–304.

9 Walter Legge, typescript of draft review of August 1965 revival, EMI.

10 In 1967, an extract from this recording of the Second Suite was slipped – unidentified as to the performers – into a discussion of the Bach Orchestral Suites in the BBC Third Programme's series *Interpretations on Record*. Roger Fiske chaired the proceedings, with panellists Professor Jack Westrup, Denis Arnold, and Stanley Sadie. The praise which was lavished on the performance was matched by the shock with which the identity of the performers was received (*Interpretations on Record*, 27 June 1967, BBC).

11 Conversation, Barone Raffaello de Banfield Tripcovich.

12 *Opera*, January 1965, 42–3. Cf. the Austrian wit who is said to have dubbed the production 'mascarpone served on Sèvres'.

13 Ibid.

14 Reprinted as 'Opera House? – Blow them up!', *Opera*, June 1968, 440–8.

15 Giulini's withdrawal took place in 1968 after a Rome production of *Le nozze di Figaro*. He was fifty-four.

He continued to make opera recordings, and conducted *Falstaff* in the theatre in Los Angeles and London in 1982.

16 *New York Times*, 20 January 1965.

17 *The Times*, 5 April 1965.

CHAPTER 57
Pilgrimage to Järvenpää
pp. 522–524

1 'Glenn Gould interviews Glenn Gould about Glenn Gould', *High Fidelity*, February 1974; Gould (ed. Page), op. cit., 321.

2 'A Desert Island Discography', *High Fidelity*, June 1970; Gould (ed. Page), op. cit., 438.

3 Canadian Broadcasting Corporation, December 1970; released on CD in 1992 as part of *Glenn Gould's Solitude Trilogy*.

4 Erik Tawaststjerna, *Sibelius*, Volume 2, translated by Robert Layton (London, 1986), 21.

5 The Anif house draws on a number of models. The airy sitting-room, with its plain wooden floors, undulating ceiling and two central pillars, is based on the design of what is now the dining-room of Salzburg's hotel Goldener Hirsch (1564).

6 'A Consummate Conductor', 21 April, 1990, BBC. In the same programme, the philosopher Bryan Magee remarked: 'There has been a tendency to denigrate Karajan, partly based on the idea that he was a seeker after perfection and that perfection necessarily meant coldness or soullessness. This strikes me as being a silly criticism, and one that is belied by one's ears. After repeated hearings, one comes to realise that beneath the surface perfection there is genuine musicianship and genuine depth of feeling.'

CHAPTER 58
Towards the Easter Festival
pp. 525–534

1 Haeusserman, 212.

2 Conversation, Günther Schneider-Siemssen.

3 Conversation, Christoph von Dohnányi.

4 *Financial Times*, 25 August 1965.
5 Ibid.
6 Walter Legge, typescript of draft review, August 1965, EMI.
7 Ibid.
8 Conversation, Sena Jurinac. It was not Karajan's way. He hated scenes and feared being confronted emotionally. After Gundula Janowitz sang what proved to be her last performance with him, there was nothing to indicate that this was so except Karajan's phrasing of his farewell greeting. Janowitz understood, and had no problems with this. Others were often less sanguine.
9 Interview with H. C. Robbins Landon, 1967, BBC.
10 The world-wide success of Klaus Heymann's budget-price Naxos label can be put down in part to the fact that, from the outset, he refused to pay such expenses.
11 'I can confirm that Karajan normally did not ask us to pay his hotel and other expenses. He always stayed at the Kempinski in Berlin, where in his later years a threshold in his apartment was removed to make walking easier for him. We were not charged "per diems".' Letter, Christoph Schmökel, Head of Legal and Business Affairs, Deutsche Grammophon, 8 September 1995.
12 Conversation, Riccardo Chailly.
13 Karajan had little or no Greek blood in his veins, contrary to a commonly held supposition. The invitation to the Berlin Philharmonic to visit Athens and Epidauros was to some extent a bridge-building exercise. I recall from my own visits to Greece in the 1960s that anti-German feeling still ran high in Athens. It was not until one travelled away from Athens, to Mycenae (excavated by Heinrich Schliemann) that one encountered German tourists in substantial numbers.
14 'A Musical Pilgrimage to Epidaurus to Hear Verdi's Requiem', *The Times*, 17 September 1965.
15 Ibid.
16 Ibid.
17 When the decision appeared to settle on Barbirolli, Glotz remarked, 'That would be to replace Olympus with a hillock [*C'ést remplacer l'Olympe par une montagnette*]'. He regretted the remark the moment he made it (he was a great admirer of Barbirolli), though he remained convinced that EMI was deluding itself if it believed it could 'sell' Barbirolli internationally in the way it was possible to 'sell' Karajan.
18 The terms of Glotz's contract were stated in two separate letters. The second, dated 8 April 1966, confirming Glotz's position with regard to the Salzburg Easter Festival and his appointment as General Secretary of the Karajan–Kirch film company Cosmotel, ended: 'You are authorised by me to conduct any negotiations which you consider necessary and also to carry out any auditions in such a way that only the final decisions devolve upon myself.' English translation of French original, EMI.
19 Conversation, Michel Glotz. See also Michel Glotz, *Révéler les dieux* (Paris, 1981), 76.
20 During a troubled recording of Aida's 'Ritorna vincitor!' Glotz both calmed Callas and roused her to action by playing a recording by Régine Crespin, which Callas promptly denounced and then challenged.
21 Conversation, Peter Alward.
22 Conversation, Michel Glotz.
23 Conversation, Michel Glotz.

CHAPTER 59

Henri-Georges Clouzot

pp. 535–544

1 '"Oh, for heaven's sake, Cynthia, there must be something else on!"', *Musical America*, April 1969; Gould (ed. Page), op. cit., 370.
2 Ibid., 371.
3 Ibid., 372.
4 In the film, the shanty town is a prison from which there is almost literally no escape. Four men do get a passage out – driving lorries laden with a suicidally unstable cargo of nitroglycerine which is needed to

isolate a disastrous fire in a distant oilfield – but they all perish.

5 Robert McKee, introduction to BBC television screening of *Le salaire de la peur*.

6 A conference 'Hommage Henri-Georges Clouzot' was held in Florence in May 1987 during which a paper on Clouzot and Karajan was presented by the writer and Clouzot biographer Solon Smith.

7 Introduction to television transmission of the Clouzot–Karajan film of Beethoven's Fifth Symphony in the series *Die Kunst des Dirigierens*, DGG.

8 Karajan and two professional guides climbed for twenty-two hours and got within eighty feet of the summit of Mont Blanc (the wind prevented them tackling the summit itself). They then skied back down in two stages. Karajan himself claimed that the twenty-seven minutes final descent was a record for a skier with guide. See Vaughan, 255.

9 Canetti, op. cit., 458–9.

10 Conversation, Ronald Wilford.

11 *Die Kunst des Dirigierens*, 'Probenarbeit zur IV. Symphonie von Robert Schumann', Cosmotel-ORF, 1965, Unitel-DGG.

12 Conversation, Lord Menuhin.

13 Conversation, Fritz Buttenstedt.

14 *Yehudi Menuhin: The Violin of the Century*, Ideale Audience-La Sept-Arte-Imalyre Groupe France Télécome-INA, EMI, 1996.

15 Conversation, Lord Menuhin.

16 Gould (ed. Page), op. cit., 372.

17 A second video version was made in 1985, with the Vienna Philharmonic. It is very tired-looking, if not at all points tired-sounding, in comparison with the 1966 film.

18 All the soloists are magnificent, with Fiorenza Cossotto very much the star of the performance, as striking to behold as she is thrilling to hear. The film is also an important record of Karajan conducting Verdi with the La Scala orchestra and the superb Benaglio-trained La Scala chorus.

19 'First of all, he was the most creative person, inventing the music at the moment, making the orchestra play very, very precisely, with soul. After that, I always followed Karajan, singing for him when I was able right to the end of my life.' Interview with David Mellor, BBC Radio 3 *Vintage Years*, 1994. Pavarotti would sing the role of Cavaradossi in Karajan's last opera performance on 24 March 1989.

20 Letter, Herbert von Karajan to Henri-Georges Clouzot, undated, copy DGG.

CHAPTER 60
The Easter Festival
pp. 545–552

1 The sessions included remakes of Bartók's *Concerto for Orchestra* and Mussorgsky's *Pictures at an Exhibition* – the latter barely a match in terms of litheness, wit and orchestral virtuosity for the recording Karajan made with the Philharmonia Orchestra in 1955–56 – and what would become a justly famous recording of Strauss's *Don Quixote*, with Pierre Fournier and Giusto Cappone as the soloists.

2 Rudolf Bing, *5000 Nights at the Opera* (London, 1972), 259.

3 Ibid., 263

4 *New York Times Magazine*, 3 December 1967, 160.

5 Conversations, 75.

6 In March, they recorded the Ninth Symphony with Karajan, a celebrated recording in its day.

7 During the sessions a concert took place consisting of Honegger's Symphony *Liturgique* and, in the second half, Ravel's *Pavane* and *Boléro*.

8 The symphony was written shortly after Stalin's death in 1953. The Eighth Symphony shares similar preoccupations. This, too, interested Karajan deeply, though he never performed it.

9 There was also the Mitropoulos connection. Mitropoulos had conducted the work's American première in 1954, and made an exceptionally fine recording of it for CBS. Karajan's performance is

different – it has its own tempi and its own solutions to the problems of transference between tempi at key points – but is equally fine, one of the finest of all recordings of the piece.

10 Beethoven's Violin Concerto with Christian Ferras and Beethoven's First Piano Concerto with the 25-year-old Christoph Eschenbach, the latter recording an earnest of Karajan's desire to use his new powers of patronage to help bring forward startling young talent. Though someone in Deutsche Grammophon put a circled '1' on the cover of the LP, there was never any plan for Karajan and Eschenbach to record a complete cycle. The idea was that Eschenbach should record the five concertos with five different orchestras and conductors. The Third Piano Concerto followed, with Henze and the LSO. The cycle was never completed.

11 Karajan had plans to record *Gurrelieder* but the publishers vetoed his request to use a slimmed-down version of Schoenberg's notoriously extravagant orchestration.

12 Conversation, Jon Vickers.

13 Conversation, Gundula Janowitz.

14 Régine Crespin, 'Karajan le magnifique', *La vie et l'amour d'une femme* (Paris, 1982), 243–55.

15 If Veasey had found the set-up surrounding Karajan hostile and intimidating, she would later have cause to think it baneful as well. Having been engaged to sing Brangäne in Karajan's EMI recording of *Tristan und Isolde* she was forced to give up a chance to sing Octavian at Covent Garden, only to be dropped by Karajan when Ludwig suddenly became free. In such circumstances, Karajan's henchmen usually blamed each other, and the apologists blamed the henchmen. But Karajan knew perfectly well what was happening. He had told Solti personally that on no account could the arrangements over Brangäne be changed. It was a time of bitter skirmishing between Karajan's camp and Solti's, and there can be little

doubt that Veasey got caught in the crossfire. Yet Karajan was kindness itself when it came to re-scheduling rehearsals in New York to fit in with holiday arrangements for Veasey's children.

16 Conversation, Josephine Veasey.

17 Conversation, Josephine Veasey.

18 Haeusserman, 213.

19 Conversation, Gundula Janowitz.

20 Conversation, Jon Vickers.

21 *Tagesanzeiger*, 25 March 1967.

22 Herbert von Karajan, interview with Robert Chesterman, 'A Salzburg Diary', Canadian Broadcasting Corporation, 1979, Archive Number DO 10 949 / 1–2.

23 'Forging the Ring', *New Yorker*, 2 December 1972; reprinted in Andrew Porter, *A Musical Season* (London, 1974), 67.

24 Ibid.

25 Quoted ORF, 1.

26 Herbert von Karajan, conversation with H. C. Robbins Landon, 1969, BBC.

27 *Opera*, June 1967, 465–6.

28 Porter, op. cit., 71.

29 Haeusserman, 228–9.

30 Conversation, Eva Schneider-Siemssen.

31 Karajan's remark 'You have brown eyes, the eyes of a traitor' was one such. This quip was widely repeated without knowledge or explanation of the context. Conversation, Günther Schneider-Siemssen.

32 Conversation, Günther Schneider-Siemssen.

CHAPTER 61
Carmen and *Pagliacci*
pp. 553–561

1 In the immediate wake of the Easter Festival Karajan and the orchestra had recorded Sibelius's Sixth Symphony and some orchestral show-stoppers: Liszt's *Les préludes* and *Hungarian Rhapsody* No.2, and two movements from Smetana's *Má vlast*, 'Vysehrad' and 'Vltava'.

2 In London, three days later, the *Brandenburg* Concerto No.6 was added by way of preface.

3 Edward Greenfield, *Manchester Guardian*, 13 May 1967.

4 *Daily Telegraph*, 15 May 1967. Henderson was also struck by the uniquely eerie quality of the bells in the 'Witches' Sabbath'. Crouching out of view beside the tubular bells was a separate group of percussionists striking small gongs.

5 When Karajan conducted Tchaikovsky's Fourth Symphony in Edinburgh later in the year, *The Times* critic William Mann suggested he made the 'fate' theme sound 'like a gang of predatory thugs'. The concert took place on 3 September, the anniversary of the outbreak of the Second World War. Again, Karajan refused to play the British and German national anthems before the concert. Mann added: 'Perhaps the old unhappy far-off things were preying on my mind – or on Mr Karajan's.'

6 Helena Matheopoulos, *Diva* (London, 1991), 263.

7 Did this seaside *Carmen* suggest to Vickers how striking a Karajan-produced *Peter Grimes* might be in Salzburg? He pestered Karajan with the idea, just as Karajan pestered him with the idea of a Vickers-led *Wozzeck*. Sadly, neither project came to pass.

8 Peter Conrad, *A Song of Love and Death: The Meaning of Opera* (London, 1987), 310–11.

9 Conversations, 80.

10 The recording Karajan made with the Berliners the following year is another gramophone classic, to be ranked alongside Koussevitzky's 1946 Boston recording and the more recent 1992 Rattle version.

11 Letter, Herbert von Karajan to George Szell, undated, CO.

12 Conversation, Christoph von Dohnányi.

13 *New York Times Magazine*, 3 December 1967, 156.

14 *Opera*, February 1969, 123.

15 Paul Robinson, *Solti* (London, 1979), 45.

16 There has been disagreement over whether Karajan would have been subject to protest from the Jewish community in Chicago. Peter Diamand believed that the idea of Karajan–Chicago was 'a complete non-starter' politically. Solti also appears to have taken an angry view of Wilford's intervention. Wilford would recall: 'Solti summoned me to his London office. "How could you ever imagine that Karajan would be interested in Chicago? How could you think it? This terrible Nazi for an American city!" He bawled me out, took me apart. At the end of the dressing-down I said, "I don't apologise for whatever it is I am meant to have done. And I don't know in what way my actions are any of your business." I've never spoken to him since.' Conversations, Ronald Wilford, Peter Diamand.

17 Caballé did not sing the role in the stage production either; it was taken over by Teresa Zylis-Gara.

18 Peter Glossop (b. Sheffield, 1928) made his name with the Sadler's Wells company in London but was roughly handled by the critics when he transferred to the Covent Garden company in 1963. Increasingly admired abroad as a singing-actor, he was engaged for *Pagliacci* by La Scala when Guelfi fell ill. He learned the role in a day and half in London with conductor John Matheson. It was a role he was born to. In a profile of Glossop in *Opera* in May 1969, Frank Granville-Barker wrote: 'As he talks – and he talks readily, vehemently – humour keeps breaking in, the Bacchus face smiles more readily, and one gradually realises there is also a shy, vulnerable side to his nature'. Karajan was so impressed with Glossop's Tonio, he promptly engaged him to sing Iago at the 1970 Salzburg Festival.

19 The films of *Cavalleria rusticana* and *Pagliacci* were bought by a number of TV companies, but they remained unavailable commercially until 1996, when they were briefly available, digitally remastered, on a Decca video cassette.

CHAPTER 62
An urge to educate
pp. 562–574

1 Haeusserman, 270.
2 Conversation, Gundula Janowitz.
3 Address to the press at the launch of the Herbert von Karajan Stiftung, Berlin, 1 October 1968.
4 *Der Tag*, 18 May 1958.
5 Paper by Professor David Epstein. See *Wo Sprache aufhört*, ed. Heinz Götze and Walther Simon (Berlin, 1988), 4–5.
6 Herbert von Karajan, 'How do people listen to music?' Panel discussion at the Berlin College of Music. January 1972, Lang, 70–1.
7 Address to the press at the launch of the Herbert von Karajan Stiftung, Berlin, 1 October 1968. Karajan's electrocardiogram was shown on screen during a Salzburg seminar on the subject. It did not, one professional observed, inspire confidence. Though Karajan lived to the age of eighty-one, it may have been in spite of, rather than because of, the state of his heart.
8 The Trust's first scholar in 1982, the Hungarian Dr T. F. Freund, was subsequently awarded the Explorer Prize of the Cajal Club, Chicago (1991), and the Demuth Prize of the Swiss Medical Research Foundation (1992).
9 Since Wunderlich had recorded all his arias in *The Creation*, it was left to Werner Krenn to record the recitatives. But the enforced delay had caused Karajan to re-think aspects of the casting of the oratorio. Rather than have Walter Berry sing both Raphael and Adam, he invited Dietrich Fischer-Dieskau to sing Adam. In his memoirs, Fischer-Dieskau recalls the pleasure of experiencing 'this splendid work in the maestro's spacious, grandly arranged interpretation' (Dietrich Fischer-Dieskau, op. cit., 177). *The Creation* has always sat well within the mainstream of nineteenth- and twentieth-century performance practice. None but the most determined authenticists would readily turn their back on celebrated recordings by Clemens Krauss, Eugen Jochum, Münchinger and Karajan. Karajan himself was very pleased with the recording. At a dinner party in St Tropez in the late 1960s, a young lad by the name of Didier de Cottignies found himself sitting next to him. Karajan, a friend of the boy's uncle, told him all about the recording and promised to send him a copy when it was released. This he later did.

10 Memorandum, Peter Andry to David Bicknell, 13 March 1969, EMI. The memorandum suggests that Glotz was in 'severe trouble with Karajan' for not having consulted with him over the Orchestre de Paris appointment and that 'Karajan is considering not renewing Glotz's contract with him which runs out in July'. This was wishful thinking by EMI. The memorandum also suggests that Glotz was hoping that Georges Prêtre would get the job. In fact, Glotz assumed that Munch's deputy, Serge Baudo, would get it.
11 Conversation, Michel Glotz.
12 James Galway, op. cit., 42–6.
13 *Opera*, May 1969, 396.
14 Ibid.
15 During the interval, the conductor David Atherton found Bing wandering around clutching a copy of the London *Evening Standard*, apparently oblivious of the fact that details of his private life were spread all over the front page. Bing said he wanted to see Karajan, so, taking his courage in both hands, Atherton lead him off to the conductor's dressing-room, where the two men fell into one another's arms.
16 *Testimony: The Memoirs of Shostakovich*, as related to and edited by Solomon Volkov (London, 1979), 144.
17 Ibid., 148–9.
18 It was for this reason, too, that no one ever managed to fix an exchange between the Berlin Philharmonic and the Leningrad Philharmonic or between Karajan and Mravinsky, in spite of the fact that each held

the other in the highest possible esteem.

19 Karajan required an advance of £10,000 and a royalty of six per cent, the three soloists would receive three per cent each, the orchestra two per cent.

20 The autumn recording schedule was even more packed. In Paris, Karajan conducted a sumptuous account of Franck's Symphony in D minor with the Orchestre de Paris. In Berlin, Honegger's Third Symphony, *Liturgique* was finally made, one of the greatest of all Karajan's records. Lothar Koch was invited to record the Strauss Oboe Concerto, and in one of those juxtapositions that was only possible in Karajan's Berlin *Götterdämmerung* was taped alongside a coruscating disc of overtures by Franz von Suppé.

21 At the first competition in 1970 the Moscow Tchaikovsky Conservatoire String Players took first prize. As a grand finale to the event, Karajan rehearsed and conducted Brahms's Second Symphony with an *ad hoc* orchestra whose members had been drawn from among all the competing groups. The horns blooped a good deal but those who attended the final concert were amazed to hear a recognisably German Brahms sound emerging from the polyglot assembly.

22 Lang, 63.

23 Hans Hirsch, as rational and circumspect an observer as one could wish to meet, told me he would not have credited the change had he not heard it with his own ears.

24 The conducting competition survived until the early 1980s, when soaring costs and the breakdown first of Ahlendorf's health and then Karajan's put the whole thing in jeopardy. Major reforms were put in place for the 1986 competition, but by now Karajan had neither the will nor the energy to sustain it further.

CHAPTER 63
Mr Andry plays his ace
pp. 575–590

1 Memorandum, Peter Andry to L. G. Wood, 7 January 1970, EMI.

2 In 1971, when an idea was being floated for Karajan to appear with Horowitz at Carnegie Hall, Karajan nominated (1) Cleveland (2) Chicago (3) Boston as the possible orchestras. Nothing came of the plan (though Horowitz talked about the possibility of recording with Karajan as late as 1987).

3 Cost per LP, according to EMI's estimates at the time were: Berlin PO £5265, Orchestre de Paris £4500, Vienna PO £4400, LSO and New Philharmonia £3500, Hallé £2800.

4 Memorandum, Peter Andry to L. G. Wood, 29 June 1978, EMI.

5 *Opera*, June 1970, 516.

6 Played in sequence on four successive evenings, Karajan's Deutsche Grammophon recording of *The Ring* has the architectural integrity of the Parthenon.

7 *Verdi's Otello and Simon Boccanegra in letters and documents*, edited and translated by Hans Busch, Vol. II (Oxford, 1988), 626.

8 Conversation, Jon Vickers. 'Black magic!' said Bernard Haitink on hearing the story, echoing the phrase Carlos Kleiber had used to describe to him Karajan's art.

9 'The sables-and-diamonds sound of Karajan's Salzburg "Cinemascope Spectacular" is undeniably seductive, but in this stately, under-articulated tone poem it is not easy to hear much of Mussorgsky's drama; an exception is the Kromy Forest scene, where all the rehearsal time and technical expertise really does pay off.' David Hamilton, 'Boris Godunov', *Opera on Record*, ed. Alan Blyth (London, 1979), 514.

10 *Fidelio* was being performed at the 1971 Salzburg Easter Festival. Deutsche Grammophon's own recent recording with Böhm precluded a remake with Karajan.

11 *The Gramophone*, September 1971, 453.

12 Ibid.

13 English-language transcript Spanish newspaper interview, 1972, EMI.

14 *The Letters of Mozart and his Family*, edited by Emily Anderson, revised by Stanley Sadie and Fiona Smart (London, 1985), 724.

15 Charles Rosen, *The Classical Style* (London, 1971), 143. On the subject of Karajan's Mozart, Charles Rosen once remarked to me, 'What I have heard of it was either very fast or very smooth which doesn't seem to me to constitute a style.'

16 Conversation, Michel Glotz.

17 EMI, SLS 809 Disc 4.

18 Maynard Solomon, *Mozart: A Life* (London, 1995), 363.

19 Conversation, Pali Meller Marcovicz. I once asked Brendel if he enjoyed his occasional excursions into writing about music. He replied, 'I think it is important now and then in one's life to try to do the impossible.'

20 Solomon, op. cit., 363, 365, 378.

21 Nicholas Spice, 'Music Lessons', *London Review of Books*, 14 December 1995, 3–6.

22 Paul Moor, 'Mozart + Karajan', annotated typescript, EMI.

23 Ibid.

24 Session report, Ronald Kinloch Anderson to Peter Andry, 10 December 1970, EMI. Some mistakes were noticed by reviewers. Andrew Porter, writing in *The Gramophone*, cited two: Donath's straightening out of the syncopated '*ohne dich*' in 'O Sachs, mein Freund', and Adam making a less than direct ascent on the words '*Und was mein Spruch*' in 'Euch macht inr's leicht'.

25 Ibid.

26 Jeannie Williams, draft typescript of interview with Helen Donath for Seattle Opera, 1989.

27 Session report, Ronald Kinloch Anderson to Peter Andry, 10 December 1970.

28 Adam's relations with Karajan were always somewhat distant. In Adam's autobiography *Ein Sängerleben in Begegnungen und Verwandlungen* (Berlin, 1996), the chapter on Karajan (130–5) is decidedly cool in tone. Adams ends by wondering how it is possible to conduct an entire Bruckner Symphony with one's eyes closed. Was it hypnosis or self-dramatisation, he asks?

29 Session report, Ronald Kinloch Anderson to Peter Andry, 10 December 1970.

30 *The Gramophone*, January 1972, 1182.

31 LP booklet note, HMV SLS957.

32 Ibid.

33 In the years that followed, Karajan invited the Staatskapelle to visit Salzburg as often as the East German authorities would allow. In 1972 he conducted them in a concert of music by Bartók and Schumann (Bartók's Third Piano Concerto, with Géza Anda as soloist, played with an altogether astonishing beauty and intensity of purpose). In 1976, Gilels was the soloist in Beethoven's Third Piano Concerto after which, in a piece of programming that was clearly emblematic, Karajan led the Dresden players in a performance of Shostakovich's Tenth Symphony.

There were to be no more studio recordings. EMI had plans to record the four Brahms symphonies with Karajan in Dresden, just as they existed, on paper at least, for Karajan to record the late Tchaikovsky symphonies in Leningrad. Gilels also repeatedly pressed to be allowed to record with Karajan, but here there were stumbling blocks on both sides. Problems on the Soviet and the East German side were compounded by the fact that Karajan was in dispute with the Soviet bloc over its pirating of Western recordings.

34 *Financial Times*, 30 March 1972.

35 Ibid.

36 Conversation, Michel Glotz.

37 Conversation, Michel Glotz.

38 Conversation, Jon Vickers. Knowing when *not* to rehearse is a gift. Vickers remembers being in Salzburg in the summer of 1962 when Franco

Corelli was working himself into a lather over the Manrico he was due to sing in Karajan's new production of *Il trovatore*. Since what was really frightening Corelli was 'Di quella pira', Karajan avoided it entirely in rehearsal. Vickers recalled: 'On the first night it was fantastic. Afterwards, Karajan just stood in the pit smiling and applauding. How many other conductors would have dared take that kind of risk?'

39 Some time later, when Erich Leinsdorf was conducting for Vickers, he was amazed that Vickers did not ask for guidance through this particular minefield; and Lorin Maazel has recalled Karajan slipping into a performance Maazel was conducting in Bayreuth just before the passage in 5/4 for the tenor.

40 English-language transcript Spanish newspaper interview, 1972, EMI.

41 Robin Holloway, 'Tristan und Isolde', *Opera on Record*, ed. Alan Blyth (London, 1979), 370. According to Vickers, both Bayreuth and the West German Government invited Karajan to take his production of *Tristan und Isolde* to Bayreuth in 1976 as part of Bayreuth's centenary celebrations. He declined the offer.

CHAPTER 64
Brave new worlds
pp. 591–600

1 These included Video Tape (the domestic version of the professional Ampex videotape machines using high-quality chromium dioxide tape), RCA's Selectavision, the high-tech Electric Video Recording, and a form of short-play, play-only Video Disc.

2 During protracted discussions in the late 1960s, Culshaw had constantly criticised Karajan for his willingness to tolerate the play-back system of film-making. He had further muddied the waters in the autumn of 1969 when, bowing to pressure from within the BBC, he used the occasion of a television interview with Karajan to resurrect the question, 'What exactly *did* you do during the war?'

3 *The Gramophone*, September 1970, 400.

4 Ibid.

5 The documentary was based on Norman Lebrecht's book *The Maestro Myth*. Objections concerning the use to which the film of the *Eroica* Symphony had been put by the BBC were lodged by the copyright holders Unitel, who subsequently withdrew permission for any of its Karajan footage to be used by the BBC. See also p. 824.

6 Symphonies nos.1, 2, 4, 5, and 8. The Ninth Symphony had been filmed in 1968 but was never released. The version of the Ninth that is in the Unitel catalogue was made in 1977, a fine performance, directed by Humphrey Burton with great cogency and flair.

7 When Russell staged *La bohème*, he set it in four different periods. After a first act set in the 1830s and a second act set *c*.1914, the third act brought us to Paris in 1944. The Barrière d'Enfer is a Nazi whorehouse and Marcello is daubing images of Hitler and Eva Braun on his walls. When he directed *Madama Butterfly*, the opera underwent a similar progressive updating, the final scene revealing the neon signs of the commercially powerful post-war Japan flashing through the nuclear haze.

8 Memorandum, 3 February 1972, EMI.

9 The 1974 Decca sound recording, conducted by Karajan, with Luciano Pavarotti as Pinkerton, was a separate production. Within months of making the recording, Karajan and the engineers returned to Vienna to tape the film soundtrack, this time with Domingo as Pinkerton. Being able to switch from Pavarotti, the Pinkerton *par excellence* on record, to Domingo, the Pinkerton *par excellence* on film, was an earnest of the depth of talent available at the time.

10 Jürgen Ponto would later fall victim to urban terrorism. He was assassinated at his home near Frankfurt on 31 July 1977. The anarchist daughter of friends of the Ponto family planned the attack.

There is an extremely strange passage in Werner Thärichen's *Paukenschläge: Furtwängler oder Karajan* in which he talks of the relationship between Karajan and the Berlin Philharmonic in terms of Ponto and his assassins. Thärichen, 172.

11 Lang, 79–80.

12 No Karajan record surpasses this for sultry beauty. As well as *La valse*, the collection included *Rapsodie espagnole*, *Alborado del gracioso*, and *Le tombeau de Couperin*.

13 The Schumann cycle includes a freshly incisive account of the *Spring* Symphony, an at times searingly beautiful performance of the neglected Second Symphony, and a stylish account of the even more neglected *Overture, Scherzo, and Finale*. The Mendelssohn cycle was similarly fresh-voiced, Karajan's intuitions working to particularly good effect in a fine recording of the *Scottish* Symphony, where the infamous peroration, robbed here of all pomposity, sails confidently home, banners streaming in the breeze.

14 The recording of *Also sprach Zarathustra* from this period is especially fine, though it would be superseded by the 1983 sound recording and Télémondial's film of a live concert in 1987.

15 In an article in *The Times* on 27 December 1963, the paper's Music Critic William Mann linked Mahler with the Beatles by drawing attention to the fact the Aeolian cadence at the end of 'Not a Second Time' was identical to that of the chord progression that ends *Das Lied von der Erde*.

16 See Norman Lebrecht, 'Mahler and his origins', *Mahler Remembered* (London, 1987), xvii–xxiii.

17 According to Peter Alward, the symphony Karajan eventually declared to be 'too Jewish' to attempt was the First. A number of commentators have remarked on the debt the symphony's 'Funeral March' owes to Jewish folk music. (Bernard

Haitink once remarked that the movement had reminded him, quite involuntarily, of the death camps of Nazi Germany.)

18 Conversations, 120.

19 Extract from text of Deutsche Grammophon advertisement, February 1975. See *The Gramophone*, February 1975, 1545.

20 *The Gramophone*, March 1975, 1647.

21 Deutsche Grammophon advertisement, February 1975.

22 It is widely acknowledged that the recording could not have been the success it was without the skills lavished on it both by Karajan and by his producer Hans Weber, whom Karajan injudiciously dropped from his recording team shortly afterwards.

23 The soloist was Jean-Bernard Pommier, who played a good deal for Karajan at around this time. The previous January in Berlin, Schoenberg's *Pelleas und Melisande* had been prefaced by Bartók's Third Piano Concerto, with Pommier as soloist. For the Berlin Festival, Karajan might have been better advised to play the programme he had devised for one of the Berlin Philharmonic's 1974 Lucerne Festival concerts: Schoenberg's *Pelleas und Melisande* and Debussy's *La mer*.

24 For the recording and the subsequent stage performances the quartet of violas was led by Sigiswald Kuijken.

CHAPTER 65
A question of image
pp. 601–605

1 Christian Steiner, *Opera People* (London, 1982), 87–89.

2 Conversation, Pali Meller Marcovicz.

3 Barrie Hall, *The Proms and the men who made them* (London, 1981), 127.

4 'Bloody wrong!' exclaimed Esa-Pekka Salonen (whose own record sleeves have never been entirely beyond reproach in this respect) discussing the marketing of Karajan (BBC TV *Omnibus*, 23 November 1993).

5 Designed by one of post-war Germany's great design gurus Hans

Domizlaff. Domizlaff had created the famously elegant LP covers of the 1950s: a vertical yellow stripe with two thinner white stripes either side of it. The yellow and white motif was inspired by his admiration for the Vatican, which he once described as 'the greatest PR triumph of all time'. (Adding for good measure that there were only two great logos in existence, the Mercedes emblem and the Cross.) When Deutsche Grammophon was finally obliged to abandon the plain sleeve, an attempt was made to retain the yellow stripe in the form of a thick horizontal band at the head of the sleeve. Domizlaff disliked this intensely and set about looking for an alternative, which he found in the form of the now famous cartouche, a strangely old-fashioned device that would have been laughed out of court had it not been proposed by the great man himself.

6 In Berlin Philharmonic concert programmes, the orchestra's name was always printed before Karajan's and in an equivalent or larger type size.

7 The most famous late photographic portraits of Karajan were by Snowdon (a portrait Karajan loathed) and the celebrated photograph of him by Gabriela Brandenstein which was first used on the cover of Mahler's Ninth Symphony and, later, on that of the anthology *Adagio*. The Brandenstein portrait is the subject of what appears to be an amusing parody on the cover of a Deutsche Grammophon Chabrier collection in which the conductor John Eliot Gardiner is similarly photographed.

8 Conversation, Pali Meller Marcovicz.

CHAPTER 66
Disc trouble
pp. 606–609

1 Charles Osborne, *The World Theatre of Wagner: a celebration of 150 years of Wagner productions* (London, 1982), 109.

2 *Opera*, June 1974, 492–5.

3 Edward Heath, *Music: A Joy for Life* (London, 1976), 117.

4 Heath's yacht had won the Sydney

to Hobart Race in 1969. Heath had also captained the British Admiral's Cup Team in 1971 during his time as Prime Minister.

5 *New York Times*, 11 November 1974.

6 *New York Times*, 12 November 1974.

7 There was a further advantage to using the Philharmonie for recording. Since it was owned and administered by the city of West Berlin, the city stood to gain financially. It was Karajan who made the connection between this and the long-standing dispute between the orchestra and the Senate over the profits the Berliner Philharmoniker (the self-governing recording orchestra) was making on the back of the state-subsidised Berliner Philharmonisches Orchester. An initial target payment of DM100,000 recompense was agreed: money from recording sessions in the Philharmonie that would go directly to the Senate.

8 Recordings included Bruckner's Ninth Symphony and *Te Deum*, Liszt's *Tasso*, Mozart's *Coronation Mass* and *Requiem*, Tchaikovsky's Fifth Symphony, and a collection of overtures and preludes by Verdi in which the Berlin Philharmonic is made by Karajan to sound uncannily like the Orchestra of La Scala, Milan.

9 Conversation, Herbert von Karajan.

CHAPTER 67
Easter 1976
pp. 613–617

1 Interview, *Welt am Sonntag*, 16 October 1977.

2 Conversations, 143.

3 Csobádi, 119.

4 'Music had been for him a means of advance; it was only later, when he began to suffer, that he underwent a sublime transfiguration.' Conversation, Lord Menuhin.

5 Since it had not been possible at short notice to get Abbado, Barenboim, Giulini, or Mehta, Stresemann had engaged Menuhin and Gerd Albrecht.

6 Conversation, David Bell.

7 The recording was with Oistrakh pupil, Gidon Kremer. He had played the concerto with Karajan

on the occasion of Karajan's return to conducting on 7 March. But this recording proved to be almost as problematic as the *Lohengrin*. Though Karajan had flown to London the previous autumn specially to hear Kremer, they had done little real work together.

8 *Opera*, July 1976, 626–9.

9 Charles Osborne, op. cit., 71.

10 Ridderbusch is said to have owned a chair from Hitler's bunker and to have had a swastika emblazoned on the bottom of his private swimming pool.

11 Böhm looked the part and sang confidently. Some critics predicted a major international career for him. It was not to be, though his Herod on Karajan's 1977 recording of *Salome* is very fine. Bridges would eventually be partly rebuilt between Karajan and Kollo.

12 *Salzburger Volksblatt*, 15 April 1976.

13 *Sunday Telegraph*, 25 April 1976.

14 Carreras, op. cit., 125–6.

CHAPTER 68
Close encounters
pp. 618–624

1 Thärichen, 73.

2 A slightly garbled argument. Weingartner wrote his book in 1906 when there were no recordings. But one sees Karajan's point.

3 Uli Märkle was born in Tübingen and studied law in Stuttgart. Interested in music, he undertook work for the Goethe Institute in places as far afield as Africa and pre-war Vietnam, before joining Deutsche Grammophon.

4 Given what Karajan had put Legge through while sledging in St Anton, the fantasy, like all good comic fantasies, was not entirely beyond the bounds of belief.

5 Interview for Karajan's 70th birthday published in *The Gramophone*, April 1978, 1681–8.

6 Anne-Sophie Mutter, interview with Canadian Broadcasting Corporation, 1989.

7 *Encounter*, May 1988, 71–5.

8 *The Times*, 3 February 1993.

CHAPTER 69
The man with the golden jug
pp. 625–635

1 The 1962 production of *Il trovatore* had recently been revived and revised by Karajan for the 1977 Salzburg Easter Festival. *Le nozze di Figaro* was seen in Jean-Pierre Ponnelle's 1972 Salzburg staging. *La bohème* was a revival of the 1963 Zeffirelli production.

2 *Opera*, July 1977, 646–9.

3 My translation. The original reads: '*Es scheisst der Herr von Karajan/bei jedem falschen Ton sich an/und wascht sein Arsch in Goldlawur/anal sein g'hört zur Hochkultur.*'

4 With Anna Tomowa-Sintow, Agnes Baltsa, René Kollo, José van Dam, and the Chorus of the Deutsche Oper, Berlin. A Unitel film issued on video cassette by Deutsche Grammophon.

5 For Bernstein's 1979 Berlin Philharmonic Mahler Nine – arranged by the orchestra, provocatively, to take place at more or less the same time as the Karajan Beethoven Ninth – Burton had just one day to prepare the lights and cameras.

6 Conversation, Humphrey Burton.

7 Memorandum, 19 December 1977, EMI.

8 Bonisolli had been a late replacement for Giacomo Aragall at the 1977 Easter Festival but in September 1977 Karajan accepted him for the EMI recording of *Il trovatore* in Berlin. It is an uneven set, musically and technically. (Karajan lent a test cassette to Walter Legge, who returned it, the air blue with some of his choicest expletives.) Karajan's conducting has a fierce beauty, typical of much of his work at this time. But Cappuccilli is a disappointing di Luna, and Price's voice lacks sap. It is the elemental power of Bonisolli's singing and the animal cunning of the Azucena, Elena Obraztsova, Karajan's great new discovery of this period, that best complements his own direction.

9 Domingo was singing *Manon Lescaut* in Madrid when he received

Karajan's SOS. Feeling himself to be in poor shape vocally after illness and a gruelling run of performance of *Otello* with Carlos Kleiber in Munich, he answered Karajan's plea with some reluctance.

10 Austrian Television had objected, among other things, to Karajan's insistence on using his own technical team and camera crews.

11 *Frankfurter Allgemeine Zeitung*, 23 April 1980.

12 Matheopoulos, op. cit., 48.

13 Haeusserman, 29.

14 *New Statesman*, 12 January 1979.

15 This worked in the theatre but severely tested even Decca's formidable resources. (In order to gain access to the Sofiensaal, EMI had agreed that Decca should do the engineering.) This, in turn, caused ructions back in London where transfer engineer Anthony Griffith's decision to remaster the Vienna tapes caused him to be given early retirement. None of Karajan's recordings at this time was plain sailing technically (something that cannot have been helped by his listening to the edited tapes on cassette). Yet, however the *Salome* was recorded or remixed, it is sumptuous and clear, the voices reaching us, as in the theatre, *through* the orchestra.

16 Matheopoulos, op. cit., 240.

17 Conversation, Frederica von Stade.

18 R. Moberly and C. Raeburn, 'Mozart's *Figaro*: the Plan of Act III', *Music and Letters*, xlvi (1965), 134–6.

19 Conversation, Christopher Raeburn.

20 Robert Tear, *Singer Beware* (London, 1995), 45–6.

21 The Brahms symphonies were re-recorded to no particular effect, though of all Karajan's recordings of the Fourth Symphony, this 1977 version is the most tragically intense. With the 150th anniversary of Schubert's death imminent, EMI pestered Karajan into recording all eight Schubert symphonies, six of which he had never previously conducted. The Fourth Symphony is

merely guessed at, but the first three symphonies go surprisingly well and the Sixth is finely done, a reading closely modelled on Beecham's. One cycle, however, was entirely desirable: the recording of the nine Bruckner symphonies, a project the Bruckner Gesellschaft had proposed Karajan undertake as long ago as 1948. The matchlessly splendid reading of the Fifth Symphony recorded in December 1976 is on another plane of excellence from the performances Karajan was giving with the Vienna Symphony in the early 1950s.

22 Stresemann, 233. Karajan referred to the passage (which Stresemann does not specify) as 'Kapellmeistermusik'. Stresemann tried to dissuade him from making the cut. He later learned that Karajan had not made it. He had, however, refused to rehearse the passage!

23 There is really no comparison to be made between this (Unitel/DG) and Karajan's 1985 (Télémondial/Sony) film of Bruckner's Ninth Symphony. Where the Berlin playing in 1985 is cool to the point of complete detachment, the 1978 Vienna performance is both memorable and moving. The 1978 account of *Te Deum* is also glorious, the excellent solo quartet finely led by tenor David Rendall. A live 1976 Salzburg Festival recording of the Ninth Symphony, again with Karajan conducting the Vienna Philharmonic, was released by Deutsche Grammophon in 1992 as part of the 150th anniversary celebrations of the founding of the orchestra. This, too, is very fine.

24 A prime mover behind the proposal was David Smith, at that time a Student (Fellow) of Christ Church and University Lecturer in Pharmacology. Smith and his wife Ingegerd, a qualified doctor, were regular visitors to the Easter Festival. The nomination had gone forward in the name of Sir John Burnett, Professor of Rural Economy, and had been unopposed.

25 Encaenia, 'Addresses', 21 June 1978, University of Oxford.

26 By the time of Girth's death in 1997 at the age of fifty-five, many of these ambitions had been realised. He remained with the Berlin Philharmonic until 1984 and was Intendant of the Düsseldorf Symphony Orchestra 1985–90. In 1988 he organised a reconstruction of the 1938 Düsseldorf *Entartete Musik* Exhibition which later toured widely. He was Intendant of the Darmstadt Opera 1991–6. He worked as a television presenter, wrote a number of librettos, including that for Wilfried Maria Danner's opera *Venetian Roulette*, and, shortly before his death, completed a play about Karajan entitled *Maestro*.

27 Conversation, Peter Girth.

28 Karajan returned to work in Berlin on 9–10 December 1978 with Stravinsky's *Apollo* and Strauss's *Also sprach Zarathustra*.

CHAPTER 70
Phoenix
pp. 636–642

1 Conversations, Peter Alward, Peter Andry.

2 Conversation, Frederica von Stade. In his chapter on *Pelléas et Mélisande* in *Opera on Record*, Felix Aprahamian describes the recording as the culminating point of Karajan's long-standing love affair with French music, though, ironically, his sole reservation about the conducting was that the divisi violas and cellos and held horn-note at 'On a brisé la glace avec des fers rougis' are too little audible beneath the violin harmonics. *Opera on Record* (London, 1979), 630–1.

3 Conversation, Frederica von Stade.

4 Edward Lockspeiser, *Debussy* (London, 1963/R1980), 225

5 Conversation, Eliette von Karajan.

6 In 1977, Karajan tried to persuade the English baritone Thomas Allen that he was a born Golaud. Allen, who was about to sing the role of Pelléas at Covent Garden, has recounted the exchange in his memoirs. Thomas Allen, *Foreign Parts: A Singer's Journal* (London, 1993), 10.

7 *Opera*, Festival Issue, 1993, 12.

8 Conversation, Günther Breest.

9 The widely held view was that, though the Karajan recording did not surpass the famous 1941 Desormière recording, it richly complemented it. The most hostile French review was Alfred Beaujean's in *HiFi Stereophonie* (1980 No.5, 604). Like a number of writers and listeners, he preferred Boulez's approach to the score. But Beaujean did not stop there. He went on to argue: 'If we compare Karajan's interpretation with Debussy's notes in the score, it is actually time to forbid this maestro to organise conducting competitions.'

10 Karajan had already re-recorded the last three symphonies in 1975–6, fine performances, even by his standards, the account of the Fourth Symphony even more electrifying than his 1953 Philharmonia version.

11 *Der Spiegel*, 12 June 1979.

12 Born in Merseburg in 1926 and educated in Leipzig, Tennstedt had spent his early years as a violinist and conductor in East Germany where he had worked alongside two of Karajan's own former acquaintants, Felsenstein and Wagner-Régeny. He made his conducting début, in Hallé in 1952, with Wagner-Régeny's *Der Günstling*. In 1971 he defected to the West and began the slow process of rebuilding his career.

13 Between 1979 and 1983 Tennstedt recorded five LPs with the Berlin Philharmonic. However, West Germany and Austria would not be happy hunting-grounds for him. The critics had not discovered him and appear to have seen this as a sufficient reason not to take him seriously. He eventually found refuge in London, where audiences and critics took him for what he was: one of the most inspiring conductors of the age.

14 In his biography of Schwarzkopf, Alan Jefferson notes that Karajan

'uncharacteristically [*sic*] burst into tears'. In fact, Karajan often wept. Jefferson cites as his source, not Schwarzkopf herself, but a passage in Norman Lebrecht's *The Maestro Myth*: 'He wept copiously on the phone to Schwarzkopf on learning of Legge's death, *having done nothing to keep him alive* [my italics].'

15 For example, Legge had been with Karajan, helping and advising, when he auditioned Thomas Allen in 1977. See note 6, above.

16 Unitel-Deutsche Grammophon. Karajan's legendary readings of these three works are best heard (for preference, in his 1964 Berlin recordings) rather than seen. The collection is primarily interesting for the insights it offers into Karajan's conducting technique. 'Jeu de vagues' and, above all, 'Pantomime' from *Daphnis et Chloé* are especially fascinating in this respect.

17 This has considerable documentary interest, Karajan revisiting the Bruckner church, where he had conducted the Eighth Symphony in 1944. The 1988 Télémondial film of the symphony, also with the Vienna Philharmonic, is more memorable musically and more expertly filmed; but no performance of Bruckner's Eighth conducted by Karajan is easily ignored.

18 *Gramophone*, April 1978, 1688.

19 *Opera*, Festival Issue, 1979, 50–3.

20 'A Salzburg Diary', compiled and presented by Robert Chesterman, Canadian Broadcasting Corporation, 1979, Archive Number DO 10 949 / 1–2.

21 '. . . this nice *Bohème* cast stays afloat longer than we'd thought when we cut the boat loose.' Conrad L. Osborne, *The Metropolitan Guide to Recorded Opera*, ed. Gruber, (London, 1993), 651.

22 'A Salzburg Diary', compiled and presented by Robert Chesterman, Canadian Broadcasting Corporation, 1979, Archive Number DO 10 949 / 1–2.

23 Conversation, Suvi Raj Grubb. Eliette and one of the daughters

were also in the audience. There is clearly more to this story than meets the eye. When I mentioned the saga to Perlman, during the course of a telephone conversation about an unrelated matter, he said, 'Oh, that!' and changed the subject.

24 This version of events is confidently recounted by Berlin journalist Klaus Lang in *The Karajan Dossier*, 141.

25 The Berlin authorities even said they might buy the organ. What no one had reckoned with was that the Congress Centre would be an acoustic disaster, fit only for pop concerts.

26 One treatment he observed was a form of foot massage, something he himself later adopted.

27 As Karajan flew back to Europe, he felt reasonably confident that permission would be given to film *Turandot* in the Forbidden City. Eighteen months later a sound-recording was made in Vienna. They were nightmarish sessions, riven by personal and musical tensions. For although the performance was a revelation orchestrally and there were some superb performances from Karajan's chosen cast (Domingo as Calaf, Raimondi's Timur, Hendricks's Liù), Katia Ricciarelli ran into serious difficulty with the title role. Since she had clearly been cast with the film in mind, all might have been well in the end had the Chinese authorities not backed out.

CHAPTER 71
Carpe diem
pp. 643–649

1 'Digital [CD] is still a long way off.' Memorandum, Richard Bradburn, 22 August 1980, EMI. There was an element of truth in this. When Morita and Karajan demonstrated the Compact Disc and its player in April 1981, they were using mock-ups; the real equipment was not ready in time. It would be a further two years before CD was officially launched on the world market.

2 Conversation, Günther Breest.

3 *New Statesman*, 21 November 1980.
4 *The Times*, 25 October 1980.
Mann had recently published his
magisterial *The Operas of Mozart*
(London, 1977). Though a great
admirer of Karajan's 1950 Vienna
recording of *Die Zauberflöte*, he
thought the Deutsche Grammophon
set the best of the newer recordings.
5 Conversation, Jeffrey Tate.
6 Karajan's re-recording (1979) of
Beethoven's Triple Concerto with
a trio of young instrumentalists –
Mark Zelster, Anne-Sophie Mutter
and YoYo Ma – has similar strengths
and weaknesses.
7 Karajan recorded Haydn's six *Paris*
symphonies in September 1980 and
the twelve *London* symphonies in
January and February 1982. Despite
a ringing endorsement for the first
set from leading Haydn scholar H.
C. Robbins Landon in the 1982
Haydn Yearbook – 'We believe
this set of the *Paris* symphonies to
be the finest recordings ever made
of these works' – the records sold
poorly, making this one of the few
Karajan/Deutsche Grammophon
projects to be continuously in deficit.
8 Mention was made of Vaughan
Williams's emotionally disruptive
Fourth Symphony and his war-torn
Sixth. It was around this time that
Karajan asked for a number of Elgar
scores. (The request was to EMI's
Peter Alward. Deutsche Grammophon
would not have been interested; nor,
sadly, was the Berlin Philharmonic.)
The scores were all returned, except,
significantly enough, that of the
Second Symphony, which Karajan
found to be of absorbing interest. The
work has its emotional peak in the
first movement, after which all is a
slow dying towards the dark: music
which audiences in 1911 neither
comprehended nor wished to hear.
9 The recording of Bruckner's Sixth
Symphony, made in the autumn of
1979, sounds as though parts of it
are being sight-read; by contrast,
symphonies nos. 1–3, recorded in
the winter of 1980–1, are played
with an electrifying intensity, albeit

in a somewhat disparate array of
performing editions.
10 Notably with Krystian Zimerman
over the Schumann and Grieg
concertos. Karajan did not win all
the battles. Against the odds, the
16-year-old Anne-Sophie Mutter
managed to talk him into conducting
a far more spacious performance
than he had originally envisaged
of the first two movements of
the Beethoven Violin Concerto, a
misjudgement on both their parts. In
the popular Bruch and Mendelssohn
concertos honours were about even.
By 1982, it was business again on
Karajan's terms. Having taught
Mutter to play the Brahms Violin
Concerto as though it was chamber
music, he threw down the gauntlet
by insisting that she record the
concerto in two complete takes in a
single three-hour session. The results
speak for themselves, intimate yet
intensely alive.
11 Robert Layton, 'Karajan's Sibelius',
Gramophone, October 1981, 523.
12 Ibid. Karajan's 1981 remake of
Shostakovich's Tenth Symphony
shows a similar preoccupation with
the composer's metronomes, with the
finale's main allegro now taken at
the uncomfortably quick crotchet =
176 indicated by the score.
13 Conversation, Robert Layton. When
Karajan's recording first appeared,
Layton ranked it second only to
the pioneering early 1950s HMV
recording by Launy Grøndahl and
the Danish State Radio Orchestra.
He later conceded, however, that
his enthusiasm for the performance
was not widely shared by Danish
listeners.
14 See Robert Simpson, *Carl Nielsen:
Symphonist* (London, 1952/R1979),
88–9.
15 Quoted by Thomas Walker in the
sleeve note to the Karajan recording.
16 Barry Millington, '*Parsifal*: a work
for our times', *Opera*, January
1988, 16.
17 Knud Martner (ed.), *Gustav Mahler,
Eindrücke und Erinnerungen aus
den Hamburger Jahren* (Hamburg,

1973), 58–9; Norman Lebrecht (ed.), *Mahler Remembered* (London, 1987), 92–4.

18 *Stereo*, No.5, 1980, 8.

19 Peter Branscombe, *Hi-Fi News*, April 1981.

20 *Financial Times*, 18 June 1981.

21 *Gramophone*, April 1981, 1367.

22 *Parsifal* was the 1982 *Gramophone* 'Record of the Year'. (It also won the opera category.) The recording of Mahler's Ninth Symphony was voted 'Orchestral Record of the Year' at the same time.

23 Karajan was fond of quoting the words of the physician Paracelsus, who died in Salzburg in 1541: 'Emperors and kings have not liked me, the powerful, those in authority have not liked me, the magistracy has not liked me – but my patients have liked me!'

CHAPTER 72
Pleasant diversions
pp. 650–657

1 Vaughan, 217.

2 Claudio Abbado conducted a concert consisting of Beethoven's Overture *The Creatures of Prometheus*, Beethoven's Fourth Piano Concerto (Maurizio Pollini), Schoenberg's *A Survivor from Warsaw* (Maximilian Schell), and Stravinsky's *The Firebird*.

3 Conversation, Joy Bryer.

4 The most expensive, I gather, was a conductor whom I remember telling me, 'There are two things in this world which are at the heart of all our problems: power and money.'

5 Lang, 153.

6 Ibid.

7 Ibid.

8 In a memorandum dated 20 June 1977, Charles Rodier, EMI's Director of Contracts and Business Affairs, suggested it might be prudent to take out insurance on the contracts of this 'superhuman but nonetheless mortal septuagenarian'.

9 *The Times*, 14 January 1981.

10 Conversation, Bryan Magee.

11 Vaughan, 256.

12 Ibid., 189.

13 *Daily Telegraph*, 1 August 1981.

14 *The Times*, 1 August 1981.

15 In fact, the film does the production no favours. The rather bland camerawork serves only to underline the essential blankness of Karajan's stage production, and the recording is poor. The prompter is occasionally audible and the orchestral sound is backward and slightly fogged. Oddly for Karajan, the cast was made up mainly of tried and tested oldies: Taddei, a less than aristocratic Falstaff, Rolando Panerai who had been Karajan's Ford back in 1956, Raina Kabaivanska as Alice, and Christa Ludwig as Mistress Quickly.

16 The photographs were later published in Dieter Blum and Emanuel Eckardt, *Das Orchester: Herbert von Karajan und die Berliner Philharmoniker* (Dortmund, 1988).

17 Lang, 178.

CHAPTER 73
1982: Anniversary
pp. 658–664

1 In 1973, Karajan had altered the Easter Festival programme to re-admit *Das Rheingold*. Believing he had a deal with Unitel to film the entire *Ring*, he needed to revive the cycle to start laying down soundtracks. But five years would elapse before the film of *Das Rheingold* would be shot, years in which an increasingly sceptical Leo Kirch would be urging his production managers to dream up ever more elaborate stratagems for delay. The film was completed in 1978 but closed in the commercial cinema after three days, a failure that helped accelerate the end of Karajan's long-standing relationship with Unitel. The only good review came posthumously. 'The best *Ring* opera on video,' wrote Michael Scott Rohan in *The Classical Video Guide* (London 1994), 139–40. This despite his being severely, and rightly, critical of the *mise-en-scène*: 'The mountain top and Nibelheim sets are stagebound, and less effort is put into even the most essential effects. Valhalla is a dim projection, looking more artificial

than it would on stage; the rainbow bridge is a colourless invisibility . . . the whole film is a museum of 1970s Wagner production style.'

2 Conversation, Ronald Wilford.

3 Vaughan, 57.

4 Ibid.

5 The sound of the anchor was simulated backstage by a box of rocks being emptied on to a wooden plank.

6 Van Dam's performance works less well on record. Memories of Hans Hotter's Dutchman or Hermann Uhde's are not erased.

7 To which one might counter, had Karajan ever heard a tenor who *could* cope with Wagner's writing here?

8 Télémondial, released on Laserdisc and video by Sony.

9 The *Eroica* had already been filmed, as Télémondial's inaugural production. It was not a particularly auspicious start. This was the film treatment very much as before; techniques not so much renewed as reapplied and set in stone.

10 Karajan also did his best to ignore a somewhat bilious article – 'Berlin Philharmonic: Notes from an Insider' – with which the magazine *HiFi-Stereophonie* had elected to mark the orchestra's centenary. The article appeared anonymously but other insiders did not need to wait for the publication five years later of Werner Thärichen's *Paukenschläge* to work out who the author was.

11 Conversation, Otto Strasser.

12 Conversations, 118.

CHAPTER 74
Pressing matters
pp. 665–669

1 This may have been better understood in the Far East. Karajan's interest in the culture of the East, and the appeal of his personality and music-making to Japanese audiences, was not – as is sometimes implied by European critics – simply a phenomenon of hi-tech consumerism.

2 It may be of little significance, but I am interested by the fact that – to the best of my knowledge – no one has ever set up a 'Karajan Society'.

3 See Ian Buruma's outstanding study, *The Wages of Guilt: memories of War in Germany and Japan* (London, 1994).

4 The issue of terminology is discussed by Professor Ian Kershaw in Chapter 5 of his book *The Nazi Dictatorship* (London, 1985/R1989), 82–3. He writes: 'The very name "the Holocaust", which acquired its specific application to the extermination of the Jews only in the late 1950s and early 1960s, when it came to be adopted (initially by Jewish writers) in preference to the accurately descriptive term "genocide", has been taken to imply an almost sacred uniqueness of terrible events exemplifying absolute evil, a specifically Jewish fate standing in effect outside the normal historical process . . .' He goes on: 'Given the highly emotive nature of the problem, non-Jewish historians face arguably even greater difficulties in attempting to find language sensitive and appropriate to the horror of Auschwitz. The sensitivity of the problem is such that over-heated reaction and counter-reaction easily spring from a misplaced or misunderstood word or sentence.'

5 The open-air Katschhof concert in Aachen in the summer of 1935, the appearances in Paris in 1941, the connection with SS-Hauptsturmführer Franz Schmidt over trainee conductors in Berlin in 1943.

6 See Appendix B.

7 Fred K. Prieberg, *Musik im NS-Staat* (Frankfurt, 1982), 19–22.

8 See Chapter 27.

9 Jim Svejda, 'The Karajan Case', 'The Record Shelf', KUSC, Los Angeles (Radio Station of the University of Southern California), National Broadcast, 11 November 1989.

10 A complaint that was often levelled against Karajan was that he had never 'apologised' for his Nazi past. (Or even '*the* Nazi past', the phrasing varied.) This was not strictly true. During the denazification hearings in 1946, he had admitted personal errors

of judgement. Yet the question continued to be put. One suspects the demands were more strategic – a way of embarrassing Karajan – than genuine. Apologising for Germany's past was a political minefield, as the President of the Lower House of the West German Parliament, Philipp Jenniger, discovered in November 1988 when he took it upon himself to deliver a speech on the fiftieth anniversary of *Kristallnacht*. His address, with its remarks about German Jews in the Weimar Republic needing to be taken down a peg or two, was a *locus classicus* of bluff tactlessness. Yet, even today, trying to subject the years 1933–45 to more normal processes of historical analysis is a risky business fraught with difficulty.

11 Culshaw, op. cit., 195; *The Times*, 2 November 1981.

12 *The Penguin Guide to Compact Discs* (London, 1996), 204.

13 London Green, 'Carmen', *The Metropolitan Opera Guide to Recorded Opera* (London, 1993), 58.

14 Karajan's 23-year-old daughter Isabel played Frasquita, very well.

15 *Gramophone*, October 1983, 526.

16 Conversation, Michel Glotz.

17 Matheopoulos, op. cit., 243.

18 Ibid.

19 D. H. Lawrence, *Etruscan Places* (London, 1932/R1972), 47.

CHAPTER 75
1982: Divisions in the kingdom
pp. 670–675

1 Conversation, Peter Girth. Girth was surprised how quickly Karajan assessed people: 'I remember a man coming on stage for an audition. Before he played a note Karajan muttered "Ein Friseur [a hairdresser]". I thought the judgement was somewhat premature. Then the man started playing in an incredibly sleazy way. Karajan had read him the moment he set eyes on him.'

2 The problems associated with living in West Berlin, its geographical isolation and its increasingly middle-aged population, meant that the Berlin Philharmonic often had fewer people auditioning for it than other leading West German orchestras.

3 Thärichen, op. cit., 111–13.

4 Herbert von Karajan, interview with Bernard Holland, *New York Times*, 22 October 1982.

5 *The New Yorker*, 8 November 1982; reprinted in Andrew Porter, *Musical Events: A Chronicle 1980–1983* (London, 1988), 337–9.

6 *New York Times*, 23 October 1982. An interesting analogy. Karajan had lately been showing an interest in Elgar, the Second Symphony. See above Chapter 71 n.8.

7 Porter, op. cit. 339.

8 Conversation, Michel Glotz. Hansjörg Schellenberger used the same phrase – 'a sense of the eternal' – about the 1981 Salzburg Easter Festival revival of *Parsifal* and the New York performances of Mahler Nine and the *Alpine* Symphony.

9 Conversation, Michel Glotz.

10 *New York Times*, 20 October 1982.

11 Conversation, Michel Glotz.

12 The film of the *Pastoral* Symphony is a particular success. The performance is urgent yet lyrical, never routine as Karajan's reading of this symphony could sometimes be. The film, atmospherically lit, uses rapid editing and cross-fading techniques, perfectly synchronised to the music's often short-breathed pulses in the quicker movements. Above all, the relationship between conductor and orchestra – between the conductor's gesture and the orchestra's sound – is most interestingly illustrated and explored.

13 Letter, Herbert von Karajan to Berlin Philharmonic, 3 December 1982; Vaughan 79–80.

14 Letter, Sir Thomas Beecham to Walter Legge, 30 January 1945, EMI.

15 Conversation, Lord Menuhin. Riccardo Chailly has recalled consulting Karajan about the difficulties he was having with the Vienna Philharmonic over a production of Rossini's *La*

Cenerentola at the 1988 Salzburg Festival. 'Grind them under your heel,' was Karajan's peremptory advice. His attitude to orchestras in his last years did seem to take on a somewhat atavistic character, as though the changes he had helped pioneer in the postwar years had never happened.

16 Conversation, Peter Girth.

CHAPTER 76
The Erlking
pp. 676–688

1 Lang, 195.

2 In 1982 the twelve cellists joined forces with other groups from within the orchestra to make a very enjoyable LP for Deutsche Grammophon. On side one, the cellists played a mainly pre-classical programme of pieces by Alessandro Scarlatti, Funck, Haydn, and Julius Klengel; on side two, eight horns played Rossini's *Rendez-vous de chasse*, the double-bass section gave an amusing account of Strauss's *The Blue Danube* arranged by their own Erich Hartmann, and timpanist Oswald Vogler came up with a witty transcription for piano, percussion, and double-bass of Khachaturian's 'Sabre Dance'.

3 *Aachener Nachrichten*, 20 April 1983.

4 The film-video version was not published.

5 Vaughan, 207.

6 Ibid.

7 Vaughan, 211–12.

8 Ibid., 217.

9 Conversation, Dame Elisabeth Legge-Schwarzkopf.

10 Conversation, Jeffrey Tate.

11 *Sunday Telegraph*, 22 September 1991.

12 Conversation, Peter Diamand.

13 Ingmar Bergman, *The Magic Lantern*, translated by Joan Tate (London, 1988), 244.

14 Bergman spares Olivier nothing: the inedible food served at a welcoming dinner, the boorish company of sottish actors, the shop-soiled elegance of Olivier's London flat, his housekeeper ('She was Irish, four feet tall, and moved crabwise'),

even his cancer. Bergman, op. cit., 237.

15 Karajan (b. 1908) and Olivier (b. 1907) died within days of one another in July 1989. This was the subject of an interesting editorial, 'Grand Finale', *Spectator*, 22 July 1989, 5. See Chapter 81, n.8.

16 Bergman, op. cit., 243.

17 Ibid., 242.

18 Ibid., 243.

19 Ibid.

20 In a cable on 2 April, 1987, Bergman said he had retired from the film and theatre business. He hadn't, but that was that.

21 Duncan Fallowell, 'The Sponge and the Monomaniac', *Spectator*, 17 May 1986, 32.

22 Settling Arabel into tertiary education had been a problem. Unlike Isabel, who was determined to act, Arabel had been at something of a loss since her childhood dream of becoming a singer had been dashed.

23 Vaughan, 198.

24 In a memoir of Karajan published in *Le Figaro* on 21 July 1989, Liebermann described Karajan as a 'black force': 'His musical genius was absolutely fabulous but the man himself was a detestable mixture of megalomania and egocentricity.' The article is riddled with false allegations (Mozart's most important operas were not, as Liebermann claims, 'supplanted by Italian operas' when Karajan took over the Salzburg Festival in 1957) and sustained by a partly fictionalised version of Karajan's Nazi past. Liebermann claims, for instance, that once Karajan had played the 'Jewish wife' card at the post-war denazification hearings in 1946, 'he left his wife immediately afterwards', which is not true. Liebermann strongly believed that Karajan's post-war successes helped 'romanticise' Nazism. What the article reveals is the dilemma facing those who, having chosen to turn Karajan into some kind of representative Nazi, were then required to live with his huge popular success.

25 Beethoven's symphonies nos 1–4, 7–8. Musically, the performances – which were prepared for immediate release on CD and for eventual release on film – have their merits, the Berlin playing stylish and fiery even when weighed down by a large string section and quadrupled winds. But Karajan's own direction often looks laboured. The conducting on the film of Tchaikovsky's Fifth Symphony made in Vienna in March 1985 is similarly laboured.

26 This turned out to be finer than Karajan's 1973 Unitel film of Tchaikovsky's Sixth Symphony. The earlier performance had been vivid and smooth-toned. The new one is a profoundly felt elegy, atmospherically filmed, and imaginatively edited with an altogether more revealing attention to instrumental detail than the earlier film, which had failed to capitalise on such obvious images as the tam-tam's baleful intervention at the symphony's close.

27 Letter, Michel Glotz to Herbert von Karajan, 20 January 1982, EMI.

28 Memorandum, Peter Alward to Peter Andry, 8 May 1984, EMI.

29 Memorandum, Peter Alward to Peter Andry, 22 March 1984, EMI.

30 Memorandum, Peter Alward to Peter Andry, 2 May 1984, EMI. The festival was given over to *Lohengrin*, works by Mozart and Strauss, and Tchaikovsky's Symphony No.6, with Beethoven's Ninth Symphony pressed into service as the festival's choral offering.

31 Ibid.

32 Conversation, Peter Girth.

CHAPTER 77
War and peace
pp. 689–699

1 'It was electrifying. Even now, it is the greatest Brahms's First I have ever heard.' Conversation, Franz Welser-Möst.

2 Lang, 201.

3 Stresemann, 131.

4 Karajan's immediate response was to instruct Télémondial's lawyers to institute legal proceedings against the orchestra. Had the case run its full course, it is doubtful whether Karajan would have won. The Berlin district court which first examined the claim concluded that Télémondial and the Berlin Philharmonic were bound by ties of 'permanent indebtedness [*Dauerschuld-Verhältnis*]'.

5 Conversation, Ronald Wilford.

6 Conversation, Ronald Wilford.

7 Conversation, Michel Glotz.

8 Hellmut Stern (b. Berlin, 1929), first violinist and celeste player, was one of Karajan's bitterest critics. During the Nazi period, Stern's family emigrated to China. He made his début as a solo violinist there in Harbin, aged fourteen. As a young man he played for six years with the Israel Philharmonic, before joining the Berlin Philharmonic in 1961. His tenacity in pursuing Karajan has been widely admired, though it has also been asked why a man with such principled objections to his Chief Conductor (to his Nazi affiliations in particular) should have elected to join the orchestra in the first place. Stern's fondness for playing the role of court jester – jumping up before Karajan came in, mimicking his movements, and so on – was a frequent source of irritation to producers and engineers who tended to find his behaviour more disruptive than funny. He could also be a thorn in the flesh of other conductors. Christoph von Dohnányi, who had problems with Stern, later described the orchestra's treatment of Karajan at this time as 'ugly, really ugly'. [Conversations David Bell, Günther Breest, Peter Alward, Christoph von Dohnányi.]

9 Conversation, Günther Breest.

10 Conversation, Pali Meller Marcovicz.

11 Stresemann, 144.

12 Sadly, no detailed transcript of the conversation exists. My information is from Michel Glotz, who was a guest at the luncheon.

13 Letter, Herbert von Karajan to

Berlin Philharmonic Orchestra, 24 August 1984, BPO. German original (extracts), Stresemann, 152.

14 Released on CD (Deutsche Grammophon) and Laserdisc (Sony Classical).

CHAPTER 78
Soldiering on
pp. 700–709

1 *Hi-Fi News and Record Review*, December 1988, 5.

2 'Certainly the Berlin PO are galvanised from the first note. Karajan's gestures are economical, even matter-of-fact, but the orchestra unfailingly delivers what is required. I cannot remember a more unremittingly anguished first movement of Brahms's First Symphony or a finale more vigorously or thrillingly pursued to its conclusion.' Barry Millington, *Musical Times*, December 1988, 676.

3 Conversation, Michel Glotz.

4 Conversation, Christopher Headington.

5 *The Art of Conducting*, BBC TV, 1993. Gardiner's comment does not appear on the re-edited commercially available Teldec video of the programme.

It should be added that in an address to the Association of British Orchestras' conference in January 1998, Gardiner remarked: 'Say what you like about Karajan and the Berlin Philharmonic in the Seventies and Eighties, there is no denying that the physical concentration, commitment and even, on occasion, the sheer arrogance and showmanship of the players, gave an added element to the audience's experience of the music that few orchestras have matched before or since.'

6 Karajan made a film and sound recording of Dvořák's Eighth Symphony with the Vienna Philharmonic in January 1985. It is the best of his recordings of the piece, a strong, vital performance notable for the Vienna Philharmonic's pungent wind and string playing.

7 Both Strauss performances were filmed. *Tod und Verklärung* is nobly done, shorn of all bombast. The camera work at the end of the film makes it look as if it is Karajan who is being transfigured and transported. *Metamorphosen* receives a rather muted performance, with little of the incandescence of the 1981 Oxford account.

8 Gardiner's father, Rolf Gardiner, was a great Germanophile and had close ties with the Austro-Germany of Karajan's youth. See Chapter 8 n.5 above.

9 Endler, 338.

10 Robert Pullen and Stephen Taylor, op. cit., 293.

11 Eleven conductors were interviewed for this feature, of whom six singled out Karajan: Vladimir Ashkenazy, Riccardo Chailly, Andrew Davis, Sir Charles Mackerras, André Previn, Jeffrey Tate, and John Whitfield. Other conductors mentioned more than once were Boulez, Haitink, and Solti.

12 Jeffrey Tate used the German word '*geil*' to describe this aspect of Karajan. It means 'physical arousal'; not, in this instance, sexual but every bit as powerful in the drives it released.

13 Memorandum, Peter Alward to Peter Andry, 3 June 1985, EMI. The works included in this concert were later filmed by Télémondial in Berlin. The Mozart is drab, but the *Also sprach Zarathustra*, like the *Ein Heldenleben* and *Don Quixote* films from this period, is memorable. The lambency and old-world warmth of the Berlin Strauss sound is married to ensemble-playing of great refinement and inner concentration. The camera-work is first-rate, with carefully chosen perspectives and much fine detail in close-ups.

14 The event was recorded for film and video by Télémondial in conjunction with Centro Televisivo Vaticano. The negotiations were long and complex.

15 It is one of the most elegantly photographed of all Karajan's late films, and a most beautiful

performance, one that has lived too much under the shadow of the earliest of Karajan's recordings, the one with Pierre Fournier as soloist. It was released on CD (Deutsche Grammophon) as well as Laserdisc (Sony Classical).

16 Conversation, Elisabeth Furtwängler.
17 Lang, 215.
18 Stresemann would give his memoir of Karajan the subtitle 'A strange man' (Bruno Walter's phrase), adding, in the preface, lines from *Hamlet*: 'A was a man, take him for all in all:/I shall not look upon his like again.' Whether this was meant as a tribute (Hamlet's sense) or an oblique reference to the Ghost (an understandably embittered but none the less brutally vengeful old man) must be a matter for speculation.
19 Lang, 217.
20 *Opera*, Autumn 1986, 46.
21 Letter, Herbert von Karajan to Peter Alward, 13 October 1986, EMI.
22 Conversations, 147.
23 Conversation, Michel Glotz.
24 Conversation, Arabel von Karajan.
25 Sony Classical video and laserdisc, a generous ninety-seven-minute compilation drawn from all three concerts, directed by Humphrey Burton. The concerts make ideal viewing, very much something to be seen as well as heard. The Deutsche Grammophon CD does not include the overture to *Der Zigeunerbaron*, The *Emperor* waltz, or *Perpetuum mobile*.
26 Omitted from film and CD versions of the concert.
27 *Gramophone*, March 1993, 29.
28 Conversation, Walter Weller.
29 In the finest traditions of the Englishman abroad, Phillips had travelled all the way to Vienna without a ticket for the concert.
30 *The Spectator*, 24 January 1987, 38–9. The response of Adrian Brown, a finalist in the 1975 Karajan Conducting Competition, suggested that Karajan's way with Strauss was not something that appealed to Austrians alone. He told me: 'At the start of *The Blue Danube*, the sense

of weight and woe at the moment when the music suddenly veers into the minor is hardly ever played with such inwardness and depth of feeling. People casually use words like 'glossy' and 'superficial' when talking of Karajan. That really does make me angry. To a *musician*, what he did was a revelation.'

CHAPTER 79
Trouble over Taiwan
pp. 710–718

1 Memorandum, Peter Alward to Peter Andry, 29 January 1987, EMI.
2 *Daily Mail*, 11 March 1987.
3 Hampe and Pagano had first worked in Salzburg in 1982. Their production of *Così fan tutte*, conducted by Muti, had charmed critics and audiences alike. Pagano died in 1988, aged thirty-seven.
4 The programme was repeated in Berlin on 30–31 December 1987, a few months short of the fiftieth anniversary of the performances of *Tristan und Isolde* ('Das Wunder Karajan') he had conducted in Berlin in 1938.
5 August Everding, '*Entdecken und zwingen und überzeugen*', July 1989, DGG source unidentified.
6 *Karajan in Salzburg*, a film by Susan Froemke and Peter Gelb, Sony Laserdisc and video cassette.
7 Conversations, 143.
8 Ibid.
9 Telex, Peter Gelb to Mr T. L. Chang, 7 October 1987; reproduced in *Der Spiegel*, 28 March 1988, 216.
10 Quoted by Tim Page, 'Capping a Career in Podium Politics', *New York Times*, 23 February 1989.
11 Pufendorf was later quoted as saying, 'What will the Taiwanese think of us?' Gelb was also reported to have conceded that tacking on the TV rights deal was an error.
12 Conversation, Ronald Wilford.
13 Letter, Max Fisher to EMI, 1 June 1981, EMI.
14 Part of a round robin of tributes to Karajan organised by Deutsche Grammophon from among its artists. Other conductors who sent greetings

were Abbado, Giulini, Levine, and
Ozawa.
15 Conversation, Eliette von Karajan.
16 *Daily Telegraph*, 1 April 1988.
17 Ibid.
18 *Der Spiegel*, 9 May 1988.
19 One of Karajan's last acts as a
member of the Festival Direktorium
was to approach Simon Rattle about
the possibility of his appearing in
Salzburg. Karajan admired Rattle
for the way he had conducted his
career and Rattle had found Karajan
bracing and interesting to be with.
('I was very happy when I met him.
It was very interesting. I had not
expected to feel so much at ease.')
The telephone call about future
Salzburg plans was amicable enough,
until Rattle raised the question of
period instruments, at which point
Karajan put the phone down on him.
20 Karajan had always ensured that
the Berliners wanted for nothing.
This included first-rate hotel
accommodation during tours. Now,
he told me, the orchestra was
demanding that they stay in the *same
hotel as him*. In Vienna, Karajan
had switched from the Imperial
Hotel to the smaller Hotel in Palais
Schwarzenberg. He laughed: 'I told
them, "I'm sure the management
will be happy to instal bunk beds
for you."' The Hotel in Palais
Schwarzenberg has only forty-two
rooms.
21 Klaus Geitel, 'New Year's Eve
Concert 1988', notes for Sony
Classical Laserdisc, SLV 45 986.

CHAPTER 80
Resignation
pp. 719–725
1 Conversation, Sumi Jo.
2 Conversation, Placido Domingo.
3 Conversation, Josephine Barstow.
4 Quoted in Julian Budden, *The Operas
of Verdi*, vol.2 (London, 1978), 423.
5 *New York Times*, 28 February 1989.
6 *New York Times*, 27 February 1989.
7 Conversation, Klaus Geitel.
8 *New York Herald Tribune*, 17
July 1989.
9 Conversation, Michel Glotz.

10 *Guardian*, 8 April 1989.
11 Conversation, Michel Glotz.
12 Conversation, Günther Breest.
13 *Die Presse*, 17 July 1989.
14 The original letter is reproduced
in Stresemann, 180; the text of the
letter is also reprinted in Endler
356–7.
15 Sabine Weissler, a spokesman on
cultural affairs for the Green Party,
was quoted as saying: 'His retirement
comes too late. The Philharmonic
had stopped developing. Its musical
progress was being inhibited. We're
pleased that he's leaving – it's better
for all sides.' *New York Times*, 25
April 1989.
16 Conversation, Herbert von Karajan.

CHAPTER 81
A necessary end
pp. 726–731
Epigraph Marguerite Yourcenar,
'Reflections on the Composition',
Memoirs of Hadrian, translated
by Grace Frick in collaboration
with the author (Martin Secker &
Warburg, 1955/R1986), 282.
1 There is a full and fascinating
discussion of the Waldheim affair
in Gordon Brook-Shepherd, *The
Austrians: a Thousand-Year Odyssey*
(London, 1996), 429–41.
2 Ibid., 436. In Britain in June 1988,
the Waldheim case and the workings
of the Holtzman Amendment were the
subject of a so-called 'International
Television Trial'. An official from the
US Department of Justice acted as
the 'prosecution', Lord Rawlinson, a
former British Attorney-General, led
the 'defence'. The prosecution case
was comprehensively defeated.
3 Eli M. Rosenbaum, Director, Office
of Special Investigations, Criminal
Division, US Department of Justice,
wrote to me on 12 August 1997:
'Although I am not at liberty to
disclose the Government's basis
for commencing the von Karajan
inquiry, I can state that this office
did *not* [his emphasis] come into
possession of substantial new
information that was not already
in the public domain. I should add

that Mr von Karajan died before our inquiry could be completed. Accordingly, no determination that he was ineligible to re-enter the United States was ever made.'

4 When Nikisch died and Furtwängler succeeded him as permanent conductor in 1922, the *Berliner Tageblatt* gave the appointment a couple of lines in a 'miscellaneous' news round-up. How different things would be in 1954, and again in 1989! Yet, with the benefit of hindsight, it is possible to think that 1989 was almost as big a watershed as 1922.

After 1922, the impress of great musical personalities, the influence of the wireless and the gramophone, new political crises in the affairs of Germany and former Austro-Hungary, the Jewish diaspora of the 1930s, a world war and its culturally complex aftermath, had given so-called 'classical' music – in reality, the Austro-German musical legacy of the years 1700–1914 – an astonishing hold over the minds of imaginations of millions of people for whom it had hitherto been distant and inhospitable territory.

By 1989, much of that was beginning to be undone. The musically literate audience of mainly Jewish refugees from 1930s Europe, which had done so much to help reshape musical life in Britain and the United States in the postwar era, was in decline. Radio and television were losing their intellectual nerve. The record industry, which had grown fat on the huge earnings generated by LP, stereo, and CD was coming more and to resemble some latter-day South Sea Bubble. One of the industry's severest critics, Norman Lebrecht, would note that in the immediate post-Karajan period it was like Lilliput the day Gulliver went home: 'a lot of people running about the beach wondering what happens next'.

Talk in the press in the summer of 1989 about the Berlin succession was almost entirely political: about the need to 'liberalise' and 'democratise'

orchestra–conductor relationships after the demise of the last of the great 'conductor megalomaniacs'. When, to many people's surprise, Claudio Abbado was elected in October 1989 there was near-universal approval. Abbado's belief in 'instinct' and 'spontaneity' – trilled one English journalist – over and above 'whatever has gone on in rehearsal', was tremendously important: it 'keeps the players on their toes'.

The players clearly thought so, too. How else could they have elected a distinguished and likeable musician whose Achilles' heel, it had long been said within the profession, was precisely his *inability* to rehearse in the kind of rigorous and systematic way the old Kapellmeisters were trained to do. Karajan had been a great orchestra *maker*, the Berlin Philharmonic a Stradivarius he and others might play. Perhaps the unhappiest consequence of his staying to the bitter end was that by 1989 too few players knew at first hand the answer to the most important question of all: how, in the first place, the orchestra had become what it was.

5 See Ch.62 n.7.

6 Conversations, Günther Schneider-Siemssen, Herbert von Karajan. When Schneider-Siemssen visited Karajan's grave, he had a *Hamlet*-like encounter with the local gravedigger. 'How deep are the graves here?' he asked. 'Three metres usually: two metres in Karajan's case.' 'Why the difference?' 'Stands to reason, doesn't it? Come the resurrection, he'll want to be first out.'

7 Conversation, Michel Glotz.

8 The most detailed comment on Karajan's death, outside his native Austria, was in France, where the provincial coverage was especially extensive. (Karajan had strong links with the country. He had a French wife, a French recording manager, a French home, flew French aircraft, and had once headed a French orchestra.)

The Italian press treated his death with high solemnity. Obituaries in the United States were, for the most part, generous and fair-minded; Karajan had always had a stronger following there than he, or we, were sometimes led to believe. The German obituaries were full and thorough, mixed as to judgement, and – a handful of personal memoirs apart – rather bored. It was if, after sixty hectic years of writing about Karajan, inspiration had finally run dry.

British judgements were more mixed than most, often within the same publication. An editorial in the *Spectator* on 22 July 1989 observed: 'What [Laurence] Olivier and Karajan possessed of greatness was more than just charisma. It was something which we really may have seen the last of: an ability to make grand gestures without seeming either self-conscious and pretentious on the one hand or self-parodying and ironic on the other.'

In the same issue, the paper's opera critic Rodney Milnes wrote: '[Karajan] was, I think, a bad man and in the final analysis a bad conductor as well. He wielded power out of all proportion to his talent, and the musical world will be a better place without him.'

The following week in the *Spectator* the Oxford Professor of Poetry and former priest Peter Levi wrote: 'Later that Saturday my wife was watching a programme about Herbert von Karajan, about whom I used to nourish doubts because he was a Nazi and used to conduct the Horsewhistle or whatever they call it. But I have decided such doubts are ridiculous, and I certainly admire him for refusing ever to discuss the subject. He just had a passion, a deep fit of devotion, for every note of German music, and why ever not? We saw him conduct Beethoven's Third Symphony, brilliantly and unrestlessly photographed for once, with his eyes tight shut from beginning to end, and an expression so rapt that I was hugely moved by it. I think it is the best film of an artist at work that I have ever seen. John Drummond introduced it with pleasant enthusiasm, but I wanted more formality until suddenly von Karajan engendered just that. You could hear the hush behind the music.'

General Index

Index of Performances, Sound Recordings & Films

This index is of works performed by Karajan and referred to in the present volume. *Italic* page numbers indicate sound recordings; the prefix F denotes a film or video recording.